Nanoengineered Therapeutics for Lung Cancer

Nanoengineered Therapeutics for Lung Cancer

Advanced Drug Delivery Strategies

Edited by

Arun Kumar Singh
University School of Pharmaceutical Sciences,
Rayat Bahra University, Mohali, Punjab, India

Meenakshi Dhanawat
Amity Institute of Pharmacy, Amity University,
Gurugram, Haryana, India

Shikha Baghel Chauhan
Centre of Industrial Pharmacy, Amity Institute of Pharmacy,
Amity University, Noida, Uttar Pradesh, India

Indu Singh
Centre of Pharmaceutics, Amity Institute of Pharmacy,
Amity University, Noida, Uttar Pradesh, India

Niraj Kumar Jha
School of Biosciences and Technology, Galgotias University,
Greater Noida, Uttar Pradesh, India

ELSEVIER

ACADEMIC PRESS
An imprint of Elsevier
elsevier.com/books-and-journals

Academic Press is an imprint of Elsevier

125 London Wall, London EC2Y 5AS, United Kingdom
50 Hampshire Street, 5th Floor, Cambridge, MA 02139, United States

Publisher's note: Elsevier takes a neutral position with respect to territorial disputes or jurisdictional claims in its published content, including in maps and institutional affiliations.

Books and Journals published by Elsevier comply with applicable product safety requirements. For any product safety concerns or queries, please contact our authorised representative, Elsevier B.V., at productsafety@elsevier.com.

For accessibility purposes, images in electronic versions of this book are accompanied by alt text descriptions provided by Elsevier. For more information, see https://www.elsevier.com/about/accessibility.

Notices
Knowledge and best practice in this field are constantly changing. As new research and experience broaden our understanding, changes in research methods, professional practices, or medical treatment may become necessary.

Practitioners and researchers must always rely on their own experience and knowledge in evaluating and using any information, methods, compounds, or experiments described herein. In using such information or methods they should be mindful of their own safety and the safety of others, including parties for whom they have a professional responsibility.

To the fullest extent of the law, neither the Publisher nor the authors, contributors, or editors, assume any liability for any injury and/or damage to persons or property as a matter of products liability, negligence or otherwise, or from any use or operation of any methods, products, instructions, or ideas contained in the material herein.

ISBN: 978-0-443-44585-9

For Information on all Academic Press publications visit our website at https://www.elsevier.com/books-and-journals

Publisher: Megan Ball
Acquisitions Editor: Linda Buschman
Editorial Project Manager: Siddharth Khattri
Production Project Manager: Jenela Priscy
Cover Designer: Mark Rogers

Typeset by Aptara, New Delhi, India

Dedication

Dedicated to the loving memory and enduring inspiration of my grandfather,
Mr. Mahendra Pal Singh.

Your wisdom, integrity, perseverance, and unwavering belief in the value of knowledge have been a guiding light throughout my life and academic journey. The principles you embodied—hard work, humility, compassion, and dedication—continue to inspire me every day.

This book is a humble tribute to your legacy and the countless lessons you imparted through your words, actions, and character. Your encouragement to pursue education, seek understanding, and contribute meaningfully to society has been a source of strength and motivation in every endeavor.

As I present this work, I do so with profound gratitude for your love, support, and the foundation of values you helped build. Though time may pass, your influence remains deeply woven into every achievement and aspiration.

May this book stand as a testament to the respect, admiration, and affection I hold for you, and may your legacy continue to inspire future generations to pursue knowledge with purpose, integrity, and compassion.

With deepest love, gratitude, and reverence, this book is dedicated to you,
Mr. Mahendra Pal Singh. 💖 📖

To the loving memory of my beloved father, Late Dr. C. B. Dhanawat

This book is lovingly dedicated to my father, whose life as a compassionate physician and an exceptional human being continues to inspire me every day. Your unwavering commitment to serving others, your integrity, and your deep respect for knowledge shaped not only my character but also my passion for learning and research.

You taught me that true success is measured by the lives we touch, the values we uphold, and the kindness we share. Your encouragement gave me the confidence to pursue my dreams, and your example remains my greatest source of strength and motivation.

Although you are no longer with us, your wisdom, love, and legacy continue to guide my journey. Every page of this book is a tribute to your enduring influence and the ideals you lived by.

With deepest love, gratitude, and everlasting respect.

Dr. Meenakshi Dhanawat

Contents

Contributors

Syed Hamza Abbas Department of Microbiology, Faculty of Biological Sciences, Quaid-i-Azam University, Islamabad, Pakistan

Malik Zainul Abdin Centre for Transgenic Plant Development, Department of Biotechnology, Jamia Hamdard, New Delhi, India

Ritish Attri Department of Pharmacology, School of Pharmaceutical Sciences, Lovely Professional University, Phagwara, Punjab, India

Anwesha Bandyopadhyay Faculty of Applied Sciences & Biotechnology, School of Biotechnology, Shoolini University, Solan, Himachal Pradesh, India

Rohit Rajendra Bhosale Department of Pharmaceutics, Krishna Charitable Trust's Krishna College of Pharmacy, Karad, Maharashtra, India

Deepak Biswas Department of Medical Sciences, Kokshetau State Medical University, Kokshetau, Kazakhstan

Sanheeta Chakrabarty Department of Pharmaceutical Engineering and Technology, Indian Institute of Technology (BHU), Varanasi, Uttar Pradesh, India

Shikha Baghel Chauhan Centre of Industrial Pharmacy, Amity Institute of Pharmacy, Amity University, Noida, Uttar Pradesh, India

Yakshit Chauhan Amity Institute of Pharmacy, Amity University, Noida, Uttar Pradesh, India

Hitesh Chopra Department of Biosciences, Saveetha Institute of Medical and Technical Sciences (SIMATS) (Deemed to be University), Chennai, Tamil Nadu, India

Sunil Choudhary Department of Radiotherapy and Radiation Medicine, Institute of Medical Sciences, Banaras Hindu University, Varanasi, Uttar Pradesh, India

Khushi Dahiya Amity Institute of Pharmacy, Amity University, Noida, Uttar Pradesh, India

Biswajit Das Department of Molecular Cell and Developmental Biology, University of California, Santa Cruz, CA, United States

Meenakshi Dhanawat Amity Institute of Pharmacy, Amity University, Gurugram, Haryana, India

Vidhyashree Sulangi Durugappa School of Basic and Applied Sciences, Dayananda Sagar University, Bengaluru, Karnataka, India

Gayathiri Ekambaram Department of Plant Biology and Plant Biotechnology, Guru Nanak College (Autonomous), Chennai, Tamil Nadu, India

Rupesh Kumar Gautam Department of Pharmacology, Amity Institute of Pharmacy, Amity University, Noida, Uttar Pradesh, India

Jashan Girdhar Department of Pharmacy Practice, Teerthanker Mahaveer College of Pharmacy, Teerthanker Mahaveer University, Moradabad, Uttar Pradesh, India

Harsh Goswami Raj Kumar Goel Institute of Technology (Pharmacy), Ghaziabad, Uttar Pradesh, India

Rakshitha Gowda School of Basic and Applied Sciences, Dayananda Sagar University, Bengaluru, Karnataka, India

Anshul Gupta Department of Pharmaceutics, Delhi Pharmaceutical Sciences and Research University, New Delhi, India

Jyoti Gupta Department of Pharmacy, Galgotias College of Pharmacy, Greater Noida, Uttar Pradesh, India

Sumeet Gupta M. M. College of Pharmacy, Maharishi Markandeshwar (Deemed to be University), Mullana, Ambala, Haryana, India

Praveen Halagali Department of Pharmaceutics, Manipal College of Pharmaceutical Sciences, Manipal Academy of Higher Education, Manipal, Karnataka, India

Nadia Ilyas Department of Microbiology, Faculty of Biological Sciences, Quaid-i-Azam University, Islamabad, Pakistan

Geetha J Department of Microbiology, Auxilium College, Vellore, Tamil Nadu, India

Chirag Jain Amity Institute of Pharmacy, Amity University, Noida, Uttar Pradesh, India

Shreyans K. Jain Department of Pharmaceutical Engineering and Technology, Indian Institute of Technology (BHU), Varanasi, Uttar Pradesh, India

Harshitha Loganathan Kamala Kannan School of Basic and Applied Sciences, Dayananda Sagar University, Bengaluru, Karnataka, India

Mayank Kashyap Department of Pharmaceutical Engineering and Technology, Indian Institute of Technology (BHU), Varanasi, Uttar Pradesh, India

Samiullah Khan Department of Microbiology, Faculty of Biological Sciences, Quaid-i-Azam University, Islamabad, Pakistan

Shahzar Khan Department of Microbiology, Faculty of Biological Sciences, Quaid-i-Azam University, Islamabad, Pakistan

Bimlesh Kumar School of Pharmaceutical Sciences, Department of Pharmacology, Lovely Professional University, Phagwara, Punjab, India

Rakesh Kumar Amity Institute of Pharmacy, Amity University, Gurugram, Haryana, India; Department of Pharmacy, Jagannath University, Bahadurgarh, Haryana, India

Shubham Kumar School of Pharmaceutical Sciences, Department of Pharmacology, Lovely Professional University, Phagwara, Punjab, India

Garima Malik Chitkara College of Pharmacy, Chitkara University, Rajpura, Punjab, India

Syed Saima Malik Centre for Transgenic Plant Development, Department of Biotechnology, Jamia Hamdard, New Delhi, India

Blessy Baby Mathew School of Basic and Applied Sciences, Dayananda Sagar University, Bengaluru, Karnataka, India

Samir Mehndiratta Department of Discipline of Pharmacy, Graduate School of Health, University of Technology Sydney, Ultimo, NSW, Australia

Neeraj Mittal Chitkara College of Pharmacy, Chitkara University, Rajpura, Punjab, India

Thirupathihalli Pandurangappa Krishna Murthy Department of Biotechnology, M.S. Ramaiah Institute of Technology, Bengaluru, Karnataka, India

Prithiviraj Nagarajan Department of Medical Biotechnology, Aarupadai Veedu Medical College & Hospital, Vinayaka Mission's Research Foundation (Deemed to be University), Puducherry, India

Sankaranarayanan Nagarajan Department of Chemistry, National Institute of Technology Manipur, Imphal, Manipur, India

Humaira Nawaz Department of Microbiology, Faculty of Biological Sciences, Quaid-i-Azam University, Islamabad, Pakistan

Pradip Nirbhavane Department of Pharmacy, Amity University, Gurugram, Haryana, India

Tarun Pal Faculty of Applied Sciences & Biotechnology, School of Bioengineering and Food Technology, Shoolini University, Solan, Himachal Pradesh, India

Sharangouda J. Patil Department of Zoology, Nagarathnamma Meda Kasturiranga Setty Rashtreeya Vidyalaya (NMKRV) College, Bengaluru, Karnataka, India

Pankaj Popli Chitkara College of Pharmacy, Chitkara University, Rajpura, Punjab, India

Shivani Prajapati Department of Radiotherapy and Radiation Medicine, Institute of Medical Sciences, Banaras Hindu University, Varanasi, Uttar Pradesh, India

Syed Naved Quadri Centre for Transgenic Plant Development, Department of Biotechnology, Jamia Hamdard, New Delhi, India

Syed Arman Rabbani RAK College of Pharmacy, RAK Medical and Health Sciences University, Ras Al Khaimah, United Arab Emirates

Nathiya Ranganathan Department of Microbiology, Auxilium College, Vellore, Tamil Nadu, India

Deepa Rani M. M. College of Pharmacy, Maharishi Markandeshwar (Deemed to be University), Mullana, Ambala, Haryana, India

Ishfaq Rashid Department of Pharmacotherapy, College of Pharmacy, University of Utah, Salt Lake City, UT, United States

Vickram S Department of Biosciences, Saveetha School of Engineering, Saveetha Institute of Medical and Technical Sciences (SIMATS) (Deemed to be University), Chennai, Tamil Nadu, India

Ritika Saha School of Pharmaceutical Sciences, Department of Pharmacology, Lovely Professional University, Phagwara, Punjab, India

Manita Saini Amity Institute of Pharmacy, Amity University, Gurugram, Haryana, India; Geeta Institute of Pharmacy, Geeta University, Panipat, Haryana, India

Nabajit Sarkar Department of Clinical Pharmacology, R G Kar Medical College, Kolkata, West Bengal, India

Gajender Sharma Department of Pharmacology, M. M. College of Pharmacy, Maharishi Markandeshwar (Deemed to be University), Mullana, Ambala, Haryana, India

Himanshu Sharma Department of Pharmacology, NIMS Institute of Pharmacy, NIMS University Rajasthan, Jaipur, Rajasthan, India

Sarita Sharma Department of Pharmacology, Amity Institute of Pharmacy, Amity University, Gwalior, Madhya Pradesh, India

Shrestha Sharma Amity Institute of Pharmacy, Amity University, Gurugram, Haryana, India

Vikram Sharma Department of Pharmacy, Galgotias College of Pharmacy, Galgotias University, Greater Noida, Uttar Pradesh, India

Indu Singh Centre of Pharmaceutics, Amity Institute of Pharmacy, Amity University, Noida, Uttar Pradesh, India

Ravinder Singh Department of Pharmacology, School of Pharmaceutical Sciences, Lovely Professional University, Phagwara, Punjab, India

Rajan Swami Chitkara College of Pharmacy, Chitkara University, Rajpura, Punjab, India

Vamshi Krishna Tippavajhala Department of Pharmaceutics, Manipal College of Pharmaceutical Sciences, Manipal Academy of Higher Education, Manipal, Karnataka, India

Megha Tonk Raj Kumar Goel Institute of Technology (Pharmacy), Ghaziabad, Uttar Pradesh, India

Preface

Lung cancer remains one of the most prevalent and deadly malignancies worldwide, posing a significant challenge to global healthcare systems. Despite remarkable advances in diagnostic technologies, molecular profiling, and therapeutic interventions, lung cancer continues to account for a substantial proportion of cancer-related morbidity and mortality. The complexity of tumor biology, late-stage diagnosis, drug resistance, tumor heterogeneity, and systemic toxicity associated with conventional treatments often limit therapeutic success. Consequently, there is a pressing need for innovative treatment approaches that can enhance therapeutic efficacy while minimizing adverse effects.

In recent decades, nanotechnology has emerged as a transformative force in oncology, offering unprecedented opportunities to overcome the limitations of traditional cancer therapies. Nanoengineered therapeutics have revolutionized the field of drug delivery by enabling precise targeting, controlled release, improved bioavailability, and enhanced accumulation of therapeutic agents at tumor sites. These advancements have opened new avenues for the treatment of lung cancer, particularly in addressing challenges related to poor drug penetration, rapid systemic clearance, multidrug resistance, and nonspecific toxicity.

The concept of nanoengineered therapeutics encompasses a broad range of nanoscale delivery systems, including lipid-based nanoparticles, polymeric nanoparticles, dendrimers, nanogels, micelles, inorganic nanoparticles, exosomes, and biomimetic nanocarriers. These sophisticated platforms are capable of carrying a diverse array of therapeutic payloads, including chemotherapeutic agents, nucleic acids, proteins, peptides, immunomodulators, and gene-editing tools. By exploiting the unique physicochemical properties of nanomaterials, researchers have developed multifunctional systems capable of targeting tumors with remarkable specificity and efficiency.

This book, *Nanoengineered Therapeutics for Lung Cancer: Advanced Drug Delivery Strategies*, has been conceived to provide a comprehensive and up-to-date overview of the rapidly evolving landscape of nanomedicine in lung cancer therapy. The volume brings together contributions from leading experts in oncology, pharmaceutical sciences, nanotechnology, molecular biology, biomedical engineering, and translational medicine. Through an interdisciplinary perspective, the book aims to bridge fundamental scientific concepts with clinical applications, offering readers valuable insights into current developments and future directions.

The chapters explore the biological and pathological foundations of lung cancer, including tumor microenvironment dynamics, molecular signaling pathways, genetic mutations, and mechanisms of therapeutic resistance. Understanding these complex interactions is essential for designing effective nanoparticle-based interventions that can selectively target cancer cells while sparing healthy tissues.

A significant focus of the book is dedicated to advanced drug delivery technologies. Readers will find detailed discussions on passive and active targeting approaches, stimuli-responsive nanocarriers, inhalable nanoparticle systems, pulmonary drug delivery platforms, and smart nanomaterials capable of responding to environmental triggers such as pH, temperature, enzymes, redox gradients, and hypoxia. These innovative strategies offer enhanced precision and therapeutic outcomes by delivering drugs directly to diseased tissues while reducing systemic exposure.

The emergence of precision medicine has further accelerated the development of personalized nanotherapeutic approaches. Nanoengineered systems can be tailored to individual patient profiles, enabling targeted delivery based on specific molecular biomarkers and genetic alterations. The integration of nanotechnology with molecular diagnostics, companion biomarkers, and artificial intelligence-driven treatment planning represents a promising paradigm shift toward individualized lung cancer management.

Beyond chemotherapy, the book examines the application of nanotechnology in immunotherapy, gene therapy, RNA-based therapeutics, photodynamic therapy, photothermal therapy, and combination treatment strategies. Nanocarriers play an increasingly important role in enhancing immune responses, improving gene transfection efficiency, and facilitating synergistic therapeutic effects that can overcome resistance mechanisms and improve long-term outcomes.

The translation of laboratory discoveries into clinical practice is another critical theme addressed throughout this volume. Regulatory considerations, safety assessments, toxicological evaluations, large-scale manufacturing challenges, quality control measures, and commercialization pathways are discussed to provide readers with a realistic understanding of the opportunities and obstacles associated with clinical implementation. Several chapters also highlight ongoing clinical trials and approved nanomedicine products that demonstrate the growing impact of nanoengineered therapeutics in cancer care.

As the field continues to advance, emerging technologies such as biomimetic nanoparticles, extracellular vesicle-based delivery systems, Clustered regularly interspaced short palindromic repeats (CRISPR)-enabled nanocarriers, and multifunctional theranostic platforms are expected to redefine the future of lung cancer treatment. These innovations have the potential not only to improve therapeutic efficacy but also to enable earlier diagnosis, real-time treatment monitoring, and personalized disease management.

This book is intended for researchers, clinicians, pharmaceutical scientists, graduate students, biomedical engineers, healthcare professionals, and industry stakeholders interested in the intersection of nanotechnology and oncology. Whether the reader seeks foundational knowledge or advanced insights into cutting-edge therapeutic strategies, the chapters provide a valuable resource for understanding the scientific principles, technological innovations, and translational opportunities shaping the future of lung cancer therapy.

We hope that *Nanoengineered Therapeutics for Lung Cancer: Advanced Drug Delivery Strategies* will serve as a catalyst for scientific innovation, interdisciplinary collaboration, and clinical advancement. By bringing together diverse perspectives and emerging technologies, this volume aims to contribute to the development of safer, more effective, and patient-centered therapeutic solutions for one of the world's most challenging diseases. The future of lung cancer treatment lies in precision, innovation, and integration, and nanoengineered therapeutics are poised to play a central role in achieving these goals.

Acknowledgments

The author (Arun Kumar Singh) gratefully acknowledges the invaluable support and encouragement provided by the Hon'ble Vice Chancellor of Rayat Bahra University, Mohali, Punjab, India. Sincere thanks are also extended to the entire team of the University School of Pharmaceutical Sciences for their continued cooperation and contributions that have significantly facilitated the research and development activities associated with this work. Finally, my deepest and most heartfelt gratitude goes to my beloved family, especially my father, Mr. Kshetra Pal Singh, whose unwavering love, patience, and encouragement have been my greatest source of strength.

I sincerely thank the Honorable Founder-President Dr. Ashok K. Chauhan, Ritnand Balved Education Foundation (RBEF), and Dr. Aseem Chauhan, Chancellor, Amity University Gurugram, for their visionary leadership and inspiration.

I gratefully acknowledge the Honorable Vice Chancellor Prof. (Dr.) P. B. Sharma for his constant guidance and support. I extend our appreciation to Pro-Vice Chancellor Prof. Vikas Madhukar for fostering a strong research environment,

I also thank my family and friends for their never ending support and trust in me.

Dr. Meenakshi Dhanawat

Introduction

Lung cancer remains one of the most significant global health challenges, accounting for a substantial proportion of cancer-related morbidity and mortality worldwide. According to recent epidemiological reports, lung cancer continues to be the leading cause of cancer deaths despite considerable advances in diagnostic technologies, surgical interventions, radiotherapy, chemotherapy, targeted therapies, and immunotherapy. The high mortality rate is largely attributed to late-stage diagnosis, aggressive tumor progression, metastatic dissemination, and the emergence of therapeutic resistance. These persistent challenges underscore the urgent need for innovative treatment strategies capable of improving therapeutic efficacy while minimizing adverse effects.

Conventional therapeutic approaches for lung cancer often suffer from several limitations. Systemically administered chemotherapeutic agents frequently exhibit poor selectivity, resulting in widespread distribution throughout the body and causing severe toxicities to healthy tissues. Additionally, biological barriers, rapid drug clearance, poor tumor penetration, and multidrug resistance mechanisms reduce the effectiveness of many anticancer drugs. Although molecularly targeted therapies and immune checkpoint inhibitors have revolutionized treatment paradigms for specific patient populations, issues related to resistance development, limited patient responsiveness, and treatment-associated toxicities continue to hinder optimal clinical outcomes.

The emergence of nanotechnology has opened new horizons in cancer therapeutics by enabling the design of advanced drug delivery systems that operate at the molecular and cellular levels. Nanoengineered therapeutics utilize materials ranging from 1 to 100 nm in size, possessing unique physicochemical characteristics that allow enhanced interaction with biological systems. These nanoscale platforms offer significant advantages over conventional drug formulations, including improved drug solubility, prolonged circulation time, enhanced bioavailability, controlled drug release, and selective tumor targeting.

One of the fundamental principles underlying nanomedicine is the ability of nanoparticles to preferentially accumulate within tumor tissues through the enhanced permeability and retention (EPR) effect. Furthermore, active targeting strategies involving ligands, antibodies, peptides, aptamers, and receptor-specific molecules enable precise delivery of therapeutic agents to cancer cells while minimizing off-target toxicity. Such targeted approaches have the potential to improve therapeutic indices and enhance treatment outcomes in lung cancer patients.

A diverse range of nanoengineered delivery systems has been investigated for lung cancer treatment. These include lipid-based nanoparticles, liposomes, polymeric nanoparticles, dendrimers, nanomicelles, solid lipid nanoparticles, nanogels, metallic nanoparticles, carbon-based nanomaterials, extracellular vesicles, and biomimetic nanocarriers. Each platform offers distinct advantages and can be tailored to accommodate various therapeutic agents, including chemotherapeutics, proteins, peptides, nucleic acids, gene-editing systems, and immunomodulatory compounds.

The complexity of the lung tumor microenvironment presents both challenges and opportunities for nanoparticle-mediated therapy. The tumor microenvironment consists of cancer cells, immune cells, stromal components, extracellular matrix proteins, cytokines, and abnormal vasculature that collectively influence tumor progression and therapeutic response. Modern nanoengineered systems are increasingly designed to interact with and modulate these components, thereby enhancing drug delivery efficiency and overcoming mechanisms of treatment resistance.

Recent advances in precision medicine have further accelerated the development of personalized nanotherapeutic strategies. By integrating molecular profiling, genomic analysis, biomarker identification, and artificial intelligence-assisted treatment planning, researchers are creating highly customized therapeutic platforms tailored to individual patient characteristics. These approaches promise to maximize treatment efficacy while minimizing unnecessary toxicity.

In addition to drug delivery, nanotechnology has expanded into diagnostic and theranostic applications. Multifunctional nanoparticles capable of simultaneous imaging and therapy enable real-time monitoring of treatment responses and facilitate personalized clinical decision-making. Such theranostic systems represent a significant step toward integrated cancer management and precision oncology.

Furthermore, nanoengineered therapeutics have demonstrated considerable potential in emerging treatment modalities, including immunotherapy, gene therapy, RNA-based therapeutics, photothermal therapy, photodynamic therapy, and combination treatment approaches. These innovations offer opportunities to overcome current therapeutic limitations and address the complex biological mechanisms underlying lung cancer progression.

Despite remarkable progress, several challenges remain before widespread clinical adoption can be achieved. Issues related to nanoparticle safety, long-term toxicity, large-scale manufacturing, reproducibility, regulatory approval, and cost-effectiveness require continued investigation. Addressing these challenges will be critical for translating promising laboratory discoveries into clinically viable therapies.

This book explores the scientific foundations, technological innovations, and clinical applications of nanoengineered therapeutics in lung cancer treatment. It provides comprehensive coverage of advanced drug delivery strategies, emerging nanomaterials, targeting mechanisms, translational considerations, and future directions in the field. By bringing together contributions from experts across multiple disciplines, this volume aims to serve as a valuable resource for researchers, clinicians, pharmaceutical scientists, biomedical engineers, and students seeking to understand the transformative role of nanotechnology in the fight against lung cancer.

As the fields of nanomedicine, molecular oncology, and precision therapeutics continue to converge, nanoengineered drug delivery systems are poised to play a pivotal role in shaping the future of lung cancer management. The advancements discussed throughout this book highlight the immense potential of these technologies to improve patient outcomes, reduce treatment-related toxicity, and contribute to the development of more effective and personalized cancer therapies.

CHAPTER 1

Introduction to Nanomedical drug delivery for lung cancer

Jyoti Gupta[a], Indu Singh[b], Shikha Baghel Chauhan[c], Pradip Nirbhavane[d] and Vikram Sharma[a]

[a]Department of Pharmacy, Galgotias College of Pharmacy, Greater Noida, Uttar Pradesh, India [b]Centre of Pharmaceutics, Amity Institute of Pharmacy, Amity University, Noida, Uttar Pradesh, India [c]Centre of Industrial Pharmacy, Amity Institute of Pharmacy, Amity University, Noida, Uttar Pradesh, India [d]Department of Pharmacy, Amity University Haryana, Gurgaon, Haryana, India

1.1 Introduction

Lung cancer is a significant global health concern and one of the deadliest forms of cancer, contributing to the highest mortality rates among tumor-related diseases (Erratum: Global Cancer Statistics 2018, 2020; Herbst et al., 2018). Therefore there is now a lot of interest in drug delivery systems that can increase therapeutic efficacy, prevent unwanted effects to healthy cells, and serve as imaging tools. The management of lung cancer involves surgical resection, chemotherapy, immunotherapy, radiation, and targeted therapy (Fig. 1.1). Novel nanomedical drug delivery systems based on the nanoscale have been developed as a result of advances in material science, giving hope to lung cancer patients. Lung cancer is primarily classified into two types: Nonsmall cell lung carcinoma (NSCLC) and small cell lung carcinoma (SCLC). NSCLCs are further classified as squamous cell carcinoma (SCC), adenocarcinoma (ADC), and large cell carcinoma (LCC) (Mukherjee et al., 2019; Semenova et al., 2015). The stage of the cancer depends on the patient's physical state, which determines the selection of treatment for lung cancer. Chemotherapy or chemoradiotherapy is commonly used to treat all stages of SCLC (Pikor et al., 2013; Sharma et al., 2022). But chemotherapy has similar cancer relapse rates to radiation therapy and has poor specificity, drug-induced adverse effects, and drug resistance. Additionally, the FDA has approved cancer immunotherapy, which can be useful even for late-stage diagnoses. Immunotherapies are limited by the host's immune system, inflammatory responses against healthy tissues, and immune-related adverse events (Doroudian et al., 2023). One of the primary challenges in lung cancer treatment is late detection, as early-stage disease has minimal or nonspecific symptoms. Main clinical manifestations identified by persistent cough, chest pain, shortness of breath, weight loss, and hemoptysis. Diagnostic approaches such as imaging techniques,

Nanoengineered Therapeutics for Lung Cancer: Advanced Drug Delivery Strategies.
DOI: https://doi.org/10.1016/B978-0-443-44585-9.00013-5

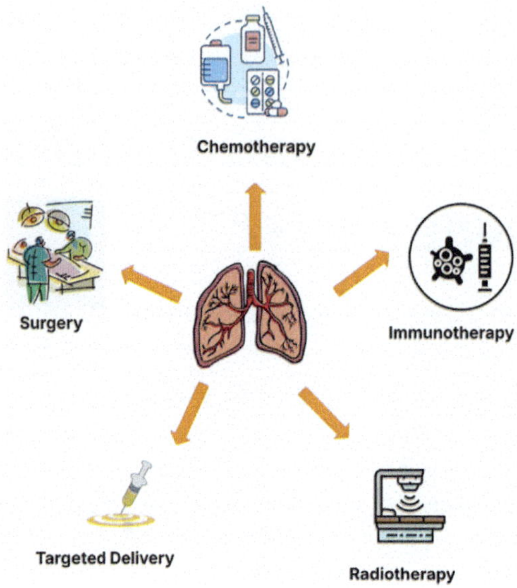

Figure 1.1: Contemporary approaches for treatment of lung cancer.
The illustrated figure represents several approaches that currently being used in the treatment of lung cancer

including computed tomography (CT) scans, along with histopathological examination and molecular profiling, have crucial roles in the diagnosis of cancer and offering treatment strategies (Mukherjee et al., 2019; Semenova et al., 2015).

Nanomedical drug delivery has a significant effect in the treatment of lung cancer and diagnosis (Xu et al., 2023). Importantly, the nanomedicines use the improved permeability and retention effect to increase drug concentration precisely at the tumor site, which can lower systemic toxicity and boost drug bioavailability (Min et al., 2015). Liposomes, polymers, organic nanoparticles, biomimetic nanoparticles, and other nanocarriers have all been developed nowadays to streamline drug delivery. These nanoplatforms make sure that antitumor drugs are targeted both passively and actively (surface functionalization with targeting ligand) to improve the therapeutic impact (Ahmad et al., 2015; Akhter et al., 2015). Moreover, nanocarriers enable the administration and targeted delivery of a wide variety of therapeutics, including drugs, genes, and other biologics, to the cancerous site.

Moreover, nanocarrier drugs facilitate the administration and targeted delivery of a wide range of therapies, containing drugs, genes, and other biologics, to the cancerous cells (Yadav et al., 2021). The pulmonary route of administration has achieved significant interest for nanocarrier-based lung cancer therapy. Lungs have a large absorptive surface area and good blood supply, which makes them an attractive target for nanoparticle-mediated drug delivery. Nanoparticle-based RNA interference strategy has emerged as a promising approach, allowing for the selective silencing of oncogenes and multidrug resistance-related genes, hence overcoming the limitations of conventional chemotherapy (Kim et al., 2015). The nanocarrier is employed to prevent drug degradation, prolong drug effect, enhance solubility, effectively drug targeting, overcome absorption barriers, and increase drug bioavailability, hence allowing for a reduction in dosage and associated side effects. Drug specificity is increased, and drug toxicity is reduced when a nanocarrier is conjugated with a targeting ligand to deliver the therapies to cancer cells or organelles rather than the general population (Alhajj et al., 2018).

Nebulizers and dry powder inhalers are typical inhalation devices used to deliver therapeutic nanomedical carriers deeper into the lung areas. Nebulizers produce liquid aerosols by using either compressed air or an ultrasonic device to break down the liquid dose form into tiny droplets for inhalation. An inhalable dry powder aerosol is produced by the user's airflow passing through a powdered drug in a dry powder inhaler. The dry powder inhalation is a choice of delivery for pulmonary drug administration, which has been promoted since the solid drug has a good physicochemical quality (Traini & Buttini, 2013).

However, the submicron size limits the distribution of nanocarriers via dry powder inhalation. Deep and peripheral lung drug deposition for cancer treatment will be limited because a significant portion of the nanocarrier will be exhaled following inhalation. The nanocarrier's high specific surface area and inter-particle forces make it aggressive. The powder becomes extremely difficult to handle, and the produced aggregates have a reduced capacity to re-distribute and release the nanocarrier. The aerocarrier has been converted into nanoagglomerates, nanocomposites, nanocarrier-loaded microparticles, and lyo-philized floccules with a mass median aerodynamic diameter of 1–5 μm to allow for dry nanopowder inhalation. But the size-dependent biological performances of nanotherapeutics may be affected by poor nanocarrier redispersibility and modifications to its nanoscale carried out by further processing. A significant amount of stabilizer is used in the case of lyophilized floccules. To regulate the nanoagglomeration and redispersibility of nanocarriers, several surfactants are used. Pulmonary inflammation could result from the ultimate effort (Lee et al., 2025; Traini & Buttini, 2013).

This chapter provides an overview of the latest developments in inhaled nanomedicine, along with various inhalation devices for lung clearance processes and drug delivery methods. Additionally, an overview of patent literature has been added to provide more information about the latest and most creative approaches to lung cancer treatment based on a nanomedical drug delivery system.

1.2 Nanomedical drug delivery system: Formulations

Nanomedical drug delivery systems provide the potential for treatment and are quite simple to develop by adjusting their structure, geometry, materials, and surface chemistry. Nanosystems appear to be an appealing answer to various cancer types presently, including both SCLC and NSCLC. Additionally, they can be developed using the genetic profiles of tumors, which leads to a more efficient drug selection for individualized patient care (Ahmad et al., 2015). Nanosystems are so attractive therapies because of a number of their properties. Size: By engineering deformability, it is possible to create perfectly sized nanosystems that are both large enough to prevent buildup in the liver and small enough to fit through the spleen's sinusoids. As a result, it may be possible to acquire a prolonged circulation of the medication. Some nanomaterials have the ability to react to both internal and external stimuli. Although the pH of tumor tissue, late endosomes, and lysosomes is lower than that of healthy tissues, some chemical connections that are fragile in acidic environments may break. Additional stimuli of interest include ultrasonic, light, magnetic fields, etc. (Alhajj et al., 2018; Kim et al., 2015; Traini & Buttini, 2013; Yadav et al., 2021).

The various nanomaterial carrier systems employed in lung cancer therapy, including polymeric nanoparticles, liposomes, dendrimers, inorganic nanoparticles, and nanoemulsions, are schematically illustrated in Fig. 1.2. These nanocarriers can encapsulate chemotherapeutic agents, nucleic acids, protein molecules, and immunotherapeutic molecules, and thereby protecting them from degradation and improve their stability in systemic circulation.

1.2.1 Polymer-based nanoparticles

Polymeric nanoparticles are commonly prepared to improve the drug delivery systems by improving the accuracy of drug administration by packing them with different bioactive compounds. The two types of polymers are synthetic polymers like poly-lactic acid (PLA), poly-lactic acid-co-glycolic acid (PLGA), poly-caprolactone (PCL), and poly-ethylene glycol (PEG), and natural polymers like proteins and polysaccharides. The improved biocompatibility and degradability properties of polymeric nanoparticles possess more potential applications in the treatment of lung cancer (Stone et al., 2007).

The use of polymeric nanoparticles encapsulation helps drug particles to diffuse more readily inside the mucus of the airways by reducing their adherence to the mucus network. With low-energy emulsification, Fornaguera et al. (2015) created polymeric nanoparticles loaded with dexamethasone for use in lung disease inhalation treatment. The biocompatibility and biodegradability of PLGA led to its selection. As a nontoxic and nonhemolytic surfactant, polysorbate 80 was used to stabilize the nanoemulsion. With the help of the low-energy emulsification method, the produced polymeric nanoparticles have a particle size of around 130 nm, which makes them suitable for delivery via the inhalation route.

Using an emulsification solvent evaporation process, Ziaei et al. (2022) produced porous PLGA microspheres loaded with celecoxib and docetaxel, a combination that is less harmful and more effective in treating various lung cancers. The rosiglitazone particles made by

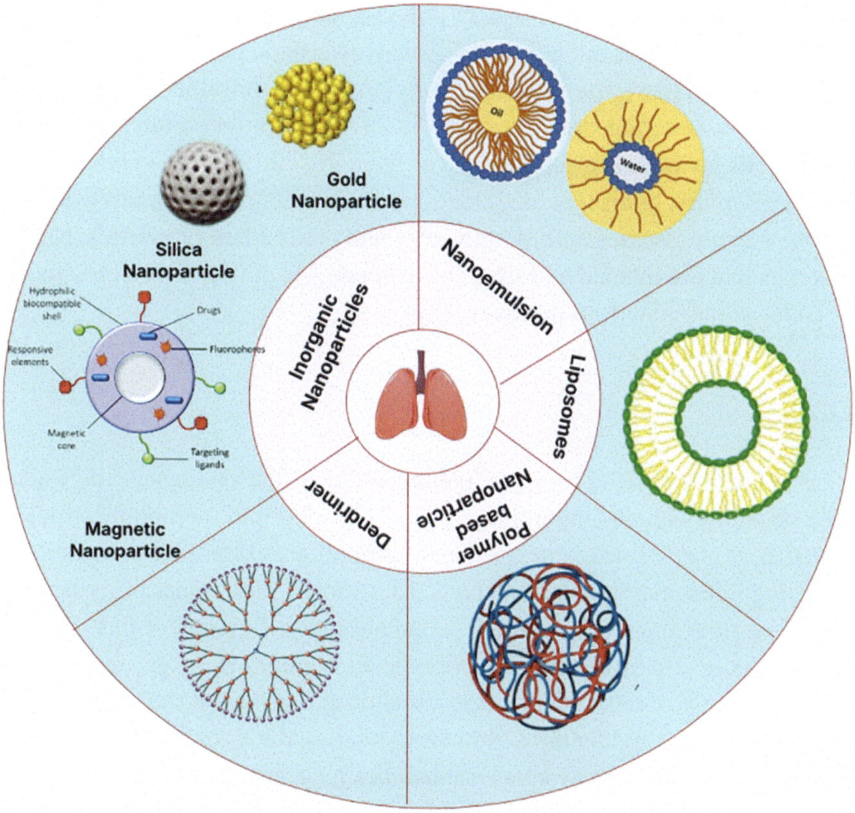

Figure 1.2: Nanomaterials carrier system.
Schematic representation of various nanomaterial carrier in the treatment of lung cancer.

Rashid et al. (2018) were based on PLGA and were designed to be spherical and microporous. They had a 24-h release rate of 87.9% ± 6.7%. Additionally, upon pulmonary injection, the rosiglitazone-loaded PLGA particles' elimination half-life was 2.5 times longer than that of the conventional formulation. The cationic polymer chitosan has a strong affinity for mucin because of electrostatic interactions. When voriconazole was encapsulated in chitosan-coated PLGA nanoparticles, it showed improved pulmonary pharmacokinetics when injected into a mouse model. As a result of the formulation, the amount of time required to attain the maximum amount of time required to attain the maximum of uncoated voriconazole particles is between 1 and 24 h (Rashid et al., 2018; Rasul et al., 2020). Bandi et al. (2005) had prepared PLGA microparticles loaded with budesonide and successfully sustained budesonide release in vitro for over 21 days. This suggests that budesonide-loaded PLGA microparticles may prevent lung tumor development and angiogenesis by reducing VEGF expression and restoring oxidative stress (Bandi et al., 2005). Furthermore, in a mouse lung tumor model, the drug levels (intratracheal injection) were greater in the lungs and bronchoalveolar lavage (BAL).

Yoo et al. (2013) developed novel antioxidant polymer nanoparticles made of a biodegradable polymeric material to treat inflammatory airway disorders, polyoxalate (HPOX) and hydroxybenzyl alcohol (HBA), used as precursor compounds. Intrathecal administration of HPOX nanoparticles was demonstrated to result in a significant reduction in the recruitment of inflammatory cells, as well as a suppression of inducible nitric oxide synthase production, strong antioxidant activity, hydrolytic degradation of this precursor drug in vivo, and the release of HBA, which possesses antiinflammatory and antioxidant properties. Numerous antiinfective drugs that are inhaled and made of nanoparticle polymers are effective in addressing the pathways of infectious diseases (Paul et al., 2018).

1.2.2 Liposomes

Liposomes are frequently utilized for drug loading and distribution because they are a kind of vesicle-like structure with an amphiphilic bilayer phospholipid membrane structure (Satta et al., 2022). It is possible to encapsulate hydrophilic and lipophilic drugs in phospholipid bilayers using liposomal delivery methods. Liposomes' biocompatibility is due to having substances that resemble lung surfactants or cell membranes. Because of this, liposomes are less harmful, may more effectively load hydrophilic and lipophilic drugs, and may develop deep deposits in the lungs. Consequently, liposomal drug-carrying systems have significant uses in respiratory research and therapy. Numerous studies were conducted on the respiratory system's liposomal drug-carrying systems. Liposomes have been utilized to deliver immunosuppressants, peptides, antisense oligonucleotides, hormones, bronchodilators, antibiotics, and anticancer drugs (LoPresti et al., 2022). Despite having superior drug encapsulation and biocompatibility, liposomes are frequently quickly eliminated by hepatocytes or macrophages when they enter the body because of the mononuclear phagocytosis system's (MPS) scavenging action (Weber et al., 2014). Liposomes are able to enhance the stability, therapeutic index, and effectiveness of the loaded drug at the target site. Additionally, it minimizes the toxicity and exposure of the loaded drug to delicate tissue. The biofunctionalized liposomes improve the effectiveness of loaded drugs in opposing lung cancer treatment through active targeting. Researchers' studies have shown that irinotecan and veliparib-loaded nanoliposomal intravenous formulations exhibit combinational synergy for PARP and topoisomerase-1 inhibition, along with improved efficacy. The limitations of liposomes include lower solubility, a shorter half-life, drug leakage from encapsulation, oxidation and hydrolysis, and increased production costs. The liposomes' advantages and limitations depend on the way liposomes interact with cells and what happens to them in vivo after injection. In 1995 the U.S FDA authorized the first liposomes, named Doxil. The use of PEGylated nanoliposomes helped to avoid RES and prolong the duration of medication circulation (Sarma et al., 2024).

The two main types of lipid matrix nanoparticles that may be effectively loaded with hydrophilic and lipophilic drugs while maintaining liposome biocompatibility are solid lipid nanoparticles (SLNs) and nanostructured lipid carriers (NLCs). SLNs have significant advantages over liposomes in terms of easier scalability and quicker manufacturing rates. However, SLNs have a limited ability to leak and encapsulate drugs effectively (Jiang et al., 2021). NLCs are improved SLNs that successfully get over the previously noted limitations. At room temperature, NLC formulations are altered by substituting liquid lipids with solid lipids while preserving their physical characteristics. More drugs were encapsulated, and storage leakage was reduced with the improved NLC formulation (Garbuzenko et al., 2019; Sakellari et al., 2021).

1.2.3 Dendrimers

Dendrimers are synthetic nanomolecules characterized by a spherical shape and a star-like topology. Their structure is hollow and amphiphilic, with many layers covering their basic core structure to symbolize each generation. A wide range of issues with drug administration, including low solubility, can be resolved by incorporating a variety of medications into the existing cavities. Dendrimers are now used to deliver chemotherapy drugs (Arora et al., 2022).

The distinctive characteristics of dendrimers are their homogeneous globular shape, excessive branching of the core, multivalent nature, and distinct molecular weight. They are on the list of fascinating novel drug delivery scaffolds because of these encouraging characteristics (Gillies & Frechet, 2005). They are a common and versatile nanocarrier system for the targeted administration of chemotherapeutics because of their propensity to accurately alter or modify their size, shape, and surface properties (ud Din et al., 2017).

Dendrimers consist of three components, i.e., the central core, surface, and branches stacked together. Dendrimers are highly branched, spherical macromolecules characterized by a well-defined structure and multifunctional properties, making them a promising candidate as an aerosol-inhaled for targeted cancer drug delivery (Xiong et al., 2018). These versatile nanocarriers can be engineered to encapsulate and deliver a variety of anticancer agents, including chemotherapeutics, genes, and photosensitizers, while also providing enhanced solubility, stability, and tumor-targeting abilities (Sharma et al., 2017). The two main categories of commercially available dendrimers on the basis of size and functional group are poly[propyleneimine] (PPI) and poly[amidoamine] (PAMAM) (Chen et al., 2016a). The PPI is discovered to be proffered for the efficient and successful delivery of peptides, such as chemotherapy drugs, to designated locations (Qin et al., 2011). The PAMAM dendrimers are nonimmunogenic, biocompatible, and hydrophilic particles. They promote their use as a drug delivery method since they can increase the bioavailability of chemical entities while lowering the frequency of administration (Palmerston Mende et al., 2017). An investigation was carried out to create a nanodrug delivery system of doxorubicin coupled to generation-4 succinamic acid (G4SA) PAMAM dendrimers and assess them using a three-dimensional in vitro lung cancer model. The dendrimer-based doxorubicin formulation was shown to have a threefold higher penetration rate and a 3.1-fold higher rate of drug aggregation in the innermost core area of cocultured spheroids when compared to free doxorubicin. PPI dendrimers are crucial for assessment in biological applications as they may also be integrated with the drug moiety using a variety of methods (Gorain et al., 2018). Rai et al. (2024) used Fucose as functionalize to produce generation 4 PAMAM dendrimers in order to improve medicine targeting to cancer cells, increase the water solubility of CRY, and overcome dendrimer toxicity. Chrysin Fucose PAMAM (CRY-FUC-PAMAM) showed reduced cancer cell colonies (Rai et al., 2024).

1.2.4 Nanoemulsions

Nanoemulsions are basically colloidal dispersions that are useful for drug delivery systems for compounds with limited water solubility that are made up of safe-grade excipients (Ganta et al., 2014; McClements, 2012). The excellent stability and solubility of this dosage form are due to the heterogeneous dispersion of a nanoscale droplet in another liquid (Gi et al., 1992). The encapsulation prolongs the drug's half-life in the plasma and protects it from deterioration (Maeda et al., 2000). Emulsifying agents stabilize the system by dispersing the droplets in an aqueous phase. Because they are made up of polar heads that often form in polar liquids and hydrophobic bicarbonate tails that tend to form in nonpolar liquids, emulsifying agents are compounds with an amphiphilic profile that lower the interfacial tension between two immiscible phases (Sánchez-López et al., 2019). Since nanoemulsions possess characteristics essential to provide an effective therapeutic effect—such as a wide surface area, superficial charge, enhanced half-life of circulation, specific targeting, and the formulation's imaging capacity—research on cancer therapy has shifted its focus to these vehicles. Nanoemulsions may readily accumulate in vascularized tissues, which surround cancer cells, and their size gives them an edge when it comes to overcoming obstacles (Arruebo et al., 2009; Tadros et al., 2004; Tiwari et al., 2006). The curcuminoids in *Curcuma longa* extract and the formulated nanoemulsion demonstrated high stability. Both the extract and nanoemulsion effectively induced apoptosis in A549 and H460 cells, potentially through mitochondria- and death receptor-mediated pathways. The treatments led to G2/M cell cycle arrest, with differing inhibition mechanisms. Additionally, caspase activation, cytochrome C expression, and CDK1 downregulation followed a dose-dependent pattern, whereas cyclin B expression exhibited cell-specific variations. These findings highlight the potential of curcuminoid-based formulations in targeted cancer therapies (Chang & Chen, 2015). Furthermore, Arbain et al. (2018) prepared a palm-based nanoemulsion for aerosol delivery of the poorly water-soluble drug quercetin. The optimized formulation, comprising palm oil ester: ricinoleic acid (1:1), lecithin, Tween 80, glycerol, and water, was developed using both low and high-energy emulsification methods. Characterization results indicated a stable nanoemulsion and suggested its potential suitability for lung cancer treatment via aerosol delivery (Arbain et al., 2018). The formulated docetaxel and curcumin-loaded nanoemulsion demonstrated nanosized, homogeneously dispersed properties with optimal pH, osmolality, and viscosity for pulmonary application. The system exhibited sustained drug release, excellent stability under extreme conditions, and effective lung deposition with an aerodynamic size below 5 μm. Notably, the combined drug formulation enhanced cytotoxicity against A549 lung cancer cells while reducing toxicity in normal lung cells (MRC-5) compared to single-drug formulations, highlighting its potential as a targeted and safer therapeutic strategy for lung cancer treatment. Kim and Park (2017) formulate hyaluronic acid-complexed paclitaxel nanoemulsions (HPNs) using high-pressure homogenization for targeted treatment of NSCLC. The incorporation of HA enabled specific binding to CD44-overexpressing cancer cells, enhancing tumor-targeting efficiency. HPN treatment significantly inhibited tumor growth, demonstrating its potential as an effective and targeted therapeutic strategy for lung cancer (Kim & Park, 2017).

1.2.5 Inorganic nanoparticles

Since inorganic nanoparticles have distinct magnetic, optical, and electrical characteristics and naturally high specific surface areas, they are utilized in the creation of drug delivery systems more often than organic nanoparticles. Through drug adsorption and penetration, they can minimize off-target negative effects while greatly increasing therapeutic effectiveness through tailored ligands (Min et al., 2023; Sarma et al., 2024). The use of inorganic nanoparticles is relatively new, emerging in the late 20th century, with their biomedical applications developing more recently. Inorganic NPs consist of two main components, i.e., a core material, which contains metals such as gold, quantum dots, or iron oxide, and a shell made of organic polymers or metals. The shell serves to protect the core from chemical interactions or acts as a substrate for conjugation with biomolecules (Chen et al., 2016b).

1.2.5.1 Gold nanoparticles

Gold nanoparticles (GNPs) are optoelectric, have mild antimicrobial activity, and are tailored drug delivery vehicles with a size range from 5 to 400 nm and have different shapes. Their ability to combat germs is contingent upon the microbial cells producing more reactive oxygen species (ROS). Additional biomedical uses for GNPs include diagnostic tools and photodynamic immunotherapy for the treatment of cancer. When exposed to laser light, electrons become excited, which causes GNPs to exhibit photothermal activity (Sarma et al., 2024).

GNPs have emerged as promising candidates for cancer-targeting multimodal drug delivery systems and tumor imaging due to their unique electrical and optical properties, ease of synthesis, and low toxicity (Kim & Jon, 2012; Yezhelyev et al., 2009). Their surface chemistry allows for easy functionalization with ligands for targeted therapy. While GNPs are generally nontoxic to certain human cell lines and have shown potential biodegradability in vivo, ultrasmall GNPs demonstrate uniform tumor distribution due to their ability to diffuse through tissues, though their cellular uptake remains limited. These findings highlight the potential of GNPs in cancer nanomedical drug delivery while underscoring the need for further optimization to enhance cellular uptake and therapeutic efficacy (Patra et al., 2010; Connor et al., 2005). One of the most attractive aspects of GNPs is the versatility with which they may be produced. GNPs' capacity to alter the surface makes them useful for both active and passive targeting. GNPs have found widespread usage as cancer theranostics due to their superior biocompatibility, multifunctional therapeutic properties, and simplicity of synthesis and functionalization (Abadeer & Murphy, 2021; Bhowmik et al., 2017). The delayed or diminished therapeutic efficacy of methotrexate (MTX) in cancer patients is caused by its typically low tumor retention ability.

Chen et al. (2007) developed an MTX–GNP conjugate that demonstrated enhanced cytotoxic and antitumor effects both in vitro and in vivo. The conjugate facilitated faster and higher accumulation of MTX in tumor cells compared to free MTX, resulting in greater cytotoxicity across multiple tumor cell lines. This enhanced efficacy is likely due to the "concentrated effect" of MTX–GNP, highlighting its potential as an improved therapeutic strategy for targeted cancer treatment (Chen et al., 2007). In an investigation, Doxorubicin-GNPs (Dox-GNPs) complexes were prepared. The study demonstrates the potential of Dox-GNP nanocomplexes stabilized with Resveratrol as an effective therapeutic approach for human cervical cancer. The strong accumulation of these nanocomplexes inside cancer cells suggests their ability to enhance cytotoxic effects even at low and safe doses. Furthermore, the combination of Dox-GNPs with X-ray irradiation presents a promising strategy to improve cancer treatment outcomes. These encouraging results pave the way for further investigations into the cellular response to nanogold complexes under varying doses and prolonged exposure, aiming to optimize their therapeutic efficacy (Tomoaia et al., 2015).

Thambiraj et al. (2019) successfully developed a GNPs-based nanocarrier for targeted drug delivery. The synthesized AuNPs exhibited well-defined optical, structural, and morphological properties, confirmed through various spectroscopic and imaging techniques. The nanoconjugates demonstrated significant anticancer activity against H520 lung cancer cells. The results highlight the potential of GNPs-based nanocarriers as a promising alternative for enhancing the efficacy of chemotherapeutic agents in cancer treatment (Thambiraj et al., 2019).

1.2.5.2 Magnetic nanoparticles

A potential and adaptable strategy for improving cancer treatments, especially for lung cancer, is the use of magnetic nanoparticles (MNPs). They are especially compatible with biological systems because of their small, manageable sizes, which enable effective circulation, cellular uptake, and tailored delivery of therapeutic substances such as genes or medications that suppress tumors. MNPs can be preferentially targeted to cancer cells that lack biological units, providing both active and passive targeting methods. MNPs' special magnetic characteristics enable external control using magnetic fields, enabling deeper penetration into injured tissues and precise targeting without sacrificing therapeutic efficacy. Because of these qualities, MNPs are positioned as an important instrument in the development of cancer treatment plans

(Fathi Karkan et al., 2016; Goya et al., 2008; Wang et al., 2016). MNPs have been used to successfully detect micro metastases in lung cancer, according to Wang et al. (2012). They conjugated MNPs with the epithelial tumor cell markers Pancytokeratin (pan-CK) and used a magnetic field to effectively separate circulating tumor cells (CTCs) from patient blood. Additionally, MNPs have drawn attention to the artificial magnetic hyperthermia process, which kills malignant cells selectively from a cluster of healthy cells. Yu et al. (2008) demonstrated that the Dox@TCL-SPION system effectively delivered anticancer drug to the tumor with high specificity since the drug was only affixed to MNPs, which internalize the tumors preferentially. MNPs have emerged as a potential drug vehicle for precise tumor targeting in an effort to lower the dosage of administration of chemotherapeutic medications and to lessen adverse effects caused by their nonuniform and nonspecific distribution. The fundamental ideas behind magnetic therapy are frequently the same as those underlying magnetic separation in other systems. By using an external magnetic field (active targeting), a compound of a lethal drug and a biocompatible MNP in the form of ferrofluid frequently targets the particular tumor (Tomoaia et al., 2015).

Yoo et al. (2012) studied and successfully developed stable and lung cancer-targeted superparamagnetic iron oxide nanoparticles (FA–PEG–SPIONs). By conjugating folic acid (FA) with poly(ethylene glycol) (PEG) and then immobilizing the FA–PEG onto aminosilane-coated SPIONs, we enhanced the stability and targeting ability of SPIONs. The inclusion of Cy5.5 allowed for optical imaging, facilitating the evaluation of intracellular uptake in both KB cells and a lung cancer mouse model, confirming the active targeting capability of FA–PEG–SPIONs. This work represents an important step in overcoming the limitations of rapid blood clearance and instability of SPIONs, offering a promising approach for targeted cancer therapy and diagnostic applications (Yoo et al., 2012).

1.2.5.3 Silica nanoparticles

A promising and adaptable class of ceramic nanomaterials, silica nanoparticles (SiNPs) are very useful in cancer treatment. They are very appealing for a variety of biological applications due to their affordability, simplicity of preparation, and biocompatibility. By making it possible to immobilize biological entities such as enzymes, proteins, and DNA, surface functionalization of SiNPs increases their usefulness and makes them perfect for gene transfection, medication delivery, sensing, and cellular imaging (Song et al., 2020). Furthermore, mesoporous silica is becoming a useful platform for the encapsulation and targeted delivery of hydrophobic chemotherapeutic medicines due to its high surface area and porous structure. This skill enhances the accuracy and efficacy of cancer therapies by assisting in overcoming the difficulties related to the erratic distribution and loss of therapeutic efficacy in the bloodstream (Zhang et al., 2010a). Zhang et al. (2010a) developed a novel molecular imaging agent utilizing miRNA-targeting oligonucleotide-functionalized nanoshells, which consist of silver shells and silica cores encapsulating fluorescent Ru(bpy3)2+ complexes. This agent is designed to detect miRNA-486, a potential biomarker for lung cancer, in positive cell lines

(H460 and H1944) with high precision through the fluorescence in situ hybridization (FISH) technique (Zhang et al., 2010a).

Myricetin (Myr) and multidrug resistance protein (MRP-1) siRNA-loaded FA-conjugated mesoporous silica nanoparticles (MSN) were successfully developed by Song et al. (2020) for the targeted therapy of NSCLC. Comparing the FA-modified nanoparticles to nontargeted nanoparticles, the former demonstrated enhanced therapeutic efficacy, prolonged drug release, and considerable cellular uptake. In vitro experiments showed that the FA-conjugated MSN formulation efficiently decreased lung cancer cell lines' cell survival, colony formation, and triggered apoptosis. Additionally, the improved tumor-targeting capability of the FA-conjugated MSN nanoparticles was validated by in vivo tests, which resulted in more efficient tumor growth inhibition with fewer adverse effects. According to these results, FA-conjugated MSN loaded with Myr and MRP-1 siRNA has a lot of potential as a remedial approach for NSCLC (Song et al., 2020).

1.2.5.4 Carbon nanotubes

Carbon nanotubes (CNTs) are lipophilic, hollow structures made of carbon atoms, with diameters varying from 4 to 100 μm, depending on the arrangement of graphene molecules. CNT resembles a singular rolled sheet of graphene, belonging to the fullerene family, which is the third allotrope of carbon. Nanotubes are categorized into two types: (1) single-walled and (22) multiwalled, with exterior diameters of 4–20 and 20–1000 Å, respectively. The first type can be made by rolling a single graphene sheet into a cylinder-like shape, whereas the latter is manufactured by rolling many concentric layers of graphene to create a cylindrical appearance (Luanpitpong et al., 2014; Madani et al., 2011). Due to their enormous potential to develop novel and improved delivery systems, their applications to distribute chemotherapeutic chemicals have been studied throughout the past few decades. But there is serious concern about their detrimental consequences on health. They are a promising drug delivery vehicle because of certain biological and physicochemical characteristics, including hollow monolith formation, improved mechanical efficiency, a higher length-to-diameter ratio, increased surface area, ultra-massive molecular weight, nanoneedle shape, elevated thermal and electrical conductivity, and surface alteration capabilities. Their needle-like characteristics allow them to penetrate the cell by endocytosis through the cellular membrane. A drug could be covalently or noncovalently bound to the surface of CNT or injected into their inner chamber. Many chemotherapeutic agents, such as doxorubicin, cisplatin, and paclitaxel, have been delivered via CNT (Sharma et al., 2022).

1.2.6 Metal oxide nanoparticle

The redox-reactive metal oxides with a size range of less than 200 nm are another choice for nanocarriers for antibiotic-resistant wound healing. An antibacterial, antifungal, and antiviral metal oxide is a porous nanoparticle with a high surface area and stable, tunable characteristics.

1.2.6.1 Zinc oxide nanoparticle

Zinc oxides are photographic catalytic metal oxides (NPs) with a diameter of less than 100 nm, which may absorb and reflect ultraviolet light. They can be rod-, hexagon-, tripod-, spherical, or other shapes. This kind of nature is useful for bio-imaging. When activated by light, zinc nanoparticles exhibit biological activities such as apoptosis. Zinc oxide nanoparticles have antimicrobial, antibacterial, and anticancer properties resulting from their overproduction of ROS. By changing the role of mitochondrial IL8 release, ZnO NPs induce cell death in colon cancer. Moreover, the precise mechanism is detrimental to NSCLC. In recent studies, it was found that zinc–organic frameworks loaded with rapamycin function by blocking the mTOR pathway. Additionally, it increases chemotherapeutic sensitivity (Earla et al., 2012; Vimercati et al., 2020).

1.2.6.2 Iron oxide nanoparticles

Iron oxide NPs are highly reactive and have applications such as targeted drug delivery, biomolecular separation, and magnetic imaging. Magnetite (Fe_3O_4), maghemite (γ-Fe_2O_3), and hematite (α-Fe_2O_3) are the three oxides of iron nanoparticles. Iron oxide nanoparticles regulate the immune response by interacting with immune cells. Iron NPs can be complexed with a carbohydrate or polysaccharide (carboxymaltose) to regulate the release of Fe ions that saturate transferrin. This NP's action mechanism begins with the RES system's absorption, which is followed by macrophages breaking down the polymeric or carbohydrate shell to either expel it by ferroportin-1 or preserve it as ferritin. Additionally, it promotes M1 macrophages to become more proinflammatory (Soetaert et al., 2020). Additionally, researchers found that superparamagnetic iron oxide polymer coated with silica monolayers inhibited the growth of lung cancer cells. Another study found that by producing hypothermia, iron oxide nanoflowers encapsulated in thermosensitive fluorescent liposomes could increase the effectiveness of cytotoxic medications against lung cancer (Iacovita et al., 2020).

1.2.7 Quantum dots

Quantum dots are nanoscale nanomaterials, colloidal electrical and fluorescent nanocrystals having a diameter ranging from 2 to 100 nm with special electronic, physical, and photophysical characteristics. The quantum dots (QDs) have unique characteristics, size, and shape, which can be used for diagnostic purposes. Its disjunctive electrical energy level is what makes it an artificial atom (Sarma et al., 2024). Disjunctive electronic energy levels distinguish manufactured atoms from isolated atoms. The quantum dot is a semiconductor heterostructure that traps electrons and holes, or charge carriers, in a volume roughly equal to the quantum mechanical wavelength of its constituent parts. These characteristics of QDs have led to an increase in interest in biomedical, biosensing, drug delivery, intracellular protein tracking, tissue engineering, and bioterrorism applications. Higher surface area improves targeting efficacy, whereas smaller QDs increase permeability. Researchers found that modified graphene QDs exhibit less systemic toxicity and greater accumulation in the oral squamous carcinoma cell microenvironment under hypoxia (Badıllı et al., 2020). In drug-resistant malignancies, internalization was enhanced by conjugating QDs with an active drug ZnO-based pH-responsive doxorubicin QD coupled with hyaluronic acid exhibits a synergistic effect on tumor development (McBain et al., 2008; Wang et al., 2017).

1.3 Targeting approach

For the development of an effective nanoparticulate system for drug delivery, the interactions between nanomaterials and biological systems must be carefully studied. Three stages must be completed before the nanoparticulate delivery system can reach the tumor. They are mostly consumed by macrophages from the reticuloendothelial system (RES) as they first move throughout the body (Zhang et al., 2021). They then continue to enter the tumor and provide medications. They eventually gather at the tumor site, where they start to have pharmacological effects.

But before nanoparticulate gets to the cancerous cells, they are more likely to engage with the RES's immune cells (neutrophils and macrophages) and deliver the drug selectively into the cell. It is necessary to use these altered innovative delivery formulations in order to lessen cell toxicity. They also contribute to the drug's increased effectiveness and retention period. The therapy of lung cancer benefits greatly from these innovative small-molecule drug delivery systems (Alshammari et al., 2023).

Targeting of nanoparticulate strategies may be broadly divided into (1) active targeting, (2) passive targeting, (3) stimulus-responsive targeting, and (4) receptor-based targeting. Over time, targeting methods have improved to enhance the preferential uptake of nanoparticles into tumor cells (Fig. 1.3).

1.3.1 Active targeting

Active targeting increases the cellular uptake of NPs at tumor sites, which enhances the efficacy of drug delivery (McBain et al., 2008; Wang et al., 2017). The NP can be surface decorated to precisely connect to tumor cell receptors, enabling the aforementioned method. The treatment's efficacy is enhanced, side effects are lessened, the quantity of the medication to be given is lowered, and the amount of drug at the tumor site is raised (Zhang et al., 2021). According to reports, a wide range of chemotherapeutics are made to target overexpressed receptors on the tumor surface in order to deliver to tumor areas employing different tailored nanodrug delivery systems.

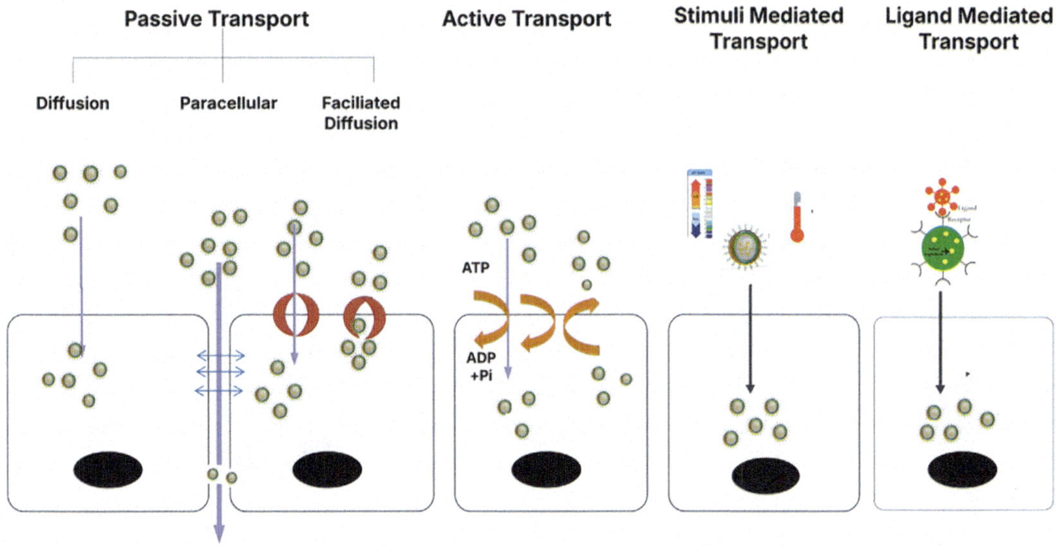

Figure 1.3: Schematic illustration of the nanoparticulate targeting strategies: (1) Active targeting, (2) passive targeting, (3) stimuli-responsive targeting, and (4) receptor-based targeting. These approaches improve the selective uptake of nanoparticles by tumor cells, enhancing the therapeutic efficiency of the drug.

List of clinical research showing the use of nanomedical carriers entrapped in chemotherapy to treat lung cancer.

Arslan et al. (2023) formulated irinotecan and stattic coloaded PLGA nanoparticles targeted to SCLC. The nanoparticles were efficiently conjugated with CD56 antibody, achieving a high conjugation efficiency. The in vitro and in vivo studies demonstrated that coloading and active targeting of irinotecan and stattic significantly enhanced cytotoxicity and anticancer efficacy in vitro. Ex vivo biodistribution studies confirmed the targeted delivery to CD56-expressing SCLC cells, with distribution primarily in tumor tissues and the lungs. The inhibition of the STAT3 pathway was effectively achieved using stattic, both in its free and nanoparticle-loaded forms. Moreover, intravenous administration of the conjugated coloaded nanoparticles reduced side effects and exhibited superior antitumor activity compared to the individual drug treatments in SCLC tumor-bearing mice (Arslan et al., 2023).

Nashaat Alnagar et al. (2024) developed nanoparticles of hyaluronic acid/lactoferrin double-coated PD/PLGA using a layer-by-layer self-assembly technique for the active targeting of CD44 receptors in lung cancer. The formulation demonstrated enhanced cytotoxicity ($IC50 = 0.57 \pm 0.02$ μg/mL) and superior cellular uptake in the A549 lung cancer cell line. A competitive inhibition study further confirmed internalization via CD44 overexpressed receptors. These results highlight the promising potential of targeted therapeutic strategies for lung cancer, laying the groundwork for future clinical applications in targeting CD44 receptors (Nashaat Alnagar et al., 2024).

1.3.2 Passive targeting

In contrast to a normal state, passive targeting techniques increase the rate of infiltration in circulatory vessels within the cancer microenvironment through the enhanced permeation and retention (EPR) effect. In comparison to healthy cells, improving permeability and retention often results in a 20%–30% increase in targeting ability (Padhi & Behera, 2020; Sharma et al., 2022). Based on intrinsic tumor features and the physicochemical properties of nanoparticles, this process causes drug accumulation at the tumor location (Alavi & Hamidi, 2019). The efficacy of drug delivery is influenced by NP characteristics such as size, shape, and surface characteristics through the EPR effect. For nanoparticles to remain in the biological milieu for an extended period of time, they should ideally be between 40 and 400 nm. Generally, tumors grow in unfavorable environments such as hypoxia or inflammation, and rapidly expanding malignant tumors obstruct newly formed blood arteries or vessels that exist in the surrounding environment (Cho et al., 2008; Lombardo et al., 2019). Nanosystems with selectively improved penetration may benefit the tumor stroma, and this improvement in penetration in newly formed vasculature may also lengthen the retention period.

Paclitaxel-loaded pluronic P123/F127 mixed micelles (PF-PTX) demonstrated superior therapeutic efficacy against NSCLC compared to Taxol, as evidenced by enhanced cytotoxicity, increased apoptosis induction, and G2/M phase cell cycle arrest in A-549 cells. The ability of pluronic mixed micelles to modulate multidrug resistance through ATP depletion and mitochondrial dysfunction further contributed to the improved anticancer effects. Additionally, PF-PTX exhibited significantly prolonged circulation time, improved pharmacokinetics, and greater tumor growth inhibition in vivo. These findings suggest that PF-PTX is a promising drug delivery system for overcoming MDR and enhancing the therapeutic potential of PTX in lung cancer treatment (Zhang et al., 2010b).

1.3.3 Stimuli-responsive based targeting

Target based on a stimuli-responsive system may offer efficient and targeted treatments. Intracellular cytosolic levels and extracellular tumor microenvironments, including temperature, pH, ATP, H_2O_2, enzyme, glutathione levels, and hypoxia, vary significantly among tumor cells. One potential method for creating such nanocarrier-inserted medications is to provide different kinds of polymers from the surroundings or to release the drug from polymers upon exposure to stimulation unique to the tumor cell microenvironment (Sarma et al., 2024). pH-responsive systems: Over time, research has investigated the direct release of a medication to the extracellular tumor microenvironment or intracellular cytosol, mitochondria, and nucleus due to the lower pH of the tumor microenvironment (4.5–6.5 pH) and lysosomes (5.5–6.8 pH). To enhance nucleic acid transfection and guarantee stability in the presence of bronchoalveolar lavage media, Liang et al. (2014) employed a pH-responsive peptide and mannitol-based spray-dried powder inhalation method, delivering payloads to tumor regions with lower pH values.

Temperature-responsive systems: Since one of the features of tumorous tissues is hyperthermia, it has been very helpful in cancer treatment to alter the pace at which medication is released to a particular region in a temperature-dependent manner (Sharma et al., 2022). Furthermore, thermoresponsive polymers may be used to alter the surface of nanocrystals. Wu et al. (2016) used thermoresponsive PNIPAM [poly(N-isopropylacrylamide)] brushes grafted with cellulose nanocrystals to encapsulate 5-fluorouracil. It has been demonstrated that PNIPAM increases drug release from the system by a factor of many when the temperature is raised from 25°C to 37–40°C. With stimulus-guided approaches, where the drug is released in response to an outside signal, the thermoresponsive release method can also be applied (Tseng et al., 2008).

Enzyme-responsive systems: Certain enzymes can be used to release medications from enzyme-responsive systems in a selective manner since they are found at the tumor site. A hybrid liposomal system composed of phospholipids and poloxamer 188 that was loaded with doxorubicin and sensitive to the phospholipase A2 (PLA2) enzyme expressed in cancer cells was reported by Tagami et al. (2017). The release of the drug increased eightfold when the PLA2 enzyme was present. For local cancer treatment, pharmaceutical nanocrystals can be encapsulated and transported via the pulmonary route using enzyme-responsive nanocarriers (Tagami et al., 2017).

Ligand-mediated-stimuli responsive system: Drug intracellular targeting in lung cancer cells can be improved with stimuli-responsive system-based drug delivery with pulmonary administered receptor-based targeting. Tseng et al. (2008) developed aerosols based on gelatin nanoparticles that target the epidermal growth factor receptor (EGFR) for mice's pulmonary administration. The chemical substance's intracellular accumulation in lung cancer cells was enhanced by the aerosolized approach. These devices might be used to administer extra therapies, such as drug nanocrystals, via the lungs. Similarly, when the intracellular concentration of small interfering RNA (siRNA) was increased with greater stability by a siRNA-loaded dextran nanogel coated with pulmonary surfactant surface and embellished with folate, the extracellular release of the payload was blocked (Yu et al., 2010).

Redox-responsive systems: In cancer treatment, redox-sensitive systems have a lot of promise and numerous benefits. It has been proven that these stimuli-responsive methods work well for selectively delivering anticancer drugs directly to the cancer cells. It is possible to use the elevated intracellular ROS found in tumors, and more specifically in cancer cells, to deliver pulmonary nanomaterials to cancer cells. In a study, Chen et al. (2017) prepared a liposome-based nanosystem that included cholesterol, soy PC (phosphatidylcholine), and a redox-sensitive cationic oligopeptide lipid with a proton sponge effect for the codelivery of paclitaxel and antisurvival siRNA. The drug and siRNA were quickly released into the cytosol by the produced liposomes via endo-lysosomal leakage, which led to a decrease in survival expression and an increase in apoptosis induction (Chen et al., 2017).

Magnetic field-responsive systems: It has also been reported that therapeutic substances can be delivered to the cytosol or extracellularly localized lung cancers using magnetic fields as an external trigger. Park et al. (2011) developed a magnetite nanocrystal cluster using PEG, polyethylenimine, and dopamine (DOPA) that demonstrated magnetically stimulated intracellular transport of loaded siRNA into cancer cells.

1.3.4 Receptor-mediated stimuli

In cancer, abnormal cellular activities are frequently caused by complex molecular interactions. Understanding the functions of receptors, including the EGFR, folate receptor, transferrin receptor, integrins, mucin-1 (MUC1), CD44, hormone receptors, and programmed death-1 receptor (PD-1), is essential to figuring out the mechanisms underlying the development of cancer (Table 1.1). Immune system evasion, unchecked cell proliferation, and survival can result from dysregulation of these receptors. Emphasizing the significance of understanding these receptors' roles in cancer biology, the next part explores the structural complexities and activities of these receptors. The development of targeted medicines, which have the potential to provide more individualized and efficient cancer treatments, is based on this concept (Sharma et al., 2022).

Drug intracellular localization in lung cancer cells can be enhanced by combining stimuli-responsive system-based drug delivery with pulmonary administered receptor-based targeting.

1.4 Applications of nanomaterials in the treatment of lung cancer

1.4.1 Nanomaterial as targeted drug delivery and chemotherapy enhancement

Nanomaterials have immense potential, with new and innovative applications being explored every day. In recent years, nanomaterials have opened up promising and advanced approaches for lung cancer treatment. To address the limitations of conventional therapy, researchers have employed a variety of nanomaterial carrier molecules that increase active or passive target selectivity and decrease cytotoxicity to the healthy cells. Treatment outcomes for lung cancer are significantly enhanced when the regimen is directed against overexpressed targets.

Nanoparticles offer a bigger surface area that results in significant improved therapeutic payload. In the previous section, we discussed various types of nanomaterials, such as SLNs, liposomes, dendrimers, micelles, magnetic nanoparticles (MNPs), inorganic nanoparticles, QDs, nanoemulsions, and polymeric nanoparticles. These nanomaterials are specially designed to act as biotherapeutic agents and improve drug target delivery (Chen et al., 2016a;

Table 1.1: Receptor targeting in cancer therapy: Key roles and contributions to tumorigenesis.

Receptor	Key role in cancer	Contribution in tumorigenesis	References
Epidermal growth factor response (EGFR)	Promotes cell survival by activating the PI3K/AKT pathway Enhances metastatic potential through epithelial–mesenchymal transition	Activation of the MAPK/ERK pathway leading to uncontrolled cell division Stimulation of the PI3K/AKT pathway promotes cell survival. Prevention of apoptosis through activation of antiapoptotic proteins Enhancement of cell cycle progression through G1/S transition	Lemos-Gonzalez et al. (2007), Martinelli et al. (2020), Licitra et al. (2013)
Folate receptor	Folate conjugates (folate linked to drugs or toxins) can specifically target cancer cells that overexpress FR. Conjugates can deliver therapeutic agents directly to the tumor, minimizing damage to normal tissues.	Enhances angiogenesis, providing a selective advantage in nutrient uptake for distant site survival and metastasis.	Cagle et al. (2013), Vergote et al. (2015), Tie et al. (2020)
Transferrin receptor	Transferrin receptors are responsible for the uptake of iron into cells. Increased iron intake supports the production of reactive oxygen species (ROS) & promote further cell growth, signaling, and tumor progression.	Upregulation is linked to the tumor microenvironment, influencing processes like DNA synthesis and repair.	Daniels et al. (2012), Habashy et al. (2010), Płoszyńska et al. (2012)

(continued on next page)

Table 1.1: Receptor targeting in cancer therapy: Key roles and contributions to tumorigenesis—cont'd

Receptor	Key role in cancer	Contribution in tumorigenesis	References
Integrins	Integrins help cancer cells degrade and remodel the ECM, facilitating their movement through tissues. For example, integrins like $\alpha v\beta 3$ and $\alpha 5\beta 1$ promote the breakdown of ECM components such as collagen and fibronectin, allowing tumor cells to invade surrounding tissues and enter the bloodstream.	Drive angiogenesis by interacting with growth factor receptors, impacting tumor vasculature and angiogenic processes.	Arias-Mejias et al. (2020), Chen et al. (2005), Suyin et al. (2013)

Ganta et al., 2014; Gi et al., 1992; Gorain et al., 2018; McClements, 2012; Palmerston Mende et al., 2017; Qin et al., 2011; Rai et al., 2024). Because it directly influences the drug's penetration and accumulation in the malignant tissue, the quality of the nanocarriers is extremely important for getting the medication to the tumor location. Over the years, many researchers have carried out extensive studies that prove nanoparticles offer significant advantages over conventional treatment approaches, particularly in terms of targeted delivery, improved drug stability, and reduced side effects.

The tumor tissue can be actively or passively targeted by the drug-conjugated nanoparticles. Nanoparticles that use passive targeting persist in tumor tissue, improving permeability while decreasing the clearance of lymphoid tissue. Active targeting precisely increases drug absorption in tumor tissues and decreases toxicity to normal tissues by binding ligands on the surface of nanoparticles to receptors on the tumor surface (Doroudian et al., 2021). The tumor cells burst when the drugs are administered to the tumor tissue, which sets off a chain reaction of immunological reactions. Antigen-presenting cells (APCs) process and display the tumor-associated antigens that are released from the ruptured tumor tissue. T cells then receive these antigens to initiate an immune response (Doroudian et al., 2021).

Nanomaterials have shown remarkable results in the treatment of cancer as an effective vehicle for the safe delivery of drugs to tumor tissues. Preclinical research and a number of clinical trials for drug conjugation with a nanomaterial carrier have produced incredible results. Lung cancer is treated either directly or indirectly by these medications based on nanoparticles (Liu et al., 2023).

1.4.2 Nanomaterials as diagnostic agents

The early detection of cancer greatly increases the survival of the patient, hence drawing the researcher's attention. Tumors may be treated if they are detected early. Consequently, the significant techniques required to detect lung cancer in its early growth phases. The correlation between early diagnosis and a much better survival pattern emphasizes the importance of accurate lung cancer staging for rational treatment regimen selection for optimal anti-cancer efficacy. Standard screening tools such as MRI, sputum cytology, CT scan, bronchial biopsy, polymerase chain reaction (PCR), fluorescence bronchoscopy, and chest radiography (CXR) are frequently used to diagnose cancer and assess the severity of the disease (Singh & Amiji, 2022).

MRI is an imaging technology capable of delivering diverse information regarding the inside structures of the body, encompassing morphological, physiological, and molecular data. Nanomaterials are acting as effective diagnostic agents, boosting imaging contrast, amplifying biosensor signals, and enabling smart monitoring of disease. They are especially advanced in cancer diagnosis; however need to address safety, standardization, and cost. With recent developments in MRI technique, the magnetic nanoparticles have led to new opportunities for specific imaging of cancer cells, which significantly contributed to the oncology field (Carrasco-Esteban et al., 2021; Singh & Amiji, 2022).

Huang et al. (2009) reported conjugated superparamagnetic nanoparticles conjugate with iron oxide, employed for MRI, having extremely sensitive nanoprobes for cancer cellular and molecular imaging. The resultant SPIO particles exhibit good T2 relaxivity and are biocompatible. MR imaging and Prussian blue staining show that the nanoprobes are selective in targeting lung cancer cells that produce $\alpha v\beta 6$. The suggested SPIO system's functional molecule offers a potent nanoplatform for lung cancer molecular diagnostics (Huang et al., 2009).

The most widely used MRI contrast compounds are gadolinium-based contrast agents (GBCAs). When GBCAs are concentrated in T1-weighted MRI images, they mainly lower the T1 in vivo to produce a stronger signal. As water proton relaxation catalysts, GBCAs are distinct from other drugs in their efficacy, as their efficacy is determined by a rate constant called relaxivity. Each GBCA's relaxivity is influenced by a variety of variables that are mentioned in relation to both current and upcoming molecular imaging agents that are being studied by researchers (Hao et al., 2012).

Guo et al. (2010) demonstrate that dendrimer-entrapped gold nanoparticles prepared by using amine-terminated generation 5 poly(amidoamine) give a highly effective platform for CT scan. The controlled complexation of $AuCl_4^-$ ions within G5.NH_2 dendrimers followed by reduction with sodium borohydride enabled the formation of uniformly dispersed Au DENPs with tunable sizes in the 2–4 nm range. The nanoparticles exhibited excellent physicochemical stability under various biological conditions, including different temperatures, pH environments, and physiological media, indicating their suitability for biomedical applications. These nanoparticles are stable, biocompatible, and highly efficient CT contrast agents, offering a promising alternative to traditional iodine-based agents and advancement in the nanoparticle-based diagnostic imaging technologies (Guo et al., 2010).

Ashton et al. (2014) studied the function of gold and iodine nanoparticles in CT scans in mice. Gold nanoparticles were injected to allow tumor accumulation, followed two days later by iodine nanoparticles to provide intravascular contrast. CT scans were performed using the single-contrast method and the dual-contrast dual-energy method. The results were found to be comparable to the single-contrast method and showed strong correlation with ex vivo validation techniques. Overall, this approach provides accurate nanoparticle quantification and represents a promising method for improved functional characterization of lung tumors using CT imaging (Ashton et al., 2014).

1.5 Clinical trial of nanomedical carriers in lung cancer

Nanomedical carriers have shown a significant role in improving lung cancer treatment by enhancing drug delivery specificity and reducing toxicity over chemotherapy and radiation therapy. Various nanocarrier systems have been explored for targeted drug delivery to lung cancer, improving bioavailability and controlling tumor growth. Advanced types of lung cancer usually require a normal course of chemotherapy and radiation therapy together with other innovative therapies, including immunotherapy or customized medications. However, resistance patterns and combination viewpoints make the use of these medicines more difficult. In an effort to forward the advancements in nanomedical carriers, a few patented nanocarriers for lung treatment are summarized in Table 1.2 . The clinical trials have assessed some of these strategies; results are pending or have been completed in different stages of clinical trials.

1.6 Challenges in drug delivery to lungs

Despite advancements in recent decades in the field of molecular biology and clinical characteristics of people with lung cancer, a genuinely successful treatment remains challenging. This is because of the numerous limitations of conventional chemotherapy regimens for lung cancer. Therefore novel, effective, and significant treatment strategies for lung cancer are desperately needed. One of the major challenges involved in the treatment of solid tumors, specifically lung cancer, is identifying a particular molecular target that is missing in healthy cells but uniformly and consistently expressed in malignant tissue. Targeted drug therapy development is made more difficult by the substantial intratumoral and intertumoral genetic variability seen in lung cancers (Carrasco-Esteban et al., 2021).

The main challenge in drug delivery is the anatomy of the lungs, which contain unique defense systems that prevent inhaled nanoparticles from penetrating, among them airway mucus, mucosal cilia clearance, peripheral degradative enzymes, and alveolar macrophages. They cause the aggregation of the nanocarrier, which causes the inhaled drug to be cleared quickly. Furthermore, drug molecules and nanoparticles cannot pass easily through epithelial tight junctions. Second, drug deposition is dependent on anatomical characteristics. Patients with lung cancer have altered lung structures, and this obstruction affects lung airflow and alters the pattern of aerosol deposition, which results in a low rate of drug deposition in lung cancer. Additionally, a number of issues related to the technology that limit the concentration of inhaled drug, including drug administration, storage, and formulation. The stability of drug substances affects the efficacy of inhalation therapy, and the selection of excipients for inhalation therapy restricts drug development and formulation techniques. Each inhalation device has advantages and limitations that need to be improved to improve drug delivery effectiveness (Singh & Amiji, 2022; Xie et al., 2024).

Cancer vaccines have limited success, primarily due to insufficient tumor-antigen expression and inappropriate mutated tumor-antigen content. Inadequate tumor-antigen presentation and mutated tumor-antigen load have also contributed to the poor success of cancer vaccinations.

Table 1.2: List of clinical research showing the use of nanomedical carriers entrapped in chemotherapy to treat lung cancer.

Nanocarrier	Intervention	Trial phase	Identifier no.	Summary	Status
Paclitaxel albumin-stabilized nanoparticle formulation and carboplatin	Drug: carboplatin Drug: paclitaxel albumin-stabilized nanoparticle formulation	II	NCT00729612	In the phase II study, nab-paclitaxel-treated NSCLC patients showed better response rates when tumor-associated stromal caveolin-1 (Cav-1) expression was elevated.	Complete
Docetaxel nanoparticles for injectable suspension	Drug: BIND-014	II	NCT02283320	Utilizing RECIST data, the tumor size change was evaluated relative to the first dose of the study drug, an expected average of 18 weeks.	Complete
Nanoparticle camptothecin with olaparib	Drug: EP0057 Drug: olaparib	II	NCT02769962	Conjugated CPT nanoparticle behavior and the mechanistically described CPT release from NLG207	Recruiting
Prostate-specific membrane antigen-targeted nanoparticles	BIND-014	II	NCT01792479	Number of patients with either a complete or partial response	Complete

(continued on next page)

Table 1.2: List of clinical research showing the use of nanomedical carriers entrapped in chemotherapy to treat lung cancer—cont'd

Nanocarrier	Intervention	Trial phase	Identifier no.	Summary	Status
Albumin-stabilized nanoparticles	Drug: paclitaxel albumin-stabilized nanoparticle formulation	II	NCT00077246	Maximum-tolerated dose (MTD) and dose-limiting toxicity (DLT) of ABI-007	Complete
Nanoparticle Cisplatin+ Gemcitabine	Drug: NC-6004 Drug: Gemcitabine	II	NCT02240238	In the expansion phase of the study will evaluate the activity, safety, and tolerability at the RPII dose.	Complete
Liposome	Drug: LY01610 (Irinotecan hydrochloride liposome injection)	II	NCT04381910	Promising clinical efficacy and manageable safety profiles in patients with relapsed SCLC	Recruiting

The efficacy of vaccines is further reduced by immune evasion strategies and an immunosuppressive tumor microenvironment (Barr et al., 2024; Li et al., 2023).

Another clinical issue is acquired resistance to targeted treatments, including tyrosine kinase inhibitors (TKIs). For instance subsequent mutations or the activation of alternate signaling pathways are mainly involved in resistance mechanisms to EGFR inhibitors. Since many resistance mechanisms have remained unknown, combination strategy development and continuous molecular profiling are necessary (Vicidomini, 2023).

1.7 Conclusion and future prospective

The use of nanoparticle-based delivery techniques has grown and developed significantly over the past decade. As mentioned previously, a nanomedical carrier for lung cancer treatment has demonstrated a significant effect. There is now a wide range of innovative therapeutic formulations being researched, each with unique properties appropriate for various lung cancer therapies. Preclinical or early-stage clinical studies are being conducted on some, while others have already received approval for clinical use. Although nanomedicine is becoming more and more common in adjuvant lung cancer treatments, a number of obstacles prevent it from being widely used. It is still necessary to resolve or improve factors, including toxicity, pharmacokinetics, mass manufacturing, biodistribution, and loading efficiency.

For lung cancer, systemic administration is the primary method of delivery for the clinically approved nanomedicines. Nanomedicines effectiveness has been constrained by nonspecific dispersion and off-target effects brought on by a lack of active targeting. In order to overcome these general obstacles, effective adjuvant therapies have been developed using flexible, focused approaches. Site-specific administration, for instance, can be made easier by surface changes employing compounds that target tumor cell receptors. In addition to significantly lowering systemic toxicity, these tumor-targeting techniques employing nanomedicines offer improved safety profiles for upcoming clinical lung cancer therapies.

Nanomaterials exhibit remarkable therapeutic benefits while simultaneously improving diagnostic platforms that have improved the field of cancer treatment by offering many functions like imaging, hyperthermia, and chemotherapy integrated with a nanoparticle system. By systemically designing nanoparticles with well-planned structures, researchers can optimize their chemical, physical, and optical properties. Such engineered techniques improve targeting ability, stability, and therapeutic performance. It can be concluded that nanotechnology holds a significant and promising approach for advancing cancer diagnosis, monitoring, and treatment in a more precise and efficient manner.

Furthermore, it is essential to investigate the biodistribution and in vivo toxicity of nanoformulations. Finally, the abundance of novel methods and compositions being published in the current patent literature offers promising effects in the treatment of lung cancer. Researchers are putting a lot of effort into creating novel nanotechnology-based combinatorial drug delivery systems that will aid in the treatment of lung cancer.

References

Abadeer, N. S., & Murphy, C. J. (2021). Recent progress in cancer thermal therapy using gold nanoparticles. *Nanomaterials and Neoplasms, 22*, 143–217.

Ahmad, J., Akhter, S., Rizwanullah, M., Amin, S., Rahman, M., Ahmad, M. Z., Rizvi, M. A., Kamal, M. A., & Ahmad, F. J. (2015). Nanotechnology-based inhalation treatments for lung cancer: State of the art. *Nanotechnology, Science and Applications, 16*, 55–66.

Akhter, S., Amin, S., Ahmad, J., Khan, S., Anwar, M., Ahmad, M. Z., Rahman, Z., & Ahmad, F. J. (2015). Nanotechnology to combat multidrug resistance in cancer. In *Resistance to targeted ABC transporters in cancer* (pp. 245–272). Springer. doi:10.1007/978-3-319-09801-2_10.

Alavi, M., & Hamidi, M. (2019). Passive and active targeting in cancer therapy by liposomes and lipid nanoparticles. *Drug Metabolism and Personalized Therapy, 34*(1), 20180032.

Alhajj, N., Chee, C. F., Wong, T. W., Rahman, N. A., Abu Kasim, N. H., & Colombo, P. (2018). Lung cancer: Active therapeutic targeting and inhalational nanoproduct design. *Expert Opinion on Drug Delivery, 15*(12), 1223–1247.

Alshammari, M. K., Almomen, E. Y., Alshahrani, K. F., Altwalah, S. F., Kamal, M., A. l-T. , M. F., Alsanad, S. H., Al-Batti, M. H., FJ, A. l-R., Alsalamah, A. Y., & Alhazza, M. B. (2023). Nano-enabled strategies for the treatment of lung cancer: Potential bottlenecks and future perspectives. *Biomedicines, 11*(2), 473.

Arbain, N. H., Basri, M., Salim, N., Wui, W. T., & Rahman, M. A. (2018). Development and characterization of aerosol nanoemulsion system encapsulating low water soluble quercetin for lung cancer treatment. *Materials Today: Proceedings, 5*, S137–S142.

Arias-Mejias, S. M., Warda, K. Y., Quattrocchi, E., Alonso-Quinones, H., Sominidi-Damodaran, S., & Meves, A. (2020). The role of integrins in melanoma: A review. *International Journal of Dermatology, 59*(5), 525–534.

Arora, V., Abourehab, M. A., Modi, G., & Kesharwani, P. (2022). Dendrimers as prospective nanocarrier for targeted delivery against lung cancer. *European Polymer Journal, 180*, 111635.

Arruebo, M., Valladares, M., & González-Fernández, Á. (2009). Antibody-conjugated nanoparticles for biomedical applications. *Journal of Nanomaterial., 2009*, 1–24. doi:10.1155/2009/439389.

Arslan, F. B., Öztürk, K., Tavukçuoğlu, E., Öztürk, S. C., Esendağlı, G., & Çalış, S. (2023). A novel combination for the treatment of small cell lung cancer: Active targeted irinotecan and static co-loaded PLGA nanoparticles. *International Journal of Pharmaceutics, 632*, 122573.

Ashton, J. R., Clark, D. P., Moding, E. J., Ghaghada, K., Kirsch, D. G., West, J. L., & Badea, C. T. (2014). Dual-energy micro-CT functional imaging of primary lung cancer in mice using gold and iodine nanoparticle contrast agents: A validation study. *PloS One, 9*(2), e88129.

Badıllı, U., Mollarasouli, F., Bakirhan, N. K., Ozkan, Y., & Ozkan, S. A. (2020). Role of quantum dots in pharmaceutical and biomedical analysis, and its application in drug delivery. *TrAC Trends in Analytical Chemistry, 131*, 116013.

Bandi, N., Ayalasomayajula, S. P., Dhanda, D. S., Iwakawa, J., Cheng, P. W., & Kompella, U. B. (2005). Intratracheal budesonide-poly(lactide-co-glycolide) microparticles reduce oxidative stress, VEGF expression, and vascular leakage in a benzo(a)pyrene-fed mouse model. *Journal of Pharmacy and Pharmacology, 57*(7), 851–860. doi:10.1211/0022357056334.

Barr, T., Ma, S., Li, Z., & Yu, J. (2024). Recent advances and remaining challenges in lung cancer therapy. *Chinese Medical Journal, 137*(05), 533–546.

Bhowmik, T., Saha, P. P., Sarkar, A., & Gomes, A. (2017). Evaluation of cytotoxicity of a purified venom protein from Naja kaouthia (NKCT1) using gold nanoparticles for targeted delivery to cancer cell. *Chemico-Biological Interactions, 261*, 35–49.

Cagle, P. T., Zhai, Q. J., Murphy, L., & Low, P. S. (2013). Folate receptor in adenocarcinoma and squamous cell carcinoma of the lung: Potential target for folate-linked therapeutic agents. *Archives of Pathology & Laboratory Medicine, 137*(2), 241–244.

Carrasco-Esteban, E., Domínguez-Rullán, J. A., Barrionuevo-Castillo, P., Pelari-Mici, L., Leaman, O., Sastre-Gallego, S., & López-Campos, F. (2021). Current role of nanoparticles in the treatment of lung cancer. *Journal of Clinical and Translational Research, 7*(2), 140.

Chang, H. B., & Chen, B. H. (2015). Inhibition of lung cancer cells A549 and H460 by curcuminoid extracts and nanoemulsions prepared from Curcuma longa Linnaeus. *International Journal of Nanomedicine, 10*, 5059–5080.

Chen, J., Sun, Y., Chen, Q., Wang, L., Wang, S., Tang, Y., Shi, X., & Wang, H. (2016a). Multifunctional gold nanocomposites designed for targeted CT/MR/optical trimodal imaging of human non-small cell lung cancer cells. *Nanoscale, 8*, 13568–13573.

Chen, S., Hao, X., Liang, X., Zhang, Q., Zhang, C., Zhou, G., Shen, S., Jia, G., & Zhang, J. (2016b). Inorganic nanomaterials as carriers for drug delivery. *Journal of Biomedical Nanotechnology, 12*(1), 1–27.

Chen, X., Sievers, E., Hou, Y., Park, R., Tohme, M., Bart, R., Bremner, R., Bading, J. R., & Conti, P. S. (2005). Integrin $\alpha\beta3$-targeted imaging of lung cancer. *Neoplasia, 7*(3), 271–279.

Chen, X., Zhang, Y., Tang, C., Tian, C., Sun, Q., Su, Z., Xue, L., Yin, Y., Ju, C., & Zhang, C. (2017). Co-delivery of paclitaxel and anti-survivin siRNA via redox-sensitive oligopeptide liposomes for the synergistic treatment of breast cancer and metastasis. *International Journal of Pharmaceutics, 529*(1-2), 102–115.

Chen, Y. H., Tsai, C. Y., Huang, P. Y., Chang, M. Y., Cheng, P. C., Chou, C. H., Chen, D. H., Wang, C. R., Shiau, A. L., & Wu, C. L. (2007). Methotrexate conjugated to gold nanoparticles inhibits tumor growth in a syngeneic lung tumor model. *Molecular Pharmaceutics, 4*(5), 713–722.

Cho, K., Wang, X. U., Nie, S., Chen, Z., & Shin, D. M. (2008). Therapeutic nanoparticles for drug delivery in cancer. *Clinical Cancer Research, 14*(5), 1310–1316.

Connor, E. E., Mwamuka, J., Gole, A., Murphy, C. J., & Wyatt, M. D. (2005). Gold nanoparticles are taken up by human cells but do not cause acute cytotoxicity. *Small, 1*(3), 325–327.

Daniels, T. R., Bernabeu, E., Rodríguez, J. A., Patel, S., Kozman, M., Chiappetta, D. A., Holler, E., Ljubimova, J. Y., Helguera, G., & Penichet, M. L. (2012). The transferrin receptor and the targeted delivery of therapeutic agents against cancer. *Biochimica et Biophysica Acta (BBA)-General Subjects, 1820*(3), 291–317.

Doroudian, M., Azhdari, M. H., Goodarzi, N., O'Sullivan, D., & Donnelly, S. C. (2021). Smart nanotherapeutics and lung cancer. *Pharmaceutics, 13*. doi:10.3390/pharmaceutics13111972.

Doroudian, M., Zanganeh, S., Abbasgholinejad, E., & Donnelly, S. C. (2023). Nanomedicine in lung cancer immunotherapy. *Frontiers in Bioengineering and Biotechnology, 11*, 1144653.

Earla, R., Cholkar, K., Gunda, S., Earla, R. L., & Mitra, A. K. (2012). Bioanalytical method validation of rapamycin in ocular matrix by QTRAP LC–MS/MS: Application to rabbit anterior tissue distribution by topical administration of rapamycin nanomicellar formulation. *Journal of Chromatography B, 908*, 76–86.

Erratum: Global Cancer Statistics 2018. (2020). GLOBOCAN estimates of incidence and mortality worldwide for 36 cancers in 185 countries. *CA – A Cancer Journal for Clinicians., 70*(4), 313.

Fathi Karkan, S., Mohammadhosseini, M., Panahi, Y., Milani, M., Zarghami, N., Akbarzadeh, A., & Davaran, S. (2016). Magnetic nanoparticles in cancer diagnosis and treatment: A review. *Artificial Cells, Nanomedicine, and Biotechnology, 45*(1), 1–5. doi:10.3109/21691401.2016.1153483.

Fornaguera, C., Llinas, M., Solans, C., & Caldero, G. (2015). Design and in vitro evaluation of biocompatible dexamethasone-loaded nanoparticle dispersions, obtained from nano-emulsions, for inhalatory therapy. *Colloids Surface B: Biointerfaces, 125*, 58–64. doi:10.1016/j.colsurfb.2014.11.006.

Ganta, S., Talekar, M., Singh, A., Coleman, T. P., & Amiji, M. M. (2014). Nanoemulsions in translational research—opportunities and challenges in targeted cancer therapy. *AAPS PharmSciTech, 15*, 694–708. doi:10.1208/s12249-014-0088-9.

Garbuzenko, O. B., Kuzmov, A., Taratula, O., Pine, S. R., & Minko, T. (2019). Strategy to enhance lung cancer treatment by five essential elements: Inhalation delivery, nanotechnology, tumor-receptor targeting, chemo- and gene therapy. *Theranostics, 9*(26), 8362–8376. doi:10.7150/thno.39816.

Gi, H. J., Chen, S. N., Hwang, J. S., Tien, C., & Kuo, M. T. (1992). Studies of formation and interface of oil-water microemulsion. *Chinese Journal of Physics, 30*, 665–678.

Gillies, E. R., & Frechet, J. M. (2005). Dendrimers and dendritic polymers in drug delivery. *Drug Discovery Today, 10*, 35–43.

Gorain, B., Choudhury, H., Pandey, M., Amin, M. C. I. M., Singh, B., Gupta, U., & Kesharwani, P. (2018). Dendrimers as effective carriers for the treatment of brain tumor. In *Nanotechnology-based targeted drug delivery systems for brain tumors* (p. 267–305). Academic Press. doi:10.1016/B978-0-12-812218-1.00010-5.

Goya, G. F., Grazu, V., & Ibarra, M. R. (2008). Magnetic nanoparticles for cancer therapy. *Current Nanoscience, 4*(1), 1–6.

Guo, R., Wang, H., Peng, C., Shen, M., Pan, M., Cao, X., Zhang, G., & Shi, X. (2010). X-ray attenuation property of dendrimer-entrapped gold nanoparticles. *The Journal of Physical Chemistry C, 114*(1), 50–56.

Habashy, H. O., Powe, D. G., Staka, C. M., Rakha, E. A., Ball, G., Green, A. R., Aleskandarany, M., Paish, E. C., Douglas Macmillan, R., Nicholson, R. I., & Ellis, I. O. (2010). Transferrin receptor (CD71) is a marker of poor prognosis in breast cancer and can predict response to tamoxifen. *Breast Cancer Research and Treatment, 119*, 283–293.

Hao, D., Ai, T., Goerner, F., Hu, X., Runge, V. M., & Tweedle, M. (2012). MRI contrast agents: Basic chemistry and safety. *Journal of Magnetic Resonance Imaging, 36*(5), 1060–1071.

Herbst, R. S., Morgensztern, D., & Boshoff, C. (2018). The biology and management of nonsmall cell lung cancer. *Nature, 553*(7689), 446–454.

Huang, G., Zhang, C., Li, S., Khemtong, C., Yang, S. G., Tian, R., Minna, J. D., Brown, K. C., & Gao, J. (2009). A novel strategy for surface modification of superparamagnetic iron oxide nanoparticles for lung cancer imaging. *Journal of Materials Chemistry, 19*(35), 6367–6372.

Iacovita, C., Fizeşan, I., Pop, A., Scorus, L., Dudric, R., Stiufiuc, G., Vedeanu, N., Tetean, R., Loghin, F., Stiufiuc, R., & Lucaciu, C. M. (2020). In vitro intracellular hyperthermia of iron oxide magnetic nanoparticles, synthesized at high temperature by a polyol process. *Pharmaceutics, 12*(5), 424.

Jiang, Z., Ma, Y., Guo, X., Remón, J., Tsang, D. C. W., Hu, C., & Shi, B. (2021). Sustainable production of lignin micro-/nano-particles (LMNPs) from biomass: Influence of the type of biomass on their self-assembly capability and physicochemical properties. *Journal of Hazardous Materials, 403*, 123701. doi:10.1016/j.jhazmat.2020.123701.

Kim, D., & Jon, S. (2012). Gold nanoparticles in image-guided cancer therapy. *Inorganica Chimica Acta, 393*, 154–164.

Kim, J. E., & Park, Y. J. (2017). Improved antitumor efficacy of hyaluronic acid-complexed paclitaxel nanoemulsions in treating non-small cell lung cancer. *Biomolecules & Therapeutics, 25*(4), 411.

Kim, Y. D., Park, T. E., Singh, B., Maharjan, S., Choi, Y. J., Choung, P. H., Arote, R. B., & Cho, C. S. (2015). Nanoparticle-mediated delivery of siRNA for effective lung cancer therapy. *Nanomedicine, 10*(7), 1165–1188.

Lee, H., Sajid, K., & Lee, J. (2025). Engineered nanocarriers for targeted lung cancer therapy: Mechanistic innovations and recent clinical progress. *Exploration of Targeted Anti-tumor Therapy, 6*, 1002339.

Lemos-Gonzalez, Y., Rodriguez-Berrocal, F. J., Cordero, O. J., Gomez, C., & Páez De La Cadena, M. (2007). Alteration of the serum levels of the epidermal growth factor receptor and its ligands in patients with non-small cell lung cancer and head and neck carcinoma. *British Journal of Cancer, 96*(10), 1569–1578.

Li, Y., Yan, B., & He, S. (2023). Advances and challenges in the treatment of lung cancer. *Biomedicine & Pharmacotherapy, 169*, 115891.

Liang, W., Kwok, P. C., Chow, M. Y., Tang, P., Mason, A. J., Chan, H. K., & Lam, J. K. (2014). Formulation of pH responsive peptides as inhalable dry powders for pulmonary delivery of nucleic acids. *European Journal of Pharmaceutics and Biopharmaceutics, 86*(1), 64–73.

Licitra, L., Störkel, S., Kerr, K. M., Van Cutsem, E., Pirker, R., Hirsch, F. R., Vermorken, J. B., von Heydebreck, A., Esser, R., Celik, I., & Ciardiello, F. (2013). Predictive value of epidermal growth factor receptor expression for first-line chemotherapy plus cetuximab in patients with head and neck and colorectal cancer: Analysis of data from the EXTREME and CRYSTAL studies. *European Journal of Cancer, 49*(6), 1161–1168.

Liu, Y., Cheng, W., Xin, H., Liu, R., Wang, Q., Cai, W., Peng, X., Yang, F., & Xin, H. (2023). Nanoparticles advanced from preclinical studies to clinical trials for lung cancer therapy. *Cancer Nanotechnology, 14*(1), 28.

Lombardo, D., Kiselev, M. A., & Caccamo, M. T. (2019). Smart nanoparticles for drug delivery application: Development of versatile nanocarrier platforms in biotechnology and nanomedicine. *Journal of Nanomaterials, 2019*(1), 3702518.

LoPresti, S. T., Arral, M. L., Chaudhary, N., & Whitehead, K. A. (2022). The replacement of helper lipids with charged alternatives in lipid nanoparticles facilitates targeted mRNA delivery to the spleen and lungs. *Journal of Controlled Release, 345*, 819–831. doi:10.1016/j.jconrel.2022.03.046.

Luanpitpong, S., Wang, L., & Rojanasakul, Y. (2014). The effects of carbon nanotubes on lung and dermal cellular behaviors. *Nanomedicine, 9*(6), 895–912.

Madani, S. Y., Naderi, N., Dissanayake, O., Tan, A., & Seifalian, A. M. (2011). A new era of cancer treatment: Carbon nanotubes as drug delivery tools. *International Journal of Nanomedicine, 6*, 2963–2979.

Maeda, H., Wu, J., Sawa, T., Matsumura, Y., & Hori, K. (2000). Tumor vascular permeability and the EPR effect in macromolecular therapeutics: A review. *Journal of Controlled Release., 65*, 271–284. doi:10.1016/S0168-3659(99)00248-5.

Martinelli, E., Ciardiello, D., Martini, G., Troiani, T., Cardone, C., Vitiello, P. P., Normanno, N., Rachiglio, A. M., Maiello, E., Latiano, T., & De, V. F. (2020). Implementing anti-epidermal growth factor receptor (EGFR) therapy in metastatic colorectal cancer: Challenges and future perspectives. *Annals of Oncology, 31*(1), 30–40.

McBain, S. C., Yiu, H. H., & Dobson, J. (2008). Magnetic nanoparticles for gene and drug delivery. *International Journal of Nanomedicine, 3*(2), 169–180.

McClements, D. J. (2012). Nanoemulsions versus microemulsions: Terminology, differences, and similarities. *Soft Matter, 6*, 1719–1729. doi:10.1039/C2SM06903B.

Min, S. H., Lei, W., Jun, C. J., Yan, Z. S., Guang, Y. X., Tong, Z., Yong, Z. P., Hui, L. Z., & Xing, H. (2023). Design strategy and research progress of multifunctional nanoparticles in lung cancer therapy. *Expert Opinion on Investigational Drugs, 32*(8), 723–739.

Min, Y., Caster, J. M., Eblan, M. J., & Wang, A. Z. (2015). Clinical translation of nanomedicine. *Chemical Reviews., 115*(19), 11147–11190.

Mukherjee, A., Paul, M., & Mukherjee, S. (2019). Recent progress in the theranostics application of nanomedicine in lung cancer. *Cancers, 11*(5), 597.

Nashaat Alnagar, A., Motawea, A., Elamin, K. M., & Abu Hashim, I. I. (2024). Hyaluronic acid/lactoferrin–coated polydatin/PLGA nanoparticles for active targeting of CD44 receptors in lung cancer. *Pharmaceutical Development and Technology, 29*(9), 1016–1032.

Padhi, S., & Behera, A. (2020). Nanotechnology based targeting strategies for the delivery of camptothecin. *Sustainable Agriculture Reviews 44*, 243–272. doi:10.1007/978-3-030-41842-7_7.

Palmerston Mende, L., Pan, J., & Torchilin, V. P. (2017). Dendrimers as nanocarriers for nucleic acid and drug delivery in cancer therapy. *Molecules, 22*, 1401.

Park, J. W., Bae, K. H., Kim, C., & Park, T. G. (2011). Clustered magnetite nanocrystals cross-linked with PEI for efficient siRNA delivery. *Biomacromolecules, 12*(2), 457–465.

Patra, C. R., Bhattacharya, R., Mukhopadhyay, D., & Mukherjee, P. (2010). Fabrication of gold nanoparticles for targeted therapy in pancreatic cancer. *Advanced Drug Delivery Reviews, 62*(3), 346–361.

Paul, P., Sengupta, S., Mukherjee, B., Shaw, T. K., Gaonkar, R. H., & Debnath, M. C. (2018). Chitosan-coated nanoparticles enhanced lung pharmacokinetic profile of voriconazole upon pulmonary delivery in mice. *Nanomedicine (Lond), 13*(5), 501–520. doi:10.2217/nnm-2017-0291.

Pikor, L. A., Ramnarine, V. R., Lam, S., & Lam, W. L. (2013). Genetic alterations defining NSCLC subtypes and their therapeutic implications. *Lung Cancer, 82*, 179–189.

Płoszyńska, A., Ruckemann-Dziurdzińska, K., Jóźwik, A., Mikosik, A., Lisowska, K., Balcerska, A., & Witkowski, J. M. (2012). Cytometric evaluation of transferrin receptor 1 (CD71) in childhood acute lymphoblastic leukemia. *Folia Histochemica et Cytobiologica, 50*(2), 304–311.

Qin, W., Yang, K., Tang, H., Tan, L., Xie, Q., Ma, M., Zhang, Y., & Yao, S. (2011). Improved GFP gene transfection mediated by polyamidoamine dendrimer-functionalized multi-walled carbon nanotubes with high biocompatibility. *Colloids and Surfaces B., 84*, 206–213.

Rai, D. B., Solanki, R., Patel, S., Pooja, D., & Kulhari, H. (2024). Designing of fucosylated dendrimers as a biocompatible carrier for the targeted delivery of chrysin to human lung cancer cells. *Next Materials, 5*, 100257.

Rashid, J., Alobaida, A., Al-Hilal, T. A., Hammouda, S., McMurtry, I. V., Nozik-Grayck, E., Stenmark, K. R., & Ahsan, F. (2018). Repurposing rosiglitazone, a PPAR-gamma agonist and oral antidiabetic, as an inhaled formulation, for the treatment of PAH. *Journal of Controlled Release, 280*, 113–123.

Rasul, R. M., Tamilarasi Muniandy, M., Zakaria, Z., Shah, K., Chee, C. F., Dabbagh, A., Rahman, N. A., & Wong, T. W. (2020). A review on chitosan and its development as pulmonary particulate anti-infective and anti-cancer drug carriers. *Carbohydrate Polymers, 250*, 116800.

Sakellari, G. I., Zafeiri, I., Batchelor, H., & Spyropoulos, F. (2021). Formulation design, production and characterisation of solid lipid nanoparticles (SLN) and nanostructured lipid carriers (NLC) for the encapsulation of a model hydrophobic active. *Food Hydrocolloids for Health, 2021*, 1.

Sánchez-López, E., Guerra, M., Dias-Ferreira, J., Lopez-Machado, A., Ettcheto, M., Cano, A., Espina, M., Camins, A., Garcia, M. L., & Souto, E. B. (2019). Current applications of nanoemulsions in cancer therapeutics. *Nanomaterials, 9*(6), 821.

Sarma, K., Akther, M. H., Ahmad, I., Afzal, O., Altamimi, A. S., Alossaimi, M. A., Jaremko, M., Emwas, A. H., & Gautam, P. (2024). Adjuvant novel nanocarrier-based targeted therapy for lung cancer. *Molecules, 29*(5), 1076.

Satta, S., Shahabipour, F., Gao, W., Lentz, S. R., Perlman, S., Ashammakhi, N., & Hsiai, T. (2022). Engineering viral genomics and nano-liposomes in microfluidic platforms for patient-specific analysis of SARS-CoV-2 variants. *Theranostics, 12*(10), 4779–4790. doi:10.7150/thno.72339.

Semenova, E. A., Nagel, R., & Berns, A. (2015). Origins, genetic landscape, and emerging therapies of small cell lung cancer. *Genes Development, 29*(14), 1447–1462.

Sharma, A., Shambhwani, D., Pandey, S., Singh, J., Lalhlenmawia, H., Kumarasamy, M., Singh, S. K., Chellappan, D. K., Gupta, G., Prasher, P., Dua, K., & Kumar, D. (2022). Advances in lung cancer treatment using nanomedicines. *ACS Omega, 8*(1), 10–41.

Sharma, A. K., Gothwal, A., Kesharwani, P., Alsaab, H., Iyer, A. K., & Gupta, U. (2017). Dendrimer nanoarchitectures for cancer diagnosis and anticancer drug delivery. *Drug Discovery Today, 22*(2), 314–326.

Singh, A., & Amiji, M. M. (2022). Application of nanotechnology in medical diagnosis and imaging. *Current Opinion in Biotechnology, 74*, 241–2416.

Soetaert, F., Korangath, P., Serantes, D., Fiering, S., & Ivkov, R. (2020). Cancer therapy with iron oxide nanoparticles: Agents of thermal and immune therapies. *Advanced Drug Delivery Reviews, 163*, 65–83.

Song, Y., Zhou, B., Du, X., Wang, Y., Zhang, J., Ai, Y., Xia, Z., & Zhao, G. (2020). Folic acid (FA)-conjugated mesoporous silica nanoparticles combined with MRP-1 siRNA improves the suppressive effects of myricetin on non-small cell lung cancer (NSCLC). *Biomedicine & Pharmacotherapy, 125*, 109561.

Stone, V., Johnston, H., & Clift, M. J. (2007). Air pollution, ultrafine and nanoparticle toxicology: Cellular and molecular interactions. *IEEE Transactions on Nanobioscience, 6*(4), 331–340. doi:10.1109/TNB.2007.909005.

Suyin, P. C., Dickinson, J. L., & Holloway, A. F. (2013). Integrins in prostate cancer invasion and metastasis. *Advances in prostate cancer*. IntechOpen. doi:10.5772/53482.

Tadros, T., Izquierdo, P., Esquena, J., & Solans, C. (2004). Formation and stability of nano-emulsions. *Advances in Colloid and Interface Science., 108–109*, 303–318. doi:10.1016/j.cis.2003.10.023.

Tagami, T., Ando, Y., & Ozeki, T. (2017). Fabrication of liposomal doxorubicin exhibiting ultrasensitivity against phospholipase A2 for efficient pulmonary drug delivery to lung cancers. *International Journal of Pharmaceutics, 517*(1-2), 35–41.

Thambiraj, S., Shruthi, S., Vijayalakshmi, R., & Shankaran, D. R. (2019). Evaluation of cytotoxic activity of docetaxel loaded gold nanoparticles for lung cancer drug delivery. *Cancer Treatment and Research Communications, 21*, 100157.

Tie, Y., Zheng, H., He, Z., Yang, J., Shao, B., Liu, L., Luo, M., Yuan, X., Liu, Y., Zhang, X., & Li, H. (2020). Targeting folate receptor β positive tumor-associated macrophages in lung cancer with a folate-modified liposomal complex. *Signal Transduction and Targeted Therapy, 5*(1), 6.

Tiwari, S., Tan, Y.-M., & Amiji, M. (2006). Preparation and in vitro characterization of multifunctional nanoemulsions for simultaneous MR imaging and targeted drug delivery. *Journal of Biomedical Nanotechnology., 2*, 217–224. doi:10.1166/jbn.2006.038.

Tomoaia, G., Horovitz, O., Mocanu, A., Nita, A., Avram, A., Racz, C. P., Soritau, O., Cenariu, M., & Tomoaia-Cotisel, M. (2015). Effects of doxorubicin mediated by gold nanoparticles and resveratrol in two human cervical tumor cell lines. *Colloids and Surfaces B: Biointerfaces, 135*, 726–734.

Traini, D., & Buttini, F. (2013). *Inhalation drug delivery: Techniques and products*. Wiley-Blackwell.

Tseng, C. L., Wu, S. Y., Wang, W. H., Peng, C. L., Lin, F. H., Lin, C. C., Young, T. H., & Shieh, M. J. (2008). Targeting efficiency and biodistribution of biotinylated-EGF-conjugated gelatin nanoparticles administered via aerosol delivery in nude mice with lung cancer. *Biomaterials, 29*(20), 3014–3022.

ud Din, F., Aman, W., Ullah, I., Qureshi, O. S., Mustapha, O., Shafique, S., & Zeb, A. (2017). Effective use of nanocarriers as drug delivery systems for the treatment of selected tumors. *International Journal of Nanomedicine., 12*, 7291.

Vergote, I. B., Marth, C., & Coleman, R. L. (2015). Role of the folate receptor in ovarian cancer treatment: Evidence, mechanism, and clinical implications. *Cancer and Metastasis Reviews, 34*, 41–52.

Vicidomini, G. (2023). Current challenges and future advances in lung cancer: Genetics, instrumental diagnosis and treatment. *Cancers, 15*(14), 3710.

Vimercati, L., Cavone, D., Caputi, A., De Maria, L., Tria, M., Prato, E., & Ferri, G. M. (2020). Nanoparticles: An experimental study of zinc nanoparticles toxicity on marine crustaceans. General overview on the health implications in humans. *Frontiers in Public Health, 8*, 192.

Wang, F., Li, C., Cheng, J., & Yuan, Z. (2016). Recent advances on inorganic nanoparticle-based cancer therapeutic agents. *International Journal of Environmental Research and Public Health, 13*, 1182. doi:10.3390/ijerph13121182.

Wang, Y., Zhang, Y., Du, Z., Wu, M., & Zhang, G. (2012). Detection of micrometastases in lung cancer with magnetic nanoparticles and quantum dots. *International Journal of Nanomedicine., 7*, 2315–2324.

Wang, Z., Qiao, R., Tang, N., Lu, Z., Wang, H., Zhang, Z., Xue, X., Huang, Z., Zhang, S., Zhang, G., & Li, Y. (2017). Active targeting theranostic iron oxide nanoparticles for MRI and magnetic resonance-guided focused ultrasound ablation of lung cancer. *Biomaterials, 127*, 25–35.

Weber, S., Zimmer, A., & Pardeike, J. (2014). Solid lipid nanoparticles (SLN) and nanostructured lipid carriers (NLC) for pulmonary application: A review of the state of the art. *European Journal of Pharmaceutics and Biopharmaceutics, 86*(1), 7–22. doi:10.1016/j.ejpb.2013.08.013.

Wu, W., Li, J., Liu, W., & Deng, Y. (2016). Temperature-sensitive, fluorescent poly (N-isopropyl-acrylamide)-grafted cellulose nanocrystals for drug release. *BioResources, 11*(3), 7026–7035.

Xie, L., Xie, D., Du, Z., Xue, S., Wang, K., Yu, X., Liu, X., Peng, Q., & Fang, C. (2024). A novel therapeutic outlook: Classification, applications and challenges of inhalable micron/nanoparticle drug delivery systems in lung cancer. *International Journal of Oncology, 64*(4), 38.

Xiong, Z., Shen, M., & Shi, X. (2018). Dendrimer-based strategies for cancer therapy: Recent advances and future perspectives. *Science China Materials, 61*(11), 1387–1403.

Xu, Y., Hsu, J. C., Xu, L., Chen, W., Cai, W., & Wang, K. (2023). Nanomedicine-based adjuvant therapy: A promising solution for lung cancer. *Journal of Nanobiotechnology, 21*(1), 211.

Yadav, K. S., Upadhya, A., & Misra, A. (2021). Targeted drug therapy in nonsmall cell lung cancer: Clinical significance and possible solutions-part II (role of nanocarriers). *Expert Opinion on Drug Delivery, 18*(1), 103–118.

Yezhelyev, M., Yacoub, R., & O 'Regan, R. (2009). Inorganic nanoparticles for predictive oncology of breast cancer. *Nanomedicine, 4*(1), 83–103.

Yoo, D., Guk, K., Kim, H., Khang, G., Wu, D., & Lee, D. (2013). Antioxidant polymeric nanoparticles as novel therapeutics for airway inflammatory diseases. *International Journal of Pharmacy, 450*(1–2), 87–94. doi:10.1016/j.ijpharm.2013.04.028.

Yoo, M. K., Park, I. K., Lim, H. T., Lee, S. J., Jiang, H. L., Kim, Y. K., Choi, Y. J., Cho, M. H., & Cho, C. S. (2012). Folate–PEG–superparamagnetic iron oxide nanoparticles for lung cancer imaging. *Acta Biomaterialia, 8*(8), 3005–3013.

Yu, B. O., Tai, H. C., Xue, W., Lee, L. J., & Lee, R. J. (2010). Receptor-targeted nanocarriers for therapeutic delivery to cancer. *Molecular Membrane Biology, 27*(7), 286–298.

Yu, M. K., Jeong, Y. Y., Park, J., Park, S., Kim, J. W., Min, J. J., Kim, K., & Jon, S. (2008). Drug-loaded superparamagnetic iron oxide nanoparticles for combined cancer imaging and therapy in vivo. *Angewandte Chemie-International Edition in English, 47*(29), 5362.

Zhang, J., Fu, Y., Mei, Y., Jiang, F., & Lakowicz, J. R. (2010a). Fluorescent metal nanoshell probe to detect single miRNA in lung cancer cell. *Analytical Chemistry, 82*(11), 4464–4471.

Zhang, M., Gao, S., Yang, D., Fang, Y., Lin, X., Jin, X., Liu, Y., Liu, X., Su, K., & Shi, K. (2021). Influencing factors and strategies of enhancing nanoparticles into tumors in vivo. *Acta Pharmaceutica Sinica B, 11*(8), 2265–2285.

Zhang, W., Shi, Y., Chen, Y., Yu, S., Hao, J., Luo, J., Sha, X., & Fang, X. (2010b). Enhanced antitumor efficacy by paclitaxel-loaded pluronic P123/F127 mixed micelles against non-small cell lung cancer based on passive tumor targeting and modulation of drug resistance. *European Journal of Pharmaceutics and Biopharmaceutics, 75*(3), 341–353.

Ziaei, E., Emami, J., Rezazadeh, M., & Kazemi, M. (2022). Pulmonary delivery of docetaxel and celecoxib by PLGA porous microparticles for their synergistic effects against lung cancer. *Anticancer Agents Medicinal Chemistry, 22*(5), 951–967. doi:10.2174/1871520621666210811111152.

CHAPTER 2

An Overview of the Anatomy and Physiology of Lung Cancers

Pankaj Popli and Rajan Swami
Chitkara College of Pharmacy, Chitkara University, Rajpura, Punjab, India

2.1 Introduction

One of the toughest global health issues is still lung cancer, causing a large share of yearly cancer deaths (Barta et al., 2019). Even with better scans, genetic analysis, and precise treatments, too many people face grim outcomes. Part of why lies in the diagnosis happening late, often after the spread begins (Nair, 2009). Just as crucial: The illness grows inside an organ built for delicate gas exchange, shaping how tumors take hold. It does not strike without warning. Changes build slowly, hidden within tissue designed for breath. The way cells turn rogue ties directly to where they live (Honish, 2021). A place made for oxygen flow becomes ground for chaos. Progress brings tools, yet survival rates stay low. Early signs are faint. Damage accumulates beneath the surface. What starts small escapes notice until harm runs deep (Tiwari et al., 2026).

Every breath pulls air deep into twisted passages ending in tiny sacs where gases move in and out (Short et al., 2024). These sacks add up to a vast zone for grabbing oxygen while pushing waste gas away. Stretchy threads weave through thin walls and blood vessels, holding shape despite endless inflation and collapse. Outside air flows straight into this fragile system without barriers or filters, slowing it down (Song et al., 2017). Every time you breathe, tiny bits of pollution, cigarette fumes, workplace particles, or germs touch lung tissue right away. Though invisible at first, ongoing contact with these invaders often sparks lasting irritation, unbalanced cell activity, plus slow damage to DNA strands (Khobragade et at., 2024). Damage that keeps coming back in the lung lining sets the stage for cancer. Cells usually fix themselves using careful cycles of growth, change, or self-removal. If genes shift their behavior, chemical tags build up incorrectly, or swelling refuses to fade, balance breaks down (Amann et al., 2011).

Lung cancers differ widely, making their biology harder to pin down. Not alike under the microscope, they split mainly into two kinds: One called NSCLC, the other SCLC. Each acts differently in patients (Larsen & Minna, 2011). Beyond that first split, smaller types emerge,

Nanoengineered Therapeutics for Lung Cancer: Advanced Drug Delivery Strategies.
DOI: https://doi.org/10.1016/B978-0-443-44585-9.00001-9

shaped by where cells come from, what genes drive them, and which part of the breathing tubes they occupy (Popper, 2016). Tumors tend to form in certain zones from the windpipe to the deep lung, likely because the surroundings there support some rogue cells more than others. So, grasping this disease means seeing how molecules interact with structure, place, and living cell networks, not just listing mutations (Macdonald et al., 2013).

What keeps lung cancer complex is not just the rogue cells. Inside tumors, there is constant chatter between cancerous tissue and its neighbors, immune fighters, structural cells, blood vessel linings, plus proteins and signals floating nearby (Vela et al., 2025). When oxygen drops low, metabolism shifts, defenses weaken, and surrounding scaffolding gets reshaped; things move forward in harmful ways. Progress happens not because of isolated mutations alone, but due to broken dialogue across entire cell communities (Paul, 2026).

Because things are so tangled, linking up body structure, organ function, shifts at the molecular level, yet also what surrounds cells matters most (Antar et al., 2023). What lungs normally look like and how they work sets the stage before spotting why diseases take hold and treatments stall or move forward. The point here is showing how lungs are built and run while tying those details to how tumors start and grow. Mixing cell architecture with events driving cancer could sharpen how we see this complex illness, perhaps pointing toward better patient results when science digs deeper.

2.2 Anatomy of the lung

The lung is an extremely specialized organ designed to carry out ventilation and gas exchange effectively. It ensures that oxygen is constantly supplied to the blood while carbon dioxide is removed at the same time, and the structural organization of the lung is represented in Fig. 2.1 (Effros, 2006). Its structural makeup mirrors this main function. The different anatomical components of the lung operate in a very coordinated way, thus forming a kind of integrated system that is optimized for respiratory efficiency (Duncker, 2004). The combination of structural redundancy and the existence of several mechanisms, such as collateral ventilation and adaptable pulmonary blood flow, significantly contributes to the lung's physiological resilience (Meduri & Torres, 2026). This allows the lung to meet the changing metabolic demands and to keep functioning even in the presence of diseases. Right at the heart of this flexibility is a very complex connective tissue network that provides a thin yet strong elastic scaffold (Guo et al., 2022).

2.2.1 External features of the lung

This meshwork accomplishes two things: It supports the lungs' shape, and it also helps in making the lungs flexible enough to be stretched and relaxed over and over again (Suki et al., 2011). Pressed in a firm chest cavity and wrapped in a sealed, pressure-controlled system, the

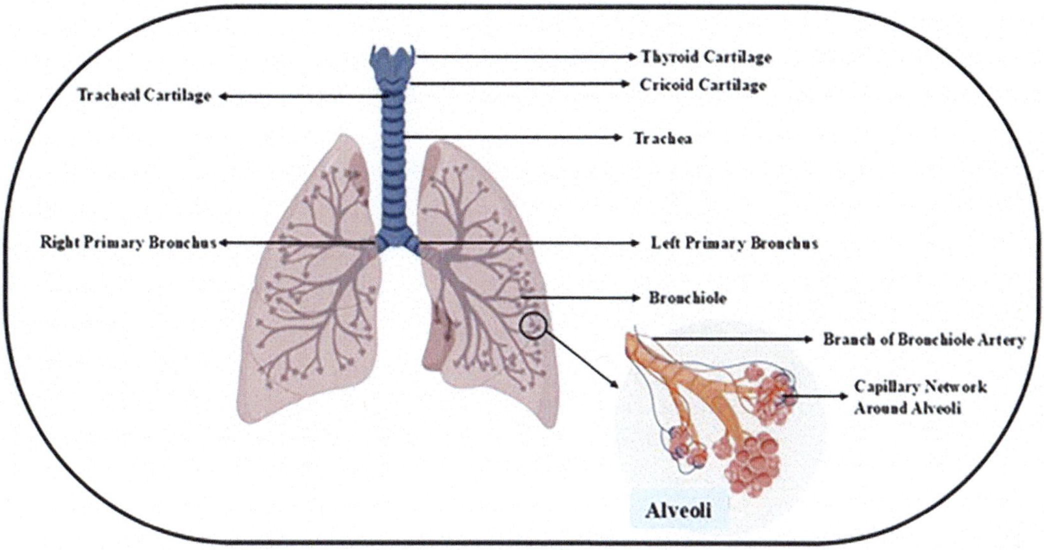

Figure 2.1
Structural organization of the human respiratory system from upper airway to alveoli.

lungs are very similar to a bellows that can expand and contract (Hagberg et al., 2014). Their steady inflation and deflation are caused by the simultaneous contraction of the diaphragm and the intercostal muscles, happening roughly 16 times per minute when at rest (De Troyer & Moxham, 2020).

The paired lungs are enveloped by the visceral pleura, and they occupy the right and left hemithoracic cavities, respectively (Suvarna & Lloyd, 2024). They are separated by the mediastinum, which contains the heart, great vessels, and other central thoracic structures, and is supported inferiorly by the dome-shaped diaphragm (Kurian, 2020). Although lung dimensions vary with respiratory phase, anatomical descriptions usually relate to lung weight rather than size, since volume is very dynamic (Aung et al., 2019). In healthy, adult individuals, each lung typically weighs between 300 and 450 g. A lung weight outside this range usually points to a pathological condition; a heavier lung may be a sign of vascular congestion, interstitial or alveolar edema, or the presence of inflammatory exudates (Bourke, 2020). Combined lung volume in adults when completely inflated has been measured using water displacement techniques to lie between 3.5 and 8.5 L (Thomas, 2015). There is a very slight asymmetry between the two lungs, with the right lung merely having about 53% of the total lung volume; thus, it is slightly larger than the left (Lutfi, 2017). The basic reason for this difference is mainly the heart's spatial accommodation in the left side of the thoracic cavity (Volpe & Makaryus, 2023). Since the lungs are naturally elastic, they will significantly shrink right after the thoracic cavity is opened, even before the chest is closed, and here the volume decreases to only about one-third of the inflated volume (Gibson, 2020). Such an elastic behavior is one of the essentials of normal respiratory mechanics, and it is the basis of both physiological ventilation and pathological changes occurring in a variety of lung diseases. The lung external surface is covered by the visceral pleura, a very thin, smooth serous membrane, giving a shiny surface (Bhana & Magan, 2023).

2.2.2 Bronchi: Branching architecture

Below the aortic arch, the windpipe splits into two large tubes, the right and left main bronchi, at a ridge called the carina (Moya Amorós & Lluveras, 2023). Where this split happens shows where the central air passage ends, and the lung branches begin. These two tubes take different paths. Off to one side, the left bronchus angles away at about 40 to 60 degrees from the centerline (Schittny, 2017). It travels farther than its counterpart, slanting sideways as it moves past the heart's left edge toward the lung's entry point. A sharper angle guides the left airway, but the right one runs nearly straight down, tilted just 20 to 30 degrees from the windpipe (Dünser et al., 2018).

Those big tubes outside the lungs stay stiff thanks to curved cartilage pieces, open at the back, that hold their shape yet let them bend behind (Brems, 2024). When these passageways reach the lung through the central opening, they split into smaller ones, each feeding a separate section inside. From the right, the main airway splits; one branch leads upward, another continues as the bronchus intermedius (Gholap et al., 2025). That lower passage then separates into two, feeding the middle and bottom sections of the lung. Up top, the upper lobe pathway sends off three smaller tubes, each serving its own area: Back, front, and tip (Tomashefski & Farver, 2008). Meanwhile, the middle section's tube breaks into inner and outer paths, handling their assigned zones. Starting low, the right lower lobe bronchus does not stretch far since the superior branch splits away sooner than usual, aiming backward close to where the middle lobe airway begins (Liyew et al., 2024). After that split, it keeps moving downward, eventually giving rise to four separate branches for the base segments.

Starting, the left main airway splits into two major branches, one serving the top part of the lung, the other heading downward (Yetkin et al., 2023). In the upper region, one branch breaks again: One path feeds both the upper, back, and front sections, while another route delivers to the tongue, like an area of the lung (Martano et al., 2022). In the lower region, the lower branch acts much like its counterpart on the right, sending out a stem for the uppermost portion prior to branching toward the bottom zones (Martano et al., 2022).

Branching deep inside, bronchi run close to pulmonary artery forks, bundled together in layers of wrapping tissue. As they split further, the tubes get narrower every time. How many times they divide changes from path to path, some take just five steps, others go as far as 25 before ending at a tiny end, branched tunnels. Usually, you cannot see these passages clearly when getting within about 2 cm of the outer lung lining, since that is where stiff, walled pipes give way to soft, flexible ones (Chen et al., 2025).

2.2.3 Connective tissue, cartilage, and smooth muscle

Kept strong by a mix of tissues working together, the breathing tubes rely on cartilage, fibers, and muscle. Around 16 to 20 stiff bands made of glassy cartilage hold up the windpipe. Curved like a C, each one wraps about two-thirds of the way around. A soft back section stays free at the rear, where the ring does not close. That flexible spot lets the food tube swell when you swallow something. Even then, airflow still moves without blockage through the passage. Over time, those clear cartilage parts can harden into bone-like areas. Stiffness creeps in slowly due to these mineral deposits building up (Chen et al., 2025).

One end of the windpipe shows different shapes compared to the other end. Split into two parts, the top ring connects firmly to the voice box's cricoid piece, linking upper and lower breathing passages through a seamless join. Instead of being round, the last cartilage widens out, forming a triangle at its base where the large tubes leading to each lung begin their split. Stretching between every pair of these stiff rings, also running down the backside of both the windpipe and major air tunnels, sits a flexible sheet made of stretchy fiber bundles mixed with tough strands. With each breath in and out, those springlike tissues help the tube snap back after getting pulled longer (Lawrence et al., 2015). Deep inside the lungs, near where big tubes split off, hard support pieces shift from neat ring shapes into broken plate forms. Moving further inward, those stiff parts get smaller and less common. Instead, soft muscle shows up more often. Around midsize branches, round bands of that flexible tissue take over most of the wall space, controlling how open or tight the passage stays. Some stretchy strands can run along the outside, though only a few show up there.

Deep inside the lungs, air passages get narrower, their smooth muscle thins out, vanishing almost completely by the time it hits the tiniest bronchioles. When diseases like Chronic Obstructive Pulmonary Disease (COPD) take hold, that same muscle sometimes grows abnormally, spreading outward and showing up where it normally would not, close to where alveoli begin (Baker, 2020). Stretchy fibers, built for bounce, back strength, travel straight through bigger tubes but twist into spiral shapes as they move inward. Coils tucked along these pathways connect directly into fragile webs lining the air sacs, helping the whole structure respond as one unit.

2.2.4 Lobes and fissures

The right lung is divided into three separate lobes, upper, middle, and lower, by two main fissures. The oblique (major) fissure runs diagonally and divides the lower lobe from the upper and middle lobes, while the horizontal (minor) fissure separates the upper lobe from the middle lobe. On the other hand, the left lung has only two lobes, upper and lower, separated by one oblique fissure. This difference in the number of lobes is due to the space taken up by the heart in the left chest (Mpolokeng et al., 2022).

One of the distinctive parts of the left upper lobe is the lingula, which is the anterior, inferior part of the lobe that lies over the left ventricle. The lingula is functionally and anatomically equivalent to the right middle lobe (Whiteman et al., 2021). Variations in the anatomy of fissures are very common, and the listing includes: Incomplete, accessory, or supernumerary fissures. On the right side in a lot of people, the anterior part of the horizontal fissure is only partly formed, which can allow collateral airflow between the right upper and middle lobes. Less frequently, the horizontal fissure very well may separate the lingula from the rest of the left upper lobe, thus making a left lung with three lobes, something that is sometimes called a pseudo-right lung. On the other hand, the absence of the horizontal fissure leads to a right lung with only two lobes.

Accessory fissures are quite common and may be detected in a large percentage of the population. These anatomical differences may lead to the partial or complete separation of certain bronchopulmonary segments. In the near vicinity of the most commonly encountered variations are the inferior accessory fissure of the right lower lobe that outlines the medial basal segment (which is commonly called the retrocardiac lobe) and a fissure that isolates the superior segment, sometimes referred to as the dorsal lobe, from the basal segments of the lower lobe. Such variations are more commonly found on the right side (Gesase, 2006).

2.2.5 Submucosal mucoserous gland

Deep inside the trachea and bronchi, tucked beneath the lining, sit unique glands filled with mucus, making and fluid, producing cells. Though different in function, these cells work together, releasing substances that blend into a shield over the airway surface. This mix builds a two-part mucus film, carefully arranged to trap invaders while helping cilia sweep debris out efficiently. Without such a structure, the lungs would struggle to stay clean and free of infection.

Slime in mucus adds thickness and catches particles; meanwhile, watery parts fight microbes. Lysozyme, lactoferrin, alongside immune protein A made nearby in plasma cells, work to slow bacterial growth. Proteins that block enzymes show up too, keeping destructive breakdown in check inside breathing passages, so harm stays low. As years pass, glands shift: Typical fluid, making cells get swapped out by oxyphil types, a change known as oxyphil metaplasia (Katrivesis et al., 2022).

2.2.6 Airway mucosa

The inside coat of the windpipe and air tubes carries on straight from the voice box lining. It is made up of tall cells with tiny waving hairs, mixed here and there with glands that make mucus. Sitting below this layer is a unique base film, giving shape and strength. Seen through a regular microscope, it looks like one even sheet. Yet in truth, that floor beneath the airway cells holds many layers, built from outside materials, about 7 μm thick when measured.

Tiny building blocks like type four collagen, fibronectin, and laminin, paired with nidogen, along with different proteoglycans, form its core structure, each part helping anchor cells, maintain directionality, and manage connections between cells and their surroundings. Seen under high magnification, this layer splits into two zones: One close to the surface, called the basal lamina, considered the real foundation, beneath which lies a denser mesh known as the lamina reticularis. When long-term irritation hits, like in persistent airway swelling seen in asthma, that lower zone grows thicker, stiffens, and reorganizes itself abnormally, a clear sign that something has gone wrong over time. Starting, the bronchial lining includes four main kinds of cells: Ciliated ones, goblet cells, basal cells, and neuroendocrine varieties. These hairs, like ciliated units, drive rhythmic movement, pushing mucus along in sync. Meanwhile, goblet cells produce mucins, pouring them out to build up the barrier gel on the surface. Deep down near the base, certain cells act as reserves, stepping in when tissue needs renewal after damage. Scattered here and there, neuroendocrine cells tune into lung signals, adjusting how airways respond. A delicate film of fluid coats the epithelial lining, working alongside rhythmic cilia motion to power mucus-based cleanup in the airways. Trapped dust, microbes, and pollutants get carried slowly upward, heading toward the voice box, where they can be cleared out. When this transport system runs smoothly, it guards against ongoing damage to lung tissue while keeping harmful invaders at bay. Without steady function here, cleanliness inside the breathing passages quickly breaks down.

2.2.7 Bronchioles

Where cartilage ends, so does the bronchus, its rigid rings fading out as the tube shrinks toward ,1 mm wide. Past that, the narrowing begins in the membranous bronchiole, lacking any skeletal scaffolding in its walls. When this passage reaches its farthest point, it earns the name terminal bronchiole. That spot sits just before airflow steps into the acinus, deep inside the lung tissue. Inside each acinus live breathing real workers: Tiny branches called respiratory bronchioles leading into hollow tunnels and clustered sacs. Those spaces, alveolar ducts, sacs, and countless small alveoli, are where oxygen slips into blood (Haddad & Sharma, 2025). About 30,000 tiny airways branch deep inside the human lung, each feeding a wide web that backs up around 10,000 air sacs. Starting here, these smallest passages have no stiff rings or hidden gland pockets, just cell layers all the way through. Lining them are tall cells with waving ends mixed in among quieter ones, once called Clara cells but now usually named club cells. Instead of rigid parts, their walls rely on shifting sheets made mostly of those beating cells plus scattered mucus, free producers. From down these narrow paths, club-shaped workers pump out shielding substances along with cleaners that break down harmful stuff. Protection comes quietly: Tools released into thin tubes where breath moves slowest. When there is no cartilage to hold them open, tiny air passages depend on nearby lung tissue for stability. From neighboring air sacs, stretchy fibers reach out and attach to the outer coat of these small tubes, pulling them outward so they stay open. That pull matters most when you breathe out, because then the pressure inside the chest goes up. If diseases like emphysema break down those elastic connections, the support weakens, causing early closure of airways and reduced airflow (Verma et al., 2015).

Downstream from the last terminal bronchiole sits the respiratory bronchiole, where tiny air sacs begin sprouting straight out of its sides. Usually, around three levels exist, though sometimes more or fewer show up. Cells with fine hairlike projections run all the way to the spot where bronchioles meet alveoli, gradually shrinking and thinning near the outer edges. Even so, those remaining cilia keep moving mucus steadily thanks to a precise layout tucked beside club-shaped cells. Here lies a shift zone where airflow paths meet gas exchange areas, part of the standard body design. Following birth, tiny air sacs grow in far sections of breathing tubes, adding up through early years. Growth slows around age 10. Airflow shortcuts exist here, too. These tiny passages linking bronchioles to nearby air sacs go by the name of Lambert's canals, offering alternate paths for air movement. When small tubes deep in the lungs get damaged, often after long-term contact with cigarette smoke, their walls grow weaker. Little bulges might form, along with small tears and changes around the tube edges. Such shifts block airflow unevenly, reshaping how air moves through distant lung zones (Tomic et al., 2013).

2.2.8 Alveolar ducts, alveolar sacs, and alveoli

Down the line, farther along the airway, bronchioles slowly give way to tiny air pockets. Where those pockets take over entirely, the tube earns a new name, alveolar duct. Branching off, these channels open into rounded chambers called alveolar sacs, each tucked behind at least four small cavities. Ending here, this setup forms the final stretch where breathing actually happens.

Tiny cup-like pockets make up the far reaches of lung tissue, known as alveoli. Ranging from 150 to 500 μm across, most hover near 250. A person weighing close to 70 kg holds nearly 300 million of these tiny chambers. Spread out, they cover a space of nearly 140 m^2, packed into just 4 or 5 L. Such tight packing reveals how well lungs handle air transfer. Later in life, the small airways deep inside the lungs begin to change shape. Starting around age 40, alveolar ducts tend to slowly widen, while nearby air sacs lose their roundness; this shift has been named alveolar duct ectasia. Some researchers question whether the walls between air spaces are actually breaking down during this process. Because it is hard to separate natural wear from disease, experts now say "aging lung" instead of the older phrase "senile emphysema," which once carried misleading implications (Moussavi, 2006).

Out here, where air finally reaches its destination, tiny pockets open up like hidden chambers. Strong threads of stretchy and tough fibers brace each entrance, carrying forward a web that began much earlier in the breathing tubes. Branching from those anchor points, thinner elastic strands reach out in fine nets, cradling each pocket within loops that tangle gently with blood vessels. On either face of this weave, flat cells just one atom thick hold position, making space so narrow that gases pass through without delay. Later in life, the small airways deep inside the lungs begin to change shape. Starting around age 40, alveolar ducts tend to slowly widen, while nearby air sacs lose their roundness; this shift has been named alveolar duct ectasia. Some researchers question whether the walls between air spaces are actually breaking down during this process. Because it is hard to separate natural wear from disease, experts now say "aging lung" instead of the older phrase "senile emphysema," which once carried misleading implications.

Out here, where air finally reaches its destination, tiny pockets open up like hidden chambers. Strong threads of stretchy and tough fibers brace each entrance, carrying forward a web that began much earlier in the breathing tubes. Branching from those anchor points, thinner elastic strands reach out in fine nets, cradling each pocket within loops that tangle gently with blood vessels. On either face of this weave, flat cells just one atom thick hold position, making space so narrow that gases pass through without delay (Patwa & Shah, 2015).

2.2.9 Bronchus-associated lymphoid tissue

Found in the airway walls, bronchus, and associated lymphoid tissue forms structured clusters beneath the mucosa. These groupings belong to a wider network known as mucosa-associated lymphoidal tissue. Included in that system are features like Peyer's patches and lymphoid areas in the appendix. Functioning at the boundary of lung tissue and the outside world, BALT supports targeted immune monitoring. Protection happens right where airborne threats enter. This setup helps mount rapid responses within the respiratory zone. Clumps of immune tissue show up across different parts of the breathing passages, especially where small airways split off. Found in a specific gut, like the lining, these structures sit near thin cover cells that let outside particles slip through easily. That unique surface allows invaders to pass into the tissue, often drawing in white blood cells ready to respond. The constant cell movement here signals it is deeply involved in defense work. Found mainly in BALT, B cells show markers like IgM, IgG, and especially IgA when tested with special stains. With its secreted form, IgA acts first against invaders, stopping them from sticking to surface layers. Most of the rest among immune cells are T types, more precisely CD4 helpers, making up around 20%. Not many plasma cells appear there, nor do organized hubs where B cells mature often crop up when things are stable. When dust, germs, or outside particles enter the airways, this tissue kicks in by making antibodies right on site (Michael Jaeger et al., 2019).

2.2.10 Thorax: Thoracic cage, inlet, diaphragm, and mediastinum

Built tough yet flexible, the chest protects key organs without limiting breath flow. At its core sits the mediastinum, holding things steady amid motion. Above, an opening called the thoracic inlet connects the upper body systems. The rib cage wraps around like a moving shield, changing shape each time air fills the lungs. Below, the diaphragm forms a dome that shifts with every inhale and exhale. Together, these parts balance strength and motion through countless cycles.

2.2.11 Thoracic cage

The thoracic cage is formed by 12 bones stacked in the back, teaming up with 12 rib pairs and a flat breastbone to build the chest's frame. Here, the collarbone sits forward of the top rib, holding space like a guardrail at the entrance to the chest, keeping big blood pipes safe. Between each backbone piece, you find springy pads made of fiber and rubbery tissue, held tight by tough bands. Alongside the run column, muscles that brace the spine while letting it bend, giving the ribcage room to stretch and snap back again (Sharara et al., 2017). From top to bottom, the breastbone holds three parts: The manubrium, body, and a tiny tip called the xiphoid. Where the upper part meets the main shaft, a slight bend forms, flexible enough to shift slightly when lungs expand. That central section grows from several blocks of bone early in life, later joining into one solid piece. Behind it, the lung lining runs close, sometimes leaving chalky marks if someone breathed in certain dusts. Odd shapes pop up now, and then, kinks where segments meet at odd angles, or a round gap down the center due to bones not fully closing; such spots might look like cracks on scans, fooling the eye into seeing harm.

2.2.12 Thoracic inlet

Overhead inside each half of the chest cavity, blood vessels and nerves pack tightly near a dome-shaped fold of membrane called the pleural cupola. Though tucked just above the upper rim of the rib cage, changes here blur lines between the chest and lower neck zones. Growths starting at the top edge of the lungs, like those known as Pancoast types, or cancers in the lining around the lungs, might spread into adjacent tissues, leading to varied signs. Nestled within this zone lie major pathways: The subclavian artery with its offshoots, the brachiocephalic vein, the phrenic nerve, bundles of sympathetic fibers, along with the lowest part of the arm's main nerve network (Fadel et al., 2002).

2.2.13 Diaphragm

Floating between the chest and belly, the diaphragm forms a curved layer made of muscle and tough tissue. From its center, a flat tendon, fibers stretch outward like spokes, springing from three zones. One set of links is behind the tip of the breastbone. Others grip the inside edges of ribs seven through 12, along with their flexible rib extensions. A third group builds two pillars near the spine, rooted to the lower back bones. These sections fold around the backbone, placing thin segments ahead and beside it. In cases tied to asbestos exposure, abnormal patches can show up exactly there. Through the middle part of the diaphragm slips the inferior vena cava, tucked into the central tendon. Moving alongside, the esophagus threads down between muscle strands from the right crus. Not cutting straight through, the aorta glides behind the diaphragm just under the arching band at the 12th thoracic segment. Openings near the breastbone, called Morgagni spaces, form softer spots where tissue might bulge out. To the back and side, gaps known as Boch dalek foramina also create thin zones prone to hernias (Palleschi et al., 2024).

2.2.14 Mediastinum

Right in the middle of your chest sits a stretchy space filled with soft tissue, which is the mediastinum. Sitting above the rib cage opening, it stretches between both lungs and touches their inner lining. At its front lies the breastbone, while behind, the spine marks its limit. This area does not stay fixed; shifts happen when forces around it change. When fluid builds up or air presses in one lung cavity, the whole pocket gets nudged sideways. On the flip side, if one lung shrinks due to scarring, collapse, or surgery, the gap tightens and drags the center along. Movement depends on what is happening inside nearby spaces. In real-world medical practice, doctors usually split the mediastinum into four parts: Upper, front, center, and back, using the central section, which holds the heart and its lining, as an anchor. Looking at growths in this area becomes easier with that layout: Issues tied to the thymus or thyroid, along with lymphomas, tend to show up higher or toward the front. Growths linked to nerves typically sit behind. Meanwhile, swollen glands or cancer commonly appear on the sides of the middle zone (Brcic & Roden, 2023).

2.2.15 Pulmonary vasculature, lymphatics, and pleural structure

One way to look at it: Lungs get blood from two separate yet linked sources. Not just one path matters here; pulmonary flow handles what comes straight from the right heart chamber. This route operates under light pressure while holding plenty of volume, taking on all the returning used blood without strain. Even when flow shifts suddenly, pressure barely rises, which helps keep breathing gases moving smoothly across membranes. On the other hand, vessels branching off the body's main arterial network bring fresh oxygen-rich fuel directly to the windpipe walls and nearby tissues. These channels push harder, feeding support layers plus lining around the outer lung surface (Brcic & Roden, 2023).

2.2.16 Pulmonary arteries and veins

From the right ventricle, a large vessel begins its path upward; this is the pulmonary trunk. It splits soon after, forming two branches that head off toward each lung. These vessels slip into openings on either side of the lungs known as hila. Once inside those regions, the artery takes a position above and just forward of the vein draining blood from the air sacs (Maki et al., 2022). Compared to arteries like the aorta, these lung-bound tubes are built with less muscle in their walls. Their design suits the gentle push of blood rather than the strong surges found elsewhere. When these blood vessels move deeper into the lung, they split off alongside the airways, following a route known as the axial path. Closer sections of the arteries travel with larger bronchi, reaching as far as the last non, gas, exchanging air passages (Chu et al., 2025). Tinyer divisions inside the acinus stretch further, reaching where oxygen exchange happens. Besides the usual paths, many extra small arteries dive straight into the lung tissue without following any airway. Big lung arteries are stretchy, built with rings of elastic tissue. Going deeper into the lungs, the tubes get smaller and shift in design. Instead of elasticity, these midsize branches rely on muscle layers. Sandwiched between two thin elastic sheets, that muscle wraps tightly around the passage. Downstream blood channels show only bits of muscle layering, while the tiniest arterioles mostly lack it, opening straight into tiny lung capillaries. Usually, those artery segments have delicate linings; yet long-term high pressure in the lungs can thicken their middle zone and alter shape. Vessels carrying blood from the lungs have less muscle compared to their arterial counterparts, built mostly of stretchy fibers instead. Not far downstream, tiny veins look nearly identical to small arteries unless viewed with specific dyes. As they grow wider, these channels travel through partitioning layers between lung segments, angling inward toward the heart's entrance chamber. Under long-term pressure stress, such veins can transform, mimicking arteries by building up more muscle beneath their lining (Zhou et al., 2023).

2.2.17 Bronchial circulation and vascular shunts

Blood for the bronchi, plus nearby lung structures like pulmonary vessels and pleura, comes from bronchial arteries. These vessels sometimes start in odd spots, yet most often branch off the lower part of the aorta or nearby rib, area arteries. As they move into the lung tissue, they follow airways right up to where breathing tubes nearly end. Normally, such arteries stay tiny, hard to spot on scans or images. When long-term inflammation hits the lungs, however, these blood lines can grow much larger than usual (Mohanka & Banga, 2023). A few bronchial veins send blood into the pulmonary veins, which adds a small natural shortcut from right to left. Blood supply might also sneak in through tiny vessels tucked inside the lower lung ligament or spread out within the chest's nerve web. Blood flow connections linking lung and airway vessels form via small bridges called bronchopulmonary anastomoses. When diseases like tumors or long-lasting infections are present, these links tend to grow stronger. Obstructed blood pathways also lead to greater development of those channels. Because of that shift, arteries from the body's main circulation start delivering more blood than usual to the lungs (Ackermann et al., 2024).

2.2.18 Pulmonary lymphatic and lymph nodes

Lying just beneath the surface, a web of vessels wraps around the outer layer of the lung. This outer network carries fluid away from the membrane, hugging the organ. Deeper inside, another set spreads along paths formed by airways and blood vessels. These inner channels lead toward clusters found at the lung's root. Connections exist between both layers, yet each moves liquid in its own direction. Their routes overlap here and there, but mostly keep apart (Egashira et al., 2025). Inside the tiny air sacs of the lungs, there are no lymph pathways at all; those show up instead near airways and blood vessels, plus between lung sections. Instead of round tubes, these drainage channels have flat lining cells, their openings uneven on purpose, so liquid and cells can slip in easily. Usually scrunched shut and nearly invisible in healthy tissue, they puff open when fluid piles up or cancer creeps through them. Their presence only stands out once swelling or disease forces them wide. Draining paths from the lungs lead through areas near the windpipe, below the airway split, close to major bronchi, and inside lung tissue. Groupings like these matter a lot when figuring out how far lung cancer has moved. Nodes within the lung itself tend to be tiny yet sometimes swell up because of immune triggers, collected particles, and ongoing irritation. Dark specks from soot often show up in grown-up nodes, especially if someone smokes. Reactions such as swollen germ centers, busy scavenger cells, and stored debris can look concerning even when harmless (Trivedi & Reed, 2023). Lymphatic spread can be unpredictable because of numerous side pathways linking vessels. Tumor cells usually enter lymphatics after moving through blood vessels and then invading nearby lymph channels. This happens more commonly than backward movement inside the lymph system alone.

2.2.19 Neural innervation

Around the arteries and airways, tiny nerves branch through the lung tissue. Coming from a large neck nerve, some of these slow airflow by tightening passages when they activate glands. Other signals start in the upper spine, traveling to control blood vessel width. Instead of typical chemical messengers, certain nerves use substances like nitric oxide to open breathing tubes wider. These pathways work without relying on the usual nervous system chemicals (Su et al., 2022).

Deep inside the lungs, tiny sensors watch for changes; some spot tightness, others catch irritation or chemical shifts. When stretch detectors fire, they help control breath depth by responding to expansion. Irritant sensors trigger coughs if smoke or dust appears. Nerve endings called C fibers react to fumes, slowing breath without warning. Together, these pathways adjust airflow, protect tissue, and maintain balance, not always noticed, yet are active every second (Yegen et al., 2023).

2.2.20 Pleural cavity and mesothelial structure

Between the two layers of pleura lies a tiny gap where lungs slide smoothly during breathing. This space holds a slick film made mostly of hyaluronic acid that keeps tissues from sticking.

The lungs themselves are wrapped by one kind of pleura, which then folds back at the root area to link with the outer type. That outer layer lines the inside of the rib cage and touches down onto the diaphragm. Movement happens without drag because surfaces glide on fluid rather than rub (Zhang et al., 2025). The pleura lining the lungs shows several coats. Mesothelium sits on top, followed by loose tissue, stretchy fibers, and then tough bands merging into lung tissue below. On the chest wall side, the sheet is sturdier, built with dense fibrous material, often sitting above fatty pockets and strips of muscle beneath. Flat or boxy, mesothelial cells shift form based on how much they are stretched or what they are doing. When you look closely, long finger-like projections cover their surface, catching slippery substances that ease movement while breathing happens. Those tiny outgrowths help spot the difference between certain cancers when doctors examine tissue samples. Water movement in the pleural space depends on push and pull forces from blood pressure and protein concentration. Instead of merging, large molecules exit via tiny lymph channels called stomata located mainly near the bottom ribs. When illness damages these pathways, drainage slows down, and fluid builds up as a result (Karpathiou, Péoc'h, Sundaralingam, Rahman, & Froudarakis, 2022).

2.3 Pulmonary physiology relevant to oncogenesis

2.3.1 Gas exchange, redox biology, and tumor microenvironment

Gas exchange stands as the lung's core job. Inside each tiny air sac, oxygen slips through a delicate wall into nearby blood vessels, whereas carbon dioxide travels back out following its own path. How well this works ties closely to how evenly air reaches those sacs, how smoothly blood flows past them, plus how intact the separating layer remains. When one part of the wobbles, breathing suffers, and at the same time, shifts begin in the lungs' inner chemistry, possibly nudging cancer toward starting or growing (Ji et al., 2023). Tiny air sacs in the lungs usually have lots of oxygen and are constantly changing. Because mitochondria use oxygen to make energy, ATP forms through oxidation. Still, some waste from cell activity becomes reactive oxygen species. When levels stay low, these molecules help control cell growth, death, and defense actions. Yet too much builds up and harms genetic material, enzymes, and fat layers in cells. That damage raises mutation risks, possibly leading to cancer changes. So breathing ties closely to how chemicals gain or lose electrons inside tissues (Viafara Garcia et al., 2023).

Lung tumors often disrupt how gases move in nearby areas. Because cancer cells multiply quickly, they sometimes lack enough blood flow, leading to low oxygen zones (Obeagu, 2025). When oxygen drops, certain proteins called Hypoxia inducible factor (HIFs) stick around longer, turning on genes linked to new blood vessels, sugar, energy use, and cell endurance. Instead of using oxygen efficiently, these tumor regions burn sugar even when air is available, spilling more lactic acid into surrounding tissue. A sour environment shifts how the body's defenses operate, while also pushing cancer cells to spread further and withstand treatment. With every breath, the way gases move ties into signals that drive tumor growth (Sobczyńska-Rak et al., 2025). Though it does not take part in normal lung gas transfer, hydrogen (H) has drawn attention due to how it affects oxidative stress. Its molecules are tiny and lack polarity, so they slip easily through cell barriers. Studies show it can clear out aggressive oxidants, like hydroxyl radicals and peroxynitrite, but leaves key redox signals untouched. Because it lessens DNA harm caused by oxidation and lowers inflammation triggers, it might alter cancer pathways fueled by long-term cellular stress. In lab animals with liver or kidney tumors, using hydrogen led to fewer tumors and quieter immune-related signals, yet exactly which proteins it interacts with is still unclear (Surate Solaligue et al., 2017). Not so simple, the link between ROS and cancer shows many layers. Higher steady levels of ROS appear in tumor cells when compared to healthy ones. Because of this, extra oxidative pressure can hit hard, yet inside that risk runs a signal boost for growth (Silva et al., 2015). So treatments split paths: Cutting ROS may reduce DNA damage plus quiet immune irritation, but pushing oxidation higher might overwhelm malignant cells instead. Even inside cells, protection against oxidative stress comes from antioxidants, some of which are enzymes like superoxide dismutase and catalase; others, such as vitamins C and E, are not (Moldoveanu et al., 2008). Yet results in patients often differ, revealing how reactive oxygen species can both help and harm tumors. Fumes, bugs, or smoke keep the body's defenses active for too long. That ongoing alarm sends chemical signals nonstop. Immune cells pile into tissue, stirring up molecular chaos along the way. Each time cells patch themselves after damage, mistakes creep into their code more easily. Low oxygen joins forces with irritation, quietly opening doors where cancer can start. The setting changes slowly, yet shifts everything (Guillot et al., 2013).

2.3.2 Role of hypoxia in tumor initiation and progression

Low oxygen pockets form in tissue areas where oxygen drops below normal. Within the lungs, such zones appear when cells need more oxygen than the blood supply can provide, especially during long-term swelling, blocked airways, scarred tissue, or initial tumor development. When present, low oxygen does not just sit idle due to weak flow; it drives changes in cell activity that support cancer formation and spread (Foster et al., 2014).

When oxygen drops, a key change happens: HIF proteins like HIF-1 and HIF-2 stop breaking down, as demonstrated in Fig. 2.2. Instead of vanishing fast under normal air levels, these molecules stick around when O gets scarce. Because they build up, gene activity shifts in response. Blood vessel growth kicks in, one result driven by signals including VEGF (Goudar & Vlahovic, 2008). Energy needs shift too; cells grab more glucose, burn it without oxygen, just to keep going. Survival mechanisms turn on, letting some cells hang in there instead of dying off. Over time, only those tough enough to handle starvation, broken DNA, and low

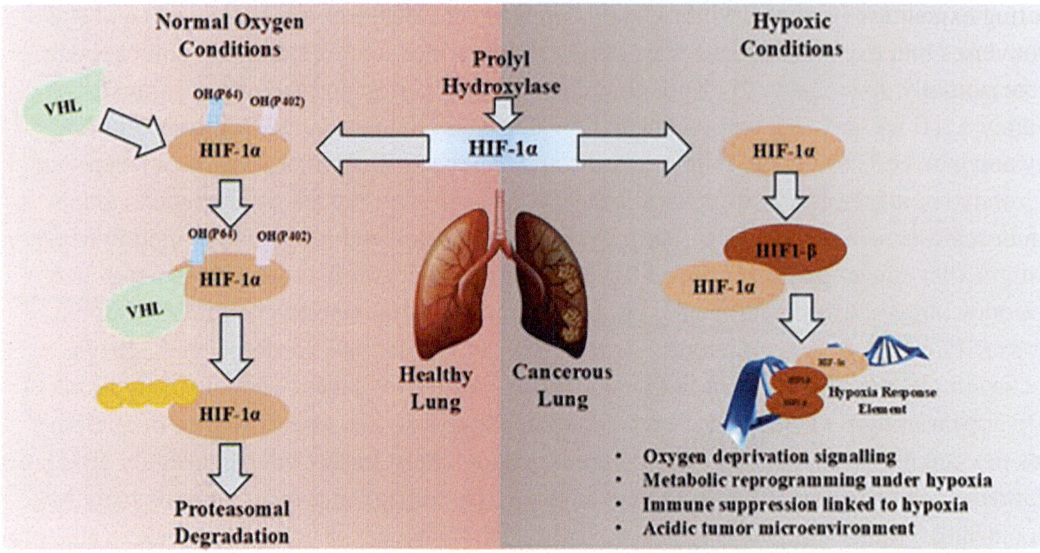

Figure 2.2
Oxygen-dependent regulation of HIF-1α in normal and hypoxic conditions in lung tissue.

fuel make it through. These resilient groups start shaping what comes next, quietly pushing evolution forward under pressure. Low oxygen pushes cells to shift how they process fuel, creating conditions that help tumors grow. Because these cells rely more on sugar breakdown, they release lactate and hydrogen ions, making the space outside more acidic (Jackson et al., 2010). This acidity changes the tissue structure around cells, turns on enzymes that break down barriers, leading to greater spread. The sour environment weakens immune attacks by hampering killer T cells while boosting types that shield tumors, like altered macrophages and control focused T cells. So, limited oxygen ties together energy shifts and the body's reduced ability to fight cancer (Camuzi & de Amorim ÍSS, 2019). It matters that low oxygen levels stir up trouble in cells. When oxygen runs short, copying DNA gets messy, and fixing errors becomes less accurate. Fluctuating between low and normal oxygen spikes harmful molecules, piling on DNA harm (Hsu et al., 2018). Slowly, these conditions open doors for genetic mistakes, reshaped chromosomes, and tougher cell types to take over. Cells under such stress may shift into a roaming state, losing grip on neighbors while moving more freely, easing their escape into nearby tissues (Tirpe et al., 2019). Hypoxic areas matter in therapy since low oxygen weakens radiation's impact; it needs oxygen to lock in DNA breaks. These zones also hinder medicine delivery, thanks to messy, faulty blood vessels inside tumors. When hypoxia switches on survival signals, cancer growth gets a boost alongside a stubborn refusal to respond to care (Herbst et al., 2005).

During exposition of cells to normal oxygen levels, HIF-1α is hydroxylated by prolyl hydroxylases that make it recognizable to the Von Hippel–Lindau (VHL) complex, which then proteasomally degrades HIF-1α. When oxygen is virtually absent, the enzyme hydroxylation is not operating, thus HIF-1α remains stable, and it dimerizes with HIF-1β. The resulting active complex binds to hypoxia response elements (HREs) and the ensuing transcriptional activities induce metabolic reprogramming, immune modulation, and the creation of an acidic tumor microenvironment that promotes lung cancer progression.

2.3.3 Pulmonary immune microenvironment

Breathing brings germs, tiny particles, and dirty air into the lungs every day, which means immunity there must act fast yet stay calm. When damage goes on too long, like from smoke, ongoing infections, or smog, the body's usual control slips, letting swelling grow unchecked. That change turns the lung's inner setting from one that blocks harm to one open to cancer growth (Altorki et al., 2019). Tumors start not just because of broken genes in lung tissue, but due to how nearby immune and support cells react: They might destroy bad cells, hold them back, or fail. Instead of a clean victory, it is a quiet tipping point shaped by context (Tan et al., 2021).

Lung cancers' surroundings mix tumor cells, immune players, CAFs, along with endothelial cells. Communication happens mostly at a distance, through crowds of signals like cytokines, chemokines, not to mention growth molecules shaping neighboring behavior. Macrophages fire up; T cells join in; both pour out substances such as IL-6 and TNF-α (Pullamsetti et al., 2017). Those compounds help tumors survive longer, split faster, while kicking off new blood vessel formation, all looping back into more inflammation. With months passing, steady messaging builds a space where damage piles up, structure shifts constantly, and division prompts never quiet down (Mittal et al., 2016). One key trait of lung cancer's environment is how it dodges immune attacks. Though CD8+ killer T cells can spot tumor markers and destroy abnormal cells if signals work right, the process often fails. Instead, cancers block defense efforts using checkpoint systems that shut down immunity (Tamminga et al., 2020). When PD-1 on T cells meets PD-L1 on tumor or support cells, the T cells wear out, losing killing power and chemical messages. Without pressure from the immune system, flawed cell lines persist, gaining more changes over time, pushing faster toward aggressive disease (Lee & Cheah, 2019).

How the lung's environment reacts to cancer hinges on early immune responses. Instead of fighting tumors, certain white blood cells help them grow. When exposed to chemicals like IL-4 or TGF-β, macrophages near tumors tend to change into a form that shields cancer. These altered cells quiet down immunity, reshape the surrounding tissue, plus boost new blood vessel growth and spread (Rusek et al., 2015). Neutrophils act much the same way, starting off hostile to tumors but switching sides when TGF steps in. Once flipped, they aid deeper infiltration and distant seeding by malignant cells. Tiny helpers around tumors lend a hand in harmful ways. Spilling out substances like TGF, FGF, and signals including CXCL8 and CXCL12, these cells push regular tissue into unstable shifts, spread deeper, form new blood routes, and, on top of pulling in quieting cell types such as Tregs and MDSCs (Genova et al., 2022). Once those calming forces arrive, they hush down CD8+ T cells, weaken how targets are shown to immunity, particularly when molecules like IL-6/STAT3, IL-10, and VEGF block key immune messengers from growing up fully. Blood vessel talks using VEGF do more than feed tumor pipelines; they tighten control on immune freedom, slowing helpful T cells from moving through, favoring the buildup of Tregs and MDSCs instead (Lim et al., 2023).

2.4 Origin and classification of lung cancer

Even now, lung cancer hits hard across the world, standing out as one of the deadliest forms of cancer. Looking at how it appears in tissue and behaves clinically, split it into two main kinds: Nonsmall cell and small cell lung cancer (Rodriguez-Canales et al., 2016). Histology plays a role in this split, yet so do real-world contrasts in where tumors grow, their biological behavior, the genes involved, and how they react to treatment (Osarogiagbon et al., 2023). Years of research have mapped countless molecular shifts behind these diseases, yet one core puzzle lingers for scientists: When harmful mutations build up, which exact healthy lung cells turn into each specific tumor type? Findings from mice altered at the genetic level show clearly that the mix of faulty genes matters just as much as the particular cell and its surroundings where changes take root, together shaping what kind of cancer emerges (Mohanty et al., 2019). Down the branching paths of the airway, location gives a hint. Closer to the center, you often find growths with squamous traits. Farther out, toward the edges, adenocarcinoma-type changes show up more. Where they sit is not random, suggesting each kind might start in a unique layer of lining. These spots differ in surroundings, damage risks, and how they heal. Place shapes what grows (Detterbeck, 2018).

2.4.1 Nonsmall cell lung cancer

Most lung cancer cases fall under NSCLC, which groups a few distinct types based on tissue appearance. Though sorted by shape under the microscope, these forms also match up with separate starting cells and genetic behaviors (Kriegsmann et al., 2020).

2.4.1.1 Adenocarcinoma

Most cases of nonsmall cell lung cancer fall under adenocarcinoma, often found in the outer parts of the lungs. Studies in mice, particularly ones with activated Kras genes, pointed to a spot called the bronchioalveolar duct junction where tumors may first form. Scientists once noticed a small group of cells producing signs of both airway, related club cells (like

CC10/SCGB1A1) and oxygen, exchanging type II alveolar cells (such as SPC). Sitting at this intersection, these dual signaling cells showed traits like low activity during normal states but sprang into division after damage occurred. Under specific lab settings, they even gave rise to different kinds of lung lining cells, leading some to suggest they act as multipotent stem units in that zone (Inamura, 2017; Moreira et al., 2020). Yet trouble followed the BASC idea just as fast. Follow-up work tracking cell lines failed to show that BASCs contribute much to daily upkeep or healing in airway linings, while trust in certain tags, Sca-1 included, wore thin because results shifted with different lab techniques, animal types, or analysis rules. Oddly enough, even without being real stem cells during normal life, BASCs might still catch mutations more easily when cancer triggers strike, particularly in fragile zones such as the BADJ. That gap, being a builder versus becoming a seed, matters deeply when reading what these experiments really mean (Detterbeck, Boffa, Kim, & Tanoue, 2017; Lim et al., 2018).

2.4.1.2 Squamous cell carcinoma

From deeper parts of the airways, squamous cell carcinoma usually arises, often mirroring the traits of tracheobronchial basal cells. These cells carry markers like KRT5 and KRT14, along with p63, especially clustering near spots such as duct openings of submucosal glands or fixed structural edges in air passages. Mouse studies tracking cell origins reveal that basal cells renew themselves, producing inner lining types postinjury, a trait suggesting they may spark SCC if cancer, driving pathways turn on (Kallini et al., 2015). Looking at DNA patterns backs up this idea. When chunks of the genome containing SOX2, tied to how early skin, type cells grow and change, get copied too much, it often comes up in talks about squamous tumors. These clues add up, pointing toward SCC starting if early, stage cells like those pick up key mutations while sitting in just the right nearby environment, yet tight lab proof tracing every step inside single cell types is still needed to confirm it (Almangush et al., 2020).

2.4.1.3 Large cell carcinoma

Something called large cell carcinoma usually gets labeled only after ruling out other types of nonsmall cell lung cancer. Not clearly glandular, like or skin, cell-like, it shows up when the tissue looks too messy under the microscope. Its biology might not follow one path; it is a unique type, other times just a broken version of known cancers. When tracing back where it begins, these tumors do not stick to one starting point. Instead, they hint at what happens when gene errors blur cellular roles (Lantuejoul et al., 2020; Rekhtman et al., 2016).

2.4.1.4 Small cell lung cancer

Lung cancers include a small yet fast-moving type called SCLC, closely tied to nerve-like cell traits. In both people and mice, this cancer tends to show proteins like CGRP and NCAM1, alongside control switches such as ASCL1 that turn on those nerve-related patterns. Out of nowhere, scientists began thinking it might come from uncommon lung cells known as PNECs, which usually sit within structures called NEBs (Rudin et al., 2021). Still, scientists have not pinned down exactly which cells start it. Instead of acting like typical stem cells, those linked to NEB might resemble limited precursor types. Whether small cell lung cancer comes from an even earlier, more flexible cell type in that area is still being argued. On top of that, certain growths display features of both small cell and nonsmall cell cancers, pointing perhaps to shifts as they grow, or sometimes hinting the source cell could be similar or connected when particular mutations are present (Bernhardt & Jalal, 2016).

2.4.1.5 Cell of origin hypothesis

Falling out of specific cells, lung cancer forms when three influences meet. Down near the lungs, branching paths, tiny areas show distinct life patterns. Where breath travels closer to the center differs from the outer zones. Tiny clusters called BADJ sit at key intersections. Nearby, NEBs monitor air quality quietly. At the base, certain cells hold space as anchors do. Each pocket follows its own biological rhythm. Kicking off with stem cells, they hold the starting point before change begins. Moving forward, progenitor types take a step closer to transformation. Not far behind, transit, amplifying cells multiply quickly on their way toward shift. Ending with mature epithelial ones, these carry out duties after full development. What changes show up in genes, oncogenes or tumor suppressors, and the order they appear. Sometimes one shifts before another. Not every shift happens at once. The path differs case by case. Which gene adjusts first can shape what follows. Patterns emerge only when tracking each step. Earlier moves may influence later ones. Sequence matters just as much as the change itself. Where cell renewal runs slowly, such as in lung tissue, cancer might start not just in durable stem cells. Some mature cells can gather mutations too, provided they keep a certain ability to divide or heal, particularly when harm strikes again and again. That is what happens in experiments using irritants to wound the lining: Hidden behaviors emerge, flexibility appears, things unseen during steady, everyday function. Now here is another piece of the puzzle: Inside both NSCLC and SCLC growths, tiny groups of cells sometimes stand out. These cells often carry tags like CD133 in lab tests. They can form little clumps in dishes. When placed into animals, they spark new tumors. On top of that, they tend to resist drugs, partly thanks to busy ABC transporters. Yet it remains unclear if these are real, long-lasting “stem” types inside actual patients. Their connection to the very first cell where cancer started? Still fuzzy. But none of this is just theory, they might be why cancers come back after therapy (Coudray et al., 2018; Megyesfalvi et al., 2023; Oser et al., 2015; Relli, Trerotola, Guerra, & Alberti, 2019).

2.4.1.6 Tumor microenvironment in lung cancer

Cancer in the lungs does not just appear out of nowhere. Inside, a busy world forms, the tumor microenvironment, where rogue cells mix with defenders, support tissue, blood vessel parts, structural scaffolding, and signaling chemicals (Golden et al., 2016). Far from sitting still, this space pushes how tumors start, grow, spread, and even react to treatment. What happens there is not background noise; it drives the entire course (Jain et al., 2014).

What stands out in the lung's surrounding tissue is long-term inflammation. Because of ongoing contact with cigarette fumes, dirty air, or repeated illness, the area fills with constant irritation marked by molecules including IL-6, TNF, and IL-1 (Bhalla et al., 2009). Inside both structural and surface cells, signals such as NFkB and STAT3 get switched on by these substances, leading to growth, longer cell life, new blood vessels, and less cell death (Kannan et al., 2025). As years pass, this irritated state encourages DNA errors while helping flawed cell groups grow stronger. Lung tissue hosts various immune players deeply involved in tumor dynamics (Karachaliou et al., 2015). CD8 killer T cells stand out by spotting abnormal cells, then destroying them. Yet cancerous spots resist attack through checkpoints like PD-L1, which wear down T cell strength (Reddy, 2016). Instead of helping, certain T regulatory cells step in, working alongside MDSCs to quiet immune responses. These types release calming signals, substances such as IL-10 and TGF-β, that reduce defense activity (Haist et al., 2021). At the same time, macrophages linked to tumors shift into a form favoring repair over attack. This M2, style behavior feeds expansion, builds blood networks, alters surroundings, helping rather than harming the mass (Swami et al., 2025). Fibroblasts tied to tumors help shape how cancers grow, both physically and through chemical signals. These altered cells release molecules, including TGF-β and FGF, along with signaling proteins such as CXCL8 and CXCL12, pushing cancer cells toward mobility and spread (Wieder, 2023). Instead of staying still, tumor cells respond by changing form and breaking away, guided by these cues. Matrix changes follow, driven by the same cells, making the surrounding tissues denser and more rigid (Mierke, 2024). That shifted environment does more than just hold space; it tweaks communication between cells while redirecting immune presence. New blood vessel growth marks a key feature of the lung's tumor environment (Forster et al., 2017). When tumors grow larger, their need for oxygen outpaces what is available, creating low oxygen conditions. In response, cells stabilize proteins called HIFs, which turn on VEGF, a signal that pushes vessels to form. Yet these newly formed vessels tend to be messy and poorly organized, so medicines do not spread evenly through tissue. This patchy flow keeps some areas starved of oxygen, fueling more invasive traits while helping cancer hide from immune attacks (Chen et al., 2023).

What stands out most is how uneven the TME can be. One part of a tumor might have more immune cells, while another has less oxygen. Changes in structure show up even inside single growths. Some spots pack tightly with support tissue, others stay loose (Chen et al., 2016). These differences help explain why treatment hits harder in certain areas. Response shifts depending on local conditions. Not every section reacts the same way to drugs aimed at specific pathways.

2.4.1.7 Molecular physiology of lung cancer

Lung cancer's inner workings are tangled, shifting in countless ways. One person's illness might look like another's on paper, yet inside the body, things run differently

(Timmermann, 2014). These differences arise through shifts across many levels: Broken DNA pieces here, genes turned silent or loud there, signals between proteins rerouted unexpectedly. Each change nudges growth speed, behavior patterns, and treatment reactions, subtly altering outcomes without warning (Chamary & Hurst, 2009). Cells start changing long before lung cancer appears. Little by little, shifts build up, switching on signals that push growth, turning off safeguards meant to stop it (Popper, 2016). With these messages stuck in motion, division happens without pause, survival ignores normal limits, and then movement into nearby areas begins almost unnoticed. Growth runs unchecked because brakes fail early, warnings go unheeded, and boundaries blur later. Spread becomes possible once barriers weaken under constant pressure from within. One big category of genetic shifts behind cancer centers on oncogenes, these genes that spur rapid cell division once turned on. Lung adenocarcinoma often shows changes in EGFR, KRAS, BRAF, MET, HER2, ALK, ROS1, or RET (Muruganantham & Veerabathiran, 2024). Instead of working normally, they show up as small DNA errors, multiplied sections, or reshuffled segments, forming faulty protein blends. Because of this, signals flow through key chains like RAS-RAF-MEK-MAPK and PI3K-AKT-mTOR, steering how cells grow, stay alive, use energy, and move around (Muruganantham & Veerabathiran, 2024). Certain cancers rely heavily on just one broken signal line to keep going, a state sometimes called being hooked on an altered gene, and that reliance explains why some people respond sharply to precise treatments.

A few things happen quietly inside lung tumors, often vital brakes, like genes, vanish without warning. Take TP53, for instance, or PTEN, RB1, LKB1 (STK11), along with p16/CDKN2A; each plays a quiet but firm role in daily cell control. Under ordinary conditions, they pause growth, fix broken DNA strands, and even order flawed cells to die on command. Once gone, chaos builds slowly: Mutations pile up while division races ahead unchecked. Mistakes survive longer now, spreading further than before, making treatment harder over time (Sharma et al., 2024). Out of all those genetic changes found in lung tumors through advanced testing, just a few actually push the cancer forward. The rest simply tag along, signs of past errors piling up inside cells. What makes it tough? These growths shift constantly, reshaped by time or squeezed by drugs, letting stubborn cell lines take over. Yet finding key flaws in their biology has shifted how doctors respond, particularly for nonsmall cell cases, aiming treatments at the main weak spots driving each tumor (Bhartiya et al., 2024).

2.5 Conclusion

Cancer in the lungs begins when tiny shifts inside cells meet certain conditions in surrounding tissues. Branching tubes for airflow, stretchy support structures, and a web of blood and lymph vessels make up the organ's design, built for breathing, but also guiding where damage piles up and healing goes off track. As years pass, ongoing swelling, chemical imbalance from oxygen byproducts, and low oxygen levels shift the area's behavior, nudging it toward unchecked growth, varied cell types, and defiance against therapy. Meanwhile, what surrounds the tumor does more than sit still: Weakened immunity, chaotic vessel formation, messages from nearby cells, and changes to structural scaffolding push the disease forward while shaping how it reacts to drugs. Because lungs work differently in each area, cancers show unique patterns depending on location, type, or how they grow. This also shapes whether targeted drugs help until resistance appears. When treatments stop working, hidden survival routes inside cells often take over. Linking physical tissue layout with starting cell types opens clearer paths to catch disease earlier. Matching these insights to specific molecules allows smarter drug pairings. Such combinations hit core mutations while disrupting nearby tissues that feed tumors growth.

References

Ackermann, M., Werlein, C., Plucinski, E., Leypold, S., Kühnel, M. P., Verleden, S. E., … Jonigk, D. D. (2024). The role of vasculature and angiogenesis in respiratory diseases. *Angiogenesis, 27*(3), 293–310.

Almangush, A., Mäkitie, A. A, Triantafyllou, A., de Bree, R., Strojan, P, Rinaldo, A., … Leivo, I. (2020). Staging and grading of oral squamous cell carcinoma: An update. *Oral Oncology, 107*, 104799.

Altorki, N. K, Markowitz, G. J, Gao, D., Port,, J. L, Saxena, A, Stiles, B, … Mittal,, V. (2019). The lung microenvironment: An important regulator of tumour growth and metastasis. *Nature Reviews Cancer, 19*(1), 9–31.

Amann, A., Corradi, M., Mazzone, P., & Mutti, A (2011). Lung cancer biomarkers in exhaled breath. *Expert Review of Molecular Diagnostics, 11*(2), 207–217.

Antar, S. A, Mahmoud, A. M, Abdo, W., Gad, C, & Al-Karmalawy, A. A. (2023). A comprehensive overview of organ inflammatory responses: Genesis, possible mechanisms, and mediators of inflammation. *Pharmaceutical Sciences, 29*(4), 397–416.

Aung, H., Sivakumar, A., Gholami, S., Venkateswaran, S., & Gorain,, B (2019). An overview of the anatomy and physiology of the lung. In *Nanotechnology-based targeted drug delivery systems for lung cancer* (pp. 1–20). Acedemic Press. doi:10.1016/B978-0-12-815720-6.00001-0.

Baker, D. J. (2020). The structure of the airways and lungs. In D. J. Baker (Ed.), *Artificial ventilation: A basic clinical guide* (pp. 27–42). Springer International Publishing.

Barta, J. A, Powell, C. A, & Wisnivesky, J. P. (2019). Global epidemiology of lung cancer. *Annals of Global Health, 85*(1), 8.

Bernhardt, E. B, & Jalal, S. I. (2016). Small cell lung cancer. In K. L. Reckamp (Ed.), *Lung cancer: Treatment and research* (pp. 301–322). Springer International Publishing.

Bhalla, D. K., Hirata, F., Rishi, A. K., & Gairola, C. G (2009). Cigarette smoke, inflammation, and lung injury: A mechanistic perspective. *Journal of Toxicology and Environmental Health, Part B, 12*(1), 45–64.

Bhana, R., & Magan, A. (2023). Lung mechanics: A review of solid mechanical elasticity in lung parenchyma. *Journal of Elasticity, 153*(1), 53–117.

Bhartiya, D., Raouf, S., Pansare, K., Tripathi, A, & Tripathi,, A (2024). Initiation of cancer: The journey from mutations in somatic cells to epigenetic changes in tissue-resident VSELs. *Stem Cell Reviews and Reports, 20*(4), 857–880.

Bourke, S. J. (2020). Lung function in specific respiratory and systemic diseases: A compendium. In *Cotes' lung function* (pp. 697–728). Wiley. doi:10.1002/9781118597309.ch38.

Brcic, L., & Roden, A. C. (2023). Histopathological features of giant mediastinal tumors-a literature review. *Mediastinum, 7*, 37.

Brems, C. (2024). Understanding the anatomy of breath and breathing. In C. Brems (Ed.), *Therapeutic breathwork: Clinical science and practice in healthcare and yoga* (pp. 41–97). Springer Nature.

Camuzi, D., de Amorim ÍSS, R. PL. F, et al. (2019). Regulation is in the air: The relationship between hypoxia and epigenetics in cancer. *Cells, 8*(4), 300.

Chamary, J., & Hurst, L. D. (2009). The price of silent mutations. *Scientific American, 300*(6), 46–53.

Chen, X., Song, M., Zhang, B., & Zhang, Y (2016). Reactive oxygen species regulate T cell immune response in the tumor microenvironment. *Oxidative Medicine and Cellular Longevity, 2016*(1), 1580967.

Chen, Y., Zhang, Q., Chen, X., Xu, Y, Guo, J, Meng, J., … Xu, Z (2025). Long noncoding RNA FGD5-AS1-encoded micropeptides improve right heart functions of pulmonary arterial hypertension through restricting the synthesis of hyaluronic acid. *International Journal of Biological Macromolecules, 320*, 146018.

Chen, Z., Zhu, L.-T., & Luo, Z.-H. (2023). Characterizing flow and transport in biological vascular systems: A review from physiological and chemical engineering perspectives. *Industrial & Engineering Chemistry Research, 63*(1), 4–36.

Chu, Y., Luo, G., Zhou, L., Cao, S, Ma, G, Meng,, X, … Gao, X (2025). Deep learning-driven pulmonary artery and vein segmentation reveals demography-associated vasculature anatomical differences. *Nature Communications, 16*(1), 2262.

Coudray, N., Ocampo, P. S, Sakellaropoulos, T., Narula, N, Snuderl, M, Fenyö, D, … Tsirigos, A. (2018). Classification and mutation prediction from non–small cell lung cancer histopathology images using deep learning. *Nature Medicine, 24*(10), 1559–1567.

De Troyer, A., & Moxham, J. (2020). Chest wall and respiratory muscles. In *Cotes' lung function* (pp. 149–176). Wiley. doi:10.1002/9781118597309.ch10.

Detterbeck, F. C. (2018). The eighth edition TNM stage classification for lung cancer: What does it mean on main street? *The Journal of Thoracic and Cardiovascular Surgery, 155*(1), 356–359.

Detterbeck, F. C, Boffa, D. J, Kim, A. W, & Tanoue, L. T. (2017). The eighth edition lung cancer stage classification. *Chest, 151*(1), 193–203.

Duncker, H.-R. (2004). Vertebrate lungs: Structure, topography and mechanics: A comparative perspective of the progressive integration of respiratory system, locomotor apparatus and ontogenetic development. *Respiratory Physiology & Neurobiology, 144*(2-3), 111–124.

Dünser, M. W, Dankl, D., Petros, S., & Mer, M. (2018). The airway and lungs. In M. W Dünser, D. Dankl, S. Petros, & M. Mer (Eds.), *Clinical examination skills in the adult critically ILL patient* (pp. 21–49). Springer.

Effros, R. M. (2006). Anatomy, development, and physiology of the lungs. *GI Motility Online*. doi:10.1038/gimo73.

Egashira, R., Yamada, D., & Jacob, J. (2025). Anatomy of pulmonary lymphatics and lymphoid tissues. *Seminars in Ultrasound, CT and MRI., 46*(4), 266–271.

Fadel, E., Missenard, G., Chapelier, A., Mussot, S, Leroy-Ladurie, F., Cerrina,, J, & Dartevelle, P. (2002). En bloc resection of non-small cell lung cancer invading the thoracic inlet and intervertebral foramina. *The Journal of Thoracic and Cardiovascular Surgery, 123*(4), 676–685.

Forster, J. C, Harriss-Phillips, W. M, Douglass, M. J, & Bezak, E. (2017). A review of the development of tumor vasculature and its effects on the tumor microenvironment. *Hypoxia*, 21–32.

Foster, J. G, Wong, S. CK., & Sharp, T. V. (2014). The hypoxic tumor microenvironment: Driving the tumorigenesis of non-small-cell lung cancer. *Future Oncology, 10*(16), 2659–2674.

Genova, C., Dellepiane, C., Carrega, P., Sommariva,, S, Ferlazzo,, G, Pronzato, P., … Croce, M (2022). Therapeutic implications of tumor microenvironment in lung cancer: Focus on immune checkpoint blockade [Review]. *Frontiers in Immunology, 12*, 2021.

Gesase, A. P. (2006). The morphological features of major and accessory fissures observed in different lung specimens. *Morphologie, 90*(288), 26–32.

Gholap, A., Pardeshi, S., Giram, P., et al. (2025). Breathing new life nanomedicines for pulmonary drug delivery: Targeting approaches, experimental models, and regulatory aspects. *Beni-Suef University Journal of Basic and Applied Sciences, 14*(1), 65.

Gibson, G. J. (2020). Lung and chest wall elasticity. In *Cotes' lung function* (pp. 187–201). Wiley. doi:10.1002/9781118597309.ch12.

Golden, S. E., Thomas, C. R., Jr., Deffebach, M. E., Nangare,, S., Sodha,, S, Kapare,, H., … Pardeshi, C (2016). "Even if I Don't Remember, I Feel Better". A qualitative study of patients with early-stage non–small cell lung cancer undergoing stereotactic body radiotherapy or surgery. *Annals of the American Thoracic Society, 13*(8), 1361–1369.

Goudar, R. K, & Vlahovic, G. (2008). Hypoxia, angiogenesis, and lung cancer. *Current Oncology Reports, 10*(4), 277–282.

Guillot, L., Nathan, N., Tabary, O., Thouvenin, G, Le Rouzic,, P, Corvol,, H., … Clement, A (2013). Alveolar epithelial cells: Master regulators of lung homeostasis. *The International Journal of Biochemistry & Cell Biology, 45*(11), 2568–2573.

Guo, T., He, C., Venado, A., & Zhou,, Y (2022). Extracellular matrix stiffness in lung health and disease. *Comprehensive Physiology, 12*(3), 3523–3558.

Haddad, M., & Sharma, S. (2025). *Physiology, lung*. StatPearls Publishing.

Hagberg, C. A, Ghouse, A. A, & Iannucci, D. G. (2014). The Development of techniques for airway management. In *The wondrous story of anesthesia* (pp. 723–744). Springer. doi:10.1007/978-1-4614-8441-7_54.

Haist, M., Stege, H., Grabbe, S., & Bros, M (2021). The functional crosstalk between myeloid-derived suppressor cells and regulatory T cells within the immunosuppressive tumor microenvironment. *Cancers, 13*(2), 210.

Herbst, R. S, Onn, A., & Sandler, A. (2005). Angiogenesis and lung cancer: Prognostic and therapeutic implications. *Journal of Clinical Oncology, 23*(14), 3243–3256.

Honish, R. L. (2021). Chest and lung diseases. In Honish R.L., (Ed). *Over, 55*, 81–100.

Hsu, Y.-L., Hung, J.-Y., Chang, W.-A., Jian, S.-F., Lin, Y.-S, Pan, Y.-C, … Kuo, P.-L. (2018). Hypoxic lung-cancer-derived extracellular Vesicle MicroRNA-103a Increases the oncogenic effects of macrophages by targeting PTEN. *Molecular Therapy, 26*(2), 568–581.

Inamura, K. (2017). Lung cancer: Understanding its molecular pathology and the 2015 WHO classification [mini review]. *Frontiers in Oncology, 7*, 2017.

Jackson, A. L, Zhou, B., & Kim, W. Y. (2010). HIF, hypoxia and the role of angiogenesis in non-small cell lung cancer. *Expert Opinion on Therapeutic Targets, 14*(10), 1047–1057.

Jain, R. K, Martin, J. D, & Stylianopoulos, T. (2014). The role of mechanical forces in tumor growth and therapy. *Annual Review of Biomedical Engineering, 16*(1), 321–346.

Ji, P., Yang, K., Xu, Q., Qin, G, Zhu, Q, Qian, Y, & Yao, W (2023). Mechanisms and application of gas-based anticancer therapies. *Pharmaceuticals, 16*(10), 1394.

Kallini, J. R, Hamed, N., & Khachemoune, A. (2015). Squamous cell carcinoma of the skin: Epidemiology, classification, management, and novel trends. *International Journal of Dermatology, 54*(2), 130–140.

Kannan, G., Paul, B. M, & Thangaraj, P. (2025). Stimulation, regulation, and inflammaging interventions of natural compounds on nuclear factor kappa B (NF-kB) pathway: A comprehensive review: G. Kannan et al. *Inflammopharmacology, 33*(1), 145–162.

Karachaliou, N., Cao, M. G, Teixidó, C., Viteri, S, Morales-Espinosa, D, Santarpia, M, & Rosell,, R (2015). Understanding the function and dysfunction of the immune system in lung cancer: The role of immune checkpoints. *Cancer Biology & Medicine, 12*(2), 79–86.

Karpathiou, G., Péoc'h, M., Sundaralingam, A., Rahman, N, & Froudarakis, M. E. (2022). Inflammation of the Pleural Cavity: A review on pathogenesis, diagnosis and implications in tumor pathophysiology. *Cancers, 14*(6), 1415.

Katrivesis, K., Elia, J., Etiz, B., Cooley-Rieders, K, Hosseinian, S, & Melucci, S. (2022). An overview of lung anatomy and physiology. In A. A. Hakimi, T. E. Milner, & G. R. Rajan, et al. (Eds.), *Mechanical ventilation amid the COVID-19 pandemic: A guide for physicians and engineers* (pp. 5–24). Springer International Publishing.

Khobragade, D. S., Agrawal, S., Potbhare, M. S., Kadiri,, S. K., & Tiwari,, P. (2024). Connecting the dots: The role of pollution in lung cancer onset. *New Emirates Medical Journal, 5*(1), E02506882350325.

Kriegsmann, M., Haag, C., Weis, C.-A., Steinbuss, G, Warth, A, Zgorzelski, C, … Klauschen, F, et al. (2020). Deep learning for the classification of small-cell and non-small-cell lung cancer. *Cancers, 12*(6), 1604.

Kurian, J. (2020). Chest wall and diaphragm. In *Pediatric body MRI: A comprehensive, multidisciplinary guide* (pp. 159–192). doi:10.1007/978-3-030-31989-2_6.

Lantuejoul, S., Fernandez-Cuesta, L., Damiola, F., Girard,, N, & McLeer, A (2020). New molecular classification of large cell neuroendocrine carcinoma and small cell lung carcinoma with potential therapeutic impacts. *Translational Lung Cancer Research, 9*(5), 2233–2244.

Larsen, J. E., & Minna, J. D. (2011). Molecular biology of lung cancer: Clinical implications. *Clinics in Chest Medicine, 32*(4), 703.

Lawrence, D. A, Branson, B., Oliva, I., & Rubinowitz, A. (2015). The wonderful world of the windpipe: A review of central airway anatomy and pathology. *Canadian Association of Radiologists Journal, 66*(1), 30–43.

Lee, S. S, & Cheah, Y. K. (2019). The interplay between MicroRNAs and cellular components of tumour microenvironment (TME) on non-small-cell lung cancer (NSCLC) progression. *Journal of Immunology Research, 2019*(1), 3046379.

Lim, J. U, Lee, E., Lee, S. Y, Cho, H. J., Ahn, D. H, Hwang,, Y, … Kim, S. J. (2023). Current literature review on the tumor immune micro-environment, its heterogeneity and future perspectives in treatment of advanced non-small cell lung cancer. *Translational Lung Cancer Research, 12*(4), 857–876.

Lim, W., Ridge, C. A, Nicholson, A. G, & Mirsadraee, S (2018). The 8(th) lung cancer TNM classification and clinical staging system: Review of the changes and clinical implications. *Quantitative Imaging in Medicine and Surgery, 8*(7), 709–718.

Liyew, W. A., Adane, F., Wondemagegn, A. T., Tsehay,, B., Deml, Y. A, Abdu, H. M, & Animaw, Z (2024). Roles of cardiac neural crest cells in cardiovascular development and associated congenital defects-an integrated review. *Translational Research in Anatomy, 36*, 100304.

Lutfi, M. F. (2017). The physiological basis and clinical significance of lung volume measurements. *Multidisciplinary Respiratory Medicine, 12*(1), 3.

Macdonald, S., Watt, G., & Macleod, U. (2013). In search of the cancer candidate: Can lay epidemiology help? *Sociology of Health & Illness, 35*(4), 575–591.

Maki, R., Miyajima, M., Ogura, K., Tada, M, Takahashi, Y, Adachi, H, & Watanabe, A (2022). Pulmonary vessels and bronchus anatomy of the left upper lobe. *Surgery Today, 52*(4), 550–558.

Martano, M., Boston, S., & Morello, E. (2022). Respiratory tract and thorax. In S. T. Kudnig, & B. Séguin (Eds.), *Veterinary surgical oncology* (pp. 393–468).

Meduri, G. U, & Torres, A. (2026). Evolutionary integration and glucocorticoid regulation of the respiratory system: Structure, function, and homeostatic adaptation. *Medical Sciences, 14*(1), 90.

Megyesfalvi, Z., Gay, C. M, Popper, H., Pirker, R, Ostoros, G, Heeke, S, … Dome, B (2023). Clinical insights into small cell lung cancer: Tumor heterogeneity, diagnosis, therapy, and future directions. *CA: A Cancer Journal for Clinicians, 73*(6), 620–652.

Michael Jaeger, J., Titus, B. J., & Blank, R. S. (2019). Essential anatomy and physiology of the respiratory system and the pulmonary circulation. In P. Slinger (Ed.), *Principles and practice of anesthesia for thoracic surgery* (pp. 65–92). Springer International Publishing.

Mierke, C. T. (2024). Extracellular matrix cues regulate mechanosensing and mechanotransduction of cancer cells. *Cells, 13*(1), 96.

Mittal, V., El Rayes, T., Narula, N., McGraw, T. E, Altorki, N. K., & Barcellos-Hoff, M. H (2016). The Microenvironment of lung cancer and therapeutic implications. In A. Ahmad, & S. M. Gadgeel (Eds.), *Lung cancer and personalized medicine: Novel therapies and clinical management* (pp. 75–110). Springer International Publishing.

Mohanka, M., & Banga, A. (2023). Alterations in pulmonary physiology with lung transplantation. *Comprehensive Physiology, 13*(1), 4269–4293.

Moldoveanu, B., Otmishi, P., Jani, P., Walker, J, Sarmiento, X, Guardiola, J, … Yu, J. (2008). Inflammatory mechanisms in the lung. *Journal of Inflammation Research, 2*, 1–11.

Moreira, A. L, Ocampo, P. SS., Xia, Y., Zhong, H, Russell, P. A, Minami, Y, … Brambilla, E, et al. (2020). A grading system for invasive pulmonary adenocarcinoma: A proposal from the international association for the study of lung cancer pathology committee. *Journal of Thoracic Oncology, 15*(10), 1599–1610.

Moussavi, Z. (2006). Anatomy and physiology of respiratory system. In Z. Moussavi (Ed.), *Fundamentals of respiratory system and sounds analysis* (pp. 1–8). Springer International Publishing.

Moya Amorós, J. A., & Lluveras, A. U. (2023). Tracheobronchial anatomy. In J. P. Díaz-Jiménez, & A. N. Rodríguez (Eds.), *Interventions in pulmonary medicine* (pp. 3–14). Springer.

Mpolokeng, K. S., Madolo, M. Y., Louw, G. J., & Gunston,, G. (2022). Anatomical variations in lung fissures leading to supernumerary lobes in the lungs. *Translational Research in Anatomy, 28*, 100209.

Muruganantham, J. K, & Veerabathiran, R (2024). Genetic variants influencing the emergence and progression of lung cancer: A comprehensive review. *Therapeutic Radiology and Oncology, 8*(pp. 2).

Nair, P. (2009). *Diagnosis: The buck starts here—The role of diagnosis in three areas of modern medicine*. The University of North Carolina at Chapel Hill.

Obeagu, E. I. (2025). Oxygen gradients in tumor tissues implications for breast cancer metastasis – A narrative review. *Annals of Medicine and Surgery, 87*(6).

Osarogiagbon, R. U, Van Schil, P., Giroux, D. J, Lim, E, Putora, P. M, Lievens, Y, … Huang, J (2023). The international association for the study of lung cancer lung cancer staging project: Overview of challenges and opportunities in revising the nodal classification of lung cancer. *Journal of Thoracic Oncology, 18*(4), 410–418.

Oser, M. G, Niederst, M. J, Sequist, L. V, & Engelman, J. A (2015). Transformation from non-small-cell lung cancer to small-cell lung cancer: Molecular drivers and cells of origin. *The Lancet Oncology, 16*(4), e165–e172.

Palleschi, A., Mattioni, G., LoMauro, A., Privitera, E, Musso, V, Morlacchi, L, … Grasselli,, G (2024). Diaphragm and lung transplantation [Review]. *Transplant International, 37*, 2024.

Patwa, A., & Shah, A. (2015). Anatomy and physiology of respiratory system relevant to anaesthesia. *Indian Journal of Anaesthesia, 59*(9), 533–541.

Paul, D. (2026). *The path to cancer cure. cancer: An integrative approach: Principles and strategies-from precision targeting to process oncology* (pp. 207–254). Springer.

Popper, H. H. (2016). Progression and metastasis of lung cancer. *Cancer and Metastasis Reviews, 35*(1), 75–91.

Pullamsetti, S. S, Kojonazarov, B., Storn, S., Gall, H, Salazar, Y, Wolf, J, … Savai,, R (2017). Lung cancer–associated pulmonary hypertension: Role of microenvironmental inflammation based on tumor cell–immune cell cross-talk. *Science Translational Medicine, 9*(416), eaai9048.

Reddy, N. KM. (2016). *Changing landscape of immuno-oncology: CAR-T therapy and PD1/PDL1 blockade*. Boston University.

Rekhtman, N., Pietanza, M. C., Hellmann, M. D., Naidoo, J, Arora, A, Won, H, … Ladanyi,, M (2016). Next-generation sequencing of pulmonary large cell neuroendocrine carcinoma reveals small cell carcinoma–like and non–small cell carcinoma–like subsets. *Clinical Cancer Research, 22*(14), 3618–3629.

Relli, V., Trerotola, M., Guerra, E., & Alberti, S (2019). Abandoning the notion of non-small cell lung cancer. *Trends in Molecular Medicine, 25*(7), 585–594.

Rodriguez-Canales, J., Parra-Cuentas, E., & Wistuba, I. I. (2016). Diagnosis and molecular classification of lung cancer. In K. L. Reckamp (Ed.), *Lung cancer: Treatment and research* (pp. 25–46). Springer International Publishing.

Rudin, C. M, Brambilla, E., Faivre-Finn, C., & Sage, J. (2021). Small-cell lung cancer. *Nature Reviews Disease Primers, 7*(1), 3.

Silva, D. M. G., Nardiello, C., Pozarska, A., & Morty,, R. E. (2015). Recent advances in the mechanisms of lung alveolarization and the pathogenesis of bronchopulmonary dysplasia. *American Journal of Physiology-Lung Cellular and Molecular Physiology, 309*(11), L1239–L1272.

Rusek, A. M, Abba, M., Eljaszewicz, A., Moniuszko, M, Niklinski, J, & Allgayer,, H (2015). MicroRNA modulators of epigenetic regulation, the tumor microenvironment and the immune system in lung cancer. *Molecular Cancer, 14*(1), 34.

Schittny, J. C. (2017). Development of the lung. *Cell and Tissue Research, 367*(3), 427–444.

Sharara, R. S, Hattab, Y., Patel, K., DiSilvio, B., Singh, A. C, & Malik, K (2017). Introduction to the anatomy and physiology of pulmonary circulation. *Critical Care Nursing Quarterly, 40*(3), 181–190.

Sharma, P., Sharma, S., & Sobti, R. C. (2024). Molecular pathogenesis of lung cancer: Evolving landscapes based on past experience. In R. C. Sobti, H. Sugimura, & A. Sobti (Eds.), *Molecular biomarkers for cancer diagnosis and therapy.* (pp. 347–380). Springer.

Short, R., Short, C., Gawlik, K. S, Teall,, A. M., Pittman, O, & Exacerbation,, A (2024). Evidence-based assessment of the lungs and respiratory system. In k. Gawlik, B. M. Melnyk, & A. Teall (Eds.), *Evidence-based physical examination: Best practices for health and well-being assessment.* (p. 247). Springer.

S. K. , L., Mohanty, S. N, K. , S., N, A, & Ramirez, G (2019). Optimal deep learning model for classification of lung cancer on CT images. *Future Generation Computer Systems, 92*, 374–382.

Sobczyńska-Rak, A., Żylińska, B., Nowicka, B., Rak, E, & Rzepka, T (2025). Role and mechanisms of angiogenesis in tumours. *Biology, 14*(7), 756.

Song, M.-A., Benowitz, N. L, Berman, M., Brasky,, T. M., Cummings, K. M., Hatsukami,, D. K., … Woroszylo, C. (2017). Cigarette filter ventilation and its relationship to increasing rates of lung adenocarcinoma. *JNCI: Journal of the National Cancer Institute, 109*(12), djx075.

Su, Y., Barr, J., Jaquish, A., Xu, J, Verheyden, J. M., & Sun, X (2022). Identification of lung innervating sensory neurons and their target specificity. *American Journal of Physiology-Lung Cellular and Molecular Physiology, 322*(1), L50–L63.

Suki, B., Stamenović, D., & Hubmayr, R. (2011). Lung parenchymal mechanics. *Comprehensive Physiology, 1*(3), 1317–1351.

Surate Solaligue, D. E., Rodríguez-Castillo, J. A., Ahlbrecht, K., & Morty, R. E. (2017). Recent advances in our understanding of the mechanisms of late lung development and bronchopulmonary dysplasia. *American Journal of Physiology-Lung Cellular and Molecular Physiology, 313*(6), L1101–L1153.

Suvarna, S. K, & Lloyd, K. L (2024). In K. S. Suvarna, G. Horne, & A. K. Sharp (Eds.), *Thorax: Heart, lungs, mediastinum, and pleura. Atlas of adult autopsy: A guide to modern practice* (pp. 83–184). Springer.

Swami, R., Popli, P., Sal, K., Challa, R. R., Vallamkonda, B, Garg, M, & Dora, C. P (2025). A review on biomacromolecular ligand-directed nanoparticles: New era in macrophage targeting. *International Journal of Biological Macromolecules, 306*, 141740.

Tamminga, M., Hiltermann, T. J. N., Schuuring, E., Timens, W, Fehrmann,, R. S. N, & Groen, H. J. M (2020). Immune microenvironment composition in non-small cell lung cancer and its association with survival. *Clinical & Translational Immunology, 9*(6), e1142.

Tan, Z., Xue, H., Sun, Y., Zhang, C., Song, Y, & Qi, Y (2021). The role of tumor inflammatory microenvironment in lung cancer [Review]. *Frontiers in Pharmacology, 12*, 2021.

Thomas, J. (2015). *A study of correlation of extravascular lung water and lung compliance in mechanically ventilated patients in the ICU of a tertiary care center*. Rajiv Gandhi University of Health Sciences (India).

Timmermann, C. (2014). Lung cancer and consumption in the nineteenth century: Bodies, tissues, cells and the making of a rare disease. In C. Timmermann (Ed.), *A history of lung cancer: The recalcitrant disease.* (pp. 11–33). Springer.

Zhou, Q., Tan, W., Li, Q., Li, B., Zhou, L, Liu, X, … Zhao, D (2023). A new segment method for pulmonary artery and vein. *Health Information Science and Systems, 11*(1), 47.

Tiwari A., Tiwari V., Kumar M. Lung cancer: Overview and therapies. 2026.

Tirpe, A. A, Gulei, D., Ciortea, S. M, Crivii,, C, & Berindan-Neagoe, I. (2019). Hypoxia: Overview on hypoxia-mediated mechanisms with a focus on the role of HIF genes. *International Journal of Molecular Sciences, 20*(24), 6140.

Tomashefski, J. F, & Farver, C. F. (2008). Anatomy and histology of the lung. In JF Tomashefski, PT Cagle, & CF Farver, et al. (Eds.), *Dail and hammar's pulmonary pathology: Volume I: Nonneoplastic lung disease* (pp. 20–48). Springer.

Tomic, R., Antonescu-Turcu, A., & Jacobs, E. R. (2013). Development, anatomy, and physiology of the lungs. In R Shaker, PC Belafsky, & GN Postma, et al. (Eds.), *Principles of deglutition: A multidisciplinary text for swallowing and its disorders* (pp. 199–214). Springer.

Trivedi, A., & Reed, H. O (2023). The lymphatic vasculature in lung function and respiratory disease [Review]. *Frontiers in Medicine, 10*, 2023.

Vela, V., Sabani, B., & Spahn, G. (2025). How cancer develops. In V. Vela, B. Sabani, & G. Spahn (Eds.), *Cancer simply explained: What is cancer and what can we do about it?* (pp. 21–73). Springer.

Verma, R. K, Ibrahim, M., & Garcia-Contreras, L. (2015). Lung anatomy and physiology and their implications for pulmonary drug delivery. In *Pulmonary drug delivery* (pp. 1–18). Wiley. doi:10.1002/9781118799536.ch1.

Viafara Garcia, S. M, Khan, M. S, Haidar, Z. S, & Acevedo Cox, J. P. (2023). Nanobubble-mediated oxygenation: Elucidating the underlying molecular mechanisms in hypoxia and mitochondrial-related pathologies. *Nanomaterials, 13*(23), 3060.

Volpe, J. K, & Makaryus, A. N. (2023). Anatomy, thorax, heart and pericardial cavity. *StatPearls [Internet].* StatPearls Publishing.

Whiteman, S., Alimi, Y., Carrasco, M., Gielecki, J, Zurada,, A, & Loukas, M (2021). Anatomy of the cardiac chambers: A review of the left ventricle. *Translational Research in Anatomy, 23*, 100095.

Wieder, R. (2023). Fibroblasts as turned agents in cancer progression. *Cancers, 15*(7), 2014.

Yegen, C.-H., Marchant, D., Bernaudin, J.-F., Planes,, C, Boncoeur, E, & Voituron, N (2023). Chronic pulmonary fibrosis alters the functioning of the respiratory neural network [Original Research]. *Frontiers in Physiology, 14*, 2023.

Yetkin, N. A, Yorgancıoğlu, A., & Cingi, C. (2023). Anatomy of upper and lower airways. In C Cingi, A Yorgancıoğlu, & N BayarMuluk, et al. (Eds.), *Airway diseases* (pp. 3–19). Springer International Publishing.

Zhang, Z., Jin, H., Liu, Z., Shi,, M, Zhang,, M., Pu,, W., ... Zhou, B. (2025). Pleural cavity macrophages promote lung tumor establishment through tissue invasion. *Protein & Cell*, pwaf078.

CHAPTER 3

Nanoparticle advancements in lung cancer: Cutting-edge diagnosis and therapy approaches

Geetha J[a], Nathiya Ranganathan[a], Vickram S[b], Hitesh Chopra[c] and Rupesh Kumar Gautam[d]

[a]Department of Microbiology, Auxilium College, Vellore, Tamil Nadu, India [b]Department of Biosciences, Saveetha School of Engineering, Saveetha Institute of Medical and Technical Sciences, (SIMATS) (Deemed to be University), Chennai, Tamil Nadu, India [c]Department of Biosciences, Saveetha Institute of Medical and Technical Sciences: SIMATS Deemed University, Chennai, Tamil Nadu, India [d]Department of Pharmacology, Amity Institute of Pharmacy, Amity University Uttar Pradesh, Noida, Uttar Pradesh, India

3.1 Introduction

Lung cancer is a highly serious disease that starts when abnormal cells grow uncontrollably and potentially cause substantial harm and death. It is a major public health issue, ranking as the second most frequently diagnosed cancer and the leading cause of cancer-related deaths worldwide. It is also a critical global burden due to its high incidence and poor survival rate. The incidence and mortality rates of lung cancer show notable variation across different geographical areas and between sexes, with the highest burden in Asia and among males. According to the data from GLOBOCAN 2020 from the International Agency for Research on Cancer (IARC), lung cancer was accountable for an estimated 1.8 million deaths (18%) in 2020. Lung cancer usually presents in two forms: One is slow-growing nonsmall cell lung cancer (NSCLC), which is the most common; the second is small cell lung cancer (SCLC), which is an aggressive form of lung cancer that spreads quickly and is much rarer. The primary risk factor is cigarette smoking, although nonsmokers can also have lung cancer due to various factors, some of which include occupational asbestos exposure, radon or certain chemical exposures, air pollution, hereditary cancer syndromes, and preexisting chronic lung disease. Symptoms include persistent coughing, pain in the chest, shortness of breath, coughing up blood, fatigue, sudden weight loss, and recurrent lung infections. Usually, the early symptoms are mild, similar to a seasonal cough, which delays the diagnosis and treatment. It is very crucial to get treatment as early as possible, and treatment options are based on personal

Nanoengineered Therapeutics for Lung Cancer: Advanced Drug Delivery Strategies.
DOI: https://doi.org/10.1016/B978-0-443-44585-9.00017-2

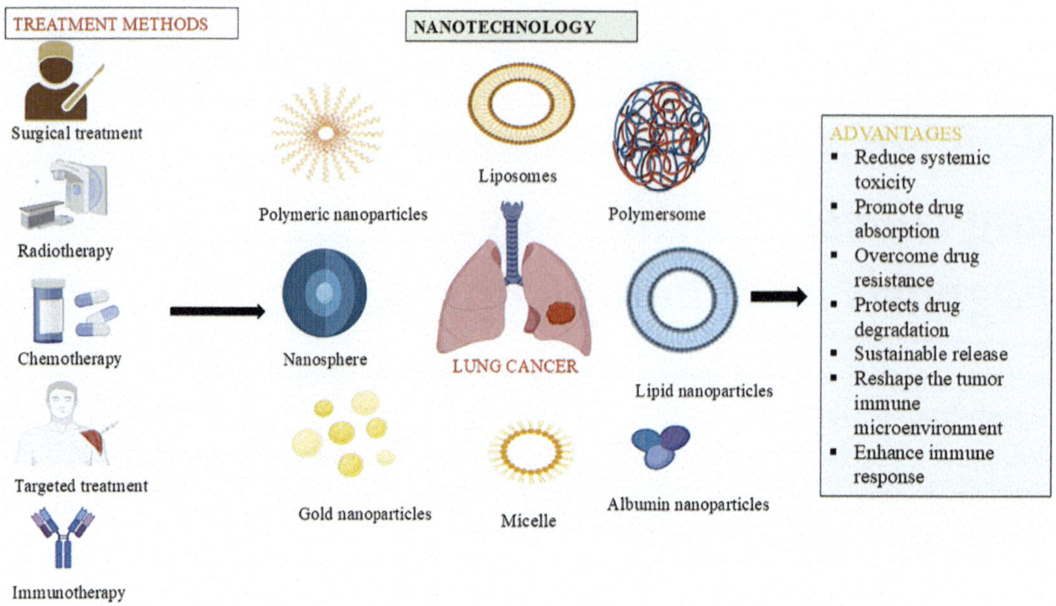

Figure 3.1
Nanotechnology enhanced lung cancer treatment: Combining conventional therapies with advanced nanocarriers (liposomes, polymeric nanoparticles, and gold nanoparticles) to improve targeting, drug absorption, controlled release, and reduce systemic toxicity.

medical history and the stage of the disease (Zhou et al., 2024; World Health Organization, 2026).

Current treatments for lung cancer include surgery, chemotherapy, radiation therapy, targeted therapy, and immunotherapy, often used in combination. The choice of treatment depends on various factors, including the type of lung cancer [SCLC or NSCLC] and the clinical stage of the disease. Treatment for lung cancer involves multiple approaches but focuses on surgery for early-stage lung cancer, chemotherapy and radiation therapy to kill cancer cells, targeted therapies tailored to mutated tumors, and immunotherapy to stimulate the immune response. Most treatment plans incorporate combinations of these approaches, and new nanotechnology-based treatments are being investigated. However, many issues exist with treatment such (Fig. 3.1) as drug resistance, side effects, treatment of metastatic disease, no effective curative options for advanced disease, and identification of cancer using early detection. There are also limitations of current treatments, including challenges in treating advanced or metastatic disease, drug resistance, and side effects from treatment (Fig. 3.1) (Barr et al., 2024; Siddiqui et al., 2023; Tamanna & Egbune, 2023).

Diagnostic approaches for lung cancer involve imaging, biopsy, and screening methods. Imaging techniques such as chest computed tomography (CT) scans are required for screening, staging, and determining tumor size, location, and spread. Positron emission tomography

(PET)-CT scans detect metabolically active cancer cells. Magnetic resonance imaging (MRI) with diffusion-weighted imaging (DWI) determines tumor response to therapy in lung cancer. Biopsy is still the gold standard for confirmation, including solid biopsies that provide histological information, but being more invasive, whereas liquid biopsies, which provide less invasive biochemical methods for circulating tumor DNA (ctDNA) and mutation detection, indicate the presence of genetic mutations in cancer, especially for advanced disease. Screening, especially with low-dose computed tomography (LDCT), is recommended for high-risk individuals and has shown potential in reducing lung cancer mortality, although its high false-positive rate necessitates careful follow-up and additional diagnostic evaluation (Duan et al., 2022; Feng et al., 2024; Nooreldeen & Bach, 2021; Park et al., 2020).

NPs are revolutionizing lung cancer research and therapy with their significant benefits related to drug delivery, diagnostic imaging, and targeted therapeutic applications. They are small enough to travel through the complex vasculature of the body to specifically deliver drugs to tumor sites, resulting in less damage to surrounding healthy tissue. This method of active targeting, along with superior drug stability and bioavailability, holds promise for producing more effective and less toxic cancer treatments (Zhang et al., 2025). It is also offering a sophisticated and targeted approach by enhancing the imaging sensitivity and biomarker detection, overcoming drug resistance, supporting multimodal therapy, reducing toxicity through controlled release, enhancing immunotherapy, and improving precision in nano-cryosurgery, ultimately facilitating earlier detection, more effective treatment, and minimal damage to healthy tissues compared to traditional methods (Baranwal et al., 2023; Feng et al., 2024).

Overall, the combination of NPs in lung cancer diagnosis and treatment is a significant improvement over traditional therapy. Nanotechnology holds the potential not only to detect lung cancer at earlier stages but also to enhance treatment efficacy and minimize the adverse effects by combining high specificity, improved imaging capabilities, and targeted therapeutic delivery. This precision-driven strategy has paved the way for more personalized, effective, and less toxic management of lung cancer than conventional diagnostic methods and therapies.

3.2 Histopathological classification of lung cancer

Histopathological classification plays a crucial role in the diagnosis, prognosis, and therapeutic management of lung cancer. The World Health Organization's (WHO) classification provides a categorization of lung tumors based on their histological (cellular) appearance and molecular features. The major groups include precursor glandular lesions, adenocarcinoma, adenosquamous carcinoma, squamous cell carcinoma, large cell carcinoma, sarcomatoid carcinoma, neuroendocrine neoplasms (including SCLC), salivary gland-type tumors, and other epithelial tumors. Histologic features, invasion depth, and spread patterns hold prognostic value. For instance, tumor spread through air spaces correlates with higher recurrence after limited resections and should be reported in pathological assessment. Immunohistochemistry (IHC) plays a pivotal role in classifying poorly differentiated tumors lacking classic light microscopy features: p40 expression indicates squamous cell carcinoma; TTF-1 positivity suggests solid adenocarcinoma; and chromogranin/synaptophysin positivity points to neuroendocrine carcinoma. Precursor glandular lesions of the lung include atypical adenomatous hyperplasia (AAH) and adenocarcinoma in situ (AIS). AAH is a small (≤5 mm) preinvasive lesion, while AIS (≤3 cm) shows a lepidic growth pattern with tumor cells spreading along alveolar walls without invasion and with intact alveolar septae. Lung adenocarcinoma shows gland formation, pneumocyte marker expression (TTF-1) with or without napsin expression, or intracytoplasmic mucin or intracellular mucin. It is divided into mucinous and nonmucinous types. Nonmucinous subtypes include acinar, papillary, micropapillary, lepidic, and solid patterns, of which the solid and micropapillary types have a poorer prognosis.

Minimally invasive adenocarcinoma (MIA) is a small tumor ≤3 cm with ≤5 mm invasion and predominant lepidic growth, while invasion >5 mm is termed lepidic-predominant adenocarcinoma. Invasive mucinous adenocarcinoma is a separate mucin-producing form, and tumors containing significant mucinous and nonmucinous components are classified as mixed adenocarcinoma. Adenosquamous carcinoma contains both glandular and squamous components, each comprising more than 10% of the tumor. This subtype is relatively uncommon but highly aggressive and is associated with increased recurrence and brain metastasis risk. Squamous cell carcinoma demonstrates keratinization and intercellular bridges and shows immunohistochemical positivity for markers such as p40, p63, CK5, and CK5/6. It may appear in nonkeratinizing, keratinizing, or basaloid forms and often exhibits central necrosis and cavitation. Some cases present as Pancoast tumors located in the superior pulmonary sulcus and may be associated with hypercalcemia. Large cell carcinoma is an undifferentiated epithelial malignancy lacking glandular, squamous, or neuroendocrine differentiation and is therefore considered a diagnosis of exclusion. The tumor is composed of large polygonal cells with abundant cytoplasm and prominent nucleoli and typically lacks TTF-1 and p40 expression. Sarcomatoid carcinomas are rare and aggressive tumors showing both epithelial and mesenchymal characteristics, including pleomorphic carcinoma, carcinosarcoma, and pulmonary blastoma. SCLC features small round/oval/fusiform cells (~2-3x lymphocyte size) with scant cytoplasm, absent nucleoli, finely granular "salt-and-pepper" chromatin, nuclear molding, Azzopardi effect, and extensive necrosis. IHC typically shows chromogranin/synaptophysin positivity. Prior WHO subtypes (oat cell, intermediate, combined SCLC-NSCLC) lack prognostic value and have been discontinued (ALQudah et al., 2021; Raso et al., 2021; Siddiqui et al., 2025).

3.3 Pathophysiology of lung cancer

Lung cancer is a multistep and heterogeneous disease characterized by the progressive accumulation of genetic and epigenetic alterations that transform normal bronchial and alveolar epithelial cells into malignant cells. The carcinogenic process develops over a prolonged period and involves genomic instability, dysregulated cell signaling, and evasion of normal growth control mechanisms. Molecular alterations include point mutations, gene amplifications, deletions, insertions, and chromosomal rearrangements, which collectively promote oncogenic signaling while suppressing tumor-inhibitory pathways. Repeated exposure to carcinogens, particularly tobacco smoke, induces dysplastic changes in the bronchial epithelium and initiates progressive genetic damage. Persistent injury results in alterations in protein synthesis, disruption of cell-cycle regulation, and malignant transformation. Distinct molecular mutations are associated with different lung cancer subtypes, including MYC, BCL2, and P53 alterations in SCLC, and epidermal growth factor receptor (EGFR), KRAS, and p16 mutations in NSCLC. The lung carcinogenesis is primarily associated with genomic instability caused by the progressive accumulation of genetic alterations. These abnormalities were the weakening of DNA integrity, thus increasing the cellular susceptibility to further mutations. Disruption of cell-cycle regulation is also a key event, primarily involving mutations in proto-oncogenes and tumor suppressor genes. The most frequently altered tumor suppressor genes in lung cancer include TP53, RB, and p16, while commonly activated proto-oncogenes belong to the MYC, RAS, and HER families. In addition, ALK gene rearrangements play a significant role, particularly in NSCLC. Growth factor signaling pathways are critically involved in tumor development. Epidermal growth factor (EGF) and its receptor EGFR are especially important in NSCLC, where receptor dysregulation promotes uncontrolled proliferation, metastasis, and resistance to inhibitory signals. Another essential event in tumor progression is angiogenesis. Tumors larger than approximately 3 mm require their own blood supply, which is achieved through persistent activation of the vascular endothelial growth factor (VEGF) pathway. VEGF released from tumor cells acts in a paracrine manner on endothelial cell receptors [vascular endothelial growth factor receptor (VEGFR)], stimulating abnormal vascular formation. These vessels are structurally irregular, fragile, and prone to bleeding, contributing to clinical symptoms such as hemoptysis. Lung cancer arises from the accumulation of genetic mutations, particularly in p53, along with alterations in Rb, MYC, RAS, and EGFR. Detecting these changes guides targeted therapy, such as EGFR inhibitors and ALK inhibitors, and may enable earlier diagnosis and improved treatment outcomes (Chen et al., 2025; Dakal et al., 2024; Kontomanolis et al., 2020; Smolarz et al., 2025).

3.3.1 Nonsmall cell lung cancer pathophysiology

NSCLC, which accounts for approximately 85% of lung cancers, arises from bronchial or alveolar epithelial cells and includes adenocarcinoma and squamous cell carcinoma. Tumor development is driven by activation of oncogenic signaling pathways due to mutations in genes such as EGFR, KRAS, and ALK rearrangements. These alterations activate receptor tyrosine kinase signaling pathways, including RAS/MAPK and PI3K/AKT, leading to increased cellular proliferation and survival. Inactivation of tumor suppressor genes such as TP53 and

PTEN impairs apoptosis and cell-cycle regulation. Tumor progression is further supported by VEGF-mediated angiogenesis and immune evasion through PD-L1 expression, allowing tumor growth within a hypoxic microenvironment (López et al., 2021).

3.3.2 Small-cell lung cancer pathophysiology

SCLC, comprising about 15% of cases, originates from pulmonary neuroendocrine cells and is characterized by rapid growth, early metastasis, and high mitotic activity. It is strongly associated with tobacco exposure and commonly shows coinactivation of TP53 and RB1, resulting in loss of cell-cycle control. SCLC cells exhibit neuroendocrine differentiation and typically express markers such as chromogranin, synaptophysin, and CD56. Histologically, the tumor consists of small cells with scant cytoplasm, finely granular chromatin, nuclear molding, and extensive necrosis (Du et al., 2020; Savchuk et al., 2025).

3.4 Stages of care in lung cancer

3.4.1 Early-stage disease

In early-stage lung cancer, where the tumor is confined to the lung without distant metastasis or major lymph node involvement, surgical resection is the standard curative treatment. Procedures include lobectomy, segmentectomy, or wedge resection depending on tumor size and location. Neoadjuvant therapy (chemotherapy and/or radiotherapy before surgery) may be administered to shrink the tumor and improve resectability. Following surgery, adjuvant chemotherapy or radiotherapy is often recommended to reduce the risk of recurrence. For patients who are not suitable surgical candidates, radiation therapy, particularly stereotactic body radiotherapy (SBRT), can serve as a definitive treatment. In selected patients, targeted therapy or immunotherapy may be considered based on molecular characteristics such as EGFR mutation or PD-L1 expression (World Health Organization, 2026).

3.4.2 Advanced disease

In advanced or metastatic lung cancer, where the tumor has spread to distant organs or lymph nodes, treatment is primarily palliative and aims to prolong survival, relieve symptoms, and improve quality of life. Systemic therapy is the mainstay of treatment and includes chemotherapy, targeted therapy, and immunotherapy. Chemotherapy uses cytotoxic drugs that circulate throughout the body and remains widely used as first-line treatment, particularly when actionable mutations are absent. Targeted therapies inhibit specific oncogenic signaling pathways in tumors harboring mutations such as EGFR or ALK rearrangements. Immunotherapy, especially immune checkpoint inhibitors (e.g., PD-1/PD-L1 inhibitors), enhances the host immune response against tumor cells and has significantly improved outcomes in many patients. Local modalities such as radiotherapy or surgery may also be employed to control specific metastatic lesions or alleviate symptoms (World Health Organization, 2026).

3.5 Limitations of current lung cancer therapy

Current lung cancer therapies, while having improved survival rates, still face significant limitations regarding efficacy, patient eligibility, and side effects. The primary, conventional treatments (surgery, chemotherapy, and radiotherapy), molecularly targeted therapies, and immunotherapies all have distinct challenges. Surgical resection is highly effective mainly in the early-stage disease; however, many patients are diagnosed late or have poor pulmonary reserve, making surgery unsuitable. Even after surgery followed by adjuvant chemotherapy in early-stage NSCLC, recurrence remains common, and long-term survival improvement is modest (about 4%–5%). Chemotherapy remains a global standard but lacks tumor selectivity, damaging healthy tissues and causing systemic toxicity, adverse effects, and resistance. Radiotherapy effectively controls local tumors yet risks injuring adjacent lung parenchyma, resulting in radiation pneumonitis and fibrosis. Targeted therapies are effective only in patients with specific genetic mutations (such as EGFR-mutated NSCLC), but their effectiveness often decreases over time as tumors develop acquired resistance through secondary mutations or activation of alternative (bypass) signaling pathways. Immunotherapy aids a minority of patients, hindered by absent predictive biomarkers, primary/secondary resistance, poor efficacy in driver-mutated tumors, immune-related adverse events, and imprecise neoadjuvant response assessment. These challenges have paved the way for NP-based drug delivery systems, which enable targeted drug delivery, controlled release, reduced systemic toxicity, and improved therapeutic effectiveness in lung cancer treatment (Glatzer et al., 2016; Jumeau et al., 2019; Meyer et al., 2026; Yang et al., 2026).

3.6 Nanoparticles in oncology

NPs are particles with at least one dimension within the nano size range, typically 1 to 100 nm. They differ from the bulk material due to their small size and high surface area when comparing properties. NPs can be categorized in multiple ways: by origin, they can be organic [made of proteins, lipids, and polymers], inorganic [made of metals, metal oxides, or ceramics], or carbon [including fullerenes, carbon nanotubes, and graphenes]. Based on size, it generally ranges from 1 to 100 nm, but some classifications may include variations in size ranges. Based on shape, it can be spherical, cylindrical, or have other complex shapes. Based on dimensionality, zero-dimensional (0D): All dimensions are in the nanoscale (quantum dots), one-dimensional (1D): 1D is in the macroscale and the other two are in the nanoscale (nanowires and nanotubes), two-dimensional (2D): 2D are in the nanoscale and 1D in the macroscale (nanosheets and thin films) and three-dimensional (3D): At least one dimension or multiple dimensions are in the nanoscale (spherical NPs). Based on chemical composition: Metal NPs, metal oxide NPs, semiconductor NPs. NPs often exhibit enhanced properties compared to their bulk counterparts, including increased surface area, higher reactivity, and altered optical and electronic properties. These properties lead to diverse applications in various fields, such as medicine (drug delivery and diagnostics), electronics, energy, and environmental science (Khan et al., 2022; Kumari & Sarkar, 2021). In oncology, NPs play a transformative role in diagnosis, drug delivery, imaging, and therapy. Their small size enables passive targeting of tumors through the enhanced permeability and retention (EPR) effect, allowing them to accumulate preferentially in tumor tissues. Surface modification with ligands, antibodies, or peptides further enables active targeting of cancer-specific receptors, enhancing treatment precision while reducing systemic toxicity. NPs improve the solubility and stability of poorly water-soluble chemotherapeutic drugs, protect drugs from premature degradation, and allow controlled or sustained release. NPs also represent a promising platform for improving early diagnosis, enhancing therapeutic efficacy, minimizing toxicity, and enabling personalized cancer treatment strategies.

3.6.1 Classification of nanoparticles used in lung cancer

The design and application of NPs in lung cancer therapy are influenced by their composition, structural properties, surface characteristics, and drug loading capabilities. Different NPs, such as liposomes, polymeric NPs, metallic NPs, and protein-based carriers, have their unique benefits associated with drug delivery, targeting, and therapeutic efficacy. Surface modifications, such as PEGylation, ligand binding, or charge modifications, allow for enhanced stability, extended circulation times, and improved tumor-specific targeting. The potential for NPs to encapsulate both hydrophilic and hydrophobic drugs makes them very versatile. The table below summarizes the major classes of NPs, their compositions, structures, functionalized modifications, encapsulations, and specific applications in lung cancer therapy (Table 3.1).

NPs have emerged as versatile platforms for both the diagnosis and treatment of lung cancer due to their tunable physicochemical properties, targeted delivery capability, and multifunctional design.

Liposomes are vesicular systems composed of phospholipids, sterols, and surfactants. Surface modification through PEGylation prolongs the circulation time by avoiding immune clearance, while ligand attachment, such as antibodies or peptides, enables selective binding to cancer cell receptors. Liposomes can encapsulate both hydrophilic and hydrophobic drugs, making them suitable for targeted and pulmonary drug delivery, improving drug solubility and bioavailability, and minimizing adverse effects. Liposome-based NPs enhance the diagnosis by improving the tumor accumulation and reducing systemic toxicity. They can encapsulate imaging agents such as gadolinium or radiolabels for MRI and PET, enabling accurate tumor detection. Surface ligands allow selective binding to receptors like EGFR, increasing imaging

Table 3.1: Classification of nanoparticles used in lung cancer.

Types of nanoparticles	Composition/ structure	Surface modification	Drug encapsulation	Lung cancer application	References
Liposomes	Phospholipids, sterols, and surfactants	PEGylation: PEG chains from the immune system extend circulation and improve tumor targeting. Ligands: antibodies and peptides enable the binding to cancer cell receptors	Both hydrophilic and hydrophobic drugs	Targeted drug delivery, pulmonary delivery, enhanced drug solubility and bioavailability, reduced toxicity	Riaz et al. (2018); Nsairat et al. (2022)
Polymeric nanoparticles	Biodegradable polymers (poly Lactic-co-glycolic acid, chitosan, PEG, and other natural or synthetic polymers)	PEGylation Ligand conjugation and peptide modification Bio membranes-coating nanoparticles enhance the tumor targeting and prolong circulation Stimuli response polymers- to control the drug release at the tumor site	Hydrophobic drugs and encapsulation (evaporation, nanoprecipitation, or emulsification)	Surface modification (e.g., folic acid conjugation) for targeted delivery to folate receptor-positive lung cancer cells; enhanced drug efficiency and solubility; reduced systemic toxicity; potential to overcome multidrug resistance; approved for NSCLC treatment	Prabhu et al. (2015); Amreddy et al. (2017)

(continued on next page)

Table 3.1: Classification of nanoparticles used in lung cancer—cont'd

Types of nanoparticles	Composition/ structure	Surface modification	Drug encapsulation	Lung cancer application	References
Metallic nanoparticles	Gold nanorods, iron oxide, silver, and other metal and metal oxide nanoparticles	PEGylation Ligand conjugation Surface charge modification Chitosan coating	Both hydrophilic and hydrophobic drugs, whereas PLGA is used to encapsulate drugs within the nanoparticles	Diagnostic applications: Enhanced imaging via MRI/CT; biosensing for early biomarker detection. Therapeutic Applications: Targeted drug delivery to lung tumors; photothermal therapy for localized tumor ablation; chemotherapy enhancement by improving solubility, stability, and bioavailability; immunotherapy support via targeted delivery and immune cell tracking; gene therapy delivery for tumor suppression	Goel et al. (2013), Goswami et al. (2024)

(continued on next page)

Dendrimers	Highly branched synthetic polymers with defined interior cavities and functionalized surface groups	**PEGylation** Attaching ligands to the dendrimer surface enables specific binding to cancer cell receptors Surface charge modification improves interactions with cell membranes and aids in gene delivery	Encapsulation in cavities to protect from degradation, surface conjugation through chemical bonds offering a route for stable drug delivery, combined with inorganic nanoparticles to enhance the drug loading capacity	Targeted chemotherapy, gene delivery, enhanced permeability and retention effect, and theranostics	Crintea et al. (2023)
Protein-based nanoparticles	Albumin-based nanoparticles, ferritin-based nanoparticles	Covalent modification-EDC/NHS coupling and thiol-mediated conjugation Noncovalent modification-electrostatic interaction, hydrophobic interaction Ligand attachment Stimuli response modification-nanoparticles can be designed to release the drug in response to TME, controlled drug release	emulsion techniques, electrospray, and desolvation	HSP-based NPs enhance solubility, targeting, and safety; folic acid–albumin NPs boost lung tumor uptake; ferritin probes enable theranostics; inhalable albumin and MAP NPs ensure direct, prolonged lung delivery	Khakpour et al. (2024), Sandra et al. (2019)

specificity. Additionally, liposomes function as theranostic systems by combining diagnostic imaging with targeted drug delivery, while PEGylation prolongs circulation and supports direct lung targeting (Nsairat et al., 2022; Riaz et al., 2018).

Polymeric NPs, synthesized from biodegradable polymers such as PLGA, chitosan, and PEG, offer a controlled and sustained release of the drug. Functionalization strategies, including ligand conjugation, peptide modification, biomembrane coating, and stimuli-responsive polymers, can enhance the tumor specificity and allow triggered drug release in response to acidic pH, enzymes, or hypoxic conditions within the tumor microenvironment. Therapeutically, these systems improve drug stability, enhance intracellular uptake, and help overcome multidrug resistance in NSCLC. The diagnosis of lung cancer is done through targeted imaging and biomarker detection using PLGA/chitosan platforms (50–200 nm). Conjugated with dyes, radiolabels, or antibodies (anti-EpCAM/EGFR), they enable sensitive PET/SPECT imaging, circulating tumor cells (CTC) capture, and multimodal probes via EPR and active targeting (Amreddy et al., 2017; Prabhu et al., 2015).

Metallic NPs, including gold nanorods (AuNRs), iron oxide, and silver NPs, possess unique optical and magnetic properties. Surface engineering through PEGylation, ligand conjugation, surface charge adjustment, or chitosan coating enhances stability and tumor targeting. These NPs can carry both hydrophilic and hydrophobic drugs and also serve diagnostic roles. They improve imaging in MRI and CT scans and enable biosensing for early biomarker detection. Gold nanoparticles enhance the detection of biomarker (e.g., EGFR) and act as strong CT imaging contrast agents, while superparamagnetic iron oxide nanoparticles (SPIONs) serve as effective MRI contrast materials with improved tumor accumulation. Silver nanoparticles have also been explored for early apoptosis detection in lung cancer cells. Therapeutically, they support targeted chemotherapy, photothermal tumor ablation, immunotherapy delivery, and gene therapy by improving drug stability, solubility, and bioavailability. Gold nanoparticles enable photothermal therapy by converting near-infrared light into heat to ablate tumor cells. Metallic nanoparticles can additionally deliver chemotherapeutic drugs, enhancing antitumor activity with reduced systemic toxicity. However, concerns regarding long-term toxicity and slow clearance remain major limitations to clinical application (Crintea et al., 2021; Kumar et al., 2022).

Dendrimers are highly branched synthetic polymers that are characterized by well-defined internal cavities and functional surface groups. PEGylation and ligand attachment allow selective receptor binding, while surface charge modification enhances cellular interaction and gene delivery. Drugs may be encapsulated within the dendrimer cavities or conjugated to the surface through chemical bonds, protecting them from degradation and enabling stable delivery. Dendrimers can also be combined with inorganic NPs to increase drug loading capacity. These dendrimer-based NPs are acting as a potential diagnostic nanocarrier because of their uniform nanoscale size and multiple functional surface groups. Poly(amidoamine)

(PAMAM) dendrimers (generation 4–6; G4–G6) conjugated with gadolinium-DOTA (Gd-DOTA) enhance T1-weighted MRI and show 2–3-fold higher retention in NSCLC lesions compared with free gadolinium. Gallium-68 (^68Ga) labeled DOTA-PAMAM systems improve PET imaging of EGFR overexpressing tumors, while EpCAM- or EGFR-targeted dendrimers can capture CTCs for liquid biopsy. Fluorescent dyes such as fluorescein isothiocyanate (FITC) or rhodamine further enable cellular-level visualization of metastasis. Their monodisperse size supports renal clearance, and multivalent binding enhances the sensitivity of imaging, thus making dendrimers a valuable tool for sensitive lung cancer diagnosis. Their applications include targeted chemotherapy, gene therapy, exploitation of the EPR effect, and theranostic (therapy + diagnostic) applications (Crintea et al., 2023).

Protein-based NPs, like albumin and ferritin-derived NPs, are biocompatible carriers with low toxicity. They can be modified through covalent methods like EDC/NHS coupling and thiol-mediated conjugation, or noncovalent approaches such as electrostatic and hydrophobic interactions. Ligand attachment and stimuli-responsive modifications allow controlled drug release within the tumor microenvironment. These NPs are typically prepared using desolvation, emulsion, or electrospray techniques. Albumin-based NPs enhance drug solubility, targeting, and safety, while folic acid-modified albumin NPs increase lung tumor uptake. Ferritin NPs function as theranostic probes, and inhalable albumin NPs enable direct and prolonged drug delivery to lung tissue. These protein-based NPs, especially albumin NPs such as nab-paclitaxel (Abraxane), are widely used in lung cancer because of their excellent biocompatibility and natural tumor targeting ability. Albumin binds gp60 receptors and SPARC proteins that are overexpressed in tumors, promoting selective accumulation. Diagnostically, albumin NPs carrying indocyanine green improve fluorescence-guided surgery, while gadolinium–albumin complexes enhance MRI imaging, and BSA–gold hybrids aid detection of EGFR and ctDNA. Therapeutically, Abraxane delivers paclitaxel efficiently to NSCLC, albumin-drug conjugates can enhance immunotherapy response, and inhalable albumin NPs enable localized cisplatin delivery with reduced systemic toxicity. Overall, their biodegradability, safety, and clinical approval make protein-based NPs promising theranostic platforms in lung cancer (Khakpour et al., 2024; Sandra et al., 2019).

Overall, the NP platforms integrate diagnostic imaging, targeted therapy, controlled drug release, and real-time treatment monitoring, representing a significant advancement toward precision medicine in lung cancer management.

3.6.2 Key physicochemical properties of nanoparticles and their impact on lung cancer

NP properties, such as size, shape, surface charge, surface properties, and agglomeration, are important to their interactions in lung tissue and tumor cells. These properties influence deposition, cellular uptake, therapeutic efficacy, and safety. The table below summarizes properties of NPs, their features, and the implications regarding treatment of lung cancer and safety (Table 3.2).

The physicochemical properties of NPs play a decisive role in determining their biological behavior, therapeutic performance, and safety in lung cancer applications. Among these characteristics, particle size is one of the most critical factors influencing biodistribution, cellular uptake, tumor penetration, and pulmonary retention. Smaller NPs generally demonstrate superior diffusion across biological barriers and are capable of penetrating deeply into tumor tissues through the intercellular spaces present within the tumor microenvironment. Their reduced dimensions facilitate internalization through endocytosis, allowing efficient intracellular drug delivery and enhanced therapeutic efficacy. However, extremely small NPs may also be cleared rapidly from the lungs or bloodstream via renal filtration or mucociliary mechanisms, thereby reducing treatment duration. Conversely, larger NPs tend to exhibit prolonged retention in lung tissues and slower systemic clearance, which may increase local drug concentration at the tumor site. Nevertheless, their larger size also increases the likelihood of recognition and uptake by alveolar macrophages, potentially triggering inflammatory responses, oxidative stress, and toxicity. Therefore, an optimal size range is essential to balance tumor penetration and retention while minimizing adverse immune reactions in pulmonary tissues (de Oliveira Cardoso et al., 2024).

Particle shape is another significant determinant that affects the NP-cell interactions, toxicity, and therapeutic efficiency. Spherical NPs are typically preferred in nanomedicine because their symmetrical geometry allows uniform cellular uptake, predictable circulation behavior, and reduced mechanical irritation to lung tissues. In contrast, elongated or fiber-shaped NPs interact differently with pulmonary defense mechanisms. Fibrous particles resist phagocytosis because macrophages cannot completely engulf their elongated structures. This phenomenon results in persistent activation of inflammatory pathways, release of cytokines, and prolonged oxidative stress within lung tissue. Continuous inflammation and tissue damage may promote fibrosis and, in certain cases, contribute to carcinogenesis. Thus, while engineered NPs for therapy are designed to be spherical or near-spherical to minimize toxicity, understanding the harmful effects of fiber-like particles provides insight into how shape directly influences lung cancer risk and treatment safety (de Oliveira Cardoso et al., 2024).

Surface charge also strongly affects NP stability, cellular interaction, and biodistribution. Cell membranes are predominantly negatively charged due to phospholipids and glycoproteins, and the positively charged NPs therefore exhibit stronger electrostatic attraction and enhanced cellular uptake. This property is advantageous for gene delivery systems because nucleic acids are negatively charged and require cationic carriers for efficient internalization. However, a highly positive surface charge may disrupt cell membranes, increase cytotoxicity, and can also damage the healthy lung epithelium. Positively charged NPs are also more readily recognized by serum proteins, leading to rapid clearance by the reticuloendothelial system

Table 3.2: Nanoparticles characteristics and lung cancer implications.

Property	Features	Impacts on lung cancer	References
Size	Smaller nanoparticles penetrate tissue and tumor more effectively; larger nanoparticles have slower clearance	Small nanoparticles can be easily taken up by cells and can penetrate deeper into tissue, including tumors, but they may also be cleared more quickly from the lungs. Larger nanoparticles have longer retention but a higher risk of macrophage clearance, inflammation, and toxicity	de Oliveira Cardoso et al. (2024)
Shape	Fiber-shaped nanoparticles (e.g., asbestos) are elongated, while spherical nanoparticles are more compact	Fiber-shaped nanoparticles are more toxic to the lungs as they resist macrophage clearance, causing prolonged inflammation, which may promote cancer development	de Oliveira Cardoso et al. (2024)
Surface charge	Surface charges affect nanoparticles' stability, bioavailability, and interactions with cells. Positive surface charge increases with negatively charged cell membranes	Positively charged nanoparticles show higher cytotoxicity, potentially damaging lung cells; neutral or negatively charged nanoparticles are safe and better for targeted delivery	de Oliveira Cardoso et al. (2024)
Surface properties	Surface reactivity and hydrophilicity influence nanoparticles' interactions with biological molecules and cells; reactive surfaces may trigger inflammation; hydrophilic surfaces enhance drug delivery	Highly reactive surfaces can promote lung inflammation, increasing cancer risk, while hydrophilic surfaces improve targeted therapy and efficacy	de Oliveira Cardoso et al. (2024)
Agglomeration	Nanoparticles tend to clump in biological fluids, affecting deposition and clearance	Agglomerated nanoparticles may be cleared more easily by macrophages but can also cause stronger inflammatory responses, impacting lung health and treatment outcomes	de Oliveira Cardoso et al. (2024)

(RES). In contrast, neutral or slightly negative NPs demonstrate improved biocompatibility, reduced nonspecific interactions, and longer circulation time. Such properties enhance tumor targeting while minimizing off-target toxicity. Consequently, surface charge must be carefully optimized to achieve efficient delivery (de Oliveira Cardoso et al., 2024).

Closely related to surface charge are surface properties such as hydrophilicity, chemical reactivity, and functionalization. The outer surface of an NP determines how it interacts with biological fluids, proteins, and immune cells. Highly reactive surfaces may catalyze the generation of reactive oxygen species, resulting in oxidative damage, inflammation, and tissue injury in the lungs. This inflammatory response can aggravate preexisting respiratory conditions and potentially promote tumor progression. Conversely, hydrophilic coatings improve dispersion in biological fluids, prevent aggregation, and reduce immune recognition. One of the most widely used modifications is polyethylene glycol (PEG) coating, which creates a hydrated layer around the NP surface. This modification reduces protein adsorption, prolongs circulation time, and improves the accumulation within tumors. Surface functionalization with targeting ligands such as antibodies, peptides, folic acid, or transferrin further enhances selective binding to lung cancer cells overexpressing specific receptors, thereby increasing therapeutic efficiency while minimizing damage to normal tissue. Thus, surface engineering transforms NPs from simple carriers into precise, targeted therapeutic platforms (de Oliveira Cardoso et al., 2024).

Agglomeration, the tendency of NPs to cluster together in biological environments, also significantly influences their pulmonary behavior. In physiological fluids, interactions with salts and proteins may cause individual NPs to aggregate into larger structures. Agglomerated particles may deposit differently within the respiratory tract, often accumulating in alveolar regions. Larger clusters are more easily recognized and cleared by macrophages, which can be beneficial for removing harmful particles but may also provoke strong inflammatory responses. Persistent inflammation can impair lung function and alter drug delivery efficiency. Additionally, agglomeration may reduce the effective surface area available for drug release, decreasing therapeutic performance. For inhalable NP formulations designed for lung cancer treatment, controlling aggregation is therefore essential to ensure uniform distribution, predictable clearance, and optimal drug availability (de Oliveira Cardoso et al., 2024).

Beyond individual properties, these characteristics interact collectively to determine the overall therapeutic outcome. For instance, a NP with optimal size but inappropriate surface charge may still exhibit rapid clearance, whereas a properly coated NP of moderate size may achieve superior tumor accumulation. Moreover, the tumor microenvironment, characterized by abnormal vasculature, hypoxia, and altered pH, further modifies NP behavior. Particles designed to respond to acidic conditions or enzymatic activity can release drugs selectively inside tumors, thereby enhancing treatment effectiveness. From a clinical perspective, understanding these physicochemical properties is crucial not only for therapy but also for safety assessment. NPs intended for lung cancer treatment must achieve sufficient retention in tumor tissue while avoiding chronic inflammation, fibrosis, or secondary toxicity. Regulatory agencies increasingly require detailed characterization of NP size distribution, surface chemistry, and stability to ensure reproducibility and patient safety. Advances in nanotechnology now allow the design of multifunctional NPs capable of simultaneous imaging and therapy (theranostics), where size influences imaging resolution, surface charge affects targeting, and surface modification controls drug release. The effectiveness of NP-based approaches in lung cancer is governed by a complex interplay of size, shape, surface charge, surface chemistry, and agglomeration behavior. Careful optimization of these parameters enables NPs to function as safe and efficient drug delivery systems, diagnostic tools, and therapeutic agents. A comprehensive understanding of these properties, therefore, forms the foundation for designing next-generation nanomedicines capable of improving lung cancer diagnosis, targeted therapy, and patient outcomes.

3.6.3 Nanoparticle targeting mechanisms in lung cancer

Nanoparticles improve lung cancer therapy by delivering the drugs specifically to the tumor tissues and also minimize the damage to normal cells. Targeting mainly occurs through two mechanisms: passive targeting and active targeting. Passive targeting of NPs in lung cancer primarily exploits the EPR effect, a pathophysiological phenomenon in which NPs preferentially accumulate in tumor tissue due to leaky vasculature and impaired lymphatic drainage. Lung tumors exhibit disorganized, hyperpermeable blood vessels with pores ranging from 100 to 780 nm, allowing NPs to extravasate into the tumor interstitium, while the lack of an effective lymphatic system prolongs their retention. Optimizing NP physicochemical properties further enhances passive targeting: Particles between 40 and 200 nm avoid rapid renal clearance, neutral or negatively charged surfaces reduce uptake by the RES, and PEGylation provides a hydrophilic coating that prolongs circulation and increases tumor accumulation. Clinically, several NP formulations leverage passive targeting in lung cancer, including Abraxane (albumin-bound paclitaxel), Genexol-PM (polymeric micelle paclitaxel), and Lipoplatin (liposomal cisplatin), which demonstrate improved antitumor efficacy and reduced toxicity. Despite these advances, passive targeting faces challenges such as tumor heterogeneity, low delivery efficiency (with typically $<1\%$ of the injected dose reaching the tumor), and discrepancies between animal models and humans, which complicate clinical translation. Active targeted NPs in lung cancer are engineered systems featuring surface-bound ligands that specifically bind receptors overexpressed on tumor cells or in the tumor microenvironment. Unlike passive targeting, which relies on the leaky vasculature of tumors (the EPR effect), active targeting enhances cellular uptake via receptor-mediated endocytosis, improving therapeutic efficacy and minimizing the off-target toxicity. Common biological targets in lung cancer include EGFR, targeted by EGF, anti-EGFR antibodies, or aptamers.

VEGFR, targeted by antibodies or tumor-homing peptides like tLYP-1), folate receptor (targeted with folic acid), transferrin receptor (exploited via transferrin or Tf-specific peptides), CD44 (hyaluronic acid-binding receptor), and integrins (e.g., $\alpha v\beta 3$, targeted by RGD peptides). Active targeting employs diverse NPs such as liposomes (e.g., Lipoplatin), polymeric NPs (PLGA, chitosan) for sustained release, inorganic NPs (gold and magnetic) for imaging or photothermal therapy, and exosome-based NPs that evade immune clearance. Thus, active targeting represents a promising approach to improve specificity, reduce systemic toxicity, and enhance therapeutic outcomes in lung cancer (Bazak et al., 2014; Holder et al., 2023; Lee et al., 2025; Muhamad et al., 2018; Vagena et al., 2025).

3.7 Nanoparticle-based diagnostic advancements

Diagnostics based on NPs are revolutionizing lung cancer treatment by providing for early diagnosis of lung cancer, advanced imaging, and integration of diagnosis with targeted therapeutics. The early stage of lung cancer is often asymptomatic, making timely detection challenging with conventional imaging techniques. Nanotechnology enhances diagnostic sensitivity by exploiting the unique optical, magnetic, and surface-modifiable properties of NPs, allowing the detection at the molecular and cellular levels. Magnetic NPs, particularly SPIONs, significantly enhance MRI by improving the contrast and tumor delineation and PET scan resolution. Engineer NPs not only detect cancer biomarkers but also deliver drugs directly to the cancer cell, reducing side effects and preventing drug resistance. old NPs are widely used in surface-enhanced Raman scattering (SERS) and colorimetric assays to detect ctDNA, microRNAs, and protein biomarkers. Liposomes carry chemotherapeutic agents like doxorubicin, quantum dots aid in sensitive fluorescence imaging, gold NPs lead to photothermal destruction of cancer cells, and magnetic NPs aid both diagnosis and targeted therapy, making lung cancer management more accurate and effective (Fig. 3.2).

3.7.1 Imaging application

Recent advancements in NP-based imaging have substantially improved lung cancer diagnostics by enhancing the specificity, sensitivity, and the detection of tumors early. Quantum dots play a vital role in the diagnosis of lung cancer due to their fluorescence properties, such as high brightness, stability, and specificity. For example, biofunctionalized graphene quantum dots in combination with gold NPs demonstrate a highly efficient fluorescent biosensor that allows for ultrasensitive detection of SCLC biomarkers such as neuron-specific enolase (NSE) (Kalkal et al., 2020). Additionally, quantum dot-based nano-biosensors have been developed that can detect circulating microRNAs for rapid, highly accurate, and minimally invasive detection beyond the standard CT imaging. There is also a DNA-functionalized quantum dot and an aptamer-based fluorescent probe that can detect tumor cells and mutations in NSCLC to improve diagnostic accuracy (Singh et al., 2018).

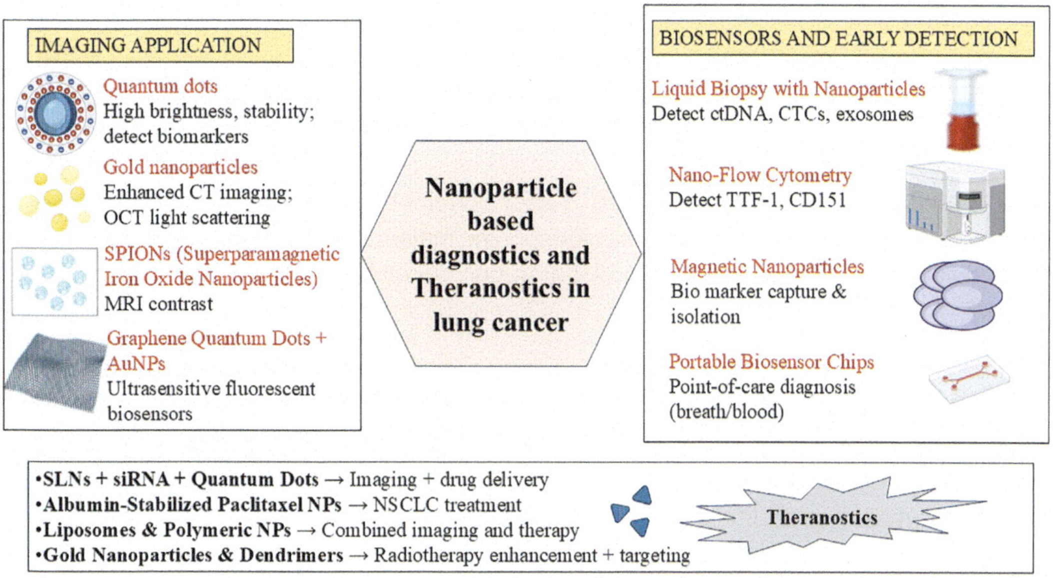

Figure 3.2
The image highlights the nanoparticles like quantum dots, gold nanoparticles, SPIONs, and graphene that enhance imaging, while biosensor technologies enable early detection through liquid biopsy, nano-flow cytometry, and theranostic approach. Combine these tools with targeted therapies for precise diagnosis; whereas TTF-1 thyroid transcription factor, OCT-optical coherence tomography, CT-computed tomography, ctDNA-circulating tumor DNA, CTC-circulating tumor cells, CD151-cluster of differentiation, NPs-nanoparticles, AuNPs-gold nanoparticles, and NSCLC-nonsmall cell lung cancer.

Gold nanoparticles have enhanced CT imaging for lung cancer by offering their greater contrast, longer circulation, and the ability to delineate a tumor accurately. SPIONs are an emerging contrast agent that enhances MRI by improving the ability to differentiate cancerous tissue from normal tissue. In optical coherence tomography (OCT), gold nanoparticles have been used because they enhance image resolution through enhanced light scattering, thus facilitating the visualization of lung cancer lesions (Duan et al., 2022). Carbon dots conjugated with anti-EGFR antibodies enable a real-time intraoperative lung tumor margin identification via near-infrared fluorescence. Silica nanoparticles carrying Raman reporters enable single-cell EGFR mutation analysis.

3.7.2 Biosensors and early detection

Liquid biopsy technologies, driven by nanoparticle-based biosensors and early detection tools, are revolutionizing the diagnostics of lung cancer. Liquid biopsy technology uses NPs to study circulating tumor components, including ctDNA, exosomes, and CTCs in body fluids (e.g., blood), making early cancer detection relatively noninvasive and real-time. Nano-flow cytometry assays have been established for detecting extracellular vesicles (exosomes) that contain lung cancer-associated proteins such as thyroid transcription factor-1 (TTF-1) and CD151 in the blood plasma of non-NSCLC patients. The assays can distinguish the person who is suffering from cancer from healthy normal controls with high sensitivity, which allows robust early detection (Zhang et al., 2024). The detection of ctDNA through liquid biopsy represents a noninvasive way to detect tumor-specific mutations in blood samples and enables a real-time molecular profile, addressing limits in traditional tissue biopsy (Bibikova & Fan, 2023).

Magnetic NPs are normally used to detect cancer biomarkers with great sensitivity and specificity, thereby facilitating the isolation and analysis of cancer-associated material derived from tumors. Nano-enabled platforms, such as nano-flow cytometry and biosensor microchips coupled with functionalized NPs, will provide rapid, accurate, and efficient detection of lung cancer biomarkers that aid in the differentiation of healthy and cancer cells. Nanotechnology-enabled point-of-care devices that include portable biosensor microchips functionalized with NPs also detect lung cancer biomarkers rapidly and accurately. These devices support rapid screening, under resource-limited conditions, with quick turnaround times, rather than expensive and extensive laboratory infrastructure. NP-based sensors incorporated into breath analysis or blood testing kits can provide noninvasive, rapid diagnostics in a point-of-care setting, which may allow for earlier detection and individualized interventions (Goswami et al., 2024; Pugazhendi et al., 2025).

Theranostic NPs, which possess both diagnostic and therapeutic functions, are rapidly becoming promising agents in the management of lung cancer by aiding in the visualization of the disease in real-time while actively treating the disease. The dual function presents an opportunity for more personalized medicine by targeting therapy, potentially reducing systemic toxicity, and improving clinical outcomes. Their diagnostic function includes advanced imaging modalities such as PET with radiotracers, MRI with contrast, SPECT, and fluorescence-based optical imaging for accurate detection, localization, and monitoring of tumors. Their therapeutic function can result in the delivery of radiopharmaceuticals, molecularly targeted drugs, immune-modulating agents, and drug carriers made with NPs such as liposomes, dendrimers, polymeric NPs, gold nanoparticles, magnetic nanoparticles, solid lipid nanoparticles (SLNs), and quantum dots. In the case of lung cancer, paclitaxel-loaded SLNs combined with siRNA and quantum dots produced synergistic anticancer effects, as well as improved cellular uptake and real-time fluorescent imaging monitoring. Clinically, NP-based formulations are being tested or are in use, such as albumin-stabilized paclitaxel NPs and irinotecan liposome injections, for NSCLC and SCLC. The integration of diagnosis, imaging, and therapy has led to theranostic NPs that provide a very targeted delivery of therapy to lung cancer. However, there are still challenges for efficient lung-specific delivery due to the organ's complex anatomical and pathological health as well as

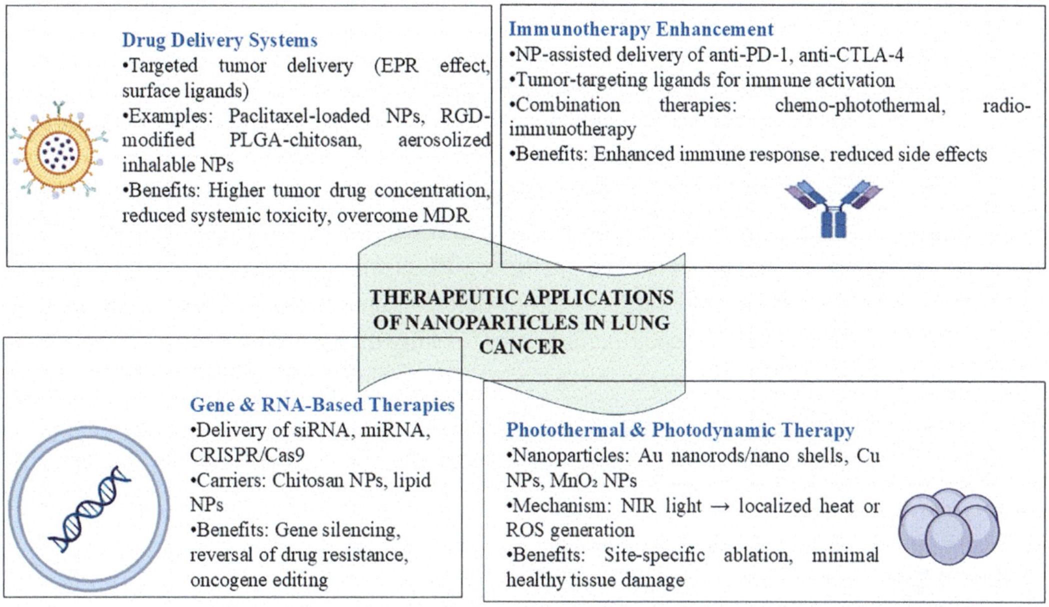

Figure 3.3

Therapeutic applications of nanoparticles in lung cancer: Includes targeted drug delivery, immunotherapy, gene/RNA therapies, and photothermal/photodynamic therapy for precise and effective treatment.

different physiological characteristics (Sharma et al., 2022; Singh et al., 2024; Wu et al., 2025).

NP-based diagnostics and theranostics offer breakthroughs in lung cancer by allowing specific and sensitive detection and targeted therapy. Using formulations such as quantum dots, gold NPs, SPIONs, and SLNs can build imaging capacity, and liquid biopsies for minimally invasive testing and monitoring of tumors in real-time without as much toxicity and exposure to patients. Even though there are challenges remaining in specific delivery and clinical validation, many advancements will be made concerning the use of these strategies in personalized care for lung cancer patients.

3.8 Therapeutic application of nanoparticles in lung cancer

NPs provide multifaceted therapeutic immunotherapeutic applications in lung cancer, including targeted delivery, gene modulation, photothermal ablation, and improved immunotherapy through selective and tumor-specific methodologies (Fig. 3.3).

3.8.1 Drug delivery systems

NPs enable targeted drug delivery in lung cancer treatment using their size, EPR effect, and their surface modification with targeting ligands to enhance selective uptake by the tumor. These particles enhance the concentration of the drug at the tumor site, which reduces systemic toxicity, bypasses the challenges of multidrug resistance by inhibiting efflux pumps, and promotes cell death. For example, paclitaxel-loaded NPs targeting the mitochondria, dual-drug hydrogel NPs including cisplatin and paclitaxel. RGD-modified PLGA-chitosan NPs and aerosolized inhalable NPs enhance targeted tumor delivery, and controlled release pharmacology and efficacy, while achieving specific targeting for lung tumors (Alshammari et al., 2023; Carrasco-Esteban et al., 2021).

Nanosized drug carrier molecules have been used in targeted drug delivery systems, including polymers, liposomes, and NPs. Drug-loaded NPs used as an inhalable form significantly inhibit lung cancer. Abraxane is the first commercial product where the albumin NPs loaded with paclitaxel (an anticancer drug) are used in an injectable form against cancer. Albumin-stabilized Abraxane is a nanoformulation of paclitaxel, which was administered with a concentration of 260 mg/m^2 every 3 weeks without premedication as a 30-min intravenous infusion in patients with advanced NSCLC. After the incubation period, a significant antitumor effect was observed. Paclitaxel-loaded lipid nanocarrier particles, paclitaxel-loaded lipid nanocapsules, have been used extensively against lung cancer, showing a significant reduction in the tumor compared to the conventional drug delivery systems (formulation) (Wang et al., 2019).

The anticancer drug docetaxel (DTX) had been loaded in NPs (PLGA-b-PEG NP), which were delivered through mesenchymal stem cells (MSC) in the lung tumors. The intracellular transportation of DTX-loaded NPs in the MSC/NP system has been studied in a lung cancer mice model (carrying a lox-stop-lox (LSL) sequence and K-ras G12D point mutation allele) by Wang et al. (2019). After 30 days of tumor induction, a PET-CT assay was observed with significant tumor inhibition for the MSC/NP/DTX lung cancer mice model group (Goel et al., 2013).

3.8.2 Gene and RNA-based therapies

NP-based gene delivery systems have emerged as powerful tools in lung cancer therapy, enabling the transport of genetic materials such as DNA, plasmid DNA (pDNA), messenger RNA (mRNA), small interfering RNA (siRNA), and microRNA (miRNA) directly to tumor cells. Gene molecules can be delivered in three primary ways: Encapsulated within NPs, electrostatically complexed through ionic interactions (e.g., forming polyplexes or lipoplexes), or conjugated onto the NP surface via chemical bonding or polymer trapping. Nanocarriers used for gene delivery are broadly classified into solid NPs, such as those composed of biodegradable polymers[poly (lactic-co-glycolic acid) (PLGA), PCL-polycaprolactone], polysaccharides (chitosan and alginate), proteins, lipids, and magnetic metal oxides, and liquid-based systems including liposomes, micelles, and emulsions formed from amphiphilic molecules. Cationic polymers like polyethylenimine (PEI) and cationic lipids such as 2-dioleoyl-3-trimethylammonium-propane (DOTAP) and 1,2-di-O-octadecenyl-3-trimethylammonium propane (DOTMA) enhance nucleic acid encapsulation and cellular uptake through electrostatic interactions. Among these, lipid-based nanoparticles (LNPs) remain the most widely used systems due to their high transfection efficiency, biocompatibility, and ease of functional modification with targeting ligands or PEG. Recent developments highlight the increasing focus on RNA-based therapeutics, particularly siRNA and miRNA, due to their high gene silencing efficiency and rapid onset of action. Compared to DNA, small RNAs are more susceptible to enzymatic degradation but demonstrate superior performance in lipid-mediated delivery, especially in nondividing cells. NPs protect these fragile molecules from nuclease degradation, enhance intracellular uptake, and promote endosomal escape. Key therapeutic strategies include silencing oncogenes such as KRAS using siRNA, restoring tumor suppressor genes like p53 through mRNA delivery, and modulating angiogenesis pathways (e.g., anti-VEGF siRNA). Combination approaches that codeliver RNA therapeutics with chemotherapeutic agents such as paclitaxel help overcome drug resistance and enhance tumor apoptosis. NP-mediated drug delivery systems have become a valuable strategy for gene and RNA therapies for lung cancer. NPs can deliver fragile molecules like siRNA and miRNA by protecting them from degradation and targeting them to tumor cells. These gene therapy strategies, using NP carriers, have been increasingly tested in preclinical models and early-stage clinical trials for lung cancer. For example, chitosan nanoparticles with RNA interference, specifically siRNA, can lead to effective gene silencing and the reversal of drug-resistant lung carcinoma cells. Other nanoparticles, such as lipid nanoparticles, deliver microRNAs and CRISPR/Cas9 components for gene editing to target oncogenes. These nanoparticles help to protect nucleic acids from degradation while also enabling them to be delivered intracellularly for modulating genes, and can be further developed in advanced lung cancer therapies (Kazmi et al., 2023; Lee et al., 2016). Despite promising preclinical outcomes demonstrating tumor growth inhibition and enhanced chemotherapy response, challenges remain, including immune clearance, off-target effects, potential toxicity of cationic materials, and large-scale manufacturing limitations. Nevertheless, a nanoparticle-mediated gene therapy represents a transformative approach in precision lung cancer treatment by enabling targeted, personalized, and minimally invasive therapeutic interventions.

3.8.3 Photothermal and photodynamic therapy

Photodynamic therapy (PDT) in lung cancer involves the administration of a photosensitizing agent that preferentially accumulates in malignant cells and is subsequently activated by a specific wavelength of light, usually in the red spectrum. Upon activation, the photosensitizer generates reactive oxygen species that induce tumor cell death, damage tumor blood vessels, and stimulate an antitumor immune response. Clinically, PDT is used for early-stage NSCLC, particularly superficial endobronchial tumors, and for palliative relief of airway obstruction. It is lung-preserving, repeatable, and suitable for patients who are not candidates for surgery, although its effectiveness is limited by shallow light penetration (approximately 1–2 cm) and temporary photosensitivity reactions. Photothermal therapy (PTT), in contrast, employs photothermal agents such as gold nanoparticles or graphene-based nanomaterials that accumulate at the tumor site and convert near-infrared light into heat, producing localized hyperthermia and tumor ablation. PTT is being explored to overcome the oxygen dependence of PDT and to improve the treatment of hypoxic lung tumors. Combining PDT and PTT offers synergistic benefits: PTT can enhance tumor oxygenation and thereby improve PDT efficiency, while PDT sensitizes tumor cells to thermal injury. Nanotechnology-based platforms capable of codelivering photodynamic and photothermal agents further improve targeting specificity and therapeutic efficacy. Additionally, both approaches can promote immunogenic cell death and antigen release, potentially trigger systemic antitumor immune responses, and support their integration with immunotherapy strategies. Metallic nanoparticles like gold (Au) nanoparticles, copper (Cu) nanoparticles, and manganese dioxide (MnO_2) nanoparticles are often used in photothermal and PDT. AuNRs and gold nanoshells are excellent in converting near-infrared light into localized heat, providing tumor cell ablation with minimal damage to the surrounding tissue. For PDT, nanoparticles containing a photosensitizer generate reactive oxygen species upon light activation. These metal-based NPs are excellent in providing controlled, site-specific tumor ablation in lung cancer. Hybrid NPs that involve polymers and metallic cores improve biocompatibility and therapeutic efficiency (Crous & Abrahamse, 2020; Guinart et al., 2020).

3.8.4 Immunotherapy enhancement

NPs improve immunotherapy by acting as vaccine adjuvants and facilitating tumor-specific delivery of immune checkpoint inhibitors. For example, polymeric NPs have been utilized to improve the delivery and efficacy of anti-PD-1 and anti-CTLA-4 antibodies with improved tumor immune responses while reducing systemic side effects. Similarly, NPs with tumor targeting ligands improve internalization by immune cells within the tumor microenvironment, leading to the reversal of immunosuppression and potentiating immunotherapeutic effects in lung cancer (Doroudian et al., 2023; Zhang et al., 2023).

NP-based combination therapies provide synergistic approaches to lung cancer through multiple treatment modalities. Strategies such as chemo-photothermal and radio-immunotherapy improve accuracy and efficacy while targeting tumors. These systems further enhance therapeutic delivery and timing, ultimately improving treatment. NBTXR3 NPs, in combination with radioimmunotherapy, greatly improve control over anti-PD-1 resistant lung tumors by stimulating a strong antitumor immune response (Hu et al., 2021). AuNRs and other plasmonic nanostructures can provide dual delivery of cytotoxics and conversion of near-infrared light into heat, resulting in an enhanced, synergistic method of killing NSCLC cells and reducing systemic doses. Paclitaxel-loaded AuNRs and AuNR-mesoporous composites demonstrate improved uptake by A549 cells and more potent effects than monotherapy in vitro; AuNR platforms are also being developed specifically for light-mediated lung cancer theranostics. Graphene-based carriers also allow for the ability to generate similar NIR-mediated chemo-photothermal effects with paclitaxel (Deinavizadeh et al., 2024; Knights & McLaughlan, 2018).

NP-based systems enhance efficacy, minimize systemic toxicities, and represent a promising avenue for more sophisticated lung cancer treatment by combining several treatment modalities.

3.9 Recent clinical trials

The translation of nanotechnology from laboratory research to clinical oncology has become increasingly evident through multiple clinical trials evaluating NP-based drug delivery systems in cancer therapy. Conventional chemotherapeutic drugs are effective anticancer agents but their clinical use is limited by poor solubility, rapid systemic clearance, nonspecific tissue distribution, and severe toxic side effects. To overcome these limitations, NP-mediated targeted drug delivery systems have been developed to improve drug pharmacokinetics, enhance tumor accumulation, and reduce systemic toxicity. Several clinical trials have investigated different NP formulations, including albumin-bound NPs, polymeric NPs, and ligand-targeted NPs. These nanocarriers enable the selective delivery of chemotherapeutic agents to tumor tissues through the EPR effect and receptor-mediated cellular uptake. Clinical studies have demonstrated improved drug solubility, prolonged circulation time, and better patient tolerance compared with conventional drug formulations.

Clinical translation of nanotechnology in lung cancer has progressed from laboratory research to human studies, and several clinical trials have evaluated NP-based chemotherapeutic formulations, particularly in NSCLC, which is summarized in Table 3.3. The safety and efficacy of platinum-based albumin-bound paclitaxel was studied in stage II B/III A patients with NSCLC and were found to be better tumor response and less toxicity in comparison with solvent-based paclitaxel (NCT02016209) https://clinicaltrials.gov/study/NCT02016209?cond=Nonsmall%20Cell%20Lung%20Cancer&term=Nanoparticle&rank=1. An improved chemotherapeutic effect and reduced toxicity were evaluated in a phase I/II study for ABI-007 (a unique protein formulation of paclitaxel). The dose-limiting toxicities (DLT) and maximum limited dose (MLD) had been evaluated in advanced NSCLC patients (stage IV) (NCT00073723). The safety and side effects have been evaluated for ABI-007 in patients with chemotherapy-naïve stage IV NSCLC patients (NCT00077246). The phase II clinical trial examines the tumor effect of Abraxane in patients with NSCLC with EGFR mutations, followed by front-line therapy with tyrosine kinase inhibitors (TKI) (NCT01620190). The multicenter phase II clinical study determined the safety and efficacy of BIND-014 (Docetaxel NPs for injectable suspension) as second-line therapy (NCT01792479). The safety and efficacy of BIND-014 (Docetaxel NPs for injectable suspension) as second-line therapy for

Table 3.3: Nanoparticles in targeted drug delivery systems used in clinical trials.

S. no.	Clinical trial id	Active drug used	Nano particles used	Clinical status	References
1	NCT02016209	Paclitaxel (PTX)	Platinum-based albumin-bound combination	Completed phase II trial	Deinavizadeh et al. (2024), National Library of Medicine (2013b)
2	NCT01620190	Paclitaxel (PTX)	Albumin-stabilized NP formulation	Completed phase II trial	Knights and McLaughlan (2018), National Library of Medicine (2011)
3	NCT00073723	Paclitaxel (PTX)	ABI-007 (a unique protein formulation)	Completed phase I and II trial	National Library of Medicine (2016c)
4	NCT00077246	Paclitaxel (PTX)	ABI-007 Albumin-stabilized NP formulation	Completed phase I and II trial	National Library of Medicine (2013a)
5	NCT01380769	camptothecin (CPT)	CRLX101 (NLG207)–nanoparticle comprised of camptothecin (CPT) conjugated to a cyclodextrin-based polymer	Completed phase II trial	National Library of Medicine (2020)
6	NCT01792479	Docetaxel	Docetaxel NPs for injectable suspension	Completed phase II trial	National Library of Medicine (2016b)
7	NCT0223320	Docetaxel	BIND-014 (Docetaxel NPs for injectable suspension)	Completed phase II trial	National Library of Medicine (2016a)
8	NCT00540514	Paclitaxel (PTX)	ABI-007 Albumin-bound PTX plus carboplatin compared with Taxol	Completed phase III trial	National Library of Medicine (2019)

patients with KARS mutation-positive or squamous cell NSCLC patients (NCT0223320). A randomized phase III clinical trial was conducted for ABI-007 Albumin-bound PTX plus carboplatin compared with Taxol was studied in an advanced NSCLC patients (NCT00540514) (National Library of Medicine, 2011, 2013a, 2013b, 2016a, 2016b, 2016c, 2019, 2020).

3.10 Challenges and limitations

Despite the promise of the NP-based strategies in lung cancer diagnosis and therapy, a significant challenge still remains that can hinder their clinical translation. The toxicity of NPs is one of the major concerns, especially with cationic polymers, heavy metal-based inorganic NPs, or high-dose formulations, which can induce systemic toxicity, inflammation, and oxidative stress. Unpredictable biodistribution and rapid clearance by the mononuclear phagocyte system (MPS) reduce the effective concentration of NPs at the site of the tumor, which limits both the diagnostic sensitivity and therapeutic efficacy. For diagnostic applications, these limitations are compounded by the difficulty in detecting low-abundance biomarkers with high specificity, as uneven NP accumulation can yield false negatives or low signal-to-noise ratios. Therapeutically, NPs face a biological barrier such as dense extracellular matrices, high interstitial pressure, hypoxic regions, and acidic tumor microenvironments, all of which can able to reduce the penetration and cellular uptake. Inefficient endosomal escape further limits the cytoplasmic delivery of therapeutics such as siRNA, miRNA, or gene editing payloads. The immune system may recognize and eliminate the NPs before they can reach their target site, thus this could lead to a potential decrease in the therapeutic efficiency of the NPs. From a translational perspective, complex and multistep synthesis protocols, batch-to-batch variability, and scalability issues are still significant manufacturing hurdles. Standardized quality control measures for NP size, surface chemistry, and drug loading efficiency are still underdeveloped, which further complicates the regulatory approval. Additionally, the regulatory framework for NP-based therapeutics remains with limited guidelines for safety, long-term toxicity, and environmental impact (Chow, 2025; Liu & Grodzinski, 2021; Zhang et al., 2019).

Addressing these challenges requires an integrated approach: advances in rational NP design to improve biocompatibility, circulation time, and penetration of NPs into the tumor. Innovations in scalable and reproducible manufacturing techniques and the establishment of robust regulatory guidelines to ensure the safety and efficacy.

3.11 Future perspectives

Future developments are likely to focus on multifunctional, stimuli-responsive NPs capable of integrating for diagnostic imaging, targeted drug delivery, and real-time monitoring into a single platform. Theranostic NPs could allow clinicians to track drug distribution, tumor response, and disease progression simultaneously, enabling more precise and timely treatment adjustments.

Personalized nanomedicine is expected to play a major role, where NPs are designed based on individual patient biomarker profiles, tumor receptor expression, and genetic characteristics. This approach promises to enhance therapeutic efficacy while minimizing the off-target effects, surpassing the limitations of conventional chemotherapy and radiotherapy.

Key challenges such as biocompatibility, biodegradability, and scalable manufacturing must be addressed to meet regulatory standards for clinical use. Advances in green synthesis methods. Standardized quality control and reproducible large-scale production are essential for successful clinical translation.

Moreover, combining NPs with immunotherapy, gene editing technologies (CRISPR/Cas systems), and artificial intelligence-driven treatment planning could transform precision oncology. Artificial intelligence can analyze the patient-specific data to optimize NP formulation, dosing schedules, and combination strategies, facilitating earlier detection, higher efficacy, and reduced toxicity.

The development of exosome-based carriers and multitargeting platforms shows potential to overcome tumor heterogeneity, multidrug resistance, and biological barriers. Collectively, these innovations could enable patient-tailored nanomedicine, offering safer, more effective, and personalized treatments for lung cancer in the future. The emerging strategies include inhalable NPs that allow direct pulmonary delivery, increasing localized drug concentration while reducing systemic side effects. This approach takes advantage of the lungs' large surface area and offers a noninvasive, targeted therapeutic option. Advanced stimuli-responsive NPs are being designed to release drugs selectively in response to tumor-specific triggers such as acidic pH, overexpressed enzymes, hypoxia, or external stimuli like near-infrared irradiation. These smart systems enhance treatment specificity and reduce damage to healthy tissues. Additionally, NPs are being engineered to overcome multidrug resistance by inhibiting efflux pumps and delivering combination therapies directly into cancer cells. Biomimetic NPs coated with cell membranes can evade immune clearance, prolong circulation time, and enhance tumor accumulation. With continued interdisciplinary research, NP-based therapies hold strong promise for safer, more personalized lung cancer treatment.

3.12 Conclusion

NPs offer a transformative potential in the management of lung cancer by improving earlier detection, targeted drug delivery, enhancing immune response, and minimizing systemic toxicity. Owing to their ultra-small size, high surface-to-volume ratio, and tunable physicochemical properties, NPs can be engineered to interact specifically with tumor tissues while sparing healthy cells. This selective targeting significantly improves therapeutic efficiency and reduces the adverse effects commonly associated with conventional chemotherapy and radiotherapy. In lung cancer, where late diagnosis and treatment resistance remain major challenges, nanotechnology provides a promising platform to overcome these clinical limitations. NPs have shown considerable value in diagnostic applications as well. They can function as contrast agents in imaging modalities such as MRI, CT, PET, and fluorescence imaging. By enhancing imaging sensitivity and specificity, NPs facilitate early tumor detection, accurate tumor localization, and the monitoring of treatment response. Early detection is particularly crucial in lung cancer because survival rates are strongly associated with the stage at diagnosis. Therefore, NP-based diagnostic systems may contribute to improved prognosis and patient survival. Their versatility in diagnostics and multimodal therapy makes NPs powerful tools for personalized medicine. Surface functionalization with ligands such as antibodies, peptides, and aptamers enables selective binding to overexpressed receptors on lung cancer cells, promoting receptor-mediated endocytosis. This targeted approach enhances intracellular drug delivery, increases drug concentration at the tumor site, and minimizes systemic exposure, thereby reducing toxicity to healthy tissues. NPs support cancer immunotherapy by enhancing immune activation and targeted delivery of therapeutic agents. Despite challenges in safety and large-scale production, their combination with conventional therapies may improve tumor targeting, overcome drug resistance, and enable more personalized lung cancer treatment. Integrating NPs with chemotherapy, radiotherapy, and immunotherapy offers strong potential to improve lung cancer treatment. These combination strategies can overcome drug resistance, enhance tumor drug penetration, and reduce recurrence. Nanotechnology offers a next-generation approach for lung cancer treatment. NPs enable early diagnosis, precise targeting, and controlled drug release while reducing toxicity. With continued research and clinical development, they are expected to transition into routine therapies and improve patient outcomes and quality of life.

References

ALQudah, M. A., ALFaqih, M. A., Hamouri, S., Al-Shaikh, A. A. F., Haddad, H. K., Al-Quran, W. Y., & Al-zoubi, K. H. (2021). Epidemiology and histopathological classification of lung cancer: A study from Jordan, retrospective observational study. *Annals of Medicine and Surgery, 65*, 102330.

Alshammari, M. K., Almomen, E. Y., Alshahrani, K. F., Altwalah, S. F., Kamal, M., Al-Twallah, M. F., Al-sanad, S. H., Al-Batti, M. H., Al-Rasheed, F. J., Alsalamah, A. Y., Alhazza, M. B., Alasmari, F. A., Abida, & Imran, M (2023). Nano-enabled strategies for the treatment of lung cancer: Potential bottlenecks and future perspectives. *Biomedicines, 11*(2), 473. https://doi.org/10.3390/biomedicines11020473.

Amreddy, N., Babu, A., Muralidharan, R., Munshi, A., & Ramesh, R. (2017). Polymeric nanoparticle-mediated gene delivery for lung cancer treatment. *Topics in Current Chemistry (Cham), 375*(2), 35. https://doi.org/10.1007/s41061-017-0128-5.

Baranwal, J., Barse, B., Di Petrillo, A., Gatto, G., Pilia, L., & Kumar, A. (2023). Nanoparticles in cancer diagnosis and treatment. *Materials, 16*(15), 5354. https://doi.org/10.3390/ma16155354.

Barr, T., Ma, S., Li, Z., & Yu, J. (2024). Recent advances and remaining challenges in lung cancer therapy. *Chinese Medical Journal, 137*(5), 533–546. https://doi.org/10.1097/CM9.0000000000002991.

Bazak, R., Houri, M., Achy, S. E., Hussein, W., & Refaat, T. (2014). Passive targeting of nanoparticles to cancer: A comprehensive review of the literature. *Molecular and Clinical Oncology, 2*(6), 904–908. https://doi.org/10.3892/mco.2014.356.

Bibikova, M., & Fan, J. (2023). Liquid biopsy for early detection of lung cancer. *Chinese Medical Journal Pulmonary and Critical Care Medicine, 1*(4), 200–206. https://doi.org/10.1016/j.pccm.2023.08.005.

Carrasco-Esteban, E., Domínguez-Rullán, J. A., Barrionuevo-Castillo, P., Pelari-Mici, L., Leaman, O., Sastre-Gallego, S., & López-Campos, F. (2021). Current role of nanoparticles in the treatment of lung cancer. *Journal of Clinical and Translational Research, 7*(2), 140–155.

Chen, T., Ashwood, L. M., Kondrashova, O., Strasser, A., Kelly, G., & Sutherland, K. D. (2025). Breathing new insights into the role of mutant p53 in lung cancer. *Oncogene, 44*(3), 115–129.

Chow, J. C. L. (2025). Nanomaterial-based molecular imaging in cancer: Advances in simulation and AI integration. *Biomolecules, 15*(3), 444. https://doi.org/10.3390/biom15030444.

Crintea, A., Dutu, A. G., Samasca, G., Florian, I. A., Lupan, I., & Craciun, A. M. (2021). The nanosystems involved in treating lung cancer. *Life (Basel, Switzerland), 11*(7), 682. https://doi.org/10.3390/life11070682.

Crintea, A., Motofelea, A. C., Şovrea, A. S., Constantin, A. M., Crivii, C. B., Carpa, R., & Duţu, A. G. (2023). Dendrimers: Advancements and potential applications in cancer diagnosis and treatment—An overview. *Pharmaceutics, 15*(5), 1406. https://doi.org/10.3390/pharmaceutics15051406.

Crous, A., & Abrahamse, H. (2020). Effective gold nanoparticle-antibody-mediated drug delivery for photodynamic therapy of lung cancer stem cells. *International Journal of Molecular Sciences, 21*(11), 3742. https://doi.org/10.3390/ijms21113742.

Dakal, T. C., Dhabhai, B., Pant, A., Moar, K., Chaudhary, K., Yadav, V., Ranga, V., Sharma, N. K., Kumar, A., Maurya, P. K., Maciaczyk, J., Schmidt-Wolf, I. G. H., & Sharma, A. (2024). Oncogenes and tumor suppressor genes: Functions and roles in cancers. *MedComm, 5*(6), e582. https://doi.org/10.1002/mco2.582.

Deinavizadeh, M., Kiasat, A. R., Shafiei, M., Sabaeian, M., Mirzajani, R., Zahraei, S. M., & Hooshmand, N. (2024). Synergistic chemo-photothermal therapy using gold nanorods supported on thiol-functionalized mesoporous silica for lung cancer treatment. *Scientific Reports, 14*(1), 4373.

de Oliveira Cardoso, V. M., Bistaffa, M. J., Sterman, R. G., de Lima, L. L. P., Toldo, G. S., Cancino-Bernardi, J., & Zucolotto, V. (2024). Nanomedicine innovations for lung cancer diagnosis and therapy. *ACS Applied Materials & Interfaces, 17*(9), 13197.

Doroudian, M., Zanganeh, S., Abbasgholinejad, E., & Donnelly, S. C. (2023). Nanomedicine in lung cancer immunotherapy. *Frontiers in Bioengineering and Biotechnology, 11*, 1144653. https://doi.org/10.3389/fbioe.2023.1144653.

Du, J., Li, Y., Wang, L., Zhou, Y., Shen, Y., Xu, F., & Chen, Y. (2020). Selective application of neuroendocrine markers in the diagnosis and treatment of small cell lung cancer. *Clinica Chimica Acta, 509*, 295–303.

Duan, Y., Shen, C., Zhang, Y., & Luo, Y. (2022). Advanced diagnostic and therapeutic strategies in nanotechnology for lung cancer. *Frontiers in Oncology, 12*, 1031000. https://doi.org/10.3389/fonc.2022.1031000.

Feng, J., Zhang, P., Wang, D., Li, Y., & Tan, J. (2024). New strategies for lung cancer diagnosis and treatment: Applications and advances in nanotechnology. *Biomarker Research, 12*(1), 136. https://doi.org/10.1186/s40364-024-00686-7.

Glatzer, M., Elicin, O., Ramella, S., Nestle, U., & Putora, P. M. (2016). Radio(chemo)therapy in locally advanced nonsmall cell lung cancer. *European Respiratory Review : An Official Journal of The European Respiratory Society, 25*(139), 65–70. https://doi.org/10.1183/16000617.0053-2015.

Goel, A., Baboota, S., Sahni, J. K., & Ali, J. (2013). Exploring targeted pulmonary delivery for treatment of lung cancer. *International Journal of Pharmaceutical investigation, 3*(1), 8.

Goswami, S., Samanta, P., & Adhikari, M. D. (2024). Nanobiotechnology: A smart platform of the future transform liquid biopsy era. *The Journal of Liquid Biopsy, 3*, 100137.

Guinart, A., Perry, H. L., Wilton-Ely, J. D. E. T., & Tetley, T. D. (2020). Gold nanomaterials in the management of lung cancer. *Emerging Topics in Life Sciences, 4*(6), 627–643. https://doi.org/10.1042/ETLS20200332.

Holder, J. E., Ferguson, C., Oliveira, E., Lodeiro, C., Trim, C. M., Byrne, L. J., & Wilson, C. M. (2023). The use of nanoparticles for targeted drug delivery in non-small cell lung cancer. *Frontiers in Oncology, 13*, 1154318.

Hu, Y., Paris, S., Barsoumian, H., Abana, C. O., He, K., Sezen, D., Wasley, M., Masrorpour, F., Chen, D., Yang, L., Dunn, J. D., Gandhi, S., Nguyen, Q. N., Cortez, M. A., & Welsh, J. W. (2021). A radioenhancing nanoparticle mediated immunoradiation improves survival and generates long-term antitumor immune memory in an anti-PD1-resistant murine lung cancer model. *Journal of Nanobiotechnology, 19*(1), 416. https://doi.org/10.1186/s12951-021-01163-1.

Jumeau, R., Vilotte, F., Durham, A. D., & Ozsahin, E. M. (2019). Current landscape of palliative radiotherapy for non-small-cell lung cancer. *Translational Lung Cancer Research, 8*(Suppl 2), S192–S201. https://doi.org/10.21037/tlcr.2019.08.10.

Kalkal, A., Pradhan, R., Kadian, S., Manik, G., & Packirisamy, G. (2020). Biofunctionalized graphene quantum dots based fluorescent biosensor toward efficient detection of small cell lung cancer. *ACS Applied Bio Materials, 3*(8), 4922–4932. https://doi.org/10.1021/acsabm.0c00427.

Kazmi, I., Shaikh, M. A. J., Afzal, O., Altamimi, A. S. A., Almalki, W. H., Alzarea, S. I., & Gupta, G. (2023). Chitosan-based nano drug delivery system for lung cancer. *Journal of Drug Delivery Science and Technology, 81*, 104196.

Khakpour, S., Hosano, N., Moosavi-Nejad, Z., Farajian, A. A., & Hosano, H. (2024). Advancing tumor therapy: Development and utilization of protein-based nanoparticles. *Pharmaceutics, 16*(7), 887. https://doi.org/10.3390/pharmaceutics16070887.

Khan, Y., Sadia, H., Shah, Ali, S. , Z., Khan, M. N., Shah, A. A., Ullah, N., Ullah, M. F., Bibi, H., Bafakeeh, O. T., Khedher, N. B., Eldin, S. M., Fadhl, B. M., & Khan, M. I (2022). Classification, synthetic, and characterization approaches to nanoparticles, and their applications in various fields of nanotechnology: A review. *Catalysts, 12*(11), 1386. https://doi.org/10.3390/catal12111386.

Knights, O. B., & McLaughlan, J. R. (2018). Gold nanorods for light-based lung cancer theranostics. *International Journal of Molecular Sciences, 19*(11), 3318. https://doi.org/10.3390/ijms19113318.

Kontomanolis, E. N., Koutras, A., Syllaios, A., Schizas, D., Mastoraki, A., Garmpis, N., Diakosavvas, M., Angelou, K., Tsatsaris, G., Pagkalos, A., Ntounis, T., & Fasoulakis, Z. (2020). Role of oncogenes and tumor-suppressor genes in carcinogenesis: A review. *Anticancer Research, 40*(11), 6009–6015. https://doi.org/10.21873/anticanres.14622.

Kumar, H., Akash, K., Bhardwaj, K., Taneja, A., Singh, S., Manickam, S., … Kuča, K. (2022). Applications of metallic nanoparticles in lung cancer treatment. In *Lung cancer diagnosis and treatment: An interdisciplinary approach* (pp. 161–184). Cham: Springer Nature Switzerland.

Kumari, S., & Sarkar, L. (2021). A review on nanoparticles: Structure, classification, synthesis & applications. *Journal of Scientific Research, 65*(8), 42–46.

Lee, H., Sajid, K., & Lee, J. (2025). Engineered nanocarriers for targeted lung cancer therapy: Mechanistic innovations and recent clinical progress. *Exploration of Targeted Anti-Tumor Therapy, 6*, 1002339. https://doi.org/10.37349/etat.2025.1002339.

Lee, H. Y., Mohammed, K. A., & Nasreen, N. (2016). Nanoparticle-based targeted gene therapy for lung cancer. *American Journal of Cancer Research, 6*(5), 1118–1134.

Liu, C. H., & Grodzinski, P. (2021). Nanotechnology for cancer imaging: Advances, challenges, and clinical opportunities. *Radiology. Imaging Cancer, 3*(3), e200052. https://doi.org/10.1148/rycan.2021200052.

López, Á., Escalera, E., Del Barco, E., Bellido, L., Cigarral, B., Barrios, B., & Cruz, J. J. (2021). Carcinoma de pulmón no microcítico. *Medicine-Programa de Formación Médica Continuada Acreditado, 13*(25), 1377–1387.

Meyer, M. L., Peters, S., Jänne, P. A., Mok, T. S., Bunn, P. A., Abdel Karim, N., Altorki, N. K., Arrieta, O., Bar, J., Cappuzzo, F., Carbone, D., Dacic, S., Diehn, M., Dziadziuszko, R., Felip, E., Flores, R., Florez, N., Forde, P. M., Gainor, J. F., Gray, J. E., … Hirsch, F. R. (2026). Global advances and future directions in lung cancer care: Expert consensus and strategic priorities. *ESMO Open, 11*(2), 106034. https://doi.org/10.1016/j.esmoop.2025.106034.

Muhamad, N., Plengsuriyakarn, T., & Na-Bangchang, K. (2018). Application of active targeting nanoparticle delivery system for chemotherapeutic drugs and traditional/herbal medicines in cancer therapy: A systematic review. *International Journal of Nanomedicine, 13*, 3921–3935. https://doi.org/10.2147/IJN.S165210.

National Library of Medicine. (2011). ClinicalTrials.gov. Retrieved August 5, 2025, from https://clinicaltrials.gov/study/NCT01620190

National Library of Medicine. (2013a). ClinicalTrials.gov. Retrieved August 5, 2025, from https://clinicaltrials.gov/study/NCT00077246

National Library of Medicine. (2013b). ClinicalTrials.gov. Retrieved August 5, 2025, from https://clinicaltrials.gov/study/NCT02016209

National Library of Medicine. (2016a). ClinicalTrials.gov. Retrieved August 5, 2025, from https://clinicaltrials.gov/study/NCT02283320

National Library of Medicine. (2016b). ClinicalTrials.gov. Retrieved August 5, 2025, from https://clinicaltrials.gov/study/NCT01792479

National Library of Medicine. (2016c). ClinicalTrials.gov. Retrieved August 5, 2025, from https://clinicaltrials.gov/study/NCT00073723

National Library of Medicine. (2019). ClinicalTrials.gov. Retrieved August 5, 2025, from https://clinicaltrials.gov/study/NCT00540514

National Library of Medicine. (2020). ClinicalTrials.gov. Retrieved August 5, 2025, from https://clinicaltrials.gov/study/NCT01380769

Nooreldeen, R., & Bach, H. (2021). Current and future development in lung cancer diagnosis. *International Journal of Molecular Sciences, 22*(16), 8661. https://doi.org/10.3390/ijms22168661.

Nsairat, H., Khater, D., Sayed, U., Odeh, F., Al Bawab, A., & Alshaer, W. (2022). Liposomes: Structure, composition, types, and clinical applications. *Heliyon, 8*(5), e09394. https://doi.org/10.1016/j.heliyon.2022.e09394.

Park, H. J., Lee, S. H., & Chang, Y. S. (2020). Recent advances in diagnostic technologies in lung cancer. *The Korean Journal of Internal Medicine, 35*(2), 257–268. https://doi.org/10.3904/kjim.2020.030.

Prabhu, R. H., Patravale, V. B., & Joshi, M. D. (2015). Polymeric nanoparticles for targeted treatment in oncology: Current insights. *International Journal of Nanomedicine, 10*, 1001–1018. https://doi.org/10.2147/IJN.S56932.

Pugazhendi, I., Agrawal, A., Sofia, A., Manoharan, M. P., Fernandes, B. C. A., & Maroules, M. (2025). Liquid biopsy for early detection and monitoring of lung cancer: A systematic review and meta-analysis. *Journal of Clinical Oncology, 43*(16_suppl), e20019.

Raso, M. G., Bota-Rabassedas, N., & Wistuba, I. I. (2021). Pathology and classification of SCLC. *Cancers, 13*(4), 820. https://doi.org/10.3390/cancers13040820.

Riaz, M. K., Riaz, M. A., Zhang, X., Lin, C., Wong, K. H., Chen, X., Zhang, G., Lu, A., & Yang, Z. (2018). Surface functionalization and targeting strategies of liposomes in solid tumor therapy: A review. *International Journal of Molecular Sciences, 19*(1), 195. https://doi.org/10.3390/ijms19010195.

Sandra, F., Khaliq, N. U., Sunna, A., & Care, A. (2019). Developing protein-based nanoparticles as versatile delivery systems for cancer therapy and imaging. *Nanomaterials, 9*(9), 1329. https://doi.org/10.3390/nano9091329.

Savchuk, S., Gentry, K. M., Wang, W., Carleton, E., Biagi-Junior, C. A., Luthria, K., & Venkatesh, H. S. (2025). Neuronal activity-dependent mechanisms of small cell lung cancer pathogenesis. *Nature, 646*(8087), 1232–1242.

Sharma, A., Shambhwani, D., Pandey, S., Singh, J., Lalhlenmawia, H., Kumarasamy, M., & Kumar, D. (2022). Advances in lung cancer treatment using nanomedicines. *ACS Omega, 8*(1), 10–41.

Siddiqui, F., Vaqar, S., & Siddiqui, A. H. (2023). *Lung cancer. In StatPearls. StatPearls Publishing* https://www.ncbi.nlm.nih.gov/books/NBK482357/.

Siddiqui, F, Vaqar, S, & Siddiqui, AH. (2025). Lung cancer. [Updated 2023 May 8]. *StatPearls [Internet]*. StatPearls Publishing https://www.ncbi.nlm.nih.gov/books/NBK482357/.

Singh, P., Semwal, P., Gargi, B., Painuli, S., Aschner, M., Alsharif, K. F., & Worku, L. A. (2024). Global research and current trends on nanotherapy in lung cancer research: A bibliometric analysis of 20 years. *Discover Oncology, 15*(1), 539.

Singh, R. D., Shandilya, R., Bhargava, A., Kumar, R., Tiwari, R., Chaudhury, K., Srivastava, R. K., Goryacheva, I. Y., & Mishra, P. K. (2018). Quantum dot based nano-biosensors for detection of circulating cell-free miRNAs in lung carcinogenesis: From biology to clinical translation. *Frontiers in Genetics, 9*, 616. https://doi.org/10.3389/fgene.2018.00616.

Smolarz, B., Łukasiewicz, H., Samulak, D., Piekarska, E., Kołaciński, R., & Romanowicz, H. (2025). Lung cancer—Epidemiology, pathogenesis, treatment and molecular aspect (review of literature). *International Journal of Molecular Sciences, 26*(5), 2049. https://doi.org/10.3390/ijms26052049.

Tamanna, M. T., & Egbune, C. (2023). Traditional Treatment Approaches and Role of Immunotherapy in Lung Malignancy and Mesothelioma. *Cancer treatment and research, 185*, 79–89. https://doi.org/10.1007/978-3-031-27156-4_5.

Vagena, I.-A., Malapani, C., Gatou, M.-A., Lagopati, N., & Pavlatou, E. A. (2025). Enhancement of EPR Effect for passive tumor targeting: Current status and future perspectives. *Applied Sciences, 15*(6), 3189. https://doi.org/10.3390/app15063189.

Wang, X., Chen, H., Zeng, X., Guo, W., Jin, Y., Wang, S., & Mei, L. (2019). Efficient lung cancer-targeted drug delivery via a nanoparticle/MSC system. *Acta Pharmaceutica Sinica B, 9*(1), 167–176.

World Health Organization. (2026, April 16). Lung cancer. World Health Organization. https://www.who.int/news-room/fact-sheets/detail/lung-cancer.

Wu, Y., Sun, C., Jin, K., & Dong, C. (2025). Theranostic role of advanced nanotechnological tools in early brain metastases in lung cancer: An updated review. *International Journal of Nanomedicine, 20*, 7215–7232. https://doi.org/10.2147/IJN.S517928.

Yang, K., Wang, L., Wang, Z., Lv, P., Cai, C., Zhao, H., & Wang, B. (2026). Neoadjuvant immunotherapy for lung cancer: Current limitations and future prospects. *Frontiers in Immunology, 17*, 1752298.

Zhang, A., Gao, Q., Tian, C., Chen, W., Pan, C., Wang, L., Huang, J., & Zhang, J. (2024). Liquid biopsy in lung cancer: Nano-flow cytometry detection of non-small cell lung cancer in blood. *Laboratory Investigation; A Journal of Technical Methods and Pathology, 104*(12), 102151. https://doi.org/10.1016/j.labinv.2024.102151.

Zhang, C., Fan, J., & Wu, L. (2025). Application of nanomaterials in precision treatment of lung cancer. *iScience, 28*(1).

Zhang, X., Wang, X., Hou, L., Xu, Z., Liu, Y., & Wang, X. (2023). Nanoparticles overcome adaptive immune resistance and enhance immunotherapy *via* targeting tumor microenvironment in lung cancer. *Frontiers in Pharmacology, 14*, 1130937. https://doi.org/10.3389/fphar.2023.1130937.

Zhang, Y., Li, M., Gao, X., Chen, Y., & Liu, T. (2019). Nanotechnology in cancer diagnosis: Progress, challenges and opportunities. *Journal of Hematology & Oncology, 12*(1), 137. https://doi.org/10.1186/s13045-019-0833-3.

Zhou, J., Xu, Y., Liu, J., Feng, L., Yu, J., & Chen, D. (2024). Global burden of lung cancer in 2022 and projections to 2050: Incidence and mortality estimates from GLOBOCAN. *Cancer Epidemiology, 93*, 102693.

CHAPTER 4

Revolutionizing lung cancer treatment: Nanoengineered enhancements in targeted drug delivery for enhanced efficacy

Shahzar Khan, Nadia Ilyas, Humaira Nawaz, Syed Hamza Abbas and Samiullah Khan

Department of Microbiology, Faculty of Biological Sciences, Quaid-i-Azam University, Islamabad, Pakistan

4.1 Introduction

Lung cancer remains the leading cause of cancer-related deaths globally, with more than 1.8 million deaths being recorded every year. Despite significant research investments, survival rates remain disappointingly low, particularly in advanced stages, where the 5-year survival rate is less than 20% (Peng et al., 2023; Shojaei et al., 2024). Moreover, approximately 85% of all instances pertain to nonsmall cell lung cancer (NSCLC), and it is challenging to treat because of its heterogeneity and the late stage at which the cancer is diagnosed. Lung cancer continues to pose a significant public health burden worldwide. Early detection remains one of the most critical factors in improving diagnosis and patient survival.

Traditional therapeutic measures, which comprise conventional surgery, radiation, and chemotherapy, have severe limitations, including nonspecific cytotoxicity, multidrug resistance (MDR), inadequate drug uptake and concentration at the tumor sites (Kazmi et al., 2023; Zhang et al., 2024). Poor selectivity of traditional treatment led patients to experience severe side effects. The existence of such difficulties poses the dire necessity to have more targeted, efficient, and less risky therapy. More focus is given to developing therapies that specifically target cancer cells while leaving healthy tissues.

Nanotechnology has captured the attention as an evolving concept in addressing the discrepancies in the field of oncology. For instance, the ability to merge drug solubility, extended pharmacokinetics (PKs), and targeted tumor delivery capability with reduced systemic toxicity has been demonstrated with nanoengineered drug delivery systems, which can take

Nanoengineered Therapeutics for Lung Cancer: Advanced Drug Delivery Strategies.
DOI: https://doi.org/10.1016/B978-0-443-44585-9.00005-6

on various structures, including liposomes, dendrimers, polymeric micelles, and solid lipid nanoparticles (NPs) (Jin et al., 2024; Kaur, Guleria, & Kumar, 2023; Min et al., 2023). Furthermore, it can be used both for diagnostic and therapeutic purposes. In short, NPs provide new possibilities in lung cancer personalized treatment (Gao, Guo, Li, Thu, & Hussain, 2018). Moreover, real-time monitoring of tumors is also possible with NPs through imaging techniques.

The chapter gives an inclusive discussion of nanoengineered platforms for lung cancer therapy. It gives special attention to the new developments in the drug delivery systems, functionalizing the surfaces to achieve targeted therapy, and removing the barriers. It also discusses new methods of stimuli-responsive systems, combination therapies, and theranostic nanocarriers. Recent clinical investigations have revealed enhanced results with the process of nanoparticle-based drug delivery systems amongst lung cancer patients. These developments demonstrate the possibility of nanotechnology overturning the treatment of lung cancer in the next few years.

4.1.1 Socioeconomic impact of lung cancer

Lung cancer is one of the most devastating malignancies in the world, given that it is one of the leading causes of cancer morbidity and mortality in both developed and developing countries. Lung cancer is the most life-threatening type of all cancers worldwide, presenting with about 2.2 million new cases and close to 1.8 million deaths per year (Sun, Zhang, Yang, & Wang, 2021). The results of the diagnosis imaging, molecular profiling, and therapeutic interventions, however, have not significantly improved the survival rates, with 5-year survival rates continuing to be less than 25% in most areas, primarily because of the late diagnosis and rapid progression of the disease (Wang, Nelson, Bogardus, & Grannis, 2010).

There are marked variations in the incidence, mortality, and survival of lung cancer across regions due to variation in health infrastructure, environmental exposures, socioeconomic status, and access to early detection and treatment services. The organized screening programs, the latest diagnostic technologies, and access to specific therapies give high-income countries (HICs) a comparatively better outcome. However, low- and middle-income countries (LMICs) still experience disproportionately higher death rates because of the delayed diagnosis of the disease, inadequate health care facilities, and inaccessibility to the most recent treatment modalities. Such disparities add to the growing global survival gap and highlight the pressing necessity of scalable and accessible therapeutic innovations (Nwagbara, Ginindza, & Hlongwana, 2020).

In addition to its clinical effect, lung cancer has an immense negative socioeconomic effect on healthcare systems and communities. The economic cost of lung cancer encompasses direct medical expenses incurred in diagnosis, hospitalization, chemotherapy, radiotherapy, immunotherapy, and long-term care, indirect expenses in terms of loss of productivity, long-term disability, and early death. Long treatment regimens, recurring hospitalization, and multimodal therapies are common in patients, which is a heavy burden on the infrastructure of healthcare and health budgets of countries, especially in resource-deficient environments.

One of the significant elements of this burden is productivity loss since lung cancer is largely common among people in economically productive ages, thus resulting in work absenteeism, premature retirement, and permanent disability. The social impacts of the disease also include the impact on families and caregivers in terms of financial instability, psychological strain, and burden of care, which add to the existing burden. The disability burden of lung cancer is cumulative and therefore is a significant source of disability-adjusted life year (DALYs), which substantiates its status as a high-priority area of concern in global populations (Vayr et al., 2019).

Late-stage diagnosis is one of the most significant issues of lung cancer treatment, where most patients come with advanced or metastatic cancers, where curative treatment is not possible, and the therapeutic prognosis is low. Lack of effective large-scale screening programs in most of the areas, along with nonspecific early symptoms, adds to delayed diagnosis and low prognosis (Scheff & Schneider, 2013). Despite mortality reduction observed to be achieved by low-dose computed tomography (LDCT) screening in high-risk groups, its spread is limited by cost and infrastructure requirements and barriers to access, especially in LMICs (Edelman et al., 2020).

The overall epidemiological, socioeconomic, diagnostic, and healthcare disparities of the disease have placed lung cancer in a very clear position of need, as new therapeutic approaches are necessary not only to be effective but also to be scalable, targeted, and cost-effective. These issues present a compelling reason to create and innovate high-tech nanoengineered drug delivery systems, which hold promise in improving treatment precision, systemic toxicity, and treatment access, and eventually lead to improved clinical outcomes and a lower burden of lung cancer in society.

4.2 Nanotechnology in oncology: Foundations and promise

4.2.1 Principles of nanomedicine

Nanomedicine is the study and implementation of nanoscale materials design and their use in diagnosis, therapy, and regeneration (Boulaiz et al., 2011). In oncology, the core concept consists of the use of the ability of NPs to have specific physicochemical properties and therefore be able to overcome major limitations of conventional cancer therapy, which can be summarized as inadequate solubility of drugs, systemic toxicity, and nonspecific distribution of drugs in the body. Nanoscale size enables passive targeting of the tumor through the enhanced permeability and retention (EPR) effect. This effect enables NPs to accumulate preferably in tumor tissues having leaky vasculature and poor lymphatic drainage. Alongside passive targeting, active targeting is also useful in the context of nanomedicine. In active targeting, ligands, antibodies, or peptides are incorporated on the nanocarriers to enable specific binding to tumor-related agents, which increases cancer cell uptake, enhances therapeutic efficacy, and minimizes the negative effects. Passive and active targeting techniques combined will enable more specific anticancer drug delivery. NPs may also be further functionalized to increase blood circulation and stability. Through functionalization, poorly vascularized tumors can be targeted by nanocarriers to enable drug uptake. Different studies have shown that NPs could be designed to react to certain stimuli in the tumor microenvironment (TME). These stimuli help in the proper, timely, and selective release of the loaded drug (Shojaei et al., 2024).

4.2.2 Advantages of nanoengineered drug delivery over traditional methods

There are several important benefits of nanoengineered systems in comparison to standard drug formulations. On one hand, they increase the solubility and bioavailability of anticancer hydrophobic drugs. On the other hand, they improve the therapeutic index and decrease the adverse effects (Kazmi et al., 2023). In addition, NPs can be designed to release drugs in a controlled and stimulus-responsive manner. The controlled release can be easily achieved by pH, redox conditions, or enzymes within the TME (Min et al., 2023). Moreover, due to their multifunctional potential, nanocarriers can be used for both treatment and diagnosis (theranostic) modules. This can help to track drug distribution in real-time and the response to treatment (Gao, Guo, Li, Thu, & Hussain, 2018). Nanoengineered drug delivery systems would be able to improve drug stability and increase blood circulation time. These systems have the ability to attack tumors with great precision and limit the destruction of healthy tissues. Nanocarriers can be stimuli-responsive to enable control in both space and time of drug release. Theranostic nanocarriers offer a combination of imaging and therapy, thus enabling a personalized treatment approach. NPs are also capable of enhancing patient compliance by lowering the dosing rate. Furthermore, nanoformulations can effectively combat MDR due to their unique cellular uptake mechanism (endocytosis). Their uptake mechanism does not involve drug efflux pumps. They are also used to codeliver different agents, such as chemotherapeutics, siRNAs, or immunomodulators, in a single nanocarrier to realize synergistic effects and a decreased dosing interval (Peng et al., 2023; Shojaei et al., 2024). Combining two or more agents in the same nanocarrier might increase therapeutic effect and decrease toxicity. NPs can be designed to overcome resistance mechanisms and regain drug sensitivity to resistant cancer cells. Advanced nanoformulations allow combination therapy to fight cancer using more than one route. These characteristics render nanoengineered systems a very promising strategy for next-generation cancer therapy.

4.2.3 Clinical significance of nanoscale drug delivery systems

In medicinal research, several nano-based therapeutics have achieved regulatory or advanced degree-of-trial status. For instance, nanoformulations having proven efficacy in enhancing the treatment of different cancers, including lung cancer, are liposomal doxorubicin, albumin-bound paclitaxel (Abraxane), and liposomal (Zhang et al., 2024). These nano-based therapeutics have been shown to have better clinical results than traditional drug formulations. These NPs are also safer in general, with lower systemic toxicity. NPs have made it possible to use drugs that have been restricted because of inadequate solubility or stability.

Moreover, NPs can be delivered in a site-specific manner, increasing the drug level at the target sites and reducing drug levels in healthy tissues. The specificity plays a significant role in decreasing adverse effects and enhancing a patient's quality of life. Clinical translation is progressing, but it is facilitated by progress in mass production, regulatory pathways, and individual cancer genome-directed and receptor-directed approaches. NPs can be delivered directly to the tumor cells. This approach is very important in ensuring the proper supply of a greater concentration of drugs reaches the tumor. It also significantly reduces the exposure of normal organs to NPs. Individualized therapy with NPs can be applied to attain optimal response through personalization of application to the tumor profile of individual patients. The approval of regulatory bodies and scalable production is a requirement that can make the difference between nanoparticle-based therapies being researched and being implemented in a clinic. The clinical trials are still underway to add to the knowledge of the safety and potential therapeutic benefits of NPs (Attia, Anton, Wallyn, Omran, & Vandamme, 2019).

4.2.4 Nanoparticles for lung cancer drug delivery

Among the different platforms that have received the most research and applications in lung cancer targeted treatment, NPs stand out. Their ability to enhance solubility, bioavailability, and tumor site-delivered drugs and minimize systemic toxicity has made them the focus of next-generation cancer chemotherapies. In general, metallic and nonmetallic classes of NPs may be utilized in lung cancer drug delivery. These NPs have different structural features, drug load, and release mechanisms. Metallic NPs, including gold (Au) and silver (Ag) NPs, have the capability of delivering therapeutic and diagnostic capabilities. The nonmetallic NPs, such as polymeric and lipid-based NPs, are usually biodegradable and biocompatible. The suitability of the type of nanoparticle can be determined by the site of the tissue and the drug release profile. NPs provide the possibilities of combination therapies in that they can transport several drugs or agents on the same platform. The design of advanced NPs is to overcome biological obstacles and enhance the penetration of drugs in tumor tissues (Singh et al., 2025).

4.3 Types of nanocarriers: Overview, advantages, and classification

4.3.1 Metallic and nonmetallic nanoparticles

Au, Ag, and iron oxide (Fe_3O_4) have also received attention as metallic NPs that have multifunctional applications. The most notable properties of AuNPs are surface plasmon resonance, their ease of surface modification, and good biocompatibility. The properties provide a possibility to conjugate with any targeting ligand or therapeutic agent with precision by virtue of surface conjugation or even photothermal therapy. It has been demonstrated that functionalized AuNPs are able to exert high tumor specificity, improve the cellular targeting performance against lung cancer cells, and alleviate off-target effects (Zhou, Vázquez-González, & Willner, 2021). In addition, AgNPs have also acquired natural anticancerous ability and have been commonly used for controlled drug delivery that helps in the TME. For instance, mesoporous silica-coated Fe_3O_4–AgNPs proved to release the drug in multiresponsive acidic and near-infrared light reactions. This release mechanism triggers cytotoxicity and can help in imaging (Sun, Zhang, Yang, & Wang, 2021). AuNPs can further be used as a contrast in imaging, which enhances early cancer detection. Photothermal treatment combined with drug delivery increases the total anticancer activity. AgNPs have demonstrated the potential to cause apoptosis in selective cancer cells.

The magnetic characteristics of Fe_3O_4 nanoparticles make them contribute to the process of treatment given with the help of magnetic fields, as well as target the tumor regions. These particles can preserve their magnetic properties with a high-level of drug loading when conjugated with polyethylene glycol (PEG) or ionic liquids. The strategy enables effective release of payloads in the cancerous intracellular environment, leading to site-specific delivery and addressing the protein adsorption problem in the bloodstream (Kuznetsova & Timerbaev, 2022). External magnetic fields enable the targeting of tumor sites by Fe_3O_4 nanoparticles, which makes them more effective at targeting tumor cells. These NPs may also be utilized in magnetic resonance imaging (MRI), which includes both diagnostic and therapeutic effects. PEGylation or surface modification suppresses immune clearance, thus permitting an increase in the period of circulation.

Conversely, nonmetallic NPs such as polymeric NPs, lipid-based NPs, and carbonate apatite systems have an advantage over their counterparts, since they are biodegradable and less toxic. Polymeric nanoparticles (PNPs) prepared based on chitosan or poly (lactic-co-glycolic acid) (PLGA) can incorporate hydrophobic and hydrophilic drugs to achieve dual-drug delivery platforms to overcome MDR. In a study, using the amphiphilic chitosan nanoparticle, coloading cisplatin and demethoxycurcumin, and functionalizing it by biofunctionalization with CD133 antibodies, has shown destruction of stem-like lung cancer cells (Huang, Larsson, Lee, Liu, & Chiou, 2016). Biodegradable NPs are less harmful to use over time because they reduce body accumulation. Dual-drug delivery systems enable the use of several cancer pathways at the same time to enhance efficacy.

Lipid nanoparticle systems have been engineered with insoluble lipid supports, including solid lipid NPs and liposomes, with the aim of loading drugs and long-term drug release. For instance, Zn^{+2} or Cu^{+2} ions can electrostatically interact with the phospholipid bilayers, making the lipids more compact, so that the drug remains more sequestered and is released slowly due to the enhanced lipid compactness (Yang et al., 2016). The encapsulation of such a drug as afatinib using carbonate apatite NPs against an NSCLC is another promising innovation with higher encapsulation efficiency, retention, and sustained release, marking its potential application and success in the preclinical circumstances (Maarof, Abdulmalek, Fakurazi, & Rahman, 2022). Lipid NPs offer sustained and regulated delivery, enhancing drug bioavailability. Apatite NPs made of carbonate show great encapsulation of hydrophilic and hydrophobic drugs.

Structural and chemical properties determine the mechanisms of drug loading and release in such systems. Common entrapment methods are physical, electrostatic binding, covalent attachment, and pH-dependent release. Precisely, the pH-responsive systems are designed to utilize the acidic TME to trigger target and regulated release. Moreover, the release of the drugs can also be initiated by some external stimuli, including light, heat, or ultrasound. For example, the lipid nanoparticle can release the payloads via ultrasound stimuli and target epidermal growth factor receptor (EGFR) positive lung cancer cells (Kim et al., 2024). Stimuli-responsive NPs also make sure that the drugs are released at the tumor site. Light or ultrasound causes the system to be triggered externally, resulting in accurate targeting of the delivery of a drug and minimizing systemic exposure. NPs targeting EGFR increase the selectivity of cancerous cells in the lung, which increases the effectiveness of the therapeutic intervention.

Generally, metallic and nonmetallic NPs have great potential in drug delivery. Their distinct loading and release capabilities, the capacity to locate tumors well, and the ability to react to the environment are compelling characteristics that make them potent agents in the pursuit of safer and better cancer treatment modalities. The combination of multifunctionality and targeted delivery positions NPs as a key tool in precision oncology. Ongoing research continues to optimize these systems for clinical translation and improved patient outcomes. There are many different types of nanocarriers that can be used in lung cancer treatment, as shown in Fig. 4.1.

4.3.2 Liposomes

Liposomes are spherical vesicles that have a phospholipid bilayer, which can entrap hydrophilic and hydrophobic drugs. Due to their dual entrapment properties, liposomes are now the most suitable nanocarriers in cancer therapy. Unlike other carriers, they can generate better PKs and targeted medication effects. PEGylation, or alteration of the surface of a liposome with PEG, has been one of the most promising findings in liposomal drug delivery. PEGylation can increase the systemic circulation lifetime by lessening the recognition and clearance of the mononuclear phagocyte system (MPS) (Shen, Ye, Kröger, & Li, 2018). Liposomes can lower systemic toxicity by sheltering drugs against premature breakdown. They can be

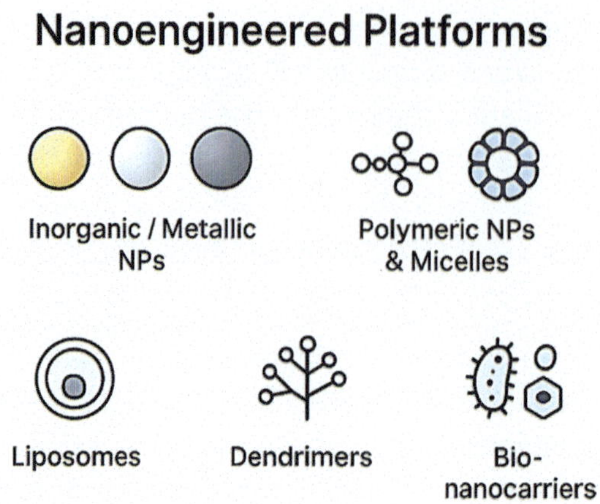

Figure 4.1
A schematic diagram of the key nanocarriers utilized in lung cancer therapy, such as liposomes, polymeric nanoparticles, dendrimers, micelles, solid lipid nanoparticles, metallic nanoparticles, and nanoemulsions, with their structural characteristics, drug-loading capabilities, targeting capabilities, and the contribution to the therapeutic functions, bioavailability, and controlled delivery of drugs to tumor cells.

designed in such a way that they deliver drugs at a controlled and sustained rate that enhances the therapeutic effect.

Liposomes can be versatile for encapsulating small-molecule drugs and biologics. PEGylated liposomes have been proven to be stable under several physiological conditions. Several findings have shown that the nebulization of PEGylated liposomes remains drug-loaded and structurally stable regardless of interacting with the pulmonary surfactant, thus making it viable for pulmonary delivery of drugs (Anabousi et al., 2006). Several types of PEGylated liposomes have been clinically approved by the FDA, such as pegylated liposomal doxorubicin (PLD), which has been used in multiple malignancies such as breast cancer and Kaposi sarcoma. Reduced cardiotoxicity and prolonged circulation of PLD increases targeting of tumors, through the EPR effect (Solomon & Gabizon, 2008).

One potential challenge is the inefficiency of the endocytosis process of liposomes. Nevertheless, strategic changes exist that equalize the long circulation and efficient cellular uptake, such as changes in PEG chain length or the use of PEGylation and targeting ligands (Papi et al., 2017). PEGylated liposomes have the EPR effect, which enables these liposomes to be concentrated selectively in tumor tissues. PEG chain length can be optimized to create a balance between stealth properties and cells that are internalized efficiently. PEGylated liposomes are used as combination vectors to enhance drug delivery to the resistant cancer cells.

Recently, the advantage of using two-drug-loaded PEGylated liposomes has been extended to a combination containing vinorelbine/quinacrine to treat NSCLC (Li et al., 2015), which shows synergistic cytotoxicity and a greater tumor specificity. Dual-drug-loaded liposomes provide the opportunity to target several pathways in cancer cells at once. This method will increase the therapeutic response and reduce the chances of drug resistance. Combination therapies that involve liposome-based therapies are proving to be promising in preclinical and clinical studies to treat lung cancer.

4.3.3 Dendrimers

Dendrimers are hyperbranched nanoscale macromolecules that offer a distinctive platform for drug delivery in lung cancer because of their multivalent surface, perfect structure, and capability to entrap therapeutic drugs. They adopt branched architecture, making them capable of multivalent targeting, increasing the efficiency of targeting and delivery of therapeutic payload. Dendrimers offer both a hydrophilic and hydrophobic platform of drug encapsulation. Their accurate and standardized structure enables predictable kinetics of loading and release of drugs. Multivalent surfaces can have targeting ligands and therapeutic agents on the same surface simultaneously.

The dendrimers, such as polyamidoamine (PAMAM), have gained a lot of attention in the development of lung cancer treatment. The binding affinity of functionalized dendrimers, including folic acid-conjugated dendrimers, increases in the presence of cancerous cells with overexpression of folate receptors (Amreddy et al., 2018). For instance, fucosylated PAMAM dendrimers boosted the aqueous solubility of poorly soluble anticancer molecules such as chrysin and increased the biocompatibility and cytotoxic effects with lung cancer cells without affecting the normal cells (Rai, Solanki, Patel, Pooja, & Kulhari, 2024). Selective uptake can be enhanced by the functionalization of folic acid or other ligands by tumor cells. Anticancer drugs that are poorly soluble in water can be improved in solubility by using dendrimers to enhance their therapeutic efficacy. Targeted dendrimers reduce off-target effects and improve safety profiles in normal tissues.

Dendrimers can become cytotoxic, particularly amine-terminated dendrimers, which disrupt the membrane of the cells. To overcome this functionalization of the surface, conjugation with sugars, peptides, PEG, or other neutral entities has been used. These changes not only decrease toxicity but also increase the targeting potential of the dendrimer and its circulation time and cellular absorption (Ghaffari et al., 2018). For instance, PEGylation conceals the charge, enhances systemic circulation, and lowers immunogenicity (Luong et al., 2016). Cytotoxicity is greatly decreased, and biocompatibility is enhanced by surface modification of dendrimers. PEGylation also prevents the quick clearance of dendrimers by the immune system. The conjugation with the targeting ligands also improves selective delivery to the cancer cells. The design of a dendrimer-based drug delivery system must consider biocompatibility, biodegradability, and drug release profiles. Release behavior has also been exhibited using stimuli-responsive dendrimers, taking advantage of modifying tumor-specific conditions, such as pH or redox conditions. Along with the high loading capacity and accurate targeting, these characteristics make dendrimers hold potential as vehicles in the development of personalized lung cancer treatment. Stimuli-responsive dendrimers enable the release of the drug under the control of the conditions of the microenvironment of the tumor. Large drug loading capacity allows the achievement of high doses of drugs using low carrier volumes. Dendrimers are now an emerging approach to personalized and precision therapy for lung cancer.

4.3.4 Nanomicelles

Self-assembled nanomaterials of polymeric micelles, which are made of the amphiphilic block copolymer, have a remarkable capacity for solubilizing different poorly soluble drugs. These micelles can have a hydrophobic core where lipophilic medications are enclosed, and a hydrophilic corona that may be of PEG, which stabilizes the micelle in aqueous conditions, increasing the interval of systemic circulating time. Polymeric micelles enhance the solubility of hydrophobic drugs, enabling them to be able to access therapeutic concentrations in the bloodstream. They are nanoscale in size, and this allows their build-up in the tumor tissue with minimal exposure in normal tissue. The hydrophilic corona prevents the degradation of the drug and increases the time of circulation.

Amphiphilic block copolymers like PEG-b-PPS and PEG-b-PCL have played a crucial role in solubilizing hydrophobic drugs. For example, PEG-b-PPS micelles were able to encapsulate cyclosporin A with good loading capacities and with maintenance over a period of 9–12 days without any burst effect, indicating that it could be effectively utilized in solubilization and release under control (Velluto, Demurtas, & Hubbell, 2008). The slow release of drugs through micelles lowers the chances of toxicity from sudden high drug concentrations. The prolonged release of drugs leads to longer therapeutic activity, which may result in fewer doses. Among the major benefits of polymeric micelles associated with a small size (generally 10,100 nm), passive targeting in tumors can be found based on the EPR effect. The property is able not only to cause an increase in drugs to accumulate on the sites of tumors, but it also enhances the minimized off-target toxicity (Torchilin, 2005). Moreover, polymeric micelles may be targeted using ligands or antibodies, and they can be designed (or altered using ligands) to react when subjected to a distinct pH, temperature, or redox stimulus in the tumor environment (Rapoport, 2007). Polymeric micelles are small enough to penetrate deep into the tumor tissues. Micelles functionalized with ligands increase the selective uptake in cancer cells and increase efficacy. On-demand drug release. Stimuli-responsive micelles enable treatment precision to a greater extent. Innovations have also resulted in the creation of hypoxia-responsive micelles and temperature-sensitive micelles, which have the capability of releasing drugs on demand. As an example, the carbon micelles formed with

N-(2-hydroxypropyl)methacrylamide showed impressive temperature-responsive self-assembly. They maintained the great capacity to deliver paclitaxel to lung cancer cells, such as the 3D spheroid models, causing the negligible toxicity of the carrier (Kasmi et al., 2016). The drugs are delivered selectively to low oxygen tumors by hypoxia-responsive delivery of micelles, resulting in increased specificity. It is possible to stimulate temperature-sensitive micelles externally, which can accurately control drug delivery. 3D tumor models show that micelles can penetrate and deliver drugs without damaging normal cells.

The use of polymeric micelles in lung cancer chemotherapy can bring a change toward safer, more effective, and more target-specific chemotherapy. Polymeric micelles are structurally flexible, biocompatible, and can be modified, making them one of the most appealing nanocarriers in nanomedicine. Polymeric micelles have been increasingly discussed in terms of being translated to clinical use because they are safe and flexible. They can be versatile, which enables the combination of several drugs or imaging agents in theranostics and combination therapy. These properties render polymeric micelles an attractive agent of targeted nanomedicine in lung cancer.

4.3.5 Bio-nanocarriers and microbiotic nanosystems

Microbiotic-based nanosystems have been receiving solid preclinical and clinical validation to be adopted in oncology. Bacteria, viruses, and fungi tend to exhibit tropism for specific cells and organs in their natural environment. Consequently, their potential as vectors for targeted tumor delivery, given their high intracellular penetration capacity is promising. Their pathogenicity has been reduced by technological advances in bioengineering, making them safer and more specific in their targeting. Existing approaches have encompassed bio-nanocarriers based on microbiome-derived tools, including oncolytic viruses (virotherapy) and genetically engineered bacteria, which are currently in development against cancers, including lung cancer. The therapeutic agents can be delivered to the tumor cells by bio-nanocarriers, selectively to reduce harm to normal tissues. Oncolytic viruses have the potential to kill cancer cells, as well as to induce antitumor immunity. Bacteria engineered genetically can be programmed to release therapeutic molecules in the TME. Microbiotic nanosystems provide a chance of combination therapy, which is the integration of immunotherapy and conventional chemotherapy. Preclinical proof that these systems can increase the specificity and therapeutic efficacy of tumors in lung cancer models has been demonstrated. Bioengineering approaches are still enhancing the level of safety, aiming at precision, and clinical utility of the microbiotic nanosystems (Rawal & Patel, 2021).

4.3.6 Bacterial bio-nanocarriers

Numerous specialized functions of bacteria, which include their ability to be motile, exhibit chemotaxis (Sharma, Nagpal, & Mishra, 2025), and evade the immune system, in addition to accumulating selectively in tumors' vasculature, make them promising therapeutic agents to be used in the treatment of cancer (Zong, Ruan, Liu, Fan, & Li, 2023). With the help of bioengineering, the production of strains with a low pathogenicity level and increased tumor-target potential is actively developing, which makes it safe and efficient to deliver drugs. . Active penetration of tumor tissue by bacteria bio-nanocarriers is possible because of their motility and chemotaxis (Zhou, Gravekamp, Bermudes, & Liu, 2018). Drug delivery can be made more specific as engineered bacteria are able to locate hypoxic tumor parts selectively. These carriers can be programmed to release therapeutic molecules in response to tumor-specific signals.

The development of bionanotechnology has allowed the development of a variety of bacterial nanocarriers (Li et al., 2024a; Li et al., 2024b), which include minicells, nanovesicle membrane-derived (Kim et al., 2017), bacterial ghosts, surface-layer components, endospores, magnetosomes, and bacterial-derived polymers, including alginate, cellulose, and hyaluronic acid. Moreover, bio composites that are nanobio-hybrids may have bacterial components. Minicells and bacterial ghosts are nonreplicating carriers, which can be used safely in vivo. The magnetic fields may be used to target the magnetosomes externally to a specific tumor. Polymers derived from bacteria are biocompatible scaffolds in drug encapsulation and release. Nanobio-hybrids combine the capability of using materials engineered to develop better therapeutic capabilities for bacteria. These innovations highlight the future potential of bacterial bio-nanocarriers in precision oncology (Farjadian et al., 2018).

4.3.7 Bacterial polymer-based nanocarriers

Bacterial polymers include polysaccharides (e.g., hyaluronic acid, dextran, alginate, starch, K30 antigen, xanthan, and glycogen), polyamides (e.g., poly-γ-glutamic acid, polypeptides and proteins), polyesters (e.g., polythioesters and polyhydroxyalkanoates), polyphosphates and polyphenols (a, (Ali, Liu, Liang, Li, & Kong, 2020). Bacterial polymers provide a versatile and biocompatible platform for nanoparticle formation. They can be functionalized to improve drug loading, stability, and targeted delivery. These polymers offer natural biodegradability, reducing long-term toxicity in vivo.

These bacterial biopolymers have been functionalized to form NPs, whereby diverse nanoparticle-based materials derived from this biopolymer have been explored broadly in biomedical applications, drug delivery, biosensors, and cancer theranostics. In cancer treatment, bacterial polymer-based nanocarriers provide a potential role in prevention/detection, imaging, targeted therapy, and integrated theranostics as the application in lung cancer (Li et al., 2024b). NPs made of bacterial polymers can be designed to release drugs in a controlled and stimulus-responsive manner. They can also be theranostic (combination of therapeutic and diagnostic functions). Such systems improve the specificity of targeting and minimize the side effects of these systems on normal lung tissues.

4.3.8 Viral bio-nanocarriers

Oncolytic viruses, and viral bio-nanocarriers are the most widely explored types of bio-engineered viruses and have received notable attention in oncology, due to their impressive transgene expression capability with tropism and cell-specificity (Dong et al., 2024; Mishra et al., 2021). The first problem is that viral vectors could not be used clinically due to their pathogenicity and virulence (Tomanin & Scarpa, 2004). Nevertheless, improvements in the field of bioengineering and molecular biotechnology have allowed us to produce modified viral platforms that are less pathogenic and have a greater level of tumor specificity. Such systems are currently being developed in cancer treatment, such as lung cancer. Tumor cells are selectively targeted by viral bio-nanocarriers because they have natural tropism. Engineering decreases the pathogenicity of the viruses, rendering them safe for clinical use. Oncolytic viruses can kill tumor cells as well as induce antitumor immunity.

Physical, chemical, or biotemplation strategies can be used to manufacture viral bio-nanocarriers. This is because they show strong chemical versatility due to the plethora of reactive surface functional groups (i.e., amide, aniline, thiol, carboxyl, and phenolic moieties), which enable easy chemical modifications (Manchester & Singh, 2006). Direct conjugations are one of the most commonly used methods in the chemical approach to it, with viral capsids being covalently associated with nanomaterials (Depienne et al., 2023). It is a technique that allows the modification of viral components with various nanocarriers such as quantum dots (Liu, Wang, Liu, & Pang, 2023), and bacteriophages (Hameed et al., 2026), thereby enhancing their stability and their ability to target the tumor. In addition, viruses have proven to be effective in bioconjugation with therapeutic compounds, imaging probes, proteins, chromophores, and nanomaterials, leading to multifunctional therapeutic and diagnostic purposes (Sun, Tian, Lian, & Cui, 2024). Precise attachment of drugs and imaging agents can be done by chemical modification of the capsids of the virus. Bioconjugated viruses integrate therapeutics and diagnostics, which allows real-time treatment monitoring. Viral bio-nanocarriers are stable in biological environments, which enhances their application in delivering drugs.

Furthermore, due to the inherent structural symmetry and self-assembly of viral capsids, biotemplation strategies can be used to create viral bio-nanocarriers whereby NPs are deposited evenly on the surface of the viral scaffolds (Aljabali et al., 2021). Beyond ensuring greater chemical stability, this unusual architecture lends high levels of control at the spatial level to the way nanomaterials are arranged, something of great benefit in the context of cancer nanomedicine. Viral capsids can self-assemble to give predictable nanocarriers. Viral nanocarriers can be biotemplated, enabling a precise spatial placement of therapeutic and imaging components. This architecture increases the targeting, stability, and treatment efficacy of nanomedicine for cancer.

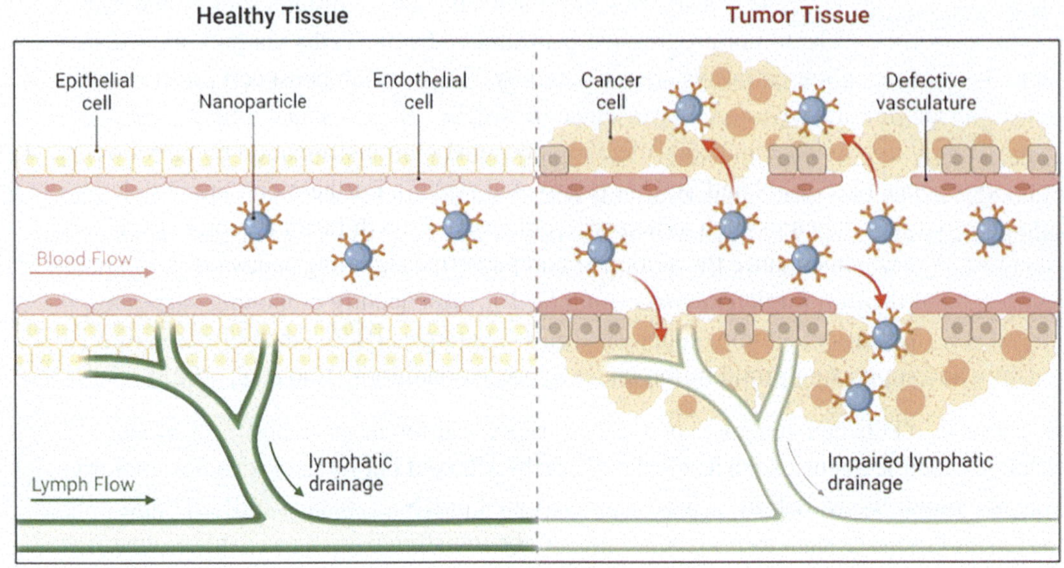

Figure 4.2
Visualization of the enhanced permeability and retention (EPR) effect in tumor tissue, showing that nanoparticles preferentially accumulate and stay longer in tumors than in healthy tissues as a result of leaky and defective tumor vasculature and defective lymphatic drainage, which enables passive targeting, increase drug concentration at the tumor site, increase therapeutic efficacy, and decrease systemic toxicity of anticancer nanomedicines (created with BioRender.com).

4.3.9 *Strategies for improving the tumor-specific targeting effect of nanoparticles*

The efficiency of nanomedicine in treating lung cancer significantly depends on the packaging of drugs in a manner that allows for the selective delivery of therapeutic payloads to tumor tissues, rather than normal cells. The drug release can be increased through the following methods: Passive targeting based on the EPR effect, active targeting based on the surface functionalization with ligands, and the means of overcoming biological barriers of the TME and the host immune system. Optimization of NPs boosts the concentration of drugs in tumor tissue and reduces the exposure of the rest of the body. Precision of delivery strategies may result in lower doses and frequency of chemotherapy. A combination of several targeting methods can also enhance therapeutic efficacy.

4.3.10 *Passive targeting: Enhanced permeability and retention effect*

Passive targeting takes advantage of the pathophysiological abnormalities of tumors, of which leaky vasculature and impaired lymphatic drainage have been most studied together, and are commonly referred to as the EPR effect, as shown in Fig. 4.2. It has an advantage that increases local concentration of drugs and minimizes systemic toxicity, as NPs that are 10–200 nm can be preferentially concentrated in tumor tissue (Danhier et al., 2010). However, relaxation is not very efficient in all cases in terms of tumor type or even within a singular tumor, especially in lung cancer, where vasculature discrepancies and the presence of a stromal barrier may be obstacles to drug distribution (Danhier, 2016). The EPR effect enables NPs to localize selectively in tumor tissue as a result of leakage vascularity. Passive targeting minimizes the off-target toxicity, enhancing the safety of patients. Heterogeneity of tumors may restrict the effectiveness of EPR-based delivery, and additional approaches should therefore be explored.

4.3.11 Surface functionalization as an active targeting approach

To enhance specificity beyond the use of EPR, there is now a greater tendency to engineer NPs to contain specifically targeted molecules (antibodies, peptides, aptamers, or small molecules) against the overexpressed receptors on lung cancer cells, as shown in Fig. 4.3. For instance, the recurrent overexpression of the EGFR and folate receptor in NSCLC makes them an interesting target of the ligand-conjugated nanocarriers (Danhier et al., 2010). Active targeting enhances the internalization of cells by receptor-mediated endocytosis, thereby boosting the efficacy of a drug compared to passive delivery methods. In preclinical experiments, ligand-modified NPs were demonstrated to promote a distinct increase in biodistribution and a cytotoxicity profile in lung malignancies, which proves the possibility of further translation of such NPs into targeted nano therapy (Huang et al., 2020). Active targeting allows specific delivery of drugs to tumor cells, providing the therapeutic effect. Passive targeting can be circumvented using ligand-functionalized NPs. This approach increases the uptake of cancer cells and spares the normal tissues, thus minimizing the side effects.

4.3.12 Overcoming the biological barriers

Although passive and active targeting have improved, it is still not possible to effectively deliver drugs to the targeted area, as biological barriers exist in lung cancer. Nanoparticle delivery into tumors is also hindered by dense extracellular matrix (ECM), hypoxia, and elevated interstitial fluid pressure (IFP), which prevent uniform drug distribution in tumors at high doses of drugs (Danhier, 2016). Moreover, the time of appearance of the NPs in circulation is shortened by systemic deposition with the help of the MPS and immune clearance. There are different ways to overcome these barriers as shown in Fig. 4.4. For instance, applying stealth coatings, e.g., PEG, to extend circulation lifetime, charge switchable nanocarriers that switch according to tumor pH-mediated penetration, as well as biomimetic NPs that are coated in cell membranes to avoid recognition by the immune system, all these are consider as possible option to increase the uptake of nanoparticle and decrease their clearance (Danhier et al., 2010). PEG-based stealth coating lowers immune clearance and increases systemic nanoparticle

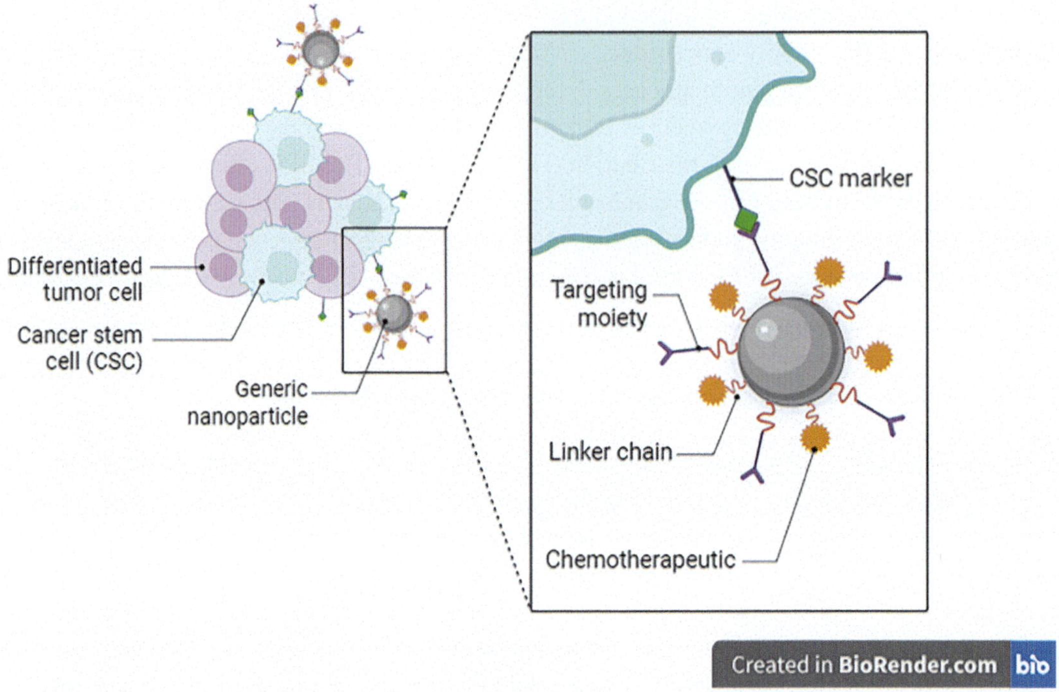

Figure 4.3
Active targeting of cancer stem cells (CSCs) with functionalized nanoparticles, which have been engineered to carry targeted ligands recognizing CSC-expressing surface antigens (antibodies, peptides, aptamers) on their surface, to selectively target CSCs, trigger cellular internalization, and deliver chemotherapeutic agents precisely to CSCs within the tumor microenvironment, thereby increasing therapeutic efficacy, overcoming drug resistance, reducing off-target effects, and limiting tumor recurrence and relapse (created with BioRender.com).

retention. Charge switchable nanocarriers increase penetration into tumor tissue depending on pH variation. Cell membrane-coated biomimetic NPs escape immunobiological recognition, enhancing bioavailability. Breaking biological barriers, in turn, makes the distribution of drugs more homogeneous and the treatment more effective. The maximization of NPs is achieved by combinations of strategies that focus on circulation time, immune evasion, and tissue penetration.

4.3.12.1 Tumor microenvironment as a barrier to effective therapy

TME is a crucial factor in the growth of lung cancer, resistance to therapy, and the inability to deliver drugs efficiently. TME is a very complex and dynamic ecosystem that comprises cancer cells, cancer-related fibroblasts (CAFs), immune cells, endothelial cells, ECM components, cytokines, and growth factors that all work together to control tumor growth, metastasis, and treatment response (Martinez-Outschoorn, Bartrons, & Bartrons, 2019). This

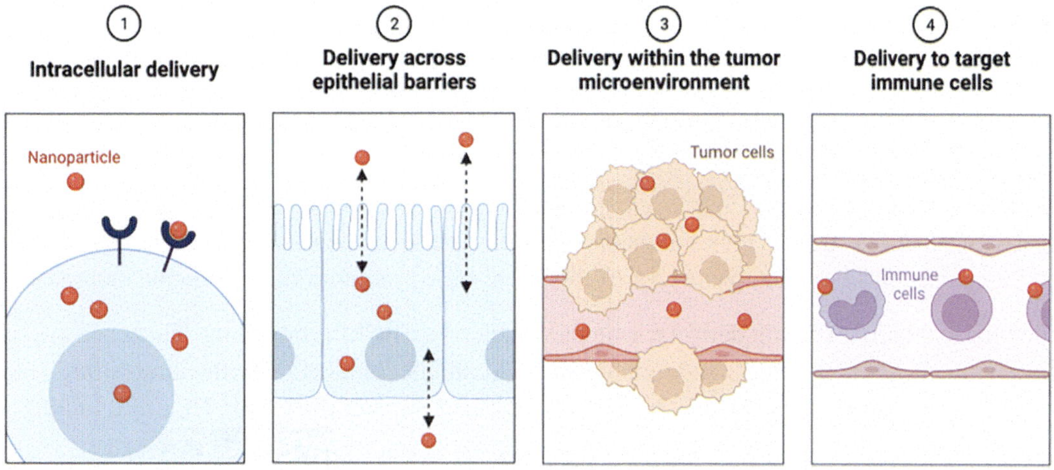

Figure 4.4
Comprehensive review of elevated nanoparticle-based solutions meant to boost targeting efficiency and counteract biological barriers, consisting of surface functionalization with targeting ligands, stimuli-responsive drug delivery systems, stealth coatings to avoid immunologic exposure, amplified cellular uptake pathways, penetration through thick tumor stroma, transport across physiologic barriers, including the endothelial membrane and cellular membrane, all to improve site-specific drug delivery, therapeutic efficacy, and treatment outcomes (created using BioRender.com).

dissimilar biological network forms a protective niche that ensures the survival of the tumor and, at the same time, provides a physical and biological shield against therapeutic penetration and effectiveness.

One of the most prominent stromal elements of the lung cancer microenvironment is CAFs, which are at the center of ECM remodeling, tumor stiffness, and resistance to therapy. CAFs are hyper-secreting collagen, fibronectin, and proteoglycans, which prompt the excessive deposition of ECM, which increases tissue density and decreases NPs diffusion and drug penetration within cancerous tissues (Suzuki et al., 2022). Cytokines and growth factors produced by CAFs also facilitate tumor growth, angiogenesis, and immune suppression, which further enhances treatment resistance as a tumor phenotype (Feng et al., 2022).

Another characteristic of the lung cancer microenvironment that has a strong negative impact on therapeutic efficacy is hypoxia. Dysplastic tumor vascularity and high tumor growth rate cause the formation of hypoxic areas in the tumor bulk, which are associated with metabolic reprogramming, angiogenic signaling, and tumor aggressiveness (Majidpoor et al., 2021). Hypoxia leads to chemotherapy and radiotherapy resistance, besides diminishing the transportation of NPs owing to inadequate perfusion and inaccessibility of the vasculature (Debnath et al., 2024). Signaling pathways due to hypoxia also increase the invasiveness and metastatic capability of tumors, aggravating the clinical outcomes.

Another significant barrier of the TME is represented by immunosuppressive cells. An immunosuppressive environment created by regulatory T cells (Tregs), tumor-associated macrophages (TAMS), and myeloid-derived suppressor cells (MDSCs) inhibits the antitumor immune response by preventing immune response and promoting immune evasion (De Cicco et al., 2020). Specifically, TAMs promote tumor progression by releasing immunosuppressive cytokines, promoting angiogenesis, and stimulating tumor cell survival signaling pathways (Dallavalasa et al., 2021). This immunosuppression decreases the usefulness of immunotherapy and constrains the effectiveness of nanoparticle-based immuno-nanomedicine methods.

The physical barrier to drug delivery is again enhanced by ECM remodeling. Thick collagen networks, stiffer matrix, and remodeled ECM architecture decrease the interstitial transport, and narrow nanoparticle diffusion into deeper parts of the tumor. High IFP in lung tumors also prevents convective uptake, which prevents even distribution of therapeutic agents and nanocarriers across the tumor mass. Such biomechanical forces greatly restrict nanoparticle penetration despite the presence of passive targeting vectors like the EPR effect (Gouarderes, Mingotaud, Vicendo, & Gibot, 2020).

Another factor that leads to therapeutic failure is angiogenesis in the TME. Neovascularization induced by the tumor results in the formation of structurally abnormal, leaky, and poorly organized blood vessels, which hinder the effective delivery of drugs and lead to heterogeneous perfusion patterns (Jászai et al., 2019). Though passive nanoparticle accumulation requires a leaky vasculature, uneven blood flow, and vessel rupture decrease the uniform distribution of NPs and limit efficient drug exposure of the tumor tissue.

There are also immune evasion mechanisms, which enhance the defense of tumor cells to therapeutic destruction. To avoid detection by the immune system, tumor cells suppress antigen presentation, increase the expression of immune checkpoint molecules, and modulate signaling pathways that cytokines mediate. These processes diminish the activity of immunotherapy and diminish the synergistic capacity of nano-immunotherapy approaches when the immune suppression is not addressed (Tufail, Jiang, & Li, 2025).

The TME in lung cancer acts as a multifactorial biological and physical barrier that highly limits the penetration of NPs, distribution of drugs, and therapeutic efficacy. The synergistic interaction of CAF activity, hypoxia, immunosuppression, ECM remodeling, high interstitial pressure, inappropriate angiogenesis, and immune evasion results in an unfavorable environment to deliver effective treatment. These obstacles directly lead to failure of nanoparticle penetration, uneven distribution of drugs, and resistance to treatment (Piwocka, Piotrowski, Suchorska, & Kulcenty, 2024).

Thus, effective nanomedicine approaches to lung cancer should combine TME control with nanoparticle engineering. ECM remodeling agents, hypoxia-responsive systems, immune-modulating nanocarriers, vessel normalization strategies, and biomimetic NPs are some of the directions that can help overcome TME-associated resistance (Choi & Jung, 2023). To maximize the efficiency of nanoparticle-based drug delivery and achieve sustained therapeutic effect in the treatment of lung cancer, it is necessary to target the TME.

4.4 Nanocarriers pharmacokinetic/pharmacodynamic modulation

The application of nanocarrier-based drug delivery systems essentially changes the pharmacodynamics (PD) and PK of therapeutic agents, allowing them to be used better in clinical practice than standard drug preparations. The usual disadvantages of traditional small-molecule chemotherapeutics are poor bioavailability, rapid systemic clearance, nonspecific distribution, and limited therapeutic windows, which all reduce their clinical efficacy and increase systemic toxicity. Nanocarriers can overcome these restrictions by reorganizing absorption, distribution, metabolism, and excretion (ADME) of drugs, improving their therapeutic efficacy and reducing off-target effects (Milewska et al., 2021).

4.4.1 Modulation of absorption, distribution, metabolism, and excretion

Encapsulated drugs in nanoparticle-based formulations exhibit a tremendous effect on ADME properties. Enhanced solubility and stability of poorly water-soluble drugs lead to improved absorption, resulting in more predictable PKs and better systemic availability. Nanocarriers also shield drugs against early enzyme breakdown and chemical degradation and enhance bioavailability and preserve drug integrity in the systemic circulation (Wilhelm et al., 2016).

Nanocarriers also significantly change distribution. Rather than free systemic diffusion, nanoparticle-based drug encapsulation is directed by carrier-mediated biosystem distribution, which allows selective tumor accumulation through passive and active targeting mechanisms (Shi, Kantoff, Wooster, & Farokhzad, 2017). This targeted delivery lowers the exposure of drugs to normal tissues and high local concentration of drugs in tumor areas, stimulating therapeutic indices and safety profiles (Danhier et al., 2010).

Physical shielding of drugs in nanocarriers results in delayed metabolism through inhibition of hepatic biotransformation and plasma enzymatic degradation. There are also changes in the excretion pathways because the renal filtration, hepatobiliary clearance, and MPS uptake depend upon the size of the NPs, their surface charge, and composition.

4.4.2 Increased bioavailability and half-life

Nanocarriers dramatically increase drug bioavailability through aqueous solubility, resistance to early degradation, and regulated release kinetics (Blanco, Shen, & Ferrari, 2015). PEGylation and surface decoration techniques minimize opsonization and immune detection, which increases systemic circulation and plasma half-life. Circulation increases the exposure time of the tumor and the accumulation by the EPR effect, leading to better therapeutic implications (Maeda, Nakamura, & Fang, 2013). Encapsulation of nanocarriers extends half-life, decreases dosing frequency, enhances patient compliance, and maintains steady plasma drug concentrations within their therapeutic ranges. These properties are especially important when used in the treatment of lung cancer, where long-term therapeutic drug levels are crucial to successful suppression of tumors (Zheng, Wang, Guo, Zhao, & Wang, 2018).

4.4.3 Controlled distribution and targeted biodistribution

Nanocarriers facilitate the spatial and temporal regulation of drug distribution. The surface-functionalized NPs are selective to tumor-associated receptors, which allows receptor-mediated endocytosis and intracellular delivery of drugs. Such targeted delivery reduces the systemic exposure of the drug and augments the drug concentration in cancerous cells, resulting in favorable pharmacodynamic actions and lesser adverse effects (Shi, Kantoff, Wooster, & Farokhzad, 2017). Controlled biodistribution also leads to less accumulation in dose-limiting organs, including heart, kidney, bone marrow, and, hence, decreases cardiotoxicity, nephrotoxicity, and myelosuppression of conventional chemotherapy (Wicki, Witzigmann, Balasubramanian, & Huwyler, 2015).

4.4.4 Clearance pathways and reticuloendothelial system interactions

The clearance of NPs is highly controlled by the reticuloendothelial system (RES), also known as the MPS, and encompasses the macrophages of the liver (Kupffer cells), the spleen, and the lymph nodes. NPs are regarded as foreign substances and eliminated via opsonization and phagocytosis, and accumulate in organs rich in RES (Blanco, Shen, & Ferrari, 2015). PEGylation and other surface modification approaches also decrease the RES internalization by reducing protein adsorption and immune detection, thus enhancing the circulation time and efficiency of tumor transportation. Nevertheless, it is still difficult to avoid immunological reactions, such that immune system interactions become central to nanoparticle PKs (Shi, Kantoff, Wooster, & Farokhzad, 2017).

4.4.5 Nano–bio interface and protein corona formation

When NPs are exposed to biological fluids, they quickly adsorb biomolecules like proteins, lipids, and glycoproteins to form a dynamic protein corona that determines the biological identity of the nanocarrier. Protein corona has a significant effect on the biodistribution, cellular uptake, immune recognition, and clearance pathways of NPs. This nano-bio interface defines the mechanism of action of nanocarriers on cell membranes, immune cells, and biological barriers and would eventually dictate the pharmacodynamic and PK profile of the nanocarrier (Waheed et al., 2022). Protein corona composition may modify its targeting efficiency, receptor binding affinity, and intracellular trafficking, thus influencing therapeutic outcomes (Panico et al., 2022).

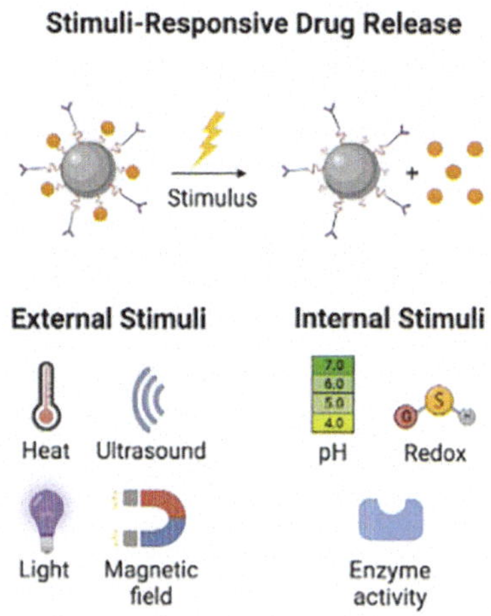

Figure 4.5
Stimulus-responsive nanoparticles is used to deliver drugs in a controlled and precise manner, where the exposure to a certain internal (pH, enzymes, and redox conditions) or external (temperature, light, magnetic field, and ultrasound) stimulus causes a change in the shape of the nanocarrier, which then releases the chemotherapeutic cargo directly into the tumor microenvironment, improving targeting into cells, therapeutic efficacy and reducing systemic toxicity and off-target effects (created with BioRender.com).

4.4.6 *Therapeutic efficacy and pharmacodynamic modulation*

Nanocarriers improve pharmacodynamic effects by elevating intracellular levels of drugs, providing better subcellular localization, and longer release profiles. Controlled release kinetics ensure that therapeutic drugs remain in tumor cells longer, increasing the effects of cytotoxicity and decreasing the development of resistance (Shi, Kantoff, Wooster, & Farokhzad, 2017). Another application of nanoparticle-mediated delivery is in combination therapy with a synergistic PD where several drugs or therapeutic modalities work together within tumor cells, with the result of greater antitumor effects compared to monotherapies. Emerging innovations in nanotherapeutics for lung cancer

4.4.7 *Stimuli-responsive nanocarriers*

One of the most significant breakthroughs in lung cancer nanomedicines is the development of stimuli-responsive nanocarriers that utilize the physiological and biochemical peculiarities of the microenvironment, as shown in Fig. 4.5. Such systems are designed to deliver drugs in a specific way, either based on intrinsic stimuli such as pH, redox potential, and enzyme activity, or upon extrinsic stimuli like temperature, light, and ultrasound. Stimuli-responsive nanocarriers enhance drug release specifically at the tumor site, minimizing off-target effects. These smart carriers reduce premature drug leakage and improve therapeutic efficiency. Selective activation in TMEs is possible with the help of intrinsic stimuli like pH, redox potential, and enzymatic activity.

For example, hypoxic glycolysis usually leads to an acidic TME, where pH-responsive nanocarriers can be created with acid-labile bonders showing acid-responsive degradation that, upon encountering lower pH, release the carried agent. Similarly, the redox-responsive systems take advantage of the higher levels of glutathione that occur in cancerous cells, where the disulfide bonds that bind drugs are cleaved to initiate the release of the drugs (Raza, Hayat, Rasheed, Bilal, & Iqbal, 2018). The enzyme used is matrix metalloproteinases (MMPs), upregulated in lung cancer, to activate the carrier site-specifically (Kiran, Kumari, Krishnamurthy, & Khaydarov, 2021). These delivery tools make them more precise due to the reduced untimely drug leakage and better therapeutic concentration at tumor locations. pH-responsive systems exploit tumor acidity for controlled release of anticancer agents. Redox-sensitive nanocarriers take advantage of the increased glutathione concentration in cancerous cells in order to release drugs. The enzyme-responsive nanocarriers are targeted to overexpressed tumor enzymes, enhancing the spatial precision of treatment. All these strategies increase drug accumulation and efficacy and reduce systemic toxicity (Bhairam, Shukla, Pande, & Gidwani, 2026).

4.4.8 Combination therapies

Currently, there is growing interest in using nanotechnology to overcome the drawbacks of monotherapy by codelivering multiple therapeutic agents in the same nanocarrier to ensure maximum effectiveness. These methods would be used to solve drug resistance and enhance synergy. In lung cancer, special interest is shown where chemotherapy is combined with either immunotherapy or gene therapy using the codelivery system. For example, the capability of nanoparticle technologies has been used to deliver simultaneous paclitaxel and siRNA against resistance-associated genes to improve chemosensitivity and inhibition of tumors (Huang et al., 2020). Additionally, coloading immunomodulatory agents with cancer-destroying agents, such as multifunctional nanocarriers loaded with antibodies targeting immune checkpoints and anti-PD-1 monoclonal antibodies, can promote both tumor cell killing and immune killing, leading to superior antitumor effects (Shi, Kantoff, Wooster, & Farokhzad, 2017). The given strategies can be utilized in addressing the intra-tumoral heterogeneity and lowering the development of resistance mechanisms. The combination of chemotherapeutics and gene therapy agents enhances sensitivity and lowers resistance. Multidrug regimens have the potential to activate multiple cancer cell pathways at the same time. The immunotherapy incorporation promotes the antitumor immune response and also kills tumor cells. Multiagent nanocarriers enhance compliance and decrease the dosing frequency of the patient.

4.4.9 Theranostics: Integration of imaging and therapy

Theranostics is another lung cancer nano-therapeutic frontier, combining both therapeutic and diagnostic operations into a combined platform. Theranostic NPs function simultaneously as drug carriers and imaging agents, enabling real-time monitoring of drug distribution, efficacy, and disease state. To clarify, nanocarriers that bear magnetic or fluorescent probes enable monitoring the biodistribution during the release of chemotherapeutic drugs in the treatment of cancer, favoring precision and personalized treatment (Kelkar & Reineke, 2011). Most recently, nanoplatforms have been introduced that combine photothermal therapy, MRI, and chemotherapy against lung cancer, with the ability to show synergetic tumor suppression and real-time control of treatment (Shi, Kantoff, Wooster, & Farokhzad, 2017). Theranostic methods can be used to potentially treat cancer on a highly individualized level by integrating diagnostics and therapy. Theranostic NPs allow both treatment and imaging, allowing real-time monitoring of therapy. Distribution and accumulation of drugs in the tumors can be visualized with magnetic and fluorescent probes. A combination of photothermal therapy, chemotherapy, and imaging leads to synergistic tumor suppression. Theranostic strategies offer a basis for personalized and precision nanomedicine in lung cancer. They are multifunctional systems where clinicians can change therapy in real-time depending on tumor response.

4.5 Preclinical and clinical studies

4.5.1 Key preclinical findings: Efficacy, biodistribution, and toxicity reduction

In lung cancer, preclinical studies based on nanomedicine have seen much success in PKs, biodistribution, and drug efficacy. Chemotherapeutics used in the form of liposomes, like doxorubicin and cisplatin, have shown increased penetration into lung tumors because of the EPR effect, as well as low systemic toxicity compared to free drugs (Maeda, Nakamura, & Fang, 2013). The solubility of the poorly water-soluble drugs has been increased due to polymeric micelles, which exhibited better antitumor activity in the xenograft lung cancer models (Shi, Kantoff, Wooster, & Farokhzad, 2017). Notably, the reduction of toxicity has been a common finding; dendrimers-based drug conjugates and PEGylated NPs have lower cardiotoxicity and nephrotoxicity with a great deal of potency against tumor cells (Wicki, Witzigmann, Balasubramanian, & Huwyler, 2015). Premedical research indicates that tumor drug delivery and efficacy are enhanced by nanocarriers. NPs improve the antitumor activity of hydrophobic drugs by increasing solubility and bioavailability. The lower toxicity of the key organs enhances the safety profile of nanoformulations. The biodistribution studies indicate the specific accumulation in the tumors without a lot of off-target accumulation.

4.5.2 Translation into clinical trials: Successes, failures

Although promising therapeutic indices have been indicated in preclinical studies, its clinical translation has received mixed responses. Albumin-bound paclitaxel (nab-paclitaxel, Abraxane) showed improved best response rates and progression-free survival relative to solvent-based paclitaxel by showing reduced hypersensitivity reactions in NSCLC (Desai, 2007). Likewise, liposome products such as liposomal cisplatin (Lipoplatin) have advanced to phase

III trials where they have demonstrated a less nephrotoxic profile compared to free cisplatin; however, they have demonstrated mixed efficacy outcomes. There are failures too; there are nanosystems based on NPs with promising preclinical performance, but that proved to be no better than conventional chemotherapy in phase III trials because of difficulties in patient stratification, the heterogeneity of TMEs, and the lack of full utilization of active targeting principles (Shi, Kantoff, Wooster, & Farokhzad, 2017). Clinical translation points out the difficulty of transferring animal models to humans. Certain nanoformulations are safer but do not necessarily enhance efficacy. One of the biggest obstacles is patient heterogeneity and differences in the microenvironment of the tumor. Active targeting strategies are essential to clinical success, especially when used properly.

4.5.3 Case studies of nanoformulations under clinical evaluation for lung cancer

Numerous nanoformulations are either in clinical trials or have been through lung cancer evaluation. Nab-paclitaxel (Abraxane 12) combined with carboplatin has been approved as a first-line treatment of advanced NSCLC, which demonstrated a successful translation of nanotechnology into standard care (Socinski et al., 2012). The NK105 micellar formulation of paclitaxel has already reached clinical testing, with the possibility of obtaining a better tumor accumulation and a lower neurotoxicity in comparison to normal paclitaxel (Hamaguchi et al., 2005). In the meantime, theranostic formulations combining diagnostic imaging and therapy are currently in the early stages of clinical testing, highlighting the potential for personalizing nanomedicine in the future (Shi, Kantoff, Wooster, & Farokhzad, 2017). Case studies indicate that certain nanoformulations are capable of making it to the clinical stage. Better tumor targeting, NK105, and such micellar systems have fewer side effects. The theranostic NPs have the potential to integrate therapy and imaging in personalized medicine. Initial clinical testing indicates that it is possible, but requires strict testing on efficacy and safety. These studies provide the road to future innovation and increased clinical use of nanomedicine in the treatment of lung cancer.

4.6 Challenges and barriers to clinical translation

4.6.1 Large-scale manufacturing and reproducibility

The barrier to commercial translation of nanomedicine to large and reproducible scale has been one of its most significant challenges. Unlike standard small-molecule drugs, nanocarriers exhibit complex formulations (e.g., liposomes, dendrimers, and polymeric micelles) and, therefore, minor differences in particle size, surface charge, or drug payload can effectively impact safety and efficacy. It is challenging to achieve compliance with good manufacturing practice (GMP) for supplies, and variable processes between batches should be addressed, restricting regulatory acceptance and commercial scale-up (Blanco, Shen, & Ferrari, 2015). More sophisticated methods, such as the use of microfluidics in synthesizing NPs, have been suggested to enhance reproducible results and automated quality-control pipelines, which are yet to be adopted in clinical practice. Large-scale production can be reproducible to provide uniform clinical results. Minor differences in the characteristics of NPs can have a great impact on therapeutic effectiveness and safety. Postmodern technologies, such as microfluidics, enable the exact size and drug loading of particles. Nanoparticle synthesis requires automation and standardization to enable it to meet regulatory expectations (Colombo et al., 2018).

4.6.2 Stability, storage, and shelf-life concerns

Physicochemical instability on storage and distribution is a common problem with nanomedicine formulations. Liposomes might experience the oxidation of the lipid and the leakage of the drug, whereas the polymeric micelles might experience premature disassembly, thus losing their therapeutic efficacy. Also, nanoparticle morphology or drug release profiles may be changed by the lyophilization and cryopreservation procedure to extend the shelf-life, which is a problem during long-term usage in hospitals and pharmacies (Wicki, Witzigmann, Balasubramanian, & Huwyler, 2015). To overcome these barriers, there is a need to optimize excipients, stabilizers, and packaging modalities that are specific to the requirements of nanocarriers. The stability of NPs is important to preserve therapeutic effects in the process of storage and transportation. Structural integrity and premature drug release could be avoided by formulation optimization. Individualized packaging and stabilizers could increase shelf-life without reducing activity. The provision of long-term stability contributes to clinical adoption and minimizes logistical issues in healthcare.

4.6.3 Safety and immunogenicity risks

Though nanocarriers have the potential to decrease the systemic toxicity of conventional chemotherapies, they may induce novel safety considerations. NPs can cause activation of complement-related pseudo-allergy (CARPA) or oxidative stress, or undesirable immune activation. PEGylated NPs were thought to be stealth agents. However, it has since been discovered that they do not act as stealth agents, as they induce anti-PEG antibodies, triggering rapid clearance and hypersensitivity reactions (Shi, Kantoff, Wooster, & Farokhzad, 2017). In addition, there is little information on long-term biodistribution and clearance of inorganic NPs, which is a potential risk of off-target accumulation in the liver, spleen, or kidneys (Hare et al., 2017). Therefore, preuse in the human population, immunotoxicology evaluations, and predictive animal models must take place. New nanomedicines can cause unintended immune reactions and complement activation. The long-term biodistribution is necessary to avoid organ build-up and organ toxicity. Preclinical immunotoxicology needs to be done to anticipate the adverse reactions in humans. Surface modification can be used as a strategy to reduce immunogenicity to improve safety profiles.

4.6.4 Regulatory and ethical hurdles in nanomedicine

Semistandardized evaluation frameworks are absent, which contributes to the difficulty of regulatory approval for nanomedicine. The FDA and EMA are among the agencies that have not established converged protocols of PKs, toxicity assay, and long-term surveillance unique to nanotherapeutics (Blanco, Shen, & Ferrari, 2015). Moral issues also make the process of translation more complex, and the consent of patients must be obtained with references to uncertainties in terms of long-term safety and possible inability to accumulate irreversibly in organs and tissues. Also, extensive development and production mean that the cost of treatment only increases the question of fair access to treatment after approval, which may become another gap in cancer care (Hare et al., 2017). Nanomedicines have yet to have an established regulatory framework that is simple to approve. The ethical considerations consist of informed consent and the long-term safety uncertainty. The cost of production could lead to equal access to high-level nanotherapeutics. Standardization of regulatory systems in different regions would ease clinical translation. Long-term surveillance would be necessary to enhance safety and effectiveness among patients.

4.7 Future perspectives

4.7.1 Artificial intelligence and computational modeling in nano-drug design

Computational modeling and artificial intelligence (AI) are novel technologies to transform the design of nanomedicines to treat lung cancer. Machine learning allows optimal nanoparticle size, shape, and surface chemistry to be predicted so that they can accumulate in tumors and limit targeting to the body at large. Prediction and screening of drug-nanocarrier interactions and preclinical trial-eliminating PKs could also be simulated in the silico environment, making it possible to reduce the necessity to conduct preclinical trials that are costly (Wilhelm et al., 2016). AI-based methods may speed up the pipeline to discover new nano-drugs and rationally design drugs based on the biology of lung tumors. Nanocarrier optimization with maximum tumor targeting can be done through AI-based optimization of nanocarrier properties in a short period of time. Traditional experimental trials may be costly and time-consuming, which can be minimized by the use of computational modeling. Potential toxicity and biodistribution patterns can be predicted before in vivo studies using machine learning algorithms. The implementation of AI in nanomedicine design helps create therapeutic development that is more rational.

4.7.2 Potential for personalized nanomedicine in lung cancer

Lung tumors' heterogeneity requires shifting at both the molecular and microenvironment levels. Depending on patient type or subtype and biomarkers (e.g., receptor expression patterns and genetic mutations), it is possible to select targeting ligands or payload complexes. Individualized nanocarriers may be designed to tailor to the individual biological environment of the patient and thus enhance efficacy and reduce toxicity. Nanocarrier design paradigms can integrate genomic and proteomic information into a novel set of personalized medicines (Shi, Kantoff, Wooster, & Farokhzad, 2017). Individualized nanomedicine allows specific targeting, depending on tumor biology. Nanocarriers can be selected using biomarkers to enhance treatment efficacy and reduce adverse side effects. A combination of genomic and proteomic information can be used to come up with patient-centered therapies. Individualized treatment options have the potential to break the tumor heterogeneity and drug resistance issues.

4.7.3 Integration with other advanced therapies

Nanomedicine is also being conceptualized more as a complementary companion to other cutting-edge treatments. For example, nanocarriers could be used to enable improved delivery and stability of oncogenic mutation-correcting CRISPR-Cas9 gene editors or enable safer CAR-T generation through codelivery of modulatory agents such as those that improve the safety of CAR-T cell therapy through cytokine release syndrome reduction. The reprogramming of the TME and immunotherapeutic resistance may be overcome using nanocarrier-based immuno-nanomedicine solutions in combination with immune checkpoint inhibitors or cytokines that have demonstrated preclinical activity in this regard. The integrations report on the opportunities of nanomedicine as a means of enabling multimodal therapy of lung cancer. Nanomedicine, together with gene and immune therapies, can be used to improve treatment accuracy and effectiveness. Nanocarriers have the ability to transport sensitive therapeutic agents and deliver them to tumor sites. Nanomedicine-based multimodal therapy can resolve resistance and enhance survival. Combination with modern therapies opens the path to synergistic treatment of lung cancer.

4.7.4 Roadmap to clinical adoption and improving patient outcomes

Making nanomedicine meaningful in terms of actual implementation in the clinical arena requires a strategic roadmap that looks at technical, regulatory, and economic limits. The key steps include standardizing the manufacturing process, aligning regulations across countries, and incorporating real-world data into the approval processes. In addition, cost-effectiveness studies will be essential to achieve equitable access to nanomedicines when they arrive in the clinic. On the one hand, translation can be supported by close interaction between academia, industry, and regulatory agencies, and adaptive clinical trial design could provide shorter approval timelines on the other hand (Hare et al., 2017). Finally, AI, personalized medicine, and immuno-nanomedicine introduce a new approach to lung cancer treatment, which may increase patients' survival and improve their quality of life in the clinical setting.

4.8 Conclusion

Lung cancer is still one of the most challenging cancers to treat because of its heterogeneity, intrinsic resistance, and limitations of conventional therapies. The emergence of nanoengineered systems (liposomes, dendrimers, polymeric micelles, mesoporous silica-based composites, bio-nanocarriers, stimuli-responsive, and theranostic nanocarriers) has facilitated an avenue to overcome these concerns. Nanomedicine has the potential to achieve an enormous increase in therapeutic efficacy combined with a reduced systemic toxicity by enhancing the solubility of drugs, enhancing tumor-specific accumulation by both passive and active targeting, and overcoming significant biological barriers. Improved biodistribution, diminishing off-target effects, and increased antitumor property of nanoformulations in preclinical experiments have been well established, with clinical trials currently demonstrating the potential and translation challenges of the technologies. Nanomedicine is a breakthrough approach to overcoming the shortcomings of traditional lung cancer treatment. The targeted delivery, controlled release, and multifunctional nanocarriers increase therapeutic outcomes. Nanomedicine has the potential to enhance survival and minimize systemic toxicity as demonstrated by preclinical and clinical evidence. Along with future integration with AI, personalized treatment, and multimodal therapy, lung cancer will be optimized further. Further studies and close clinical translation must be conducted to achieve the full potential of nanomedicine in treating patients.

References

Ali, M. K., Liu, Q., Liang, K., Li, P., & Kong, Q. (2020). Bacteria-derived minicells for cancer therapy. *Cancer Letters, 491*, 11–21.

Aljabali, A. A., Hassan, S. S., Pabari, R. M., Shahcheraghi, S. H., Mishra, V., Charbe, N. B., … Tambuwala, M. M. (2021). The viral capsid as novel nanomaterials for drug delivery. *Future science OA, 7*(9), FSO744.

Amreddy, N., Babu, A., Panneerselvam, J., Srivastava, A., Muralidharan, R., Chen, A., … Ramesh, R. (2018). Chemo-biologic combinatorial drug delivery using folate receptor-targeted dendrimer nanoparticles for lung cancer treatment. *Nanomedicine: Nanotechnology, Biology and Medicine, 14*(2), 373–384.

Anabousi, S., Kleemann, E., Bakowsky, U., Kissel, T., Schmehl, T., Gessler, T., … Ehrhardt, C. (2006). Effect of PEGylation on the stability of liposomes during nebulisation and in lung surfactant. *Journal of nanoscience and nanotechnology, 6*(9–10), 3010–3016.

Attia, M. F., Anton, N., Wallyn, J., Omran, Z., & Vandamme, T. F. (2019). An overview of active and passive targeting strategies to improve the nanocarriers efficiency to tumour sites. *journal of Pharmacy and Pharmacology, 71*(8), 1185–1198.

Bazak, R., Houri, M., El Achy, S., Kamel, S., & Refaat, T. (2015). Cancer nanomedicine: Is targeting our future? *Journal of Controlled Release, 213*, 108–122.

Bhairam, M., Shukla, S. S., Pande, R. K., & Gidwani, B. (2026). Emerging frontiers of responsive nanomaterials in drug delivery systems: from design to clinical translation. *OpenNano, 100299*.

Blanco, E., Shen, H., & Ferrari, M. (2015). Principles of nanoparticle design for overcoming biological barriers to drug delivery. *Nature biotechnology, 33*(9), 941–951.

Boulaiz, H., Alvarez, P. J., Ramirez, A., Marchal, J. A., Prados, J., Rodríguez-Serrano, F., … Aranega, A. (2011). Nanomedicine: application areas and development prospects. *International journal of molecular sciences, 12*(5), 3303–3321.

Boulikas, T. (2009). Clinical overview on Lipoplatin™: a successful liposomal formulation of cisplatin. *Expert opinion on investigational drugs, 18*(8), 1197–1218.

Choi, Y., & Jung, K. (2023). Normalization of the tumor microenvironment by harnessing vascular and immune modulation to achieve enhanced cancer therapy. *Experimental & molecular medicine, 55*(11), 2308–2319.

Colombo, S., Beck-Broichsitter, M., Bøtker, J. P., Malmsten, M., Rantanen, J., & Bohr, A. (2018). Transforming nanomedicine manufacturing toward Quality by Design and microfluidics. *Advanced drug delivery reviews, 128*, 115–131.

Dallavalasa, S., Beeraka, N. M., Basavaraju, C. G., Tulimilli, S. V., Sadhu, S. P., Rajesh, K., … Madhunapantula, S. V. (2021). The role of tumor associated macrophages (TAMs) in cancer progression, chemoresistance, angiogenesis and metastasis-current status. *Current medicinal chemistry, 28*(39), 8203–8236.

Danhier, F. (2016). To exploit the tumor microenvironment: Since the EPR effect fails in the clinic, what is the future of nanomedicine? *Journal of Controlled Release, 244*, 108–121.

Danhier, F., Feron, O., & Préat, V. é (2010). To exploit the tumor microenvironment: Passive and active tumor targeting of nanocarriers for anti-cancer drug delivery. *Journal of Controlled Release, 148*(2), 135–146. doi:10.1016/j.jconrel.2010.08.027.

De Cicco, P., Ercolano, G., & Ianaro, A. (2020). The new era of cancer immunotherapy: Targeting myeloid-derived suppressor cells to overcome immune evasion. *Frontiers in Immunology, 11*. doi:10.3389/fimmu.2020.01680.

Debnath, S. K, Debnath, M., Ghosh, A., Srivastava, R., & Omri, A. (2024). Targeting tumor hypoxia with nanoparticle-based therapies: Challenges, opportunities, and clinical implications. *Pharmaceuticals, 17*(10), 1389. doi:10.3390/ph17101389.

Depienne, S., Bouzelha, M., Courtois, E., Pavageau, K., Lalys, P. A., Marchand, M., … Gouin, S. G. (2023). Click-electrochemistry for the rapid labeling of virus, bacteria and cell surfaces. *Nature communications, 14*(1), 5122.

Desai, N. (2007). Nab technology: a drug delivery platform utilising endothelial gp60 receptor-based transport and tumour-derived SPARC for targeting. *Drug Delivery Report, 16*, 37–41.

Dong, W., Luo, Y., He, D., Zhang, M., Zeng, J., & Chen, Y. (2024). Oncolytic virotherapy against lung cancer: key receptors and signaling pathways of viral entry. *Frontiers in Immunology, 15*, 1473288.

Edelman Saul, E., Guerra, R. B., Saul, M. E., Lopes da Silva, L., Aleixo, G. F. P., Matuda, R. M. K., & Lopes, G. (2020). The challenges of implementing low-dose computed tomography for lung cancer screening in low- and middle-income countries. *Nature Cancer, 1*(12), 1140–1152. doi:10.1038/s43018-020-00142-z.

Farjadian, F., Moghoofei, M., Mirkiani, S., Ghasemi, A., Rabiee, N., Hadifar, S., … Hamblin, M. R. (2018). Bacterial components as naturally inspired nano-carriers for drug/gene delivery and immunization: Set the bugs to work? *Biotechnology advances, 36*(4), 968–985.

Feng, B., Wu, J., Shen, B, Jiang, F., & Feng, J. (2022). Cancer-associated fibroblasts and resistance to anti-cancer therapies: Status, mechanisms, and countermeasures. *Cancer Cell International, 22*(1). doi:10.1186/s12935-022-02599-7.

Gao, X., Guo, L., Li, J., Thu, H. E., & Hussain, Z. (2018). Nanomedicines guided nanoimaging probes and nanotherapeutics for early detection of lung cancer and abolishing pulmonary metastasis: Critical appraisal of newer developments and challenges to clinical transition. *Journal of Controlled Release, 292*, 29–57.

Ghaffari, M., Dehghan, G., Abedi-Gaballu, F., Kashanian, S., Baradaran, B., Dolatabadi, J. E. N., & Losic, D. (2018). Surface functionalized dendrimers as controlled-release delivery nanosystems for tumor targeting. *European Journal of Pharmaceutical Sciences, 122*, 311–330.

Gouarderes, S., Mingotaud, A. F., Vicendo, P., & Gibot, L. (2020). Vascular and extracellular matrix remodeling by physical approaches to improve drug delivery at the tumor site. *Expert opinion on drug delivery, 17*(12), 1703–1726.

Hamaguchi, T., Matsumura, Y., Suzuki, M., Shimizu, K., Goda, R., Nakamura, I., … Kakizoe, T. (2005). NK105, a paclitaxel-incorporating micellar nanoparticle formulation, can extend in vivo antitumour activity and reduce the neurotoxicity of paclitaxel. *British journal of cancer, 92*(7), 1240–1246.

Hameed, M., Hu, Y., Khan, A., Yu, L., Saghir, A., Hong, W., … Li, P. (2026). Chemically mediated modification of bacteriophages: Strategies, functionalities and applications in precision medicine. *Nanomedicine: Nanotechnology, Biology and Medicine, 102944.*

Hare, J. I., Lammers, T., Ashford, M. B., Puri, S., Storm, G., & Barry, S. T. (2017). Challenges and strategies in anti-cancer nanomedicine development: An industry perspective. *Advanced drug delivery reviews, 108*, 25–38.

Huang, W. T., Larsson, M., Lee, Y. C., Liu, D. M., & Chiou, G. Y. (2016). Dual drug-loaded biofunctionalized amphiphilic chitosan nanoparticles: Enhanced synergy between cisplatin and demethoxycurcumin against multidrug-resistant stem-like lung cancer cells. *European Journal of Pharmaceutics and Biopharmaceutics, 109*, 165–173.

Huang, X., Wu, J., He, C., & Tang, Y. (2020). Targeted nanomedicine for lung cancer therapy: Recent advances and future prospects. *Acta Pharmaceutica Sinica B, 10*(11), 2019–2034.

Jászai, J. ó, & Schmidt, M. (2019). Trends and challenges in tumor anti-angiogenic therapies. *Cells, 8*(9), 1102. doi:10.3390/cells8091102.

Jin, X., Heidari, G., Nezhad, S. M., Shao, M., Hua, Z., Lei, Y., … Xu, Y. (2024). Progress in translating bioinorganic nanoplatform discoveries into clinical lung cancer care: Overcoming limitations, targeted drug delivery and imaging. *Alexandria Engineering Journal, 99*, 271–281.

Kasmi, S., Louage, B., Nuhn, L., Van Driessche, A., Van Deun, J., Karalic, I., Risseeuw, M., Van Calenbergh, S., Hoogenboom, R., De Rycke, R., De Wever, O., Hennink, W. E., & De Geest, B. G. (2016). Transiently responsive block copolymer micelles based on N-(2-hydroxypropyl)methacrylamide engineered with hydrolyzable ethylcarbonate side chains. *Biomacromolecules, 17*(1), 119–127. http://pubs.acs.org/journal/bomaf6. doi:10.1021/acs.biomac.5b01252.

Kaur, M., Guleria, P., & Kumar, V. (2023). Nanomaterials for diagnosis and treatment of lung cancer: a review of recent patents. *Recent Patents on Anti-Cancer Drug Discovery, 18*(2), 114–124.

Kazmi, I., Shaikh, M. A. J., Afzal, O., Alfawaz Altamimi, A. S., Almalki, W. H., Alzarea, S. I., … Gupta, G. (2023). Chitosan-based nano drug delivery system for lung cancer. *Journal of Drug Delivery Science and Technology, 81*.

Kelkar, S. S., & Reineke, T. M. (2011). Theranostics: combining imaging and therapy. *Bioconjugate chemistry, 22*(10), 1879–1903.

Kim, M. W., Moon, S., Park, Y. I., Kim, J., Kim, S. I., & Lee, R. (2024). Ultrasound-Responsive Lipid Nanoparticles for Targeted Therapy and Controlled Drug Release in Non-Small Cell Lung Cancer. *Advanced Therapeutics, 7*(12), 2400248.

Kim, O. Y., Dinh, N. T. H., Park, H. T., Choi, S. J., Hong, K., & Gho, Y. S. (2017). Bacterial protoplast-derived nanovesicles for tumor targeted delivery of chemotherapeutics. *Biomaterials, 113*, 68–79.

Kiran, A. V. R., Kumari, G. K., Krishnamurthy, P. T., & Khaydarov, R. R. (2021). Tumor microenvironment and nanotherapeutics: intruding the tumor fort. *Biomaterials science, 9*(23), 7667–7704.

Kuznetsova, O. V., & Timerbaev, A. R. (2022). Magnetic nanoparticles for highly robust, facile and efficient loading of metal-based drugs. *Journal of Inorganic Biochemistry, 227*, 111685.

Li, M., Zhao, L., & Chen, H. (2024a). The application of bacteria-nanomaterial hybrids in antitumor therapy. *Journal of Nanobiotechnology, 22*(1), 536.

Li, Z., Chen, X., & Zhang, H. (2024b). Advances in bacterial biopolymers for nanomedicine and cancer therapy. *Advanced Drug Delivery Reviews, 205*, 114376.

Li, X. T., Zhou, Z. Y., Jiang, Y., He, M. L., Jia, L. Q., Zhao, L., … Jia, T. Z. (2015). PEGylated VRB plus quinacrine cationic liposomes for treating non-small cell lung cancer. *Journal of drug targeting, 23*(3), 232–243.

Liu, H. Y., Wang, Z. G., Liu, S. L., & Pang, D. W. (2023). Single-virus tracking with quantum dots in live cells. *Nature Protocols, 18*(2), 458–489.

Luong, D., Kesharwani, P., Deshmukh, R., Amin, M. C. I. M., Gupta, U., Greish, K., & Iyer, A. K. (2016). PEGylated PAMAM dendrimers: Enhancing efficacy and mitigating toxicity for effective anticancer drug and gene delivery. *Acta biomaterialia, 43*, 14–29.

Maarof, N. N., Abdulmalek, E., Fakurazi, S., & Rahman, M. B. A. (2022). Biodegradable carbonate apatite nanoparticle as a delivery system to promote afatinib delivery for non-small cell lung cancer treatment. *Pharmaceutics, 14*(6), 1230.

Maeda, H., Nakamura, H., & Fang, J. (2013). The EPR effect for macromolecular drug delivery to solid tumors: Improvement of tumor uptake, lowering of systemic toxicity, and distinct tumor imaging in vivo. *Advanced drug delivery reviews, 65*(1), 71–79.

Majidpoor, J., & Mortezaee, K. (2021). Angiogenesis as a hallmark of solid tumors - clinical perspectives. *Cellular Oncology, 44*(4), 715–737. doi:10.1007/s13402-021-00602-3.

Manchester, M., & Singh, P. (2006). Virus-based nanoparticles (VNPs): Platform technologies for diagnostic imaging. *Advanced Drug Delivery Reviews, 58*(14), 1505–1522.

Martinez-Outschoorn, U. E., Bartrons, M., & Bartrons, R. (2019). Cancer ecosystems. *Frontiers in oncology, 9*, 718.

Milewska, S., Niemirowicz-Laskowska, K., Siemiaszko, G., Nowicki, P., Wilczewska, A. Z., & Car, H. (2021). Current trends and challenges in pharmacoeconomic aspects of nanocarriers as drug delivery systems for cancer treatment. *International journal of nanomedicine*, 6593–6644.

Min, S. H., Lei, W., Jun, C. J., Yan, Z. S., Guang, Y. X., Tong, Z., … Xing, H. (2023). Design strategy and research progress of multifunctional nanoparticles in lung cancer therapy. *Expert opinion on investigational drugs, 32*(8), 723–739.

Mishra, Y. K., Aljabali, A. A., Hassan, S. S., Pabari, R. M., Shahcheraghi, S. H., Mishra, V., … Tambuwala, M. M. (2021). The viral capsid as novel nanomaterials for drug delivery. *Future Science OA, 7*(9).

Nwagbara, U. I., Ginindza, T. G., & Hlongwana, K. W. (2020). Health systems influence on the pathways of care for lung cancer in low-and middle-income countries: a scoping review. *Globalization and health, 16*(1), 23.

Panico, S., Capolla, S., Bozzer, S., Toffoli, G., Dal Bo, M., & Macor, P. (2022). Biological features of nanoparticles: protein corona formation and interaction with the immune system. *Pharmaceutics, 14*(12), 2605.

Papi, M., Caputo, D., Palmieri, V., Coppola, R. O. S. S. E. L. L. A., Palchetti, S., Bugli, F., … Caracciolo, G. (2017). Clinically approved PEGylated nanoparticles are covered by a protein corona that boosts the uptake by cancer cells. *Nanoscale, 9*(29), 10327–10334.

Peng, L., Xu, Q., Yin, S., Zhang, Y., Wu, H., Liu, Y., … Lin, Q. (2023). The emerging nanomedicine-based technology for non-small cell lung cancer immunotherapy: how far are we from an effective treatment. *Frontiers in Oncology, 13*, 1153319.

Piwocka, O., Piotrowski, I., Suchorska, W. M., & Kulcenty, K. (2024). Dynamic interactions in the tumor niche: how the cross-talk between CAFs and the tumor microenvironment impacts resistance to therapy. *Frontiers in Molecular Biosciences, 11*, 1343523.

Rai, D. B., Solanki, R., Patel, S., Pooja, D., & Kulhari, H. (2024). Designing of fucosylated dendrimers as a biocompatible carrier for the targeted delivery of chrysin to human lung cancer cells. *Next Materials, 5*, 100257.

Rapoport, N. (2007). Physical stimuli-responsive polymeric micelles for anti-cancer drug delivery. *Progress in Polymer Science, 32*(8–9), 962–990.

Rawal, S., & Patel, M. (2021). Bio-nanocarriers for lung cancer management: befriending the barriers. *Nano-Micro Letters, 13*(1), 142.

Raza, A., Hayat, U., Rasheed, T., Bilal, M., & Iqbal, H. M. (2018). Redox-responsive nano-carriers as tumor-targeted drug delivery systems. *European journal of medicinal chemistry, 157*, 705–715.

Scheff, R. J., & Schneider, B. J. (2013, June). Non–small-cell lung cancer: treatment of late stage disease: chemotherapeutics and new frontiers. In Seminars in interventional radiology*: (Vol. 30, No. 02,* (pp. 191–198). Thieme Medical Publishers.

Sharma, I., Nagpal, S., & Mishra, A. K. (2025). Navigating bacterial motility through chemotaxis: from molecular mechanisms to physiological perspectives. *Folia Microbiologica, 70*(4), 753–777.

Shen, Z., Ye, H., Kröger, M., & Li, Y. (2018). Aggregation of polyethylene glycol polymers suppresses receptor-mediated endocytosis of PEGylated liposomes. *Nanoscale, 10*(9), 4545–4560.

Shi, J., Kantoff, P. W., Wooster, R., & Farokhzad, O. C. (2017). Cancer nanomedicine: progress, challenges and opportunities. *Nature reviews cancer, 17*(1), 20–37.

Shojaei, S., Pourmadadi, M., Homayoonfal, M., Behnamrad, P., Fathi-karkan, S., Rahdar, A., … Pandey, S. (2024). Revolutionizing lung cancer treatment: Nanotechnology-driven advances in targeted drug delivery and novel therapeutic strategies. *Journal of Drug Delivery Science and Technology, 101.*

Singh, P., Pandit, S., Mokkapati, V. R. S. S., Garg, A., Ravikumar, V., & Mijakovic, I. (2025). Advanced nanomaterials for cancer therapy: Gold, silver, and iron oxide nanoparticles in oncological applications. *Advanced Healthcare Materials, 14*(3), e2403059.

Socinski, M. A., Bondarenko, I., Karaseva, N. A., Makhson, A. M., Vynnychenko, I., Okamoto, I., … Renschler, M. F. (2012). Weekly nab-paclitaxel in combination with carboplatin versus solvent-based paclitaxel plus carboplatin as first-line therapy in patients with advanced non–small-cell lung cancer: final results of a phase III trial. *Journal of clinical oncology, 30*(17), 2055–2062.

Solomon, R., & Gabizon, A. A. (2008). Clinical pharmacology of liposomal anthracyclines: focus on pegylated liposomal doxorubicin. *Clinical lymphoma and myeloma, 8*(1), 21–32.

Sun, X., Tian, T., Lian, Y., & Cui, Z. (2024). Current advances in viral nanoparticles for biomedicine. *ACS nano, 18*(50), 33827–33863.

Suzuki, J., Tsuboi, M., & Ishii, G. (2022). Cancer-associated fibroblasts and the tumor microenvironment in non-small cell lung cancer. *Expert Review of Anticancer Therapy, 22*(2), 169–182. doi:10.1080/14737140.2022.2019018.

Tomanin, R., & Scarpa, M. (2004). Why do we need new gene therapy viral vectors? Characteristics, limitations and future perspectives of viral vector transduction. *Current gene therapy, 4*(4), 357–372.

Torchilin, V. P. (2005). Block copolymer micelles as a solution for drug delivery problems. *Expert opinion on therapeutic patents, 15*(1), 63–75.

Tufail, M., Jiang, C. H., & Li, N. (2025). Immune evasion in cancer: mechanisms and cutting-edge therapeutic approaches. *Signal transduction and targeted. therapy, 10*(1), 227.

Vayr, F., Savall, F., Bigay-Game, L., Soulat, J. M., Chouaid, C., & Herin, F. (2019). Lung cancer survivors and employment: a systematic review. *Lung Cancer, 131*, 31–39.

Velluto, D., Demurtas, D., & Hubbell, J. A. (2008). PEG-b-PPS diblock copolymer aggregates for hydrophobic drug solubilization and release: cyclosporin A as an example. *Molecular pharmaceutics, 5*(4), 632–642.

Waheed, S., Li, Z., Zhang, F., Chiarini, A., Armato, U., & Wu, J. (2022). Engineering nano-drug biointerface to overcome biological barriers toward precision drug delivery. *Journal of Nanobiotechnology, 20*(1), 395.

Wang, T., Nelson, R. A., Bogardus, A., & Grannis, F. W., Jr. (2010). Five-year lung cancer survival: which advanced stage nonsmall cell lung cancer patients attain long-term survival? *Cancer: Interdisciplinary International Journal of the American Cancer Society, 116*(6), 1518–1525.

Wicki, A., Witzigmann, D., Balasubramanian, V., & Huwyler, J. (2015). Nanomedicine in cancer therapy: challenges, opportunities, and clinical applications. *Journal of controlled release, 200*, 138–157.

Wilhelm, S., Tavares, A. J., Dai, Q., Ohta, S., Audet, J., Dvorak, H. F., & Chan, W. C. (2016). Analysis of nanoparticle delivery to tumours. *Nature reviews materials, 1*(5), 16014.

Yang, C., Lv, J., Lv, T., Pan, Y., Han, Y., Zhao, S., & Wang, J. (2016). Metal ion-assisted drug-loading model for novel delivery system of cisplatin solid lipid nanoparticles with improving loading efficiency and sustained release. *Journal of Microencapsulation, 33*(3), 292–298.

Zhang, J., Li, Y., Guo, S., Zhang, W., Fang, B., & Wang, S. (2024). Moving beyond traditional therapies: the role of nanomedicines in lung cancer. *Frontiers in Pharmacology, 15*, 1363346.

Zheng, D., Wang, J., Guo, S., Zhao, Z., & Wang, F. (2018). Formulations, pharmacodynamic and clinical studies of nanoparticles for lung cancer therapy-an overview. *Current drug metabolism, 19*(9), 759–767.

Zhou, S., Gravekamp, C., Bermudes, D., & Liu, K. (2018). Tumour-targeting bacteria engineered to fight cancer. *Nature Reviews Cancer, 18*(12), 727–743.

Zhou, Z., Vázquez-González, M., & Willner, I. (2021). Stimuli-responsive metal–organic framework nanoparticles for controlled drug delivery and medical applications. *Chemical Society Reviews, 50*(7), 4541–4563.

Zong, R., Ruan, H., Liu, C., Fan, S., & Li, J. (2023). Bacteria and bacterial components as natural bio-nanocarriers for drug and gene delivery systems in cancer therapy. *Pharmaceutics, 15*(10), 2490.

Sun, X., Zhang, X., Yang, H., & Wang, X. (2021). Mesoporous silica encapsulated iron oxide-silver heterodimeric nanoparticles and their applications in multi-responsive drug release.

CHAPTER 5

Exosome-Mediated precision targeting: A paradigm shift in lung cancer theranostics

Sanheeta Chakrabarty[a], Mayank Kashyap[a], Shivani Prajapati[b], Sunil Choudhary[b] and Shreyans K. Jain[a]

[a]Department of Pharmaceutical Engineering and Technology, Indian Institute of Technology (BHU), Varanasi, Uttar Pradesh, India [b]Department of Radiotherapy and Radiation Medicine, Institute of Medical Sciences, Banaras Hindu University, Varanasi, Uttar Pradesh, India

5.1 Introduction

Lung cancer (LC) has become one of the deadliest cancers, contributing to 18% of the cancer-related deaths in 2020. One of the two histological subtypes of LC is nonsmall cell LC (NSCLC), which comprises adenocarcinoma, squamous cell carcinoma, and large cell carcinoma. NSCLC accounts for 85% of the LC cases, whereas the remaining 15% are due to the other subtype, small cell LC (SCLC) (Smolarz et al., 2025). Despite advanced therapeutic approaches such as surgery, targeted therapy, chemotherapy, and radiotherapy, the success rate of treatment is still low due to late diagnosis. About 75% of the patients are diagnosed at the advanced metastatic stage; hence, the 5-year survival rate is less than 15% (Wild et al., 2020). Conventional diagnostic procedures, including X-ray, computed tomography, bronchoscopy, and lung biopsy, are some of the practical and economical approaches, but have some demerits. X-ray examination fails to fully analyze the pulmonary lesions and may give false negative reports (Bradley et al., 2019). Computed tomography has better sensitivity than X-ray but still possesses the risk of radiation exposure (The National Lung Screening Trial Research Team, 2011). Bronchoscopy is the primary diagnostic and therapeutic method, but with various complications (Ernst et al., 2008). Hence, there is an urgent need for better diagnostic procedures with higher sensitivity and specificity to allow early diagnosis and better treatment. To achieve this goal, studying biomarkers like exosomes is an excellent theranostic approach.

Exosomes are the nanosized extracellular vesicles (EVs) ranging from 30 to 100 nm in diameter. Initially, in 1985 they were identified as cellular wastes, but later, with the help of enhanced isolation techniques such as ultracentrifugation, microfluidics, immunoaffinity capturing, size exclusion, and exosomal precipitation, researchers discovered that exosomes

Nanoengineered Therapeutics for Lung Cancer: Advanced Drug Delivery Strategies.
DOI: https://doi.org/10.1016/B978-0-443-44585-9.00010-X

play a critical role in the pathology of numerous diseases, including cancer, by facilitating intercellular communication (Chen et al., 2024a). Exosomes are found in all major body fluids, such as blood, semen, breast milk, bronchoalveolar lavage, urine, cerebrospinal fluid, pleural fluid, saliva, tears, nasal secretion, synovial fluid, amniotic fluid, lymph, bile, and gastric acid. Thus this high natural abundance of exosomes in the human body makes them an ideal biomarker for disease theranostics (Mukerjee et al., 2025).

5.2 Biology of exosomes

5.2.1 Classifications of exosomes

Most cells naturally release some membranous vesicles, called EVs. These are of different types, which include exosomes, apoptotic bodies, and microvesicles (Crescitelli et al., 2013). Since they function as crucial messengers in both physiological and pathological circumstances, all three subtypes have the potential to be therapeutic. All EVs have the potential to target immune cells and facilitate immunotherapy deliberately (Debs et al., 2019; Sun et al., 2020; Welsh et al., 2024; Wu et al., 2017; Xie et al., 2020). They differ mainly in their size, biogenesis, and physiological roles. Exosomes are the smallest EVs (30–150 nm) originating from the endosomal system through inward budding of the plasma membrane and subsequent release of intraluminal vesicles (ILVs) upon fusion of multivesicular bodies (MVBs) with the plasma membrane (Perrin et al., 2021; Qiu et al., 2021). In contrast, microvesicles (100–1000 nm) are formed by direct outward blebbing and fission of the plasma membrane (Kakarla et al., 2020). Apoptotic bodies are larger vesicles (50–5000 nm) generated during apoptosis because of membrane blebbing and cellular fragmentation (Wen et al., 2023).

All three vesicle types possess a lipid bilayer and carry proteins, lipids, and nucleic acids reflective of their parent cells, but their cellular targets and functions differ (Arandjelovic & Ravichandran, 2015). Exosomes and microvesicles exhibit broad targeting capabilities, often mediating intercellular communication, immune modulation, and drug delivery, whereas apoptotic bodies primarily interact with phagocytes such as macrophages and dendritic cells, influencing immune polarization (Liu et al., 2020). Notably, both exosomes and microvesicles express CD47, which can confer resistance to phagocytosis and prolong circulation time. Despite the functional overlap among these EVs, apoptotic bodies remain less studied than exosomes and microvesicles, though they possess significant immunomodulatory potential (Hus et al., 2005; Wen et al., 2023).

5.2.2 Biogenesis of exosomes

The biogenesis of exosomes has been known to follow multiple mechanisms. The best described mechanism is the endosomal sorting complex required for transport (ESCRT) dependent mechanism (Fig. 5.1). It initiates with the invagination of the endosomal mem-

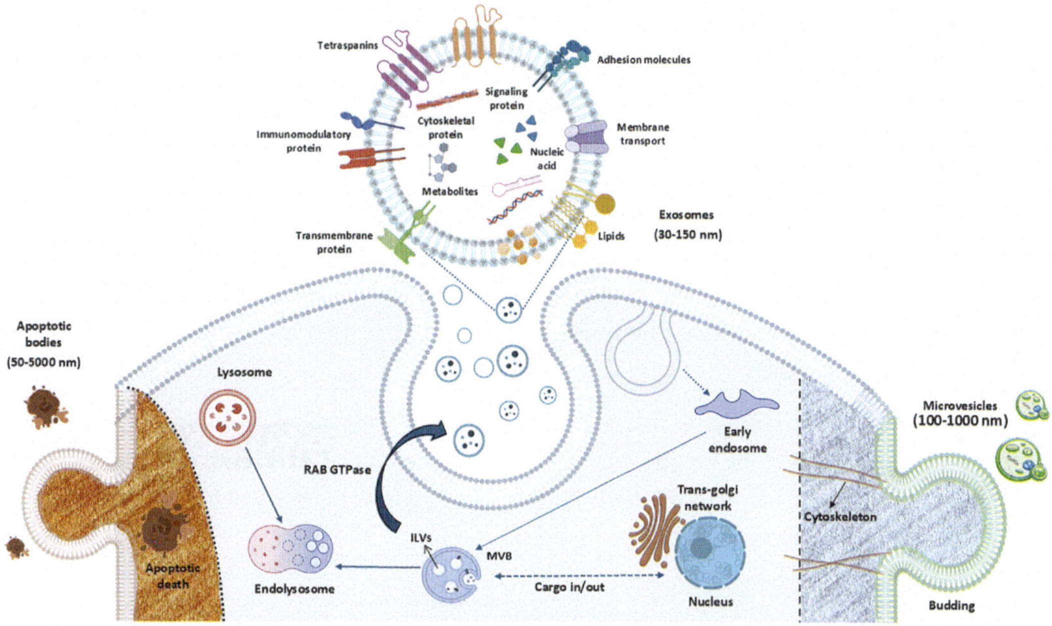

Figure 5.1: Endosomal sorting complex required for transport (ESCRT)-dependent biogenesis and release of exosomes.

The schematic illustrates the classical endosomal pathway of exosome biogenesis. Invagination of the plasma membrane leads to the formation of early endosomes, which mature into late endosomes or multivesicular bodies (MVBs) containing multiple intraluminal vesicles (ILVs). The sorting of biologically active cargo, including proteins, lipids, nucleic acids (DNA, mRNA, miRNA), and metabolites, into ILVs is primarily mediated by the ESCRT machinery and associated proteins. MVBs have three possible fates: recycling via the trans-Golgi network, degradation through lysosomal fusion, or fusion with the plasma membrane. Fusion of MVBs with the plasma membrane results in the release of ILVs into the extracellular space as exosomes. Exosomes are enriched in endocytic and cytosolic proteins, such as Rab GTPases, TSG101, and tetraspanins, which regulate vesicle trafficking, cargo sorting, and secretion, thereby enabling their role in intercellular communication.

brane, resulting in the formation of early endosomes. The early endosomes then matured into MVBs, also known as late endosomes, containing numerous ILVs. Various biologically active molecules, such as proteins, lipids, nucleic acids (DNA, mRNA, miRNA), and some small molecules such as metabolites, are stored in these ILVs with the aid of ESCRT machinery, comprised of four protein complexes and accessory proteins that sequentially bind future exosome cargoes and form the ILVs. The MVBs containing these cargo boxes have three fates: trans-Golgi network (TGN) mediated recycling, degradation of ILVs constituents by lysosomes, or fusion with the internal membrane of the cell (Crescitelli et al., 2013). This fusion causes an outward budding and expulsion of the ILVs into the extracellular space via exocytosis in the form of exosomes.

The process begins with the formation of early endosomes from the plasma membrane. These mature into late endosomes, within which parts of the limiting membrane bud inward to generate ILVs, forming MVBs. When MVBs fuse with the plasma membrane, ILVs are released into the extracellular space as exosomes (Kalluri & LeBleu, 2020).

Exosomes are not simple fragments of the plasma membrane, as they lack many surface proteins but are enriched in endocytic and cytosolic proteins such as annexin II, RAB5, RAB7, and TSG101, which are key regulators of endosomal trafficking. Protein sorting into these vesicles involves ubiquitin-dependent mechanisms mediated by TSG101 and c-CBL, as well as ubiquitin-independent pathways involving tetraspanins and lipid microdomains (Chen et al., 2024a; Lee et al., 2024).

Exosome secretion occurs through fusion of MVBs with the plasma membrane, a process that can be constitutive (in B cells, dendritic cells, epithelial cells) or Ca^{2+}-regulated (in mast cells and T-cells). This fusion involves SNARE proteins and synaptotagmins, which coordinate vesicle docking and release (van Niel et al., 2022).

5.2.3 Composition and cargo

Exosomes are small, membrane-bound EVs characterized by a lipid bilayer and a typical saucer-like morphology under an electron microscope. They generally range from 30 to 100 nm in diameter, with B-cell-derived exosomes being particularly uniform (60–80 nm) (van Niel et al., 2022). The standard procedure for isolating exosomes from cell culture supernatants involves sequential centrifugation steps to remove cells, debris, and large vesicles, followed by high-speed ultracentrifugation to pellet the exosomes. Further purification is often achieved by sucrose density-gradient flotation, where exosomes display a buoyant density between 1.13 and 1.19 g mL^{-1}, helping to distinguish them from contaminating protein aggregates or apoptotic fragments (Welsh et al., 2024). Since larger vesicular structures such as ectosomes, prostasomes, or platelet-derived vesicles (>100 nm) may also be secreted, filtration through 0.22 μm membranes is commonly used to minimize contamination. Because fetal calf serum (FCS) used in cell culture contains bovine exosomes, it is essential to prevent their inclusion in preparations. This can be done by culturing cells in media supplemented with exosome-depleted FCS or with defined supplements such as insulin–transferrin–selenite, or bovine serum albumin. Radiolabeling studies have further confirmed that exosomal proteins originate from the producer cells themselves and not from serum-derived contaminants (Mathieu et al., 2019; Welsh et al., 2024).

Exosomes are enriched in proteins associated with endosomal trafficking and membrane organization. These include membrane transport and fusion proteins (GTPases, Annexins, Flotillins), tetraspanins (CD9, CD63, CD81, CD82), heat shock proteins (Hsc70, Hsp90), and MVB biogenesis proteins (Alix, TSG101). Such proteins are considered hallmark exosomal

Table 5.1: Molecular composition of exosomes and their biological relevance.

Component	Representative molecules	Functional significance
Membrane proteins	CD9, CD63, CD81, CD82	Exosome identification and targeting
Endosomal proteins	Alix, TSG101, Rab5, Rab7	MVB biogenesis and trafficking
Stress proteins	Hsc70, Hsp90	Protein stabilization and folding
Lipids	Cholesterol, ceramide, sphingolipids	Membrane rigidity and vesicle stability
Glycans	Mannose, N-linked glycans	Cell-specific recognition
Nucleic acids	mRNA, miRNA, ncRNA	Gene regulation and signaling
Metabolites	Prostaglandins	Intercellular communication

mRNA, messenger RNA; *miRNA*, microRNA; *MVB*, multivesicular body; *ncRNA*, noncoding RNA.

markers. Additionally, exosomes carry lipid-related enzymes such as phospholipases and proteins involved in signaling and antigen presentation. Proteomic studies have identified over 4400 proteins across various exosome types, with composition varying according to the cell of origin and physiological state (Keerthikumar et al., 2016; Pegtel & Gould, 2019).

Exosomes are also rich in raft-associated lipids, conferring stability and rigidity to their bilayer membrane. Key lipids include cholesterol, ceramide, sphingolipids, and phosphoglycerides with long, saturated fatty acyl chains. Notably, ceramide plays a vital role in the biogenesis of exosomes by differentiating exosomal MVBs from lysosomal ones. Exosomes derived from mast and dendritic cells show enrichment in phosphatidylethanolamines and exhibit higher lipid bilayer flipping activity than cellular membranes. They also contain surface glycosylation, enriched in mannose, polylactosamine, α-2,6 sialic acid, and complex N-linked glycans, contributing to cell-specific targeting and recognition (Skotland et al., 2023; Trajkovic et al., 2008).

Exosomes contain a diverse set of nucleic acids, including mRNAs, miRNAs, and other noncoding RNAs. Although many RNA molecules appear fragmented (<200 nt), full-length mRNAs capable of in vitro translation have also been reported. The RNA cargo differs markedly from that of the parent cells, indicating selective packaging mechanisms (Schwarz et al., 2025). In cancer-derived exosomes, however, the miRNA content often mirrors that of the originating tumor cells, suggesting diagnostic potential for liquid biopsy applications. While less extensively characterized, exosomes also carry small metabolites and bioactive molecules, such as prostaglandins, which may contribute to intercellular communication and signaling in physiological and pathological conditions (Kumar, 2025a). The major molecular constituents of exosomes and their functional roles in intercellular communication are summarized in Table 5.1.

5.2.4 Mechanisms of uptake and intercellular communication

Exosomes undergo diverse intracellular trafficking routes that determine their functional fate within recipient cells. They can directly fuse with the plasma membrane to release cargo into the cytosol or interact with surface receptors to trigger downstream signaling cascades. Once internalized, exosomes typically follow the endosomal maturation pathway from early endosomes to late endosomes or MVBs, and ultimately fuse with lysosomes for degradation. This trafficking depends on cytoskeletal transport, lipid composition, SNARE proteins, and intracellular pH regulation (Mohamed et al., 2025; Patat et al., 2025).

However, not all exosomes are destined for degradation. Cargoes may bypass lysosomal breakdown to exert functional effects, as evidenced by sustained signaling through pH-sensitive molecules like latent TGF-β1, which becomes activated in acidic endosomal compartments. Exosome-endosome fusion and acidification can facilitate cargo uncoating and cytosolic release, a process aided by anionic lipids such as lysobisphosphatidic acid (LBPA) (Liu et al., 2024). Moreover, interactions between Rab5/Rab7-positive endosomes and the endoplasmic reticulum (ER) suggest that exosomal mRNAs and miRNAs may be released near ER sites for efficient translation and gene regulation (Solinger et al., 2025).

Alternative routes, including retrograde trafficking to the TGN, recycling through early endosomes, or partial release from ruptured endo-lysosomal membranes, allow cargo escape and intercellular dissemination. In some specialized cells, such as dendritic cells, exosomes can avoid lysosomal degradation via CD81-positive compartments, such as viral trafficking mechanisms. Conversely, certain exosomes, such as those from oligodendrocytes internalized by microglia, are targeted for degradation, contributing to membrane turnover in a silent clearance process. Despite advances in exosome labeling and imaging, direct visualization of cargo release remains limited. Understanding the precise intracellular fate and communication routes of exosome cargoes remains crucial for elucidating their role in intercellular signaling and therapeutic potential (Gilleron et al., 2024; Toshima & Toshima, 2024).

5.3 Exosomes in lung cancer biology

5.3.1 Tumor-derived exosomes and their role in tumor progression

Exosomes are secreted by all kinds of cells in our body, including tumor cells. The exosomes released by tumor cells are called tumor-derived exosomes (TDEs). These EVs are highly abundant in cancer patients. Though both types follow the same mechanistic approach, i.e., Endocytosis → Early endosome → MVB formation → Fusion with plasma membrane → Exosome release, there are some major differences between the two types of exosomes, as explained in Table 5.2. The TDEs serve as critical mediators of intercellular communication in LC. Hence, they are also called molecular messengers (Manap et al., 2024). These nanobodies encapsulate a diverse bioactive cargo, including lipids, proteins, mRNAs, miRNAs, DNA fragments, and metabolites that are crucial messengers for cell proliferation. The TDEs are largely heterogeneous, implying nonuniformity, diversity, or variation in characteristics and

Table 5.2: Comparison between physiological and tumor-derived exosomes.

Feature	Physiological exosomes	Tumor-derived exosomes (TDEs)
Biogenesis	Biosynthesized in healthy cells such as epithelial cells, immune cells, endothelial cells, fibroblasts, and neurons under physiological conditions.	Released by malignant cells in virtually all tumor types, including lung, breast, and colorectal cancers.
Natural abundance	Moderate amount for routine intercellular communication and tissue homeostasis.	Produced in extreme amounts, often correlating with tumor aggressiveness and stage.
Bioactive cargoes	Transfer regular cellular components, such as proteins, lipids, mRNA, and regulatory miRNAs, reflecting the physiological state of the donor cell.	Augmented with oncogenic proteins (e.g., EGFRvIII, KRAS), pro-angiogenic and immunosuppressive factors, and tumor-promoting noncoding RNAs (miR-21, miR-23a, lncRNA MALAT1).
Physiological functions	Regulate homeostasis: maintain immune function, aid tissue repair, mediate normal signaling between cells, and remove cellular waste.	Promote tumor progression: enhance proliferation, angiogenesis, metastasis, immune evasion, and therapy resistance.

composition. Some TDEs have a slightly larger size and carry a different set of oncogenic proteins and RNAs. The tumor progression is promoted by the TDEs via multiple mechanisms. Various signaling pathways are mediated by TDEs, which boost cell proliferation, metastasis, and immune evasion. For instance in NSCLC, the exosomal miR-21 and miR-155 are recurrently upregulated and contribute to oncogenic biotransformation by targeting tumor suppressor genes like PTEN and SOCS1 (Fang et al., 2025). Furthermore, the vesicles transfer various signaling molecules such as activated epidermal growth factor receptor (EGFR) and mutant KRAS, which enhance the autocrine and paracrine signaling pathways in the neighboring cells of the tumor microenvironment (TME), subsequently promoting aggressive tumor cell growth. In addition, a tumor suppressor miR-23a targets PTEN, thereby activating AKT signaling and supporting proliferation under hypoxic conditions (Rao et al., 2023).

Furthermore, TDEs can generate chemoresistance via different mechanisms. Various chemotherapeutic agents, such as cisplatin, can be effluxed out by the exosomes, thereby decreasing their bioavailability. Numerous exosomal miRNAs, such as miR-222 and miR-100-5p, and proteins such as p-glycoprotein can be transferred from resistant to sensitive cells, conferring multidrug resistance. Also, apoptotic-related genes can be suppressed by long noncoding RNAs such as H19 and MALAT1, sustaining tumor survival during therapy. So these findings establish TDEs not only as the byproducts of tumor cells but as active mediators promoting malignancy and chemoresistance (Liu et al., 2025).

Table 5.3: Immunomodulatory mechanisms mediated by tumor-derived exosomal components.

Exosomal component	Immune target	Mechanism
PD-L1	CD8+ T-cells	PD-1 binding
miR-214	Dendritic cells	↓ Antigen presentation
TGF-β	T-cells	↑ Tregs, tolerance

5.3.2 Modulation of the tumor microenvironment

A dynamic ecosystem called the TME is composed of tumor cells, stromal fibroblasts, immune cells, endothelial cells, and extracellular matrix (ECM). The TDEs serve as a communication link between these components, regulating tumor–stroma interactions and facilitating tumor progression (Wang et al., 2025).

5.3.2.1 Angiogenesis

Angiogenesis is the process by which new blood vessels form from preexisting ones. These newly formed blood vessels provide oxygen and an essential nutrient supply to the growing tumor mass for further proliferation. Multiple growth factors are associated with angiogenesis, such as VEGF, FGF, and angiopoietin, which are transported by the TDEs and activate the downstream signaling pathways of VEGFR and FGFR present in the endothelial cells. Another mechanism of stimulating angiogenesis by transferring pro-angiogenic miRNA, miR-23a, to its target prolyl hydroxylase and tight junction proteins in endothelial cells, improving vascular permeability and increasing vessel production. Another miRNA, miR-210, produced due to hypoxia, also promotes the endothelial migration and tubologenesis under hypoxic stress (Rao et al., 2023; Tan et al., 2020). These mechanisms collectively contribute to the development of metastatic cancer.

5.3.2.2 Immune evasion

The T-cells of the immune system continuously do surveillance to protect the body from major threats such as tumor cells. This activity can be inhibited by TDEs expressing PD-L1 that directly suppress CD8+ by binding with the PD-1 receptors. In addition to this, the exosomes carry miR-214 and TGF-β that inhibit the dendritic cell maturation and antigen presentation. The immune system can be further suppressed by TDE-induced differentiation of myeloid-derived suppressor cells (MDSCs) and regulatory T-cells (Tregs) (Table 5.3; Dragu et al., 2025; Wu et al., 2024). Hence, exosomes can be labeled as immunomodulatory vesicles, creating a tolerogenic atmosphere conducive to tumor survival.

5.3.2.3 Epithelial–mesenchymal transition

The epithelial–mesenchymal transition (EMT) is a dynamic cellular process in which stationary epithelial cells are transformed into mobile, migratory, and invasive mesenchymal cells.

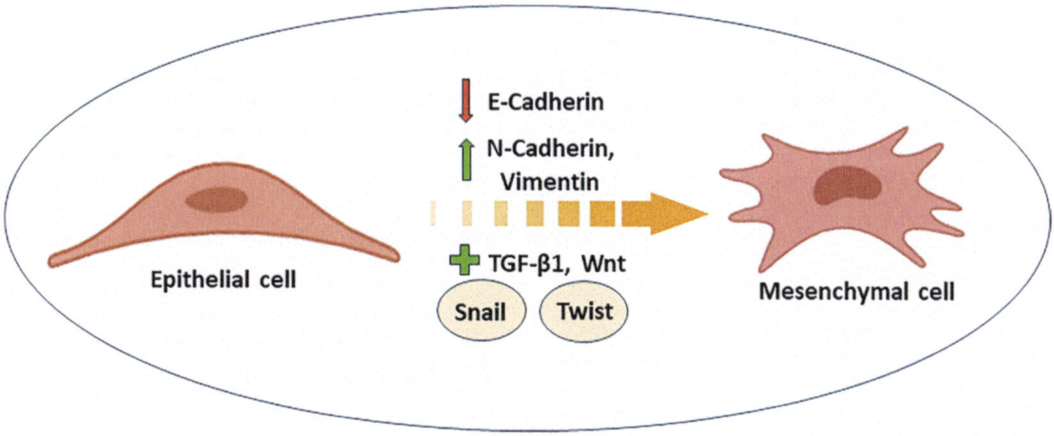

Figure 5.2
Exosome-induced epithelial-mesenchymal transition (EMT). Exosomal signaling promotes downregulation of the epithelial marker E-cadherin and upregulation of mesenchymal markers N-cadherin and vimentin through activation of TGF-β1 and Wnt signaling pathways, leading to induction of EMT-associated transcription factors such as Snail and Twist.

This transition aids the tumor cells in undergoing invasion and metastasis. Exosomes mediate this process through downregulation of the E-cadherin, an epithelial marker, by exosomal miR-21, miR-210, and miR-499a-5p, and simultaneous upregulation of mesenchymal markers N-cadherin and vimentin. The EMT process can also be activated by TGF-β1 and Wnt ligands that trigger SMAD and β-catenin signaling cascades, driving EMT transcription factors such as Twist and Snail. The tumor invasion can further be enhanced by STAT3-mediated transcriptional activation caused by IL-6 delivered by the TDEs (Fig. 5.2; Li et al., 2025).

5.3.2.4 Metastasis and premetastatic niche formation

Metastasis is the propagation of cancer cells from their original location to other parts of the body. All cancer types follow the same basic procedure of metastasis (invasion, intravasation, circulation, extravasation, colonization). First, the cancer cells penetrate the surrounding tissue by degrading the ECM with proteolytic enzymes. This process, i.e., invasion, exposes the blood vessels to cancer cells and allows them to follow the next step, intravasation, in which they enter the bloodstream to travel to other organs of the body (Alshahrani et al., 2025). During the third phase (circulation), the cancer cells need to survive the physical stress and immune predation. To overcome these barriers and reach the target location, they often form clusters with platelets or evade immune recognition. In the last two stages, extravasation and colonization, the migrated cancer cells adhere to the walls of blood vessels and migrate through the vessel lining into new tissue, a process facilitated by tissue-specific adhesion molecules, and adapt to the new microenvironment. Then they begin to proliferate and produce secondary tumors depending on different factors like angiogenesis and immune evasion.

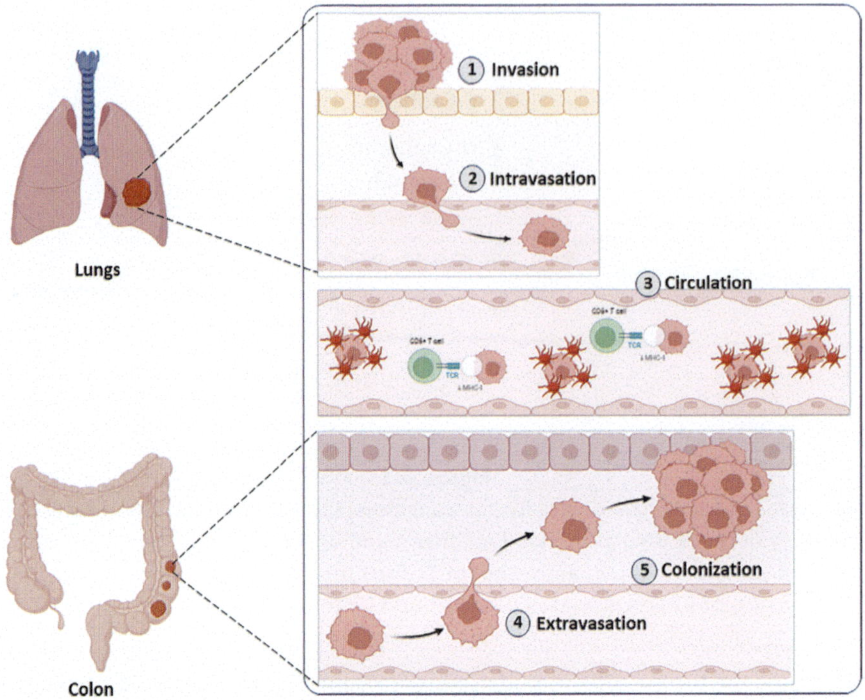

Figure 5.3
Exosome-regulated metastatic cascade and premetastatic niche formation. Schematic illustration of the multistep metastatic process in lung cancer, including invasion, intravasation, circulation, extravasation, and colonization at distant organs.

The resultant metastatic cancer is of the original cancer type, i.e., metastatic LC in the colon is still LC, not colorectal cancer (Fig. 5.3; Lambert et al., 2017; Simonetta et al., 2020).

Exosomal integrins ($\alpha6\beta4$, $\alpha6\beta1$, $\alpha v\beta5$) determine metastatic organ specificity. LC exosomes enriched with $\alpha6\beta4$ promote lung colonization by interacting with resident fibroblasts and epithelial cells. Exosomes can carry matrix metalloproteinases (MMPs), specifically MMP-2 and MMP-9, which then degrade the ECM to break down barriers, allowing cancer cells to invade and metastasize. This remodeling of the ECM creates a permissive environment for tumor growth by degrading structural components and can also release signaling molecules that promote cancer progression. Exosomes can establish a supportive microenvironment for metastasis, known as a premetastatic niche, by carrying S100 proteins and cytokines that attract progenitor cells to distant sites. This allows the cancer cells to prepare the distant organs for colonization before actual metastasis occurs (Hoshino et al., 2015; Peinado et al., 2012). The major exosomal cargoes involved in organ-specific metastasis and their functional consequences are summarized in Table 5.4.

Table 5.4: Organotropism and functional roles of tumor-derived exosomal cargo in metastatic progression.

Exosomal cargo	Target organ	Function
$\alpha 6\beta 4$, $\alpha 6\beta 1$	Lung	Fibroblast activation
$\alpha v\beta 5$	Liver	Kupffer cell interaction
MMP-2, MMP-9	ECM	Invasion
S100 proteins	Distant organs	Premetastatic niche

5.3.3 Exosomal biomarkers in lung cancer: Diagnostic and prognostic potential

Exosomes possess robust stability and reflection of tumor molecular profiles. Hence, they are being extensively explored as liquid biopsy biomarkers in LC.

5.3.3.1 Diagnostic applications

Exosomes are present in all bodily fluids, such as blood, saliva, urine, pleural effusions, and bronchoalveolar lavage fluid. The exosomal miRNA profile is particularly informative for early cancer detection. In NSCLC patients, there are observed to be elevated serum levels of miR-21, miR-17-5p, miR-126, and miR-486-5p are observed, distinguishing them from healthy individuals. Detection of mutant EGFR, ALK rearrangements, or KRAS mutations within exosomes allows for noninvasive tumor genotyping. These exosomal signatures are increasingly integrated into clinical workflows to monitor tumor evolution and therapeutic response (Zhang et al., 2022).

5.3.3.2 Prognostic applications

There is a strong correlation of exosomal molecules with tumor stage, metastasis, and patient survival. Elevated levels of miR-222, miR-196a, and PD-L1 are associated with advanced disease, drug resistance, and poor prognosis. The resistance to tyrosine kinase inhibitors (TKIs) can be revealed by detecting exosomal KRAS mutations and EGFR T790M. The tumor's immune-suppressive activity can be monitored by analyzing PD-L1 levels in the blood. The TDEs carry PD-L1, which can bind to the T-cells of the immune system and suppress their activity, mirroring immune evasion. The elevated levels of PD-L1 are often associated with poor response to PD-L1/PD-1 checkpoint inhibitors, whereas a decline in these levels correlates with better therapeutic response to the immunotherapy. Hence, measuring circulating exosomal PD-L1 levels provides a noninvasive, dynamic indicator of immunotherapy response and resistance (Wu et al., 2024).

5.3.4 Cross talk between tumor and stromal cells via exosomes

Stromal cells have a key role in the development of cancer cells. They are noncancerous cells present in the TME that can promote cancer growth and metastasis by releasing various growth factors and stimulating angiogenesis, remodeling the ECM, and suppressing the

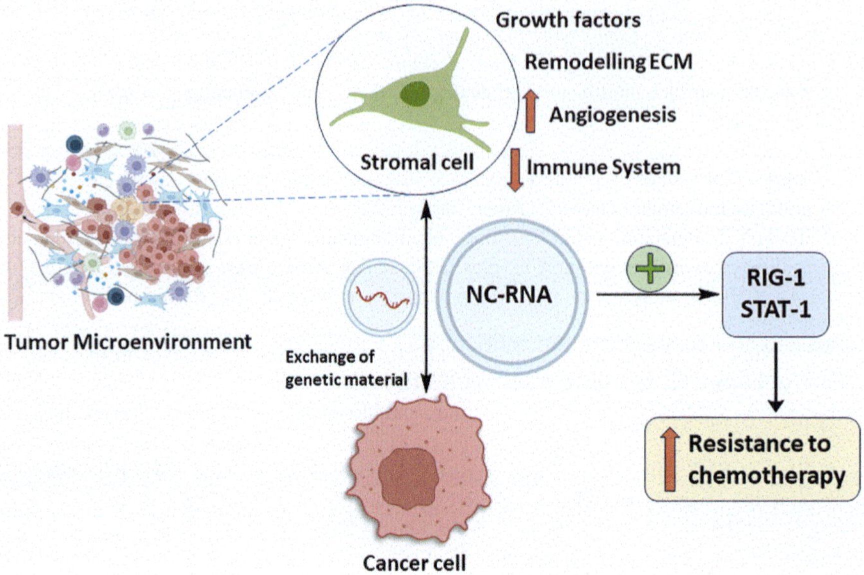

Figure 5.4
Exosome-mediated crosstalk between cancer cells and stromal cells in the tumor microenvironment. Schematic showing exosome-driven exchange of genetic material between cancer cells and stromal cells within the tumor microenvironment, leading to stromal reprogramming, activation of RIG-I/STAT-1 signaling, enhanced angiogenesis, immune suppression, and increased resistance to chemotherapy.

immune system. Exosomes are crucial mediators of this interaction. They allow exchange of different genetic materials between cancer cells and stromal cells, promoting cell proliferation. Exosomes also transfer noncoding RNA that activate signaling pathways such as RIG-I and STAT1, in cancer cells, leading to increased resistance to chemotherapy and radiation. The TDEs can also get taken up by stromal cells such as fibroblasts, endothelial cells, and immune cells, changing their function and making them more supportive of tumor growth. After getting internalized, the exosomes alter the metabolic pathways such as glycolysis and glutamine metabolism, making nutrients more accessible to the tumor cells. These deviations collectively render stromal cells more supportive of cancer proliferation, metastasis, and resistance to cancer treatment and help establish and inflate the TME (Fig. 5.4; Zhang et al., 2019).

5.4 Exosomes in lung cancer diagnostics

5.4.1 Exosomal microRNAs, long noncoding RNAs, and proteins as noninvasive biomarkers

Exosomes, nanosized EVs ranging between 30 and 150 nm, are secreted by nearly all cell types and serve as critical mediators of intercellular communication. Their unique composition includes proteins, lipids, DNA, messenger RNA, and noncoding RNAs such as microRNAs (miRNAs) and long noncoding RNAs (lncRNAs) that reflect the physiological and pathological status of the parent cells. Because exosomes are stable in circulation and can be isolated from various body fluids, such as serum, plasma, urine, saliva, and cerebrospinal fluid, their molecular cargo offers a promising avenue for noninvasive biomarker discovery (Kalluri & LeBleu, 2020; Théry et al., 2018).

Among the exosomal components, miRNAs (exomiRs) have gained considerable attention due to their regulatory roles in gene expression and their stability against enzymatic degradation, temperature fluctuations, and pH variations. The selective packaging of miRNAs into exosomes involves sophisticated mechanisms mediated by the ESCRT, RNA-binding proteins such as Y-box protein 1 (YBX1), and heterogeneous nuclear ribonucleoprotein A2B1 (hnRNPA2B1). Alterations in exosomal miRNA profiles have been linked to a wide range of noncommunicable diseases (NCDs), including cancer, cardiovascular, renal, and neurodegenerative disorders. For instance elevated exosomal miR-21 and miR-155 are associated with tumor progression and chemoresistance, whereas circulating exosomal miR-92b serves as an early diagnostic marker in colorectal and hepatocellular cancers. Similarly, miR-145 and miR-210 have been correlated with hypertensive and hypoxic conditions in cardiovascular pathologies, and urinary exosomal miR-21, miR-192, and miR-200 families are indicative of renal injury and diabetic nephropathy. In neurological diseases, altered exosomal miR-19b, miR-195, and let-7 family members have been reported in Parkinson's and Alzheimer's disease, highlighting their diagnostic and prognostic potential (Kalluri & LeBleu, 2020; O'Brien et al., 2020).

In parallel, exosomal lncRNAs have emerged as valuable biomarkers due to their involvement in transcriptional regulation, chromatin remodeling, and RNA splicing. Differential expression of lncRNAs within exosomes correlates with cancer metastasis, cardiovascular remodeling, and inflammatory responses, suggesting their role in disease monitoring and therapeutic targeting. Similarly, exosomal proteins include tetraspanins (CD9, CD63, CD81), heat shock proteins, and enzymes that provide additional diagnostic cues. Their presence can reflect pathological processes such as tumor aggressiveness, immune modulation, and metabolic reprogramming (Martiniano et al., 2016).

Collectively, exosomal miRNAs, lncRNAs, and proteins constitute a complex, cell-specific signature that mirrors pathological alterations with high fidelity. Their accessibility from noninvasive samples, coupled with their molecular stability, positions them as next-generation biomarkers for early diagnosis, disease stratification, and therapeutic monitoring across diverse clinical settings. Continued advancements in high-throughput sequencing, proteomics, and bioinformatics will further refine their clinical translation, enabling precision medicine approaches through exosome-based diagnostics and targeted therapy development (Kalluri & LeBleu, 2020; Xu et al., 2018).

5.4.2 Techniques for exosome isolation and characterization

Isolation and characterization of exosomes are crucial steps for exploring their biological and diagnostic potential. Given their small size (30–150 nm) and heterogeneity, efficient, reproducible, and nondestructive techniques are essential for obtaining intact, pure exosomes. Conventional isolation methods are mainly based on physical properties such as size, density, and surface markers, whereas emerging nanotechnological and microfluidic approaches have enabled higher precision and throughput. Ultracentrifugation remains the "gold standard" for exosome isolation. It separates vesicles by sequentially increasing centrifugal forces (from 300 × *g* to over 100,000 × *g*) to eliminate cells, debris, and larger vesicles. Although cost-effective and widely accessible, it often results in co-precipitation of protein aggregates and mechanical damage to vesicles. Density-gradient centrifugation refines this method by layering sucrose or iodixanol gradients, achieving higher purity (1.10–1.18 g/mL) and better removal of contaminants. However, it is labor-intensive, time-consuming, and requires trained personnel and specialized equipment (Théry et al., 2018). Ultrafiltration utilizes membranes with defined molecular weight cut-offs (MWCOs) to separate exosomes based on their size. It is simpler, faster, and avoids high-speed centrifugation, but can cause vesicle loss or deformation due to membrane clogging. SEC, which passes samples through porous gel matrices, separates particles by size without high pressure or force, preserving vesicle integrity and bioactivity. Combinations of ultrafiltration and SEC have been shown to improve exosome yield and purity compared to traditional centrifugation methods. Hydrophilic polymers such as polyethylene glycol (PEG) reduce exosomal solubility, enabling precipitation followed by low-speed centrifugation. This easy, scalable approach is widely used in commercial kits (e.g., ExoQuick, Total Exosome Isolation Kit). Although suitable for large sample volumes, it often co-precipitates lipoproteins and protein contaminants, limiting downstream omics applications. This approach exploits antibody–antigen interactions targeting exosomal surface markers such as CD9, CD63, CD81, and EpCAM. Magnetic beads, chromatography matrices, or microfluidic chips functionalized with antibodies allow the selective isolation of specific exosome subpopulations. The resulting purity is high, but the method is costly, time-consuming, and limited by antibody specificity and sample type. Recent advances integrate nanomaterials and microfluidics for rapid, label-free, and high-throughput exosome isolation. Techniques, such as deterministic lateral displacement (nano-DLD), resistive pulse sensing (RPS), and surface plasmon resonance (SPR)-based nanosensors, enable size-selective separation and real-time quantification at the single-vesicle level. Acoustofluidic and electric field-driven devices have further enhanced recovery efficiency from microliter-scale biofluids. These integrated platforms minimize sample loss, allow automation, and facilitate direct downstream analysis, offering a promising route for clinical translation (Li et al., 2017).

Comprehensive characterization of exosomes is essential to confirm their identity, purity, size distribution, and molecular composition before any biological or diagnostic application. A combination of complementary physical, biochemical, and molecular approaches is employed to ensure reliable exosome profiling. Electron microscopy techniques are the gold standard for visualizing exosome morphology. Transmission electron microscopy (TEM) reveals their characteristic cup-shaped or spherical vesicular structure enclosed by a lipid bilayer, providing direct evidence of vesicle integrity and purity. Scanning electron microscopy (SEM) offers topographical details, while cryo-electron microscopy (cryo-EM) enables high-resolution imaging of hydrated, native vesicles without chemical fixation or staining artifacts. Atomic force microscopy (AFM) has also been utilized to analyze exosome surface roughness, stiffness, and mechanical properties under near-physiological conditions. These techniques, when combined, confirm vesicle morphology and distinguish exosomes from microvesicles or cellular debris (Théry et al., 2018). Nanoparticle tracking analysis (NTA) and dynamic light scattering (DLS) are widely applied to determine the size distribution and concentration of exosomes in suspension. NTA visualizes Brownian motion of individual vesicles under a laser beam, providing particle-by-particle analysis with high accuracy within the 40–300 nm range. DLS, on the other hand, estimates the average hydrodynamic diameter of vesicles by measuring light scattering fluctuations caused by particle motion. Although DLS offers quick measurements, it can be influenced by sample polydispersity. Tunable RPS (TRPS) offers an alternative method, where individual vesicles passing through a nanopore are detected as transient changes in resistance, yielding precise size and concentration data. The protein and lipid composition of exosomes serves as a molecular fingerprint for validation. Western blotting, enzyme-linked immunosorbent assay (ELISA), and flow cytometry are used to detect canonical exosomal markers such as tetraspanins (CD9, CD63, CD81), Alix, TSG101, flotillin, and heat shock proteins (HSP70, HSP90). These confirm the endosomal origin of exosomes, while negative markers such as calnexin, GM130, or cytochrome C verify the absence of cellular contaminants. Immunogold labeling combined with TEM offers ultrastructural confirmation of marker localization on the vesicle surface. More recently, bead-based flow cytometry and microfluidic immunoassays have enabled multiplexed detection of exosomal surface proteins from minimal sample volumes (Dragovic et al., 2011). High-throughput "omics" techniques have revolutionized exosome cargo profiling. Proteomic analysis via LC–MS/MS or MALDI–TOF identifies functional proteins and signaling molecules. RNA sequencing (RNA-Seq) and qRT-PCR detect and quantify encapsulated miRNAs, mRNAs, and lncRNAs, providing insights into exosome-mediated gene regulation. Lipidomics further characterizes membrane composition, identifying phosphatidylserine, sphingomyelin, and cholesterol as key structural components influencing exosome stability and fusion. Together, these molecular analyses reveal disease-specific cargo signatures and form the basis for biomarker discovery. Advancements in optical and nanotechnological methods have introduced rapid, label-free exosome characterization techniques. SPR, Raman spectroscopy, and Fourier-transform infrared spectroscopy (FTIR) enable molecular fingerprinting based on unique vibrational or optical properties. Microfluidic chips integrated with impedance spectroscopy, interferometric imaging, or nanoplasmonic sensors allow real-time detection of exosome size, concentration, and molecular composition at the single-vesicle level. These platforms offer high sensitivity, minimal sample requirement, and compatibility with clinical applications (Xu et al., 2015; Yang et al., 2020).

While ultracentrifugation remains the benchmark for exosome isolation, its limitations in purity and yield have driven the development of advanced nanotechnological and microfluidic systems. The integration of isolation and characterization on microdevices promises reproducibility, minimal sample requirement, and automation, paving the way for standardized exosome-based diagnostics and therapeutic applications (Yang et al., 2020).

5.4.3 Clinical utility in early detection and disease monitoring

Exosomes have emerged as promising tools for early disease detection and real-time monitoring of disease progression due to their unique ability to encapsulate and transport biomolecules that reflect the physiological or pathological state of their parental cells. The molecular cargo of exosomes reflects the molecular signatures of their originating cells, which makes them particularly useful in distinguishing disease states from normal physiology. For example, tetraspanins (CD9, CD63, CD81), tumor susceptibility gene 101 (TSG101), and Alix are frequently identified as exosomal markers associated with cancer progression. Elevated plasma CD63 and exosomes have been detected in melanoma patients, whereas CD81 expression correlates with fibrosis and inflammation in hepatitis C. Similarly, glypican-1 (GPC1)-positive exosomes have been proposed as early diagnostic markers in pancreatic cancer, demonstrating high specificity and sensitivity compared to traditional serum biomarkers. In neurodegenerative disorders, exosome-derived proteins such as LRRK2 and α-synuclein in cerebrospinal fluid and plasma serve as indicators for Parkinson's disease, highlighting their role in early neurological diagnosis (Kalluri & LeBleu, 2020; Melo et al., 2015; Shi et al., 2014).

Clinical studies have extended these findings, integrating exosome profiling with imaging and molecular diagnostics. For instance exosomal microRNA signatures, including let-7 and miR-21, have been associated with oncogenic transformation and disease recurrence. In LC, combined computed tomography (CT) imaging with exosomal microRNA detection enhanced diagnostic accuracy in early-stage disease. Similarly, urinary exosome profiling has revealed potential biomarkers such as CD26, CD81, and LAMP1 for hepatic and renal dysfunctions, facilitating noninvasive organ health assessments. Beyond early detection, exosomes play a critical role in disease monitoring and treatment response evaluation. Blood exosome levels and their cargo composition fluctuate with disease progression, therapeutic efficacy, and relapse, providing a dynamic reflection of patient status. Clinical trials, including those targeting cancer, brain, and cardiovascular diseases, are investigating exosome-based assays as longitudinal monitoring tools. For instance plasma-derived exosomes have been utilized to monitor response to immunotherapies in NSCLC and to evaluate drug efficacy in soft-tissue sarcoma and thyroid cancer. The translation of exosome research into clinical practice offers substantial advantages such as minimally invasive sampling, molecular precision, and real-time monitoring. However, to achieve standardized diagnostic use, harmonized protocols for exosome isolation, characterization, and data interpretation are essential. Despite these challenges, current evidence strongly supports the clinical potential of exosomes as next-generation biomarkers for early detection, prognosis, and therapeutic monitoring across a spectrum of diseases, including cancer, neurodegeneration, and metabolic disorders (Chen et al., 2018; Sun et al., 2020b).

5.4.4 Comparative analysis of exosomes with conventional biomarkers

In recent years, exosomes have emerged as a transformative class of biomarkers, offering distinct advantages over traditional circulating biomarkers such as proteins, metabolites, and free nucleic acids. Conventional biomarkers are derived from serum proteins (e.g., C-reactive protein, prostate-specific antigen), circulating tumor cells (CTCs), or cell-free DNA (cfDNA), which have long been used in clinical diagnostics for disease detection and monitoring. However, their sensitivity and specificity are often limited by biological variability, instability in circulation, and a lack of direct cellular origin information. In contrast, exosomes, as nano-sized EVs (30–150 nm) secreted by nearly all cell types, encapsulate a rich and protected molecular cargo reflective of the physiological and pathological status of their parent cells. This unique origin and structure confer several advantages for diagnostic and prognostic applications. One of the most significant differences lies in molecular stability. Conventional biomarkers such as cfDNA and soluble proteins are highly susceptible to enzymatic degradation and environmental fluctuations. Exosomes, by contrast, possess a lipid bilayer that shields their internal contents, including proteins, lipids, mRNAs, microRNAs, and DNA fragments, from degradation, thereby maintaining molecular integrity even in harsh biological conditions, such as serum or urine. This inherent stability enables exosomes to serve as reliable carriers of disease-specific information for extended periods, making them highly suitable for longitudinal and noninvasive monitoring. Exosomes also offer superior cellular specificity. The molecular composition of exosomes is defined by tetraspanins (CD9, CD63, CD81), Alix, TSG101, and other surface proteins, which mirrors the molecular phenotype of their parent cells. This enables precise identification of the tissue or cell of origin, which is not possible with most conventional biomarkers. For example, glypican-1 (GPC1)-positive exosomes specifically indicate pancreatic cancer, whereas neuron-derived exosomes in cerebrospinal fluid or plasma are valuable for early diagnosis of neurodegenerative disorders such as Alzheimer's and Parkinson's diseases. Traditional serum biomarkers, in contrast, often lack such cell-type specificity and can be elevated in multiple unrelated pathological conditions, reducing diagnostic precision (Kalluri & LeBleu, 2020; Melo et al., 2015; Shi et al., 2014).

Moreover, exosomes facilitate multiplexed molecular profiling. Unlike conventional biomarkers that generally reflect a single biochemical change, exosomes carry diverse classes of molecules, including proteins, lipids, and various RNA species, enabling integrative analyses of cellular signaling, gene regulation, and metabolic status. This multifactorial data offers a more comprehensive view of disease mechanisms, supporting precision medicine approaches. For instance exosomal miRNAs (miR-21, miR-155, and let-7 family) have demonstrated higher diagnostic accuracy in cancer detection compared to conventional serum-based markers due to their combined regulatory and signaling roles. In clinical translation, exosomes have shown promise in improving early detection and real-time disease monitoring. While conventional biomarkers are often limited to detecting advanced disease stages when tissue damage has already occurred, exosomes can reveal subtle cellular alterations at preclinical stages. Additionally, changes in exosome concentration or molecular composition can reflect therapeutic responses and disease recurrence, offering continuous insight into disease dynamics, which is an attribute not shared by most traditional markers. Despite these advantages, exosome-based diagnostics face challenges, particularly in standardizing isolation, purification, and quantification methods, as well as ensuring reproducibility across laboratories. Nevertheless, the integration of exosome analysis with existing biomarker platforms enhances overall diagnostic performance, providing both molecular depth and clinical relevance (Kalluri & LeBleu, 2020; Li et al., 2017).

5.5 Exosomes as therapeutic tools

The ability of exosomes to transport nucleic acids, lipids, proteins, and small molecules across various biological barriers has made them an emerging class of biological nanoparticles for targeted drug delivery that synthetic nanoparticles have long sought to achieve. In the context of LC, exosomes provide a natural means of communication that can be co-opted for treatment. Since exosomes are derived from cell membranes and carry native molecules, they exhibit high biocompatibility, low immunogenicity, and efficient cellular uptake, which makes them ideal candidates for drug carriers, gene delivery vehicles, and even therapeutic agents themselves (Ha et al., 2016).

5.5.1 Exosomes as drug delivery vehicles: Advantages over synthetic nanoparticles

Conventional nanoparticle systems, including liposomes, polymeric nanoparticles, and inorganic nanocarriers, often encounter issues such as immune clearance, poor biodistribution, and toxicity. Exosomes, by contrast, are nanosized MVBs produced endogenously that circulate naturally in the body and participate in cellular communication due to their intrinsic biocompatibility unmatched by artificial systems (Ha et al., 2016).

Numerous significant benefits highlight the therapeutic potential of exosomes. They contain membrane proteins like tetraspanins (CD9, CD63, CD81) and adhesion molecules, which enable receptor-mediated absorption by target cells. This permits effective transportation of therapeutic agents with limited off-target toxicity. In addition to this, their lipid bilayer configuration offers robust safeguarding for nucleic acids and sensitive medications from enzymatic breakdown. For example, miRNAs enclosed in exosomes exhibit stability in circulation compared to unprotected RNA molecules. Furthermore, exosomes demonstrate inherent tissue affinity based on their originating cells. Exosomes from tumor cells typically target metastatic sites, whereas exosomes from mesenchymal stem cells (MSCs) preferentially move toward inflamed or damaged tissues. This characteristic can be utilized to guide therapeutic agents to specific targets inside the lung microenvironment (Ha et al., 2016; Li et al., 2016).

Synthetic nanoparticles are recognized as xenobiotics by the human body, thus activating immune clearance, which reduces their bioavailability. Exosomes easily overcome this obstacle as they are naturally occurring. Their nano size and deformable membrane enable them to penetrate deeply into the dense tumor matrices and cross endothelial barriers effectively. Nevertheless, these advantages are accompanied by challenges like low yield, difficulty in large-scale production, and possible co-packaging of undesirable biomolecules if sourced from tumor cells. Even with these hurdles, the natural biological complexity of exosomes positions them ahead of solely synthetic systems in the pursuit of clinically applicable nanotherapeutics (Li et al., 2016).

5.5.2 Strategies for exosome engineering: Surface modification, genetic modification, and cargo loading

Transforming exosomes into therapeutic tools functionally involves engineering them to carry specific cargo and, in many cases, targeting specific cell types. Two principal avenues make this engineering, which involves genetically or metabolically reprogramming the producer cells before exosome harvest and exogenous engineering, wherein isolated exosomes are altered after they have been secreted (Fig. 5.5). Within these approaches, donor cells receive material that codes for therapeutic agents, such as Small Interfering RNA (siRNA), miRNA, or proteins. As the cells naturally generate exosomes, these agents become incorporated into the vesicles during their formation. For example, transfecting cells with a plasmid encoding miR-34a raises the miRNA's abundance in the released exosomes, which can then restore tumor-suppressing signals in lung-cancer cells. The exosomal surface can likewise be genetically programmed by fusing a targeting ligand to membrane proteins such as Lamp2b or CD63. In 2011 Alvarez-Erviti et al. (2011) demonstrated that fusing the protein Lamp2b to an RVG peptide yields exosomes that home in on neurons, enabling truly tissue-specific delivery (Kalluri & LeBleu, 2020; Ha et al., 2016).

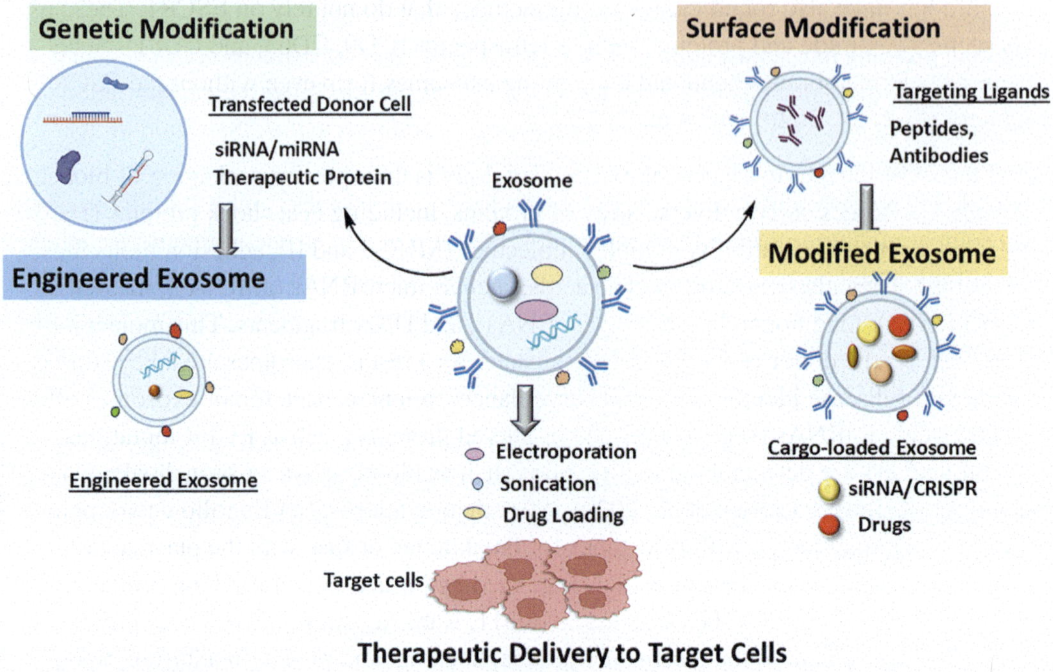

Figure 5.5

Engineering strategies for therapeutic exosome-based drug delivery. Schematic illustration of exosome engineering approaches, including genetic modification of donor cells for endogenous cargo loading, exogenous cargo incorporation via electroporation or sonication, and surface modification with targeting ligands such as peptides or antibodies.

In engineering therapeutic cargoes are ushered into purified exosomes. Hydrophobic agents like paclitaxel, doxorubicin can diffuse across the lipid bilayer during incubation, though this passive route usually yields modest efficiency. To coax molecules and nucleic acids inside the exosomal membrane is briefly rendered permeable by techniques such as electroporation, sonication, or repeated freeze-thaw cycles. Electroporation, a choice for loading siRNA or CRISPR components, demands fine-tuning; otherwise, vesicle aggregation and cargo damage become significant concerns (Kalluri & LeBleu, 2020; Lamichhane et al., 2015).

Another important facet of exosome engineering is tweaking the particle's surface. By harnessing covalent coupling through "click chemistry," targeting ligands, PEG, or antibodies can be affixed, a maneuver that lengthens circulation time and sharpens specificity. Lately, hybrid exosomes created by fusing exosomes with liposomes have emerged as a trending strategy aimed at marrying the innate recognition of biological vesicles with the scalability and controlled-release advantages of synthetic carriers. In short, these hybrid systems preserve the targeting prowess of exosomes while delivering the manufacturing benefits of vesicles.

In the end, any engineering approach must preserve exosome integrity, retain the native surface proteins, and guarantee stability throughout storage and delivery. Before use, thorough characterization using NTA, blotting for exosomal markers such as TSG101, CD63, CD9, and CD81, and RNA quantification is essential (Kooijmans et al., 2016a; Timin et al., 2018).

5.5.3 Exosome-mediated delivery of chemotherapeutics, siRNA, microRNA, and CRISPR/Cas9

Exosomes have found use as delivery trucks for a mix of therapies spanning modest small-molecule drugs to sophisticated genetic and genome-editing agents. Their knack for shuttling these cargoes into cells in LC has sparked a deal of research interest. One of the most intuitive uses of exosomes is for chemotherapy delivery. For example, macrophage-derived exosomes loaded with paclitaxel have been shown to penetrate tumors and kill lung carcinoma cells more effectively than free paclitaxel. By embedding the hydrophobic drug within the lipid bilayer, it is guarded against metabolism and can be released in a sustained fashion, right at the tumor site. Likewise, exosomes carrying doxorubicin exhibit uptake by cancer cells, allowing them to bypass efflux-pump–mediated resistance. These benefits stem from exosomes' knack for hijacking the cell's native entry routes, especially endocytosis and membrane fusion (Tian et al., 2014; Timin et al., 2018).

Beyond chemotherapeutics, exosomes have emerged as efficient couriers for RNA-based therapies. Loading siRNA into these vesicles enables a highly specific gene-silencing effect while keeping immune stimulation to a minimum. In LC models, exosome-mediated delivery of siRNA aimed at mutant KRAS or EGFR has produced marked dampening of signaling pathways. In a vein, reintroducing tumor-suppressive miRNA and miR-145, through exosome-mediated delivery, has been shown to curb cell proliferation and trigger apoptosis in NSCLC cells. Conversely, exosomes can also be employed to ferry antagomirs that silence oncogenic miRNAs driving metastasis or drug-resistance (Alvarez-Erviti et al., 2011).

The CRISPR/Cas9 toolbox has slipped into the emerging arena of exosome therapeutics, offering an angle on gene editing. Researchers are now reshaping exosomes so they ferry Cas9-laden cargo, whether that be messenger RNA, the nuclease protein, or the whole ribonucleoprotein complex together, together with the matching guide RNAs, effectively turning these nanoscale parcels into precision-guided editing drones. Still, the sheer bulk of Cas9 and its potential to stir the system remain issues. Nonetheless, early proof-of-concept work hints that exosomal delivery of CRISPR components can indeed patch mutations. For instance consider an exosome-encapsulated Cas9 RNP directed against PD-L1. These engineered vesicles have been shown to suppress checkpoint protein expression. As a result, it makes lung tumors more receptive to immunotherapy. This evidence underscores the flexibility of exosomes as carriers for next-generation therapeutics that can act at both the genomic layers (Giraldo et al., 2021; Liu et al., 2019).

Combining strategies adds advantages. Exosomes can co-package a drug and an siRNA, launching a dual-mode attack on tumors. For instance loading doxorubicin with an siRNA that silences multidrug-resistance genes can cripple efflux pumps and amplify drug potency. In the vein, exosomes bearing both agents and checkpoint-blocking antibodies have been trialed as cancer vaccines, merging pinpoint delivery with an immune boost (Chen et al., 2018; Tian et al., 2014; Timin et al., 2018).

5.5.4 Overcoming biological barriers and targeting specificity in lung cancer

With their promise, exosome-based therapies still confront hefty biological obstacles before they can leap into clinical use, especially in LC, where the tangled tumor architecture and the peculiarities of pulmonary physiology turn drug delivery into a real conundrum. Once administered systemically, exosomes are swiftly swept up by the mononuclear phagocyte system, chiefly the liver and spleen. To prolong their stay in circulation, researchers have turned to approaches such as PEGylation. Adorning the vesicles with self-recognition markers such as CD47, which essentially flashes a "don't eat me" signal to macrophages. However, it is a tightrope walk; excessive PEGylation can blunt the uptake by the target cells (Ha et al., 2016; Kooijmans et al., 2016a).

Targeting specificity remains a goal in exosome engineering. Although exosomes already exhibit tropism, affinity can be sharpened by adorning their surfaces with ligands or peptides that recognize tumor-associated receptors. In LC, overexpressed targets such as EGFR, various integrins, and folate receptor-α serve as docking sites for engineered exosomes. For example, exosomes displaying an EGFR-binding peptide or an scFv antibody fragment have shown uptake by NSCLC cells while largely sparing tissues. Dual-targeting designs, such as exosomes loaded with ligands that engage both targets, can enhance accumulation within the heterogeneous TME (Kooijmans et al., 2016a; Ohno et al., 2013).

Delivery routes have an impact on outcomes. While systemic administration still holds merit for disease, inhalation therapy provides a focused, localized strategy for primary lung tumors. By aerosolizing or nebulizing exosomes, drugs can be deposited onto the epithelium, achieving high local concentrations while curbing systemic side effects. The principal hurdles of this approach are preserving vesicle integrity during nebulization (Ha et al., 2016; Smyth et al., 2015; Zhuang et al., 2011).

At the cellular level, exosomes are forced to surmount another obstacle. After internalization, they frequently become trapped within endosomes. To achieve delivery of nucleic acid cargo, scientists are now outfitting exosomes with fusogenic peptides or pH-responsive lipids that spring into action under the low pH conditions characteristic of tumor cells, thereby prompting endosomal escape. Moreover, these vesicles can be engineered as sentinels releasing their payload, preferentially when they encounter the hallmark acidity, altered redox gradients, or specific enzymatic activity of the TME (Liu et al., 2019; Rollyson et al., 2014).

Safety continues to be the concern. Employing exosomes derived from tumors as delivery vectors carries the danger of conveying cargo or immunosuppressive cues. Consequently, most exosome platforms now draw on stem cells, dendritic cells, or engineered nontumorigenic cell lines as safer origins. Stringent purification methods, batch testing, and good manufacturing practice (GMP)-aligned production pipelines are being assembled to ensure reproducibility and satisfy benchmarks (Ha et al., 2016).

5.6 Exosomes in theranostics

5.6.1 Concept of theranostics

Theranostics represent an integrated biomedical strategy that unifies diagnostic and therapeutic functionalities within a single platform, enabling disease detection, targeted intervention, and real-time monitoring of treatment response. Within this framework, exosomes and other nanocarrier systems have gained significant scientific interest due to their unique biological characteristics and translational applicability. Theranostic approaches benefit from the intrinsic capacity of nanoscale systems to deliver drugs and diagnose diseases. This dual capability allows for precision medicine strategies in which patient-specific molecular profiles guide therapeutic decisions and enable continuous evaluation of therapeutic efficacy (Chen et al., 2025; Gulati et al., 2022; Shahraki et al., 2023).

Exosomes in particular offer a natural and biomimetic theranostic vehicle owing to their endogenous origin, excellent biocompatibility, and intrinsic tropism toward specific tissues. Their capacity to encapsulate nucleic acids, proteins, and bioactive lipids provides opportunities for targeted therapy, whereas their cargo can also serve as biomarkers for early detection, disease stratification, and treatment monitoring. Engineered exosomes further expand their theranostic utility through surface modification with targeting ligands, imaging probes, or reporter molecules, thus enhancing specificity for TMEs, inflammatory sites, or neurological tissues. Importantly, exosome-based theranostic systems overcome limitations associated with synthetic nanocarriers, such as immunogenicity and rapid systemic clearance, by exploiting endogenous vesicle-mediated communication pathways. Advances in imaging technologies, molecular profiling, and exosome engineering are accelerating the development of clinically relevant theranostic applications, including cancer detection and drug delivery, neurodegenerative disease monitoring, and cardiovascular therapy. Despite promising progress, clinical translation remains challenged by the need for standardized isolation protocols, scalable production systems, and comprehensive safety evaluation (Gulati et al., 2022; Shahraki et al., 2023).

5.6.2 Exosome-based imaging agents and biosensors

Exosomes have emerged as transformative tools in biomedical imaging and diagnostics, owing to their endogenous stability, biocompatibility, and ability to transport molecular signatures reflective of disease states. Their natural enrichment in disease-specific proteins, nucleic acids, and lipids has catalyzed interest in their application as imaging vectors and biosensor targets for precision diagnostics and real-time monitoring. In vivo imaging of exosomes enables spatiotemporal assessment of vesicular trafficking, biodistribution, and therapeutic responses, facilitating translation toward precision medicine. Diverse visualization platforms, including optical imaging, magnetic resonance imaging (MRI), radionuclide imaging, and emerging hybrid modalities, have been optimized for tracking exosome dynamics. Optical imaging methodologies, including fluorescence and bioluminescence imaging, offer high sensitivity and real-time resolution. Luciferase-based systems such as Renilla luciferase (RLuc), NanoLuc (Nluc), and BRET-based reporters (e.g., Antares2) have been integrated into exosome membrane proteins, enabling long-term quantitative tracking in cancer and cardiac models. These strategies permit deep-tissue monitoring and reveal distinct accumulation profiles of TDEs within TMEs. Complementary advances in near-infrared and hybrid fluorescence/bioluminescence systems further enhance tissue penetration and sensitivity. MRI-based exosome imaging leverages contrast agents and magnetically responsive labeling to achieve high spatial resolution, although sensitivity remains limited relative to optical platforms. Continued development of magnetic nanoprobes and signal-amplification approaches seeks to overcome low molecular sensitivity and high operational cost constraints. Additionally, radionuclide-based positron emission tomography (PET) and single-photon emission computed tomography (SPECT) allow highly sensitive and quantitative whole-body tracking, although radiotracer stability and safety remain concerns. Beyond systemic tracking, exosome-based biosensors represent a rapidly advancing frontier for noninvasive early disease detection. Biosensor platforms utilize electrochemical, optical (fluorescence, colorimetric, plasmonic), and electrochemiluminescence interfaces to detect exosome-associated biomarkers with exceptional sensitivity and rapid turnaround. These sensors offer key advantages, including miniaturization and portability, enabling exosome quantification in blood, saliva, and urine during early oncogenic transformation. Electrochemical biosensors employing aptamers or immuno-probes can detect cancer-associated exosomes with ultra-low limits of detection, reaffirming their utility in precision oncology. Optical biosensors such as surface-enhanced Raman scattering (SERS) platforms further permit molecular fingerprinting and multiplex detection of tumor-derived vesicles with superior specificity. Collectively, exosome-based imaging and biosensing technologies are reshaping the landscape of disease monitoring, enabling sensitive visualization and quantification of vesicle trafficking, tumor burden, and therapeutic outcomes. However, challenges persist, including standardized labeling protocols, in vivo safety validation, and assay reproducibility. Future innovations integrating multimodal imaging, nanomaterial engineering, and machine learning-based signal analytics are expected to yield robust, clinically translatable systems that harness exosomes as dynamic, real-time indicators of disease physiology and treatment response. As research progresses, these platforms hold promise to facilitate early detection, targeted intervention, and personalized medicine (Karjoo et al., 2016; Shao et al., 2018; Zhang et al., 2018 , 2021).

5.6.3 Smart exosome platforms for simultaneous drug delivery and real-time monitoring

Smart exosome platforms represent a rapidly advancing frontier in precision nanomedicine, enabling simultaneous therapeutic delivery and real-time monitoring of cellular responses. Exosomes, as naturally secreted EVs enriched with proteins, lipids, and nucleic acids, offer intrinsic advantages as drug carriers, including biocompatibility, immune-evasive behavior, and inherent targeting capabilities. Emerging engineering strategies have transformed exosomes from passive carriers into intelligent theranostic systems capable of transporting therapeutic payloads while concurrently reporting on treatment efficacy and disease progression at the single-cell and tissue levels. This dual functionality is critical for precision oncology, regenerative medicine, and immune modulation, where continuous feedback can guide dosing, minimize toxicity, and enhance clinical outcomes. Integration of biosensing modalities into engineered exosomes has enabled real-time visualization and quantification of exosome-mediated communication and drug release dynamics. Novel nanopore-based platforms, for instance, allow continuous monitoring of exosome secretion and molecular cargo exchange at the single-cell level, providing high-resolution mechanistic insight into disease-relevant signaling pathways. Dual nanopore biosensors permit electrophoretic characterization of exosomes and real-time assessment of vesicle trafficking and release kinetics, advancing our understanding of how exosome-mediated drug payloads propagate therapeutic effects in target cells. These breakthroughs highlight the capacity of smart platforms to decode nanoscale communication events that govern cellular response to therapy, enabling dynamic and personalized treatment strategies. Smart exosomes have also been functionalized with fluorescent, bioluminescent, and electrochemical reporters to enable spatiotemporal analysis of drug delivery pathways and therapeutic biodistribution. Such platforms facilitate direct tracking of exosome internalization, drug release, and downstream cellular responses, while maintaining payload integrity and minimizing off-target accumulation. Moreover, biosensor-integrated exosomes can quantify microenvironmental changes, including pH variations, enzymatic activity, and effector molecule levels, serving as early indicators of therapeutic response or drug resistance. Combined with molecular imaging and computational signal analytics, these technologies deliver actionable insights into treatment efficacy and disease dynamics at unprecedented resolution. Despite the promise of smart exosome systems, translational challenges persist, including standardization of exosome isolation, scalable manufacturing, and long-term safety evaluation of engineered vesicles. Advances in microfluidics, bio-nanofabrication, and genetic engineering are increasingly addressing these limitations, enabling controlled exosome loading, surface functionalization, and biosensor integration with improved stability and reproducibility. Future developments are expected to incorporate multiplexed sensing, artificial intelligence (AI)-driven signal interpretation, and adaptive drug release systems responsive to real-time biomolecular feedback (Ahmadi et al., 2020; Im et al., 2014; Jo & Lee, 2020; Lee et al., 2018; Shao et al., 2012).

5.6.4 Clinical translation challenges and case studies

The clinical translation of exosome-based diagnostics and therapeutics has advanced substantially in recent years, driven by their roles in intercellular communication, intrinsic cargo-carrying capacity, and favorable biocompatibility. Preclinical studies have demonstrated the utility of exosomes in regenerative medicine, oncology, inflammatory disorders, and infectious diseases. MSC-derived and dendritic cell (DC)-derived exosomes are the most investigated platforms in clinical settings, reflecting their regenerative and immunomodulatory potential. Clinical trial databases indicate multiple ongoing human studies focusing on exosomes as biomarkers, cell-free therapeutic agents, drug delivery vehicles, and cancer vaccines, with 50% of trials dedicated to biomarker discovery and 28% investigating therapeutic functions (Mirgh et al., 2024; Rahnama et al., 2024; Redkin & Turubanova, 2025).

Case studies support the translational promise of exosomes. MSC-derived exosomes have been evaluated for tissue repair, inflammation control, and COVID-19-related lung injury, with around 60% of reported exosome-therapy trials using MSC sources. Clinical studies have also explored plant-derived exosomes for oral mucositis prevention and delivery of curcumin in inflammatory bowel disease and colorectal cancer therapy. In addition, trials evaluating exosome-mediated delivery of therapeutic nucleic acids such as siRNA against the KRAS G12D mutation in pancreatic cancer and miR-124 for stroke recovery represent notable case examples of precision exosome therapeutics. Despite compelling early promise, clinical translation faces critical challenges. Manufacturing quality, including GMP-grade production, purification, and batch-to-batch consistency, remains a major barrier. Exosomes exhibit heterogeneity in size, cargo, and biological effects, necessitating robust characterization pipelines. Regulatory frameworks require stringent identity, purity, potency, and safety validation, supported by guidelines such as MISEV and EV-TRACK. Additionally, reproducible large-scale production is hindered by low vesicle yield and variable efficiency across isolation platforms. Drug loading remains technically challenging, and loading methods such as electroporation, sonication, or parental cell engineering must be optimized to preserve exosome integrity and function. Safety concerns, including potential immunomodulatory risks and tumor-promoting properties of some sources, require careful evaluation. Regulatory alerts have been issued regarding unapproved exosome products associated with adverse effects, emphasizing the need for controlled, ethically regulated clinical deployment. Standardization of storage, dosing, biodistribution tracking, and long-term follow-up frameworks remains an unmet need in the translational pipeline (Kamerkar et al., 2017; Sengupta et al., 2020; Théry et al., 2018; Xin et al., 2013; Zhang et al., 2016).

5.7 Engineering strategies for precision targeting

The rapid advancement in nanobiotechnology has transformed exosomes from passive biological messengers to actively engineered, precision-targeted tools of drug delivery. Unlike conventional nanoparticles, which rely mainly on physicochemical tuning, exosomes can be engineered at various levels on the surface molecule, inside the cargo, and at the parent-cell genome. These various strategies improve their specificity against LC cells, circulation time, and therapeutic payload delivery.

5.7.1 Ligand-directed targeting: Peptides, antibodies, and aptamers

It has been reported that the surface functionalization of exosomes, with targeting ligands, works well for tumor delivery. The surface functionalization of exosomes, with targeting ligands, adds a guide that points the exosomes to the tumor. The ligand-directed engineering approach aims to raise the exosome uptake by the receptors that are overexpressed in the LC cells (Gabaran et al., 2025; Rahimian et al., 2024).

Peptide ligands are among the most frequently studied methods for targeting exosomes due to their specificity, low immunogenic response, and simplicity in chemical or genetic attachment. Numerous peptides have been evaluated for their potential in cancer-specific delivery systems. The GE11 peptide exhibits selective binding to the EGFR, which is often overexpressed in NSCLC, rendering it a useful ligand for directing exosomal delivery to tumors. RGD peptides bind to integrins associated with tumor angiogenesis and metastasis, particularly the $\alpha v\beta 3$ integrins, thus enabling focused targeting of tumor blood vessels and invasive cancer cells. Furthermore, neuropilin-1 receptor, which is linked to tumor infiltration and vascular permeability, is present to which certain peptides, such as tLyp-1 and iRGD, bind and enhance penetration into tumors, allowing exosomes to reach more profound tumor areas. Antibodies and their fragments are another significant category of targeting ligands used in exosomal engineering. These macromolecules are genetically fused or chemically linked to the exosomal membrane, thus providing selective uptake of certain antibodies, such as anti-EGFR or anti-HER2, improving target specificity. In addition to this, exosomes bound with anti-PD-L1 antibodies have been explored for delivering immunomodulators, facilitating localized regulation of immune checkpoints within the TME (Ackaert et al., 2021; Kooijmans et al., 2016a; Ohno et al., 2013; Sugahara et al., 2009).

Another effective approach for targeted exosome-based delivery is the use of an aptamer, a short single-stranded DNA or RNA molecule with a specific 3D structure, capable of binding to a specific cancer-related surface marker with very high affinity. The widely investigated

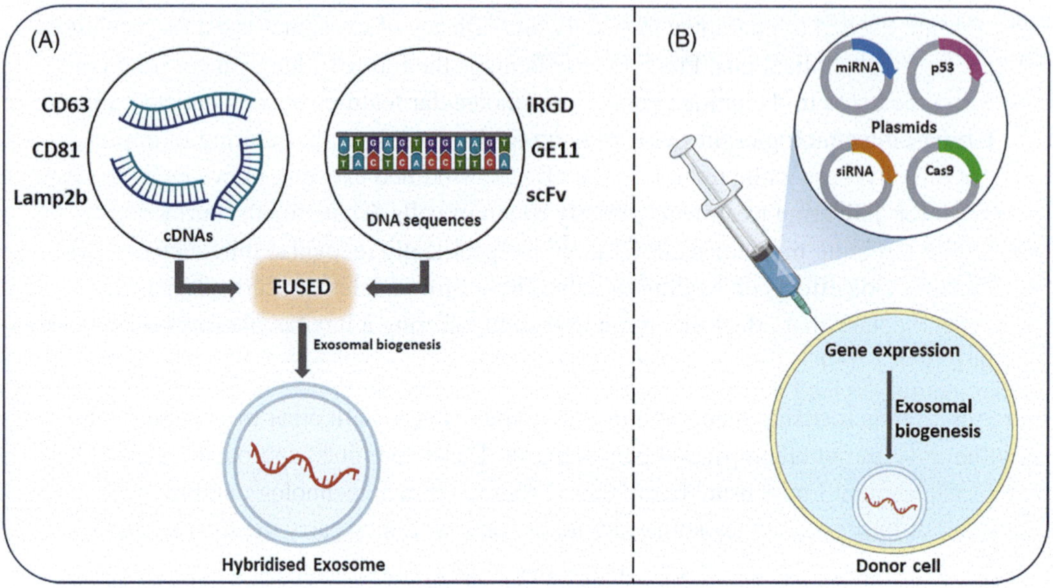

Figure 5.6
Genetic engineering of donor cells for therapeutic exosome production. (A) Surface engineering of exosomes via fusion of targeting ligands with exosomal membrane proteins (CD63, CD81, Lamp2b) to enable receptor-specific targeting. (B) Cargo engineering through donor cell transfection with plasmids encoding therapeutic nucleic acids or proteins, resulting in endogenous loading of functional cargo into secreted exosomes.

AS1411 aptamer targets nucleolin protein, which is overexpressed in LC cells. Aptamers offer various benefits like precision targeting, chemical stability, and low immunogenicity, making them appealing alternatives to antibodies (Bates et al., 2009; Soundararajan et al., 2008).

5.7.2 Genetic engineering of donor cells

A more integrated approach involves the genetic modification of donor cells so that they naturally secrete exosomes possessing desired properties. This produces biologically compatible exosomes with high stability, target specificity, and uniformity.

One widely used approach involves genetic level fusion between cDNAs encoding exosomal membrane proteins such as CD63, CD81, or Lamp2b, and targeting moieties such as iRGD, GE11, antibody fragments such as single-chain variable fragments (scFv), or other tumor-homing ligands. These fusion proteins get naturally incorporated into the exosomal membrane during their biogenesis, enabling the released exosomes to selectively bind LC-associated receptors and thereby improve targeted delivery and cellular uptake (Fig. 5.6; Alvarez-Erviti et al., 2011; Kooijmans et al., 2016b; Ohno et al., 2013; Tian et al., 2014).

Cargo engineering is another crucial strategy involving transfected donor cells to overexpress therapeutic genetic materials or proteins that are subsequently and efficiently loaded into the exosomes, like siRNAs or miRNAs targeting key oncogenic pathways such as KRAS, EGFR, and ALK. CRISPR/Cas9 components for genome editing and tumor suppressor proteins such as p53 and PTEN can also be transfected via plasmid. This approach allows direct modulation of oncogenic signaling in recipient LC cells, leading to enhanced therapeutic efficacy (Fig. 5.6; Kamerkar et al., 2017; Lin et al., 2018; Munagala et al., 2016).

Additionally, an advanced genetic engineering approach involving reprogramming of exosomal content regulates both exosome yield and cargo composition. It aids in increasing the exosome production while selectively altering cargo sorting mechanisms by modulating key regulators of exosome biogenesis and secretion, including Rab GTPases, neutral sphingomyelinase 2 (sSMase2), and ESCRT-associated proteins. A major advantage of this strategy is the generation of highly reproducible exosome populations with reduced batch-to-batch variability, making it particularly attractive for scalable manufacturing and clinical translation (Bavafa et al., 2025; Zhao et al., 2025).

5.7.3 Synthetic hybrid exosomes (biohybrids)

Biohybrid exosomes combine the advantages of exosomes with those of synthetic nanoparticles. These are engineered by the fusion of exosomal membranes with different synthetic models, such as liposomes, polymeric nanoparticles, or inorganic nanomaterials, and based on the type of synthetic material fused with the exosomal membrane, the hybrid exosomes can be classified into three types.

In exosome-liposome hybrids, the biocompatibility and biological recognition of exosomes are retained, and the advantages of high drug-loading capacity and formulation flexibility of liposomes are also incorporated. PLGA and PEG are the most typically used polymers in exosome-polymer hybrids, since these polymers prolong the circulation time and reduce premature clearance by the reticuloendothelial system, resulting in enhanced systemic stability. For theranostic approaches, incorporating gold nanoparticles for photothermal therapy, magnetic nanoparticles for guided targeting and navigation, and quantum dots for high-resolution imaging, exosome-inorganic hybrids are developed. Altogether, these hybrid models aid in overcoming the individual barriers of synthetic systems and exosomes (Liu et al., 2022; Palakurthi et al., 2024; Sonar et al., 2026).

5.7.4 Computational and artificial intelligence-assisted design of exosome-based nanocarriers

Exosome engineering is a very time-consuming, iterative, and technical process with high experimental trial and error. Fortunately, AI and computational modeling have emerged as powerful tools for predicting optimized designs for target specificity, drug loading, and biodistribution patterns by integrating large biological datasets with different predictive algorithms to speed up this process and develop exosomes with high precision for theranostic applications (Schwarz et al., 2025).

Various machine learning models are being used to analyze the sequence motifs, physicochemical, and structural features of RNAs and proteins to predict which RNAs/proteins will be efficiently packaged into exosomes. Thus allowing better selection of therapeutic agents to subsequently improve the reproducibility and efficiency of exosome-guided drug delivery (Palakurthi et al., 2024).

Another crucial role of AI-driven models is in the rational design of targeting ligands using different techniques such as molecular docking, virtual screening, and structure-activity relationship (SAR) development. These strategies help in identifying which peptides or aptamer sequences will possess better binding affinity toward tumor-associated receptors such as EGFR, VEGFR, FGFR, MET, and PD-L1. Such approaches will result in improved specificity and cellular uptake of the engineered exosomes (Palakurthi et al., 2024).

Simultaneously, computational modeling approaches such as the prediction of pharmacokinetic profiles can help in estimating the transport, accumulation, and clearance of the engineered exosomes across various organ systems of the body and metastatic niches. Thus providing valuable insights into dose optimization, route of administration, therapeutic efficacy, and off-target side effects (Kumar et al., 2023).

In addition, AI is being increasingly used to monitor quality control and manufacturing processes. To identify impurities, structural defects, and damaged exosomes during large-scale production, deep learning algorithms are used, thereby facilitating process standardization and ensuring consistency. Such AI-driven monitoring systems are crucial for achieving GMP requirements in clinical translation (Zhu, 2025).

And lastly, AI-driven computational tools help in combining CRISPR/Cas9-based genome editing with exosomal delivery formulations. The predictive models assisted the design of CRISPR constructs that maximize the desired pharmacological effectiveness while minimizing off-target toxic effects. This mutualism between AI, genome editing, and exosome engineering holds substantial potential for developing safe and precise gene-based therapeutics (Zhu et al., 2023).

5.8 Preclinical and clinical studies

5.8.1 Overview of in vitro and in vivo models in exosome research

In vitro and in vivo models serve as essential platforms for elucidating exosome biogenesis, function, and therapeutic potential. In vitro systems provide controlled environments for dissecting the molecular mechanisms of exosome generation, cargo loading, and cellular communication. They enable high-throughput mechanistic studies that are not feasible in animal models due to complexity, cost, and limitations on exosome yield. For example, exosomes can be rapidly purified from cultured cells for downstream molecular and functional assays, facilitating exploration of exposure-induced alterations in exosome signaling and bioactivity. Primary cultures, cancer cell lines, neuronal cells, and emerging organ-on-chip systems allow precise manipulation of signaling pathways, toxic exposures, and genetic perturbations to delineate exosome-mediated mechanisms of disease, such as neurodegeneration and pulmonary inflammation. In vitro models have been especially informative in identifying pathogenic exosome transfer of proteins and miRNAs in neurotoxicity and carcinogenesis, providing insight into early disease-associated communication signatures. In vivo models remain indispensable for validating exosome biodistribution, pharmacokinetics, and therapeutic efficacy. Exosome-based delivery systems have been evaluated in murine models, in which dendritic-cell-derived exosomes demonstrated efficient, tissue-specific delivery of small interfering RNA to the brain with minimal immunogenicity. Animal studies have also shown biodistribution patterns following systemic administration, with accumulation in the liver, spleen, kidneys, and inflamed neural tissues. Radio- and fluorescence-labeled exosomes have enabled real-time tracking in animals, supporting assessment of absorption, metabolism, and clearance. These models further establish safety considerations, such as avoiding immune activation by selecting syngeneic exosome sources for in vivo delivery. Together, in vitro and in vivo systems offer complementary insights into exosome biology. While in vitro models provide mechanistic resolution and scalability, animal models validate physiological relevance, biodistribution, and translational feasibility. The integration of these platforms continues to accelerate understanding of exosome-mediated signaling and therapeutic applications across disease settings (Bowers et al., 2020; Chen et al., 2024b; Choi et al., 2021; Kim et al., 2019).

5.8.2 Notable preclinical findings in lung cancer models

Preclinical studies have increasingly highlighted the pivotal role of exosomes in the initiation, progression, and therapeutic response of LC. These nanosized vesicles derived from tumor cells, immune cells, and the TME act as carriers of oncogenic proteins, miRNAs, lncRNAs, circRNAs, and metabolites, significantly influencing cellular communication and disease trajectory. Exosomes isolated from LC tissues and cell lines have been shown to promote tumor proliferation, EMT, angiogenesis, and metastatic colonization, particularly to the brain and lymph nodes. Tumor-derived exosomal miR-21, miR-155, and miR-210 have been implicated in regulating pathways associated with hypoxia adaptation, immune evasion, and drug resistance. Additionally, exosomal PD-L1 has been reported to inhibit T-cell activity, thereby facilitating immune escape and correlating with aggressive tumor phenotypes (Chen et al., 2018; Pan et al., 2025; Tomasetti et al., 2017).

Experimental models, including xenograft mice and 3D co-culture systems, have also revealed the role of exosomes in drug-resistance mechanisms. For example, exosomal transfer of ALK-related resistance genes and EGFR-mutant cargo induces resistance to targeted therapies. Importantly, preclinical interventions targeting exosome biogenesis or release, such as neutral sphingomyelinase inhibitors or exosome uptake blockers, have reduced tumor growth and metastatic burden. Engineered exosomes loaded with siRNAs, miRNAs, or chemotherapeutic drugs like paclitaxel represent a promising therapeutic strategy, showing enhanced tumor targeting and reduced systemic toxicity in murine models. Collectively, these findings underscore the diagnostic, prognostic, and therapeutic potential of exosomes in LC and support their translation toward precision oncology approaches (Ghosh et al., 2024; Kim et al., 2016; Zhu et al., 2020).

5.8.3 Ongoing and completed clinical trials on exosome-based therapies in lung cancer

In LC, particularly NSCLC, exosome-based approaches hold potential for targeted drug delivery, immunotherapy, and predictive biomarker use, although most clinical efforts remain in early stages.

5.8.3.1 Completed exosome-related clinical trials

One of the earliest translational efforts involved dendritic cell-derived exosomes (Dex) used as a maintenance immunotherapy following induction chemotherapy in advanced unresectable NSCLC. The phase II trial (ClinicalTrials.gov Identifier NCT01159288) evaluated a vaccination regimen of tumor antigen-loaded Dex in patients stabilized after initial therapy. The trial aimed to boost antitumor immunity via NK cell and T-cell activation. Although the primary endpoint of improved progression-free survival was not met, the study established the feasibility and safety of Dex-based immunomodulation in LC patients and documented immunologic activity in a subset of treated individuals. Additional exosome-related clinical investigations have explored plasma exosomal biomarkers rather than therapeutics. For example, observational studies such as NCT05854030 examine the utility of serum exosomal miRNAs to predict treatment responses in squamous cell carcinoma of the lung, reflecting the dual role of exosomes in both therapy and precision oncology (Besse et al., 2016).

5.8.3.2 Ongoing clinical trials

Recent developments have seen the entry of engineered exosome platforms into first-in-human testing. A notable example is SOB100, an HLA-G targeted exosome therapy engineered with nanobody (anti-HLA-G VHH) technology. This platform is designed to selectively deliver therapeutic agents to TMEs exhibiting elevated HLA-G expression, an immunosuppressive molecule frequently upregulated in solid tumors. In 2025 the U.S. Food and Drug Administration (FDA) cleared a Phase I dose-escalation study (NCT07219940) to evaluate SOB100's safety, tolerability, and pharmacokinetics in healthy subjects, with subsequent plans to extend into cancer populations, including LC. Although detailed results have yet to be published, this trial represents the first FDA-approved clinical evaluation of an engineered exosome for cancer therapy. Beyond SOB100, numerous exosome-centric clinical activities are registered globally. As of 2024 ~18 clinical studies focused on exosomes in LC settings have been reported, encompassing diagnostic and therapeutic endpoints. These include early screening, disease monitoring, and exosome-based vehicles for immunomodulatory agents such as dendritic cell-derived vaccines (Xiao et al., 2025).

5.8.4 Regulatory and manufacturing challenges

Despite significant advances in preclinical and early clinical studies, the clinical translation of exosome-based therapies for LC is constrained by substantial regulatory and manufacturing challenges. One of the primary obstacles is the lack of standardized protocols for exosome isolation, purification, characterization, and storage. Currently employed techniques such as ultracentrifugation, size-exclusion chromatography, polymer-based precipitation, and microfluidic approaches vary considerably in yield, purity, scalability, and reproducibility. This methodological heterogeneity complicates cross-study comparisons and poses difficulties in meeting regulatory expectations for product consistency and quality control (Serrano et al., 2025; Sharma et al., 2024).

From a manufacturing perspective, large-scale production of clinical-grade exosomes remains a critical bottleneck. Exosomes are inherently heterogeneous and sensitive to variations in cell source, culture conditions, and isolation methods. Scaling up production while preserving their biological integrity, functional cargo, and batch-to-batch uniformity is technically demanding. Moreover, the selection of appropriate parent cells, such as MSCs, dendritic cells, or tumor cells, raises additional concerns regarding safety, immunogenicity, and oncogenic potential. Regulatory agencies require rigorous demonstration that exosome preparations are free from contaminating proteins, nucleic acids, viruses, or other EV subtypes, necessitating robust and validated analytical assays (Hu et al., 2025; Sha et al., 2025).

Another major challenge lies in drug-loading efficiency and targeting specificity. While exosomes possess natural homing abilities, efficient and reproducible loading of therapeutic agents (e.g., small-molecule drugs, siRNAs, miRNAs, or proteins) remains suboptimal. Both endogenous loading strategies (via donor cell engineering) and exogenous methods (such as electroporation or sonication) suffer from limitations, including low encapsulation efficiency, cargo degradation, and structural damage to vesicles. Additionally, ensuring precise tumor targeting while minimizing off-target biodistribution is essential for regulatory approval, particularly in LC, where systemic delivery may lead to accumulation in non-target organs such as the liver or spleen. From a regulatory standpoint, the classification of exosome-based therapeutics remains ambiguous, as they share characteristics with biologics, drug delivery systems, and advanced therapy medicinal products. Regulatory frameworks from agencies such as the U.S. FDA and EMA are still evolving, with no universally accepted guidelines specific to exosome-based medicines. This uncertainty complicates the design of clinical trials, the definition of critical quality attributes, and the establishment of release criteria. Furthermore, long-term safety data, including immunotoxicity, biodistribution, and potential horizontal gene transfer, are required to support regulatory approval but are currently limited (Luan et al., 2017; Wiklander et al., 2019).

Despite these challenges, the field is witnessing encouraging translational momentum. The progression of exosome platforms from preclinical proof-of-concept to FDA-cleared early-phase clinical trials reflects growing regulatory engagement and technological maturity. Future regulatory strategies are likely to emphasize the harmonization of manufacturing standards, implementation of GMP-compliant production pipelines, and development of consensus guidelines for exosome characterization. Importantly, combining exosome-based systems with established LC therapies such as chemotherapy, targeted agents, and immune checkpoint inhibitors may enhance therapeutic efficacy while facilitating regulatory acceptance (Herrmann et al., 2021; Witwer et al., 2019).

5.9 Future perspectives and challenges

Exosome-based research has advanced considerably in LC over the past decade, with exosomes representing the interface between diagnostics, targeted therapy, and precision medicine. Biological advantages notwithstanding, scientific, technical, ethical, and regulatory obstacles still exist that seriously challenge the clinical translation of exosomes.

5.9.1 Standardization of isolation, characterization, and quantification

One of the most fundamental translational obstacles pertains to the lack of uniformity and reproducibility in approaches used for exosome isolation and characterization. Protocols currently in use, including ultracentrifugation, size-exclusion chromatography, precipitation kits, and microfluidic platforms, often result in exosome populations with variable purity, size distribution, and cargo composition. As exosomes often overlap in size and biochemical characteristics with microvesicles and apoptotic bodies, they fail to achieve the intrinsic homogeneity of EVs. Additionally, the yield and purity of exosomes highly depend on the isolation technique employed, which leads to batch variability. Furthermore, there is a lack of exosome-exclusive markers; although tetraspanins such as CD9, CD63, and CD81 are extensively used for exosome identification, they are not specifically expressed on exosomes. There are inconsistencies in quantification and characterization, also due to differences in analytical tools, including NTA, flow cytometry, TRPS, and protein-based assays, each of which measures distinct physical or biochemical parameters. Altogether, there is an urgent need for standardized isolation, characterization, and reporting guidelines to enable reliable clinical translation of exosome-based therapeutics (Lobb et al., 2015; Théry et al., 2018; Van der Pol et al., 2012).

5.9.2 Large-scale production and purity issues

Translational and industrial applications of exosomes require scalable biomanufacturing, which is still in its infancy. Clinical-grade manufacturing of exosomes requires reproducibility of yield, batch-to-batch consistency, and strict adherence to GMP. Most donor cells possess low exosome secretion rates, resulting in low yield and making it insufficient for large-scale production. Another challenge, especially in precipitation-based and ultracentrifugation methods, is the co-isolation of contaminants like lipoproteins, protein aggregates, and residual isolation reagents. Batch-to-batch variation further complicates the situation due to differences in donor cell states, transfection efficiency, and culture conditions. Moreover, improper storage conditions also affect the exosomal membrane integrity, cargo composition, and biological activity. Collectively, these limitations highlight the need for improved production strategies, purification technologies, and standardized storage protocols to facilitate the reliable clinical application of exosome-based therapeutics (Busatto et al., 2018; Gardiner et al., 2013; Görgens et al., 2022; Lener et al., 2015).

5.9.3 Immunogenicity, toxicity, and clearance concerns

While exosomes naturally occur, their safety profile is not fully predictable, especially when engineered or derived from tumor cells. The immune system could potentially get activated by exosomes depending on the surface antigens, glycosylation patterns, or contaminating proteins. The TDEs could also transport oncogenic proteins or nucleic acids that may further enhance the tumor growth and other promoting effects. The exosomes can also disturb the normal gene regulation process by off-target delivery of siRNA, miRNA, or CRISPR components, while accumulation of exosomes in metabolic organs like the liver can cause localized toxicity. On the other hand, rapid uptake by the mononuclear phagocyte system can limit the therapeutic efficacy of the exosomes. Also, the biodistribution of exosomes significantly depends on the route of administration. IV injection leads to liver accumulation, while intranasal delivery may be better for the targeting of the lungs (El Andaloussi et al., 2013; Kalluri & LeBleu, 2020; Wiklander et al., 2015).

5.9.4 Ethical and regulatory considerations

Because exosomes lie at the junction of biologics, cell-based therapies, and nanomedicine, regulatory pathways are complicated and usually not well defined. Stem cells and tumor-derived cells are the major sources of donor cells and raise ethical concerns related to consent, safety, and traceability. In the case of genetically engineered exosomes, there are strict safety evaluations as the regulatory agencies classify them together with the gene therapy vectors. The clinical trial approval highly depends on the purity, potency assays, and release criteria. The lack of these parameters slows down the approval process. The integration of patient data and AI models also raises some ethical concerns, particularly with informed consent and long-term data storage. The AI models can generate inaccurate results if incomplete or small datasets are used. Ensuring data security is also crucial to prevent non-confidentiality and misuse of personal records. Hence, strict guidelines need to be followed to maintain the maximum safety, reproducibility, and ethical compliance throughout the development, characterization, and clinical translation of exosome-based therapeutics (Lener et al., 2015; Topol, 2019; Wiklander et al., 2019).

5.9.5 Integration of multiomics and artificial intelligence in exosome theranostics

Ultimately, the future of exosome-based management of LC will involve the integration of high-throughput multi-omics technologies together with AI-driven predictive models to eventually enable personalized and precision medicine approaches. The genomics and transcriptomics will help in the identification of tumor-specific miRNA/lncRNA cargo signatures and allow more accurate stratification of patients and rational design of therapeutic exosomes. Proteomics and lipidomics will improve the characterization of membrane and cargo components for the discovery of diagnostic, prognostic, and predictive biomarkers. To improve our understanding of vesicle subpopulations with distinct biological functions, single-vesicle omics can be employed to decipher exosome heterogeneity at unparalleled resolution (Witwer & Théry, 2019; Yáñez-Mó et al., 2015; Yang et al., 2020).

AI and computational biology can also contribute to the development of better exosome delivery systems by using AI models based on precise algorithms to predict the optimal cargo packaging, receptor-ligand interactions, and stability, whereas machine learning algorithms can identify disease-specific exosomal signatures for liquid biopsy–based diagnosis and monitoring. The simulation models can help predict the biodistribution, pharmacokinetics, and tumor penetrability of exosomes to calculate the optimum dose and decide the route of administration. Furthermore, to improve target specificity and reduce toxicity, AI-driven strategies can be applied to modify the exosomes. Altogether, AI and computational biology can play a central role in yielding precision-engineered exosomes matched to specific tumor profiles (Herrmann et al., 2021; Kumar, 2025b; Li et al., 2024; Yang et al., 2020).

5.10 Conclusion

Exosomes have emerged as pivotal mediators of intercellular communication, fundamentally reshaping our understanding of LC biology, diagnosis, and treatment. Their unique biogenesis, molecular composition, and inherent ability to reflect the physiological and pathological state of their parent cells position them as powerful tools in the evolving landscape of precision oncology. This chapter highlights how TDEs orchestrate critical processes in LC progression, including immune evasion, angiogenesis, EMT, metastasis, and therapy resistance, thereby actively shaping the TME rather than serving as passive byproducts of malignancy.

From a diagnostic standpoint, exosomes offer unprecedented advantages as noninvasive platforms for liquid biopsies. Their remarkable stability in biological fluids and enrichment with disease-specific nucleic acids and proteins enable early detection, prognostic stratification, and real-time monitoring of therapeutic responses in LC patients. Compared with conventional biomarkers, exosomal cargo provides superior molecular fidelity and cellular specificity, reinforcing their value in personalized disease management. Advances in isolation, characterization, and microfluidic technologies are further accelerating the clinical translation of exosome-based diagnostics.

Therapeutically, exosomes represent a paradigm shift in drug delivery and theranostics. Their endogenous origin, low immunogenicity, and intrinsic targeting capabilities make them superior to many synthetic nanocarriers. Engineered exosomes capable of delivering chemotherapeutics, RNA-based therapeutics, and genome-editing tools such as CRISPR/Cas9 offer promising avenues to overcome biological barriers, enhance targeting specificity, and reduce systemic toxicity in LC therapy. Moreover, the integration of diagnostic and therapeutic functionalities within a single exosome-based platform underscores their potential as next-generation theranostic agents. Despite these advances, several challenges must be addressed before widespread clinical implementation can be achieved. Standardization of isolation and characterization protocols, scalable and GMP-compliant manufacturing, cargo heterogeneity, and long-term safety concerns remain critical hurdles. Addressing these limitations through interdisciplinary collaboration, technological innovation, and rigorous clinical validation will be essential for translating exosome research into routine clinical practice.

In conclusion, exosome-mediated precision targeting represents a transformative approach in LC theranostics. Continued exploration of exosomal biology, coupled with advances in nanotechnology and molecular engineering, holds immense promise for enabling early diagnosis, personalized treatment, and improved clinical outcomes. As our understanding deepens, exosomes are poised to transition from experimental tools to integral components of precision medicine in LC and beyond.

References

Ackaert, C., Smiejkowska, N., Xavier, C., Sterckx, Y. G., Denies, S., Stijlemans, B., et al. (2021). Immunogenicity risk profile of nanobodies. *Frontiers in Immunology, 12*, 632687.

Ahmadi, S., Rabiee, N., Bagherzadeh, M., Elmi, F., Fatahi, Y., Farjadian, F., et al. (2020). Stimulus-responsive sequential release systems for drug and gene delivery. *Nano Today, 34*, 100914.

Alshahrani, A., Alsubait, A., Asiri, Z., Alghamdi, S., Saqyah, S. B., Alqahtani, T., et al. (2025). Deciphering molecular pathways driving cancer invasion and metastasis: Advances and therapeutic prospects. *Frontiers in Oncology, 15*, 1684896.

Alvarez-Erviti, L., Seow, Y., Yin, H., Betts, C., Lakhal, S., & Wood, M. J. (2011). Delivery of siRNA to the mouse brain by systemic injection of targeted exosomes. *Nature Biotechnology, 29*(4), 341–345.

Arandjelovic, S., & Ravichandran, K. S. (2015). Phagocytosis of apoptotic cells in homeostasis. *Nature Immunology, 16*(9), 907–917.

Bates, P. J., Laber, D. A., Miller, D. M., Thomas, S. D., & Trent, J. O. (2009). Discovery and development of the G-rich oligonucleotide AS1411 as a novel treatment for cancer. *Experimental and Molecular Pathology, 86*(3), 151–164.

Bavafa, A., Izadpanahi, M., Hosseini, E., Hajinejad, M., Abedi, M., Forouzanfar, F., et al. (2025). Exosome: An overview on enhanced biogenesis by small molecules. *Naunyn-Schmiedeberg's Archives of Pharmacology, 398*(6), 6473–6508.

Besse, B., Charrier, M., Lapierre, V., Dansin, E., Lantz, O., Planchard, D., et al. (2016). Dendritic cell-derived exosomes as maintenance immunotherapy after first line chemotherapy in NSCLC. *Oncoimmunology, 5*(4), e1071008.

Bowers, E. C., Hassanin, A. A., & Ramos, K. S. (2020). In vitro models of exosome biology and toxicology: New frontiers in biomedical research. *Toxicology in Vitro, 64*, 104462.

Bradley, S. H., Abraham, S., Callister, M. E., Grice, A., Hamilton, W. T., Lopez, R. R., et al. (2019). Sensitivity of chest X-ray for detecting lung cancer in people presenting with symptoms: A systematic review. *British Journal of General Practice, 69*, bjgp19X706853.

Busatto, S., Vilanilam, G., Ticer, T., Lin, W.-L., Dickson, D. W., Shapiro, S., et al. (2018). Tangential flow filtration for highly efficient concentration of extracellular vesicles from large volumes of fluid. *Cells, 7*(12), 273.

Chen, G., Huang, A. C., Zhang, W., Zhang, G., Wu, M., Xu, W., et al. (2018). Exosomal PD-L1 contributes to immunosuppression and is associated with anti-PD-1 response. *Nature, 560*(7718), 382–386.

Chen, Y., Qi, W., Wang, Z., & Niu, F. (2025). Exosome source matters: A comprehensive review from the perspective of diverse cellular origins. *Pharmaceutics, 17*(2), 147.

Chen, Y.-F., Luh, F., Ho, Y.-S., & Yen, Y. (2024a). Exosomes: A review of biologic function, diagnostic and targeted therapy applications, and clinical trials. *Journal of Biomedical Science, 31*(1), 67.

Chen, Z., Xiong, M., Tian, J., Song, D., Duan, S., & Zhang, L. (2024b). Encapsulation and assessment of therapeutic cargo in engineered exosomes: A systematic review. *Journal of Nanobiotechnology, 22*(1), 18.

Choi, H., Choi, Y., Yim, H. Y., Mirzaaghasi, A., Yoo, J.-K., & Choi, C. (2021). Biodistribution of exosomes and engineering strategies for targeted delivery of therapeutic exosomes. *Tissue Engineering and Regenerative Medicine, 18*(4), 499–511.

Crescitelli, R., Lässer, C., Szabó, T. G., Kittel, A., Eldh, M., Dianzani, I., et al. (2013). Distinct RNA profiles in subpopulations of extracellular vesicles: Apoptotic bodies, microvesicles and exosomes. *Journal of Extracellular Vesicles, 2*(1), 20677.

Debs, S., Cohen, A., Hosseini-Beheshti, E., Chimini, G., Hunt, N. H., & Grau, G. E. (2019). Interplay of extracellular vesicles and other players in cerebral malaria pathogenesis. *Biochimica et Biophysica Acta (BBA)-General Subjects, 1863*(2), 325–331.

Dragovic, R. A., Gardiner, C., Brooks, A. S., Tannetta, D. S., Ferguson, D. J., Hole, P., et al. (2011). Sizing and phenotyping of cellular vesicles using nanoparticle tracking analysis. *Nanomedicine: Nanotechnology, Biology and Medicine, 7*(6), 780–788.

Dragu, L. D., Chivu-Economescu, M., Pitica, I. M., Matei, L., Bleotu, C., Diaconu, C. C., et al. (2025). Targeting exosomal PD-L1 as a new frontier in cancer immunotherapy. *Current Issues in Molecular Biology, 47*(7), 525.

El Andaloussi, S., Mäger, I., Breakefield, X. O., & Wood, M. J. (2013). Extracellular vesicles: Biology and emerging therapeutic opportunities. *Nature Reviews Drug Discovery, 12*(5), 347–357.

Ernst, A., Simoff, M., Ost, D., Goldman, Y., & Herth, F. J. (2008). Prospective risk-adjusted morbidity and mortality outcome analysis after therapeutic bronchoscopic procedures: Results of a multi-institutional outcomes database. *Chest, 134*(3), 514–519.

Fang, H., Chi, X., Wang, M., Liu, J., Sun, M., Zhang, J., et al. (2025). M2 macrophage-derived exosomes promote cell proliferation, migration and EMT of non-small cell lung cancer by secreting miR-155-5p. *Molecular and Cellular Biochemistry, 480*(5), 3019–3032.

Gabaran, S. G., Ghasemzadeh, N., Rahnama, M., Karatas, E., Akbari, A., & Rezaie, J. (2025). Functionalized exosomes for targeted therapy in cancer and regenerative medicine: Genetic, chemical, and physical modifications. *Cell Communication and Signaling, 23*(1), 265.

Gardiner, C., Ferreira, Y. J., Dragovic, R. A., Redman, C. W., & Sargent, I. L. (2013). Extracellular vesicle sizing and enumeration by nanoparticle tracking analysis. *Journal of Extracellular Vesicles, 2*(1), 19671.

Ghosh, S., Rajendran, R. L., Mahajan, A. A., Chowdhury, A., Bera, A., Guha, S., et al. (2024). Harnessing exosomes as cancer biomarkers in clinical oncology. *Cancer Cell International, 24*(1), 278.

Gilleron, J., Chafik, A., Lacas-Gervais, S., Tanti, J.-F., & Cormont, M. (2024). Golgi-associated retrograde protein (GARP) complex-dependent endosomes to trans Golgi network retrograde trafficking is controlled by Rab4b. *Cellular & Molecular Biology Letters, 29*(1), 54.

Giraldo, E., Nebot, V., Đorđević, S., Requejo-Aguilar, R., Alastrue-Agudo, A., Zagorodko, O., et al. (2021). A rationally designed self-immolative linker enhances the synergism between a polymer-rock inhibitor conjugate and neural progenitor cells in the treatment of spinal cord injury. *Biomaterials, 276*, 121052.

Görgens, A., Corso, G., Hagey, D. W., Jawad Wiklander, R., Gustafsson, M. O., Felldin, U., et al. (2022). Identification of storage conditions stabilizing extracellular vesicles preparations. *Journal of Extracellular Vesicles, 11*(6), e12238.

Gulati, R., Nandi, D., Sarkar, K., Venkataraman, P., Ramkumar, K., Ranjan, P., et al. (2022). Exosomes as theranostic targets: Implications for the clinical prognosis of aggressive cancers. *Frontiers in Molecular Biosciences, 9*, 890768.

Ha, D., Yang, N., & Nadithe, V. (2016). Exosomes as therapeutic drug carriers and delivery vehicles across biological membranes: Current perspectives and future challenges. *Acta Pharmaceutica Sinica B, 6*(4), 287–296.

Herrmann, I. K., Wood, M. J. A., & Fuhrmann, G. (2021). Extracellular vesicles as a next-generation drug delivery platform. *Nature Nanotechnology, 16*(7), 748–759.

Hoshino, A., Costa-Silva, B., Shen, T.-L., Rodrigues, G., Hashimoto, A., Tesic Mark, M., et al. (2015). Tumour exosome integrins determine organotropic metastasis. *Nature, 527*(7578), 329–335.

Hu, M., Han, Y., Zhang, X., Tian, S., Shang, Z., Yuan, Z., et al. (2025). Extracellular vesicles for targeted drug delivery: Advances in surface modification strategies and therapeutic applications. *Journal of Translational Medicine, 23*(1), 1028.

Hus, I., Roliński, J., Tabarkiewicz, J., Wojas, K., Bojarska-Junak, A., Greiner, J., et al. (2005). Allogeneic dendritic cells pulsed with tumor lysates or apoptotic bodies as immunotherapy for patients with early-stage B-cell chronic lymphocytic leukemia. *Leukemia, 19*(9), 1621–1627.

Im, H., Shao, H., Park, Y. I., Peterson, V. M., Castro, C. M., Weissleder, R., et al. (2014). Label-free detection and molecular profiling of exosomes with a nano-plasmonic sensor. *Nature Biotechnology, 32*(5), 490–495.

Jo, Y. K., & Lee, D. (2020). Biopolymer microparticles prepared by microfluidics for biomedical applications. *Small, 16*(9), 1903736.

Kakarla, R., Hur, J., Kim, Y. J., Kim, J., & Chwae, Y.-J. (2020). Apoptotic cell-derived exosomes: Messages from dying cells. *Experimental & Molecular Medicine, 52*(1), 1–6.

Kalluri, R., & LeBleu, V. S. (2020). The biology, function, and biomedical applications of exosomes. *Science, 367*(6478), eaau6977.

Kamerkar, S., LeBleu, V. S., Sugimoto, H., Yang, S., Ruivo, C. F., Melo, S. A., et al. (2017). Exosomes facilitate therapeutic targeting of oncogenic KRAS in pancreatic cancer. *Nature, 546*(7659), 498–503.

Karjoo, Z., Chen, X., & Hatefi, A. (2016). Progress and problems with the use of suicide genes for targeted cancer therapy. *Advanced Drug Delivery Reviews, 99*, 113–128.

Keerthikumar, S., Chisanga, D., Ariyaratne, D., Al Saffar, H., Anand, S., Zhao, K., et al. (2016). ExoCarta: A web-based compendium of exosomal cargo. *Journal of Molecular Biology, 428*(4), 688–692.

Kim, D. H., Kothandan, V. K., Kim, H. W., Kim, K. S., Kim, J. Y., Cho, H. J., et al. (2019). Noninvasive assessment of exosome pharmacokinetics in vivo: A review. *Pharmaceutics, 11*(12), 649.

Kim, M. S., Haney, M. J., Zhao, Y., Mahajan, V., Deygen, I., Klyachko, N. L., et al. (2016). Development of exosome-encapsulated paclitaxel to overcome MDR in cancer cells. *Nanomedicine: Nanotechnology, Biology and Medicine., 12*(3), 655–664.

Kooijmans, S., Fliervoet, L., Van Der Meel, R., Fens, M., Heijnen, H., PvB, H., et al. (2016a). PEGylated and targeted extracellular vesicles display enhanced cell specificity and circulation time. *Journal of Controlled Release, 224*, 77–85.

Kooijmans, S. A., Aleza, C. G., Roffler, S. R., van Solinge, W. W., Vader, P., & Schiffelers, R. M. (2016b). Display of GPI-anchored anti-EGFR nanobodies on extracellular vesicles promotes tumour cell targeting. *Journal of Extracellular Vesicles, 5*(1), 31053.

Kumar, P., Mehta, D., & Bissler, J. J. (2023). Physiologically based pharmacokinetic modeling of extracellular vesicles. *Biology, 12*(9), 1178.

Kumar, R. M. R. (2025a). Exosomal microRNAs: Impact on cancer detection, treatment, and monitoring. *Clinical and Translational Oncology, 27*(1), 83–94.

Kumar, R. M. R. (2025b). Exosome-machine learning integration in biomedicine: Advancing diagnosis and biomarker discovery. *Current Medicinal Chemistry, 32*(27), 5760–5771.

Lambert, A. W., Pattabiraman, D. R., & Weinberg, R. A. (2017). Emerging biological principles of metastasis. *Cell, 168*(4), 670–691.

Lamichhane, T. N., Raiker, R. S., & Jay, S. M. (2015). Exogenous DNA loading into extracellular vesicles via electroporation is size-dependent and enables limited gene delivery. *Molecular Pharmaceutics, 12*(10), 3650–3657.

Lee, K., Fraser, K., Ghaddar, B., Yang, K., Kim, E., Balaj, L., et al. (2018). Multiplexed profiling of single extracellular vesicles. *ACS Nano, 12*(1), 494–503.

Lee, Y. J., Shin, K. J., & Chae, Y. C. (2024). Regulation of cargo selection in exosome biogenesis and its biomedical applications in cancer. *Experimental & Molecular Medicine, 56*(4), 877–889.

Lener, T., Gimona, M., Aigner, L., Börger, V., Buzas, E., Camussi, G., et al. (2015). Applying extracellular vesicles based therapeutics in clinical trials–an ISEV position paper. *Journal of Extracellular Vesicles, 4*(1), 30087.

Li, B., Kugeratski, F. G., & Kalluri, R. (2024). A novel machine learning algorithm selects proteome signature to specifically identify cancer exosomes. *Elife, 12*, RP90390.

Li, H. Q., Wu, Y. B., Yin, C. S., Chen, L., Zhang, Q., & Hu, L. Q. (2016). Obestatin attenuated doxorubicin-induced cardiomyopathy via enhancing long noncoding Mhrt RNA expression. *Biomedicine & Pharmacotherapy, 81*, 474–481.

Li, J., Huang, Y., Fu, L., Shi, M., Hu, G., Du, F., et al. (2025). Role of exosomal non-coding RNAs in cancer-associated fibroblast-mediated therapy resistance. *International Journal of Oncology, 67*(2), 68.

Li, P., Kaslan, M., Lee, S. H., Yao, J., & Gao, Z. (2017). Progress in exosome isolation techniques. *Theranostics, 7*(3), 789.

Lin, Y., Wu, J., Gu, W., Huang, Y., Tong, Z., Huang, L., et al. (2018). Exosome–liposome hybrid nanoparticles deliver CRISPR/Cas9 system in MSCs. *Advanced Science, 5*(4), 1700611.

Liu, A., Yang, G., Liu, Y., & Liu, T. (2022). Research progress in membrane fusion-based hybrid exosomes for drug delivery systems. *Frontiers in Bioengineering and Biotechnology, 10*, 939441.

Liu, C., Zhang, W., Li, Y., Chang, J., Tian, F., Zhao, F., et al. (2019). Microfluidic sonication to assemble exosome membrane-coated nanoparticles for immune evasion-mediated targeting. *Nano letters, 19*(11), 7836–7844.

Liu, G., Liu, J., Li, S., Zhang, Y., & Ren, H. (2025). Exosome-mediated chemoresistance in cancers: Mechanisms, therapeutic implications, and future directions. *Biomolecules, 15*(5), 685.

Liu, J., Qiu, X., Lv, Y., Zheng, C., Dong, Y., Dou, G., et al. (2020). Apoptotic bodies derived from mesenchymal stem cells promote cutaneous wound healing via regulating the functions of macrophages. *Stem Cell Research & Therapy, 11*(1), 507.

Liu, M., Wen, Z., Zhang, T., Zhang, L., Liu, X., & Wang, M. (2024). The role of exosomal molecular cargo in exosome biogenesis and disease diagnosis. *Frontiers in Immunology, 15*, 1417758.

Lobb, R. J., Becker, M., Wen, S., Wong, C. S., Wiegmans, A. P., Leimgruber, A., et al. (2015). Optimized exosome isolation protocol for cell culture supernatant and human plasma. *Journal of Extracellular Vesicles, 4*(1), 27031.

Luan, X., Sansanaphongpricha, K., Myers, I., Chen, H., Yuan, H., & Sun, D. (2017). Engineering exosomes as refined biological nanoplatforms for drug delivery. *Acta Pharmacologica Sinica, 38*(6), 754–763.

Manap, A. S. A., Ngwenya, F. M., Selvan, M. K., Arni, S., Hassan, F. H., Rudy, A. D. M., et al. (2024). Lung cancer cell-derived exosomes: Progress on pivotal role and its application in diagnostic and therapeutic potential. *Frontiers in Oncology, 14*, 1459178.

Martiniano, R., Caffell, A., Holst, M., Hunter-Mann, K., Montgomery, J., Müldner, G., et al. (2016). Genomic signals of migration and continuity in Britain before the Anglo-Saxons. *Nature Communications, 7*(1), 10326.

Mathieu, M., Martin-Jaular, L., Lavieu, G., & Théry, C. (2019). Specificities of secretion and uptake of exosomes and other extracellular vesicles for cell-to-cell communication. *Nature Cell Biology, 21*(1), 9–17.

Melo, S. A., Luecke, L. B., Kahlert, C., Fernandez, A. F., Gammon, S. T., Kaye, J., et al. (2015). Glypican-1 identifies cancer exosomes and detects early pancreatic cancer. *Nature, 523*(7559), 177–182.

Mirgh, D., Sonar, S., Ghosh, S., Adhikari, M. D., Subramaniyan, V., Gorai, S., et al. (2024). Landscape of exosomes to modified exosomes: A state of the art in cancer therapy. *RSC Advances, 14*(42), 30807–30829.

Mohamed, A. H., Abaza, T., Youssef, Y. A., Rady, M., Fahmy, S. A., Kamel, R., et al. (2025). Extracellular vesicles: From intracellular trafficking molecules to fully fortified delivery vehicles for cancer therapeutics. *Nanoscale Advances, 7*(4), 934–962.

Mukerjee, N., Bhattacharya, A., Maitra, S., Kaur, M., Ganesan, S., Mishra, S., et al. (2025). Exosome isolation and characterization for advanced diagnostic and therapeutic applications. *Materials Today Bio, 31*, 101613.

Munagala, R., Aqil, F., Jeyabalan, J., & Gupta, R. C. (2016). Bovine milk-derived exosomes for drug delivery. *Cancer Letters, 371*(1), 48–61.

O'Brien, K., Breyne, K., Ughetto, S., Laurent, L. C., & Breakefield, X. O. (2020). RNA delivery by extracellular vesicles in mammalian cells and its applications. *Nature Reviews Molecular Cell Biology, 21*(10), 585–606.

Ohno, S., Takanashi, M., Sudo, K., Ueda, S., Ishikawa, A., Matsuyama, N., Fujita, K., Mizutani, T., Ohgi, T., Ochiya, T., Gotoh, N., & Kuroda, M. (2013). Systemically injected exosomes targeted to EGFR deliver antitumor microRNA to breast cancer cells. *Molecular Therapy, 21*(1), 185–191.

Palakurthi, S. S., Shah, B., Kapre, S., Charbe, N., Immanuel, S., Pasham, S., et al. (2024). A comprehensive review of challenges and advances in exosome-based drug delivery systems. *Nanoscale Advances, 6*, 5803–5806.

Pan, W., Gao, X., Zhang, X., Li, Y., Zhao, Q., Wang, D., et al. (2025). Exosomes promote pre-metastatic niche formation in lung cancer. *Cancer Cell International, 25*(1), 379.

Patat, J., Schauer, K., & Lachuer, H. (2025). Trafficking in cancer: From gene deregulation to altered organelles and emerging biophysical properties. *Frontiers in Cell and Developmental Biology, 12*, 1491304.

Pegtel, D. M., & Gould, S. J. (2019). Exosomes. *Annual Review of Biochemistry, 88*(1), 487–514.

Peinado, H., Alečković, M., Lavotshkin, S., Matei, I., Costa-Silva, B., Moreno-Bueno, G., et al. (2012). Melanoma exosomes educate bone marrow progenitor cells toward a pro-metastatic phenotype through MET. *Nature Medicine, 18*(6), 883–891.

Perrin, P., Janssen, L., Janssen, H., van den Broek, B., Voortman, L. M., van Elsland, D., et al. (2021). Retrofusion of intralumenal MVB membranes parallels viral infection and coexists with exosome release. *Current Biology, 31*(17), 3884–3893.

Qiu, P., Zhou, J., Zhang, J., Dong, Y., & Liu, Y. (2021). Exosome: The regulator of the immune system in sepsis. *Frontiers in Pharmacology, 12*, 671164.

Rahimian, S., Najafi, H., Afzali, B., & Doroudian, M. (2024). Extracellular vesicles and exosomes: Novel insights and perspectives on lung cancer from early detection to targeted treatment. *Biomedicines, 12*(1), 123.

Rahnama, M., Heidari, M., Poursalehi, Z., & Golchin, A. (2024). Global trends of exosomes application in clinical trials: A scoping review. *Stem Cell Reviews and Reports, 20*(8), 2165–2193.

Rao, D.-Y., Huang, D.-F., Si, M.-Y., Lu, H., Tang, Z.-X., & Zhang, Z.-X. (2023). Role of exosomes in non-small cell lung cancer and EGFR-mutated lung cancer. *Frontiers in Immunology, 14*, 1142539.

Redkin, T., & Turubanova, V. (2025). Dendritic cell-derived exosomes as anti-cancer cell-free agents: New insights into enhancing immunogenic effects. *Frontiers in Immunology, 16*, 1586892.

Rollyson, W. D., Stover, C. A., Brown, K. C., Perry, H. E., Stevenson, C. D., McNees, C. A., et al. (2014). Bioavailability of capsaicin and its implications for drug delivery. *Journal of Controlled Release, 196*, 96–105.

Schwarz, G., Ren, X., Xie, W., Guo, H., Jiang, Y., & Zhang, J. (2025). Engineered exosomes: A promising drug delivery platform with therapeutic potential. *Frontiers in Molecular Biosciences, 12*, 1583992.

Sengupta, V., Sengupta, S., Lazo, A., Woods, P., Nolan, A., & Bremer, N. (2020). Exosomes derived from bone marrow mesenchymal stem cells as treatment for severe COVID-19. *Stem Cells and Development, 29*(12), 747–754.

Serrano, D. R., Juste, F., Anaya, B. J., Ramirez, B. I., Sánchez-Guirales, S. A., Quispillo, J. M., et al. (2025). Exosome-based drug delivery: A next-generation platform for cancer, infection, neurological and immunological diseases, gene therapy and regenerative medicine. *Pharmaceutics, 17*(10), 1336.

Sha, M., Gao, Y., Yin, X., Li, X., Liu, C., & Li, S. (2025). Engineered exosomes: A promising approach for overcoming challenges in pancreatic cancer therapy. *Journal of Nanobiotechnology, 23*(1), 1–25.

Shahraki, K., Boroumand, P. G., Lotfi, H., Radnia, F., Shahriari, H., Sargazi, S., et al. (2023). An update in the applications of exosomes in cancer theranostics: From research to clinical trials. *Journal of Cancer Research and Clinical Oncology, 149*(10), 8087–8116.

Shao, H., Chung, J., Balaj, L., Charest, A., Bigner, D. D., Carter, B. S., et al. (2012). Protein typing of circulating microvesicles allows real-time monitoring of glioblastoma therapy. *Nature Medicine, 18*(12), 1835–1840.

Shao, H., Im, H., Castro, C. M., Breakefield, X., Weissleder, R., & Lee, H. (2018). New technologies for analysis of extracellular vesicles. *Chemical Reviews, 118*(4), 1917–1950.

Sharma, A., Yadav, A., Nandy, A., & Ghatak, S. (2024). Insight into the functional dynamics and challenges of exosomes in pharmaceutical innovation and precision medicine. *Pharmaceutics, 16*(6), 709.

Shi, M., Liu, C., Cook, T. J., Bullock, K. M., Zhao, Y., Ginghina, C., et al. (2014). Plasma exosomal α-synuclein is likely CNS-derived and increased in Parkinson's disease. *Acta Neuropathologica, 128*(5), 639–650.

Simonetta, I., Tuttolomondo, A., Daidone, M., & Pinto, A. (2020). Biomarkers in Anderson–Fabry disease. *International Journal of Molecular Sciences, 21*(21), 8080.

Skotland, T., Llorente, A., & Sandvig, K. (2023). Lipids in extracellular vesicles: What can be learned about membrane structure and function? *Cold Spring Harbor Perspectives in Biology, 15*(8), a041415.

Smolarz, B., Łukasiewicz, H., Samulak, D., Piekarska, E., Kołaciński, R., & Romanowicz, H. (2025). Lung cancer—epidemiology, pathogenesis, treatment and molecular aspect (review of literature). *International Journal of Molecular Sciences, 26*(5), 2049.

Smyth, T., Kullberg, M., Malik, N., Smith-Jones, P., Graner, M. W., & Anchordoquy, T. J. (2015). Biodistribution and delivery efficiency of unmodified tumor-derived exosomes. *Journal of Controlled Release, 199*, 145–155.

Solinger, J. A., Ott, D. P., & Spang, A. (2025). ESCRTing the RABs through conversion. *Biochemical Society Transactions, 53*(02), 431–445.

Sonar, S., Das, A., Nyahatkar, S., Dhar, R., Kalele, K., Balasubramaniam, V. R., et al. (2026). Hybrid exosomes: A rising horizon for precision cancer therapy. *RSC Advances, 16*(2), 1292–1309.

Soundararajan, S., Chen, W., Spicer, E. K., Courtenay-Luck, N., & Fernandes, D. J. (2008). The nucleolin targeting aptamer AS1411 destabilizes Bcl-2 messenger RNA in human breast cancer cells. *Cancer Research, 68*(7), 2358–2365.

Sugahara, K. N., Teesalu, T., Karmali, P. P., Kotamraju, V. R., Agemy, L., Girard, O. M., et al. (2009). Tissue-penetrating delivery of compounds and nanoparticles into tumors. *Cancer Cell, 16*(6), 510–520.

Sun, H., Burrola, S., Wu, J., & Ding, W.-Q. (2020a). Extracellular vesicles in the development of cancer therapeutics. *International Journal Of Molecular Sciences, 21*(17), 6097.

Sun, L., Yu, Y., Niu, B., & Wang, D. (2020b). Red blood cells as potential repositories of microRNAs in the circulatory system. *Frontiers in Genetics, 11*, 442.

Tan, S., Xia, L., Yi, P., Han, Y., Tang, L., Pan, Q., et al. (2020). Exosomal miRNAs in tumor microenvironment. *Journal of Experimental & Clinical Cancer Research, 39*(1), 67.

The National Lung Screening Trial Research Team. (2011). Reduced lung-cancer mortality with low-dose computed tomographic screening. *New England Journal of Medicine, 365*(5), 395–409.

Théry, C., Witwer, K. W., Aikawa, E., Alcaraz, M. J., Anderson, J. D., Andriantsitohaina, R., et al. (2018). Minimal information for studies of extracellular vesicles 2018 (MISEV2018): A position statement of the International Society for Extracellular Vesicles and update of the MISEV2014 guidelines. *Journal of Extracellular Vesicles, 7*(1), 1535750.

Tian, Y., Li, S., Song, J., Ji, T., Zhu, M., Anderson, G. J., et al. (2014). A doxorubicin delivery platform using engineered natural membrane vesicle exosomes for targeted tumor therapy. *Biomaterials, 35*(7), 2383–2390.

Timin, A. S., Muslimov, A. R., Lepik, K. V., Epifanovskaya, O. S., Shakirova, A. I., Mock, U., et al. (2018). Efficient gene editing via non-viral delivery of CRISPR–Cas9 system using polymeric and hybrid microcarriers. *Nanomedicine: Nanotechnology, Biology and Medicine., 14*(1), 97–108.

Tomasetti, M., Lee, W., Santarelli, L., & Neuzil, J. (2017). Exosome-derived microRNAs in cancer metabolism: Possible implications in cancer diagnostics and therapy. *Experimental & Molecular Medicine, 49*(1), e285.

Topol, E. J. (2019). High-performance medicine: The convergence of human and artificial intelligence. *Nature Medicine, 25*(1), 44–56.

Toshima, J. Y., & Toshima, J. (2024). Transport mechanisms between the endocytic, recycling, and biosynthetic pathways via endosomes and the trans-Golgi network. *Frontiers in Cell and Developmental Biology, 12*, 1464337.

Trajkovic, K., Hsu, C., Chiantia, S., Rajendran, L., Wenzel, D., Wieland, F., et al. (2008). Ceramide triggers budding of exosome vesicles into multivesicular endosomes. *Science, 319*(5867), 1244–1247.

Van der Pol, E., Böing, A. N., Harrison, P., Sturk, A., & Nieuwland, R. (2012). Classification, functions, and clinical relevance of extracellular vesicles. *Pharmacological Reviews, 64*(3), 676–705.

van Niel, G., Carter, D. R., Clayton, A., Lambert, D. W., Raposo, G., & Vader, P. (2022). Challenges and directions in studying cell–cell communication by extracellular vesicles. *Nature Reviews Molecular Cell Biology, 23*(5), 369–382.

Wang, X., Liu, Y., Jiang, Y., & Li, Q. (2025). Tumor-derived exosomes as promising tools for cancer diagnosis and therapy. *Frontiers in Pharmacology, 16*, 1596217.

Welsh, J. A., Goberdhan, D. C., O'Driscoll, L., Buzas, E. I., Blenkiron, C., Bussolati, B., et al. (2024). Minimal information for studies of extracellular vesicles (MISEV2023): From basic to advanced approaches. *Journal of Extracellular Vesicles, 13*(2), e12404.

Wen, J., Creaven, D., Luan, X., & Wang, J. (2023). Comparison of immunotherapy mediated by apoptotic bodies, microvesicles and exosomes: Apoptotic bodies' unique anti-inflammatory potential. *Journal of Translational Medicine, 21*(1), 478.

Wiklander, O. P., Brennan, M. Á., Lötvall, J., Breakefield, X. O., & El Andaloussi, S. (2019). Advances in therapeutic applications of extracellular vesicles. *Science Translational Medicine, 11*(492), eaav8521.

Wiklander, O. P., Nordin, J. Z., O'Loughlin, A., Gustafsson, Y., Corso, G., Mäger, I., et al. (2015). Extracellular vesicle in vivo biodistribution is determined by cell source, route of administration and targeting. *Journal of Extracellular Vesicles, 4*(1), 26316.

Wild, C. P., Weiderpass, E., & Stewart, B. W. (2020). World Cancer Report.

Witwer, K. W., & Théry, C. (2019). Extracellular vesicles or exosomes? On primacy, precision, and popularity influencing a choice of nomenclature. *Journal of Extracellular Vesicles, 8*, 1648167.

Witwer, K. W., Van Balkom, B. W., Bruno, S., Choo, A., Dominici, M., Gimona, M., et al. (2019). Defining mesenchymal stromal cell (MSC)-derived small extracellular vesicles for therapeutic applications. *Journal of Extracellular Vesicles, 8*(1), 1609206.

Wu, K., Xing, F., Wu, S.-Y., & Watabe, K. (2017). Extracellular vesicles as emerging targets in cancer: Recent development from bench to bedside. *Biochimica et Biophysica Acta (BBA)-Reviews on Cancer, 1868*(2), 538–563.

Wu, Y., Fu, H., Hao, J., Yang, Z., Qiao, X., Li, Y., et al. (2024). Tumor-derived exosomal PD-L1: A new perspective in PD-1/PD-L1 therapy for lung cancer. *Frontiers in Immunology, 15*, 1342728.

Xiao, Q., Tan, M., Yan, G., & Peng, L. (2025). Revolutionizing lung cancer treatment: Harnessing exosomes as early diagnostic biomarkers, therapeutics and nano-delivery platforms. *Journal of Nanobiotechnology, 23*(1), 1–19.

Xie, M., Xiong, W., She, Z., Wen, Z., Abdirahman, A. S., Wan, W., et al. (2020). Immunoregulatory effects of stem cell-derived extracellular vesicles on immune cells. *Frontiers in Immunology, 11*, 13.

Xin, H., Li, Y., Liu, Z., Wang, X., Shang, X., Cui, Y., et al. (2013). MiR-133b promotes neural plasticity and functional recovery after treatment of stroke with multipotent mesenchymal stromal cells in rats via transfer of exosome-enriched extracellular particles. *Stem Cells, 31*(12), 2737–2746.

Xu, R., Greening, D. W., Rai, A., Ji, H., & Simpson, R. J. (2015). Highly-purified exosomes and shed microvesicles isolated from the human colon cancer cell line LIM1863 by sequential centrifugal ultrafiltration are biochemically and functionally distinct. *Methods, 87*, 11–25.

Xu, R., Rai, A., Chen, M., Suwakulsiri, W., Greening, D. W., & Simpson, R. J. (2018). Extracellular vesicles in cancer—Implications for future improvements in cancer care. *Nature Reviews Clinical Oncology, 15*(10), 617-6 38.

Yáñez-Mó, M., Siljander, P. R.-M., Andreu, Z., Bedina Zavec, A., Borràs, F. E., Buzas, E. I., et al. (2015). Biological properties of extracellular vesicles and their physiological functions. *Journal of Extracellular Vesicles, 4*(1), 27066.

Yang, D., Zhang, W., Zhang, H., Zhang, F., Chen, L., Ma, L., et al. (2020). Progress, opportunity, and perspective on exosome isolation-efforts for efficient exosome-based theranostics. *Theranostics, 10*(8), 3684.

Zhang, G., Yang, Y., Shi, J., Yao, X., Chen, W., Wei, X., et al. (2021). Near-infrared light II-assisted rapid biofilm elimination platform for bone implants at mild temperature. *Biomaterials, 269*, 120634.

Zhang, H., Freitas, D., Kim, H. S., Fabijanic, K., Li, Z., Chen, H., et al. (2018). Identification of distinct nanoparticles and subsets of extracellular vesicles by asymmetric flow field-flow fractionation. *Nature Cell Biology, 20*(3), 332–343.

Zhang, M., Viennois, E., Prasad, M., Zhang, Y., Wang, L., Zhang, Z., et al. (2016). Edible ginger-derived nanoparticles: A novel therapeutic approach for the prevention and treatment of inflammatory bowel disease and colitis-associated cancer. *Biomaterials, 101*, 321–340.

Zhang, W., Jiang, Z., & Tang, D. (2022). The value of exosome-derived noncoding RNAs in colorectal cancer proliferation, metastasis, and clinical applications. *Clinical and Translational Oncology, 24*(12), 2305–2318.

Zhang, Y., Liu, Y., Liu, H., & Tang, W. H. (2019). Exosomes: Biogenesis, biologic function and clinical potential. *Cell & Bioscience, 9*(1), 19.

Zhao, P., Tian, R., Song, D., Zhu, Q., Ding, X., Zhang, J., et al. (2025). Rab GTPases are evolutionarily conserved signals mediating selective autophagy. *Journal of Cell Biology, 224*(5), e202410150.

Zhu, L., Sun, H.-T., Wang, S., Huang, S.-L., Zheng, Y., Wang, C.-Q., et al. (2020). Isolation and characterization of exosomes for cancer research. *Journal of Hematology & Oncology, 13*(1), 152.

Zhu, X., Gao, M., Yang, Y., Li, W., Bao, J., & Li, Y. (2023). The CRISPR/Cas9 system delivered by extracellular vesicles. *Pharmaceutics, 15*(3), 984.

Zhu, Z. (2025). Intelligent information management enables quality-by-design in pharmaceutical production. *Scientific Reports, 15*(1), 44201.

Zhuang, X., Xiang, X., Grizzle, W., Sun, D., Zhang, S., Axtell, R. C., et al. (2011). Treatment of brain inflammatory diseases by delivering exosome encapsulated anti-inflammatory drugs from the nasal region to the brain. *Molecular Therapy, 19*(10), 1769–1779.

CHAPTER 6

Exosome-mediated precision immunotherapy in lung cancer: Harnessing smart drug delivery vehicles

Syed Naved Quadri, Syed Saima Malik and Malik Zainul Abdin

Centre for Transgenic Plant Development, Department of Biotechnology, Jamia Hamdard, New Delhi, India

6.1 Introduction

Lung cancer is the most common cause of cancer-related fatalities across the world, which puts a lot of pressure on health care systems. According to the Global Cancer Observatory (GLOBOCAN 2024), lung cancer is the second most common cancer after breast cancer. An estimated 2.4 million new cases add up, whereas roughly 1.9 million deaths occur each year due to lung cancer. The disease exists in two primary forms: nonsmall cell lung cancer (NSCLC), which makes up around 85% of all cases, and small cell lung cancer, which is notorious for being aggressive and spreading quickly (Bray et al., 2024). Several sophisticated diagnostic imaging techniques, surgical procedures, chemotherapy regimens, and targeted medicines have been developed so far, but the general outlook of the disease is still very poor. Late diagnosis of lung cancer is the main cause of early death within the first 5 years. Early symptoms are either not very distinct or not there at all, which might make people wait too long to consult a doctor. In almost 70% of cases, lung cancer has already spread by the time it is diagnosed, making curative treatments less effective (Deng & Zhang, 2025). Tissue biopsy, computed tomography (CT), positron emission tomography (PET), and bronchoscopy are some commonly employed ways to diagnose cancer. These invasive technologies are costly, but not good enough for early-stage detection. Platinum-based chemotherapy, immunotherapy, and tyrosine kinase inhibitors (TKIs) are some other treatment options that have shown promise, but they often do not work because some tumors develop resistance, and they can be toxic to the whole body (Godoy et al., 2023). Innovative strategies are the need of the hour, which may enable earlier diagnosis, provide precise molecular characterization, and deliver targeted therapies with minimal adverse effects.

Nanoengineered Therapeutics for Lung Cancer: Advanced Drug Delivery Strategies.
DOI: https://doi.org/10.1016/B978-0-443-44585-9.00003-2

Standard treatments for lung cancer comprise surgery, chemotherapy, and radiotherapy. Although survival rates have improved, a major challenge remains the lack of treatment selectivity. Chemotherapy targets rapidly dividing cells but often harms healthy cells, causing side effects such as fatigue, hair loss, nausea, and organ damage. Drugs, such as cisplatin and paclitaxel, are commonly employed in lung cancer therapy; nevertheless, their administration is often linked to toxicity and problems (Zafar et al., 2025). Radiotherapy is a significant treatment alternative, particularly for individuals ineligible for surgery. Radiation not only affects tumor tissues but may also harm adjacent healthy lung cells. This may lead to chronic problems such as inflammation or fibrosis of lung tissue. A significant constraint is the emergence of drug resistance. Numerous lung cancers initially exhibit responsiveness to chemotherapy or targeted therapy but progressively develop resistance over time. For example, certain patients with epidermal growth factor receptor (EGFR) inhibitors ultimately acquire mutations that diminish the drug's efficacy. Moreover, traditional medicines frequently do not eradicate tumor cells or inhibit the spread. Due to these challenges, there is a growing necessity for more specific and targeted treatment procedures that can enhance therapeutic outcomes while reducing adverse side effects (Verginadis et al., 2025).

Precision immunotherapy has become a revolutionary method for treating lung cancer. It works by boosting the immune system's ability to find and kill tumor cells while causing as little harm as possible to healthy tissues. Specific biochemical and immunological pathways are being targeted, which makes it possible to create more tailored therapy plans. Immune checkpoint inhibitors, cancer vaccines, and adoptive cell treatments are important examples that have shown promise in increasing antitumor responses. Precision immunotherapy has the promise to provide more effective, targeted, and long-lasting cancer treatments by customizing therapy to the specific characteristics of each patient's tumor and immune profile (Padinharayil et al., 2022).

Conventional cancer treatments typically have problems, including not being able to target the right cells, not being stable, and being very harmful to the body as a whole, which makes them less successful. Biological barriers and the fact that tumors are made up of many types of cells make it even harder for drugs to get to cancer cells. Advanced delivery systems, such as nanoparticles and exosomes, can protect drugs, make them more stable, and help them reach their exact targets. These technologies improve treatment effectiveness while reducing adverse effects by delivering medications directly to tumor locations. This makes them essential for developing next-generation lung cancer therapies that work better.

6.2 Biology of exosomes: Biogenesis and release

Exosomes are small, membrane-bound extracellular vesicles (EVs) about 30–150 nm in diameter. They were once thought to be simple waste-disposal units for cells. In the last two decades, scientists have grown interested in exosomes for their key role in cell-to-cell communication. Almost all cell types, such as immune cells, epithelial cells, neurons, and tumor cells, release exosomes. These vesicles carry proteins, fats, and nucleic acids. Their cargo enables exosomes to affect the healthy and diseased states of recipient cells. In oncology, especially lung cancer, exosomes play important roles in tumor growth, immune system changes, metastasis, and drug resistance. This makes them promising for targeted diagnosis and therapy (Bunggulawa et al., 2018; Fordjour et al., 2022; Lin et al., 2020)

Exosomes are distinguished from other EVs, such as microvesicles and apoptotic bodies, by their distinct production process via the endosomal route. Exosome formation begins with the invagination of the plasma membrane and the production of early endosomes. These eventually develop into late endosomes, called multivesicular bodies (MVBs). During this maturation, the limiting membrane of the endosome invaginates, forming intraluminal vesicles (ILVs) within MVBs. Once released into the external environment, these ILVs are known as exosomes (Xie et al., 2022; Yokoi & Ochiya, 2021). The procedure for loading cargo into ILVs is highly controlled and selective. It is not just a random collection of cytosolic material. There are two ways that this sorting can happen: ESCRT-dependent and ESCRT-independent. The Endosomal Sorting Complex Required for Transport (ESCRT) system consists of protein complexes (ESCRT-0, -I, -II, and -III). These complexes identify and sequester ubiquitinated proteins into specific membrane domains. These regions then bud inward to create ILVs. ESCRT-III is crucial for the final step in the budding vesicle's journey into the endosome lumen. Studies have also found cargo-sorting methods that do not rely on ESCRT. These use lipids such as ceramide and proteins, such as tetraspanins (CD9, CD63, and CD81). Such substances help membranes bend and bud, letting exosomes form even without the ESCRT machinery (Fu et al., 2020; Wei et al., 2021).

One of the most intriguing aspects of exosome biology is their precise packaging of bioactive chemicals. Exosomes carry a diverse array of proteins, including heat shock proteins (Hsp70, Hsp90), major histocompatibility complex molecules (MHC-I and II), adhesion molecules, and enzymes. They also transport nucleic acids, such as microRNAs (miRNAs), messenger RNAs (mRNAs), long noncoding RNAs (lncRNAs), and DNA fragments. This molecular payload reflects the donor cell's physiological state. As a result, exosomes are a key source of biomarkers for disease identification and surveillance. In lung cancer, tumor exosomes often carry oncogenic miRNAs (such as miR-21) or altered proteins (such as EGFR mutations). These biomarkers are detectable in bodily fluids such as blood, saliva, or bronchoalveolar lavage fluid (Kalluri & LeBleu et al., 2020). After their synthesis, MVBs follow two main pathways. They may merge with lysosomes for breakdown, or fuse with the plasma membrane to release exosomes. This process is regulated by intracellular trafficking proteins, including Rab family small GTPases such as Rab11, Rab27a, and Rab27b. These proteins control MVB movement to the plasma membrane, docking, and fusion. In addition, SNARE proteins (soluble NSF attachment protein receptors) enable fusion of the MVB membrane with the plasma membrane, which releases ILVs as exosomes. Calcium signaling and other intracellular pathways also influence exosome release (Papoutsoglou & Morillon, 2024). After their release, exosomes interact with recipient cells in several ways. They may fuse directly with the plasma membrane, be internalized by endocytosis, or bind to surface receptors and activate signaling cascades. Interaction mechanisms often depend on the exosome's surface composition and the target cell's surface composition (Xu et al., 2023). For example, integrins and tetraspanins on exosomal surfaces can confer tissue- or cell-specificity, promoting selective uptake by target cells. This built-in targeting ability is critical for the development of exosome-based drug delivery in precision medicine. For cancers such as lung cancer, local targeting can enhance treatment efficacy and limit off-target effects (Hu et al., 2020).

In diseases such as cancer, the production and release of exosomes often increase. Tumor cells release many exosomes filled with oncogenic proteins, miRNAs, and signaling molecules. These can alter adjacent stromal cells, disrupt immune function, and promote angiogenesis and metastasis (He et al., 2022; Ingenito et al., 2019). Exosomes help tumors resist treatment by releasing chemotherapeutic agents or by secreting compounds that make other tumor cells resistant. Exosomes have been linked to transmitting cancerous traits and forming premetastatic niches in distant organs in people with lung cancer. Overall, the creation, release, and function of exosomes involve a well-coordinated, dynamic system essential for both normal and abnormal cellular communication (Azmi et al., 2013). Exosomes are powerful tools for lung cancer theranostics because they can carry and protect physiological substances, target them naturally, and offer biocompatibility. Understanding exosome biology helps explain tumorigenesis and supports the development of new diagnostic and therapeutic approaches using this natural nanocarrier system (Li et al., 2025a).

6.3 Exosomes in cell–cell communication and tumor dynamics

Exosomes essentially serve intercellular communication, functioning as nanocarriers. These tiny structures help in the transportation of the physiologically active materials, such as proteins, RNAs, lipids, and DNA, between cells. Unlike soluble signaling molecules that rely on receptor–ligand interactions, exosomes transport their cargo directly into recipient cells, facilitating a more comprehensive control of physiological activities. This mechanism facilitates long-range communication among cells and supports systemic control throughout tissues. In lung cancer, tumor-derived exosomes (TDEs) markedly modify the tumor microenvironment (TME) to facilitate cancer progression (Rajput et al., 2022). They affect multiple biological elements within the TME, such as fibroblasts, endothelial cells, immune cells, and the extracellular matrix, by transmitting oncogenic chemicals that promote angiogenesis, immunological suppression, extracellular matrix remodeling, and the establishment of metastatic niches. Exosomes containing VEGF or miR-210 promote angiogenesis. Those enriched in

PD-L1 or immunosuppressive cytokines reduce T-cell function and weaken antitumor immunity. Exosomes also drive epithelial-to-mesenchymal transition (EMT) by delivering factors that change tumor cell phenotype. They promote drug resistance by transferring signaling molecules and RNAs associated with efflux pumps to nearby tumor cells. Additionally, they recruit and reprogram stromal cells, including cancer-associated fibroblasts (CAFs), to boost tumor survival and invasion (Wei et al., 2020). Significantly, these communication functions extend beyond the local area. Circulating exosomes can access remote organs, where they deliver specific molecular cargo, such as proteins, lipids, and nucleic acids, to recipient cells. There, these contents can modulate cellular signaling pathways, priming tissues for metastatic colonization by establishing a premetastatic habitat. This process often promotes EMT in recipient cells. Through such targeted interactions, exosomes orchestrate a supportive environment for tumor proliferation, immune evasion, and therapeutic resistance. Thus exosomes are a crucial target and an effective tool in lung cancer theranostics (Guo et al., 2019).

TDEs often regulate immunity by weakening the body's innate defenses. They reduce the effectiveness of cytotoxic T cells and natural killer cells, which identify and destroy cancer cells. These exosomes also promote the growth of regulatory T cells and myeloid-derived suppressor cells, both of which create an immunosuppressive environment that allows tumors to grow and persist. However, exosomes do not always suppress immune responses. Exosomes from immune cells, especially dendritic cells, can enhance anticancer responses by delivering tumor antigens and activating T lymphocytes. Because of this dual role, researchers are actively studying exosomes as tools for cancer immunotherapy, aiming to enhance immune activation and improve lung cancer treatment outcomes (Truong et al., 2020; Wang et al., 2025).

6.4 Immunotherapy strategies in lung cancer

Immune checkpoint inhibitors have become an important treatment for cancer, especially lung cancer. Normally, immune checkpoints control the immune system. They keep it balanced and stop it from overreacting and harming healthy tissues. Cancer cells often take advantage of these checkpoints. This helps them avoid being noticed and destroyed by the immune system. The most studied immune checkpoint involves a protein called PD-1 on T cells and its partner, PD-L1, found on tumor cells. When PD-1 connects with PD-L1, T cells stop working properly. This lets cancer cells live and grow. Immune checkpoint inhibitors are drugs made to block this connection. These drugs help T cells find and attack tumor cells again. Another checkpoint molecule, CTLA-4, also controls T-cell activity and can be blocked by certain drugs (Chen et al., 2025; Jain et al., 2018; Mejía-Guarnizo et al., 2023). In lung cancer treatment, drugs that target PD-1, PD-L1, and CTLA-4 have shown good results by helping the immune system kill tumors. But not all patients respond well, and side effects related to the immune system can happen. Because of this, research is now focusing on better ways to

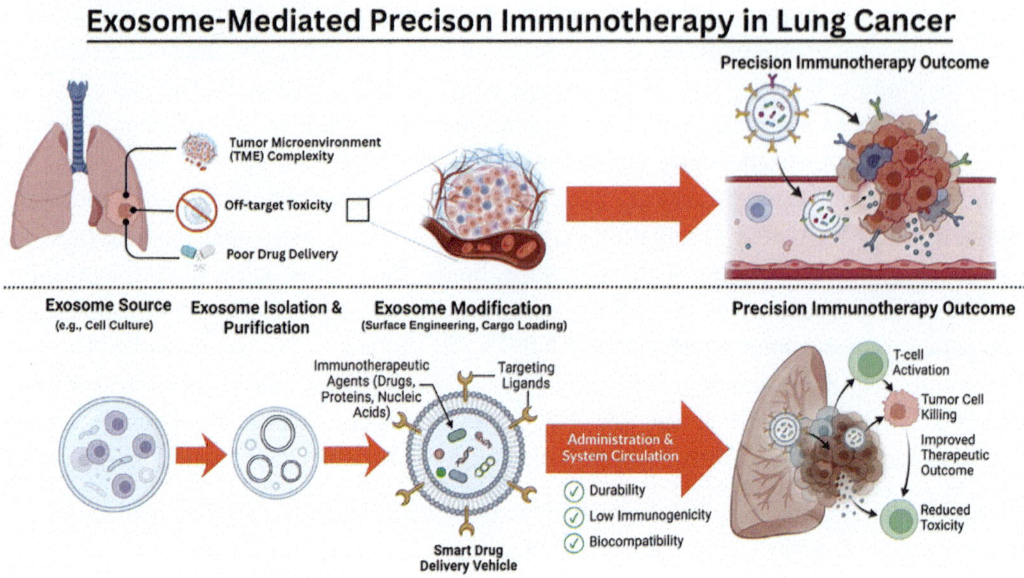

Figure 6.1
Exosome-mediated precision immunotherapy.

deliver these drugs, combining treatments, and personalizing approaches to make immune checkpoint therapy safer and more effective (Fig. 6.1; Wojtukiewicz et al., 2021).

Cancer vaccines and adoptive cell therapy are new types of immunotherapies. Their goal is to help the immune system find and destroy tumor cells. Cancer vaccines work by teaching the immune system to recognize specific markers on tumor cells. These vaccines can include small proteins, genetic material, or parts of tumor cells. They help certain immune cells activate T cells, which increases attacks on cancer cells (Garg et al., 2024; Jou et al., 2021; Rota et al., 2025).

Adoptive cell therapy means taking a patient's own immune cells, usually T cells, out of the body. These cells are then grown or changed in a lab. After that, they are put back into the patient. The changed cells can better recognize and fight cancer cells. Scientists are studying immune cells that enter tumors and modified T-cell treatments. These methods aim to improve lung cancer immunotherapy results (Qian & Liu, 2025; Pu et al., 2024). Lung cancer treatment has advanced, but many challenges remain. Tumor heterogeneity is a major issue. Cancer cells within the same tumor vary in their genetic and functional profiles. This leads to different responses to the same treatments. Cancers can also develop resistance to chemotherapy, targeted therapy, or immunotherapy. As a result, the long-term success of these options decreases. Another challenge is the complex environment around the tumor. Lung tumors interact with nearby cells, chemical signals, and parts of the immune system.

These interactions can weaken the immune response and help tumors grow. This immune-suppressing environment can reduce how well modern immunotherapies, such as immune checkpoint inhibitors, work. It can also be hard to get drugs to reach all parts of the tumor. Some medicines may not reach every cancer cell. Side effects and harmful reactions to the whole body are still big problems in traditional cancer treatments. Many treatments affect healthy tissue as well as cancer, causing side effects and lowering patients' quality of life. It is also still difficult to find reliable markers to predict if a therapy will work. These problems show the need for more focused and new treatments to improve lung cancer care (Lahiri et al., 2023; Liu et al., 2025; Oh et al., 2025).

6.5 Exosomes as smart drug delivery vehicles

Exosomes are widely studied as potential drug carriers because they offer advantages over traditional man-made nanoparticles. Exosomes are tiny, membrane-bound vesicles naturally released by various cell types that help cells communicate. Because they come from living cells, the body readily accepts exosomes, and they are less likely to trigger immune reactions. This makes them attractive for medical treatments (Butreddy et al., 2021; Ferreira et al., 2022). Exosomes transport many biological materials, including proteins, fats, small medicines, and genetic molecules such as miRNA (which controls gene activity) and mRNA (which carries genetic instructions from DNA to the cell's protein-making parts). Their flexibility lets researchers add different treatment agents for various medical goals. Proteins on the exosome surface help them connect with target cells and deliver their contents (Mukerjee et al., 2025; Tenchov et al., 2022).in human fluids than artificial nanoparticles. They remain in the bloodstream for longer periods (Dikici et al., 2025; Sen et al., 2023,). Their small size and natural structure may help them cross some biological barriers. These traits make exosomes promising for direct and effective drug delivery in cancer treatment (Rana et al., 2025; Yang et al., 2024).

Exosomes, naturally released by cells, can target specific cells and interact well with living tissues, making them effective for delivering drugs in cancer treatment. Since they are natural, they cause less immune response than many manmade nanoparticles, reducing the risk of harmful effects or rejection (Chen et al., 2021; Serrano et al., 2025). Exosomes bind to specific target cells via surface proteins and other molecules, allowing them to adhere and enter. Scientists can modify these signals to improve targeting, focusing on proteins abundantly expressed in lung cancer cells or delivering small molecules that can turn off genes or deliver anticancer drugs to tumors. Exosomes from dendritic cells have also been used to carry tumor markers that can start immune responses. These features help make exosomes useful for precise and safe drug delivery (Chao et al., 2025; Kalluri & LeBleu, 2020). Exosomes are attracting attention as drug carriers because they are stable in the body. Their lipid membrane, similar to that of cell membranes, protects their contents from degrading enzymes in bodily fluids. Therapeutic molecules, such as exosomes, are gaining interest as drug carriers because they are stable in the body. Their fat-based membrane, like cell membranes, protects what's inside from enzymes that break down substances in body fluids. Treatment molecules, such as RNA, proteins, or small drugs, remain intact longer in the blood (Butreddy et al., 2021; Chavda et al., 2023). They bind to membranes and enter target cells (Li et al., 2025b).

6.6 Engineering and functionalization of exosomes

Before being studied or used for treatment, exosomes must be carefully removed and cleaned from biological samples. They are very small and are often found together with other particles in fluids such as blood, urine, or cell culture media. Because of this, special methods are needed to separate them. Over time, scientists have developed many methods to isolate exosomes with sufficient purity (Yang et al., 2020). Differential ultracentrifugation is a common method. The sample is spun at different speeds in a centrifuge. The first spins remove cells and large debris. Faster spins collect smaller particles, such as exosomes. This method needs costly equipment and may sometimes collect similar particles (Coughlan et al., 2020). Density gradient centrifugation separates particles based on their density, using substances like sucrose or iodixanol. This method gives purer exosomes than regular centrifugation. Scientists also use size-exclusion chromatography to separate particles by size and keep exosomes intact (Yu et al., 2018). Other methods include filtering, using polymers to make particles clump, and capturing with antibodies. Many studies show that combining these methods yields more reliable and purer exosome samples (Dilsiz, 2024). After isolating and purifying exosomes, they can be loaded with therapeutic substances. To deliver drugs effectively, therapeutic molecules must be encapsulated in exosomes. Scientists have developed methods to load drugs, proteins, and genetic materials, such as siRNA and miRNA, into exosomes. These methods are called passive or active loading (Volpini et al., 2023; Bunggulawa et al., 2018). Passive loading is simple. Exosomes are grown with the drug under controlled conditions. Small, water-repelling drug molecules can pass through the exosome membrane and get enclosed. This method is easy but may result in low drug loading (Gul et al., 2024; Zeng et al., 2023).

Active methods are often used to improve how much of the drug gets loaded. Electroporation is a common technique. It uses a short electrical pulse to make temporary holes in the exosome membrane (the outer surface). This helps genetic materials like siRNA (short pieces of RNA that block gene activity) and miRNA (small RNA molecules that help control gene function) enter the exosomes. Other physical methods include using sound waves (sonication), pushing exosomes through a filter (extrusion), and freezing and thawing them several times. These methods help get more therapeutic agents inside exosomes (Pomatto et al., 2019). An alternative approach involves modifying donor cells to intrinsically produce exosomes preloaded with therapeutic compounds. This cell-based strategy improves loading efficiency while maintaining the exosomes' natural structure and stability. Surface modification is commonly used to enhance exosome targeting. Although exosomes naturally contain membrane proteins that mediate interactions with other cells, engineered surface modifications can further increase the specificity of cargo delivery. This approach is especially beneficial in cancer therapy. Here, the goal is to deliver therapeutic agents directly to tumor cells and minimize effects on healthy tissues (Kim et al., 2024; Sadeghi et al., 2023). A common method is to attach molecules, such as ligands, peptides, or antibodies, that bind to specific targets on the exosome surface. Exosomes are small membrane-covered particles released by cells. These molecules bind receptors, which are proteins on cell surfaces that receive signals and are often abundant on cancer cells. For example, if lung cancer cells have many specific receptors, exosomes can carry ligands that stick to those receptors. This allows targeted delivery to tumor areas (Yang et al., 2022). Another way is to genetically modify donor cells so their exosomes naturally have targeting proteins. This helps them recognize certain cell types. These methods let exosomes deliver drugs or genetic material directly to diseased tissues. This leads to better treatment results and fewer side effects in healthy cells (Choi et al., 2021; Sha et al., 2025).

6.7 Therapeutic applications of exosome-mediated immunotherapy

Exosomes are increasingly studied as vehicles for delivering immunomodulatory drugs in cancer treatment. Immunomodulatory drugs either stimulate or control the immune system. This enhances its ability to recognize and fight cancer cells. A main advantage of using exosomes is their natural ability to interact with immune cells. They also enable the transfer of biological substances between cells (Chen et al., 2022; Feng et al., 2025; Hussain et al., 2022). Researchers have found that exosomes can carry many immunomodulatory compounds. These include cytokines, small interfering RNA, miRNA, and immune checkpoint inhibitors. After delivery, these compounds can affect immune cells in the tumor microenvironment. This helps restore or boost the body's anticancer immune response. For example, exosomes with certain RNA molecules can inhibit genes that promote tumor growth. Others may activate immune cells that attack cancer cells (Kumar et al., 2024). Exosomes can also protect therapeutic compounds from breaking down in the body. This helps ensure that these chemicals reach their target cells more effectively. Because of their stability, biological compatibility, and ability to interact with immune cells, exosomes are attractive options for administering immunomodulatory drugs. They can also enhance the effectiveness of cancer immunotherapy. Exosome-based vaccines are gaining attention as a promising strategy in cancer immunotherapy (Li et al., 2022). This approach uses exosomes, which are small vesicles produced by cells, to deliver tumor antigens to the immune system. This differs from traditional vaccination methods. Exosomes enable cell-to-cell communication and efficiently transmit signals. These signals help immune cells recognize and fight cancer

(Huda & Nurunnabi, 2022; Lu et al., 2024; Sheikhhossein et al., 2024). Early research used exosomes from dendritic cells. These exosomes contain important molecules, such as major histocompatibility complex (MHC) proteins and tumor-associated antigens. These molecules help activate immune cells, including T lymphocytes and natural killer cells. Clinical trials in patients with NSCLC show that dendritic cell-derived exosome vaccines are mostly safe. They can also cause immune responses. However, their effectiveness still needs improvement (Coelho et al., 2025; Liu et al., 2017). Recent studies focus on changing exosomes to improve their effectiveness as vaccines. Scientists have engineered exosomes with tumor antigens, specific peptides, or mRNA linked to lung cancer cells. Some preclinical research has shown that these modified exosomes improve antigen presentation. They also stimulate stronger cytotoxic T-cell responses against tumor cells (Sheikhhossein et al., 2024). Exosomes are stable, biocompatible, and interact well with immune cells. For these reasons, they are widely studied as new platforms for developing stronger cancer vaccines. Exosomes play key roles in immune pathways and help shape the tumor microenvironment. This makes them valuable in cancer immunotherapy. The tumor microenvironment is a complex network of cancer cells, immune cells, stromal cells, and signaling chemicals. Often, it becomes immunosuppressive. This lets tumor cells grow and evade the immune system (Aakel et al., 2025; Li et al., 2025b). Exosomes naturally carry proteins, lipids, and nucleic acids. They can be used to change signaling pathways and strengthen immune responses to tumors. Delivering immune-controlling chemicals through modified exosomes is an interesting tactic. For example, exosomes with miRNA or short-interfering RNA can block genes that help tumors escape the immune system or grow. Likewise, exosomes might carry substances that boost immune cell activity, such as natural killer cells or cytotoxic T lymphocytes. This can help these cells find and destroy cancer cells (Qin et al., 2023; Essola et al., 2024).

6.8 Challenges, clinical translation, and future perspectives

Although interest in exosome-based therapies is growing, using them in clinics and producing them on a large-scale faces big challenges. Exosomes are usually collected from cultured cells or body fluids in lab studies. But the amount collected is often very small. Clinical treatments need much larger and more reliable amounts. Keeping exosomes biologically intact while making these amounts is a major challenge. Consistency is also a big issue. Exosomes from different cell types, or even the same cell under different conditions, can differ in size, makeup, and activity. These differences can affect how well treatments work and make standardization difficult. Exosome batches must be consistent and repeatable to help move treatments into clinics.

Current methods to isolate and purify exosomes have limitations. Techniques, such as ultracentrifugation, common in labs, require a lot of work, are expensive, and cannot easily be scaled up for large production. Keeping exosome quality high is very important because contamination with proteins, cell fragments, or other particles can reduce safety and effectiveness. Also, storage, stability, and transport need careful handling to keep exosomes active. Researchers are working on scalable production systems, including better bioreactors and purification methods. Solving these problems is key to moving exosome therapies from experiments to reliable medical treatments.

Although exosome-based therapies look promising for cancer treatment, there are still major safety and regulatory challenges. These problems need to be solved before these therapies can be widely used in clinics. One main difficulty is that the rules for exosome therapies are still changing. Since exosomes come from living cells and act as natural carriers, they do not fit easily into usual drug or biological product categories, making it harder for health authorities to regulate them.

Keeping exosome preparations consistent and controlled is still very important. Exosome features change based on the cell type, how cells are grown, and how exosomes are isolated, which can affect how safe and effective treatments are. So, having standard production methods and strict quality checks is necessary for medical use. Safety concerns go beyond the main compounds because exosomes may also carry fats, proteins, or genetic material from the original cells. If these are not properly cleaned, they could harm normal cell functions or cause unwanted effects. For example, some exosomes from tumors can weaken the immune system or help tumors grow. These issues highlight the importance of comprehensive characterization, careful purification, and well-designed clinical studies. Such steps are needed to guarantee the safety and efficacy of exosome-based therapeutics for future medical applications. Precision medicine is the future of lung cancer treatment by tailoring therapies to the unique genetic and molecular features of each patient's tumor. Exosome-based technologies are set to play an important role in this, aiming to improve treatment effectiveness while reducing side effects. Modified exosomes have become promising carriers for delivering treatments directly to tumor cells. Changing the surface of exosomes with targeting molecules allows them to specifically recognize lung cancer cells, which reduces side effects on healthy tissues. These tiny vesicles can carry drugs, small RNAs, or molecules that affect the immune system, offering a flexible platform for precise treatment.

Future research is focusing on combining exosome delivery with other treatments such as chemotherapy, immunotherapy, and gene therapy. These combined approaches may help overcome resistance that limits usual treatments. Progress in nanotechnology and bioengineering is expected to improve how exosomes are made, how well they carry treatments, and how precisely they target cells. These advances make large-scale clinical use more possible. The goal is to create personalized exosome therapies based on each patient's tumor. These precise methods could improve treatment success, lower side effects, and provide new options for lung cancer patients. This leads to highly targeted next-generation treatments.

References

Aakel, N., Mohammed, R., Fathima, A., Kerzabi, R., Abdallah, A., & Ibrahim, W. N. (2025). Role of exosome in solid cancer progression and its potential therapeutics in cancer treatment. *Cancer Medicine, 14*(9), e70941.

Azmi, A. S., Bao, B., & Sarkar, F. H. (2013). Exosomes in cancer development, metastasis, and drug resistance: A comprehensive review. *Cancer and Metastasis Reviews, 32*(3), 623–642.

Bray, F., Laversanne, M., Sung, H., Ferlay, J., Siegel, R. L., Soerjomataram, I., & Jemal, A. (2024). Global cancer statistics 2022: GLOBOCAN estimates of incidence and mortality worldwide for 36 cancers in 185 countries. *CA: A Cancer Journal for Clinicians, 74*(3), 229–263.

Bunggulawa, E. J., Wang, W., Yin, T., Wang, N., Durkan, C., Wang, Y., & Wang, G. (2018). Recent advancements in the use of exosomes as drug delivery systems. *Journal of Nanobiotechnology, 16*(1), 81.

Butreddy, A., Kommineni, N., & Dudhipala, N. (2021). Exosomes as naturally occurring vehicles for delivery of biopharmaceuticals: Insights from drug delivery to clinical perspectives. *Nanomaterials, 11*(6), 1481.

Chao, T., Zhao, J., Gao, R., Wang, H., Guo, J., Gao, Z., & Wang, Y. (2025). Exosome surface modification and functionalization: A narrative review of emerging technologies and their application potential in precision medicine. *Advanced Technology in Neuroscience, 2*(1), 27–33.

Chavda, V. P., Pandya, A., Kumar, L., Raval, N., Vora, L. K., Pulakkat, S., & Tang, B. Z. (2023). Exosome nanovesicles: A potential carrier for therapeutic delivery. *Nano Today, 49*, 101771.

Chen, H., Wang, L., Zeng, X., Schwarz, H., Nanda, H. S., Peng, X., & Zhou, Y. (2021). Exosomes, a new star for targeted delivery. *Frontiers in Cell and Developmental Biology, 9*, 751079.

Chen, H., Yang, H., Guo, L., & Sun, Q. (2025). The role of immune checkpoint inhibitors in cancer therapy: Mechanism and therapeutic advances. *MedComm, 6*(10), e70412.

Chen, L., Wang, L., Zhu, L., Xu, Z., Liu, Y., Li, Z., Zhou, J., & Luo, F. (2022). Exosomes as drug carriers in anti-cancer therapy. *Frontiers in Cell and Developmental Biology, 10*, 728616. doi:10.3389/fcell.2022.728616.

Choi, H., Choi, Y., Yim, H. Y., Mirzaaghasi, A., Yoo, J. K., & Choi, C. (2021). Biodistribution of exosomes and engineering strategies for targeted delivery of therapeutic exosomes. *Tissue Engineering and Regenerative Medicine, 18*(4), 499–511.

Coelho, M. O., Quintas, S. T., Sarmento, B., De Wever, O., & Castro, F. (2025). Engineered dendritic cells-derived extracellular vesicles for cancer immunotherapy. *Journal of Controlled Release, 381*, 113620.

Coughlan, C., Bruce, K. D., Burgy, O., Boyd, T. D., Michel, C. R., Garcia-Perez, J. E., & Potter, H. (2020). Exosome isolation by ultracentrifugation and precipitation and techniques for downstream analyses. *Current Protocols in Cell Biology, 88*(1), e110.

Deng, Y., & Zhang, X. (2025). Multidimensional predictive model of survival risk in small cell lung cancer patients: A comprehensive analysis based on clinical characteristics and treatment strategies. *Current Problems in Surgery, 66*, 101759.

Dikici, E., Acet, B. Ö., Gül, D., Kummer, N., Stauber, R. H., Odabaşı, M., & Acet, Ö. (2025). Bringing exosomes into the game: Current situation, opportunities, limitations and future perspectives. *Materials Today Advances, 28*, 100623.

Dilsiz, N. (2024). A comprehensive review on recent advances in exosome isolation and characterization: Toward clinical applications. *Translational Oncology, 50*, 102121.

Essola, J. M., Zhang, M., Yang, H., Li, F., Xia, B., Mavoungou, J. F., & Huang, Y. (2024). Exosome regulation of immune response mechanism: Pros and cons in immunotherapy. *Bioactive Materials, 32*, 124–146.

Feng, P., Zhang, X., Gao, J., Jiang, L., & Li, Y. (2025). The roles of exosomes in anti-cancer drugs. *Cancer Medicine, 14*(9), e70897.

Ferreira, D., Moreira, J. N., & Rodrigues, L. R. (2022). New advances in exosome-based targeted drug delivery systems. *Critical Reviews in Oncology/Hematology, 172*, 103628.

Fordjour, F. K., Guo, C., Ai, Y., Daaboul, G. G., & Gould, S. J. (2022). A shared, stochastic pathway mediates exosome protein budding along plasma and endosome membranes. *Journal of Biological Chemistry, 298*(10), 102394.

Fu, S., Wang, Y., Xia, X., & Zheng, J. C. (2020). Exosome engineering: Current progress in cargo loading and targeted delivery. *NanoImpact, 20*, 100261.

Garg, P., Pareek, S., Kulkarni, P., Horne, D., Salgia, R., & Singhal, S. S. (2024). Next-generation immunotherapy: Advancing clinical applications in cancer treatment. *Journal of Clinical Medicine, 13*(21), 6537.

Godoy, L. A., Chen, J., Ma, W., Lally, J., Toomey, K. A., Rajappa, P., Sheridan, R., Mahajan, S., Stollenwerk, N., Phan, C. T., & Cheng, D. (2023). Emerging precision neoadjuvant systemic therapy for patients with resectable non-small cell lung cancer: Current status and perspectives. *Biomarker Research, 11*(1), 7.

Gul, R., Bashir, H., Sarfraz, M., Shaikh, A. J., Jardan, Y. A. B., Hussain, Z., & Amirzada, M. I. (2024). Human plasma derived exosomes: Impact of active and passive drug loading approaches on drug delivery. *Saudi Pharmaceutical Journal, 32*(6), 102096.

Guo, Y., Ji, X., Liu, J., Fan, D., Zhou, Q., Chen, C., Wang, W., Wang, G., Wang, H., Yuan, W., Ji, Z., & Sun, Z. (2019). Effects of exosomes on pre-metastatic niche formation in tumors. *Molecular Cancer, 18*(1), 39. doi:10.1186/s12943-019-0995-1.

He, J., Ren, W., Wang, W., Han, W., Jiang, L., Zhang, D., & Guo, M. (2022). Exosomal targeting and its potential clinical application. *Drug Delivery and Translational Research, 12*(10), 2385–2402.

Hu, Q., Su, H., Li, J., Lyon, C., Tang, W., Wan, M., & Hu, T. Y. (2020). Clinical applications of exosome membrane proteins. *Precision Clinical Medicine, 3*(1), 54–66.

Huda, M. N., & Nurunnabi, M. (2022). Potential application of exosomes in vaccine development and delivery: Huda, Walker and Nurunnabi. *Pharmaceutical Research, 39*(11), 2635–2671.

Hussain, M. W. A., Jahangir, S., Ghosh, B., Yesmin, F., Anis, A., Satil, S. N., & Rashid, M. H. (2022). Exosomes for regulation of immune responses and immunotherapy. *Journal of Nanotheranostics, 3*(1), 55–85.

Ingenito, F., Roscigno, G., Affinito, A., Nuzzo, S., Scognamiglio, I., Quintavalle, C., & Condorelli, G. (2019). The role of exo-miRNAs in cancer: A focus on therapeutic and diagnostic applications. *International Journal of Molecular Sciences, 20*(19), 4687.

Jain, P., Jain, C., & Velcheti, V. (2018). Role of immune-checkpoint inhibitors in lung cancer. *Therapeutic Advances in Respiratory Disease, 12*, 1753465817750075.

Jou, J., Harrington, K. J., Zocca, M. B., Ehrnrooth, E., & Cohen, E. E. (2021). The changing landscape of therapeutic cancer vaccines—novel platforms and neoantigen identification. *Clinical Cancer Research, 27*(3), 689–703.

Kalluri, R., & LeBleu, V. S. (2020). The biology, function, and biomedical applications of exosomes. *Science, 367*(6478), eaau6977. doi:10.1126/science. aau6977.

Kim, H. I., Park, J., Zhu, Y., Wang, X., Han, Y., & Zhang, D. (2024). Recent advances in extracellular vesicles for therapeutic cargo delivery. *Experimental & Molecular Medicine, 56*(4), 836–849.

Kumar, M. A., Baba, S. K., Sadida, H. Q., Marzooqi, S. A., Jerobin, J., Altemani, F. H., & Bhat, A. A. (2024). Extracellular vesicles as tools and targets in therapy for diseases. *Signal Transduction and Targeted Therapy, 9*(1), 27.

Lahiri, A., Maji, A., Potdar, P. D., Singh, N., Parikh, P., Bisht, B., & Paul, M. K. (2023). Lung cancer immunotherapy: Progress, pitfalls, and promises. *Molecular Cancer, 22*(1), 40.

Li, J., Peng, J., Wang, J., & Chen, Z. (2025a). The dual role of exosomes in the tumor microenvironment: From pro-tumorigenic signaling to immune modulation. *Medical Research, 1*(2), 257–284.

Li, J., Wang, J., & Chen, Z. (2025b). Emerging role of exosomes in cancer therapy: Progress and challenges. *Molecular Cancer, 24*(1), 13.

Li, T., Li, X., Han, G., Liang, M., Yang, Z., Zhang, C., & Yu, S. (2022). The therapeutic potential and clinical significance of exosomes as carriers of drug delivery system. *Pharmaceutics, 15*(1), 21.

Lin, Y., Anderson, J. D., Rahnama, L. M., Gu, S. V., & Knowlton, A. A. (2020). Exosomes in disease and regeneration: Biological functions, diagnostics, and beneficial effects. *American Journal of Physiology-Heart and Circulatory Physiology, 319*(6), H1162–H1180.

Liu, H., Chen, L., Peng, Y., Yu, S., Liu, J., Wu, L., & Liu, T. (2017). Dendritic cells loaded with tumor derived exosomes for cancer immunotherapy. *Oncotarget, 9*(2), 2887.

Liu, L., Yang, L., Li, H., Shang, T., & Liu, L. (2025). The tumor microenvironment in lung cancer: Heterogeneity, therapeutic resistance and emerging treatment strategies. *International Journal of Oncology, 68*(1), 11.

Lu, M., Xing, H., Zhao, X., Huang, Y., Zheng, A., & Liang, X. J. (2024). Engineered extracellular vesicles as a next-generation vaccine platform. *Matter, 7*(12), 4180–4205.

Mejía-Guarnizo, L. V., Monroy-Camacho, P. S., Turizo-Smith, A. D., & Rodríguez-García, J. A. (2023). The role of immune checkpoints in antitumor response: A potential antitumor immunotherapy. *Frontiers in Immunology, 14*, 1298571.

Mukerjee, N., Bhattacharya, A., Maitra, S., Kaur, M., Ganesan, S., Mishra, S., & Thorat, N. D. (2025). Exosome isolation and characterization for advanced diagnostic and therapeutic applications. *Materials Today Bio, 31*, 101613.

Oh, M. S., Abascal, J., Rennels, A. K., Salehi-Rad, R., Dubinett, S. M., & Liu, B. (2025). Tumor heterogeneity and the immune response in non-small cell lung cancer: Emerging insights and implications for immunotherapy. *Cancers, 17*(6), 1027.

Padinharayil, H., Alappat, R. R., Joy, L. M., Anilkumar, K. V., Wilson, C. M., George, A., & Ganesan, R. (2022). Advances in the lung cancer immunotherapy approaches. *Vaccines, 10*(11), 1963.

Papoutsoglou, P., & Morillon, A. (2024). Extracellular vesicle lncRNAs as key biomolecules for cell-to-cell communication and circulating cancer biomarkers. *Non-Coding RNA, 10*(6), 54.

Pomatto, M. A. C., Bussolati, B., D'Antico, S., Ghiotto, S., Tetta, C., Brizzi, M. F., & Camussi, G. (2019). Improved loading of plasma-derived extracellular vesicles to encapsulate antitumor miRNAs. *Molecular Therapy Methods & Clinical Development, 13*, 133–144.

Pu, J., Liu, T., Sharma, A., Jiang, L., Wei, F., Ren, X., & Hou, J. (2024). Advances in adoptive cellular immunotherapy and therapeutic breakthroughs in multiple myeloma. *Experimental Hematology & Oncology, 13*(1), 105.

Qian, J., & Liu, Y. (2025). Recent advances in adoptive cell therapy for cancer immunotherapy. *Frontiers in Immunology, 16*, 1665488.

Qin, S., Cao, J., & Ma, X. (2023). Function and clinical application of exosome—how to improve tumor immunotherapy? *Frontiers in Cell and Developmental Biology, 11*, 1228624.

Rajput, A., Varshney, A., Bajaj, R., & Pokharkar, V. (2022). Exosomes as new generation vehicles for drug delivery: Biomedical applications and future perspectives. *Molecules, 27*(21), 7289.

Rana, R., Devi, S. N., Bhardwaj, A. K., Yashavarddhan, M. H., Bohra, D., & Ganguly, N. K. (2025). Exosomes as nature's nano carriers: Promising drug delivery tools and targeted therapy for glioma. *Biomedicine & Pharmacotherapy, 182*, 117754.

Rota, M., Torresan, I., Palmerio, S., Tasselli, E., Rossi, A., Zivi, A., & Zacchi, F. (2025). The role of therapeutic cancer vaccines in the modern immunotherapy era: State of the art with recent progress and future challenges. *Critical Reviews in Oncology/Hematology, 217*, 105068.

Sadeghi, S., Tehrani, F. R., Tahmasebi, S., Shafiee, A., & Hashemi, S. M. (2023). Exosome engineering in cell therapy and drug delivery. *Inflammopharmacology, 31*(1), 145–169.

Sen, S., Xavier, J., Kumar, N., Ahmad, M. Z., & Ranjan, O. P. (2023). Exosomes as natural nanocarrier-based drug delivery system: Recent insights and future perspectives. *3 Biotech, 13*(3), 101.

Serrano, D. R., Juste, F., Anaya, B. J., Ramirez, B. I., Sánchez-Guirales, S. A., Quispillo, J. M., & Lalatsa, A. (2025). Exosome-based drug delivery: A next-generation platform for cancer, infection, neurological and immunological diseases, gene therapy and regenerative medicine. *Pharmaceutics, 17*(10), 1336.

Sha, M., Gao, Y., Yin, X., Li, X., Liu, C., & Li, S. (2025). Engineered exosomes: A promising approach for overcoming challenges in pancreatic cancer therapy. *Journal of Nanobiotechnology, 23*(1), 619.

Sheikhhossein, H. H., Iommelli, F., Di Pietro, N., Curia, M. C., Piattelli, A., Palumbo, R., & De Rosa, V. (2024). Exosome-like systems: From therapies to vaccination for cancer treatment and prevention—Exploring the state of the art. *Vaccines, 12*(5), 519.

Tenchov, R., Sasso, J. M., Wang, X., Liaw, W. S., Chen, C. A., & Zhou, Q. A. (2022). Exosomes–nature's lipid nanoparticles, a rising star in drug delivery and diagnostics. *ACS Nano, 16*(11), 17802–17846.

Truong, N. C., Huynh, T. N., Pham, K. D., & Van Pham, P. (2020). The role of tumor-derived exosomes in tumor immune escape: A concise review. *Biomedical Research and Therapy, 7*(11), 4132–4137.

Verginadis, I. I., Citrin, D. E., Ky, B., Feigenberg, S. J., Georgakilas, A. G., Hill-Kayser, C. E., & Lin, A. (2025). Radiotherapy toxicities: Mechanisms, management, and future directions. *The Lancet, 405*(10475), 338–352.

Volpini, L., Monaco, F., Santarelli, L., Neuzil, J., & Tomasetti, M. (2023). Advances in RNA cancer therapeutics: New insight into exosomes as miRNA delivery. *Aspects of Molecular Medicine, 1*, 100005.

Wang, W., Qiao, S., Kong, X., Zhang, G., & Cai, Z. (2025). The role of exosomes in immunopathology and potential therapeutic implications. *Cellular & Molecular Immunology, 22*(9), 975–995.

Wei, H., Chen, Q., Lin, L., Sha, C., Li, T., Liu, Y., Yin, X., Xu, Y., Chen, L., Gao, W., & Li, Y. (2021). Regulation of exosome production and cargo sorting. *International Journal of Biological Sciences, 17*(1), 163.

Wei, R., Liu, S., Zhang, S., Min, L., & Zhu, S. (2020). Cellular and extracellular components in tumor microenvironment and their application in early diagnosis of cancers. *Analytical Cellular Pathology*, 6283796. doi:10.1155/2020/6283796.

Wojtukiewicz, M. Z., Rek, M. M., Karpowicz, K., Górska, M., Polityńska, B., Wojtukiewicz, A. M., & Honn, K. V. (2021). Inhibitors of immune checkpoints—PD-1, PD-L1, CTLA-4—new opportunities for cancer patients and a new challenge for internists and general practitioners. *Cancer and Metastasis Reviews, 40*(3), 949–982.

Xie, S., Zhang, Q., & Jiang, L. (2022). Current knowledge on exosome biogenesis, cargo-sorting mechanism and therapeutic implications. *Membranes, 12*(5), 498.

Xu, M., Ji, J., Jin, D., Wu, Y., Wu, T., Lin, R., Zhu, S., Jiang, F., Ji, Y., Bao, B., & Li, M. (2023). The biogenesis and secretion of exosomes and multivesicular bodies (MVBs): Intercellular shuttles and implications in human diseases. *Genes & Diseases, 10*(5), 1894–1907.

Yang, D., Zhang, W., Zhang, H., Zhang, F., Chen, L., Ma, L., & Wang, T. (2020). Progress, opportunity, and perspective on exosome isolation-efforts for efficient exosome-based theranostics. *Theranostics, 10*(8), 3684.

Yang, K., Jia, M., Cheddah, S., Zhang, Z., Wang, W., Li, X., & Yan, C. (2022). Peptide ligand-SiO2 microspheres with specific affinity for phosphatidylserine as a new strategy to isolate exosomes and application in proteomics to differentiate hepatic cancer. *Bioactive Materials, 15*, 343–354.

Yang, Q., Li, S., Ou, H., Zhang, Y., Zhu, G., Li, S., & Lei, L. (2024). Exosome-based delivery strategies for tumor therapy: An update on modification, loading, and clinical application. *Journal of Nanobiotechnology, 22*(1), 41.

Yokoi, A., & Ochiya, T. (2021). Exosomes and extracellular vesicles: Rethinking the essential values in cancer biology. In *Seminars in cancer biology: 74* (pp. 79–91). Academic Press. doi:10.1016/j.semcancer.2021.03.032.

Yu, L. L., Zhu, J., Liu, J. X., Jiang, F., Ni, W. K., Qu, L. S., & Xiao, M. B. (2018). A comparison of traditional and novel methods for the separation of exosomes from human samples. *BioMed Research International, 2018*(1), 3634563.

Zafar, A., Khatoon, S., Khan, M. J., Abu, J., & Naeem, A. (2025). Advancements and limitations in traditional anti-cancer therapies: A comprehensive review of surgery, chemotherapy, radiation therapy, and hormonal therapy. *Discover Oncology, 16*(1), 607.

Zeng, H., Guo, S., Ren, X., Wu, Z., Liu, S., & Yao, X. (2023). Current strategies for exosome cargo loading and targeting delivery. *Cells, 12*(10), 1416.

CHAPTER 7

Gold nanoparticles in the battle against lung cancer: Biomedical applications and therapeutic innovations

Sarita Sharma[a], Gajender Sharma[b], Deepa Rani[c], Sumeet Gupta[d] and Samir Mehndiratta[e]

[a]Department of Pharmacology, Amity Institute of Pharmacy, Amity University Madhya Pradesh, Gwalior, India [b]Department of Pharmacology, M.M. College of Pharmacy, Maharishi Markandeshwar (Deemed to be University), Ambala, Haryana, India [c]M.M. College of Pharmacy, Maharishi Markandeshwar (Deemed to be University), Ambala, Haryana, India [d]M. M. College of Pharmacy, Maharishi Markandeshwar (Deemed to be University), Ambala, Haryana, India [e]Department of Discipline of Pharmacy, Graduate School of Health, University of Technology Sydney, Ultimo, NSW, Australia

7.1 Introduction

7.1.1 Lung cancer burden and treatment limitations

Cancer of the lung is the number one primary cause of cancer-related deaths, contributing to almost 1.8 million deaths globally per year. Lung cancer also ranks as one of the most prevalent malignancies in the world, with over 2 million new cases reported annually (WHO). Late diagnosis, aggressive tumors, and limited access to early lung cancer screening have contributed to the high rate of lung cancer deaths in many settings.

There are two types of lung cancer: Nonsmall cell lung cancer (NSCLC, 85%) and small cell lung cancer (SCLC, 15%). NSCLC represents most lung cancers; SCLC tends to be the more aggressive type of lung cancer and has a more rapid growth rate. The principal cause of lung cancer is smoking, accounting for over 85% of all lung cancers. Lung cancer can also strike nonsmokers from second-hand smoke exposure, exposure to radon, asbestos, and/or air pollution, carcinogenic risk factors in their workplaces, or inherited genetic susceptibility to developing cancer.

Nanoengineered Therapeutics for Lung Cancer: Advanced Drug Delivery Strategies.
DOI: https://doi.org/10.1016/B978-0-443-44585-9.00016-0

In recent years, rising levels of air pollution in urban and industrialized regions have further contributed to global incidence rates. Symptoms often do not appear until the disease has progressed to an advanced stage. Early signs may include a persistent cough, coughing up blood (hemoptysis), chest pain, hoarseness, fatigue, unexplained weight loss, recurrent respiratory infections, and shortness of breath. Because these symptoms can resemble less severe respiratory conditions, diagnosis is frequently delayed (Schabath & Cote, 2019).

The severity of lung cancer as a global public health threat is evident from the fact that the World Health Organization and International Organization for Cancer Research estimate that there are approximately 2.2 million new cases of lung cancer diagnosed around the world each year. This represents more than 12% of all new cases of cancer diagnosed globally, making it the largest cause of cancer-related deaths, accounting for around 1.8 million total deaths due to lung cancer globally every year, accounting for almost 18% of all cancer deaths globally.

7.1.2 Lung cancer's incidence and mortality rates show substantial geographical variation

Historically, more advanced nations, such as the United States, Canada, and the majority of Western Europe, have reported significantly higher rates of lung cancer than less developed countries. Possible reasons for this higher rate of lung cancer incidence and mortality include:

- Widespread use of tobacco (continued high rates of lifetime smoking)
- Significant industrial exposure to carcinogenic agents
- Age-related elevated chance of lung cancer development
- Improved methods of diagnosis and reporting

In the United States alone, lung cancer is the number one cancer killer for both men and women and causes more deaths from cancer than breast, prostate, and colorectal cancers combined (Howlader et al., 2020).

The difficulties associated with early detection of lung cancer make it a significant burden, in addition to the high mortality rate associated with the disease. One must make an effort to decrease their use of tobacco as well as their exposure to other risk factors to contribute to the reduction of the burden that society bears. Although survival rates have recently increased, lung cancer continues to be a significant public health concern on a global scale (Dela Cruz et al., 2011).

Lung cancer presents major therapeutic restrictions that affect not only the availability of medications but also the success rate of therapy. Surgery on those with limited lung capacity or tumors in the middle of the chest is either risky or impossible (Sharma et al., 2023).

Even though radiation treatment is often successful, it may cause severe adverse effects and is not appropriate for a large number of individuals. Immunotherapy, on the other hand, shows promise, despite the fact that it only helps a limited number of patients. Furthermore, nanomedicines have a difficult time precisely targeting tumor cells, which would increase the likelihood that they are less effective (Sharma et al., 2023).

When all these limits are considered together, it becomes clear that individualized treatment plans and continued research into more effective treatments are required to improve the results for lung cancer patients. Despite these obstacles, early diagnosis and stopping smoking continue to be of the utmost importance in terms of lowering the incidence of lung cancer and increasing the percentage of people who survive the disease (Sharma et al., 2023).

7.1.3 Nanomedicine and gold nanoparticles

Nanomedicine is a multifaceted field that contributes to the improvement of healthcare via the combination of medical applications and nanotechnology. Imaging, drug delivery, diagnosis, and therapy are some of the medical applications that potentially gain from the application of nanoscale technologies and materials. These applications range from 1 to 100 nm in size (Vangijzegem et al., 2023).

7.1.4 Significant applications for nanomedicine

Among the conditions perhaps treatable using nanomedicine are diabetes, cancer, cardiovascular disease, and neurological disorders. This branch of medicine has great potential (Saha, 2009). Its ability to provide concentrated and customized medications while also lowering the possibility of side effects helps to completely overhaul the healthcare system. Though it is still in its infancy, it is expected that nanomedicine will become quite important in the evolution of future medical procedures. Besides enhancing human health, nanomedicine will provide innovative approaches to curing diseases (Sim & Wong, 2021).

7.1.5 Gold nanoparticles have become prevalent in nanomedicine owing to a number of significant properties they possess

Biocompatibility and inertness: AuNPs fit for use in biological systems because of their chemical inertness and nontoxic character (Sim & Wong, 2021).

Flexibility in functioning: They may be readily changed to include other molecules, including drugs or antibodies, therefore enabling more focused delivery and more powerful therapeutic effects (Carabineiro, 2017; Sweeney, 2015).

Optical properties: Surface plasmon resonance (SPR) and other optical characteristics of AuNPs allow photothermal treatment and imaging applications (Sweeney, 2015).

High surface area: Their small size and great surface area allow them to interact with biological molecules and cells enough (Carabineiro, 2017; Malik et al., 2023).

7.2 Objectives and scope

7.2.1 Objectives

The remarkable properties of nanoparticles of gold nanoparticles (AuNPs) have led to a lot of research on them. In the realm of biomedicine, these nanoparticles are quite flexible and fit for many uses. Mostly, the use of AuNPs is meant to achieve the following:

Biomedical diagnostics: AuNPs are used in biological sensors, immunoassays, and medicinal chemistry under improved imaging techniques such as optical bioimaging and computed tomography (CT) scans to detect disorders, including cancer (Milan et al., 2022).

Targeted drug delivery: They act as carriers to deliver drugs, antigens, and DNA to specific locations, thereby reducing adverse effects and improving effectiveness (Arvizo et al., 2010; Milan et al., 2022).

Therapeutic uses: Through their capacity to absorb and transform light into heat, AuNPs are used in photodynamic and photothermal therapies to treat cancer (Arvizo et al., 2010; Milan et al., 2022).

Monitoring and magnification: Their optical properties enable the imaging and detection of tissues and cells, supporting the investigation of biological mechanisms and processes like endocytosis (Milan et al., 2022).

7.2.2 Scope

Among the many fields where AuNPs find use are the following:

Medical applications: In a variety of medical specialties, they are employed in evaluation, therapy, prevention, and cleanliness (Khlebtsov & Dykman, 2011).

Nanomedicine: AuNPs play a crucial role in nanomedicine, particularly in cancer treatment and diagnostics, by offering targeted and noninvasive therapies (Arvizo et al., 2010; Khlebtsov & Dykman, 2011).

Biotechnology: Its uses in clinical chemistry, biosensorics, and genomics enable breakthroughs in these domains (Arvizo et al., 2010b; Khlebtsov & Dykman, 2011).

Scanning technologies: AuNPs improve contrast in techniques for imaging like magnetic resonance imaging (MRIs) and CT scans, making tissues and malignancies easier to identify (Arvizo et al., 2010; Khlebtsov & Dykman, 2011).

7.3 Gold nanoparticles-properties and biomedical potential

7.3.1 Physicochemical properties

AuNPs have attracted a lot of attention from many different fields and may be employed in a wide spectrum of biological applications because of their different physicochemical properties. Among them include their shape, scale, stability, optical properties, and biocompatibility.

7.3.2 Shape and size

Variability: From 1 nm to several 100 nm, AuNPs may have very different diameters and show spherical, octahedral, decahedral, nanorods, and nano prisms (Tkachenko et al., 2003).

Effect on properties: The form and size of AuNPs change their optical and electrical characteristics. Bigger nanoparticles, for instance, absorb light at longer wavelengths, whereas smaller ones often grab light in the green and blue spectrum (Tkachenko et al., 2003).

7.3.3 Surface chemistry

Modification: The surface of AuNPs may be changed using various distinct molecules. Among these compounds are biological recognition molecules, small molecules, and polymers. This makes them appropriate for use in medicinal delivery systems as well as imaging ones (Tkachenko et al., 2003).

Stability: By keeping the same surface charge throughout the process, surface modification helps to prevent aggregation. This is very important to protect optical features and lower the unwanted contact count in biological environments (Tkachenko et al., 2003).

7.3.4 Stability and biocompatibility

Noncytotoxicity: Because AuNPs are typically noncytotoxic, they can be used in biological applications (Tkachenko et al., 2003).

Stability: Surface variations that stop aggregation and guarantee consistent performance in multiple environments improve their stability (Tkachenko et al., 2003).

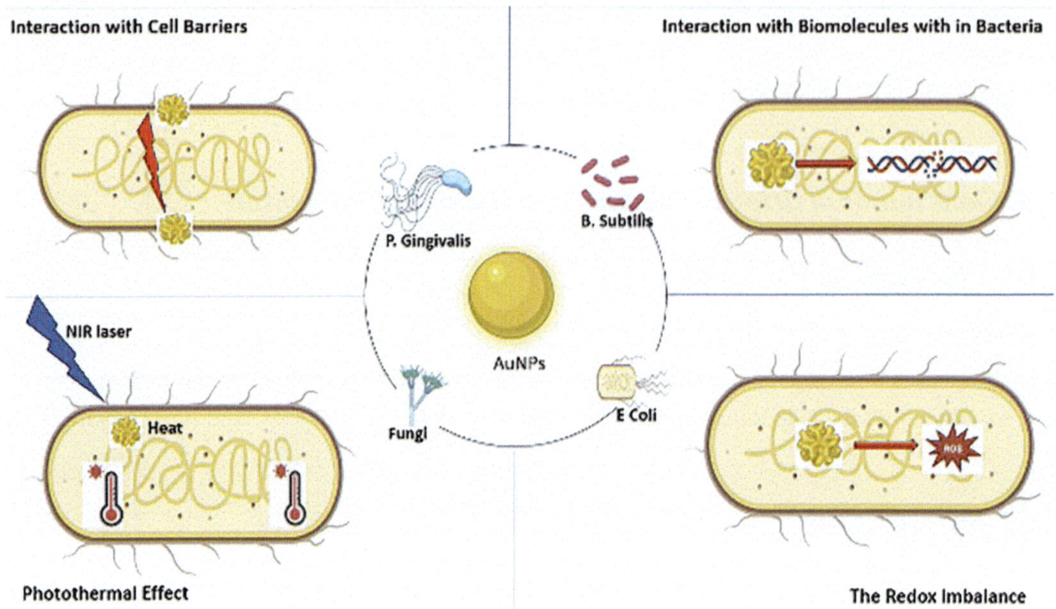

Figure 7.1
Mechanism of interactions of gold nanoparticles (AuNPs) with biological systems.

7.4 Mechanism of interactions with biological systems

Their uses in the realms of biotechnology and medicine depend much on the many ways in which AuNPs interact with biological systems. Important elements engaged in these interactions are the ones listed later and represented in Fig. 7.1.

Protein adsorption and surface modification: The proteins in the surrounding region rapidly adsorb onto the surface of the AuNPs when they are added to a biological medium, therefore changing the hydrodynamic radius and charge of the proteins. This mechanism shapes both the cellular uptake and the toxicity of these compounds (Alkilany & Murphy, 2010).

Cellular uptake: Under certain conditions, such as the charge of the surface, the hydrophobicity of the ligand, and the structure of the ligand, AuNPs may enter cells by endocytosis or through direct transmembrane penetration. Numerous instances involve the use of cationic and electrostatic interactions between nanoparticles and a cell with negatively charged membranes (Alkilany & Murphy, 2010).

Interactions with biological molecules: AuNPs may be used as templates to build ordered arrays that are useful for biosensors and catalysis. This can be accomplished via the use of biological molecules. Additionally, they have the potential to serve as a building block for ligands that are attached, thus enhancing essential activities that are associated with biological molecules (Alkilany & Murphy, 2010; Arvizo et al., 2010).

Toxicity considerations: The nanoparticles themselves are not always to blame for the toxicity of AuNPs; rather, it is the residual surfactants, such as Cetyltrimethylammonium Bromide (CTAB), that end up being culpable. It is vital to have good filtration to reduce toxicity (Alkilany & Murphy, 2010; Arvizo et al., 2010).

7.5 Advantages of gold nanoparticles in cancer therapy

Biological compatibility and minimal toxicity: AuNPs are safe for usage in the human body due to their great biocompatibility and low toxicity (Nisha et al., 2024).

Size tunability: Their efficacy in delivering drugs can be raised by adjusting their size to maximize delivery and contact with cancer cells (Nisha et al., 2024).

Diagnostic and therapeutic uses: AuNPs can be applied to therapies such as photothermal treatment and radio sensitization, as well as diagnostic imaging (Nisha et al., 2024).

Targeted delivery: By integrating them with targeting ligands, medications can be delivered to cancer cells solely, limiting negative effects on healthy tissues (Nisha et al., 2024).

Immunotherapy synergistic effects: By increasing immune responses and enhancing tumor management, AuNPs can improve immunotherapy (Nisha et al., 2024).

Passive and active tumor targeting: Due to their tiny size, AuNPs can passively aggregate in tumors. They can also be altered for active targeting through the use of certain molecules (Nisha et al., 2024).

7.6 Diagnostic applications of gold nanoparticles in lung cancer

The likelihood of surviving and having your treatments succeed is greatly influenced by finding and treating lung cancer early. Cases of lung cancer have a much higher rate of survival, measured at 5 years from the time of diagnosis, if they are diagnosed early enough to be treated before they have spread beyond the lungs, than if they are diagnosed at a later stage. For example, the survival rate after 5 years for stage 1 patients may be above 60%–80% compared with stage 4 patients, who have a survival rate under 10% after 5 years. Additionally, because lung cancers that are detected early are less likely to have invades (metastasized) into the surrounding lymph nodes or other organs, patients diagnosed at an earlier stage are likely to have access to less invasive treatment options (e.g., surgery and targeted therapy) which may lead to fewer and less severe treatment-related complications and allow the patient to have a better quality of life after treatment (Guinart et al., 2021).

7.7 Biomarker-based methods

Serum tumor markers: Sensors based on AuNPs technology might detect many among the biomarkers, including carcinoembryonic antigen (CEA) and neuron-specific enolase (NSE). These signals help to identify lung cancer early on and track the development of the illness (Guinart et al., 2021; Ostrin et al., 2020).

Multiplex detection: Techniques incorporating AuNPs allow for the simultaneous identification of many biomarkers, increasing diagnostic precision and reducing processing time (Guinart et al., 2021; Ostrin et al., 2020).

Electrochemical biosensors: Clinical applications can benefit from the excellent sensitivity and quick, label-free detection provided by electrochemical biosensors (Bhardwaj et al., 2024; Ostrin et al., 2020).

7.8 Biosensing and imaging techniques

AuNPs represent a useful instrument for lung cancer diagnostics. AuNPs exhibit unique physical and chemical attributes like extremely high SPR, very large surface area-to-volume ratio, highly efficient electrical conductivity, and biocompatibility, making them ideally suited to detect small amounts of lung cancers. The optical and electrical characteristics of AuNPs allow them to produce enhanced signals from absorbed and scattered light, making AuNPs excellent contrast enhancers in imaging methods, including CT and photoacoustic imaging. Target-specific binding improves sensitivity and specificity for detecting lung cancer-related indicators like epidermal growth factor receptor (EGFR), circulating tumor DNA, and specific protein signatures. AuNPs possess significant potential for early-stage detection of malignant disease, with targeted binding improving sensitivity and specificity using CT versus conventional imaging modalities. AuNPs can also be developed as biosensors for the quantitative measurement of very small quantities of tumor markers in blood, sputum, or breath samples, thus enabling diagnostic techniques that minimally invade or do not invade the patient's body. The high electrical conductivity of AuNPs also facilitates the incorporation of AuNPs into an electrochemical platform for real-time biomarker monitoring. The difficulty in diagnosing early-stage lung cancer, because they frequently present asymptomatically, makes AuNPs an important addition to diagnostic systems for increasing the accuracy of lung cancer screening and promoting personalized treatment approaches, ultimately resulting in improved patient outcomes (Guinart et al., 2021).

7.9 Biosensing techniques

Immunosensors: By modifying AuNPs with antibodies, it is possible to identify certain antigens in blood samples, strengthening the sensitivity and speed of lung cancer diagnosis (Guinart et al., 2021; Usman et al., 2021).

Electrochemical biosensors: AuNPs are used in electrochemical biosensors for the purpose of signal amplification. This permits the rapid and independent detection of biomarkers, such as NSE, without the need for labeling (Guinart et al., 2021; Usman et al., 2021).

7.9.1 Imaging techniques

CT scans: By enhancing X-ray attenuation, AuNPs can improve CT image contrast and enable upgraded tumor visibility with lower radiation dosages (Guinart et al., 2021; Usman et al., 2021).

Plasmonic sensors: AuNPs offer great specificity as well as sensitivity in the detection of lung cancer by using SPR technology to find biomarkers (Guinart et al., 2021; Usman et al., 2021).

7.9.2 Role of nanoparticles of gold in early detection of lung cancer

At both the University of Colorado Cancer Center and Technion—Israel Institute of Technology, researchers are working together on a highly sensitive breath-analysis instrument that uses functionalized AuNPs to characterize and measure volatile organic compounds (VOC) found within exhaled air. Functionalized AuNPs have specific organic ligands that will only respond to certain patterns of VOCs within exhaled breath. When a subject exhales into the instrument, the VOC molecules will attach to the AuNPs' surface, leading to a change in the electrical resistance measured across a nano sensor array. This resistance change produces an individual "breath print" which will be further analyzed with pattern recognition algorithms and machine learning models to determine whether or not the sample is malignant.

Due to their large ratio of AuNPs' surface area to volume are well suited for this type of application. Their chemical stability, biocompatibility, and tunable surface chemistry further enhance their utility as an effective means of diagnosing VOCs at extremely low levels (in the parts per billion [ppb] range) with minimal patient discomfort. Breath analysis has the ability to replace traditional diagnostic methods, such as imaging or biopsy, by being painless, much quicker, and much cheaper than traditional methods, while exposing the patient to no radiation. Because of these characteristics, breath analysis has the potential to be a viable screening method for at-risk populations like individuals who have smoked for long periods of time (Guinart et al., 2021).

Breath diagnostics and other treatments for lung cancer using AuNPs have been investigated as a possible multi-purpose imaging and biosensor platform to support the detection of lung cancer. With their high atomic number ($Z = 79$) and excellent X-ray attenuation ability, AuNPs provide an alternative source of contrast material for CT imaging of lung cancers. AuNPs will stay in the vascular space longer [especially if they are surface-modified with biocompatible coatings such as polyethylene glycol (PEG)] because they create less friction and are cleared by the reticuloendothelial system more slowly than other traditional CT contrast materials. Because AuNPs are limited to the blood supply, they can accumulate at greater levels within tumors due to the increased retention and permeability (EPR) effect, which occurs when AuNPs preferentially accumulate in tumors because of the permeable vascular networks and inadequate lymphatic drainage typically seen within tumor tissue. As such, targeted accumulation of AuNPs within tumors by the EPR effect creates greater contrast between malignant and nonmalignant lung tissues, which aids in the ease of identifying tumors and determining their margins on CT images.

AuNPs provide advantages over traditional iodinated contrast agents in terms of contrast enhancement and assessment time. Their high attenuation properties may also permit high-resolution imaging at lower doses of radiation and ultimately minimize total radiation exposure to patients receiving multiple CT scans. Additionally, AuNPs can be functionalized with tumor-specific ligands (for example, antibodies against EGFR, peptides, or small molecules), thus allowing for both anatomic imaging and molecular imaging of tumor-associated pathways.

In addition to their use in imaging techniques, biosensor systems that use AuNP technology are being investigated for sensitive detection of lung cancer, using patient samples (e.g., blood, sputum, and exhaled breath condensate) containing lung cancer biomarker molecules. The AuNPs' inherent optical, electrical, and plasmonic properties can be utilized to enable biosensor systems to facilitate assay procedures. When treated with specific recognition elements (e.g., antibodies, aptamers, or nucleic acid probes), AuNPs can selectively bind to lung cancer biomarkers, including: Circulating tumor DNA (ctDNA), specific microRNAs (e.g., miR-21), CEA, cytokeratin fragments (CYFRA 21-1), as well as other protein signatures indicative of lung cancer. Binding events involving AuNPs induce detectable changes in one (or more) of the following optical properties: Absorbance, the visible color of the AuNP solution, fluorescence quenching, and/or conductivity, thus facilitating a rapid and minimally intrusive technique for finding biomarkers for lung cancer (Guinart et al., 2021; Liu et al., 2014).

In addition to their established uses for diagnosing patients through imaging and detecting diseases through biosensing, AuNPs are also beginning to be investigated for therapeutic applications, particularly in cancer therapy. One of the most promising ways to use AuNPs in the treatment of tumors is through photothermal therapy (PTT). PTT is a minimally invasive therapy that takes advantage of the optical properties of AuNPs. AuNPs can vibrate when they are irradiated with light at a specific wavelength, which is most commonly in the near-infrared (NIR) region. The vibration or oscillation of the AuNPs generates an immense amount of heat. The localized application of heat is able to destroy cancerous cells without causing significant harm to the surrounding healthy tissue. Preclinical evidence demonstrates that AuNP-mediated PTT induces either apoptosis or necrosis in various types of cancer cells, reduces the volume of a tumor, and increases the effectiveness of traditional cancer treatments, including chemotherapy and radiation therapy, via an additive or synergistic effect.

Although there are some encouraging results from therapeutic studies using AuNPs, how they interact biologically is still somewhat complicated and sometimes even contradictory. For instance, it has been shown that AuNPs at various sizes, surface modifications, and concentrations can increase the uptake of materials via cellular processes such as enhanced cellular migration and/or invasion in particular situations. There are also examples using in vivo lung cancer models where, after exposure to AuNPs, various changes were seen in signaling pathways associated with cell signaling, leading to epithelial–mesenchymal transition (EMT), oxidative stress, and pro-inflammatory signaling changes. These changes would be expected to influence the rate of tumor growth, but in an unpredictable manner. In addition to particle size, the shape of the particles (e.g., nanorods vs. nanospheres), surface functionalization, dosage, and length/time of exposure are some additional factors that have been shown to have an influence over cellular behavior and cell toxicity. Lastly, the tumor (i.e., cancer) microenvironment also has an important impact on how effective the treatment will be because of the presence of hypoxia (i.e., lack of oxygen) and the presence of immune cells.

For AuNPs to be clinically translated as dual agent diagnostic and therapeutic applications (theranostics), they must first undergo careful optimization and thorough safety evaluation. Before therapeutic implementation can take place on a widespread basis, thorough investigations of AuNPs' dose-dependent effects, long-term biocompatibility, routes of biodistribution and clearance, and potential promotion of metastasis must all occur (Liu et al., 2014).

When all these aspects are taken into consideration, AuNPs offer a great deal of potential to improve the methods of lung cancer diagnosis and treatment. Scientists expect that by using these unique characteristics, they will be able to develop more individualized therapies as well as diagnostic methods that are more precise and straightforward. This may result in an increase in survival rates and a decrease in the expenses of healthcare. To overcome the challenges that present themselves in the process of integrating new technology into clinical practice, it is imperative that more research be conducted (Liu et al., 2014).

7.10 Contrast enhancement in imaging (computed tomography, magnetic resonance imaging, and positron emission tomography)

7.10.1 Computed tomography scans

Contrast enhancement: Particularly at clinical imaging energies, AuNPs are better than conventional contrast agents such as iodine and barium sulfate. AuNPs have a high atomic number, which causes a significant decrease in the quantity of X-rays absorbed by the medium (Carbone et al., 2025; Dreaden et al., 2012a).

Radio sensitization: In addition to boosting contrast, AuNPs have the potential to boost the efficiency of radiation by increasing the local dosage deposition around tumors, which in turn improves the results of treatment (Dreaden et al., 2012a; Rajeshkumar, 2016).

7.10.2 Magnetic resonance imaging

Even though AuNPs do not provide great contrast for MRI, they do serve an important function in applications where contrast may be needed, since they provide a template for creating multiple functions on hybrid nanostructures that contain MRI-active materials. Since gold, being diamagnetic, does not significantly affect relaxation times (T1 or T2) of protons, it cannot be used as an independent source of contrast; nevertheless, AuNPs have several unique physicochemical characteristics, which include a large surface-area ratio, tunable particle size and form, easy functionalization of surfaces, and great compatibility with biological reagents, thus, they make excellent templates for developing composite/hybrid nanostructures featuring MRI technologies.

Combining AuNPs with other MRI-compatible materials [such as gadolinium (Gd^{3+}) chelates, manganese, or superparamagnetic iron oxide nanoparticles (SPION)] produces composite systems that can indirectly improve MRI signal detection. The magnetic component in such composites provides the contrast effect (T1 enhancement in the case of Gd or Mn, T2 shortening in the case of Fe oxide), while the Au core of the composite contributes stability/structure, longer circulation time, and targeting capability. Surface modification of AuNPs with PEG may enhance biocompatibility and decrease immune clearance; these nanoparticles can also be functionalized with antibodies, peptides, or small molecules for tumor-targeted or biological marker-targeted imaging applications.

This indirect way of therapy and diagnostics using nanotechnology aligns with the definitions of Theragnostic, which means an integrated method to perform both therapies and diagnostics using one nano-platform. In these types of systems, AuNPs can perform many different functions all at the same time (e.g., enhance MRI signal through the use of incorporated magnetic agents, CT imaging because of the high atomic number of the gold, and to provide PTT by exploiting localized SPR). An example of this application would be using hybrid Au/Fe2O3 nanoparticles to perform MRI-guided photothermal cancer treatment; in this case, MRIs would monitor the accumulation of nanoparticles at the tumor site, while activation of the AuNPs with NIR light would generate localized heating to destroy the tumor cells.

Moreover, adding AuNPs into larger nanostructures (e.g., liposomes, polymeric micelles, silica shells, or dendrimers) can also improve MRI efficiency. Nanostructures enable higher local concentrations of magnetic ions, enhanced relaxivity, and controlled drug release. Additionally, the spatial arrangement of the magnetic components around a gold core may influence the accessibility of water protons to these magnetic components and enhance MRI contrast (Liu et al., 2013; Sukumar et al., 2013).

7.10.3 Positron emission tomography

Positron emission tomography (PET) and other nuclear imaging techniques may finally make use of doped AuNPs with radioactive isotopes. High degrees of sensitivity and specificity in the diagnosis of cancer may be obtained by use of the outstanding targeting ability of AuNPs (Gao et al., 2017; Sardar et al., 2009).

7.11 Therapeutic applications of gold nanoparticles

AuNPs possess unique physical, chemical, and biological characteristics that make them suitable candidates for use in targeted drug delivery systems. One of the factors leading to increased interest in AuNPs is the ability to control their size, shape, and surface properties with precision, allowing for customization based on specific therapeutic requirements. For example, AuNPs have high surface-to-volume ratios, providing the ability to carry large quantities of therapeutics, targeting ligands, and imaging agents on their surfaces, resulting in greater efficacy. Additionally, gold is biocompatible and nontoxic; thus, it can be used with little concern for adverse immune reactions and, therefore, is a good candidate for in vivo studies. In addition, molecules may be added (i.e., functionalized) to the surface of AuNPs to enhance circulation time (e.g., PEG), maintain targeted therapy (e.g., targeting antibodies), or provide for imaging (e.g., fluorescent dyes).

Researchers have had great success with the development of AuNPs because of the simple nature of modifying the surface of these particles. Researchers can design multifunctional nanoparticles that can be used to diagnose and deliver drugs while also monitoring the outcome of therapy. AuNPs have a wide range of optical and electronic properties, such as localized SPR. Due to this property, AuNPs can be imaged using noninvasive techniques, which can further assist with precision medicine efforts. The overall characteristics of AuNPs make them an excellent platform for developing targeted drug delivery systems that may provide better efficacy and a reduced incidence of side effects (Dreaden et al., 2012b; Vines et al., 2019).

7.11.1 Key features of gold nanoparticles conjugated with chemotherapeutic agents

Targeted delivery: It is possible that AuNPs are able to target cancer cells by interacting with tumor-specific ligands such as folic acids, transferrin, or monoclonal antibodies (Dreaden et al., 2012b; Vines et al., 2019).

Drug loading and release: Chemotherapeutic medications such as doxorubicin and 5-fluorouracil may be transported atop AuNPs, which subsequently release these chemicals intracellularly when cancer cells integrate them always (Dreaden et al., 2012b; Vines et al., 2019).

Enhanced efficacy: Coupling with AuNPs may increase the therapeutic effectiveness of chemotherapeutic medicines by raising their concentration in tumors and lowering their systemic toxicity (Dreaden et al., 2012b; Mohd-Zahid et al., 2021).

Multimodal therapy: By serving as photothermal agents, GNPs may increase the success rate of cancer treatment by combining chemo-PTT (Morărașu et al., 2021; Siddique & Chow, 2020; Yahyaei & Pourali, 2019).

7.11.2 Reduction of off-target toxicity

AuNPs have a lot of potential as promising candidates for cancer treatment because they can help to reduce the toxic effect of the target. Unlike typical chemotherapeutic agents, AuNPs are also inherently low in their toxicity and therefore have a lower chance of causing the bad side effects associated with other chemotherapeutics. AuNPs also show a very high level of biocompatibility, or they are very compatible with biological systems, which is important for any type of drug or material that will be used within a living system. In addition, another important aspect of AuNPs is that researchers can easily modify their surfaces chemically. This gives researchers the ability to covalently link a variety of functional molecules, such as drug or targeting ligands or imaging agents, on the surface of AuNPs, which increases their potential.

Due to their properties, AuNPs are highly suitable for both drug delivery applications and advanced imaging methods (e.g., CT, MRI, photoacoustic imaging). AuNPs are able to selectively bind to cancerous cells due to their surface being modified with different ligands, antibodies, and/or peptides, and will preferentially concentrate within the tumor while avoiding healthy tissues. This mechanism prevents the development of systemic toxicity while improving treatment efficacy. Additionally, AuNPs have physical properties (size, shape, and surface charge) that can be controlled throughout the synthesis process; this allows for the optimization of the circulation time of AuNPs, cellular uptake of AuNPs, and tissue distribution of AuNPs. Thus, AuNPs are considered to be a flexible platform for developing new types of multifunctional cancer therapies [i.e., targeted therapy, imaging in real time, and possibly using a photothermal or photodynamic treatment (PDT) approach] as a complete approach to combating cancer (Arvizo et al., 2010).

To further improve specificity, AuNPs can also be designed to react to the tumor microenvironment (TME), releasing therapeutic compounds in response to conditions including acidity and hypoxia (Jain et al., 2012).

It is not only feasible to reduce the amount of phototoxicity that is caused to healthy tissues as a result of their ability to raise the quantum efficiency of singlet oxygen formation in PDT, but it also makes it possible to eliminate tumors in a more efficient manner. When it comes to cancer therapy, the use of AuNPs is a promising technique that has the potential to mitigate the adverse effects of conventional drugs. In the field of medicine, AuNPs provide therapeutic administration that is not only targeted but also controlled (Arvizo et al., 2010; Goddard et al., 2020).

7.12 Photothermal therapy and photodynamic therapy

7.12.1 Gold nanoparticles are able to produce heat and light absorption

The unique optical properties of AuNPs account for their characteristic behavior and suitability for applications. They have a unique optical absence of light (Abs), which occurs when light interacts with conduction electrons of an AuNP and generates a collective oscillation of those electrons. As a result, light is absorbed and scattered abundantly at certain wavelengths due to the creation of collective electron oscillations resulting from the interaction between light and an AuNP's electrons. Surface plasmons are collectively oscillating conduction electrons caused by such an interaction, making them exist at a predictable resonant frequency within the AuNP and are therefore generally understood as being very sensitive to the size, shape, and composition of the nanoparticles. Spherical AuNPs tend to have a surface plasmon peak around 520 nm within the visible range, whereas for the larger-sized AuNPs or AuNPs with nonsymmetrical shapes (i.e., nanorods and nanoshells), the frequency of surface plasmon oscillation increases into the NIR range. The NIR region is highly desirable for use in medicine and other biological applications because NIR light penetrates through biological tissue much better than visible light, as it is absorbed only minimally by other biological materials.

The phenomenon of SPR is involved in the photothermal effect, in which absorbed light is converted into localized heat. This property allows for many applications, including high contrast imaging and targeted PTT. Gold nanorods and gold nano shells are particularly useful in these applications due to their tunable SPR in the NIR region, which enables selective, focused heating. This ability to selectively apply heat with a photothermal effect makes it possible to destroy cancerous cells or pathogens, while causing little to no harm to healthy tissue nearby, making AuNP promising therapeutic and diagnostic agents for use in medicine. In addition to therapy, the tunability of SPR provides additional contrast for imaging techniques, biosensing, and even drug delivery systems, demonstrating that there are a variety of uses for AuNPs in nanomedicine today (Jain et al., 2006; Pattani & Tunnell, 2012).

7.12.2 Synergistic effects of gold nanoparticles with traditional treatments

Improved drug delivery and effectiveness: Using AuNPs helps one to distribute and utilize anticancer medications such as botulinic acid more effectively. By improving the solubility, stability, and targeted transfer to tumor sites, they raise local drug concentrations and therefore enhance the therapeutic benefits of the medicine (Gottesman, 2002).

Multimechanism action: AuNPs and anticancer medications like botulinic acid boost the killing of cancer cells by destroying mitochondria and generating reactive oxygen species (Jain et al., 2006; Gottesman, 2002).

Photothermal and PDT: The production of cancer cells that are thermally inhibited may be accomplished by heating AuNPs in the context of PTT using NIR light. If this activity is combined with the death that is brought about by pharmaceuticals that are used to treat cancer, the efficacy of tumor treatment is increased (Gottesman, 2002).

7.13 Gene therapy and immunotherapy applications of gold nanoparticles

7.13.1 Gold nanoparticles in gene delivery

Targeted gene therapy: AuNPs may be made to target certain cells or tissues by affixing molecules to their surface that recognize and bind to specific biological markers. This targeted approach increases the efficacy of gene therapy by guaranteeing that therapeutic genes are delivered precisely to the intended location, therefore lowering side effects and improving results (Kanu et al., 2022).

Editing and gene silencing: Nucleic acids—especially short interfering RNA (siRNA)—have been carried in AuNPs to silence genes. Once the necessary elements reach the nucleus, they might also be used in technologies for gene editing like CRISpen-Cas9 to correct defects in genes (Bahadur et al., 2014; Huang et al., 2023).

Cancer treatment: AuNPs may be used to silence genes encouraging tumor development or to transmit genes causing cancer cells to die. Their ability to access the nucleus makes them helpful for delivering therapeutic nucleic acids directly to the cell nucleus, especially considering their minuscule nature (Bahadur et al., 2014; Gottesman, 2002).

Drug and gene co-delivering: Combination therapy has become feasible as a result of the ability of AuNPs to concurrently disseminate both medicines and genes. Increasing the effectiveness of treatment by combining the advantages of chemotherapy and gene therapy will assist in improving the situation (Eker et al., 2024; Huo et al., 2014).

7.13.2 Role of gold nanoparticles in overcoming immune evasion

Enhancing antigen delivery and presentation: Gold nanoparticles (AuNPs) have the potential to serve as adjuvants by facilitating the delivery of antigens to immune cells, particularly dendritic cells, which ultimately activate T cells, so enhancing the immune response (Dykman & Khlebtsov, 2017; Salazar-González et al., 2015).

Targeted delivery: By conjugating with specific ligands or antigens to target certain cells or organs, AuNPs may improve the transport of immunomodulators and antigens (Chauhan et al., 2021; Huang et al., 2023; Salazar-González et al., 2015).

Synergistic effects: There is a possibility that the immune response to cancers may be enhanced by the use of AuNPs in conjunction with other therapy techniques, such as moderate hyperthermia or CRISpen/Cas9 gene editing. This multimodal strategy helps combat immune evasion by concentrating on a number of different pathways that are associated with the growth and survival of tumors (Chauhan et al., 2021; Huang et al., 2023; Zhou et al., 2021).

7.14 Preclinical and clinical studies

7.14.1 Recent preclinical findings on gold nanoparticles in lung cancer models

7.14.1.1 Imaging and diagnosis

Improved imaging: By increasing contrast, AuNPs can increase the accuracy of CT scans, enabling fewer radiation dosages and better tumor and normal tissue distinction (Guinart et al., 2021).

Biosensors: By using their optical characteristics for early detection, AuNPs are being investigated for noninvasive diagnostic instruments (Guinart et al., 2021).

7.14.1.2 Targeted therapy

Gold nanoparticle—silibinin conjugates: Conjugates of AuNPs and silibinin have the potential to kill lung cancer cells (A549) by means of pH-responsive release mechanisms (Ravi et al., 2022).

DNA-tagged AuNPs: Researchers have produced DNA-tagged AuNPs for focused cancer treatment by delivering therapeutic nucleic acids and applying photothermal treatment, hence improving accuracy (Ravi et al., 2022).

Plant-mediated AuNPs: Studies have shown that plant-mediated AuNPs can induce apoptosis in lung cancer cells by modulating key proteins involved in cell survival and death pathways (Ravi et al., 2022).

7.14.1.3 Photodynamic and photothermal therapy

Gold nanoparticle–antibody conjugates: The effects of PDT on lung cancer stem cells have been enhanced using gold nanoparticle–antibody conjugates, which significantly raise cell toxicity and mortality (Crous & Abrahamse, 2020a).

PTT: Nanoparticles of gold are being investigated for customized treatments depending on nanoparticle form and size preferences. They are effective at turning light into heat and destroying cancer cells (Crous & Abrahamse, 2020).

7.14.1.4 Drug delivery

Targeted drug delivery: By effectively delivering drugs to tumor regions, AuNPs may reduce systemic adverse effects and enhance therapeutic results (Nisha et al., 2024; Sardar et al., 2009).

7.15 Current clinical trials

AuroShells: Participants get an intravenous PEG-coated nanomedicine injection over the course of 6 months, and laser irradiation demonstrates a reduction in tumor development without causing thermal burns. AuroShells, which are nano shells made of gold, were recently employed in a clinical study to treat lung cancers, both primary and metastatic (Guinart et al., 2021).

CYT-6091: Phase 1 clinical trials are underway for this formulation of gold nanomaterial. It is used to increase the lung's permeability, which boosts the effectiveness of later chemotherapy (Guinart et al., 2021; Nisha et al., 2024).

7.16 General nanoparticle studies

Most clinical trials are not specifically designed to measure the effect of AuNPs, with only limited mention of their use in the treatment of lung carcinoma; however, this area is gaining credence in the literature, as shown by increasing numbers of studies examining alternative forms of nanotechnology for potential therapeutic application in lung cancer. In particular, early phase clinical trials (i.e., Phase I and II) have produced findings related to safety, tolerability, and preliminary efficacy of various types (polymers, lipid-based nanoparticles) of nanoparticles in the treatment of lung cancer and other malignant tumors. For example, BIND-014, which is a polymeric nanoparticle that contains the chemotherapeutic agent docetaxel, was originally developed for overall delivery to solid tumors; therefore, it will also have potential application in lung cancer. Not only will these studies document/monitor cytotoxicity as a basis for the safety and tolerability of using nanoparticles to deliver drugs, but they will also document/utilize improvements in targeted delivery, reductions in systemic toxicity, as well as overcoming common mechanisms of drug resistance in the approval and acceptance of such products as therapeutic agents for the treatment of lung cancer. A few examples of nanoparticles that are currently being investigated as treatment options for lung cancer include, but are not limited to: Liposomal formulations, polymeric micelles, and metal-based nanoparticles; all three of these types of nanoparticles were developed to improve solubility, circulation time, and accumulation in tumor tissues of therapeutic agents. Collectively, these studies illustrate increasing interest and potential for enhanced precision and efficacy of lung cancer therapies using nanomedicine, ultimately leading to greater treatment options

Table 7.1: Applications of gold nanoparticles.

Sr no.	Application	Description	Status
1.	Photothermal therapy (PTT)	Gold nanomaterials, such gold-silica nano shells are made (AuroShells), are utilized to increase the effectiveness of chemotherapy and radiotherapy by causing localized heat in cancer upon laser irradiation	Clinical trials (e.g., NCT01679470)
2.	Drug delivery	To improve delivery and effectiveness against lung cancer cells, gold nanoparticles can be coupled with medications such as silibinin	Preclinical studies
3.	Imaging and diagnosis	Because of their optical characteristics, gold nanoparticles are being investigated for their capacity in lung cancer imaging and diagnosis	Preclinical and research stages
4.	Radio sensitization	As radiosensitizers, gold nanoparticles may increase the efficacy of radiation treatment	Preclinical studies

for patients who have not been responsive to traditional treatment modalities (Guinart et al., 2021; Nisha et al., 2024) (Table 7.1).

7.16.1 Challenges in bridging lab research to human applications

Biodistribution and pharmacokinetics: Understanding the pharmacokinetic qualities and the manner in which AuNPs are distributed throughout the body is one of the primary issues. Consequently, this has an impact on their ability to deliver medications or diagnostics to the target tissues in a manner that is both safe and effective (Kumarasamy et al., 2024).

Scalability and consistency: It is occasionally necessary to scale up the laboratory-scale synthesis procedures that are employed in clinical settings. This might result in variations in particle size, shape, and surface chemical properties. Maintaining consistency is necessary for dependable performance (Kumarasamy et al., 2024; Sharma et al., 2023).

Public perception and acceptability: The adoption and acceptability of nanoparticles in medical therapies may be affected by public skepticism or concerns (Arvizo et al., 2010; Anik et al., 2022).

7.16.2 Safety, regulatory, and clinical translation challenges

7.16.2.1 Toxicity concerns

The use of AuNPs in medical applications has raised concerns about their potential to elicit harmful effects on living systems. The properties of bulk gold are considered biocompatible and have an established history of use in medicine and dentistry; however, AuNPs have unique physical and chemical properties due to their extremely small size and high surface area. AuNPs, therefore, may behave differently from their bulk counterpart when interacting with cells and tissues. One of the major reasons for this difference in biological interaction is through the process of functionalization. Functionalization is the deliberate or unintentional attachment of molecules onto the surface of AuNPs, which may result in altered biological activities, distribution patterns, and overall behaviors in vivo. For example, surface modifications of AuNPs can influence cellular uptake, circulation time within the organism, and immune responses.

It is essential to conduct an extensive evaluation of safety prior to the use of gold nanoparticles (AuNPs) for human consumption. This could consist of performing in vitro cytotoxicity studies (to determine AuNPs damage to the cell) and in vivo studies (to determine how the body distributes, accumulates, and potentially causes toxicity), as well as pharmacokinetic studies (to understand how the body processes and eliminates AuNPs). The US Food and Drug Administration (FDA) and the European Medicines Agency (EMA) have established regulations for assessing the safety of AuNPs in biomedical uses. Only after adequate safety profiles exist can researchers or industry users evaluate the use of AuNPs for human products such as dietary supplements, drug delivery systems, and medical diagnostics (Eker et al., 2024).

Regulatory hurdles for AuNPs-based treatments: The rules controlling nanomaterials vary often and may be somewhat difficult. One major challenge is guaranteeing adherence to safety and efficacy criteria for human usage (Gao et al., 2017; Talarska, et al., 2021).

7.16.2.2 Future perspectives in nanomedicine for lung cancer

Targeted therapies: The development of nanoparticles that target specific receptors that are overexpressed in lung cancer cells has the potential to increase the effectiveness of therapies while simultaneously reducing the number of unexpected side effects (Fitzmaurice et al., 2015).

Immunotherapy integration: Treating lung cancer using nanomedicines alongside immunotherapies, such as checkpoint inhibitors, could provide a possibility for synergistic effects (Wang et al., 2022).

Early diagnosis and detection: To greatly increase survival rates, nanoplatforms for early lung cancer diagnosis and detection are being created (Carrasco-Esteban et al., 2021; Wang et al., 2022).

Clinical translation challenges: Despite improvements, there are still problems with large-scale production, toxicity, and nano bio-interactions that must be resolved for clinical translation to be effective (Carrasco-Esteban et al., 2021).

7.17 Conclusion and future directions

7.17.1 Potential of gold nanoparticles as adjunctive therapy

AuNPs have great potential as adjuvant therapies for a range of medical conditions, including the treatment of cancer and other conditions. AuNPs are being investigated in the following important areas:

7.17.2 Cancer

Radio sensitization: By improving the absorption of irradiation within the tissues of tumors, NPs can increase the efficacy of radiation treatment and improve the death of cancer cells (Carbone et al., 2025).

PTT: AuNPs may be engineered to disperse drugs in a precise way and absorb NIR light, producing localized heat that kills cancer cells (Carbone et al., 2025).

Imaging contrast agents: They are better than traditional iodine-based contrast agents for imaging because of their exceptionally high atomic number and X-ray absorption coefficient, resulting in higher contrast at lower radiation doses (Carbone et al., 2025; Vines et al., 2019).

7.17.3 Diabetes management

Therapeutic results: AuNPs have demonstrated antioxidant, antiinflammatory, and anti-hyperglycemic properties, which could assist with treating diabetes and its adverse effects (Alomari et al., 2021; Vines et al., 2019).

7.17.4 General medical application

Drug delivery: AuNPs can deliver medications and anticancer agents accurately, as well as possibly reducing negative effects (Alomari et al., 2021).

Biocompatibility and safety: AuNPs are usually safe and biocompatible, which makes them appropriate for a range of in vivo applications (Alomari et al., 2021; Gao et al., 2017).

7.17.5 Limitations

Toxicity issues: Despite their promising properties, AuNPs can trigger inflammation and oxidative stress based on their size and surface chemistry (Siddique & Chow, 2020).

Clinical translation: Because of the sensitivity of the lung, most studies are still in their earliest stages, and there are still challenges in using these technologies in clinical settings (Siddique & Chow, 2020).

Standardization: To assess the efficiency and safety of AuNPs in different forms and applications, standard processes are required (Sztandera et al., 2019; Siddique & Chow, 2020).

7.18 Future research needs for clinical implementation

7.18.1 Optimization of nanoparticles formulation

Stability and scalability: For consistent and large production, AuNP formulations have to be made more stable and scalable. This involves refining synthesis techniques to guarantee consistent particle sizes and forms (Guinart et al., 2021; Sztandera et al., 2019).

Surface modifications: It is crucial to enhance surface modifications to reduce possible immunogenicity and increase targeted efficiency. Conjugating AuNPs with certain binders aimed at lung cancer cells will achieve this (Guinart et al., 2021; Sharma et al., 2023).

7.18.2 Enhanced target efficiency

Active targeting: By developing ways of actively targeting cancer cells in the lung using AuNPs coupled to peptides or antibodies that bind to markers of cancer with preference, outcomes from therapy can be enhanced (Chehelgerdi et al., 2023; Kumarasamy et al., 2024; Peng et al., 2009).

Combination medicines: Exploring how AuNPs may improve the effectiveness of treatment and lessen negative effects when used in conjunction with other medicines, such as immunotherapy (Chehelgerdi et al., 2023; Guinart et al., 2021).

7.18.3 Safety and toxicity evaluation

Long-term toxicity studies: To evaluate the safety characteristics of AuNPs in humans, thorough long-term toxicity studies must be performed. This involves evaluating systemic toxicity and any off-target consequences (Crous & Abrahamse, 2020; Nisha et al., 2024).

7.18.4 Clinical translation

Clinical investigations: Establishing and carrying out detailed clinical studies to assess the safety and efficacy of AuNP-based therapies for patients with lung cancer. This will help with the conversion of promising preclinical findings into clinical practice (Crous & Abrahamse, 2020; Sardar et al., 2009).

7.18.5 Personalized medication

Biomarker identification: Discovering certain lung cancer biomarkers that AuNPs can target to enable personalized therapy plans that enhance patient outcomes (Chehelgerdi et al., 2023; Daraee et al., 2016; Sharma et al., 2023).

References

Alkilany, A. M., & Murphy, C. J. (2010). Toxicity and cellular uptake of gold nanoparticles: What we have learned so far? *Journal of Nanoparticle Research, 12*(7), 2313–2333. doi:10.1007/s11051-010-9911-8.

Alomari, G., Hamdan, S., & Al-Trad, B. (2021). Gold nanoparticles as a promising treatment for diabetes and its complications: Current and future potentials. *Brazilian Journal of Pharmaceutical Sciences, 57*. doi:10.1590/s2175-97902020000419040.

Anik, M. I., Mahmud, N., Masud, A. Al, & Hasan, M. (2022). Gold nanoparticles (AuNPs) in biomedical and clinical applications: A review. *Nano Select, 3*(4), 792–828. doi:10.1002/nano.202100255.

Arvizo, R., Bhattacharya, R., & Mukherjee, P. (2010). Gold nanoparticles: Opportunities and challenges in nanomedicine. *Expert Opinion on Drug Delivery, 7*(6), 753–763. doi:10.1517/17425241003777010.

Bhardwaj, H., Archana, N., Noumani, A., Himanshu, J. K., Chakravorty, S., & Solanki, P. R. (2024). Recent advancement in the detection of potential cancer biomarkers using the nanomaterial integrated electrochemical sensing technique: A detailed review. *Materials Advances, 5*(2), 475–503. doi:10.1039/d3ma00621b.

Carabineiro, S. (2017). Applications of gold nanoparticles in nanomedicine: Recent advances in vaccines. *Molecules, 22*(5), 857. doi:10.3390/molecules22050857.

Carbone, G. G., Mariano, S., Gabriele, A., Cennamo, S., Primiceri, V., Aziz, M. R., Panzarini, E., & Calcagnile, L. (2025). Exploring the potential of gold nanoparticles in proton therapy: Mechanisms, advances, and clinical horizons. *Pharmaceutics, 17*(2). doi:10.3390/pharmaceutics17020176.

Carrasco-Esteban E., Domínguez-Rullán J.A, Barrionuevo-Castillo P., Pelari-Mici L., Leaman O., Sastre-Gallego S., López-Campos F. Current role of nanoparticles in the treatment of lung cancer. Journal of Clinical and Translational Research, 7(2), 140.

Chauhan, A., Khan, T., & Omri, A. (2021). Design and encapsulation of immunomodulators onto gold nanoparticles in cancer immunotherapy. *International Journal of Molecular Sciences, 22*(15), 8037. doi:10.3390/ijms22158037.

Chehelgerdi, M., Chehelgerdi, M., Allela, O. Q. B., Pecho, R. D. C., Jayasankar, N., Rao, D. P., Thamaraikani, T., Vasanthan, M., Viktor, P., Lakshmaiya, N., Saadh, M. J., Amajd, A., Abo-Zaid, M. A., Castillo-Acobo, R. Y., Ismail, A. H., Amin, A. H., & Akhavan-Sigari, R. (2023). Progressing nanotechnology to improve targeted cancer treatment: Overcoming hurdles in its clinical implementation. *Molecular Cancer, 22*(1). doi:10.1186/s12943-023-01865-0.

Crous, A., & Abrahamse, H. (2020). Effective gold nanoparticle-antibody-mediated drug delivery for photodynamic therapy of lung cancer stem cells. *International Journal of Molecular Sciences, 21*(11), 3742. doi:10.3390/ijms21113742.

Daraee, H., Pourhassanmoghadam, M., Akbarzadeh, A., Zarghami, N., & Rahmati-Yamchi, M. (2016). Gold nanoparticle–oligonucleotide conjugate to detect the sequence of lung cancer biomarker. *Artificial Cells, Nanomedicine and Biotechnology, 44*(6), 1417–1423. doi:10.3109/21691401.2015.1031905.

Dela Cruz, C. S., Tanoue, L. T., & Matthay, R. A. (2011). Lung cancer: Epidemiology, etiology, and prevention. *Clinics in Chest Medicine, 32*(4), 605–644. doi:10.1016/j.ccm.2011.09.001.

Dreaden, E. C., Alkilany, A. M., Huang, X., Murphy, C. J., & El-Sayed, M. A. (2012a). The golden age: Gold nanoparticles for biomedicine. *Chemical Society Reviews, 41*(7), 2740–2779. doi:10.1039/c1cs15237h.

Dreaden, E. C., Austin, L. A., MacKey, M. A., & El-Sayed, M. A. (2012b). Size matters: Gold nanoparticles in targeted cancer drug delivery. *Therapeutic Delivery, 3*(4), 457–478. doi:10.4155/tde.12.21.

Dykman, L. A., & Khlebtsov, N. G. (2017). Immunological properties of gold nanoparticles. *Chemical Science, 8*(3), 1719–1735. doi:10.1039/c6sc03631g.

Eker, F., Akdaşçi, E., Duman, H., Bechelany, M., & Karav, S. (2024). Gold nanoparticles in nanomedicine: Unique properties and therapeutic potential. *Nanomaterials, 14*(22), 1854. doi:10.3390/nano14221854.

Fitzmaurice, C., Dicker, D., Pain, A., Hamavid, H., Moradi-Lakeh, M., MacIntyre, M. F., Allen, C., Hansen, G., Woodbrook, R., Wolfe, C., Hamadeh, R. R., Moore, A., Werdecker, A., Gessner, B. D., Te Ao, B., McMahon, B., Karimkhani, C., Yu, C., Cooke, G. S., … Naghavi, M. (2015). The global burden of cancer 2013. *JAMA Oncology, 1*(4), 505–527. doi:10.1001/jamaoncol.2015.0735.

Gao, W., Wang, W., Yao, S., Wu, S., Zhang, H., Zhang, J., Jing, F., Mao, H., Jin, Q., Cong, H., Jia, C., Zhang, G., & Zhao, J. (2017). Highly sensitive detection of multiple tumor markers for lung cancer using gold nanoparticle probes and microarrays. *Analytica Chimica Acta, 958*, 77–84. doi:10.1016/j.aca.2016.12.016.

Goddard, Z. R., Marín, M. J., Russell, D. A., & Searcey, M. (2020). Active targeting of gold nanoparticles as cancer therapeutics. *Chemical Society Reviews, 49*(23), 8774–8789. doi:10.1039/d0cs01121e.

Gottesman, M. M. (2002). Mechanisms of cancer drug resistance. *Annual Review of Medicine, 53*, 615–627. doi:10.1146/annurev.med.53.082901.103929.

Guinart, A., Perry, H. L., Wilton-Ely, J. D. E. T., & Tetley, T. D. (2021). Gold nanomaterials in the management of lung cancer. *Emerging Topics in Life Sciences, 4*(6), 627–643. doi:10.1042/ETLS20200332.

Howlader, N., Forjaz, G., Mooradian, M. J., Meza, R., Kong, C. Y., Cronin, K. A., Mariotto, A. B., Lowy, D. R., & Feuer, E. J. (2020). The effect of advances in lung-cancer treatment on population mortality. *New England Journal of Medicine, 383*(7), 640–649. doi:10.1056/NEJMoa1916623.

Huang, H., Liu, R., Yang, J., Dai, J., Fan, S., Pi, J., Wei, Y., & Guo, X. (2023). Gold nanoparticles: Construction for drug delivery and application in cancer immunotherapy. *Pharmaceutics, 15*(7), 1868. doi:10.3390/pharmaceutics15071868.

Huo, S., Jin, S., Ma, X., Xue, X., Yang, K., Kumar, A., Wang, P. C., Zhang, J., Hu, Z., & Liang, X. J. (2014). Ultrasmall gold nanoparticles as carriers for nucleus-based gene therapy due to size-dependent nuclear entry. *ACS Nano, 8*(6), 5852–5862. doi:10.1021/nn5008572.

Jain, P. K., Lee, K. S., El-Sayed, I. H., & El-Sayed, M. A. (2006). Calculated absorption and scattering properties of gold nanoparticles of different size, shape, and composition: Applications in biological imaging and biomedicine. *Journal of Physical Chemistry B, 110*(14), 7238–7248. doi:10.1021/jp057170o.

Jain, S., Hirst, D. G., & O'Sullivan, J. M. (2012). Gold nanoparticles as novel agents for cancer therapy. *British Journal of Radiology, 85*(1010), 101–113. doi:10.1259/bjr/59448833United Kingdom.

Kanu, G. A., Parambath, J. B. M., Abu Odeh, R. O., & Mohamed, A. A. (2022). Gold nanoparticle-mediated gene therapy. *Cancers, 14*(21). doi:10.3390/cancers14215366.

Khlebtsov, N., & Dykman, L. (2011). Biodistribution and toxicity of engineered gold nanoparticles: A review of in vitro and in vivo studies. *Chemical Society Reviews, 40*(3), 1647–1671. doi:10.1039/c0cs00018c.

Kumarasamy, R. V., Natarajan, P. M., Umapathy, V. R., Roy, J. R., Mironescu, M., & Palanisamy, C. P. (2024). Clinical applications and therapeutic potentials of advanced nanoparticles: A comprehensive review on completed human clinical trials. *Frontiers in Nanotechnology, 6*. doi:10.3389/fnano.2024.1479993.

Kumar Sukumar, U., Bhushan, B., Dubey, P., Matai, I., Sachdev, A., & Packirisamy, G. (2013). Emerging applications of nanoparticles for lung cancer diagnosis and therapy. *International Nano Letters, 3*(1). doi:10.1186/2228-5326-3-45.

Liu, M., Gu, X., Zhang, K., Ding, Y., Wei, X., Zhang, X., & Zhao, Y. (2013). Gold nanoparticles trigger apoptosis and necrosis in lung cancer cells with low intracellular glutathione. *Journal of Nanoparticle Research, 15*(8). doi:10.1007/s11051-013-1745-8.

Liu, Z., Wu, Y., Guo, Z., Liu, Y., Shen, Y., Zhou, P., Lu, X., & Munshi, H. G. (2014). Effects of internalized gold nanoparticles with respect to cytotoxicity and invasion activity in lung cancer cells. *PLoS ONE, 9*(6), e99175. doi:10.1371/journal.pone.0099175.

Malik, S., Muhammad, K., & Waheed, Y. (2023). Emerging applications of nanotechnology in healthcare and medicine. *Molecules, 28*(18), 6624. doi:10.3390/molecules28186624.

Milan, J., Niemczyk, K., & Kus-Liśkiewicz, M. (2022). Treasure on the earth—Gold nanoparticles and their biomedical applications. *Materials, 15*(9), 3355. doi:10.3390/ma15093355.

Mohd-Zahid, M. H., Zulkifli, S. N., Che Abdullah, C. A., Lim, J., Fakurazi, S., Wong, K. K., Zakaria, A. D., Ismail, N., Uskoković, V., Mohamud, R., & Iskandar, Z. A. (2021). Gold nanoparticles conjugated with anti-CD133 monoclonal antibody and 5-fluorouracil chemotherapeutic agent as nanocarriers for cancer cell targeting. *RSC Advances, 11*(26), 16131–16141. doi:10.1039/d1ra01093j.

Morărașu, Ș, Iacob, Ș, Tudorancea, I., & Luncă, S. (2021). Mihail-gabriel dimofte, targeted chemotherapy delivery via gold nanoparticles: A scoping review of in vivo studies. *Crystals, 11*(10), 1169. doi:10.3390/cryst11101169.

Nisha, R. S. K. S., Singh, A., Karnwal, A., Shidiki, A., & Kumar, G. (2024). Plant-mediated gold nanoparticles in cancer therapy: Exploring anti-cancer mechanisms, drug delivery applications, and future prospects. *Frontiers in Nanotechnology, 6*. doi:10.3389/fnano.2024.1490980.

Ostrin, E. J., Sidransky, D., Spira, A., & Hanash, S. M. (2020). Biomarkers for lung cancer screening and detection. *Cancer Epidemiology Biomarkers and Prevention, 29*(12), 2411–2415. doi:10.1158/1055-9965.EPI-20-0865.

Pattani, V. P., & Tunnell, J. W. (2012). Nanoparticle-mediated photothermal therapy: A comparative study of heating for different particle types. *Lasers in Surgery and Medicine, 44*(8), 675–684. doi:10.1002/lsm.22072.

Peng, G., Tisch, U., Adams, O., Hakim, M., Shehada, N., Broza, Y. Y., Billan, S., Abdah-Bortnyak, R., Kuten, A., & Haick, H. (2009). Diagnosing lung cancer in exhaled breath using gold nanoparticles. *Nature Nanotechnology, 4*(10), 669–673. doi:10.1038/nnano.2009.235.

Rajeshkumar, S. (2016). Anticancer activity of eco-friendly gold nanoparticles against lung and liver cancer cells. *Journal of Genetic Engineering and Biotechnology, 14*(1), 195–202. doi:10.1016/j.jgeb.2016.05.007.

Ravi, R., Zeyaullah, M., Ghosh, S., Khan Warsi, M., Baweja, R., AlShahrani, A. M., Mishra, A., & Ahmad, R. (2022). Use of gold nanoparticle-silibinin conjugates: A novel approach against lung cancer cells. *Frontiers in Chemistry, 10*. doi:10.3389/fchem.2022.1018759.

Remant Bahadur, K. C., Thapa, B., & Bhattarai, N. (2014). Gold nanoparticle-based gene delivery: Promises and challenges. *Nanotechnology Reviews, 3*(3), 2191–9097. doi:10.1515/ntrev-2013-0026.

Saha M. Nanomedicine: Promising tiny machine for the healthcare in future-a review. Oman Medical Journal, 24(4), 242.

Salazar-González, J. A., González-Ortega, O., & Rosales-Mendoza, S. (2015). Gold nanoparticles and vaccine development. *Expert Review of Vaccines, 14*(9), 1197–1211. doi:10.1586/14760584.2015.1064772.

Sardar, R., Funston, A. M., Mulvaney, P., & Murray, R. W. (2009). Gold nanoparticles: Past, present, and future. *Langmuir, 25*(24), 13840–13851. doi:10.1021/la9019475United States.

Schabath, M. B., & Cote, M. L. (2019). Cancer progress and priorities: Lung cancer. *Cancer Epidemiology Biomarkers and Prevention, 28*(10), 1563–1579. doi:10.1158/1055-9965.EPI-19-0221.

Sharma, A., Shambhwani, D., Pandey, S., Singh, J., Lalhlenmawia, H., Kumarasamy, M., Singh, S. K., Chellappan, D. K., Gupta, G., Prasher, P., Dua, K., & Kumar, D. (2023). Advances in lung cancer treatment using nanomedicines. *ACS Omega, 8*(1), 10–41. doi:10.1021/acsomega.2c04078.

Siddique, S., & Chow, J. C. L. (2020). Gold nanoparticles for drug delivery and cancer therapy. *Applied Sciences, 10*(11), 3824. doi:10.3390/app10113824.

Sim, S., & Wong, N. (2021). Nanotechnology and its use in imaging and drug delivery (Review). *Biomedical Reports, 14*(5), 2049–9434. doi:10.3892/br.2021.1418.

Sweeney, A. (2015). Nanomedicine concepts in the general medical curriculum: Initiating a discussion. *International Journal of Nanomedicine, 10*, 7319. doi:10.2147/ijn.s96480.

Sztandera, K., Gorzkiewicz, M. ł, & Klajnert-Maculewicz, B. (2019). Gold nanoparticles in cancer treatment. *Molecular Pharmaceutics, 16*(1), 1–23. doi:10.1021/acs.molpharmaceut.8b00810.

Talarska, P., Boruczkowski, M., & Żurawski, J. (2021). Current knowledge of silver and gold nanoparticles in laboratory research—Application, toxicity, cellular uptake. *Nanomaterials, 11*(9), 2454. doi:10.3390/nano11092454.

Tkachenko, A. G., Xie, H., Coleman, D., Glomm, W., Ryan, J., Anderson, M. F., Franzen, S., & Feldheim, D. L. (2003). Multifunctional gold nanoparticle-peptide complexes for nuclear targeting. *Journal of the American Chemical Society, 125*(16), 4700–4701. doi:10.1021/ja0296935.

Usman, F., Dennis, J. O., Aljameel, A. I., Ali, M. K. M., Aldaghri, O., Ibnaouf, K. H., Zango, Z. U., Beygisangchin, M., Alsadig, A., & Meriaudeau, F. (2021). Plasmonic biosensors for the detection of lung cancer biomarkers: A review. *Chemosensors, 9*(11). doi:10.3390/chemosensors9110326.

Vangijzegem, T., Lecomte, V., Ternad, I., Van Leuven, L., Muller, R. N., Stanicki, D., & Laurent, S. (2023). Superparamagnetic iron oxide nanoparticles (SPION): From fundamentals to state-of-the-art innovative applications for cancer therapy. *Pharmaceutics, 15*(1). doi:10.3390/pharmaceutics15010236.

Vines, J. B., Yoon, J. H., Ryu, N. E., Lim, D. J., & Park, H. (2019). Gold nanoparticles for photothermal cancer therapy. *Frontiers in Chemistry, 7*. doi:10.3389/fchem.2019.00167.

Wang, J., Zhou, T., Liu, Y., Chen, S., & Yu, Z. (2022). Application of Nanoparticles in the Treatment of Lung Cancer With Emphasis on Receptors. *Frontiers in Pharmacology, 12*. doi:10.3389/fphar.2021.781425.

Yahyaei, B., & Pourali, P. (2019). One step conjugation of some chemotherapeutic drugs to the biologically produced gold nanoparticles and assessment of their anticancer effects. *Scientific Reports, 9*(1). doi:10.1038/s41598-019-46602-0.

Zhou, L., Liu, H., Liu, K., & Wei, S. (2021). Gold compounds and the anticancer immune response. *Frontiers in Pharmacology, 12*. doi:10.3389/fphar.2021.739481.

CHAPTER 8

Nanoparticle chemotherapy via the pulmonary route: Addressing challenges, exploring opportunities in lung cancer treatment

Prithiviraj Nagarajan[a], Sankaranarayanan Nagarajan[b], Sharangouda J. Patil[c] and Gayathiri Ekambaram[d]

[a]Department of Medical Biotechnology, Aarupadai Veedu Medical College & Hospital, Vinayaka Mission's Research Foundation (Deemed to be university), Puducherry, India [b]Department of Chemistry, National Institute of Technology Manipur, Imphal, Manipur, India [c]Department of Zoology, Nagarathnamma Meda Kasturiranga Setty Rashtreeya Vidyalaya (NMKRV) College, Bangalore, Karnataka, India [d]Department of Plant Biology and Plant Biotechnology, Guru Nanak College (Autonomous), Chennai, Tamil Nadu, India

8.1 Introduction

8.1.1 Epidemiology and clinical rationale for pulmonary delivery

Lung cancer is the leading cause of cancer-related deaths worldwide, and its advanced stages are catastrophic (Luo et al., 2022). Nonsmall cell lung cancer (NSCLC) comprises approximately 84% of all cases of lung cancer, and the remaining 16% is small cell lung cancer (SCLC), which has unsatisfactory survival rates after diagnosis and treatment (Rajasegaran et al., 2023). The survival rate of patients with lung cancer is also extremely low over a 5-year period, indicating the necessity of new approaches for the treatment of this disease (Luo et al., 2022). Existing treatment paradigms primarily involve the use of systemic chemotherapy along with surgery and radiotherapy; however, these two traditional treatment methods are limited by dose-limiting toxicity and low levels of tumor accumulation (Akhter et al., 2015). To date, SCLC has not been identified at its earliest stage, and most patients with SCLC are diagnosed at stage IIIb or IV; therefore platinum-based chemotherapy is the primary mode of treatment (Huber & Tufman, 2012). Targeted therapy in the context of NSCLC has demonstrated benefits in selected genetic subtypes; however, resistance mechanisms, such as the translocation of Anaplastic Lymphoma Kinase (ALK) and epidermal growth factor receptor

Nanoengineered Therapeutics for Lung Cancer: Advanced Drug Delivery Strategies.
DOI: https://doi.org/10.1016/B978-0-443-44585-9.00007-X

(EGFR) mutations, have remained an obstacle to prolonged survival (Spitaleri et al., 2023). The presence of an inflammatory microenvironment in NSCLC is both an opportunity and a hindrance to intervention (Rajasegaran et al., 2023).

8.1.2 Limitations in systemic chemotherapy and first-pass metabolism

Classical intravenous chemotherapy is limited by fundamental limitations that limit its therapeutic capability. Due to the limited accumulation of systemically injected drugs at the tumor site and the dose-limiting toxicity of normal tissues, therapeutic efficacy is limited (Akhter et al., 2015). Hepatic first-pass metabolism and rapid systemic clearance also considerably decrease the bioavailability of chemotherapeutic agents, thereby increasing the systemic dose and off-target toxicity (Al Khatib et al., 2023). Side effects such as hair loss, nausea, vomiting, and immunosuppression significantly affect the quality of life of patients and their adherence to treatment. Another serious concern is multidrug resistance (MDR), in which chemotherapeutic agents are actively pumped out of cancer cells by efflux pumps, especially P-glycoprotein and other ATP-binding cassette (ABC) transporters (Shi et al., 2023). This increases DNA repair mechanisms and epithelial–mesenchymal transition (EMT), which favors survival and metastatic capacity, and reduces the efficacy of conventional chemotherapy (Shi et al., 2023), especially in cases of relapse and refractory disease.

8.1.3 Advantages of the pulmonary route and increase in bioavailability

The lungs represent a unique and advantageous route for drug delivery, offering several physiological benefits beyond systemic barriers. The numerous surfaces of the alveoli (approximately 70 m^2), high level of vascularization, and thin epithelial barrier facilitate drug absorption (Khatib et al., 2023). Direct pulmonary delivery circumvents hepatic first-pass metabolism, resulting in a significant decrease in systemic exposure and high local drug concentrations (Akhter et al., 2015). The delivery selectivity of this local delivery enables the achievement of therapeutic drug levels at the tumor site with minimal systemic toxicity, which is crucial in patients undergoing chemotherapy. The pulmonary route also permits the inhalation of NP preparations that are otherwise inappropriate for parenteral administration, thereby expanding the therapeutic arsenal of oncologists. Direct deposition of the NP formulation into tumor-bearing lung areas ensures the maximal efficiency of treatment and allows the implementation of combination-based approaches with immunotherapy and radiation sensitization (Khatib et al., 2023).

8.1.4 Clinical signs and staging of the disease

Pulmonary nanochemotherapy is especially applicable to primary lung tumors, including NSCLC and SCLC, in various clinical settings, such as adjuvant, neoadjuvant, and palliative

(Khatib et al., 2023). Direct pulmonary delivery in localized lesions ensures high localization, whereas aerosol deposition in the respiratory areas in diffuse lung disease causes the tumor to be more covered than in traditional lobar chemotherapy (Akhter et al., 2015). This method has specific potential in recurrent or refractory diseases, where damaging systemic tolerability has become a dose-limiting element.

8.2 Nanoparticle deposition, pulmonary anatomy, and physiology

8.2.1 Mechanisms of airway microenvironment and clearance

Certain regions of the respiratory tract have multiple clearance mechanisms that are essential for NP behavior. The columnar epithelium lines the airways (trachea-terminal bronchioles), and mucus clearance is highly effective in the airways due to the synchronous beating of cilia and mucus (Khatib et al., 2023). The respiratory space (respiratory bronchioles and alveoli) is less permissive and contains fewer mechanical clearance mechanisms but more alveolar macrophage uptake. Pulmonary surfactants are multifaceted lipoprotein lipid phospholipid protein complexes that control NP aggregation, opsonization, and cellular uptake and must be considered in the design of NPs. Mucociliary clearance is the greatest defense mechanism, and in this process, intact layers of mucus clear particles within a few hours (Khatib et al., 2023). Nevertheless, lung cancer and treatment may impact cilia functionality and mucus structure, which could prolong the residence time of fundi NPs. The most prominent component of innate immunity is alveolar macrophages, which can absorb opsonized particles via phagocytosis, a process that depends on the size of the particle, surface chemistry, and protein corona composition (Fig. 8.1; Akhter et al., 2015).

8.2.2 Deposition determinants in aerosol science

Aerodynamic principles governing the action of NPs in the respiratory tract dictate whether they are deposited in the conducting airways, terminal bronchioles, or alveolar areas. Deposition is not based on physical particle size but rather on aerodynamic diameter or the diameter of a comparable-density sphere with the same settling velocity because porous or hollow particles settle deeper than predicted based on morphological evaluation alone (Akhter et al., 2015). Particles with aerodynamic diameters between 5 and 10 mm were deposited mainly in conducting airways, impaction, and sedimentation. Particles between 1 and 5 mm can reach the distal respiratory areas, and the smallest (<1 mm) particles are deposited via Brownian diffusion, which allows alveolar deposition (Khatib et al., 2023). Hygroscopicity, that is, the ability of particles to absorb moisture from the atmosphere, is an important factor that influences deposition. Particles with hygroscopic properties experience size growth when passing through the moist respiratory system, which can alter their settling locations (Akhter et al., 2015). PEGylation and coating with hydrophobic surfactants are formulation

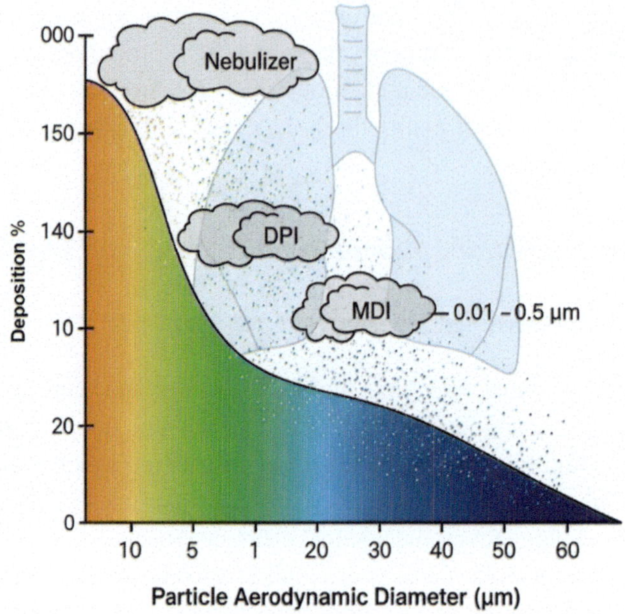

Figure 8.1
Map of pulmonary deposition versus particle aerodynamic diameter and device type. The figure shows a plot of the efficiency of pulmonary deposition (*y*-axis) versus the aerodynamic diameter of the particles (*x*-axis). This demonstrates that large particles affect the nasopharynx (*orange*), medium particles affect the tracheobronchial airways (*green*), and nanoparticle suspensions (0.01–0.5 μm, *deep blue* mist) reach the peak of alveolar deposition through diffusion. The overlays display the delivery of intermediate sizes by the conventional devices (nebulizer, DPI, MDI), whereas nanoparticles are distinctive specifically in delivering to the deep lung. *DPI*, dry powder inhaler; *MDI*, metered-dose inhaler.

methods that have been used to reduce hygroscopicity and increase residence time in target areas.

8.2.3 Comparison of carrier properties to the localization of diseases

Effective pulmonary nanochemotherapy would necessitate a logical correspondence between Np characteristics and the desired locations of deposition and disease spread. Particles with larger aerodynamic diameters (5–10 mm) can facilitate impactor delivery in the case of central airway tumors affecting the bronchi and bronchioles (Khatib et al., 2023). For peripheral lung cancers localized to the alveolar areas, particle deposition of (1–5 mm aerodynamic diameter) can be achieved through a combination of sedimentation and Brownian diffusion. Ultrafine particles can be used to treat diffuse metastatic disease or lymphangitic carcinomatosis, where a wide distribution to the alveoli is required. The functionalization of tumor-homing ligands (e.g., RGD peptides, transferrin, and folate) increases cancer cell uptake after alveolar deposition (Akhter et al., 2015). Deposition, as well as cellular internalization and cellular internalization, depends on the interaction of particle size, density, shape, and surface properties.

8.3 Nanoparticle formulations and carriers

8.3.1 The liposomal and lipid-based carriers

Liposomes are among the best-investigated nanocarrier platforms for pulmonary delivery, which are inherently biocompatible, have tunable surface properties, and have established manufacturing pathways (Franco et al., 2021). They are spherical lipid-based vesicles that contain hydrophobic chemotherapeutic agents and hydrophilic drugs within the lipid and aqueous phases, respectively. Liposomal formulations can be used to codeliver various agents to the lungs, which decreases the required systemic concentration by maximizing local concentration (Akhter et al., 2015). Stimulus-responsive liposomes represent a more developed version, which includes pH- or temperature-sensitive lipids that undergo phase changes/destabilization under tumor microenvironmental conditions (Franco et al., 2021). Such systems are resistant to degradation in normal pH-conducting airways but extracellularly release the payload quickly in acidic tumor-infiltrating cell endosomes, offering selective chemotherapy delivery and resulting in minimal off-target exposure.

8.3.2 Polymeric nanoparticles and poly(lactic-co-glycolic acid)-based systems

Polymeric NPs, particularly poly(lactic-co-glycolic acid) (PLGA), exhibit the best adaptability for delivering cancer drugs (Ding et al., 2024). PLGA is an FDA-approved biodegradable polymer with adjustable degradation kinetics that allow for days to weeks of sustained drug release based on molecular weight and lactate/glycolate ratio (Alsaab et al., 2022). The polymer has been shown to easily entrap hydrophobic and hydrophilic chemotherapeutic agents using various synthesis strategies, such as emulsion-based and nanoprecipitation methods (Ding et al., 2024). In the case of pulmonary administration, PLGA NPs allow for the controlled release of drugs, such as cisplatin, paclitaxel, or doxorubicin, along with their degradation products (lactic acid and glycolic acid), which can be metabolized by normal metabolic processes (Akhter et al., 2015). PEGylation as a surface functional group prolongs circulation duration and decreases uptake by macrophages, and active tumor cell targeting is possible by conjugating targeting ligands to PEGylation (Alsaab et al., 2022). Inorganic NPs based on hybrid PLGA NPs (mesoporous silica, gold NPs, and iron oxide) provide multifunctional platforms for drug delivery, imaging, and photothermal or photodynamic therapy.

8.3.3 Mesoporous silica and inorganic nanocarriers

Mesoporous silica NPs (MSNs) are a unique category of inorganic carriers, whose prominent drug-loading capacity and pore architecture can be controlled (Rastegari et al., 2021). Their high pore volume allows high drug-loading ratios for encapsulation with chemotherapeutic agents and selective pore capping with stimuli-responsive gatekeepers to be released on demand based on pH, enzyme, or redox conditions (Rastegari et al., 2021). Silanol hydrolysis of the amorphous silica framework breaks down into orthosilicic acid, thereby reducing systemic accumulation. In the case of lung cancer, MSN-based preparations can be designed to focus on chemotherapy and nucleic acid therapeutics so that gene silencing with resistance-mediating proteins can be conducted concomitantly with chemotherapy. PEGylation of surfaces suppresses protein corona generation and macrophage elimination and increases the length of stay and passive nutrient accumulation in tumors via the enhanced permeability and retention effect (Rastegari et al., 2021).

8.3.4 Perfluorocarbon nanoparticle oxygen-carrying systems

Perfluorocarbon (PFC) NPs represent a novel and rapidly emerging platform with specific applications in pulmonary cancer treatment. These fluorinated carriers possess an exceptional oxygen-carrying capacity of up to 50% of oxygen by volume, facilitating the direct intratumoral delivery of oxygen that sensitizes hypoxic tumors to chemotherapy and radiation. PFCs exhibit unique liquid-like properties and can be formulated into stable nanoemulsions with pharmaceutical excipients. Hypoxia-driven resistance mechanisms of PFC systems in solid tumors, where low oxygen density inhibits the activity of chemotherapy, enhance EMT and metastasis. PFC NPs integrate the effects of oxygen delivery with chemotherapeutic cargo, allowing oxygenation of hypoxic areas and chemotherapy of dividing cells to occur synergistically. In addition, PFC NPs are acoustically active and therefore offer natural imaging capabilities through magnetic resonance (MR) imaging and ultrasound contrast enhancement.

1. Nanocarrier platforms for inhaled chemotherapy
   Nanocarrier platforms for inhaled chemotherapy have been rapidly developed as promising delivery vehicles to improve lung cancer treatment by facilitating the targeted delivery of suitable drugs to the respiratory tract, maximizing local drug concentration, and reducing systemic toxicity. These platforms mainly consist of lipid-based systems, such as liposomes, solid lipid NPs (SLNs), and nanostructured lipid carriers (NLCs), providing versatility in the encapsulation of both hydrophilic and hydrophobic drugs, improved stability in surfactant-rich pulmonary environments, and compatibility with inhalation devices (dry powder inhalers [DPI], nebulizer). Biodegradable polymers, including PLGA and chitosan, can be manipulated to exhibit mucoadhesive and mucopenetrating characteristics to enhance lung retention and cell uptake, and their NPs can be controlled in terms of rate and thus controlled to release at specific rates. Other benefits of hybrid constructs containing lipids and polymers are greater stability and functionality, including oxygen delivery and imaging (when PFC cores are included). The NPs of PFC that are administered through the pulmonary route have a number of exclusive characteristics, including high oxygen solubility, visibility under ultrasound/magnetic resonance imaging

(MRI), and the ability to regulate hypoxia in tumor-supportive theranostic therapies. The key considerations about the formulation design are optimization of the particle size to achieve efficient deposition in the lungs, optimization of the surface chemistry through the targeting of ligands (e.g., EGFR and PD-L1), and the selection of an appropriate aerosol device to maintain the integrity of the NPs and delivery efficiency. The most recent research has demonstrated the possibility of such nanocarrier platforms to enhance drug bioavailability, therapeutic efficacy, and reduce off-target effects, which is a significant accomplishment in personalized and precision medicine of lung cancer (Gandhi & Roy, 2023; Kakaei et al., 2023a; Panovich et al., 2025).

2. Lipid-based systems
   Lipid-based systems have received considerable attention as effective nanocarriers for inhaled chemotherapy in the treatment of lung cancer because of their biocompatibility, ease of production, and ability to accommodate both hydrophilic and hydrophobic drugs.
   a. Liposomes: Liposomes are one of the most studied lipid-based nanocarriers in lung cancer chemotherapy due to their physicochemical properties, which address most of the issues of the pulmonary drug delivery process. Liposomes are phospholipid vesicles composed of phospholipid-based bilayers that have hydrophilic drugs inside the aqueous core and hydrophobic drugs inside the lipid bilayer; therefore they can be used to deliver a wide range of anticancer drugs (Gandhi & Roy, 2023). PEGylation, which refers to the attachment of polyethylene glycol (PEG) chains to the liposome face, is one of the significant enhancements of the liposomal technology. This alteration is credited with the stabilization of liposomes by steric hindrance, decreased opsonization, and clearance of the alveoli by macrophages of the lungs, leading to increased circulation times and increased tumor deposition (Kassaee et al., 2024). PEGylation also enhances the stability of liposomes against aggregation and fusion, which is relevant in surfactant-rich pulmonary pathways in which proteins and phospholipids that destabilize lipid structures are found.
      The behavior of liposomes during inhalation therapy is important for the surface charge. Uncharged and negatively charged liposomes are more dispersible and stable than positively charged liposomes, with little toxicity and no specific affinity to lung cells or mucus (Rajoriya et al., 2024). This type of tuning is required to attain optimum aerosol functionality, in which the liposomes can penetrate the deepest part of the alveoli and reach the tumor microenvironment. In addition, it can be used in conjunction with the framework of surface charge modification to enhance targeting; for example, anionic liposomes have a reduced clearance rate but may require additional targeting ligands.
      Liposomes can encapsulate a wide variety of chemotherapeutic agents. Hydrophilic drugs (cisplatin, gemcitabine) are confined to the inner aqueous compartment, and hydrophobic drugs (paclitaxel, docetaxel) are incorporated into the lipid bilayer, which guarantees the stability and bioavailability of the drugs

(Gandhi & Roy, 2023). Drug release can be controlled through the achievement of lipid composition and membrane fluidity, and sustained therapeutic levels in the lung tissues can be maintained. This extended drug release reduces the number of dosing schedules and systemic side effects, which is particularly advantageous in the treatment of patients who require long-term treatment.

Liposomal inhalation has been proven to be more effective than systemic chemotherapy in the treatment of lung cancer. PEGylated liposomal doxorubicin and paclitaxel preparations have been proven to result in tumor death, systemic toxicity, and survival in preclinical models of lung cancer (Kassaee et al., 2024; Rajoriya et al., 2024). Moreover, modification of inhalable liposomes by surface functionalization with targeting ligands (e.g., antibodies and peptides against overexpressed receptors on lung cancer cells: EGFR and PD-L1) can improve drug selectivity and therapeutic efficacy (Gandhi & Roy, 2023).

Lung formulation problems emerge owing to the abundance of surfactants in the environment, which can destabilize liposomes. Nevertheless, recent improvements in the optimization of lipid composition, including the addition of cholesterol and sphingomyelin to liposomes, have increased the mechanical properties of liposomes, including rigidity and resistance to surfactant disruption (Rajoriya et al., 2024). All these enhancements are aimed at maintaining the integrity of liposomes following aerosolization and deposition of the substance in the lungs, such that the maximum therapeutic payload is delivered into the tumor (Table 8.1).

b. Solid lipid NPs and nanostructured lipid carriers: SLN and NLCs are new forms of lipid-based nanocarrier systems that have found significant application in pulmonary chemotherapy of lung cancer due to excellent biocompatibility, enhanced drug stability, and controlled and sustained drug delivery. The common SLNs are made with fully crystalline lipids; thus they have low drug loading and a high likelihood of drug expulsion during storage. The common SLNs are made with fully crystalline lipids, thus low drug loading and the likelihood of drug expulsion during storage. NLCs, on the contrary, are a mixture of solid and liquid lipids and less-ordered lipid matrices, allowing a greater drug loading and reduced loss of drugs, as well as increased drug therapeutic activity in lung cancer models (Viegas et al., 2023). Crystallinity was also fine-tuned in the lipid matrices to deliver a balance between structural strength and controlled release, allowing the controllable long-term release of chemotherapeutics, e.g., paclitaxel and docetaxel, to sustain therapeutic drug concentrations in the lungs over extended periods.

Moreover, SLNs and NLCs can be easily used with pulmonary administration devices, primarily DPIs and NP nebulizers. Their insolubility and controllable size make them ideal for aerosol-like behavior, capable of being deposited into the deep lung, and the emergence of novel spray-drying and freeze–drying methods has led to inhalable (dry powder) NP forms

Table 8.1: Comparison of nanocarrier platforms for inhalation.

Nanocarrier type	Drug loading	Stability in the lungs	Release profile	Delivery devices	Targeting ability	References
Liposomes	High	Stable with PEGylation	Sustained, controlled	Mesh nebulizers, DPIs	Ligand-modified for EGFR, PD-L1	Gandhi and Roy (2023), Rajoriya et al. (2024)
Solid lipid nanoparticles	Moderate	Good with surfactants	Sustained	DPIs, jet nebulizers	Surface modifiable	Safdar et al. (2025)
Nanostructured lipid carriers	High	High stability	Sustained	DPIs, nebulizers	Functionalize	Rajoriya et al. (2024)
Polymeric nanoparticles	High	Stable; mu-coadhesive	Tunable (immediate to stimuli-responsive)	Mesh nebulizers, DPIs	Responsive coatings	Panovich et al. (2025)
Lipid–polymer hybrids	High	Enhanced stability	Controlled, stimuli-responsive	Mesh nebulizers, DPIs	Dual targeting & imaging	Kassaee et al. (2024)
Perfluorocarbon nanoparticles	Moderate	Stable emulsions	Sustained, oxygen-enhanced	Mesh nebulizers	Hypoxia targeting, imaging	Kakaei et al. (2023)
Protein/enzyme carriers	Variable	Less stable, needs stabilization	Immediate or enzyme-triggered	Experimental nebulizers	Highly specific	

DPI, dry powder inhaler; *EGFR*, Epidermal growth factor receptor; *PD-L1*, programmed death-ligand 1.

that preserve the structure of the NPs and the properties of the drug (Weber et al., 2013). This compatibility is useful for enhancing patient compliance because it allows chemotherapeutic agents to be delivered to lung tumors via noninvasive and targeted delivery. Inhaled NLC formulations have recently been demonstrated to enhance systemic toxicity and anticancer activity and enhance systemic retention of tumors by drugs by avoiding clearance activity (Kim et al., 2023). Dual-drug-loaded NLCs can be used in combination chemotherapy to realize synergism and avoid multidrug resistance in lung cancer cells.

SLN and NLC surfaces can be further functionalized with targeting ligands or hydrophilic polymers to increase muco-adhesion or muco-penetration, thereby maximizing tumor targeting and increasing therapy. In addition, they have demonstrated enhanced resistance to pulmonary surfactants and their structural integrity upon inhalation (Rajoriya et al., 2024). All these features render SLNs and NLCs prospective nanocarrier systems for future inhaled chemotherapy of lung cancer, where the synergistic benefits of increased pharmacokinetics, precise targeting, and straightforward delivery to patients are combined.

8.3.5 Hybrid systems: Polymeric systems

The development of polymeric and hybrid nanocarriers has also led to the development of promising and effective drug delivery systems for pulmonary chemotherapy in the treatment of lung cancer, with the advantage of better drug-release kinetics, stability, and targeted delivery. Mucoadhesive (improving the residence time in the lungs) or mucopenetrating (enhancing tissue penetration) polymeric NPs can be prepared based on biodegradable polymers, including poly(lactic-co-glycolic acid) (PLGA), chitosan, and PEG derivatives. These systems offer the possibility of accurately modulating drug release patterns (immediate to sustained release or stimuli-responsive release) by changing the composition of polymers, molecular weight, and degradation rates, and achieving an optimum level and distribution of therapeutics locally at the location of the tumor and reducing side effects on other body regions (Panovich et al., 2025). Hybrid nanocarriers, in particular lipid–polymer hybrids, are polymers that combine the stability and controlled-release characteristics of polymers with the biocompatibility and versatile functionality of lipids. One of the factors that leads to lung cancer resistance to chemotherapy and radiotherapy is the use of PFC (n) cores incorporated into core-shell hybrid NPs that offer core-shell NPs-specific oxygen-carrying and imaging properties for theranostic applications (Kakaei et al., 2023Kassaee et al., 2024). Moreover, these hybrid systems can be used to co-deliver chemotherapeutic agents with nucleic acid or immune-regulating agents, which have a synergistic anticancer effect. It is also important to note the versatility and excellent scalability of polymeric and hybrid systems and their ability to interact with pulmonary delivery devices, including nebulizers and DPI, and the way in which they can inform the creation of personalized and precise therapeutics to treat lung cancer (Fig. 8.2).

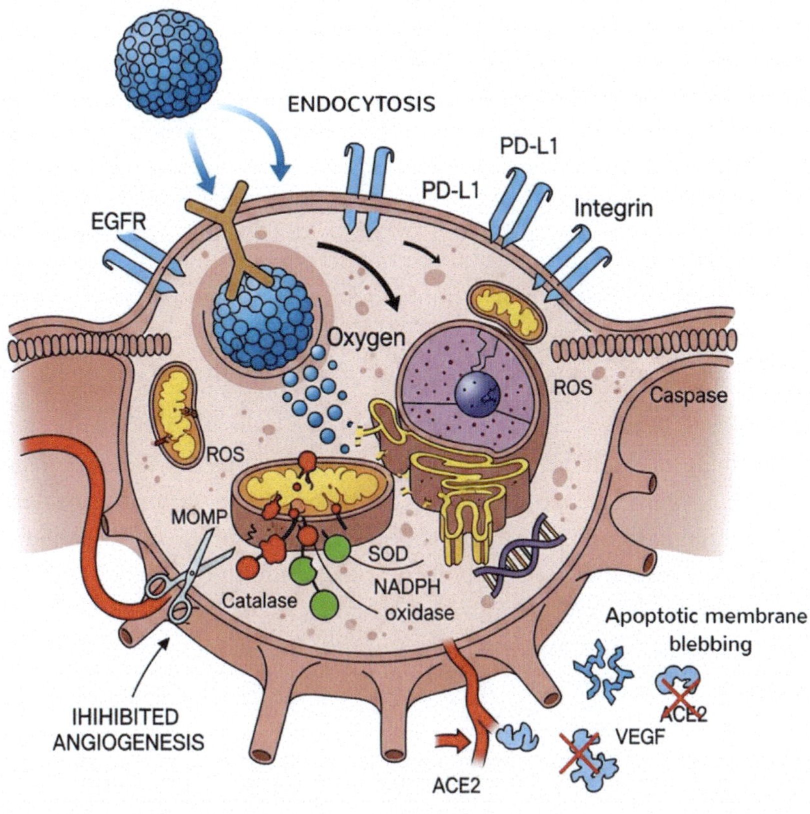

Figure 8.2

PFC nanoparticle design and oxygen-mediated tumor sensitization. This illustration represents a specific treatment nanoparticle with an oxygen carrier PFC core covered with EGFR, PD-L1, and integrin antibodies. The nanoparticles release oxygen upon endocytosis by tumor cells to form reactive oxygen species (ROS). Such ROS bursts result in mitochondrial outer membrane permeabilization (MOMP), caspase release, DNA damage, and apoptotic cell blebbing, thus attaining tumor sensitization to chemotherapy and radiotherapy. In addition, oxygen counteracts hypoxia, which causes the downregulation (strike-through) of Hypoxia-inducible factor 1-alpha (HIF-1α), Vascular Endothelial Growth Factor (VEGF), and Angiotensin-converting enzyme 2 (ACE2), and eventually suppresses angiogenesis. *EGFR*, Epidermal growth factor receptor; *PD-L1*, programmed death-ligand 1; *PFC*, perfluorocarbon.

1. Polymeric NPs: Polymeric NPs such as PLGA, chitosan, and PEG variants are being increasingly used in the chemotherapy of lung cancers because of their tunable properties that allow the triggering of drugs into the lungs in a controlled manner. For lung cancer treatment, these two types of NPs are engineered either as mucoadhesive systems, which attach to the mucosal surface of the lungs to increase the retention and local concentration of the drug, or as mucopenetrating systems, which can overcome the mucus barrier and penetrate deeper into the tumor tissues. PLGA-based NPs provide a sustained drug

release effect due to hydrolytic degradation and help provide long-term therapeutic levels of chemotherapeutics, such as doxorubicin and paclitaxel. Reducing the frequency of dosages and systemic toxicity (Kapoor et al., 2025). Wang et al. found that chitosan NPs show mucoadhesive properties due to their positive charge to interact electrostatically with mucus negatively charged surfaces, leading to an increase in residence time and absorption of the drug in the lung tissue. Further stabilization, decreased clearance, and extension of circulation time by PEGylation of polymeric NPs enable deep penetration into lung tissues. The results showed that the release can be controlled by adjusting the polymer molecular weight, composition, and degradation rates to maintain effective drug concentrations in the tumor microenvironment for a longer time to enhance chemotherapeutic efficacy. These novel systems can be used with pulmonary delivery devices (e.g., DPI and nebulizers) to ensure a noninvasive route of administration with high patient compliance (Zhang et al., 2024). Recent studies have highlighted the importance of polymeric NPs with optimized mucoadhesive or mucopenetrating properties in lung cancer treatment, particularly in terms of improved drug bioavailability, tumor targeting capability, and therapeutic response, especially for the use of multiple agents or gene co-delivery found that polymeric NPs with optimized mucoadhesive or mucopenetrating properties enhance drug bioavailability, tumor targeting ability, and therapeutic response in lung cancer treatment, particularly when applied for co-delivery of multiple agents or gene therapy (Da Silva Gündel et al., 2025).

2. Lipid–polymer hybrid NPs combine the mechanical strength and controlled-release properties of polymers, such as PLGA, with the biocompatibility and tunable surface chemistry of lipids for vehicles with improved stability, high drug-loading capacity, and cellular uptake. Lipid–polymer hybrid NPs are a combination of the mechanical strength and controlled-release properties of polymers, such as PLGA, biocompatibility, and tunable surface chemistry of lipids for vehicles with improved stability, high drug-loading capacity, and cellular uptake. These hybrids can be used to co-deliver chemotherapeutics and gene therapeutics, which can achieve synergistic anticancer abilities that can overcome drug resistance in lung tumors (Kassaee et al., 2024).

The development of PFC cores is a further step toward lung cancer chemotherapy, given their ability to carry oxygen extremely well and overcome tumor hypoxia, which is a major contributor to therapeutic resistance and poor prognosis. Oxygenated PFC cores cause a local increase in the oxygen level of the tumor, which sensitizes cancer cells to chemotherapy and radiotherapy, while simultaneously enabling noninvasive imaging modalities, such as ^{19}F-MRI and ultrasound, for real-time treatment monitoring and diagnosis (Kakaei et al., 2023). This theranostic feature enables the optimization of treatment regimens at both the efficacy and side effect levels, while offering the opportunity for personalization. The core-shell structure results in a protective shell that improves PFC stability and subsequently controls the release of encapsulated drugs to maintain sustained delivery to the lung tumor site. Collectively, these hybrid platforms have tremendous scope for innovations in inhaled chemotherapy regarding enhanced oxygen delivery and specific targeting, and combined therapeutic and diagnostic capabilities, which are fundamental in the effective control of lung cancer (Kakaei et al., 2023; Sobol et al., 2025).

8.3.6 Perfluorocarbon nanoparticles via intratracheal route

PFC NPs administered via the intratracheal (IT) route offer a novel and promising approach for lung cancer treatment by combining the advantages of localized drug delivery with the unique physicochemical properties of PFCs. These NPs can efficiently deliver chemotherapeutics to lung tumors (and other sites), increasing the concentration of drugs at the site of action and reducing systemic exposure and associated toxicities. PFCs are characterized by their high solubility in oxygen; thus PFC NPs can be used to modulate tumor hypoxia, which is a major obstacle to effective chemotherapy and radiotherapy in lung cancer. By increasing the oxygen supply in the tumor microenvironment, PFC NPs render cancer cells vulnerable to cancer therapy, which could help overcome resistance mechanisms (Kakaei et al., 2023).

IT delivery of PFC NPs allows for deep deposition in the lungs and tumor-selective retention owing to the optimized particle size and surfactant compatibility, which also helps circumvent rapid elimination by alveolar macrophages. In addition, PFC NPs can be used as contrast agents for innovative imaging techniques, such as ^{19}F-MRI and ultrasound, which can allow noninvasive theranostics-based monitoring of tumor response and NP biodistribution in real time. Formulation strategies are concerned with the stability of emulsions, droplet sizes, and surfactant–surfactant interactions to guarantee the integrity of the NPs and their maximum effect on delivering them to the lung. All these features predispose intratracheally delivered PFC NPs as a flexible device to be used in improving targeted chemotherapy, oxygenation, and diagnostic imaging in the treatment of lung cancer (Kassaee et al., 2024; Shi et al., 2023).

1. Local high dose, tumor selective, retained, and systemic low exposure
   Chemotherapeutics contained in PFC NPs can be delivered directly to the lung, which contains lung tumors, via the pulmonary route. Such local delivery will assist in delivering high levels of the drug to the tumor site, which will increase its effectiveness against malignancies and decrease systemic uptake and related toxicities, which occur in most cases with intravenous chemotherapy. Optimization of the particle size and surface properties achieves tumor-selective retention of these NPs and, therefore preferential accumulation within tumor tissue through the effects of enhanced permeability and retention and interaction with tumor microenvironment components. This approach achieves maximum tumor suppression while sparing healthy tissues, making the treatment process less severe and ensuring improvement in the patient's quality of life (Kakaei et al., 2023; Weber et al., 2013).

2. Physical and chemical properties: Oxygen solubility, ultrasound/MR visibility, hypoxia modulation, and theranostics
   PFC NPs exhibit excellent oxygen solubility and can transport and deliver oxygen directly to hypoxic tumor areas. Hypoxia plays a role in increasing the aggressiveness and resistance of tumors to treatment, representing a major challenge in lung cancer therapy. By alleviating hypoxia, PFC NPs render tumors more sensitive to chemotherapy and radiotherapy. In addition, PFCs possess inherent imaging properties and can be used as contrast agents in both ultrasound and 19F-MRI, facilitating the identification of tumor locations and real-time tracking of therapeutic delivery. This theranostic capability combines treatment and diagnosis in a single system, enabling personalized adjustments to therapy and enhancing clinical outcomes (Kakaei et al., 2023; Kassaee et al., 2024).
3. Formulation notes
   Formulating PFC NPs for pulmonary delivery, to maintain a uniform droplet size, must consider the stability of the emulsification to avoid droplet size coalescence, which could affect the efficiency of delivery and lung deposition. Surfactants are used to stabilize emulsions and increase compatibility with lung surfactants to avoid clumping of NPs and aid in the passage through mucus barriers. Droplet and particle size (usually <200 nm for NPs and aerodynamic diameters in the range of 1–5 mm for inhalable droplets) should be controlled to achieve efficient deep lung penetration and retention at the tumor sites. These novel technologies include high-pressure homogenization and microfluidization, which are employed in the manufacture of stable monodisperse PFC NPs for the formulation of nebulized or DPI.

8.3.7 Formulation design principles: Pulmonary delivery

The design principles for the formulation of NPs for pulmonary delivery in lung cancer chemotherapy include optimizing particle characteristics and surface properties to achieve the greatest therapeutic efficacy with minimal off-target effects.

1. Particles with aerodynamic diameters of 1–5 μm are efficient for deposition in the lower airways and alveolar areas, which are key to targeting lung tumors. Density tuning by material choice or particle porosity allows for the control of aerodynamic behavior; porous or low-density particles have lower aerodynamic diameters than they are geometrically, which improves deep lung deposition. Nanosized inhalable microparticles are aggregated in aggregated microstructures and nanocomposites in the form of microparticles and disaggregates upon administration, combining attributes of deep lung delivery and NP release, i.e., increasing cellular uptake and controlled release. The strategies also lead to successful tumor targeting through the elimination of barriers to the immune system (mucus entrapment and clearance by alveolar macrophage) (Weber et al., 2013; Winer et al., 2018).

2. Surface chemistry: This is a balance between hydrophilicity and hydrophobicity on the surface of nanoparticles and determines mucous and immune recognition penetration. The presence of zwitterionic coating offers a neutral charge and hydration shell that develops an antifouling effect and minimizes protein adsorption and uptake by the macrophages, thus enhancing the residence time in the lungs. PEG or polysaccharide coating is also used as an antifouling coating, hence enhancing the stealth characteristics of the nanoparticles. Selective binding and uptake of drugs and therapeutic properties in lung cancerous tumor cells can be achieved after incorporation of targeting ligands specific to lung cancer markers (e.g., EGFR, programmed death-ligand 1 [PD-L1], and integrins). These types of surface modifications are crucial for addressing tumor heterogeneity and delivering payloads to the exact locations where they are required, with reduced side effects throughout the body (Singh et al., 2025; Swaminathan & Ehrhardt, 2011).
3. Immediate-release formulations enable the high-speed availability of the drug in lung tissues, which is useful for acute intervention in which the drug must quickly kill the tumor. However, lung tumors are often heterogeneous and have complex microenvironments such as hypoxia, acidic microenvironments, and high expression of certain enzymes, which weaken the efficacy of traditional chemotherapy. To overcome this, the concept of sustained-release systems has been introduced to ensure that the levels of therapeutic drugs are maintained for longer periods, thereby avoiding rapid elimination of the therapeutic drug and reducing the frequency of dosing, which will improve the level of adherence and patient compliance. Sustained-release formulations of inhaled chemotherapy are frequently used based on matrix materials, such as PLGA and lipid-based polymers, to provide a uniform anticancer effect in lung tumors over an extended period (Panovich et al., 2025).

   More sophisticated stimuli-responsive release systems respond to specific cues in the tumor microenvironment, such as acidic pH, elevated glutathione concentration, or overexpressed enzymes, such as matrix metalloproteinases. These systems locally release their payload in the vicinity of the tumor, thereby improving drug concentration in the tumor and reducing systemic toxicity. For example, pH-sensitive polymer coatings can degrade in the acidic environment of tumors (pH $\sim$ 6.5), which triggers the release of the drug directly at the location where it is required. In addition, chemoselective linkages are abrogated by high intracellular glutathione levels to guarantee intracellular drug release after nanoparticle internalization into cancer cells. In addition to enhancing targeting accuracy, stimuli-responsive structures facilitate drug resistance by achieving effective intracellular drug concentrations (Kassaee et al., 2024; Singh et al., 2025). The release pattern of this smart release system is in accordance with the physiological conditions of lung tumors; thus it permits a dynamic and personalized chemotherapy schedule according to the specific tumor profile of the patient. In addition to nanoparticle surface modifications for targeting and pulmonary routes for drug delivery, carrier systems with fine-tuned release profiles are major innovations in lung cancer chemotherapy. They can optimize treatment effects, decrease side effects, and surmount the limitations of traditional systemic chemotherapy.

4. Optimal combination of devices and formulations: Pulmonary chemotherapy of lung cancer depends on the optimal combination of devices and formulations that directly influence the efficacy of drug delivery, stability, and patient adherence based on nanoparticles. Nebulizers (jet, ultrasonic, and mesh) are widely used to disperse nanoparticles in liquids. Jet nebulizers are characterized by the formation of aerosols with the aid of compressed air; however, they also cause comparatively high levels of shear forces that can destabilize delicate nanoparticles, resulting in aggregation or breakdown of the drug substance. Ultrasonic nebulizers apply high-frequency vibrations that may cause heating and alteration of nanoparticle integrity. In contrast, mesh nebulizers utilize vibrating mesh technology, which is less harsh aerosolizing, has low shear stress, and concomitantly maintains nanoparticle stability, bioactivity, and dose reproducibility; therefore it is particularly advantageous for fragile nanoparticle formulations (Safdar et al., 2025).

Aerosolized drugs are delivered through pressurized metered-dose inhalers (pMDIs), which propel the drugs; therefore they should be formulated with care to ensure that nanoparticles are not collected or sedimented in the device. Because nanoparticles can be shear-sensitive during actuation, this can affect homogeneity or re-dispersibility, so stabilizer excipients or surfactants may be needed in the formulation. DPI devices have the benefit of being stable and portable, since they provide the drug powder for inhalation by the patient. The formulation of DPIs is optimized for particle size, flowability, and dispersibility to achieve deep lung deposition. Currently, nanomedicines are frequently prepared in the form of porous or hollow microparticles to improve aerosolization and redispersibility after inhalation. Ensuring the integrity of nanoparticles and avoiding irreversible aggregation are important criteria for therapeutic efficiency. Overall, matching the device type with formulation characteristics (such as shear sensitivity, particle size, and physical state) is key to targeted effective pulmonary chemotherapy with high patient compliance (Table 8.2; Lee et al., 2025; Rajoriya et al., 2024).

8.4 Drug resistance: Mechanisms of action and overcoming

8.4.1 Intracellular delivery and endosomal escape

After being deposited in the alveoli and internalized by cells, the most significant challenge faced by nanoparticles is the delivery of cargo to therapeutic targets. The main route of uptake is endocytosis, and nanoparticles enter via clathrin-mediated, caveolin-mediated, or macropinocytic pathways based on their surface characteristics and size (Akhter et al., 2015). Nevertheless, conventional endosomal trafficking pathways entrap nanoparticles in increasingly acidic compartments (early endosomes to late endosomes to lysosomes), which

Table 8.2: Key enzyme and protein pathways in lung cancer.

Enzyme/protein pathway	Role in lung cancer pathophysiology	Therapeutic targeting strategy	Therapeutic agents	References
EGFR signaling pathway	Regulates cell proliferation; often mutated in lung tumors	Tyrosine kinase inhibitors block EGFR activity	Gefitinib, erlotinib	Rajoriya et al. (2024)
phosphatidylinositol 3-kinase (PI3K/AKT)/ Mechanistic Target of Rapamycin (mTOR) pathway	Controls cell growth, survival, metabolism	Inhibitors induce apoptosis and growth arrest	Everolimus, buparlisib	Qiang et al. (2025), Singh et al. (2025)
PD-1/PD-L1 immune checkpoint	Tumor immune evasion by inhibiting T-cell activation	Immune checkpoint inhibitors restore the immune response	Nivolumab, pembrolizumab	Alsaab et al. (2017), Alsaab et al. (2017)
Matrix metallo-proteinases (MMPs)	ECM degradation facilitates tumor invasion and metastasis	MMP inhibitors reduce metastasis and invasiveness	Marimastat, prinomastat	Lee et al. (2025)

EGFR, epidermal growth factor receptor; *PD-1*, programmed death-ligand 1; *PD-L1*, programmed death-ligand 1.

in turn degrades or traps chemotherapeutic agents out of the location of action. pH-reactive polymers, including ionizable groups (histidine and imidazole), are gated in acidic endosomal compartments where they are protonated, resulting in an enhanced positive charge and osmotic swelling that destabilizes endosomal membranes via the proton sponge mechanism (Ding et al., 2024). In other cases, cell-penetrating peptides (CPPs) and fusogenic lipids incorporated into the surface of nanoparticles directly disrupt the lipid bilayers via membrane disruption pathways. Effective cytosolic delivery allows chemotherapeutic agents to reach cytoplasmic targets (mitochondria and microtubule networks) and subsequently accumulate in the nucleus, where DNA-interactive agents exert their effects (Akhter et al., 2015). Nanoparticles that feature both endosomal escape and nuclear targeting sequences (nuclear localization sequences) are even more effective in that they result in direct nuclear importation as opposed to passive diffusion into the cell.

8.4.2 Hypoxia and oxygenation tumor microenvironment modulation

Hypoxia in tumors is one of the greatest impediments to successful chemotherapy as it promotes inherent drug resistance and favors aggressive tumor phenotypes. Hypoxic areas in tumors are less susceptible to chemotherapy because of reduced drug metabolism, altered cell physiology, and induction of hypoxia-inducible factors (HIFs), leading to survival signaling. Hypoxia also promotes EMT, which promotes metastatic capacity and the development of cancer stem cell features. Other complementary approaches to managing tumor acidity, another characteristic of the hypoxic microenvironment, involve pH-buffering nanoparticles that counteract lactate-mediated acidification, restore antitumor immune responses, and sensitize tumors to pH-sensitive chemotherapeutic drugs. Microenvironment-targeted approaches represent a paradigm shift from agent-centric cancer therapy to ecosystem-centric cancer therapy.

8.4.3 Combinations logic: Chemotherapy, immunotherapy, and gene therapy

In complicated tumor ecologies in which both resistance mechanisms occur, monotherapy strategies have fundamental constraints. Combination strategies facilitate simultaneous targeting of tumor cells and immunosuppressive microenvironmental factors. Pulmonary delivery allows direct priming of lung-associated lymphoid tissue (LALT), which is a large immune reservoir with the potential to develop powerful antitumor responses (Donkor & Jones, 2021). Inhibitors of PD-1/PD-L1 are introduced through the pulmonary route and directly reach tumor-infiltrating lymphocytes, overcoming the suppressive effect of exhaustion (Puglisi et al., 2025). Immunotherapy can be augmented by chemotherapy using immunogenic cell death (ICD), in which damaged tumor cells secrete damage-associated molecular patterns (DAMPs) that stimulate dendritic cell maturation and T-cell priming. Therefore checkpoint blockade in combination with chemotherapy provides synergistic antitumor immunity. There are numerous ways in which gene therapy supplements chemotherapy. Multidrug resistance gene (MDR1/P-glycoprotein) siRNAs can be co-loaded into polymeric nanoparticles with chemotherapy-inducing sensitization of tumors to chemotherapy (Akhter et al., 2015). Pro-survival pathway anti-miR-21 (anti-miR-155) microRNA therapeutics increase chemotherapy-induced apoptosis (Petrek & Yu, 2019). CRISPR-Cas9 can be permanently silenced using nanoparticles, which is a fundamentally curative method for permanently silencing the resistance mechanisms of selected resistance drivers (Le et al., 2021).

8.4.4 Multidrug resistance mechanisms and inhibition of efflux pumps

Efflux pumps are the major mechanism underlying acquired chemotherapy resistance, actively pumping out drugs from cells to maintain sub-therapeutic intracellular levels. MDR1/P-glycoprotein and MRP1 are ABC transporters that are often overexpressed in resistant tumors. These pumps recognize a variety of chemotherapy structures, which explains the cross-resistance between multiple classes of drugs (Shi et al., 2023). Two solutions may be considered to overcome resistance resulting from efflux. First, resistant tumors may be chemosensitized by direct inhibition of pump function via competitive antagonists or allosteric modulators (Akhter et al., 2015). Second, encapsulation of chemotherapy agents with nanoparticles is a highly efficient method for protecting the agent against pump recognition, as conjugated or encapsulated drugs do not bind to pump ATPase-binding sites (Ding et al., 2024). Hybrid solutions involving the two therapies, encapsulation of chemotherapy and simultaneous transfection with MDR1 inhibitors or siRNA, result in complete chemosensitization in resistant models (Akhter et al., 2015). In addition to efflux pumps, DNA repair amplification is a vital mechanism of resistance, and the upregulation of nucleotide excision repair (NER), mismatch repair (MMR), and homologous recombination (HR) pathways can help tumor cells endure DNA damage. Synthetic lethality can be achieved by co-delivering DNA repair inhibitors (PARP inhibitors, checkpoint kinase inhibitors) with chemotherapy targets, which are tumors that require certain repair pathways (Akhter et al., 2015).

8.5 Obstacles and hindrances to clinical translation

8.5.1 Physiological barriers: Macrophage interactions, surfactant, and mucus

The respiratory distress barrier is the mucus of the respiratory system, and it is a significant impediment to efficient nanoparticle delivery. The mucus layer, which consists of a viscoelastic gel (mucins, immunoglobulins, and antimicrobial proteins), physically traps inhaled particles and quickly clears them (Akhter et al., 2015). In cancer patients, epithelial damage caused by chemotherapy can result in increased mucus production as a regenerative mechanism, which further hinders nanoparticle deposition (Khatib et al., 2023). Mucopenetrating formulas can overcome this barrier by coating the surface of the particles with PEG or other hydrophilic polymers that fail to permit mucus adhesion and afford diffusion of particles through mucus networks. PEGylation is, however, a very harsh tradeoff, as PEG coating reduces cellular uptake due to a lack of ligand–receptor interaction and opsonization with surfactant proteins. This necessitates careful consideration of PEG density and chain length to balance mucus penetration and cellular interactions. Pulmonary surfactants present a challenge and a chance. Pattern recognition receptors (surfactant protein [SP-A] and dendritic cell [SP-D]) are expressed by alveolar macrophages and dendritic cells and mediate the recognition and clearance of opsonized nanoparticles (Akhter et al., 2015). Nevertheless, nanoparticles can be biologically coated with surfactant-phospholipids, which form biomimetic carriers with increased lung retention and decreased immunogenicity in endogenous surfactant mimicry (Akhter et al., 2015). Another drawback is macrophage interactions. The clearance of pathogens and debris depends on alveolar macrophages, which cannot completely clear nanoparticles in the systemic space; therefore their rapid uptake and subsequent processing of nanoparticles favor the clearance of delivered carriers. Evasion of macrophage uptake and avoidance of inflammatory activation include PEGylation of the surface, the addition of CD47 to deliver do not eat me signals, and targeting properties that redirect particle–surface markers on pattern recognition receptors to a particular cancer cell surface receptor (Akhter et al., 2015).

8.5.2 Scale-up, process development, and manufacturing

Transitioning promising laboratory-scale nanochemotherapy formulations into clinical-grade products presents significant challenges. The fact that reproducibility among manufacturing batches is a demand that cannot be met without regulatory approval serves as an indication of why nanoemulsions and polymeric nanoparticles are highly sensitive to process parameters, such as temperature, mixing rate, and residence time (Alsaab et al., 2022). Any changes in a small parameter can significantly alter the particle size distribution, drug loading, and encapsulation efficiency, with downstream implications for efficacy and safety. Ethanol separation is one such bottleneck in the production of nanoparticle polymers. Traditional emulsion-based practices have a lengthy evaporation of solvents or dialysis step to eliminate organic solvents, which raises concerns about the quantity of solvents that remain and inter-lot variability (Alsaab et al., 2022). These needs can be satisfied by solvent-free techniques, including supercritical fluid technology, spray drying, and nanoprecipitation in aqueous solutions; however, these processes must be optimized and validated (Akhter et al., 2015). Direct delivery of pulmonary products that are targeted to lung tissues must be sterilized. Traditional methods of gamma radiation or ethylene oxide terminal sterilization have been shown to destroy thermolabile nanoparticles or interfere with drug filling and release kinetics (Akhter et al., 2015). This requires the application of aseptic production by sterile filtration and lyophilization with the respective cryoprotectants, adding considerable costs and complexity (Alsaab et al., 2022). Continuous manufacturing methods, such as microfluidic synthesis and inline ultrasonic mixing, are more reproducible and less wasteful of solvents than batch processes; however, they require a large capital outlay and adjustments to the regulatory framework (Akhter et al., 2015). The integration of quality by design (QbD) and process analytical technology (PAT) is becoming a mandatory requirement of regulatory agencies when developing a nanoparticle product. In QbD, critical process parameters and critical quality attributes should be identified prospectively, and the design space and control strategy should be developed (Alsaab et al., 2022). The implementation of PAT allows the monitoring of key parameters in real-time by employing inline analytical techniques, such as particle size, polydispersity, and zeta potential, and automatically adjusts the processes to meet the specifications (Akhter et al., 2015).

8.5.3 Stability and storage requirements

Nanoparticle formulations have many stability issues during manufacturing, storage, and administration, which significantly impair their efficacy. Physical instability mechanisms, such as Ostwald ripening (the increase in large particles at the cost of small ones), coalescence, and aggregation, may cause drastic changes in the particle size distribution and drug release rates during storage (Akhter et al., 2015). These phenomena are thermodynamically driven and occur irrespective of formulation elegance in the absence of proper stabilization measures (Akhter et al., 2015). Lyophilization (freeze–drying) is an ideal stabilization method for nanoparticles, as it transforms aqueous suspensions into dry powders with a significantly increased shelf life (Akhter et al., 2015). Nevertheless, freeze–drying causes damage to nanoparticles due to ice crystal development and osmotic stress during freezing and collapse effects during drying. During freezing, cryoprotectants (usually sugars [trehalose, mannitol] or polymers [PVP, dextran]) form amorphous glass, which protects the particles against ice crystal destruction (Akhter et al., 2015). This process requires optimization of cryoprotectants, concentration, and freeze–drying conditions (cooling rate, primary drying time, and shelf temperature) to ensure that the nanoparticles remain intact (Akhter et al., 2015). The cold chain required for labile formulations makes these products expensive and complicated, especially when used in resource-constrained environments. Formulations that are stable at room temperature are desirable and can be achieved by spray drying, supercritical fluid technology, or new formulations that provide intrinsic stability (Akhter et al., 2015). Specifically, with pulmonary delivery, preparations of DPI are stable and enable the simple delivery of dosages and administration to a patient without the use of electricity or water (Akhter et al., 2015).

8.5.4 Safety, toxicology, and long-term biocompatibility

Nanoparticles are directly deposited in the lungs and occur at much lower systemic concentrations than systemically administered drugs and have distinct safety hazards that must be carefully considered. Local irritation and inflammation can reduce lung functionality and patient tolerance to repeated doses. The inflammatory response of lipid-based nanoparticles can be minimized through smaller endotoxin loading and simplification of surface chemistry; however, more detailed characterization is necessary (Akhter et al., 2015). Nanoparticle products must undergo immunogenicity testing because direct intrapulmonary deposition of a substance triggers a stronger innate immune response than systemic delivery. Recurrent exposure can cause adaptive immune responses to nanoparticle components (especially polymers and proteins), thus decreasing efficacy owing to immune clearance or causing hypersensitivity reactions. The study of immunogenicity in animal models should be conducted on a comprehensive level to evaluate antibody formation, complement activation, and infiltration of immune cells into lung tissues (Akhter et al., 2015). Off-target deposition is a safety concern because inhaled nanoparticles can be deposited in unintended areas of the airways and subsequently cleared, entering the bloodstream. Radiolabeled or fluorescently labeled nanoparticles can be utilized in comprehensive studies of biodistribution, which is required to define the fate of particles after pulmonary delivery and measure the deposition in the lungs, systemic bioavailability, organ distribution, and tissue retention (Akhter et al., 2015). Repeated dosing is likely to be used in the treatment of cancer, and chronic toxicity assessment is essential in this case. The investigation of the long-term pulmonary exposure associated with repeated doses of nanoparticles is vital to Good Laboratory Practice (GLP), as it can be used to determine safety margins, describe dose-response curves, and reveal target organ toxicity. The risk of pulmonary fibrosis should be given special attention, with chronic inflammation or the continued accumulation of nanoparticles potentially favoring fibrotic remodeling (Akhter et al., 2015).

8.5.5 Regulatory path and chemistry, manufacturing, and control requirements

The regulatory pathways for inhaled nanoparticle formulations are complicated, as they are viewed as combination drug-device products in which coordination between the review divisions of pharmaceuticals and medical devices is required. The Chemistry, Manufacturing, and Controls (CMC) sections are required to provide a comprehensive description of the formulation composition, manufacturing operations (with explanations of the development rationale), process controls, and analytical procedures used to evaluate product quality (Alsaab et al., 2022). Particular attention is given to nanoparticle size distribution, morphology, drug loading, and stability. Regulatory agencies are increasingly requiring in vitro–in vivo correlation (IVIVC) development of products containing nanoparticles (Akhter et al., 2015). IVIVC connects laboratory dissolution and release testing to systemic absorption and clinical efficacy, allowing rational bridging between formulation development and clinical performance (Alsaab et al., 2022). In particular, for pulmonary products, in vitro simulations of artificial respiratory fluids (modeling the lung lining fluid) and three-dimensional lung tissues must be matched with in vivo deposition, clearance, and absorption. The bioequivalence of nanoparticle products remains debatable because classic pharmacokinetic biomarkers (area under the curve and peak concentration) may not adequately reflect efficacy dissimilarities due to altered deposition or interactions with cells (Akhter et al., 2015). Regulatory advice is moving toward more mechanistic bioequivalence strategies that include a complete description of in vitro behavior (dissolution and cellular uptake), in vivo deposition, and systemic absorption. Pulmonary-specific clinical efficacy endpoints should include pulmonary functional evaluation (FEV1, forced vital capacity [FVC]), tumor burden evaluation (CT, positron emission tomography [PET]/CT), and pulmonary safety biomarkers. Such adverse pulmonary events as inflammation by nanoparticles, bronchospasm, or fibrosis should be given special consideration as part of clinical monitoring procedures (Akhter et al., 2015).

8.6 Preclinical and clinical assessment system (PCAS)

8.6.1 In vitro model systems: Air–liquid interfaces and barrier systems

Conventional two-dimensional (2D) monolayer cell culture systems fail to reproduce the complicated three-dimensional structure and special physiology of the respiratory epithelium, thereby limiting their predictive capability with respect to inhaled nanoparticle behavior. Air–liquid interface (ALI) models constitute significant improvements that expand human respiratory epithelial cells (or primary cells obtained from patient bronchial brushings) at the border between apical air exposure and basolateral culture medium. The culture system enables physiological air exposure, which promotes the development of mucociliary epithelium that develops into functional tight junctions, beating cilia, and gland-producing goblet cells (Akhter et al., 2015). The ALI model also allows the analysis of nanoparticle deposition, the movement of substances across epithelial barriers, and cell–cell interactions, which are more physiologically realistic than conventional submerged cell cultures (Akhter et al., 2015). It can be mucus-mimetic by co-culture with mucin-secreting cells or exogenous application of a mucus layer, whereby mucopenetrating formulation designs can be evaluated (Akhter et al., 2015). Objective functional measurements applied to assess epithelial integrity and barrier properties of the transport are ciliary beat frequency and transepithelial electrical resistance (TEER). It is possible to introduce immune cell migration—macrophages and dendritic cells—into ALI models to assess the reaction of the inflammatory response and antigen presentation upon exposure to nanoparticles (Akhter et al., 2015). These coupled models provide fast and cost-effective ways of optimizing formulations and investigating nanoparticle–epithelial interactions.

8.6.2 Ex vivo and in vivo models

Precision-cut lung slices (PCLS) are a new ex vivo model that maintains three-dimensional tissue architecture and cellular heterogeneity and physiological capability, as well as in situ exposure to nanoparticles. Slices of thin tissues (200–250 mm) maintain viable and functional epithelial tissue over many days in culture, and in this way, nanoparticle transport, cellular uptake, and inflammatory responses can be determined in real-time (Akhter et al., 2015). PCLS preserves the natural structure of the surfactants and the alveolar macrophage population, which has more physiological benefits compared to isolated cell models. The gold standard in vivo efficacy testing is performed using orthotopic lung tumor models, in which tumor cells are implanted on the lung tissue rather than under the skin. These models can be used to measure the deposition profiles of nanoparticles in tumor-bearing lungs, drug release, and antitumor activity with respect to systemic delivery. The distribution and exposure of drugs in the locations of cancer are determined through pharmacokinetic measurements of imaging drugs conducted with micro-CT, PET/MRI in fluorescent or radiolabeled nanoparticles, and ex vivo analysis of tissues (Akhter et al., 2015). Radiolabeled or near-infrared fluorescent nanoparticles' biodistribution can be used to investigate the fate of the particles after they have been administered into the lungs, which determines the clearance half-life, organ retention, and peripheral deposition. This type of data can be utilized to choose the most appropriate formulations to be applied in clinical development and to develop dosing schedules that are effective and reduce systemic toxicity (Akhter et al., 2015).

8.6.3 Dynamics of advanced imaging and analytics

Micro-computed tomography (mCT) is a technique that allows noninvasive visualization of aerosol deposition patterns in intact lungs at a high spatial resolution on a micrometer scale (Akhter et al., 2015). When combined with PET and labeling of nanoparticles with fluorine-18 or copper-64, deposition patterns and pharmacokinetics can be measured simultaneously (Akhter et al., 2015). In the case of theranostic PFC nanoparticles, there is an inherent MRI functionality that allows the tracking of oxygen delivery and tumor accumulation without any extra labeling (Donkor & Jones, 2021). Mass spectrometry imaging (MSI) is a compelling new method for spatial quantification of drugs in intact tissue sections. High-resolution secondary ion mass spectrometry (SIMS) or matrix-assisted laser desorption ionization (MALDI) can be used to measure local drug concentrations with cellular-scale spatial resolution to study drug delivery using nanoparticles. Pharmacokinetic/pharmacodynamics (PK/PD) modeling combines in vitro and in vivo data to forecast clinical doses and dosing schedules, and considers issues unique to nanoparticles, such as macrophage clearance, surfactant effects, and pH-dependent drug release (Akhter et al., 2015).

8.6.4 Clinical endpoint and biomarker evaluation

Pulmonary nanochemotherapy clinical efficacy outcomes must include both conventional tumor burden outcome measures and pulmonary outcome measures. Endpoints based on imaging, such as the Response Evaluation Criteria in Solid Tumors (RECIST), modified RECIST considered for diffuse pulmonary disease, and volume-based metrics, provide objective tumor assessments. PET/CT functional imaging, including fluorodeoxyglucose and other metabolic tracers, provides an earlier sign of efficacy than size-based thresholds

(Akhter et al., 2015). The safety and tolerability of repeated inhaled dosing were measured using pulmonary function tests, namely forced expiratory volume in 1 s (FEV1), FVC, and diffusion capacity of carbon monoxide (DLCO). These objective findings help differentiate treatment-related pulmonary toxicity and disease progression and quantitatively evaluate lung functional reserve (Akhter et al., 2015). The actual safety biomarkers that are applied to pulmonary drug delivery are the measurement of proinflammatory cytokines (IL-6, TNF-α, IL-8) in bronchoalveolar lavage (BAL) fluid or sputum, circulating neutrophil counts, and imaging-based measurements of pulmonary infiltrates. Circulating tight junction proteins (biomarkers of epithelial and endothelial barrier dysfunction) could provide early detection of unfavorable pulmonary events (Akhter et al., 2015).

8.7 Smart and responsive pulmonary nanomedicines

8.7.1 Responsive drug delivery systems

Stimuli-responsive nanocarriers represent a paradigm shift in cancer nanomedicine, providing the opportunity to use productive formulations in which ionizable polymers remain inactive during systemic delivery and respond to the tumor microenvironment through structural changes at a pH below 6.5 (Rahim et al., 2021). These systems are highly stable at physiological pH (7.4) but quickly destabilize at acidic pH in tumor tissues or within acidic endosomal compartments, thereby enabling selective drug release (Zhou et al., 2018a, 2018b). Redox-responsive nanocarriers exploit the varying reducing conditions of cells, involving the use of disulfide bonds that can be hydrolyzed by reducing agents such as glutathione (GSH), which is present in millimolar concentrations in tumor cells and is insignificant in the extracellular environment (Zhou et al., 2018a). This specificity allows drugs to be released into the intracellular space and preserved when circulating or in the oxidizing tumor interstitium (Zhou et al., 2018b). Enzyme-reactive systems with either peptide sequences or polysaccharide substrates are cleaved to release enzymes that are particularly up-regulated in tumors (matrix metalloproteinases, cathepsin B) or in tumor microenvironments (Rahim et al., 2021). Reactive oxygen species (ROS)-responsive systems represent a novel solution for managing high oxidative stress levels in tumors. Nanoparticles containing ROS-labile bonds (boronic acids and selenium compounds) degrade because of increased tumor-specific ROS, thereby releasing tumor-selective payloads (Rahim et al., 2021). To enable hypoxia-specific activation, hypoxia-inducible transcription factor-binding domains or azide groups are reduced in hypoxic environments, which are present in well-oxygenated tumor regions to achieve hypoxia-responsive activation (Zhou et al., 2018a).

8.7.2 External-initiated delivery systems

Externally controlled systems allow for fine control of drug release, independent of the timing of nanoparticle biodistribution (Zhou et al., 2018a). Systems with ultrasound-induced acoustic cavitation utilize the acoustic cavitation phenomenon to rupture nanoparticle membranes and cargo on demand, specifically for PFC nanoparticles, whose acoustic properties provide highly effective energy absorption. The concentration of ultrasound applicators allows targeting of the tumor region and reduces the release of drugs into healthy tissues, offering a new level of control over space (Akhter et al., 2015). Deep tissues can be delivered using light-activated delivery with near-infrared (NIR) wavelengths with minimal photodamage to healthy tissues (Ai et al., 2016). Nanoparticles loaded with photosensitizers absorb light and undergo a conformational change or heat (photothermal effect), which disrupts lipid membranes and triggers drug release (Ai et al., 2016). Light-responsive systems can be combined with photothermal or photodynamic therapy, and synergistic cytotoxicity of chemotherapy and thermal/phototherapy can be achieved (Ai et al., 2016). A magnetic field-responsive system employing superparamagnetic iron oxide nanoparticles (SPIONs) enables the control of targeting and drug release by applying an external magnetic field to a particle, either by heating the particle (magnetic hyperthermia) or dislodging the nanoparticle structure. In pulmonary applications, external magnetic coils permit preferential deposition in the lung areas, resulting in improved tumor location buildup (Akhter et al., 2015).

8.7.3 Individualized medicine and biomarker-directed targeting

The identification of patient-specific driver mutations and therapeutic targets through genomic and proteomic profiling of individual tumors enables the selection of nanoparticle chemotherapy regimens tailored to the molecular profiles of individual patients (Le et al., 2021). Nanochemotherapy could be useful for tumors containing EGFR mutations with the delivery of EGFR inhibitor nanoparticles, whereas ALK-directed nanochemotherapy is effective for tumors with ALK translocations (Spitaleri et al., 2023). miRNA profiles can be used to select patients who are most likely to respond to miRNA-based therapies and to encourage the rational choice of co-delivered siRNA or anti-miRNA agents (Petrek & Yu, 2019). Patient-specific aerosol profiles, which consider the airway anatomy of the patient, breathing patterns, and disease distribution, can optimize nanoparticle deposition, allowing customized device choices and inhalation education (Akhter et al., 2015). Sensors and wireless connectivity in digital inhalers can offer real-time compliance and monitoring of inhalation techniques and automatic scheduling of doses. In combination with electronic health records, continuous therapy optimization of clinical response and monitoring of adverse events can be achieved (Akhter et al., 2015).

8.7.4 Case studies and new clinical candidates

The clinical development of several therapeutic candidates for pulmonary nanochemotherapy has halted. Cisplatin nanoparticle formulations allow direct delivery to the lungs in high amounts of this DNA-crosslinking agent, with significantly less systemic toxicity than in the case of intravenous administration. Polymeric nanoparticles carrying paclitaxel avoid resistance mediated by efflux pumps and allow for targeted release in the tumor microenvironment. Liposomal formulations of doxorubicin circumvent the issue of cardiotoxicity related to its systemic delivery and have superior local exposure to the tumor (Akhter et al., 2015). PD-L1 checkpoint inhibitor combination immunotherapy, which co-delivers PD-L1 inhibitors with either chemotherapy or therapeutic vaccines, allows local immune priming of LALT (Donkor & Jones, 2021). Gene therapy using siRNA to silence MDR1 with chemotherapy can be used to chemosensitize multidrug-resistant tumors (Akhter et al., 2015). Next-generation nanoparticle systems of PFC can simultaneously perform tumor sensitization by oxygen delivery, imaging-guided therapy by inherent MR and ultrasound contrast enhancement, and co-delivery of chemotherapy agents (Donkor & Jones, 2021).

8.8 Conclusion

The pulmonary nanochemotherapy field is at the crossroads of decades of formulation science and preclinical validation, combined with the dire clinical requirement for better lung cancer therapeutics. The most promising avenues of research are the preparation of effective mucopenetrating surfaces that do not allow mucus adhesion but have limited inflammatory potential, which is a delicate balance that should be optimized in terms of surface chemistry. Nanocomposite microparticles that contain lipid and polymeric components and are stable, or inorganic imaging agents injected with organic drug carriers, have improved functionality and are easier to manufacture. A new approach involves responsive and combination therapies, in which stimuli-responsive release systems allow selective activation of drugs in tumors, and combinations of immunotherapy, gene therapy, and oxygen delivery can be used against multiple resistance mechanisms simultaneously. More sophisticated characterization techniques, such as in situ transmission electron microscopy, cryo-EM on particles in biological fluids, and real-time imaging of drug release kinetics with microfluidic instruments, will hasten the optimization of the formulations. Artificial intelligence (AI) applications to CMC will simplify regulatory pathways and use machine learning to predict the best formulation compositions and process parameters. Practical clinical trial designs based on adaptive enrollment, biomarker-based stratification, and early indication of efficacy will be used to expedite the reporting of promising candidates to clinical validation. The long-term aim is to clinically validate pulmonary nanochemotherapy, which enhances the survival of lung cancer and reduces the systemic side effects of the treatment, which currently limit the standards of care. With the strategic integration of the inherent benefits of pulmonary delivery and sound formulation science, responsive mechanisms, and the logic of combinations, the discipline has the potential to change the treatment outcomes of patients with this debilitating illness. To achieve this vision, more funding is needed in translational research, adapting regulatory frameworks, and pragmatic clinical trials partnerships that bridge the gap that has persistently existed in the past in developing potential new treatments into life-saving modalities.

References

Ai, X., Mu, J., & Xing, B. (2016). Recent advances in light-mediated theranostics. *Theranostics, 6*(13), 2439–2457. doi:10.7150/thno.16088.

Akhter, S., Ahmad, J., Rizwanullah, M., Rahman, M., Ahmad, M. Z., Rizvi, M. A., Ahmad, F. J., Amin, S., & Kamal, M. A. (2015). Nanotechnology-based inhalation treatments for lung cancer: State of the art. *Nanotechnology Science and Applications, 8*, 55. doi:10.2147/nsa.s49052.

Al Khatib, A. O., El-Tanani, M., & Al-Obaidi, H. (2023). Inhaled medicines for targeting non-small cell lung cancer. *Pharmaceutics, 15*(12), 2777. doi:10.3390/pharmaceutics15122777.

Alsaab, H. O., Alharbi, F. D., Alhibs, A. S., Alanazi, N. B., Alshehri, B. Y., Saleh, M. A., Alshehri, F. S., Algarni, M. A., Almugaiteeb, T., Uddin, M. N., & Alzhrani, R. M. (2022). PLGA-based nanomedicine: History of advancement and development in clinical applications of multiple diseases. *Pharmaceutics, 14*(12). doi:10.3390/pharmaceutics14122728.

Alsaab, H. O., Sau, S., Alzhrani, R., Tatiparti, K., Bhise, K., Kashaw, S. K., & Iyer, A. K. (2017). PD-1 and PD-L1 checkpoint signaling inhibition for cancer immunotherapy: Mechanism, combinations, and clinical outcome. *Frontiers in Pharmacology, 8*. doi:10.3389/fphar.2017.00561.

Da Silva Gündel, S., De Cristo Soares Alves, A., Dallemole, D. R., Guterres, S. S., & Pohlmann, A. R. (2025). Surface-modified organic nanoparticles for lung cancer targeted therapy. *Colloids and Surfaces B: Biointerfaces, 257*, 115175. doi:10.1016/j.colsurfb.2025.115175.

Ding, L., Agrawal, P., Singh, S. K., Chhonker, Y. S., Sun, J., & Murry, D. J. (2024). Polymer-based drug delivery systems for cancer therapeutics. *Polymers, 16*(6). doi:10.3390/polym16060843.

Donkor, M., & Jones, H. P. (2021). The proposition of the pulmonary route as an attractive drug delivery approach of nano-based immune therapies and cancer vaccines to treat lung tumors. *Frontiers in Nanotechnology, 3*. doi:10.3389/fnano.2021.635194.

Franco, M. S., Gomes, E. R., Roque, M. C., & Oliveira, M. C. (2021). Triggered drug release from liposomes: Exploiting the outer and inner tumor environment. *Frontiers in Oncology, 11*. doi:10.3389/fonc.2021.623760.

Gandhi, S., & Roy, I. (2023). Lipid-based inhalable micro- and nanocarriers of active agents for treating non-small-cell lung cancer. *Pharmaceutics, 15*(5), 1457. doi:10.3390/pharmaceutics15051457.

Huber, R. M., & Tufman, A. (2012). Update on small cell lung cancer management. *Breathe, 8*(4), 314–330. doi:10.1183/20734735.013211.

Kakaei, K., Mirzaei, E., & Akbarzadeh, A. (2023a). Theranostic polymeric-lipid hybrid nanoparticles in lung cancer. *Bioengineering & Translational Medicine, 8*(4), e10456. doi:10.1002/btm2.10456.

Kakaei, N., Amirian, R., Azadi, M., Mohammadi, G., & Izadi, Z. (2023b). Perfluorocarbons: A perspective of theranostic applications and challenges. *Frontiers in Bioengineering and Biotechnology, 11*. doi:10.3389/fbioe.2023.1115254.

Kapoor, D. U., Gandhi, S. M., Swarn, S., Lal, B., Prajapati, B. G., Khondee, S., Mangmool, S., Singh, S., & Chittasupho, C. (2025). Polymeric nanoparticles for targeted lung cancer treatment: Review and perspectives. *Pharmaceutics, 17*(9). doi:10.3390/pharmaceutics17091091.

Kassaee, S. N., Richard, D., Ayoko, G. A., & Islam, N. (2024). Lipid polymer hybrid nanoparticles against lung cancer and their application as inhalable formulation. *Nanomedicine, 19*(25), 2113–2133. doi:10.1080/17435889.2024.2387530.

Kim, S.-J., Puranik, N., Yadav, D., Jin, J.-O., & Lee, P. C. W. (2023). Lipid nanocarrier-based drug delivery systems: Therapeutic advances in the treatment of lung cancer. *International Journal of Nanomedicine, 18*, 2659–2676. doi:10.2147/ijn.s406415.

Le, P., Romano, G., Nana-Sinkam, P., & Acunzo, M. (2021). Non-coding RNAs in cancer diagnosis and therapy: Focus on lung cancer. *Cancers, 13*(6), 1372. doi:10.3390/cancers13061372.

Lee, H., Sajid, K., & Lee, J. (2025). Engineered nanocarriers for targeted lung cancer therapy: Mechanistic innovations and recent clinical progress. *Exploration of Targeted Anti-tumor Therapy, 6*, 1002339. doi:10.37349/etat.2025.1002339.

Luo, Y.-H., Liang, K.-H., Huang, H.-C., Shen, C.-I., Chiang, C.-L. u, Wang, M.-L., Chiou, S.-H., & Chen, Y.-M. (2022). State-of-the-art molecular oncology of lung cancer in Taiwan. *International Journal of Molecular Sciences, 23*(13), 7037. doi:10.3390/ijms23137037.

Panovich, P. M., Ganesan, A., Angadi, A. R., & Piotrowski-Daspit, A. S. (2025). Recent advances in the application of polymeric nanoparticles to the pulmonary delivery of mRNA. *Nanomedicine*. doi:10.1080/17435889.2025.2509477.

Petrek, H., & Yu, A.-M. (2019). MicroRNAs in non-small cell lung cancer: Gene regulation, impact on cancer cellular processes, and therapeutic potential. *Pharmacology Research & Perspectives, 7*(6), e00528. doi:10.1002/prp2.528.

Puglisi, M., May, L., Gardiyehewa, T., & Landry, J. W. (2025). Sex differences in the response to lung cancer and its relation to programmed cell death protein-1/programmed death-ligand-1 checkpoint therapies. *Cancers, 17*(24). doi:10.3390/cancers17243953.

Qiang, M., Chen, Z., Liu, H., Dong, J., Gong, K., Zhang, X., Huo, P., Zhu, J., Shao, Y., Ma, J., Zhang, B., Liu, W., & Tang, M. (2025). Targeting the PI3K/AKT/mTOR pathway in lung cancer: Mechanisms and therapeutic targeting. *Frontiers in Pharmacology, 16*. doi:10.3389/fphar.2025.1516583.

Rahim, M. A., Jan, N., Khan, S., Shah, H., Madni, A., Khan, A., Jabar, A., Khan, S., Elhissi, A., Hussain, Z., Aziz, H. C., Sohail, M., Khan, M., & Thu, H. E. (2021). Recent advancements in stimuli responsive drug delivery platforms for active and passive cancer targeting. *Cancers, 13*(4), 1–52. doi:10.3390/cancers13040670.

Rajasegaran, T., How, C. W., Saud, A., Ali, A., & Lim, J. C. W. (2023). Targeting inflammation in non-small cell lung cancer through drug repurposing. *Pharmaceuticals, 16*(3). doi:10.3390/ph16030451.

Rajoriya, V., Gupta, R., Vengurlekar, S., & Singh, U. S. (2024). Nanostructured lipid carriers (NLCs): A promising candidate for lung cancer targeting. *International Journal of Pharmaceutics, 655*, 123986. doi:10.1016/j.ijpharm.2024.123986.

Rastegari, E., Hsiao, Y. J., Lai, W. Y., Lai, Y. H., Yang, T. C., Chen, S. J., Huang, P. I., Chiou, S. H., Mou, C. Y., & Chien, Y. (2021). An update on mesoporous silica nanoparticle applications in nanomedicine. *Pharmaceutics, 13*(7). doi:10.3390/pharmaceutics13071067.

Safdar, I., Mahmood, S., Abdulwahab, M. K., Mohd Noor, S., Ge, Y., & Sofian, Z. M. (2025). Inhalable nanomaterial discoveries for lung cancer therapy: A review. *Pharmaceutics, 17*(8). doi:10.3390/pharmaceutics17080996.

Shi, H., Gou, X., Zhang, S., Zhang, X., Huang, H., Wang, W., & Gao, X. (2023). Nanodelivery systems as a novel strategy to overcome treatment failure of cancer. *Small Methods, 8*(1). doi:10.1002/smtd.202301127.

Singh, R., Patel, S., & Kumar, A. (2025). Surface-modified nanocarriers for precision oncology: Addressing tumor heterogeneity. *Journal of Nanomedicine and Nanotechnology, 16*(2), 112–124.

Sobol, Ż., Chiczewski, R., & Wątróbska-Świetlikowska, D. (2025). Advances in liposomal drug delivery: Multidirectional perspectives on overcoming biological barriers. *Pharmaceutics, 17*(7), 885. doi:10.3390/pharmaceutics17070885.

Spitaleri, G., Trillo Aliaga, P., Attili, I., Del Signore, E., Corvaja, C., Corti, C., Crimini, E., Passaro, A., & de Marinis, F. (2023). Sustained improvement in the management of patients with non-small-cell lung cancer (NSCLC) harboring ALK translocation: Where are we running? *Current Oncology, 30*(5), 5072–5092. doi:10.3390/curroncol30050384.

Swaminathan, J., & Ehrhardt, C. (2011). Liposomes for pulmonary drug delivery. In H. Smyth, & A Hickey (Eds.), *Controlled pulmonary drug delivery. Advances in delivery science and technology*. Springer. doi:10.1007/978-1-4419-9745-6_14.

Viegas, C., Patrício, A. B., Prata, J. M., Nadhman, A., Chintamaneni, P. K., & Fonte, P. (2023). Solid lipid nanoparticles vs. nanostructured lipid carriers: A comparative review. *Pharmaceutics, 15*(6). doi:10.3390/pharmaceutics15061593.

Weber, S., Zimmer, A., & Pardeike, J. (2013). Solid lipid nanoparticles (SLN) and nanostructured lipid carriers (NLC) for pulmonary application: A review of the state of the art. *European Journal of Pharmaceutics and Biopharmaceutics, 86*(1), 7–22. doi:10.1016/j.ejpb.2013.08.013.

Winer, A., Adams, S., & Mignatti, P. (2018). Matrix metalloproteinase inhibitors in cancer therapy: Turning past failures into future successes. *Molecular Cancer Therapeutics, 17*(6), 1147–1155. doi:10.1158/1535-7163.mct-17-0646.

Zhang, C., Fan, J., & Wu, L. (2024). Application of nanomaterials in precision treatment of lung cancer. *iScience, 28*(1), 111704. doi:10.1016/j.isci.2024.111704.

Zhou, L., Wang, H., & Li, Y. (2018b). Stimuli-responsive nanomedicines for overcoming cancer multidrug resistance. *Theranostics, 8*(4), 1059–1074. doi:10.7150/thno.22679.

Zhou, Q., Zhang, L., Yang, T. H., & Wu, H. (2018). Stimuli-responsive polymeric micelles for drug delivery and cancer therapy. *International Journal of Nanomedicine, 13*, 2921–2942. doi:10.2147/IJN.S158696.

CHAPTER 9

Targeted therapeutics: Harnessing polymeric nanoparticles for lung cancer treatment

Praveen Halagali[a], Rohit Rajendra Bhosale[b], Himanshu Sharma[c], Deepak Biswas[d] and Vamshi Krishna Tippavajhala[a]

[a]Department of Pharmaceutics, Manipal College of Pharmaceutical Sciences, Manipal Academy of Higher Education, Manipal, Karnataka, India [b]Department of Pharmaceutics, Krishna Charitable Trust's Krishna College of Pharmacy, Karad, Maharashtra, India [c]Department of Pharmacology, NIMS Institute of Pharmacy, NIMS University Rajasthan, Jaipur, Rajasthan, India [d]Department of Medical Sciences, Kokshetau State Medical University, Kokshetau, Kazakhstan

9.1 Introduction

9.1.1 Overview of lung cancer

Tobacco use is the primary cause of 90% of lung cancer cases, which is the world's biggest cause of cancer-related deaths. Non-small cell lung cancer (NSCLC) and small cell lung cancer (SCLC) are the two main histologic subtypes of lung cancer, each having unique biological characteristics, genetic changes, and treatment approaches. Only over 25% of individuals with NSCLC have early-stage, curable cancer; most patients with both NSCLC and SCLC have signs of either metastatic or locally advanced disease. For patients with stage I or II NSCLC, surgical resection is the recommended course of treatment; in 60%–80% of instances, it results in long-term survival, whereas in 40%–50% of cases, it does so. Subsets of lung cancer patients have now demonstrated notable clinical advantages from some of these molecularly targeted treatments. The molecular biology of lung cancer has recently improved, leading to new treatment approaches that target important pathways that control the growth and/or spread of the disease. Aggressive chemotherapy and radiation therapy can cure 20%–25% of patients with limited-stage SCLC, locally advanced NSCLC, or stage III. In patients with extensive-stage SCLC and stage IV, or metastatic, NSCLC, which are incurable conditions, treatment can increase survival and reduce symptoms (Gadgeel & Kalemkerian, 2010).

Nanoengineered Therapeutics for Lung Cancer: Advanced Drug Delivery Strategies.
DOI: https://doi.org/10.1016/B978-0-443-44585-9.00009-3

9.1.2 Importance of targeted therapeutics

Systemic cytotoxic chemotherapy was utilized to treat any kind of cancer before the development of targeted treatment. This one-size-fits-all strategy, however, has only been effective for some types of cancer. To prevent the significant toxicities associated with conventional chemotherapy and to produce a long-lasting response, researchers have been looking for new ways to treat a variety of tumors. Small cell lung tumors, which make-up 15% of all lung cancers, are still treated with standard cytotoxic chemotherapy. But when it comes to treating NSCLC, which makes up 85% of all lung cancers, it has not worked. Because of this revelation, lung cancer treatments based on histology and molecular profiling have been developed (Mayekar & Bivona, 2017).

Targeted therapy showed promise in treating lung cancer when gefitinib treatment proved successful in treating patients with epidermal growth factor receptor (EGFR) inhibitor-sensitizing mutations. The early EGFR inhibitor therapy studies underscored the need to understand the oncogenic drivers. Later EGFR inhibitor research employed this clinical trial strategy to investigate the efficacy of targeted medications in certain patient populations with genetic defects responsive to inhibitors. Due to the design's efficacy, it was included in subsequent targeted treatment studies targeting other actionable oncogenic drivers of lung cancer. Smoking is the main risk factor for lung cancer, and it is connected to the disease's genetic heterogeneity. By systematically examining the genomes of several hundred malignant lung tumors, it has been possible to filter out passenger mutations and progressively identify the primary oncogenic drivers and rare oncogenic genetic abnormalities (Campbell et al., 2016; The Cancer Genome Atlas Research Network, 2014). The US Food and Drug Administration (FDA) approved small molecule inhibitors have been successfully used to target the oncogenic drivers listed in Table 9.1 to provide superior therapeutic interventions to standard chemotherapy. These oncogenic drivers are currently being further investigated to be directly targeted with monotherapy or combination therapy for the treatment of lung cancers.

9.2 Polymeric nanoparticles: Fundamentals

9.2.1 Definition and types of polymeric nanoparticles

Polymeric nanoparticles (PNPs), which are particles with a size range of 1–1000 nm, can include active ingredients that are confined inside the polymeric core or surface-adsorbed onto it. Recent years have seen a significant increase in interest in PNPs due to their small size-related characteristics. Using PNPs as drug carriers has several advantages, including the potential for regulated release, the ability to protect physiologically active substances from the environment, increased bioavailability, and an improved therapeutic index. While they

Table 9.1: FDA-approved and potential targeted therapies to treat lung cancer with oncogenic drivers that can be targeted.

FDA-approved drugs	Targeted oncogenic driver	Drugs under study	% NSCLC patients
	MET	Capmatinib, MGCD265, cabozantinib, Crizotinib	4%–5%
Trametinib and dabrafenib combination	BRAF	Selumetinib, PLX8394, Vemurafenib,	1%–4%
	NTRK	LOXO-195, larotrectinib (LOXO-101), Entrectinib,	1%–2%
	RET	Regorafenib, cabozantinib, RXDX-105, vandetanib, sorafenib, alectinib, sunitinib, nintedanib, ponatinib, lenvatinib	1%–2%
Crizotinib	ROS1	entrectinib, lorlatinib, cabozantinib, ceritinib,	1%–2%
	HER2	Trastuzumab, dacomitinib, Afatinib,	1%–2%
Brigatinib, ceritinib, crizotinib, alectinib,	ALK	Lorlatinib, entrectinib, Ensartinib,	3%–7%
Erlotinib, osimertinib gefitinib, afatinib,	EGFR	HS-10296, ASP8273, avitinib, olmutinib (HM61713), PF-06747775, dacomitinib, nazartinib (EGF816)	10%–15%

ALK, anaplastic lymphoma kinase; *EGFR*, epidermal growth factor receptor; *FDA*, Food and Drug Administration; *NSCLC*, non-small cell lung cancer; *ROS*, reactive oxygen species; BRAF, B-Raf proto-oncogene; NTRK, Neurotrophic Tyrosine Receptor Kinase;RET, Rearranged During Transfection.

have various shapes, the word "nanoparticle" encompasses both nanospheres and nanocapsules (Schaffazick et al., 2003). Usually, the drug dissolves in the oily core of nanocapsules, which is surrounded by a polymeric shell that controls the drug's release profile from the core (Seenivasan et al., 2026). Drugs can be retained within the continuous polymeric network of nanospheres or adsorbed onto their surface (Halagali et al., 2025; Inamdar et al., 2025; Nayak et al., 2025; Pathak et al., 2025; R et al., 2023). The two types of PNPs, referred to as matrix systems (nanosphere) and reservoir systems (nanocapsule), are shown in Fig. 9.1 (Christoforidis et al., 2012).

9.2.2 Methods of preparation of polymeric nanoparticles

Various preparation methods may be employed, depending on the kind of drug to be added to the PNPs and their requirements for a specific delivery method (Jawahar & Meyyanathan, 2012). There are two main methods that are frequently employed: dispersing

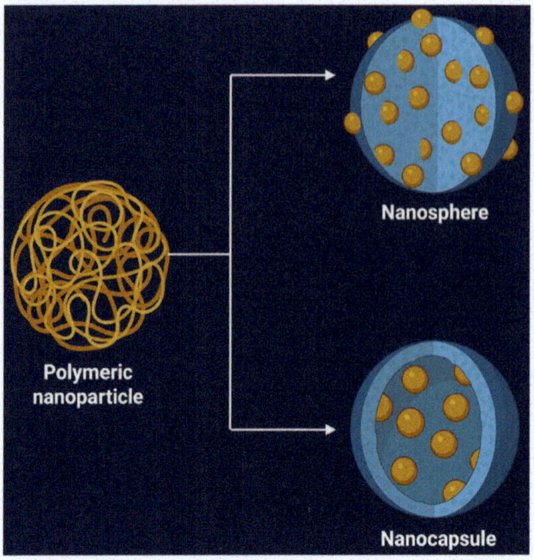

Figure 9.1
Diagrammatic representation of structure of nanosphere and nanocapsule.

readymade polymers or polymerization of monomers (Amgoth et al., 2020; Pinto Reis et al., 2006).

9.2.2.1 Solvent evaporation

PNPs were initially prepared using this technique (Desgouilles et al., 2003;Jose et al., 2014; Vieira et al., 2019). An organic phase is first created, consisting of a polar organic solvent in which the polymer is dissolved, in order to include the active component through dispersion or dissolution. Although they were used more often in the past, dichloromethane and chloroform are nevertheless routinely employed today (Grumezescu, 2017). Ethyl acetate (Bohrey et al., 2016) has replaced them due of their toxicity. An aqueous phase containing a surfactant is a basic preparation. The organic solution can frequently be treated using high-speed homogenization or ultrasonication to produce a dispersion of nanodroplets after being emulsified in the aqueous phase using a surfactant (Sharma et al., 2016). The nanoparticles (NPs) are suspended when the polymer solvent evaporates and is permitted to enter the emulsion's continuous phase. The solvent can be evaporated using either progressive, reduced pressure, or continuous magnetic stirring at room temperature. Centrifugation can be used to gather and purify the formed NPs once the solvent has evaporated. They can then be freeze-dried for long-term preservation. This technique allows for the creation of nanospheres (Szczech & Szczepanowicz, 2020). Diagrammatic representation of the solvent evaporation method is given in Fig. 9.2.

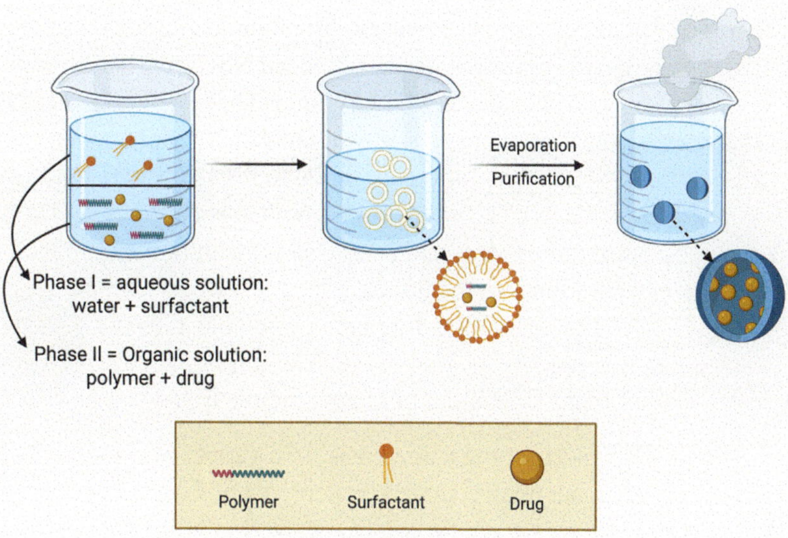

Figure 9.2
Diagrammatic representation of solvent evaporation method.

9.2.2.2 *Emulsification/solvent diffusion*

Using an aqueous phase (water), a surfactant, and a miscible organic solvent containing the drug and polymer, a process is conducted to generate an emulsion of the oil-in-water (o/w) type (Kumar et al., 2012; Souto et al., 2019) with the organic solvent forming the internal phase or continuum of the emulsion. To achieve a first thermodynamic equilibrium between the two phases at ambient conditions, this was achieved by first saturating the organic phase with water (Souto et al., 2012). Through the difference in concentration of the solute between the internal and external phases, the solvent from the dispersed droplets will diffuse into the external phase when diluted with a considerable amount of water, producing colloidal particles. This method is frequently used to create nanospheres; nanocapsules may also be formed by the introduction of a minor amount of oil into the organic phase. Final removal of this final step may be accomplished through either filtration or evaporation, depending on the boiling point of the organic solvent (Guterres et al., 2007). A schematic diagram of the process can be found in Fig. 9.3 (Quintanar-Guerrero et al., 1998; Vasile, 2018).

9.2.2.3 *Emulsification/reverse salting-out*

One approach to making nanospheres is to use the emulsification/solvent diffusion method discussed earlier. By removing a hydrophilic solvent (water-miscible liquid) from an aqueous solution, this method takes advantage of a phenomenon known as the salting-out effect to produce nanospheres (Wang et al., 2016). For example, in creating an o/w emulsion, a

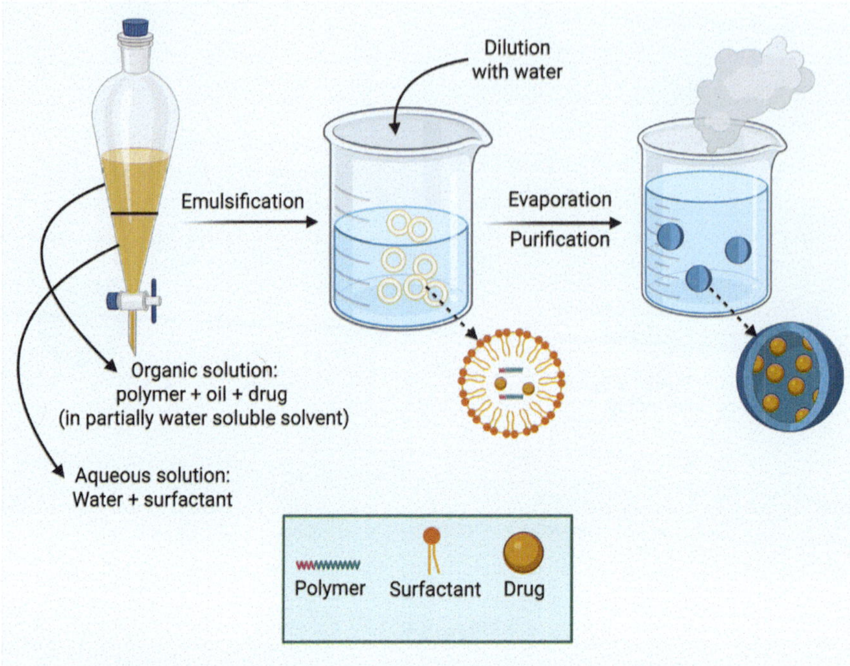

Figure 9.3
Diagrammatic representation of emulsification/solvent diffusion method.

hydrophilic solvent (e.g., ethanol or acetone) is used as the organic phase and will contain a polymer, a water-soluble gel, and a colloidal stabilizer that has salting-out agents (Lim & Hamid, 2018). When the water phase is saturated with respect to the solute(s) contained within the o/w emulsion, the remaining miscible phases will form an o/w emulsion, which will result in decreased miscibility of acetone and water (Vauthier & Bouchemal, 2009). At room temperature, when the two phases (aqueous and organic) are vigorously stirred together, they form an o/w emulsion. By dilution of the nanoemulsion with enough DI water or aqueous solution, the diffusion of the organic solvent to the external aqueous phase is facilitated, and consequently, the polymer precipitates out, resulting in nanosphere formation from the emulsions. The final product will have all residual organic solvents and salting-out agents removed via cross-flow filtration. The fact that organic solvents and water will mix well will make this easier; however, they do not have to be completely miscible (Krishnamoorthy & Mahalingam, 2015).

9.2.3 Characterization of polymeric nanoparticles

Polymeric NPs have diverse characteristics, including composition, shape, dispersion, concentration, surface properties, crystallinity, and size. To characterize the NPs, many different techniques are used. Commonly used techniques for this purpose include photon correlation spectroscopy (PCS), electrophoresis, electron microscopy, chromatography, dynamic light scattering (DLS), and near infrared spectroscopy. Polymeric NP characterization is important to evaluate nanotoxicology and exposure risks in the workplace related to health and safety hazards (Andreani et al., 2015). Additionally, characterizing polymer NPs is an essential step in determining their potential utility (Doktorovova et al., 2014).

9.2.3.1 Morphology

PNPs have been extensively studied with respect to size and morphology using transmission electron microscopy (TEM) and scanning electron microscopy (SEM). In general, cryofractures are commonly used to assess the morphology of PNPs. One frequently used technique to examine the wall thickness of nanocapsules and differentiate between nanocapsules and nanospheres is TEM. Nanocapsules contain an oily core surrounded by a very thin (~5 nm) polymeric membrane; whereas, nanospheres are spherical and made of solid polymeric materials. The surface morphology of PNPs has also been characterized using atomic force microscopy (AFM) (Andreani et al., 2015). AFM provides three-dimensional and nanometric resolutions of surface features and has been used to map features on a nanometric scale (Mathurin et al., 2018). AFM results confirm that polymer nanocapsules have very complex topographies and reveal the presence of small pores and voids on the surface of the polymer NPs (Crucho & Barros, 2017).

9.2.3.2 Particle size distribution

PNPs manufactured using certain methods commonly have mean diameters between 100 and 300 nm. The polydispersity of these NPs should have an almost uniform distribution (or a value near zero). However, NPs can be smaller than 50 nm, down to sizes of 60 or 70 nm (Hickey et al., 2015). Even though other techniques, such as SEM, AFM, and TEM, are used, static laser light scattering (SLS) and DLS are the most common methods for determining NP size (Brar & Verma, 2011). Different methods can lead to differing measured sizes. DLS is able to provide information on the hydrodynamic radius of the particle in solution, while electron microscopy offers only a picture of the NP without surrounding materials. DLS will provide better measurement with larger-sized particles and give comparative measurements of the particle size distribution; the measurement from DLS will thus provide information regarding NP aggregation in solution and complement TEM (Carvalho et al., 2018). The various qualitative and quantitative compositions of the polymeric NPs, for example, influence how large a polymeric NP will be. There are variations in hydrophobicity, viscosity, and interfacial tension of different liquid phases that contribute to the type of oil that is used as the core for the production of nanocapsules; this will impact the diameter of the particles. Additionally, if the drug's concentration is changed, this could also result in a change in the average diameter of the NPs due to potential increases in the size of the particles and larger distributions in the sizes of the NPs (Crucho & Barros, 2017; Guterres et al., 2007).

9.2.3.3 Molar mass distribution of the polymer

After the synthesis has been completed, information about how the formulation components affect polymerization, if there are chemical interactions between drug and polymer formulations, and any degradation of the polymer can be assessed by examining the polymer's molar mass distribution data (Doncom et al., 2017). Currently, the most common method for measuring the molar mass distribution of polymers is size-exclusion chromatography (SEC) (Podzimek, 2011; Stals et al., 2014).

9.2.3.4 Chemical composition and crystal structure

Chemical composition is made up of the elemental make-up of the NPs and natural or synthetic functional groups. The chemical composition of any particle can be determined through the use of ensemble or individual particle elemental analysis methods. The most widely used of these is y (AAS). This technique is based on the principle that when atoms are in their ground state, they can "jump" from the ground state to the excited state by absorbing certain amounts of energy from light at particular wavelengths (Mourdikoudis et al., 2018). The amount of energy absorbed by a particular atom can also be affected by the types and numbers of atoms that the light passes through on its way to the atom, if the intensity of the light reaching the atom is compared to that of known concentrations of calibration standards, the mass concentration of the sample can be calculated. Time-of-flight mass spectrometry (TOFMS) is one method used to analyze the chemical composition of solids. TOFMS involves vaporizing small to large organic solids and analyzing them in the gas phase by either measuring the time it takes them to travel through a TOFMS or measuring the flight time and distance and then converting these values into mass (Lu et al., 2017). The crystallographic or noncrystallographic layout of the elements in an NP will be specified either through Powder XRD or via selective area electron diffraction (SAED) using TEM. The use of X-ray diffraction generally requires that at least 1 gm of material be available for the testing, whereas testing can be performed at the individual NP level using electron diffraction methods (Dazon et al., 2019; Zielińska et al., 2020).

9.2.3.5 Surface area and chemistry

The surface area of NPs is important because it provides information about the reactivity of the NPs and the surface interactions with ligands. There are multiple ways to measure the surface area of NPs, including the use of inert gases via gas adsorption at a variety of pressure conditions until a monolayer of the gas becomes adsorbed onto the surface of the NP (Mansfield et al., 2017). The total surface area of the adsorbate gas molecules is derived from a comparison of the cross-sectional area and number of gas molecules required to make a monolayer of gas (Dumitriu & Popa, 2013). Additionally, using this method with porous materials allows a judgment on morphology because of the way an inert gas attaches itself to the internal pores/cracks (Dumitriu & Popa, 2013). Elemental or molecular chemistry at the surface of a particle is referred to as the surface chemistry of that particle. Because of the higher surface area/volume ratio, there will be a higher fraction of atoms at the surface of NP layers than at the core of those layers. Interactions between the atoms at the surface of the NPs and the solvents have an effect on the interactions between the solvents of other molecules and the other molecules themselves (Baer et al., 2013). The atoms that constitute NPs, such as nanocapsules at the inner core, may be different from the atoms at the outer surface due to their core-shell structure. Methods such as X-ray photoelectron spectroscopy and secondary ion mass spectroscopy can help characterize surface chemistry (Simonet & Valcárcel, 2009).

9.2.3.6 Zeta potential

Zeta potential is based on changes at the interface between superfluid/aqueous solution and dispersed medium (saline), solvation or hydration of drug, dissociation of ionizable groups on particle surface, and/or adsorption of dissolved ionic species (salt ions) in parent drug and/or dispersion medium contact with the items measured (either superfluid, aqueous or other) (Honary & Zahir, 2013). These changes in charge are used to calculate the zeta potential by analyzing the use of Doppler imaging to identify particles' movement as related to applied voltage (Ostolska & Wiśniewska, 2014). Following these measurements, one can determine the zeta potential from electrophoresis when matching solvent conditions are used to measure phospholipids, poloxomers, and/or polymers in used polymeric NPs concerning other component materials' inclusion in their formulation. Such double-blind testing indicates that a zeta potential value should be $|\pm 30 \text{ mV}|$ to provide optimal physicochemical stability for NP solutions, as it has been shown that there are strong electro-repulsive forces acting between two or more colloidal NP particles, preventing aggregation due to temporary attraction to other colloids near them. The measurement of the zeta potential provides insight into the way that drug action takes place against NPs (Zielińska et al., 2019).

Calvo et al. (1997) found that the zeta potential helped to load albumin onto chitosan NPs with Poly(ethylene oxide)-Poly(propylene oxide) (PEO-PPO) diblock copolymers; they also looked at the effects of various formulations on zeta potential. They demonstrated that NPs could be coated with surfactant or coating materials having different molecular weights [e.g., polyethylene glycol (PEG)] to alter zeta potential for specific uses (Doktorovová et al., 2014).

9.2.3.7 pH of suspensions

Monitoring the pH of an NP suspension will tell how stable the suspension is over time. If the pH shifts from neutral to either acidic or basic, it indicates a change in the protonation of the particle surface, which can indicate that the polymer has degraded (thus affecting the texture of the NPs). The study by Calvo et al. indicated that there was a decrease in the pH of the formulations of nanocapsules/nanospheres as a result of a decrease in the molar weight of the suspensions after they had been stored for 6 months (Calvo et al., 1997; Guterres et al., 2007).

The pH drop of the suspensions could have also been affected by the ionization of carboxylic acid groups in the polymer chain and the release of protons into the solution, as well as by the degree of hydrophobicity of the overall polymer molecule. At the same time, the influence of pH on electrostatic stability and the zeta potential are both important for formulation, so pH measurements must be closely monitored.

9.2.3.8 Stability of polymeric nanoparticle suspensions

On average, colloids will tend to form separate phases over time, particularly in on the order of months, due in part to the fact that the rate at which the particles will settle (sedimentation) is very slow when the size of the particle is less than 1 micron, and additionally because of brownian movement of the particle, which will further slow the rate at which sedimentation occurs. However, the settling and agglomerating of these particles can still occur over time (Rahman & Asiri, 2016). Stability of the colloidal suspension can also be negatively impacted depending on the type of chemical or biological adsorbent being used, as well as the adsorption of other surface-bound substances from the surface of the NP. The stability of the colloidal suspension may be assessed using physicochemical properties (such as pH, drug concentration, polymer mean molecular weight distribution, zeta potential, and size distribution of the particles) of the polymer colloids. However, colloidal PNPs used in the industrial application of aqueous dispersions may present an issue due to limited physicochemical stability over an extended period of time during storage (Lazzari et al., 2012). These present as particle agglomeration and/or the degradation of the drug and or other raw materials that were used to manufacture the nanostructure; the chemical stability or integrity of the polymer; or the initial release of the therapeutic agent from the product. Another consideration when assessing a liquid pharmaceutical formulation will be the addition of a preservative due to the potential for microbial growth (Heinz et al., 2017). Drying methods such as spray drying or lyophilization are usually suggested to avoid these microbiological and physicochemical problems. Lyophilization, a popular method for drying nanosphere suspensions, entails sublimating water (Abdelwahed et al., 2006). Spray drying, an alternative to lyophilization, involves sending the solution through an atomizing nozzle and into the drying chamber as droplets in order to maximize the stability of solid lipid-formed NPs. A co-current, counter-current, or mixed flow of hot air causes the droplets to dry rapidly. Following their separation and collection, the dry solid particles may appear as fine powders, granules, or agglomerates (Wanning, Süverkrüp, & Lamprecht, 2015; Ziaee et al., 2019).

9.2.3.9 Determination of the drug association

Due to their small size, it is very difficult to quantify the amount of drug associated with NPs because it is impossible to distinguish between the free and associated fractions for measures of NPs (De Jong & Borm, 2008). To measure the amount of free drug in a combination of drugs, ultracentrifugation (the standard separation method) is carried out to separate out the drug from the NPs; after ultracentrifugation, the supernatant will contain all of the free drug;

therefore, the amount of drug measured after ultracentrifugation and the total amount of drug from fully dissolving the NPs gives the total concentration of drug in the solution; therefore, the difference between the total and free drug concentrations is used to calculate the amount of drug that is associated with the NPs (Bohnert & Gan, 2013; Wallace et al., 2012). One method to isolate the portion of the dispersion aqueous phase from the colloidal suspension is ultrafiltration-centrifugation, which uses a membrane. Calculation of the fraction of drug that is bound to the nanostructured systems and the quantity of free drug in the ultrafiltrate is made by subtracting the total and free concentrations. The amount of drug added to the nanostructures, the order of drug addition to the formulation, the type of oil used (for nanocapsules), the type of surfactant that is adsorbed on the surface of the polymer, the pH of the medium, the size and characteristics of the NP, and the physicochemical properties of the drug will affect the amount of drug associated with the nanostructured formulations (Khan et al., 2019; Patra et al., 2018). Different surface properties of the NPs enable different rates of adsorption for the same initial drug concentration. This is a critical aspect of determining whether the drug has the potential to extend its effect. Determining the drug adsorption isotherm with the particle's surface is critical because it describes the distribution of the drug on the surface of the particle and its association capacity (Khan et al., 2019). There are several types of drug association described with respect to nanospheres; the drug may be adsorbed to the polymeric material or dissolved or dispersed in the polymeric matrix. Conversely, the polymeric film providing the nanocapsule oily/solvent core will provide maximum loading of lipophilic drugs (Guterres et al., 2007).

Another factor and complicating factor will be the existing techniques used for characterizing how drugs associating with NPs, as these techniques measure only the concentration of drug that is associated with NPs but do not provide information that can be used to develop the different associations (it does not differentiate whether the drug has been adsorbed or immobilized within the polymeric matrix of the nanospheres; or dissolved in the oil of the nanocapsules or adsorbing into the polymeric wall of the nanocapsules) (Sumana et al., 2020). Because of this, we can only estimate the mode of drug association with NPs, based on available methods like zeta potential studies, desorption of drug from NP studies, polymer molecular weight studies, drug desorption rate from NPs, or via fluorescent probes (Singh & Lillard, 2009). Additionally, we may use DSC, IR spectroscopy, or XRD techniques (Mourdikoudis et al., 2018).

9.2.3.10 Pharmaceutical in vitro release kinetics

According to Soppimath et al. (2001), the release of drugs from polymeric NPs (Bohrey et al., 2016; Kamaly et al., 2016) depends on: drug desorption from particle surface, drug diffusion through the NPs or the walls of the nanocapsule, or a combination of these.

Methods such as dialysis bag diffusion and then further separations via ultracentrifugation, low-pressure filtration, or by using ultrafiltration with a centrifuge have all been described for drug release from PNPs (Shen & Burgess, 2013). Prior studies have shown that drug release from nanosphere-type delivery vehicles often follows an exponential (first-order) kinetic profile. This is likely due to either the drug diffusing into the environment from the polymeric matrix or the polymer matrix deteriorating and releasing the drug (Kamaly et al., 2016; Lee & Yeo, 2015). When a drug is dissolved into the oily core of a nanocapsule, it will then diffuse through the polymeric wall of the nanocapsule and be released from the vesicular structure via zero-order kinetics (Fu & Kao, 2010); therefore, the drug's release from a nanocapsule should behave similarly to that of a nanoemulsion due to the similarity of these methods of drug release; thus, Calvo et al. (1997) concluded that the polymer walls of nanocapsules do not influence how rapidly drugs are released but instead only influence how rapidly drugs can diffuse between oil droplets and the surrounding aqueous medium.

9.2.3.11 Fluorescence imaging

Fluorescence imaging is an essential technique for polymer NP characterization as it allows researchers to obtain noninvasive data regarding the properties and interactions of these materials in real-time. Fluorescence imaging can be used to track the location of fluorescently tagged NPs within biological systems and to observe the dynamic processes of cellular uptake, biodistribution, and drug release (Reisch & Klymchenko, 2016). In addition, since researchers can identify specific components of the NP(s), they can then evaluate how the core-shell design and dynamic properties of the core-shell structures behave in complex biological systems.

Albertazzi and Meijer's initial investigations showed that the properties of the benzene-1,3,5-tricarboxamide (BTA)-derived supermolecular polymeric materials include the characteristic exchange of building blocks (Fig. 9.4A and B) via homogeneous exchange as evidenced by using the STORM technique (Albertazzi et al., 2014). Homogeneous exchange is expected due to the presence of disorder in the ordered hydrogen-bonded structure (there are regions in which the hydrogen-bond networks are cohesively intact), making the exchange process easier as a result of the weaker interaction between monomeric units (Albertazzi et al., 2014; Bakker et al., 2016). There was no evidence of fragmentation, fusion, or polymerization–depolymerization at the polymer chain ends; therefore, the use of the STORM technique for analyzing polymer chains indicates that the homogeneous exchanges are consistent throughout the polymer backbone and suggest that we can better study the dynamic characteristics of supramolecular fibers (da Silva et al., 2016). According to Cox et al., AFM and STORM were employed to examine the assembly of peptide surfactants, revealing the presence of helical fibrils ranging from 5 to 10 μm in length, as per Fig. 9.4C and D. After mixing peptide surfactants, the dynamic assembly of peptides could be characterized using two-color STORM. Perrier et al. elaborated on Cox et al.'s work by demonstrating how dual labels could be applied via STORM to visualize the creation of supramolecular bi-blocks or tubular structures

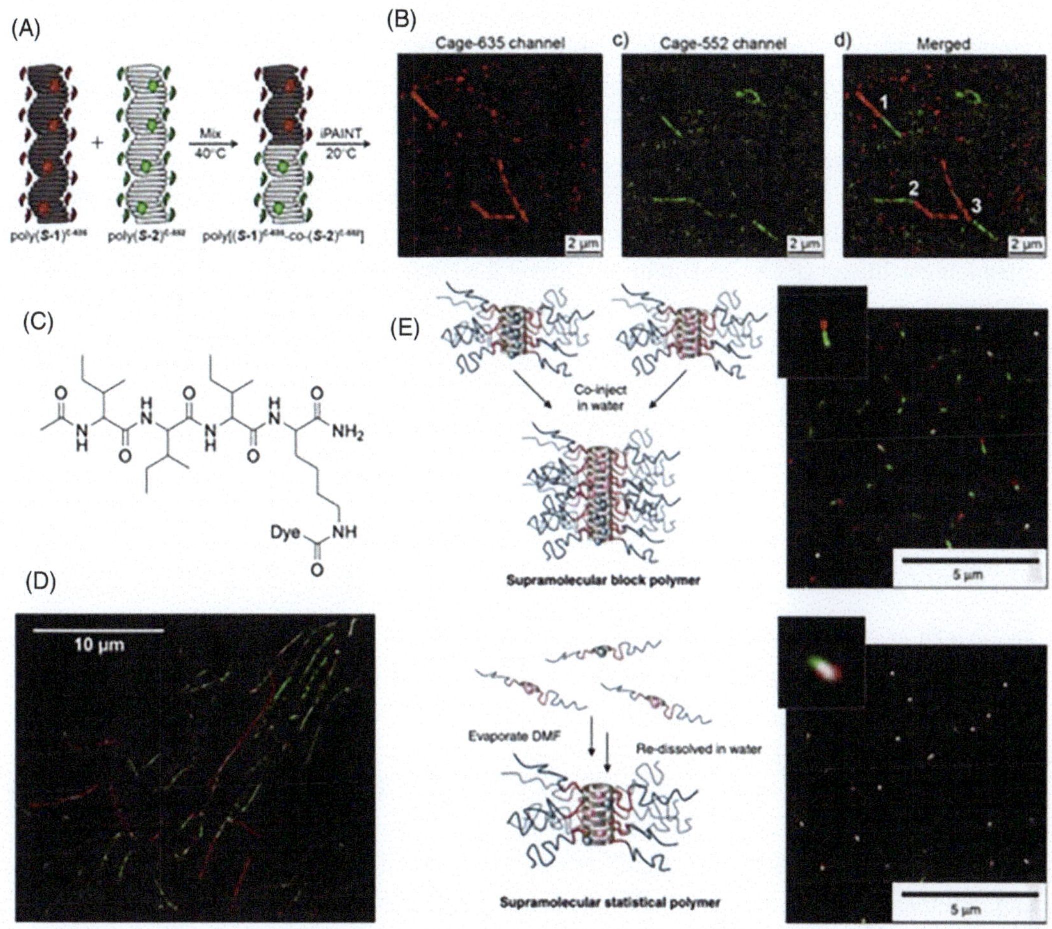

Figure 9.4

(A) Diagrammatic illustration of supramolecular polymers based on copolymerized BTA, (B) Cage-635, Cage-552, and combined (*left* to *right*) channels show the resultant copolymer in iPAINT imaging. (C) Chemical structure and (D) STORM image showing peptide-dye conjugates that self-assemble to produce nanofibers. (E) Metastable supramolecular peptide-dye conjugated nanotubes: schematic depiction and STORM images.

caused by fusing two independent metastable polymer-peptide nanotubes (Floyd et al., 2025; Fig. 9.4E.

9.3 Applications in lung cancer treatment

Polymeric NPs are changing the way to treat lung cancer by increasing drug delivery, improving systemic toxicity, and utilizing multi-functional therapies. Polymeric NPs are based on the use of biodegradable polymers such as poly lactic-co-glycolic acid (PLGA) and PEG because they improve the targeted action, bioavailability, and stability. Some of the applications of PNPs are (1) active targeting ligands: Polymeric NPs are functionalized with ligands, Arginylglycylaspartic acid (RGD) peptides, folic acid (FA), and epidermal growth factor (EGF), to attach to receptors that are overexpressed in lung cancer. (2) Dendrimer- based NPs can co-deliver cisplatin and small interfering RNA (siRNA) to silence drug resistance genes such as Bcl-2 to overcome chemotherapy resistance in NSCLC. (3) Hybrid lipid-polymer NPs co-encapsulate paclitaxel (PTX) and quantum dots (QDs) that provide real-time tracking of the particles and provide synergistic tumor suppression. (4) PLGA NPs are loaded with PTX and cisplatin and show notably improved cytotoxicity in vitro and improved tumor inhibition in vivo compared to free drugs. (5) PLGA and PEG-PLGA NPs have extended drug release kinetics that achieve local therapeutic concentrations.

9.3.1 Case studies of polymeric nanoparticles for drug delivery in lung cancer treatment

The use of PLGA-polyethyleneimine (PEI) NPs as a method to co-deliver both PTX and an siRNA therapeutic for treating lung cancer in vivo has been investigated in this study. PTX is an anticancer drug that has a hydrophobic formulation, so the researchers used PLGA NPs to form a carrier for PTX. The researchers used an electrostatic binding to attach stat3 siRNA to the exterior of the PLGA-PEI NPs. The researchers employed fluorescence measurements to ascertain that Stat3 siRNA and PTX were delivered concurrently to A549 lung cancer cells by PLGA-PEI NPs. The data show that Stat3 was activated in both A549 and A549/T12 lung cancer cell lines, while using PLGA-PEI-TAX-S3SI NPs silenced the Stat3 gene, utilizing Stat3 siRNA, and increased cell death through greater sensitivity to PTX when compared to PLGA-PEI-TA NPs (Su et al., 2012).

In a recent study, antisense oligonucleotides (DNA/RNA) were successfully delivered to lung cancer cells using chitosan-modified PLGA NPs. The chitosan-modified PLGA NPs had a positive surface charge that could be adjusted and had a size of 130 nm. Chitosan-PLGA NPs were electrostatically linked to antisense oligonucleotides and 2′-O-methyl-RNA (OMR) for the human telomerase gene, and effective cellular absorption was noted (Nafee et al., 2007). In a follow-up investigation, the same group assessed the stability, binding effectiveness, chitosan content, and cell absorption efficiency of the chitosan-PLGA nanoplexes for OMR delivery (Taetz et al., 2009). The researchers found that the amount of chitosan in the NP affected both the transfection effectiveness and the cellular uptake of OMR. The NPs effectively reduced telomerase activity and were nontoxic.

A PEI-based polymer combination including Hyaluronic Acid (HA) and PEG (HA-PEI/AH-PEG) was created by Mattheolabakis et al. (2016). By simply combining the siRNA, anionic HA, and cationic PEI, a polyplex was created. This polyplex demonstrated effective transfection and siRNA encapsulation. The cytotoxic activity of cisplatin (cis-diamminedichloroplatinum(II)) CDDP-C8 and CDDP-C6 compounds was reportedly enhanced in A549/DDP cells by survivin-silencing siRNA pretreatment. Furthermore, co-treatment with CDDP-C8 and the survivin-silencing siRNA suppressed tumor development more than CDDP alone in a model of CDDP-resistant lung cancer.

Taetz et al. (2009) demonstrated how emulsion-solvent evaporation was used to combine PLGA with different amounts of cationic chitosan to produce chitosan-PLGA nanoparticles (CPNPs). These CPNPs were used to deliver an antisense 2OMR that targeted a human telomerase RNA template. They found that although the complex stability and binding efficacy of CPNP with 2OMR were weak in physiologically relevant media, they were strong in water and positively correlated with the particles' chitosan concentration. According to their flow cytometry data, the amount of chitosan employed in the complex determined how well it inhibited telomerase activity, and transfecting A549 lung cancer cells with CPNP significantly increased the uptake of 2OMR into the cells.

The siRNA-PPI-dendrimer system was presented in a report (Taratula et al., 2009). Using dithiol crosslinkers, the siRNA-PPI system was incorporated with a PEG polymer coat after crosslinking to increase stability and circulation time. The luteinizing hormone-releasing hormone (LHRH) peptide was added to the distal end of the PEG polymer to enhance targeting properties to specific types of cancer cells. These layer-by-layer PPI-targeted NPs were used to achieve selective uptake by tumors and to silence the target gene in A549 human lung cancer cell lines expressing the LHRH receptor. Additionally, in vivo biodistribution supports the targeted delivery of siRNAs to tumors with reduced side effects on adjacent healthy tissues (Taratula et al., 2009).

Ragelle et al. (2015) developed PEG-grafted chitosan-PEI NPs that had RGD peptide ligand or an RGD peptidomimetic (RGDp) attached to their surface to target gene delivery to αvb3 receptors in lung cancer cells. The NPs containing GFP siRNA showed that they displayed a 90% gene silencing level for green fluorescent protein (GFP) gene silencing in the human lung cancer H1299 cell line. Additionally, the RGD-modified NPs displayed two-fold greater cellular uptake than RGDp and had enhanced endo-lysosomal escape. The level of eGFP gene silencing and cellular uptake by the chitosan-PEI/siGFP NPs was dependent upon the concentration of the RGD on their surfaces.

Sundaram et al.'s (2009) research involved the development and use of an RGD-conjugated NP, which was targeted for administration in lung cancer in order to examine the efficacy of a new docetaxel-deslorelin (D-D) derivative, in vitro using H1299 human NSCLC cells, and in vivo using an H1299 xenograft mouse model of NSCLC. The application of the RGD conjugation PLGA NP containing the D-D conjugate improved the efficacy of the drug at inhibiting vascular endothelial growth factor (VEGF) in vivo when delivered in combination with an anti-VEGF intraceptor plasmid (RGD-Flt23k-NP). The co-delivery of Flt23k-NP and D-D to neovascular tissues via RGD conjugation resulted in an increase in the therapeutic efficacy of a combination treatment for lung cancer.

9.4 Challenges in polymer nanoparticle delivery

Polymeric NPs hold potential for drug delivery; however, realizing that potential will require overcoming a number of barriers. One significant challenge is understanding how the characteristics of the polymeric NPs change throughout their process in the body. For example, when interacting with biological components, the NP shape, surface charge, size, and presence of targeting moieties can all change. A recent review by Mitchell et al. (2021) has shown that changes in characteristics of the nanomaterials can significantly affect their systemic delivery, circulation stability, biodistribution, and eventual clearance. One of the biggest information gaps at the moment is determining the final characteristics of NPs once they have reached their cellular target. But it is important to note that the article also mentions a few FDA-approved nanomedicine treatments, and there are a number of exciting novel treatments that make use of NPs that are presently being used in clinical settings (Anselmo & Mitragotri, 2019).

The infrastructure of the pharmaceutical business is primarily designed for conventional distribution methods and small molecule medicines. Making the switch to polymer-based drug delivery vectors would require a large financial outlay for new production techniques, legal frameworks, and technology. Adoption of these cutting-edge solutions is being delayed by logistical and financial obstacles brought forth by this structural change. Complex structures are often required for polymer-based NPs to provide optimal targeting, controlled release, and stability in physiological conditions. However, this increased intricacy comes at a greater cost. Are the increases in efficiency and efficacy greater than the extra expenses incurred in developing and producing these treatments? This remains a vital subject. A balance between affordability and innovation is necessary for these systems to be scalable and available.

Polymer NPs' complex designs significantly reduce their efficacy in drug delivery. Some NPs are so persistent that they cannot release their pharmacological cargo even after effective cellular uptake, which undermines the system's therapeutic efficacy. However, the benefits of their protective structure and nanoscale shape could be lost if the NPs are too unstable and disintegrate before they can reach their goal. Their ability to shield the drug or biologic from deterioration is compromised by premature disassembly, which reduces their therapeutic effectiveness.

These issues necessitate an interdisciplinary approach that considers developments in systems biology, pharmacology, and material science/characterization. Polymer-based drug delivery systems may be able to overcome inefficiencies and fulfill their potential as next-generation therapies if cost and complexity are balanced, our knowledge of NP transformations is improved, and pharmaceutical infrastructure is rethought.

9.4.1 Biological and toxicity concerns

The topic of drug delivery using NPs has advanced significantly in the last few years. NPs, often composed of several different components carefully organized in a precise three-dimensional arrangement, are engineered to deliver therapeutic agents effectively. However, even small adjustments in their composition or structure can have unintended consequences due to the delicate balance of interactions between the different elements. Nanotechnology has one of its greatest challenges in producing NPs that are the ideal size to both carry the therapeutic cargo and accurately deliver it to specified sites in the body. When NPs are administered into the body, there are several challenges they may encounter when navigating through the biological environment. These challenges may include irregular morphology, incorrectly sized particles, limited biocompatibility, and unwanted surface properties. Biological challenges with NPs include routes of administration, biodistribution, controlling biological compartments, and degradation and toxicity of the NP. NPs are typically administered parenterally (for example, intravenously), and are circulated rapidly, and essentially are excreted from biological compartments, as it is difficult to retain them in the biological compartment long enough to act on the intended target. For this reason, higher concentrations of the drug are required, and at times, the dose does not achieve the therapeutic effect. The biological behavior of the NPs is critically important to manage, and many factors need to be closely observed. Although NPs are made from biocompatible materials and have been modified to enhance their retention time and half-life, it is still possible to cause injury to the organs such as the lungs, liver, and kidneys. The potential toxic effects associated with NP technology have been observed to be influenced by the particle size and shape, their surface area, their solubility properties, and their tendency to agglomerate.

NPs accumulate higher concentrations in the lung, imparting inflammation, oxidative stress, and cytotoxicity. It has been noted that healthy cells could be harmed by the free radicals caused by the introduction of the NPs. Developing NPs of more biocompatible materials, like chitosan, or incorporating materials that break down when exposed to near infrared light, could yield highly effective options. Because of the varying physical, chemical, and biological properties of NPs, developing delivery systems that function effectively and deliver therapeutics to specific targets (i.e., to the lungs) remains an ongoing challenge. As these particles proceed from preclinical to clinical stages of drug development, they must also contend with other challenges such as clearance, immune responses, biological barriers, and targeting. Nanocarrier system design for clinical use must be conscious of the many factors that will be involved in the process. One must also understand the core materials and interactions of those materials together. The system must be able to effectively target specific sites by overcoming biological barriers. In addition, it is important to develop an understanding of the underlying attributes that dictate the behavior of the system and ensure it can be produced consistently. Nanocarriers should be stable over time, easy to store, and to administer. This is true while at the same time being developed in a sterile manner with an emphasis on production timelines.

Effective delivery of chemotherapeutic medications to the alveolar region necessitates careful consideration of a number of parameters. Most importantly, it is crucial to produce NPs of the right size to enhance tumor retention, maximize avoidance of enzymatic breakdown, and circumvent obstacles like mucus and epithelial absorption that can impede medication absorption. To evaluate these NPs' behavior in biological systems, it is essential to comprehend their physicochemical characteristics, which include their propensity to aggregate, the ways in which proteins may stick to their surfaces, and how they move within cells. Significant changes to any of these characteristics could reduce the amount of medication delivered to the target or result in unfavorable side effects, which could compromise the therapeutic success. Additionally, because bigger particles tend to be quickly removed from the bloodstream, they are generally not the best candidates for intravenous administration (Floyd et al., 2025). PNPs must be made using exacting, meticulously regulated procedures in order to reach a consistent size, usually less than 200 nm. By using standard extrusion techniques, the particle size distribution can be modified. The surface charge of nanocarriers has a significant impact on their behavior in in vivo experiments. The zeta potential plays a significant role in determining the interactions and propensity for aggregation of NPs. Positively charged NPs typically have a greater affinity for the negatively charged cell membranes. However, before utilizing these NPs in living systems, it is crucial to conduct a complete assessment (Hubbs et al., 2011).

Generally, adding multiple functionalities to NPs increases their complexity. While metallic and inorganic NPs have shown promise in cancer treatment, they also carry the potential risk of harming healthy cells. For instance, amorphous silica NPs may provoke inflammatory responses at the targeted site (Hubbs et al., 2011). Titanium dioxide plays an important role in various biomedical applications due to its biological significance; however, its potential toxicity to healthy cells remains a critical concern that must be addressed (McCarthy et al., 2012). Furthermore, NPs have the potential to produce unique effects that may not occur with larger particles, such as damage to mitochondria, absorption via the olfactory epithelium, platelet aggregation, and potential cardiovascular impacts. Using NPs as drug carriers has the potential to reduce the toxicity of the drug being delivered; however, toxicity assessments often focus on the entire formulation, without clearly distinguishing the effects of the NPs themselves. Therefore, it is challenging to dissociate the toxicity of the drug from the toxicity of the NP. It is very important to specifically investigate the toxicity of empty NPs without a drug in them. This is especially relevant when using particles that are slowly degrading or nondegradable because these particles may accumulate in high quantities at the drug delivery site and can feasibly cause long-term inflammation or some other permanent response (McCarthy et al., 2012; Sharma et al., 2022).

Research is exploring alternate ways to transport NPs to tumors in lung cancer due to the densely packed stroma, irregular blood vessels, and various barriers that the dense tissue creates. One potential approach is to use tumor-penetrating peptides (TPPs) bound to NPs. These peptides target receptors overexpressed on tumor cells, which allows for targeted delivery and deeper penetration through the tumors (Floyd et al., 2025). Another approach is enzyme-responsive NPs, where the NPs may change size or charge upon exposure to tumor-specific enzymes.

Consequently, even if promising approaches are being explored and coming into the limelight, it is essential to conduct thorough safety evaluations of each nanocarrier system before clinical application through both in vitro and in vivo toxicity studies. Moreover, NPs must undergo careful analysis before being approved for use in medical treatments, including for the treatment of various cancer types (Crintea et al., 2021), and they must be tested across different tissue or cell types to assess their potential positive and negative effects on the human body (Jin et al., 2020). Therefore, advancements in the bioavailability, biocompatibility, and safety profiles of nanotechnology-based delivery systems are required to fully realize their potential in a variety of biomedical sectors, such as gene therapy and cancer treatment.

9.4.2 Regulatory concerns

Treatments with NPs have a complex and continually evolving regulatory framework. Agencies like the FDA and European Medicines Agency (EMA) are still developing their strategies for regulating the effectiveness and safety of nanomedicines. As nanomaterials possess unique qualities, they are all likely to challenge already-existing regulatory approaches. A primary issue is that different regulatory regions lack standard definitions for nanomaterials and even standard characterization techniques result in differing classifications and reviews of nanomedicines. Progress is being made to harmonize regulatory pathways, but there still remains a long way to go. Existing preclinical testing regimens for nanomaterials-based therapies still face challenges, namely that existing toxicology regimens need to be considered when looking at the unique biological interactions that nanomaterials have with biological systems. Subsequently, there is increasing pressure from regulatory agencies to conduct specific studies; in addition to biodistribution studies, comprehensive studies of long-term toxicity are examples where there appears to be increasing regulatory emphasis for the application of nanomedicine. Regulatory issues pertaining to nanomaterial-based combination products, which can include both drugs and devices, are significant. These products are typically subject to two or more regulatory categories and would need concurrent reviews by multiple divisions of a regulatory agency. Regardless of these challenges, it is a positive development that there are continuing efforts to establish more distinct regulatory pathways for nanomedicines (Zhang et al., 2025).

9.4.3 Manufacturing scalability concerns

The development of applicable nanomaterial-based therapies from studies in the laboratory will encounter a number of important requirements with regard to scaling up and manufacturing of nanomaterials. The majority of NP formulations that show promising effects in laboratory models are difficult, if not impossible, to manufacture at the scale or standardized quality required for clinical trials and larger-scale commercial production. One challenge with any nanomaterial-based therapy is that the physicochemical properties, including surface charge, size distribution, and drug loading, may vary from production batch to production batch. This might seem trivial, but small changes can greatly influence biodistribution, efficacy, and safety of nanomedicines. For goods that include nanomaterials, regulatory bodies have been creating strict quality control measures to reduce quality problems. Businesses are investigating cutting-edge production methods to increase the scalability and repeatability of NPs. In contrast to a conventional batch process, these techniques offer improved control over reaction conditions and yield NPs with more repeatable characteristics. The difficulty of creating analytical techniques that can accurately capture the intricacy of nanomaterial compositions must be addressed in order to maintain current developments. Conventional methods may not capture the properties unique to nanomedicines, and therefore, new methods have been developed that are specialized (Bian et al., 2023; Ramirez et al., 2021).

It is critical to overcome the technical challenges facing NPs, such as scaling up production, maximizing formulations, and quantitatively predicting their effectiveness to ensure their success in clinical settings. Most NPs used in in vitro and in vivo studies are generally produced in limited amounts, making it hard to scale production into larger quantities due to equipment limitations, among others. Moreover, the best clinical candidates that do well in animal studies are very often not systematically optimized during the development process for larger clinical use. To address this, approaches can be adopted that allow testing of multiple nanoformulations and, through selective iterations, identify the most optimized version for further development. However, these promising candidates should not be rushed into human trials without further evaluation. Predicting the efficacy and performance of NPs is challenging and translating in vivo results to human trials remains a significant hurdle. To address this, computational models and experimental data can be combined to replicate the conditions of physiological tissues and their environments. For example, organs-on-chips are being actively explored as a tool to enhance the prediction of NP efficacy and performance (Dobrovolskaia et al., 2008; Xia et al., 2020). Designing studies for NP therapies presents challenges related to factors like study size, objectives, and the timing of treatment. Many clinical studies rely on cell and animal models, which often fail to fully replicate human responses. Relying on a single model makes it difficult to adequately represent how the real body responds to treatment. Furthermore, there is a need for greater study into cancer metastasis models, because metastasis is a crucial feature of cancer that considerably impacts treatment outcomes (Love et al., 2010; Schork, 2015).

9.5 Future directions

9.5.1 Innovations in nanotechnology

Innovative drug delivery systems are being developed for a variety of purposes, with substantial potential for enhancing treatment safety, efficacy, and precision. These systems address traditional medicines' fundamental drawbacks, such as a lack of targeted administration, decreased therapeutic efficacy, undesirable side effects, and drug resistance. They also outperform previous approaches in detecting early stages of metastasis. NPs, for example, can deliver medications directly to certain tissues using techniques such as peptide targeting, PEGylation, or receptor-ligand interaction, resulting in more concentrated drug delivery at the target region. This approach typically requires lower doses and reduces cytotoxicity compared to applying the free drug topically. Numerous studies have identified encapsulation of chemotherapy into nanocarriers to be effective for reducing cytotoxicity compared to using free drug solutions. These advancements in nano-based delivery systems now provide a novel way to treat lung cancer. However, there are still some significant challenges to overcome before using these systems as desired. Drug resistance can occur when medications do not release enough from the nanocarrier into the environment to harm the cancer cell. Solutions to the challenge of drug resistance include studying multifunctionalized nanocarriers for accurate targeting of tumors, endosomal disruption for immediate the cytoplasm and applying combination therapies with multiple chemotherapeutic drugs. As particles progress from micro to nano size, their surface area and particle count increase as their total size decreases. This increased surface area boosts their chemical reactivity, making it more difficult to anticipate how NPs will behave in various situations. The increased reactivity of NPs can result in the generation of reactive oxygen species (ROS), which can induce inflammation, DNA damage, and oxidative stress, ultimately leading to cell death. Despite its potential, only a small number of liposome and NP-based formulations have been approved by the FDA to yet (Crintea et al., 2021).

While most lung tumors are detected at an advanced stage, there is an increasing demand for effective drug delivery methods. These systems should employ nanocarriers capable of delivering medication to both peripheral and central lung tissues, as well as the circulation, in order to target primary and metastatic tumor locations. More research is needed in designing carriers capable of controlling the release of chemotherapeutic medicines in response to precise triggers. Cancer theranostics, which combines diagnosis and targeted therapy in one, is based on flexible nanocarriers that carry both screening agents and chemotherapeutic medicines. This approach could play a key role in the future of cancer treatment, offering the ability to detect tumor cells and selectively destroy them with minimal side effects. Additionally, it could enable real-time in vivo screening and provide immediate insights into treatment effectiveness (Babu et al., 2013; Crintea et al., 2021).

Future research should focus on assessing NPs that are sufficiently stable, allow for better de-agglomeration, and have increased tissue infiltration. Particle stability and the issue of clumping during storage may be improved by changing the physical properties, such as mass median diameter and porosity, and altering the chemical properties, such as amphiphilic nature, targeting ligands, or permanent polymers. Apart from the challenges that come with the original design and manufacture of nanocarriers for drug delivery, researchers often also have to deal with a lack of standardized methods for assessing the manufacture of nanomedicines. This includes variability in manufacturing processes, evaluation of function, and safety regulations. The fact that there are often multiple active compounds in NPs also complicates matters. The complexity involved in NPs requires an update to current ways of pharmacokinetics, bioequivalence, and safety evaluation. Replacing traditional dosing with drug delivery systems using nanotechnology approaches will take a significant amount of research into new types of development of nanoproducts built on the rationale of enhancing drug delivery, and a regulatory authority must apply a toolbox of testing supporting an expedited clearance process (Babu et al., 2013; Zhang et al., 2025).

9.5.2 Personalized medicine approach

Personalized medicine has emerged as an area for investigation to enhance traditional forms of practice by recognizing a patient's illness on their terms, their account of their illness, their disease from their past medical history, and most importantly, in identifying custom drugs and medical devices for them. Personalized medicine will transform medical care, providing personalized medical care ahead of traditional norms. Many clinicians will shift care objectives from predicting diseases to anticipating illness and protecting health through the implementation of personalized medicines, personal laboratory tests, and individualized treatment based on global genetics. Not only does personalized medicine present a leap from traditional treatment, but it also programs therapies as capable of being modified from unique assessments of the individual's genetic profile. It is now possible to study tumor DNA simply, rapidly, and affordably through new forms of next-generation sequencing technology, and develop targeted treatments based on the patient's immune system, which considers the complete unique genetics of the patient, including diverse medical treatments or medicines, including pharmaceutical, herbal, and also characterized by the cancer stage, type of cancer and is considered a better management of care. The integration of personalized medicine into cancer research holds the potential for major breakthroughs in the battle against cancer. However, healthcare practitioners encounter problems such as the need for lengthy treatment plans, the complexities of cancer stages, and the unpredictability in how different individuals respond to treatments. One of the most important advancements in personalized medicine has been the discovery of specific molecular alterations that can be used as therapy targets. A variety of molecular changes have been revealed through genomic, proteomic, and metabolomic studies, providing new potential for personalizing therapy to particular patients (Singh et al., 2024).

Lung cancer is still one of the leading causes of cancer mortality worldwide. The disease's complexity, with its various tumor features, development of resistance to treatment, and limited efficacy of existing medicines, makes successful treatment difficult. Although progress has been achieved with targeted treatments such as tyrosine kinase inhibitors (TKIs) and monoclonal antibodies, the establishment of medication resistance remains a substantial hurdle to increasing patients' long-term survival chances. One of the significant advancements in cancer treatment has been the use of pharmacogenomics, which customizes therapies for specific genes, such as anaplastic lymphoma kinase (ALK), Kirsten rat sarcoma viral oncogene homolog, v-raf murine sarcoma viral oncogene homolog B1, Mesenchymal-Epithelial Transition (MET) proto-oncogene, and EGFR. While the tailored method has considerable potential, it is limited by problems such as tumor adaptation, a lack of validated biomarkers for predicting responses, and poor solo outcomes. Combination therapies (targeted medicines, immunotherapy, and chemotherapy) have the potential to significantly improve treatment and resistance mechanisms (Namini et al., 2025).

9.6 Patents on using polymeric nanoparticles for lung cancer treatment

Magnetic NPs based on trimethyl chitosan have been engineered with a diameter of approximately 300 nm and contain the drug gemcitabine in order to deliver the drug via a magnetically guided, mucoadhesive route directly to lung tumors. This is expected to increase drug concentration at the tumor site while decreasing the possibility of systemic side effects. These NPs are used to formulate either lipid or lipid-polymer systems that are coated with PEG and ligands for receptors that are overexpressed in NSCLCs in order to co-encapsulate chemotherapeutics and surface-bound siRNA against EGFR1-4 and have been developed for use by inhalation. This will facilitate the active targeting of the drug to the tumor via the bypassing of the normal delivery systems (i.e., the respiratory tract and/ or circulation) and passive deposition into the lungs. Dendritic or hyperbranching biodegradable polymer NPs that form micelle-like structures (i.e., a hydrophobic interior and a hydrophilic exterior) can be utilized for the encapsulation of Bi-DOTA complexes and any additional drugs to provide both a theranostic imaging method and a therapeutic method for solid tumors, including lung cancer. Less complex biodegradable block-copolymer delivery systems that can encapsulate anticancer poly-peptides, nucleic acids, or chemotherapeutics and have been functionalized on the surface with vitamins, ligands, antibodies, or aptamers can be used to formulate modular drug formulations that can be utilized against lung tumors. The use of polymer-based

Table 9.2: Patents on using polymeric nanoparticles for lung cancer treatment.

Patent (Pub. no., Year)	Title	Nanoparticle/polymer system	Targeting strategy
WO2022125031A1 (2022)	Trimethyl chitosan nanoparticles containing magnetic-targeted gemcitabine	Trimethyl chitosan polymeric nanoparticles incorporating magnetic material and gemcitabine	Magnetic targeting plus chitosan-based mucoadhesion; size ≈294 nm for enhanced deposition
US20220125728A1 / US11896713B2 (2022–2024)	Strategies to enhance lung cancer treatment	Lipid-based nanoparticle (non-liposomal) with PEG chains and surface-attached ligands; may carry siRNA and drug	Active receptor-mediated targeting via ligands to receptors overexpressed on NSCLC cells; inhalation delivery for passive lung targeting
EP3900743A1 / US20210236665A1 (2021)	Bi-DOTA complex-loaded dendritic polymer nanoparticles	Dendritic/hyperbranched biodegradable polymer nanoparticles with internal hydrophobic pockets, loaded with Bi-DOTA complexes and optional drugs	Tumor targeting via enhanced permeability and retention plus optional functionalization; suitable for solid tumor targeting
EP3778696A1 (2021)	Polymeric nanoparticles and a process of preparation thereof	Biodegradable block-copolymer nanoparticles (30–120 nm) produced without emulsifiers	Surface conjugation of targeting moieties: vitamins, ligands, peptides, antibodies, aptamers etc.
WO2021102279A1 (2021)	Anti-cancer compositions and methods	Lipid-polymer hybrid (LPH) nanoparticles encapsulating miriplatin ultrasmall dots (uPtD) and/or lomitapide, optionally paclitaxel	Nanoparticle surface "decorated with a targeting agent" for tumor-specific delivery
US20210228564A1 (2021)	Pyrvinium pamoate therapies and methods of use	Polymer-based nanoparticles including PLGA; may include targeting agents such as peptide ligands or hyaluronic acid	Targeting via ligands and hyaluronic acid (CD44-mediated uptake) on cancer cells

NSCLC, non-small cell lung cancer; *PEG*, polyethylene glycol; *PLGA*, poly lactic-co-glycolic acid;DOTA, 1,4,7,10-tetraazacyclododecane-1,4,7,10-tetraacetic acid.

or lipid-polymer composite nanoparticles to transport cytotoxic medicines (e.g., pyrvinium pamoate, miriplatin small dots, and lomitapide) and targeted at specific tumors, including lung cancer, indicates a growing trend of using biodegradable surface-modified nanotechnology containing targeting ligands, dual-drug payloads, and/or imaging agents to enhance the accuracy/effectiveness of therapy for lung cancer (Bian et al., 2023). Patents on using PNPs for lung cancer treatment are given in Table 9.2 (Bian et al., 2023).

9.7 Conclusion

Lung cancer remains a global health concern due to the disease's high incidence and mortality rate. Treating lung cancer has evolved over the years; however, traditional approaches, namely chemotherapy and radiotherapy, are often constrained by systemic toxicity, tumor heterogenicity, the development of resistance to conventional drugs, and the lack of specificity in targeting tumors. PNPs, a branch of nanomedicine still in development, hold promise in mitigating drug resistance and improving efficacy by taking properties of nanoscale materials and applying them to drug delivery and combination therapy to overcome drug resistance and leverage immune modulation. Applications of nanomaterials, such as immunotherapy, phototherapy, and chemotherapy, have shown considerable efficacy in the research domain, especially in resistant cancers in human clinical research. While nanomedicine-based approaches hold much potential, it can be emphasized that issues like biological barriers, innate and adaptive immune response, standard manufacturing processes (upscaling), and regulation used as a barrier to clinical application must be resolved. Additionally, pharmacogenomics technology can also play a role in personalizing medical therapy by understanding the biochemical and genetic make-up of persons. However, there are still limitations on the universal and cost-effective application of pharmacogenomics given the lack of full testing, and knowledge of all of the biomarkers involved. It remains challenging to realize its full potential until such issues are resolved. To overcome these issues and make it easier to include nanomedicine into lung cancer therapy, future studies should focus on innovative design techniques, the creation of sophisticated manufacturing techniques, and multidisciplinary cooperation. NPs have the ability to alter the course of lung cancer treatment, perhaps leading to increased patient survival and quality of life despite this uncertainty.

Abbreviations

PNPs	Polymeric nanoparticles
NSCLC	Non-small cell lung cancer
SCLC	Small cell lung cancer
EGFR	Epidermal growth factor receptor
FDA	Food and Drug Administration
NPs	Nanoparticles
PLGA	Poly lactic-co-glycolic acid
FA	Folic acid
EGF	Epidermal growth factor
QDs	Quantum dots
TPPs	Tumor-penetrating peptides
MMPs	Matrix etalloproteinases
EMA	European medicines agency
ROS	Reactive oxygen species
TKIs	Tyrosine kinase inhibitors
ALK	Anaplastic lymphoma kinase

Refrences

Abdelwahed, W., Degobert, G., Stainmesse, S., & Fessi, H. (2006). Freeze-drying of nanoparticles: Formulation, process and storage considerations. *Advanced Drug Delivery Reviews, 58*, 1688–1713.

Albertazzi, L., Van Der Zwaag, D., Leenders, C. M. A., Fitzner, R., Van Der Hofstad, R. W., & Meijer, E. W. (2014). Probing exchange pathways in one-dimensional aggregates with super-resolution microscopy. *Science, 344*(6183), 491–495. doi:10.1126/science.1250945.

Amgoth, C., Phan, C., Banavoth, M., Rompivalasa, S., & Tang, G. (2020). Polymer properties: Functionalization and surface modified nanoparticles. *Role of novel drug delivery vehicles in nanobiomedicine*. IntechOpen. doi:10.5772/intechopen.84424.

Andreani, T., Kiill, C. P., de Souza, A. L. R., Fangueiro, J. F., Doktorovová, S., Garcia, M. L., et al. (2015). Effect of cryoprotectants on the reconstitution of silica nanoparticles produced by sol–gel technology. *Journal of Thermal Analysis and Calorimetry, 120*(1), 1001–1007. doi:10.1007/s10973-014-4275-4.

Anselmo, A. C., & Mitragotri, S. (2019). Nanoparticles in the clinic: An update. *Bioengineering & Translational Medicine, 4*(3), e10143. doi:10.1002/btm2.10143.

Babu, A., Templeton, A. K., Munshi, A., & Ramesh, R. (2013). Nanoparticle-based drug delivery for therapy of lung cancer: Progress and challenges. *Journal of Nanomaterials, 2013*(1), 863951. doi:10.1155/2013/863951.

Baer, D. R., Engelhard, M. H., Johnson, G. E., Laskin, J., Lai, J., Mueller, K., et al. (2013). Surface characterization of nanomaterials and nanoparticles: Important needs and challenging opportunities. *Journal of Vaccum Science & Technology Vac Surf Films, 31*(5), 050820. doi:10.1116/1.4818423.

Bakker, M. H., Lee, C. C., Meijer, E. W., Dankers, P. Y. W., & Albertazzi, L. (2016). Multicomponent supramolecular polymers as a modular platform for intracellular delivery. *ACS Nano, 10*(2), 1845–1852. doi:10.1021/acsnano.5b05383.

Bian, J., Gobalasingham, N., Purchel, A., & Lin, J. (2023). The power of field-flow fractionation in characterization of nanoparticles in drug delivery. *Molecules, 28*, 4169. https://patentscope.wipo.int/search/en/search.jsf.

Bohnert, T., & Gan, L. S. (2013). Plasma protein binding: From discovery to development. *Journal of Pharmaceutical Sciences, 102*(9), 2953–2994. doi:10.1002/jps.23614.

Bohrey, S., Chourasiya, V., & Pandey, A. (2016). Polymeric nanoparticles containing diazepam: Preparation, optimization, characterization, in-vitro drug release and release kinetic study. *Nano Convergence, 3*(1), 3. doi:10.1186/s40580-016-0061-2.

Brar, S. K., & Verma, M. (2011). Measurement of nanoparticles by light-scattering techniques. *TrAC Trends in Analytical Chemistry, 30*(1), 4–17. doi:10.1016/j.trac.2010.08.008.

Calvo, P., Remuñán-López, C., Vila-Jato, J. L., & Alonso, M. J. (1997). Novel hydrophilic chitosan-polyethylene oxide nanoparticles as protein carriers. *Journal of Applied Polymer Science, 63*(1), 125–132. doi:10.1002/(SICI)1097-4628(19970103)63:1⟨125.

Campbell, J. D., Alexandrov, A., Kim, J., Wala, J., Berger, A. H., Pedamallu, C. S., et al. (2016). Distinct patterns of somatic genome alterations in lung adenocarcinomas and squamous cell carcinomas. *Nature Genetics, 48*(6), 607–616. doi:10.1038/ng.3564.

Carvalho, P. M., Felício, M. R., Santos, N. C., Gonçalves, S., & Domingues, M. M. (2018). Application of light scattering techniques to nanoparticle characterization and development. *Frontiers in Chemistry, 6*, 237. doi:10.3389/fchem.2018.00237.

Christoforidis, J. B., Chang, S., Jiang, A., Wang, J., & Cebulla, C. M. (2012). Intravitreal devices for the treatment of vitreous inflammation. *Mediators of Inflammation, 2012*(1), 126463. doi:10.1155/2012/126463.

Crintea, A., Dutu, A. G., Samasca, G., Florian, I. A., Lupan, I., & Craciun, A. M. (2021). The nanosystems involved in treating lung cancer. *Life, 11*(7), 682. doi:10.3390/life11070682.

Crucho, C. I. C., & Barros, M. T. (2017). Polymeric nanoparticles: A study on the preparation variables and characterization methods. *Materials Science and Engineering C, 80*, 771–784. doi:10.1016/j.msec.2017.06.004.

da Silva, R. M. P., van der Zwaag, D., Albertazzi, L., Lee, S. S., Meijer, E. W., & Stupp, S. I. (2016). Super-resolution microscopy reveals structural diversity in molecular exchange among peptide amphiphile nanofibres. *Nature Communications, 7*(1), 11561. doi:10.1038/ncomms11561.

Dazon, C., Witschger, O., Bau, S., Fierro, V., & Llewellyn, P. L. (2019). Nanomaterial identification of powders: Comparing volume specific surface area, X-ray diffraction and scanning electron microscopy methods. *Environmental Science: Nano, 6*(1), 152–162. doi:10.1039/C8EN00760H.

De Jong, W. H., & Borm, P. J. A. (2008). Drug delivery and nanoparticles:applications and hazards. *International Journal of Nanomedicine, 3*(2), 133–149. doi:10.2147/ijn.s596.

Desgouilles, S., Vauthier, C., Bazile, D., Vacus, J., Grossiord, J. L., Veillard, M., et al. (2003). The design of nanoparticles obtained by solvent evaporation: A comprehensive study. *Langmuir, 19*(22), 9504–9510. doi:10.1021/la034999q.

Dobrovolskaia, M. A., Aggarwal, P., Hall, J. B., & McNeil, S. E. (2008). Preclinical studies to understand nanoparticle interaction with the immune system and its potential effects on nanoparticle biodistribution. *Molecular Pharmaceutics, 5*(4), 487–495. doi:10.1021/mp800032f.

Doktorovová, S., Santos, D. L., Costa, I., Andreani, T., Souto, E. B., & Silva, A. M. (2014). Cationic solid lipid nanoparticles interfere with the activity of antioxidant enzymes in hepatocellular carcinoma cells. *Int J Pharm, 471*(1–2), 18–27. doi:10.1016/j.ijpharm.2014.05.011.

Doktorovova, S., Souto, E. B., & Silva, A. M. (2014). Nanotoxicology applied to solid lipid nanoparticles and nanostructured lipid carriers – A systematic review of *in vitro* data. *European Journal of Pharmaceutics and Biopharmaceutics, 87*(1), 1–18. doi:10.1016/j.ejpb.2014.02.005.

Doncom, K. E. B., Blackman, L. D., Wright, D. B., Gibson, M. I., & O'Reilly, R. K. (2017). Dispersity effects in polymer self-assemblies: A matter of hierarchical control. *Chemical Society Review, 46*(14), 4119–4134. doi:10.1039/C6CS00818F.

Dumitriu, S., & Popa, V. (2013). In *Polymeric biomaterials: Medicinal and pharmaceutical applications: 2* (p. 843). CRC Press.

Floyd, T. G., Gurnani, P., & Rho J. , Y. (2025). Characterisation of polymeric nanoparticles for drug delivery. *Nanoscale, 17*(13), 7738–7752. doi:10.1039/D5NR00071H.

Fu, Y., & Kao, W. J. (2010). Drug release kinetics and transport mechanisms of non-degradable and degradable polymeric delivery systems. *Expert Opinion on Drug Delivery, 7*(4), 429–444. doi:10.1517/17425241003602259.

Gadgeel, S. M., & Kalemkerian, G. P. (2010). Lung cancer: Overview. In V. Keshamouni, D. Arenberg, & G. Kalemkerian (Eds.), *Lung cancer metastasis: Novel biological mechanisms and impact on clinical practice* (pp. 1–27). Springer. doi:10.1007/978-1-4419-0772-1_1.

Grumezescu, A. M. (2017). *Design and development of new nanocarriers* (p. 769). William Andrew.

Guterres, S. S., Alves, M. P., & Pohlmann, A. R. (2007). Polymeric nanoparticles, nanospheres and nanocapsules, for cutaneous applications. *Drug Target Insights, 2*. doi:10.1177/117739280700200002.

Halagali, P., Nayak, D., Tippavajhala, V. K., Rathnanand, M., Biswas, D., & Sharma, H. (2025). Navigating the nanoscopic frontier: Ethical dimensions in developing nanocarriers for neurodegenerative diseases. In *The neurodegeneration revolution* (pp. 399–420). Academic Press. emerging therapies and sustainable solutions. doi:10.1016/B978-0-443-28822-7.00011-8.

Heinz, H., Pramanik, C., Heinz, O., Ding, Y., Mishra, R. K., Marchon, D., … Ziolo, R. F. (2017). Nanoparticle decoration with surfactants: Molecular interactions, assembly, and applications. *Surface Science Reports, 72*(1), 1–58.

Hickey, J. W., Santos, J. L., Williford, J. M., & Mao, H. Q. (2015). Control of polymeric nanoparticle size to improve therapeutic delivery. *Journal of Controlled Release, 219*, 536–547. doi:10.1016/j.jconrel.2015.10.006.

Honary, S., & Zahir, F. (2013). Effect of zeta potential on the properties of nano-drug delivery systems - A review (Part 1). *Tropical Journal of Pharmaceutical Resarch, 12*(2), 255–264. doi:10.4314/tjpr.v12i2.19.

Hubbs, A. F., Mercer, R. R., Benkovic, S. A., Harkema, J., Sriram, K., Schwegler-Berry, D., et al. (2011). Nanotoxicology—A pathologist's perspective. *Toxicologic Pathology, 39*(2), 301–324. doi:10.1177/0192623310390705.

Inamdar, A., Gurupadayya, B., Halagali, P., Tippavajhala, V. K., Khan, F., Pathak, R., et al. (2025). Unraveling neurological drug delivery: Polymeric nanocarriers for enhanced blood-brain barrier penetration. *Current Drug Targets, 26*(4), 243–266. doi:10.2174/0113894501339455241101065040.

Jawahar, N., & Meyyanathan, S. (2012). Polymeric nanoparticles for drug delivery and targeting: A comprehensive review. *International Journal of Health & Allied Science, 1*(4), 217.

Jin, C., Wang, K., Oppong-Gyebi, A., & Hu, J. (2020). Application of nanotechnology in cancer diagnosis and therapy—A mini-review. *International Journal of Medical Sciences, 17*(18), 2964–2973. doi:10.7150/ijms.49801.

Jose, S., Sowmya, S., Cinu, T. A., Aleykutty, N. A., Thomas, S., & Souto, E. B. (2014). Surface modified PLGA nanoparticles for brain targeting of Bacoside-A. *European Journal of Pharmaceutical Sciences, 63*, 29–35. doi:10.1016/j.ejps.2014.06.024.

Kamaly, N., Yameen, B., Wu, J., & Farokhzad, O. C. (2016). Degradable controlled-release polymers and polymeric nanoparticles: Mechanisms of controlling drug release. *Chemical Review, 116*(4), 2602–2663. doi:10.1021/acs.chemrev.5b00346.

Khan, I., Saeed, K., & Khan, I. (2019). Nanoparticles: Properties, applications and toxicities. *Arabian Journal of Chemistry, 12*(7), 908–931. doi:10.1016/j.arabjc.2017.05.011.

Krishnamoorthy, K., & Mahalingam, M. (2015). Selection of a suitable method for the preparation of polymeric nanoparticles: Multi-criteria decision making approach. *Advanced Pharmaceutical Bulletin, 5*(1), 57–67. doi:10.5681/apb.2015.008.

Kumar, S., Dilbaghi, N., Saharan, R., & Bhanjana, G. (2012). Nanotechnology as emerging tool for enhancing solubility of poorly water-soluble drugs. *BioNanoScience, 2*(4), 227–250. doi:10.1007/s12668-012-0060-7.

Lazzari, S., Moscatelli, D., Codari, F., Salmona, M., Morbidelli, M., & Diomede, L. (2012). Colloidal stability of polymeric nanoparticles in biological fluids. *Journal of Nanoparticle Research, 14*(6), 920. doi:10.1007/s11051-012-0920-7.

Lee, J. H., & Yeo, Y. (2015). Controlled drug release from pharmaceutical nanocarriers. *Chemical Engineering Science, 125*, 75–84. doi:10.1016/j.ces.2014.08.046.

Lim, K., & Hamid, Z. A. A. (2018). Polymer nanoparticle carriers in drug delivery systems. In *Applications of nanocomposite materials in drug delivery* (pp. 217–237). Woodhead Publishing. doi:10.1016/B978-0-12-813741-3.00010-8.

Love, K. T., Mahon, K. P., Levins, C. G., Whitehead, K. A., Querbes, W., Dorkin, J. R., et al. (2010). Lipid-like materials for low-dose, in vivo gene silencing. *PNAS, 107*(5), 1864–1869. doi:10.1073/pnas.0910603106.

Lu, M., Yang, X., Yang, Y., Qin, P., Wu, X., & Cai, Z. (2017). Nanomaterials as assisted matrix of laser desorption/ionization time-of-flight mass spectrometry for the analysis of small molecules. *Nanomaterials, 7*(4), 87. doi:10.3390/nano7040087.

Mansfield, E., Kaiser, D. L., Fujita, D., & Van de Voorde, M. . (2017). *Metrology and standardization for nanotechnology: Protocols and industrial innovations* (p. 589). John Wiley & Sons.

Mathurin, J., Pancani, E., Deniset-Besseau, A., Kjoller, K., Prater, C. B., Gref, R., & Dazzi, A. (2018). How to unravel the chemical structure and component localization of individual drug-loaded polymeric nanoparticles by using tapping AFM-IR. *Analyst, 143*(24), 5940–5949. doi:10.1039/C8AN01239C.

Mattheolabakis, G., Ling, D., Ahmad, G., & Amiji, M. (2016). Enhanced anti-tumor efficacy of lipid-modified platinum derivatives in combination with survivin silencing siRNA in resistant non-small cell lung cancer. *Pharmaceutical Research, 33*(12), 2943–2953. doi:10.1007/s11095-016-2016-z.

Mayekar, M. K., & Bivona, T. G. (2017). Current landscape of targeted therapy in lung cancer. *Clinical Pharmacology & Therapeutics, 102*(5), 757–764. doi:10.1002/cpt.810.

McCarthy, J., Inkielewicz-Stępniak, I., Corbalan, J. J., & Radomski, M. W. (2012). Mechanisms of toxicity of amorphous silica nanoparticles on human lung submucosal cells in vitro: Protective effects of fisetin. *Chemical Research in Toxicology, 25*(10), 2227–2235. doi:10.1021/tx3002884.

Mitchell, M. J., Billingsley, M. M., Haley, R. M., Wechsler, M. E., Peppas, N. A., & Langer, R. (2021). Engineering precision nanoparticles for drug delivery. *Nature Reviews Drug Discovery, 20*(2), 101–124. doi:10.1038/s41573-020-0090-8.

Mourdikoudis, S., Pallares, R. M., & Thanh, N. T. K. (2018). Characterization techniques for nanoparticles: Comparison and complementarity upon studying nanoparticle properties. *Nanoscale, 10*(27), 12871–12934. doi:10.1039/C8NR02278J.

Nafee, N., Taetz, S., Schneider, M., Schaefer, U. F., & Lehr, C. M. (2007). Chitosan-coated PLGA nanoparticles for DNA/RNA delivery: Effect of the formulation parameters on complexation and transfection of antisense oligonucleotides. *Nanomedicine: Nanotechnology, Biology and Medicine, 3*(3), 173–183. doi:10.1016/j.nano.2007.03.006.

Namini, M., Bhagya, G., & Sharma, M. (2025). Personalized approaches to lung cancer treatment: A review of targeted therapies, pharmacogenomics, and combination strategies. *Aspects of Molecular Medicine, 5*, 100073. doi:10.1016/j.amolm.2025.100073.

Nayak, U., Halagali, P., Panchal, K. N., Tippavajhala, V. K., Mudgal, J., Radhakrishnan, R., & Manikkath, J. (2025). Nanoparticles in CNS therapeutics: Pioneering drug delivery advancements. *Current Pharmaceutical Design, 31*(6), 443–460. doi:10.2174/0113816128328722240828184410.

Ostolska, I., & Wiśniewska, M. (2014). Application of the zeta potential measurements to explanation of colloidal Cr_2O_3 stability mechanism in the presence of the ionic polyamino acids. *Colloid and Polymer Science, 292*(10), 2453–2464. doi:10.1007/s00396-014-3276-y.

Pathak, R., Halagali, P., Tippavajhala, V. K., Dodakallanavar, J., Ramachandra, H. D., & Sharma, H. (2025). Recent advances in targeted nanocomposite-based therapeutics for cancer therapy. *Current Drug Research Reviews, 17*(3), 428–449. doi:10.2174/0125899775367848250226063700.

Patra, J. K., Das, G., Fraceto, L. F., Campos, E. V. R., Rodriguez-Torres, M., del, P., Acosta-Torres, L. S., et al. (2018). Nano based drug delivery systems: Recent developments and future prospects. *Journal of Nanobiotechnology, 16*(1), 71. doi:10.1186/s12951-018-0392-8.

Podzimek, S. (2011). *Light scattering, size exclusion chromatography and asymmetric flow field flow fractionation: Powerful tools for the characterization of polymers, proteins and nanoparticles* (p. 325). John Wiley & Sons.

Quintanar-Guerrero, D., Allémann, E., Doelker, E., & Fessi, H. (1998). Preparation and characterization of nanocapsules from preformed polymers by a new process based on emulsification-diffusion technique. *Pharmaceutical Research, 15*(7), 1056–1062. doi:10.1023/A:1011934328471.

R, S., Halagali, P., Preethi.s, P., Vikram P R, H. (2023). Quality by design (QBD) approach in processing of nanoparticles loading antifungal drugs. 2023. https://www.researchgate.net/publication/368986206_Quality_By_Design_QBD_Approach_in_Processing_of_Nanoparticles_Loading_Antifungal_Drugs.

Ragelle, H., Colombo, S., Pourcelle, V., Vanvarenberg, K., Vandermeulen, G., Bouzin, C., et al. (2015). Intracellular siRNA delivery dynamics of integrin-targeted, PEGylated chitosan–poly(ethylene imine) hybrid nanoparticles: A mechanistic insight. *Journal of Controlled Release, 211*, 1–9. doi:10.1016/j.jconrel.2015.05.274.

Rahman, M., & Asiri, A. M. (2016). *Advances in colloid science* (p. 286). IntechOpen.

Ramirez, L. M. F., Rihouey, C., Chaubet, F., Le Cerf, D., & Picton, L. (2021). Characterization of dextran particle size: How frit-inlet asymmetrical flow field-flow fractionation (FI-AF4) coupled online with dynamic light scattering (DLS) leads to enhanced size distribution. *Journal of Chromatography A, 1653*, 462404. doi:10.1016/j.chroma.2021.462404.

Reis, C. P., Neufeld, R. J., Ribeiro António, A. J., & Veiga, F. (2006). Nanoencapsulation I. Methods for preparation of drug-loaded polymeric nanoparticles. *Nanomedicine: Nanotechnology, Biology and Medicine, 2*(1), 8–21. doi:10.1016/j.nano.2005.12.003.

Reisch, A., & Klymchenko, A. S. (2016). Fluorescent polymer nanoparticles based on dyes: Seeking brighter tools for bioimaging. *Small, 12*(15), 1968–1992. doi:10.1002/smll.201503396.

Schaffazick, S. R., Pohlmann, A. R., Dalla-Costa, T., & Guterres, S. S. (2003). Freeze-drying polymeric colloidal suspensions: Nanocapsules, nanospheres and nanodispersion. A comparative study. *European Journal of Pharmaceutics and Biopharmaceutics, 56*(3), 501–505. doi:10.1016/S0939-6411(03)00139-5.

Schork, N. J. (2015). Personalized medicine: Time for one-person trials. *Nature, 520*(7549), 609–611. doi:10.1038/520609a.

Seenivasan, R., Halagali, P., Pachiyappan, J. K., Marimuthu, A., Sharma, H., Somanna, P., et al. (2026). Introduction to polymer nanocomposites. In N. Kothawade, V. Pande, S. Gattani, & R. Sumbe (Eds.), *Polymer nanocomposites: Advances in design, synthesis, and applications* (pp. 1–21). Springer Nature Switzerland. doi:10.1007/978-3-032-00365-2_1.

Sharma, A., Tonk, R., Shekhar, R., Dohare, S., & Kumar, D. (2022). Need to focus on inhibitory activity of benzimidazole analogues against indolamine 2,3-dioxygenase-1 (IDO-1). *EXCLI Journal, 21*, 904–905. doi:10.17179/excli2022-4988.

Sharma, N., Madan, P., & Lin, S. (2016). Effect of process and formulation variables on the preparation of parenteral paclitaxel-loaded biodegradable polymeric nanoparticles: A co-surfactant study. *Asian Journal of Pharmaceutical Sciences, 11*(3), 404–416. doi:10.1016/j.ajps.2015.09.004.

Shen, J., & Burgess, D. J. (2013). In vitro dissolution testing strategies for nanoparticulate drug delivery systems: Recent developments and challenges. *Drug Delivery and Translational Research, 3*(5), 409–415. doi:10.1007/s13346-013-0129-z.

Simonet, B. M., & Valcárcel, M. (2009). Monitoring nanoparticles in the environment. *Analytical and Bioanalytical Chemistry, 393*(1), 17–21. doi:10.1007/s00216-008-2484-z.

Singh, D., Dhiman, V. K., Pandey, M., Dhiman, V. K., Sharma, A., Pandey, H., et al. (2024). Personalized medicine: An alternative for cancer treatment. *Cancer Treatment and Research Communications, 42*, 100860. doi:10.1016/j.ctarc.2024.100860.

Singh, R., & Lillard, J. W. (2009). Nanoparticle-based targeted drug delivery. *Experimental and Molecular Pathology, 86*(3), 215–223. doi:10.1016/j.yexmp.2008.12.004.

Soppimath, K. S., Aminabhavi, T. M., Kulkarni, A. R., & Rudzinski, W. E. (2001). Biodegradable polymeric nanoparticles as drug delivery devices. *Journal of Controlled Release, 70*(1–2), 1–20. doi:10.1016/S0168-3659(00)00339-4.

Souto, E. B., Severino, P., & Santana, M. H. A. (2012). Preparação de nanopartículas poliméricas a partir da polimerização de monômeros: Parte I. *Polímeros, 22*, 96–100. doi:10.1590/S0104-14282012005000006.

Souto, E. B., Souto, S. B., Campos, J. R., Severino, P., Pashirova, T. N., Zakharova, L. Y., et al. (2019). Nanoparticle delivery systems in the treatment of diabetes complications. *Molecules, 24*(23), 4209. doi:10.3390/molecules24234209.

Stals, P. J. M., Gillissen, M. A. J., Paffen, T. F. E., De Greef, T. F. A., Lindner, P., Meijer, E. W., et al. (2014). Folding polymers with pendant hydrogen bonding motifs in water: The effect of polymer length and concentration on the shape and size of single-chain polymeric nanoparticles. *Macromolecules, 47*(9), 2947–2954. doi:10.1021/ma500273g.

Su, W. C., Su, W. P., Cheng, S., & Yeh (2012). PLGA nanoparticles codeliver paclitaxel and Stat3 siRNA to overcome cellular resistance in lung cancer cells. *International Journal of Nanomedicine*, 4269. doi:10.2147/IJN.S33666.

Sumana, M., Alagu, T., Muthukumaran, P., & Anand, K. (2020). Biodegradable natural polymeric nanoparticles as carrier for drug delivery. In *Integrative nanomedicine for new therapies* (pp. 231–246). Springer Nature. doi:10.1007/978-3-030-36260-7_8.

Sundaram, S., Trivedi, R., Durairaj, C., Ramesh, R., Ambati, B. K., & Kompella, U. B. (2009). Targeted drug and gene delivery systems for lung cancer therapy. *Clinical Cancer Research, 15*(23), 7299–7308. doi:10.1158/1078-0432.CCR-09-1745.

Szczech, M., & Szczepanowicz, K. (2020). Polymeric core-shell nanoparticles prepared by spontaneous emulsification solvent evaporation and functionalized by the layer-by-layer method. *Nanomaterials, 10*, 496. https://www.mdpi.com/2079-4991/10/3/496.

Taetz, S., Nafee, N., Beisner, J., Piotrowska, K., Baldes, C., Mürdter, T. E., et al. (2009). The influence of chitosan content in cationic chitosan/PLGA nanoparticles on the delivery efficiency of antisense 2′-*O*-methyl-RNA directed against telomerase in lung cancer cells. *European Journal of Pharmaceutics and Biopharmaceutics, 72*(2), 358–369. doi:10.1016/j.ejpb.2008.07.011.

Taratula, O., Garbuzenko, O. B., Kirkpatrick, P., Pandya, I., Savla, R., Pozharov, V. P., et al. (2009). Surface-engineered targeted PPI dendrimer for efficient intracellular and intratumoral siRNA delivery. *Journal of Controlled Release, 140*(3), 284–293. doi:10.1016/j.jconrel.2009.06.019.

The Cancer Genome Atlas Research Network. (2014). Comprehensive molecular profiling of lung adenocarcinoma. *Nature, 511*(7511), 543–550. doi:10.1038/nature13385.

Vasile, C. (2018). *Polymeric nanomaterials in nanotherapeutics* (p. 561). Elsevier.

Vauthier, C., & Bouchemal, K. (2009). Methods for the preparation and manufacture of polymeric nanoparticles. *Pharmaceutical Research, 26*(5), 1025–1058. doi:10.1007/s11095-008-9800-3.

Vieira, R., Souto, S. B., Sánchez-López, E., López Machado, A., Severino, P., Jose, S., et al. (2019). Sugar-lowering drugs for type 2 diabetes mellitus and metabolic syndrome—review of classical and new compounds: Part-I. *Pharmaceuticals, 12*(4), 152. doi:10.3390/ph12040152.

Wallace, S. J., Li, J., Nation, R. L., & Boyd, B. J. (2012). Drug release from nanomedicines: Selection of appropriate encapsulation and release methodology. *Drug Delivery and Translational Research, 2*(4), 284–292. doi:10.1007/s13346-012-0064-4.

Wang, Y., Li, P., Truong-Dinh Tran, T., Zhang, J., & Kong, L. (2016). Manufacturing techniques and surface engineering of polymer based nanoparticles for targeted drug delivery to cancer. *Nanomaterials, 6*(2), 26. doi:10.3390/nano6020026.

Wanning, S., Süverkrüp, R., & Lamprecht, A. (2015). Pharmaceutical spray freeze drying. *Int J Pharm, 488*(1–2), 136–153. doi:10.1016/j.ijpharm.2015.04.053.

Xia, Y., Rao, L., Yao, H., Wang, Z., Ning, P., & Chen, X. (2020). Engineering macrophages for cancer immunotherapy and drug delivery. *Advanced Materials, 32*, e2002054. doi:10.1002/adma.202002054.

Zhang, C., Fan, J., & Wu, L. (2025). Application of nanomaterials in precision treatment of lung cancer. *Iscience, 28*(1), 111704. doi:10.1016/j.isci.2024.111704.

Ziaee, A., Albadarin, A. B., Padrela, L., Femmer, T., O'Reilly, E., & Walker, G. (2019). Spray drying of pharmaceuticals and biopharmaceuticals: Critical parameters and experimental process optimization approaches. *European Journal of Pharmaceutical Sciences, 127*, 300–318. doi:10.1016/j.ejps.2018.10.026.

Zielińska, A., Ferreira, N. R., Durazzo, A., Lucarini, M., Cicero, N., Mamouni, S. E., et al. (2019). Development and optimization of alpha-pinene-loaded solid lipid nanoparticles (SLN) using experimental factorial design and dispersion analysis. *Molecules, 24*(15), 2683. doi:10.3390/molecules24152683.

Zielińska, A., Ferreira, N. R., Feliczak-Guzik, A., Nowak, I., & Souto, E. B. (2020). Loading, release profile and accelerated stability assessment of monoterpenes-loaded solid lipid nanoparticles (SLN). *Pharmaceutical Development and Technology, 25*(7), 832–844. doi:10.1080/10837450.2020.1744008.

CHAPTER 10

Solid lipid nanoparticles: Revolutionizing lung cancer therapy through targeted drug delivery

Shikha Baghel Chauhan[a], Indu Singh[b] and Chirag Jain[c]

[a]Centre of Industrial Pharmacy, Amity Institute of Pharmacy, Amity University, Noida, Uttar Pradesh, India [b]Centre of Pharmaceutics, Amity Institute of Pharmacy, Amity University, Noida, Uttar Pradesh, India [c]Amity Institute of Pharmacy, Amity University, Noida, Uttar Pradesh, India

10.1 Introduction to lung cancer

10.1.1 Global epidemiology and molecular classification of lung cancer

Lung cancer, often mentioned as bronchogenic carcinoma, which labels tumors that start in the bronchi or lung parenchyma, is one of the foremost causes of cancer-linked fatalities in the United States. Lung cancer has slayed more women than breast cancer since 1987. In the US, there are approximately 160,000 lung cancer deaths and 225,000 new occurrences of lung cancer acknowledged year. Lung cancer was a very rare disease before the start of the 20th century, and the core reason of its theatrical rise in succeeding decades was intensifying smoking rates among both men and women. Concluded the past 5 years, there have been yearly increases in 2-year comparative survival of 1.4%, with diminutions in lung cancer mortality actually much larger than falls in occurrence among women (4.3% vs. 1.1% yearly) and males (5.0% vs. 2.6% yearly). Increased admittance to care under the **Patient Protection and Affordable Care Act**, better-quality treatment, and prior stage identification are perhaps the causes of these gains; for example, the rate of localized-stage disease rose by 3.6% yearly (Kratzer et al., 2024).

Lung cancer, as it is commonly defined by physicians when they talk about it in a medical context, can be divided into two main categories: nonsmall cell lung cancer (NSCLC), which accounts for 85% of all cases, and small cell lung cancer (SCLC), which accounts for the remaining 15%. NSCLC, in turn, can be divided into three main subtypes: adenocarcinoma,

Nanoengineered Therapeutics for Lung Cancer: Advanced Drug Delivery Strategies.
DOI: https://doi.org/10.1016/B978-0-443-44585-9.00006-8

squamous cell carcinoma, and large cell carcinoma (Smolarz et al., 2025). Currently, adenocarcinoma is the most prevalent form of NSCLC, and it is predominantly found in people who are nonsmokers and women. The game changer here has been the use of molecular profiling. By analyzing the genetic fingerprint of the cancer, we have identified actionable mutations in several genes: epidermal growth factor receptor (EGFR), KRAS, ALK, BRAF, MET, and TP53. This has completely turned around the way we treat the disease. For example, EGFR mutations are particularly prevalent in Asian patients, and KRAS mutations are more common in smokers. But cancer finds a way to resist treatment. New mutations emerge, other pathways are activated, and the cancer's natural heterogeneity keeps it one step ahead (Caliman et al., 2023)

10.1.2 Limitation for conventional lung cancer therapies

The current scenario in lung cancer therapy is a combination of surgery, chemotherapy, targeted therapy, radiotherapy, and immunotherapy, which are administered in combination depending on the stage of advancement of the disease and the molecular characteristics of the tumor. In advanced NSCLC, platinum-based doublet chemotherapy, consisting of cisplatin or carboplatin in combination with paclitaxel or gemcitabine, remains a cornerstone of therapy (Zhang et al., 2024). Targeted therapies such as Erlotinib and Osimertinib, which selectively inhibit EGFR tyrosine kinase activity, have significantly improved progression-free survival in patients harboring the respective mutations. Similarly, tumors with ALK rearrangements are sensitive to crizotinib and alectinib. Immunotherapy with Pembrolizumab and checkpoint inhibitors can harness the power of the immune system to target cancer cells, thereby completely changing the management of advanced NSCLC. However, there are still challenges in these therapies (Barr et al., 2024). Systemic chemotherapy is associated with dose-limiting toxicities, including myelosuppression, renal and peripheral neurotoxicity, and gastrointestinal symptoms. Targeted therapies are prone to resistance due to the emergence of secondary mutations, such as EGFR T790M. Immunotherapy, although promising, is of limited benefit to only a subset of patients and is associated with immune-related adverse events. Moreover, poor penetration into the tumor, off-target effects, and rapid systemic clearance can result in low concentrations of the drug being available at the tumor site. Thus, the need for nanotechnology-based delivery systems, such as solid lipid nanoparticles (SLNs), is imperative to improve tumor targeting and minimize systemic toxicity (Lahiri et al., 2023).

Patients may not find therapy succeeding a diagnosis for a variety of reasons. Some of these factors might be unavoidable, but no one should be deprived of treatment due to unawareness on the part of the patient or breadwinner, the stigma devoted to lung cancer, postdiagnosis resignation, or the expenditure of therapy. A total of 26% of cases countrywide were left unprocessed. Rates were lowermost in New Mexico (31.5%) and highest in North Dakota (14.3%), with a 2% development over the preceding 5 years. In 2020, taxes on nontreatment rose by 5%, most probably as a consequence of the COVID-19 pandemic's belongings on admission to healthcare, as shown in Fig. 10.1.

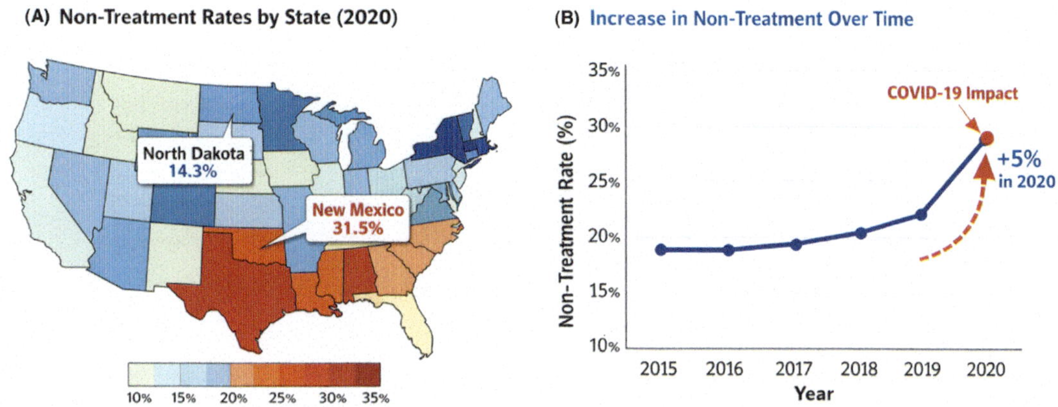

Figure 10.1

Impact of the COVID-19 pandemic on lung cancer nontreatment rates in the United States (A) State-wise distribution of lung cancer nontreatment rates in the United States for the year 2020, illustrating geographic variability, with selected examples highlighting lower rates in North Dakota (14.3%) and higher rates in New Mexico (31.5%). (B) Temporal trend of lung cancer nontreatment rates from 2015 to 2020, demonstrating a gradual increase over time and a marked rise in 2020, corresponding to the COVID-19 pandemic. The data indicate an approximate 5% increase in nontreatment rates during 2020 compared to preceding years, emphasizing the pandemic's impact on access to oncology care and treatment continuity.

10.1.3 Emergence of nanotechnology in cancer treatment

Usage of nanotechnology to recover therapeutics is no longer original; in fact, there has been a stable upsurge in nanotechnology research as the assistances become additional apparent. Currently accepted cancer nanomedicines are mainly liposomal preparations and drug conjugates (protein, polymer, and/or antibody) which focused on refining the pharmacokinetics and pharmacodynamics (PK/PD) of the free drug and using passive targeting. There are numerous clinical studies presently examining nanomaterials for therapeutic and diagnostic requests, including imaging modalities. Passive targeting for tumors is founded upon the improved enhanced permeability and retention (EPR) effect, where nanoparticles can specifically collect within tumor vasculature (Kemp & Kwon, 2021).

10.2 Solid lipid nanoparticles

10.2.1 Definition

SLNs represent a major advancement in lipid-based drug delivery systems and are widely regarded as the first-generation of solid lipid nanocarriers. They were developed to combine the advantages of traditional colloidal carriers, such as emulsions and liposomes, while minimizing their limitations, particularly issues related to stability and large-scale production.

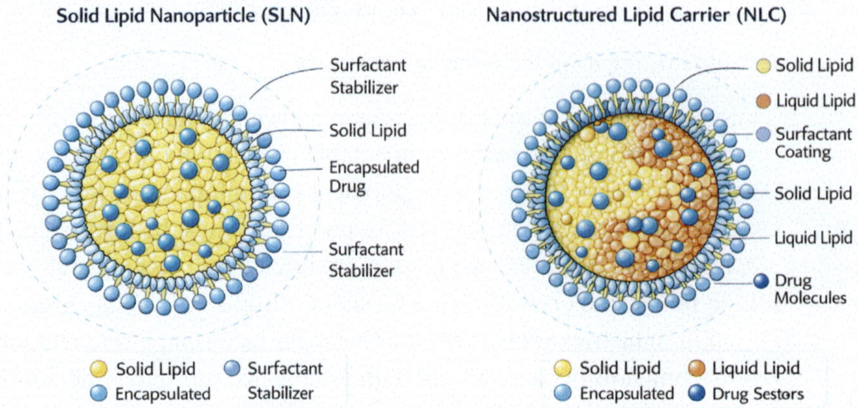

Figure 10.2

Schematic representation comparing the structural organization of solid lipid nanoparticles (SLNs) and nanostructured lipid carriers (NLCs). The SLN structure consists of a solid lipid core matrix uniformly encapsulating drug molecules and surrounded by a surfactant stabilizing layer. In contrast, NLCs contain a mixed lipid matrix composed of both solid and liquid lipids, resulting in a less ordered internal structure that enhances drug loading capacity and reduces drug expulsion during storage. Both systems are stabilized by a surfactant coating that improves colloidal stability and bioavailability. The diagram highlights differences in internal lipid arrangement, drug distribution, and structural flexibility between SLNs and NLCs.

SLNs are submicron colloidal carriers typically ranging in size from 50 to 1000 nm and are composed of physiologically compatible lipids that remain solid at both room and body temperature (Ghasemiyeh & Mohammadi-Samani, 2018; Satapathy et al., 2021). The solid lipid core is stabilized by surfactants in an aqueous dispersion medium, forming a thermodynamically stable and biocompatible nanosystem suitable for diverse therapeutic applications.

The defining structural characteristic of SLNs is their solid lipid matrix, which distinguishes them from liquid lipid-based systems such as nanoemulsions. The lipid core may consist of triglycerides, fatty acids, waxes, or partial glycerides that remain crystalline or semicrystalline under physiological conditions. This solid matrix enables the incorporation of both lipophilic and, to a certain extent, hydrophilic drugs through various entrapment models, including homogeneous matrix dispersion, drug-enriched core, and drug-enriched shell structures (Akanda et al., 2023). The rigid lipid framework not only encapsulates active pharmaceutical ingredients (APIs) but also provides physical protection against chemical and enzymatic degradation, photolysis, and hydrolysis, thereby enhancing drug stability during storage and after administration (Montoto et al., 2020). Fig. 10.2 describes a schematic representation of SLNs and nanostructured lipid carriers (NLCs), illustrating differences in internal lipid organization and drug incorporation patterns.

A significant advantage of SLNs lies in their ability to improve the bioavailability of poorly water-soluble drugs. Many new chemical entities exhibit low aqueous solubility, leading to limited dissolution and absorption. By incorporating such drugs into a nanosized lipid matrix, SLNs enhance surface area, promote intimate contact with biological membranes, and facilitate improved dissolution in physiological fluids. Furthermore, the lipidic nature of SLNs enhances interaction with cell membranes, potentially increasing cellular uptake and improving therapeutic efficacy. The nanoscale size also enables passive targeting through the EPR effect in tumor tissues, making SLNs particularly attractive for oncology applications (Duan et al., 2020). Another important aspect of SLNs is their controlled and sustained drug release behavior. The crystalline lipid matrix acts as a diffusion barrier, allowing gradual drug release over extended periods. This feature can reduce dosing frequency, minimize peak plasma fluctuations, and decrease systemic side effects. The release profile can be modulated by altering lipid composition, surfactant concentration, particle size, and preparation method. As a result, SLNs offer considerable formulation flexibility and can be tailored for oral, topical, pulmonary, and parenteral routes of administration. In addition to therapeutic applications, SLNs are valued for their relatively low toxicity and high biocompatibility. The lipids used in their formulation are often derived from physiological or food-grade materials, which are generally recognized as safe (GRAS). This enhances their acceptability in pharmaceutical development and facilitates regulatory approval compared to polymeric nanoparticles that may involve synthetic and potentially toxic materials. Consequently, SLNs have emerged as a promising nanocarrier system bridging the gap between conventional dosage forms and advanced nanomedicine platforms (Viegas et al., 2023).

10.2.2 Comparison with other nanocarriers

SLNs have been extensively investigated as versatile drug delivery systems across multiple administration routes, including topical, parenteral, oral, and pulmonary pathways. Their structural and compositional flexibility enables precise adjustment of physicochemical characteristics according to therapeutic requirements. Compared with other nanocarriers such as liposomes, polymeric nanoparticles, dendrimers, and nanoemulsions, SLNs offer a unique balance between stability, drug protection, scalability, and cost-effectiveness. However, like any delivery system, they present certain formulation challenges that must be carefully addressed.

One of the major advantages of SLNs over liposomes is improved physical stability. Liposomes, which are composed of phospholipid bilayers, often suffer from issues such as leakage of encapsulated drugs, fusion, and phospholipid oxidation during storage. In contrast, the solid lipid core of SLNs provides a more rigid and stable matrix that reduces drug leakage and enhances shelf-life. Moreover, the production of SLNs using high-pressure homogenization or microemulsion techniques is generally more amenable to industrial scale-up compared to the relatively delicate preparation processes of liposomes. When compared with polymeric nanoparticles, SLNs demonstrate superior biocompatibility due to the use of physiological lipids rather than synthetic polymers. Polymeric systems may raise concerns regarding polymer toxicity, residual monomers, and long-term biodegradation products. SLNs avoid many of these issues by employing biodegradable lipids that are metabolized through natural lipid pathways. Furthermore, lipid excipients often have regulatory approval and established safety profiles, facilitating smoother translation from laboratory research to clinical application (Ghasemiyeh & Mohammadi-Samani, 2018).

Despite these advantages, SLNs also present specific limitations related to their crystalline structure. The solid state of the lipid core plays a crucial role in determining drug loading capacity and release characteristics. Crystallization behavior and physicochemical transitions within the lipid matrix significantly influence drug incorporation and stability. During storage, lipids may undergo polymorphic transitions from less ordered α-forms to more stable β-forms. These transitions can lead to the rearrangement of lipid molecules, resulting in the expulsion of the incorporated drug and reduction of encapsulation efficiency. Such phenomena have been reported as delayed or incomplete crystallization, ultimately causing suboptimal pharmacological payload retention (Jaiswal et al., 2016; Sgorla et al., 2016).

Physicochemical transformations such as matrix molecule relocation are common in lipid-based systems. As the lipid matrix reorganizes into a more thermodynamically stable form, it may become more densely packed and highly ordered. This increased crystallinity reduces the available space within the matrix for drug molecules, potentially forcing them toward the particle surface. Consequently, some drugs may exhibit undesirable surface localization, which can result in burst release upon administration. In extreme cases, poor compatibility between the drug and lipid may lead to phase separation or drug crystallization outside the matrix, compromising formulation stability and therapeutic performance (Viegas et al., 2022). Another critical factor influencing SLN performance is the physicochemical compatibility between the drug molecule and the lipid matrix. The solubility of the drug in the melted lipid, its partition coefficient, and its molecular structure collectively determine loading efficiency. Drugs with limited solubility in the selected lipid may not be effectively incorporated and instead may adsorb onto the nanoparticle surface. Surface-associated drug molecules are more susceptible to degradation and rapid release, potentially diminishing sustained delivery advantages. Therefore, rational lipid selection and thorough preformulation studies are essential to optimize drug-lipid compatibility and maximize therapeutic payload.

In comparison to second-generation NLCs, SLNs may exhibit relatively lower drug loading capacity due to their highly ordered crystalline matrix. NLCs incorporate a mixture of solid and liquid lipids, creating structural imperfections that accommodate higher drug quantities and reduce the risk of drug expulsion. Nevertheless, SLNs maintain advantages in terms of structural simplicity, ease of characterization, and established formulation strategies, making them a foundational platform in lipid nanotechnology. Overall, SLNs occupy a distinct position among nanocarrier systems. They combine the safety and biocompatibility of lipid-based formulations with the advantages of nanoscale delivery, including enhanced bioavailability, controlled release, and potential targeting capabilities. Although challenges related to crystallization, drug expulsion, and polymorphic transitions persist, ongoing advancements in lipid engineering, surfactant optimization, and hybrid nanostructures continue to improve their performance. With careful formulation design and comprehensive characterization, SLNs remain a robust and promising nanocarrier system for diverse pharmaceutical applications (Ghasemiyeh & Mohammadi-Samani, 2018; Jaiswal et al., 2016; Sgorla et al., 2016; Viegas et al., 2022).

10.2.3 Tumor microenvironment and solid lipid nanoparticles interaction

The tumor microenvironment (TME) is known to influence the efficacy of treatments and the failure of drug delivery. In lung cancers, there is low oxygen, an acidic extracellular pH of 6.5–6.8, irregular blood vessels, high interstitial fluid pressure (IFP), and a high matrix content that is rich in collagen and fibronectin. The hypoxic regions promote angiogenesis and make drugs less effective, while the acidic environment affects the ionization state and diffusion of drugs. To add to that, tumor-associated macrophages and cancer-associated fibroblasts form an immunosuppressive microenvironment that helps the tumor grow. SLNs provide strategies to overcome these challenges. For example, pH-sensitive SLNs, which contain linkers that degrade in an acidic environment, can target chemotherapy to the tumor site. Sensitivity to reactive oxygen species (ROS) can be utilized to target SLNs to degrade mainly in regions of high oxidative stress, which is a characteristic of tumors. PEGylation of SLNs can help them evade opsonization and remain in the bloodstream longer, enhancing their accumulation through the EPR effect. With these modifications, SLNs can transform from being drug carriers to being smart nanoplatforms that respond to tumor-specific stimuli (Nalawade et al., 2025).

10.2.4 Comparison of solid lipid nanoparticles with nanostructured lipid carriers in lung cancer therapy

NLCs were developed as a second-generation lipid nanocarrier system to overcome certain limitations associated with SLNs, particularly low drug loading capacity and drug expulsion during storage due to lipid polymorphic transitions. While SLNs consist entirely of solid lipids forming a highly ordered crystalline matrix, NLCs incorporate a mixture of solid and liquid lipids, creating structural imperfections within the matrix. These imperfections provide additional space for drug accommodation, thereby increasing drug loading efficiency and reducing the likelihood of drug expulsion. In lung cancer therapy, where chemotherapeutic agents such as paclitaxel, erlotinib, and gemcitabine require stable encapsulation and sustained release, the structural differences between SLNs and NLCs directly influence therapeutic performance. Despite the enhanced loading capacity of NLCs, SLNs continue to hold significant relevance in lung cancer applications due to their structural simplicity, predictable release kinetics, and well-established formulation methodologies. The highly crystalline matrix of SLNs offers controlled and sustained drug release, which can be advantageous for maintaining therapeutic concentrations within tumor tissues over prolonged periods. In contrast, the less ordered structure of NLCs may lead to comparatively faster release profiles depending on lipid composition. For inhalable formulations targeting primary lung tumors, the physical stability and reproducibility of SLNs remain particularly advantageous, especially when aerosolization and spray-drying processes are involved.

From a translational perspective, SLNs benefit from a longer history of investigation and relatively standardized production methods such as high-pressure homogenization and microemulsion techniques. Their composition often includes lipids that are GRAS, facilitating regulatory evaluation. Although NLCs demonstrate improved drug loading in some cases, their more complex lipid composition may introduce additional variability in crystallization behavior and large-scale production. In lung cancer therapy, where precise dosing and reproducibility are critical to minimize systemic toxicity, the robustness of SLNs offers a practical advantage. Preclinical studies comparing paclitaxel-loaded SLNs and NLCs in lung tumor models have demonstrated comparable tumor accumulation via the EPR effect, with slight variations in release kinetics and stability profiles. Therefore, while NLCs represent an evolution in lipid nanocarrier design, SLNs remain a foundational and clinically promising platform for lung cancer drug delivery, particularly when formulation simplicity, scalability, and controlled release are prioritized.

10.3 Formulation and characterization of solid lipid nanoparticles

10.3.1 Composition of solid lipid nanoparticles: Lipid, surfactants, and active ingredients composition

Solid lipids, surfactants or cosurfactants, and active medication molecules form SLNs (Jamous et al., 2023). Since they protect medications from hostile conditions, are biocompatible and decomposable, and are modest to create on a large scale, they provide a potential drug delivery mechanism (Ghasemiyeh & Mohammadi-Samani, 2018). The therapeutic performance of SLNs depends on their composition. Traditional solid lipids such as glyceryl monostearate, tripalmitin, stearic acid, and Compritol 888 ATO influence the amount of drug that can be incorporated and the rate of release. The packing of these lipids into various polymorphic forms, such as α, β', and β, has a direct effect on the crystallinity and the amount of drug that is pushed out during storage. Specifically, the β-forms, which have a high degree of order, may leave less space for the drug, leading to leakage. To ensure that SLNs remain stable and that particles do not agglomerate, surfactants like Tween 80, Poloxamer 188, lecithin, and PEGylated emulsifiers are used to coat the surface. The surface charge or zeta potential should remain outside ±30 mV to ensure colloidal stability. Moreover, PEGylation assists the particles in avoiding the reticuloendothelial system, increasing their residence time in systemic circulation (Duong et al., 2020).

Incorporation of the drug can take three different forms: the homogeneous matrix formulation, the drug-loaded shell formulation, and the drug-loaded core formulation. In the homogeneous formulation, the drug is evenly distributed throughout. In the shell formulation, there is a possibility of a burst release if the drug is concentrated near the surface. This depends on the lipophilicity of the drug and whether its melting point is compatible with the carrier. Analysis would involve dynamic light scattering to determine the size of the particles (which should target less than 200 nm for tumor targeting), transmission electron microscopy to determine shape and morphology, and differential scanning calorimetry to determine crystallinity. Release kinetics can be modeled in vitro using the Higuchi model or the Korsmeyer-Peppas model. In the case of anticancer applications, it is generally preferred that the entrapment efficiency be greater than 70% (Khezri et al., 2020). The method of preparation, including hot homogenization, cold homogenization, and solvent evaporation are explained thoroughly in Table 10.1 .

10.4 Mechanisms of targeted drug delivery using solid lipid nanoparticles

Targeted drug delivery aims to enhance therapeutic efficacy while minimizing systemic toxicity by selectively directing anticancer agents to tumor tissues. In lung cancer therapy, this approach is particularly critical because conventional chemotherapy distributes nonselectively throughout the body, affecting rapidly dividing normal cells and leading to dose-limiting toxicities. SLNs, owing to their nanoscale size, biocompatible lipid matrix, modifiable surface chemistry, and controlled drug release properties, serve as an advanced platform capable of achieving both passive and active targeting. These mechanisms function either independently or synergistically to maximize tumor accumulation and intracellular drug delivery (Mohammed et al., 2023).

10.4.1 Active vs. passive targeting in lung cancer therapy

10.4.1.1 Passive targeting via the enhanced permeability and retention effect

Passive targeting is predominantly governed by the EPR effect, a hallmark feature of solid tumors. Rapid tumor growth necessitates aggressive angiogenesis; however, tumor neovasculature is structurally abnormal, characterized by irregular endothelial alignment, widened inter-endothelial junctions (100–800 nm), defective basement membrane architecture, and

Table 10.1: Method of preparation for hot homogenization, cold homogenization, solvent evaporation along with their advantages and disadvantages.

Method	Process description	Advantages	Disadvantages	References
Hot homogenization	The process operates at high temperature, which is above the lipids' melting point. Lipid and drug are combined together with an aqueous surfaced at the same temperature. A high sheer mixing device creates a hot preemulsion, which is oil in water type. The mixture is cold and leading to lipid crystallization and SLN formation. 3–5 cycles of homogenization, 500–1500 bar ensures a proper SLN production. Increased cycle of pressure may increase the particle size due to the attractive force.	It is suitable for a lipophilic drug The duration of production time is shorter It is a simple and widely used process.	It has a high risk of drug degradation at higher temperatures It shows a polymorphic changes in lipid In aqueous phase, there is a loss of drug	Pathak and Nagarsenker (2009), Sastri et al. (2020), Waters et al. (2011)

(continued on next page)

Cold homogenization	Developed to overcome issues in hot homogenization, such as drug degradation and lipid polymorphism. The drug is soluble in the lipid (melted). Rapid cooling with solid carbon dioxide or liquid nitrogen ensures the drug is homogenized for the distribution in the lipid matrix. The solidified lipid is ground into fine dust (50–100 μm) using ball mill. The fine lipid dust is dispersed in the aqueous surface, which is chilled. High-pressure homogenization is then applied to form SLNs.	It prevents thermal degradation of thermo-sensitive drugs. Reduce drug loss in the aqueous phase	It produces larger particles comparing with hot homogenization process. Results in broader distribution size.	Mehnert and Mäder (2012)

(*continued on next page*)

Table 10.1: Method of preparation for hot homogenization, cold homogenization, solvent evaporation along with their advantages and disadvantages—cont'd

Method	Process description	Advantages	Disadvantages	References
Solvent emulsification	Lipophilic material, hydrophobic drugs are dissolved in water, immiscible organic solvent, like cyclohexane, or chloroform. High speed causes a proper homogenization of a mixture into aqueous phase. The organic solvent is evaporated by using the rotary evaporated under a mechanical education at the room temperature and the pressure is reduced.	Avoids thermal stress, making it suitable for thermostable drugs.	Usage of organic solvents may cause drug instability or toxicity concerns	Ramteke and Joshi (2012), Sjöström and Bergenståhl (1992)

From[ELS-LE06]:AU: Per style guide (edit credit lines for stylistic consistency), we have reworded the source lines as 'From' in this chapter. Please confirm whether this change in word for consistency is correct or we should follow different text as supplied originally in this chapter. (Reprinted, reused, or etc).
Sjöström, B., & Bergenståhl, B. (1992). Preparation of submicron drug particles in lecithin-stabilized o/w emulsions I. Model studies of the precipitation of cholesteryl acetate. International Journal of Pharmaceutics, 88 (1–3), 53–62. https://doi.org/10.1016/0378-5173(92)90303-J.
SLN, solid lipid nanoparticle.

poor pericyte coverage. These abnormalities result in significantly enhanced vascular permeability compared to normal tissues. Furthermore, tumors exhibit impaired lymphatic drainage, which restricts nanoparticle clearance from the tumor interstitium. SLNs with particle sizes typically below 150–200 nm can exploit these leaky vasculature structures and preferentially extravasate into tumor tissue through diffusion and convection mechanisms (Li et al., 2023). Once within the TME, the deficient lymphatic system promotes prolonged retention, allowing sustained drug release directly at the tumor site. This passive accumulation increases local drug concentration while reducing systemic exposure.

In lung cancer specifically, highly vascularized non-small cell lung cancer (NSCLC) lesions demonstrate significant EPR-mediated nanoparticle uptake. For example, paclitaxel-loaded SLNs have shown enhanced tumor deposition compared to free paclitaxel due to prolonged systemic circulation and preferential tumor retention. Moreover, surface PEGylation of SLNs reduces opsonization by plasma proteins and minimizes uptake by the mononuclear phagocyte system (MPS), thereby increasing blood half-life and improving EPR-driven tumor accumulation. However, the EPR effect exhibits heterogeneity across patients and tumor types. Hypoxic tumor regions with elevated IFP may limit deep nanoparticle penetration. Therefore, while passive targeting enhances tumor localization, it often requires complementary active targeting strategies to optimize intracellular drug delivery (Li et al., 2023).

10.4.1.2 Active targeting via ligand-receptor interactions

Active targeting involves surface functionalization of SLNs with specific ligands that recognize and bind to overexpressed receptors on lung cancer cells. This mechanism enhances selective cellular uptake through receptor-mediated endocytosis. One of the most extensively studied pathways is transferrin receptor-mediated targeting. Transferrin receptors are frequently overexpressed in rapidly proliferating tumor cells due to increased iron demand. SLNs conjugated with transferrin ligands bind specifically to these receptors, triggering clathrin-mediated endocytosis and facilitating intracellular drug delivery (Shojaei et al., 2024). This approach not only increases tumor selectivity but also improves cytoplasmic drug concentration, which is crucial for chemotherapeutics that act on intracellular targets such as microtubules or DNA. Similarly, mannose receptor targeting has been employed in lung cancer therapy. Mannosylated SLNs loaded with gemcitabine have demonstrated enhanced cellular internalization in lung cancer cells expressing mannose-binding receptors. The conjugation promotes selective uptake and increases cytotoxic efficacy compared to nonfunctionalized SLNs. This strategy significantly enhances the therapeutic index while reducing systemic toxicity.

Another clinically relevant example includes targeting the EGFR, which is frequently overexpressed or mutated in NSCLC. Although core-shell lipid-polymer hybrid nanoparticles loaded with erlotinib have shown improved cellular uptake and bioavailability compared to conventional formulations (Colaco et al., 2024), SLNs can similarly be engineered to incorporate anti-EGFR antibodies or peptides, enabling dual targeting—both molecular and nanocarrier-mediated. Additionally, luteinizing hormone-releasing hormone (LHRH) receptor-targeted NLCs have demonstrated effective pulmonary targeting of paclitaxel via inhalation delivery (Sharma et al., 2023). LHRH receptors are overexpressed in certain lung cancer subtypes, allowing ligand-modified nanoparticles to selectively bind tumor cells following pulmonary deposition. Thus, active targeting enhances tumor cell specificity beyond the vascular-level targeting achieved through the EPR effect. While passive targeting improves tumor localization, active targeting ensures receptor-mediated internalization and intracellular drug release.

10.4.2 Enhanced permeability and retention effect in tumors

10.4.2.1 Conceptual foundation of the enhanced permeability and retention effect in nanomedicine

The EPR effect remains one of the most fundamental principles guiding the development of nanocarrier-based drug delivery systems in oncology. First conceptualized as a passive targeting mechanism, the EPR effect describes the preferential accumulation of macromolecules and nanoparticles within tumor tissues due to abnormal tumor vasculature and impaired lymphatic drainage. In contemporary nanomedicine design, the EPR effect is considered a cornerstone concept, particularly in the engineering of lipid-based nanosystems such as SLNs (Wu, 2021).

Tumor growth beyond a few millimeters in diameter necessitates the formation of new blood vessels through angiogenesis. However, tumor-induced angiogenesis produces structurally abnormal and highly disorganized vasculature. These vessels are characterized by wide endothelial gaps, defective basement membranes, irregular pericyte coverage, and chaotic branching architecture. As a result, vascular permeability in tumors is significantly higher than in normal tissues. Nanoparticles within an optimal size range can extravasate through these leaky vessels and accumulate in the tumor interstitium. Simultaneously, tumors typically lack efficient lymphatic drainage, preventing the rapid clearance of accumulated nanoparticles. The combined effect of enhanced permeability and impaired retention mechanisms gives rise to the EPR phenomenon.

10.4.2.2 Physiological determinants of enhanced permeability and retention in lung tumors

Several physiological and molecular factors contribute to the manifestation of the EPR effect in lung tumors. One of the primary drivers is increased vascular permeability due to abnormal angiogenesis. Tumor-associated endothelial cells form fenestrations that may range from 100 to 800 nm, depending on tumor type and progression stage. This fenestrated vasculature allows nanoparticles within the nanometer scale to escape systemic circulation and localize within tumor tissue. Overexpression of vascular endothelial growth factor (VEGF) further enhances vascular leakiness. VEGF disrupts endothelial tight junctions and increases transendothelial transport, amplifying nanoparticle extravasation. In lung adenocarcinomas, elevated VEGF expression correlates with increased microvascular density and permeability, favoring nanoparticle deposition (Islam et al., 2022).

Reduced lymphatic drainage represents another defining feature. In healthy tissues, interstitial fluid and macromolecules are efficiently cleared via lymphatic vessels. In contrast, tumors often exhibit dysfunctional or absent lymphatic networks within the tumor core. Consequently, once nanoparticles accumulate in the tumor interstitium, they are retained for prolonged durations. This retention enhances local drug concentration and sustained release. Elevated tumor IFP also influences nanoparticle transport. Tumor IFP arises from leaky vasculature combined with poor lymphatic clearance, generating a pressure gradient that may limit deep penetration of nanoparticles into tumor cores. While EPR promotes accumulation near vascular regions, high IFP may hinder uniform distribution throughout the tumor mass. Altered extracellular matrix (ECM) architecture further modulates nanoparticle diffusion. Dense stromal components, such as collagen and hyaluronic acid, can create physical barriers restricting nanoparticle movement. In lung tumors, especially desmoplastic adenocarcinomas, stromal density may limit intratumoral diffusion despite efficient vascular extravasation (Sharifi et al., 2022).

10.4.2.3 Enhanced permeability and retention in primary and metastatic lung cancer

The EPR effect is observed not only in primary lung tumors but also in metastatic lesions and inflammatory tissues. Metastatic nodules in the lung, derived from breast or colorectal cancer, similarly exhibit abnormal vasculature and VEGF-driven permeability. Inflammatory microenvironments associated with tumor progression can further enhance vascular leakiness, facilitating nanoparticle deposition. Preclinical murine xenograft models often demonstrate pronounced EPR effects. Nanoparticles sized between 100 and 150 nm frequently show substantial tumor accumulation in mice due to their rapid tumor growth and highly permeable vasculature. However, clinical translation remains inconsistent. Human tumors exhibit greater heterogeneity in vascular density, stromal composition, and perfusion patterns. Inter-patient variability, tumor subtype differences, and prior treatments such as chemotherapy or radiation may alter vascular integrity, affecting EPR efficiency (Wu, 2021). This discrepancy between animal models and human tumors has prompted researchers to reconsider reliance solely on passive targeting. While EPR remains a valuable mechanism, combining it with active targeting strategies enhances reproducibility and therapeutic efficacy.

10.4.2.4 Optimization of solid lipid nanoparticle design for maximizing enhanced permeability and retention

To maximize EPR-mediated accumulation, careful optimization of SLN physicochemical properties is essential. Particle size plays a central role; nanoparticles smaller than 50 nm may undergo rapid renal clearance, whereas particles larger than 200 nm may be sequestered by the reticuloendothelial system. A size range of 100–150 nm is often considered optimal for balancing circulation time and tumor extravasation. Surface charge neutrality or a slight negative charge improves systemic stability and reduces nonspecific protein adsorption. Highly cationic nanoparticles may interact with plasma proteins and be rapidly cleared. Hydrophilic surface modification, particularly PEGylation, enhances circulation half-life by reducing opsonization and macrophage uptake. By fine-tuning these parameters, SLNs can exploit the EPR effect more effectively in lung cancer therapy. Nonetheless, given the variability in EPR responsiveness, integration with receptor-mediated targeting remains critical (Musielak et al., 2022).

10.4.3 Functionalization of solid lipid nanoparticles for lung-specific delivery

10.4.3.1 Rationale for surface engineering

While passive targeting via the EPR effect enhances tumor accumulation, it does not guarantee cellular internalization or specificity. Surface functionalization of SLNs provides an additional layer of targeting precision by enabling receptor-mediated interactions. Surface engineering modifies nanoparticle behavior in systemic circulation, tissue distribution, and cellular uptake. Functionalization strategies include PEGylation for stealth properties, ligand conjugation for receptor targeting, mucoadhesive coatings for pulmonary retention, and stimuli-responsive modifications for controlled release (Seidu et al., 2022). These approaches are particularly relevant for lung cancer therapy, where local delivery and molecular specificity significantly influence therapeutic outcomes.

10.4.3.2 PEGylation and stealth properties

PEGylation involves the attachment of polyethylene glycol chains to the nanoparticle surface. This hydrophilic polymer creates a steric barrier that reduces protein adsorption and prevents recognition by macrophages. As a result, PEGylated SLNs exhibit prolonged systemic circulation and improved tumor accumulation. In lung cancer chemotherapy, PEGylated SLNs loaded with paclitaxel or doxorubicin have demonstrated increased plasma half-life and enhanced tumor deposition compared to non-PEGylated formulations. By evading rapid clearance, these nanoparticles maintain sufficient systemic exposure to exploit EPR-mediated targeting.

10.4.3.3 Ligand-conjugated solid lipid nanoparticles for receptor-mediated targeting

Receptor overexpression in lung cancer cells provides molecular docking sites for ligand-functionalized SLNs. Transferrin receptors are frequently upregulated in rapidly proliferating cancer cells due to increased iron demand. Transferrin-conjugated SLNs can selectively bind to these receptors, triggering receptor-mediated endocytosis and enhanced intracellular drug delivery. EGFR is another prominent target in NSCLC. Antibody-conjugated SLNs targeting EGFR have shown improved cellular uptake and cytotoxic efficacy in EGFR-overexpressing tumor cells. Similarly, folate receptors and integrins are commonly overexpressed in lung malignancies, allowing folate- or peptide-modified SLNs to achieve selective tumor targeting (Seidu et al., 2022). These ligand-receptor interactions facilitate active targeting beyond passive accumulation, improving therapeutic index and reducing off-target toxicity.

10.4.3.4 Chitosan coating and pulmonary mucoadhesion

For inhalable SLN formulations, mucoadhesion enhances residence time in the pulmonary epithelium. Chitosan, a cationic biopolymer, is widely used as a coating material due to its biocompatibility and mucoadhesive properties. Chitosan-coated SLNs interact electrostatically with negatively charged mucosal surfaces, prolonging retention and improving drug absorption. In pulmonary lung cancer therapy, inhalable SLNs with aerodynamic diameters between 1 and 5 μm ensure deep alveolar deposition. Once deposited, the nanoparticles may disintegrate into smaller units capable of penetrating tumor tissue. Chitosan coatings also transiently open tight junctions, enhancing paracellular transport (Liu et al., 2022).

10.4.3.5 Stimuli-responsive functionalization

TMEs exhibit distinct characteristics, including acidic pH, elevated glutathione levels, and hypoxia. Stimuli-responsive SLNs are engineered to release drugs selectively under such conditions. pH-sensitive linkers degrade in acidic tumor environments, triggering drug release. Redox-sensitive modifications respond to intracellular glutathione concentrations, enabling cytosolic drug delivery. For example, redox-responsive SLNs coloaded with chemotherapeutic agents and small interfering RNA (siRNA) targeting multidrug resistance (MDR) genes have demonstrated enhanced intracellular release and gene silencing efficiency. Such multifunctional systems simultaneously deliver cytotoxic drugs and genetic modulators (Seidu et al., 2022).

10.4.3.6 Overcoming multidrug resistance through functionalized solid lipid nanoparticles

MDR in lung cancer is often mediated by P-glycoprotein (P-gp) efflux pumps that expel chemotherapeutic agents from cancer cells. Functionalized SLNs can bypass these efflux mechanisms by promoting endocytosis-mediated uptake rather than passive diffusion. Once internalized, nanoparticles release drugs intracellularly, reducing the likelihood of efflux. Codelivery strategies further enhance efficacy. SLNs encapsulating paclitaxel alongside siRNA targeting P-gp expression have shown synergistic effects in resistant lung cancer cell lines. By suppressing resistance gene expression while delivering cytotoxic agents, these systems restore drug sensitivity (Seidu et al., 2022).

10.4.3.7 Toward multifunctional nanotherapeutics

Modern SLNs are increasingly designed as multifunctional platforms integrating passive targeting, active receptor-mediated uptake, controlled release, and resistance modulation.

These next-generation nanotherapeutics can be engineered to carry imaging agents for theranostic applications, enabling simultaneous diagnosis and therapy. By combining EPR-based accumulation with ligand-mediated targeting and stimuli-responsive release, SLNs achieve enhanced selectivity and efficacy in lung cancer therapy. Although challenges such as tumor heterogeneity and translational variability persist, continued refinement of functionalization strategies promises to improve clinical outcomes (Liu et al., 2022).

10.4.4 Pulmonary route optimization: Inhalable solid lipid nanoparticle formulations

The pulmonary route offers a highly attractive strategy for lung cancer therapy, as it enables direct drug deposition at the tumor site while minimizing systemic exposure and associated toxicities. For inhalable SLN formulations, optimization of aerodynamic properties is critical. Nanoparticles themselves are typically below 200 nm in size; however, for effective deep lung deposition, the mass median aerodynamic diameter (MMAD) of aerosolized particles should range between 1 and 5 μm. This is often achieved by incorporating SLNs into microparticulate carriers through spray-drying or freeze-drying techniques, forming inhalable dry powder systems suitable for delivery via dry powder inhalers (DPIs) or nebulizers.

A major consideration in pulmonary SLN formulation is maintaining nanoparticle stability during aerosolization. Shear stress generated during nebulization or inhaler actuation may induce aggregation or alter particle size distribution. Therefore, stabilizers such as surfactants and cryoprotectants are incorporated to preserve colloidal integrity. Additionally, pulmonary clearance mechanisms must be carefully considered. Particles deposited in the upper respiratory tract are removed via mucociliary clearance, whereas particles reaching the alveolar region may be internalized by alveolar macrophages. Surface modification strategies, including PEGylation or chitosan coating, can modulate interactions with mucus and immune cells, thereby enhancing pulmonary retention time and improving therapeutic outcomes.

Another important factor is the balance between lung retention and systemic absorption. While localized therapy is desirable for primary lung tumors, excessive systemic absorption may increase off-target toxicity. Controlled release from the solid lipid matrix of SLNs helps maintain sustained local drug concentrations within tumor tissue. Inhalable SLN systems have demonstrated improved lung tissue drug levels compared to intravenous administration in preclinical models, highlighting their potential as a lung-specific therapeutic platform. Nevertheless, challenges such as large-scale production, device compatibility, and long-term pulmonary safety evaluation remain areas requiring further investigation.

10.5 Therapeutic applications in lung cancer

Lung cancer remains one of the most therapeutically challenging malignancies due to late-stage diagnosis, high metastatic potential, tumor heterogeneity, and rapid development of resistance to systemic chemotherapy. SLNs have emerged as a promising nanotechnological intervention for improving the delivery and therapeutic performance of anticancer agents in lung cancer. Owing to their biocompatible lipid matrix, controlled drug release properties, scalability, and surface functionalization capability, SLNs are increasingly being investigated as carriers for chemotherapeutics, targeted agents, gene therapeutics, and combination regimens (Girigoswami and Girigoswami, 2023).

Unlike conventional drug formulations that exhibit nonspecific biodistribution and systemic toxicity, SLNs improve PK profiles, enhance tumor accumulation via passive and active targeting, protect labile drugs from degradation, and facilitate intracellular drug delivery. Lipid-based nanocarriers are not only being investigated for lung cancer chemotherapy but also for vaccine development and immunomodulatory strategies (Kim et al., 2023). Their versatility enables administration through multiple routes, including intravenous, oral, pulmonary (inhalation), intranasal, dermal, and transdermal pathways. Among these, pulmonary delivery is particularly advantageous for primary lung malignancies, allowing direct tumor exposure while minimizing systemic adverse effects.

10.5.1 Solid lipid nanoparticles for chemotherapy delivery: Case studies

Chemotherapy remains the backbone of treatment for advanced NSCLC and SCLC. However, the clinical efficacy of many chemotherapeutic agents is limited by poor solubility, rapid systemic clearance, dose-limiting toxicity, and MDR. SLNs address these limitations through enhanced drug loading, sustained release, tumor-targeted delivery, and improved cellular uptake.

10.5.1.1 Paclitaxel-loaded solid lipid nanoparticles

Paclitaxel, a microtubule-stabilizing agent, is widely used in lung cancer but is poorly water-soluble and requires Cremophor EL for solubilization, which contributes to hypersensitivity reactions. Encapsulation into SLNs enhances its aqueous dispersibility, improves PK stability, and reduces systemic toxicity. Preclinical studies have demonstrated that paclitaxel-loaded SLNs exhibit prolonged circulation time, increased tumor accumulation via the EPR effect, and reduced IC50 values in lung cancer cell lines compared to free paclitaxel. Sustained release from the solid lipid matrix ensures continuous cytotoxic exposure to tumor cells. When administered via inhalation, paclitaxel SLNs have shown significantly higher lung tissue concentrations with lower plasma exposure, suggesting improved therapeutic index and reduced off-target toxicity.

10.5.1.2 Gemcitabine-loaded solid lipid nanoparticles

Gemcitabine, a nucleoside analog, is frequently used in NSCLC but suffers from rapid plasma degradation and a short half-life. SLN encapsulation protects gemcitabine from enzymatic breakdown and enhances tumor-specific delivery. Mannosylated gemcitabine-loaded SLNs exploit mannose receptor overexpression in lung cancer cells, increasing receptor-mediated endocytosis and intracellular drug accumulation. Studies demonstrate enhanced tumor growth inhibition and reduced systemic toxicity compared to free drug formulations (Apostolou et al., 2024).

10.5.1.3 Erlotinib-loaded nanoparticles

Erlotinib, an EGFR tyrosine kinase inhibitor (TKI), is particularly effective in EGFR-mutant NSCLC. However, oral administration results in variable bioavailability and gastrointestinal toxicity. Nanoparticle-based systems, including lipid-polymer hybrids, have demonstrated improved cellular uptake and enhanced antitumor efficacy (Wang et al., 2022). Similar strategies using SLNs can improve solubility, control release kinetics, and facilitate tumor-specific targeting through ligand conjugation.

10.5.1.4 Vascular endothelial growth factor receptor-targeted nanoparticles

Angiogenesis plays a central role in lung tumor progression. Vascular endothelial growth factor receptor (VEGFR) targeting has been explored as a strategy to disrupt tumor vascularization. Nanoparticles functionalized with VEGFR ligands demonstrate enhanced binding to tumor endothelium and improved internalization into tumor microvasculature. This targeted binding increases tumor inhibition while minimizing systemic exposure (Wang et al., 2022). SLNs engineered with VEGFR-targeting peptides or antibodies can therefore function as dual-action systems—delivering cytotoxic drugs while simultaneously interfering with angiogenic signaling.

10.5.1.5 Combination therapy using solid lipid nanoparticles

One of the most promising applications of SLNs is the codelivery of multiple therapeutic agents. For instance, coencapsulation of paclitaxel with siRNA targeting resistance genes enhances apoptosis induction and suppresses tumor growth more effectively than monotherapy. Such combinational nanoplatforms address tumor heterogeneity and reduce the likelihood of resistance development.

10.5.2 Overcoming multidrug resistance in lung cancer

10.5.2.1 Introduction: The clinical burden of multidrug resistance

MDR represents one of the most formidable obstacles in the successful treatment of lung cancer, particularly NSCLC. Despite initial responsiveness to platinum-based chemotherapy, taxanes, or targeted therapies, many patients eventually develop resistance, resulting in disease progression and reduced survival. MDR is not a single-pathway phenomenon but rather a complex, multifactorial process involving cellular, genetic, epigenetic, and microenvironmental alterations. The emergence of resistance severely compromises intracellular drug accumulation and diminishes cytotoxic efficacy, ultimately leading to therapeutic failure (Wang et al., 2022).

One of the most well-characterized mechanisms of MDR involves the overexpression of ATP-binding cassette (ABC) transporters, particularly P-gp, which actively pump chemotherapeutic agents out of cancer cells. However, additional mechanisms such as oncogenic mutations, enhanced DNA repair capacity, epithelial–mesenchymal transition (EMT), tumor hypoxia, altered apoptosis signaling, and tumor heterogeneity also contribute to resistance development (Emran et al., 2022). Given this complexity, therapeutic strategies must address multiple resistance pathways simultaneously rather than targeting a single molecular mechanism. SLNs have emerged as promising multifunctional nanocarriers capable of overcoming MDR through diverse and synergistic mechanisms. By modifying cellular uptake pathways, codelivering gene modulators, and enhancing tumor-specific drug accumulation, SLNs provide a comprehensive platform for restoring chemosensitivity in resistant lung cancer cells (Wang et al., 2022).

10.5.2.2 Molecular basis of multidrug resistance in lung cancer

ABC transporter overexpression is among the earliest and most studied contributors to MDR. P-gp, encoded by the MDR1 gene, is an ATP-dependent efflux pump located on the plasma membrane. It recognizes a wide range of hydrophobic chemotherapeutic agents, including paclitaxel, doxorubicin, vincristine, and etoposide, and actively expels them from cells. This reduces intracellular drug concentration below cytotoxic thresholds, enabling tumor cell survival despite drug exposure. Beyond efflux-mediated resistance, oncogenic mutations in pathways such as EGFR, KRAS, and ALK may alter therapeutic responsiveness. Mutations can modify drug-binding sites, activate bypass signaling pathways, or enhance survival signaling cascades. Additionally, enhanced DNA repair mechanisms enable cancer cells to repair chemotherapy-induced damage more efficiently. For example, increased expression of excision repair cross-complementation group 1 (ERCC1) is associated with resistance to platinum-based drugs (Wang et al., 2022).

The TME further complicates resistance. Hypoxia induces the stabilization of hypoxia-inducible factor-1α (HIF-1α), which upregulates genes associated with angiogenesis, glycolysis, and survival. Acidic extracellular pH and high IFP can limit drug penetration. Tumor heterogeneity ensures that subpopulations of resistant clones survive initial treatment and repopulate the tumor mass (Emran et al., 2022). Given these interlinked mechanisms, overcoming MDR requires innovative delivery systems capable of bypassing efflux transporters, modulating gene expression, and sustaining cytotoxic pressure within tumor cells.

10.5.2.3 Endocytosis-mediated uptake: Bypassing efflux pumps

One of the primary advantages of SLNs in overcoming MDR lies in their cellular uptake mechanism. Conventional small-molecule drugs enter cells predominantly via passive diffusion across the plasma membrane. Once inside, they are vulnerable to recognition and extrusion by P-gp and other ABC transporters. In contrast, SLNs are internalized through energy-dependent endocytic pathways, including clathrin-mediated endocytosis, caveolae-mediated uptake, and macropinocytosis. This vesicular internalization allows the nanoparticle to bypass direct interaction with efflux pumps located on the plasma membrane. After internalization, SLNs are trafficked to endosomes and lysosomes, where gradual degradation of the lipid matrix releases the encapsulated drug intracellularly.

This mechanism ensures higher intracellular drug retention compared to free drug administration. For example, paclitaxel-loaded SLNs have demonstrated significantly increased intracellular accumulation in resistant lung cancer cell lines compared to free paclitaxel. By avoiding immediate recognition by P-gp transporters, SLNs effectively circumvent one of the central mechanisms of MDR. Furthermore, receptor-mediated targeting strategies enhance endocytosis. Functionalization of SLNs with ligands targeting transferrin receptors or EGFR overexpressed in lung cancer cells further promotes receptor-triggered internalization, enhancing drug delivery efficiency and minimizing efflux susceptibility (Gorachinov et al., 2023).

10.5.2.4 Codelivery of efflux inhibitors and gene silencing agents

SLNs offer the unique advantage of coencapsulating multiple therapeutic agents within a single nanocarrier. This enables simultaneous delivery of a cytotoxic drug and a molecular modulator targeting resistance pathways. One strategy involves codelivery of chemotherapeutics with P-gp inhibitors such as verapamil or tariquidar. These inhibitors block efflux pump activity, allowing higher intracellular drug concentrations. However, systemic administration of P-gp inhibitors alone may produce off-target toxicity. Encapsulation within SLNs localizes their effect primarily to tumor cells, reducing systemic adverse effects.

An even more sophisticated approach involves codelivery of siRNA targeting MDR-related genes. For instance, SLNs can be engineered to deliver siRNA against the MDR1 gene alongside paclitaxel. The siRNA downregulates P-gp expression at the transcriptional level, while the chemotherapeutic induces cytotoxicity. This dual-action approach has demonstrated significant restoration of drug sensitivity in resistant lung cancer models. Similarly, SLNs may codeliver agents targeting antiapoptotic proteins such as Bcl-2 or survivin, further sensitizing tumor cells to chemotherapy-induced apoptosis. Such multifunctional nanocarriers exemplify how SLNs can address resistance at both protein activity and gene expression levels (Omidian et al., 2024).

10.5.2.5 Controlled and sustained drug release

Another key feature of SLNs in overcoming MDR is their ability to provide controlled and sustained drug release. The solid lipid matrix encapsulating the drug ensures gradual diffusion and release over time. Unlike free drugs, which may reach peak intracellular concentrations quickly and then decline rapidly, SLNs maintain therapeutic drug levels within tumor cells for extended periods. Sustained cytotoxic exposure reduces the opportunity for cancer cells to activate adaptive survival pathways. Continuous intracellular drug presence may overwhelm DNA repair mechanisms and apoptotic evasion strategies. Additionally, prolonged exposure at submaximal but consistent concentrations may reduce the selective pressure that promotes the survival of highly resistant clones. The lipid composition and crystallinity of SLNs influence release kinetics. By adjusting lipid types such as glyceryl monostearate or stearic acid, researchers can fine-tune drug release profiles to maintain optimal cytotoxic levels. This controlled PK behavior contributes to improved therapeutic outcomes in resistant lung cancer (Patel et al., 2025).

10.5.2.6 Integration with targeted molecular therapies

Modern lung cancer treatment increasingly relies on targeted molecular therapies, including TKIs, monoclonal antibodies, PARP inhibitors, and mTOR inhibitors. These agents act on specific signaling pathways involved in tumor proliferation, angiogenesis, and survival (Garg et al., 2024). However, resistance to targeted therapies also develops through secondary mutations or pathway reactivation. SLNs enhance the therapeutic index of targeted agents by improving their bioavailability and tumor specificity. For example, encapsulation of EGFR-targeting TKIs within SLNs can increase solubility and reduce systemic toxicity. Targeted SLNs functionalized with antibodies may further concentrate these agents within tumor tissue. PARP inhibitors used in DNA repair-deficient tumors may also benefit from SLN-mediated delivery, ensuring sustained intracellular concentrations that maximize DNA damage accumulation. Similarly, mTOR inhibitors delivered via SLNs may achieve improved tumor penetration and reduced off-target exposure. By integrating targeted molecular therapies within nanocarrier systems, SLNs contribute to multipathway inhibition strategies that address both intrinsic and acquired resistance mechanisms (Haider et al., 2022).

10.5.2.7 Multifunctional platforms for restoring chemosensitivity

The true strength of SLNs in overcoming MDR lies in their multifunctionality. They are capable of bypassing efflux transporters, modulating gene expression, sustaining cytotoxic pressure, and enhancing tumor-specific delivery simultaneously. This multipronged approach is essential given the complex and adaptive nature of lung cancer resistance. In resistant lung cancer cell models, SLN formulations have demonstrated restored chemosensitivity, reduced tumor growth, and improved survival in preclinical studies. The ability to codeliver chemotherapeutics with genetic modulators or targeted agents represents a paradigm shift from single-drug approaches toward integrated nanotherapeutic strategies.

10.6 Pharmacokinetics and biodistribution

PK profiling is essential for understanding the in vivo behavior of SLNs and optimizing therapeutic performance. Absorption, distribution, metabolism, and excretion (ADME) studies determine how nanocarriers interact with biological systems, influence systemic circulation, and accumulate in target tissues. Biodistribution studies—often performed using radiolabeled or fluorescently labeled nanoparticles—are considered the gold standard for evaluating tissue-specific accumulation. Small animal models, particularly mice and rats, are commonly employed to quantify plasma concentration, tumor uptake, and organ distribution patterns (Deol & Khuller 1997).

10.6.1 Absorption, distribution, metabolism, and excretion of solid lipid nanoparticles

Understanding the ADME profile of SLNs is essential for optimizing their therapeutic performance in lung cancer treatment. ADME studies provide crucial insights into how SLN-based formulations behave once administered, influencing bioavailability, therapeutic efficacy, toxicity, and dosing frequency. Unlike conventional drug formulations, SLNs alter the PK profile of encapsulated drugs due to their nanoscale size (50–1000 nm), lipid matrix composition, surface modification, and ability to evade biological barriers. In lung cancer therapy, SLNs may be administered via intravenous, oral, pulmonary (inhalational), or intranasal routes, and each route significantly affects their PKs. Biodistribution studies, often conducted in small animals using radiolabeled nanoparticles or fluorescent probes, remain the gold standard for evaluating tissue accumulation and clearance patterns. Parameters such as area under the curve (AUC), half-life ($t½$), clearance (CL), and volume of distribution (Vd) are critical in assessing the in vivo fate of SLNs (Shahrivar et al., 2023). Table 10.2 is a detailed representation of ADME processes specifically for SLNs

10.6.2 Lung-specific accumulation: In vitro and in vivo studies

The lungs are highly perfused organs with dense capillary networks, making them favorable for nanoparticle accumulation following systemic administration. Additionally, inhalation delivery directly deposits nanoparticles in pulmonary tissues, maximizing local concentration. Cell-penetrating peptides (CPPs) and ligand-functionalized SLNs demonstrate rapid distribution to lung tissue after intravenous injection. CPPs exhibit a biphasic PK profile characterized by a rapid distribution phase followed by slower elimination (Reveret et al., 2023). Their central Vd often exceeds plasma volume, indicating extensive tissue penetration.

Table 10.2: Detailed ADME profile of solid lipid nanoparticles.

Pharmacokinetic process	Detailed description in context of SLNs	Mechanism and influencing factors	Examples in lung cancer therapy
Absorption	Absorption refers to the entry of SLNs into systemic circulation or local lung tissue after administration. SLNs enhance drug solubility and protect labile drugs from degradation, improving bioavailability.	• Route-dependent (oral, IV, pulmonary) • Particle size (<200 nm improves uptake) • Surface charge (cationic particles enhance cellular uptake) • Surface modification (PEGylation improves stability) • Lipid composition (glyceryl monostearate, stearic acid) • Endocytosis mechanisms (clathrin- or caveolae-mediated uptake).	• Inhalable SLNs loaded with paclitaxel show enhanced pulmonary absorption compared to the free drug. • Oral SLNs improve lymphatic uptake, bypassing first-pass metabolism.
Distribution	Distribution describes the transport of SLNs from circulation to tissues, including tumor accumulation. SLNs can exploit the enhanced permeability and retention (EPR) effect in tumors.	• Particle size influences tumor penetration. • Surface ligands (antibodies, aptamers) enable active targeting. • Hydrophobicity affects plasma protein binding. • PEGylation prolongs circulation time. • Tumor microenvironment characteristics (leaky vasculature).	• VEGFR-targeted SLNs accumulate preferentially in lung tumor vasculature. • PEGylated SLNs show prolonged blood circulation and improved tumor localization.

(*continued on next page*)

Table 10.2: Detailed ADME profile of solid lipid nanoparticles—cont'd

Pharmacokinetic process	Detailed description in context of SLNs	Mechanism and influencing factors	Examples in lung cancer therapy
Metabolism	Metabolism involves the degradation of the lipid matrix and release of the drug. SLNs are composed of physiological lipids that undergo enzymatic breakdown.	• Lipase-mediated hydrolysis in liver and plasma. • Reticuloendothelial system (RES) uptake (liver, spleen macrophages). • Lipid crystallinity influences drug release rate. • Biodegradable lipid matrix ensures safe metabolism.	• SLNs containing doxorubicin demonstrate controlled release due to gradual lipid degradation. • Lipid core is metabolized into fatty acids, entering normal metabolic pathways.
Excretion	Excretion refers to the elimination of SLN components and released drug from the body via renal or hepatobiliary pathways.	• Small degraded lipid fragments eliminated via urine. • Larger particles cleared via biliary route. • Surface charge affects renal filtration. • Plasma protein binding influences elimination rate.	• Radiolabeled SLNs show hepatic clearance followed by fecal excretion. • Reduced systemic toxicity due to controlled elimination.

ADME, absorption, distribution, metabolism, and excretion; *SLNs*, solid lipid nanoparticles; *VEGFR*, vascular endothelial growth factor receptor.

In vivo imaging studies using fluorescently labeled SLNs reveal enhanced lung tumor accumulation compared to free drugs. Inhalable SLNs achieve high alveolar deposition, prolonged residence time, and improved tumor penetration. Importantly, pulmonary SLNs reduce systemic toxicity by limiting drug exposure to nontarget organs. In vitro studies using lung cancer cell lines demonstrate enhanced cellular uptake via receptor-mediated endocytosis and increased apoptosis induction compared to conventional formulations. Together, these findings confirm that SLNs provide superior lung-specific targeting, sustained drug release, and improved therapeutic index.

10.6.3 Immunological interactions and tumor immune modulation by solid lipid nanoparticles

Beyond PK enhancement and tumor targeting, SLNs interact dynamically with the immune system, influencing both therapeutic efficacy and safety. Upon systemic administration, SLNs encounter immune cells, including macrophages, dendritic cells, and components of the complement system. The formation of a protein corona around nanoparticles can modulate immune recognition, affecting biodistribution and clearance. While rapid uptake by macrophages in the liver and spleen may limit systemic circulation time, surface modifications such as PEGylation reduce opsonization and prolong blood half-life.

In the context of lung cancer, immunological interactions are particularly relevant due to the increasing use of immune checkpoint inhibitors such as Pembrolizumab. SLNs have the potential to function synergistically with immunotherapy by modulating the TME. For instance, SLNs can be engineered to codeliver chemotherapeutic agents alongside immunomodulatory molecules, promoting immunogenic cell death and enhancing antigen presentation. Controlled release of cytotoxic drugs within tumors may increase tumor-associated antigen exposure, thereby potentiating immune responses.

Moreover, lipid-based nanoparticles have demonstrated potential as carriers for mRNA, peptides, or tumor antigens, opening avenues for therapeutic cancer vaccines. In lung tumors characterized by an immunosuppressive microenvironment, SLNs may facilitate localized delivery of immune-stimulating agents while minimizing systemic inflammation. However, careful evaluation of complement activation and hypersensitivity reactions is necessary to ensure safety, particularly for repeated dosing regimens. Thus, understanding and harnessing immunological interactions represent a promising frontier in SLN-based lung cancer therapy.

10.7 Safety and toxicological evaluations of solid lipid nanoparticles

The rapid advancement of lipid-based nanocarriers, particularly SLNs, has significantly expanded their application in oncology, including lung cancer therapy. Their successful use in modern platforms such as mRNA vaccine delivery systems has reinforced confidence in lipid nanocarriers as safe and efficient drug delivery vehicles. However, despite their promising therapeutic potential, rigorous safety and toxicological evaluations remain essential before clinical translation. Toxicity profiling of SLNs encompasses in vitro cytotoxicity screening, in vivo preclinical safety studies, immunogenicity assessment, organ-specific toxicity evaluation, and long-term exposure monitoring. Given that SLNs are designed to alter PKs and biodistribution, their interaction with biological systems must be carefully examined to avoid unintended toxicological consequences.

10.7.1 Cytotoxicity studies on solid lipid nanoparticles

Cytotoxicity assessment is the first and most fundamental step in evaluating the safety of SLNs. In vitro proliferation assays are widely employed for both adherent and nonadherent cell lines to determine the dose-dependent effects of nanoparticle formulations on cellular viability. These assays typically include MTT, XTT, WST-1, trypan blue exclusion, and flow cytometry-based apoptosis analyses. Such assays not only measure direct cytotoxic effects but also provide insights into mechanisms such as oxidative stress induction, mitochondrial dysfunction, membrane disruption, and apoptosis activation (Syama et al., 2022).

In oncology research, cytotoxicity studies are particularly critical because SLNs are engineered to maximize toxicity toward cancer cells while minimizing effects on normal cells. For example, bio-conjugate-loaded SLNs have demonstrated enhanced cellular internalization in brain cancer cell lines. Jain et al. (2022) reported that SLN-C, a formulation loaded with a flavin adenine dinucleotide (FAD) conjugate, exhibited strong anticancer activity with a half-maximal inhibitory concentration (IC50) of 2.5 μg/mL in brain cancer cells. The nanoparticles had an average particle size of 220.4 nm, a range favorable for endocytic uptake. This study confirmed that lipid-based nanosystems can facilitate efficient intracellular drug delivery and enhance cytotoxic activity against tumor cells while maintaining structural stability.

In lung cancer models, similar principles apply. SLNs encapsulating chemotherapeutic agents such as paclitaxel, doxorubicin, or cisplatin are frequently tested on A549 and H1299 lung carcinoma cell lines. These studies often demonstrate improved cytotoxic effects compared to free drugs due to enhanced cellular uptake and sustained drug release. Importantly, selective cytotoxicity is evaluated by comparing effects on normal bronchial epithelial cells, ensuring therapeutic specificity. Surface modifications, such as PEGylation or ligand conjugation, can further influence cytotoxic profiles by altering cellular uptake pathways. Nanoparticle internalization mechanisms significantly affect toxicity outcomes. SLNs are typically internalized through clathrin-mediated endocytosis, caveolae-mediated pathways, or macropinocytosis. Once internalized, the lipid matrix gradually degrades, releasing the encapsulated drug intracellularly. Excessive accumulation, however, may trigger lysosomal stress or ROS generation, underscoring the need for dose optimization. Therefore, cytotoxicity studies are not merely preliminary safety screenings but critical tools for formulation refinement.

10.7.2 Biocompatibility and long-term safety

Biocompatibility is defined as the ability of a material to perform its intended function while eliciting an appropriate host response in a specific application. For SLNs, this involves ensuring that lipid components, surfactants, and surface modifiers do not provoke adverse inflammatory, immunological, or systemic reactions. Since SLNs are composed of physiological lipids such as stearic acid, glyceryl monostearate, and triglycerides, they are generally regarded as safe. However, nanoscale properties can alter biological interactions, necessitating a comprehensive evaluation. Long-term safety assessment involves examining both cancer and noncancer endpoints. Toxicological evaluation begins with reviewing discovery data from foundational studies used to establish noncancer health guidelines, followed by analysis of more recent investigations to assess evolving evidence. Toxicity benchmarks such as inhalation unit risk (IUR) and cancer slope factor (CSF) are considered when evaluating potential carcinogenic risk. When such reference values are unavailable, risk assessment relies on dose-response relationships derived from animal and human studies (Crawford et al., 2021).

In preclinical toxicology, SLNs are administered to rodents to evaluate acute, subacute, and chronic toxicity. Parameters assessed include hematologic indices, liver and kidney function markers, histopathological examination of organs, and inflammatory cytokine levels. Necropsy PKs and tissue biodistribution analyses help identify potential accumulation in target organs such as the liver, spleen, or lungs. Comparing observed tissue concentrations with levels of significant exposure (LSE) data assists in determining safety margins. For pulmonary delivery systems, long-term inhalation toxicity studies are particularly important. Chronic exposure may lead to inflammation, fibrosis, or altered lung function if particle clearance is impaired. Macrophage uptake and mucociliary clearance mechanisms play crucial roles in determining lung biocompatibility. Studies evaluating oxidative stress markers, alveolar integrity, and cytokine expression profiles help characterize pulmonary safety. Importantly, the concept of "safe exposure" does not imply zero risk but rather an acceptable risk threshold based on regulatory standards. Determining safe human exposure levels requires extrapolation from animal models, incorporating uncertainty factors to account for interspecies variability. Thus, long-term safety evaluation is a continuous process that evolves alongside clinical data accumulation.

10.7.3 Regulatory challenges in clinical translation

Translating SLNs from laboratory research to clinical practice presents significant regulatory challenges. Regulatory authorities require extensive safety pharmacology, toxicokinetic data, and standardized manufacturing protocols before approving investigational new drug applications. Preclinical animal studies are conducted to identify target organ toxicity, determine no-observed-adverse-effect levels (NOAEL), and establish dosage guidelines for human trials.

However, translational gaps often arise between preclinical findings and clinical outcomes. Traditional animal models may fail to predict certain adverse effects, particularly neurobehavioral or immunological reactions. For example, some drug-induced symptoms, such as nausea or dizziness, are difficult to detect accurately in rodents, raising concerns regarding predictive validity (Berridge et al., 2024). These limitations highlight the need for improved safety pharmacology models incorporating quantitative neurological screening and standardized protocols. Another regulatory challenge involves nanoparticle characterization. Agencies require precise data on particle size distribution, zeta potential, lipid polymorphism, encapsulation efficiency, and batch-to-batch reproducibility. Minor variations in production parameters can significantly alter biological behavior. Therefore, harmonized guidelines for nanomedicine evaluation are essential. Moreover, immunogenicity assessment remains critical, especially for repeated dosing regimens. Lipid-based systems may activate complement pathways or induce hypersensitivity reactions. Regulatory frameworks must balance innovation with patient safety by ensuring thorough evaluation without unnecessarily delaying therapeutic advancement.

10.8 Current challenges and future prospects

SLNs have emerged as versatile and promising nanocarriers for lung cancer therapy, offering advantages such as improved drug solubility, controlled release, enhanced tumor targeting, and the potential to overcome MDR. However, despite encouraging preclinical outcomes, their transition from bench to bedside remains limited. The clinical translation of SLNs faces several technical, regulatory, biological, and translational challenges that must be addressed systematically. At the same time, emerging technologies—particularly artificial intelligence (AI), precision medicine, and advanced manufacturing platforms—offer transformative opportunities to overcome these barriers and redefine the future of nanomedicine in oncology.

10.8.1 Technical challenges in large-scale production

10.8.1.1 Scale-up complexity and process reproducibility

One of the most critical barriers to SLN commercialization lies in the complexity of scaling up production from laboratory-scale batches to industrial manufacturing. At the research level, SLNs are commonly prepared using high-pressure homogenization, microemulsion techniques, solvent emulsification–evaporation, ultrasonication, or hot and cold homogenization methods. These methods are optimized under tightly controlled small-scale conditions, where parameters such as homogenization pressure, sonication time, lipid-to-surfactant ratio, cooling rate, and stirring speed are carefully regulated.

However, when production is scaled up, these parameters do not behave linearly. For example, homogenization pressure that yields a uniform 120 nm particle size in a 50 mL laboratory batch may produce broader size distributions when applied to multiliter industrial reactors.

Similarly, cooling rates influence lipid crystallization behavior. In large-scale vessels, uneven heat transfer may result in heterogeneous nucleation and polymorphic transitions, altering particle size distribution and encapsulation efficiency. Achieving consistent particle size distribution across batches remains a significant technical challenge, as size directly affects biodistribution, tumor penetration, and clearance kinetics. Drug loading efficiency and encapsulation stability also vary during scale-up. Minor variations in mixing efficiency or surfactant dispersion can lead to drug expulsion from the lipid matrix. Since lung cancer therapy often requires precise dosing to avoid systemic toxicity, maintaining batch-to-batch consistency is crucial (Chauhan et al., 2023).

10.8.1.2 Lipid polymorphism and stability concerns

SLNs are composed of solid lipids that can exist in multiple polymorphic forms, including α, β', and β crystalline states. During storage, lipids may transition from less ordered to more stable crystalline forms. These polymorphic transitions can cause drug expulsion from the lipid matrix and modify release kinetics. For chemotherapeutic agents requiring sustained intracellular exposure, such instability can compromise therapeutic outcomes. Long-term storage stability is influenced by temperature, humidity, lipid composition, and packaging materials. Aggregation, gelation, or particle growth may occur over time. Lyophilization is often employed to enhance stability, but this introduces additional challenges such as cryoprotectant selection and reconstitution efficiency. Ensuring that reconstituted SLNs maintain original particle size and drug loading is critical for clinical reliability (Rajendran et al., 2022).

10.8.1.3 Integration into existing manufacturing infrastructure

Introducing SLNs into established pharmaceutical manufacturing systems requires adaptation of existing infrastructure. Conventional tablet or injectable production lines are not necessarily optimized for nanosuspensions. Specialized equipment for high-pressure homogenization, sterile filtration, nanoparticle characterization, and aseptic filling must be integrated. The incorporation of advanced lipid matrixes may require modification of heating and cooling systems to control melting points and crystallization behavior. Similar to challenges encountered in material substitution in industries such as automotive manufacturing, introducing innovative materials demands compatibility assessment with established processes and workflows (Jose et al., 2025). Workforce training, quality assurance upgrades, and equipment validation further increase complexity and cost.

10.8.1.4 Regulatory and quality control requirements

From a regulatory perspective, SLNs must comply with good manufacturing practices (GMP) and demonstrate robust quality control. Critical quality attributes include particle size distribution, zeta potential, lipid polymorphism, drug encapsulation efficiency, sterility, endotoxin levels, and in vitro release profiles. Minor variations in any of these attributes can significantly alter PKs and biodistribution. Regulatory agencies often require detailed characterization of nanomedicines beyond conventional drug formulations. Establishing standardized guidelines for nanoparticle evaluation remains an ongoing challenge. Additionally, long-term toxicological data are necessary before approval for chronic use in lung cancer therapy (Mehta et al., 2023).

10.8.2 Integration of solid lipid nanoparticles with emerging technologies: Artificial intelligence and precision medicine

10.8.2.1 Data-driven nanomedicine design

The rapid expansion of biomedical data—from genomics and proteomics to imaging and electronic health records—has created unprecedented opportunities for integrating nanotechnology with data science. AI and machine learning (ML) algorithms can analyze complex datasets to identify patterns that inform nanoparticle design and therapeutic optimization. For SLNs, AI can predict how physicochemical properties such as particle size, lipid composition, and surface charge influence PKs, tumor accumulation, and toxicity. ML models trained on experimental datasets can establish correlations between formulation variables and biological outcomes. This predictive modeling significantly reduces reliance on trial-and-error experimentation.

For instance, AI algorithms may identify that a 130 nm PEGylated SLN composed of glyceryl monostearate provides optimal tumor retention with minimal hepatic accumulation. By analyzing multiparameter datasets, AI-driven platforms can recommend formulation adjustments before experimental validation, accelerating development timelines and reducing cost. Predictive analytics can also enhance supply chain management and manufacturing logistics. Forecasting raw material shortages or equipment downtime ensures uninterrupted production (Bajwa et al., 2021; Johnson et al., 2021). Such integration improves operational efficiency and sustainability in pharmaceutical manufacturing.

10.8.2.2 Artificial intelligence in clinical decision-making

Beyond formulation design, AI plays a transformative role in the clinical implementation of SLN-based therapies. Lung cancer is characterized by substantial genetic heterogeneity. Tumor mutations in EGFR, KRAS, ALK, and BRAF influence therapeutic response. AI-assisted systems can integrate genomic sequencing data with PK modeling to personalize SLN-based treatment regimens. For example, patients with mutations affecting drug-metabolizing enzymes may require sustained release SLN formulations to maintain therapeutic drug levels. AI algorithms can simulate PK profiles based on patient-specific variables such as age, liver function, tumor burden, and genetic polymorphisms. AI tools in clinical practice also assist in the early detection of resistance patterns. By analyzing imaging data and biomarker trends, predictive models may signal impending therapeutic failure, prompting timely modification of SLN formulations or combination strategies (Carini et al., 2024).

10.8.2.3 Precision medicine and molecular targeting

Precision medicine complements SLN technology by tailoring therapy according to individual tumor biology. Functionalization of SLNs with antibodies, aptamers, or peptides targeting overexpressed receptors enhances specificity. In lung cancer, receptors such as EGFR, transferrin receptor, folate receptor, and integrins provide molecular docking sites. For instance, antibody-conjugated SLNs targeting EGFR-overexpressing tumors enable selective drug delivery while minimizing systemic exposure. Aptamer-functionalized SLNs may recognize specific cancer stem cell markers, addressing tumor heterogeneity. By integrating molecular diagnostics with nanocarrier engineering, precision medicine ensures that each patient receives a formulation optimized for their tumor profile. Furthermore, SLNs can codeliver chemotherapeutic drugs and gene-editing components such as CRISPR-Cas systems or siRNA targeting resistance genes. Such combination strategies align with personalized therapeutic approaches aimed at simultaneously suppressing oncogenic drivers and restoring drug sensitivity (Alwani et al., 2024).

10.8.2.4 Sustainability and future outlook

The convergence of nanotechnology, AI, and precision medicine represents a paradigm shift in oncology therapeutics. AI-driven optimization reduces resource consumption, minimizes experimental redundancy, and enhances sustainability in drug development. Personalized SLN formulations may improve therapeutic outcomes while reducing adverse effects, ultimately lowering healthcare costs. Future research directions include the development of smart SLNs capable of real-time response to TME signals, integration with wearable monitoring devices for adaptive dosing, and utilization of digital twins to simulate patient-specific therapeutic responses (Younis et al., 2025).

10.9 Discussion and conclusion

Certain SLN formulations, counting paclitaxel-loaded tripalmitin SLNs, have demonstrated improved in vitro anticancer effectiveness. This is because they allow for a lengthy announcement of the medicine and inferior the IC50 of paclitaxel, which upsurges cytotoxicity in breast as well as lung cancer tissues. Lung cancer has efficiently helped from the synergistic anticancer activity of therapeutic medicines such as paclitaxel and siRNA full in SLNs. The result of the medicine may be assessed by detecting improved in vivo cellular acceptance of the drug on-site while declining off-site cancer cell uptake thanks to the practice of quantum dots (QDs) in SLNs (Sharma et al., 2023).

SLNs for the delivery of several anticancer treatments. The therapeutic efficacy and safety profile of gemcitabine in the treatment of lung cancer are better-quality by gemcitabine-loaded mannosylated SLNs (Gemcitabine-SLNs), which usage the mannosylation to recover drug delivery selectively to lung cancer cells. Inhalation delivery of methotrexate/chitosan-coated SLNs comprehending methotrexate (CS-SLN-MTX) has been established to upsurge apoptosis in lung cancer cells and reach advanced concentrations of methotrexate in the lungs. This proposes that by enhancing local drug concentration at the tumor site, this route could importantly recover therapeutic outcomes. The aptitude of tretinoin-loaded lipid core nanocapsules (TTN-LNC) to overwhelmed drug resistance, trigger apoptosis, and break the cell cycle in lung adenocarcinoma cells proposes a workable method to combat confrontation and recover tretinoin's therapeutic efficacy in giving lung cancer (Omidian et al., 2024).

References

Akanda, M., Mithu, M. S. H., & Douroumis, D. (2023). Solid lipid nanoparticles: An effective lipid-based technology for cancer treatment. *Journal of Drug Delivery Science and Technology, 86*. http://www.editionsdesante.fr/category.php?id_category=48. doi:10.1016/j.jddst.2023.104709.

Alwani, S., Wasan, E. K., & Badea, I. (2024). Solid lipid nanoparticles for pulmonary delivery of biopharmaceuticals: A review of opportunities, challenges, and delivery applications. *Molecular Pharmaceutics, 21*(7), 3084–3102. doi:10.1021/acs.molpharmaceut.4c00128.

Apostolou, M., Fatokun, A. A., Assi, S., & Khan, I. (2024). Targeted lipid-based drug delivery systems for lung cancer therapy. *Applied Sciences, 14*(15), 6759. doi:10.3390/app14156759.

Bajwa, J., Munir, U., Nori, A., & Williams, B. (2021). Artificial intelligence in healthcare: Transforming the practice of medicine. *Future Healthcare Journal, 8*(2), e188. doi:10.7861/fhj.2021-0095.

Barr, T., Ma, S., Li, Z., & Yu, J. (2024). Recent advances and remaining challenges in lung cancer therapy. *Chinese Medical Journal, 137*(5), 533–546. doi:10.1097/cm9.0000000000002991.

Berridge, B. R., Baran, S. W., Kumar, V., Bratcher-Petersen, N., Ellis, M., Liu, C. N., & Robertson, T. L. (2024). Digitalization of toxicology: Improving preclinical to clinical translation. *Frontiers in Toxicology, 6*. doi:10.3389/ftox.2024.1377542.

Caliman, E., Fancelli, S., Petroni, G., Gatta Michelet, M. R., Cosso, F., Ottanelli, C., Mazzoni, F., Voltolini, L., Pillozzi, S., & Antonuzzo, L. (2023). Challenges in the treatment of small cell lung cancer in the era of immunotherapy and molecular classification. *Lung Cancer, 175*, 88–100. doi:10.1016/j.lungcan.2022.11.014.

Carini, C., & Seyhan, A. A. (2024). Tribulations and future opportunities for artificial intelligence in precision medicine. *Journal of Translational Medicine, 22*(1). doi:10.1186/s12967-024-05067-0.

Chauhan, G., Wang, X., Yousry, C., & Gupta, V. (2023). Scalable production and in vitro efficacy of inhaled erlotinib nanoemulsion for enhanced efficacy in non-small cell lung cancer (NSCLC). *Pharmaceutics, 15*(3), 996. doi:10.3390/pharmaceutics15030996.

Colaco, V., Roy, A. A., Naik, G. A. R. R., Mondal, A., Mutalik, S., & Dhas, N. (2024). Advancement in lipid-based nanocomposites for theranostic applications in lung carcinoma treatment. *OpenNano, 15*. doi:10.1016/j.onano.2023.100199.

Crawford, L., Wyatt, M., Bryers, J., & Ratner, B. (2021). Biocompatibility evolves: Phenomenology to toxicology to regeneration. *Advanced Healthcare Materials., 10*(11). doi:10.1002/adhm.202002153.

Deol, P., & Khuller, G. K. (1997). Lung specific stealth liposomes: Stability, biodistribution and toxicity of liposomal antitubercular drugs in mice. *Biochimica et Biophysica Acta - General Subjects, 1334*(2-3), 161–172. doi:10.1016/S0304-4165(96)00088-8.

Duan, Y., Dhar, A., Patel, C., Khimani, M., Neogi, S., Sharma, P., Siva Kumar, N., & Vekariya, R. L. (2020). A brief review on solid lipid nanoparticles: Part and parcel of contemporary drug delivery systems. *RSC Advances, 10*(45), 26777–26791. doi:10.1039/d0ra03491f.

Duong, V. A., Nguyen, T. T. L., & Maeng, H. J. (2020). Preparation of solid lipid nanoparticles and nanostructured lipid carriers for drug delivery and the effects of preparation parameters of solvent injection method. *Molecules, 25*(20). doi:10.3390/molecules25204781.

Emran, T. B., Shahriar, A., Mahmud, A. R., Rahman, T., Abir, M. H., Siddiquee, M. F.-R., Ahmed, H., Rahman, N., Nainu, F., Wahyudin, E., Mitra, S., Dhama, K., Habiballah, M. M., Haque, S., Islam, A., & Hassan, M. M. (2022). Multidrug resistance in cancer: Understanding molecular mechanisms, immunoprevention and therapeutic approaches. *Frontiers in Oncology, 12*. doi:10.3389/fonc.2022.891652.

Garg, P., Malhotra, J., Kulkarni, P., Horne, D., Salgia, R., & Singhal, S. S. (2024). Emerging therapeutic strategies to overcome drug resistance in cancer cells. *Cancers, 16*(13). doi:10.3390/cancers16132478.

Ghasemiyeh, P., & Mohammadi-Samani, S. (2018). Solid lipid nanoparticles and nanostructured lipid carriers as novel drug delivery systems: Applications, advantages and disadvantages. *Research in Pharmaceutical Sciences, 13*(4), 288–303. doi:10.4103/1735-5362.235156.

Girigoswami, A., & Girigoswami, K. (2023). Potential applications of nanoparticles in improving the outcome of lung cancer treatment. *Genes, 14*(7), 1370. doi:10.3390/genes14071370.

Gorachinov, F., Mraiche, F., Moustafa, D. A., Hishari, O., Ismail, Y., Joseph, J., Crcarevska, M. S., Dodov, M. G., Geskovski, N., & Goracinova, K. (2023). Nanotechnology – A robust tool for fighting the challenges of drug resistance in non-small cell lung cancer. *Beilstein Journal of Nanotechnology, 14*, 240–261. doi:10.3762/bjnano.14.23.

Haider, M., Elsherbeny, A., Pittalà, V., Consoli, V., Ali Alghamdi, M., Hussain, Z., Khoder, G., & Greish, K. (2022). Nanomedicine strategies for management of drug resistance in lung cancer. *International Journal of Molecular Sciences, 23*(3), 1853. doi:10.3390/ijms23031853.

Islam, W., Niidome, T., & Sawa, T. (2022). Enhanced permeability and retention effect as a ubiquitous and epoch-making phenomenon for the selective drug targeting of solid tumors. *Journal of Personalized Medicine, 12*(12). doi:10.3390/jpm12121964.

Jain, P., Pandey, V., & Soni, V. (2022). Bioconjugate-loaded solid lipid nanoparticles for enhanced anticancer drug delivery to brain cancer cells: An in vitro evaluation. *Indian Journal of Medical Research, 156*(1), 139–148. doi:10.4103/ijmr.ijmr_514_19.

Jaiswal, P., Gidwani, B., & Vyas, A. (2016). Nanostructured lipid carriers and their current application in targeted drug delivery. *Artificial Cells, Nanomedicine and Biotechnology, 44*(1), 27–40. doi:10.3109/21691401.2014.909822.

Jamous, Y. F., Altwaijry, N. A., Saleem, M. T. S., Alrayes, A. F., Albishi, S. M., & Almeshari, M. A. (2023). Formulation and characterization of solid lipid nanoparticles loaded with troxerutin. *Processes, 11*(10). doi:10.3390/pr11103039.

Johnson, K. B., Wei, W.-Q. i, Weeraratne, D., Frisse, M. E., Misulis, K., Rhee, K., Zhao, J., & Snowdon, J. L. (2021). Precision medicine, AI, and the future of personalized health care. *Clinical and Translational Science, 14*(1), 86–93. doi:10.1111/cts.12884.

Jose, S. A., Tonner, A., Feliciano, M., Roy, T., Shackleford, A., & Menezes, P. L. (2025). Smart manufacturing for high-performance materials: Advances, challenges, and future directions. *Materials, 18*(10). doi:10.3390/ma18102255.

Kemp, J. A., & Jik Kwon, Y. (2021). Cancer nanotechnology: Current status and perspectives. *Nano Convergence, 8*(1). doi:10.1186/s40580-021-00282-7.

Khezri, K., Saeedi, M., Morteza-Semnani, K., Akbari, J., & Rostamkalaei, S. S. (2020). An emerging technology in lipid research for targeting hydrophilic drugs to the skin in the treatment of hyperpigmentation disorders: Kojic acid-solid lipid nanoparticles. *Artificial Cells, Nanomedicine and Biotechnology, 48*(1), 841–853. doi:10.1080/21691401.2020.1770271.

Kim, S. o-J., Puranik, N., Yadav, D., & Lee, P. C. W. (2023). Lipid nanocarrier-based drug delivery systems: Therapeutic advances in the treatment of lung cancer. *International Journal of Nanomedicine, 18*, 2659–2676. doi:10.2147/ijn.s406415.

Kratzer, T. B., Bandi, P., Freedman, N. D., Smith, R. A., Travis, W. D., Jemal, A., & Siegel, R. L. (2024). Lung cancer statistics, 2023. *Cancer., 130*(8), 1330–1348. doi:10.1002/cncr.35128.

Lahiri, A., Maji, A., Potdar, P. D., Singh, N., Parikh, P., Bisht, B., Mukherjee, A., & Paul, M. K. (2023). Lung cancer immunotherapy: Progress, pitfalls, and promises. *Molecular Cancer, 22*(1). doi:10.1186/s12943-023-01740-y.

Li, J., Wang, Q., Xia, G., Adilijiang, N., Li, Y., Hou, Z., Fan, Z., & Li, J. (2023). Recent advances in targeted drug delivery strategy for enhancing oncotherapy. *Pharmaceutics, 15*(9). doi:10.3390/pharmaceutics15092233.

Liu, H., Li, Y., Zhang, X., Shi, M., Li, D., Wang, Y., & Corlateanu, A. (2022). Chitosan-coated solid lipid nanoencapsulation improves the therapeutic antiairway inflammation effect of berberine against COPD in cigarette smoke-exposed rats. *Canadian Respiratory Journal, 2022*, 1–13. doi:10.1155/2022/8509396.

Mehnert, W., & Mäder, K. (2012). Solid lipid nanoparticles: Production, characterization and applications. *Advanced Drug Delivery Reviews, 64*, 83–101. doi:10.1016/j.addr.2012.09.021.

Mehta, M., Bui, T. A., Yang, X., Aksoy, Y., Goldys, E. M., & Deng, W. (2023). Lipid-based nanoparticles for drug/gene delivery: An overview of the production techniques and difficulties encountered in their industrial development. *ACS Materials Au, 3*(6), 600–619. doi:10.1021/acsmaterialsau.3c00032.

Mohammed, H. A., Khan, R. A., Singh, V., Yusuf, M., Akhtar, N., Sulaiman, G. M., Albukhaty, S., Abdellatif, A. A. H., Khan, M., Mohammed, S. A. A., & Al-Subaiyel, A. M. (2023). Solid lipid nanoparticles for targeted natural and synthetic drugs delivery in high-incidence cancers, and other diseases: Roles of preparation methods, lipid composition, transitional stability, and release profiles in nanocarriers' development. *Nanotechnology Reviews, 12*(1). doi:10.1515/ntrev-2022-0517.

Montoto, S. S., Muraca, G., & Ruiz, M. íaE. (2020). Solid lipid nanoparticles for drug delivery: Pharmacological and biopharmaceutical aspects. *Frontiers in Molecular Biosciences, 7*. doi:10.3389/fmolb.2020.587997.

Musielak, E., Feliczak-Guzik, A., & Nowak, I. (2022). Optimization of the conditions of solid lipid nanoparticles (SLN) synthesis. *Molecules, 27*(7), 2202. doi:10.3390/molecules27072202.

Nalawade, S., Narwade, M., Deshmukh, V., Nasir, N., Wahab, S., Kesharwani, P., & Gajbhiye, K. R. (2025). Surface-modified nintedanib-loaded solid lipid nanoparticles for effective targeting of non-small cell lung cancer. *Colloids and Surfaces B: Biointerfaces, 251*, 114622. doi:10.1016/j.colsurfb.2025.114622.

Omidian, H., Gill, E. J., & Cubeddu, L. X. (2024). Lipid Nanoparticles in Lung Cancer Therapy. *Pharmaceutics, 16*(5). doi:10.3390/pharmaceutics16050644.

Patel, P., Patel, M., Dua, K., Singh, S. K., & Patel, R. (2025). Unraveling the potential of curcumin-based nanoformulations: Advancing against multidrug resistance in lung cancer. In *Fighting multidrug resistance with herbal extracts, essential oils and their components* (pp. 499–518). Elsevier. doi:10.1016/B978-0-443-29044-2.00021-7.

Pathak, P., & Nagarsenker, M. (2009). Formulation and evaluation of lidocaine lipid nanosystems for dermal delivery. *AAPS PharmSciTech, 10*(3), 985–992. doi:10.1208/s12249-009-9287-1.

Rajendran, J. V., Thomas, S., Jafari, Z., Fariborzi, N., Khorasani, S., Mofrad, Z. K., Katouzian, I., & Mozafari (2022). Recent advances on large-scale manufacture of curcumin and its nanoformulation for cancer therapeutic application. *Biointerface Research in Applied Chemistry, 12*(6), 7863–7885. doi:10.33263/briac126.78637885.

Ramteke, K. H., & Joshi, S. A. (2012). Solid lipid nanoparticle: A review. *OSR Journal of Pharmacy, 2*(6), 34–44. doi:10.9790/3013-26103444.

Reveret, L., Leclerc, L., Morin, F., Emond, V., & Calon, F. (2023). Pharmacokinetics, biodistribution and toxicology of novel cell-penetrating peptides. *Scientific Reports, 13*(1). doi:10.1038/s41598-023-37280-0.

Sastri, K. T., Radha, G. V., Pidikiti, S., & Vajjhala, P. (2020). Solid lipid nanoparticles: Preparation techniques, their characterization, and an update on recent studies. *Journal of Applied Pharmaceutical Science, 10*(6), 126–141. doi:10.7324/JAPS.2020.10617.

Satapathy, M. K., Yen, T.-L., Jan, J.-S., Tang, R.-D., Wang, J.-Y. i, Taliyan, R., & Yang, C.-H. (2021). Solid lipid nanoparticles (Slns): An advanced drug delivery system targeting brain through bbb. *Pharmaceutics, 13*(8). doi:10.3390/pharmaceutics13081183.

Seidu, T. A., Kutoka, P. T., Asante, D. O., Farooq, M. A., Alolga, R. N., & Bo, W. (2022). Functionalization of nanoparticulate drug delivery systems and its influence in cancer therapy. *Pharmaceutics, 14*(5). doi:10.3390/pharmaceutics14051113.

Sgorla, D., Bunhak, É. J., Cavalcanti, O. A., Fonte, P., & Sarmento, B. (2016). Exploitation of lipid-polymeric matrices at nanoscale for drug delivery applications. *Expert Opinion on Drug Delivery, 13*(9), 1301–1309. doi:10.1080/17425247.2016.1182492.

Shahrivar, R. Y., Fakhr, Z. A., Abbasgholinejad, E., & Doroudian, M. (2023). Smart lipid-based nanoparticles in lung cancer treatment: Current status and future directions. *Advanced Therapeutics, 6*(12). doi:10.1002/adtp.202300275.

Sharifi, M., Cho, W. C., Ansariesfahani, A., Tarharoudi, R., Malekisarvar, H., Sari, S., Bloukh, S. H., Edis, Z., Amin, M., Gleghorn, J. P., Ten Hagen, T. L. M., & Falahati, M. (2022). An updated review on EPR-based solid tumor targeting nanocarriers for cancer treatment. *Cancers, 14*(12). doi:10.3390/cancers14122868.

Sharma, A., Shambhwani, D., Pandey, S., Singh, J., Lalhlenmawia, H., Kumarasamy, M., Singh, S. K., Kumar Chellappan, D., Gupta, G., Prasher, P., Dua, K., & Kumar, D. (2023). Advances in lung cancer treatment using nanomedicines. *ACS Omega, 8*(1), 10–41. doi:10.1021/acsomega.2c04078.

Shojaei, S., Pourmadadi, M., Homayoonfal, M., Behnamrad, P., Fathi-karkan, S., Rahdar, A., Gerayli, S., & Pandey, S. (2024). Revolutionizing lung cancer treatment: Nanotechnology-driven advances in targeted drug delivery and novel therapeutic strategies. *Journal of Drug Delivery Science and Technology, 101*, 106186. doi:10.1016/j.jddst.2024.106186.

Sjöström, B., & Bergenståhl, B. (1992). Preparation of submicron drug particles in lecithin-stabilized o/w emulsions I. Model studies of the precipitation of cholesteryl acetate. *International Journal of Pharmaceutics, 88*(1-3), 53–62. doi:10.1016/0378-5173(92)90303-J.

Smolarz, B., Łukasiewicz, H., Samulak, D., Piekarska, E., Kołaciński, R. ł, & Romanowicz, H. (2025). Lung cancer—Epidemiology, pathogenesis, treatment and molecular aspect (review of literature). *International Journal of Molecular Sciences, 26*(5), 2049. doi:10.3390/ijms26052049.

Syama, K., Jakubek, Z. J., Chen, S., Zaifman, J., Tam, Y. Y. iC., & Zou, S. (2022). Development of lipid nanoparticles and liposomes reference materials (II): Cytotoxic profiles. *Scientific Reports, 12*(1). doi:10.1038/s41598-022-23013-2.

Viegas, C., Patrício, A. B., Prata, J. M., Nadhman, A., Chintamaneni, P. K., & Fonte, P. (2023). Solid lipid nanoparticles vs. nanostructured lipid carriers: A comparative review. *Pharmaceutics, 15*(6). doi:10.3390/pharmaceutics15061593.

Viegas, C. lá, Seck, F., & Fonte, P. (2022). An insight on lipid nanoparticles for therapeutic proteins delivery. *Journal of Drug Delivery Science and Technology, 77*, 103839. doi:10.1016/j.jddst.2022.103839.

Wang, J., Zhou, T., Liu, Y., Chen, S., & Yu, Z. (2022). Application of nanoparticles in the treatment of lung cancer with emphasis on receptors. *Frontiers in Pharmacology, 12*. doi:10.3389/fphar.2021.781425.

Waters, L. J., Bedford, S., & Parkes, G. M. B. (2011). Controlled microwave processing applied to the pharmaceutical formulation of ibuprofen. *AAPS PharmSciTech, 12*(4), 1038–1043. doi:10.1208/s12249-011-9671-5.

Wu, J. (2021). The enhanced permeability and retention (Epr) effect: The significance of the concept and methods to enhance its application. *Journal of Personalized Medicine, 11*(8). doi:10.3390/jpm11080771.

Younis, M. A., Alsogaihi, M. A., Abdellatif, A. A. H., & Saleem, I. (2025). Nanoformulations in the treatment of lung cancer: Current status and clinical potential. *Drug Development and Industrial Pharmacy, 51*(9), 1088–1104. doi:10.1080/03639045.2024.2437562.

Zhang, J., Li, Y., Guo, S. a, Zhang, W., Fang, B., & Wang, S. (2024). Moving beyond traditional therapies: The role of nanomedicines in lung cancer. *Frontiers in Pharmacology, 15*. doi:10.3389/fphar.2024.1363346.

CHAPTER 11

Dendrimers: Promising nanocarriers for targeted delivery in lung cancer treatment

Shikha Baghel Chauhan, Indu Singh, Khushi Dahiya and Yakshit Chauhan
Amity Institute of Pharmacy, Amity University, Noida, Uttar Pradesh, India

11.1 Introduction

Highly branching polymeric macromolecules with consistent, well-defined sizes and forms are called dendrimers (Almuqbil et al., 2020). Since their infancy, dendrimers have been thought to be promising as novel drug delivery vehicles because of their nanometric size. Drugs and dendrimers can associate in a variety of ways, including covalent and noncovalent interactions. Simple encapsulation inside dendrimers that increases the solubility of lipophilic medications in water or electrostatic interactions between the surface and charged drugs are examples of noncovalent interactions (Caminade & Turrin, 2014).

The word "dendrimer" comes from the Greek word "dendron," which means "tree." This makes sense given that they usually have a lot of branching units in their structure and the word "mer," which means "segment," which characterizes the synthetic (Schlüter & Rabe, 2000). Three primary parts make up their basic structure: a central core, repeating branching units, and terminal groups, which offer surface functionality that can be changed. The creation of a globular structure and the generation of the dendrimer are determined by the rise in the number of repeated branching units (Almuqbil et al., 2020).

11.1.1 Overview of lung cancer

Dendrimers being used for pulmonary medication administration. Due to their high density and diverse range of functional groups on their surface, dendrimers are multifunctional and offer a great deal of potential for drug delivery applications. An intriguing architecture for dendrimers is provided by their segmental spherical construction and well-defined molecular structure. The other segment can be identified as the target group if the active drug molecule is connected to one of these segments. This double functional group increases the

Nanoengineered Therapeutics for Lung Cancer: Advanced Drug Delivery Strategies.
DOI: https://doi.org/10.1016/B978-0-443-44585-9.00014-7

pharmaceutical efficiency of the medicine by ensuring that its plasma level remains at the correct level for a longer period of time (Wilkins et al., 2005).

Lung cancer remains one of the leading causes of cancer-related mortality worldwide, accounting for nearly one in five cancer deaths annually. The disease is broadly classified into nonsmall cell lung cancer (NSCLC), which constitutes approximately 85% of cases, and small cell lung cancer (SCLC), which accounts for the remaining 15%. NSCLC itself is further subdivided into adenocarcinoma, squamous cell carcinoma, and large cell carcinoma, each with distinct histopathological and molecular features (Sasaki et al., 2024). In recent years, molecular profiling has transformed the therapeutic landscape of lung cancer, revealing actionable mutations such as epidermal growth factor receptor (EGFR) mutations, ALK rearrangements, KRAS mutations, and BRAF alterations. These molecular drivers not only influence prognosis but also determine responsiveness to targeted therapies (Harada et al., 2023). However, despite advances in precision medicine, challenges such as tumor heterogeneity, acquired resistance, and poor drug penetration into tumor tissues continue to limit therapeutic success. The integration of nanotechnology-based platforms such as dendrimers provides a promising avenue to overcome these biological barriers by enabling molecularly guided and receptor-specific drug delivery (Ramos et al., 2025).

11.1.2 Limitations of conventional therapies

Various strategies have been used to reduce the impact of resistance and manage this threat, but their effectiveness and safety remain a mystery. New anti-infectious strategies to combat multidrug resistance (MDR) are being investigated in this context. One such promising strategy for combating bacterial resistance is the use of novel antibiotics and their combination with new β-lactamase inhibitors, phage treatment, antimicrobial peptides, nanoparticles, and antisense antimicrobial therapies (Rhodes et al., 2017). For patients with few treatment options and unmet needs—such as those who cannot endure the status quo or have not achieved their goals with traditional therapy—novel therapies may provide alternatives. A crucial part of health technology assessment (HTA) evaluations, cost-effectiveness studies, must take into consideration the particular risks, expenses, and advantages of different patient subgroups. Ensuring that the event risk and benefit profile is representative of the actual population is crucial (Lai et al., 2020).

11.1.3 Role of nanotechnology in cancer treatment

Cancer has grown to be a major global menace to humanity. With the highest death rate, this illness is the second most prevalent. It has been more obvious in recent years that advancements in pharmacological therapy cannot be guaranteed only by the creation of new medications. Therefore, the primary objective of anticancer drug delivery is to attain a high intratumor drug concentration while minimizing drug exposure to healthy tissue. By delivering them via nanoparticles, these issues can be resolved. In contrast to healthy cells, it increases permeability and retention in malignant cells. It also aids in providing the targeted cells with a gradual and regulated release. By reducing their toxicity to physiological tissues and maintaining long-term, controlled therapeutic levels of the drug, drug carriers at the nanoscale present opportunities to improve the therapeutic index of pharmacological molecules. It would optimize the absorption, biodistribution, metabolism, and excretion (ADME) profile while reducing the concentration of drug intake (Levine & Kroemer, 2008).

11.1.4 Tumor microenvironment in lung cancer

The tumor microenvironment (TME) in lung cancer plays a pivotal role in disease progression, metastasis, and therapeutic resistance. It comprises cancer-associated fibroblasts, immune cells such as tumor-associated macrophages (TAMs), extracellular matrix (ECM) components, abnormal vasculature, and hypoxic regions. Hypoxia-inducible factors (HIFs) promote angiogenesis and metabolic reprogramming, while acidic pH conditions and elevated glutathione levels create a distinct biochemical environment. These pathological features significantly influence drug distribution and cellular uptake (Genova et al., 2022). Dendrimers can be strategically engineered to respond to these microenvironmental cues, such as acidic pH or redox gradients, allowing selective drug release within tumor tissue. Furthermore, dendrimers functionalized with ligands targeting overexpressed receptors within the TME, such as folate receptors or EGFR, can enhance tumor-specific accumulation. A comprehensive understanding of the lung cancer microenvironment therefore strengthens the rationale for dendrimer-based targeted delivery systems (Madeddu et al., 2022).

11.2 Dendrimers: Structure and characteristics

The systemic disposition and biomedical performance of dendrimers are governed by a complex interplay of architectural and physicochemical parameters that collectively define their in vivo behavior. Unlike conventional linear polymers, dendrimers possess a highly ordered and monodisperse structure that allows precise control over molecular weight, size distribution, and surface functionality. However, even within this controlled framework, subtle variations in core composition, branching density, terminal functional groups, and surface modifications can dramatically influence pharmacokinetics, biodistribution, cellular uptake, and toxicity. For instance, the attachment of polyethylene glycol (PEG) chains to surface amine groups does not merely neutralize positive charge; it simultaneously increases hydrodynamic diameter, enhances steric stabilization, reduces protein adsorption, and modifies hydrophilicity. Such interdependence of properties makes it difficult to attribute biological outcomes to a single structural feature (Zhang et al., 2007).

Although dendrimers are often described as structurally uniform, the field has evolved to include diverse chemical backbones such as polyamidoamine, polypropylene imine (PPI), carbosilane, polylysine, and phosphorus-based dendrimers. Compared to other nanoscale synthetic constructs such as carbon nanotubes or fullerene derivatives, dendrimers offer superior architectural precision, lower structural heterogeneity, and greater tunability of surface chemistry. This controlled multivalency enables simultaneous conjugation of drugs, targeting ligands, imaging agents, and stealth polymers within a single nanosystem. Importantly, their pharmacokinetic characteristics—including circulation half-life, renal clearance threshold, plasma protein binding, and tissue penetration—are tightly correlated with molecular size and surface charge density. Smaller dendrimers below approximately 5–6 nm tend to undergo rapid renal filtration, whereas higher-generation dendrimers exhibit prolonged systemic retention and enhanced tumor accumulation via the enhanced permeability and retention (EPR) effect.

The versatility of dendrimers has expanded their applications beyond drug delivery into imaging, gene therapy, photodynamic therapy, and neutron capture therapy. For example, boron-containing dendrimers have been investigated as carriers for boron neutron capture therapy, where precise tumor targeting is essential for therapeutic selectivity. Similarly, dendrimer-based imaging probes conjugated with gadolinium ions have demonstrated enhanced contrast efficiency in magnetic resonance imaging. Another significant advancement includes the development of dendritic "boxes," in which peripheral functional groups are engineered to entrap guest molecules within internal cavities, thereby improving drug stability and controlled release. Antibody–dendrimer and peptide–dendrimer conjugates further exemplify the adaptability of these systems, enabling receptor-specific targeting in oncological applications (Abbasi et al., 2014).

11.2.1 Definition and unique structural features of dendrimers

Dendrimers are synthetic, highly branched macromolecules characterized by a central core, repeated branching units organized in successive layers known as generations, and terminal functional groups located on the periphery. The synthesis of dendrimers follows either divergent or convergent strategies, allowing stepwise growth with precise architectural control. Each generational increase results in exponential growth in the number of surface groups and near-linear growth in molecular diameter. This predictable scaling distinguishes dendrimers from hyperbranched polymers, which lack strict structural uniformity. The generation number directly determines molecular weight, globular diameter, surface charge density, and drug loading capacity. Lower-generation dendrimers typically display flexible, open conformations with fewer terminal groups, whereas higher generations exhibit compact, globular structures with dense surface functionalities (Yang et al., 2021).

The concentric, tree-like architecture creates internal void spaces capable of accommodating small molecules through hydrogen bonding, hydrophobic interactions, or electrostatic forces. This internal cavity structure is particularly advantageous for solubilizing poorly water-soluble drugs such as paclitaxel or camptothecin. Additionally, the multivalent presentation of functional groups enhances binding affinity toward biological targets through cooperative interactions, a phenomenon known as the multivalency effect. In biological systems, multivalency can significantly amplify receptor–ligand interactions, enabling stronger and more selective cellular targeting compared to monovalent ligands (Senapati et al., 2018).

While the central core is often considered structurally passive, it can impart unique physicochemical and biological properties depending on its chemical composition. For example, porphyrin-core dendrimers exhibit intrinsic photodynamic activity due to the light-absorbing properties of the porphyrin moiety, making them suitable for photodynamic cancer therapy. Upon irradiation, these dendrimers generate reactive oxygen species capable of inducing tumor cell apoptosis. Similarly, cores derived from cyclophane structures enable host–guest chemistry, facilitating selective encapsulation of aromatic compounds and improving drug stability (Abbas et al., 2022; Trewyn et al., 2007). Other core variations, such as ethylenediamine or ammonia cores in poly(amidoamine) (PAMAM) dendrimers, influence overall symmetry and internal packing density. Multifunctional cores containing imaging isotopes or fluorescent chromophores further extend dendrimer functionality into theranostic applications.

The branching units serve as the structural backbone of dendrimers and are crucial determinants of flexibility, degradability, and synthetic feasibility. Amine-based branching units, such as those in PAMAM dendrimers, confer hydrophilicity and positive surface charge, facilitating electrostatic interaction with negatively charged nucleic acids for gene delivery applications. Ester-based branches, in contrast, may introduce hydrolytic degradability, enabling controlled biodegradation under physiological conditions. Ether-based or aromatic branches provide structural rigidity and enhanced thermal stability, which may be advantageous for imaging or diagnostic applications requiring structural robustness. The synthetic route selected—whether Michael addition reactions, amidation steps, or click chemistry—depends heavily on the chemical nature of branching units (Percec et al., 1996).

Flexibility of dendrimers is another crucial structural parameter influencing biological interaction. Flexible aliphatic branches allow conformational adaptation upon interaction with cellular membranes, potentially enhancing cellular internalization through endocytosis. Conversely, rigid aromatic branches yield compact and stable architectures that may reduce nonspecific membrane interactions. The degree of flexibility also impacts the ability of dendrimers to encapsulate drugs within internal cavities, as more flexible frameworks can expand slightly to accommodate guest molecules (Naji et al., 2022).

Stability considerations are equally important, particularly for biomedical applications requiring predictable degradation profiles. Dendrimers containing amide linkages typically exhibit strong chemical stability, whereas ester-containing dendrimers may undergo hydrolysis under physiological conditions, providing controlled biodegradability. Enzymatically cleavable linkages can be strategically incorporated to allow site-specific degradation within TMEs rich in proteases or esterases. Thermal stability varies depending on backbone chemistry; carbosilane dendrimers, for instance, demonstrate exceptional resistance to thermal and oxidative degradation due to the strength of silicon–carbon bonds. In contrast, polycaprolactone-based dendritic structures may undergo hydrolytic degradation, rendering them suitable for temporary therapeutic applications (Woodruff & Hutmacher, 2010).

Beyond classic examples, phosphorus-containing dendrimers represent another emerging class characterized by P=N and P–O linkages, offering intrinsic flame retardancy and unique coordination properties. These dendrimers have been investigated for immunomodulatory effects and metal ion chelation. Similarly, glycodendrimers incorporating carbohydrate moieties on their surface mimic biological glycocalyx structures and enhance selective targeting of lectin receptors on cancer cells (Wang et al., 2022). Such structural diversity demonstrates that dendrimers are not merely spherical nanocarriers but highly programmable molecular platforms capable of being tailored for specific therapeutic objectives. Collectively, the intricate structural design of dendrimers—defined by core composition, generational growth, branching chemistry, and terminal functionalization—provides unmatched control over size, shape, multivalency, and functional density. This architectural precision enables rational engineering of dendrimers for targeted drug delivery, imaging, gene therapy, and combination therapeutic strategies while maintaining tunable pharmacokinetic and safety profiles (Zaman et al., 2023).

11.2.2 Types of dendrimers in drug delivery

The classification of dendrimers used in drug delivery is generally based on their generational architecture, chemical backbone composition, surface functionalization, and physicochemical behavior. The concept of "generation" refers to the number of repeated branching cycles emanating from the central core toward the periphery. Each successive generation adds a new layer of branching units, resulting in exponential growth in the number of surface functional groups and a predictable increase in molecular diameter. Although some inconsistencies exist in the literature regarding generation numbering, the most widely accepted definition considers the number of cascade or focal points between the core and terminal surface. Accordingly, a fifth-generation (G5) dendrimer contains five branching layers between its core and outer surface (Brandenburg, 2001).

The generational increase produces profound structural and biological consequences. With each higher-generation, the dendrimer transitions from a relatively open, flexible structure to a compact, globular nanosphere with densely packed terminal functionalities. For instance, a G0 dendrimer derived from an ethylenediamine core may possess four terminal groups, whereas a G5 analog can exhibit up to 128 terminal functional groups depending on branching multiplicity. This exponential amplification of surface groups enhances multivalency, drug conjugation capacity, and targeting ligand density. Simultaneously, the hydrodynamic diameter increases from approximately 1–2 nm in lower generations to 5–10 nm or higher in

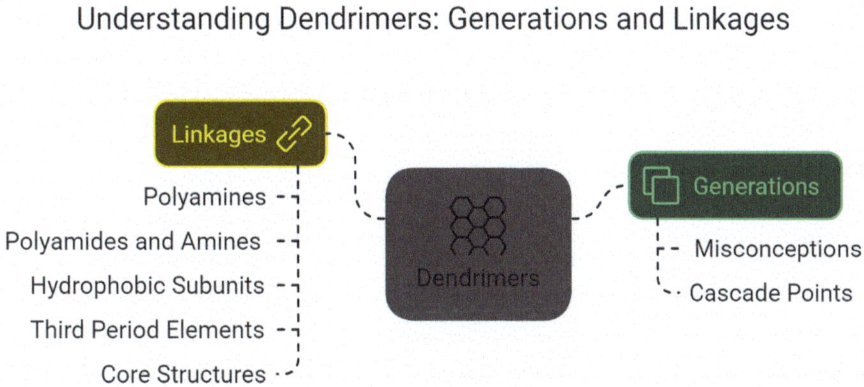

Figure 11.1
Schematic representation of dendrimer architecture highlighting linkages and generational growth. Conceptual illustration of dendrimers showing key structural components, including core structures and linkages (polyamines, polyamides/amines, hydrophobic subunits, and third-period elements) and their hierarchical generational expansion, with cascade branching points and common misconceptions indicated.

advanced generations, placing dendrimers within the optimal size range for tumor targeting through the EPR effect. However, increased surface charge density, especially in amine-terminated dendrimers, may also elevate cytotoxicity, necessitating careful generational selection during formulation design.

Beyond generational classification, dendrimers are distinguished by their chemical backbone linkages. Polyamine-based dendrimers such as PPI possess tertiary amine branching points, while PAMAM dendrimers incorporate both amide and amine linkages. Hydrophobic dendrimers constructed from poly(aryl ether) frameworks exhibit rigid backbones and enhanced structural stability. More advanced designs include carbosilane dendrimers containing silicon–carbon bonds and phosphorus-based dendrimers incorporating P=N or P–O linkages. Additionally, carbohydrate-based dendrimers and calixarene-centered dendrimers introduce biologically inspired recognition elements and host–guest properties into the system (Jang & Kataoka, 2005). The diversity of chemical scaffolds allows researchers to tailor dendrimers for specific therapeutic objectives, ranging from hydrophilic drug solubilization to gene delivery and imaging applications. Fig. 11.1 is a schematic representation of dendrimer architecture highlighting linkages and generational growth.

11.2.2.1 Poly(amidoamine)

PAMAM dendrimers are among the most extensively studied and commercially available dendrimer systems in biomedical research. They are synthesized through a divergent growth method, typically beginning with an ethylenediamine or ammonia core. The synthesis involves repeated Michael addition reactions between amine groups and methyl acrylate, followed by amidation with ethylenediamine, producing alternating layers of tertiary amine branching points and amide linkages. Each full synthetic cycle doubles the number of surface amine groups, leading to exponential surface functionality growth and predictable increases in molecular weight and size (Svenson & Tomalia, 2012).

PAMAM dendrimers are highly water-soluble due to their abundant amine and amide groups, which enable hydrogen bonding with aqueous environments. The presence of primary amine termini at physiological pH results in a positive surface charge, facilitating electrostatic interaction with negatively charged biological membranes and nucleic acids. This property makes PAMAM dendrimers particularly suitable for gene delivery applications, where they form stable complexes known as dendriplexes with DNA or small interfering ribonucleic acid (siRNA). However, this same cationic nature may disrupt cellular membranes, highlighting the importance of surface modification strategies such as acetylation or PEGylation to reduce cytotoxicity (Oledzka et al., 2023). Structurally, PAMAM dendrimers adopt a spherical conformation at higher generations due to intramolecular hydrogen bonding and back-folding of terminal groups. This globular morphology creates internal nanocavities capable of encapsulating hydrophobic drugs such as paclitaxel, camptothecin, and doxorubicin. The ability to both encapsulate drugs internally and conjugate them covalently to surface groups provides dual drug loading strategies. In lung cancer therapy, PAMAM-based systems have been explored for targeted delivery of chemotherapeutic agents, siRNA molecules targeting oncogenic pathways, and imaging agents for theranostic applications (Zenze et al., 2023).

Atomic force microscopy (AFM) and transmission electron microscopy (TEM) studies have provided valuable insights into the morphology and assembly behavior of PAMAM dendrimers. Investigations into self-assembled multilayer films formed by alternating deposition of oppositely charged PAMAM dendrimers and metal complexes such as K2PtCl4 demonstrated linear increases in film thickness with each deposited layer, confirming controlled multilayer ordering. High-generation PAMAM dendrimers such as G9 have exhibited entangled microfiber-like networks under tapping-mode AFM, indicating the ability of dendrimers to participate in supramolecular assembly processes (Carrière et al., 2009). These structural properties underscore the adaptability of PAMAM dendrimers in drug delivery and nanofabrication contexts.

11.2.2.2 Polypropylene imine

PPI dendrimers represent another important class of polyamine-based dendrimers widely investigated for drug and gene delivery applications. Their synthesis typically follows a divergent growth approach beginning with an ethylenediamine core. The process involves a double Michael addition of acrylonitrile to primary amine groups, generating nitrile-terminated half generations. Subsequent catalytic hydrogenation using Raney nickel converts nitrile groups into primary amines, completing one full generation cycle. Repetition of these steps allows synthesis of higher-generation PPI dendrimers such as PPI-5.0G (Kesharwani et al., 2014).

Compared to PAMAM dendrimers, PPI dendrimers possess a more hydrophobic internal structure due to the absence of amide linkages and the presence of tertiary amine branching units. This structural difference results in distinct physicochemical properties, including altered flexibility and higher internal hydrophobicity. Consequently, PPI dendrimers may demonstrate enhanced capacity for encapsulating hydrophobic drugs while still maintaining surface amine groups suitable for conjugation or nucleic acid binding. Purification of PPI dendrimers is critical to ensure monodispersity and complete reaction conversion. Techniques such as Sephadex G25 gel filtration chromatography and high-performance liquid chromatography (HPLC) using C18 columns are commonly employed. The presence of a single chromatographic peak confirms structural uniformity and purity. In lung cancer therapy, PPI dendrimers have been explored for the targeted delivery of gemcitabine and siRNA molecules. Surface functionalization with targeting ligands such as mannose or folic acid enhances tumor specificity and reduces off-target toxicity. However, as with other cationic dendrimers, unmodified PPI systems may exhibit membrane-disruptive behavior, necessitating careful surface engineering (Prasher et al., 2026).

11.2.2.3 Carbosilane dendrimers

Carbosilane dendrimers are characterized by a backbone composed of alternating carbon and silicon atoms linked via strong C–Si bonds. These dendrimers exhibit exceptional thermal stability, oxidative resistance, and structural rigidity due to the high bond dissociation energy of silicon–carbon linkages. The hydrophobic nature of carbosilane frameworks makes them particularly suitable for applications requiring stable, nondegradable scaffolds (Kovalev & Fujii, 2005).

Although inherently hydrophobic, carbosilane dendrimers can be rendered hydrophilic through surface modification with polar functional groups such as hydroxyl, carboxyl, or amine moieties. Functional groups such as Si–Cl, Si–H, and allylsilane ($Si–CH_2CH=CH_2$) allow versatile chemical transformations, enabling conjugation of bioactive molecules, peptides, or imaging agents. In drug delivery applications, carbosilane dendrimers have demonstrated utility in gene therapy due to their ability to condense DNA and protect it from enzymatic degradation. Their structural robustness also makes them suitable for applications involving photodynamic therapy or magnetic nanoparticle hybrid systems. Additionally, the incorporation of silicon confers unique optical and electronic properties that may be exploited in theranostic platforms combining drug delivery with imaging capabilities. However, their hydrophobic core necessitates careful formulation strategies to ensure biocompatibility and efficient dispersion in aqueous biological environments.

11.2.3 Physicochemical properties relevant to targeted delivery

The success of dendrimer-based targeted drug delivery systems depends heavily on their physicochemical characteristics, which dictate biodistribution, cellular uptake, clearance pathways, and therapeutic efficacy. Particle size plays a central role in determining tumor accumulation and systemic circulation time. Dendrimers within the 5–10 nm range exhibit prolonged blood circulation while avoiding rapid renal filtration, thereby enhancing passive tumor targeting via the EPR effect. Conversely, smaller dendrimers may be rapidly eliminated through glomerular filtration, reducing systemic exposure but limiting tumor accumulation. Surface charge significantly influences interactions with biological membranes and serum proteins. Positively charged dendrimers readily interact with negatively charged cell membranes, promoting endocytosis but also increasing cytotoxic potential. Neutral or slightly negative surface modifications reduce nonspecific protein adsorption and prolong circulation time. Hydrophobicity affects membrane permeability and internal drug encapsulation capacity, while hydrophilicity enhances systemic compatibility and solubility (Ezhilarasan et al., 2022).

Active targeting strategies involve conjugating specific ligands such as folic acid, peptides, antibodies, or aptamers to dendrimer surfaces. These ligands bind selectively to overexpressed receptors on cancer cells, enabling receptor-mediated endocytosis. Passive targeting, on the other hand, relies on intrinsic nanoparticle properties such as size, surface charge, and shape to achieve preferential tumor accumulation through vascular permeability differences (Shi et al., 2010). Ultimately, the therapeutic performance of dendrimer systems arises from a synergistic integration of structural design, surface chemistry, generational architecture, and physicochemical optimization. Through rational engineering of these parameters, dendrimers can be customized to achieve precise targeting, controlled drug release, minimized systemic toxicity, and enhanced anticancer efficacy in lung cancer therapy (Ezhilarasan et al., 2022).

11.3 Dendrimers in targeted lung cancer therapy

The therapeutic management of lung cancer continues to face major limitations, including poor tumor selectivity, systemic toxicity of chemotherapeutic agents, MDR, and inadequate penetration of drugs into dense tumor tissues. Conventional chemotherapy distributes cytotoxic drugs nonspecifically throughout the body, affecting both malignant and healthy proliferating cells, which results in dose-limiting toxicities such as myelosuppression, cardiotoxicity, and gastrointestinal damage. Therefore, precise spatial and temporal control over drug distribution has become a fundamental objective in modern oncology. The development of advanced drug delivery systems capable of site-specific accumulation and controlled release is critical for improving therapeutic outcomes.

Polymer-based nanocarriers have significantly enhanced drug pharmacokinetics and biodistribution by prolonging circulation time, reducing rapid renal clearance, and enabling sustained release. However, traditional polymeric systems often suffer from polydispersity, limited surface functional control, and unpredictable degradation behavior. In contrast, dendrimers offer an unprecedented level of structural precision, monodispersity, and multivalent functionality. Their well-defined molecular weight, globular nanoscale size, high aqueous solubility, and tunable surface chemistry make them particularly attractive for lung cancer therapy. The polyvalent surface enables simultaneous attachment of therapeutic agents, targeting ligands, imaging probes, and stealth polymers, creating multifunctional nanoplatforms capable of precise tumor targeting (Senapati et al., 2018).

An important aspect in evaluating dendrimers for pulmonary oncology is their biopermeability across biological barriers. Lung tumors are often surrounded by abnormal vasculature and ECM components that limit drug penetration. Dendrimers, owing to their nanoscale dimensions and modifiable surface charge, can traverse endothelial gaps and penetrate tumor interstitium more efficiently than larger polymeric carriers. Moreover, their ability to interact with cellular membranes via electrostatic interactions facilitates internalization through endocytic pathways. Nevertheless, excessive positive surface charge may disrupt cellular membranes, underscoring the necessity of surface engineering strategies to balance cellular uptake with safety.

11.3.1 Mechanisms of targeted drug delivery

Targeted drug delivery in lung cancer aims to maximize intratumoral drug concentration while minimizing systemic exposure and toxicity. Dendrimer-based targeting strategies are broadly categorized into passive and active mechanisms, both of which exploit unique pathological features of tumor tissues. Due to their nanoscale size, dendrimers can accumulate preferentially in tumor tissues through passive mechanisms, while surface modification enables receptor-specific active targeting. The combination of these mechanisms enhances therapeutic precision and reduces off-target effects.

At the cellular level, dendrimers can enter tumor cells primarily through endocytosis, including clathrin-mediated, caveolae-mediated, and macropinocytosis pathways. Once internalized, dendrimers may escape endosomal compartments via the "proton sponge" effect, particularly in the case of amine-rich systems such as PAMAM dendrimers. The buffering capacity of tertiary amines leads to osmotic swelling and rupture of endosomes, releasing the therapeutic payload into the cytoplasm. This mechanism is especially advantageous in gene therapy applications targeting oncogenic pathways in lung cancer. Passive and active targeting strategies therefore operate in synergy, ensuring both preferential tumor localization and efficient intracellular drug release (Rajani et al., 2019).

11.3.2 Passive targeting: Enhanced permeability and retention effect

Passive targeting relies on the EPR effect, a hallmark of solid tumors, including lung carcinoma. Rapid tumor growth results in the formation of irregular, poorly aligned, and highly permeable blood vessels with fenestrations ranging from 100 to 800 nm. These abnormal vascular structures permit extravasation of nanoscale carriers such as dendrimers into the tumor interstitium. Simultaneously, deficient lymphatic drainage within tumor tissues prevents efficient clearance of accumulated nanoparticles, resulting in prolonged retention.

Dendrimers are particularly well-suited to exploit the EPR effect due to their controllable size and surface characteristics. Generations typically ranging from G4 to G6 exhibit diameters compatible with optimal tumor accumulation while avoiding rapid renal elimination. Surface modifications such as PEGylation further enhance circulation time by reducing opsonization and recognition by the mononuclear phagocyte system. In lung cancer models, PEGylated dendrimer–doxorubicin conjugates have demonstrated prolonged systemic half-life and increased tumor uptake compared to free drug formulations. However, it is important to recognize that the magnitude of the EPR effect varies between patients and tumor types, particularly in heterogeneous lung tumors with dense stromal components. Hypoxic and fibrotic regions may restrict nanoparticle penetration. Therefore, optimizing dendrimer size, flexibility, and surface hydrophilicity is essential for maximizing passive tumor accumulation. Adjustments in surface charge can influence vascular interaction and tissue diffusion, further improving therapeutic index (Caminade & Turrin, 2014).

11.3.3 Active targeting: Functionalization with ligands and antibodies

Active targeting enhances selectivity by decorating dendrimer surfaces with ligands that recognize receptors overexpressed on lung cancer cells. This strategy exploits molecular differences between malignant and healthy tissues to achieve receptor-mediated endocytosis. The high density of terminal functional groups on dendrimers enables multivalent presentation of targeting ligands, significantly increasing binding affinity through cooperative interactions. Folate receptor alpha is frequently overexpressed in certain subtypes of NSCLC. Dendrimers functionalized with folic acid exhibit enhanced uptake in folate receptor-positive cells via receptor-mediated endocytosis. Similarly, EGFR, commonly overexpressed in lung adenocarcinoma, represents an important therapeutic target. Dendrimer conjugation with antiEGFR antibodies or peptide fragments allows selective binding to EGFR-positive tumor cells, improving intracellular drug delivery and reducing nonspecific toxicity (Sarma et al., 2024).

Beyond folate and EGFR targeting, other ligands such as transferrin, arginine–glycine–aspartic acid (RGD) peptides targeting integrins, and aptamers specific to tumor-associated antigens have been investigated. For example, integrin $\alpha v\beta 3$ is highly expressed in tumor angiogenic vessels; dendrimers modified with RGD peptides can bind selectively to these receptors, enhancing vascular targeting and tumor penetration. Antibody-conjugated dendrimers further provide specificity toward human epidermal growth factor receptor 2 (HER2) or programmed death-ligand 1 (PD-L1) expressing tumor cells. Such targeted systems reduce systemic exposure and improve therapeutic selectivity by minimizing uptake in nonmalignant tissues (Thanh & Green, 2010). The multivalency of dendrimers allows simultaneous attachment of multiple ligand types, enabling targeting of heterogeneous tumor cell populations. This is particularly valuable in lung cancer, where intratumoral heterogeneity contributes to therapeutic resistance.

11.3.4 Dual and multifunctionalized dendrimers for enhanced targeting

The integration of passive and active targeting strategies has led to the development of dual and multifunctionalized dendrimer systems capable of addressing complex tumor biology. These advanced platforms combine tumor-homing ligands, stimuli-responsive linkers, imaging agents, and therapeutic payloads within a single nanoscale construct. By exploiting both the EPR effect and receptor-mediated endocytosis, dual-targeted dendrimers achieve superior tumor accumulation and cellular internalization compared to single-mode systems.

For instance, a dendrimer may be PEGylated to prolong circulation and exploit passive accumulation, while simultaneously conjugated with folic acid or antiEGFR antibodies to facilitate active targeting. Incorporation of pH-sensitive hydrazone linkers allows drug release specifically within the acidic TME or endosomal compartments. Redox-sensitive disulfide bonds can enable intracellular drug release in response to elevated glutathione concentrations in cancer cells. This multilevel targeting ensures that the drug remains stable during systemic circulation but is released efficiently upon reaching tumor tissue. Furthermore, dendrimers can serve as theranostic agents by codelivering chemotherapeutic drugs and imaging molecules such as fluorescent dyes or magnetic resonance contrast agents. This approach allows simultaneous tumor visualization and therapy monitoring, facilitating personalized treatment strategies (Wang et al., 2018). In lung cancer management, such systems hold promise for real-time assessment of drug delivery efficiency and early detection of therapeutic response.

Multifunctional dendrimers also offer potential in overcoming MDR, a common obstacle in advanced lung cancer. By codelivering chemotherapeutic agents with siRNA targeting resistance-related genes such as MDR1 or Bcl-2, dendrimers can restore drug sensitivity and enhance apoptosis. This combinatorial strategy addresses tumor heterogeneity and adaptive resistance mechanisms more effectively than monotherapy approaches. Overall, dendrimer-based targeted systems represent a sophisticated evolution in nanomedicine, integrating structural precision, biological responsiveness, and multifunctionality. Their ability to navigate TME barriers, selectively bind to cancer cells, and release therapeutic agents in a controlled manner underscores their transformative potential in lung cancer therapy. Continued optimization of surface chemistry, ligand density, and release mechanisms will further enhance their clinical applicability and therapeutic efficacy.

11.3.5 Dendrimer generations and structural considerations in lung cancer targeting

Following the discussion of dual and multifunctional dendrimers, it is important to elaborate on how dendrimer generation and architecture influence their performance in targeted lung cancer therapy. Dendrimers are synthesized in successive layers called generations, and each generation increases molecular weight, diameter, surface functional groups, and internal cavity volume. These structural parameters directly impact pharmacokinetics, tumor accumulation, and cellular uptake. Lower-generation dendrimers such as G2 and G3 typically exhibit smaller diameters and faster renal clearance, which may limit their tumor retention but reduce systemic toxicity. In contrast, higher generations such as G5 or G6 possess larger sizes and increased surface amine density, which enhance drug loading capacity and multivalent ligand attachment but may increase cytotoxicity due to strong positive surface charge. In lung cancer therapy, selecting an optimal generation is crucial for balancing tumor accumulation and safety. For example, a G4 or G5 PAMAM dendrimer often demonstrates sufficient nanoscale dimensions to exploit the EPR effect while maintaining manageable toxicity after surface modification. The internal cavities of higher-generation dendrimers also allow encapsulation of hydrophobic chemotherapeutics such as paclitaxel or docetaxel, which are frequently used in NSCLC. Therefore, inserting a section discussing generation-dependent behavior will help readers understand how structural tuning directly affects therapeutic performance and clinical translation potential (Kedar et al., 2025).

11.3.6 Surface engineering and biocompatibility enhancement

To expand the chapter further, a detailed discussion on surface engineering strategies is essential, particularly in the context of lung cancer therapy where pulmonary tissues are highly sensitive to inflammatory responses. Native amine-terminated dendrimers often exhibit cytotoxicity due to membrane disruption caused by strong electrostatic interactions with negatively charged cell membranes. Consequently, surface modification plays a pivotal role in improving biocompatibility while preserving targeting efficiency (Sharma et al., 2023).

PEGylation is one of the most widely employed strategies to reduce immunogenicity and prolong systemic circulation. PEG chains create a hydrophilic steric barrier that reduces protein adsorption and opsonization, thereby minimizing rapid clearance by macrophages. In lung cancer models, PEGylated dendrimer–drug conjugates have shown improved pharmacokinetic profiles and reduced off-target toxicity compared to unmodified dendrimers. Acetylation and hydroxylation of terminal amine groups also reduce cytotoxicity by neutralizing positive charge while maintaining adequate drug loading capacity. Another promising strategy is the incorporation of biodegradable linkages into the dendrimer backbone. Biodegradable dendrimers degrade into smaller, nontoxic fragments that can be eliminated via renal pathways, reducing long-term accumulation risks. Including this section after multifunctional dendrimers will provide a logical progression from targeting efficiency to safety optimization, which is critical for lung cancer therapeutics (Sharmila et al., 2025).

11.3.7 Stimuli-responsive dendrimers in lung cancer therapy

An additional section that significantly enhances chapter depth is the incorporation of stimuli-responsive dendrimer systems. Lung tumors exhibit distinct microenvironmental features such as acidic pH, elevated glutathione levels, hypoxia, and overexpression of specific enzymes. These characteristics can be exploited to design smart dendrimer systems that release drugs selectively in tumor tissues. pH-responsive dendrimers utilize acid-labile linkers such as hydrazone or imine bonds to ensure drug release under acidic tumor conditions while remaining stable in physiological blood pH. For example, doxorubicin conjugated via hydrazone linkage to a dendrimer remains stable in circulation but releases rapidly in acidic endosomal compartments of lung cancer cells. Redox-responsive systems incorporate disulfide bonds that are cleaved in the presence of high intracellular glutathione concentrations, enabling cytoplasmic drug release. Enzyme-responsive dendrimers can be designed to degrade in the presence of tumor-associated proteases, enhancing site-specific activation. These smart systems improve therapeutic index and reduce systemic toxicity, making them highly relevant for lung cancer treatment, where minimizing pulmonary and cardiac side effects is essential. This section should be placed after surface engineering, as it builds upon the concept of controlled and selective release (Lin et al., 2022).

11.3.8 Dendrimers for gene therapy and RNA interference in lung cancer

To further expand the chapter toward 10,000 words, a comprehensive discussion on dendrimer-mediated gene delivery should be included. Lung cancer progression is driven by genetic mutations such as KRAS mutations, EGFR alterations, ALK rearrangements, and overexpression of antiapoptotic genes. Dendrimers, particularly amine-rich PAMAM systems, are excellent candidates for gene delivery due to their ability to complex negatively charged nucleic acids through electrostatic interactions. Dendrimer–siRNA complexes can silence oncogenes or drug resistance genes in lung cancer cells. For example, siRNA targeting vascular endothelial growth factor (VEGF) can reduce tumor angiogenesis, while siRNA against Bcl-2 enhances apoptosis. The proton sponge effect of dendrimers facilitates endosomal escape, ensuring efficient cytoplasmic delivery of genetic material. Similarly, dendrimer-mediated clustered regularly interspaced short palindromic repeats–CRISPR-associated protein 9 (CRISPR-Cas9) delivery represents an emerging strategy for gene editing in lung tumors. Gene therapy integration into dendrimer platforms is particularly relevant in overcoming resistance to tyrosine kinase inhibitors in EGFR-mutated lung cancer. This section can follow stimuli-responsive systems to demonstrate how dendrimers are not limited to chemotherapy but extend into molecular-level therapeutic interventions (Liu et al., 2023).

11.3.9 Pulmonary route of administration and inhalable dendrimer systems

Considering that lung cancer affects the respiratory system directly, a dedicated section on pulmonary delivery of dendrimer-based systems would substantially enrich the chapter. Inhalation therapy provides localized drug delivery directly to lung tumors, potentially reducing systemic toxicity. Dendrimers can be formulated into aerosolizable nanoparticles or dry powder inhalers for targeted deposition in bronchial and alveolar regions. Particle size plays a crucial role in pulmonary deposition, with aerodynamic diameters between 1 and 5 μm being optimal for deep lung delivery. Dendrimer-based nano-in-microparticle formulations can achieve this deposition profile. Additionally, surface modifications can enhance mucus penetration and reduce clearance by alveolar macrophages. Localized dendrimer delivery may be particularly beneficial for early-stage lung tumors or postsurgical adjuvant therapy. This section logically follows gene therapy discussions and highlights route-specific advantages unique to lung cancer treatment (Aggarwal et al., 2026).

11.3.10 Overcoming multidrug resistance in lung cancer

MDR represents one of the most critical barriers to successful chemotherapy in both NSCLC and SCLC. Despite initial responsiveness to platinum-based chemotherapy, taxanes, or targeted tyrosine kinase inhibitors, many patients eventually develop acquired resistance that leads to tumor progression and poor prognosis. MDR arises from multiple interrelated mechanisms, including overexpression of ATP-binding cassette (ABC) transporters, dysregulation of apoptotic pathways, enhanced DNA repair capacity, epithelial–mesenchymal transition (EMT), cancer stem cell enrichment, and altered TMEal signaling. A comprehensive understanding of these resistance pathways is essential to appreciate the unique role dendrimers can play in overcoming therapeutic failure.

One of the most extensively studied mechanisms of resistance in lung cancer is the overexpression of efflux transporters such as P-glycoprotein (P-gp, encoded by MDR1), MDR-associated proteins (MRPs), and breast cancer resistance protein (BCRP). These transporters actively pump chemotherapeutic agents out of tumor cells, reducing intracellular drug accumulation below cytotoxic thresholds. Drugs such as paclitaxel, doxorubicin, and vinorelbine are particularly susceptible to efflux-mediated resistance. Dendrimer-based nanocarriers can bypass this limitation by facilitating endocytosis-mediated cellular entry rather than relying on passive diffusion. Once internalized, dendrimer–drug conjugates are compartmentalized within endosomes and subsequently released into the cytoplasm, thereby partially evading immediate recognition by efflux pumps (Park et al., 2023).

More importantly, dendrimers provide a platform for combinatorial delivery strategies aimed at silencing efflux transporter expression at the genetic level. For instance, PAMAM dendrimers complexed with siRNA targeting MDR1 can effectively reduce P-gp expression in resistant lung cancer cells. When codelivered with paclitaxel, this approach not only increases intracellular drug retention but also restores drug sensitivity. The multivalent surface of dendrimers enables simultaneous conjugation of chemotherapeutic drugs and nucleic acids, ensuring synchronized intracellular release. Such dual-delivery systems can be engineered using stimuli-responsive linkers that release siRNA in the cytosol and cytotoxic agents in proximity to their molecular targets, thereby maximizing therapeutic synergy. Alterations in apoptotic signaling pathways also contribute significantly to drug resistance. Overexpression of anti-apoptotic proteins such as Bcl-2, Bcl-xL, and survivin inhibits programmed cell death, even in the presence of DNA damage induced by cisplatin or other chemotherapeutics. Dendrimers can be designed to codeliver platinum drugs and gene-silencing agents directed against these antiapoptotic proteins. For example, cisplatin-loaded dendrimers combined with antisurvivin siRNA have demonstrated enhanced induction of caspase activation and increased apoptotic cell death in resistant lung tumor models. This strategy addresses resistance at both the cytotoxic and molecular regulatory levels, providing a multipronged therapeutic intervention (Ge et al., 2025).

Enhanced DNA repair capacity is another hallmark of chemoresistant lung cancer. Upregulation of nucleotide excision repair proteins and homologous recombination pathways enables tumor cells to repair platinum-induced DNA crosslinks efficiently. Dendrimer-mediated delivery of small molecule inhibitors targeting DNA repair enzymes, in combination with DNA-damaging agents, offers a rational approach to sensitize tumors. For example, coencapsulation of cisplatin with PARP inhibitors within a dendrimer platform can potentiate DNA damage accumulation and trigger apoptosis in resistant NSCLC cells. Additionally, dendrimers can be utilized to target cancer stem cells (CSCs), a subpopulation believed to drive relapse and resistance. CSCs exhibit high expression of drug transporters and robust self-renewal capacity. Surface-functionalized dendrimers targeting stem cell markers such as CD44 or CD133 can selectively deliver cytotoxic agents or gene-silencing molecules to this resistant fraction, potentially preventing tumor recurrence. The high drug loading capacity, precise structural control, and ability to incorporate multiple therapeutic modalities position dendrimers as sophisticated tools to counteract the multifactorial nature of MDR in lung cancer. By simultaneously modulating efflux mechanisms, apoptotic pathways, DNA repair systems, and CSC survival, dendrimer-based systems move beyond conventional monotherapy and embody a systems-level therapeutic strategy (Zheng et al., 2024).

11.3.11 Tumor microenvironment modulation by dendrimers

The TME in lung cancer plays a decisive role in disease progression, metastasis, immune evasion, and therapeutic resistance. It consists of a complex network of cancer-associated fibroblasts, immune cells, endothelial cells, ECM components, and soluble signaling molecules. Hypoxia, acidic extracellular pH, abnormal vasculature, elevated interstitial fluid pressure, and dense stromal barriers collectively hinder effective drug delivery and promote tumor survival. Therefore, successful lung cancer therapy increasingly requires not only direct cytotoxicity against cancer cells but also modulation of the TME. Hypoxia is a defining feature of rapidly growing lung tumors due to inadequate vascularization. Low oxygen levels activate HIFs, which upregulate angiogenic factors such as VEGF and promote metabolic reprogramming, invasion, and resistance to radiotherapy and chemotherapy. Dendrimers can be engineered to deliver hypoxia-responsive agents or oxygen-generating compounds to counteract this hostile microenvironment. For instance, dendrimers loaded with nitric oxide donors can transiently enhance tumor blood flow and vascular permeability, improve oxygenation, and facilitate deeper drug penetration. Nitric oxide also exerts direct cytotoxic and antiangiogenic effects at controlled concentrations, contributing to tumor growth inhibition (Srinivasarao et al., 2025).

The acidic extracellular pH of lung tumors, typically ranging from 6.5 to 6.9, results from increased glycolytic metabolism and lactic acid production. This acidic environment can reduce the efficacy of weakly basic chemotherapeutic drugs by limiting cellular uptake. Dendrimers equipped with pH-responsive moieties can exploit this feature to achieve site-specific drug release. Moreover, dendrimers can be designed to buffer extracellular acidity, thereby improving drug stability and cellular penetration. Such adaptive systems enhance therapeutic precision by responding dynamically to TME conditions. Immune suppression within the lung TME significantly impairs antitumor immunity. TAMs often adopt an M2 phenotype that promotes angiogenesis, tissue remodeling, and immune evasion. Reprogramming TAMs toward a proinflammatory M1 phenotype has emerged as a promising immunotherapeutic strategy. Dendrimer-based platforms can selectively target TAMs using ligands that recognize macrophage surface receptors and deliver immunomodulatory agents such as Toll-like receptor agonists or cytokine genes. This reprogramming enhances antigen presentation, stimulates cytotoxic T cell activation, and shifts the immune balance toward tumor rejection (Chen et al., 2025).

In addition to macrophage modulation, dendrimers can serve as carriers for immune checkpoint inhibitors or small interfering RNAs targeting PD-L1 expression in tumor cells. By reducing PD-L1 levels locally within the TME, dendrimer systems may enhance T cell-mediated cytotoxicity while minimizing systemic immune-related adverse effects. This localized immunomodulation aligns with modern immunotherapy paradigms and may complement existing monoclonal antibody therapies. The dense ECM in lung tumors also presents a physical barrier to drug penetration. Collagen fibers and hyaluronic acid accumulation increase interstitial pressure and restrict nanoparticle diffusion. Dendrimers can be functionalized with ECM-degrading enzymes or matrix-modulating agents to transiently remodel stromal barriers, thereby enhancing intratumoral distribution of therapeutic payloads. Collectively, dendrimers extend beyond their conventional role as passive drug carriers and function as dynamic modulators of the TME. By improving perfusion, reversing hypoxia, neutralizing acidity, reprogramming immune cells, and remodeling stromal barriers, dendrimer-based systems address the biological complexity of lung cancer at multiple levels. Incorporating these microenvironment-focused strategies into therapeutic design provides a comprehensive framework that integrates chemotherapy, gene therapy, and immunotherapy within a single multifunctional nanoplatform, thereby advancing the paradigm of precision oncology (Edirisinghe et al., 2025).

11.3.12 Architecturally engineered and hybrid dendrimers in drug delivery

Beyond conventional classifications such as PAMAM, PPI, carbosilane, and polyester dendrimers, recent advances in nanotechnology have led to the development of architecturally engineered and hybrid dendritic systems that expand the functional capabilities of dendrimers in drug delivery. These advanced dendrimers are not defined solely by their chemical composition but by deliberate structural modifications that tailor their biological performance, mechanical properties, and therapeutic behavior. Such innovations represent a shift from simply "what dendrimer is used" to "how the dendrimer architecture is engineered" for a specific therapeutic objective.

One important category includes Janus dendrimers, which possess two chemically distinct faces within the same molecule. This asymmetric structure allows simultaneous incorporation of hydrophilic and hydrophobic domains, enabling self-assembly into dendrimersomes—vesicle-like nanostructures resembling liposomes but with enhanced stability and structural precision. These systems can encapsulate both hydrophilic and hydrophobic drugs within a single carrier, making them particularly useful for combination therapy. Their membrane-like organization also allows better mimicry of biological systems, facilitating cellular uptake and controlled release.

Another innovative class is core-shell dendrimers, where the core and surface are engineered with different functional properties. For example, a hydrophobic core may enhance drug encapsulation efficiency, while a hydrophilic or PEGylated shell improves circulation time and reduces immunogenicity. This spatial separation of functions allows precise control over pharmacokinetics and biodistribution. Core engineering can also involve the incorporation of stimuli-sensitive moieties, transforming the dendrimer into a programmable nanocarrier capable of responding to pathological conditions.

Dendronized polymers represent a hybrid architecture in which dendrons (wedge-shaped dendritic segments) are grafted onto linear polymer backbones. This design combines the flexibility and mechanical strength of polymers with the multivalency of dendrimers. Such systems exhibit enhanced drug loading capacity and improved stability compared to conventional dendrimers. Their semiflexible structure also reduces steric hindrance, potentially lowering cytotoxicity while maintaining high surface functionality.

In addition, metallodendrimers have emerged as a unique subclass in which metal ions are incorporated either within the core or along the branches. These systems provide dual functionality—serving both as drug carriers and as therapeutic or imaging agents. For example, metal-containing dendrimers may exhibit intrinsic anticancer, antimicrobial, or catalytic activity. Their ability to participate in redox reactions or generate reactive oxygen species adds a therapeutic dimension beyond passive drug transport. Furthermore, self-immolative dendrimers represent a novel concept in which the dendritic structure undergoes cascade disassembly after a specific trigger, leading to rapid and amplified drug release. Unlike gradual diffusion-based release systems, these dendrimers provide sharp and controlled therapeutic bursts, which can be advantageous in diseases requiring immediate pharmacological action.

Collectively, architecturally engineered and hybrid dendrimers demonstrate that modern dendrimer classification extends beyond traditional chemical families. By manipulating symmetry, core composition, branching patterns, and hybridization with other nanomaterials, researchers can design highly specialized drug delivery systems with tunable properties. This architectural evolution underscores the adaptability of dendrimers and highlights their expanding role in next-generation nanomedicine.

11.4 Drug loading and release mechanisms

11.4.1 Encapsulation and conjugation strategies

The two main methods for loading drugs into dendrimers are encapsulation and conjugation, each of which has special benefits for targeted drug delivery in the treatment of lung cancer. Encapsulation is the process of physically trapping drug molecules inside the dendritic structure. Both hydrophobic and hydrophilic pharmaceuticals can be accommodated by using the interior cavities and surface functional groups of dendrimers. For example, the hydrophilic surface of dendrimers like PAMAM ensures stability in aqueous environments, making them suitable for intravenous administration, while the hydrophobic core of these dendrimers can encapsulate hydrophobic chemotherapeutic agents like doxorubicin or paclitaxel. Dendrimer formation, size, and the drug's physicochemical characteristics are some of the variables that affect encapsulation efficiency (Wang et al., 2011). Contrarily, conjugation entails the covalent bonding of drug molecules to the functional groups on the surface of dendrimers, frequently via enzymatically cleavable or pH-sensitive connections such as amide, hydrazone, or ester bonds. Because the medicine is only released under specified circumstances, like the acidic TME or in the presence of particular enzymes, this approach enables controlled

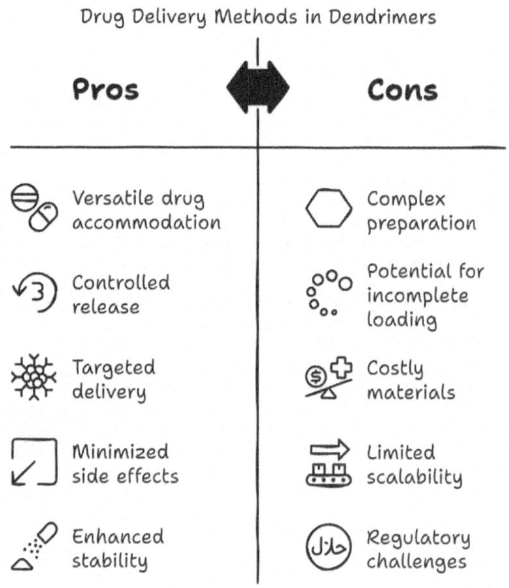

Figure 11.2

Advantages and limitations of dendrimer-based drug delivery systems.
Summary of the major pros and cons of dendrimers in pharmaceutical applications. Advantages include versatile drug accommodation, controlled release, targeted delivery, minimized side effects, and enhanced solubility, while limitations include complex preparation, potential toxicity upon high loading, high material cost, limited scalability, and regulatory challenges.

drug release, enhanced stability, and decreased systemic toxicity. Conjugating methotrexate and cisplatin to dendrimers, for instance, allows for tailored distribution while reducing off-target effects. The specificity of drug delivery to cancer cells is further improved by conjugation, which makes it easier for targeting ligands like folic acid or antibodies to adhere. Fig. 11.2 lists down advantages and limitations of dendrimer-based drug delivery systems.

11.4.2 pH-responsive and stimuli-triggered release mechanisms

Because they allow the controlled release of therapeutic drugs in response to particular physiological circumstances or external stimuli, pH-responsive and stimuli-triggered release mechanisms are essential for attaining site-specific medication delivery in lung cancer therapy. In contrast to normal tissues (pH 7.4), tumor tissues frequently have a slightly acidic pH (6.5–7.0), which can be used to trigger pH-responsive medication release. It is possible to build dendrimers with pH-sensitive connections, including hydrazone, acetal, or imine bonds, which hydrolyze in the acidic TME and release the medication while remaining stable at physiological pH. For instance, doxorubicin conjugated to dendrimers via hydrazone bonds ensures targeted administration and reduces systemic toxicity by remaining stable in the bloodstream while releasing in the acidic environment of cancer cells. Apart from pH-responsive systems, dendrimers can be engineered to release medications in response to enzyme activity, temperature, or redox potential (Li et al., 2015).

Disulfide bonds used by redox-responsive dendrimers are stable in the extracellular environment but cleave when high intracellular glutathione levels, which are present in cancer cells, are present. This improves the effectiveness of treatment by enabling the selective release of medications within cancer cells. To improve drug delivery in cancer treatment, thermoresponsive dendrimers can be engineered to release medications in reaction to localized hyperthermia. When exposed to mild hyperthermia (40°C–42°C), which can be created with external heat sources, thermoresponsive dendrimers, for example, can be incorporated with chemotherapeutic drugs and made to release their payload. The usage of enzyme-cleavable bonds, including peptide bonds, that are broken down by particular enzymes that are overexpressed in tumor tissues, like matrix metalloproteinases (MMPs) or cathepsins, is a component of enzymatically induced release mechanisms. By accurately releasing the medication at the intended location, these stimuli-triggered release mechanisms maximize therapeutic efficacy and reduce off-target effects (Fernandes et al., 2018). Overall, dendrimers are very effective nanocarriers for targeted lung cancer therapy because of their pH-responsive and stimuli-triggered release mechanisms, which offer complex techniques for controlled drug delivery.

11.4.3 Codelivery of drugs and genes using dendrimers

Dendrimers' special structure allows them to transmit genetic material like siRNA or MicroRNA (miRNA) and chemotherapeutic agents concurrently, making codelivery of medications and genes a viable approach in lung cancer therapy. Caitic dendrimers, like PAMAM, electrostatically bind nucleic acids to create stable complexes known as dendriplexes, whereas dendrimers can conjugate hydrophilic medications to their surface or encapsulate hydrophobic drugs within their core. By functionalizing with ligands like folic acid or antibodies, these complexes prevent the payload from degrading and enable targeted delivery to cancer cells. The medication and gene are released into the acidic endosomal environment after being ingested through receptor-mediated endocytosis, allowing for synergistic effects such as increased cytotoxicity and gene silence. By codelivering medications like doxorubicin with siRNA that targets MDR genes, this strategy is very successful in reducing MDR and regaining drug sensitivity. Furthermore, combination treatments such as delivering cisplatin with miRNA to block carcinogenic pathways are made possible by codelivery, which improves therapeutic efficacy while lowering systemic toxicity. There are still difficulties, nevertheless, such as the possible cytotoxicity of cationic dendrimers, synthesis scalability problems, and regulatory barriers to clinical translation (Pan et al., 2019). Future research aims to fully utilize dendrimer-based codelivery systems in tailored and targeted lung cancer treatments by reducing toxicity by surface modifications, enhancing manufacturing procedures, and advancing preclinical and clinical investigations. Table 11.1 lists the therapeutic applications of different dendrimers in lung cancer.

11.5 Biological evaluation and safety considerations of dendrimers in lung cancer

The successful translation of dendrimer-based nanocarriers from laboratory research to clinical lung cancer therapy requires comprehensive biological evaluation, including in vitro cytotoxicity studies, in vivo pharmacokinetics, biodistribution profiling, pulmonary compatibility assessment, and long-term safety analysis. Although dendrimers exhibit remarkable versatility in drug loading and targeting, their biological behavior is highly influenced by generation number, surface charge, size, and functional modifications. Therefore, understanding their interactions with cancer cells, normal lung tissue, immune components, and systemic organs is critical for safe and effective therapeutic application (Li et al., 2022).

In vitro evaluation represents the first stage of biological validation. Cytotoxicity studies are commonly performed using lung cancer cell lines such as A549 (adenocarcinoma), NCI-H460 (large cell carcinoma), and H1299 (nonsmall cell lung carcinoma). For instance, PAMAM dendrimer–doxorubicin conjugates have demonstrated significantly enhanced cytotoxicity in A549 cells compared to free doxorubicin due to improved intracellular uptake and prolonged retention. In another example, miR-34a-loaded PAMAM dendrimers exhibited strong antiproliferative effects by restoring tumor suppressor gene expression and inducing apoptosis. Similarly, camptothecin conjugated to generation 3.5 PAMAM dendrimers reduced cell survival and migration more effectively than the free drug, illustrating the advantage of dendrimer-mediated intracellular drug delivery. Cellular uptake studies using fluorescence microscopy and flow cytometry have further confirmed that cationic dendrimers efficiently enter lung cancer cells via receptor-mediated endocytosis, especially when functionalized with targeting ligands such as folic acid or antiEGFR antibodies. However, these studies also reveal that high-generation cationic dendrimers may disrupt cell membranes due to strong electrostatic interactions, leading to nonspecific toxicity, which underscores the need for careful surface engineering.

Beyond anticancer efficacy, hemocompatibility and membrane interaction studies are essential. Native amine-terminated PAMAM dendrimers, particularly higher generations (G5–G7), have been associated with hemolysis and plasma protein aggregation because of their strong positive charge. To mitigate this issue, surface modifications such as PEGylation or acetylation have been employed. PEGylated dendrimers demonstrate reduced protein adsorption, prolonged circulation time, and decreased immune recognition. For example, PEG-modified polylysine dendrimers carrying doxorubicin via pH-sensitive linkers have shown improved tumor targeting while minimizing systemic toxicity. These findings illustrate that minor chemical modifications can dramatically alter biological responses.

Table 11.1: Therapeutic applications of different dendrimers in lung cancer.

S.no.	Drug/carrier	Dendrimer type	Applications	References
1	**Doxorubicin**	PAMAM dendrimer (G4)	Increased cytoxic action.	Almuqbil et al. (2020)
2	**Bcl-xL shRNA**	PAMAM dendrimer	PAMAM demonstrated no toxicity to cells and a robust binding with the protection of genetic materials.	Fox et al. (2018)
3	**miR-34a**	PAMAM dendrimer	Outstanding antiproliferative and intracellular gene transfection capabilities.	Pooja et al. (2020)
4	**Camptothecin (CPT)**	PAMAM dendrimer (G3.5)	The conjugation with CPT reduced cell survival and motility and boosted toxicity against A549 malignant cells by 4.5 times compared to natural CPT.	Pooja et al. (2020)
5	Cisplatin (cis-diammine-dichloroplatinum(II) (**HuR siRNA and CDDP)codelivery**	PAMAM dendrimer (G4)	The cells showed higher levels of apoptosis as a result of their efficient absorption of Den-PEI-CDDPsiGLO Nanoparticles (NPs).	(Kedar et al., 2025)
6	**Gadolinium (III)**	PAMAM dendrimer (G5)	Conjugate successfully displayed high antifouling ability, cytocompatibility, and good biosafety.	(Genova et al., 2022)
7	**AntiEGFR**	PAMAM dendrimer (G7)	Significant therapeutic benefit and stable binding of antiEGFR-dendrimer immobilized surface with cancer cells.	(Levine & Kroemer, 2008; Li et al., 2022)
8	**EndoNt**	PAMAM dendrimer (G7)	Compared to aEpCAM-immobilized surfaces, EndoNt exhibited capture efficiencies of more than 1.8 times in SW2 cells and 2.5 times in NCI-H69 cells.	Fox et al. (2018)

(continued on next page)

Table 11.1: Therapeutic applications of different dendrimers in lung cancer—cont'd

S.no.	Drug/carrier	Dendrimer type	Applications	References
9	**Paclitaxel (PTX)**	PAMAM dendrimer	Compared to the PAMAMPTX combination and PTX alone, GE-PAMAM-PTX exhibited a strong antiproliferative effect and a cellular uptake capacity that was 2.5 times greater.	(Kharwade et al., 2022)
10	**PTX**	PAMAM dendrimer (G4)	These dendrimer conjugates have shown remarkable efficacy in both cellular internalization and cell death.	(Oledzka et al., 2023)
11	**PTX**	PAMAM dendrimer (G4)	VES was successful in making PTX more soluble.	Almuqbil et al. (2020)
12	**Gold NP**	PAMAM dendrimer	The probe's sensitivity increases two to three times.	Kim et al. (2009)
13	**Guanidinylated PPI dendrimers**	PPI dendrimer	Following incubation, the dendrimeric derivatives reduced cell viability by 80%, according to the cytotoxic assay.	Tsogas et al. (2007)
14	**Gemcitabine**	PPI dendrimer	GmcH loading in the mannosylated PPI dendritic system may improve the ability to target anticancer drugs in the lungs for effective lung cancer treatment.	Kim et al. (2009)
15	**siRNA**	PPI dendrimer	The delivery system's formulation enhances cisplatin's antitumor activity in vivo.	Tsogas et al. (2007)
16	**Doxorubicin**	PLL dendrimer	Compared to other inhalable drug delivery systems that contain nonbiodegradable pieces, the Complex is an attractive inhalable drug delivery vector.	(Liu et al., 2023)

(*continued on next page*)

Table 11.1: Therapeutic applications of different dendrimers in lung cancer—cont'd

S.no.	Drug/carrier	Dendrimer type	Applications	References
17	"KG6E" with glutamic acid modification	PLL dendrimer (G6)	The conjugate's binding affinity for the cell line is strong.	Fox et al. (2018)
18	Doxorubicin	Magnetic dendrimer	The carrier's entrapment efficiency was 84.28% and its drug loading potential was 8.4%.	Almuqbil et al. (2020)
19	siRNA		A total of 70% of MDM2 could be silenced by the delivery technique, which also effectively bonded with siRNA.	Tsogas et al. (2007)

EGFR, epidermal growth factor recepto; *G5*, fifth-generation; *PAMAM*, poly(amidoamine); *PPI*, polypropylene imine.

In vivo pharmacokinetics and biodistribution studies further determine therapeutic feasibility. Dendrimer size plays a crucial role in circulation and clearance pathways. Lower-generation dendrimers (≤G3) are rapidly cleared via renal filtration due to their small hydrodynamic diameter, whereas higher-generation dendrimers accumulate preferentially in tumors via the EPR effect. In lung cancer models, G4 and G5 PAMAM dendrimers have demonstrated prolonged systemic half-life and enhanced tumor deposition compared to free drugs. Biodistribution studies using radiolabeled or fluorescently tagged dendrimers reveal accumulation in the liver and spleen due to uptake by the reticuloendothelial system, a common challenge for nanocarriers. Surface neutralization and PEGylation significantly reduce this off-target accumulation, thereby enhancing tumor specificity. Magnetic dendrimer formulations have also been investigated to further improve targeted localization using external magnetic guidance, demonstrating promising tumor-selective drug accumulation in experimental models (Kharwade et al., 2022).

Because lung cancer therapy may involve inhalational delivery, pulmonary compatibility is particularly relevant. Dendrimers can be engineered for aerosolization by optimizing particle aerodynamic diameter within the respirable range (1–5 μm) through formulation into dry powder inhalers or nebulizable solutions. Poly(L-lysine) dendrimers have been studied as inhalable carriers, showing acceptable deposition in alveolar regions and improved local drug concentration. However, interaction with lung surfactant, mucus barriers, and alveolar macrophages significantly influences performance. Studies indicate that excessive positive surface charge may trigger macrophage activation and inflammatory cytokine release. Therefore, partially neutralized or PEG-coated dendrimers exhibit better mucus penetration and reduced inflammatory responses. Redox-responsive dendrimers have also shown promise in pulmonary delivery, where intracellular glutathione levels in cancer cells trigger drug release while maintaining extracellular stability.

Toxicity and immunogenicity remain critical challenges. Generation-dependent toxicity is one of the most widely reported concerns in dendrimer research. High-generation amine-terminated dendrimers can induce oxidative stress, mitochondrial damage, and apoptosis in normal cells. Complement activation and cytokine release have also been observed in some formulations, raising concerns regarding systemic inflammatory responses. To overcome these limitations, biodegradable dendrimers incorporating ester or disulfide linkages have been developed, enabling controlled degradation and reduced long-term accumulation. Additionally, carbohydrate-modified dendrimers and hydroxyl-terminated surfaces exhibit significantly lower cytotoxicity compared to primary amine-terminated variants. For example, N-acetyl-D-glucosamine-conjugated PAMAM dendrimers have demonstrated improved biocompatibility while maintaining targeting efficiency in lung cancer models.

Codelivery systems further highlight both the potential and complexity of dendrimer-based therapy. Simultaneous delivery of chemotherapeutic agents and siRNA targeting MDR genes has shown synergistic tumor suppression. In particular, PAMAM-based systems delivering cisplatin alongside MDR-targeted siRNA have restored drug sensitivity in resistant lung cancer cells. However, ensuring stability of nucleic acid complexes in circulation while preventing off-target gene-silencing remains a delicate balance requiring optimized charge ratios and surface shielding. Despite encouraging preclinical findings, clinical translation of dendrimers in lung cancer remains limited. Regulatory challenges include reproducibility of large-scale synthesis, batch-to-batch consistency, long-term toxicity profiling, and comprehensive immunogenicity evaluation. Nevertheless, advancements in surface engineering, biodegradable dendrimer platforms, and multifunctional theranostic systems continue to move the field closer to clinical applicability (Tsogas et al., 2007).

11.6 Future perspectives and challenges

Dendrimers have emerged as highly versatile nanoplatforms with the potential to transform the therapeutic landscape of lung cancer. Their precisely defined architecture, tunable surface functionality, and multivalent binding capacity provide significant advantages over conventional drug delivery systems. As highlighted by Scherpereel et al. (2010), dendrimers offer improved accuracy in tumor targeting and the capacity to integrate therapeutic agents with diagnostic probes, enabling multimodal and personalized treatment approaches. However, despite encouraging preclinical findings, the translation of dendrimer-based systems into routine clinical practice remains limited. Bridging this gap requires addressing scientific, regulatory, manufacturing, and translational challenges while capitalizing on emerging technological innovations.

11.6.1 Advancement toward personalized and precision nanomedicine

One of the most promising future directions for dendrimers in lung cancer therapy lies in their integration with precision oncology. Lung cancer is a molecularly heterogeneous disease characterized by genetic alterations such as EGFR mutations, ALK rearrangements, KRAS mutations, and mesenchymal–epithelial transition factor (MET)amplifications. Dendrimer systems can be engineered to target specific molecular subtypes by conjugating ligands or antibodies directed against these biomarkers. For instance, dendrimers functionalized with antiEGFR moieties could selectively deliver chemotherapeutic agents or siRNA to EGFR-mutant tumors, thereby enhancing therapeutic specificity while minimizing systemic toxicity. In addition, the multivalency of dendrimers enables simultaneous delivery of multiple agents tailored to a patient's tumor profile. A single dendrimer platform could codeliver a tyrosine kinase inhibitor, a gene-silencing construct targeting resistance pathways, and an imaging probe for real-time monitoring. Such combinatorial precision strategies align with the growing emphasis on individualized cancer treatment and adaptive therapeutic regimens.

11.6.2 Expansion into gene editing and advanced nucleic acid delivery

Beyond conventional chemotherapy, dendrimers are expected to play an increasingly important role in nucleic acid therapeutics. Their cationic surface groups facilitate electrostatic complexation with DNA, siRNA, mRNA, and CRISPR-Cas gene editing systems. In lung cancer, gene editing technologies targeting oncogenic drivers such as KRAS or correcting tumor suppressor gene mutations represent an exciting frontier. Dendrimer-mediated CRISPR delivery could enable localized gene editing within tumor tissues, reducing systemic exposure and off-target genetic alterations. Furthermore, dendrimers may enhance the stability and intracellular delivery of mRNA-based therapeutics, which have gained significant attention in recent years. The ability to shield nucleic acids from enzymatic degradation while promoting efficient endosomal escape underscores their value as next-generation gene delivery vehicles. As noted by Almuqbil et al. (2020), optimizing dendrimer formulations to enhance bioavailability and transfection efficiency remains a key research priority.

11.6.3 Theranostics and real-time treatment monitoring

The concept of theranostics, integrating therapy and diagnostics within a single nanoplatform, represents a transformative application of dendrimers. Their branched architecture permits the simultaneous conjugation of imaging agents such as fluorescent dyes, radionuclides, or magnetic resonance contrast agents alongside therapeutic payloads. In lung cancer management, this approach may facilitate early tumor detection, real-time monitoring of drug distribution, and assessment of therapeutic response. For example, a dendrimer carrying both a cytotoxic drug and a radiolabeled imaging probe could allow clinicians to visualize tumor accumulation using positron emission tomography while administering targeted chemotherapy. This dual functionality enhances treatment precision and enables rapid adjustments to therapeutic regimens based on observed biodistribution patterns. The development of such image-guided nanotherapeutics may significantly improve clinical outcomes by reducing ineffective treatments and optimizing dosing strategies.

11.6.4 Overcoming toxicity and biocompatibility concerns

Despite their promise, dendrimers face substantial challenges related to toxicity, particularly those associated with their cationic surface groups. Positively charged dendrimers can disrupt cellular membranes, induce hemolysis, and trigger inflammatory responses, especially within delicate pulmonary tissues. Surface modification strategies such as PEGylation, acetylation, or conjugation with biocompatible polymers are critical to mitigating these adverse effects. Future research must focus on developing biodegradable dendrimer backbones that degrade into nontoxic metabolites after fulfilling their therapeutic function. Such degradable systems would reduce long-term accumulation risks and enhance safety profiles. Additionally, comprehensive in vivo toxicological evaluations, including chronic exposure studies and immunogenicity assessments, are necessary to establish clinical safety standards (Chen et al., 2025).

11.6.5 Regulatory and translational barriers

Nanomedicines, including dendrimer-based systems, are subject to rigorous regulatory scrutiny due to their complex structures and multifaceted mechanisms of action. Regulatory agencies require detailed characterization of physicochemical properties, stability, biodistribution, pharmacokinetics, and long-term toxicity. The absence of standardized guidelines for nanocarrier evaluation further complicates approval pathways. Batch-to-batch reproducibility remains a major challenge because even minor variations in dendrimer synthesis can influence therapeutic performance. Establishing robust quality control measures and scalable manufacturing protocols is essential for regulatory approval. Moreover, translating promising preclinical findings into clinical success requires well-designed clinical trials that account for interpatient variability in tumor vascularization and EPR effect magnitude.

11.6.6 Scaling up and cost-effective manufacturing

The synthesis of higher-generation dendrimers involves multiple iterative reaction steps, purification processes, and stringent control of reaction conditions. These complex procedures increase production costs and limit large-scale commercialization. Developing simplified synthetic routes, automated manufacturing technologies, and green chemistry approaches could significantly improve scalability. Industrial translation also requires optimization of formulation stability, storage conditions, and shelf-life. Ensuring that dendrimer-based therapeutics maintain structural integrity and drug loading efficiency over extended periods is crucial for practical deployment. Economic feasibility will ultimately determine their accessibility in clinical settings, particularly in low- and middle-income healthcare systems.

11.6.7 Pulmonary delivery challenges and opportunities

For lung cancer therapy, direct pulmonary administration represents a logical and potentially transformative approach. However, delivering dendrimer systems effectively through the lung epithelium presents biological challenges, including mucociliary clearance, alveolar macrophage uptake, and enzymatic degradation. Future innovations may involve surface engineering strategies that enhance mucus penetration and reduce immune clearance. The development of inhalable dry powder formulations or nebulized dendrimer aerosols with optimized aerodynamic properties could improve localized deposition within tumor-bearing lung regions. Such targeted pulmonary delivery may reduce systemic toxicity and increase drug concentration at the disease site (Chen et al., 2025).

11.6.8 Market acceptance and clinical adoption

Beyond scientific and regulatory hurdles, successful clinical implementation depends on acceptance by healthcare providers and patients. Educational initiatives highlighting the safety, efficacy, and advantages of dendrimer-based therapies will be essential for widespread adoption. Collaboration among academic researchers, pharmaceutical industries, and regulatory authorities can accelerate translational progress. Moreover, integrating dendrimer systems with existing therapeutic modalities, including immunotherapy and targeted small molecule inhibitors, may facilitate gradual clinical introduction rather than complete therapeutic replacement. Demonstrating clear clinical superiority in terms of survival benefits, reduced toxicity, or improved quality of life will ultimately determine their market success.

11.7 Conclusion

Dendrimers represent a cutting-edge advancement in nanotechnology, offering significant potential as nanocarriers for targeted lung cancer therapy. Their unique branched architecture, high drug loading capacity, and surface modifiability enable precise delivery to tumor sites while minimizing systemic toxicity. Dendrimer-based systems have shown promise in enhancing the efficacy of chemotherapeutics, improving pharmacokinetics, and overcoming MDR in lung cancer. Despite certain limitations such as toxicity at higher generations and challenges in large-scale production, ongoing research and surface engineering strategies are rapidly addressing these concerns. As innovations continue, dendrimers stand poised to revolutionize lung cancer treatment, paving the way for safer, more effective, and patient-specific therapeutic approaches that could significantly improve clinical outcomes and quality of life.

References

Abbas, M., Ovais, M., Atiq, A., Ansari, T. M, Xing, R., Spruijt, E., & Yan, X. (2022). Tailoring supramolecular short peptide nanomaterials for antibacterial applications. *Coordination Chemistry Reviews, 460*, 214481. https://doi.org/10.1016/j.ccr.2022.214481.

Abbasi, E., Aval, S. F., Akbarzadeh, A., Milani, M., Nasrabadi, H. T., Joo, S. W., Hanifehpour, Y., Nejati-Koshki, K., & Pashaei-Asl, R. (2014). Dendrimers: Synthesis, applications, and properties. *Nanoscale Research Letters, 9*(1), 1–10. https://doi.org/10.1186/1556-276X-9-247.

Aggarwal, P., Ishan, Chawla, P. A., & Chawla, V. (2026). *Dendrimers for the management of COPD* (pp. 247–265). Elsevier BV. https://doi.org/10.1016/b978-0-443-43946-9.00011-2.

Almuqbil, R. M., Heyder, R. S., Bielski, E. R., Durymanov, M., Reineke, J. J., & Da Rocha, S. R. P. (2020). Dendrimer conjugation enhances tumor penetration and efficacy of doxorubicin in extracellular matrix-expressing 3D lung cancer models. *Molecular Pharmaceutics, 17*(5), 1648–1662. https://doi.org/10.1021/acs.molpharmaceut.0c00083.

Brandenburg, A. (2001). The inverse cascade and nonlinear alpha-effect in simulations of isotropic helical hydromagnetic turbulence. *The Astrophysical Journal, 550*(2), 824–840. https://doi.org/10.1086/319783.

Caminade, A. M., & Turrin, C. O. (2014). Dendrimers for drug delivery. *Journal of Materials Chemistry B, 2*(26), 4055–4066. https://doi.org/10.1039/c4tb00171k.

Carrière, D., Belloni, L., Demé, B., Dubois, M., Vautrin, C., Meister, A., & Zemb, T. (2009). In-plane distribution in mixtures of cationic and anionic surfactants. *Soft Matter, 5*(24), 4983. https://doi.org/10.1039/b912286a.

Chen, Q., Sun, J., Ling, S., Yang, H., Li, T., Yang, X., Li, M., Du, M., Zhang, Y., Li, C., & Wang, Q. (2025). Tumor microenvironment-responsive nano-immunomodulators for enhancing chimeric antigen receptor-T cell therapy in lung cancer. *ACS Nano, 19*(8), 8212–8226. https://doi.org/10.1021/acsnano.4c17899.

Edirisinghe, D. T., Kaur, J., Lee, Y. Q., Lim, H. X., Lo, S. W. T., Vishupriyaa, S., Tan, E. W., Wong, R. S. Y., & Goh, B. H. (2025). The role of the tumour microenvironment in lung cancer and its therapeutic implications. *Medical Oncology, 42*(6). https://doi.org/10.1007/s12032-025-02765-7.

Ezhilarasan, D., Lakshmi, T., & Mallineni, S. K. (2022). Nano-based targeted drug delivery for lung cancer: Therapeutic avenues and challenges. *Nanomedicine, 17*(24), 1855–1869. https://doi.org/10.2217/nnm-2021-0364.

Fernandes, C., Suares, D., & Yergeri, M. C. (2018). Tumor microenvironment targeted nanotherapy. *Frontiers in Pharmacology, 9*. https://doi.org/10.3389/fphar.2018.01230.

Fox, L. J., Richardson, R. M., & Briscoe, W. H. (2018). PAMAM dendrimer - cell membrane interactions. *Advances in Colloid and Interface Science, 257*, 1–18. https://doi.org/10.1016/j.cis.2018.06.005.

Ge, M., Chen, X. Y., Huang, P., Fleishman, J. S., Yang, D. H., Wu, Z. X., Ke, Z. F., & Chen, Z. S. (2025). Understanding and overcoming multidrug resistance in cancer. *Nature Reviews Clinical Oncology, 22*(10), 760–780. https://doi.org/10.1038/s41571-025-01059-1.

Genova, C., Dellepiane, C., Carrega, P., Sommariva, S., Ferlazzo, G., Pronzato, P., Gangemi, R., Filaci, G., Coco, S., & Croce, M. (2022). Therapeutic implications of tumor microenvironment in lung cancer: Focus on immune checkpoint blockade. *Frontiers in Immunology, 12*. https://doi.org/10.3389/fimmu.2021.799455.

Harada, G., Yang, S.-R., Cocco, E., & Drilon, A. (2023). Rare molecular subtypes of lung cancer. *Nature Reviews Clinical Oncology, 20*(4), 229–249. https://doi.org/10.1038/s41571-023-00733-6.

Jang, W. D., & Kataoka, K. (2005). Bioinspired applications of functional dendrimers. *Journal of Drug Delivery Science and Technology, 15*(1), 19–30. https://doi.org/10.1016/s1773-2247(05)50003-0.

Kaminskas, L. M., Kelly, B. D., McLeod, V. M., Sberna, G., Owen, D. J., Boyd, B. J., & Porter, C. J. H. (2011). Characterisation and tumour targeting of PEGylated polylysine dendrimers bearing doxorubicin via a pH labile linker. *Journal of Controlled Release, 152*(2), 241–248. https://doi.org/10.1016/j.jconrel.2011.02.005.

Kedar, P., Saraf, A., Maheshwari, R., & Sharma, M. (2025). Advances in dendritic systems and dendronized nanoparticles: Paradigm shifts in cancer targeted therapy and diagnostics. *Molecular Pharmaceutics, 22*(1), 28–57. https://doi.org/10.1021/acs.molpharmaceut.4c00856.

Kesharwani, P., Tekade, R. K., & Jain, N. K. (2014). Formulation development and in vitro-in vivo assessment of the fourth-generation PPI dendrimer as a cancer-targeting vector. *Nanomedicine, 9*(15), 2291–2308. https://doi.org/10.2217/nnm.13.210.

Kharwade, R., Badole, P., Mahajan, N., & More, S. (2022). Toxicity and surface modification of dendrimers: A critical review. *Current Drug Delivery, 19*(4), 451–465. https://doi.org/10.2174/1567201818666211021160441.

Kim, D. M., Noh, H. B., Park, D. S., Ryu, S. H., Koo, J. S., & Shim, Y. B. (2009). Immunosensors for detection of Annexin II and MUC5AC for early diagnosis of lung cancer. *Biosensors and Bioelectronics, 25*(2), 456–462. https://doi.org/10.1016/j.bios.2009.08.007.

Kovalev, D., & Fujii, M. (2005). Silicon nanocrystals: Photosensitizers for oxygen molecules. *Advanced Materials, 17*(21), 2531–2544. https://doi.org/10.1002/adma.200500328.

Lai, C. C., Shih, T. P., Ko, W. C., Tang, H. J., & Hsueh, P. R. (2020). Severe acute respiratory syndrome coronavirus 2 (SARS-CoV-2) and coronavirus disease-2019 (COVID-19): The epidemic and the challenges. *International Journal of Antimicrobial Agents, 55*(3). https://doi.org/10.1016/j.ijantimicag.2020.105924.

Levine, B., & Kroemer, G. (2008). Autophagy in the pathogenesis of disease. *Cell, 132*(1), 27–42. https://doi.org/10.1016/j.cell.2007.12.018.

Li, X., Naeem, A., Xiao, S., Hu, L., Zhang, J., & Zheng, Q. (2022). Safety challenges and application strategies for the use of dendrimers in medicine. *Pharmaceutics, 14*(6), 1292. https://doi.org/10.3390/pharmaceutics14061292.

Li, J., Ke, W., Li, H., Zha, Z., Han, Y. u, & Ge, Z. (2015). Endogenous stimuli-sensitive multistage polymeric micelleplex anticancer drug delivery system for efficient tumor penetration and cellular internalization. *Advanced Healthcare Materials, 4*(15), 2206–2219. https://doi.org/10.1002/adhm.201500379.

Lin, X. u, Wu, J., Liu, Y., Lin, N., Hu, J., & Zhang, B. (2022). Stimuli-responsive drug delivery systems for the diagnosis and therapy of lung cancer. *Molecules, 27*(3), 948. https://doi.org/10.3390/molecules27030948.

Liu, J., Li, G., Guo, H., Ni, C., Gao, Y., Cao, X., Xia, J., Shi, X., & Guo, R. (2023). Dual-responsive core-shell tecto dendrimers enable efficient gene editing of cancer cells to boost immune checkpoint blockade therapy. *ACS Applied Materials and Interfaces, 15*(10), 12809–12821. https://doi.org/10.1021/acsami.2c22584.

Madeddu, C., Donisi, C., Liscia, N., Lai, E., Scartozzi, M., & Macciò, A. (2022). EGFR-mutated non-small cell lung cancer and resistance to immunotherapy: Role of the tumor microenvironment. *International Journal of Molecular Sciences, 23*(12), 6489. https://doi.org/10.3390/ijms23126489.

Naji, G., Fareed, N., & Al-Zheery, W. (2022). Dendrimer as a recent drug delivery system: An overview. *Journal of Biomedicine and Biochemistry*. https://doi.org/10.57238/jbb.2022.20109.

Oledzka, E., Paśnik, K., Domańska, I., Zielińska-Pisklak, M., Piotrowska, U., Sobczak, M., Szeleszczuk, Ł, & Laskowska, A. (2023). Poly(amidoamine) dendrimer/camptothecin complex: From synthesis to in vitro cancer cell line studies. *Molecules, 28*(6), 2696. https://doi.org/10.3390/molecules28062696.

Pan, J., Mendes, L. P., Yao, M., Filipczak, N., Garai, S., Thakur, G. A., Sarisozen, C., & Torchilin, V. P. (2019). Polyamidoamine dendrimers-based nanomedicine for combination therapy with siRNA and chemotherapeutics to overcome multidrug resistance. *European Journal of Pharmaceutics and Biopharmaceutics, 136*, 18–28. https://doi.org/10.1016/j.ejpb.2019.01.006.

Park, J. Y., Lee, G. H., Yoo, K. H., & Khang, D. (2023). Overcoming multidrug-resistant lung cancer by mitochondrial-associated ATP inhibition using nanodrugs. *Journal of Nanobiotechnology, 21*(1). https://doi.org/10.1186/s12951-023-01768-8.

Percec, V., Johansson, G., Ungar, G., & Zhou, J. (1996). Fluorophobic effect induces the self-assembly of semifluorinated tapered monodendrons containing crown ethers into supramolecular columnar dendrimers which exhibit a homeotropic hexagonal columnar liquid crystalline phase. *Journal of the American Chemical Society, 118*(41), 9855–9866. https://doi.org/10.1021/ja9615738.

Pooja, D., Reddy, T. S., Kulhari, H., Kadari, A., Adams, D. J., Bansal, V., & Sistla, R. (2020). N-acetyl-d-glucosamine-conjugated PAMAM dendrimers as dual receptor-targeting nanocarriers for anticancer drug delivery. *European Journal of Pharmaceutics and Biopharmaceutics, 154*, 377–386. https://doi.org/10.1016/j.ejpb.2020.07.020.

Prasher, P., Sharma, M., Kaur, I. P, Macloughlin, R., Loebenberg, R., Davies, N., & Dua, K. (2026). *Nanotechnology and drug delivery innovations in lung cancer treatment*. CRC Press https://doi.org/10.1201/9781003595830.

Rajani, C., Borisa, P., Karanwad, T., Borade, Y., Patel, V., Rajpoot, K., & Tekade, R. K. (2019). Cancer-targeted chemotherapy: Emerging role of the folate anchored dendrimer as drug delivery nanocarrier. In *Pharmaceutical applications of dendrimers* (pp. 151–198). Elsevier. https://doi.org/10.1016/B978-0-12-814527-2.00007-X.

Ramos, R., Moura, C. çãoS., Costa, M., Lamas, N. J, Castro, L. íP. e, Correia, R., Garcez, D., Pereira, J. éM., Sousa, C., & Vale, N. (2025). Heterogeneity of lung cancer: The histopathological diversity and tumour classification in the artificial intelligence era. *Pathobiology, 92*(4), 239–250. https://doi.org/10.1159/000544892.

Rhodes, A., Evans, L. E., Alhazzani, W., Levy, M. M., Antonelli, M., Ferrer, R., Kumar, A., Sevransky, J. E., Sprung, C. L., Nunnally, M. E., Rochwerg, B., Rubenfeld, G. D., Angus, D. C., Annane, D., Beale, R. J., Bellinghan, G. J., Bernard, G. R., Chiche, J. D., Coopersmith, C., … Dellinger, R. P. (2017). Surviving sepsis campaign: International guidelines for management of sepsis and septic shock: 2016. *Intensive Care Medicine, 43*(3), 304–377. https://doi.org/10.1007/s00134-017-4683-6.

Sarma, K., Akther, M. H., Ahmad, I., Afzal, O., Altamimi, A. S. A., Alossaimi, M. A., Jaremko, M., Emwas, A. H., & Gautam, P. (2024). Adjuvant novel nanocarrier-based targeted therapy for lung cancer. *Molecules, 29*(5). https://doi.org/10.3390/molecules29051076.

Sasaki, T., Kuno, H., Hiyama, T., Oda, S., Masuoka, S., Miyasaka, Y., Taki, T., Nagasaki, Y., Jeong-yoo Ohtani-Kim, S., Ishii, G., Kaku, S., Shroff, G. S., & Kobayashi, T. (2024). 2021 WHO classification of lung cancer: Molecular biology research and radiologic-pathologic correlation. *RadioGraphics, 44*(3). https://doi.org/10.1148/rg.230136.

Scherpereel, A., Astoul, P., Baas, P., Berghmans, T., Clayson, H., De Vuyst, P., Dienemann, H., Galateau-Salle, F., Hennequin, C., Hillerdal, G., Le Péchoux, C., Mutti, L., Pairon, J. C., Stahel, R., Van Houtte, P., Van Meerbeeck, J., Waller, D., & Weder, W. (2010). Guidelines of the European Respiratory Society and the European Society of Thoracic Surgeons for the management of malignant pleural mesothelioma. *European Respiratory Journal, 35*(3), 479–495. https://doi.org/10.1183/09031936.00063109.

Schlüter, A. D., & Rabe, J. P. (2000). Dendronized polymers: Synthesis, characterization, assembly at interfaces, and manipulation. *Angewandte Chemie International Edition, 39*(5), 864–883. https://doi.org/10.1002/(sici)1521-3773(20000303)39:5⟨864::aid-anie864⟩3.0.co;2-e.

Senapati, S., Mahanta, A. K., Kumar, S., & Maiti, P. (2018). Controlled drug delivery vehicles for cancer treatment and their performance. *Signal Transduction and Targeted Therapy, 3*(1). https://doi.org/10.1038/s41392-017-0004-3.

Sharma, A., Shambhwani, D., Pandey, S., Singh, J., Lalhlenmawia, H., Kumarasamy, M., Singh, S. K, Kumar Chellappan, D., Gupta, G., Prasher, P., Dua, K., & Kumar, D. (2023). Advances in lung cancer treatment using nanomedicines. *ACS Omega, 8*(1), 10–41. https://doi.org/10.1021/acsomega.2c04078.

Sharmila, S., Karthikeyan, C., Faiyazuddin, M. d, Arthi, S., Das, U., Maqsood, S., Chakraborty, A., & Gowri, S. (2025). *Surface modification of lipid based drug delivery for lungs* (pp. 319–335). Elsevier BV. https://doi.org/10.1016/b978-0-443-22374-7.00014-1.

Shi, J., Votruba, A. R., Farokhzad, O. C., & Langer, R. (2010). Nanotechnology in drug delivery and tissue engineering: From discovery to applications. *Nano Letters, 10*(9), 3223–3230. https://doi.org/10.1021/nl102184c.

Srinivasarao, D. A., Shah, S., Famta, P., Vambhurkar, G., Jain, N., Pindiprolu, S. KS. S., Sharma, A., Kumar, R., Padhy, H. P, Kumari, M., Madan, J., & Srivastava, S. (2025). Unravelling the role of tumor microenvironment responsive nanobiomaterials in spatiotemporal controlled drug delivery for lung cancer therapy. *Drug Delivery and Translational Research, 15*(2), 407–435. https://doi.org/10.1007/s13346-024-01673-z.

Svenson, S., & Tomalia, D. A. (2012). Dendrimers in biomedical applications-reflections on the field. *Advanced Drug Delivery Reviews, 64*, 102–115. https://doi.org/10.1016/j.addr.2012.09.030.

Thanh, N. T. K., & Green, L. A. W. (2010). Functionalisation of nanoparticles for biomedical applications. *Nano Today, 5*(3), 213–230. https://doi.org/10.1016/j.nantod.2010.05.003.

Trewyn, B. G., Slowing, I. I., Giri, S., Chen, H.-T., & Lin, V. S.-Y. (2007). Synthesis and functionalization of a mesoporous silica nanoparticle based on the sol-gel process and applications in controlled release. *Accounts of Chemical Research, 40*(9), 846–853. https://doi.org/10.1021/ar600032u.

Tsogas, I., Sideratou, Z., Tsiourvas, D., Theodossiou, T. A., & Paleos, C. M. (2007). Interactive transport of guanidinylated poly(propylene imine)-based dendrimers through liposomal and cellular membranes. *ChemBioChem, 8*(15), 1865–1876. https://doi.org/10.1002/cbic.200700289.

Wang, B., An, J., Zhang, H., Zhang, S., Zhang, H., Wang, L., Zhang, H., & Zhang, Z. (2018). Personalized cancer immunotherapy via transporting endogenous tumor antigens to lymph nodes mediated by nano Fe_3O_4. *Small, 14*(38). https://doi.org/10.1002/smll.201801372.

Wang, J., Li, B., Qiu, L. i, Qiao, X., & Hu, Y. (2022). Dendrimer-based drug delivery systems: History, challenges, and latest developments. *Journal of Biological Engineering, 16*(1). https://doi.org/10.1186/s13036-022-00298-5.

Wang, Y., Cao, X., Guo, R., Shen, M., Zhang, M., Zhu, M., & Shi, X. (2011). Targeted delivery of doxorubicin into cancer cells using a folic acid-dendrimer conjugate. *Polymer Chemistry, 2*(8), 1754–1760. https://doi.org/10.1039/c1py00179e.

Wilkins, M. R., Paul, G. A., Strange, J. W., Tunariu, N., Gin-Sing, W., Banya, W. A., Westwood, M. A., Stefanidis, A., Ng, L. L., Pennell, D. J., Mohiaddin, R. H., Nihoyannopoulos, P., & Gibbs, J. S. R. (2005). Sildenafil versus endothelin receptor antagonist for pulmonary hypertension (SERAPH) study. *American Journal of Respiratory and Critical Care Medicine, 171*(11), 1292–1297. https://doi.org/10.1164/rccm.200410-1411OC.

Woodruff, M. A, & Hutmacher, D. W (2010). The return of a forgotten polymer - Polycaprolactone in the 21st century. *Progress in Polymer Science, 35*(10), 1217–1256. https://doi.org/10.1016/j.progpolymsci.2010.04.002.

Yang, D., Liu, M., Xiao, X., Tao, Z., & Redshaw, C. (2021). Polymeric self-assembled cucurbit[n]urils: Synthesis, structures and applications. *Coordination Chemistry Reviews, 434*, 213733. https://doi.org/10.1016/j.ccr.2020.213733.

Zaman, S., Ullah, A., & Shafaqat, A. (2023). Structural modeling and topological characterization of three kinds of dendrimer networks. *The European Physical Journal E, 46*(5). https://doi.org/10.1140/epje/s10189-023-00297-4.

Zenze, M., Daniels, A., & Singh, M. (2023). Dendrimers as modifiers of inorganic nanoparticles for therapeutic delivery in cancer. *Pharmaceutics, 15*(2), 398. https://doi.org/10.3390/pharmaceutics15020398.

Zhang, L., Gu, F. X, Chan, J. M, Wang, A. Z, Langer, R. S, & Farokhzad, O. C (2007). Nanoparticles in medicine: Therapeutic applications and developments. *Clinical Pharmacology & Therapeutics, 83*(5), 761–769. https://doi.org/10.1038/sj.clpt.6100400.

Zheng, X., Song, X., Zhu, G., Pan, D., Li, H., Hu, J., Xiao, K., Gong, Q., Gu, Z., Luo, K., & Li, W. (2024). Nanomedicine combats drug resistance in lung cancer. *Advanced Materials, 36*(3). https://doi.org/10.1002/adma.202308977.

CHAPTER 12

Targeting lung cancer: Aerosol delivery of star polymer-small interfering RNA nanoparticles for tumor inhibition

Garima Malik[a], Neeraj Mittal[a], Meenakshi Dhanawat[b], Ishfaq Rashid[c] and Jashan Girdhar[d]

[a]Chitkara College of Pharmacy, Chitkara University, Rajpura, Punjab, India [b]Amity Institute of Pharmacy, Amity University, Gurugram, Haryana, India [c]Department of Pharmacotherapy, College of Pharmacy, University of Utah, Salt Lake City, UT, United States [d]Department of Pharmacy Practice, Teerthanker Mahaveer College of Pharmacy, Teerthanker Mahaveer University, Moradabad, Uttar Pradesh, India

12.1 Introduction

The cancer that is responsible for the death of the greatest number of people worldwide is lung cancer, which also has the highest mortality rate of all malignancies. Every single year, lung cancer is responsible for the deaths of 1.8 million individuals, as stated by the World Health Organization. This number keeps going up even though surgery, chemotherapy, and radiation are getting better (Wang et al., 2024). There are no specific signs of lung cancer; however, if it is diagnosed early and if it is treated in a specialized way, lung cancer can be combated without harming healthy surrounding tissue. Currently, advanced nanomedicine techniques revolutionize tumor therapies through targeted drug and genetic delivery to tumors of cancer cells, with experts particularly focused on lung cancer cells.

Small interfering RNA (siRNA) molecules, which are short interfering RNA molecules, are being investigated by researchers as a possible therapeutic approach for the treatment of noninvasive lung cancer in older patients. Cellular RNA interference (RNAi) functions as a vital regulatory mechanism that can impede tumor progression and advanced malignancy by targeting oncogenes (Hattab et al., 2021). The suggested therapy paradigm shows promise for effective lung cancer treatment by using siRNA molecules to inhibit drug-resistant behavior, metastasis, and cancer cell survival pathways. For siRNA therapies to work in the clinic, there needs to be a good way to get these compounds to lung tissues. These molecules are also

Nanoengineered Therapeutics for Lung Cancer: Advanced Drug Delivery Strategies.
DOI: https://doi.org/10.1016/B978-0-443-44585-9.00008-1

unstable when they can not cross biological barriers like cell membranes, which means that effective ways to deliver therapeutic siRNA need to be found. Biocompatible nanoparticles are great for delivering siRNA because they can wrap it up and send it to specific parts of the body, like lung tumors and other areas that have been chosen. Star polymers are the best way to use nanoparticles to get siRNA to cancer cells. There is a central core and several polymeric arms that stick out from it in a special way that makes star polymers. These polymers have a branching structure that makes them better at absorbing cells, holding drugs, and resisting damage. Star polymer nanoparticles are the best way to get RNA-based treatments like siRNA to where they need to go (McCarroll et al., 2019). Nanoparticles in aerosol delivery systems have made it easier to treat lung cancer, which is aimed at certain areas. Doctors can give drugs directly to the lungs with medical aerosols. This is better than surgery because it lowers the chance of side effects and helps the body take in the drugs better. Medical research (George et al., 2025) demonstrates that aerosol delivery technologies facilitate the targeting of siRNA to lung tissues, thereby enhancing the efficacy of gene silencing in lung cancer cells. This shows a new way to deal with this disease. This chapter talks about how to make nanoparticles that are based on star polymers and can deliver siRNA to lung cancer cells. It also talks about their characteristics and the problems with using them in hospitals. Also, talk about how to give aerosols in a way that better targets the lungs, as well as the possible uses and therapeutic uses of RNA-based cancer treatments.

12.2 Star polymer-small interfering RNA nanoparticles

12.2.1 Overview of star polymers

Star polymers, categorized as branched macromolecules, substantially improve drug delivery owing to their distinctive structural properties. The polymers are star-shaped, featuring several polymer chains radiating from a singular central core. These nanoparticles have a wide variety of core radii and arm counts to allow researchers to control their properties (Wu et al., 2015). Based on the structural benefits of star polymers, the engineering of various therapeutic agents, such as small molecules, proteins, and nucleic acids, including siRNA, can be efficiently encapsulated and delivered. Being branched, it provides a higher stability and better biologic media compatibility than linear polymers, important parameters to deliver fragile molecules such as siRNA (Fig. 12.1). In addition to giving high loading capacities, multiple functional groups present in the branched structure allow for the insertion of targeting ligands for nanoparticle direction to specific tissues, such as the lung.

12.2.2 Advantages of star polymers for small interfering RNA delivery

The distribution of siRNA to lung cancer cells is enhanced by employing star polymer-based nanoparticles due to their fulfillment of numerous critical attributes (Table 12.1). These include the following:

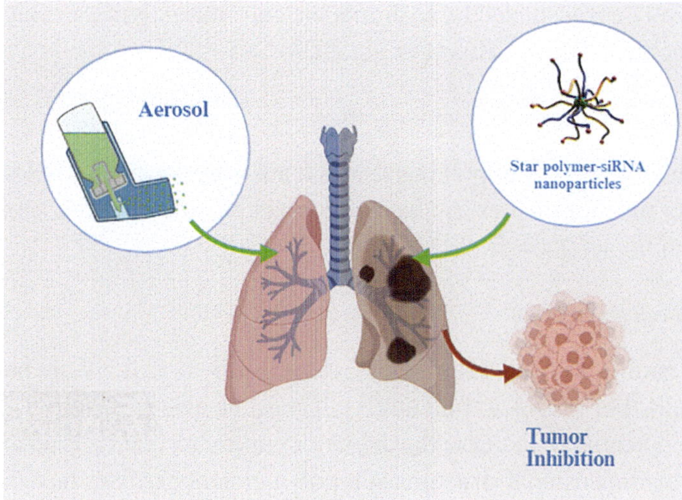

Figure 12.1
Schematic illustration of aerosol-based pulmonary delivery of star polymer-siRNA nanoparticles for lung cancer therapy. *siRNA*, Small interfering RNA.

Table 12.1: Commonly used siRNA targets in lung cancer therapy.

Gene target	Function	Relevance in lung cancer	Outcome upon silencing
KRAS	Oncogene	Frequently mutated in NSCLC	Reduced proliferation, increased apoptosis
EGFR	Growth receptor	Overexpressed in NSCLC	Tumor regression, sensitization to TKIs
VEGF	Angiogenesis	Promotes tumor vascularization	Inhibition of angiogenesis
BCL-2	Antiapoptotic protein	Promotes cell survival	Induces apoptosis

12.2.2.1 More stability and protection

Star polymers keep siRNA from breaking down quickly in the fluids that flow through the body. Star polymers are made in such a way that they form a protective capsule around siRNA, which keeps it safe from enzymes that break it down and other things that could happen too soon. Because of its star-shaped structure, the nanoparticle is robust enough to withstand environmental changes, which increases the stability of siRNA (Lara et al., 2024).

12.2.2.2 High encapsulation efficiency

Due to their large number of polymeric arms, star polymers are excellent at encapsulating siRNA molecules. Research has indicated that the administration of siRNA in significant amounts through star polymer nanoparticles improves the effectiveness of treatment. The siRNA was effectively encapsulated by hydrophobic core star polymers, which facilitated its accessibility in specific locations (Huang et al., 2024).

12.2.2.3 Controlled release of small interfering RNA

One effective method is to use star polymers, which are made to release siRNA at tumor sites gradually. The drug functions better and has fewer negative side effects when it is released under regulated conditions (Dowdy, 2023).

12.2.2.4 Improved cellular uptake

By repeatedly interacting with cell membranes, the star polymers facilitate nanoparticles' entry into target cells. For siRNA to function, cells must be able to absorb it. Star polymers appear to have the potential to increase the amount of nutrients that cells absorb. Because of their unique three-dimensional structure, star polymer nanoparticles have been shown to absorb more than linear polymers (Yao et al., 2020).

12.2.2.5 Endosomal escape

Getting siRNA to exit endosomes after entering a cell is the most difficult part of its delivery. According to the study, gene silencing occurs when siRNA escapes endosomes through the breakdown of their membranes, which is facilitated by star polymers (Beck et al., 2021). The effectiveness of RNA-based treatments depends on this particular trait.

12.2.3 Aerosol delivery of star polymer-small interfering RNA nanoparticles

Aerosol-based delivery methods for lung cancer treatment using star polymer-siRNA nanoparticles have been the focus of a lot of research in the past few years. Aerosol devices let doctors give medicines directly to the lung tissues, which reduces the amount of drug in the rest of the body and increases the concentration of the drug at the target site (Singh et al., 2024). To make aerosol delivery work, star polymer-siRNA nanoparticles need to be made into stable aerosol forms that keep their ability to deposit in the lungs. To get nanoparticles to the alveoli and through lung tissue, you need to come up with optimization strategies for particle size, surface charge, and aerosolization conditions (Ding et al., 2021). The best size range for delivering particles deep into the lungs is 1–5 microns. This is because these particles can pass through the lower respiratory tract but are too heavy to leave the lungs or spread throughout the body. Researchers have shown that aerosolizing star polymer-siRNA nanoparticles makes it easier to target lung cancers. Aerosolized star polymer-siRNA nanoparticles exhibited efficient target gene silencing mechanisms through their accumulation in pulmonary tissues, leading to diminished tumor sizes and improved survival rates in animal models (Teo et al., 2016). Aerosol systems are a good option for people who can not use regular injectable treatments because they do not have to cut into their skin. The aerosol delivery system allows patients to administer their own drugs, which is beneficial for those suffering from chronic conditions such as lung cancer (Ma et al., 2022).

12.3 Aerosol delivery systems for lung targeting

Drugs can be administered effectively through the pulmonary route, particularly to patients with lung conditions like lung cancer. The alveolar region has a large surface area (roughly 100 m^2), a thin epithelial barrier, numerous blood vessels, and no first-pass metabolism. This is an excellent method for delivering medications to specific body parts, such as siRNA, as well as to the entire body (Patton & Byron, 2007). When used with an advanced nanocarrier system like star polymer-based nanoparticles, the aerosol delivery route is a safe way to turn off genes that cause lung cancer. Direct inhalation of siRNA into the lungs presents considerable advantages over systemic administration. There are many problems with systemic delivery, such as degradation by nucleases, clearance by the kidneys, immune activation, and off-target effects. On the other hand, aerosol-based delivery sends the therapeutic agent straight to the lungs, increases its concentration at the tumor site, lowers systemic exposure, and lowers side effects (Kanasty et al., 2013). Additionally, lung cancers frequently arise in the epithelial lining, rendering direct contact via aerosol delivery optimal for therapeutic efficacy. The small size of siRNA (about 21–23 nucleotides) makes it easy to put inside nanoparticles that can go deep into the lungs and get to the alveolar regions, where lung cancer cells can take it up and silence genes (Lai et al., 2009).

12.3.1 Aerosol devices for small interfering RNA delivery

For siRNA to be delivered effectively to the lungs, devices must be able to make aerosol particles of the right size and keep siRNA-containing nanoparticles stable. There are three main types of devices used for pulmonary delivery:

12.3.1.1 Nebulizers

These tools turn liquid formulations into very fine aerosols. Mesh nebulizers, in particular, have become popular for delivering nucleic acids because they can keep molecules intact and get a lot of them into the lungs (Kumar et al., 2020).

12.3.1.2 Dry powder inhalers

These devices give medicine in the form of dry powder. Dry powder inhalers (DPIs) work well with formulations that are stable at high temperatures and stay stable while being stored. To make star polymer-siRNA nanoparticles easier to flow and disperse, they can be spray-dried or freeze-dried with excipients like mannitol and leucine (Seville et al., 2007).

12.3.1.3 Pressurized metered dose inhalers

Pressurized metered dose inhalers (pMDIs) are often used for asthma medications, but they are not as good for siRNA because propellants make it hard to dissolve and make the right formulation (Schultheis et al., 2014).

12.3.2 Size of particles and aerodynamic properties

For the best delivery to the deep lungs, the aerodynamic diameter of aerosolized particles should be between 1 and 5 μm. Particles that are less than 1 μm in size may be exhaled before they settle, but particles that are more than 5 μm in size usually settle in the upper respiratory tract. The mass median aerodynamic diameter (MMAD) is an important number that needs to be improved during the development of formulations (Hickey, 2003). Star polymer-siRNA nanoparticles are usually between 50 and 200 nm in size. Still, these primary particles are often mixed with excipients or made into microparticles to make them work better with airflow. When these microparticles reach the lungs, they break down into nanoparticles that can get into tissues and target cells.

12.3.3 Formulation strategies

Developing stable and respirable formulations of siRNA with star polymer carriers involves:

12.3.3.1 Lyophilization or spray drying

These methods are employed to create dry powders compatible with DPI systems. Trehalose and mannitol are two examples of protectants that help keep siRNA stable while it is being processed and stored (Seville et al., 2007).

12.3.3.2 Formulations for nebulizers in suspension

In this case, star polymer-siRNA nanoparticles are kept from clumping together by being suspended in a buffered solution with stabilizers. The solution has the right viscosity, osmolarity, and surface tension for making aerosols (Byron & Patton, 1994).

12.3.3.3 Properties of mucus penetration

Mucus lines the respiratory tract, which can make it harder for nanoparticles to move through it. Adding PEG or a similar polymer to the surface makes it more hydrophilic and protects the charge, which helps mucus get through (Lai et al., 2009).

12.3.4 Deposition, absorption, and transfection in the lungs

Nanoparticles must effectively settle postinhalation, traverse the mucus barrier in the airway, and be absorbed by target cells to inhibit gene expression. The primary mechanism by which star polymer-siRNA nanoparticles enter cells is endocytosis. The polymer is more likely to interact with the anionic cell membrane because of its cationic characteristics

(Kanasty et al., 2013). Endosomal escape is a serious problem. Star polymers can be created with pH-sensitive or proton-absorbing components, which weaken the endosomal membrane. This facilitates siRNA's entry into the cytoplasm, the site of RNAi (Schultheis et al., 2014). Once in the cytoplasm, the siRNA complex combines with the RNA-induced silencing complex (RISC). As a result, mRNA is broken down, and genes function less.

12.4 Applications of star polymer-small interfering RNA nanoparticles

A crucial strategy in oncology is the creation of siRNA therapies, which target and eliminate harmful genes precisely. Because siRNA can target genetic alterations and malfunctioning signaling pathways that cause tumors to grow and become resistant to treatment, it holds great promise for the treatment of lung cancer. Notwithstanding these issues, siRNA is not effective in treating illnesses because it is rapidly broken down by nucleases, is poorly absorbed by cells, and is poorly transported to tumor sites. Nanoparticles based on star polymers have drawn a lot of interest as improved siRNA delivery systems to address these problems. Because of their distinctive, highly branched structures, star polymers can form numerous functional arms that can encircle and shield siRNA molecules. Multivalency improves binding for surfaces and makes it stronger and more stable. Additionally, it allows for size modification and improves the material's compatibility with living organisms, extending its circulation time. Important characteristics of these nanoparticles also enable them to pass through biological barriers, be absorbed by cells, and exit endosomes. For gene silencing to work, all of these things are necessary. To treat lung cancer, star polymer-siRNA nanoparticles can be designed to target malignant cells by adding ligands to their surface that only bind to receptors associated with tumors. It also makes the drug work better by lowering its off-target effects and increasing the amount of drug that builds up in the tumor tissues. They can also be delivered with chemotherapy drugs because they are modular, which makes them work better and helps them get around drug resistance. Overall, star polymer-siRNA nanoparticles represent a versatile and powerful platform to advance gene therapy in lung cancer with the capability for clinical translation both in isolation and in conjunction with other treatments.

12.4.1 Gene silencing in lung cancer therapy

The pathogenesis of lung cancer involves multiple genetic alterations, such as the overexpression of oncogenes [e.g., KRAS, MYC, and epidermal growth factor receptor (EGFR)] and the downregulation of tumor suppressor genes (e.g., p53 and PTEN). The ability of siRNA to block certain mRNA transcripts offers a way to fix these molecular problems (Sen & Blau, 2006). Star polymer nanoparticles improve the delivery of siRNA to lung carcinoma cells, enabling intracellular gene silencing without the use of viral vectors, which carry risks of immunogenicity and insertional mutagenesis. In preclinical studies, siRNA-loaded star polymer nanoparticles targeting mutant KRAS mRNA significantly inhibited tumor growth

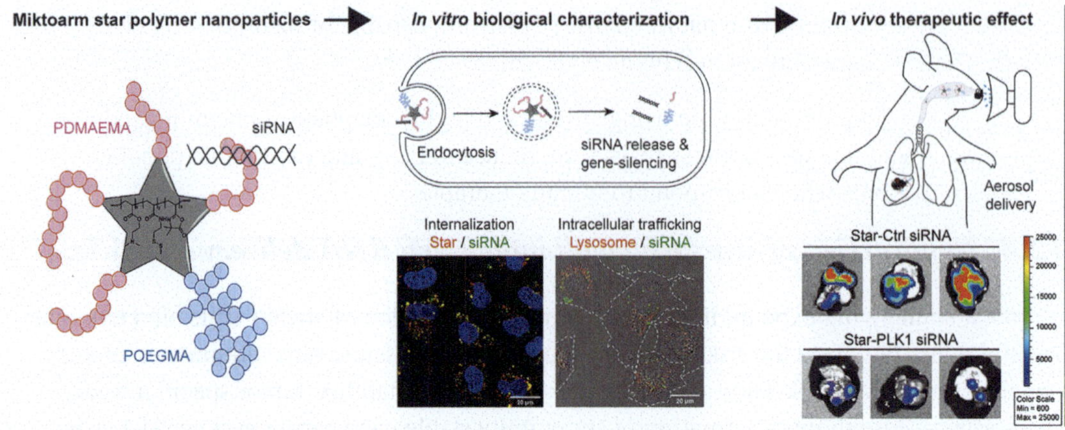

Figure 12.2

Schematic illustration of miktoarm star polymer-siRNA nanoparticles for aerosol delivery in lung cancer therapy. *Source: Reprinted Ma et al. (2022) with permission from Elsevier.*

and reduced metastatic spread (Hong et al., 2020). Ma et al. (2022) examined the capacity of nebulized star-siRNA nanoparticles to localize within orthotopic mouse lung tumors to suppress the expression of two genes. In vitro, star polymer-siRNA nanoparticles exhibit effective cellular uptake and gene silencing in lung cancer cell lines, generally diminishing target oncogene expression by more than 70%, resulting in significant reductions in proliferation and the initiation of apoptosis. The nanoparticles demonstrate negligible cytotoxicity in noncancerous lung cells, signifying favorable biocompatibility. In vivo, aerosolized delivery enables direct deposition into the lungs of mouse tumor models, achieving high local nanoparticle accumulation with sustained gene knockdown effects. Treated tumors exhibit significant growth inhibition—commonly over 60% reduction in volume compared to controls—with histological analysis revealing decreased proliferation markers and increased apoptosis. This delivery method significantly reduces systemic exposure, hence minimizing off-target effects and immunological activation, making it a viable approach for targeted lung cancer therapy (Fig. 12.2) (Ma et al., 2022).

12.4.2 Targeted delivery and tumor selectivity

To achieve tumor-specific delivery, surface functionalization of star polymers with tumor-targeting ligands is a commonly employed strategy. Sometimes ligands like folic acid, transferrin, RGD peptides, or antibodies are attached to the surface of the nanoparticle. This makes it possible for tumor cells that overexpress certain surface markers to undergo receptor-mediated endocytosis (Ma et al., 2022). The overexpression of the EGFR is one of the most important molecular traits of nonsmall cell lung cancer (NSCLC). The researchers have used this property to attach anti-EGFR antibody fragments or epidermal growth factor (EGF) peptide tags to star-shaped polymer nanoparticles. This has made it possible for the nanoparticles to find and attach to cancer cells more easily. This customized approach not only enhances the uptake of therapeutic nanoparticles by tumor cells but also increases their retention within tumor tissue while concurrently reducing unwanted accumulation in healthy areas. Also, passive delivery methods like the increased permeability and retention (EPR) effect help nanoparticles selectively build up in tumor areas. This is in addition to the targeting that was done before. This happens because the blood vessels in tumors are often too leaky and do not drain lymphatic fluid well, which keeps nanoparticles concentrated in malignant tissue (Allen & Cullis, 2013). Using these ideas as a starting point, Zhao and his team created a noninvasive inhalable nanoparticle system called siKRAS@GCLPP NPs to treat NSCLC with KRAS mutations. These nanoparticles that assemble themselves stay stable when they are aerosolized and tend to stay in areas of the lung that have tumors after they are inhaled. In preclinical studies utilizing an orthotopic mouse model of KRAS-mutant NSCLC, inhaled siKRAS@GCLPP nanoparticles demonstrated robust tumor-targeting efficacy and markedly inhibited cancer proliferation. The aerosol therapy significantly decreased mutant KRAS expression in the lungs without causing any discernible side effects, demonstrating a superior safety profile relative to traditional systemic treatments. In summary, these results show that inhalable siRNA-based therapies could be a good way to treat KRAS-mutant NSCLC and maybe other lung diseases as well (Maeda et al., 2000).

12.4.3 Overcoming multidrug resistance

Multidrug resistance continues to pose a significant challenge in the treatment of lung cancer. One method is to make efflux transporters, like P-glycoprotein (P-gp), work too hard, which pushes chemotherapeutic drugs out of cancer cells and makes them less effective. Star polymer-siRNA nanoparticles can be engineered to deliver siRNA that targets genes linked to multidrug resistance. Using siRNA to turn off genes like MDR1 or ABCB1 lowers the levels of efflux proteins, making tumors more sensitive to chemotherapy (Zhao et al., 2023). Preclinical research has demonstrated that star polymer systems co-delivering MDR1 siRNA and paclitaxel produced markedly elevated intracellular drug concentrations and enhanced apoptosis of tumor cells in resistant lung cancer models (Rabanel et al., 2014).

12.4.4 Immunomodulation in the tumor microenvironment

In addition to directly attacking cancer cells, siRNA can also change the tumor microenvironment (TME). Star polymer-siRNA nanoparticles can transport siRNA to stromal cells, immune cells, or cancer-associated fibroblasts (CAFs) within the TME, thereby modifying the tumor's supportive framework. For example, blocking TGF-β (transforming growth factor-beta) signaling with siRNA has been shown to lower tumor fibrosis, increase immune infiltration, and make immune checkpoint blockade therapies like antiPD-1 work better in lung tumors (Begines et al., 2020). Star polymers facilitate complex and localized delivery while avoiding immune responses, making them suitable for combinatorial immunotherapy strategies.

12.4.5 Diagnostic and theranostic applications

Nanomedicine has made a big leap forward with the development of theranostic systems, which are nanoparticles that can both diagnose and treat diseases. Star polymers can be connected to fluorescent dyes, radioisotopes, or MRI contrast agents to track drug delivery, biodistribution, and how well a tumor responds in real time (Mariathasan et al., 2018). A theranostic star polymer system that carries siRNA and quantum dots let researchers see tumor buildup and gene knockdown in living organisms. This told them how well the therapy worked and how the drugs worked in the body. Dual-function systems are especially helpful for lung cancer because they make it easier to monitor patients without hurting them and come up with personalized treatment plans. Taratula and his team made a good inhalable nanocarrier system that uses nanostructured lipid carriers (NLCs) to deliver MRP1 siRNA, BCL2 siRNA, and the cancer-fighting drug paclitaxel (TAX) all at once. To enhance selectivity, researchers modified the surface of these NLCs by incorporating luteinizing hormone-releasing hormone (LHRH) analog peptides. These peptides only bind to receptors that are too many lung cancer cells. This targeted approach ensured that the therapeutic agents were confined to tumor regions, sparing healthy tissues. Research on animals demonstrated that the NLC-siRNA platform facilitated the direct delivery of drugs to the lungs, resulting in a significant reduction in tumors without causing damage to adjacent organs (Gao et al., 2013). Jensen and his team made a poly(lactic-co-glycolic acid) (PLGA)-based carrier that held siRNA by using a spray drying method. This was a big step in the right direction. We could still control how siRNA got to the lungs and make it work. PLGA nanoparticles that can be inhaled were shown to help siRNA stay in lung tissue longer and lower the amount of medicine needed. Adding dipalmitoyl phosphatidylcholine (DPPC) to PLGA made it easier for the lungs to use, helped it get through the mucus barrier in the airways, and helped lung epithelial cells take it up, all without causing inflammation (Taratula et al., 2013). Hanafy and his team were able to put siRNA that targets PD-1 into solid lipid nanoparticles (SLNs) with an impressive 98.9% success rate. Researchers in labs and on animals found that this formulation slowed the growth of tumors a lot by blocking PD-1. Researchers made dry powder forms of SLN that contained TNF-α siRNA. They used a thin-film freeze-drying method to make it easier for the drugs to get into the lungs. This method preserved essential physical properties such as particle size, polydispersity index, zeta potential, and gene silencing efficacy postprocessing. Simulated experiments demonstrated that the dry powder particles can readily traverse the mucus layer. The likely reason for this was that polyethylene glycol (PEG) was on the surface of the SLN, which lowered the negative zeta potential. These data collectively indicate that SLN dry powder formulations may constitute a viable approach for the direct delivery of siRNA therapies to the lungs (Jensen et al., 2010).

12.5 Challenges and future directions

There have been big improvements in making star polymer-siRNA nanoparticles for treating lung cancer, but the technology, biology, and translation still have a lot of problems that need to be fixed before they can be used in hospitals. This part talks about the main problems and gives suggestions for how this field could improve and grow in the future.

12.5.1 Delivery barriers and overcoming limitations

One major issue with administering siRNA to the lungs is overcoming the extracellular barriers. One of these is mucociliary clearance. It clears the airways of things that do not belong there. Therapeutic nanoparticles can be eaten and broken down by alveolar macrophages. Nanoparticle formulations may become less stable when pulmonary surfactants are present. All of these things make it harder for siRNA to stay in lung tissue and make it harder for the body to get to it (Ding et al., 2021; Hanafy et al., 2021). Scientists have come up with some new ways to get around these biological barriers. Adding PEG to the surfaces of nanoparticles is a common way to do this. This makes it harder for the immune system to find them and easier for them to get through the thick mucus in the lungs. Another new idea is to make nanoparticles that are muco-inert or mucus-penetrating by carefully changing their surface properties, such as their charge and how well they absorb water, so that they can move through the mucus layer without getting stuck. Scientists are also trying to make biodegradable polymer carriers that work well in the lungs, which are a special place. These materials can break down when the pH changes or certain enzymes are active, for example. This makes it possible to release siRNA in a controlled and site-specific way, right where it is needed (Ding et al., 2021).

But pulmonary gene therapy will not work just because it can get past mucus barriers. After nanoparticles enter the respiratory tract, they must enter the target cells and release their siRNA cargo into the cytoplasm, where gene silencing occurs. This requires overcoming two major intracellular challenges: Enhancing cellular uptake and promoting endosomal escape, which allows the therapeutic siRNA to avoid degradation pathways and reach its functional site within the cell.

But endosomal entrapment is still a common problem that often causes siRNA to break down in lysosomes. To fight this, delivery systems often use proton sponge agents like polyethylenimine (PEI) to keep the pH of endosomes stable and cause osmotic swelling, pH-sensitive linkers or polymers that break down in acidic endosomal environments, and membrane-disruptive peptides or surfactants that help endosomes break open. However, achieving effective cytosolic delivery without causing significant cell damage is challenging (Wang et al., 2024). One significant barrier to siRNA therapy is the intrinsic heterogeneity of lung cancer. The structure, genetic mutations, microenvironment, and location of lung cancer tumors vary greatly from one another. Because of this complexity, highly customized siRNA designs that are based on the genomic sequencing of individual tumors are required, as are multivalent or multiplexed delivery systems that can target multiple oncogenes at once (Ma et al., 2022). Scientists are also developing dynamic nanoparticles that can react to the TME and allow siRNA therapeutics to be activated on demand in a certain area. In this complicated and varied disease landscape, this will make treatment more effective and targeted.

12.5.2 Biocompatibility and toxicology concerns

The fact that cationic polymers like PEI and polyamidoamine (PAMAM) can harm cells is a major issue with using star polymers to deliver siRNA. Due primarily to their strong positive surface charge, which can rupture cell membranes and prevent mitochondria from functioning, these substances are toxic in a dose-dependent manner. Many techniques have been employed by researchers to address this issue, including PEGylation of the surface to neutralize the surface charge and increase its biocompatibility, low-molecular-weight polymers that are typically less harmful to cells, and the addition of biodegradable or cleavable linkers to the polymer backbone to accelerate degradation and facilitate the removal of the carrier after delivery (Ren et al., 2025).

Immunogenicity and inflammatory responses, in addition to cytotoxicity, are significant safety concerns. Although SiRNA is usually thought to be nonimmunogenic, the nanoparticle carriers used to deliver it to the lungs may cause immune cells and lung epithelial cells to activate their toll-like receptors (TLRs), which could lead to cytokine storms or inflammatory cascades. Therefore, comprehensive preclinical evaluations are crucial, such as extended exposure studies to evaluate chronic safety profiles, immunotoxicity tests like cytokine profiling for indicators like IL-6 and TNF-α, and in-depth histological analysis of pulmonary tissues (Lam et al., 2011). Additionally, you should consider the likelihood that particles will accumulate and become difficult to remove. Ineffectively dissolving or removing nanoparticles from lung tissue can cause them to accumulate in the lungs or other organs, such as the liver and spleen. Concerns regarding long-term toxicity are raised by this. The best way to address this is to use biodegradable polymers, such as polyesters, poly(oxazoline)s, and poly(caprolactone). Additionally, enzyme-sensitive links in systems that respond to stimuli can help the body get rid of siRNA faster. Making nanoformulations better by keeping particle sizes under 200 nm and making sure they are hydrophilic enough makes it harder for the reticuloendothelial system to absorb them and keeps them from building up (Ma et al., 2022).

12.5.3 Future clinical applications and translation to humans

If you want to use inhaled siRNA therapies in hospitals, you need to make sure that the formulations can be made again and again. Nanoparticles made using scalable manufacturing methods must always be the same size, have the same siRNA loading efficiency, and be the same from batch to batch. Microfluidic mixing, spray drying, and lyophilization are some of the methods that are being improved to make them better for making things on a large scale. All drugs that use nanoparticles must follow the rules of good manufacturing practice (GMP). This guarantees that both the patient and the product are safe. Comprehensive stability tests under different storage and environmental conditions are necessary to figure out the right shelf life and packaging standards (Hanafy et al., 2021).

It is even harder to understand the rules for siRNA treatments because these products usually fit into more than one category, such as drug-device or drug-biologic. This means that you need to look at them very closely. The FDA, EMA, and other regulatory bodies want to know a lot about the safety of devices before they can be used in inhalation systems. They also want to know a lot about how drugs work and how they get into the body. It is important to set clear key quality characteristics (CQAs) for nanoparticle formulations to get regulatory approval. As RNA-based therapies progress, successful instances such as Patisiran (Onpattro) and Inclisiran establish a robust foundation for forthcoming approvals. The increasing focus on tailored and precise medicine significantly impacts the advancement of siRNA-based therapies. Advancements in genomics and molecular profiling may facilitate the development of novel therapies utilizing patient-specific siRNA libraries tailored to individual mutational landscapes. AI tools will probably be very important for making delivery system designs better by making them more precise and less toxic. Theranostic platforms, which combine therapeutic and diagnostic functions, could also make it possible to keep an eye on how well treatment is working in real time. This would allow for personalized care plans that change based on how well the treatment is working. This connection between siRNA drugs and precision oncology is very promising for lung cancer patients who do not respond to standard treatments. There are not many clinical trials of inhaled siRNA therapies yet, even though the preclinical data look good. There are only a few trials going on right now that are looking into these drugs, and even fewer that are looking into delivery systems that use star polymers. To connect the bench and bedside, Phase I/II clinical trials must begin to test safety, tolerability, and the best dose in humans. Biomarker analyses are essential for validating the efficacy of gene silencing and therapeutic effects at the molecular level, while patient-reported outcomes provide significant insights into quality of life, treatment adherence, and satisfaction with inhalation-based systems (Ismail & Chou, 2025). To fix problems with translation, academic researchers, biotechnology companies, and government agencies will have to work together. These partnerships can accelerate the transfer of new ideas from the lab to the real world and stay up to date with changes in the law. They can help solve long-standing issues like biological barriers, the safety of nanoparticles, and the efficacy of pulmonary deposition. Inhaled star polymer-siRNA nanoparticles may eventually prove to be very effective in the fight against lung cancer as polymer chemistry, aerosol drug delivery, and precision medicine platforms continue to progress (Ma et al., 2022).

12.6 Conclusion

An innovative and promising treatment option for lung cancer is aerosolized star polymer-siRNA nanoparticles. These innovative nanocarrier systems offer numerous advantages over conventional therapies. They enable the local and direct administration of medications to the respiratory system, lowering systemic toxicity and raising drug concentrations at the tumor site. They are perfect for chronic, progressive diseases like lung cancer that need repeated, noninvasive treatments because they work well with patient-friendly inhalation devices like nebulizers and DPIs. The modular and programmable nature of star polymer architectures allows for the precise control of key nanoparticle properties such as size, surface charge, and release kinetics. All of these are necessary to overcome the lungs' biological barriers. Because siRNA can be given with small-molecule drugs, immunotherapies, or imaging agents, they are more useful for treating diseases. This is because it gives doctors more options for treatment and lets them see how well the treatments are working right away.

These delivery systems are very important because they work well with the new ideas about personalized and precise medicine. Combining genetic and molecular data that is specific to each patient may make it possible for future treatments to use custom siRNA mixtures and delivery technologies that are made just for that person's tumor profile. Integrating artificial intelligence into treatment design and optimization could speed up the process of finding successful siRNA sequences, predicting off-target effects, and improving the processes for making nanoparticles, which would improve clinical outcomes. Nonetheless, other major problems need to be fixed before these technologies can be used in hospitals. Cationic polymers' cytotoxicity, problems with endosomal escape, biological clearance, scaling up production, formulation stability, and unclear regulations are still major problems. To solve these problems, we need to make strategic progress in biodegradable, stimuli-responsive materials, AI-assisted development, personalized medicine integration, combination medicines, and large scale clinical trials. With continued scientific innovation, clinical research, and interdisciplinary collaboration, aerosol-delivered star polymer-siRNA nanoparticle systems could change the way lung cancer is treated. Their ability to provide targeted, less harmful, and highly customizable therapies makes them a game-changing tool in the next generation of cancer treatments. They give patients around the world hope for better survival rates and a better quality of life.

References

Allen, T. M., & Cullis, P. R. (2013). Liposomal drug delivery systems: From concept to clinical applications. *Advanced Drug Delivery Reviews, 65*, 36–48. https://doi.org/10.1016/J.ADDR.2012.09.037.

Beck, J. D., Reidenbach, D., Salomon, N., Sahin, U., Türeci, Ö., Vormehr, M., & Kranz, L. M. (2021). mRNA therapeutics in cancer immunotherapy. *Molecular Cancer, 20*, 1–24. https://doi.org/10.1186/S12943-021-01348-0.

Begines, B., Ortiz, T., Pérez-Aranda, M., Martínez, G., Merinero, M., Argüelles-Arias, F., & Alcudia, A. (2020). Polymeric nanoparticles for drug delivery: Recent developments and future prospects. *Nanomaterials, 10*, 1–41. https://doi.org/10.3390/NANO10071403.

Byron, P. R., & Patton, J. S. (1994). Drug delivery via the respiratory tract. *Journal of Aerosol Medicine: Deposition, Clearance, and Effects in the Lung, 7*, 49–75. https://doi.org/10.1089/JAM.1994.7.49.

Ding, L., Tang, S., Wyatt, T. A., Knoell, D. L., & Oupický, D. (2021). Pulmonary siRNA delivery for lung disease: Review of recent progress and challenges. *Journal of Controlled Release, 330*, 977–991. https://doi.org/10.1016/J.JCONREL.2020.11.005.

Dowdy, S. F. (2023). Endosomal escape of RNA therapeutics: How do we solve this rate-limiting problem? *RNA, 29*, 396–401. https://doi.org/10.1261/RNA.079507.122.

Gao, W., Hu, C. M. J., Fang, R. H., & Zhang, L. (2013). Liposome-like nanostructures for drug delivery. *Journal of Materials Chemistry B: Materials for Biology and Medicine, 1*. https://doi.org/10.1039/C3TB21238F.

George, M., Boukherroub, R., Sanyal, A., & Szunerits, S. (2025). Treatment of lung diseases via nanoparticles and nanorobots: Are these viable alternatives to overcome current treatments? *Materials Today Bio, 31*, 101616. https://doi.org/10.1016/J.MTBIO.2025.101616.

Hanafy, M. S., Hufnagel, S., Trementozzi, A. N., Sakran, W., Stachowiak, J. C., Koleng, J. J., & Cui, Z. (2021). PD-1 siRNA-encapsulated solid lipid nanoparticles downregulate PD-1 expression by macrophages and inhibit tumor growth : PD-1 siRNA-encapsulated solid lipid nanoparticles. *Aaps Pharmscitech [Electronic Resource], 22*. https://doi.org/10.1208/S12249-021-01933-Y.

Hattab, D., Gazzali, A. M., & Bakhtiar, A. (2021). Clinical advances of sirna-based nanotherapeutics for cancer treatment. *Pharmaceutics, 13*. https://doi.org/10.3390/PHARMACEUTICS13071009.

Hickey, A. J. (2003). Pharmaceutical inhalation aerosol technology. *Pharmaceutical Inhalation Aerosol Technology*. https://doi.org/10.1201/9780203912898.

Hong, D. S., Fakih, M. G., Strickler, J. H., Desai, J., Durm, G. A., Shapiro, G. I., Falchook, G. S., Price, T. J., Sacher, A., Denlinger, C. S., Bang, Y.-J., Dy, G. K., Krauss, J. C., Kuboki, Y., Kuo, J. C., Coveler, A. L., Park, K., Kim, T. W., Barlesi, F., … Li, B. T. (2020). KRAS G12C inhibition with sotorasib in advanced solid tumors. *New England Journal of Medicine, 383*, 1207–1217. https://doi.org/10.1056/NEJMOA1917239.

Huang, Y., Zhang, J., Wang, X., Jing, H., & Li, H. (2024). Aerosol inhalation of gene delivery therapy for pulmonary diseases. *Biomolecules, 14*. https://doi.org/10.3390/BIOM14080904.

Ismail, A., & Chou, S. F. (2025). Polyethylenimine carriers for drug and gene delivery. *Polymers (Basel), 17*, 2150. https://doi.org/10.3390/POLYM17152150.

Jensen, D. M. K., Cun, D., Maltesen, M. J., Frokjaer, S., Nielsen, H. M., & Foged, C. (2010). Spray drying of siRNA-containing PLGA nanoparticles intended for inhalation. *Journal of Controlled Release, 142*, 138–145. https://doi.org/10.1016/J.JCONREL.2009.10.010.

Kanasty, R., Dorkin, J. R., Vegas, A., & Anderson, D. (2013). Delivery materials for siRNA therapeutics. *Nature Materials, 12*, 967–977. https://doi.org/10.1038/nmat3765.

Kumar, A., Kumar, P., Saumya, K. U., Kapuganti, S. K., Bhardwaj, T., & Giri, R. (2020). Exploring the SARS-CoV-2 structural proteins for multi-epitope vaccine development: An in-silico approach. *Expert Review of Vaccines., 19*, 887–898. https://doi.org/10.1080/14760584.2020.1813576.

Lai, S. K., Wang, Y. Y., & Hanes, J. (2009). Mucus-penetrating nanoparticles for drug and gene delivery to mucosal tissues. *Advanced Drug Delivery Reviews, 61*, 158–171. https://doi.org/10.1016/J.ADDR.2008.11.002.

Lam, J. K. W., Liang, W., & Chan, H. K. (2011). Pulmonary delivery of therapeutic siRNA. *Advanced Drug Delivery Reviews, 64*, 1. https://doi.org/10.1016/J.ADDR.2011.02.006.

Lara, P., Quiñonero, F., Ortiz, R., Prados, J., & Melguizo, C. (2024). Nanoparticles bounded to interfering RNAs as a therapy for pancreatic cancer: A systematic review. *Wiley Interdisciplinary Reviews: Nanomedicine Nanobiotechnology, 16*. https://doi.org/10.1002/WNAN.2013.

Ma, Z., Wong, S. W., Forgham, H., Esser, L., Lai, M., Leiske, M. N., Kempe, K., Sharbeen, G., Youkhana, J., Mansfeld, F., Quinn, J. F., Phillips, P. A., Davis, T. P., Kavallaris, M., & McCarroll, J. A. (2022). Aerosol delivery of star polymer-siRNA nanoparticles as a therapeutic strategy to inhibit lung tumor growth. *Biomaterials, 285*, 121539. https://doi.org/10.1016/J.BIOMATERIALS.2022.121539.

Maeda, H., Wu, J., Sawa, T., Matsumura, Y., & Hori, K. (2000). Tumor vascular permeability and the EPR effect in macromolecular therapeutics: A review. *Journal of Controlled Release, 65*, 271–284. https://doi.org/10.1016/S0168-3659(99)00248-5.

Mariathasan, S., Turley, S. J., Nickles, D., Castiglioni, A., Yuen, K., Wang, Y., Kadel, E. E., Koeppen, H., Astarita, J. L., Cubas, R., Jhunjhunwala, S., Banchereau, R., Yang, Y., Guan, Y., Chalouni, C., Ziai, J., Şenbabaoğlu, Y., Santoro, S., Sheinson, D., … Powles, T. (2018). TGFβ attenuates tumour response to PD-L1 blockade by contributing to exclusion of T cells. *Nature, 554*, 544–548. https://doi.org/10.1038/NATURE25501.

McCarroll, J. A., Sharbeen, G., Kavallaris, M., & Phillips, P. A. (2019). The use of star polymer nanoparticles for the Delivery of siRNA to mouse orthotopic pancreatic tumor models. *Methods in Molecular Biology, 1974*, 329–353. https://doi.org/10.1007/978-1-4939-9220-1_23.

Patton, J. S., & Byron, P. R. (2007). Inhaling medicines: Delivering drugs to the body through the lungs. *Nature Reviews Drug Discovery, 6*, 67–74. https://doi.org/10.1038/NRD2153.

Rabanel, J. M., Hildgen, P., & Banquy, X. (2014). Assessment of PEG on polymeric particles surface, a key step in drug carrier translation. *Journal of Controlled Release, 185*, 71–87. https://doi.org/10.1016/J.JCONREL.2014.04.017.

Ren, L., Wang, S., Li, B. C., & Bin Ding, G. (2025). Research progress on polymer-based nanocarriers for tumor-targeted delivery of survivin siRNA. *Polymers, 17*, 2279. https://doi.org/10.3390/POLYM17172279.

Schultheis, B., Strumberg, D., Santel, A., Vank, C., Gebhardt, F., Keil, O., Lange, C., Giese, K., Kaufmann, J., Khan, M., & Drevs, J. (2014). First-in-human phase I study of the liposomal RNA interference therapeutic Atu027 in patients with advanced solid tumors. *Journal of Clinical Oncology, 32*, 4141–4148. https://doi.org/10.1200/JCO.2013.55.0376.

Sen, G. L., & Blau, H. M. (2006). A brief history of RNAi: The silence of the genes. *Faseb Journal, 20*, 1293–1299. https://doi.org/10.1096/FJ.06-6014REV.

Seville, P. C., Li, H. Y., & Learoyd, T. P. (2007). Spray-dried powders for pulmonary drug delivery. *Critical Reviews in Therapeutic Drug Carrier Systems, 24*, 307–360. https://doi.org/10.1615/CRITREVTHERDRUGCARRIERSYST.V24.I4.10.

Singh, S., Malviya, R., & Awasthi, R. (2024). STAR particles as potential game-changer in drug delivery and biological processes: Moving beyond conventional nanoparticles. *Journal of Drug Delivery Science and Technology, 93*, 105413. https://doi.org/10.1016/J.JDDST.2024.105413.

Taratula, O., Kuzmov, A., Shah, M., Garbuzenko, O. B., & Minko, T. (2013). Nanostructured lipid carriers as multifunctional nanomedicine platform for pulmonary co-delivery of anticancer drugs and siRNA. *Journal of Controlled Release, 171*, 349–357. https://doi.org/10.1016/J.JCONREL.2013.04.018.

Teo, J., McCarroll, J. A., Boyer, C., Youkhana, J., Sagnella, S. M., Duong, H. T. T., Liu, J., Sharbeen, G., Goldstein, D., Davis, T. P., Kavallaris, M., & Phillips, P. A. (2016). A rationally optimized nanoparticle system for the delivery of RNA interference therapeutics into pancreatic tumors in vivo. *Biomacromolecules, 17*, 2337–2351. https://doi.org/10.1021/ACS.BIOMAC.6B00185.

Wang, Q., Bu, C., Dai, Q., Chen, J., Zhang, R., Zheng, X., Ren, H., Xin, X., & Li, X. (2024a). Recent progress in nucleic acid pulmonary delivery toward overcoming physiological barriers and improving transfection efficiency. *Advancement of Science, 11*, 2309748. https://doi.org/10.1002/ADVS.202309748.

Wang, X., Shi, J., & Liu, Z. (2024b). Advancements in the diagnosis and treatment of sub-centimeter lung cancer in the era of precision medicine (Review), Mol. *Clinical Oncology, 20*. https://doi.org/10.3892/MCO.2024.2726.

Wu, W., Wang, W., & Li, J. (2015). Star polymers: Advances in biomedical applications. *Progress in Polymer Science, 46*, 55–85. https://doi.org/10.1016/J.PROGPOLYMSCI.2015.02.002.

Yao, Y., Zhou, Y., Liu, L., Xu, Y., Chen, Q., Wang, Y., Wu, S., Deng, Y., Zhang, J., & Shao, A. (2020). Nanoparticle-based drug delivery in cancer therapy and its role in overcoming drug resistance. *Frontiers in Molecular Biosciences, 7*. https://doi.org/10.3389/FMOLB.2020.00193.

Zhao, G., Ho, W., Chu, J., Xiong, X., Hu, B., Boakye-Yiadom, K. O., Xu, X., & Zhang, X. Q. (2023). Inhalable siRNA nanoparticles for enhanced tumor-targeting treatment of KRAS-mutant non-small-cell lung cancer. *ACS Applied Materials & Interfaces, 15*, 31273–31284. https://doi.org/10.1021/ACSAMI.3C05007.

CHAPTER 13

Revolutionizing lung cancer immunotherapy: Small interfering RNA-based gene silencing for immune checkpoint blockade

Ritika Saha, Shubham Kumar, Ravinder Singh, Ritish Attri and Bimlesh Kumar

Department of Pharmacology, School of Pharmaceutical Sciences, Lovely Professional University, Phagwara, Punjab, India

13.1 Introduction

Lung cancer has continued to be the major cause of mortality related to cancer even though with the developed screening, diagnosis, and treatment methods (Thai et al., 2021). Its incidence is very high and the fact that the disease has a poor prognosis is an indication that more elaborate therapeutic methods are lacking (Siegel &Miller, 2022). The various methods include the cancer immunotherapy that has proved to be a paradigm shift since it uses the immunity system of the body to destroy malignancies (Ribas & Wolchok, 2018; Topalian et al., 2015). immune checkpoint inhibitors (ICI), specifically, programmed death receptor-1 (PD-1), programmed death ligand-1 (PD-L1), and cytotoxic T-lymphocyte-associated antigen 4 (CTLA-4) have also shown sustainable improvements in a section of lung cancer subjects (Reck et al., 2016). But issues including intrinsic and acquired resistance, immune-related toxicity and inappropriate responsiveness in some patients have hindered their universal effectiveness (Sharma et al., 2017; Wang et al., 2018).

An interesting technology called gene silencing has picked up steam as a new therapeutic approach to overcome these deficiencies, mainly in the form of small interfering ribonucleic acid (RNA) (siRNA) (Fire et al., 1998). siRNAs act by degraded mRNAs with complementary sequences, resulting in the downregulation of target proteins (Castanotto & Rossi, 2009). Such specificity will provide distinctive benefits compared to conventional ICIs where dual molecular blocking of immune checkpoints is possible, and blockade of adaptive resistance mechanisms that tumors use to evade immune recognition may be possible (Huang, 2014).

Nanoengineered Therapeutics for Lung Cancer: Advanced Drug Delivery Strategies.
DOI: https://doi.org/10.1016/B978-0-443-44585-9.00011-1

Novel technologies in nanotechnology-based siRNA delivery methods have already hastened the translational charging of the method even further (Kanasty et al., 2013). To increase stability of the siRNA, its bioavailability and tumor specificity, the polymeric carriers, lipid nanoparticles (LNPs) and tumor specific delivery systems are under intensive investigation (Babu et al., 2013). Combined with currently used immunotherapies and standard of care approaches (chemotherapy, radiotherapy), siRNA-based immune checkpoint blockade (ICB) will combine to render a synergistic and sustained antitumor immune response (Galluzzi et al.,2015; Twomey & Zhang, 2021).

The chapter presents the overview of global burden of lung cancer, reviews the current situation with immunotherapy and develops the rationale why the use of siRNA in an immune checkpoint silencing of target cells is a revolutionary treatment option.

13.1.1 Global burden of lung cancer

Lung cancer is still considered one of the most important issues of the global public health and the primary cause of cancer-associated deaths. The burden of the disease is still high despite improved treatment methods especially in the early detection stages, surgical procedures, radiation, chemotherapy and immunotherapy. As per the global statistics of cancer, lung cancer is known to cause millions of new diagnoses every year and is the leading cause of cancer related mortality in both the developed and the developing world. This is evidenced by a high mortality-to-incidence ratio which represents a forceful biological behavior of the disease and the bulk of patients being diagnosed at advanced stages.

Nonsmall cell lung cancer (NSCLC) occupies approximately 80–85 in the entire cases of lung cancer and the remaining cases a small cell lung cancer (SCLC). NSCLC in its turn is further sub-classified into adenocarcinoma, squamous cell carcinoma, and large cell carcinoma all with dissimilar molecular and clinical features. Irrespective of the development in the field of molecular profiling and targeted therapies, patients with metastatic disease have low chances of surviving over the long-term (Sung et al., 2021).

Tobacco smoking is the major etiological cause of lung cancer and this cause is the one that contributes to majority of cases worldwide. Nevertheless, there are also environmental health and occupational exposures to environmental pollution, radon gas, asbestos, and occupational carcinogens. Over the last few years, a growing proportion of lung cancer in never-smokers especially women and those in urban populations with heavy air pollution has provoked interest in other risk factors and complicated interactions between genes and the environment.

Geographical differences in incidence and mortality represent variations in prevalence of smoking, health care facilities and screening facilities, and socioeconomic status. Though smoking-related lung cancer cases are decreasing gradually in high-income nations because of tobacco control measures, in a number of low and middle-income nations, the trends are on the increase. Aging populations also increase the burden bearing in mind that the incidence of lung cancer is age-dependent (Siegel & Miller, 2022).

Lung cancer has a very low prognosis despite the fact that it has a high prognosis with other malignancies. The 5-year survival rates are diverse on the basis of the stage at which it is diagnosed but low in general. Disease at its earlier stage identified through screening programs like low dose computed tomography is much better treated but most people have not been able to uphold the use of screening programs on a wide scale.

In addition to mortality rates, lung cancer has huge economic and social costs. Long-term systemic therapies, hospitalizations, and supportive care is a financial burden to both the health care system and the patient. Also, the disease has severe effects on the quality of life as it results in respiratory dysfunction, toxicities during treatment, and mental distress.

Lung cancer is the disease with a high incidence, low prognosis, and complicated pathobiology that needs to be a focus of therapeutic innovation. The introduction of immunotherapy has changed the paradigm of management, but the weaknesses of the existing strategies make it necessary to consider next-generation strategies. The knowledge of the prevalence and the bio-pathology of lung cancer in the world highlights the necessity of new, specific, and sustainable therapeutic manipulation like siRNA-based immune checkpoint modulation (Thai et al., 2021).

13.1.2 Significant ongoing trends in the immunotherapy of lung cancer

Immunotherapy has now altered the treatment paradigm of advanced NSCLC and long-term overall survival and protracted response has been seen in a population of patients (Herbst et al., 2018). The most impactful one has been the development of ICIs, i.e., the PD-1/PD-L1 axis and CTLA-4 agents. The modern treatment methods have been revolutionized through PD-1/PD-L1 and CTLA-4 blockers such as nivolumab and atezolizumab, and ipilimumab and tremelimumab. These agents restore the T-cell-mediated cytotoxicity by suppressing the inhibitory effects which the tumor cells have tried to employ to escape the immune system.

The PD-1/PD-L1 inhibitors have been interesting as option of treatment of the patient with increased PD-L1 expression as a mono-agent treatment or a combination with the chemotherapy (Reck et al., 2022). Another important trend is the introduction of immunotherapy into earlier disease stages such as neoadjuvant and adjuvant. Clinical trials show there is better event free survival and pathological response rate with the use of immunotherapy before the surgical resection. Combination regimens that combine the ICIs with chemotherapy, radiotherapy or antiangiogenic agents are also utilized more in order to increase the immunogenicity of the tumor and boost response rates.

Notwithstanding these developments, it still has some critical clinical shortcomings. Response rates in response to objective are low, with about 20%–30% of the patients realizing sustained benefit. A high percentage of patients are primary resistant, and the other patients acquire resistance during treatment. In most instances of adaptive resistance, tumors can evade PD-1 blockade by upregulating alternative immune checkpoints T-cell immunoglobulin and the mucin-domain containing-3 (TIM-3) and lymphocyte activation gene-3 (LAG-3), (Bagchi et al., 2021). Destruction of antigen presentation apparatus and interferon signaling pathway dysregulations are additional causes of therapeutic failure.

Another critical problem is the immune-related adverse events (irAEs). Activation of systemic immune may lead to inflammatory toxicities like pneumonitis, colitis, dermatitis, endocrinopathies, and hepatitis (Martins et al., 2019). Pneumonitis is of paramount concern in patients of lung cancer because of preexisting pulmonary vulnerability. These toxicities can require immunosuppressive therapy and restrict the continued maintenance of therapy.

Thus, although immunotherapy has transformed an important breakthrough in the treatment of lung cancer, its drawbacks indicate the necessity of the next-generation approaches with higher specificity, lower systemic toxicity, and resistance to resistance mechanisms. Future directions are actively pursued in the form of emerging technologies such as multiplex checkpoint targeting, biomarker-based precision immunotherapy, and gene silencing platforms that can be considered as the extension of the current ICIs.

13.1.3 Limitations of current immune checkpoint inhibitors

PD-1, PD-L1, and CTLA-4 ICIs have completely changed the treatment paradigm of lung cancer and enhanced the survival of some patients. Although these have been made, their clinical utility is still limited by a number of significant limitations. The response rates are quite different, and a large percentage of patients are resistant in the first place, which is usually because of poor tumor immunogenicity, inefficient antigen presentation, or insufficient T-cell infiltration in the tumor microenvironment (TME).

Acquired resistance often occurs even in those patients who respond initially. The tumors can also evolve by increasing the expression of other inhibitory receptors like TIM-3, LAG-3 or T-cell immunoreceptor with Ig and immunoreceptor tyrosine-based inhibitory motif (ITIM) domains (TIGIT) thus avoiding the scale of the inhibited pathway. Immune escape is also caused by genetic changes in interferon signaling, or elements of the antigen presentation machinery. These mechanisms of adaptation underscore the dynamic aspect of tumor immune interactions and can imply that single-pathway blockade might not be effective in long-term control.

A serious clinical problem is also irAEs. Checkpoint inhibitors may be used to destabilize immune tolerance and initiate inflammatory toxicities in various body organs, including lungs, gastrointestinal tract, endocrine glands, and liver, by enhancing systemic immune activation. Even though most of the adverse events can be controlled, some serious complications can be treated by corticosteroid therapy or even the irreversible termination of treatment. Monoclonal antibodies (mAbs) are characterized by a long half-life, which prolongs immune activation to an undesired therapeutic period.

Other drawbacks are also heterogeneous PD-L1 expression in tumors, limited penetration of large antibody molecules to poorly vascularized tumor regions, and the high cost of biologic treatment of tumors over the long-term. All these challenges and issues, in turn, highlight the necessity of alternative or complementary methods that offer more accurate, flexible, and controllable control over the immune checkpoint pathways.

13.1.4 Reason to silence gene

Immune checkpoint molecules are dynamically regulated transcriptional proteins which expression levels are controlled by oncogenic signaling pathways, inflammatory cytokines and microenvironmental stressors. Due to the transcription of these proteins, the fact that checkpoint expression can be targeted at the messenger RNA level offers an alternative solution to the standard antibody-based therapy. siRNA technology represents an approach with a mechanistically different approach through which gene expression is suppressed prior to protein production. The strategy has a number of conceptual and translational benefits compared to monoclonal antibody therapy, which are as follows and elaborated in Table 13.1.

(1) Precise specificity: siRNA molecules are specific and strong binding molecules that can induce selective degradation of target transcripts, including PD-L1, CTLA-4, LAG-3, or TIM-3. Sanctioned contrary to antibodies reacting with extracellular protein domains, siRNA inhibits the expression of the checkpoint protein completely. This level of accuracy at transcript level minimizes the requirement of protein conformation, density of the receptors or localization of the epitopes. Moreover, rational sequence design and computational screening can be used to increase specificity at minimal unnecessary interaction with any other gene (Pecot et al., 2011).

(2) Multi-target potential: Compensatory upregulation of alternative inhibitory pathways following single-checkpoint blockade is commonly used as a mechanism of tumor immune escape. Simultaneous silencing of multiple checkpoint genes with a single platform of therapeutic formulation is made possible by siRNA platforms (Postow et al., 2015) .The strategies of dual or multiplex targeting can overcome redundant immunosuppressive signals and, therefore, minimize the chances of adaptive resistance. Such multi-target functionality offers a major benefit in lung cancer, in which co-expression of inhibitory receptors is prevalent in tumor infiltrating lymphocytes (TILs).

(3) Reduced systemic toxicity: Typically, mAbs can trigger systemic immune response with irAEs. SiRNA on the other hand can be targeted to tumor tissue locally or selectively

Table 13.1: Comparison of conventional immunotherapy vs. siRNA-based approaches.

Feature	Conventional ICIs (mAbs)	siRNA-based approaches	References
Mechanism of action	Blocks surface protein interaction (PD-1/PD-L1, CTLA-4)	Silences gene expression at mRNA level	Setten et al. (2019), Pardoll (2012)
Specificity	High, but limited to protein–protein interactions	High, programmable against any gene sequence	Mansoori et al. (2014),Ribas and Wolchok (2018)
Resistance issues	Adaptive resistance, alternate pathway activation	Can silence multiple checkpoints simultaneously	Sharma et al. (2017), Lee et al. (2016)
Delivery challenges	Intravenous infusion, systemic exposure	Requires nanocarriers for stability and targeting	Sharma et al. (2020), Postow et al. (2015)
Toxicity profile	Immune-related adverse events (irAEs)	Reduced systemic toxicity (if targeted efficiently)	Kim et al. (2016), Michot et al. (2016)
Cost	High (biologic manufacturing)	Potentially lower (synthetic, scalable production)	Wittrup and Lieberman (2015), Prasad et al. (2018)
Future potential	Limited by toxicity and resistance	Highly versatile; combinable with other therapies	Zottel et al. (2019), Havel et al. (2019)

CTLA-4, cytotoxic T-lymphocyte- associated antigen 4; *PD-1*, programmed death receptor-1; *PD-L1*, programmed death ligand-1; *siRNA*, small interfering RNA.

with the use of nanocarrier systems (Zhuang et al., 2011). Deliberate delivery minimizes overall immune stimulation and possibly the occurrence and intensity of immune-related toxicities. Moreover, the temporal quality of the silencing mechanism mediated by siRNA enables a regulation of immune responses to limit the long-term overstimulation of the immune system.

(4) Flexibility: siRNA therapeutics have a high level of flexibility, and they can be combined with chemotherapy, radiotherapy, immune checkpoint blockers, or other RNA-based constructs (Kim et al., 2016). SiRNA has the potential to increase tumor sensitivity to current therapeutic agents by modulating immune checkpoint on the genetic scale to develop synergies. Additionally, siRNA-based technology can be redesigned in a very short time to curb such resistance mechanisms and this provides flexibility which is not similar in traditional biologics.

The use of siRNA in immunotherapy against lung cancer is a solution to two significant unmet clinical problems: immune escape in solids and durability of response without excessive systemic toxicity (Kim et al., 2016; Pandey et al., 2022; Setten et al., 2019). Increasing the gene expression level by targeting it upstream, siRNA-based approaches provide a next-generation solution that can supplement -and potentially enhance the effects of antibody-based checkpoint blockade.

13.2 Immune checkpoints in lung cancer

Tolerance and autoimmune prevention are the checkpoints that are closely regulating the adaptive immune system. However, tumor cells almost always exploit these mechanisms of inhibition to escape the surveillance (Pardoll, 2012). Checkpoint molecules, which include CTLA-4, PD-1 and PD-L1, are involved in tumor immune interplay in lung cancer. Checkpoint molecules (CTLA-4, PD-1, and PD-L1) are a component of the tumor immune interaction of lung cancer (Keir et al., 2008). More current checkpoint proteins are also found to be playing a considerable role toward immunological resistance, such as T-cell immunoglobulin/mucin domain containing-3/TTIM3, lymphocyte activation gene-3/LAG-3 and T-cell immunoreceptor with Ig/ITIM domains/TIGIT.

The biological history of such pathways is important to be comprehended with a view to designing specific treatment modalities, such as siRNA-mediated silencing, which can directly suppress the expression of immune checkpoint genes, and stop the development of adaptive resistances.

13.2.1 Overview of immune checkpoints

The immunological checkpoints are inhibitory and stimulatory regulation receptors found on the surface of the activated T-cells and other immune subsets that act as vital regulators of immune homeostasis. These receptors serve like physiological brakes or accelerators of the immune system that make sure that immune activation is well regulated. Although the checkpoint signaling plays a critical role in the prevention of autoimmunity and peripheral tolerance, its aberrant regulation in cancer augments immune escape and tumor progression in the TME (Pardoll, 2012).

Immune checkpoints may be divided into two major groups:

(1) TIM-3, LAG-3, and TIGIT inhibitory checkpoints regulate and suppress T-cell activity and effector responses. Constant stimulation of such suppressive receptors helps in the T-cell exhaustion and immune tolerance in cancer.

(2) Stimulatory receptors, including, CD28, OX40, and 4-1BB, stimulate T- cell activation, proliferation and survival. These co-stimulatory signaling pathways are necessary conditions of strong antitumor immune responses and are frequently not adequately utilized in the immunosuppressive TME.

Oncology therapy strategies typically aim at inhibiting the inhibitory checkpoint signaling of TILs and tumor cells to reinstate T-cell activity, prevent T-cell exhaustion and tumor immune escape (Dong et al., 2002; Sun et al., 2018). The key to designing the next-generation immunotherapies is to understand the balance between inhibitory and stimulatory pathways.

13.2.2 PD-1/PD-1 axis

PD-1 is an immune receptor on activated natural killer cells, B cells, and T-cells, which is coded by PDCD1. It has ligands, PD-L1 (CD274) and PD-L2, which are commonly expressed on tumor cells and antigen-presenting cells in the TME (Freeman et al., 2000; Keir et al., 2008). The interaction of PD-1 with PD-L1 triggers negative intracellular signaling pathways which inhibit the T-cell receptor (TCR) signal as well as diminish cytokine and cause T-cell anergy or apoptosis. This relationship is the dominant type of immune suppression in lung cancer (Brahmer et al., 2012).

The expression of PD-L1 in NSCLC is linked to poor survival and has beneficial prognostic predictive value in response to PD-1/PD-L1 inhibitors. Antibodies against this pathway (nivolumab and pembrolizumab) have also shown prolonged clinical response. Nevertheless, objective response rates are still minimal at about 20%–30% of the number of patients which implies that a significant percentage of patients do not respond or ultimately develop resistance (Hellmann et al., 2019).

The resistance mechanisms that develop to adapt to PD-1 blockade are major limiting factors to blockade duration. PD-1 blockage can increase the expression of other inhibitory checkpoints, including TIM-3 and LAG-3 by tumors, therefore maintaining immune suppression (Koyama et al., 2016a; Sharma et al., 2017). Also, depletion of antigen presentation apparatus such as major histocompatibility complex molecules downregulation makes tumors less visible to cytotoxic lymphocytes. Such compensatory mechanisms underscore the significance of multi-target therapeutic mechanisms that have the ability of surmounting dynamic immune escape.

13.2.3 Cytotoxic T-lymphocyte-associated antigen-4 and other emerging targets

CTLA-4 is located on stimulated T-cells and suppress the binding of CD80 and CD86 on antigen-presenting cells with CD28 CTLA-4 is efficient to suppress T-cell activation and co-stimulatory signaling because of its increased affinity with such ligands. In contrast to PD-1 which mostly controls the activity of the effector T-cell in peripheral tissues, CTLA-4 is a key regulator of the priming stage of T-cells in lymph nodes (Buchbinder & Desai, 2016).

Antibodies that block the inhibitory interaction like ipilimumab are therapeutic antibodies that can be used to treat CTLA-4 in order to stimulate T-cell reactivation. PD-1 inhibitors used in combination with each other have shown to be better than monotherapy in improving the survival of advanced NSCLC at the expense of increased immune toxicity (Hellmann et al., 2019). The complementary mechanisms of action between CTLA-4 and PD-1 are highlighted by this synergy.

On top of PD-1, CTLA-4, there are a few different emerging immune checkpoints involved in tumor immune evasion. LAG-3 also binds major histocompatibility complex class II molecules and is often co-expressed with PD-1 on exhausted T-cells, which develops inhibitory signal (Anderson et al., 2016). TIM-3 interacts with galectin-9 and is linked to immune evasion and poor prognosis of lung cancer. TIGIT inhibits the natural killer and T-cells by binding to CD155, which weakens the cytotoxic reaction.

The prevalent co-expression of PD-1 and LAG-3, TIM-3, and TIGIT on TILs are indicative of single-agent immunotherapy checkpoint blockade being not fully able to reverse immune silencing in lung cancer. These studies demonstrate the use of multi-specific/ multi-plex targeting approaches that have the potential to regulate multiple inhibitory pathways at the same time.

13.2.4 Immune evasion mechanisms

The various mechanisms through which lung cancer exploits the checkpoint pathways in the evasion of immune responses include:

(1) Checkpoint overexpression and PD-L1 amplification: The overexpression of PD-L1 on tumor and stromal cells is one of the most striking immune evasions in lung cancer. There is the possibility of an adaptive induction of PD-L1 by released interferon-g of activated T-cells, a process referred to as adaptive immune resistance. Also, oncogenic intrinsic pathways including epidermal growth factor receptor (EGFR mutations, KRAS stimulation, and ALK rearrangements have the capacity to directly transcriptionally regulate PD-L1, not reliant on immune signaling. Epigenetic alterations and gene amplification also augment the expression of PD-L1 in some subsets of tumors. The PD-L1 upregulation is also encouraged by hypoxic conditions in the TME as a result of transcription via hypoxia-inducible factor-1a. Continued overexpression of PD-L1 enhances PD-1 unleashing abilities of cytotoxic T-cells and enabling tumor survival (Jia et al., 2025; Lin et al., 2024; Yamaguchi et al., 2022).

(2) T-cell exhaustion and inhibitory receptors co-expression: T-cell exhaustion in chronic exposure to the antigen in the TME develops progressively. Tumor infiltrating Lymphocytes often have a high rate of co-expression of PD-1, LAG-3, TIM-3 and other inhibitory receptors. This expression pattern of multi-receptors is linked with a decrease in proliferative potential, dysfunctional cytokine release, and less cytotoxic efficacy. T-cells experience transcriptional and metabolic reprogramming, stabilizing their dysfunctional phenotype, when exhausted, to only a limited level of responsiveness to

single-checkpoint blockade. Deeply exhausted populations of T-cells play a role in therapeutic resistance in advanced lung cancer (Andrews et al., 2024; Jiang et al., 2015; Xiang et al., 2025).

(3) Checkpoint blockade resistant to adaptive response: In reaction to immunotherapy, tumors show considerable flexibility. After PD-1 inhibition, other checkpoints like TIM-3, LAG-3 or TIGIT can be upregulated, and the immunological response can still be suppressed. This dynamic regulation change is a kind of adaptive resistance where the inhibition of a specific pathway results in the activation of other redundant inhibitory pathways. Moreover, a decrease in immune-mediated cytotoxicity can be caused by changes in interferon signaling pathways or the antigen presentation apparatus. These adaptation mechanisms highlight the intricacy of immune escape in lung cancer (Koyama et al., 2016).

(4) Immune-related toxicities therapeutic constrains: Even though checkpoint inhibitors reestablish antitumor immunity, their global induction of immune responses can lead to irAEs. Pneumonitis in patients with lung cancer is an especially worrying complication, as the underlying pulmonary pathology in this group of patients is of some concern. Colitis, dermatitis, endocrinopathies and hepatitis are also seen. These toxicities reduce the extensive and chronic administration of checkpoint inhibitors, and can lead to the requirement of immunosuppressive treatment, which can reverse therapeutic efficacy. Therefore, although the checkpoint blockade has revolutionized the clinical management, there is a challenge in safety constraint (Yin et al., 2023).

All these mechanisms represent that lung cancer is a dynamic immunologic environment with redundancy, adaptation, and multifaceted regulatory processes. The multifaceted immune evasion observed here demonstrates the possible benefit of siRNA-based approaches that would have the potential to silence two or more checkpoint genes at once. Gene silencing strategies can help decrease adaptive resistance by inhibiting multiple inhibitory receptors sets on the transcriptional level, leading to more durable antitumor immune response.

13.3 Small interfering RNA technology: Fundamentals and advantages

siRNA technology has been found to be highly functional molecular tool in silencing disease-associated genes through the process of RNA interference (RNAi). Researchers have pursued the potential therapeutic uses of siRNAs to include treatment of cancer or viral disease (Fire et al., 1998). The key mechanism behind siRNA therapy is the sequence-specific degraded messenger ribonucleic acid (mRNA) target resulting in the post-transcriptional gene silencing (Meister & Tuschl, 2004).

In lung cancer immunotherapy, the siRNA way to shut down immune checkpoint gene expression may offer a more tightly-focused approach to the overriding of immune checkpoint-regulated inhibition of antitumor immunity. Relative to antibody-based checkpoint

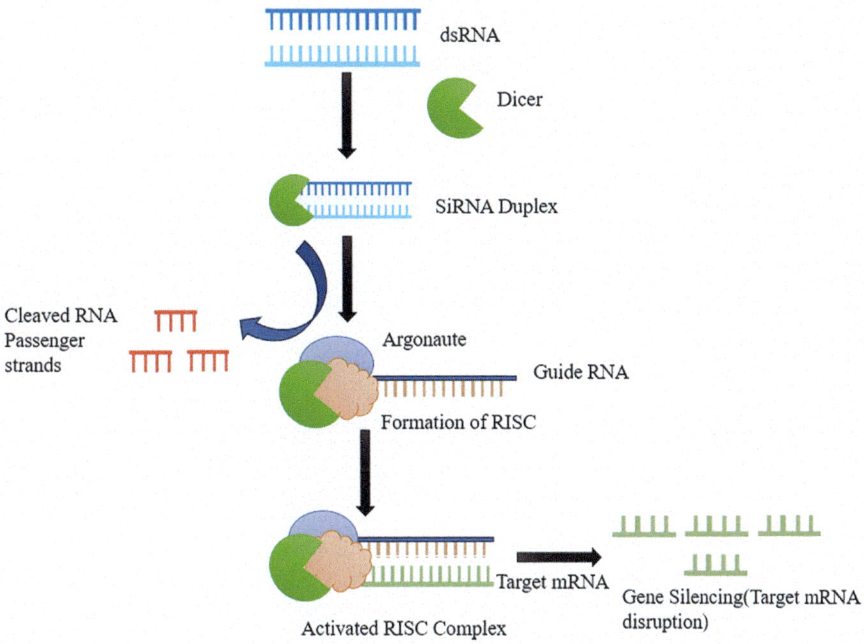

Figure 13.1
Mechanism of RNA interference (RNAi).

inhibitors, siRNA has unique benefits, such short-term effects, modularity, decreased immunogenicity, and potential multiplexed targeting (Davidson & McCray, 2011; Kim & Rossi, 2007).

13.3.1 Mechanism of RNA interference

RNA interference is a common cell pathway which is involved in sequence-specific RNA degradation. The process starts by the introduction of the molecules of RNA (doubled strands) in the cytoplasm. Within mammalian cells, RNase III protein Dicer processes long double-stranded RNA into small interfering fragments of RNA about 21–23 bases long. These siRNA dups are further integrated into the RNA-induced silencing complex (RISC) which is a multiprotein complex that has the Argonaute proteins which take part in target recognition and cleavage shown in Fig. 13.1 (Meister & Tuschl, 2004).

In RISC, the siRNA duplex passenger strand is cleaved off and the guide strand is available to mediate sequence-specific binding to complementary mRNA transcripts. During binding, Argonaute-2 triggers endo nucleolytic cleavage of the target mRNA and causes the target protein synthesis to be rapidly degraded and suppressed. Since the mechanism is based on complementarity of nucleotides and not protein structure, RNA interference has enabled very specific targeting of any gene whose sequence is known.

Synthetic siRNA molecules can bypass the Dicer processing step and normally enter the RISC pathway, used in therapeutics. After they enter the cytoplasm, they work in a similar manner as endogenous small RNAs. Notably, genomic DNA is not permanently disturbed by RNA interference. The silencing effect is temporary, as long as siRNA molecules are in place, and the effect is available to be reversed and regulated. This is a highly beneficial characteristic in immunotherapy where too much or too long immune activation can lead to toxicity (Kim & Rossi, 2007).

13.3.2 Design and synthesis of small interfering RNA molecules

Rational design and chemical optimization are important in the success of the therapeutic activity of siRNA. Good siRNAs have a duplex length of 19-base pairs and three overhangs, which are two nucleotides, which improve stability and RISC internalization. Bioinformatic algorithms are used in sequence choice by predicting accessibility of the target and reducing homology with unrelated transcripts. Repetitive or immunostimulatory motifs should be avoided as much as possible in order to minimize unwanted biological responses.

Native RNA molecules in biological fluids are also unstable by nature because of the presence of nucleases. Hence, chemical alterations are regularly introduced in order to improve the pharmacokinetics. Replacements include 2 -O methyl and 2 -fluoro at the ribose backbone, which improve stability against enzymatic degradation without disrupting gene silencing activity. Stability is further enhanced by phosphorothioate linkages which modify the chemistry of the backbone and increase plasma protein binding. These augment systemic half-life and enhance the therapeutic persistence.

Strategies of conjugation further help in better delivery and biodistribution. Lipophilic group or polyethylene glycol group or targeting ligand attachment can increase cellular uptake and defer quick renal elimination. Stability, specificity and functional activity should be balanced carefully to ensure the efficient RISC loading and target recognition. These developments in solid-phase oligonucleotide synthesis have made it possible to manufacture oligonucleotides in large quantities in a scalable and reproducible way, allowing clinical utility of RNAi-based therapeutics (Reynolds et al., 2004).

13.3.3 Off-target effects and immune activation

Even though siRNA therapeutics provide extremely sequence-specific gene silencing, undesired biological effects can be detected as they partially complement, are recognized by innate immunity or are delivered. These factors need to be carefully considered during safe and effective clinical translation, especially in immunotherapy where excessive immune response may have severe outcomes.

Off-target gene silencing is one of the major concerns. Although siRNA molecules are engineered to fit one messenger RNA sequence, partial sequence similarity between the siRNA and other transcripts may lead to unintentional silencing. It can be common with interactions between the seed region, whereby nucleotides 2-8 of the guide strand interact with off-target mRNAs in a microRNA-like fashion that is imperfect. Gene expression networks outside the target can also change as a result of such interactions, and may have an impact on cell viability, immune signaling pathways, or metabolic processes. Computational algorithms and transcriptome-wide screening methodologies are consequently used in the process of siRNA design in an attempt to decrease unintended complementarity as well as off-target risk (Hu et al., 2020).

Specificity is further increased by chemical modification. The 2′-O-methyl or 2′-fluoro modifications incorporated into the seed region result in decreased unintended microRNA-like activity without decreasing silencing activity. Also, target sites are carefully chosen to ensure that they do not have homology with other transcripts. All these measures minimize nonspecific modulation of the genes and increase the therapeutic safety (Kaushal, 2023).

In addition to the effects that are dependent on the sequence, siRNA molecules have the potential to stimulate innate immune responses. Pattern recognition receptors that identify double-stranded RNA include toll-like receptor 3, toll-like receptor 7, toll-like receptor 8 and cytosolic sensors (RIG-I and MDA5). These receptors upon activation evoke the production of type I interferons and proinflammatory cytokines. Although minor immune stimulation is effective in cancer treatment, it can cause a systemic inflammatory reaction, cytokine discharge, or unintentional toxicity when overstimulated (Choi et al., 2024).

The activation of immune is determined by various factors such as siRNA length, sequence motifs, delivery route and chemical composition. genitourinary (GU)-rich motifs are especially likely to be recognized by toll-like receptor. This immunostimulatory potential is greatly decreased by structural optimization and alteration of the backbone. Nanoparticles also shield siRNA by encapsulation, which prevents immune sensors (activation due to lack of specificity) of the siRNA when in circulation .

The carrier of delivery is also another protective factor in immune responses. Polymeric lipids and cationic lipids can activate complement or disrupt the membrane at very high concentrations. Thus, biodegradable and ionizable substances are used to eliminate inflammatory responses as much as possible. Cytokine monitoring and dose optimization are also important when conducting preclinical and clinical trials.

Notably, the fleeting character of RNA interference grants there is some control of safety. In comparison with permanently genome editing methods, the effect of siRNA-mediated decays due to the degradation of the molecule. The ability to reverse this enables the dosing schedules to be modulated to ensure therapeutic use and at the same time allow immune safety. Controlled gene silencing in the case of ICB could decreases the chances of chronic immune overstimulation and still induce antitumor effect. All in all, although off-target effects and immune stimulation is a critical problem, the development of molecular design, chemical modification and delivery technology has greatly enhanced the safety profile of siRNA therapeutics. Continued improvements in the selection algorithms of the sequence and options of biomarkers surveillance will also improve the accuracy and clinical viability of RNA interference in immunotherapy of lung cancer (Ali Zaidi et al., 2023; Robbins et al., 2009).

13.3.4 Benefits over traditional immunotherapy

Even though ICI like mAbs against PD-1, PD-L1, and CTLA-4 have transformed the treatment of lung cancer, their clinical potential is hindered by poor response, immune-like adverse event, resistance, and high cost of production. The response rates in NSCLC are usually objective (ranging 20%–30%), and more flexible and targeted immunotherapeutic methods are necessary. Against this context, the siRNA-based gene silencing has a number of conceptual and translational advantages as compared to the traditional antibody-based methods.

(1) Increased specificity: siRNA molecules have their effect by complementary messenger RNA sequence-specific degradation, which has enabled high accuracy in targeting immunosuppressive genes. Unlike mAbs, which attach themselves to extracellular proteins and can be affected by the receptor density, the protein changes in shape, as well as by masking the epitopes, siRNA acts at the transcript level, halting the production of the target protein. This upstream intervention is more probable to decrease the chance of incomplete blockade and possibly structural heterogeneity in checkpoint proteins. Moreover, the rational sequence design and computational screening optimize unwanted interactions between the genes, and improve therapeutic specificity (Bumcrot et al., 2006).

(2) Reduced systemic toxicity: The effect of checkpoint inhibitors usually causes systemic immune activation, which results in irAEs of the lungs, gastrointestinal tract, endocrine organs, and liver. By comparison, the knockdown method of siRNAs facilitates the blockage of the checkpoint gene expression in a localized and controlled manner . Since the effect of siRNA is temporary and dose-dependent, immune modulation can be controlled to minimize the chances of excessive immune stimulation. Delivery systems that are specifically designed also limit gene silencing to tumor tissues, which could reduce off-target immune responses as well as the intensity of systemic toxicities that are typically involved in antibody therapy (Setten et al., 2019).

(3) Multiplex targeting and versatility: The ability of the RNA interference to silence multiple genes at a time is one of the greatest advantages of RNA interference technology. Dual or multi-siRNA systems may be used to suppress multiple immune checkpoint pathways by inhibiting PD-L1 and CTLA-4 at the same time or by integrating the inhibition of immune checkpoint pathways with oncogenic or angiogenic signaling pathways. The ability is specifically significant in lung cancers, where the tumor tends to develop adaptive resistance mechanisms of upregulating alternative inhibitory receptors. Multiplex targeting enables extensive modulation of the immunosuppressive TME and this can result in more prolonged and endearing antitumor responses than single-agent blockade (Wittrup & Lieberman, 2015).

(4) Flexibility to the emerging resistance mechanisms: Production of mAbs is a multidimensional procedure that has taken a long time to optimize its structure and be verified in clinical use. However, siRNA sequences can then be speedily redesigned to attack new pathways or resistance mechanisms. With the development of tumor biology and the discovery of new immune escape mechanisms, siRNA platforms can with relative ease be modified to include new gene targets. Such flexibility gives RNA interference especially good application in dynamic oncologic settings where molecular heterogeneity and therapeutic resistance are the norm (Castanotto & Rossi, 2009).

(5) Manufacturing efficiency and cost-effectiveness: mAbs are recombinant biologics that need elaborate cell-based manufacturing systems, purification procedures, and cold-chain logistics, which drive it up in terms of manufacturing costs. In comparison, synthetic siRNAs are synthesized by solid-phase oligonucleotide synthesis, which can be scaled and reproducibly manufactured at what may be low cost (Deng et al., 2014). With the further development of synthesis technologies, it is possible that large-scale synthesis of siRNA therapeutics will be more cost-effective and more accessible, not only economically but also socially, decreasing the financial load on medical systems.

Combined with these strengths, these advantages make siRNA-based therapeutics a next-generation immunotherapy platform. Due to their increased specificity, controlled immune modulation, the ability to multiplex, adapt to changes in tumor biology, and, in some settings, better therapeutic responses, siRNA-mediated strategies can supplement the existing ICIs or deliver superior therapeutic responses in some situations. Further development of delivery system and clinical testing will dictate the level of RNA interference in the future of immunotherapy of lung cancer.

13.4 Small interfering RNA-mediated immune checkpoint blockade

ICB has revolutionized the field of cancer therapy, and they have developed antibodies against PD-1, PD-L1, and CTLA-4 which have clinically validated usage against a variety of tumors. However, there are inherent limitations to monoclonal antibody-based therapies regarding irAEs, long half-life, poor tumor penetration, and expense (Ribas & Wolchok, 2018; Topalian et al., 2015). siRNA represents a viable alternative to checkpoint inhibition in that it can offer transient mRNA gene silencing, and further, potentially support combination therapies and/or tumor specificity (Ribas & Wolchok, 2018).

13.4.1 Targeting PD-1/PD-L1 with small interfering RNA

The PD-1/PD-L1 axis is among the best-validated immune checkpoint axes in lung cancer. Conventional mAbs that yield PD-1 (nivolumab, pembrolizumab) and PD-L1 (atezolizumab, durvalumab) have transformed clinical practice, yet need to address the deprived pieces together with high prices, irAEs (irAEs), and primary/secondary resistance which requires further strategy (Meng & Lu, 2017; Sristi et al., 2025).

Direct genetic manipulation using siRNA-mediated silencing can be used to downregulate the PD-1 or PD-L1 expression at transcript level once again restoring T-cell effector functions. In vitro studies on PD-L1, PD-L1 can also be effectively silenced using nanocarriers loaded with siRNA to treat the PD-L1 target NSCLC, in vitro, the silencing mechanism can increase the infiltration of CD8+ T-cells to promote tumor regression. Notably, as opposed to a systemic antibody, the effect of siRNA-based modalities is reversible and can be adjusted, therefore the chance of persistent immune stimulation can be limited (Tran & Phuong Tran, 2022).

The next virtue is that it may circumvent the heterogeneity toward PD-L1 expression in tumor tissue. SiRNA has the advantage over antibodies in that post-translational modified epitopes can contribute to variability; siRNA can be directed toward conserved sequences of mRNA to overcome this issue. In addition, siRNA may be designed to target both tumor and stromal PD-L1, interfering with immunosuppressive signaling in the TME.

13.4.2 Dual and multi-targeting strategies (PD-L1 + CTLA-4)

One mechanism of resistance commonly seen with ICIs relates to adaptive upregulation of other inhibitory receptors like CTLA-4, TIM-3, or LAG-3, in response. To counter this, siRNA technology can support dual or multiplex silent of two or more checkpoints in one delivery system (Sristi et al., 2025).

As one example, siRNAs encapsulated using LNPs to PD-L1 and CTLA-4 demonstrated synergistic antitumor effects in the models of lung cancer in mice. The combined blockade boosted expansion of memory T-cells, production of interferon-γ (IFN-γ), and reduced the infiltration of regulatory T-cell (Treg). This dual-targeting strategy can also overcome the mechanism of adaptive resistance that is evident with monotherapies (Gu et al., 2025).

Moreover, siRNA cocktails may be tailor-made to hit simultaneously activation pathways of tumor cells (e.g. STAT3, VEGF) along with immune checkpoints. This makes a possibility of undulating the immune evasion signals and tumor proliferation signals together. One major strength in this approach is specificity and modularity siRNA can be readily re-programmed to incorporate additional targets as new immune escape mechanisms are mapped.

13.4.3 Synergistic effects with existing immunotherapies

siRNA-based approaches are not planned to substitute but to complement other immunotherapy approaches. It is possible that simultaneous inhibition of siRNA checkpoint silencing with mAbs, cancer vaccines, or adoptive cell transfer (chimeric antigen aeceptor t-cell therapy (CAR-T), TIL therapy) might be synergistic.

As an example, preclinical data indicate that PD-L1 siRNA can increase the utility of antiPD-1 antibodies to the point where they can be administered at reduced antibody doses, but still retain their therapeutic effects, thereby lessening immune-related toxicity. Correspondingly, in situ priming of dendritic cell using CTLA-4 siRNA has been used to augment vaccine induced T-cell response in lung tumor models (Barati et al., 2022).

The dual-modality approaches radiotherapy and chemotherapy, which augment tumor antigen release and immune recognition also have a synergistic effect with siRNA checkpoint blockade. The postchemotherapy effect is the derepression of PD-L1 signaling, silencing of which allows elimination of checkpoint rebound inhibitory signaling so frequently seen after administration of a cytostatic agent. Formally, siRNA-engineered exosomes of immune cells are showing promise as a natural delivery platform capable of incorporating checkpoint silencing and immune activation (Huynh et al., 2025).

In summary, checkpoint inhibition using siRNA is a highly adaptable, containing and a potent form of treatment that may address resistance, reduce toxicity and expand the population of lung cancer patients who can respond to immunotherapies.

13.5 Nanocarrier systems for small interfering RNA delivery

The most challenging expounding factor in clinical translation of siRNA is its effective delivery. Naked siRNAs face the risk of enzyme degradation, possible rapid elimination in kidneys and poor uptake by cells. Thus, there is a need to enhance stability, tumor specificity and endosomal release through formation of structurally stable nano carrier systems (Jackson & Linsley, 2010). Classes of delivery vehicles have been evolved and include those built on lipids, polymers and inorganic systems, along with hybrids, each with its own advantages and drawbacks.

13.5.1 Challenges in small interfering RNA delivery

Although the therapeutic potential of the immune checkpoint inhibition is clear by using siRNA, there are a number of intrinsic limitations hindering its clinical application. A naked siRNA molecule has a short half-life (<10 minutes) which is highly vulnerable to degradation by bloodstream nucleases. They are also poorly taken up because they are negatively charged and repel the cell membrane and can stimulate inappropriate immune response through toll-like receptors (TLRs). Moreover, enhanced targeting of the tumor with minimal accumulation to the hepatic, renal or splenic regions poses a major stumbling block. These challenges highlight the need of delivering nanocarrier-based delivery systems that can increase the stability of siRNA, shield it against degradation in enzymes, and release it in tumor specific areas (Jackson & Linsley, 2010; Wittrup & Lieberman, 2015).

13.5.2 Lipid-based nanoparticles

LNPs are the most clinically developed siRNA delivery technology with patrician (an FDA-approved RNAi drug) showing the translational potential of the platform. LNPs are composed of ionizable lipids, cholesterol, helper lipids and polyethylene glycol (PEG)-lipids. Ionizable lipids promote escape of the endosomes through the generation of a positive charge in low pH conditions and allow the release of siRNA into the cytoplasm (Hou et al., 2021; Kulkarni et al., 2018).

LNP-based PD-L1 siRNA has also demonstrated potent antitumor effects in lung cancer patient murine models, increasing effective infiltration of T-cells and T-cell cytotoxicity. LNPs are also amenable to surface conjugation with ligands (i.e., transferrin, folic acid, antibodies) to enhance tumor specificity. Nevertheless, hepatotoxicity, which varies according to dose, and complement activation still hold back application (Ge et al., 2025).

13.5.3 Polymer-based carriers

Cationic polymers such as polyethyleneimine (PEI), poly(L-lysine), and dendrimers are widely studied for siRNA delivery. Their high density of positive charges facilitates strong siRNA binding and endosomal escape via the "proton sponge effect."

Recent advances include biodegradable polymers [poly(beta-amino esters), chitosan derivatives, and poly(2-dimethylaminoethyl methacrylate, PDMAEMA)] that reduce cytotoxicity while maintaining delivery efficiency. In lung cancer, polymeric nanoparticles co-delivering PD-L1 siRNA and cisplatin demonstrated synergistic tumor inhibition by reversing immunosuppression and inducing apoptosis (Kim et al., 2016).

The major limitation is dose-dependent toxicity and nonspecific interactions with serum proteins, which require chemical modifications to improve biocompatibility.

13.5.4 Inorganic and hybrid delivery platforms

Nanoparticles of inorganic compounds, including gold nanoparticle (AuNPs), mesoporous silica nanoparticle (MSNs), and calcium phosphate nanoparticle, allow structural stability, size-adjustability, and surface modifications. Thiol-linked PD-1 silencing siRNA with aggregate AuNPs has been used in silencing PD-1 in cancerous lung cells to enhance T-cell cytotoxicity (Baker et al., 2023).

Hybrid nanoparticles that are composed of a combination of lipids, polymers and inorganic substances combine the benefit of each. Indeed, the tumor targeting of lipid-coated MSNs carrying PD-L1 siRNA compared to drug-free lipid-coated MSNs and naked PD-L1 siRNA was improved, and off-target distribution was reduced in xenografts. Such hybrid carriers can also enable stimuli-responsive design (e.g. pH-, redox- or enzyme- triggered release of siRNA in the TME) (Hao et al., 2024; Mieszawska et al., 2013).

13.5.5 Tumor-targeted and stimuli-responsive systems

Targeting tumor specific approaches enhance the effectiveness of exchange at the expense of systemic side effects. This can be either through active targeting (e.g., antibody- or aptamer-conjugated nanoparticles which target EGFR or PD-L1 on lung cancer cells) or passive targeting via the enhanced permeability and retention (EPR) effect present in tumor vasculature (Xiong et al., 2025)

The challenge of next-generation smart siRNA delivery is stimuli-responsive systems.

For example: pH-responsive delivery systems allow the liberation of siRNA in acidic tumor micro environments.

The redox-activated carriers take advantage of the abundance of glutathione in cancer cells to liberate siRNA in tumor cells.

Enzyme-responsive carriers (also known as tumor-activated drug delivery) The release of targeted products is triggered by cleavage by tumor-overexpressed proteins, such as tumor-activated drug delivery using protease-sensitive prodrugs. siRNA carriers also undergo specific release of their contents upon cleavage by tumor-overexpressed proteins.

These systems hold great promise as a precision immunotherapy and may be used in patient specific targeting of siRNA-based therapies in lung cancer as shown in Table 13.2.

13.6 Pharmacokinetics and biodistribution

The pharmacokinetic characteristics of siRNA drugs are quite similar to the behavior of the usual small-molecule drugs and mAbs. The siRNAs have short degradation rates, low membrane permeability, and a large exposure to biological clearance mechanisms because of their nucleic acid structure. Effective ICB siRNA-based translation thus requires that in addition to specific targeting, it should be able to generate an appropriate circulation time, tumor accumulation, intracellular release, and minimal and tolerated systemic toxicity. It is

Table 13.2: Comparative overview of nanocarrier platforms for siRNA delivery in lung cancer.

Nanocarrier type	Key features	Advantages	Limitations	Examples in lung cancer	References
Lipid nanoparticles (LNPs)	Ionizable lipids + PEG	High transfection efficiency, clinically validated	Hepatotoxicity, complement activation	PD-L1 siRNA-loaded LNPs enhancing T-cell infiltration	Hou et al. (2021)
Polymer-based carriers	PEI, chitosan, dendrimers	Strong binding, proton sponge effect	Cytotoxicity, nonspecific interactions	PD-L1 siRNA + cisplatin polymeric nanoparticles	Ge et al. (2025)
Inorganic nanoparticles	Gold, silica, calcium phosphate	Stability, tunable size, multifunctionality	Accumulation, long-term safety concerns	AuNPs delivering PD-1 siRNA to NSCLC cells	Mieszawska et al. (2013), An et al. (2024)
Hybrid nanocarriers	Lipid-polymer, lipid-silica	Combine best of multiple systems	Complex formulation	Lipid-coated silica delivering PD-L1 siRNA	Jürgens et al. (2024)
Stimuli-responsive carriers	pH, redox, enzyme-triggered	Tumor-selective release, high precision	Early stage of development	Redox-sensitive PD-L1 siRNA nanoplatform	Xiong et al. (2025)

NSCLC, nonsmall cell lung cancer; *PEI*, polyethyleneimine; *PD-1*, programmed death receptor-1; *PD-L1*, programmed death ligand-1; *siRNA*, small interfering RNA.

vital to understand the nature of absorption, distribution, metabolism and elimination in order to promote the efficacy of therapy in lung cancer.

13.6.1 Circulation stability and clearance

Native siRNA molecules are very prone to disintegration by endonucleases and exonucleases, which exist in serum. The plasma half-life of unmodified duplexes is a few minutes; this is because of a quick enzyme cleavage and renal filtration. They are hydrophilic and due to their small size, they are rapidly cleared by glomerular filtration and so there is limited systemic exposure, and they are less likely to reach tumor tissue.

The circulation is greatly improved through chemical modification. Resistance to nuclease activity is enhanced by substitution like 2′-O-methyl and 2′-fluoro that maintain RNA interference activity. Backbone modifications to phosphorothioate further enhance stability by enhancing resistance to enzyme attack, and increasing the plasma protein binding, which increases half-life. Another technique, conjugation in which lipophilic moieties or polyethylene glycosylation of the conjugate is used, also regards renal clearance and enhances systemic persistence (Mainini & Eccles, 2020; Zhang et al., 2023).

Pharmacokinetic behavior is significantly changed in case of encapsulation in nanocarrier systems. LNPs and polymeric particles protect siRNA against enzymatic degradation and ensure it is not eliminated by the kidneys. The ensuing rise in the circulation time contributes to the likelihood of mass accumulation of tumor, especially via the passive targeting capacity, including the EPR effect present in solid tumors. The duration of circulation should, however, be compromised against the risk of retention in clearance organs such as the liver and the spleen which may decrease therapeutic availability through uptake by the reticuloendothelial system (Park et al., 2016).

13.6.2 Cellular uptake and endosomal escape

Once inside one of the tumor tissues, the siRNA has to pass through the cellular membrane and avoid the intracellular vesicular compartments in order to have gene silencing effects. Since siRNA molecules assume a negative charge, they cannot diffuse across the lipid bi-layer and they rely instead on being carried into the cell by a carrier. Nanoparticles enter the cell via the internalization process by endocytosis, or clathrin-mediated and caveolae-mediated endocytosis .

After the internalization process, complexes of siRNA are internalized in the endosomes. Absence of efficient escape to the endosomes means that the therapeutic payload is transported to lysosomes and degraded. Thus, endosomal release can be considered a bottleneck rate in RNA interference therapy. The positively charged LNPs generated in acidic conditions in endosomes destabilize the membrane and release into the cytoplasm. In the same manner, cationic polymers utilize the proton sponge principle, in which buffering capacity causes the osmotic swelling of the endosomal membrane and its rupture.

There is a direct correlation of gene knockdown power with endosomal escape efficiency. Poor escape leads to the poor cytoplasmic retention and reduction in therapeutic efficacy, and superior delivery systems increase RISC loading and long-term maintenance of immune checkpoint transcripts suppression. One of the key design challenges in controlled intracellular release is to avoid cytotoxic membrane disruption while achieving controlled intracellular release (Hu et al., 2020).

13.6.3 Tumor accumulation and off-target distribution

Tumor physiology and carrier design have a role in the distribution of siRNA therapeutic. Passive targeting through the EPR effect enables the nanoparticles to be preferentially accumulated in tumors which have leaky vessels and poor lymphatic drainage. Nevertheless, the extent of this effect differs across patients and subtypes of tumors, and it is a cause of interindividual differences in therapeutic response.

Selectivity can be enhanced using active targeting techniques where ligands (i.e., antibodies, peptides, or aptamers) that identify tumor-associated receptors are used. The epidermal growth factor receptor or PD-L1 itself have been used as a target in lung cancer to enhance tumor localization. These strategies will improve uptake in the malignant cells and decrease nonspecific distribution.

Although targeting, extensive uptake of TB happens in the liver, spleen and kidneys because of the recognition by macrophages and filtration systems. These organs can accumulate a lot resulting in decreased therapeutic effectiveness and possible toxicity. Close attention should be paid to optimization of the size of particles, surface charge, and hydrophilicity to minimize off-target deposition and enhance penetration of the tumor (Sarett et al., 2017).

Heterogeneity of tumor also has an impact on distribution. Areas of hypoxia, hypertensive interstitial pressure and dense extracellular matrix may hinder diffusion of nanoparticles, preventing access to deeper layers of tumor. Enhanced formulations aim at increasing the level of penetration and homogenous dispersion within the TME in order to obtain uniform gene silencing (Mainini & Eccles, 2020).

13.6.4 Safety and toxicological issues

The safety testing of siRNA therapeutics includes sequence-effect and carrier- effect. Unintended silencing of an off-target gene can happen when unintended transcript silencing is caused by a portion of the sequence complementing. Such risk can be mitigated by rational design and computational screening although extensive preclinical evaluation is necessary.

Another issue is that of innate immune activation. TLRs are able to detect the presence of double-stranded RNA, which leads to the release of inflammatory cytokines. This reaction is addressed by chemical derivation and selection of the sequence in such a way that immune activation is mainly due to checkpoint modulation and not nonspecific stimulation.

There should be carrier-associated toxicity as well. High concentrations of cationic lipids and polymers are able to destabilize cell membranes causing dose-dependent cytotoxicity. Hepatic tissue build-up can lead to short-lived increases in liver enzymes whereas complement activation can result in infusion-related reaction. Biodegradable and ionizable materials have been produced in order to minimize these effects and still deliver effectively.

Notably, RNA interference can be turned off which provides a safety benefit over more permanent technologies of genome editing. A gradual restoration of gene expression with the degradation of siRNA allows the duration of immune modulation to be regulated. Immunological biomarkers and dose-titration as well as close observation of the blood improve clinical safety (Sajid et al., 2020).

13.7 Preclinical and clinical evidence

A close relationship between conceptual framework and therapeutic application of siRNA-mediated ICB requires stringent preclinical validation and early clinical study. There are in vitro and in vivo experimental studies, which have given evidence of concept data to support the viability, efficacy and safety of gene silencing strategies in lung cancer. Despite the fact that clinical translation is a relatively new field, the growing literature indicates that siRNA-based immunotherapy is a potential next-generation approach.

13.7.1 In vitro studies

The initial phase in assessing siRNA-mediated immune checkpoint modulation in lung cancer is in vitro experiments. Human NSCLC cell lines include A549, H1975, and H1299 that have been extensively used to determine the efficacy of PD-L1, PD-1 and CTLA-4 gene silencing with synthetic siRNA constructs (Du et al., 2021). Through these models, one is able to investigate in detail target knockdown, downstream changes, and immune functional restoration in a controlled condition.

PD-L1 silencing by siRNA has always shown a high percentage of reduction in the mRNA and level of protein expression. Quantitative polymerase chain reaction and Western blot result in the effective suppression of transcript and the following reduction in protein abundance. Flow cytometry also confirms suppressive expression of surface PD-L1 after treatment.

The checkpoint gene silencing in the functional co-culture assays between tumor cells and activated T lymphocytes show recovery of T-cell-mediated cytotoxicity (Abounar et al., 2024). Enhanced Secretion of interferon-g and augmented CD8+ T- cell activity is commonly seen which represents reversal of cellular immune suppression.

Constructs of multiplex siRNA with more than one checkpoint gene have been found to be more effective than single genes silencing. Indicatively, PD-L1/CTLA-4 or LAG-3 dual-targeting therapy has been shown to have better suppressive effect of immune evasion processes in cell cultures. These results confirm the hypothesis that combined inhibition of several pathways can be more effective in dealing with tumor-induced immune tolerance. Besides, in vitro toxicity testing validates that optimized siRNA preparations have the ability to induce strong gene knockdown without causing toxicity in normal epithelial or immune cells.

Together, in vitro experiments offer a good mechanistic argument that suppression of immunity through siRNA can rescue at least some immune function and lower tumor immunosuppression, which warrants the development of animal studies.

13.7.2 In vivo animal models

In vivo testing is very important in the determination of systemic delivery, pharmacokinetics, biodistribution, and immunological effects of siRNA-based therapies. The therapeutic efficacy is usually studied in murine models of NSCLC, such as xenograft systems and syngeneic systems. The models that are especially useful are syngeneic ones as they maintain a natural immune system intact and therefore, immunomodulatory effects can be evaluated.

Nanoparticle-based lipid nanoparticle lipid-based formulations with siPD-L1 have proven to have significant tumor growth inhibitory effects against murine lung cancer models. The tumors undergoing treatment have lower PD-L1 expression, higher penetration of CD8+ cytotoxic T lymphocytes and lower populations of Treg in the TME. Histology usually shows an increased apoptosis and less proliferation index than control groups. Such results establish that transcript level gene silencing can also have significant immunological and antitumor effects in vivo.

Similar effectiveness in delivering siRNA was demonstrated by polymeric and inorganic nanocarriers. Optimism nanoparticle sizes and surface characteristics studies have shown that biodistribution favors tumor tissue when used. Notably, systemic toxicity is usually reduced in the event that biodegradable and ionizable materials are employed. Cytokine profiling of serum and organ histopathology results prove that there are acceptable safety margins in most preclinical models.

Combinative strategies have had some very good outcomes. mAbs, including nivolumab or atezolizumab, used as checkpoint blockade alongside siRNA-based checkpoint blockade have been shown to have additive or synergistic tumor immunotherapies in animals (Elzoghby et al., 2024). Complementary This is indicated by the fact that siRNA-mediated PD-L1 expression decreases responsiveness to antibody therapy in certain instances. Such preclinical results give strong reasons to support translational development.

13.7.3 Continuing and conducted clinical trials

The siRNA-based immunotherapy in lung cancer is yet to be assessed clinically, yet there is a gradual development of the same. Although not many studies have specifically studied the use of checkpoint gene silencing in NSCLC, a number of studies are examining siRNA-based nanomedicines against oncogenic and angiogenic pathways associated with lung cancer biology.

In solid tumors, including NSCLC, siRNA-based therapeutic platforms have been investigated in clinical trials in NCT03020017 and NCT04675996 and focus on vascular endothelial growth factor (VEGF) and KRAS, and PD-L1-associated signaling pathways (Kumthekar et al., 2021). The main aim of these initial trials is to determine safety, dose-effect, pharmacokinetics, as well as initial efficacy. Analysis of biomarkers can involve analysis of linkage to target knockdown of tumor biopsies and immune activation markers in peripheral blood.

The successful clinical demonstration of siRNA therapeutics like patisiran and givosiran on nononcolytic diseases give valuable evidence of concept that RNA interference is safety translatable into human therapy. Though these are not targeting agents, their approval shows that it is possible to deliver siRNA systemically, produce them in large quantities, and be accepted by the regulatory authorities.

In the case of lung cancer, a continuous phase I and II trial is being conducted assessing siRNA-based preparations as monotherapy or as a combination of chemotherapy and ICIs (Cheng et al., 2024; Hattab et al., 2021).Combination strategies are of interest especially because gene silencing can increase responsiveness to established immunotherapies, and lower dosing can be used along with possible immune-related toxicity. Preclinical evidence highlights the importance of close surveillance of immune activation biomarker and cytokine profiles and organ conditions to be safe. Even though large randomized trials have not been done yet, there is growing support in the early stages of evidence to proceed with the development of siRNA-mediated checkpoint modulation. With the advancement of delivery technologies and the development of improved patient selection, siRNA-based immunotherapy could advance to larger clinical application.

13.8 Advantages and limitations of small interfering RNA-based immunotherapy

Lung cancer therapy by siRNA-based immunotherapy has also been found to be a revolutionary approach in the management of lung cancer mainly by complementing the effect of ICB explained in Table 13.3 . This is because siRNA has the capability of silencing oncogenic and immunosuppressive genes selectively thus permitting a more specific control of the TME. Nevertheless, similar to other therapies that are based on siRNA technology, there are present translational challenges that hinder its clinical power. This chapter contains a critical identification of benefits and shortcomings of siRNA-based immunotherapy in lung cancer.

13.9 Future perspectives and challenges

The field of immunotherapy of lung cancer has reached a revolutionary stage, the combination of siRNA notched ligand-based ICB may be a feasible direction of research in the next-generation of lung cancer immunotherapy. A number of scientific, translational and regulatory issues must be solved before it can be widely adopted clinically. The chapter identifies the major directions and challenges concerning the siRNA-based immunotherapy in the future.

13.9.1 Personalized small interfering RNA therapies

Personalized therapeutic strategies in precision oncology entail designing therapeutics in relation to the genetic, epigenetic, and immunological characteristics of a single patient. siRNAs can be tailored according to a specific immune checkpoint or tumor-related target as defined by next-generation sequencing (NGS). This personalization enables patient specific inhibition of immune evasion pathways, which can increase therapeutic success.

Nonetheless, tumor heterogeneity in the lung and changing immune topography form obstacles. One of the limitations is creating effective biomarker-based platforms that can predict the patient groups who would most gain benefits of siRNA-based therapy. Synthesis of multi-omics (genomics, transcriptomics, and proteomics) with computational modeling is likely to lead to such personalization (Yang et al., 2012).

13.9.2 Combination strategies with chemo- and radiotherapy

Monotherapy with ICIs and often yield only partial responses, in part because they are accompanied by compensatory immune evasion mechanisms. Synergistic combinations can be envisioned with standard therapies like chemotherapy and radiotherapy using siRNA-based therapeutics (Ganesh et al., 2013).

Chemotherapy treatment may increase the release of tumor antigen, and synergize with an siRNA targeting PD-L1 or CTLA-4 (Gu et al., 2017).

Table 13.3: Advantages and limitations of siRNA-based immunotherapy.

Category	Description	References
1. High specificity and precision	siRNA mediates sequence-specific mRNA degradation, silencing immune checkpoints (e.g., PD-1, PD-L1, CTLA-4) with higher precision than small-molecule inhibitors, reducing systemic off-target effects.	Setten et al. (2019), Alshaer et al. (2021)
2. Targeting nondruggable genes	siRNA expands therapeutic reach to transcription factors, intracellular regulators, or proteins inaccessible to antibodies and small molecules.	Bobbin and Rossi (2016), Jackson and Linsley (2010)
3. Synergy with ICIs	siRNA knockdown of PD-L1 augments activity of antiPD-1 antibodies. siRNA can also reprogram tumor-associated macrophages (TAMs) and dendritic cells, enhancing responsiveness to immunotherapy.	Markov et al. (2019), Liu et al. (2015)
4. Reduced systemic toxicity	Tumor-selective nanocarrier delivery (LNPs, exosomes) improves localization of siRNA, minimizing adverse effects (e.g., pneumonitis, autoimmunity) seen with systemic ICIs.	Ubanako et al. (2024), Hou et al. (2021)
5. Rapid and reversible action	siRNA silencing is transient, unlike clustered regularly interspaced short palindromic repeats (CRISPR)-based permanent edits, enabling dynamic tuning of checkpoint expression with better safety controls.	Setten et al. (2019), Kim and Rossi (2007)
Limitations		
1. Delivery challenges	Naked siRNA is unstable in blood, degrades rapidly, and clears via kidneys. Even with nanocarriers, barriers like immune clearance, poor tumor vasculature, and tissue penetration reduce efficacy.	Kanasty et al. (2013), Hou et al. (2021)
2. Off-target effects & immune activation	siRNA can silence unintended mRNAs via partial complementarity; dsRNA can also activate innate immunity through TLR3/7/8, causing inflammation.	Jackson and Linsley (2010b), Robbins et al. (2008)
3. Tumor microenvironment barriers	Hypoxia, dense extracellular matrix, and suppressor cells (Tregs, myeloid-derived suppressor cells (MDSCs)) impede siRNA delivery and uptake; adaptive tumor resistance can restore checkpoint expression.	Quail and Joyce (2013)
4. Manufacturing & stability issues	Production requires specialized modifications for nuclease resistance and formulations (e.g., lipid nanoparticles). Scaling up stable, reproducible nanocarriers is costly.	Setten et al. (2019)

(*continued on next page*)

Table 13.3: Advantages and limitations of siRNA-based immunotherapy—cont'd

Category	Description	References
5. Limited clinical evidence	Most FDA-approved siRNA drugs (patisiran, givosiran) treat genetic/metabolic disorders, not cancer. Clinical translation for lung cancer faces additional hurdles (heterogeneity, immune suppression).	Hoy (2018)
6. Risk of immune-related toxicity	Excessive checkpoint silencing risks unleashing autoimmune reactions, mirroring immune-related adverse events with ICIs.	Postow et al. (2018)

CTLA-4, cytotoxic T-lymphocyte- associated antigen 4; *ICIs*, immune checkpoint inhibitors; *LNPs*, lipid nanoparticles; *PD-1*, programmed death receptor-1; *PD-L1*, programmed death ligand-1; *siRNA*, small interfering RNA; *Treg*, regulatory T-cell.

Radiotherapy causes the immunogenic cell death that makes the microenvironment more accessible to siRNA-induced checkpoint blockade. Whether the sequence, time, and dosage of siRNA are optimized in combination with conventional therapy remains a prospective area of investigation. Clinical translation will involve trial design to reduce the toxicity and generate the maximum synergy (Xue et al., 2014).

13.9.3 Regulatory and ethical considerations

The regulation environment of siRNA therapeutic is in the transition phase (Ebbesen et al., 2008). After the approval of the first several siRNA-based drugs in noncancer indications (e.g., patisiran, givosiran), the base has been laid. However, in case of lung cancer, there are some other issues:

(1) Nonhomogeneous group of patients.
(2) Intricate tumor biology.
(3) Safety problems of long-term immune modulation.

Regulatory authorities require that off-target impacts are highly scrutinized as well as permanence of silencing, together with immunostimulatory potentials (Vervaeke et al., 2022). The ethics also come to the fore when we address the personalized siRNA therapies, especially when it comes to the patient privacy in the context of the organization of genomic and transcriptomic data. Further concerns have been about cost of siRNA manufacturing and delivery platforms which will pose equity in the low resource (Ebenezer et al., 2025; Hu et al., 2020).

13.9.4 Technological innovations in delivery and targeting

Effective transportation is the limiter to siRNA-based lung cancer therapeutics. The tumor tissues have impediments that include dense stroma, hypoxia, and immune suppressions. New advancement aims:

(1) Nanoparticles based on a lipid optimized to deliver by pulmonary route (Kim et al., 2015).
(2) Polymeric systems that are relatively biodegradable and have pH-responsive (release) tumor, or tumor matrix enzyme-reactive features.
(3) Exosome-mimetic vesicles capable of taking advantage of in vivo trafficking.
(4) CRISPR/siRNA hybrid systems, in which siRNAs perform the role of precision regulators in addition to genome editing systems.

Synthesis of synthetical nanomaterials Synthesizing nanomaterials to deliver siRNA or synthetic nanomaterials involves integrating AI-enhanced drug development and nanomaterials to potentially maximize delivery efficiencies, mitigate off-target effects, and target a specific environment in the tumor. The third frontier is the creation of smart nanocarriers to perform in real time drug release and to produce therapeutic response (Bardoliwala et al., 2019; Chen et al., 2014).

13.10 Conclusion

Lung cancer is one of the most challenging problems in oncology with a significant incidence, late-stage diagnosis, and a high mortality rate in the global arena. The introduction of ICIs against PD-1/PD-L1 and CTLA-4 has reshaped the treatment environment, which provides long-term responses and increased survival in a small number of patients. However, with this paradigm shift, there are still some serious constraints. The general clinical efficacy of existing immunotherapies is still limited by primary and acquired resistance, compensatory activation of alternative inhibitory pathways, heterogeneous expression of biomarkers and immune-related toxicities.

In this ever-changing treatment paradigm, gene silencing through siRNA is an attractive next-generation intervention. The siRNA therapeutics suppress the immune checkpoint proteins by inhibiting their expression at the transcript level instead of inhibiting their extracellular association. This is an upstream intervention that offers better accuracy and the possibility of overcoming structural variability, epitope masking, and adaptive overexpression systems that restrain the effects of mAbs. Further, the scale of siRNA technology by design allows targeting multiple checkpoints or other oncogenic pathways, and this feature provides a strategic benefit in dealing with tumor heterogeneity and redundant immune escape pathways.

The nanotechnology breakthroughs have enhanced the translational viability of siRNA as immunotherapy further. Polymer-based carriers, hybrid platforms, LNPs and inorganic systems have shown tremendous stability, effective circulation, tumor accumulation, and efficient intracellular delivery. Tumor specific and stimuli-responsive delivery systems are a promising advancement in the reduction of systemic toxicity and the reduction of therapeutic specificity, respectively. All of these technological advances have brought RNA interference out of experimental idea and into clinically practicable platform.

Though this is most likely to happen, there are a few obstacles that need to be overcome before the siRNA-based ICB can see mass clinical adoption. Unintended activation of innate immunity, off-target gene silencing, pharmacokinetic optimization, complexity of TME, and regulatory factors need further research. Strict preclinical validation, patient selection using biomarkers and well-planned clinical trials will be necessary to determine long-term safety and therapeutic durability.

In the future, the process of incorporating siRNA-based approaches with standard chemotherapy, radiotherapy, current immunomodulators in the form of immune checkpoints, and new immunomodulators provides an excellent combinatorial platform. Genomic and transcriptomic profiling can be used to design personalized RNA therapeutics, which may be precision immunotherapy based on the tumor biology of the individual. Spanning the long-term, it allows siRNA to facilitate immune checkpoint modulation, which could not just supplement existing treatments, but could also be the future of lung cancer treatment the disease that has long been a deadly killer, increasingly manageable and, perhaps, cured.

References

Abounar, S. A., El-Nikhely, N. A., Turkowski, K., Savai, R., & Saeed, H. (2024). CRISPR/Cas-mediated knockdown of PD-L1 and KRAS in Lung Cancer Cells. *International Journal of Molecular Sciences, 25*(16). doi:10.3390/ijms25169086.

Ali Zaidi, S. S., Fatima, F., Ali Zaidi, S. A., Zhou, D., Deng, W., & Liu, S. (2023). Engineering siRNA therapeutics: Challenges and strategies. *Journal of Nanobiotechnology, 21*(1). doi:10.1186/s12951-023-02147-z.

Alshaer, W., Zureigat, H., Karaki, A. A. l, Al-Kadash, A., Gharaibeh, L., Hatmal, M. a'M., Aljabali, A. A. A., & Abdalla, A. (2021). siRNA: Mechanism of action, challenges, and therapeutic approaches. *European Journal of Pharmacology, 905*, 174178. doi:10.1016/j.ejphar.2021.174178.

An, X., Gao, Y., Liu, X., Yin, Q., Meng, L., & Wei, L. (2024). Gold nanoparticles green-mediated by Descurainia sophia extract for the treatment of ovalbumin-induced asthma in rats. *Inorganic Chemistry Communications, 161*, 112011. doi:10.1016/j.inoche.2023.112011.

Anderson, A. C., Joller, N., & Kuchroo, V. K. (2016). Lag-3, Tim-3, and TIGIT: Co-inhibitory receptors with specialized functions in immune regulation. *Immunity, 44*(5), 989–1004. doi:10.1016/j.immuni.2016.05.001.

Andrews, L. P., Butler, S. C., Cui, J., Cillo, A. R., Cardello, C., Liu, C., Brunazzi, E. A., Baessler, A., Xie, B., Kunning, S. R., Ngiow, S. F., Huang, Y. J., Manne, S., Sharpe, A. H., Delgoffe, G. M., Wherry, E. J., Kirkwood, J. M., Bruno, T. C., & Workman, C. J. (2024). LAG-3 and PD-1 synergize on CD8+ T-cells to drive T-cell exhaustion and hinder autocrine IFN-γ-dependent antitumor immunity. *Cell, 187*(16), 4355. doi:10.1016/j.cell.2024.07.016.

Babu, A., Templeton, A. K., Munshi, A., & Ramesh, R. (2013). Nanoparticle-based drug delivery for therapy of lung cancer: Progress and challenges. *Journal of Nanomaterials, 2013*, 11. doi:10.1155/2013/863951.

Bagchi, S., Yuan, R., & Engleman, E. G. (2021). Immune checkpoint inhibitors for the treatment of cancer: Clinical impact and mechanisms of response and resistance. *Annual Review of Pathology: Mechanisms of Disease, 16*, 223–249. doi:10.1146/annurev-pathol-042020-042741.

Baker, A., Lorch, J., VanderWeele, D., & Zhang, B. (2023). Smart nanocarriers for the targeted delivery of therapeutic nucleic acid for cancer immunotherapy. *Pharmaceutics, 15*(6), 1743. doi:10.3390/pharmaceutics15061743.

Barati, M., Mirzavi, F., Atabaki, M., Bibak, B., Mohammadi, M., & Jaafari, M. R. (2022). A review of PD-1/PD-L1 siRNA delivery systems in immune T-cells and cancer cells. *International Immunopharmacology, 111*, 109022. doi:10.1016/j.intimp.2022.109022.

Bardoliwala, D., Patel, V., Javia, A., Ghosh, S., Patel, A., & Misra, A. (2019). Nanocarriers in effective pulmonary delivery of siRNA: Current approaches and challenges. *Therapeutic Delivery, 10*(5), 311–332. doi:10.4155/tde-2019-0012.

Bobbin, M. L., & Rossi, J. J. (2016). RNA interference (RNAi)-based therapeutics: Delivering on the promise? *Annual Review of Pharmacology and Toxicology, 56*, 103–122. doi:10.1146/annurev-pharmtox-010715-103633.

Brahmer, J. R., Tykodi, S. S., Chow, L. Q. M., Hwu, W. J., Topalian, S. L., Hwu, P., Drake, C. G., Camacho, L. H., Kauh, J., Odunsi, K., Pitot, H. C., Hamid, O., Bhatia, S., Martins, R., Eaton, K., Chen, S., Salay, T. M., Alaparthy, S., Grosso, J. F., … Wigginton, J. M. (2012). Safety and activity of anti-PD-L1 antibody in patients with advanced cancer. *New England Journal of Medicine, 366*(26), 2455–2465. doi:10.1056/NEJMoa1200694.

Buchbinder, E. I., & Desai, A. (2016). CTLA-4 and PD-1 Pathways. *American Journal of Clinical Oncology, 39*(1), 98–106. doi:10.1097/coc.0000000000000239.

Bumcrot, D., Manoharan, M., Koteliansky, V., & Sah, D. W. Y. (2006). RNAi therapeutics: A potential new class of pharmaceutical drugs. *Nature Chemical Biology, 2*(12), 711–719. doi:10.1038/nchembio839.

Castanotto, D., & Rossi, J. J. (2009). The promises and pitfalls of RNA-interference-based therapeutics. *Nature, 457*(7228), 426–433. doi:10.1038/nature07758.

Chen, Y., Gu, H., Zhang, D. S. Z., Li, F., Liu, T., & Xia, W. (2014). Highly effective inhibition of lung cancer growth and metastasis by systemic delivery of siRNA via multimodal mesoporous silica-based nanocarrier. *Biomaterials, 35*(38), 10058–10069. doi:10.1016/j.biomaterials.2014.09.003.

Cheng, Z., Fobian, S. F., Gurrieri, E., Amin, M., D'Agostino, V. G., Falahati, M., Zalba, S., Debets, R., Garrido, M. J., Saeed, M., Seynhaeve, A. L. B., Balcioglu, H. E., & ten Hagen, T. L. M. (2024). Lipid-based nanosystems: The next-generation of cancer immune therapy. *Journal of Hematology and Oncology, 17*(1). doi:10.1186/s13045-024-01574-1.

Choi, Y., Seok, S. H., Yoon, H. Y., Ryu, J. H., & Kwon, I. C. (2024). Advancing cancer immunotherapy through siRNA-based gene silencing for immune checkpoint blockade. *Advanced Drug Delivery Reviews, 209*. doi:10.1016/j.addr.2024.115306.

Davidson, B. L., & McCray, P. B. (2011). Current prospects for RNA interference-based therapies. *Nature Reviews Genetics, 12*(5), 329–340. doi:10.1038/nrg2968.

Deng, Y., Wang, C. C., Choy, K. W., Du, Q., Chen, J., Wang, Q., Li, L., Chung, T. K. H., & Tang, T. (2014). Therapeutic potentials of gene silencing by RNA interference: Principles, challenges, and new strategies. *Gene, 538*(2), 217–227. doi:10.1016/j.gene.2013.12.019.

Dong, H., Strome, S. E., Salomao, D. R., Tamura, H., Hirano, F., Flies, D. B., Roche, P. C., Lu, J., Zhu, G., Tamada, K., Lennon, V. A., Cells, E., & Chen, L. (2002). Tumor-associated B7-H1 promotes T-cell apoptosis: A potential mechanism of immune evasion. *Nature Medicine, 8*(8), 793–800. doi:10.1038/nm730.

Du, F., Qi, X., Zhang, A., Sui, F., Wang, X., Proud, C. G., Lin, C., Fan, X., & Li, J. (2021). MRTF-A-NF-κB/p65 axis-mediated PDL1 transcription and expression contributes to immune evasion of non-small-cell lung cancer via TGF-β. *Experimental and Molecular Medicine, 53*(9), 1366–1378. doi:10.1038/s12276-021-00670-3.

Ebbesen, M., Jensen, T. G., Andersen, S., & Pedersen, F. S. (2008). Ethical perspectives on RNA interference therapeutics. *International Journal of Medical Sciences, 5*(3), 159–168. doi:10.7150/ijms.5.159.

Ebenezer, O., Oyebamiji, A. K., Olanlokun, J. O., Tuszynski, J. A., & Wong, G. K. S. (2025). Recent update on siRNA therapeutics. *International Journal of Molecular Sciences, 26*(8). doi:10.3390/ijms26083456.

Elzoghby, A. O., Samir, O., Emam, H. E., Soliman, A., Abdelgalil, R. M., Elmorshedy, Y. M., Elkhodairy, K. A., & Nasr, M. L. (2024). Engineering nanomedicines for immunogenic eradication of cancer cells: Recent trends and synergistic approaches. *Acta Pharmaceutica Sinica B, 14*(6), 2475–2504. doi:10.1016/j.apsb.2024.03.022.

Fire, A., Xu, S., Montgomery, M. K., Kostas, S. A., Driver, S. E., & Mello, C. C. (1998). Potent and specific genetic interference by double-stranded RNA in caenorhabditis elegans. *Nature, 391*(6669), 806–811. doi:10.1038/35888.

Freeman, G., Long, A., Iwai, Y., Bourque, K., Chernova, T., Nishimura, H., Fitz, L. J., Malenkovich, N., Okazaki, T., Byrne, M. C., Horton, H. F., Fouser, L., Carte, L, Ling, V., Bowman, M. R., Carreno, B. M., Collins, M., Wood, C. R., & Honjo, T. (2000). Engagement of the PD-1 immunoinhibitory receptor by a novel B7 family member leads to negative regulation of lymphocyte activation. *Journal of Experimental Medicine, 192*(7), 1027–1034. https://rupress.org/jem/article-abstract/192/7/1027/8251.

Galluzzi, L., Buque, A., Kepp, O., & Zitvogel, L. (2015). Immunological effects of conventional chemotherapy and targeted anticancer agents. *Cancer cell, 28*, 690–714. https://www.cell.com/cancer-cell/fulltext/S153561081500389X.

Ganesh, S., Iyer, A. K., Weiler, J., Morrissey, D. V., & Amiji, M. M. (2013). Combination of siRNA-directed gene silencing with cisplatin reverses drug resistance in human non-small cell lung cancer. *Molecular Therapy Nucleic Acids, 2*, e110. doi:10.1038/mtna.2013.29.

Ge, Y., Zhou, Q., Pan, F., & Wang, R. (2025). Utilizing nanoparticles to overcome anti-PD-1/PD-L1 immunotherapy resistance in non-small cell lung cancer: A potential strategy. *International Journal of Nanomedicine, 20*, 2371–2394. doi:10.2147/ijn.s505539.

Gu, L., Deng, Z. J., Roy, S., & Hammond, P. T. (2017). A combination RNAi-chemotherapy layer-by-layer nanoparticle for systemic targeting of KRAS/P53 with cisplatin to treat non-small cell lung cancer. *Clinical Cancer Research, 23*(23), 7312–7323. doi:10.1158/1078-0432.CCR-16-2186.

Gu, X., Yu, T., Nie, W., Shi, H., Jin, K., Zhang, W., & Cai, J. (2025). Intelligent nanoparticles loaded simultaneously with anti-PD-L1 and anti-CTLA-4 for photothermal immunotherapy of lung cancer. *Advanced Composites and Hybrid Materials, 8*(4). doi:10.1007/s42114-025-01335-9.

Hao, Y., Yang, J., Liu, D., Zhang, H., Ou, T., Xiao, L., & Chen, W. (2024). Construction of aptamer-siRNA chimera and glutamine modified carboxymethyl-β-cyclodextrin nanoparticles for the combination therapy against lung squamous cell carcinoma. *Biomedicine & Pharmacotherapy, 174*, 116506. doi:10.1016/j.biopha.2024.116506.

Hattab, D., Gazzali, A. M., & Bakhtiar, A. (2021). Clinical advances of sirna-based nanotherapeutics for cancer treatment. *Pharmaceutics, 13*(7). doi:10.3390/pharmaceutics13071009.

Havel, J. J., Chowell, D., & Chan, T. A. (2019). The evolving landscape of biomarkers for checkpoint inhibitor immunotherapy. *Nature Reviews Cancer, 19*(3), 133–150. doi:10.1038/s41568-019-0116-x.

Hellmann, M. D., Paz Ares, L., Bernabe Caro, R., Zurawski, B., Kim, S. W., Carcereny Costa, E., Park, K., Alexandru, A., Lupinacci, L., De La Mora Jimenez, E., Sakai, H., Albert, I., Vergnenegre, A., Peters, S., Syrigos, K., Barlesi, F., Reck, M., Borghaei, H., Brahmer, J. R., … Ramalingam, S. S. (2019). Nivolumab plus ipilimumab in advanced non-small-cell lung cancer. *New England Journal of Medicine, 381*(21), 2020–2031. doi:10.1056/NEJMoa1910231.

Herbst, R. S., Morgensztern, D., & Boshoff, C. (2018). The biology and management of non-small cell lung cancer. *Nature, 553*(7689), 446–454. doi:10.1038/nature25183.

Hou, X., Zaks, T., Langer, R., & Dong, Y. (2021). Lipid nanoparticles for mRNA delivery. *Nature Reviews Materials, 6*(12), 1078–1094. doi:10.1038/s41578-021-00358-0.

Hoy, S. M. (2018). Patisiran: First global approval. *Drugs, 78*(15), 1625–1631. doi:10.1007/s40265-018-0983-6.

Hu, B., Zhong, L., Weng, Y., Peng, L., Huang, Y., Zhao, Y., & Liang, X.-J. (2020). Therapeutic siRNA: State of the art. *Signal Transduction and Targeted Therapy, 5*(1). doi:10.1038/s41392-020-0207-x.

Huynh, T. M. H., Huang, P. X., Wang, K. L., Tran, N. T., Iao, H. M., Pan, W. C., Chang, Y. H., Lien, H. W., Lee, A. Y. L., Chou, T. C., Chiang, W. H., & Hu, S. H. (2025). Reprogramming immunodeficiency in lung metastases via PD-L1 siRNA delivery and antigen capture of nanosponge-mediated dendritic cell modulation. *ACS Nano, 19*(27), 25134–25153. doi:10.1021/acsnano.5c05395.

Jackson, A. L., & Linsley, P. S. (2010). Recognizing and avoiding siRNA off-target effects for target identification and therapeutic application. *Nature Reviews Drug Discovery, 9*(1), 57–67. doi:10.1038/nrd3010.

Jia, D., Wang, P., Zheng, S., Lei, Z., Xu, W., Wang, Y., Pan, X., Feng, Q., & Yang, J. (2025). KRAS mutations promote PD-L1-mediated immune escape by ETV4 in lung adenocarcinoma. *Translational Oncology, 61*. doi:10.1016/j.tranon.2025.102525.

Jiang, Y., Li, Y., & Zhu, B. (2015). T-cell exhaustion in the tumor microenvironment. *Cell Death and Disease, 6*(6). doi:10.1038/cddis.2015.162.

Jürgens, D. C., Müller, J. T., Nguyen, A., & Merkel, O. M. (2024). Tailoring lipid nanoparticles for T-cell targeting in allergic asthma: Insights into efficacy and specificity. *European Journal of Pharmaceutics and Biopharmaceutics, 198*. doi:10.1016/j.ejpb.2024.114242.

Kanasty, R., Dorkin, J., Vegas, A., & Anderson, D. (2013). Delivery materials for siRNA therapeutics. *Nature Materials, 12*, 967–977. https://www.nature.com/articles/nmat3765.

Kaushal, A. (2023). Innate immune regulations and various siRNA modalities. *Drug Delivery and Translational Research, 13*(11), 2704–2718. doi:10.1007/s13346-023-01361-4.

Keir, M. E., Butte, M. J., Freeman, G. J., & Sharpe, A. H. (2008). PD-1 and its ligands in tolerance and immunity. *Annual Review of Immunology, 26*(1), 677–704. doi:10.1146/annurev.immunol.26.021607.090331.

Kim, D. H., & Rossi, J. J. (2007). Strategies for silencing human disease using RNA interference. *Nature Reviews Genetics, 8*(3), 173–184. doi:10.1038/nrg2006.

Kim, H. J., Kim, A., Miyata, K., & Kataoka, K. (2016). Recent progress in development of siRNA delivery vehicles for cancer therapy. *Advanced Drug Delivery Reviews, 104*, 61–77. doi:10.1016/j.addr.2016.06.011.

Kim, Y. D., Park, T. E., Singh, B., Maharjan, S., Choi, Y. J., Choung, P. H., Arote, R. B., & Cho, C. S. (2015). Nanoparticle-mediated delivery of siRNA for effective lung cancer therapy. *Nanomedicine, 10*(7), 1165–1188. doi:10.2217/nnm.14.214.

Koyama, S., Akbay, E. A., Li, Y. Y., Herter-Sprie, G. S., Buczkowski, K. A., Richards, W. G., Gandhi, L., Redig, A. J., Rodig, S. J., Asahina, H., Jones, R. E., Kulkarni, M. M., Kuraguchi, M., Palakurthi, S., Fecci, P. E., Johnson, B. E., Janne, P. A., Engelman, J. A., Gangadharan, S. P., … Hammerman, P. S. (2016). Adaptive resistance to therapeutic PD-1 blockade is associated with upregulation of alternative immune checkpoints. *Nature Communications, 7*. doi:10.1038/ncomms10501.

Kulkarni, J. A., Cullis, P. R., & Van Der Meel, R. (2018). Lipid nanoparticles enabling gene therapies: From concepts to clinical utility. *Nucleic Acid Therapeutics, 28*(3), 146–157. doi:10.1089/nat.2018.0721.

Kumthekar, P., Ko, C. H., Paunesku, T., Dixit, K., Sonabend, A. M., Bloch, O., Tate, M., Schwartz, M., Zuckerman, L., Lezon, R., Lukas, R. V., Jovanovic, B., McCortney, K., Colman, H., Chen, S., Lai, B., Antipova, O., Deng, J., Li, L., … Stegh, A. H. (2021). A first-in-human phase 0 clinical study of RNA interference-based spherical nucleic acids in patients with recurrent glioblastoma. *Science Translational Medicine, 13*(584). doi:10.1126/scitranslmed.abb3945.

Lee, S. J., Kim, M. J., Kwon, I. C., & Roberts, T. M. (2016). Delivery strategies and potential targets for siRNA in major cancer types. *Advanced Drug Delivery Reviews, 104*, 2–15. doi:10.1016/j.addr.2016.05.010.

Lin, X., Kang, K., Chen, P., Zeng, Z., Li, G., Xiong, W., Yi, M., & Xiang, B. (2024). Regulatory mechanisms of PD-1/PD-L1 in cancers. *Molecular Cancer, 23*(1). doi:10.1186/s12943-024-02023-w.

Liu, B., Qu, J., Xu, F., Guo, Y., Wang, Y. u, Yu, H., & Qian, B. (2015). MiR-195 suppresses non-small cell lung cancer by targeting CHEK1. *Oncotarget, 6*(11), 9445–9456. doi:10.18632/oncotarget.3255.

Mainini, F., & Eccles, M. R. (2020). Lipid and polymer-based nanoparticle siRNA delivery systems for cancer therapy. *Molecules, 25*(11). doi:10.3390/molecules25112692.

Mansoori, B., Shotorbani, S. S., & Baradaran, B. (2014). RNA interference and its role in cancer therapy. *Advanced Pharmaceutical Bulletin, 4*(4), 313–321. doi:10.5681/apb.2014.046.

Markov, O., Oshchepkova, A., & Mironova, N. (2019). Immunotherapy based on dendritic cell-targeted/-derived extracellular vesicles—A novel strategy for enhancement of the antitumor immune response. *Frontiers in Pharmacology, 10*. doi:10.3389/fphar.2019.01152.

Martins, F., Sofiya, L., Sykiotis, G. P., Lamine, F., Maillard, M., Fraga, M., Shabafrouz, K., Ribi, C., Cairoli, A., Guex-Crosier, Y., Kuntzer, T., Michielin, O., Peters, S., Coukos, G., Spertini, F., Thompson, J. A., & Obeid, M. (2019). Adverse effects of immune checkpoint inhibitors: Epidemiology, management and surveillance. *Nature Reviews Clinical Oncology, 16*(9), 563–580. doi:10.1038/s41571-019-0218-0.

Meister, G., & Tuschl, T. (2004). Mechanisms of gene silencing by double-stranded RNA. *Nature, 431*(7006), 343–349. doi:10.1038/nature02873.

Meng, Z., & Lu, M. (2017). RNA interference-induced innate immunity, off-target effect, or immune adjuvant? *Frontiers in Immunology, 8*. doi:10.3389/fimmu.2017.00331.

Michot, J. M., Bigenwald, C., Champiat, S., Collins, M., Carbonnel, F., Postel-Vinay, S., Berdelou, A., Varga, A., Bahleda, R., Hollebecque, A., Massard, C., Fuerea, A., Ribrag, V., Gazzah, A., Armand, J. P., Amellal, N., Angevin, E., Noel, N., Boutros, C., … Lambotte, O. (2016). Immune-related adverse events with immune checkpoint blockade: A comprehensive review. *European Journal of Cancer, 54*, 139–148. doi:10.1016/j.ejca.2015.11.016.

Mieszawska, A. J., Mulder, W. J. M., Fayad, Z. A., & Cormode, D. P. (2013). Multifunctional gold nanoparticles for diagnosis and therapy of disease. *Molecular Pharmaceutics, 10*(3), 831–847. doi:10.1021/mp3005885.

Pandey, P. R., Young, K. H., Kumar, D., & Jain, N. (2022). RNA-mediated immunotherapy regulating tumor immune microenvironment: Next wave of cancer therapeutics. *Molecular Cancer, 21*(1). doi:10.1186/s12943-022-01528-6.

Pardoll, D. M. (2012). The blockade of immune checkpoints in cancer immunotherapy. *Nature Reviews Cancer, 12*(4), 252–264. doi:10.1038/nrc3239.

Park, J., Park, J., Pei, Y., Xu, J., & Yeo, Y. (2016). Pharmacokinetics and biodistribution of recently-developed siRNA nanomedicines. *Advanced Drug Delivery Reviews, 104*, 93–109. doi:10.1016/j.addr.2015.12.004.

Pecot, C. V., Calin, G. A., Coleman, R. L., Lopez-Berestein, G., & Sood, A. K. (2011). RNA interference in the clinic: Challenges and future directions. *Nature Reviews Cancer, 11*(1), 59–67. doi:10.1038/nrc2966.

Postow, M. A., Callahan, M. K., & Wolchok, J. D. (2015). Immune checkpoint blockade in cancer therapy. *Journal of Clinical Oncology, 33*(17), 1974–1982. doi:10.1200/JCO.2014.59.4358.

Postow, M. A., Sidlow, R., & Hellmann, M. D. (2018). Immune-related adverse events associated with immune checkpoint blockade. *New England Journal of Medicine, 378*(2), 158–168. doi:10.1056/NEJMra1703481.

Prasad, V., Kaestner, V., & Mailankody, S. (2018). Cancer drugs approved based on biomarkers and not tumor type - FDA approval of pembrolizumab for mismatch repair-deficient solid cancers. *JAMA Oncology, 4*(2), 157–158. doi:10.1001/jamaoncol.2017.4182.

Quail, D. F., & Joyce, J. A. (2013). Microenvironmental regulation of tumor progression and metastasis. *Nature Medicine, 19*(11), 1423–1437. doi:10.1038/nm.3394.

Reck, M., Remon, J., & Hellmann, M. D. (2022). First-line immunotherapy for non-small-cell lung cancer. *Journal of Clinical Oncology, 40*(6), 586–597. doi:10.1200/JCO.21.01497.

Reck, M., Rodríguez-Abreu, D., Robinson, A. G., Hui, R., Csőszi, T., Fülöp, A., Gottfried, M., Peled, N., Tafreshi, A., Cuffe, S., O'Brien, M., Rao, S., Hotta, K., Leiby, M. A., Lubiniecki, G. M., Shentu, Y., Rangwala, R., & Brahmer, J. R. (2016). Pembrolizumab versus chemotherapy for PD-L1–Positive non-small-cell lung cancer. *New England Journal of Medicine, 375*(19), 1823–1833. doi:10.1056/nejmoa1606774.

Huang, L., & Liu, Y. (2011). In vivo delivery of RNAi with lipid-based nanoparticles. Annual Review of Biomedical Engineering, 13, 507–530. https://cir.nii.ac.jp/crid/1370285712534033289.

Reynolds, A., Leake, D., Boese, Q., Scaringe, S., Marshal, W. S., & Khvorova, A. (2004). Rational siRNA design for RNA interference. *Nature Biotechnology, 22*(3), 326–330. doi:10.1038/nbt936.

Ribas, A., & Wolchok, J. D. (2018). Cancer immunotherapy using checkpoint blockade. *Science, 359*(6382), 1350–1355. doi:10.1126/science.aar4060.

Robbins, M., Judge, A., Ambegia, E., Choi, C., Yaworski, E., Palmer, L., McClintock, K., & MacLachlan, I. (2008). Misinterpreting the therapeutic effects of small interfering RNA caused by immune stimulation. *Human Gene Therapy, 19*(10), 991–999. doi:10.1089/hum.2008.131.

Robbins, M., Judge, A., & MacLachlan, I. (2009). SiRNA and innate immunity. *Oligonucleotides, 19*(2), 89–101. doi:10.1089/oli.2009.0180.

Sajid, M. I., Moazzam, M., Tiwari, R. K., Kato, S., & Cho, K. Y. (2020). Overcoming barriers for siRNA therapeutics: From bench to bedside. *Pharmaceuticals, 13*(10), 1–25. doi:10.3390/ph13100294.

Sarett, S. M., Werfel, T. A., Lee, L., Jackson, M. A., Kilchrist, K. V., Brantley-Sieders, D., & Duvall, C. L. (2017). Lipophilic siRNA targets albumin in situ and promotes bioavailability, tumor penetration, and carrier-free gene silencing. *Proceedings of the National Academy of Sciences of the United States of America, 114*(32), E6490. doi:10.1073/pnas.1621240114.

Setten, R. L., Rossi, J. J., & Han, S. (2019). The current state and future directions of RNAi-based therapeutics. *Nature Reviews Drug Discovery, 18*(6), 421–446. doi:10.1038/s41573-019-0017-4.

Sharma, A., Jha, N. K., Dahiya, K., Singh, V. K., Chaurasiya, K., Jha, A. N., Jha, S. K., Mishra, P. C., Dholpuria, S., Astya, R., Nand, P., Kumar, A., Ruokolainen, J., & Kesari, K. K. (2020). Nanoparticulate RNA delivery systems in cancer. *Cancer Reports, 3*(5). doi:10.1002/cnr2.1271.

Sharma, P., Hu-Lieskovan, S., Wargo, J. A., & Ribas, A. (2017). Primary, adaptive, and acquired resistance to cancer immunotherapy. *Cell, 168*(4), 707–723. doi:10.1016/j.cell.2017.01.017.

Siegel, R., & Miller, K. (2022). Cancer statistics. *CA: A Cancer Journal of Clinicians*. doi:10.3322/caac.21708.

Sristi, G. G., Abourehab, M. A. S., Sahebkar, A., & Kesharwani, P. (2025). Recent advances in PD-L1 siRNA nanocarriers for cancer therapy. *International Journal of Biological Macromolecules, 311*. doi:10.1016/j.ijbiomac.2025.143994.

Sun, C., Mezzadra, R., & Schumacher, T. N. (2018). Regulation and function of the PD-L1 checkpoint. *Immunity, 48*(3), 434–452. doi:10.1016/j.immuni.2018.03.014.

Sung, H., Ferlay, J., Siegel, R. L., Laversanne, M., Soerjomataram, I., Jemal, A., & Bray, F. (2021). Global Cancer Statistics 2020: GLOBOCAN estimates of incidence and mortality worldwide for 36 cancers in 185 countries. *CA Cancer Journal for Clinicians, 71*(3), 209–249. doi:10.3322/caac.21660.

Thai, A. A., Solomon, B. J., Sequist, L. V., Gainor, J. F., & Heist, R. S. (2021). Lung cancer. *The Lancet, 398*(10299), 535–554. doi:10.1016/S0140-6736(21)00312-3.

Topalian, S. L., Drake, C. G., & Pardoll, D. M. (2015). Immune checkpoint blockade: A common denominator approach to cancer therapy. *Cancer Cell, 27*(4), 450–461. doi:10.1016/j.ccell.2015.03.001.

Tran, T. H., & Tran, T. T. P. (2022). Targeting the PD-1/PD-L1 axis for cancer treatment: A review on nanotechnology. *Royal Society Open Science, 9*(4). doi:10.1098/rsos.211991.

Twomey, J. D., & Zhang, B. (2021). Cancer immunotherapy update: FDA-approved checkpoint inhibitors and companion diagnostics. *The AAPS Journal, 23*(2). doi:10.1208/S12248-021-00574-0.

Ubanako, P., Mirza, S., Ruff, P., & Penny, C. (2024). Exosome-mediated delivery of siRNA molecules in cancer therapy: Triumphs and challenges. *Frontiers in Molecular Biosciences, 11*. doi:10.3389/fmolb.2024.1447953.

Vervaeke, P., Borgos, S. E., Sanders, N. N., & Combes, F. (2022). Regulatory guidelines and preclinical tools to study the biodistribution of RNA therapeutics. *Advanced Drug Delivery Reviews, 184*, 114236. doi:10.1016/j.addr.2022.114236.

Wang, D. Y., Salem, J. E., Cohen, J. V., Chandra, S., Menzer, C., Ye, F., Zhao, S., Das, S., Beckermann, K. E., Ha, L., Rathmell, W. K., Ancell, K. K., Balko, J. M., Bowman, C., Davis, E. J., Chism, D. D., Horn, L., Long, G. V., Carlino, M. S., … Johnson, D. B. (2018). Fatal toxic effects associated with immune checkpoint inhibitors: A systematic review and meta-analysis. *JAMA Oncology, 4*(12), 1721–1728. doi:10.1001/jamaoncol.2018.3923.

Wittrup, A., & Lieberman, J. (2015). Knocking down disease: A progress report on siRNA therapeutics. *Nature Reviews Genetics, 16*(9), 543–552. doi:10.1038/nrg3978.

Xiang, S., Li, S., & Xu, J. (2025). Unraveling T-cell exhaustion through co-inhibitory receptors and its transformative role in cancer immunotherapy. *Clinical and Translational Medicine, 15*(5). doi:10.1002/ctm2.70345.

Xiong, L., Chen, S., Li, S., He, D., Wang, Y., Zhang, Q., He, Z., Li, M., & He, Q. (2025). ATP-responsive tumor-targeted lipid nanoparticle for enhanced siRNA delivery and improved treatment efficacy in melanoma. *Journal of Controlled Release, 382*, 113622. doi:10.1016/j.jconrel.2025.113622.

Xue, W., Dahlman, J. E., Tammela, T., Khan, O. F., Sood, S., Dave, A., Cai, W., Chirino, L. M., Yang, G. R., Bronson, R., Crowley, D. G., Sahay, G., Schroeder, A., Langer, R., Anderson, D. G., & Jacks, T. (2014). Small RNA combination therapy for lung cancer. *Proceedings of the National Academy of Sciences of the United States of America, 111*(34), E3553. doi:10.1073/pnas.1412686111.

Yamaguchi, H., Hsu, J. M., Yang, W. H., & Hung, M. C. (2022). Mechanisms regulating PD-L1 expression in cancers and associated opportunities for novel small-molecule therapeutics. *Nature Reviews Clinical Oncology, 19*(5), 287–305. doi:10.1038/s41571-022-00601-9.

Yang, Y., Hu, Y., Wang, Y., Li, J., Liu, F., & Huang, L. (2012). Nanoparticle delivery of pooled siRNA for effective treatment of non-small cell lung caner. *Molecular Pharmaceutics, 9*(8), 2280–2289. doi:10.1021/mp300152v.

Yin, Q., Wu, L., Han, L., Zheng, X., Tong, R., Li, L., Bai, L., & Bian, Y. (2023). Immune-related adverse events of immune checkpoint inhibitors: A review. *Frontiers in Immunology, 14*. doi:10.3389/fimmu.2023.1167975.

Zhang, J., Chen, B., Gan, C., Sun, H., Zhang, J., & Feng, L. (2023). A comprehensive review of small interfering RNAs (siRNAs): Mechanism, therapeutic targets, and delivery strategies for cancer therapy. *International Journal of Nanomedicine, 18*, 7605–7635. doi:10.2147/IJN.S436038.

Zhuang, X., Xiang, X., Grizzle, W., Sun, D., Zhang, S., Axtell, R. C., Ju, S., Mu, J., Zhang, L., Steinman, L., Miller, D., & Zhang, H. G. (2011). Treatment of brain inflammatory diseases by delivering exosome encapsulated anti-inflammatory drugs from the nasal region to the brain. *Molecular Therapy, 19*(10), 1769–1779. doi:10.1038/mt.2011.164.

Zottel, A., Paska, A. V., & Jovčevska, I. (2019). Nanotechnology meets oncology: Nanomaterials in brain cancer research, diagnosis and therapy. *Materials, 12*(10). doi:10.3390/ma12101588.

CHAPTER 14

Overcoming drug resistance in nonsmall cell lung cancer: Small interfering RNAs-guided gene silencing combined with cisplatin therapy

Blessy Baby Mathew[a], Harshitha Loganathan Kamala Kannan[a], Vidhyashree Sulangi Durugappa[a], Rakshitha Gowda[a] and Thirupathihalli Pandurangappa Krishna Murthy[b]

[a]*School of Basic and Applied Sciences, Dayananda Sagar University, Bengaluru, Karnataka, India*
[b]*Department of Biotechnology, M.S. Ramaiah Institute of Technology, Bengaluru, Karnataka, India*

14.1 Introduction

Small interfering RNAs (siRNAs) arise from the processing of long double-stranded RNAs, whether introduced from outside the cell or generated internally, and they are central to RNA interference (RNAi) (7–10). A protein of the ribonuclease III (RNase III) type called Dicer cleaves long dsRNAs (Gavrilov & Saltzman, 2012). Dicer produces SiRNA that has an overhang at each of its three ends. It is a short (~22-nt) RNA duplex. Every strand has a 3-hydroxyl group with a 5-phosphate group. The RNA-induced silencing complex (RISC), into which siRNA integrates, is a nuclease complex that targets and cleaves complementary mRNA (Zhang et al., 2023). RISC is first inactive, carrying a siRNA duplex (Dana et al., 2017; Lee et al., 2013) before it changes into an active form (RISC*). This change includes the loss of one strand from the duplex by an RNA helicase activity. RNAi, cosuppression (PTGS), and quelling are among the gene silencing processes that are now collectively referred to as RNA silencing (Dana et al., 2017). RNA, at 21–28 nucleotides (nt) long, often acts as the main player during RNA silencing. MicroRNAs (miRNAs) as well as siRNAs are considered the two kinds of short RNAs. RNA silencing involves each of these two kinds (Hong & Nam, 2016). Because of its extraordinary effectiveness along with specificity (Chang et al., 2009), RNAi has gained a lot of interest as a powerful gene knockdown method. The biogenesis of siRNAs is the process by which these small RNA molecules are created.

Nanoengineered Therapeutics for Lung Cancer: Advanced Drug Delivery Strategies.
DOI: https://doi.org/10.1016/B978-0-443-44585-9.00004-4

siRNAs are single-stranded RNAs that measure 21–25 nt in length. The enzyme DICER1 produces them by cutting longer double-stranded RNAs within the RISC loading complex, which includes DICER1, an argonaute protein (humans have four Argonaute proteins), and either TARBP2 or PRKRA (PACT) (Kim et al., 2004). siRNA-loaded AGO2 is found mainly on the cytosolic surface of the rough endoplasmic reticulum, although it has also been observed in the nucleus, which recognizes and cleaves long dsRNA into short siRNA duplexes. The cleavage occurs at specific intervals, resulting in siRNAs with 2-nucleotide 3' overhangs and 5' phosphate groups, which are important for subsequent steps (Bernstein et al., 2001). The siRNA duplex is loaded into RISC, a multiprotein complex that mediates gene silencing. Within RISC, one strand (the passenger strand) is discarded, while the other strand (the guide strand) remains and directs the complex to its target mRNA (Macrae et al., 2006). The guide strand within RISC base pairs with a complementary mRNA sequence, leading to the cleavage and degradation of the target mRNA. This results in gene silencing, preventing the synthesis of the corresponding protein (Bernstein et al., 2001). In some organisms (especially plants), siRNA biogenesis is amplified through the activity of RNA-dependent RNA polymerases (RDRs). RDRs use cleaved mRNA fragments as templates to generate new dsRNAs, which are processed into secondary siRNAs, amplifying the silencing effect (Macrae et al., 2006). siRNA biogenesis can be divided into endogenous and exogenous pathways. Endogenous siRNAs are usually 21 to 24 nt long and are generated from perfectly complementary double-stranded RNA precursors. They contain 2-nucleotide 3' overhangs due to Dicer cleavage, which is critical for their inclusion into the RISC (Carthew & Sontheimer, 2009). Endo-siRNAs are produced from the action of Dicer, an RNase III enzyme, on canonical dsRNA precursors. Subsequently, the siRNA duplexes are partitioned into RISC, where one strand, termed the guide strand, is spared while the other, the passenger strand, undergoes degradation (Piatek & Werner, 2014). The strand within RISC guides the complex to corresponding mRNA targets, facilitating their cleavage and degradation, thus silencing gene activity (Piatek & Werner, 2014). In the context of regulatory pathways, endogenously generated short interfering RNAs (endo-siRNAs, 18–30 nt) are critical because they function to recruit Argonaute effector proteins that target and hybridize to nucleic acid filaments within a functional ribonucleoprotein complex known as RISC, the RISC. Following the 1993 discovery of the first microRNA, the endo-siRNAs saturation in all three life kingdoms was made possible by advancements in high-throughput sequencing technology (Snead & Rossi, 2010). siRNA can cancel the gene expression of target sequences by degrading the mRNA in a very precise and efficient manner. This kind of gene silencing does not compromise the effect on target genes. The therapeutics concerning siRNA could be based on a target slightly or completely changed depending on the need (Hu et al., 2020). siRNA can be synthesized as short sets of sequences in an exogenous manner in cancer therapeutics and can be delivered by using nanocarriers. This can trigger RNAi, which can mute the gene expression (Zhang et al., 2023). siRNA was initially believed to be directly coming from the virus or transposon and later it was understood to be a part of long RNA that is double-stranded in nature. This dual-stranded nature of

Table 14.1: siRNA-guided gene silencing strategies in lung cancer.

S. no.	siRNA delivery	Outcome
1	Lipid nanoparticles, polymeric nanoparticles, viruses as vectors	Reduced cell growth, increased apoptosis
2	Polyethyleneimine (PEI)-based nanoparticles, aptamer conjugates	Reduced angiogenesis, diminished tumor growth
3	Nanoparticle formulations and liposomes	Inhibition of tumor growth, enhanced sensitivity

the precursors belonging to siRNA categorizes them physiologically, giving a prospect of its close knitted relationship with their similar kind (Carthew & Sontheimer, 2009). The growing range of cellular processes that are regulated by RNAi-related short RNA pathways has been significantly increased at the same time. This chapter will highlight interesting current advances in endo-siRNA pathways, building a solid foundation of RNAi, endogenous siRNA guides, and the functional outcomes of key pathways in well-established model systems have been central to advances in short RNA research.

14.2 The role of small interfering RNAs in targeting cancer progression and chemoresistance

14.2.1 Small interfering RNAs-mediated oncogene silencing in cancer therapy

siRNA technology has become a promising strategy for cancer therapy because it can selectively silence oncogenes that drive tumor cell growth and survival. Knocking down genes like Kirsten rat sarcoma virus oncogene homologue (KRAS) and **MYC Proto-Oncogene, BHLH Transcription Factor** (MYC) with siRNA is capable of preventing cancer cell proliferation and increasing the effectiveness of chemotherapeutic drugs. KRAS gene mutations occur frequently in many cancers, like pancreatic cancer, colorectal cancer, and lung cancer, and as a result, it leads to uncontrollable cell growth and tumor formation. Studies have shown that silencing of KRAS using siRNA is effective enough to suppress tumor cell proliferation. For example, in a pancreatic cancer cell, the delivery of KRAS-targeted siRNA through gold nanoparticles caused substantial growth inhibition, which highlights the therapeutic value of this method (Küçükekmekci & Budak Yıldıran, 2024). MYC oncogene is essential for the regulation of cell cycle, metabolism, and apoptosis. MYC overexpression correlates with aggressive tumor behavior and poor prognosis. Studies have shown that cotargeting KRAS and MYC by chimeric siRNAs significantly reduced the viability and tumor-forming capacity in lung cancer models (Chareddy et al., 2023). A few strategies of siRNA-guided gene silencing in lung cancer are presented in Table 14.1.

14.2.2 Small interfering RNAs strategies to overcome chemo resistance

Chemo resistance remains a major challenge in cancer treatment and often leads to treatment failure, arising from mechanisms such as enhanced DNA repair and overexpression of drug efflux pumps. siRNA-based treatments present approaches to reverse the resistance mechanisms. In mechanisms of DNA repair, cancer cells may become resistant to DNA-damaging agents by upregulating DNA damage response (DDR) pathways. siRNA-mediated targeting of the most important DDR components can sensitize tumor cells to chemotherapy. Silencing DDR components, for instance, has been demonstrated to increase the efficacy of treatments by inhibiting the repair of chemotherapeutically induced DNA damage (Jurkovicova et al., 2022). In drug efflux pumps, overexpression of the ATP-binding cassette (ABC) transporters like P-glycoprotein (P-gp) results in the extrusion of the chemotherapeutic drugs from cancer cells and lessens the efficacy of treatment. siRNA-induced downregulation of the transporters was shown to restore multidrug resistance (MDR) by enhancing the intracellular levels of the chemotherapeutic agents and reestablishing their cytotoxic activity (Jurkovicova et al., 2022). Antiapoptotic genes code for proteins that suppress apoptosis, the process of programmed cell death that is vital for cellular homeostasis and development. Through the suppression of pro-apoptotic signals, these genes ensure cell survival. Dysregulation of these genes, however, may result in pathological states, such as cancer, through the inability of abnormal cells to undergo death.

14.2.3 Targeting antiapoptotic genes: B cell lymphoma-2 and X-linked inhibitor of apoptosis protein

B cell lymphoma-2 (BCL-2) is a founding member of the BCL-2 protein family and functions by binding to and inhibiting pro-apoptotic proteins like BAX and BAK, thereby preventing mitochondrial outer membrane permeabilization (MOMP) and subsequent cytochrome c release, a critical step in the intrinsic apoptosis pathway. BCL-2 is an antiapoptotic protein that contributes to chemotherapy resistance by inhibiting cell death mechanisms. Studies have shown that silencing BCL-2 using siRNA can significantly reduce tumor growth and enhance the effectiveness of chemotherapeutic agents. In breast cancer studies, the estrogen receptor-negative (ER−) MDA-MB-231 breast cancer cells, systemic administration of nano-liposomal BCL-2 siRNA led to a marked decrease in tumor growth. When combined with doxorubicin, a commonly used chemotherapeutic agent, this approach resulted in better reduction of tumor cells, which indicates a synergistic effect between the BCL-2 silencing and chemotherapy (Tekedereli et al., 2013). X-linked inhibitor of apoptosis protein (XIAP) directly inhibits caspases-3, -7, and -9, key executors of apoptosis. By binding to these caspases, XIAP prevents the apoptotic cascade, thereby promoting cell survival. Targeting antiapoptotic genes such as BCL-2 and XIAP using siRNA has demonstrated significant potential in sensitizing cancer cells to chemotherapeutic agents like paclitaxel and etoposide. When these genes are sliced, the apoptotic pathway gets reactivated, enhancing the efficacy of chemotherapy and promoting programmed cell death in resistant cancer cells. XIAP binds to the suppressive caspases and inhibits apoptotic cell death. In nonsmall cell lung cancer (NSCLC), a small molecule inhibitor of XIAP induced apoptosis (Dean et al., 2010).

14.2.4 Caspase activation and its therapeutic modulation

A set of conserved cysteine proteases that cleave after finding an aspartate residue in their substrate comes under the class of caspases. These take part in apoptosis and are divided into two distinct groups: the initiators, such as caspase-9, which consist of 20–30 residues in the pro-domain sequence, and the second group is the effector, such as caspase-7 and caspase-3, which consist of 20–30 residues in the pro-domain sequence. During apoptosis, the initiator caspase is activated instantly (Adams & Cory, 2002). The mitochondrial pathway, also called the apoptotic intrinsic pathway, begins with the damage of DNA, followed by the activation of the tumor suppressor protein p53, which results in a cascade of events that eventually leads to mitochondrial permeabilization of the outer membrane. This results in the cessation of ATP synthesis in the mitochondria and arrests the related transport activities. This is also regulated by the members of the BCL-2 protein family, involving both pro-apoptotic and antiapoptotic proteins. Heterodimeric interactions among the BCL-2 proteins decide the destiny of the cells. Antiapoptotic associates in the BCL-2 family contain 4BH domains. Once the death signal BH3 domain is activated, the proteins within the domain can only neutralize the antiapoptotic BCL-2 proteins. The changes in the membrane potential of mitochondria are due to the pro-apoptotic proteins such as Bax and Bak. The internal proteins that are usually found in the inner membrane space of mitochondria are released into the cytosol, and the overexpression of the antiapoptotic BCL-2 proteins results in chronic lymphocytic leukemia. Extracellular death ligands bind to their respective death receptors on the cell surface, resulting in the formation of the death-inducing signaling complex (DISC). DISC facilitates the oligomerization and activation of procaspase-8, another initiator caspase. Activated initiator caspases (e.g., caspase-8 and caspase-9) cleave and activate executioner caspases, such as caspase-3 and caspase-7. Once activated, these executioner caspases degrade key cellular components, leading to the morphological and biochemical changes characteristic of apoptosis. siRNA targeting caspase inhibitors (e.g., XIAP) can lead to the activation of caspase-dependent apoptosis pathways, thereby sensitizing cancer cells to apoptotic stimuli (Cheng et al., 2010).

14.2.5 Cell cycle regulation and tumor suppression

The cell cycle is tightly regulated, and dysregulation of cell cycle checkpoints is a hallmark of cancer. Several cyclins, cyclin-dependent kinases (CDKs), and checkpoint proteins promote uncontrolled cell division. siRNA- mediated silencing of these genes can halt the progression of the cell cycle and lead to cancer cell death, as depicted in Fig. 14.1. Experimentally defined

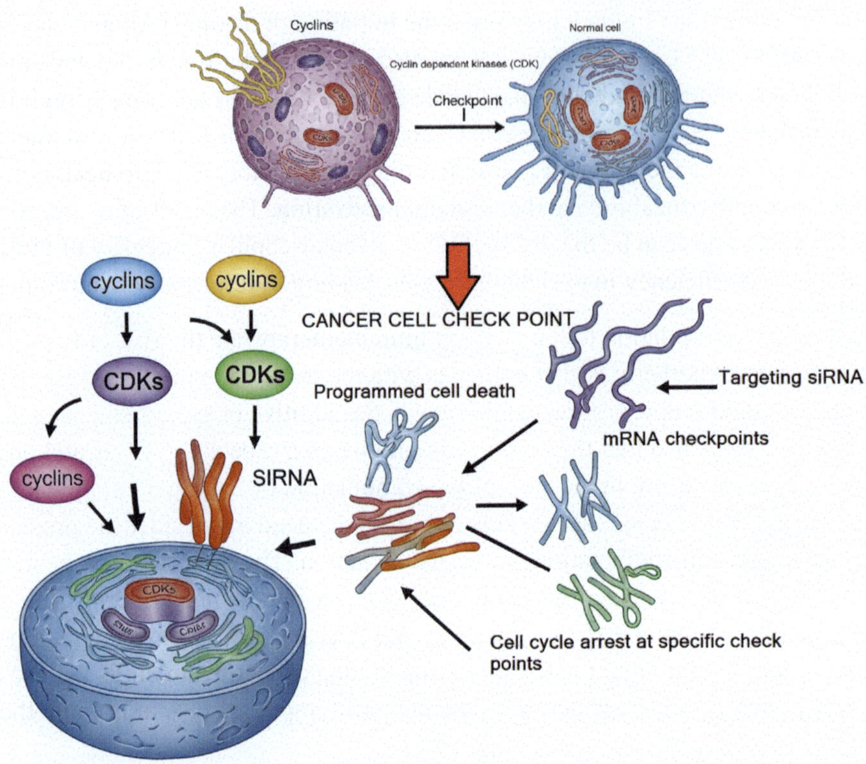

Figure 14.1
Cell cycle control. Cell cycle regulation and tumor suppression.

periods during which cells get ready and subsequently divide their genome equally between two daughter cells are called the cell cycle. The four successive phases are the G1 phase, when the cell grows and builds up the materials needed for DNA replication; the S phase, when the DNA is replicated; the G2 phase, when the cell checks that replication is complete and prepares for division; and the M phase, when the cell divides, and the duplicated DNA is separated into two daughter cells. Most adult cells are kept in a resting stage called G0. In this state, cells are not actively dividing and are often either postmitotic or moving toward terminal differentiation. When cells do reenter the cell cycle, the early steps help determine whether they will continue to proliferate and divide. Cell cycle progression is controlled by cyclins and CDKs. CDKs only become active when they pair with the right cyclin, which switches them on. This pairing depends on a conserved region in cyclins called the cyclin box, a roughly 100 amino acid segment that forms the binding surface for the matching CDK. CDKs define which partner kinases bind to their cognate cyclins to become activated due to their significance in biology. Cyclins D1, D2, and D3 are among the D cyclins that form active complexes with either CDK4 or CDK6, which phosphorylate the retinoblastoma protein

(Rb) and cause the passage of the G1 to S phase. D cyclins work with external stimuli (such as the availability of growth factors and nutrients) to coordinate cell cycle growth. The deregulation of cyclin D1 in human malignancies has garnered a lot of interest (Qie & Diehl, 2016). p21, which codes for the cyclin-dependent kinase inhibitor, is commonly known as CDKN1A. P53 and induced G1 cell cycle arrest are mediated by p21. Its p53-induced induction and simultaneous CDK inhibition are believed to be critical for the tumor-suppressive activity of p21 (Warfel & El-Deiry, 2013). p21 controls RB phosphorylation as a tumor suppressor. The phosphorylation status of RB governs the assembly of the RB-E2F complexes. This protein contains many phosphorylation sites that cyclins D-CDK4/6, E-CDK2, A-CDK2, and B-CDK1 can use as substrates. RB that has been hypo-phosphorylated attaches itself to E2F transcription factor dimers. Many cell cycle genes, especially those needed for the G1 to S transition, have their transcription suppressed by RB-E2F complexes (Sherr & Roberts, 1995). The kinase activity of cyclin-CDK complexes can change the hypo-phosphorylated state of RB to hyperphosphorylation. p21 has the ability to inhibit several kinases. Thus, p21 can promote the development of the RB-E2F complex (Sdek et al., 2005). p53 is the most well-known factor that is important for avoiding cancer. The best studied tumor suppressor is the p53 protein. Cell cycle arrest as well as induction of apoptosis are among its main functions. Additionally, p53 functions in the senescence of cells, repair of DNA, embryo implantation, and regulation of metabolic pathways (Narasimha et al., 2014). Various viral oncoproteins inactivate p53. Numerous genes, some of which code for BCL-2 (Gonzalez-Avila et al., 2019) and surviving and MCL-1, all of which inhibit apoptosis, and MDR-1, which confers the MDR phenotype, have their transcription inhibited by p53.

14.3 Inhibition of metastasis and epithelial-to-mesenchymal transition through small interfering RNAs

Metastasis is the spreading and diffusion of cancerous cells from their original site to reach a distant or nearby organ. It has an important role in the prognosis of cancer patients. At first, the cancer cell detachment occurs from the primary site, and later it gets disseminated within the tissues, after which the cancer cells get into the vascular channels and then into the lymphatic system. The key players in this process include matrix metalloproteinases (MMPs), E-cadherin, and vimentin. Utilizing siRNA to target these genes offers a promising strategy to inhibit cancer cell migration and invasion, as shown in Fig. 14.2.

14.3.1 Matrix metalloproteinases

The zinc-dependent endopeptidases are known as MMPs. They are essential for many physiological functions, including organ development and tissue remodeling, the control of inflammatory processes, and the development of illnesses like cancer. The architectural characteristics of the 23 MMPs expressed in humans are grouped (Gross & Lapiere, 1962). Functional

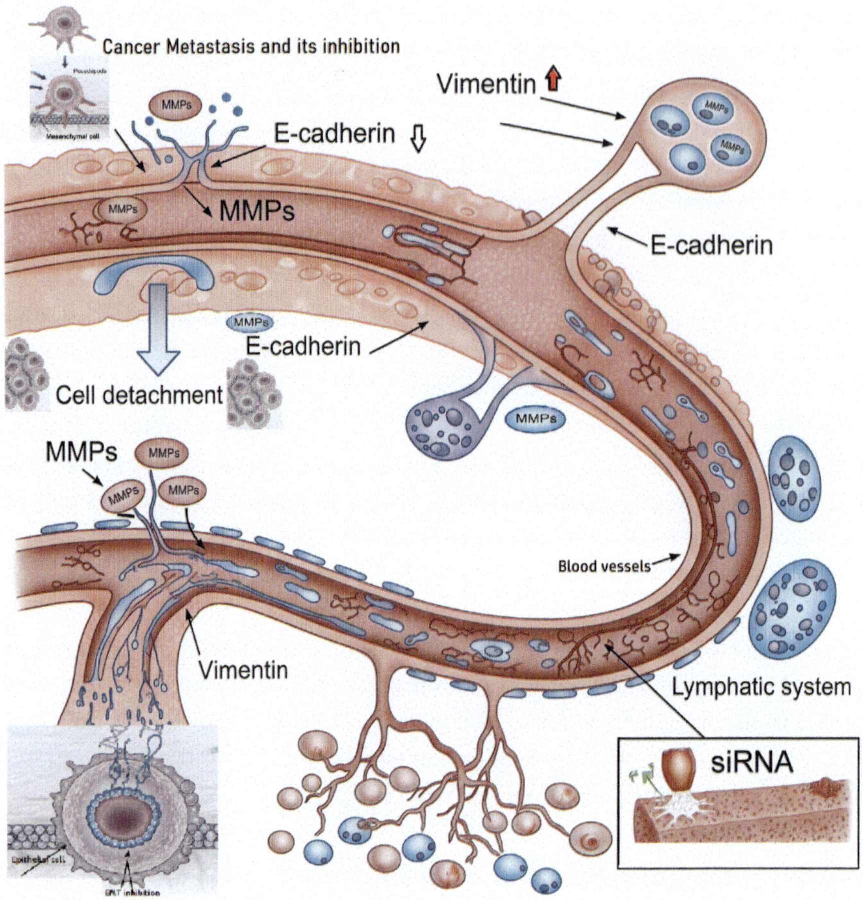

Figure 14.2
Role of siRNA. Inhibition of metastasis through siRNA.

proteins operate some crucial proteins that take part in several events (Satelli & Li, 2011). Three domains are shared by nearly all MMPs, according to their basic structural blueprint: Most MMPs share the same basic structure, with a propeptide, a catalytic domain, and a hemopexin-like C-terminal domain connected to the catalytic region by a flexible hinge. They are produced first as inactive enzymes because a cysteine in the pro domain binds to the zinc ion in the catalytic site and blocks activity (Cabral-Pacheco et al., 2020). MMPs become active only when this interaction is disrupted in a process known as the cysteine switch, usually after the pro domain is cleaved by proteolysis or when the cysteine residue is chemically modified. The consensus sequence in the pro-domain necessitates proteolytic cleavage by convertases, which can happen extracellularly by serine proteinases like plasmin or intracellularly by furin, depending on the sequences (Egeblad & Werb, 2002). Different subdomains make up the composition and expression of MMPs in the Stroma MMPs. The "minimal domain," which is shared by all MMPs, is composed of three main regions: the catalytic domain, which contains a zinc binding site (Zn2+), and a pro domain that includes a thiol group (SH) as well as a furin cleavage site, and an amino-terminal signal sequence (Pre) that the signal peptidase will cleave upon entry into the endoplasmic reticulum. The enzyme remains an inactive zymogen when the pro-domain's -SH group interacts with the catalytic domain's zinc ion (Sternlicht & Werb, 2001). Intracellular furin-like proteinases are frequently responsible for zymogen activation by cleaving the furin recognition motif (Fu) located between the pro domain and the catalytic domain. The majority of MMPs have a hemopexin-like region in addition to the minimum domain. This region contains four hemopexin-like repeats, with a disulfide bond (S–S) linking the first and the last subdomains. It is attached to the catalytic domain through a flexible hinge region (Costa et al., 2024). The tumor microenvironment has a wide range of metalloproteinase and inhibitory expression. TIMPs and members of the MMP and ADAM families can be expressed by cancer cells from different organs, although stromal cells that infiltrate the tumor are the main source of these proteinases. The milieu around the tumor is specifically changed by the distinct set of proteinases and proteinase inhibitors that are produced by the various types of stromal cells and discharged into the extracellular space (Deryugina & Quigley, 2006).

14.3.2 Vimentin and E-cadherin

A functional protein with multiple roles that can regulate the interaction with other proteins is Vimentin. It has the ability to control various physiological functions, preserve cellular shape, protect cytoplasm and its integrity, together with providing stability to the interactions of the cytoskeleton that take part in any immune response. It operates several crucial proteins that take part in cellular attachment, signaling, and migration, and is highly expressed in mesenchymal cells and is positively correlated with increased metastasis (Satelli & Li, 2011). E-cadherin, on the other hand, is a transmembrane glycoprotein that acts as a cell-cell junction protein, takes an active part in cellular adhesion, maintains tissue architecture, and is a conventional marker of epithelial cells that is important for epithelial cell adhesion and for maintaining normal tissue architecture.

14.3.3 Epithelial-to-mesenchymal transition and its regulators

Epithelial-to-mesenchymal transition (EMT) is an evolutionarily conserved process that changes the expression of many genes in epithelial cells, enabling them to acquire mesenchymal-like characteristics. In the pathogenic stage, E-cadherin and vitexin biomarkers are responsible for setting the level of EMT markers. EMT is responsible for the morphogenesis and stem cell plasticity necessary for normal gastrulation and organ formation in early human development (Škovierová et al., 2018). Circulating tumor cells (CTCs) and CTC clusters are two of the various cell types that can be found in the blood during tumor growth. After significant changes in cell morphology induced by EMT, they are released from the primary tumors. Identification of cancer can be achieved by a process of cell dedifferentiation using EMT. EMT is required for the initiation of the migration of tumor cells and metastasis formation. Proteins that include cytokeratins and E-cadherin are typically expressed in epithelial cells, and one of the important features of EMT is that the expression is decreased (Yeung & Yang, 2017).

14.4 Mechanisms of chemo resistance and small interfering RNAs-based therapeutic targets

Chemo resistance is one of the major obstacles in the treatment of cancer. The issue of treatment for cancer is because of a huge number of intrinsic or extrinsic invaders that keep increasing in number. The limitation of chemotherapy, where a single drug is used, was addressed by employing polychemotherapy that allows the administration of more than a single drug, which addresses the problem of drug resistance in chemotherapy (Wang et al., 2024). Making use of siRNA in drug delivery can make the disease-linked genes go silent by specific binding behavior.

14.4.1 ATP-binding cassette transporters (drug efflux)

One of the biggest protein families is made up of proteins known as ABCs. ABC proteins can regulate membrane channels by opening or closing them, such as ion channels. They can also act as primary active transporters that move substrates across membranes in a directed manner, or function as part of multiprotein channel complexes, such as receptors, by using energy from ATP hydrolysis (Wang et al., 2024). ATP hydrolysis in the nucleotide-binding domains (NBDs) is essential for ABC transport activity, as these proteins function as major primary active transporters. The functional link between these two distinct domains is provided by a close association between these cytoplasmic domains and the intracellular areas of the TMDs. The nucleotide-binding domains bind cytoplasmic ATP, and ATP hydrolysis powers active transport by providing the energy to move substrates against their concentration gradient. Close coupling between binding domains of nt and transmembrane domains acts as the transmission system that converts substrate binding and ATP hydrolysis into the conformational changes required for transport (Hristos et al., 2004).

14.4.2 Targeting drug metabolism enzymes (CYPs and glutathione S transferases)

Phase I metabolizing enzymes, including cytochrome P450 monooxygenases (P450) and carboxylesterases (CarEs), mainly process xenobiotics and endobiotics through hydroxylation and other oxidation reactions. The superfamily of mixed function oxidases, which includes cytochrome P450 1B1 (CYP1B1), is involved in the metabolic activation of numerous structurally varied substances as well as cell detoxification (Gavrilov & Saltzman, 2012; Zhang et al., 2023). One important extrahepatic enzyme involved in the metabolism of xenobiotics and estrogen is CYP1B1. Heme-thiolate proteins called P450s are present in all living beings. This also catalyzes the stereospecific and regio-specific transformation of a variety of lipophilic substances into more hydrophilic forms. The metabolism of aliphatic, alicyclic, and aromatic compounds has been demonstrated to involve P450s collectively in reactions with in situ selectivity in hydroxylation, epoxidation, dealkylation, sulfoxydation, deamination, desulphuration, dehalogenation, and nitro reduction (Borst, 2020). The components belonging to the group of phase II detoxification enzymes are glutathione S transferases (GSTs) that can protect cellular macromolecules from electrophiles that are highly reactive in nature. They do this by catalyzing the conjugation of glutathione (GSH) to a broad range of electrophilic compounds, including both endogenous and exogenous substrates, which is the initial step in the mercapturic acid pathway that results in the removal of toxic compounds. GSH and GSTs have evolved together, and they are found in most life forms. GSTs are generally divided into two main super families, microsomal membrane-bound GSTs and cytosolic GSTs. In addition to detoxification, GSTs contribute to cellular defense against oxidative stress and a range of toxic compounds, and they are also involved in the metabolism of leukotrienes and prostaglandins. By reducing oxidative stress, GSTs help protect DNA from damage and mutations that can promote carcinogenesis (Li et al., 2009).

14.4.3 Regulation of apoptosis by p53 and B cell lymphoma-2 family in chemo resistance

p53, a tumor suppressor, and BCL-2, a proto-oncogene, were among the first cancer-related genes to be identified. Mutant p53 proteins were first detected in transformed murine cell lines, whereas BCL-2 translocations were first identified in human follicular lymphoma. p53 was proposed to activate cell cycle checkpoints, whereas BCL-2 was shown to inhibit cell death. Early studies also suggested that BCL-2 overexpression was largely restricted to hematopoietic malignancies, while p53 mutations were more commonly reported in solid tumors. In response to cellular stresses such as DNA damage, p53 accumulates in the nucleus and either pauses the cell cycle to allow time for DNA repair or triggers apoptosis when the damage cannot be repaired (Kale et al., 2018). The BCL-2 family regulates apoptosis and includes proteins that either promote or block cell death. These proteins control mitochondrial outer MOMP and, as a result, the release of apoptogenic factors from mitochondria. BCL-2 is an antiapoptotic protein. BCL-XL preserves mitochondrial integrity by inhibiting pro-apoptotic members, thereby preventing apoptosis. Pro-apoptotic proteins such as BAX and BAK mediate MOMP, causing the release of cytochrome c and activation of the caspase cascade with a culmination in cell death (Hardwick & Soane, 2013). BH3-only proteins like

BID and BIM function as cellular stress sensors and induce apoptosis by inhibiting antiapoptotic proteins or activating pro-apoptotic proteins (Kelly et al., 2010). p53 helps regulate the expression of different members of the BCL-2 family, by shifting the balance in favor of cell survival or death depending upon the cellular component. For example, p53 can induce pro-apoptotic proteins such as BAX and PUMA, and induce apoptosis when there is any severe DNA damage. Mutations in p53 can, on the other hand, disturb the regulation, which results in uncontrolled cell division and tumor growth. Inhibition of BCL-2 and recovery of p53 function by siRNA methods have been found to make chemotherapy-resistant cancer cells sensitive to apoptosis (Fatemian et al., 2014).

14.4.4 Cisplatin mechanism of action

Cisplatin is a platinum (Pt)-based chemotherapeutic agent that has been extensively studied for its efficacy in treating various cancers. The molecular structure of cisplatin features a central Pt atom coordinated in a square planar geometry by two chloride (Cl^-) ligands and two ammonia (NH_3) molecules positioned adjacent to each other. Cisplatin's reactivity is primarily attributed to its Cl^- ligands, which can be displaced in an aqueous environment to form a highly reactive, positively charged Pt complex. These activated complexes exhibit a strong affinity for nucleophilic functional groups, including phosphate, amino, sulfhydryl, carboxyl, and hydroxyl groups (Chen & Chang, 2019). Upon the administration, cisplatin undergoes hydrolysis, which leads to the replacement of its Cl^- ligands with water molecules, resulting in the formation of reactive species. These species can form bonds with guanine and adenine bases in DNA, leading to the formation of intra-strand and interstrand cross-links. Additionally, cisplatin can also interact with the functional groups on proteins, particularly the sulfur atoms in cysteine and methionine side chains, forming additional compound that disrupts the protein function (Kiss et al., 2021). Cisplatin primarily exerts its toxic effects by forming cross-links in DNA, which interrupt the replication process and lead to cell death. However, some cancer cells counteract this damage by activating the DNA repair pathways. The nucleotide excision repair (NER) system plays a crucial role in this process, with proteins like ERCC1 facilitating the removal of cisplatin-induced DNA adducts. Higher ERCC1 expression has been linked to reduced cisplatin effectiveness, particularly in NSCLC (Ayrton & Morgan, 2001). Transport proteins are integral proteins present in the membrane that can facilitate the movement of substances across cellular membranes, playing crucial roles in the absorption, distribution, and excretion of various compounds, including drugs (Uppal et al., 2014).

14.4.5 Role of transport proteins

ABC transporters use the energy released by ATP hydrolysis to move substrates across membranes against their concentration gradients. P-gp, also known as MDR, is an efflux pump that expels a wide range of xenobiotics and drugs out of cells, contributing to MDR in cancer therapy. Cancer cells can develop resistance to chemotherapy through MDR mechanisms (Wood et al., 2007). The ABC family includes about 48 energy-dependent membrane transporters that function as efflux pumps. All three proteins belong to the ABC transporter family and are expressed in epithelial cells of the adrenal cortex, the gastrointestinal tract, and the placenta. It is also seen in the hepatobiliary tract, renal tubules, and in the blood-brain barrier (BBB) membranes (Devarajan et al., 2002). ABC transporters export sterols, peptides, lipids, and other potentially toxic compounds from the cytoplasm and are essential for normal physiological function (Wood et al., 2007).

14.4.6 Apoptotic pathways and cisplatin resistance

Apoptosis, or programmed cell death, is a vital process that enables organisms to eliminate damaged, infected, or unnecessary cells, thereby maintaining tissue homeostasis and development. This highly regulated mechanism involves a cascade of molecular events leading to characteristic cellular changes, such as chromatin condensation, DNA fragmentation, and membrane blebbing (Caroppi et al., 2009). There are two primary pathways through which apoptosis is initiated: the intrinsic pathway and the extrinsic pathway. The intrinsic pathway describes apoptosis that begins inside the cell and is triggered by internal signals such as DNA damage, oxidative stress, and hypoxia (Devarajan et al., 2002). The intrinsic pathway, also known as the mitochondrial pathway, is triggered by increased mitochondrial membrane permeability, which leads to the release of pro-apoptotic factors such as cytochrome c into the cytoplasm (Caroppi et al., 2009). This pathway is controlled by the BCL-2 family of proteins. The family is named after the BCL-2 gene, which was first discovered at the chromosomal breakpoint of the t(14;18) translocation in follicular nonHodgkin lymphoma (Wood et al., 2007). Antiapoptotic BCL-2 family members, such as BCL-2, BCL-XL, BCL-W, BFL-1, and MCL-1, inhibit apoptosis by preventing the mitochondrial release of cytochrome c. In contrast, pro-apoptotic members, including BAX, BAK, BAD, BCL-XS, BID, BIK, BIM, and HRK, promote cytochrome c release from mitochondria and thereby drive apoptosis. In contrast, the extrinsic or death receptor pathway is triggered when death ligands bind to their corresponding death receptors on the cell surface (Park et al., 2003). Many tumor cells overexpress Pgp, which recognizes several chemotherapeutic agents as foreign and pumps them out of the cell, lowering the intracellular drug level and reducing treatment effectiveness. Several death receptors, including TNF receptor 1 (TNFR1) and Fas (CD95), are involved in this apoptotic pathway (Iizasa et al., 2012). These receptors contain an intracellular death domain that recruits adaptor proteins such as TRADD and FADD, along with caspase 8 (Searles et al., 1999). Ligand receptor binding promotes the assembly of the DISC (Wood et al., 2007), which leads to the activation of procaspase 8. Activated caspase 8 then initiates apoptosis by cleaving and activating downstream executioner caspases (LaCasse et al., 2008).

DR3, DR4, DR5, and DR6 are some examples of known death receptors, along with ectodysplasin A receptor (EDAR) and NGFR (nerve growth factor receptor (Lee et al., 2003).

14.4.7 Role and structure of high-mobility group box 1 in cancer resistance

High-mobility group box 1 (HMGB1) is a nuclear protein that is highly conserved, a non-histone chromatin-associated protein that plays crucial roles in various cellular processes, including DNA organization, transcription regulation, and the modulation of inflammatory responses (Ruggieri et al., 2024). It is expressed differently in tumor tissues and normal tissues, and thus it has been closely related to the divisional stages and prognosis of tumor mutational studies and resistance to drugs in various pathways. It has a crucial role in microsatellite instability and immune cell infiltration. C-Terminal acidic tail is rich in glutamic and aspartic acids, and this negatively charged region modulates the protein's DNA-binding affinity and interactions with other proteins (Martinotti et al., 2015). High expression of HMGB1 has been correlated with enhanced resistance to cisplatin since this protein may augment drug efflux and hinder apoptotic signals. Research reveals that HMGB1 overexpression has been implicated in tumor development and chemotherapy resistance in NSCLC (Ma et al., 2023). HMGB1 supports tumor development by controlling cell death and survival signals. It plays a two-faced role, functioning as both an oncogene and a tumor suppressor, depending on the situation. HMGB1 overexpression is associated with increased proliferation, invasion, and metastasis in cancer cells. Its involvement in DNA repair processes also contributes to the survival of cancer cells under genotoxic stress (Wu et al., 2016). HMGB1 is located in nucleus, may interact with TLR2 and TLR-4 and consists of 215 amino acids and features three primary domains: Two DNA-binding domains (HMG Boxes A and B) A-box (residues 9–79) and B-box (residues 95–163)-and an acidic C-terminal tail (residues 186–215), with nuclear localization signals (NLS1 at residues 28–44 and NLS2 at residues 179–185) that regulate its intracellular transport (Lv et al., 2024), these tandem HMG-box motifs enable HMGB1 to bind nonsequence-specifically to the minor groove of DNA, inducing bending and facilitating interactions with other nuclear proteins. Overexpression of HMGB1 has been linked to increased drug resistance to chemotherapy. In osteosarcoma, for example, elevated levels of HMGB1 were correlated with drug resistance to agents such as doxorubicin, cisplatin, and methotrexate. Knockdown of HMGB1 in these cells increased drug-induced cell death, suggesting that HMGB1 promotes chemo-resistance by inhibiting apoptosis and possibly through the induction of autophagy (Guan et al., 2023).

14.5 Combination of small interfering RNAs and cisplatin

The main molecular mechanism is thought to involve activation of both the intrinsic and extrinsic apoptotic pathways. This is driven by the generation of reactive oxygen species

(ROS) through peroxidation of lipids, initiation of manifold pathways contributing to signal transduction, beginning of p53 signaling and cell cycle arrest, pouring in of pro-apoptotic genes and proteins, and lowering of proto-oncogenes along with lesser antiapoptotic genes and proteins. As neurotoxicity, ototoxicity, renal toxicity, and various other side effects have been noted, treatment success has been difficult to achieve beyond thorough drug research. Therefore, methods for addressing drug resistance and toxicity associated with cisplatin must be devised. The side effects can be mitigated by a thorough look at lower toxicity in cisplatin analogs, conjugated therapy along with the other cancer medications, and nanotechnology (Tchounwou et al., 2021).

14.5.1 Targeting resistance pathways

Combining siRNA-mediated gene silencing with cisplatin chemotherapy has emerged as a promising strategy to overcome drug resistance in cancers. Copper transporters such as ATP7A and ATP7B have a unique and critical role to play in Pt drug resistance, and this depends on the type of cancer. ATP7B is involved in the regulation of cisplatin resistance by drug efflux via a secretory vesicle, and ATP7A regulates intracellular sequestration. In an ovarian cancer model, it has been observed that expression of ATP7B is highly upregulated in a resistant cell line, and its downregulation resulted in a 2.5-fold decrease in IC50 of cisplatin and an increase in DNA adduct formation. On the other hand, ATP7A silencing showed no significant effect in an ovarian cancer but demonstrated a partial resistance reversal in esophageal squamous cell carcinoma. ATP7B, a copper-transporting P-type ATPase, contributes to cisplatin resistance across multiple cancer types, primarily through two mechanisms that are enhanced in drug efflux and intracellular sequestration, though its clinical impact varies by the type of tumor. ATP7B overexpression in NSCLC is linked to cisplatin resistance, especially in adenocarcinomas. Resistant tumors have higher ATP7B mRNA levels, and ATP7B reduces intracellular cisplatin accumulation by promoting drug efflux. Adenocarcinomas have significantly higher ATP7B expression (Inoue et al., 2010). ATP7B expression increases in cisplatin-resistant oral squamous cell carcinoma (OSCC) cell lines, leading to acquired resistance. Silencing ATP7B with siRNA restores cisplatin sensitivity by 10.6-fold in resistant OSC-19-R cells, highlighting its crucial role in efflux-mediated resistance (Yoshizawa et al., 2007). ATP7B transports cisplatin into extracellular secretory vesicles, reducing drug bioavailability. In some models, ATP7B mediates transient Pt sequestration in vesicles, delaying DNA damage.

14.5.2 Sensitizing tumor cells

siRNAs have a major role in sensitizing tumor cells to cisplatin by targeting proteins involved in DNA repair and apoptosis regulation. Cisplatin mainly damages DNA through the formation of DNA crosslinks, which results in the death of the cell if the damages irreversible.

Although many cancer cells develop resistance to cisplatin by enhancing their DNA repair mechanisms or evading apoptosis. siRNAs can target DNA repair proteins, such as REV1 and REV3L, to impair the cell's ability to repair cisplatin-induced DNA damage. This can increase cancer cells' sensitivity to chemotherapy, as they become less capable of repairing the damage caused by cisplatin. This mode of action can be used for the treatment of various cancer types (Xu et al., 2013). This is possible by employing siRNA, which can be used for the targeting of proteins that play key roles in the regulation of apoptosis, especially anti-apoptotic proteins such as BCL-2. This can be achieved by reducing the expression of such proteins, which can be helpful for the promotion of apoptosis, especially during treatment with cisplatin. Studies suggest that the knockdown of BCL-2 can increase the sensitivity of breast cancer cells to chemotherapy, which can be helpful for improving treatment outcomes (Thiel et al., 2012). The use of siRNA technology, coupled with traditional chemotherapy such as cisplatin, is believed to be helpful for cancer treatment. This mode of treatment can be achieved by selectively knocking down genes that can cause resistance during cancer treatment.

14.5.3 Nanoparticle delivery systems

Some of these recent innovations include the development of nanoparticle platforms for the coadministration of siRNAs and cisplatin. This not only enhances the delivery of siRNAs but also allows for the simultaneous targeting of different drug resistance pathways (Xu et al., 2013). The effects of siRNA treatment can be sustained over a period of time, thus providing a prolonged sensitization of tumor cells. This is a desirable feature for long-term treatment regimens. By employing siRNAs that target specific proteins in DNA repair and apoptosis, the sensitivity of tumor cells to cisplatin can be increased significantly. This approach has the potential to be effective in improving the results of cancer therapy by overcoming drug resistance and improving the effectiveness of existing drugs (Geis et al., 2010). Due to the utilization of siRNAs, which have the potential for cancer therapy, there is increased attention for the treatment of cancer by gene silencing. The improvement of target delivery of siRNAs can be achieved by the utilization of nanoparticles, which increases the effectiveness of treatment while minimizing the side effects. The nanoparticles of transferrin (TF) can specifically transport siRNAs to the tumor site. This is achieved by the use of the transferrin receptor (TfR), which is often overexpressed on the surface of tumor cells. The nanoparticles are formed by the chemical modification of both TF and siRNA. Studies have shown that the TF nanoparticles can specifically silence genes in tumor cells with minimal toxicity. In vivo research supports their potential as an "effective delivery system" for cancer therapies, which "may enhance their efficacy while reducing their adverse effects" (Yhee et al., 2013). This technique of delivery has been tested by using peptides such as "RGDK" that can target particular receptors on cancer cells, such as "neuropilin-1" and "integrins." This technique avoids the healthy cells of the body while enhancing the delivery of siRNA into cancer cells, improving their efficacy without increasing the "chances of tissue damage."

Another emerging form of lipid-based triblock PAMAM hybrid nanocarriers that can deliver chemotherapeutic agents as well as siRNA has been developed. These hybrid carriers have been shown to have improved loading efficiency, reduced cytotoxicity, and the ability to suppress the expression of oncogenes in different models of cancer (Goyal et al., 2022). The administration of siRNA by using nanoparticles has shown significant promise in terms of in vivo safety and efficacy. Since the blood circulation times are between 5 and 10 hours, there is great stability in these systems, and there is a sustained therapeutic effect and retention in the tumor tissue. Targeted nanoparticles are effective in silencing genes in the body in clinical trials in patients with tumors. For instance, siRNA that is targeted to ribonucleotide reductase inhibition is delivered by nanoparticles, and there has been significant knockdown in the tumor tissue. This shows that the effectiveness of siRNA therapies can be increased by the use of nanoparticle systems in a clinical setting (Khan et al., 2023). Targeted nanoparticle delivery systems are shown to enhance the therapeutic effectiveness of siRNA, and there are significant benefits in the use of siRNA in the treatment of cancer. Research is showing a bright future in the use of nanoparticles in siRNA therapies.

14.6 Challenges and considerations

When treating lung cancer with cisplatin and siRNA-mediated gene silencing, there are a few factors that must be considered. The efficient delivery of siRNA into tumor cells is one of the major challenges. Because siRNA is large, negatively charged, and rapidly degraded by enzymes, it has difficulty entering cell membranes and silencing genes. To improve the stability of siRNA and its ability of tumor targeting, different nanoparticle delivery methods, including lipid carriers, polymeric nanoparticles, and inorganic nanoparticles, have been investigated. Although siRNA is designed to target a specific gene, it sometimes suppresses other genes in an undesirable way, which can have unexpected implications, for example, cell toxicity or a reaction from the immune system. To deal with these issues and maintain its specificity, scientists have added chemical modifications such as 2'-O-methylation and phospho-rothioate couplings. These modifications enhance the safety and effectiveness of siRNA-based treatments.

Battling drug resistance to cisplatin therapy is still a large hurdle in having cancer therapy work effectively. In NSCLC, the ERCC1 gene, involved in DNA repair, is a key factor in drug resistance. Targeting ERCC1 with siRNA has promise for making cancer cells more sensitive to cisplatin, though there are still some practical hurdles to iron out before it can be employed efficiently. siRNA is rapidly degraded in the body and tends to have difficulty traveling to and being effective within tumor cells. Furthermore, the stressful environment of the tumor, including low oxygen and high acidity, can further hinder the entry of siRNA and nanoparticles into the cells, thereby hindering the efficacy of treatment. A second difficulty with siRNA therapies is the possibility of triggering immune responses within the body. Some siRNA sequences may have the potential to stimulate the body's immune system via toll-like receptors (TLRs), which would initiate the release of inflammatory molecules and cause side effects throughout the body. Scientists have looked into methods such as creating stealth nanocarriers, delivering certain chemical changes, and carefully choosing siRNA sequences to reduce immune response. Moreover, siRNA has a short half-life and is quickly eliminated from the bloodstream, reducing the amount of time it can circulate and reach the cancer. To counteract this drawback, scientists are working toward establishing shielded coatings for nanoparticles. These coatings are created to increase the stability of siRNA, make it more bioavailable in the body, and allow it to accumulate more efficiently within tumor tissue. Another reason the potential of siRNA therapy is reduced is because of the difficulty it has in entering the cells and escaping from the endosomes when it is inside. After entering the cell, siRNA tends to become stuck in endosomes, where it can be degraded before reaching the cytoplasm, which is the location it must be in to silence genes. To overcome this problem, scientists have developed pH-responsive nanocarriers and endosomal release agents, which greatly enhance the delivery of siRNA to the cytoplasm, increasing the efficiency of the process. To improve the targeting of tumor cells and reduce side effects to normal tissues, scientists are employing selective ligands such as folic acid, transferrin, or anticancer-related receptor antibodies, such as EGFR, to target siRNA specifically to cancer cells. Though there has been substantial progress, bringing siRNA-cisplatin combination therapies to clinical application continues to be a serious challenge. Issues such as scale-up production, batch-to-batch consistency, and compliance with regulatory standards remain challenges. To bring these therapies forward to clinical application successfully, it is important to standardize production protocols, provide consistent and reproducible outcomes, and perform careful investigations of their long-term safety.

Further innovation in gene silencing technologies, nanomedicine, and treatments for cancer will be needed to solve these difficulties and improve patient outcomes in lung cancer treatment (Paul et al., 2022). When combined with cisplatin therapy, siRNA delivery via nanoparticles has demonstrated the ability to increase cancer cells' sensitivity to the medication, providing a potentially effective method of treating lung cancer. One of the primary treatments for advanced NSCLC is cisplatin, a Pt-based chemotherapy. But with time, cancer cells become resistant to Pt medicines, which is a major difficulty in treatment. Proteins like ERCC1 and XPF are essential for this resistance because they aid cells in repairing the drug-induced damage to DNA. Studies have shown that lowering ERCC1/XPF levels can increase the sensitivity of cancer cells, especially those from ovarian and lung malignancies, to Pt-based therapies. To address this issue, researchers are investigating the use of short interfering RNA (siRNA) to target and inhibit the ERCC1/XPF genes, which could increase cisplatin's efficacy and improve patient outcomes. Administering siRNA is challenging because of its small instability and negative charge, which both limit its passage through the cell membrane and result in enzymatic degradation. Nonviral vectors, particularly polymeric delivery systems, offer an ideal choice due to their variable chemical composition and ability to overcome biological barriers. One such system uses amphiphilic triblock copolymers, like polyethyleneimine-polycaprolactone-polyethene glycol. While PEG reduces toxicity and extends the particles' time in circulation, PCL helps in the formation of micelles and allows the polymer to gradually break down. In meanwhile, PEI increases the amount of genetic material that penetrates cells. These elements combine to generate PEI-PCL-PEG micelle complexes, which have been demonstrated in experiments to efficiently deliver siRNA in both lab and animal settings. In one study, scientists employed microfluidic assembly to produce PEI-PCL-PEG nanoparticles loaded with siRNA that targets XPF and ERCC1. It was found that these nanoparticles reduced ERCC1/XPF protein levels in A549 lung cancer cells, in addition to the widely used transfection agent, Lipofectamine. Also, these siRNA-loaded nanoparticles enhanced susceptibility to Pt-based medicines in laboratory experiments in a p53 wildtype model of NSCLC. These findings imply that targeting ERCC1/XPF with nanoparticles may be an effective and potentially new technique to address cisplatin resistance in lung cancer. Another significant factor in this circumstance is the microfluidic technique, which produces consistent, dependable nanoparticles that improve the efficiency and consistency of siRNA delivery (Feldmann et al., 2020). By introducing siRNA-guided gene silencing, nanoparticle-mediated delivery systems emerged as a promising approach for enhancing cisplatin's therapeutic efficacy in lung cancer treatment. This method uses nanoparticles as carriers to codeliver siRNA and cisplatin molecules that target specific oncogenes or genes associated with treatment resistance, increasing the sensitivity of cancer cells to chemotherapy. Another example is the use of polyethyleneimine-polycaprolactone-polyethene glycol nanoparticles to deliver siRNA, which target excision repair cross-complementation group 1 (ERCC1), a gene associated with cisplatin resistance in NSCLC. These nanoparticles enhance cisplatin-induced cytotoxicity by preventing ERCC1, which disrupts cancer cells' DNA repair processes. Another strategy delivers siRNA against mitotic arrest deficient-2 (Mad2), an essential regulator of cell cycle checkpoints, utilizing chitosan nanoparticles that are targeted to the EGFR. Mad2 inhibition increases cisplatin's apoptotic effects and stops tumor growth.

In addition, gelatin nanoparticles functionalized with tyrosine kinase inhibitors (TKIs) and siRNA against AXL, a receptor tyrosine kinase that triggers drug resistance and epithelial-mesenchymal transition, cause tumor regression in NSCLC models, and cisplatin has a combined effect greater than either treatment alone. These nanoparticle-based codelivery systems not only improve the stability and bioavailability of siRNA but also enable customized delivery to tumor cells, reducing systemic toxicity and off-target effects. The enhanced cellular absorption and endosomal escape that these nanoparticles facilitate further increase their effectiveness. Intra-tumoral heterogeneity is a major biological barrier. NSCLC tumors are made up of subclonal populations with a variety of genetic and phenotypic characteristics that can change in response to treatment pressure (Swanton, 2012). Cisplatin and other chemotherapeutic drugs exert pressure on selection by eliminating sensitive cells while allowing resistant clones to survive and multiply (Dagogo-Jack & Shaw, 2018). Smaller subclones that depend on other resistance mechanisms can survive and eventually repopulate the tumor even when siRNA-mediated ERCC1 silencing improves the primary tumor cell population's sensitivity to cisplatin (Swanton, 2012). This continuous clonal change may lessen the long-term effects of focusing on a single gene, indicating that multiplex targeting or treatment plans that may be modified over time may be necessary for long-term management (Dagogo-Jack & Shaw, 2018).

DNA repair networks exhibit significant overlap and crosstalk, which is directly linked to tumor heterogeneity. While homologous recombination (HR) and nonhomologous end joining (NHEJ) can also aid in maintaining genomic integrity, NER is the primary mechanism for fixing cisplatin-induced DNA crosslinks. NER can be weakened by lowering ERCC1 levels, but tumor cells may respond by boosting HR activity, for instance, by upregulating proteins like BRCA1 or RAD51. The long-term impact of ERCC1 silencing may be lessened by this compensation, which also aids in maintaining total DNA repair capability (Lord & Ashworth, 2012). Due to this, techniques that block several DNA repair pathways simultaneously can result in more potent chemosensitization than targeting a single gene (O'Connor, 2015). Epigenetic plasticity, in addition to genetic redundancy, enables rapid transcriptional adaptation of cancer cells. They can experience reversible chromatin remodeling under therapeutic stress, which modifies the expression of stress response mediators, antiapoptotic proteins, and DNA repair genes. Tumor cells may thereby remodel epigenetically, activate alternate survival pathways, and regain resistance even after targeted gene silencing (Sharma et al., 2010). This adaptability highlights how important it is to include epigenomic analysis in treatment planning. siRNA delivery introduces an additional level of complexity at the intracellular level. siRNA must be loaded into the RNA-induced silencing complex RISC to have a therapeutic effect. RISC then controls the degradation of mRNA. RISC components may become saturated by high intracellular siRNA levels, interfering with endogenous microRNA processing and potentially disrupting normal gene regulation (Grimm et al., 2006).

Off-target changes in gene expression or unwanted stress reactions may result from this saturation. Furthermore, partial sequence complementarity may result in off-target regulation of other transcripts similar to microRNA (Jackson et al., 2003). These arguments emphasize that to preserve efficacy without sacrificing genomic stability, rigorous siRNA sequence design, suitable chemical modifications, and dose optimization are required. The in vivo behavior of systemically administered nanoparticles has an important effect on therapeutic efficacy in addition to processes occurring within the cell. Nanoparticles rapidly adsorb plasma proteins after injection, creating a "protein corona" that modifies the proteins' surface characteristics and radically affects their biological identity. Particularly in the liver and spleen, this corona can change surface charge, disguise targeted ligands, and speed up reticuloendothelial system clearance. To counter this, researchers are exploring advanced surface modifications like biomimetic membrane cloaking and zwitterionic coatings, which reduce protein binding and boost tumor specificity. RNA can become unstable due to additional biochemical stresses introduced by the tumor microenvironment. ROS produced by cisplatin therapy both increase cytotoxicity and produce a highly oxidative intracellular environment. RNA is particularly susceptible to this oxidative damage, affecting the integrity of siRNA and impairing gene silencing. In addition, stabilizing techniques might be required to protect siRNA activity in such severe tumor settings, even with chemical modifications like 2'-O-methylation and phosphorothioate links increasing nuclease resistance (Kanasty et al., 2013). Increasing concern links DNA damage signaling to immune checkpoint regulation. DNA damage from cisplatin can activate pathways that increase expression of immune checkpoint proteins such as PD-L1. Thus, although silencing ERCC1 results in enhanced DNA damage and drug efficacy, it may inadvertently assist tumors in evading the immune system (Sato et al., 2017). This suggests synergetic delivery of siRNA to chemo-sensitize treatment with PD-1/PD-L1 inhibitors. But patient-to-patient variability poses major barriers to real-world clinic use. In particular, pharmacogenomic variations, such as variations in DNA repair genes, can significantly affect drug responsiveness to cisplatin. Variation in ERCC1 expression levels or genetic polymorphism in ERCC1 can affect the level of DNA repair capacity before drug treatment, regardless of how effectively siRNA targets the gene (Bao et al., 2020). Hence, incorporation of genomic screening in drug design can aid in identifying target populations that are most likely to respond to drug treatment and increase overall drug responsiveness. Despite encouraging preclinical data, several barriers to clinical application still exist. For example, for the large-scale manufacturing of nanoparticle siRNA formulations, it should be reproducible, stable, and compliant with "good manufacturing practices." Long-term evaluation of safety is particularly crucial, as there is the possibility of untoward effects arising due to genomic changes or immune system activation. Additionally, the approval of such complex nanomedicines is often more challenging than traditional small molecules (Kanasty et al., 2013).

These biological and translational challenges collectively indicate that, in addition to achieving successful siRNA-mediated gene silencing, the successful application of siRNA and cisplatin combination therapy is a task that is much more complex and multifaceted than simply achieving successful siRNA-mediated gene silencing. Successful application of siRNA and cisplatin combination therapy will likely involve successful intervention in multiple genes, immunotherapy, pharmacogenomic screening, better design in nanotechnology, and analysis of the evolutionary changes in tumors over time to adapt the therapy accordingly (Dagogo-Jack & Shaw, 2018). It is likely that successful application and solution of all these issues and problems will be crucial in the successful translation and application of siRNA and cisplatin combination therapies from experimental systems into human clinics. Thus, in overcoming the issue of resistance and improving the effectiveness of chemotherapy and siRNA, the application and use of cisplatin chemotherapy and siRNA in lung cancer is a significant improvement in the management and treatment of this type of cancer. Intra-tumoral genetic variability can lead to distinct gene expression patterns that shape how tumors respond to therapy. Therefore, detailed molecular profiling of the tumors, which can be achieved by the use of next-generation sequencing technology, may aid in the identification of the major resistance-associated target genes within individual patients (Malone et al., 2020). This may, in turn, aid in the design of siRNA constructs that can be tailored to the specific alterations within the patient cells, which may enhance the efficacy of the treatment (Kanasty et al., 2013; Whitehead et al., 2009). Moreover, there is also a need for further research on the pharmacodynamics of siRNA-loaded nanocarriers, as the escape of the siRNA from the endosomes is one of the key factors that determine the success of the treatment, as it has to reach the cytoplasm of the cell where it can interact with the RNA induced silencing complex RISC (Dominska & Dykxhoorn, 2010; Watts & Corey, 2012). Further strategies using pH buffering polymers, disruptive peptides in membranes, or proton sponges could increase cytoplasmic delivery and thus increase efficacy (Behr, 1997; Whitehead et al., 2009). Quantitative in vitro and in vivo models are still needed to support mechanistic understanding and evaluate gene knockdown efficacy, apoptosis induction, and changes in downstream targets (Sui et al., 2002; Tekedereli et al., 2013). Safety profiles for long-term use are also important, especially for immunogenicity, off-target gene suppression, and toxicity (Judge et al., 2005; Robbins et al., 2009). Therefore, preclinical toxicology studies will be necessary, followed by appropriate phase I and phase II clinical trials, which will be necessary for defining the optimal dosing regimens, therapeutic windows, and toxicity profiles (Setten et al., 2019). Concurrently, monitoring biomarkers of response and resistance during treatment may provide valuable predictive information, which can be used for making appropriate changes in the treatment regimen, if necessary. The use of molecular target-based therapies, coupled with traditional chemotherapy, can be seen as part of the trend toward mechanism-based cancer treatment (Holohan et al., 2013; Shi et al., 2017).

14.7 Conclusion

Combining cisplatin therapy with siRNA-mediated gene silencing to overcome chemo resistance is an effective way to treat lung cancer, especially NSCLC. Although acquired resistance mechanisms frequently limit its long-term efficiency, cisplatin is still one of the most effective chemotherapeutic drugs. These include MDR1 overexpression, TP53 mutations, activation of survival pathways like EGFR signaling, and upregulation of antiapoptotic proteins, e.g., BCL-2 and survivin. By specifically targeting these resistance-associated genes, siRNA-mediated silencing increases cisplatin sensitivity. Several challenges must be addressed before siRNA therapy can transition to clinical applications. A primary obstacle in cancer treatment is the development of efficient and targeted delivery systems for siRNA to tumor cells. Naked siRNA is highly susceptible to nuclease degradation, exhibits poor cellular uptake, and is rapidly cleared from the bloodstream. Researchers have developed different delivery systems, including viral vectors, polymeric micelles, and lipid-based nanoparticles, to deal with these issues. By increasing siRNA stability and effectively delivering both siRNA and cisplatin simultaneously, liposomal formulations have improved siRNA's ability to penetrate tumors while reducing harmful side effects. Lentiviruses and adenoviruses are examples of viral vector-based delivery systems that can produce persistent gene silencing. However, because siRNA molecules sometimes unintentionally silence the wrong genes and interfere with normal cell functions, off-target effects remain a significant concern. These issues involve the possibility of immunological reactions and unwanted integration into the genome. To improve siRNA selectivity and minimize these unwanted interactions, chemical modifications such as locked nucleic acids and 2'-O-methylation have been employed alongside computational techniques. Additionally, siRNA molecules can activate TLRs, leading to the release of inflammatory cytokines and the initiation of immune responses. Researchers have explored ways to reduce immune activation and enhance treatment safety, including modifying the siRNA backbone and utilizing stealth delivery techniques. Preclinical research has shown that siRNA therapy can elevate the cisplatin sensitivity of lung cancer cells. For instance, it has been shown that EGFR-targeted siRNA significantly decreases tumor migration and proliferation while increasing cisplatin cytotoxicity. Similarly, siRNA-mediated MDR1 knockdown reverses chemo resistance by preventing drug efflux and increasing intracellular cisplatin accumulation. Furthermore, siRNA-based therapy that targets mutant p53 has shown potential in promoting the efficacy of cisplatin and causing apoptosis, particularly in TP53-mutant NSCLC cases. Even though these results are beneficial, more studies need to be done, especially in clinical trials, to determine the most efficient ways of siRNA delivery, evaluate long-term safety profiles, and confirm the therapeutic advantages in human patients. Further research should focus on developing more accurate tumor-targeting techniques, improving siRNA formulations, and combining siRNA therapy with personalized medicine methods. If these difficulties succeed, combining cisplatin therapy with siRNA-guided gene silencing may transform lung cancer treatment by providing a more focused and effective alternative to overcome drug resistance and improve patient survival. Translating siRNA-enhanced cisplatin therapy from experimental models to standardized clinical practices in NSCLC management will require continuous interdisciplinary research, including oncology, molecular biology, pharmaceutical sciences, and nanotechnology.

References

Adams, J. M., & Cory, S. (2002). Apoptosomes: Engines for caspase activation. *Current Opinion in Cell Biology, 14*, 715–720.

Ayrton, A., & Morgan, P. (2001). Role of transport proteins in drug absorption, distribution and excretion. *Xenobiotica, 31*(8-9), 469–497. https://doi.org/10.1080/00498250110060969.

Bao, Y., Yang, B., Zhao, J., Shen, S., & Gao, J. (2020). Role of common ERCC1 polymorphisms in cisplatin-resistant epithelial ovarian cancer patients: A study in Chinese cohort. *International Journal of Immunogenetics, 47*(5), 443–453.

Behr, J. P. (1997). The proton sponge: A trick to enter cells the viruses did not exploit. *Chimia, 51*(1-2), 34.

Bernstein, E., Caudy, A., Hammond, S., & Hannon, G. J. (2001). Role for a bidentate ribonuclease in the initiation step of RNA interference. *Nature, 409*, 363–366. https://doi.org/10.1038/35053110.

Borst, P. (2020). Looking back at multidrug resistance (MDR) research and ten mistakes to be avoided when writing about ABC transporters in MDR. *Febs Letters, 594*, 4001–4011. https://doi.org/10.1002/1873-3468.13972.

Cabral-Pacheco, G. A., Garza-Veloz, I., Castruita-De la Rosa, C., Ramirez-Acuña, J. M., Perez-Romero, B. A., Guerrero-Rodriguez, J. F., Martinez-Avila, N., & Martinez-Fierro, M. L. (2020). The roles of matrix metalloproteinases and their inhibitors in human diseases. *International Journal of Molecular Sciences, 21*(24), 9739. https://doi.org/10.3390/ijms21249739.

Caroppi, P., Sinibaldi, F., Fiorucci, L., & Santucci, R. (2009). Apoptosis and human diseases: Mitochondrion damage and lethal role of released cytochrome C as proapoptotic protein. *Current Medicinal Chemistry, 16*(31), 4058–4065.

Carthew, R. W., & Sontheimer, E. J. (2009). Origins and Mechanisms of miRNAs and siRNAs. *Cell, 136*(4), 642–655. https://doi.org/10.1016/j.cell.2009.01.035.

Chang, C. I., Yoo, J. W., Hong, S. W., Lee, S. E., Kang, H. S., Sun, X., Rogoff, H. A., Ban, C., Kim, S., Li, C. J., & Lee, D. K. (2009). Asymmetric shorter-duplex siRNA structures trigger efficient gene silencing with reduced nonspecific effects. *Molecular Therapy, 17*(4), 725–732. https://doi.org/10.1038/mt.2008.298.

Chareddy, Y., Huggins, H. P., Gutierrez-Ford, C., Azam, S. H., Im, J., Bowers, A. A., Egli, M., & Pecot, C. V. (2023). P2. 11-03 Synergistic co-targeting of MYC and KRAS in lung cancer by novel ligand-directed inverted chimeric RNAi molecules. *Journal of Thoracic Oncology, 18*(11), S360–S361.

Chen, S.-H., & Chang, J.-Y. (2019). New insights into mechanisms of cisplatin resistance: From tumor cell to microenvironment. *International Journal of Molecular Sciences, 20*, 4136. https://doi.org/10.3390/ijms20174136.

Cheng, Y. J., Jiang, H. S., Hsu, S. L., Lin, L. C., Wu, C. L., Ghanta, V. K., & Hsueh, C. M. (2010). XIAP-mediated protection of H460 lung cancer cells against cisplatin. *European journal of pharmacology, 627*(1-3), 75–84.

Costa, D., Scalise, E., Ielapi, N., Bracale, U. M., Andreucci, M., & Serra, R. (2024). Metalloproteinases as biomarkers and sociomarkers in human health and disease. *Biomolecules, 14*(1), 96.

Dagogo-Jack, I., & Shaw, A. T. (2018). Tumour heterogeneity and resistance to cancer therapies. *Nature Reviews Clinical Oncology, 15*(2), 81–94. https://doi.org/10.1038/nrclinonc.2017.166.

Dana, H., Chalbatani, G. M., Mahmoodzadeh, H., Karimloo, R., Rezaiean, O., Moradzadeh, A., Mehmandoost, N., Moazzen, F., Mazraeh, A., Marmari, V., & Ebrahimi, M. (2017). Molecular mechanisms and biological functions of siRNA. *International Journal of Biomedical Science: IJBS, 13*(2), 48.

Dean, E. J., Ward, T., Pinilla, C., Houghten, R., Welsh, K., Makin, G., Ranson, M., & Dive, C. (2010). A small molecule inhibitor of XIAP induces apoptosis and synergises with vinorelbine and cisplatin in NSCLC. *British Journal of Cancer, 102*(1), 97–103. https://doi.org/10.1038/sj.bjc.6605418.

Deryugina, E. I., & Quigley, J. P. (2006). Matrix metalloproteinases and tumor metastasis. *Cancer and Metastasis Reviews, 25*, 9–34.

Devarajan, E., Sahin, A. A., Chen, J. S., Krishnamurthy, R. R., Aggarwal, N., Brun, A. M., & Mehta, K. (2002). Down-regulation of caspase 3 in breast cancer: A possible mechanism for chemoresistance. *Oncogene, 21*, 8843–8851. https://doi.org/10.1038/sj.onc.1206044.

Dominska, M., & Dykxhoorn, D. M. (2010). Breaking down the barriers: siRNA delivery and endosomal escape. *Journal of Cell Science, 123*, 1183–1189.

Egeblad, M., & Werb, Z. (2002). New functions for the matrix metalloproteinases in cancer progression. *Nature Reviews Cancer, 2*(3), 161–174.

Fatemian, T., Othman, I., & Chowdhury, E. H. (2014). Strategies and validation for siRNA-based therapeutics for the reversal of multi-drug resistance in cancer. *Drug Discovery Today, 19*(1), 71–78.

Feldmann, D. P., Heyza, J., Zimmermann, C. M., Patrick, S. M., & Merkel, O. M. (2020). Nanoparticle-mediated gene silencing for sensitization of lung cancer to cisplatin therapy. *Molecules, 25*(8), 1994. https://doi.org/10.3390/molecules25081994.

Gavrilov, K., & Saltzman, W. M. (2012). Therapeutic siRNA: Principles, challenges, and strategies. *The Yale Journal of Biology and Medicine, 85*(2), 187.

Geis, N., Zell, S., Rutz, R., Li, W., Giese, T., Mamidi, S., Schultz, S., & Kirschfink, M. (2010). Inhibition of membrane complement inhibitor expression (CD46, CD55, CD59) by siRNA sensitizes tumor cells to complement attack in vitro. *Current Cancer Drug Targets, 10*(8). https://doi.org/10.2174/156800910793357952.

Gonzalez-Avila, G., Sommer, B., Mendoza-Posada, D. A., Ramos, C., Armando Garcia-Hernandez, A., & Falfan-Valencia, R. (2019). Matrix metalloproteinases participation in the metastatic process and their diagnostic and therapeutic applications in cancer. *Critical Reviews in Oncology/Hematology, 137*, 57–83. https://doi.org/10.1016/j.critrevonc.2019.02.010.

Goyal, R., Chopra, H., Singh, I., Dua, K., & Gautam, R. K. (2022). Insights on prospects of nano-siRNA based approaches in treatment of Cancer. *Frontiers in Pharmacology, 13*, 985670.

Grimm, D., Streetz, K. L., Jopling, C. L., Storm, T. A., Pandey, K., Davis, C. R., Marion, P., Salazar, F., & Kay, M. A. (2006). Fatality in mice due to oversaturation of cellular microRNA/short hairpin RNA pathways. *Nature, 441*(7092), 537–541. https://doi.org/10.1038/nature04791.

Gross, J., & Lapiere, C. M. (1962). Collagenolytic activity in amphibian tissues: A tissue culture assay. *Proceedings of the National Academy of Sciences, 48*(6), 1014–1022.

Guan, H., Zhong, M., Ma, K., Tang, C., Wang, X., Ouyang, M., & Zheng, Z. (2023). The comprehensive role of high mobility group box 1 (HMGB1) protein in different tumors: A pan-cancer analysis. *Journal of Inflammation Research, 16*, 617–637. https://doi.org/10.2147/JIR.S386898.

Hardwick, J. M., & Soane, L. (2013). Multiple functions of BCL-2 family proteins. *Cold Spring Harbor Perspectives in Biology, 5*(2), a008722.

Holohan, C., Van Schaeybroeck, S., Longley, D. B., & Johnston, P. G. (2013). Cancer drug resistance: An evolving paradigm. *Nature Reviews Cancer, 13*, 714–726.

Hong, C. A., & Nam, Y. S. (2016). Reducible dimeric conjugates of small internally segment interfering RNA for efficient gene silencing. *Macromolecular Bioscience, 16*(10), 1442–1449. https://doi.org/10.1002/mabi.201600137.

Hristos, G., Peter, K., Judit, C., & Balazs, S. (2004). The role of ABC transporters in drug resistance metabolism and toxicity. *Current Drug Delivery, 1*(1). https://doi.org/10.2174/1567201043480036.

Hu, B., Zhong, L., Weng, Y., Peng, L., Huang, Y., Zhao, Y., & Liang, X. J. (2020). Therapeutic siRNA: State of the art. *Signal Transduction and Targeted Therapy, 5*(1), 101.

Iizasa, H., Nanbo, A., Nishikawa, J., Jinushi, M., & Yoshiyama, H. (2012). Epstein-barr virus (EBV)-associated gastric carcinoma. *Viruses, 4*, 3420–3439. https://doi.org/10.3390/v4123420.

Inoue, Y., Matsumoto, H., Yamada, S., Kawai, K., Suemizu, H., Gika, M., Takanami, I., Nakamura, M., & Iwazaki, M. (2010). ATP7B expression is associated with in vitro sensitivity to cisplatin in non-small cell lung cancer. *Oncology Letters, 1*(2), 279–282. https://doi.org/10.3892/ol_00000049.

Jackson, A. L., Bartz, S. R., Schelter, J., Kobayashi, S. V., Burchard, J., Mao, M., Li, B., Cavet, G., & Linsley, P. S. (2003). Expression profiling reveals off-target gene regulation by RNAi. *Nature Biotechnology, 21*(6), 635–637. https://doi.org/10.1038/nbt831.

Judge, A. D., Sood, V., Shaw, J. R., Fang, D., McClintock, K., & MacLachlan, I. (2005). Sequence-dependent stimulation of the mammalian innate immune response by synthetic siRNA. *Nature Biotechnology, 23*, 457–462.

Jurkovicova, D., Neophytou, C. M., Gašparović, A. Č., & Gonçalves, A. C. (2022). DNA damage response in cancer therapy and resistance: Challenges and opportunities. *International Journal of Molecular Sciences, 23*, 14672. https://doi.org/10.3390/ijms232314672.

Kale, J., Osterlund, E., & Andrews, D. (2018). BCL-2 family proteins: Changing partners in the dance towards death. *Cell Death and Differentiation, 25*, 65–80. https://doi.org/10.1038/cdd.2017.186.

Kanasty, R., Dorkin, J. R., Vegas, A., & Anderson, D. (2013). Delivery materials for siRNA therapeutics. *Nature Materials, 12*(11), 967–977. https://doi.org/10.1038/nmat3765.

Kelly, P. N., White, M. J., Goschnick, M. W., Fairfax, K. A., Tarlinton, D. M., Kinkel, S. A., Bouillet, P., Adams, J. M., Kile, B. T., & Strasser, A. (2010). Individual and overlapping roles of BH3-only proteins Bim and Bad in apoptosis of lymphocytes and platelets and in suppression of thymic lymphoma development. *Cell Death & Differentiation, 17*(10), 1655–1664.

Khan, S., Rehman, U., Parveen, N., Kumar, S., Baboota, S., & Ali, J. (2023). siRNA therapeutics: Insights, challenges, remedies and future prospects. *Expert Opinion on Drug Delivery, 20*(9), 1167–1187.

Kim, M., Krogan, N., Vasiljeva, L., Rando, O. J., Nedea, E., Greenblatt, J. F., & Buratowski, S. (2004). The yeast Rat1 exonuclease promotes transcription termination by RNA polymerase II. *Nature, 432*, 517–522. https://doi.org/10.1038/nature03041.

Kiss, R. C., Xia, F., & Acklin, S. (2021). Targeting DNA damage response and repair to enhance therapeutic index in cisplatin-based cancer treatment. *International Journal of Molecular Sciences, 22*(15), 8199. https://doi.org/10.3390/ijms22158199.

Küçükekmekci, B., & Budak Yıldıran, F. A. (2024). Investigation of the efficacy of siRNA-mediated KRAS gene silencing in pancreatic cancer therapy. *PeerJ, 12*, e18214. https://doi.org/10.7717/peerj.18214.

LaCasse, E. C., Mahoney, D. J., Cheung, H. H., Plenchette, S., Baird, S., & Korneluk, R. G. (2008). IAP-targeted therapies for cancer. *Oncogene, 27*, 6252–6275. https://doi.org/10.1038/onc.2008.302.

Lee, B. S., Connole, M., Tang, Z., Harris, N. L., & Jung, J. U. (2003). Structural analysis of the Kaposi's sarcoma-associated herpesvirus K1 protein. *Journal of Virology, 77*, 8072–8086. https://doi.org/10.1128/JVI.77.14.8072-8086.2003.

Lee, S. J., Son, S., Yhee, J. Y., Choi, K., Kwon, I. C., Kim, S. H., & Kim, K. (2013). Structural modification of siRNA for efficient gene silencing. *Biotechnology Advances, 31*(5), 491–503. https://doi.org/10.1016/j.biotechadv.2012.09.002.

Li, Y. S., Hung, S. C., Wei, Y. H., & Tarng, D. C. (2009). GST M1 polymorphism associates with DNA oxidative damage and mortality among hemodialysis patients. *Journal of the American Society of Nephrology, 20*, 405–415. https://doi.org/10.1681/ASN.2008020227.

Lord, C. J., & Ashworth, A. (2012). The DNA damage response and cancer therapy. *Nature, 481*(7381), 287–294. https://doi.org/10.1038/nature10760.

Lv, G., Yang, M., Gai, K., Jia, Q., Wang, Z., Wang, B., & Li, X. (2024). Multiple functions of HMGB1 in cancer. *Frontiers in oncology, 14*, 1384109.

Ma, Y., Feng, Q., Han, B., Yu, R., & Jin, Z. (2023). Elevated HMGB1 promotes the malignant progression and contributes to cisplatin resistance of non-small cell lung cancer. *Hereditas, 160*, 33. https://doi.org/10.1186/s41065-023-00294-9.

Macrae, I. J., Zhou, K., Li, F., Repic, A., Brooks, A. N., Cande, W. Z., Adams, P. D., & Doudna, J. A. (2006). Structural basis for double-stranded RNA processing by Dicer. *Science, 311*(5758), 195–198. https://doi.org/10.1126/science.1121638.

Malone, E. R., Oliva, M., Sabatini, P. J., Stockley, T. L., & Siu, L. L. (2020). Molecular profiling for precision cancer therapies. *Genome Medicine, 12*, 8.

Martinotti, S., Patrone, M., & Ranzato, E. (2015). Emerging roles for HMGB1 protein in immunity, inflammation, and cancer. *ImmunoTargets and therapy, 4*, 101–109.

Narasimha, A. M., Kaulich, M., Shapiro, G. S., Choi, Y. J., Sicinski, P., & Dowdy, S. F. (2014). Cyclin D activates the Rb tumor suppressor by mono-phosphorylation. *Elife, 3*, e02872.

O'Connor, M. J. (2015). Targeting the DNA damage response in cancer. *Molecular Cell, 60*(4), 547–560. https://doi.org/10.1016/j.molcel.2015.10.040.

Park, J., Cho, N. H., Choi, J. K., Feng, P., Choe, J., & Jung, J. U. (2003). Distinct roles of cellular Lck and p80 proteins in herpesvirus saimiri Tip function on lipid rafts. *Journal of Virology, 77*, 9041–9051. https://doi.org/10.1128/JVI.77.16.9041-9051.2003.

Paul, A., Muralidharan, A., Biswas, A., Kamath, B. V., Joseph, A., & Alex, A. T. (2022). siRNA therapeutics and its challenges: Recent advances in effective delivery for cancer therapy. *OpenNano, 7*, 100063. https://doi.org/10.1016/j.onano.2022.100063.

Piatek, M. J., & Werner, A. (2014). Endogenous siRNAs: Regulators of internal affairs. *Biochemical Society Transactions, 42*(4), 1174–1179.

Qie, S., & Diehl, J. A. (2016). Cyclin D1, cancer progression, and opportunities in cancer treatment. *Journal of Molecular Medicine (Berlin, Germany), 94*(12), 1313–1326. https://doi.org/10.1007/s00109-016-1475-3.

Robbins, M., Judge, A., & MacLachlan, I. (2009). siRNA and innate immunity. *Oligonucleotides, 19*, 89–102.

Ruggieri, E., Domenico, E. D., Locatelli, A. G., Isopo, F., Damanti, S., Lorenzo, R. D., Milan, E., Musco, G., Rovere-Querini, P., Cenci, S., & Vénéreau, E. (2024). HMGB1, an evolving pleiotropic protein critical for cellular and tissue homeostasis: Role in aging and age-related diseases. *Ageing Research Reviews, 102*, 102550. https://doi.org/10.1016/j.arr.2024.102550.

Satelli, A., & Li, S. (2011). Vimentin in cancer and its potential as a molecular target for cancer therapy. *Cellular and Molecular Life Sciences, 68*, 3033–3046. https://doi.org/10.1007/s00018-011-0735-1.

Sato, H., Niimi, A., Yasuhara, T., Permata, T. B. M., Hagiwara, Y., Isono, M., Nuryadi, E., Sekine, R., Oike, T., Kakoti, S., & Nakano, T. (2017). DNA double-strand break repair pathway regulates PD-L1 expression in cancer cells. *Clinical Cancer Research, 23*(14), 3656–3666. https://doi.org/10.1158/1078-0432.CCR-16-3213.

Sdek, P., Ying, H., Chang, D. L., Qiu, W., Zheng, H., & Touitou, R. (2005). MDM2 promotes proteasome- dependent ubiquitin-independent degradation of retinoblastoma protein. *Molecular Cell, 20*, 699–708. https://doi.org/10.1016/j.molcel.2005.10.017.

Searles, R. P., Bergquam, E. P., Axthelm, M. K., & Wong, S. W. (1999). Sequence and genomic analysis of a Rhesus macaque rhadinovirus with similarity to Kaposi's sarcoma-associated herpesvirus/human herpesvirus 8. *Journal of Virology, 73*, 3040–3053.

Setten, R. L., Rossi, J. J., & Han, S. P. (2019). The current state and future directions of RNAi therapeutics. *Nature Reviews Drug Discovery, 18*, 421–446.

Sharma, S. V., Lee, D. Y., Li, B., Quinlan, M. P., Takahashi, F., Maheswaran, S., McDermott, U., Azizian, N., Zou, L., Fischbach, M. A., Wong, K. K., Brandstetter, K., Wittner, B., Ramaswamy, S., Classon, M., & Settleman, J. (2010). A chromatin-mediated reversible drug-tolerant state in cancer cell subpopulations. *Cell, 141*(1), 69–80. https://doi.org/10.1016/j.cell.2010.02.027.

Sherr, C. J., & Roberts, J. M. (1995). Inhibitors of mammalian G1 cyclin-dependent kinases. *Genes & Development, 9*, 1149–1163. https://doi.org/10.1101/gad.9.10.1149.

Shi, J., Kantoff, P. W., Wooster, R., & Farokhzad, O. C. (2017). Cancer nanomedicine: Progress, challenges and opportunities. *Nature Reviews Cancer, 17*, 20–37.

Škovierová, H., Okajčeková, T., Strnádel, J., Vidomanová, E., & Halašová, E. (2018). Molecular regulation of epithelial-to-mesenchymal transition in tumorigenesis (Review). *International Journal of Molecular Medicine, 41*(3), 1187–1200. https://doi.org/10.3892/ijmm.2017.3320.

Snead, N. M., & Rossi, J. J. (2010). Biogenesis and function of endogenous and exogenous siRNAs. *Wiley Interdisciplinary Reviews: RNA, 1*(1), 117–131.

Sternlicht, M. D., & Werb, Z. (2001). How matrix metalloproteinases regulate cell behavior. *Annual Review of Cell and Developmental Biology, 17*(1), 463–516.

Sui, G., Soohoo, C., Affar, E. B., Gay, F., Shi, Y., Forrester, W. C., & Shi, Y. (2002). A DNA vector-based RNAi technology to suppress gene expression in mammalian cells. *Proceedings of the National Academy of Sciences, 99*(8), 5515–5520.

Swanton, C. (2012). Intratumor heterogeneity: Evolution through space and time. *Cancer Research, 72*(19), 4875–4882. https://doi.org/10.1158/0008-5472.CAN-12-2217.

Tchounwou, P. B., Dasari, S., Noubissi, F. K., Ray, P., & Kumar, S. (2021). Advances in our understanding of the molecular mechanisms of action of cisplatin in cancer therapy. *Journal of Experimental Pharmacology, 13*, 303–328. https://doi.org/10.2147/JEP.S267383.

Tekedereli, I., Alpay, S. N., Akar, U., Yuca, E., Ayugo-Rodriguez, C., Han, H. D., Sood, A. K., Lopez-Berestein, G., & Ozpolat, B. (2013). Therapeutic silencing of Bcl-2 by systemically administered siRNA nanotherapeutics inhibits tumor growth by autophagy and apoptosis and enhances the efficacy of chemotherapy in orthotopic xenograft models of ER (-) and ER (+) breast cancer. *Molecular Therapy Nucleic Acids, 2*(9), e121. https://doi.org/10.1038/mtna.2013.45.

Thiel, K. W., Hernandez, L. I., Dassie, J. P., Thiel, W. H., Liu, X., Stockdale, K. R., Rothman, A. M., Hernandez, F. J., McNamara, J. O., & Giangrande, P. H. (2012). Delivery of chemo-sensitizing siRNAs to HER2+-breast cancer cells using RNA aptamers. *Nucleic Acids Research, 40*(13), 6319–6337. https://doi.org/10.1093/nar/gks294.

Uppal, T., Banerjee, S., Sun, Z., Verma, S. C., & Robertson, E. S. (2014). KSHV LANA– the master regulator of KSHV latency. *Viruses, 6*, 4961–4998. https://doi.org/10.3390/v6124961.

Wang, Y., Tu, M. J., & Yu, A. M. (2024). Efflux ABC transporters in drug disposition and their posttranscriptional gene regulation by microRNAs. *Frontiers in pharmacology, 15*, 1423416. https://doi.org/10.3389/fphar.2024.1423416.

Warfel, N. A., & El-Deiry, W. S. (2013). p21WAF1 and tumourigenesis: 20 years after. *Current Opinion in Oncology, 25*, 52–58. https://doi.org/10.1097/CCO.0b013e32835b639e.

Watts, J. K., & Corey, D. R. (2012). Silencing disease genes in the laboratory and the clinic. *Journal of Pathology, 226*, 365–379.

Whitehead, K. A., Langer, R., & Anderson, D. G. (2009). Knocking down barriers: Advances in siRNA delivery. *Nature Reviews Drug Discovery, 8*, 129–138.

Wood, V. H., O'neil, J. D., Wei, W., Stewart, S. E., Dawson, C. W., & Young, L. S. (2007). Epstein-Barr virus-encoded EBNA1 regulates cellular gene transcription and modulates the STAT1 and TGFbeta signaling pathways. *Oncogene, 26*, 4135–4147. https://doi.org/10.1038/sj.onc.1210496.

Wu, T., Zhang, W., Yang, G., Li, H., Chen, Q., Song, R., & Zhao, L. (2016). HMGB1 overexpression as a prognostic factor for survival in cancer: A meta- analysis and systematic review. *Oncotarget, 7*(31), 50417–50427. https://doi.org/10.18632/oncotarget.10413.

Xu, X., Xie, K., Zhang, X., Pridgen, E. M., Park, G. Y., Cui, D. S., Shi, J., Wu, J., Kantoff, P. W., Lippard, S. J., Langer, R., Walker, G. C., & Farokhzad, O. C. (2013). Enhancing tumor cell response to chemotherapy through nanoparticle-mediated codelivery of siRNA and cisplatin prodrug. *Proceedings of the National Academy of Sciences of the United States of America, 110*(46), 18638–18643. https://doi.org/10.1073/pnas.1303958110.

Yeung, K. T., & Yang, J. (2017). Epithelial-mesenchymal transition in tumor metastasis. *Molecular Oncology, 11*, 28–39. https://doi.org/10.1002/1878-0261.12017.

Yhee, J. Y., Lee, S. J., Lee, S., Song, S., Min, H. S., Kang, S. W., Son, S., Jeong, S. Y., Kwon, I. C., Kim, S. H., & Kim, K. (2013). Tumor-Targeting Transferrin Nanoparticles for Systemic Polymerized siRNA Delivery in Tumor-Bearing Mice. *Bioconjugate Chemistry, 24*(10), 1850–1860. https://doi.org/10.1021/bc400226b127.

Yoshizawa, K., Nozaki, S., Kitahara, H., Ohara, T., Kato, K., Kawashiri, S., & Yamamoto, E. (2007). Copper efflux transporter (ATP7B) contributes to the acquisition of cisplatin-resistance in human oral squamous cell lines. *Oncology Reports, 18*(4), 987–991. https://doi.org/10.3892/or.18.4.987.

Zhang, J., Chen, B., Gan, C., Sun, H., Zhang, J., & Feng, L. (2023). A comprehensive review of small interfering RNAs (siRNAs): Mechanism, therapeutic targets, and delivery strategies for cancer therapy. *International Journal of Nanomedicine, 18*, 7605–7635. https://doi.org/10.2147/IJN.S436038.

CHAPTER 15

Navigating toxicity in lung cancer immunotherapy: Challenges and advances in nanomedicine drug delivery

Anwesha Bandyopadhyay[a], Tarun Pal[b], Nabajit Sarkar[c] and Biswajit Das[d]

[a]Faculty of Applied Sciences & Biotechnology, School of Biotechnology, Shoolini University, Solan, Himachal Pradesh, India [b]Faculty of Applied Sciences & Biotechnology, School of Bioengineering and Food Technology, Shoolini University, Solan, Himachal Pradesh, India [c]Department of Clinical Pharmacology, R G Kar Medical College, Kolkata, West Bengal, India [d]Department of Molecular Cell and Developmental Biology, University of California, Santa Cruz, CA, United States

15.1 Introduction

Globally, cancer is the leading cause of death, outpacing cardiometabolic morbidities such as heart disease and cerebral blood flow disturbance. To understand and find a cure for cancer, extensive research and clinical trials have been conducted. Despite progress, cancer remains a serious global issue. Effective prevention and treatment methods are urgently needed, as it is expected that by 2030 there will be 13.2 million deaths and 22.2 million new cases (Cardoso et al., 2024; Norouzi et al., 2021; Sung et al., 2021). Lung cancer accounts for 18.0% of cancer deaths globally. Early diagnosis is a primary factor influencing the survival rates of lung cancer affected individuals (Song et al., 2023). Due to the greater rates of smoking history and chronic lung pathologies, for example, emphysema or Interstitial Lung Disease (ILD), individuals with lung cancer may be more susceptible to developing drug-mediated respiratory complications. According to Binder et al. (2011) 15′s meta-analysis of individuals treated with gemcitabine and docetaxel for various cancer types, individuals with lung cancer had a much-increased susceptibility to pulmonary toxicity than those with breast cancer. These days, nanomedicine can be used to reduce the toxicity of lung cancer immunotherapy. Clinical applications of nanomedicine have already advanced significantly, offering unique opportunities to develop platforms for lung disease diagnosis, treatment, and prevention. Current biological issues, particularly in oncology, can be addressed in innovative and revolutionary ways through this exciting area of research and technology. Researchers are looking into

Nanoengineered Therapeutics for Lung Cancer: Advanced Drug Delivery Strategies.
DOI: https://doi.org/10.1016/B978-0-443-44585-9.00015-9

nanotechnology as a viable and efficient alternative to conventional treatments for lung cancer because it presents many opportunities, including pharmacokinetics, targeted approaches, and pharmacodynamic characteristics in nanoparticles by lowering toxicity (Cryer et al., 2019; Maliyakkal et al., 2021; Moreno et al., 2010; Norouzi et al., 2021). Only two nanoparticle-based treatments—Genexol-PM (Cynviloq) and Abraxane (nab-paclitaxel)—are currently clinically available, even though there are currently over 50 nanomedicines developed for lung cancer (Farjadian et al., 2019). Genexol-PM and Abraxane are the first albumin-containing chemotherapeutic nanoparticles in South Korea to receive FDA approval. Overcoming physiological and immunological system obstacles is a major issue for modern nanomedicine techniques, notwithstanding the benefits of nanotechnology in oncology (Marangoni et al., 2016). The stability, biodistribution, and physicochemical characteristics of nanoparticles can be significantly impacted by the complex process of aggregating with a serum protein layer, known as the "protein corona," that occurs when the particles come into contact with biological fluids.

To achieve clinical advancement in the case, one should be aware of the disease and physicochemical properties of the nano systems. Moreover, the property of these nanoparticles to escape the immune defense cells, cross biological barriers, and accumulate also deserves attention (Parodi et al., 2013). Revolving around the latest developments in nanotechnology about containing such toxicity in the early stages of the diseases, this chapter aims at highlighting the challenges of toxicity of immunotherapy to lung cancer. The concepts discussed under this section are also relevant in the development of new methods of cancer treatment that enhance clinical efficacy by minimizing toxicity-related issues and, ultimately, positively affecting the health-related quality of life of patients. Immuno-checkpoints inhibition and personalized treatment have advanced greatly, though there is still a disparity in the long-term survival rates of patients with advanced lung cancer. The complexity of the molecular interactions between tumors and immune cells is emphasized by the high rate of individuals who fail to respond to immunotherapy or subsequently develop acquired resistance. Even though immune blockers such as CTLA-4 blockers and PD-1/PD-L1 have altered therapy regimens, their benefits are often accompanied by immune-related side effects that occur unexpectedly. This dichotomy is focused on immune dysregulation and therapeutic activation, whereby better methods are needed to enhance accuracy without heightening the harm. Another area of great concern is the changing clinical environment of lung cancer. Immunotherapy has been extended to the neoadjuvant and adjuvant treatment setting, and the low-dose CT scanning has allowed the diagnosis of earlier-stage disease, thus increasing the population exposed to immunomodulating drugs. This has allowed the provision of toxicity treatment to patients who have diseases that could be treated, as well as those with metastatic disease. Even the mild immune-related side effects in such cases may have a significant impact on endocrine balance and long-term pulmonary performance and overall quality of life. Moreover, the genetic, metabolic, and immunological diversity of lung tumors complicates the predictability of treatment. Tumor mutational burden, neoantigen expression, stromal composition, and underlying inflammatory condition differ according to treatment response and toxicity susceptibility. Innovative delivery systems that can control immune activation both geographically and temporally are required to address these multifactorial factors. Therefore nanotechnology-based approaches are a paradigm shift toward precision-guided immunomodulation rather than just supplementary tools. Nanomedicine has the potential to change immunotherapy from widely systemic activation to precisely regulated immune orchestration by combining tumor-targeted delivery with regulated pharmacodynamics.

15.2 Lung cancer immunotherapy

Lung cancer immunotherapy is now a reality and is being applied in clinical settings. The acceptability of immunotherapy for lung cancer, however, may be constrained by a variety of factors. The targeting of the response to programmed cell-death protein-1 (PD-1) blockage remains unclear. The dynamic expression of programmed death-ligand-1 (PD-L1) and taking into consideration the fact that some patients did not show any evidence that PD-L1 responded to the PD-1 blocking, however, makes using PD-L1 as a diagnostic tool appears interesting. Tumor mutational burden (TMB), instability of microsatellites (MSI), and unique genetic changes, such as TP53 and KRAS, are associated with improved responses to ICIs. Additionally, peripheral blood markers, like circulating tumor DNA (ctDNA) and immune cell profiles, are being investigated for their potential to predict treatment response (Wang et al., 2023). ICIs are linked to irAEs that can impact several organ systems, despite their increased survival rates. With an incidence of roughly 2.7%, pneumonitis is especially worrying irAE in NSCLC patients. If this illness is not identified and treated very quickly, it may become serious and even deadly. Colitis, hepatitis, endocrinopathies, and dermatological responses are additional irAEs. Management typically involves immunosuppressive therapies, such as corticosteroids, and may necessitate discontinuation of ICIs, potentially compromising cancer control (Brahmer et al., 2018). Vaccines against lung cancer have also been investigated in the past, with varying degrees of effectiveness. Identifying the most promising neoantigens could enhance the effectiveness of cancer vaccines and pave the way for personalized lung cancer immunological intervention, either alone or in combination with other immunotherapies, like immune checkpoint inhibition. To understand why lung cancer immunotherapies failed earlier and how to make the best use of contemporary medicines, it is essential to comprehend the steps involved in immune detection and destruction of lung cancer cells (Steven et al., 2017).

15.3 Toxicity in lung cancer immunotherapy

Lung cancer is a very complicated and rarely known pathophysiology (Islam et al., 2025). It is essential to comprehend the complexities of this illness to prevent and treat it in a planned manner that will work. Based on histological classification, WHO divides lung cancer in two types: (1) small cell lung cancer (SCLC), which comprising about 13%, and (2) nonsmall cell lung cancer (NSCLC), which comprising for about 85% among total cases and is a highly heterogeneous type with almost 5 year survival rate (Cryer et al., 2019; Mukherjee et al., 2019). Many patients with progressive-stage NSCLC have shown a considerable improvement in response to lung cancer immunotherapy, especially ICIs. Although these treatments have shown promise, several issues remain with their related hazard profiles. irAEs are common and adverse as they are caused by immune systems of the uncontrolled activity against healthy tissues and tumors (Tang et al., 2022). The immune-related toxicities may impact several tissues, including skin, liver, gastrointestinal system, and endocrine glands. These adverse events may be mild or life-threatening and should be recognized early, followed closely, and well-managed. They are toxicities intertwined with underlying mechanisms. By blocking immunosuppressive signals such as PD-1/PD-L1 interactions, which are important for maintaining immune-autoantigen tolerance (Kroschinsky et al., 2017; Wang et al., 2023). However, autoimmunity triggered by this loss of tolerance can lead to the inflammation of the normal tissues. Studies show that dermatitis, pneumonitis, and colitis, all of which range in severity, are the top irAEs among patients with lung cancer treated with immunotherapy. The pace and severity of these toxicities can be influenced by the patient's underlying health, the presence of comorbidities, and prior treatments like radiation or chemotherapy, which may change immune responses (Kroschinsky et al., 2017). Given the variety of possible toxicities linked to immunotherapy, early detection is necessary to improve patient outcomes. Research on biomarkers that forecast the onset and severity of irAEs is crucial. Furthermore, creating individualized treatment plans that strike a balance between toxicity and efficacy is still difficult. Cytokine-release syndrome (CRS) refers to a group of symptoms that include skin responses, fever, hypotension, and abnormal test results. CRS is a serious issue for recipients of chimeric antigen receptor (CAR) modified T-lymphocytes and can happen following the infusion of monoclonal or bispecific antibodies (MABs, BABs) that target immune effectors and lung tumor cells. Additionally, central nervous system (CNS) toxicities such as cerebral dysfunction, impaired consciousness, or seizures may jeopardize the effectiveness of BAB and CAR-T-cell therapy—this is also due to the toxicity in the lung cancer immunotherapy (Kroschinsky et al., 2017).

The most prominent issues dealing with lung cancer immunotherapy are the chances of toxicities related to combination therapy. Additive or synergistic adverse effects are also a risk that increases with the increased use of immunotherapy alongside radiation, chemotherapy, or targeted therapies. The risk of severe adverse events associated with immunotherapy, particularly colitis and pneumonitis, has been proven to be higher when ICIs are combined with other treatment methods (Wargo et al., 2015). This reiterates the importance of contemplating the advantages and disadvantages of combining regimens with keen carefulness. The analysis of how nanomedicine may help to allow regulated drug delivery within the combination drugs may become a guiding principle to reduce the unwanted, undesired side effects and increase the therapeutic outcomes. The advancements in nanotechnology may enhance the safety and efficacy of immunotherapies, which will provide a potential route to solving the toxicity problem in the treatment of lung cancer (Borghaei et al., 2015; Deng et al., 2020; Han et al., 2021; Pardoll et al., 2012). The molecular pathophysiology of toxicity in immune therapy of lung cancer is the disruption of immune homeostasis that goes beyond the clinically observable side effects of the immune system. In physiological conditions, immune checkpoints, such as PD-1 and CTLA-4, can stop the activation of autoreactive T-cells. When these inhibitory pathways are suppressed, cytotoxic lymphocytes revert to their effector activity against cancerous cells, though this activity is not tumor-specific. The reactivation of the inactive autoreactive clones can lead to the immune system invasion in the nonmalignant tissue, which leads to inflammatory harm, akin to the classic autoimmune diseases. Most importantly, this phenomenon marks the actual shift in immune regulation and not merely an increase in immunological activity. In recent research by immunologists, it has been found that in the case of afflicted organs, tumor-infiltrating lymphocytes and T-cell receptor (TCR) repertoires often overlap, which is a sign of cross-reactive recognition of antigens. This observation supports the theory of antigenic mimicry, where the host tissues and the tumor antigens have peptide motifs that result in undesirable immune targeting. In addition, neoantigens generated by the death of tumor cells can enhance the possibility of systemic inflammation by promoting the immune response through the process known as epitope spreading. The processes contribute to explaining why certain toxicities appear during the intervals of several treatment cycles rather than immediately upon the initiation of therapy (Altan et al., 2024; Cottrell et al., 2021). The cytokine environment also plays a major role in the development of toxicity. Patients who respond with high-grade adverse reactions are usually high in proinflammatory mediators, such as interleukin-6 (IL-6), tumor necrosis factor-a, and interferon-g. These cytokines promote the influx of additional immune effector cells into healthy tissues, an increased vascular permeability, and endothelial activation. The result of overproduction of inflammatory cascades can be the destruction of alveolar-capillary integrity of pulmonary tissue and decreased efficiency in exchanging gases, leading to respiratory compromise.

The greatest concerns in relation to lung cancer immunotherapy are the risk of toxicity from combination therapy. Another risk that escalates with the increase in immunotherapy use with radiation, chemotherapy, or targeted therapy is the additive or synergistic adverse effects. It has been established that the risk of immunotherapy, especially colitis and pneumonitis, becomes more severe in the case of the combination of immunotherapy with other types of treatment (Wargo et al., 2015). This reiterates the need to consider the pros and cons of using regimens in combination with critical caution. The discussion of the means of making nanomedicine to enable controllable drug delivery in combination drugs can become a working principle to minimize the undesirable side effects and maximize the therapeutic effects. The proposed solution to the toxicity issue in lung cancer treatment is the use of nanotechnology, which can be enhanced by the powerful improvements in immunotherapies

(Borghaei et al., 2015; Deng et al., 2020; Han et al., 2021; Pardoll et al., 2012). The molecular pathophysiology of immune therapy of lung cancer is the loss of immune homeostasis beyond the clinically manifested side effects of the immune system. In physiological settings, immune checkpoints, including PD-1 and CTLA-4, have the potential to prevent the activation of autoreactive T-cells. Once these inhibitory pathways are damped, the cytotoxic lymphocytes resume their role as effector cells against cancer cells, but this is not tumor-selective. The induction of the dormant inactive clones of the immune system may result in the invasion by the immune system of the nonmalignant tissue, which causes inflammatory damage, similar to prototypical autoimmune diseases. Above all, this phenomenon represents the real change of immune regulation and not only the rise of immunological activity. It has also been discovered that in the afflicted organs, in the latest study by immunologists, Tumor-infiltrating lymphocytes and TCR repertoires frequently overlap, which is an indication of cross-reactive recognition of antigens in the case. The given observation is in line with the theory of antigenic mimicry, according to which the tissues of the host and the tumor antigens possess peptide motifs that lead to the unwanted immune targeting. Moreover, neoantigens that are produced after tumor cells are killed may also increase the likelihood of systemic inflammation stimulating the immune response through the process called epitope spreading. The processes also help to understand why some toxicities are observed within the intervals of multiple treatment cycles instead of right after the therapy begins (Altan et al., 2024; Cottrell et al., 2021). A significant part of the development of toxicity is also taken up by the cytokine environment. The high-grade adverse reactions typically are the response of patients who have a high concentration of proinflammatory mediators, including interleukin-6 (IL-6), tumor necrosis factor-a, and interferon-g. These cytokines facilitate the inflammation of more immune effector cells in healthy tissues, increased vascular permeability, and endothelial activation. Excessive production of the inflammatory cascade may occur, which may destroy the alveolar-capillary integrity of the pulmonary tissue and result in reduced efficiency of gas exchange, causing respiratory compromise. Such amplification to inflammatory agents may also render the lung tissue especially vulnerable due to the compromised immunological response of such tissue, especially in people who have previously gone through fibrotic remodeling or have been previously exposed to smoking (Table 15.1 ; Wang et al., 2021bb).

15.4 Nanomedicine and its role in immunotherapy

Nanomedicine has developed into a ground-breaking technique that offers a promising strategy to mitigate immune-related toxicities, typically by enabling delivery of checkpoint blockade agents to neoplastic tissues, to alleviate these limitations, toxicity, and improve the safety and efficacy of lung cancer immunotherapy. Nanoparticle-based solutions minimize systemic adverse effects by reducing off-target immune activation through improved tumor accumulation and regulated release. This targeting strategy leverages specific ligand and

Table 15.1: Incidence, mechanisms, and management of organ-specific immune-related adverse events in lung cancer immunotherapy.

Affected organ system	Common clinical manifestations	Approximate incidence in NSCLC (%)	Underlying immunological mechanism	Severity (CTCAE grade 3–4 risk)	Standard management strategy	References
Pulmonary	Pneumonitis, dyspnea, cough, hypoxia	3%–5% (higher in lung cancer vs. melanoma)	$CD8^+$ T-cell infiltration, alveolar macrophage activation, and IFN-γ-mediated inflammation	High	Immediate ICI interruption; corticosteroids; oxygen support; severe cases require infliximab or mycophenolate	Naidoo et al. (2017)
Gastrointestinal	Colitis, diarrhea, abdominal pain	5%–10% (higher with combination ICI)	TNF-α-mediated mucosal damage; Th17-driven inflammation	Moderate–high	Corticosteroids; infliximab for steroid-refractory colitis	Wang et al. (2018)
Hepatic	Immune-mediated hepatitis, elevated ALT/AST	3%–9%	Cytotoxic T-cell-induced hepatocyte injury; loss of immune tolerance	Moderate	Steroids; mycophenolate in refractory cases	De Martin et al. (2018)
Endocrine	Hypophysitis, thyroiditis, and adrenal insufficiency	5%–15% (thyroid dysfunction is most common)	Autoantibody formation; lymphocytic infiltration of endocrine glands	Usually mild–moderate (often permanent)	Hormone replacement; steroids in acute inflammation	Barroso-Sousa et al. (2018)

(continued on next page)

Table 15.1: Incidence, mechanisms, and management of organ-specific immune-related adverse events in lung cancer immunotherapy—cont'd

Affected organ system	Common clinical manifestations	Approximate incidence in NSCLC (%)	Underlying immunological mechanism	Severity (CTCAE grade 3–4 risk)	Standard management strategy	References
Cardiac	Myocarditis, arrhythmia, heart failure	<1% (rare but severe)	Shared antigen cross-reactivity; T-cell-mediated myocardial inflammation	Very high (high mortality)	High-dose steroids; cardiac monitoring; immunosuppressants	Mahmood et al. (2018)
Dermatologic	Rash, pruritus, vitiligo	10%–20%	Cutaneous immune activation; increased Th1/Th17 signaling	Low–moderate	Topical steroids; systemic steroids if severe	Geisler et al. (2020)
Hematologic	Autoimmune anemia, thrombocytopenia	Rare (<1%)	Autoantibody-mediated cytopenias	Variable	Immunosuppression; hematology consultation	Delanoy et al. (2019)
Systemic (CRS-like)	Fever, hypotension, elevated IL-6	Rare (more common in CAR-T cells)	Cytokine surge (IL-6, IFN-γ, TNF-α)	High	Tocilizumab; steroids; intensive care unit if severe	Lee et al. (2014)

CRS, Cytokine-release syndrome; *NSCLC*, nonsmall cell lung cancer; CTCAE, Common Terminology Criteria for Adverse Events; ALT, Alanine Aminotransferase; AST, Aspartate Aminotransferase; IFN, Interferon; ICI, Immune Checkpoint Inhibitor; TNF, Tumor Necrosis Factor; NIR, Near-Infrared.

receptor interactions that are overly expressed in lung cancer cells, enabling precise lung cancer recognition (Wathoni et al., 2022). Nanoimmunotherapy has already shown promising outcomes in ongoing and finished clinical trials, and preclinical research has shown notable increases in treatment effectiveness (Sun et al., 2020). Studies reported that ICI therapy targeting PD-1 and PD-L1 can increase NSCLC patients' chances of survival. Since ICIs worked in a small percentage of NSCLC patients, better immunotherapy is needed. To amplify the potency of the PD-L1 inhibitor, Reda et al. (2022) developed the checkpoint inhibitor and antigen release agent, which is a nanoparticle-based immunotherapy system. The PD-L1 antibody and Volasertib, an inhibitor of Polo-like kinase 1 (PLK1), are codelivered by a nanoparticle in the antibiotic resistance awareness and control platform (ARAC platform). By selectively killing carcinogenic cells and upregulating PD-L1 expression in lung cancer cells that survive, PD-L1 antibody-conjugated nanoparticles enable the feed-forward targeted delivery of ARAC. By primarily affecting CD8+ T-cells, it decreases the effective dosages of Volasertib and PD-L1 antibody by five times in a metastatic lung tumor model (LLC-JSP). Additionally, ARAC has been demonstrated to work in the model of lung tumor - KLN-205, which resists the combination of two inhibitors, PD-1 and CTLA-4 (Islam et al., 2021; Liu et al., 2017; Zhang et al., 2020). Wang et al. (2021) created a unique nanocarrier, which is mesoporous with a core composed of big mesoporous pores of silica (UCMS) that is also loaded with photosensitizer particles. They studied the nanocarrier in a mouse model and the lung carcinoma cell line of Lewis murine. This was done to alleviate intractable tumor microenvironments. It was demonstrated that the elements of the created UCMS@Pep-aPDL1 could enhance immunity against tumors by triggering the death of tumor cells that showed IDO, causing immunogenic cell death (ICD), and encouraging effector T-cell infiltration (Chen et al., 2022; Wang et al., 2021). Meraz et al. (2022) have demonstrated using a humanized mouse model that TUSC2, a tumor suppressor gene, eliminates tumor development in the majority of animals, whereas carboplatin and pembrolizumab only mildly and temporarily limit tumor growth. TUSC2 modulates a pro-immune milieu in the tumor, increasing the sensitivity of KRAS/LKB1 tumors (Meraz et al., 2018, 2022). Toll-like receptor (TLR) agonists, a type of immunomodulator, have attracted attention in early clinical studies as potential therapeutic anticancer agents based on their ability to activate innate immunity and influence the adaptive immune system. As a TLR9 agonist, CpG (cytosine-phosphate-guanine dinucleotide) oligodeoxynucleotides attach to TLR9 and trigger a series of innate and adaptive immunological reactions. Particle replication in non-wetting templates (PRINT) nanoparticles were used by Perry et al. (2020) to administer CpG by orotracheal instillations into two mouse metastatic lung tumors (KAL-LN2E1 and NSCLC-344SQ). Large tumor shrinkage, resistance to tumor rechallenge, a prolonged increase in antitumor cytokine levels, an extended residence period of CpG in the lungs, and reduced toxicity in comparison to soluble CpG. Small endogenous noncoding RNAs known as microRNAs (miR) have a key role in regulating immunomodulation. In a model of subcutaneous EL4 tumor, tumoricidal activity is improved by either a direct oncocidal effect or an indirect reduction in their proliferation.

Intraperitoneal delivery of macrophage-targeting HA-PEI nanoparticles into the lung tissues of both naïve mice and a genetically engineered NSCLC mouse model with KRAS/p53 double mutations led to effective TAM repolarization. This was demonstrated by miR-125b transfection, which increased the M1/M2 macrophage ratio by more than sixfold and elevated the iNOS (M1 marker) to Arg-1 (M2 marker) ratio in TAMs by 300-fold compared to untreated groups (Gharavi et al., 2022; Zanganeh et al., 2022). Various viral vectors have been further employed as part of nanotechnology-based strategies for cancer immunotherapy. In addition, Feldmann et al. (2018) created an adenovirus-based synthetic polymer system promoting endosomal escape mechanisms, connected this nanoparticle to siRNA, administered it to human NSCLC cell line NCI-H1299 cells, and knocked down the genes implicated in the initiation or spread of cancer (Carrasco-Esteban et al., 2021; Lizotte et al., 2016). Yang et al. (2020) have created a combination therapy that can get past the desynchronized pharmacokinetic pattern limitations of metformin and cisplatin that arise when the drugs are used in their free form. Chiang et al. (2018) combined T-cell activators, checkpoint inhibitors, and iron oxide (magnetic) nanoparticles with fucoidan and aldehyde-functionalized dextran (Dex). In order to function as an immune system activator, the animals' median survival rate increased, their immune responses improved, their infiltration of T (CD4+ and CD8+) cells increased, and the number of metastatic nodules decreased (Chiang et al., 2018; Sanaei et al., 2021). Au@PG nanoparticles made of gold and glycostructures based on polyaniline were shown by Su et al. (2022). When used in conjunction with PD-1 therapy, Au@PG nanoparticles in lung cancer immunotherapy produced the encouraging polarization activity of M1 macrophages, and upregulation of immunostimulatory cytokines starts (Su et al., 2022). By enhancing the therapeutic index of ICIs and lowering irAEs, which are frequently linked to systemic administration, these nanocarriers can be surface modified to enable targeted drug delivery (Kiaie et al., 2023). Additionally, because the tumor microenvironment is complex and varied in lung cancer, nanomedicine can increase dissolution rate, biological absorption, and formulation stability of immunotherapeutic drugs. By utilizing many ways to boost medication delivery and modify the immune response, nanomedicine improves immune-modulated therapy for lung cancer. Activating the immune response against lung cancer cells, nanoparticles can be engineered to deliver immune checkpoint inhibitors (ICIs), such as anti-PD-1 and anti-CTLA-4 antibodies, and release them in a targeted manner at the tumor site (Singh et al., 2020). To achieve greater specificity and limit nonspecific effects, nanoparticles can be conjugated with targeting ligands or antibodies to selectively bind to specific immunological or lung cancer cells. Additionally, nanomedicines can enhance the presentation of tumor-associated antigens (TAAs) to immune cells, boosting the immune response. Lipid-based nanoparticles, including liposomes and micelles, have shown potential in delivering immunotherapeutic medicines and facilitating the entry of immune-modulating chemicals into the tumor microenvironment to circumvent the tumor's immune evasion mechanisms (Table 15.2 , Fig. 15.1; Liu et al., 2019).

Table 15.2: Overview of various nanomedicine platforms used in lung cancer immunotherapy.

Sl. No.	Nanomedicine type	Immunotherapy agent	Combination therapy	Toxicities observed	Toxicity severity	Outcome	References
1.	Liposomes	Pembrolizumab, Nivolumab	Anti-PD-1 monotherapy	Reduced systemic inflammation, mild skin rash	Mild to moderate	Improved efficacy, reduced adverse events compared to the free drug	Conniot et al. (2014)
2.	Dendrimers	Atezolizumab (anti-PD-L1)	ICI monotherapy	Mild pneumonitis, low gastrointestinal issues	Mild	Enhanced immune response, reduced risk of pneumonitis	Cryer et al. (2019)
3.	Polymeric nanoparticles	Pembrolizumab + Carboplatin	Combination of ICI + chemotherapy	Mild liver toxicity, mild colitis	Mild to moderate	Improved tumor response, reduced liver toxicity	Farjadian et al. (2022)
4.	Gold nanoparticles	Pembrolizumab, Nivolumab	Anti-PD-1/CTLA-4 combination	No significant increase in immune-related toxicity	Low	Increased T-cell activation, reduced skin rash	de Oliveira Cardoso et al. (2022)
5.	PLGA nanoparticles	Nivolumab (anti-PD-1)	ICI monotherapy	Mild pneumonitis, mild fever	Mild	Enhanced pharmacokinetics, reduced rash and toxicity	Dinauer et al. (2024)
6.	pH-sensitive nanoparticles	Pembrolizumab + CTLA-4 inhibitors	Combination with checkpoint blockade	Mild diarrhea, mild rash	Moderate	Tumor-targeted delivery, reduced colitis	Deng et al. (2020)

(continued on next page)

Table 15.2: Overview of various nanomedicine platforms used in lung cancer immunotherapy—cont'd

Sl. No.	Nanomedicine type	Immunotherapy agent	Combination therapy	Toxicities observed	Toxicity severity	Outcome	References
7.	Lipid-polymer hybrid nanoparticles	Atezolizumab (anti-PD-L1)	ICI monotherapy	Mild fever, slight rash, mild hepatotoxicity	Mild to moderate	Lower toxicity profile, improved ICI efficacy	Dobrovolskaia et al. (2016)
8.	Mesoporous silica nanoparticles	Pembrolizumab, Nivolumab	Combination with immunochemotherapy	Mild fever, low incidence of rash	Mild	Enhanced targeting, reduced systemic toxicity	Feldmann et al. (2018)
9.	Exosome-based nanoparticles	Nivolumab (anti-PD-1)	ICI monotherapy	Minimal fatigue, transient low-grade fever	Mild	Prolonged circulation, targeted delivery, improved immunomodulation	Kamerkar et al. (2017)
10.	Carbon nanotubes (functionalized)	Anti-PD-L1 antibody	ICI with photothermal therapy	Mild local inflammation, no systemic toxicity	Mild	Enhanced tumor ablation and checkpoint blockade synergy	Yang et al. (2020)
11.	Albumin-bound nanoparticles	Atezolizumab	Combined with paclitaxel chemotherapy	Moderate neutropenia, mild rash	Moderate	Increased drug accumulation in the tumor, reduced off-target toxicity	He et al. (2019)

PD-1, programmed cell-death protein-1; *PD-L1*, programmed death-ligand-1.

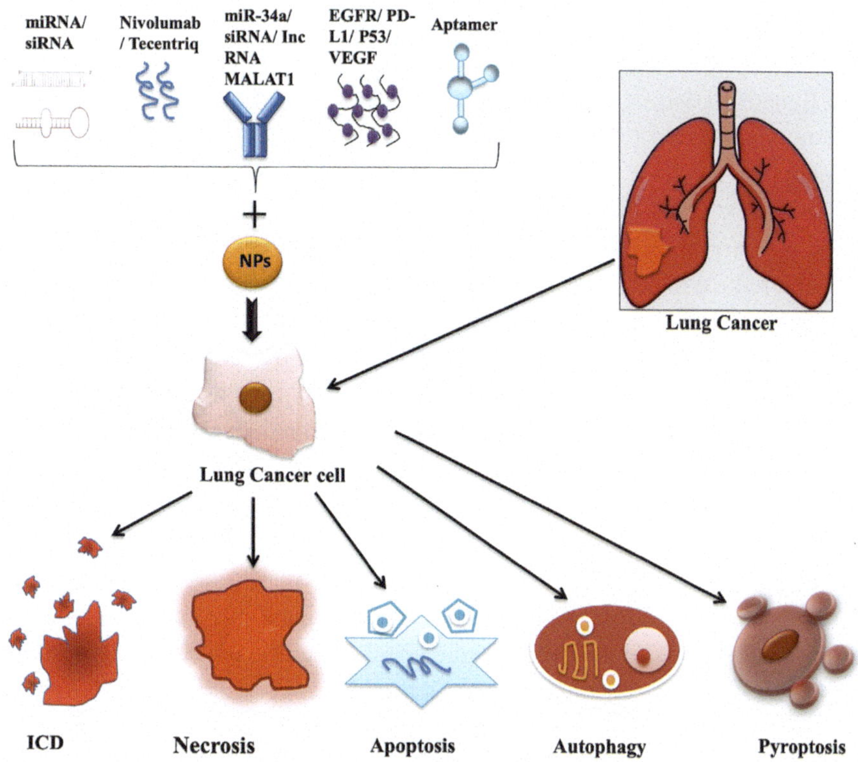

Figure 15.1
Nanoparticle-mediated targeted delivery and cell death mechanisms in lung cancer immunotherapy. This schematic diagram shows how immune checkpoint inhibitors (such as Nivolumab), nucleic acids (such as miR-34a, siRNA, and lncRNA), and targeting ligands (such as aptamers) are delivered to tumour cells by nanoparticles (NPs) to improve lung cancer immunotherapy. These functionalized NPs enhance drug localization, decrease off-target toxicity, and trigger several pathways of cancer cell death, such as necrosis, apoptosis, autophagy, pyroptosis, and immunogenic cell death (ICD). Nanocarriers improve therapeutic efficacy in the treatment of lung cancer by addressing issues of systemic toxicity and immune-related side events through the promotion of localized and controlled drug release.

15.5 Nanocarrier-based approaches for targeted immunotherapy and immune modulation in lung cancer

Building on the foundational role of nanomedicine in enhancing immunotherapy efficacy and safety, advanced nanocarrier-based strategies now offer even greater precision in targeting immune pathways and tumor-specific mechanisms in lung cancer. Nanosystems can exhibit better pharmacokinetics and tissue and cell targeting to increase efficacy, selectivity, and reduce toxicity, as reported by Chow et al. (2013). These nanoparticles are often engineered to have specific surface properties, such as antibodies or ligands, which will identify and attach to cancer-specific markers or receptors, enabling the site-specific delivery of pharmacological agents directly at the tumor site (Wang et al., 2021). Because nanoparticles can actively target several ligands to deliver them into the tumor region, they exhibit extraordinary tumor selectivity. Hence, lung cancer nanomedicine lowers the systemic toxicity of administered medications and shows greater therapeutic efficacy. The antitumor effects of many lung cancer medications can be enhanced by administering them in the same application, which can carry heavy loads. Certain ligands may be added to nanoparticles to increase the targeted to tumor tissues and reduce general toxicity (Zein et al., 2020). When small interfering RNA (siRNA)-containing nanoparticles are used to suppress TGF-β, the number of Treg cells decreases, and CD8+ T-cells rise, which results in a 52% inhibition of tumor growth (Xu et al., 2014). An analogous method for suppressing the growth and spread of lung cancer has been developed, employing polyethylenimine-capped silica nanoparticles delivering VEGF siRNA (Chen et al., 2014b). The tumor microenvironment has also been discovered to have high amounts of indoleamine 2,3-dioxygenase, which lowers the concentration of tryptophan and stops the cell cycle (Ahmad et al., 2004). When compared to healthy tissues, this region presents a number of unique traits that impact the designed tumor-targeted systems (Fernald et al., 2013; Torchilin et al., 2011). Angiogenesis ensures that tumor cells receive oxygen and other nutrients. It is caused by a variety of causes, including matrix metalloproteinases, extracellular matrix proteins, and pro-angiogenic proteins. According to Torchilin (2011), this process is essential to the disease's evolution and has influenced the creation of several targeted nanocarriers because of the unique architecture of the blood vessels. Because of the so-called enhanced permeability and retention (EPR), the aberrant blood vessel architecture resulting from inadequate angiogenesis allows for the prolonged retention of various nanodelivery systems precisely at this specific tumor location. By allowing them to escape from endo-lysosomal compartments, nanoparticle-based carriers can also enhance the cytosolic distribution of biomolecules such as siRNA and miRNA, which are crucial regulators of gene expression. miRNAs are short oligonucleotides (18–22 nucleotides) that are an important target since they are implicated in several pathways linked to cell formation and differentiation as well as the pathophysiology of cancer (Chen et al., 2014b; Gajos-Michniewicz et al., 2014). However, its in vivo use necessitates the creation of targeted cellular delivery strategies to enhance their biological impact, which are presently inadequately understood. Numerous polymers from various sources have already been identified as valuable resources for the creation of polymeric nanoparticles and employed in preclinical research. There is one more example - chitosan is a natural polymer, while polylactic acid and poly-lactic-co-glycolic acid (PLGA) are synthetic polymers (Krishnamachari et al., 2011). Nanoparticles, such as PCL and PLGA nanoparticles, attract huge attention because of their mechanical strength. An excellent assessment of the primary characteristics and uses of PLGA-based nanocarriers was provided by Danhier et al. (2012). The most researched polymer for vaccine formulation is really PLGA, which has been used for human health purposes for decades. It has been demonstrated to boost cellular and antibody responses to PLGA nanoparticle loaded with antigen (Chen et al., 2014a; Johansen et al., 2000; Shen et al., 2006). Because of its hydrophobicity, low rate of degradation, excellent permeability, lower toxicity, and stability in vitro, PCL has a lot of potential for creating antigen-mediated controlled systems. Numerous investigations have previously demonstrated that PCL nanoparticles have the adjuvant effect of inducing immunological responses against infectious diseases (Benoit et al., 1999; Florindo et al., 2008,2009; Labet et al., 2009). More recent research has been conducted to improve peptide-based cancer nanovaccines employing innovative polymeric nanoparticles systems, despite the lack of effectiveness in clinical trials (Conniot et al., 2014). Since the physicochemical characteristics of nanoparticles seem to play a significant role in determining how nanocarriers work with tumors (Dobrovolskaia et al., 2016), it is crucial to consider the transnational effects of newly developed materials (Navarro-Ocon et al., 2022). Therefore designing novel cancer immunotherapeutics with nanomaterials is a potential strategy that needs more research (Doroudian et al., 2020; Farjadian et al., 2022; Velpurisiva et al., 2017). Even for late-stage diagnoses, cancer immunotherapy has been authorized for use by the FDA. Clinical research indicates that successful integration of cancer immunotherapies within nanoparticle systems offers a considerably more potent and sustained anticancer effect than when administered as free medications, making them a versatile and durable therapeutic approach (Chen et al., 2022). nanoparticles exhibit a significant development in the delivery of immunostimulatory medicines for cancer-directed immune treatments through physicochemical manipulation (Fig. 15.2).

15.6 Clinical and preclinical case studies on nanomedicine in immunotherapy

Preclinical models also show the synergistic potential of combining nanomedicine with traditional lung immunotherapeutic medications, such as ICIs and monoclonal antibodies (Sun et al., 2020). Research indicates that immune-stimulating agents such as cytokines or antibodies can be encapsulated by nanoparticles and released directly into the tumor site, thereby reducing systemic adverse effects and boosting immune cell activation. Additionally, the use of nanomedicine in lung cancer immunotherapy improves immune checkpoint inhibitor penetration into lung tumor tissue, an area where conventional treatments often fail. Nanoparticles can overcome these challenges and greatly improve tumor control and overall survival rates, according to both in vitro and in vivo research (Xu et al., 2020). Gold nanoparticles have been widely used in cancer theranostics applications because of their multifunctional theranostics properties, good biocompatibility, and ease of synthesis and post-synthetic functionalization (Balakrishnan et al., 2017; Liu et al., 2018; Meka et al., 2019). Several research organizations employed Au nanoparticles for lung cancer theranostics (Knights et al., 2018). For example, nanospectra has developed silica-gold nanoshells stabilized by (poly)ethylene glycol (PEG) for photothermal therapy of solid tumors using an NIR light source (Singh et al., 2018).

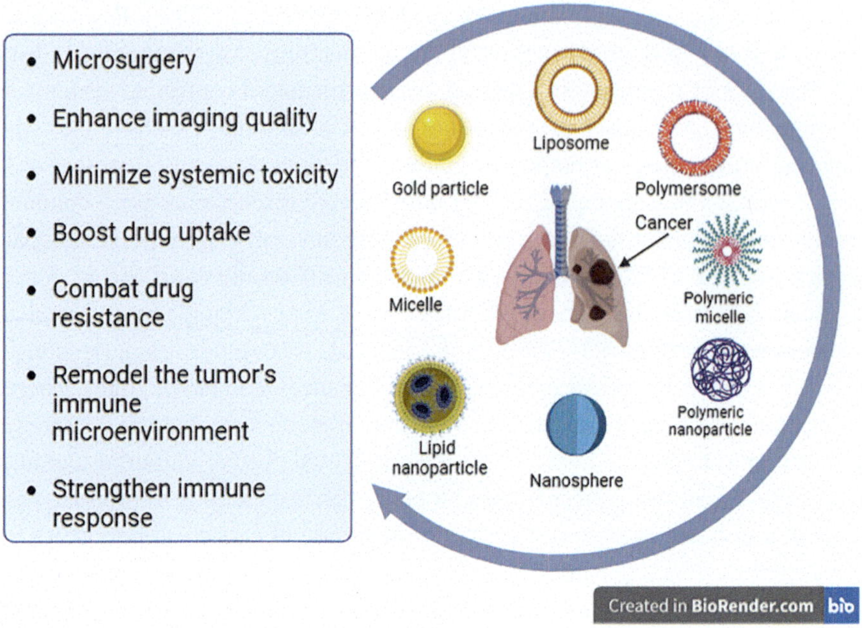

Figure 15.2
Nanocarrier systems in lung cancer immunotherapy. Various nanocarriers, including liposomes, micelles, gold particles, polymersomes, and lipid nanoparticles, enhance drug delivery, decrease systemic toxicity, and modulate the tumor immune microenvironment to improve therapeutic efficacy.

More importantly, a recent clinical trial (NCT01679470) used AuroLase for photothermal therapy of primary or metastatic lung tumors (Singh et al., 2018). In a recent study, Knights et al. (2018) demonstrated the size-governed properties of gold nanorods (AuNRs) on the photoacoustic (PA) imaging response and pulsed-wave photothermal treatment (PW-PPTT) efficacy. This is crucial for AuNRs' clinical translation (Knights et al., 2018). It is interesting to note that the PA intensity increased as the AuNR size increased due to the overall mass of the nanoparticles. The toxicity of all the various-sized AuNRs to lung cancer cells upon laser fluence revealed the therapeutic potential of AuNRs in conjunction with PW lasers in lung cancer, with the smallest AuNR treatment showing the greatest cell death. Using polyvinylpyrrolidone functionalized gold nanoparticles (Dox@PVP-AuNPs), Ramalingam et al. (2018) demonstrated the increased anticancer activity of doxorubicin (DOX) in lung cancer cells. The administration of Dox@PVP-AuNPs to lung cancer cells has been shown through mechanistic studies to increase the formation of reactive oxygen species (ROS), stimulate tumor-suppressive pathways while destabilizing mitochondrial membrane potential, and further promote apoptosis (Ramalingam et al., 2018). Peng et al. (2009) demonstrated that a new sensor-based technique utilizing gold nanoparticles might be employed as a low-cost, noninvasive lung cancer diagnostic tool. Because of their small size, high surface-to-area ratio, ease of synthesis and scaling up, affordability, multifunctional theragnostic applications, and intriguing physicochemical properties, metal nanoparticles have recently piqued the interest of scientists and researchers (Mukherjee et al., 2019). However, in comparison to their other counterparts, the clinical translation of these nanomaterials remains limited due to inadequate understanding of their long-term toxicity, pharmacokinetics, pharmacodynamics, and degradability (Mukherjee et al., 2016). For the delivery of paclitaxel and cisplatin in NSCLC, albumin-based nanoparticles are being used in various stages of clinical trials (Socinski et al., 2013a, 2013b). The immunosuppressive tumor microenvironment, systemic toxicity, and insufficient drug delivery are some of the primary barriers to lung cancer treatment that preclinical research on nanomedicine has shown promising results in tackling. Case studies indicate that nanoparticles can provide lung cancer cells with tailored therapy while minimizing the off-target effects commonly linked to conventional chemotherapy (Anderson et al., 2020). The ability of liposomes, dendrimers, and gold nanoparticles to carry immunomodulators or chemotherapeutic drugs, which can boost the immune system's defenses against tumors, has been investigated. These advances in nanomedicine have led to preclinical models where ICIs were effectively delivered by nanoparticles, boosting the immune response against tumors (Liu et al., 2019). Further research is needed to optimize the formulation of nanomedicines for immunotherapy against lung cancer. Recent preclinical research has highlighted the importance of modifying particle diameters, zeta potential, and surface functionalization of nanoparticles to enhance tumor targeting and immune activation. For example, nanoparticles functionalized with ligands or antibodies that target tumor-specific antigens have shown improved selectivity for cancer cells and reduced detrimental effects on healthy tissues (Zhao et al., 2020). This approach is expected to improve patient outcomes and reduce immune-related adverse effects. It is still challenging to use these insights in clinical settings, despite the encouraging preclinical outcomes. Research is currently focused on the safety, biocompatibility, and efficacy of nanomedicines in human trials to ensure their potential as a practical therapeutic method in lung cancer immunotherapy (Table 15.3; Ezhilarasan et al., 2022).

15.7 Limitations of the nanoparticle-based drug delivery

15.7.1 Safety concerns and toxicological limitations

Even if nanocarriers have the potential to improve lung cancer immunotherapy, it is crucial to understand the drawbacks and safety issues of drug delivery systems based on nanoparticles (Gettinger et al., 2018). It is expected that nanoparticles will employ existing platforms as advanced drug delivery agents to enhance the targeting of subpopulations and the synchronized delivery of costimulatory signals. Chemotherapy and radiation are two commonly observed traditional lung cancer treatments that are often hampered by serious side effects and toxicity because of their nonspecific drug delivery. However, immunotherapeutic drugs can be encapsulated in nanoparticles and delivered straight to the tumor site, avoiding healthy tissues

Table 15.3: Clinical and preclinical case studies on nanomedicine in immunotherapy.

Sl. no.	Study	Key findings	References
	Nanoparticle-encapsulated cytokines & antibodies	Enhances immune activation and reduces systemic side effects by targeted delivery of immune-stimulating substances to tumors.	Zhang et al. (2014)
	Nanomedicine for immune checkpoint inhibitors in lung cancer	Improves penetration into tumor tissue, overcoming stroma-related limitations of traditional therapies.	Xu et al. (2020)
	Gold nanoparticles (AuNPs) in cancer theranostics	High biocompatibility and multifunctional properties make them effective for lung cancer treatment.	Balakrishnan et al. (2017), Liu et al. (2018), Meka et al. (2019)
	Silica-gold nanoshells for photothermal therapy	PEG-stabilized nanoshells developed for solid tumor treatment using NIR light.	Singh et al. (2018)
	AuroLase in clinical trials	Used to treat primary and metastatic lung tumors with photothermal therapy (NCT01679470).	Singh et al. (2018)
	Gold nanorods (AuNRs) in photoacoustic (PA) imaging & photothermal therapy	Size-dependent effects improve PA imaging and PW-PPTT efficacy, demonstrating significant tumor cell death.	Knights et al. (2018)
	Dox@PVP-AuNPs for enhanced chemotherapy	Functionalized AuNPs enhance DOX efficacy by increasing ROS formation and promoting apoptosis in lung cancer cells.	Ramalingam et al. (2018)
	Gold nanoparticle-based lung cancer diagnosis	A novel sensor-based technique for low-cost, noninvasive lung cancer diagnostics.	Peng et al. (2009)
	Metal nanoparticles in cancer therapy	Small size and multifunctional properties make them attractive, but clinical translation remains limited due to toxicity concerns.	Mukherjee et al. (2019)
	Albumin-based nanoparticles in clinical trials	Used for delivering paclitaxel and cisplatin in NSCLC.	Green et al. (2018), Socinski et al. (2013a, 2013b), Zheng et al. (2006)
	Targeted drug delivery by nanoparticles	Nanoparticles reduce off-target effects of traditional chemotherapy while improving lung cancer treatment.	Zhang et al. (2020)

DOX, doxorubicin; NSCLC, nonsmall cell lung cancer; *PEG*, (poly)ethylene glycol; *PW-PTT*, pulsed-wave photothermal treatment; *ROS*, reactive oxygen species; NIR, Near-Infrared.

and reducing systemic toxicity (Zhao et al., 2020). Certain nanoparticles have been shown to be harmful to healthy cells, with a focus on inorganic and metal-based nanoparticles. For instance amorphous silica nanoparticles may induce inflammatory responses in target organs, which may lead to apoptotic cell death (McCarthy et al., 2012). As a result, silica-based nanoparticles can only be used in vitro at modest doses (0.1 mg/mL) for cancer treatment. Given its biological applications, titanium oxide (TiO2) nanoparticle's toxicity to normal cells is also a cause for concern (Trouiller et al., 2009). Additionally, reports of carbon nanotubes (CNTs) damaging healthy cells have been made. Lipid peroxidation and mitochondrial dysfunction are caused by ROS generated when CNTs come into contact with live cells (Manke et al., 2013). Therefore thorough research must be done to ensure safety before the innovative nanoparticle systems are employed in humans (Babu et al., 2013).

15.7.2 Biological barriers and translational challenges in nanomedicine

In addition to shielding medications from premature inactivation or biodegradation, these characteristics allow nano systems to get past physiological barriers. They also help them overcome efflux transporters and multidrug resistance, extend circulatory persistence, improve lipid solubility, and increase the ability to traverse physiological barriers (Tzogani et al., 2020; Yuan et al., 2016). Although nanomedicine has great promise in lung cancer immunotherapy, there are still multiple barriers to overcome before it can be used in a healthcare setting. TME variability is one of the main obstacles, since it might impact the effectiveness of medication delivery using nanoparticles (Huang et al., 2020). High hydrostatic pressure in the tumor interstitium, the presence of strong extracellular matrix, and the diverse nature of tumors can all make it difficult for nanoparticles to effectively penetrate tumor tissue. To increase their ability to penetrate the cancerous area and deliver the drug, research is focusing on developing nanoparticles that can actively respond to the tumor microenvironment, such as pH-sensitive or enzyme-triggered nanoparticles (Swain et al., 2016). Moreover, concerns remain with respect to toxicity risks and prolonged biocompatibility of nanoparticles. Ongoing research aims to minimize side effects while optimizing the therapeutic effectiveness of lung cancer therapies based on nanoparticles (Shao et al., 2020).

15.7.3 Immunological barriers and interference with the immune system

Despite being designed to improve targeted medication administration, nanocarriers' interactions with the immune system continue to be a challenging regimen. When administered systemically, nanoparticles come into direct contact with plasma proteins, which causes a protein corona to form quickly (Monopoli et al., 2020). This dynamic biomolecular layer has the power to drastically change the surface properties of nanoparticles, impacting immunological recognition, cellular uptake, and biodistribution. Protein corona development can sometimes improve opsonization, which speeds up the mononuclear phagocyte system's

(MPS) clearance, especially in the liver and spleen (Blanco et al., 2015). Therapeutic accumulation in tumor tissue may be significantly decreased as a result. Another crucial issue is complementing activation. Complement activation-related pseudoallergy (CARPA), which results in hypersensitive reactions marked by inflammatory reactions and cardiac discomfort, can be triggered by specific nanoparticle formulations. This effect is especially pertinent to intravenous administration of liposomal and polymeric systems. Although the design of stealth nanoparticles using PEGylation or biomimetic coatings has demonstrated promise in lowering immune recognition, repeated administration may result in the production of anti-PEG antibodies, which would reduce therapeutic efficacy and perhaps cause immunological problems (Blanco et al., 2015; Monopoli et al., 2020).

Furthermore, the bioactivity and functional antibody orientation of ICIs administered by nanoparticles must be maintained. Therapeutic binding affinity may be compromised by structural instability or incorrect surface conjugation, which could change immunological results. A recurring technological problem is thus maintaining structural integrity throughout formulation, storage, and in vivo circulation (Dobrovolskaia et al., 2016).

15.7.4 Heterogeneity of tumor of vasculature and enhanced permeability and retention variability

The foundation of cancer treatment based on nanoparticles has long been thought to be the EPR effect. Nevertheless, a growing body of studies indicates that EPR varies greatly between patients and even within distinct tumor areas. Nanoparticle extravasation in lung cancer is restricted by tumor vascular architecture that may be asymmetrical, compacted, or inadequately perfused. Nanoparticle penetration is further limited by interstitial fluid pressure in solid tumors. The outward fluid flow caused by high hydrostatic pressure prevents therapeutic particles from diffusing inward. Collagen fibers and hyaluronic acid, two dense extracellular matrix constituents, also create physical barriers that prevent deep tumor invasion. As a result, nanoparticles might build up peri-vascularily without making it to hypoxic tumor cores, which are home to resistant cell populations. Future remedies could include vascular normalization techniques, enzymatic ECM breakdown tactics, or the coadministration of matrix-modulating medicines. However, there is a significant translational challenge in incorporating these tactics without raising systemic toxicity (Maeda et al., 2000).

15.7.5 Pharmacokinetic and biodistribution uncertainty

The pharmacokinetics of nanoparticles are very different from those of traditional small molecules. Tissue distribution and circulation half-life are influenced by factors such as hydrophobicity, size distribution, surface charge, and shape. Significant differences in in vivo behavior might result from small manufacturing errors. Furthermore, preclinical research consistently shows accumulation in nontarget tissues such as the liver, spleen, and bone marrow. Reticuloendothelial sequestration raises questions about long-term organ toxicity in addition to limiting the effectiveness of tumor targeting. The long-term effects of oxidative stress or subclinical inflammation brought on by chronic nanoparticle deposition are still unclear. Dosage scaling from animal models to people is another factor to consider. When compared to human tumors, rodent tumor models frequently overestimate EPR-mediated delivery. As a result, there are still many difficulties in translating preclinical achievement into clinical results (Decuzzi et al., 2007).

15.7.6 Complexity and reproducibility in manufacturing

The challenges to be faced in the way of expansion of the production of nanoparticles from the lab facilities to the industrial facilities, following good manufacturing practice (GMP), are numerous. The performance of the therapy could be influenced by variations between batches of particles in terms of size, surface functionalization, the effectiveness of encapsulation, and release kinetics. The other important issue is the question of keeping the nanoparticles sterile and not destroying the structure itself. Lipid or polymeric-based systems can be destabilized by the conventional means of sterilization, such as heat or radiation. The use of alternative sterile filtration methods is limited by the cost of particle size constraints. Moreover, the large-scale reproducibility requires stringent quality control requirements such as zeta potential, polydispersity index, morphology, and surface chemical characterization. Regulatory bodies need comprehensive physicochemical profiling and toxicological information before clearance, and this increases the development costs and delays (Desai et al., 2012).

15.7.7 Biodegradability and bioaccumulation long term

Although most polymeric nanoparticles are designed to be biodegradable, the degradation rate depends on the situation of the local tissues and the type of polymer. Examples of inorganic nanoparticles that may remain for a long time in tissues include metal oxides, silica, and gold. Bioaccumulation raises concerns regarding delayed toxicity, particularly of immune-privileged tissues. There is a theoretical possibility that long-term exposure will either influence immune functioning or lead to minor levels of inflammation. Long-term human data are still lacking, indicating the need for longitudinal safety trials and extended postmarketing surveillance. The investigation of the metabolic fate of nanoparticle components, their excretion pathways, and potential mechanisms of interaction with the cellular organelles remains one of the priorities (Danhier et al., 2012; Hirn et al., 2011).

15.7.8 Regulatory and ethical consideration

The laws governing nanomedicine are still being developed. In contrast to traditional pharmaceuticals, nanoparticle systems frequently blend biologic, device, and medication properties, making classification and approval processes more difficult. Regulators frequently need more information on biodistribution, immunotoxicity, and stability than they do for conventional treatments. Long-term exposure dangers and fair access to cutting-edge nanoimmunotherapies also raise ethical questions. In low-resource areas, access may be restricted by high production costs, which could exacerbate inequities in the treatment of lung cancer. The development of standardized protocols tailored to nanoimmunotherapeutics is still ongoing. Accelerating patient access and enabling international clinical trials will depend on the harmonization of global regulatory standards (Tinkle et al., 2014).

15.7.9 Economic and clinical adoption barriers

Nanoparticle-based immunotherapies may encounter obstacles pertaining to healthcare infrastructure and cost-effectiveness even after they have been clinically validated. Production costs rise with complex industrial processes. Widespread adoption may also be constrained by certain administration procedures and storage conditions. Healthcare professionals must also receive training on how to identify and handle side effects unique to nanoparticles. Despite encouraging efficacy evidence, adoption can be sluggish in the absence of a strong pharmacovigilance infrastructure and physician education.

15.7.10 Integration with personalized medicine

Precision oncology and nanomedicine are conceptually compatible; there are practical difficulties in incorporating customized methods into standard practice. Validated diagnostic systems are necessary to find biomarkers predictive of nanoparticle toxicity or response. Treatment complexity may rise if immune surveillance, molecular profiling, and customized nanoparticle formulation are coordinated. Long-term goals include creating adaptive treatment algorithms that combine nanoparticle design with tumor biology unique to each patient. It will take interdisciplinary cooperation and substantial technological advancement to do this.

15.8 Future perspectives

The next stage of immunotherapy for lung cancer will probably be characterized by precise management of immune-mediated toxicity in addition to enhanced antitumor activity. Predictive modeling of adverse events and spatially limited immune activation is becoming more important as ICIs and cellular treatments are incorporated into first-line and combo regimens (Sun et al., 2020). As a result, future approaches will focus on systems-level immune surveillance, microenvironment-responsive nanocarriers, and biomarker-guided patient selection (Shao et al., 2020).

Predictive immunoprofiling prior to therapy beginning is a significant frontier. There is growing evidence that baseline immunological tone, TCR diversity, cytokine profiles, and microbiome composition affect the likelihood of immune-related adverse events as well as the therapeutic response (Naqash et al., 2021). By discovering intricate relationships between immunological markers and organ-specific problems, artificial intelligence-driven analytics applied to substantial clinical datasets should improve these models even more (Shao et al., 2020). In the end, these prediction frameworks might enable physicians to customize preventive measures, surveillance intervals, and dosage levels.

The creation of tumor-microenvironment-responsive nanomedicine platforms is another exciting avenue. When checkpoint inhibitors are administered systemically, circulating immune activation signals are exposed to nonmalignant tissues. Future nanocarriers could lower systemic exposure while maintaining intratumoral immune activation if they are made to release payloads only in acidic, hypoxic, or enzyme-rich tumor habitats. To attain spatiotemporal accuracy in drug release, stimuli-responsive systems such as protease-cleavable linkers, pH-sensitive liposomes, and redox-responsive polymers are being developed.

Additionally, the idea of localized immune regulation is becoming more popular. Concentrating immunotherapeutic drugs inside lung tumors while reducing systemic circulation is possible with inhalable nanoparticle formulations made especially for pulmonary administration (Sun et al., 2020). Since direct regional administration is made possible by tumor accessibility through the respiratory route, such techniques may be especially helpful in the case of non-SCLC. Aerosolized nanoimmunotherapeutics may reduce the occurrence of distant organ inflammation while increasing cytotoxic lymphocyte infiltration of tumors. To successfully implement this strategy in clinical settings, it will be crucial to keep improving the particle size, surface charge, and mucosal penetration characteristics (Dobrovolskaia et al., 2016).

Another significant avenue is the development of combined nanoimmunotherapy. Multiple immune pathways may be synchronized, whereas dose control is maintained by rationally built nanocarriers that can codeliver checkpoint inhibitors with immunostimulatory nucleic acids, tumor antigens, or small-molecule kinase inhibitors. If release kinetics are properly regulated, such coordinated delivery may improve therapeutic synergy without correspondingly increasing toxicity. Parallel to this, immunomodulatory drugs delivered by nanoparticles that target particular cytokine pathways may act as built-in safety switches, reducing excessive inflammatory cascades upon reaching predetermined thresholds (Wang et al., 2021).

There are more options when lipid nanoparticles and mRNA technology are combined. Knowledge gained from the production of vaccines shows that lipid nanoparticle systems can produce strong immune responses and safely deliver nucleic acids at scale (Pardi et al., 2018). Highly programmable immune activation with controlled duration may be possible if this technology is modified for tumor-specific neoantigen vaccines or temporary immune checkpoint manipulation. Theoretically, mRNA constructions have the benefit of reversible immunostimulation, which may lessen chronic autoimmune sequelae because they naturally fade over time. Long-term safety surveillance will continue to be essential. Future studies should concentrate on clarifying the long-term immunological effects of persistent checkpoint inhibition, especially in survivors with long-term disease control. Delayed or cumulative toxicities that might not be completely recorded in clinical trials can be described with the aid of prospective registries and real-world pharmacovigilance databases (Sun et al., 2020). Digital health surveillance techniques, circulating immunological biomarkers, and sophisticated imaging modalities may all help detect subclinical inflammation earlier, before irreparable tissue damage happens.

The design of nanoimmunotherapies may be redefined by the incorporation of spatial multiomics technology. Tumor stromal architecture, cytokine gradients, and immune cell distribution can all be mapped using advanced imaging and spatial transcriptomics. The creation of nanoparticles designed to react to specific microanatomical stimuli may be guided by these discoveries. Such spatial accuracy may lessen collateral damage to nearby healthy tissue while increasing intratumoral immune activation. Another important direction is the study of noninvasive delivery systems, i.e., transdermal, inhaled, and ultrasound-mediated nanoparticle activation systems. As an example, ultrasound-triggered nanocarriers can potentially be used to release drugs to the lung tissue without systemic drug increase. Such a plan might reduce systemic immune-related injury and significantly reduce the treatment window. Finally, flexible treatment algorithms are likely to be a requirement in the future of immunotherapy for lung cancer. Dynamic protocols based on immune surveillance in response to alterations in toxicity markers can enable targeted immunosuppression, dose adjustment, or suspension rather than prescribed treatment regimens (Shao et al., 2020). This set of strategies coupled with the accurate nanodelivery platforms may redefine the index of drug therapy and immunotherapy and transform the toxicity into a debilitating side effect into a variable. Taken altogether, it can be suggested that in the future, the treatment of lung cancer will focus on coordinated immune activation and not on indiscriminate activation of immunity. Possibly, biomarker-driven prediction, microenvironment-targeted nanotechnology, programmable mRNA platforms, and adaptive clinical monitoring could be combined to maintain anticancer immunity and physiological tolerance.

15.9 Conclusion

Advancement of integrated nanoplatforms has immense clinical implications in the future of biomedicine because it can allow theragnostic use in a single nanostructure. The various treatment challenges posed by the complexity of lung cancer and other microenvironment tumors have been mitigated in this chapter. It further offers an integrative vision in nano systems, which are aimed at preclinical diagnostics. The development of viable treatment options requires a comprehensive knowledge of the disease, the clinical outcomes, physicochemical properties of nanomaterials, nano–bio interactions, regulatory compliance, and the nanotoxicity to guarantee a safe clinical use of the nanomaterials. Nanomedicine is revolutionarily poised to change the manner in which cancer is therapeutically handled and provide the infected and the medical care personnel with renewed hope. Importantly, the interdisciplinary collaboration is indicated by the integration of immunotherapy and nanotechnology. This field is now in need of the integration of cancer, immunology, materials science, pharmacology, and regulatory science. A careful understanding of nano–bio interactions, protein corona dynamics, biodistribution patterns, and immunological signaling pathways is necessary to ensure safety and repeatability. In addition, strict preclinical modeling and standardized immunotoxicity testing, and carefully designed clinical trials with toxicity biomarkers and long-term follow-ups will all be needed to translate into success. It is also likely that the paradigm of future therapy will be shifted to personalization. Better risk prediction of the toxicity could be achieved in case people are stratified by the molecular tumor characteristics, immunological profile, genetic predispositions, and microbiome composition. Nanocarrier-based immunotherapies could be tailored to the individual immunological profile of a specific patient by altering release kinetics or tactical release to different vulnerable levels. This personalized approach is consistent with the broader trend of precision oncology, where treatment is conditioned to the immunological context of the host, on top of the tumor genetics. Other factors are also long-term survival and sustainability. Increased patients with prolonged response require chronic immunological consequences, quality of life, and maintenance of organ functioning, along with the acute toxicity treatment. Surveillance systems that use imaging, circulating biomarkers, and digital health technology can potentially enable the early detection of subclinical inflammation. This would allow timely management before it is too late to cause irreparable damage. Eventually, such proactive surveillance methods could shift the approach of toxicity management, which is currently reactive to preventive. Conclusively, immunotherapy of lung cancer is one of the red lines in prudence and innovation. The immune checkpoint blockade and related methods have redefined the clinical outcomes, and their maximum effectiveness is attainable only through simultaneous enhancement of mitigation of toxicity. Nanomedicine could be a potential way to reach this balance through regulated, specific, and adaptive immunological regulation. In order to maintain the balance between safety and efficacy, the research in the field of translational optimization, predictive identification of biomarkers, and the explanation of the mechanism will require additional studies. Ensuring good immunity against cancer without compromising the physiological equilibrium needed to sustain good health in patients over time may be achieved through scientific endeavors.

References

Ahmad, M., Rees, R. C., & Ali, S. A. (2004). Escape from immunotherapy: Possible mechanisms that influence tumor regression/progression. *Cancer Immunology, Immunotherapy, 53*, 844–854.

Altan, M., Li, R., Li, Z., Chen, R., Sheshadri, A., Tran, H. T., & Zhang, J. (2024). High peripheral T cell diversity is associated with lower risk of toxicity and superior response to dual immune checkpoint inhibitor therapy in patients with metastatic NSCLC. *Journal for Immunotherapy of Cancer, 12*(12), e008950.

Anderson, C. F., Grimmett, M. E., Domalewski, C. J., & Cui, H. (2020). Inhalable nanotherapeutics to improve treatment efficacy for common lung diseases. *Wiley Interdisciplinary Reviews: Nanomedicine and Nanobiotechnology, 12*(1), e1586.

Babu, A., Templeton, A. K., Munshi, A., & Ramesh, R. (2013). Nanoparticle-based drug delivery for therapy of lung cancer: Progress and challenges. *Journal of Nanomaterials, 2013*(1), 863951.

Balakrishnan, S., Mukherjee, S., Das, S., Bhat, F. A., Singh, R., P. , P., C. , R., & Arunakaran, J. (2017). Gold nanoparticles–conjugated quercetin induces apoptosis via inhibition of EGFR/PI3K/Akt–mediated pathway in breast cancer cell lines (MCF-7 and MDA-MB-231). *Cell Biochemistry and Function, 35*(4), 217–231.

Barroso-Sousa, R., Barry, W. T., Garrido-Castro, A. C., Hodi, F. S., Min, L., Krop, I. E., & Tolaney, S. M. (2018). Incidence of endocrine dysfunction following the use of different immune checkpoint inhibitor regimens: A systematic review and meta-analysis. *JAMA Oncology, 4*(2), 173–182.

Benoit, M. A., Baras, B., & Gillard, J. (1999). Preparation and characterization of protein-loaded poly (ε-caprolactone) microparticles for oral vaccine delivery. *International Journal of Pharmaceutics, 184*(1), 73–84.

Binder, D., Hübner, R. H., Temmesfeld-Wollbrück, B., & Schlattmann, P. (2011). Pulmonary toxicity among cancer patients treated with a combination of docetaxel and gemcitabine: A meta-analysis of clinical trials. *Cancer Chemotherapy and Pharmacology, 68*, 1575–1583.

Blanco, E., Shen, H., & Ferrari, M. (2015). Principles of nanoparticle design for overcoming biological barriers to drug delivery. *Nature Biotechnology, 33*(9), 941–951.

Borghaei, H., Paz-Ares, L., Horn, L., Spigel, D. R., Steins, M., Ready, N. E., & Brahmer, J. R. (2015). Nivolumab versus docetaxel in advanced nonsquamous non–small-cell lung cancer. *New England Journal of Medicine, 373*(17), 1627–1639.

Brahmer, J. R., Lacchetti, C., Schneider, B. J., Atkins, M. B., Brassil, K. J., & Caterino, J. M.National Comprehensive Cancer Network. (2018). Management of immune-related adverse events in patients treated with immune checkpoint inhibitor therapy: American Society of Clinical Oncology Clinical Practice Guideline. *Journal of Clinical Oncology, 36*(17), 1714–1768.

Cardoso, V. M. D. O., Bistaffa, M. J., Sterman, R. G., Lima, L. L. P. D., Toldo, G. S., Cancino-Bernardi, J., & Zucolotto, V. (2024). Nanomedicine innovations for lung cancer diagnosis and therapy. *ACS Applied Materials & Interfaces, 17*, 13197–13220.

Carrasco-Esteban, E., Domínguez-Rullán, J. A., Barrionuevo-Castillo, P., Pelari-Mici, L., Leaman, O., Sastre-Gallego, S., & López-Campos, F. (2021). Current role of nanoparticles in the treatment of lung cancer. *Journal of Clinical and Translational Research, 7*(2), 140.

Chen, M., Ouyang, H., Zhou, S., Li, J., & Ye, Y. (2014a). PLGA-nanoparticle mediated delivery of anti-OX40 monoclonal antibody enhances anti-tumour cytotoxic T cell responses. *Cellular Immunology, 287*(2), 91–99.

Chen, Y., Gu, H., Zhang, D. S. Z., Li, F., Liu, T., & Xia, W. (2014b). Highly effective inhibition of lung cancer growth and metastasis by systemic delivery of siRNA via multimodal mesoporous silica-based nanocarrier. *Biomaterials, 35*(38), 10058–10069.

Chen, Z., Yue, Z., Yang, K., & Li, S. (2022). Nanomaterials: Small particles show huge possibilities for cancer immunotherapy. *Journal of Nanobiotechnology, 20*(1), 484.

Chiang, C. S., Lin, Y. J., Lee, R., Lai, Y. H., Cheng, H. W., Hsieh, C. H., & Chen, S. Y. (2018). Combination of fucoidan-based magnetic nanoparticles and immunomodulators enhances tumor-localized immunotherapy. *Nature Nanotechnology, 13*(8), 746–754.

Chow, E. K. H., & Ho, D. (2013). Cancer nanomedicine: From drug delivery to imaging. *Science Translational Medicine, 5*(216), 216rv4.

Conniot, J., Silva, J. M., Fernandes, J. G., Silva, L. C., Gaspar, R., Brocchini, S., & Barata, T. S. (2014). Cancer immunotherapy: Nanodelivery approaches for immune cell targeting and tracking. *Frontiers in Chemistry, 2*, 105.

Cottrell, T., Zhang, J., Zhang, B., Kaunitz, G. J., Burman, P., Chan, H. Y., & Smith, K. N. (2021). Evaluating T-cell cross-reactivity between tumors and immune-related adverse events with TCR sequencing: Pitfalls in interpretations of functional relevance. *Journal for Immunotherapy of Cancer, 9*(7), e002642.

Cryer, A. M., & Thorley, A. J. (2019). Nanotechnology in the diagnosis and treatment of lung cancer. *Pharmacology & Therapeutics, 198*, 189–205.

Danhier, F., Ansorena, E., Silva, J. M., Coco, R., Le Breton, A., & Préat, V. (2012). PLGA-based nanoparticles: An overview of biomedical applications. *Journal of Controlled Release, 161*(2), 505–522.

De Martin, E., Michot, J. M., Papouin, B., Champiat, S., Mateus, C., Lambotte, O., & Samuel, D. (2018). Characterization of liver injury induced by cancer immunotherapy using immune checkpoint inhibitors. *Journal of Hepatology, 68*(6), 1181–1190.

de Oliveira Cardoso, Ferreira, L. M. B., Comparetti, E. J., Sampaio, I., Ferreira, N. N., … Zucolotto, V. (2022). Stimuli-responsive polymeric nanoparticles as controlled drug delivery systems. In L. S. Milane, & M. M. Amiji (Eds.), *Stimuli-responsive nanocarriers* (pp. 87–117). Academic Press. https://doi.org/10.1016/B978-0-12-824456-2.00011-4.

Decuzzi, P., & Ferrari, M. (2007). The role of specific and non-specific interactions in receptor-mediated endocytosis of nanoparticles. *Biomaterials, 28*(18), 2915–2922.

Delanoy, N., Michot, J. M., Comont, T., Kramkimel, N., Lazarovici, J., Dupont, R., & Lambotte, O. (2019). Haematological immune-related adverse events induced by anti-PD-1 or anti-PD-L1 immunotherapy: A descriptive observational study. *The Lancet Haematology, 6*(1), e48–e57.

Deng, S., Yang, Q., Shu, X., Lang, J., & Lu, S. (2020). The relative risk of immune-related liver dysfunction of PD-1. *Evidence-based Advance and Management of Adverse Events of Immunotherapy for Cancer*, 1254054.

Desai, N. (2012). Challenges in development of nanoparticle-based therapeutics. *The AAPS Journal, 14*(2), 282–295.

Dinauer, N., Balthasar, S., Weber, C., Kreuter, J., Langer, K., & von Briesen, H. (2005). Selective targeting of antibody-conjugated nanoparticles to leukemic cells and primary T-lymphocytes. *Biomaterials, 26*(29), 5898–5906.

Dobrovolskaia, M. A., Shurin, M., & Shvedova, A. A. (2016). Current understanding of interactions between nanoparticles and the immune system. *Toxicology and Applied Pharmacology, 299*, 78–89.

Doroudian, M., O'Neill, A., O'Reilly, C., Tynan, A., Mawhinney, L., McElroy, A., & Donnelly, S. C. (2020). Aerosolized drug-loaded nanoparticles targeting migration inhibitory factors inhibit Pseudomonas aeruginosa-induced inflammation and biofilm formation. *Nanomedicine, 15*(30), 2933–2953.

Ezhilarasan, D., Lakshmi, T., & Mallineni, S. K. (2022). Nano-based targeted drug delivery for lung cancer: Therapeutic avenues and challenges. *Nanomedicine, 17*(24), 1855–1869.

Farjadian, F., Ghasemi, A., Gohari, O., Roointan, A., Karimi, M., & Hamblin, M. R. (2019). Nanopharmaceuticals and nanomedicines currently on the market: Challenges and opportunities. *Nanomedicine, 14*(1), 93–126.

Farjadian, F., Ghasemi, S., Akbarian, M., Hoseini-Ghahfarokhi, M., Moghoofei, M., & Doroudian, M. (2022). Physically stimulus-responsive nanoparticles for therapy and diagnosis. *Frontiers in Chemistry, 10*, 952675.

Feldmann, D. P., Cheng, Y., Kandil, R., Xie, Y., Mohammadi, M., Harz, H., & Merkel, O. M. (2018). *In vitro* and *in vivo* delivery of siRNA via VIPER polymer system to lung cells. *Journal of Controlled Release, 276*, 50–58.

Fernald, K., & Kurokawa, M. (2013). Evading apoptosis in cancer. *Trends in Cell Biology, 23*(12), 620–633.

Florindo, H. F., Pandit, S., Gonçalves, L. M. D., Alpar, H. O., & Almeida, A. J. (2008). Streptococcus equi antigens adsorbed onto surface modified poly-ε-caprolactone microspheres induce humoral and cellular specific immune responses. *Vaccine, 26*(33), 4168–4177.

Florindo, H. F., Pandit, S., Lacerda, L., Gonçalves, L. M. D., Alpar, H. O., & Almeida, A. J. (2009). The enhancement of the immune response against S. equi antigens through the intranasal administration of poly-ε-caprolactone-based nanoparticles. *Biomaterials, 30*(5), 879–891.

Gajos-Michniewicz, A., Duechler, M., & Czyz, M. (2014). MiRNA in melanoma-derived exosomes. *Cancer Letters, 347*(1), 29–37.

Geisler, A. N., Phillips, G. S., Barrios, D. M., Wu, J., Leung, D. Y., Moy, A. P., & Lacouture, M. E. (2020). Immune checkpoint inhibitor–related dermatologic adverse events. *Journal of the American Academy of Dermatology, 83*(5), 1255–1268.

Gettinger, S., Horn, L., Jackman, D., Spigel, D., Antonia, S., Hellmann, M., & Brahmer, J. (2018). Five-year follow-up of nivolumab in previously treated advanced non–small-cell lung cancer: Results from the CA209-003 study. *Journal of Clinical Oncology, 36*(17), 1675–1684.

Gharavi, A. T., Hanjani, N. A., Movahed, E., & Doroudian, M. (2022). The role of macrophage subtypes and exosomes in immunomodulation. *Cellular & Molecular Biology Letters, 27*(1), 83.

Green, M. R., Manikhas, G. M., Orlov, S., Afanasyev, B., Makhson, A. M., Bhar, P., & Hawkins, M. J. (2006). Abraxane®, a novel Cremophor®-free, albumin-bound particle form of paclitaxel for the treatment of advanced non-small-cell lung cancer. *Annals of Oncology, 17*(8), 1263–1268 109.

Han, J., Goodman, J. B., & Zhang, M. (2021). Cardiovascular drug delivery. In L. S. Milane, & M. M. Amiji (Eds.), *Organelle and molecular targeting* (pp. 279–306). CRC Press.

He, C., Lu, J., Lin, W., & Wang, X. (2019). Albumin-based nanoparticles for cancer therapy. *Cancer Letters, 456*, 50–58.

Hirn, S., Semmler-Behnke, M., Schleh, C., Wenk, A., Lipka, J., Schäffler, M., & Kreyling, W. G. (2011). Particle size-dependent and surface charge-dependent biodistribution of gold nanoparticles after intravenous administration. *European Journal of Pharmaceutics and Biopharmaceutics, 77*(3), 407–416.

Huang, Y., Zhang, X., & Li, J. (2020). Targeted nanomedicines for cancer immunotherapy. *Advanced Drug Delivery Reviews, 158*, 28–47.

Islam, A., Rahat, I., Rejeeth, C., Sharma, D., & Sharma, A. (2025). Recent advcances on plant-based bioengineered nanoparticles using secondary metabolites and their potential in lung cancer management. *Journal of Future Foods, 5*(1), 1–20.

Islam, M. K., & Stanslas, J. (2021). Peptide-based and small molecule PD-1 and PD-L1 pharmacological modulators in the treatment of cancer. *Pharmacology & Therapeutics, 227*, 107870.

Johansen, P., Estevez, F., Zurbriggen, R., Merkle, H. P., Glück, R., Corradin, G., & Gander, B. (2000). Towards clinical testing of a single-administration tetanus vaccine based on PLA/PLGA microspheres. *Vaccine, 19*(9-10), 1047–1054.

Kamerkar, S., LeBleu, V. S., Sugimoto, H., Yang, S., Ruivo, C. F., Melo, S. A., & Kalluri, R. (2017). Exosomes facilitate therapeutic targeting of oncogenic KRAS in pancreatic cancer. *Nature, 546*(7659), 498–503.

Kiaie, S. H., Salehi-Shadkami, H., Sanaei, M. J., Azizi, M., Shokrollahi Barough, M., Nasr, M. S., & Sheibani, M. (2023). Nano-immunotherapy: overcoming delivery challenge of immune checkpoint therapy. *Journal of nanobiotechnology, 21*(1), 339.

Knights, O. B., & McLaughlan, J. R. (2018). Gold nanorods for light-based lung cancer theranostics. *International Journal of Molecular Sciences, 19*(11), 3318.

Krishnamachari, Y., Geary, S. M., Lemke, C. D., & Salem, A. K. (2011). Nanoparticle delivery systems in cancer vaccines. *Pharmaceutical Research, 28*, 215–236.

Kroschinsky, F., Stölzel, F., von Bonin, S., Beutel, G., Kochanek, M., & Kiehl, M.Intensive Care in Hematological and Oncological Patients (iCHOP) Collaborative Group. (2017). New drugs, new toxicities: Severe side effects of modern targeted and immunotherapy of cancer and their management. *Critical Care, 21*, 1–11.

Labet, M., & Thielemans, W. (2009). Synthesis of polycaprolactone: A review. *Chemical Society Reviews, 38*(12), 3484–3504.

Lee, D. W., Gardner, R., Porter, D. L., Louis, C. U., Ahmed, N., Jensen, M., & Mackall, C. L. (2014). Current concepts in the diagnosis and management of cytokine release syndrome. *Blood, 124*(2), 188–195.

Liu, B., Song, Y., & Liu, D. (2017). Clinical trials of CAR-T cells in China. *Journal of Hematology & Oncology, 10*, 1–10.

Liu, Y., Ma, W., & Wang, J. (2018). Theranostics of gold nanoparticles with an emphasis on photoacoustic imaging and photothermal therapy. *Current Pharmaceutical Design, 24*(23), 2719–2728.

Liu, Y., Zhang, P., & Wang, L. (2019). Advances in nanoparticles for immunotherapy: Strategies to enhance immune response in cancer. *Advanced Drug Delivery Reviews, 153*, 79–92.

Lizotte, P. H., Wen, A. M., Sheen, M. R., Fields, J., Rojanasopondist, P., Steinmetz, N. F., & Fiering, S. (2016). In situ vaccination with cowpea mosaic virus nanoparticles suppresses metastatic cancer. *Nature Nanotechnology, 11*(3), 295–303.

Maeda, H., Wu, J., Sawa, T., Matsumura, Y., & Hori, K. (2000). Tumor vascular permeability and the EPR effect in macromolecular therapeutics: A review. *Journal of Controlled Release, 65*(1-2), 271–284.

Mahmood, S. S., Fradley, M. G., Cohen, J. V., Nohria, A., Reynolds, K. L., Heinzerling, L. M., & Neilan, T. G. (2018). Myocarditis in patients treated with immune checkpoint inhibitors. *Journal of the American College of Cardiology, 71*(16), 1755–1764.

Maliyakkal, N., Beeran, A. A., & Udupa, N. (2021). Nanoparticles of cisplatin augment drug accumulations and inhibit multidrug resistance transporters in human glioblastoma cells. *Saudi Pharmaceutical Journal, 29*(8), 857–873.

Manke, A., Wang, L., & Rojanasakul, Y. (2013). Mechanisms of nanoparticle-induced oxidative stress and toxicity. *BioMed Research International, 2013*(1), 942916.

Marangoni, V. S. (2016). *Theranostic nanomaterials applied to the cancer diagnostic and therapy and nanotoxicity studies* (Doctoral dissertation, Universidade de São Paulo).

McCarthy, J., Inkielewicz-Stepniak, I., Corbalan, J. J., & Radomski, M. W. (2012). Mechanisms of toxicity of amorphous silica nanoparticles on human lung submucosal cells *in vitro*: Protective effects of fisetin. *Chemical Research in Toxicology, 25*(10), 2227–2235.

Meka, R. R., Mukherjee, S., Patra, C. R., & Chaudhuri, A. (2019). Shikimoyl-ligand decorated gold nanoparticles for use in ex vivo engineered dendritic cell based DNA vaccination. *Nanoscale, 11*(16), 7931–7943.

Meraz, I. M., Majidi, M., Cao, X., Lin, H., Li, L., Wang, J., & Roth, J. A. (2018). TUSC2 immunogene therapy synergizes with anti–PD-1 through enhanced proliferation and infiltration of natural killer cells in syngeneic Kras-mutant mouse lung cancer models. *Cancer Immunology Research, 6*(2), 163–177.

Meraz, I. M., Majidi, M., Shao, R., Meng, F., Ha, M. J., Shpall, E., & Roth, J. A. (2022). TUSC2 immunogene enhances efficacy of chemo-immuno combination on KRAS/LKB1 mutant NSCLC in humanized mouse model. *Communications Biology, 5*(1), 167.

Monopoli, M. P., Aberg, C., Salvati, A., & Dawson, K. A. (2020). Biomolecular coronas provide the biological identity of nanosized materials, *Nature Nanotechnology* (7, pp. 205–229).

Moreno, D., Zalba, S., Navarro, I., de Ilarduya, C. T., & Garrido, M. J. (2010). Pharmacodynamics of cisplatin-loaded PLGA nanoparticles administered to tumor-bearing mice. *European Journal of Pharmaceutics and Biopharmaceutics, 74*(2), 265–274.

Mukherjee, A., Paul, M., & Mukherjee, S. (2019). Recent progress in the theranostics application of nanomedicine in lung cancer. *Cancers, 11*(5), 597.

Mukherjee, S., & Patra, C. R. (2016). Therapeutic application of anti-angiogenic nanomaterials in cancers. *Nanoscale, 8*(25), 12444–12470.

Naidoo, J., Wang, X., Woo, K. M., Iyriboz, T., Halpenny, D., Cunningham, J., & Hellmann, M. D. (2017). Pneumonitis in patients treated with anti programmed death-1/programmed death ligand 1 therapy. *Journal of Clinical Oncology, 35*(7), 709–717.

Naqash, A. R., Kihn-Alarcón, A. J., Stavraka, C., Kerrigan, K., Vareki, S. M., Pinato, D. J., & Puri, S. (2021). The role of gut microbiome in modulating response to immune checkpoint inhibitor therapy in cancer. *Annals of Translational Medicine, 9*(12), 1034.

Navarro-Ocon, A., Blaya-Canovas, J. L., López-Tejada, A., Blancas, I., Sánchez-Martín, R. M., Garrido, M. J., & Granados-Principal, S. (2022). Nanomedicine as a promising tool to overcome immune escape in breast cancer. *Pharmaceutics, 14*(3), 505.

Norouzi, M., & Hardy, P. (2021). Clinical applications of nanomedicines in lung cancer treatment. *Acta Biomaterialia, 121*, 134–142.

Pardi, N., Hogan, M. J., Porter, F. W., & Weissman, D. (2018). mRNA vaccines—A new era in vaccinology. *Nature Reviews Drug Discovery, 17*(4), 261–279.

Pardoll, D. M. (2012). The blockade of immune checkpoints in cancer immunotherapy. *Nature Reviews Cancer, 12*(4), 252–264.

Parodi, A., Quattrocchi, N., Van De Ven, A. L., Chiappini, C., Evangelopoulos, M., Martinez, J. O., & Tasciotti, E. (2013). Synthetic nanoparticles functionalized with biomimetic leukocyte membranes possess cell-like functions. *Nature Nanotechnology, 8*(1), 61–68.

Peng, G., Tisch, U., Adams, O., Hakim, M., Shehada, N., Broza, Y. Y., & Haick, H. (2009). Diagnosing lung cancer in exhaled breath using gold nanoparticles. *Nature Nanotechnology, 4*(10), 669–673.

Perry, J. L., Tian, S., Sengottuvel, N., Harrison, E. B., Gorentla, B. K., Kapadia, C. H., & Pecot, C. V. (2020). Pulmonary delivery of nanoparticle-bound toll-like receptor 9 agonist for the treatment of metastatic lung cancer. *ACS Nano, 14*(6), 7200–7215.

Ramalingam, V., Varunkumar, K., Ravikumar, V., & Rajaram, R. (2018). Target delivery of doxorubicin tethered with PVP stabilized gold nanoparticles for effective treatment of lung cancer. *Scientific Reports, 8*(1), 3815.

Reda, M., Ngamcherdtrakul, W., Nelson, M. A., Siriwon, N., Wang, R., Zaidan, H. Y., & Yantasee, W. (2022). Development of a nanoparticle-based immunotherapy targeting PD-L1 and PLK1 for lung cancer treatment. *Nature Communications, 13*(1), 4261.

Sanaei, M. J., Pourbagheri-Sigaroodi, A., Kaveh, V., Abolghasemi, H., Ghaffari, S. H., Momeny, M., & Bashash, D. (2021). Recent advances in immune checkpoint therapy in non-small cell lung cancer and opportunities for nanoparticle-based therapy. *European Journal of Pharmacology, 909*, 174404.

Shao, Z., Lu, Y., & Zhang, Q. (2020). Personalized immunotherapy for cancer: Integration with nanomedicine. *Frontiers in Pharmacology, 11*, 611392.

Shen, H., Ackerman, A. L., Cody, V., Giodini, A., Hinson, E. R., Cresswell, P., & Hanlon, D. J. (2006). Enhanced and prolonged cross-presentation following endosomal escape of exogenous antigens encapsulated in biodegradable nanoparticles. *Immunology, 117*(1), 78–88.

Singh, A., Soni, R., & Soni, R. (2020). Nanoparticles in cancer immunotherapy: A review of strategies and applications. *Drug Delivery and Translational Research, 10*(1), 43–54.

Singh, P., Pandit, S., Mokkapati, V. R. S. S., Garg, A., Ravikumar, V., & Mijakovic, I. (2018). Gold nanoparticles in diagnostics and therapeutics for human cancer. *International Journal of Molecular Sciences, 19*(7), 1979.

Socinski, M. A., Langer, C. J., Okamoto, I., Hon, J. K., Hirsh, V., Dakhil, S. R., & Renschler, M. F. (2013a). Safety and efficacy of weekly nab®-paclitaxel in combination with carboplatin as first-line therapy in elderly patients with advanced non-small-cell lung cancer. *Annals of Oncology, 24*(2), 314–321.

Socinski, M. A., Okamoto, I., Hon, J. K., Hirsh, V., Dakhil, S. R., Page, R. D., & Renschler, M. F. (2013b). Safety and efficacy analysis by histology of weekly nab-paclitaxel in combination with carboplatin as first-line therapy in patients with advanced non-small-cell lung cancer. *Annals of Oncology, 24*(9), 2390–2396.

Song, Z., Ma, H., Sun, H., Li, Q., Liu, Y., Xie, J., & Wang, J. (2023). Construction and validation of a prognostic nomogram model for SCLC patients in Shandong Province, China, *BMC Cancer* p. 1182.

Steven, A., Fisher, S. A., & Robinson, B. W. (2016). Immunotherapy for lung cancer. *Respirology, 21*(5), 821–833.

Su, W. P., Chang, L. C., Song, W. H., Yang, L. X., Wang, L. C., Chia, Z. C., & Yeh, C. S. (2022). Polyaniline-based glyco-condensation on Au nanoparticles enhances immunotherapy in lung cancer. *ACS Applied Materials & Interfaces, 14*(21), 24144–24159.

Sun, Q., Bai, X., Sofias, A. M., van der Meel, R., Ruiz-Hernandez, E., Storm, G., & Shi, Y. (2020). Cancer nanomedicine meets immunotherapy: Opportunities and challenges. *Acta Pharmacologica Sinica, 41*(7), 954–958.

Sung, H., Ferlay, J., Siegel, R. L., Laversanne, M., Soerjomataram, I., Jemal, A., & Bray, F. (2021). Global cancer statistics 2020: GLOBOCAN estimates of incidence and mortality worldwide for 36 cancers in 185 countries. *CA: A Cancer Journal for Clinicians, 71*(3), 209–249.

Swain, S., Kumar Sahu, P., Beg, S., & Manohar Babu, S. (2016). Nanoparticles for cancer targeting: Current and future directions. *Current Drug Delivery, 13*(8), 1290–1302.

Tang, S., Qin, C., Hu, H., Liu, T., He, Y., Guo, H., & Zhou, H. (2022). Immune checkpoint inhibitors in non-small cell lung cancer: Progress, challenges, and prospects. *Cells, 11*(3), 320.

Tinkle, S., McNeil, S. E., Mühlebach, S., Bawa, R., Borchard, G., Barenholz, Y., & Desai, N. (2014). Nanomedicines: Addressing the scientific and regulatory gap. *Annals of the New York Academy of Sciences, 1313*(1), 35–56.

Torchilin, V. (2011). Tumor delivery of macromolecular drugs based on the EPR effect. *Advanced Drug Delivery Reviews, 63*(3), 131–135.

Trouiller, B., Reliene, R., Westbrook, A., Solaimani, P., & Schiestl, R. H. (2009). Titanium dioxide nanoparticles induce DNA damage and genetic instability *in vivo* in mice. *Cancer Research, 69*(22), 8784–8789.

Tzogani, K., Penttilä, K., Lapveteläinen, T., Hemmings, R., Koenig, J., Freire, J., & Pignatti, F. (2020). EMA review of daunorubicin and cytarabine encapsulated in liposomes (Vyxeos, CPX-351) for the treatment of adults with newly diagnosed, therapy-related acute myeloid leukemia or acute myeloid leukemia with myelodysplasia-related changes. *The Oncologist, 25*(9), e1414–e1420.

Velpurisiva, P., Gad, A., Piel, B., Jadia, R., & Rai, P. (2017). Nanoparticle design strategies for effective cancer immunotherapy. *Journal of Biomedicine (Sydney, NSW), 2*(2), 64.

Wang, L., Yang, Z., Guo, F., Chen, Y., Wei, J., Dai, X., & Zhang, X. (2023). Research progress of biomarkers in the prediction of anti-PD-1/PD-L1 immunotherapeutic efficiency in lung cancer. *Frontiers in Immunology, 14*, 1227797.

Wang, M., Zhai, X., Li, J., Guan, J., Xu, S., Li, Y., & Zhu, H. (2021a). The role of cytokines in predicting the response and adverse events related to immune checkpoint inhibitors. *Frontiers in Immunology, 12*, 670391.

Wang, S., Liu, J., & Wang, L. (2021b). Nanoparticle-based drug delivery systems for cancer immunotherapy. *Therapeutic Advances in Medical Oncology, 13*, 1–13.

Wang, Y., Wiesnoski, D. H., Helmink, B. A., Gopalakrishnan, V., Choi, K., DuPont, H. L., & Jenq, R. R. (2018). Fecal microbiota transplantation for refractory immune checkpoint inhibitor-associated colitis. *Nature Medicine, 24*(12), 1804–1808.

Wang, Z., Chen, L., Ma, Y., Li, X., Hu, A., Wang, H., & Dong, J. (2021c). Peptide vaccine-conjugated mesoporous carriers synergize with immunogenic cell death and PD-L1 blockade for amplified immunotherapy of metastatic spinal. *Journal of Nanobiotechnology, 19*, 1–16.

Wargo, J. A., Reuben, A., Cooper, Z. A., Oh, K. S., & Sullivan, R. J. (2015). Immune Effects of Chemotherapy, Radiation, and Targeted Therapy and Opportunities for Combination With Immunotherapy. *Seminars in oncology, 42*(4), 601–616. https://doi.org/10.1053/j.seminoncol.2015.05.007.

Wathoni, N., Puluhulawa, L. E., Joni, I. M., Muchtaridi, M., Mohammed, A. F. A., Elamin, K. M., & Gozali, D. (2022). Monoclonal antibody as a targeting mediator for nanoparticle targeted delivery system for lung cancer. *Drug Delivery, 29*(1), 2959–2970.

Xu, L., Wang, Y. Y., Huang, J., Chen, C. Y., Wang, Z. X., & Xie, H. (2020). Silver nanoparticles: Synthesis, medical applications and biosafety. *Theranostics, 10*(20), 8996.

Xu, Z., Wang, Y., Zhang, L., & Huang, L. (2014). Nanoparticle-delivered transforming growth factor-β siRNA enhances vaccination against advanced melanoma by modifying tumor microenvironment. *ACS Nano, 8*(4), 3636–3645.

Yang, T., Yu, S., Liu, L., Sun, Y., Lan, Y., Ma, X., & Liu, Y. (2020). Dual polymeric prodrug co-assembled nanoparticles with precise ratiometric co-delivery of cisplatin and metformin for lung cancer chemoimmunotherapy. *Biomaterials Science, 8*(20), 5698–5714.

Yuan, Y., Cai, T., Xia, X., Zhang, R., Chiba, P., & Cai, Y. (2016). Nanoparticle delivery of anticancer drugs overcomes multidrug resistance in breast cancer. *Drug Delivery, 23*(9), 3350–3357.

Zanganeh, S., Goodarzi, N., Doroudian, M., & Movahed, E. (2022). Potential COVID-19 therapeutic approaches targeting angiotensin-converting enzyme 2; an updated review. *Reviews in Medical Virology, 32*(4), e2321.

Zein, R., Sharrouf, W., & Selting, K. (2020). Physical properties of nanoparticles that result in improved cancer targeting. *Journal of Oncology, 2020*(1), 5194780.

Zhang, S., Bai, X., & Shan, F. (2020). The progress and confusion of anti-PD1/PD-L1 immunotherapy for patients with advanced non-small cell lung cancer. *International Immunopharmacology, 80*, 106247.

Zhang, W., Wang, L., Liu, Y., Chen, X., Liu, Q., Jia, J., & Ma, G. (2014). Immune responses to vaccines involving a combined antigen–nanoparticle mixture and nanoparticle-encapsulated antigen formulation. *Biomaterials, 35*(23), 6086–6097.

Zhao, X., Xie, Y., & Liu, X. (2020). Nanomedicine strategies in enhancing the efficacy of cancer immunotherapy. *Biomaterials Science, 8*(1), 15–34.

CHAPTER 16

Nanotechnology in lung cancer therapy: Recent advancements and future perspectives in drug delivery systems

Rakesh Kumar[a,b], Shrestha Sharma[a], Manita Saini[a,c] and Syed Arman Rabbani[d]

[a]Amity Institute of Pharmacy, Amity University, Gurugram, Haryana, India [b]Department of Pharmacy, Pharmaceutics, Jagannath University, Bahadurgarh, Haryana, India [c]Geeta Institute of Pharmacy, Geeta University, Panipat, Haryana, India [d]RAK College of Pharmacy, RAK Medical and Health Sciences University, Ras Al Khaimah, United Arab Emirates

16.1 Introduction

Cancer continues to be one of the most pernicious diseases in the world, accounting for about 18 million new cases and 9.6 million fatalities each year. According to the International Agency for Research on Cancer, there will be 13.2 million cancer-related deaths and 22.2 million new cases worldwide by 2030, which is a concerning trend. Lung cancer accounts for 19% of cancer fatalities worldwide, making it the most common subtype of cancer and the leading cause of cancer mortality. Furthermore, lung cancer has the worst prognosis, with a 5-year survival rate of only about 19%, making it the cancer with the second-worst prognosis after pancreatic cancer (Kiely et al., 2012). It indicates that our knowledge of the illness does not correspond with our capacity to cure it because most lung tumors are discovered at an advanced stage. It is difficult to administer treatment regimens to the tumor at high enough concentrations without causing collateral harm to good tissue. An ideal therapeutic scenario would be one in which a curative treatment could be delivered to the tumor cells in the very early phases of their malignant metamorphosis with high selectivity (Cheng et al., 2016). The idea of a "magic bullet" has existed in Paul Ehrlich's immunological research, and with the development of nanotechnology, it now has the potential to become a reality. The primary risk factor was determined to be tobacco use, and other variables like home & environmental air pollution also play a crucial role. The preliminary treatment pillars for lung cancer are surgery, radiation, and oncological medicines (Thandra et al., 2021).

Nanoengineered Therapeutics for Lung Cancer: Advanced Drug Delivery Strategies.
DOI: https://doi.org/10.1016/B978-0-443-44585-9.00002-0

16.1.1 Early diagnosis of lung cancer

The medicinal medicines that nanoparticles (NPs) carry can have their pharmacokinetics, biodistribution, and activity changed. These characteristics enable scientists to create targeted nanotechnology approaches that enhance the anticancer medications' therapeutic effectiveness. When nanomaterials and probes are used together, they can target tumor tissues specifically, opening the door to the diagnosis and therapy of cancer. Traditional techniques for detecting lung cancer, such as computed tomography (CT), magnetic resonance imaging (MRI), sputum cytology, bronchial biopsy, and chest radiographs (CXRs), are highly dependent on the size and course of the tumor and may require additional specialist medical equipment (Li et al., 2021). The National Lung Screening Trial (NLST) in the United States has demonstrated that the rate of false-positive results from low-dose computed tomography (LDCT) is as high as 96.4%. The most common treatment choices for lung cancer are still chemotherapy, radiation therapy, and surgery; these methods differ depending on the stage and subtype of the disease (Ning et al., 2021).

16.1.2 Limitations of conventional drug delivery methods

The primary causes of lung cancer's continued dominance in cancer-related mortality worldwide are its high heterogeneity, late diagnosis, and the inadequacy of traditional treatment delivery methods. Despite being essential components of contemporary treatment plans, traditional systemic chemotherapy and radiation therapy have significant limitations in providing efficient and focused care. Chemotherapy has an efficacy rate of less than 30% because of its nonspecific nature in treating cancer, which can also result in side effects such as myelosuppression, gastrointestinal problems, and drug resistance. In contrast, radiotherapy mostly uses the stereotactic ablative radiotherapy (SABR) technique (Sullivan et al., 2021).

16.1.2.1 Poor tumor selectivity and off-target toxicity

Conventional chemotherapy's lack of tumor selectivity is one of its main drawbacks. Drugs that are delivered systemically, such as docetaxel, paclitaxel, and cisplatin, cause serious harm to healthy tissues and organs because they spread nonselectively throughout the body. This nonspecific biodistribution is especially problematic for lung cancer because of the high vascularization of the lungs and the potential for pulmonary damage. The effectiveness of treatment is diminished since these off-target effects frequently require dose lowering (Ouyang et al., 2021).

16.1.2.2 Rapid drug clearance and short circulation time

Conventional medications frequently have poor pharmacokinetics, with quick hepatic or renal metabolism that reduces their plasma half-life and narrows their therapeutic window. This is made worse in the pulmonary environment, where drug retention is decreased, especially in inhalation-based therapy, by the alveolar–capillary barrier and mucociliary clearance mechanisms. As a result, several dosage schedules are needed, which raises the potential of systemic toxicity and patient burden (Li et al., 2022).

16.1.2.3 Inefficient penetration into tumor tissue

When employing standard administration methods, deep medication penetration is impeded by the aberrant vasculature, high interstitial pressure, and dense extracellular matrices (ECM) found in solid lung tumors. These physiological barriers lead to uneven drug distribution, as cells near the periphery of the tumor get higher drug concentrations than those at the center. Therapeutic failure results from this geographical diversity, which also helps resistant clones survive.

16.1.2.4 Drug resistance and tumor adaptation

Multidrug resistance (MDR), which is caused by increased DNA repair mechanisms and overexpression of efflux pumps like P-glycoprotein (P-gp), is frequently the result of repeated exposure to traditional chemotherapeutics. Overall survival in lung cancer is greatly decreased by resistance to platinum-based therapy, particularly in nonsmall cell lung cancer (NSCLC). Furthermore, adaptive resistance is caused by intratumoral heterogeneity and cancer stem cell populations, both of which are not sufficiently addressed by traditional treatment approaches (Ezhilarasani et al., 2022).

16.1.2.5 Limited capability for combination or sequential therapy

The structural flexibility needed to codeliver several agents with regulated pharmacokinetics and ratios is not present in traditional drug delivery. Separate dosing is frequently used in combination regimens, such as chemotherapy with immunotherapy or targeted medicines, which might result in mismatched bioavailability and less than ideal synergy. Inaccurate control could lead to higher toxicity or therapeutic antagonism.

16.1.2.6 Lack of real-time monitoring and response evaluation

Integrated diagnostic capabilities are not available with traditional delivery methods. To assess treatment response, clinicians must rely on imaging and biomarkers that are acquired independently. This fragmented strategy hinders real-time monitoring of therapy efficacy and delays therapeutic modifications, especially in dynamic tumor settings (Kapoor et al., 2025).

16.1.3 Emergence of nanomedicine in lung cancer

In recent years, nanocomposite-based drug delivery systems have emerged as a promising strategy for enhancing therapeutic efficacy and diagnostic precision. These nanoformulations offer the potential for targeted delivery, controlled release, and improved bioavailability, making them highly attractive for treating lung cancer. Among various applications, their role in lung cancer therapy has gained particular interest due to the limitations of conventional treatment modalities (Alexandru et al., 2024). Its powerful targeting and high modifiability make it an important tool in the field of tumor diagnostics and treatment. For example, MRI-guided breast cancer immunoferroptosis synergistic therapy can be employed with FeGd-HN@TA-Fe (2+)-SN38 NPs, an activator of the STING pathway. Furthermore, the repolarization process from M2 to M1 macrophages is measured by MRI utilizing a molecular imaging nanoprobe-based on superparamagnetic iron oxide NPs and employing redox-active nitric oxide as a chemical target. Despite significant progress, the development of efficient nanocarriers remains challenging. The fabrication of NPs with uniform size, well-defined morphology, and consistent surface chemistry is critical for their functional performance but remains technically demanding. Common obstacles include nonuniform size distribution, structural inconsistency, suboptimal biocompatibility, and difficulties in achieving scalable reproducibility (Yin et al., 2021).

To boost the effectiveness of targeted therapy and immunotherapy, NPs can also enhance immune responses and overcome drug resistance due to their editable and adjustable characteristics. Moreover, nanodelivery systems can also deliver CRISPR/Cas9, noncoding RNA, and RNAi, improving the efficiency of gene therapy and inhibiting tumor progression (Baig et al., 2025). This chapter presents an in-depth exploration of the key nanoparticle platforms employed in the diagnosis and treatment of lung cancer. It synthesizes current research findings on the role of nanotechnology in early detection, diagnostic imaging, standard therapies, targeted drug delivery, and immunotherapy.

16.2 Pathophysiology of lung cancer relevant to nanomedicine

Lung cancer is primarily categorized into small cell lung cancer (SCLC) and NSCLC, with NSCLC accounting for roughly 85% of cases and SCLC about 15%. The histopathological features, molecular profiles, clinical behavior, and response to therapy of these subtypes vary significantly, and these differences have a direct impact on the development and use of therapeutic approaches based on nanomedicine (Haider et al., 2022.

16.2.1 Molecular subtypes (nonsmall cell lung cancer vs. small cell lung cancer) and their implications

About 85% of all instances of lung cancer are classified as NSCLC, which comprises big cell carcinoma, squamous cell carcinoma, and adenocarcinoma. Compared to SCLC, NSCLC usually advances more slowly and frequently has actionable genetic changes. The development of molecularly targeted medicines has been made possible by mutations and rearrangements in genes, including the epidermal growth factor receptor (EGFR), anaplastic lymphoma kinase (ALK), KRAS, ROS1, and BRAF (Smolarz et al., 2025). These particular alterations also support the use of nanocarriers functionalized with ligands or antibodies for active targeting, which minimizes off-target damage while enabling targeted medication delivery to cancerous cells. Furthermore, NSCLC's heterogeneity encourages the application of tailored nanomedicine techniques, in which NPs are designed to deliver many medicines or combined therapeutic/imaging payloads to enhance treatment response and diagnostic accuracy (Schwendenwein et al., 2021).

About 15% of lung cancer cases are SCLC, which is distinguished by its aggressiveness, quick development, early metastasis, and neuroendocrine origin. The effectiveness of precision treatments is limited in SCLC due to the absence of distinct, targetable mutations, in contrast to NSCLC. However, nanoparticle-based methods that use the increased permeability and retention (EPR) effect for passive targeting can take advantage of the high proliferation index and high vascularization that are common in SCLC (Padinharayil et al., 2023). The necessity for novel nanomedicine solutions that can administer chemotherapeutics in a sustained or stimuli-responsive manner is further highlighted by the rapid progression and chemoresistance frequently observed in SCLC. These solutions may increase treatment efficacy and lower systemic toxicity (Crintea et al., 2023). Customized nanomedicine approaches are required because of the unique biological and molecular features of NSCLC and SCLC. Designing NPs with the right size, surface chemistry, and targeting ligands requires a thorough understanding of the vascular architecture, receptor expression patterns, and tumor microenvironment (TME) of each subtype. In patients with NSCLC and SCLC, this level of precision in nanoparticle creation can improve clinical outcomes, overcome medication resistance, and increase therapeutic index (Lee et al., 2025).

16.2.2 Tumor microenvironment-barriers and opportunities

Treatment efficacy, therapeutic resistance, and disease progression are all significantly influenced by the lung cancer TME. The TME, which is made up of a dynamic and intricate network of cancer cells, stromal cells, immunological components, extracellular matrix (ECM), and aberrant vasculature, offers both special opportunities and major obstacles for treatments based on nanomedicine (Shah et al., 2025).

16.2.2.1 Barriers presented by the tumor microenvironment

The aberrant tumor vasculature present in lung cancer tissues is one of the biggest problems in nanomedicine. The structure of tumor vasculature is chaotic, leaky, and inadequately perfused, in contrast to the ordered and selective architecture of normal blood arteries. This irregularity causes restricted penetration of NPs into the tumor core and heterogeneous medication distribution, even though it can promote the EPR effect. Deep tissue penetration is further limited by the tumor mass's high interstitial fluid pressure (IFP), which prevents NPs from moving convectively (Arandhara et al., 2025). Collagen, fibronectin, and hyaluronic acid make up the thick ECM, which forms a physical barrier that prevents the dispersion of NPs and cellular uptake. This is especially important for desmoplastic cancers, such as some NSCLC subtypes, where ECM remodeling leads to resistance to treatment

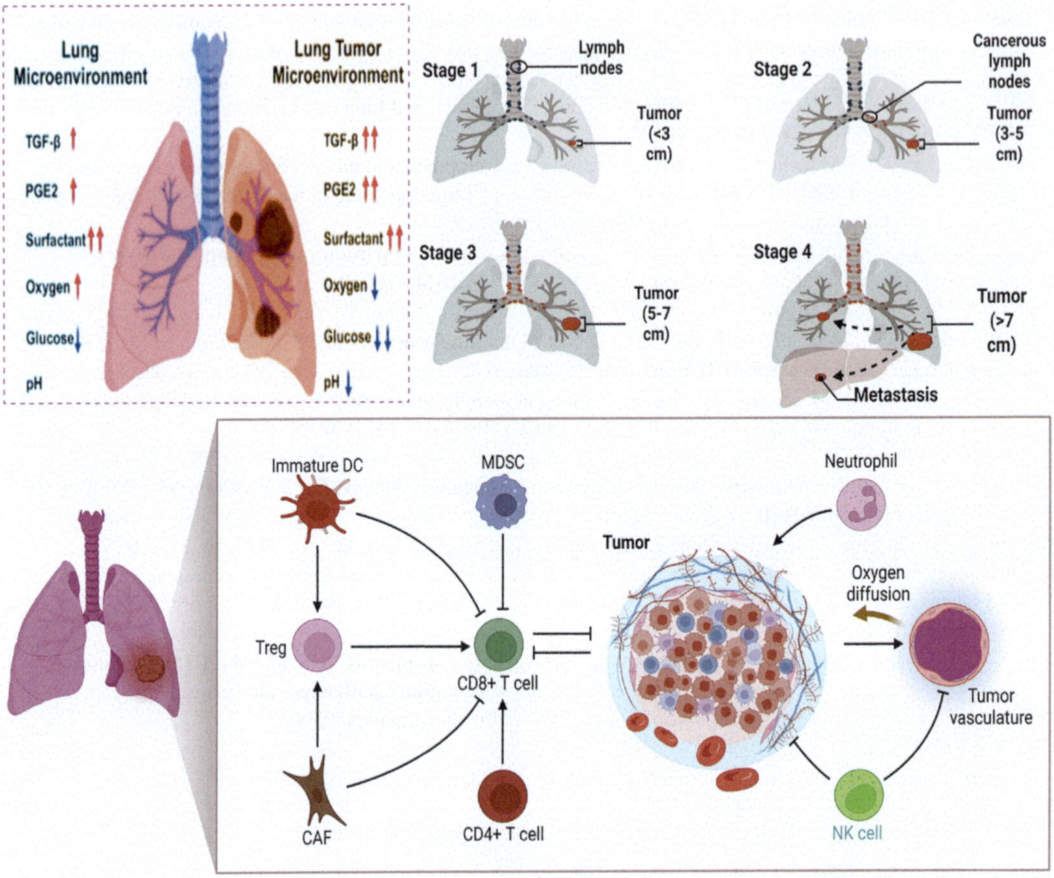

Figure 16.1

Tumor microenvironment and progression of lung cancer. Long description: The lung tumor microenvironment is characterized by altered cytokines (TGF-β and PGE2), reduced oxygen and glucose levels, and acidic pH, which collectively support tumor survival and immune evasion. Progressive stages of lung cancer (stages 1–4) highlight tumor growth and metastasis. The tumor immune landscape involves immune-suppressive cells (Tregs, CAFs, and MDSCs) and reduced CD8 + T-cell activity, along with dysregulated oxygen diffusion and abnormal vasculature, ultimately facilitating tumor progression and immune escape.

(Gupta et al., 2023). Tumor-associated macrophages (TAMs), myeloid-derived suppressor cells (MDSCs), and regulatory T cells (Tregs) all contribute to tumor immune evasion, which is another significant barrier: Immune suppression within the TME. These substances have the potential to reduce the effectiveness of immune-stimulating nanotherapies by causing sequestration or clearance of NPs (Sabit et al., 2025). Overview of lung tumor microenvironmental alterations and immune regulation in cancer progression, as depicted in Fig. 16.1.

In spite of these obstacles, the TME offers strategic benefits for the design of nanomedicine. NPs (usually 100–200 nm in size) can concentrate preferentially in tumor areas over healthy tissues by using the EPR effect to passively target tumor tissues' leaky vasculature and inadequate lymphatic drainage (Thomas et al., 2025). Furthermore, the distinct biochemical characteristics of the TME, including its acidic pH, high glutathione (GSH) levels, hypoxia, and upregulated enzymes (such as matrix metalloproteinases (MMPs), provide opportunities for the development of stimuli-responsive NPs. Controlled and targeted medication delivery is made possible by these intelligent systems' ability to release their payload in response to particular triggers in the TME (Linton et al., 2016). Opportunities for active targeting, in which NPs are functionalized with ligands, peptides, or antibodies to improve specificity and cellular uptake, are presented by the overexpression of specific tumor-specific receptors (such as EGFR, integrins, and folate receptors) on cancer cells or endothelial cells (Mendes et al., 2021). To improve subsequent nanoparticle penetration and therapeutic efficacy, nanocarriers can also be designed to modify the TME itself by delivering substances that normalize tumor vasculature, break down the ECM, or rewire immune-suppressive cells. In addition to enhancing medication delivery, this strategy works in concert with immunotherapies and traditional chemotherapies (Peng et al., 2022).

16.2.3 Hallmarks of cancer exploited by nanocarriers

The use of nanomedicine in lung cancer treatment is based on taking advantage of several distinctive characteristics of tumor biology that set cancerous tissues apart from healthy ones. These distinct pathophysiological characteristics offer vital chances for creating NPs that precisely deliver therapeutic payloads, selectively accumulate in tumor tissues, and penetrate the TME. As functional triggers or passive targets for nanocarrier systems, the EPR effect, hypoxia, acidic pH, and aberrant signaling pathways are some of the most exploited characteristics (Parker et al., 2016).

16.2.3.1 Enhanced permeability and retention effect

The EPR effect, which results from the disordered and leaky vasculature of tumors along with compromised lymphatic drainage, is one of the most basic concepts in tumor-targeted nanomedicine. Abnormal angiogenesis causes vascular fenestrations and irregular blood flow in lung tumors, especially NSCLC. This allows NPs, which are usually between 100 and 200 nm in size, to passively collect within tumor tissues (Sirvi et al., 2025).

16.2.3.2 Tumor hypoxia

When oxygen demand and blood supply are out of balance, hypoxia, a characteristic of quickly growing solid tumors like lung cancer, occurs. In addition to promoting aggressive behavior and resistance to treatment, tumor hypoxia serves as a metabolic trigger for stimuli-responsive NPs. By using hypoxia-activated prodrugs or hypoxia-cleavable linkers, hypoxia-sensitive nanocarriers are designed to release their payload selectively in low oxygen environments (Chen et al., 2018).

16.2.3.3 Acidic tumor microenvironment

In contrast to normal tissues (pH 7.4), the extracellular pH in lung tumors is often more acidic (pH 6.5–6.8) due to increased glycolytic activity (Warburg effect) and inadequate perfusion. pH-sensitive nanocarriers that stay stable in circulation but experience structural alterations or drug release within the acidic TME can take advantage of this pH difference. This method lessens early medication leakage and enhances site-specific drug delivery (Garbuzenko et al., 2019).

16.2.3.4 Overexpression of tumor-specific receptors

Numerous surface receptors, including the folate receptor, transferrin receptor, integrins (including $\alpha v\beta 3$), and EGFR, are frequently overexpressed in lung cancer cells. Active targeting is made possible by functionalizing nanocarriers with targeting ligands (such as aptamers, peptides, and antibodies) that bind to these receptors specifically. This increases intracellular medication delivery while protecting healthy tissues by improving cellular uptake through receptor-mediated endocytosis (Alshammari et al., 2023).

16.2.3.5 Oxidative stress and redox imbalance

Increased intracellular GSH and reactive oxygen species (ROS) are frequently seen in tumor cells, particularly those found in lung cancer. Redox-sensitive NPs, which are stable in the bloodstream but break down or release their payload in the oxidative or reductive environment of the tumor, can take advantage of these redox imbalances to activate therapeutic medicines at specific sites.

16.2.3.6 Enzyme overexpression

In lung cancer, especially in the invasive and metastatic stages, MMPs, cathepsins, and other tumor-associated enzymes are frequently increased. Enzyme-cleavable linkers or coatings on nanocarriers can react to these enzymes to release medications or enter the tumor stroma more deeply, increasing the efficacy of treatment (Hani et al., 2022).

16.2.3.7 Aberrant cell signaling and genetic mutations

Genes including EGFR, KRAS, ALK, and TP53 are commonly mutated in lung cancer, which leads to unchecked growth, resistance to apoptosis, and metastasis. To specifically mute or fix these genetic abnormalities, nanocarriers can be employed to carry gene editing tools (like CRISPR-Cas9) or RNA interference (RNAi) agents (like siRNA and miRNA). The protective and targeting properties of nanoscale systems make this type of molecular precision medicine possible (Sharma et al., 2023; Sharma, 2023b).

16.3 Nanotechnology-enabled drug delivery systems: Classification and mechanisms

16.3.1 Lipid-based nanocarriers

In nanomedicine, lipid-based nanocarriers have become one of the most therapeutically sophisticated and adaptable platforms, especially for the targeted administration of imaging agents, nucleic acids, and chemotherapeutics. These systems enhance the pharmacokinetics, stability, and therapeutic index of anticancer drugs by utilizing the biocompatibility, structural diversity, and effective encapsulation ability of lipid materials. By improving tumor-specific delivery and lowering systemic side effects, lipid-based nanocarriers provide significant benefits in the setting of lung cancer, where biological barriers and off-target toxicity restrict traditional therapy (Babu et al., 2013).

16.3.1.1 Liposomes drug delivery

Liposomes are spherical vesicles with an aqueous core surrounded by one or more phospholipid bilayers. They can include both hydrophilic (in the core) and hydrophobic (in the bilayer) medications due to their amphiphilic nature. Through the EPR effect, liposomes passively accumulate in tumors. For active targeting, they can be functionalized with ligands. The encapsulated medication is released either by lysosomal breakdown or pH-triggered lipid membrane instability following cellular uptake, usually through endocytosis (Gonsalves et al., 2023). Liposomes are characterized by their low immunogenicity, good biocompatibility, regulated and sustained release profiles, and surface modification capacity (e.g., PEGylation for extended circulation). For instance, Onivyde (Irinotecan liposome injection) is approved for pancreatic cancer, and Doxil (a PEGylated liposomal doxorubicin), with possible application in lung and other solid tumors, is under trial (Desai et al., 2025). Immunoliposomes functionalized with monoclonal antibodies for improved specificity are recent developments in the management of lung cancer (Hajiaghapour et al., 2023).

16.3.1.2 Solid lipid nanoparticles

The solid lipid core of SLNs is maintained by surfactants, and maintains its solid state at body temperature as well as room temperature. They shield labile medications and are usually 50–1000 nm in size. By releasing hydrophobic medications via lipid matrix erosion or diffusion, SLNs increase the bioavailability and stability of these medications. Their solid matrix provides regulated drug release, resistance to enzymatic breakdown, long-term physical stability, biodegradability, and low cytotoxicity, compatibility with sterilization, and scalable manufacture (Bhatia et al., 2016). In preclinical lung cancer models, SLNs have demonstrated potential in the delivery of medicines with poor solubility, such as docetaxel and paclitaxel. Lung carcinoma is one of the tumors for which several SLN formulations are presently undergoing early-stage clinical studies(Table 16.1).

16.3.1.3 Nanostructured lipid carriers

Second-generation lipid NPs, or NLCs, were created to get beyond SLN drawbacks such as poor drug loading and expulsion during storage. They are made up of a mixture of liquid and solid lipids, which results in an imperfect lipid matrix that enhances drug loading and trapping. NLCs' amorphous nature enables controlled and prolonged drug release (Essa et al., 2020). They make intracellular delivery more effective and are especially well-suited to target malignancies with intricate vasculature, such as lung cancers. NLCs are adaptable for the pulmonary route, having a high drug loading capacity and very little drug leakage during storage (Hani et al., 2022). In clinical trials for lung cancer, NLCs are now being studied for the targeted delivery of chemotherapeutics like cisplatin and gemcitabine. With the potential to lower systemic toxicity and increase local drug concentration, pulmonary delivery of NLCs for the localized treatment of lung cancers is an area that is currently undergoing active development (Parker et al., 2016).

Nanocarrier-mediated strategies for targeted lung cancer therapy improve bioavailability, solubility, and tumor-specific delivery, while minimizing systemic toxicity and modulating immune responses, ultimately contributing to cancer cell eradication and preservation of healthy lung tissue, as depicted in Fig. 16.2.

Long description: NPs enable regulation of drug release, deep tumor penetration, and encapsulation for enhanced stability. These attributes promote sustained release, improved bioavailability, targeted tumor delivery, and protection against degradation, ultimately resulting in reduced systemic toxicity, immune modulation, and restoration of healthy lung function.

16.3.2 Polymeric nanoparticles

Polymeric nanocarriers, which provide a highly adjustable platform for regulated, targeted, and sustained drug delivery, have proven essential to the development of nanomedicine. In the treatment of lung cancer, where conventional chemotherapeutics frequently have issues with poor selectivity, quick clearance, and systemic toxicity, these methods hold great promise (Ashique et al., 2023). By using biocompatible and biodegradable materials, polymeric nanocarriers can be designed to react to particular physiological cues and administer medications in a site-specific way, increasing effectiveness and reducing side effects (Jawahar et al., 2012).

Table 16.1: Main nanoparticles applied in the field of lung cancer and their advantages and disadvantages.

Nanoparticle type	Key advantages	Primary limitations	Representative example	References
Lipid-based nanoparticles	Dual delivery capability for hydrophilic and hydrophobic drugs; high drug loading capacity; biocompatible; stable in serum	Variability in production batches; potential for systemic toxicity and hepatic side effects; high manufacturing costs	GSDM-DENG circRNA-LNPsa	Majumder et al. (2021)
Protein-based nanoparticles	Easily modifiable; supports dual-drug delivery; biodegradable	Source variability (e.g., HSA); cost-intensive; may elicit immunogenic responses (BSA)	Albumin nanoparticles (ALB-NPs)b	Zare-Zardini et al. (2025)
Viral nanoparticles	High encapsulation efficiency; scalable production; excellent transfection potential	Immunogenicity; liver-associated toxicity	PPE-Ad conjugates	Carrasco-Esteban et al. (2021)
Apoferritin nanocarriers	Exceptional surface modifiability; thermal stability; abundant in blood; low toxicity profile	Limited drug encapsulation can impair efficacy and stability	Ferritin nanocages (FTn)d	Dostalova et al. (2017)
Polymeric nanoparticles	Thermodynamically stable; biocompatible; cost-effective; easily synthesized; suitable for endothelial delivery	Aggregation risks; suboptimal targeting; potential cytotoxicity	CMNP(@Osi)e	Zhao et al. (2021)
Metal-based nanoparticles	Multifunctional theranostic potential; tunable surfaces; compatible with imaging modalities	Risk of hemolysis, nephrotoxicity, and inefficient endosomal escape	SPION-CCPMsf	Hheidari et al. (2024)

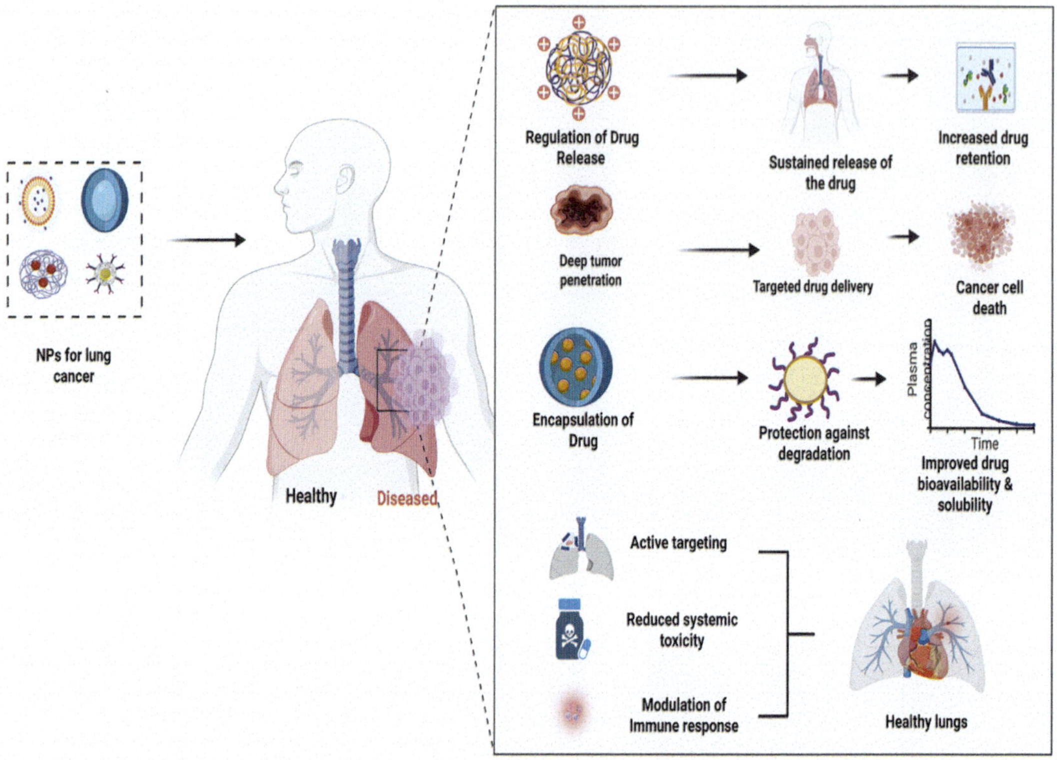

Figure 16.2

Schematic representation of nanocarrier-based drug delivery for lung cancer therapy. Long description: Nanoparticles enable regulation of drug release, deep tumor penetration, and encapsulation for enhanced stability. These attributes promote sustained release, improved bioavailability, targeted tumor delivery, and protection against degradation, ultimately resulting in reduced systemic toxicity, immune modulation, and restoration of healthy lung function.

16.3.2.1 Biodegradable polymeric nanocarriers

Since biodegradable polymers can encapsulate a variety of medications and have controlled degradation rates, they are frequently utilized in the creation of nanocarriers. Chitosan, polyethylene glycol (PEG), and poly(lactic-co-glycolic acid) (PLGA) are the most widely used biodegradable polymers (Doppalapudi et al., 2016).

16.3.2.2.1 Poly(lactic-co-glycolic acid)

The lactic to glycolic acid ratio can be changed to modify the tunable degradation kinetics of PLGA, an FDA-approved copolymer. It breaks down into glycolic acid and lactic acid, which are both broken down by natural processes. PLGA NPs shield labile medications from enzymatic breakdown and offer a prolonged release profile. PLGA nanocarriers are perfect for long-term chemotherapy treatments because they release drugs by a combination of polymer erosion and diffusion (Banik et al., 2016). Paclitaxel, cisplatin, and siRNA targeting EGFR mutations in NSCLC have been delivered via PLGA-based NPs, which have demonstrated enhanced tumor accumulation and decreased systemic toxicity in lung cancer. To transport sorafenib to lung cancer cells, a chitosan-PLGA-FA nanocarrier was created.

16.3.2.2.2 Polyethylene glycol

PEG is frequently utilized to alter the surface of NPs (PEGylation) to prolong circulation, lessen plasma protein opsonization, and avoid detection by the mononuclear phagocyte system (MPS). PEG-based systems in lung cancer have made it possible for longer circulation, improved tumor accumulation through the EPR effect, and more effective administration of gene therapies and chemotherapeutics (Begines et al., 2020). By forming a hydrophilic "stealth" corona surrounding nanocarriers, PEGylation considerably increases the half-life of therapeutic medicines by lowering immune cell detection and clearance.

16.3.2.2.3 Chitosan

Chitosan, a naturally occurring cationic polymer that is generated from chitin, is particularly appealing for pulmonary medication delivery because of its exceptional mucoadhesive qualities. Chitosan NPs can be chemically altered to enhance solubility, targeting, or stimuli-responsiveness, and they aid in medication absorption via epithelial barriers. Its positive charge facilitates endocytosis by improving its contact with negatively charged cell membranes. By adding various functional groups to its surface through chemical processes, including acylation, alcoholization, and amination, chitosan's solubility can be changed. Chitosan has been utilized extensively as a nonviral medication delivery system (Shi et al., 2015). Because of its mucoadhesive qualities, chitosan can be applied to tight epithelial junctions. As a result, chitosan-based NPs are frequently employed in continuous medication release systems for pulmonary, intestinal, nasal, and buccal epithelia. In addition to altering the metabolism of tumor cells by causing apoptosis and preventing cell division, chitosan nanoparticles (ChNPs) also successfully stop tumor cell growth by raising the drug concentration in tumor tissues (Jawahar et al., 2012).

16.3.2.2.4 Alginate

Alginate is another biopolymeric substance that has been utilized to transport drugs. When compared to cationic and neutral polymers, this biopolymer exhibits higher mucoadhesive strength due to its final carboxyl groups, which make it an anionic mucoadhesive polymer. To increase blood insulin levels and decrease serum glucose levels in diabetic rats, Patil and Devarajan (n.d.) created insulin-containing alginate nanoparticles using nicotinamide as a penetration agent. When given sublingually (5 IU/kg) with nicotinamide present, nanoparticles demonstrated great pharmacological availability (>100%) and bioavailability (>80%) (Patil & Devarajan, 2016). By attaining a pharmacological high potential of 20.2% and a bioavailability of 24.1% in comparison to the subcutaneous injection at 1 IU/kg, NPs have demonstrated their promise as insulin carriers via the sublingual route in the streptozotocin-induced diabetic mouse model (Chen et al., 2022).

16.3.2.2 Stimuli-responsive polymeric nanocarriers

By reacting to particular endogenous or external triggers, stimuli-responsive polymeric nanocarriers have become a next-generation platform in lung cancer therapy, providing spatiotemporal precision in medication delivery. By allowing the controlled release of genetic material or chemotherapeutics at tumor locations, these "smart" delivery devices enhance therapeutic efficacy and reduce systemic toxicity. Engineering these carriers to react to tumor-specific stimuli like pH, redox potential, enzymes, and temperature has advanced significantly over the past 10 years, which is in line with the biological complexity of lung cancer (Alshammari et al., 2023).

16.3.2.3 PH-responsive systems

In contrast to normal physiological pH (7.4), tumor tissues usually have an extracellular pH that is somewhat acidic (6.5–6.8). pH-sensitive polymers are made to break down or modify their structure in acidic environments. These systems, such as poly(β-amino esters), poly(histidine), and chitosan derivatives, stay stable in blood circulation but release the medication quickly when they come into contact with the acidic TME or within acidic endosomal/lysosomal compartments after cellular uptake. Because of hypoxia and altered metabolism, lung tumors, like many solid malignancies, have an extracellular environment that is slightly acidic (Warburg effect).

16.3.2.4 Temperature-responsive systems

These systems make use of polymers that, at particular temperatures, exhibit structural rearrangements or phase transitions. Temperature-sensitive carriers can take advantage of the mild hyperthermia that may exist in inflammatory or tumorous tissues. On-demand medication release is made possible by polymers like [poly(N-isopropyl acrylamide) PNIPAM], which expand or collapse in response to local temperature variations. These are used in conjunction with local hyperthermia therapy to cause a fast release of drugs at the tumor site.

16.3.2.5 Redox-responsive systems

Intracellular GSH levels in tumor cells are frequently 100–1000 times greater than those in the extracellular environment. Disulfide bonds that are broken down in the reductive intracellular environment are used by redox-sensitive systems (Jorgenson et al., 2013). High GSH concentrations cause disulfide bonds to be broken down when internalized by cancer cells, which causes the encapsulated medication or therapeutic nucleic acids—such as disulfide-crosslinked PEG, PLGA derivatives, and thiolated chitosan to be released quickly. GSH levels are up to 1000 times greater in the intracellular milieu of tumor cells than in the extracellular areas. Disulfide linkages are added to the polymeric backbone to take advantage of this redox gradient (Banik et al., 2016).

16.3.3 Inorganic nanocarriers

In the realm of nanomedicine, inorganic nanocarriers have attracted a lot of interest because of their special physicochemical characteristics, which include high surface area-to-volume ratios, customizable size and shape, optical activity, magnetic responsiveness, and structural rigidity. These characteristics make them ideal for theranostic and diagnostic imaging applications in addition to drug administration, providing real-time monitoring of therapeutic efficacy. Their incorporation into lung cancer treatment has great promise for facilitating multimodal approaches such as imaging-guided precision medicine, magnetic hyperthermia, and photothermal therapy (PTT) (Chen et al., 2016).

16.3.3.1 Gold nanoparticles

Usually produced in spherical, rod-shaped, or cage-like shapes, gold nanoparticles all have surface plasmon resonance (SPR), which causes intense light absorption and scattering in the near-infrared (NIR) spectrum. Covalent or noncovalent interactions can be used to functionalize AuNPs with medicinal drugs. Long-term circulation and active targeting to lung tumor cells are made possible by surface modification using PEG, antibodies, or aptamers. AuNPs transform light into heat when exposed to NIR lasers, causing localized hyperthermia that kills cancer cells while preserving healthy tissue (Guinart et al., 2021).

16.3.3.2 Silica nanoparticles

Mesoporous silica nanoparticles (MSNs) are very effective carriers for loading both hydrophobic and hydrophilic drugs because of their large surface area, adjustable pore diameters, and distinct shape. High drug loading is made possible by the porous matrix, and controlled and targeted release is achieved through surface functionalization with polymers or ligands. It is possible to design MSNs to release cargo in reaction to external stimuli such as light and ultrasound, redox conditions, or pH. SiNPs doped with radionuclides or fluorescent dyes can be used as multimodal imaging agents for MRI, positron emission tomography (PET), or fluorescence (Gao et al., 2020).

16.3.3.3 Magnetic nanoparticles

The superparamagnetic characteristics of magnetic nanoparticles, which are mostly made of iron oxide (FeO_4 or γ-FeO_3), allow for magnetic field-guided administration and hyperthermia treatment (Sadhukha et al., 2013). An external magnetic field can be used to direct MNPs to the tumor site, increasing accumulation and reducing off-target dissemination. MNPs produce localized heat when exposed to an alternating magnetic field, which causes cancer cells to undergo apoptosis. In MRI, MNPs serve as contrast agents, making it easier to observe biodistribution in real-time (Agnihotri et al., 2022).

16.3.3.4 Photothermal and imaging-guided therapy: An integrated strategy

The versatility of using magnetic and light-responsive devices to guide accumulation, inorganic nanocarriers for lung cancer, offers simultaneous administration, imaging, and treatment. Effective medication distribution is ensured by the excellent stability and structural integrity of inorganic nanocarriers under physiological circumstances. Because inorganic nanocarriers combine therapeutic molecules with imaging capabilities on a single platform, they are advantageously positioned for theranostics, or the combination of therapy and diagnostics (Muthukrishnan et al., 2022).

16.3.4 Hybrid and biomimetic systems

A revolutionary development in nanomedicine, hybrid and biomimetic nanocarrier systems combine biological functioning with synthetic nanotechnology to address issues with drug delivery, including lack of selectivity, poor tumor penetration, and immune clearance. To achieve improved biocompatibility, immune evasion, targeted distribution, and extended circulation time, these systems combine synthetic nanomaterials with the structural and functional benefits of natural biological components, such as cell membranes and extracellular vesicles (EVs). These next-generation platforms hold the potential for more effective and individualized treatment approaches in the context of lung cancer therapy (Han et al., 2024; Peng et al., 2021).

16.3.4.1 Cell membrane-coated nanoparticles

Core-shell nanostructures known as cell membrane-coated nanoparticles (CMNPs) are made up of a synthetic nanoparticle core (such as PLGA, silica, or gold) covered with plasma membranes from different cell types, such as immune, cancer, platelet, and red blood cells (RBCs). Because the membrane coating protects the source cells' surface proteins and antigens, nanoparticles are able to evade immune surveillance and lessen the MPS clearance (Rezaei et al., 2024). Paclitaxel or doxorubicin-loaded RBC membrane-coated nanoparticles have demonstrated increased tumor accumulation and decreased toxicity. Membrane adhesion molecules give cancer CMNPs their homotypic targeting capacity, allowing them to preferentially accumulate in tumors of the same origin (Desai et al., 2024).

16.3.4.2 Exosomes and natural vesicle-mimicking platforms

Most cell types secrete exosomes, which are nanoscale (30–150 nm) EVs that contain bioactive substances such as proteins, lipids, and nucleic acids. They inherently promote transport across biological barriers, such as the pulmonary and blood-brain barriers, and intercellular communication. It is possible to separate exosomes from particular donor cells (such as immune cells, tumor cells, or mesenchymal stem cells) while keeping the membrane proteins that highly specifically guide them to recipient cells (Ansa-Addo et al., 2012). Through parent cell transfection, electroporation, or passive incubation, drugs, RNA, and proteins can be loaded into exosomes.

16.3.4.3 Natural vesicle-mimicking platforms (synthetic exosome-mimetics)

These synthetic vesicles, which have the benefits of consistency and scalability, are made to resemble the size, shape, and surface protein makeup of natural exosomes. Usually, they are created by assembling lipids and functional proteins in vitro or by serially extruding cells through microfluidic devices (Huang et al., 2022). Preserve targeting and immune-evasive characteristics while overcoming the drawbacks of natural exosomes, such as batch variability and low production. Macrophage-mimetic vesicles that deliver doxorubicin and antiinflammatory drugs have shown improved tumor penetration and immune regulation, while lung-targeted synthetic vesicles have been designed to deliver microRNAs (miRNA) or CRISPR-Cas9 components for gene editing in refractory cancers (Tiruneh et al., 2021).

A new area in lung cancer treatment is represented by hybrid and biomimetic nanocarriers, which have clear benefits over conventional synthetic systems. These platforms combine synthetic nanoparticle cores with the structural and functional characteristics of biological membranes, such as those found in immune, cancer, or RBCs, to provide bioinspired systems with extremely effective drug delivery capabilities. Improved biocompatibility is one of the main benefits of biomimetic nanocarriers (Alinejad et al., 2023).

16.4 Targeted drug delivery in lung cancer

16.4.1 Passive targeting

One of the fundamental tactics in nanomedicine is passive targeting, which uses the distinct pathophysiological properties of tumor tissues to improve medication accumulation at the disease site without the need for active ligand-based targeting. Through leaky vasculature and compromised lymphatic drainage, the EPR effect primarily controls this mechanism, allowing nanocarriers to preferentially collect in solid tumors like lung cancer. EPR passive targeting is a promising way to increase therapeutic efficacy and reduce off-target effects in lung cancers, where conventional chemotherapies frequently have systemic toxicity and poor tumor specificity (Attia et al., 2019).

16.4.2 Active targeting

By improving the specificity of nanocarriers for tumor cells, active targeting is a complex method in nanomedicine that aims to get beyond the drawbacks of passive targeting. This tactic uses targeting ligands, like aptamers, peptides, or antibodies, to modify the surface of nanoparticles. These ligands bind selectively to overexpressed receptors on lung cancer cells, increasing cellular uptake, decreasing off-target toxicity, and improving therapeutic efficacy. In the treatment of SCLC and NSCLC, where tumor heterogeneity and resistance mechanisms frequently diminish the efficacy of traditional therapies, active targeting is especially advantageous (Huynh et al., 2010). Ongoing research focuses on multiligand strategies, dual-targeting systems, and stimuli-responsive nanocarriers to address these limitations and further refine active targeting approaches.

16.4.3 Organelle-specific targeting

A state-of-the-art development in nanomedicine, organelle-specific targeting seeks to improve the accuracy and effectiveness of therapeutic treatments at the subcellular level. Targeting certain organelles like mitochondria, nuclei, and lysosomes has become a powerful method to increase cytotoxicity, trigger apoptosis, and get beyond treatment barriers in lung cancer, where traditional treatments frequently have trouble delivering their medications intracellularly and cause drug resistance (Singh et al., 2024). By guaranteeing that chemotherapeutics, nucleic acids, or photosensitizers accumulate at intracellular locations that are crucial for tumor development and survival, nanocarriers designed for organelle-specific delivery might enhance their pharmacodynamics.

16.5 Recent breakthroughs and clinical advances

16.5.1 Nanomedicine platforms in ongoing or completed clinical trials

A new era in lung cancer treatment has been brought about by nanotechnology, which provides creative answers to persistent problems such as systemic toxicity, medication resistance, and low therapeutic specificity. Nanoengineered platforms have the potential to completely transform the way that lung cancer, especially NSCLC, is treated, according to recent preclinical and clinical research (Wang et al., 2020). The use of mRNA-based vaccinations to treat lung cancer is among the most exciting advancements. Clinical trials for BioNTech's BNT116, an mRNA vaccine that targets NSCLC, have begun in seven countries, including the UK, the USA, and Germany. By exposing the immune system to tumor-specific antigens, this vaccine seeks to strengthen the body's defenses against the spread of cancer by teaching it to identify and fight cancer cells. The vaccine's capacity to elicit a strong immune response with a favorable safety profile has been shown in early-phase trials, which represents a major advancement in tailored cancer immunotherapy (Feng et al., 2024). Simultaneously, patients with advanced lung cancer and melanoma have demonstrated promising outcomes in early trials of Moderna's mRNA-4359 vaccine. Like their COVID-19 vaccine, mRNA-4359 uses mRNA technology to help the immune system identify and eliminate cancer cells while preserving healthy tissue (Li et al., 2018).

Clinical studies have shown that it works well when combined with paclitaxel to treat NSCLC, providing a viable substitute for conventional cisplatin-based therapy plans. There has also been promise in combining radiation therapy with nanotechnology (Kumaravelu et al., 2025). Made of gadolinium-based polysiloxane, AGuIX nanoparticles function as radiosensitizers and MRI contrast agents. Their application in conjunction with stereotactic body radiation treatment (SBRT) for lung cancers is being investigated in clinical trials. According to preliminary findings, AGuIX improves radiation therapy efficacy while offering real-time imaging capabilities that enable accurate tumor targeting. Researchers have created antibody-functionalized nanoparticles in the field of immunotherapy to target particular proteins that are produced by lung cancers (Badrzadeh et al., 2016).

16.5.2 Personalized nanomedicine in lung cancer (genomic profiling + nanoparticle therapy)

Personalized therapy for lung cancer, especially NSCLC, has entered a new age thanks to the combination of precision oncology and nanotechnology. Researchers want to improve therapeutic efficacy, reduce systemic toxicity, and combat drug resistance by fusing genomic profiling with drug delivery methods based on nanoparticles (Hussain, 2015).

16.5.2.1 Genomic profiling and nanoparticle design

The detection of certain mutations and molecular abnormalities in patients with lung cancer has been made possible by developments in genomic sequencing (Lee et al., 2019). Targeted therapy selection is made easier by methods like enhanced performance integrated cancer sequencing (EPIC-Seq) and cancer personalized profiling by deep sequencing (CAPP-Seq), which enable the identification of circulating tumor DNA (ctDNA) and the categorization of NSCLC subtypes (Tiruneh et al., 2021).

16.5.2.2 mRNA-based nanovaccines

By creating mRNA-based nanovaccines, personalized nanomedicine has also extended into immunotherapy. Encapsulated in lipid nanoparticles, Moderna's mRNA-4157/V940 vaccine encodes neoantigens unique to each patient that were discovered through genetic profiling. When paired with immune checkpoint inhibitors, clinical trials have shown that it can generate strong immunological responses (Rabbani et al., 2025).

16.5.2.3 Polymer-based nanocarriers

Nanoparticles-based on polymers have been developed to deliver gene treatments and chemotherapeutic drugs simultaneously. Huang et al. (2022) created a dendritic polymer system coated with hyaluronic acid and loaded with YAP-siRNA and gefitinib (an EGFR-TKI) for targeted delivery to NSCLC cells that overexpress CD44. In vitro, this system showed increased cytotoxicity and apoptosis induction.

16.5.2.4 Clinical translation and trials

Numerous compositions of nanoparticles have advanced to clinical testing. Phase II trials for advanced NSCLC have shown promise for CRLX101, a cyclodextrin-based nanoparticle that delivers camptothecin. Likewise, in clinical settings, Genexol-PM, a polymeric micelle version of paclitaxel, has shown enhanced safety and effectiveness characteristics (Verma et al., 2024).

16.5.3 Combination nanotherapy

The treatment of lung cancer, especially NSCLC, has changed dramatically as a result of the application of nanotechnology in oncology. Nanoengineered platforms have made it possible to codeliver several therapeutic drugs, facilitating combination therapies that reduce systemic toxicity while simultaneously increasing anticancer activity. Combining chemotherapy, immunotherapy, radiation, and photodynamic treatment (PDT) in a single nanocarrier has shown promise in recent years, providing a multimodal strategy to address the variability and adaptability of lung cancers (Zhang et al., 2024).

16.5.3.1 Chemo-immunotherapy nanoplatforms

A promising method for boosting anticancer immune responses is the combination of immunotherapy and chemotherapy. By codelivering immune modulators and chemotherapeutic drugs, nanoparticles have been developed to increase tumor cells' immunogenicity and foster a strong immune response. By triggering apoptosis and altering the TME, hyaluronic acid-modified polydopamine nanoparticle coloaded with ursolic acid (UA) and astragaloside IV (AS-IV), for example, demonstrated a notable suppression of tumor growth and spread in NSCLC models (Singh et al., 2024).

16.5.3.2 Radio-chemotherapy nanoconstructs

Chemotherapy and radiation therapy have long been a mainstay of cancer treatment, but their effectiveness is limited by their concurrent toxicity. By facilitating the regulated release and targeted distribution of chemoradiotherapeutic drugs, nanotechnology provides an answer. Recent research has investigated the use of nanoparticles as radiosensitizers to deliver chemotherapeutic medications and improve the effectiveness of radiation therapy. For instance, the potential of GSH-protected gold nanoclusters to increase the therapeutic index by sensitizing tumor cells to radiation has been studied.

16.5.3.3 Photodynamic therapy integration

PDT uses particular light wavelengths to activate photosensitizers, which produce ROS that kill tumor cells. The transport and selectivity of photosensitizers have been enhanced through the use of nanoparticles. Furthermore, PDT has demonstrated synergistic benefits when combined with immunotherapy or chemotherapy on a single nanoplatform. Zhang et al. (2021) described the creation of self-adjuvanting photosensitizer nanoparticles that codeliver immune adjuvants and photosensitizers, leading to improved antitumor immunity and tumor regression.

16.6 Overcoming drug resistance using nanotechnology

One major obstacle to the successful treatment of lung cancer, especially NSCLC, is drug resistance. The overexpression of efflux pumps and the activity of intracellular enzymes are important factors among the many mechanisms causing this resistance. By improving drug delivery and altering resistance pathways, nanotechnology provides creative solutions to get around these obstacles (Ashrafi et al., 2022).

16.6.1 Targeting efflux pumps and intracellular enzymes

Chemotherapeutic drugs are actively transported out of cancer cells by efflux pumps, such as P-gp, MDR-associated proteins (MRPs), and breast cancer resistance protein (BCRP), which lowers intracellular drug concentrations and efficacy. Drug accumulation within tumor cells can be improved by engineering nanoparticles to block or avoid these pumps. For example, it has been shown that carbon nanotube-based nanodrugs can effectively inhibit tumors by avoiding efflux pathways in SCLC cells that are resistant to many drugs. These nanodrugs cause damage to the mitochondria, which depletes ATP and inhibits the efflux pump. Drug resistance may also be overcome by multifunctional nanoparticles functionalized with ATP-binding cassette (ABC) transporter inhibitors (Nakanishi et al., 2018). These nanoparticles improve medication retention and cytotoxicity in resistant cancer cells by codelivering efflux pump inhibitors and chemotherapeutic drugs. Intracellular enzymes that metabolize and inactivate chemotherapeutic drugs, such as GSH S-transferases and cytochrome P450s, contribute to drug resistance (Sun et al., 2023). Enzyme inhibitors can be delivered using nanocarriers in conjunction with anticancer medications, limiting drug degradation and improving therapeutic efficacy.

16.6.2 Nanocarriers for codelivery of small interfering RNA/microRNA and chemotherapeutics

One major barrier to the successful treatment of lung cancer, especially NSCLC, is drug resistance. Apoptosis evasion and changes in drug targets are two mechanisms that lead to chemotherapeutic drugs' decreased effectiveness (Parida et al., 2025). By enabling the codelivery of chemotherapeutic medications and gene-silencing molecules like small interfering RNA (siRNA) or miRNA, nanotechnology provides creative ways to get around these obstacles and improve therapeutic results (Mishra et al., 2024).

16.6.3 Heterogeneity and tumor plasticity

Significant intratumoral heterogeneity and cellular plasticity are hallmarks of lung cancer, especially NSCLC, and they play a key role in the development of treatment resistance. When different subpopulations of cancer cells with unique genetic, epigenetic, and phenotypic characteristics exist inside a single tumor, this is referred to as tumor heterogeneity (Sheng et al., 2018). Due to this variability, certain subclones can withstand therapeutic efforts, which cause the disease to progress and recur. The ability of cancer cells to dynamically change their phenotypes due to cellular plasticity, which includes processes like the epithelial-to-mesenchymal transition (EMT), makes treatment plans even more challenging. By making it possible to create multifunctional nanocarriers that can target several tumor subpopulations at once, nanotechnology provides creative solutions to these problems (Mir et al., 2022). To address the various processes driving drug resistance, these nanocarriers can be designed to transport combinations of chemical inhibitors, gene-silencing molecules (such as siRNA or miRNA), and chemotherapeutic drugs. Stimuli-responsive nanoparticles, for example, can improve the specificity and effectiveness of medication administration by releasing their payload in response to particular tumor microenvironmental cues (such as pH or redox potential) (Xiao et al., 2019).

16.7 Nanotechnology for early diagnosis and theranostics

Improving patient outcomes depends critically on the early detection and accurate characterization of lung cancer. For diagnostic and treatment planning, traditional imaging techniques, including CT, MRI, and PET, are essential. Nevertheless, the sensitivity, specificity, and resolution of these methods are constrained. By creating specific nanoparticles, nanotechnology improves the capabilities of existing imaging modalities and provides creative solutions (Waerzeggers et al., 2012).

16.7.1 Nanoparticles for computed tomography/magnetic resonance imaging/positron emission tomography enhancement

CT imaging creates contrast between tissues by using variations in X-ray attenuation. Among the drawbacks of conventional iodinated contrast agents are their quick elimination and possible nephrotoxicity (Chenchula et al., 2026). Because of their superior X-ray attenuation properties, nanoparticles, especially those made of high atomic number elements like gold, bismuth, and tantalum, have been investigated as substitute contrast agents. MRI has a low sensitivity yet provides good soft tissue contrast without ionizing radiation (Liu et al., 2020). As contrast agents, nanoparticles can improve MRI signals. Among the most researched for this purpose are gadolinium-based nanoparticles and superparamagnetic iron oxide nanoparticles (SPIONs). The use of magnetic resonance-guided focused ultrasonic surgery (MRgFUS) in noninvasive cancer treatment has been restricted by the insensitivity of MRI and the low efficiency of ultrasound energy deposition (Mishra et al., 2025). Targeting EGFR-overexpressing lung cancer and surface-modified with anti-EGFR antibodies, PEG SPIO nanoparticles not only improve MRI contrast at the tumor site but also greatly increase the efficiency of ultrasound energy deposition, which aids in the development of MRgFUS (Forte et al., 2019). The specificity of MRI in identifying lung cancer lesions can be increased by engineering these nanoparticles to target particular tumor markers. Through the detection of radiolabeled tracers, PET imaging offers functional information. To act as PET tracers, nanoparticles can be labeled with positron-emitting isotopes like ^{18}F, ^{6}4Cu, or ^{68}Ga. By targeting particular molecular processes linked to lung cancer, these radiolabeled nanoparticles can improve the sensitivity and specificity of PET imaging (Liu et al., 2024).

Theranostics, the combination of medicinal and diagnostic properties into a single nanoparticle platform, has drawn a lot of interest. Multimodal nanoparticles can improve CT, MRI, and PET imaging all at once, giving detailed anatomical and functional data. The creation of multimodal, targeted nanoparticles has the potential to improve patient outcomes and management by enabling early diagnosis and accurate characterization of lung cancer. For these nanotechnological advancements to reach their full potential in oncological diagnostics and theranostics, more study and clinical application are required.

16.7.2 Nanosensors for liquid biopsy and circulating tumor DNA detection

They can detect volatile organic molecules in lung cancer biomarkers when combined with solid-phase microextraction, gas chromatography, or mass spectrometry. This could make them a low-cost, noninvasive lung cancer diagnostic method. Because of their remarkable catalytic activity, nanomaterials like Ni-OTC NPs and PdCuB MNs have greatly increased the sensitivity of biosensors in identifying low-abundance biomarkers like PD-L1 exosomes and EGFR exon 21 mutations. These nanomaterials have also improved the sensors' electron transfer efficiency through electropolymerization and functional modification, resulting in a quick response. With their unique chemical and physical characteristics, nanocomposite materials such as rGO/f-OMC and NG-THI-AuNPs give the sensors great selectivity while successfully lowering the possibility of cross-reactivity and false positives. Giving lung cancer patients more accurate diagnostic tools, this helps to improve the speed and accuracy. As evidenced by the electrochemical gene biosensors' 21-day stability, the addition of nanomaterials not only improves the stability and durability of biosensors but also lowers the detection limit to 120 nm due to their large surface area and surface effects, increasing detection sensitivity (Guo et al., 2016).

16.8 Future perspectives and innovations

The field of nanoengineered drug delivery systems for lung cancer is changing due to emerging technologies that promise improved safety, efficacy, and precision. To speed up nanoparticle design and optimize formulation parameters, artificial intelligence (AI) and machine learning (ML) have emerged as indispensable technologies (Rabbani et al., 2025). AI/ML systems can anticipate nanoparticle behavior, toxicity, and therapeutic effects by combining large datasets from physicochemical features and biological reactions (Rakaee et al., 2025). This reduces trial-and-error testing and speeds up translational workflows.

A new era in lung cancer treatment is being ushered in by the combination of nanotechnology and genome editing techniques like CRISPR-Cas9. Targeted gene editing within tumor cells is made possible by nanocarriers designed for the accurate delivery of CRISPR components, which may provide treatments for genetically driven lung malignancies with few side effects. By simulating patient-specific tumor biology and medication response, these methods enable customized nano-formulation testing, enabling customized treatment plans that optimize efficacy while reducing toxicity (Rabbani et al., 2025). The combination of genome editing nanodelivery, AI/ML, sophisticated preclinical models, and customized platforms puts nanoengineered medicine at the forefront of lung cancer treatment (Aryal et al., 2023). With accurate, efficient, and adaptable treatments, these breakthroughs have the potential to revolutionize patient care. Transforming these innovative technologies into clinical realities will require sustained interdisciplinary cooperation and thorough validation, which will ultimately improve lung cancer patients' quality of life and survival rates. Ongoing and completed clinical trials involving nab-paclitaxel-based regimens in lung cancer are demonstrated in Table 16.2 .

Table 16.2: Ongoing and completed clinical trials involving nab-paclitaxel-based regimens in lung cancer.

Trial id	Phase	Start date	Status	Cancer type (N)	Intervention/ combination	Primary endpoint(s)	Secondary endpoints
UMIN000030994	II	Feb 2018	Completed	NSCLC (~30)	PD-(L)1 inhibitors + nab-paclitaxel	ORR (55.2%)	–
UMIN000014764	I	Mar 2019	Completed	NSCLC (~19)	Nab-paclitaxel + carboplatin + thoracic radiotherapy	FDLT, TCR (100%)	–
NCT04338620	II	Apr 2020	Completed	NSCLC (~94)	Camrelizumab + nab-paclitaxel + platinum (vs. control)	pCR	–
ChiCTR2300068627	II	Nov 2022	Unknown	SCLC	Nab-paclitaxel + anlotinib	PFS	OS, DCR, ORR, and safety
ChiCTR2300072520	IV	Jun 2023	Recruiting	SCLC	Adbelimab + apatinib + nab-paclitaxel	1-yr OS rate	ORR, PFS, OS, and duration of therapy
ChiCTR2300077241	II	Nov 2023	Recruiting	Lung cancer	Cadonilimab + nab-paclitaxel + platinum chemotherapy	6-month PFS	OS, 1-year OS, ORR, QOL, and AEs
ChiCTR2300077236	II	Nov 2023	Recruiting	Lung cancer	Envafolimab + Nab-Paclitaxel + platinum chemotherapy	6-month PFS	ORR, OS, QOL, and AEs
ChiCTR2300078968	IV	Nov 2023	Recruiting	SCLC	Group A: Ateolimab + apatinib + nab-paclitaxel (plus arms B & C)	ORR	OS, DCR, DOR, AEs, tumor markers, and QOL

(continued on next page)

Table 16.2: Ongoing and completed clinical trials involving nab-paclitaxel-based regimens in lung cancer—cont'd

Trial id	Phase	Start date	Status	Cancer type (N)	Intervention/ combination	Primary endpoint(s)	Secondary endpoints
ChiCTR2400082754	II	Apr 2024	Recruiting	NSCLC	Atezolizumab + Nab-Paclitaxel + platinum chemotherapy	Pathologic complete response	R0 rate, EFS, OS, ORR, and safety
ChiCTR2400083693	II	Mar 2024	Recruiting	SCLC	Irinotecan liposome (± platinum or famitinib)	PFS	ORR, OS, DCR, and safety
Nab-paclitaxel-based lung cancer trials							
CRB7180005	II	Apr 2022	Recruiting	TTF-1 neg, advanced NSCLC	Atezolizumab + carboplatin + nab-paclitaxel	PFS	OS, DOR, TTF, and safety
CRB4180010	II	Jun 2021	Recruiting	NSCLC	Atezolizumab + carboplatin + nab-paclitaxel	ORR	OS, safety, tolerability, and PFS
jRCTs071200102	II	Feb 2021	Recruiting	Advanced NSCLC (renal dys-function)	Atezolizumab + carboplatin + nab-paclitaxel	RR	PFS, OS, DOR, TTF, and safety
jRCTs041180110	III	Mar 2019	Recruiting	Elderly advanced squamous NSCLC	Docetaxel vs. carboplatin + nab-paclitaxel	OS	PFS, RR, toxicity,and QOL
jRCTs042180077	I	Nov 2019	Recruiting	Unresectable NSCLC	CBDCA + nab-paclitaxel	DLT, treatment completion	Safety, RR, and OS
jRCTs071180037	III	Nov 2019	Recruiting	NSCLC	Nab-paclitaxel vs. DTX	OS	PFS, RR, and QOL
jRCTs031180214	II	Mar 2019	Recruiting	Advanced NSCLC	Nab-paclitaxel (100 vs. 70 mg/m^2)	PFS	OS, AEs, and ORR

(continued on next page)

ChiCTR2400085724	I	Jun 2024	Registered	NSCLC	Carboplatin + nab-paclitaxel	PFS	ORR, OS, iORR, and iPFS
NCT04826913	–	Feb 2021	Unknown	NSCLC	Organoid testing of anticancer drugs	Drug response evaluation	–
NCT03967652	–	Mar 2019	Unknown	Cancer (Dx)	Nanomaterial-based diagnostic sensor	Diagnostic database development	Gene-breath link profiling
Nab-paclitaxel trials in combination and perioperative settings							
Trial id	Phase	Start date	Status	Cancer type (N)	Intervention/ combination	Primary endpoint(s)	Secondary endpoints
NCT06421298	II	May 2024	Recruiting	Lung cancer (~30)	Nab-paclitaxel + sintilimab + gemcitabine + docetaxel	PFS	ORR, OS, DOR, and AEs
NCT06357598	III	Jan 2024	Recruiting	NSCLC (~30)	Surgery + platinum-based chemo + tislelizumab	R0 resection rate	MPR, PFS, resectability, and safety
NCT06299371	II	Apr 2024	Not recruiting	NSCLC	Adebrelimab + platinum + nab-paclitaxel	pCR	MPR, R0, EFS, and AEs
CTR20231113	III	–	Not recruiting	Metastatic NSCLC	Multiple chemo + immunotherapy combinations	ORR	PFS, OS, DOR, and AEs
NCT05766800	II	Mar 2023	Recruiting	Locally advanced NSCLC (~100)	Serplulimab-based multimodal treatment	EFS	ORR, DFS, OS, R0, and QOL
NCT05407155	–	Jun 2022	Not recruiting	Metastatic NSCLC	Bevacizumab + nab-paclitaxel + platinum	ORR	PFS and OS

(continued on next page)

Table 16.2: Ongoing and completed clinical trials involving nab-paclitaxel-based regimens in lung cancer—cont'd

Trial id	Phase	Start date	Status	Cancer type (N)	Intervention/ combination	Primary endpoint(s)	Secondary endpoints
NCT04865250	II	Jan 2021	Recruiting	Stage II-IIIB NSCLC (~20)	Atezolizumab + carboplatin + nab-paclitaxel	MPR	EFS and OS
NCT04213937	II	Jan 2020	Unknown	Extensive SCLC (~386)	Nab-paclitaxel vs. topotecan	OS	ORR and AEs
NCT04056949	II	Aug 2019	Unknown	Extensive SCLC (~30)	IBI308 + nab-paclitaxel	PFS	OS, ORR, and DOR
NCT04541251	II	Aug 2020	Unknown	NSCLC (~27)	Camrelizumab + nab-paclitaxel + carboplatin	MPR	pCR, R0, DFS, OS, AEs, and SAEs
NCT04015778	II	Aug 2019	Unknown	NSCLC (~48)	Nivolumab (± platinum + nab-paclitaxel)	MPR	AEs and resection delay

16.9 Conclusion

The incorporation of nanotechnology into medication delivery systems has revolutionized the treatment of lung cancer in recent decades. Clinical results are frequently jeopardized by traditional medicines' poor absorption, systemic toxicity, and inadequate specificity. By providing targeted, regulated, and multipurpose drug delivery platforms that maximize therapeutic efficacy while reducing side effects, the development of nanoengineered therapies has overcome these constraints. Improved pharmacokinetics and biodistribution are provided by nanocarriers like liposomes, polymeric nanoparticles, and inorganic nanostructures, which use phenomena like the EPR effect to preferentially accumulate in tumor tissues.

The management of lung cancer has undergone a dramatic paradigm change with the switch from traditional drug delivery to nanoengineered therapies. Nanoformulations have revolutionized therapeutic approaches by combining controlled release, multifunctionality, and targeted delivery, leading to better patient outcomes and the development of customized medicine. Nanomedicine's position as a key component of lung cancer treatment will be further cemented by ongoing research aimed at reducing toxicity, improving clinical translation, and overcoming tumor heterogeneity.

AI disclosure

During the preparation of this work, the author(s) used Open AI Chatgpt in order to Chatgpt by OpenAI were used to assist with language enhancement and grammar correction during the preparation of this chapter. After using this tool/service, the author(s) reviewed and edited the content as needed and take(s) full responsibility for the content of the publication.

References

Agnihotri, T. G., Gomte, S. S., & Jain, A. (2022). Emerging theranostics to combat cancer: A perspective on metal-based nanomaterials. *Drug Development and Industrial Pharmacy, 48*(11), 585–601. doi:10.1080/03639045.2022.2153862.

Alexandru, I., Davidescu, L., Cătălin Motofelea, A., Ciocarlie, T., Motofelea, N., Costachescu, D., Marc, M. S, Suppini, N., Simona Șovrea, A., Coșeriu, R.-L., Bondor, D.-A., Bobeică, L.-G., & Crintea, A. (2024). Emerging nanomedicine approaches in targeted lung cancer treatment. *International Journal of Molecular Sciences, 25*(20), 11235. doi:10.3390/ijms252011235.

Alinejad, T., Modarressi, S., Sadri, Z., Hao, Z., & Chen, C. S. (2023). Diagnostic applications and therapeutic option of Cascade CRISPR/Cas in the modulation of miRNA in diverse cancers: Promises and obstacles. *Journal of Cancer Research and Clinical Oncology, 149*(12), 9557–9575. doi:10.1007/s00432-023-04747-6.

Alshammari, M. K., Almomen, E. Y., Alshahrani, K. F., Altwalah, S. F., Kamal, M., Al-Twallah, M. F., Al-sanad, S. H., Al-Batti, M. H., Al-Rasheed, F. J., Alsalamah, A. Y., Alhazza, M. B., Alasmari, F. A., & Abida, M. I. (2023). Nano-enabled strategies for the treatment of lung cancer: Potential bottlenecks and future perspectives. *Biomedicines, 11*(2). doi:10.3390/biomedicines11020473.

Ansa-Addo, E. A., Stratton, D., Jorfi, S., Kholia, S., Krige, L., Lange, S., & Inal, J. (2012). Isolation of microvesicles and exosomes by filtration and estimation of normal reference range in blood plasma. *International society for extracellular vesicles 1st annual meeting: ISEV meeting*.

Arandhara, A., Bhuyan, P., & Das, B. K. (2025). Exploring lung cancer microenvironment: Pathways and nanoparticle-based therapies. *Discover Oncology, 16*(1). doi:10.1007/s12672-025-01902-y.

Aryal, S., Park, S., Park, H., Park, C., Kim, W. C, Thakur, D., Won, Y.-J., & Key, J. (2023). Clinical trials for oral, inhaled and intravenous drug delivery system for lung cancer and emerging nanomedicine-based approaches. *International Journal of Nanomedicine, 18*, 7865–7888. doi:10.2147/ijn.s432839.

Ashique, S., Garg, A., Mishra, N., Raina, N., Ming, L. C., Tulli, H. S., Behl, T., Rani, R., & Gupta, M. (2023). Nano-mediated strategy for targeting and treatment of non-small cell lung cancer (NSCLC). *Naunyn-Schmiedeberg's Archives of Pharmacology, 396*(11), 2769–2792. doi:10.1007/s00210-023-02522-5.

Ashrafi, A., Akter, Z., Modareszadeh, P., Modareszadeh, P., Berisha, E., Alemi, P. S., Chacon Castro, M. D. C., Deese, A. R., & Zhang, L. (2022). Current landscape of therapeutic resistance in lung cancer and promising strategies to overcome resistance. *Cancers, 14*(19). doi:10.3390/cancers14194562.

Attia, M. F., Anton, N., Wallyn, J., Omran, Z., & Vandamme, T. F. (2019). An overview of active and passive targeting strategies to improve the nanocarriers efficiency to tumour sites. *Journal of Pharmacy and Pharmacology, 71*(8), 1185–1198. doi:10.1111/jphp.13098.

Babu, A., Templeton, A. K., Munshi, A., Ramesh, R., & Chen, H. (2013). Nanoparticle-based drug delivery for therapy of lung cancer: Progress and challenges. *Journal of Nanomaterials, 2013*(1). doi:10.1155/2013/863951.

Badrzadeh, F., Rahmati-Yamchi, M., Badrzadeh, K., Valizadeh, A., Zarghami, N., Farkhani, S. M., & Akbarzadeh, A. (2016). Drug delivery and nanodetection in lung cancer. Artificial Cells. *Nanomedicine and Biotechnology, 44*(2), 618–634. doi:10.3109/21691401.2014.975237.

Baig, M. M. F. A., Chien, W. T., & Chair, S. Y. (2025). Nanotechnological approaches for the targeted delivery of CRISPR-Cas systems for genomic modifications, biomolecular sensing, and precision medicine. *Biomaterials Science, 13*(17), 4597–4638. doi:10.1039/d5bm00711a.

Banik, B. L., Fattahi, P., & Brown, J. L. (2016). Polymeric nanoparticles: The future of nanomedicine. *Wiley Interdisciplinary Reviews: Nanomedicine and Nanobiotechnology, 8*(2), 271–299. doi:10.1002/wnan.1364.

Begines, B., Ortiz, T., Pérez-Aranda, M., Martínez, G., Merinero, M., Argüelles-Arias, F., & Alcudia, A. (2020). Polymeric nanoparticles for drug delivery: Recent developments and future prospects. *Nanomaterials, 10*(7), 1403. doi:10.3390/nano10071403.

Bhatia, S. (2016). Nanoparticles types, classification, characterization, fabrication methods and drug delivery applications. In *Natural polymer drug delivery systems: Nanoparticles, plants, and algae* (pp. 33–93). Springer International Publishing.

Carrasco-Esteban, D.-R., Barrionuevo-Castillo, P.-M., Leaman, S.-G., & López-Campos, F. (2021). Current role of nanoparticles in the treatment of lung cancer. *Journal of Clinical and Translational Research, 7*(2).

Chen, J., Yang, X., Huang, L., Lai, H., Gan, C., & Luo, X. (2018). Development of dual-drug-loaded stealth nanocarriers for targeted and synergistic anti-lung cancer efficacy. *Drug Delivery, 25*(1), 1932–1942. doi:10.1080/10717544.2018.1477856.

Chen, P, Liu, Y, Wen, Y, & Zhou, C (2022). Non-small cell lung cancer in China. *Cancer Commun, 42*, 937–970. https://doi.org/10.1002/cac2.12359.

Chen, S., Hao, X., Liang, X., Zhang, Q., Zhang, C., Zhou, G., Shen, S., Jia, G., & Zhang, J. (2016). Inorganic nanomaterials as carriers for drug delivery. *Journal of Biomedical Nanotechnology, 12*(1), 1–27. doi:10.1166/jbn.2016.2122.

Chenchula, S., Sharma, S. S. K., Aditya, C., Ghanta, M. K., & Chavan, M. (2026). Theranostics in lung cancer. In K. Anitha, S. Bhatt, & S. Chenchula (Eds.), *Theranostics in cancer management* (pp. 111–132). Academic Press.

Cheng, T. Y. D., Cramb, S. M., Baade, P. D., Youlden, D. R., Nwogu, C., & Reid, M. E. (2016). The international epidemiology of lung cancer: Latest trends, disparities, and tumor characteristics. *Journal of Thoracic Oncology, 11*(10), 1653–1671. doi:10.1016/j.jtho.2016.05.021.

Crintea, A., Constantin, A. M., Motofelea, A. C., Crivii, C. B., Velescu, M. A., Coşeriu, R. L., Ilyés, T., Crăciun, A. M., & Silaghi, C. N. (2023). Targeted EGFR nanotherapy in non-small cell lung cancer. *Journal of Functional Biomaterials., 14*(9). doi:10.3390/jfb14090466.

Desai, N., Rana, D., Patel, M., Bajwa, N., Prasad, R., & Vora, L. K. (2025). Nanoparticle therapeutics in clinical perspective: Classification, marketed products, and regulatory landscape. *Small, 21*(29). doi:10.1002/smll.202502315.

Desai, N., Tambe, V., Pofali, P., & Vora, L. K. (2024). Cell membrane-coated nanoparticles: A new frontier in immunomodulation. *Advanced NanoBiomed Research, 4*(8). doi:10.1002/anbr.202400012.

Doppalapudi, S., Jain, A., Domb, A. J., & Khan, W. (2016). Biodegradable polymers for targeted delivery of anti-cancer drugs. *Expert Opinion on Drug Delivery, 13*(6), 891–909. doi:10.1517/17425247.2016.1156671.

Dostalova, S., Vasickova, K., Hynek, D., Krizkova, S., Richtera, L., Vaculovicova, M., Eckschlager, T., Stiborova, M., Heger, Z., & Adam, V. (2017). Apoferritin as an ubiquitous nanocarrier with excellent shelf life. *International Journal of Nanomedicine, 12*, 2265–2278. doi:10.2147/ijn.s130267.

Essa, M. L, El-Kemary, M. A, Saied, E. ME., Leporatti, S., & Nemany Hanafy, N. A. (2020). Nano targeted therapies made of lipids and polymers have promising strategy for the treatment of lung cancer. *Materials, 13*(23), 5397. doi:10.3390/ma13235397.

Ezhilarasan, D., Lakshmi, T., & Mallineni, S. K. (2022). Nano-based targeted drug delivery for lung cancer: Therapeutic avenues and challenges. *Nanomedicine, 17*(24), 1855–1869. doi:10.2217/nnm-2021-0364.

Feng, J., Zhang, P., Wang, D., Li, Y., & Tan, J. (2024). New strategies for lung cancer diagnosis and treatment: Applications and advances in nanotechnology. *Biomarker Research, 12*(1). doi:10.1186/s40364-024-00686-7.

Forte, E., Fiorenza, D., Torino, E., Di Polidoro, A. C., Cavaliere, C., Netti, P. A., Salvatore, M., & Aiello, M. (2020). Radiolabeled PET/MRI nanoparticles for tumor imaging. *Journal of Clinical Medicine, 9*(1). doi:10.3390/jcm9010089.

Gao, Y., Gao, D., Shen, J., & Wang, Q. (2020). A review of mesoporous silica nanoparticle delivery systems in chemo-based combination cancer therapies. *Frontiers in Chemistry, 8*. doi:10.3389/fchem.2020.598722.

Garbuzenko, O. B., Kuzmov, A., Taratula, O., Pine, S. R., & Minko, T. (2019). Strategy to enhance lung cancer treatment by five essential elements: Inhalation delivery, nanotechnology, tumor-receptor targeting, chemo- and gene therapy. *Theranostics, 9*(26), 8362–8376. doi:10.7150/thno.39816.

Gonsalves, A., Sorkhdini, P., Bazinet, J., Ghumman, M., Dhamecha, D., Zhou, Y., & Menon, J. U. (2023). Development and characterization of lung surfactant-coated polymer nanoparticles for pulmonary drug delivery. *Biomaterials Advances, 150*, 213430. doi:10.1016/j.bioadv.2023.213430.

Guinart, A., Perry, H. L., Wilton-Ely, J. D. E. T., & Tetley, T. D. (2021). Gold nanomaterials in the management of lung cancer. *Emerging Topics in Life Sciences, 4*(6), 627–643. doi:10.1042/ETLS20200332.

Guo, N., Lou, F., Ma, Y., Li, J., Yang, B., Chen, W., Ye, H., Zhang, J.-B., Zhao, M.-Y., Wu, W.-J., Shi, R., Jones, L., Chen, K. S., Huang, X. F., Chen, S.-Y., & Liu, Y. (2016). Circulating tumor DNA detection in lung cancer patients before and after surgery. *Scientific Reports, 6*(1). doi:10.1038/srep33519.

Gupta, C., Jaipuria, A., & Gupta, N. (2023). Inhalable formulations to treat non-small cell lung cancer (NSCLC): Recent therapies and developments. *Pharmaceutics, 15*(1), 139. doi:10.3390/pharmaceutics15010139.

Haider, M., Elsherbeny, A., Pittalà, V., Consoli, V., Ali Alghamdi, M., Hussain, Z., Khoder, G., & Greish, K. (2022). Nanomedicine strategies for management of drug resistance in lung cancer. *International Journal of Molecular Sciences, 23*(3), 1853. doi:10.3390/ijms23031853.

Hajiaghapour Asr, M., Dayani, F., Segherloo, F. S., Kamedi, A., Neill, A. O., MacLoughlin, R., & Doroudian, M. (2023). Lipid nanoparticles as promising carriers for mRNA vaccines for viral lung infections. *Pharmaceutics, 15*(4), 1127. doi:10.3390/pharmaceutics15041127.

Han, X., Gong, C., Yang, Q., Zheng, K., Wang, Z., & Zhang, W. (2024). Biomimetic nano-drug delivery system: An emerging platform for promoting tumor treatment. *International Journal of Nanomedicine, 19*, 571–608. doi:10.2147/ijn.s442877.

Hani, U., Yasmin Begum, M., Wahab, S., Siddiqua, A., Osmani, R. A. M., & Rahamathulla, M. (2022). A comprehensive review of current perspectives on novel drug delivery systems and approaches for lung cancer management. *Journal of Pharmaceutical Innovation, 17*(4), 1530–1553. doi:10.1007/s12247-021-09582-1.

Hheidari, A., Mohammadi, J., Ghodousi, M., Mahmoodi, M., Ebrahimi, S., Pishbin, E., & Rahdar, A. (2024). Metal-based nanoparticle in cancer treatment: Lessons learned and challenges. *Frontiers in Bioengineering and Biotechnology, 12*. doi:10.3389/fbioe.2024.1436297.

Hussain, S. (2015). Nanomedicine for treatment of lung cancer. In A. Ahmad, & S. M. Gadgeel (Eds.), *Lung cancer and personalized medicine: Novel therapies and clinical management* (pp. 137–147). Springer.

Huang, L., Liao, Z., Liu, Z., Chen, Y., Huang, T., & Xiao, H. (2022). Application and prospect of CRISPR/Cas9 technology in reversing drug resistance of non-small cell lung cancer. *Frontiers in Pharmacology, 13*. doi:10.3389/fphar.2022.900825.

Huynh, N. T., Roger, E., Lautram, N., Benoît, J. P., & Passirani, C. (2010). The rise and rise of stealth nanocarriers for cancer therapy: Passive versus active targeting. *Nanomedicine, 5*(9), 1415–1433. doi:10.2217/nnm.10.113.

Jawahar, N., & Meyyanathan, S. N. (2012). Polymeric nanoparticles for drug delivery and targeting: A comprehensive review. *International Journal of Health & Allied Sciences, 1*(4), 217. doi:10.4103/2278-344X.107832.

Jorgenson, T. C., Zhong, W., & Oberley, T. D. (2013). Redox imbalance and biochemical changes in cancer. *Cancer Research, 73*(20), 6118–6123. doi:10.1158/0008-5472.CAN-13-1117.

Kapoor, D. U., Gandhi, S. M., Swarn, S., Lal, B., Prajapati, B. G., Khondee, S., Mangmool, S., Singh, S., & Chittasupho, C. (2025). Polymeric nanoparticles for targeted lung cancer treatment: Review and perspectives. *Pharmaceutics, 17*(9). doi:10.3390/pharmaceutics17091091.

Kiely, B. E., Alam, M., Blinman, P., Tattersall, M. H. N., & Stockler, M. R. (2012). Estimating typical, best-case and worst-case life expectancy scenarios for patients starting chemotherapy for advanced non-small-cell lung cancer: A systematic review of contemporary randomized trials. *Lung Cancer, 77*(3), 537–544. doi:10.1016/j.lungcan.2012.04.017.

Kumaravelu, P., Shanmugam, R., & Jayakodi, S. (2025). Advances in nanoparticle-based mechanisms and therapeutic applications for lung cancer. *BioNanoScience, 15*(3). doi:10.1007/s12668-025-02132-w.

Lee, A. Y., Cho, M. H., & Kim, S. (2019). Recent advances in aerosol gene delivery systems using non-viral vectors for lung cancer therapy. *Expert Opinion on Drug Delivery, 16*(7), 757–772. doi:10.1080/17425247.2019.1641083.

Lee, H., Rho, W. Y., Kim, Y. H., Chang, H., & Jun, B. H. (2025). CRISPR-Cas9 gene therapy: Non-viral delivery and stimuli-responsive nanoformulations. *Molecules, 30*(3). doi:10.3390/molecules30030542.

Li, M. Y., Liu, L. Z., & Dong, M. (2021). Progress on pivotal role and application of exosome in lung cancer carcinogenesis, diagnosis, therapy and prognosis. *Molecular Cancer, 20*(1). doi:10.1186/s12943-021-01312-y.

Li, Q., Zhou, T., Wu, F., Li, N., Wang, R., Zhao, Q., Ma, Y. M., Zhang, J. Q., & Ma, B. L. (2018). Subcellular drug distribution: Mechanisms and roles in drug efficacy, toxicity, resistance, and targeted delivery. *Drug Metabolism Reviews, 50*(4), 430–447. doi:10.1080/03602532.2018.1512614.

Li, W., Liu, J. B., Hou, L. K., Yu, F., Zhang, J., Wu, W., Tang, X. M., Sun, F., Lu, H. M., Deng, J., Bai, J., Li, J., Wu, C. Y., Lin, Q. L., Lv, Z. W., Wang, G. R., Jiang, G. X., Ma, Y. S., & Fu, D. (2022). Liquid biopsy in lung cancer: Significance in diagnostics, prediction, and treatment monitoring. *Molecular Cancer, 21*(1). doi:10.1186/s12943-022-01505-z.

Linton, S. S., Sherwood, S. G., Drews, K. C., & Kester, M. (2016). Targeting cancer cells in the tumor microenvironment: Opportunities and challenges in combinatorial nanomedicine. *Wiley Interdisciplinary Reviews: Nanomedicine and Nanobiotechnology, 8*(2), 208–222. doi:10.1002/wnan.1358.

Liu, H., Wang, R., Gao, H., Chen, L., Li, X., Yu, X., Wu, Y., Bai, Y., Wei, W., & Wang, M. (2024). Nanoprobes for PET/MR imaging. *Advanced Therapeutics., 7*(2). doi:10.1002/adtp.202300232.

Liu, M., Anderson, R. C., Lan, X., Conti, P. S., & Chen, K. (2020). Recent advances in the development of nanoparticles for multimodality imaging and therapy of cancer. *Medicinal Research Reviews, 40*(3), 909–930. doi:10.1002/med.21642.

Majumder, J., & Minko, T. (2021). Multifunctional lipid-based nanoparticles for codelivery of anticancer drugs and siRNA for treatment of non-small cell lung cancer with different level of resistance and EGFR mutations. *Pharmaceutics, 13*(7), 1063. doi:10.3390/pharmaceutics13071063.

Mendes, B. B., Sousa, D. P., Conniot, J., & Conde, J. (2021). Nanomedicine-based strategies to target and modulate the tumor microenvironment. *Trends in Cancer, 7*(9), 847–862. doi:10.1016/j.trecan.2021.05.001.

Mir, S. A., Hamid, L., Bader, G. N., Shoaib, A., Rahamathulla, M., Alshahrani, M. Y., Alam, P., & Shakeel, F. (2022). Role of nanotechnology in overcoming the multidrug resistance in cancer therapy: A review. *Molecules, 27*(19). doi:10.3390/molecules27196608.

Mishra, L., Kumari, L., Sharma, Y., Chahar, K., Kumar, M., Patel, P., Gupta, G. D., & Kurmi, B. D. (2024). Recent nanotechnological aspects and molecular targeting strategies for lung cancer therapy. *Journal of Nanoparticle Research, 26*(5). doi:10.1007/s11051-024-06008-0.

Mishra, V., Kumari, N., Vyas, M., Aljabali, A. A. A., Chattaraj, A., & Mishra, Y. (2025). Advances in multimodal imaging techniques in nanomedicine: Enhancing drug delivery precision. *RSC Advances, 15*(33), 27187–27209. doi:10.1039/d5ra03255e.

Muthukrishnan, S., Anand, A. V., Palanisamy, K., Gunasangkaran, G., Ravi, A. K., & Balasubramanian, B. (2022). *Novel organic and inorganic nanoparticles as a targeted drug delivery vehicle in cancer treatment nanotechnology in the life sciences* (pp. 117–161). Springer Science and Business Media B.V. doi:10.1007/978-3-030-80371-1_4.

Nakanishi, T., Menju, T., Nishikawa, S., Takahashi, K., Miyata, R., Shikuma, K., Sowa, T., Imamura, N., Hamaji, M., Motoyama, H., Hijiya, K., Aoyama, A., Sato, T., Chen-Yoshikawa, T. F., Sonobe, M., & Date, H. (2018). The synergistic role of ATP -dependent drug efflux pump and focal adhesion signaling pathways in vinorelbine resistance in lung cancer. *Cancer Medicine, 7*(2), 408–419. doi:10.1002/cam4.1282.

Ning, J., Ge, T., Jiang, M., Jia, K., Wang, L., Li, W., Chen, B., Liu, Y., Wang, H., Zhao, S., & He, Y. (2021). Early diagnosis of lung cancer: Which is the optimal choice? *Aging, 13*(4), 6214–6227. doi:10.18632/aging.202504.

Ouyang, R., Wu, S., Zhang, B., Wang, T., Yin, B., Huang, J., Wei, W., Huang, M., Zhang, M., Wang, Y., Wang, F., & Hou, H. (2021). Clinical value of tumor-associated antigens and autoantibody panel combination detection in the early diagnostic of lung cancer. *Cancer Biomarkers, 32*(3), 401–409. doi:10.3233/cbm-210099.

Padinharayil, H., Varghese, J., John, M. C., Rajanikant, G. K., Wilson, C. M., Al-Yozbaki, M., Renu, K., Dewanjee, S., Sanyal, R., Dey, A., Mukherjee, A. G., Wanjari, U. R., Gopalakrishnan, A. V., & George, A. (2023). Non-small cell lung carcinoma (NSCLC): Implications on molecular pathology and advances in early diagnostics and therapeutics. *Genes and Diseases, 10*(3), 960–989. doi:10.1016/j.gendis.2022.07.023.

Parida, R. C., Thamizhanban, D., Lakshmi, K., & Jena, G. K. (2025). Polymeric nano-carrier based drug delivery: The recent development and their applications on colon, breast, and lung cancer. *Biomedical Materials and Devices*. doi:10.1007/s44174-025-00415-0.

Parker, J. P., Ude, Z., & Marmion, C. J. (2016). Exploiting developments in nanotechnology for the preferential delivery of platinum-based anti-cancer agents to tumours: Targeting some of the hallmarks of cancer. *Metallomics, 8*(1), 43–60. doi:10.1039/c5mt00181a.

Patil, N. H., & Devarajan, P. V. (2016). Insulin-loaded alginic acid nanoparticles for sublingual delivery. *Drug delivery, 23*(2), 429–436. https://doi.org/10.3109/10717544.2014.916769.

Peng, Q., Li, H., Deng, Q., Liang, L. U, Wang, F., Lin, Y., Yang, L., Zhang, Y., Yu, X., & Zhang, L. (2021). Hybrid artificial cell-mediated epigenetic inhibition in metastatic lung cancer. *Journal of Colloid and Interface Science, 603*, 319–332. doi:10.1016/j.jcis.2021.06.066.

Peng, S., Xiao, F., Chen, M., & Gao, H. (2022). Tumor-microenvironment-responsive nanomedicine for enhanced cancer immunotherapy. *Advanced Science, 9*(1). doi:10.1002/advs.202103836.

Rabbani, S., El-Tanani, M., Sharma, S., El-Tanani, Y., Kumar, R., Saini, M., … Parvez, S. (2025). RNA-Based Therapies for Neurodegenerative Diseases Targeting Pathogenic Proteins. *Eur J Neurosci, 61*, e70110. https://doi.org/10.1111/ejn.70110.

Rabbani, S. A., El-Tanani, M., El-Tanani, Y., Kumar, R., Sharma, S., Khan, M. A., … Rizzo, M. (2025). Advances in Adoptive Cell Therapies in Cancer: From Mechanistic Breakthroughs to Clinical Frontiers and Overcoming Barriers. *Medical sciences (Basel, Switzerland), 13*(3), 190. https://doi.org/10.3390/medsci13030190.

Rabbani, SA, El-Tanani, M, Sharma, S, Rabbani, SS, El-Tanani, Y, Kumar, R, & Saini, M (2025). Generative Artificial Intelligence in Healthcare: Applications, Implementation Challenges, and Future Directions. *BioMedInformatics, 5*(3), 37. https://doi.org/10.3390/biomedinformatics5030037.

Rakaee, M., Tafavvoghi, M., Ricciuti, B., Alessi, J. V., Cortellini, A., Citarella, F., Nibid, L., Perrone, G., Adib, E., Fulgenzi, C. A. M., Hidalgo Filho, C. M., Di Federico, A., Jabar, F., Hashemi, S., Houda, I., Richardsen, E., Rasmussen Busund, L. T., Donnem, T., Bahce, I., … Kwiatkowski, D. J. (2025). Deep learning model for predicting immunotherapy response in advanced non-small cell lung cancer. *JAMA Oncology, 11*(2), 109–118. doi:10.1001/jamaoncol.2024.5356.

Rezaei, B., Harun, A., Wu, X., Iyer, P. R., Mostufa, S., Ciannella, S., Karampelas, I. H., Chalmers, J., Srivastava, I., Gómez-Pastora, J., & Wu, K. (2024). Effect of polymer and cell membrane coatings on theranostic applications of nanoparticles: A review. *Advanced Healthcare Materials, 13*(26). doi:10.1002/adhm.202401213.

Sabit, H., Pawlik, T. M., Radwan, F., Abdel-Hakeem, M., Abdel-Ghany, S., Wadan, A. H. S., Elzawahri, M., El-Hashash, A., & Arneth, B. (2025). Precision nanomedicine: Navigating the tumor microenvironment for enhanced cancer immunotherapy and targeted drug delivery. *Molecular Cancer, 24*(1). doi:10.1186/s12943-025-02357-z.

Sadhukha, T., Wiedmann, T. S., & Panyam, J. (2013). Inhalable magnetic nanoparticles for targeted hyperthermia in lung cancer therapy. *Biomaterials, 34*(21), 5163–5171. doi:10.1016/j.biomaterials.2013.03.061.

Schwendenwein, A., Megyesfalvi, Z., Barany, N., Valko, Z., Bugyik, E., Lang, C., Ferencz, B., Paku, S., Lantos, A., Fillinger, J., Rezeli, M., Marko-Varga, G., Bogos, K., Galffy, G., Renyi-Vamos, F., Hoda, M. A, Klepetko, W., Hoetzenecker, K., Laszlo, V., … Dome, B. (2021). Molecular profiles of small cell lung cancer subtypes: Therapeutic implications. *Molecular Therapy - Oncolytics, 20*, 470–483. doi:10.1016/j.omto.2021.02.004.

Shah, K. A., Razzaq, A., Ali, T., Ullah, S., You, B., Iqbal, H., & Cui, J. H. (2025). Role of nanomedicines in lung cancer treatment and diagnosis: Opportunities and challenges. *Medical Oncology, 42*(8). doi:10.1007/s12032-025-02862-7.

Sharma, A., Shambhwani, D., Pandey, S., Singh, J., Lalhlenmawia, H., Kumarasamy, M., Singh, S. K., Chellappan, D. K., Gupta, G., Prasher, P., Dua, K., & Kumar, D. (2023a). Advances in lung cancer treatment using nanomedicines. *ACS Omega, 8*(1), 10–41. doi:10.1021/acsomega.2c04078.

Sharma, P. (2023b). Nanostructured biomaterials in drug delivery: Current trends and upcoming possibilities. In *In Engineered Biomaterials: Synthesis and Applications* (pp. 261–280). Singapore: Springer Nature Singapore.

Sheng, S., Bernardo, M. M., Dzinic, S. H., Chen, K., Heath, E. I., & Sakr, W. A. (2018). Tackling tumor heterogeneity and phenotypic plasticity in cancer precision medicine: Our experience and a literature review. *Cancer and Metastasis Reviews, 37*(4), 655–663. doi:10.1007/s10555-018-9767-4.

Shi, C., Yu, H., Sun, D., Ma, L., Tang, Z., Xiao, Q., & Chen, X. (2015). Cisplatin-loaded polymeric nanoparticles: Characterization and potential exploitation for the treatment of non-small cell lung carcinoma. *Acta Biomaterialia, 18*, 68–76. doi:10.1016/j.actbio.2015.02.009.

Singh, D. (2024). Organelle targeted drug delivery: Key challenges, recent advancements and therapeutic implications. *Endocrine, Metabolic & Immune Disorders - Drug Targets, 24*(13), 1480–1487. doi:10.2174/0118715303282573240112104035.

Sirvi, P. K., Jadhav, V., Paul, G., Jain, R., & Yadav, A. K. (2025). *Therapeutic hallmarks of cancer and immunology nanotechnology based strategies for cancer immunotherapy: Concepts, design, and clinical applications* (pp. 21–53). Springer Nature. doi:10.1007/978-981-97-7022-9_2.

Smolarz, B., Łukasiewicz, H., Samulak, D., Piekarska, E., Kołaciński, R., & Romanowicz, H. (2025). Lung cancer—epidemiology, pathogenesis, treatment and molecular aspect (review of literature). *International Journal of Molecular Sciences, 26*(5), 2049. doi:10.3390/ijms26052049.

Sullivan, F. M., Mair, F. S., Anderson, W., Armory, P., Briggs, A., Chew, C., Dorward, A., Haughney, J., Hogarth, F., Kendrick, D., Littleford, R., McConnachie, A., McCowan, C., McMeekin, N., Patel, M., Rauchhaus, P., Ritchie, L., Robertson, C., Robertson, J., … Schembri, S. (2021). Earlier diagnosis of lung cancer in a randomised trial of an autoantibody blood test followed by imaging. *European Respiratory Journal, 57*(1). doi:10.1183/13993003.00670-2020.

Sun, X., Zhao, P., Lin, J., Chen, K., & Shen, J. (2023). Recent advances in access to overcome cancer drug resistance by nanocarrier drug delivery system. *Cancer Drug Resistance, 6*(2), 390–415. doi:10.20517/cdr.2023.16.

Thandra, K. C., Barsouk, A., Saginala, K., Aluru, J. S., & Barsouk, A. (2021). Epidemiology of lung cancer. *Wspolczesna Onkologia, 25*(1), 45–52. doi:10.5114/wo.2021.103829.

Thomas, M. R., Badekila, A. K., Pai, V., Nijil, S., Bhandary, Y., Rai, A., & Kini, S. (2025). Navigating tumor microenvironment barriers with nanotherapeutic strategies for targeting metastasis. *Advanced Healthcare Materials, 14*(7). doi:10.1002/adhm.202403107.

Tiruneh G/Medhin, M., Abebe, E. C, Sisay, T., Berhane, N., Bekele, T., & Asmamaw Dejenie, T. (2021). Current applications and future perspectives of CRISPR-Cas9 for the treatment of lung cancer. *Biologics: Targets and Therapy, 15*, 199–204. doi:10.2147/btt.s310312.

Verma, R., Rao, L., Nagpal, D., Yadav, M., Kumar, V., Kumar, V., Kumar, H., Parashar, J., Bansal, N., Kumar, M., Pandey, P., Mittal, V., & Kaushik, D. (2024). Emerging nanotechnology-based therapeutics: A new insight into promising drug delivery system for lung cancer therapy. *Recent Patents on Nanotechnology, 18*(4), 395–414. doi:10.2174/1872210517666230613154847.

Waerzeggers, Y., Monfared, P., Ullrich, R., Viel, T., & Jacobs, A. H. (2012). *Multimodality imaging: Overview of imaging techniques (CT, MRI, PET, optical imaging) and impact of multimodality imaging on drug development trends on the role of PET in drug development* (pp. 319–382). World Scientific Publishing Co. doi:10.1142/9789814317740_0013.

Wang, X., Qiu, Y., Wang, M., Zhang, C., Zhang, T., Zhou, H., Zhao, W., Xia, G., & Shao, R. (2020). Endocytosis and organelle targeting of nanomedicines in cancer therapy. *International Journal of Nanomedicine, 15*, 9447–9467. doi:10.2147/IJN.S274289.

Xiao, Y., Shi, K., Qu, Y., Chu, B., & Qian, Z. (2019). Engineering nanoparticles for targeted delivery of nucleic acid therapeutics in tumor. *Molecular Therapy - Methods & Clinical Development, 12*, 1–18. doi:10.1016/j.omtm.2018.09.002.

Yin, W., Pan, F., Zhu, J., Xu, J., Gonzalez-Rivas, D., Okumura, M., Tang, Z., & Yang, Y. (2021). Nanotechnology and nanomedicine: A promising avenue for lung cancer diagnosis and therapy. *Engineering, 7*(11), 1577–1585. doi:10.1016/j.eng.2020.04.017.

Zare-Zardini, H., Dehghanpour, F., Saberian, E., Petrášová, A., Jenča, A., Jenča, A., Jenčová, J., Nodoshan, A. J., Hedayati-Goudarzi, M. T., Soltaninejad, H., Ghorani-Azam, A., & Imani, M. (2025). Protein nanoparticles: A promising frontier in reducing lung complications from chemotherapy in pediatric oncology. *BioMedical Engineering Online, 24*(1). doi:10.1186/s12938-025-01489-z.

Zhang, G., Wang, N., Sun, H., Fu, X., Zhai, S., & Cui, J. (2021). Self-adjuvanting photosensitizer nanoparticles for combination photodynamic immunotherapy. *Biomaterials Science, 9*(20), 6940–6949. doi:10.1039/d1bm01139a.

Zhang, J., Li, Y., Guo, S. A., Zhang, W., Fang, B., & Wang, S. (2024). Moving beyond traditional therapies: The role of nanomedicines in lung cancer. *Frontiers in Pharmacology, 15*. doi:10.3389/fphar.2024.1363346.

Zhao, Y., Liu, K., Li, J., Liao, J., & Ma, L. i (2021). Engineering of hybrid anticancer drug-loaded polymeric nanoparticles delivery system for the treatment and care of lung cancer therapy. *Drug Delivery, 28*(1), 1539–1547. doi:10.1080/10717544.2021.1934187.

CHAPTER 17

Conclusion: Future directions and emerging trends in nanomedical drug delivery for lung cancer

Megha Tonk[a], Harsh Goswami[a], Anshul Gupta[b], Shikha Baghel Chauhan[c] and Indu Singh[d]

[a]Raj Kumar Goel Institute of Technology (Pharmacy), Ghaziabad, Uttar Pradesh, India [b]Department of Pharmaceutics, Delhi Pharmaceutical Sciences and Research University, New Delhi, India [c]Centre of Industrial Pharmacy, Amity Institute of Pharmacy, Amity University, Noida, Uttar Pradesh, India [d]Centre of Pharmaceutics, Amity Institute of Pharmacy, Amity University, Noida, Uttar Pradesh, India

17.1 Introduction

Across the globe, cancer is one of the biggest health issues in both developed and developing nations. Over 100 distinct cancer types may be identified based on the organ and tissue of origin. Lung cancer (LC) has the highest mortality rate when it comes to cancer-related deaths around the world. According to current cancer statistics, by 2022 LC accounted for 2.48 million new cases annually, or 11.7% of all cancer cases globally. It also contributed to over one-fifth of all cancer-related fatalities (Ji et al., 2023). LC is primarily caused by tobacco use, environmental exposures (including radon, air pollution, and passive smoking), occupational exposures (such as asbestos and arsenic), and epigenetic modifications (Norouzi & Hardy, 2021).

LC has two main categories: nonsmall cell lung cancer (NSCLC) and small cell lung cancer (SCLC). SCLC is treated more quickly because it spreads fast. NSCLC is usually detected in later stages and is less aggressive. NSCLC can be divided into types like adenocarcinoma, squamous cell carcinoma, bronchioalveolar carcinoma, and large cell carcinoma, making up about 80% of all LCs. The other 20% are linked to neuroendocrine features (Haider et al., 2022). The treatment options for LC are surgery, immunotherapy, oncogene-targeted therapy, or systemic chemotherapy. The most successful treatment option is surgery to remove the tumor, which is frequently performed as a lobectomy or pneumonectomy for stage I and II NSCLCs. However, tumor resectability is frequently restricted in advanced stages, especially when LC has progressed metastatically (Wang et al., 2021). Among different

Nanoengineered Therapeutics for Lung Cancer: Advanced Drug Delivery Strategies.
DOI: https://doi.org/10.1016/B978-0-443-44585-9.00012-3

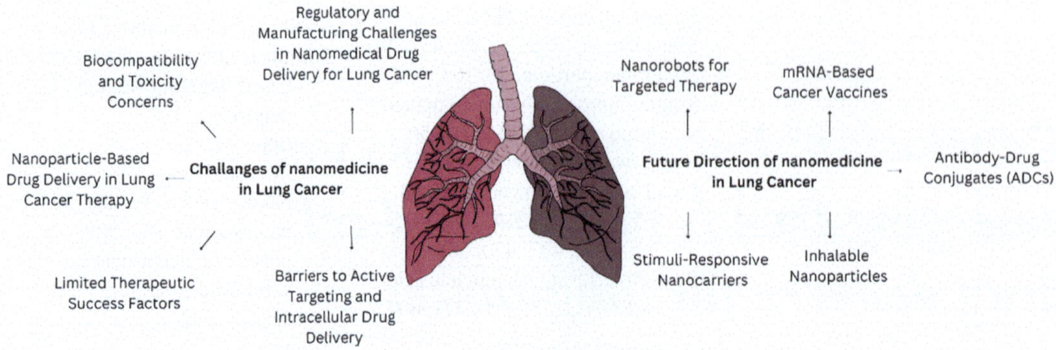

Figure 17.1
Challenges and future directions of nanomedicine in lung cancer therapy.

therapeutic options for patients with NSCLC, systemic chemotherapy with platinum-based cytotoxic chemotherapy is the most commonly used. But platinum-based chemotherapy can cause a variety of adverse effects, such as intestinal damage, peripheral neuropathy, anemia, nephrotoxicity, and cardiotoxicity. Furthermore, the use of chemotherapy is restricted by the poor water solubility of many drugs, and the issue that tumor resistance frequently results in chemotherapy failure remains unresolved (Doroudian et al., 2021). Recent years have seen the development of immunotherapy, a revolutionary approach to cancer treatment that has shown remarkable clinical effectiveness by modifying the patient's immune system and indirectly eliminating cancer cells. However, the objective response rate of single-agent immune checkpoint inhibitors in NSCLC was just 20%. Many patients have little to no benefit from this treatment, even though significant remission rates have been documented in clinical situations (Taefehshokr et al., 2022). The application of nanotechnology in drug delivery has motivated several studies and provided novel approaches to treating lung cancer. Nanocarriers can efficiently enhance the quantity of medications at the tumor location by using the enhanced permeability and retention (EPR) effect (Ezhilarasan et al., 2022). As a result, they have been used in clinical treatment for LC and many other cancers because of their ability to enhance drug solubility, in vivo stability, drug distribution in the body, and sustained and targeted delivery. They can also effectively improve the effect of drug treatment and reduce toxic side effects (Li et al., 2021a). This chapter provides an overview of the challenges in treating LC using nanotechnology and the issues with biocompatibility and toxicity. It also highlights emerging trends and future directions in the delivery of drugs for LC using nanomedicine, as displayed in Fig. 17.1.

17.2 Challenges in nanotechnology-based treatments

One of the most difficult obstacles in the field of medicine at the nanoscale is achieving affordable technology and mass manufacturing. The advanced formulations of nanoparticles (NPs) have performed well during preclinical trials, but applying these scientific breakthroughs to large-volume production that is both readily reproducible and cost-effective is challenging (Rosière et al., 2019). The complexity associated with NP synthesis, including stability issues and formulation credibility, often caps the likelihood of commercial success. On top of that, compliance with stringent regulatory guidelines known as Good Manufacturing Practices (GMP) adds burdensome costs while taking a long time to be fulfilled, making mass commercialization more difficult. Another major hurdle is earning the right biosafety and biological compatibility. While nanocarriers are carefully formulated to limit some systemic side effects, certain materials, especially inorganic NPs, carry the risk of causing long-term toxicity due to bioaccumulation within tissues. Recognizing the way such NPs interact with biological systems—including immunogenicity, clearance processes, and critical organ damage—is essential. This knowledge is essential for protecting patients' health and safety (Crintea et al., 2021). Furthermore, because each patient's immune system is unique, it is difficult to predict how each patient will respond to treatment, which makes it difficult to consistently achieve therapeutic goals. The diversity in LC is such that achieving a single treatment outcome is tremendously challenging. LC comes with multiple components, such as NSCLC and SCLC, both of which have their own distinct molecular features and cancer pathology. There is a need to create personalized treatment strategies, and yet, the personalization of nanomedicine therapies is incredibly difficult due to the vast variability within microenvironments of tumors, genetic mutations, and individual patient responses (Thakkar et al., 2022). These compound factors highlight the necessity of individualized attempts due to the complexity of each patient's condition. Achieving effective treatment for LC is challenging due to the mechanisms of drug resistance. Tumor cells develop resistance to chemotherapy and targeted treatments through several complicated steps, including activating drug efflux pumps that discard the therapeutic medications from the cell, developing mutations that change the target site of the drug, and changing the level of autophagy, which is a mechanism that enables cancer cells to survive in unfavorable conditions. By improving the retention of drugs within carcinoma cells and successfully avoiding biological obstacles linked to drug efflux, nanocarriers offer a possible solution to these problems. However, sustained success in combating drug resistance will necessitate further developments in combination therapies, which work in concert to improve treatment efficacy, as well as novel gene-editing techniques that may be able to address particular genetic modifications causing resistance to the virus (Cao et al., 2024).

17.2.1 Biocompatibility and toxicity concerns

The toxicity of nanocarriers remains a significant concern, particularly regarding their impact on the respiratory tract and lung tissues. Certain chemotherapeutics, such as irinotecan, gemcitabine, and paclitaxel, have been observed to trigger inflammatory responses when overexposed to the pulmonary tract (Gao et al., 2018). Surface charge plays a crucial role in the fate of NPs in vivo, influencing particle interactions, aggregation tendencies, and stability, which are largely dictated by the zeta potential of nanocomposites (Younis et al., 2025).

Cationic polymers, such as N-[1-(2,3-dioleyloxy) propyl]-N, N, N-trimethylammonium chloride and dioleoyl phosphatidylcholine (DOPE), are sometimes used to enhance drug delivery to cancer cells. However, these polymers often induce hemolytic effects, raising concerns about safe drug administration. Another critical challenge is the instability of nanocarriers, as NPs tend to accumulate in physiological environments, forming aggregates that are difficult to redisperse once clumped together. This aggregation can lead to drug leaching, reducing drug loading efficiency and therapeutic effectiveness. Functional groups are now being added to NP surfaces to enable drug and biomolecule attachment, but this complex modification process is difficult to replicate in a controlled manner (Mohtar et al., 2021).

17.2.1.1 Challenges for nanoparticle-based drug delivery in lung cancer therapy

Over the past decade, drug delivery technology using NP systems has experienced remarkable advancements. Ongoing research in nanomedicine is anticipated to drive the development of safer, more efficient, and practical drug delivery methods, along with highly sensitive imaging agents for diagnostics and disease monitoring. However, despite rapid innovation, translating novel nanomedicine concepts into clinical applications remains a significant challenge (see Table 17.1). The synthesis of NP-based drug delivery systems is particularly complex, requiring precise control over size to ensure an optimal drug or gene payload while achieving targeted delivery (Doroudian et al., 2019). In the biological environment, factors such as inappropriate size distribution, undefined structure or shape, poor biocompatibility, and improper surface chemistry pose potential risks. Designing an optimal NP system for lung drug delivery has been particularly challenging due to variations in the physicochemical properties and biological behavior of the particles (Yao et al., 2020). Once these NP systems enter preclinical and clinical testing, they encounter multiple obstacles, including immune reactions, clearance rates from circulation, targeting efficiency, and the ability to cross biological barriers. A thorough understanding of NP biological behavior is essential to maximize drug delivery efficiency. Identifying key physicochemical parameters is crucial for determining particle-particle interactions within the biological environment, NP aggregation tendencies, protein adsorption on the NP surface, and intracellular trafficking (Mangla et al., 2025). Any significant variation in these factors can lead to ineffective drug delivery, reduced therapeutic efficiency, or potential toxicity. Therefore the balance between efficacy and toxicity in NP systems is largely governed by their physicochemical properties. Particles larger than 500 nm are unsuitable for intravenous administration, as they are rapidly cleared from circulation. For effective drug delivery to solid tumors, NPs should ideally be less than 200 nm in size, with a spherical shape and smooth surface, enabling efficient transport through tumor vasculature and cellular uptake. These physical characteristics enhance the NPs' ability to exploit the EPR effect, a phenomenon associated with solid tumors (Shojaei et al., 2024).

Nanomedicines must navigate numerous biological barriers within the body, including the dense extracellular matrix, elevated interstitial pressure, protein corona formation, lysosomal phagocytosis, and drug efflux pumps (Xie et al., 2024). The tumor microenvironment

Table 17.1: Challenges and regulatory barriers in nanomedical drug delivery in lung cancer.

Challenge	Description	Current solutions	Regulatory barriers	Patient safety concerns	References
Drug delivery	Targeting cancer cells without harming healthy tissue is complex.	Targeted nanoparticles (liposomes, dendrimers).	Slow approval for novel delivery methods.	Potential toxicity from accumulation in organs.	Soares et al. (2018)
Immune response	Nanoparticles may trigger immune system activation.	Surface modifications like PEGylation (coating to "hide" particles).	Safety protocols for immune-modulating nanomedicine.	Allergic reactions, cytokine storms.	Kendall and Holgate (2012)
Tumor heterogeneity	Lung tumors vary in genetic makeup, size, and environment.	Combination therapies with multiple drugs in one nanoparticle.	Guidelines missing for personalized nano treatments.	Ineffective in some tumor subtypes.	Wouters (2005)
Nanoparticle stability	Nanoparticles may degrade or aggregate in the blood or tissues.	Coatings to improve stability in biological environments.	Regulations unclear for novel nanoparticle structures.	Particle breakdown leading to toxicity.	Bur et al. (2009)

(*continued on next page*)

Table 17.1: Challenges and regulatory barriers in nanomedical drug delivery in lung cancer—cont'd

Challenge	Description	Current solutions	Regulatory barriers	Patient safety concerns	References
Penetration into the tumor	Dense tumor tissues and abnormal vasculature block nanoparticle entry.	Smaller nanoparticles, surface modifications for better penetration.	Lack of testing standards for penetration efficiency.	Poor drug diffusion in large tumors.	Mukherjee et al. (2019)
Toxicity and clearance	Nanoparticles may accumulate in organs (e.g., liver, spleen).	Biodegradable nanoparticles (e.g., lipid-based).	Slow regulatory acceptance of new clearance approaches.	Potential chronic toxicity, unknown long-term effects.	Zheng et al. (2024)
Production and scalability	Difficult to consistently produce nanoparticles at a large scale.	Standardized synthesis methods, automation.	Approval barriers for scaled-up production methods.	Variability in nanoparticle size and composition.	Babu et al. (2013)
Patient-specific factors	Differences in genetics, lung environment, and health status.	Companion diagnostics for patient profiling.	No regulatory path for personalized nanodrugs.	Ineffectiveness or severe side effects in certain patients.	Tran et al. (2017)

is highly complex, and its composition and intricate interactions remain poorly understood. Different tumor types exhibit varying responses to nanomedicines, and immune reactions also differ accordingly. Achieving precise tumor treatment is challenging without a comprehensive understanding of the underlying biological mechanisms (Duan et al., 2022). One critical aspect requiring further validation is whether nanomedicines accumulate in tumors primarily through the EPR effect, which has long been credited for their therapeutic efficacy (Alshammari et al., 2023). However, recent findings suggest that the actual delivery efficiency of nanomedicines may be less than 1%. For instance, studies have shown that up to 97% of PEGylated gold NPs enter tumors via trans-endothelial pathways rather than the EPR effect. The variability of the EPR effect has also been significantly observed. For example, Doxil has been shown to achieve greater drug accumulation in AIDS-related Kaposi sarcoma compared to other solid tumors (Thakur & Kesharwani, 2019).

Despite having a substantial understanding of nanomedicines, progress in comprehending the biological mechanisms and developing effective cancer treatments remains slow due to the absence of an appropriate animal model. Although the mouse xenograft cancer model is widely used, it is an artificial representation. Human tumors consist of cells with diverse mutations, whereas mouse models tend to be largely homogeneous (Tonk et al., 2025). Additionally, subcutaneous tumor models fail to accurately replicate the immune landscape of orthotopic tumors. Therefore an ideal tumor animal model should possess a fully functional immune system, which can be achieved through gene editing. However, numerous technical challenges still need to be addressed (Li et al., 2021b).

17.2.1.2 Toxicity concerns with inhalational nanomedicines

Toxicity remains the key challenge in the clinical transition of nanomedicines, often stemming from their physical and chemical properties, such as size and composition. Therefore it is essential to thoroughly characterize each type of nanoagent, along with assessing the interactions between NPs and different cell types. Increasingly, researchers are concentrating on FDA-approved or biodegradable nanomaterials, which can simplify the regulatory approval process (Bur et al., 2009). The lungs are highly specialized with a large surface area, thin epithelial layer, and high vascularization, making them highly vulnerable targets for NP-induced injury. Although the route offers the benefits of site-specific targeting and decreased systemic toxicity, it also presents a set of safety concerns that need to be addressed in a particular manner.

17.2.1.2.1 Local physiological response and pulmonary inflammation

In the context of particulate drug carriers (nano- or microsized) used as inhaled dispersed systems, a local physiological response, such as an increase in macrophages, is commonly observed due to the deposition of carriers with poor solubility or insoluble properties (Middleton et al., 2016). While this response is often considered nonthreatening, prolonged exposure can lead to increased deposition, particularly if the carriers are nonbiodegradable, potentially resulting in more severe inflammatory responses. These include irritation, cellular damage, edema, phagocytic dysfunction, and compromised defense mechanisms. Oxidative stress and inflammation-mediated functional disturbances are among the primary toxic effects associated with inhalational NPs (Wouters, 2005).

17.2.1.2.2 Inflammatory response and exposure-related effects

Various in vivo studies have highlighted that the inflammatory effects of NPs are often temporary, with investigations assessing whether the severity of inflammation correlates with NP exposure dose. Lung inflammation has been observed following inhalation or instillation exposure to different nanomaterials (Landsiedel et al., 2014). These studies have demonstrated the localized recruitment of leukocytes, an increased presence of inflammatory cells in bronchoalveolar lavage fluid, elevated lactate dehydrogenase (LDH) levels, and enhanced cytokine production. Furthermore, characteristic granulomatous reactions have been identified following pulmonary exposure to carbon nanotubes (Kendall & Holgate, 2012).

17.2.1.2.3 Deposition and distribution of inhaled nanoparticles

Inhaled NPs distribute throughout the respiratory tract, although larger particles are typically removed from the upper airways, whereas smaller ones penetrate deeper into the distal airways. Specific particle size ranges show distinct deposition patterns, such as 90% of 1 nm NPs accumulating in the nasopharyngeal region, while only 10% reach the tracheobronchial region, with almost none reaching the alveolar area. Conversely, for 20 nm NPs, approximately 15% accumulate in both the nasopharyngeal and tracheobronchial areas, while nearly 50% deposit in the alveolar region (Feng et al., 2024). The deposition pattern of inhaled particulate matter is further influenced by disease conditions, with significantly higher deposition occurring in asthmatic lungs compared to healthy ones. This increased deposition may intensify local inflammation, exacerbating preexisting inflammatory conditions such as asthma and chronic obstructive pulmonary disease (COPD) (Rogueda & Traini, 2007).

17.2.1.2.4 Pulmonary retention and systemic toxicity

Additionally, regardless of their biocompatibility, insoluble or slow-degrading particles can induce pulmonary inflammation upon alveolar deposition. It has been established that incorporating pulmonary-endogenous chemicals, such as dipalmitoylphosphatidylcholine (DPPC), into formulations can significantly reduce toxicity (Landsiedel et al., 2014). A critical concern regarding inhaled NPs is their potential migration into systemic circulation and subsequent diffusion into other organs. Once absorbed through the lung epithelium, these NPs can enter the bloodstream and lymphatic system, distributing to various organs, including the bone marrow, lymph nodes, spleen, heart, central nervous system, and ganglia. Ultrafine particles are recognized as more toxic than larger particles of the same chemical composition due to their increased surface area, which contributes to cytotoxicity, allergic reactions, and inflammation (Osman et al., 2020).

17.2.1.2.5 Preclinical studies and carcinogenicity concerns

Beyond epidemiological and controlled clinical studies, the effects of NPs on the respiratory tract have been extensively examined through inhalation studies in rodents and in vitro cell culture systems. Rodent studies have demonstrated that ultrafine particles induce mild pulmonary inflammation and can impact extrapulmonary organs. The shape and structure of NPs also influence inhalational toxicity; for example, carbon nanotubes exhibit different pulmonary effects compared to carbon black and graphite, despite having similar chemical compositions (Patel et al., 2021). However, limited epidemiological studies on human exposure prevent a direct correlation between engineered nanomaterials and LC risk. The mechanisms underlying NP-induced carcinogenicity remain unclear and may involve either direct genotoxic insult or secondary genotoxic responses resulting from particle-induced inflammation. Despite the promise of nanomedicine in cancer treatment, concerns regarding toxicity, immunogenicity, and biocompatibility remain significant barriers to widespread clinical application. NPs interact with various biological barriers, including the mononuclear phagocyte system (MPS), leading to rapid clearance and potential toxicity (Dobrovolskaia, 2015).

17.2.2 Regulatory and manufacturing challenges in nanomedical drug delivery for LC

17.2.2.1 Manufacturing challenges

Over the past decade, nanocomposite-based drug delivery systems have experienced remarkable advancements. Current research efforts focus on developing safe, effective, and practical nano-based drug delivery methods to improve imaging precision and therapeutic outcomes. However, the transition of NPs from experimental studies to clinically approved nanomedicines remains challenging (Sharma et al., 2019). The synthesis of these carrier systems involves significant difficulties in designing particles with an optimal size for efficient drug or gene delivery. Major developmental obstacles include variability in particle size, irregular morphology, biocompatibility concerns, undefined surface properties, and difficulties in ensuring consistent production. Specifically, NP-based drug delivery faces additional challenges when it comes to treating LC (Halwani, 2022). For local drug delivery to the lungs, inhalation devices like pressurized metered-dose inhalers, nebulizers, and dry powder inhalers are required. Typically, nano-sized drug formulations are delivered via nebulized colloidal dispersions or solid-state formulations using these inhalation devices. However, physical instability (such as agglomeration and poor dispersibility) remains a challenge (Nirmala et al., 2023). Additionally, chemical instability, including hydrolysis or degradation of the drug and carrier material, poses further complications. Achieving a uniform NP size below 200 nm in polymeric formulations requires precise control over every stage of synthesis, presenting a significant challenge. The size distribution of liposomes and vesicular NPs can be narrowed using extrusion techniques, but issues such as burst drug release and poor stability introduce additional complications (Sharma et al., 2024). The surface charge of NPs is another critical factor determining their in vivo behavior. Particle-particle interactions and aggregation tendencies are largely influenced by the zeta potential. Positively charged NPs exhibit a strong affinity for the negatively charged cellular membranes throughout the body (Soares et al., 2018). Many NPs designed for gene delivery incorporate positively charged polymers or lipids to enhance DNANP interaction. However, certain cationic NPs display high hemolytic properties, raising safety concerns in gene delivery. For instance, cationic lipid formulations containing N-[1-(2,3-dioleyloxy) propyl]-N,N,N-trimethylammonium chloride and dioleoylphosphatidylethanolamine (DOTMA/DOPE) are highly hemolytic, whereas 3-beta-[N-(N,N-dimethylaminoethane)-carbamoyl]-cholesterol (DC-chol)/DOPE liposomes exhibit moderate hemolysis (Foulkes et al., 2020).

Biocompatible polymeric NPs serve as an alternative to cationic lipids for charge-specific drug and gene delivery. However, in lung tumor models, limited information is available regarding the impact of surface charge on NP biodistribution. PEGylation is a widely used strategy to mask surface charge, effectively camouflaging NPs from opsonin proteins and significantly extending their circulation half-life (Goel et al., 2024). NP stability is another crucial aspect of drug delivery, as poor stability can lead to aggregation in physiological environments. Once aggregation occurs, re-dispersing NPs into their original size distribution becomes extremely difficult. While shear forces may help redisperse the particles, this process can cause increased drug leakage and negatively impact drug loading and therapeutic efficiency. Actively targeted nano-formulations designed for macromolecule delivery face additional physiological barriers due to their interactions with target cells (Hussain, 2016). One of the major challenges encountered is escaping the endocytic pathway. Following endocytosis, intracellular trafficking mechanisms direct nanocarriers (NCs) to specific subcellular compartments, which can significantly impact their fate. For example, transferrin-targeted nano-formulations internalized via clathrin-mediated endocytosis are directed toward the degradative pathway, ultimately leading to their breakdown in lysosomes (De Jong et al., 2022). Various strategies have been investigated to facilitate the escape of nano-formulations from endosomes and ensure their entry into the cytosol, including the use of pore-forming peptides, specialized proteins, and pH-buffering compounds that exploit the "proton sponge effect." However, achieving effective endosomal escape of NCs in vivo remains an immense challenge (Mühlebach et al., 2015). The complexity of tumors, including their high degree of heterogeneity and the presence of stroma that supports tumor growth and metastasis, further complicates active targeting. Many actively targeted, cell-specific nano-formulations fail to account for tumor heterogeneity, often selecting a single cancer cell-surface receptor, which inadvertently allows more resilient clones to survive (Fateh et al., 2024). Consequently, many therapies initially produce partial or even complete responses, only to be followed by tumor recurrence and resistance, ultimately leading to patient mortality. Compared to passive targeting, active targeting strategies are significantly more complex. Understanding the challenges associated with physiological barriers and tumor heterogeneity is further complicated by the intricate design and manufacturing processes of these nano-formulations, which pose difficulties in large-scale production (Bawa et al., 2016). The synthesis and purification steps involved in the conjugation of targeting ligands to nanocarriers are substantially more complex than those required for passively targeted formulations. While this complexity is not the primary obstacle preventing the clinical translation of actively targeted nanocarriers, it presents a significant hurdle in moving from laboratory research to clinical application. This is due to the increased need for quality control measures, higher production costs, and extended manufacturing timelines (Mukherjee et al., 2019). To address these challenges, researchers have developed a lipidated single-chain Fv-based linker technology that enables self-assembly into lipid-based nanocarriers while binding immunoglobulin G (IgG) antibodies of a specific isotype. This innovative approach overcomes the complexities associated with chemically conjugating antibodies to nanocarriers and eliminates the need to remove unbound antibodies. Additionally, by incorporating linkers capable of binding various targeting moieties, a single adaptable nanocarrier platform can be designed to target multiple cellular receptors (Wicki et al., 2015). Such strategies could provide a meaningful breakthrough in overcoming tumor heterogeneity without further complicating nanocarrier production. The development and commercialization of nanomedicines face significant regulatory hurdles due to their complex nature. Pharmaceutical companies and industrial vendors often exhibit limited motivation to invest in nanomedicine-based therapies due to high production costs compared to conventional treatments (Hare et al., 2017). The reproducibility and large-scale production of complex nanoplatforms pose significant technical challenges, along with maintaining sterility and ensuring regulatory compliance. Regulatory frameworks for nanomedicines require careful assessment of pharmacokinetics, biodistribution, and potential long-term toxicities. The transition of nanotheranostics from laboratory research to clinical application is further hindered by a lack of collaboration between basic and clinical scientists. Many researchers and clinicians lack awareness of regulatory requirements, contributing to the delays in clinical translation. However, the FDA is actively revising guidelines to expedite the approval process for nanotherapeutics (Chan, 2006).

17.2.2.2 Regulatory challenges

Significant progress has been made in nanomedicines during the last ten years, with the introduction of several nanocarriers into clinical practice. Despite these advancements, stakeholders in the pharmaceutical and healthcare sectors face significant obstacles due to the lack of a clear regulatory framework (Sainz et al., 2015).

17.2.3 Limited therapeutic success factors

During the clinical stage, nanomedicine-based systems encounter significant obstacles, such as immune reactions, rapid clearance from circulation, and reduced targeting efficiency. Thus an in-depth understanding of the biological behavior of nanodrug carriers is essential to achieving optimal drug delivery efficiency. Optimization of physicochemical parameters is crucial for determining particle-particle interactions, agglomeration tendencies, macromolecule adsorption on the NP surface, and intracellular uptake. NPs with a spherical shape can navigate through tumor vasculature, leveraging the EPR effect. However, NPs smaller than 50 nm are more likely to exit tumor tissues quickly, limiting their retention. Active targeting of NPs involves modifying their surfaces with specific ligands to facilitate binding with overexpressed receptors on tumor cells (Farjadian et al., 2019). Despite various techniques for size optimization, maintaining a particle size of up to 200 nm remains challenging. Exhalation and rapid clearance in tumor tissues contribute to increased NP retention. Multifunctional NPs are a growing area of interest in nanomedicine, enabling targeted drug delivery and diagnostic applications for LC. However, these systems must undergo thorough evaluation before in vivo testing (Feng et al., 2024). Cancer nanomedicine faces immunological and hematologic concerns, including endotoxin contamination and complications like immune activation and fever. The toxicity of NPs is a critical consideration, as it significantly hinders their clinical translation.

17.2.3.1 Challenges in clinical translation of nanomedicines

Despite the significant progress made in developing NPs as potential therapeutic agents, most still fail to meet the stringent clinical requirements. Even clinically approved NPs have shown effectiveness in reducing drug toxicity, yet their use has not consistently resulted in improved clinical outcomes. The clinical translation of nanomedicines faces several obstacles, including limited understanding of biochemical pathways, structural complexity, inadequate characterization techniques, and the high cost of production. As a result, many NPs remain in the preclinical phase, as achieving nano-formulations with multifunctionality and uniform size distribution for enhanced performance remains a challenge (Landesman-Milo et al., 2015).

17.2.3.2 Limitations of passive targeting and the enhanced permeability and retention effect

Passive targeting holds considerable therapeutic potential; however, its clinical application is restricted by physiological challenges, particularly the unpredictability of the EPR effect. To accurately assess the EPR effect, advanced quantitative imaging techniques need to be developed. Applying these imaging modalities to patients could be a practical approach for obtaining crucial data to optimize the next generation of nano-formulations. Additionally, these tools could serve as diagnostic aids, assisting clinicians in the early identification of patients who may benefit from EPR-based therapies, thereby improving treatment effectiveness (Mukherjee et al., 2019).

17.2.3.3 Barriers to active targeting and intracellular drug delivery

Actively targeted nano-formulations also present challenges, particularly in overcoming cellular barriers to efficient intracellular drug delivery. The formation of a protein corona under biological conditions and its influence on pharmacokinetics and pharmacodynamics must be carefully considered when designing both passively and actively targeted nano-formulations. To facilitate clinical translation, innovative approaches are required to develop nano-formulations with adjustable biological identities. Furthermore, factors such as responsiveness to stimuli, large-scale manufacturing, and potential toxicity must be meticulously addressed when designing stimuli-responsive nano-systems to prevent premature drug release (Haider et al., 2022).

17.2.3.4 Need for in vivo toxicity and biodistribution studies

Before advancing to clinical trials, extensive research into the in vivo toxicity and biodistribution of nano-formulations is essential. As tumor biology becomes better understood and reliable biomarkers are identified to predict treatment responders and nonresponders, the successful integration of novel nano-formulations into clinical practice is expected to improve. Encouragingly, recent patent filings highlight promising developments, with numerous innovative approaches and formulations being patented (Zheng et al., 2024). Researchers are actively exploring combinatorial drug delivery systems utilizing nanotechnology, particularly in the fight against LC. A phase-III clinical trial was conducted to evaluate the impact of atezolizumab in combination with nab-paclitaxel versus a placebo with nab-paclitaxel in patients with previously untreated metastatic triple-negative breast cancer (TNBC). The study focused on two primary endpoints: progression-free survival (PFS) and overall survival, with patients continuing treatment until disease progression or intolerable toxicity occurred. The findings indicated that the combination of atezolizumab and nab-paclitaxel led to sustained PFS in patients with metastatic TNBC, both in the intention-to-treat population and the programmed death ligand-1 (PD-L1)-positive subgroup (Bölükbas & Meiners, 2015).

17.3 Future directions and emerging trends in nanomedicine drug delivery for lung cancer

Currently, LC is one of the most dangerous and highly rated diseases in the world. Recent novel treatments like radiation therapy, chemotherapy, and immunotherapy are frequently hindered by drug resistance, systemic toxicity, and nonspecific targeting. Nanomedicine is transforming the site of cancer treatment by harnessing nanotechnology to develop modern drug delivery systems. These systems suggestively enhance the therapeutic efficacy while minimizing side effects. In the advanced research regarding the medicine of LC, Nano-based drug delivery for LC is conclusively shaping the future of personalized and precision medicine (Doroudian et al., 2023).

17.3.1 Advanced nanocarrier designs

One of the most significant future directions in nanomedicine for LC treatment is the development of stimuli-responsive nanocarriers. Now, these smart trucks are designed to respond specifically to certain physical things happening directly in a tumor's microenvironment. Things like whether the local environment is less or more acidic, how much energy local cells have to cope with oxidative influences, and even how enzymes work. Pac men with tuned pH know when to unleash drugs into the tumors' sour stomachs so they can act super specifically. Similarly, redox-sensitive NPs exploit high intracellular glutathione levels in tumor cells to trigger drug release (Hussain et al., 2024). Additionally, enzyme-responsive nanocarriers are being developed to degrade and release therapeutic agents in response to tumor-specific enzymes such as matrix metalloproteinases. Another really exciting development these days is the emergence of hybrids and super-practical NPs that do more than one thing at a time. These carriers integrate different materials, such as lipid-polymer hybrids, to optimize stability, biocompatibility, and controlled drug release. Magnetic NPs, for instance, allow for externally controlled drug delivery under magnetic fields, improving targeting accuracy. Moreover, gold and silver nanostructures are gaining traction for their dual role in imaging (theranostics) and drug delivery. Future nanocarriers also emphasize biodegradability and biocompatibility. Many of the researchers are developing special squishy particles called NPs made from a mix of polylactic acid and glycolic acid (PLGA) and chitosan. Researchers are trying to boost these particles' length of time in circulation and reduce their risk. Furthermore, the use of exosome-based nanocarriers derived from natural biological vesicles is being explored for enhanced cellular uptake and immune evasion (Youn & Bae, 2018).

17.3.2 Targeted drug delivery strategies

Researchers are stressing active targeting strategies to improve specificity and reduce off-target impacts. Developed to bind preferentially to overexpressed receptors on LC cells, including epidermal growth factor receptor (EGFR) and vascular endothelial growth factor receptor (VEGFR), functionalized NPs bearing monoclonal antibodies, peptides, or ligands are especially those with RGD peptides, peptide-conjugated NPs help to increase medication retention and enable deeper tumor penetration (Kaufman et al., 2021). Apart from active targeting, passive targeting methods using the improved permeability and retention (EPR) effect are being optimized. Drug accumulation in tumors is increased by designing NPs with surface changes extending circulation time and enhancing stability. Additionally, under investigation is the tuning of surface charge and size of NPs to enable deeper tumor penetration. In precision medicine, intracellular and subcellular targeting is a developing trend. Scientists are creating NPs able to specifically target organelles such as mitochondria to induce death or the nucleus to impede DNA replication. The development of mitochondria-targeting liposomes would allow medications like doxorubicin to reach the mitochondrial membrane directly, hence improving therapeutic efficacy. Likewise, nuclear-targeting peptides are under investigation as a means of selectively delivering chemotherapeutic drugs into the nucleus, hence reducing resistance systems (Mottaghitalab et al., 2019).

17.3.3 Emerging RNA-based nanomedicine

A stimulating afterward is ahead in LC treatment when RNA-based nanomedicine is encompassed. Therapeutics based on small interfering RNA, also known as siRNA, and microRNA (miRNA) have shown promise in the silencing of oncogenes and gene expression modification. Emerging as the main carriers for RNA-based treatment, lipid NPs (LNPs) provide stability and effective intracellular distribution. Furthermore, attracting interest is exosome-mediated RNA transfer because of its better biocompatibility and capacity to avoid immune detection, thereby offering a potential approach for individualized LC treatment (Tiwade et al., 2025).

17.3.4 Clustered Regularly Interspaced Short Palindromic Repeats (CRISPR)/Cas9 and gene-editing approaches

LC treatment is being transformed in nanomedicine by the use of genome editing based on CRISPR/Cas9. Scientists are aiming at precision editing of oncogenes accountable for LC growth by combining CRISPR technology with NP delivery technologies. NPs carrying CRISPR/Cas9 complexes can be engineered for selective gene knockout, leading to personalized and durable treatment outcomes. However, efforts are ongoing to enhance specificity and minimize off-target effects to ensure clinical safety (Fatima et al., 2025).

17.3.5 Theranostic nanoparticles for lung cancer

Theranostic NPs, which effectively integrate therapeutic and imaging abilities within a single platform, are progressively recognized as dynamic components of personalized medicine. For example, gold NPs are utilized both as mediators for photothermal therapy and as accompaniments of imaging contrast. Quantum dots are also being developed to make it easier to visualize tumors in real time, which will enable accurate drug biodistribution monitoring. Additionally, drug delivery methods are seamlessly incorporating positron emission tomography/magnetic resonance imaging contrast-enhancing NPs, allowing for noninvasive monitoring of treatment outcomes (Dufort et al., 2015).

17.3.6 Overcoming drug resistance in lung cancer

Resistance to treatment is a challenge that significantly diminishes the effectiveness of traditional therapies. It is one of the largest hurdles in LC treatment. In various approaches, nanomedicine is addressing this issue. One pivotal strategy involves the co-delivery of multiple drugs within a single NP. This allows for the combination therapies aimed at several mechanisms of resistance to be administered simultaneously. For instance, NPs that impair drug efflux pumps can encapsulate both P-glycoprotein inhibitors and chemotherapeutic agents, enhancing the retention of drugs within the tumor cells (Ashrafi et al., 2022). Additionally, RNA interference techniques, especially those that use siRNA-loaded NPs, are being used to target genes linked to drug resistance. By targeting the resistance genes, these NPs can make cancer cells less resistant and, consequently, more sensitive to the chemotherapeutic drugs. Also, there is work aimed at changing autophagic pathways by using nanocarriers that control autophagy. Also, these autophagy-regulating nanocarriers are intended to target and modify other pathways that could lead to drug resistance to enhance the effectiveness of the therapy (Zhang et al., 2024).

17.3.7 Inhalable nanomedicine for lung cancer

A new approach to treating LC is the creation of inhalable nanomedicine, which provides an effective and noninvasive way to deliver medication straight to the lungs. To increase drug bioavailability while reducing systemic adverse effects, diffused combinations of NP-based medications and dry powder inhalation systems are being developed. To ensure continuous medication release and an enhanced therapeutic response, mucoadhesive NPs are being researched to extend retention duration in lung tissues (Bandyopadhyay et al., 2015).

17.4 Conclusion

One of the most difficult obstacles in the field of medicine at the nanoscale is achieving affordable technology and mass manufacturing. The advanced formulations of NPs have performed well during preclinical trials, but applying these scientific breakthroughs to large-volume production that is both readily reproducible and cost-effective is challenging. The complexity associated with NP synthesis, including stability issues and formulation credibility, often caps the likelihood of commercial success. On top of that, compliance with stringent regulatory guidelines known as GMP adds burdensome costs while taking a long time to be fulfilled, making mass commercialization more difficult. Another major hurdle is in earning the right biosafety and biological compatibility (Bregoli et al., 2016). While nanocarriers are carefully formulated to limit some systemic side effects, certain materials, especially inorganic NPs, carry the risk of causing long-term toxicity due to bioaccumulation within tissues. Recognizing the way such NPs interact with biological systems—including immunogenicity, clearance processes, and critical organ damage—is essential. This knowledge is essential for protecting patients' health and safety (Xie et al., 2019). Furthermore, because each patient's immune system is unique, it is difficult to predict how each patient will respond to treatment, which makes it difficult to consistently achieve therapeutic goals. The diversity in LC is such that achieving a single treatment outcome is tremendously challenging. LC comes with multiple components, such as NSCLC and SCLC, both of which have their own distinct molecular features and cancer pathology (Rasool et al., 2022). There is a need to create personalized treatment strategies, and yet, the personalization of nanomedicine therapies is incredibly difficult due to the vast variability within microenvironments of tumors, genetic mutations, and individual patient responses. These compound factors highlight the necessity of individualized attempts due to the complexity of each patient's condition (Gupta et al., 2017). Achieving effective treatment for LC is challenging due to the mechanisms of drug resistance. Tumor cells develop resistance to chemotherapy and targeted treatments through several complicated steps, including activating drug efflux pumps that discard the therapeutic medications from the cell, developing mutations that change the target site of the drug, and changing the level of autophagy, which is a mechanism that enables cancer cells to survive in unfavorable conditions. By improving the retention of drugs within carcinoma cells and successfully avoiding biological obstacles linked to drug efflux, nanocarriers offer a possible solution to these problems. However, sustained success in combating drug resistance will necessitate further developments in combination therapies, which work in concert to improve treatment efficacy, as well as novel gene-editing techniques that may be able to address particular genetic modifications causing resistance to the virus (Chen et al., 2024).

References

Alshammari, M. K., Almomen, E. Y., Alshahrani, K. F., Altwalah, S. F., Kamal, M., Al-Twallah, M. F., Al-sanad, S. H., Al-Batti, M. H., Al-Rasheed, F. J., Alsalamah, A. Y., Alhazza, M. B., Alasmari, F. A., & Abida, M. I. (2023). Nano-enabled strategies for the treatment of lung cancer: Potential bottlenecks and future perspectives. *Biomedicines, 11*(2). doi:10.3390/biomedicines11020473.

Ashrafi, A., Akter, Z., Modareszadeh, P., Berisha, E., Alemi, P. S., Chacon Castro Maria, D., Deese Alexander, R., & Zhang, L. (2022). Current landscape of therapeutic resistance in lung cancer and promising strategies to overcome resistance. *Cancers, 14*(19), 4562. doi:10.3390/cancers14194562.

Babu, A., Templeton, A. K., Munshi, A., Ramesh, R., & Chen, H. (2013). Nanoparticle-based drug delivery for therapy of lung cancer: Progress and challenges. *Journal of Nanomaterials, 2013*(1). doi:10.1155/2013/863951.

Bandyopadhyay, A., Das, T., & Yeasmin, S. (2015). Nanoparticles in lung cancer therapy - recent trends. *Briefs in molecular science*. Springer. doi:10.1007/978-81-322-2175-3.

Bawa, R., Barenholz, Y., & Owen, A. (2016). *The challenge of regulating nanomedicine: Key issues nanomedicines: Design, delivery and detection*. The Royal Society of Chemistry. doi:10.1039/9781782622536-00290.

Bölükbas, D. A., & Meiners, S. (2015). Lung cancer nanomedicine: Potentials and pitfalls. *Nanomedicine, 10*(21), 3203–3212. doi:10.2217/nnm.15.155.

Bregoli, L., Movia, D., Gavigan-Imedio, J. D., Lysaght, J., & Reynolds, J. (2016). Adriele Prina-Mello, Nanomedicine applied to translational oncology: A future perspective on cancer treatment. *Nanomedicine: Nanotechnology, Biology and Medicine, 12*(1), 81–103. doi:10.1016/j.nano.2015.08.006.

Bur, M., Henning, A., Hein, S., Schneider, M., & Lehr, C.-M. (2009). Inhalative nanomedicine—Opportunities and challenges. *Inhalation Toxicology, 21*(sup1), 137–143. doi:10.1080/08958370902962283.

Cao, Z., Zhu, J., Chen, X., Chen, Z., Wang, W., Zhou, Y., Hua, Y., Shi, J., & Chen, J. (2024). Resistance mechanisms of non-small cell lung cancer and improvement of treatment effects through nanotechnology: A narrative review. *Journal of Thoracic Disease, 16*(11). https://journals.lww.com/jtd/fulltext/2024/11000/resistance_mechanisms_of_non_small_cell_lung.68.aspx.

Chan, V. S. W. (2006). Nanomedicine: An unresolved regulatory issue. *Regulatory Toxicology and Pharmacology, 46*(3), 218–224. doi:10.1016/j.yrtph.2006.04.009.

Chen, Y., Ye, Z., Chen, H., & Li, Z. (2024). Breaking barriers: Nanomedicine-based drug delivery for cataract treatment. *International Journal of Nanomedicine, 19*, 4021–4040. doi:10.2147/IJN.S463679.

Crintea, A., Dutu, A. G., Samasca, G., Florian, I. A., Lupan, I., & Craciun, A. M. (2021). The nanosystems involved in treating lung cancer. *Life, 11*(7). doi:10.3390/life11070682.

De Jong, W. H., Geertsma, R. E., & Borchard, G. (2022). Regulatory safety evaluation of nanomedical products: Key issues to refine. *Drug Delivery and Translational Research, 12*(9), 2042–2047. doi:10.1007/s13346-022-01208-4.

Dobrovolskaia, M. A. (2015). Pre-clinical immunotoxicity studies of nanotechnology-formulated drugs: Challenges, considerations and strategy. *Journal of Controlled Release, 220*, 571–583. doi:10.1016/j.jconrel.2015.08.056.

Doroudian, M., Zanganeh, S., Abbasgholinejad, E., & Donnelly, S. C. (2023). Nanomedicine in lung cancer immunotherapy. *Frontiers in Bioengineering and Biotechnology, 11*. doi:10.3389/fbioe.2023.1144653.

Doroudian, M., Azhdari, M. H., Goodarzi, N., O'sullivan, D., & Donnelly, S. C. (2021). Smart nanotherapeutics and lung cancer. *Pharmaceutics, 13*(11). doi:10.3390/pharmaceutics13111972.

Doroudian, M., MacLoughlin, R., Poynton, F., Prina-Mello, A., & Donnelly, S. C. (2019). Nanotechnology based therapeutics for lung disease. *Thorax, 74*(10), 965. doi:10.1136/thoraxjnl-2019-213037.

Duan, Y., Shen, C., Zhang, Y., & Luo, Y. (2022). Advanced diagnostic and therapeutic strategies in nanotechnology for lung cancer. *Frontiers in Oncology, 12*. doi:10.3389/fonc.2022.1031000.

Dufort, S., Bianchi, A., Henry, M., Lux, F., Le Duc, G., Josserand, V., Louis, C., Perriat, P., Crémillieux, Y., Tillement, O., & Coll, J. L. (2015). Nebulized gadolinium-based nanoparticles: A theranostic approach for lung tumor imaging and radiosensitization. *Small, 11*(2), 215–221. doi:10.1002/smll.201401284.

Ezhilarasan, D., Lakshmi, T., & Mallineni, S. K. (2022). Nano-based targeted drug delivery for lung cancer: Therapeutic avenues and challenges. *Nanomedicine, 17*(24), 1855–1869. doi:10.2217/nnm-2021-0364.

Farjadian, F., Ghasemi, A., Gohari, O., Roointan, A., Karimi, M., & Hamblin, M. R. (2019). Nanopharmaceuticals and nanomedicines currently on the market: Challenges and opportunities. *Nanomedicine., 14*(1), 93–126. doi:10.2217/nnm-2018-0120.

Fateh, S. T., Fateh, S. T., Salehi-Najafabadi, A., Aref, A. R., Barabadi, H., Mostafavi, E., & Chaudhery, M. H. (2024). Chapter 26—Commercial and regulatory challenges in cancer nanomedicine. In *Functionalized nanomaterials for cancer research* (pp. 579–601). Academic Press. doi:10.1016/B978-0-443-15518-5.00009-4.

Fatima, H., Singh, D., Muhammad, H., Acharya, S., & Aziz, M. A. (2025). Improving the use of CRISPR/Cas9 gene editing machinery as a cancer therapeutic tool with the help of nanomedicine. *3 Biotech, 15*(1). doi:10.1007/s13205-024-04186-1.

Feng, X., Shi, Y., Zhang, Y., Lei, F., Ren, R., & Tang, X. (2024). Opportunities and challenges for inhalable nanomedicine formulations in respiratory diseases: A review. *International Journal of Nanomedicine, 19*, 1509–1538. doi:10.2147/IJN.S446919.

Foulkes, R., Man, E., Thind, J., Yeung, S., Joy, A., & Hoskins, C. (2020). The regulation of nanomaterials and nanomedicines for clinical application: Current and future perspectives. *Biomaterials Science, 8*(17), 4653–4664. doi:10.1039/D0BM00558D.

Gao, X., Guo, L., Li, J., Ei Thu, H., & Hussain, Z. (2018). Nanomedicines guided nanoimaging probes and nanotherapeutics for early detection of lung cancer and abolishing pulmonary metastasis: Critical appraisal of newer developments and challenges to clinical transition. *Journal of Controlled Release, 292*, 29–57. doi:10.1016/j.jconrel.2018.10.024.

Goel, S., Singh, R., & Tonk, M. (2024). Polymersomes as next generation nanocarriers for drug delivery: Recent advances, patents, synthesis and characterization. *Current Nanoscience, 20*(6), 753–768. doi:10.2174/0115734137271094231101062844.

Gupta, S., Gupta, P. K., Dharanivasan, G., & Verma, R. S. (2017). Current prospects and challenges of nanomedicine delivery in prostate cancer therapy. *Nanomedicine, 12*(23), 2675–2692. doi:10.2217/nnm-2017-0236.

Haider, M., Elsherbeny, A., Pittalà, V., Consoli, V., Ali Alghamdi, M., Hussain, Z., Khoder, G., & Greish, K. (2022). Nanomedicine strategies for management of drug resistance in lung cancer. *International Journal of Molecular Sciences, 23*(3), 1853. doi:10.3390/ijms23031853.

Halwani, A. A. (2022). Development of pharmaceutical nanomedicines: From the bench to the market. *Pharmaceutics, 14*(1). doi:10.3390/pharmaceutics14010106.

Hare, J. I., Lammers, T., Ashford, M. B., Puri, S., Storm, G., & Barry, S. T. (2017). Challenges and strategies in anti-cancer nanomedicine development: An industry perspective. *Advanced Drug Delivery Reviews, 108*, 25–38. doi:10.1016/j.addr.2016.04.025.

Hussain, I., Hadi Umam, A., Borah, L., Papi, D., Nath, D., Bordoloi, T., Gogoi, H., Hoque, M., & Kalita, N. (2024). Nanomedicine for the treatment of lungs cancer: Its challenges and future perspective-a review. *Journal of Advanced Zoology, 45*. doi:10.53555/jaz.v45i2.3899.

Hussain, S. (2016). Nanomedicine for treatment of lung cancer. *Advances in Experimental Medicine and Biology, 890*, 137–147 Springer International Publishing. doi:10.1007/978-3-319-24932-2_8.

Ji, X., Chen, J., Ye, J., Xu, S., Lin, B., & Hou, K. (2023). Epidemiological analysis of global and regional lung cancer mortality: Based on 30-year data analysis of global burden disease database. *Healthcare, 11*(22), 2920. doi:10.3390/healthcare11222920.

Kaufman, N. E. M., Dhingra Simran, J., Seetharama, D., & Vicente Maria da Graça, H. (2021.). Molecular targeting of epidermal growth factor receptor (EGFR) and vascular endothelial growth factor receptor (VEGFR). *Molecules*. doi:10.3390/molecules26041076 1420-3049 4.

Kendall, M., & Holgate, S. (2012). Health impact and toxicological effects of nanomaterials in the lung. *Respirology, 17*(5), 743–758. doi:10.1111/j.1440-1843.2012.02171.x.

Landesman-Milo, D., Ramishetti, S., & Peer, D. (2015). Nanomedicine as an emerging platform for metastatic lung cancer therapy. *Cancer and Metastasis Reviews, 34*(2), 291–301. doi:10.1007/s10555-015-9554-4.

Landsiedel, R., Sauer, U. G., Ma-Hock, L., Schnekenburger, J., & Wiemann, M. (2014). Pulmonary toxicity of nanomaterials: A critical comparison of published in vitro assays and in vivo inhalation or instillation studies. *Nanomedicine, 9*(16), 2557–2585. doi:10.2217/nnm.14.149.

Li, S., Xu, S., Liang, X., Xue, Y., Mei, J., Ma, Y., Liu, Y., & Liu, Y. (2021a). Nanotechnology: Breaking the current treatment limits of lung cancer. *Advanced Healthcare Materials, 10*(12). doi:10.1002/adhm.202100078.

Li, Z., Feiyue, Z., & Gaofeng, L. (2021b). Traditional Chinese medicine and lung cancer——From theory to practice. *Biomedicine & Pharmacotherapy, 137*, 111381. doi:10.1016/j.biopha.2021.111381.

Mangla, B., Kumar, P., Javed, S., Pathan, T., Ahsan, W., & Aggarwal, G. (2025). Regulating nanomedicines: Challenges, opportunities, and the path forward. *Nanomedicine, 20*(15), 1911–1927. doi:10.1080/17435889.2025.2533107.

Middleton, E. A., Weyrich, A. S., & Zimmerman, G. A. (2016). Platelets in pulmonary immune responses and inflammatory lung diseases. *Physiological Reviews, 96*(4), 1211–1259. doi:10.1152/physrev.00038.2015.

Mohtar, N., Parumasivam, T., Gazzali, A. M., Tan Chu, S., Tan Mei, L., Othman, R., Fazalul Rahiman Siti, S., & Wahab, H. A. (2021). Advanced nanoparticle-based drug delivery systems and their cellular evaluation for non-small cell lung cancer treatment. *Cancers*. doi:10.3390/cancers13143539 2072-6694 14.

Mottaghitalab, F., Farokhi, M., Fatahi, Y., Atyabi, F., & Dinarvand, R. (2019). New insights into designing hybrid nanoparticles for lung cancer: Diagnosis and treatment. *Journal of Controlled Release, 295*, 250–267. doi:10.1016/j.jconrel.2019.01.009.

Mühlebach, S., Borchard, G., & Yildiz, S. (2015). Regulatory challenges and approaches to characterize nanomedicines and their follow-on similars. *Nanomedicine, 10*(4), 659–674. doi:10.2217/nnm.14.189.

Mukherjee, A., Paul, M., & Mukherjee, S. (2019). Recent progress in the theranostics application of nanomedicine in lung cancer. *Cancers, 11*(5), 597. doi:10.3390/cancers11050597.

Nirmala, M. J., Kizhuveetil, U., Johnson, A., Balaji, G., Nagarajan, R., & Muthuvijayan, V. (2023). Cancer nanomedicine: A review of nano-therapeutics and challenges ahead. *RSC Advances, 13*(13), 8606–8629. doi:10.1039/D2RA07863E.

Norouzi, M., & Hardy, P. (2021). Clinical applications of nanomedicines in lung cancer treatment. *Acta Biomaterialia, 121*, 134–142. doi:10.1016/j.actbio.2020.12.009.

Osman, N. M., Sexton, D. W., & Saleem, I. Y. (2020). Toxicological assessment of nanoparticle interactions with the pulmonary system. *Nanotoxicology, 14*(1), 21–58. doi:10.1080/17435390.2019.1661043.

Patel, M., Patel, R., & Rai, M. (2021). Nanomedicines. In *Nanotechnology in medicine: Toxicity and safety* (pp. 1–28). Wiely. doi:10.1002/9781119769897.ch1.

Rasool, M., Malik, A., Waquar, S., Arooj, M., Zahid, S., Asif, M., Shaheen, S., Hussain, A., Ullah, H., & Gan, S. H. (2022). New challenges in the use of nanomedicine in cancer therapy. *Bioengineered, 13*(1), 759–773. doi:10.1080/21655979.2021.2012907.

Rogueda, P. G. A., & Traini, D. (2007). The nanoscale in pulmonary delivery. Part 1: Deposition, fate, toxicology and effects. *Expert Opinion on Drug Delivery, 4*(6), 595–606. doi:10.1517/17425247.4.6.595.

Rosière, R., Amighi, K., Wauthoz, N., & Kesharwani, P. (2019). Chapter 10—Nanomedicine-based inhalation treatments for lung cancer. *Nanotechnology-based targeted drug delivery systems for lung cancer*, 249–268. doi:10.1016/B978-0-12-815720-6.00010-1.

Sainz, V., Conniot, J. oão, Matos, A. I., Peres, C., Zupanǒiǒ, E., Moura, L., Silva, L. C., Florindo, H. F., & Gaspar, R. S. (2015). Regulatory aspects on nanomedicines. *Nanomedicine, 468*(3), 504–510. doi:10.1016/j.bbrc.2015.08.023.

Sharma, P., Dasputre, N., & Jain, V. (2024). *Nanomedicine: Concepts, characteristics, and regulatory challenges smart nanocarrier for effective drug delivery* (pp. 1–16). CRC Press. doi:10.1201/9781003438953-1.

Sharma, P., Mehta, M., Singh Dhanjal, D., Kaur, S., Gupta, G., Singh, H., Thangavelu, L., Rajeshkumar, S., Tambuwala, M., Bakshi, H. A., Kumar Chellappan, D., Dua, K., & Satija, S. (2019). Emerging trends in the novel drug delivery approaches for the treatment of lung cancer. *Chemico-Biological Interactions, 309*, 108720. doi:10.1016/j.cbi.2019.06.033.

Shojaei, S., Pourmadadi, M., Homayoonfal, M., Behnamrad, P., Fathi-karkan, S., Rahdar, A., Gerayli, S., & Pandey, S. (2024). Revolutionizing lung cancer treatment: Nanotechnology-driven advances in targeted drug delivery and novel therapeutic strategies. *Journal of Drug Delivery Science and Technology, 101*, 106186. doi:10.1016/j.jddst.2024.106186.

Soares, S., Sousa, J., Pais, A., & Vitorino, C. (2018). Nanomedicine: Principles, properties, and regulatory issues. *Frontiers in Chemistry, 6*. doi:10.3389/fchem.2018.00360.

Taefehshokr, S., Parhizkar, A., Hayati, S., Mousapour, M., Mahmoudpour, A., Eleid, L., Rahmanpour, D., Fattahi, S., Shabani, H., & Taefehshokr, N. (2022). Cancer immunotherapy: Challenges and limitations. *Pathology - Research and Practice, 229*, 153723. doi:10.1016/j.prp.2021.153723.

Thakkar, A. B., Subramanian, R. B., Thakkar, V. R., Thakor, P., Egbuna, C., Găman, M.-A., & Jeevanandam, J. (2022). Chapter 13 — Applications of nanotechnology in lung cancer. In *Drug discovery update* (pp. 329–343). Elsevier. doi:10.1016/B978-0-12-824408-1.00010-7.

Thakur, C., & Kesharwani, P. (2019). An overview, current challenges of drug resistance, and targeting metastasis associated with lung cancer. In *Nanotechnology-based targeted drug delivery systems for lung cancer* (pp. 21–38). Academic Press. doi:10.1016/B978-0-12-815720-6.00002-2.

Tiwade, P. B., Fung, V., VanKeulen-Miller, R., Amruth Narasipura, E., Ma, Y., & Fenton, O. S. (2025). Non-viral RNA therapies for non-small cell lung cancer and their corresponding clinical trials. *Molecular Pharmaceutics, 22*(4), 1752–1774. doi:10.1021/acs.molpharmaceut.4c00871.

Tonk, M., Singh, I., Sharma, R. J., & Chauhan, S. B. (2025). A revolutionary approach for combating efflux transporter-mediated resistant epilepsy: Advanced drug delivery systems. *Current Pharmaceutical Design, 31*(2), 95–106. doi:10.2174/0113816128332345240823111524.

Tran, S., DeGiovanni, P.-J., Piel, B., & Rai, P. (2017). Cancer nanomedicine: A review of recent success in drug delivery. *Clinical and Translational Medicine, 6*(1). doi:10.1186/s40169-017-0175-0.

Wang, W., Hao, Y., Liu, Y., Li, R., Huang, D. B., & Pan, Y. Y. (2021). Nanomedicine in lung cancer: Current states of overcoming drug resistance and improving cancer immunotherapy. *Wiley Interdisciplinary Reviews: Nanomedicine and Nanobiotechnology, 13*(1). doi:10.1002/wnan.1654.

Wicki, A., Witzigmann, D., Balasubramanian, V., & Huwyler, J. ö (2015). Nanomedicine in cancer therapy: Challenges, opportunities, and clinical applications. *Journal of Controlled Release, 200*, 138–157. doi:10.1016/j.jconrel.2014.12.030.

Wouters, E. F. M. (2005). Local and systemic inflammation in chronic obstructive pulmonary disease. *Proceedings of the American Thoracic Society, 2*(1), 26–33. doi:10.1513/pats.200408-039MS.

Xie, X., Zhang, Y., Li, F., Lv, T., Li, Z., Chen, H., Jia, L., & Gao, Y. (2019). Challenges and opportunities from basic cancer biology for nanomedicine for targeted drug delivery. *Current Cancer Drug Targets, 19*(4), 257–276. doi:10.2174/1568009618666180628160211.

Xie, L., Xie, D., Du, Z., Xue, S., Wang, K., Yu, X., Liu, X., Peng, Q., & Fang, C. (2024). A novel therapeutic outlook: Classification, applications and challenges of inhalable micron/nanoparticle drug delivery systems in lung cancer (review). *International Journal of Oncology, 64*(4), 38. doi:10.3892/ijo.2024.5626.

Yao, S., Wang, R., Qian, K., & Zhang, Y. i (2020). Real world study for the concordance between IBM Watson for Oncology and clinical practice in advanced non-small cell lung cancer patients at a lung cancer center in China. *Thoracic Cancer, 11*(5), 1265–1270. doi:10.1111/1759-7714.13391.

Youn, Y. uS., & Bae, Y. H. (2018). Perspectives on the past, present, and future of cancer nanomedicine. *Perspectives and review articles on nanomedicine from NanoDDS 2017, 130*, 3–11. doi:10.1016/j.addr.2018.05.008.

Younis, M. A., Alsogaihi, M. A., & Abdellatif, A. A. H. (2025). Imran Saleem, Nanoformulations in the treatment of lung cancer: Current status and clinical potential. *Drug Development and Industrial Pharmacy, 51*(9), 1088–1104. doi:10.1080/03639045.2024.2437562.

Zhang, J., Li, Y., Guo, S., Zhang, W., Fang, B., & Wang, S. (2024). Moving beyond traditional therapies: The role of nanomedicines in lung cancer. *Frontiers in Pharmacology, 15*. doi:10.3389/fphar.2024.1363346.

Zheng, X., Song, X., Zhu, G., Pan, D., Li, H., Hu, J., Xiao, K., Gong, Q., Gu, Z., Luo, K., & Li, W. (2024). Nanomedicine combats drug resistance in lung cancer. *Advanced Materials, 36*(3). doi:10.1002/adma.202308977.

Index

Page numbers followed by "*f*" and "*t*" indicate, figures and tables respectively.

Printed and bound by CPI Group (UK) Ltd, Croydon, CR0 4YY
18/08/2026
02199344-0002

CONTEMPORARY MATHEMATICS

700

Centre de Recherches Mathématiques Proceedings

CRM

Geometric and Computational Spectral Theory

Séminaire de Mathématiques Supérieures
Geometric and Computational Spectral Theory
June 15–26, 2015
Centre de Recherches Mathématiques,
Université de Montréal, Montréal, Québec

Alexandre Girouard
Dmitry Jakobson
Michael Levitin
Nilima Nigam
Iosif Polterovich
Frédéric Rochon
Editors

American Mathematical Society
Providence, Rhode Island

Centre de Recherches Mathématiques
Montréal, Québec, Canada

2010 *Mathematics Subject Classification.* Primary 58Jxx, 35Pxx, 65Nxx.

Library of Congress Cataloging-in-Publication Data

Names: Girouard, Alexandre, 1976- editor.
Title: Geometric and computational spectral theory : Séminaire de Mathématiques Supérieures, June 15-26, 2015, Centre de Recherches Mathématiques, Université de Montréal, Montréal, Quebec, Canada / Alexandre Girouard, Dmitry Jakobson, Michael Levitin, Nilima Nigam, Iosif Polterovich, Frédéric Rochon, editors.
Description: Providence, Rhode Island : American Mathematical Society ; Montréal, Quebec, Canada : Centre de Recherches Mathématiques, [2017] | Series: Contemporary mathematics ; volume 700 | Includes bibliographical references.
Identifiers: LCCN 2017030037 | ISBN 9781470426651 (alk. paper)
Subjects: LCSH: Metric spaces–Congresses. | Spectral geometry–Congresses. | Geometry, Differential–Congresses. | AMS: Global analysis, analysis on manifolds – Partial differential equations on manifolds; differential operators – Partial differential equations on manifolds; differential operators. msc | Partial differential equations – Spectral theory and eigenvalue problems – Spectral theory and eigenvalue problems. msc | Numerical analysis – Partial differential equations, boundary value problems – Partial differential equations, boundary value problems. msc
Classification: LCC QA611.28 .G46 2015 | DDC 515/.353–dc23
LC record available at https://lccn.loc.gov/2017030037
DOI: http://dx.doi.org/10.1090/conm/700

∞ The paper used in this book is acid-free and falls within the guidelines established to ensure permanence and durability.
Visit the AMS home page at http://www.ams.org/

10 9 8 7 6 5 4 3 2 1 22 21 20 19 18 17

Contents

Preface

The 2015 edition of the *Séminaire de Mathématiques Supérieures* (SMS) took place on June 15-26, 2015, at the Université de Montréal. The topic of the meeting was *Geometric and computational spectral theory*, and it was perhaps the largest school in spectral geometry since the late nineties. The event was sponsored by the Centre de recherche mathématiques, as well as by the Fields Institute (Toronto), the Pacific Institute for the Mathematical Sciences (Vancouver), the Mathematical Sciences Research Institute (Berkeley), the Institut des sciences mathématiques (Montréal) and the Canadian Mathematical Society.

The summer school brought together students and internationally renowned experts in the geometric and computational aspects of spectral theory. The area of spectral theory has fascinated mathematicians and physicists for centuries, and recent years have seen remarkable progress in several branches of the field. The scientific program consisted of twelve minicourses in four main themes: geometry of eigenvalues, geometry of eigenfunctions, computational spectral theory, and spectral theory on singular spaces. A particular emphasis was made on the interplay between these topics, notably between the computational and the geometric part — which was one of the most novel aspects of the school. The minicourses were complemented by exercise sessions, computer labs and short presentations by selected junior participants who have already made important contributions to the subject. The school featured about 90 participants from 13 countries spanning five continents. The current volume contains the lecture notes and survey papers based on nine minicourses delivered at the summer school.

The lecture notes by Bruno Colbois (Neuchâtel) begin with an overview of some basic facts on the spectrum of the Laplace operator on Euclidean domains and Riemannian manifolds. The main part of the notes is concerned with the geometric eigenvalue inequalities, notably the Cheeger lower bound on the first eigenvalue and the Korevaar's method for estimating from above the eigenvalues of the Laplacian on a Riemannian manifold in a fixed conformal class. The last two sections cover some related recent results obtained by the author and his collaborators. In particular, bounds on the eigenvalues of hypersurfaces are discussed, as well as the notions of the topological and conformal spectra.

The lecture notes by Gregory Berkolaiko (Texas A & M) provide an introduction to spectral theory of Schrödinger operators on metric graphs, which in this setting are known as quantum graphs. A number of illuminating examples are treated in detail. A particular emphasis is made on the count of zeros of the eigenfunctions of quantum graphs.

A survey paper by Dorin Bucur (Chambéry) and Pedro Freitas (Lisbon) focusses on the celebrated Faber-Krahn inequality for the fundamental tone of the

Dirichlet Laplacian from the viewpoint of free boundary problems. The proof of the Faber-Krahn inequality which is presented is purely variational and, surprisingly, does not use rearrangement arguments. The advantage of this approach is its adaptability to extremal problems for higher eigenvalues and to more general Robin boundary conditions.

The paper by Pierre Bérard (Institut Fourier) and Bernard Helffer (Nantes and Orsay) is concerned with the nodal properties of the quantum harmonic oscillator and other Schrödinger operators on a Euclidean plane. In particular, the authors show that for the two-dimensional isotropic quantum harmonic oscillator there exists an infinite sequence of eigenfunctions with exactly two nodal domains. For the spherical Laplacian and the Dirichlet Laplacian on a square a similar result has been proved long time ago by A. Stern and H. Lewy. Other questions in nodal geometry are also discussed, such as bounds on the length of the zero set of a Schrödinger eigenfunction in the classically permitted region.

The next three contributions to the volume deal with various computational aspects of spectral theory. The paper by Jessica Bosch and Chen Greif (UBC) provides a review of the numerical methods for computing eigenvalues of matrices. A number of methods are discussed in detail, including the power method, the divide-and-conquer algorithms for tridiagonal matrices, as well as several approaches to compute the eigenvalues of large and sparce matrices, such as Lanczos, Arnoldi and Jacobi-Davidson methods.

The notes by Guido Kanschat (Heidelberg) give an introduction to the finite element methods for variational eigenvalue problems. In particular, Galerkin approximation is discussed in detail. Several eigenvalue problems are considered, including the standard boundary value problems for the Laplacian, as well as problems arising in the study of Maxwell and Stokes equations. In the appendix, some computer programs for experiments are presented.

The lecture notes by Alexander Strohmaier (Leeds) provide a link between the "numerical" and the "geometric" themes of this volume. The notes focus on the method of particular solutions and its applications to the computation of eigenvalues of the Laplace operator on Riemannian manifolds, including hyperbolic surfaces. Several Mathematica programs are included for illustration, which is most helpful. Computations of various spectral quantities, such as the spectral zeta function and the zeta-regularized determinant of the Laplace operator, are also discussed.

The remaining two contributions are based on minicourses requiring more advanced analytic background. The lecture notes by Daniel Grieser (Oldenburg) give an introduction to analysis on manifolds with corners in the spirit of R. Melrose. Its tools are used to construct quasimodes (i.e. approximate eigenfunctions) for degenerating families of domains, including adiabatic limit families and families exhibiting certain types of sclaing behaviour.

The notes by Colin Guillarmou (ENS) are concerned with geometric inverse problems on surfaces with boundary, such as the lens rigidity problem and its special case, the boundary rigidity problem. These problems naturally arise when one needs to recover the Riemannian metric on a surface from the boundary measurements. A closely related notion of the X-ray transform is also discussed.

The Proceedings of the *2015 Séminaire de Mathématiques Supérieures* on *Geometric and Computational Spectral Theory* cover a large variety of topics and methods, combining geometric, analytic and numerical ideas. We hope that this volume will serve both as a useful reference for experts and as an inspiring reading for young mathematicians who would like to learn more about this fascinating and rapidly developing area of mathematics. The editors would like to express their gratitude to all the contributing authors, as well as to all the speakers at the summer school. Last but not least, it is our pleasure to thank the SMS coordinator, Sakina Benhima, for all her hard work and help with the organization of this event.

Contemporary Mathematics
Volume **700**, 2017
http://dx.doi.org/10.1090/conm/700/14181

The spectrum of the Laplacian: A geometric approach

Bruno Colbois

Preamble: These notes correspond to a 4-hour lecture and one exercise session given in Montréal in June 2015 during the summer school *Geometric and Computational Spectral Theory*. The goal was to introduce the subject, that is to present various aspects of the spectrum of the Laplacian on a compact Riemannian manifold from a geometric viewpoint, and also to prepare the audience for some of the following lectures.

In the first part, I recall without proof some classical facts, I try to illustrate the theory with examples and I discuss open questions. The aim is to give an intuition to the students discovering the subject, without being too formal. The exercise session was very useful, revealing that things which are obvious for the people of the field are far from being simple for those looking at the question for the first time. This is the reason why I decided to present in these notes really simple examples with a lot of details.

In the second part, I focus mainly on a specific problem: the estimates of the spectrum in the conformal class of a given Riemannian metric. This is the opportunity to present recent developments on the subject and to explain some very interesting geometrical methods in order to get upper bounds for the spectrum.

As already mentioned, I have tried not to be too formal, and the price for that is that things may sometimes lack precision. I have tried to give all needed references, and for the basics, I will mainly refer to the following books. The book of A. Henrot [**He**] constitutes a very good reference for the study of the spectrum of the Laplacian for Euclidean domains, and the books of I. Chavel [**Ch1**] and P. Bérard [**Be**] are very convenient for the spectrum of the Laplacian on Riemannian manifolds. They contain a lot of basic and important results. More recent references are the book of Rosenberg [**Ro**] (but rather far from the goal of this lecture) and the lecture notes about Spectral Theory and Geometry edited by B. Davies and Y. Safarov [**ST**]. Last but not least, it is always interesting to look at the famous book of Berger-Gauduchon-Mazet [**BGM**], who played an important role in the development of the Geometrical Spectral Theory. At the moment when the summer school took place, the book by O. Lablée [**La**] appeared. I did not use it to write these notes but it is an interesting introduction to the subject.

2010 *Mathematics Subject Classification.* Primary 35P15, 58J50.

1. Introduction, basic results and examples

In this section, I will describe without proof some classical results and examples concerning the spectrum of the Laplacian on domains and on Riemannian manifolds. Most of the time, I will introduce the different notions rather informally and refer to classical texts for more details. The aim is to give a very rough first idea of a part of the "landscape" of the geometrical spectral theory thanks to a couple of examples and results. It is as well an opportunity to introduce some of the other lectures of the summer school.

1.1. The Laplacian for Euclidean domains with Dirichlet boundary conditions.

Let $\Omega \subset \mathbb{R}^n$ be a bounded, open, connected domain with Lipschitz boundary. The *Laplacian* we will consider is given by

$$\Delta f = -\sum_{i=1}^{n} \frac{\partial^2 f}{\partial x_i^2}$$

where $f \in C^2(\Omega)$. We investigate the spectrum of the Laplacian Δ on Ω with the *Dirichlet boundary condition*, that is we study the eigenvalue problem

$$\Delta f = \lambda f \tag{1}$$

under the Dirichlet condition

$$f_{|\partial\Omega} = 0. \tag{2}$$

This problem has a discrete and real spectrum

$$0 < \lambda_1(\Omega) < \lambda_2(\Omega) \le \lambda_3(\Omega) \le ... \to \infty,$$

with the eigenvalues repeated according to their multiplicity.

EXAMPLE 1. If Ω is the interval $]0,\pi[\subset \mathbb{R}$, the Laplacian is given by $\Delta f = -f''$ and the spectrum, for the Dirichlet boundary condition, is given by $\lambda_k = k^2$, $k = 1, 2, ...$ The eigenfunction corresponding to $\lambda_k = k^2$ is $f_k(x) = \sin kx$.

However, it is exceptional to be able to calculate explicitly the spectrum. In dimensions greater than one, it is generally not possible (apart from a few exceptions like the ball or a product of intervals) to calculate the spectrum of a domain. The calculation of the spectrum of a ball is classic, but not easy. It is done with enough details, for example, in the introduction of the Ph. D. thesis of A. Berger [**Ber**].

Given that, physically, the Dirichlet problem is a modelization of the *vibration of a fixed membrane*, it can be hoped to have connections between the *geometry* (or *shape*) of a domain Ω and its spectrum. By *fixed* membrane is understood a membrane whose boundary is fixed, like a drum. This leads to the following very classical image for two types of problems in the context of geometrical spectral theory:

The direct problems. When we see a drum, we have an idea of how it would sound. The mathematical translation is: if we have some information about the geometry (or the shape) of a domain Ω, we can hope to get information (or estimates) about its spectrum. By *information about the geometry* can be understood for example the volume, the diameter of Ω, the mean curvature of its boundary, the inner radius. By *estimates of the spectrum*, we understand lower or upper bounds for some or all of the eigenvalues, with respect to the geometrical information we have.

The inverse problems. If we hear a drum, even if we do not see it, we have an idea of its shape. The mathematical translation is: If we have information about the spectrum of a domain, we can hope to get information about its geometry. The most famous question is whether the shape of a domain is determined by its spectrum (question of M. Kac in 1966: can one hear the shape of a drum?). In other words: if we know all the spectrum of a domain, are we able to reconstruct the domain? The formal answer is no: There are a lot of domains having the same spectrum without being isometric. However, in some sense, this is often true, which makes things complicated. I will not go further in this direction in these notes, see [**Go**] for a survey of the subject.

1.1.1. *The Faber-Krahn inequality.* This is an old but very enlightening result found independently by Faber and Krahn in the 1920's: More explanations and a sketch of the proof can be found in [**As**, p. 102–103]. The proof uses the isoperimetric inequality and is not easy. In his lecture, D. Bucur will offer an approach for a new proof of this inequality (see [**BF**]).

THEOREM 2. *Let $\Omega \subset \mathbb{R}^n$ be a bounded open domain in $\mathbb{R}^n$ and $B \subset \mathbb{R}^n$, a ball with the same volume as Ω. If λ_1 denotes the first eigenvalue for the Dirichlet boundary conditions, then*

$$\lambda_1(B) \leq \lambda_1(\Omega),$$

with equality if and only if Ω is equal to B up to a displacement.

Firstly, the theorem gives a lower bound for the first Dirichlet eigenvalue of a domain Ω which is a typical direct problem. If the volume of Ω is known, then one gets immediately information about the spectrum: a lower bound for the first eigenvalue. But the *equality case* can be understood as an inverse result. If Ω and B have the same volume and if $\lambda_1(\Omega) = \lambda_1(B)$, then Ω is a ball.

This result is also very interesting because it allows very modern questions to be asked. We will mention a few of them, without going into much detail. The same type of questions could also be asked in other situations (other boundary conditions, Laplacian on Riemannian manifolds, other differential operators, etc.).

(1) **The stability.** If a domain $\Omega \subset \mathbb{R}^n$ has the same volume as a ball B and if, moreover, $\lambda_1(\Omega)$ is close to $\lambda_1(B)$, can one say that Ω is *close* to the ball B? Of course, a difficulty is to state what is meant by "close". There are a lot of results around this problem that I will not describe in detail, but see [**FMP**] for a recent and important contribution and [**BP**] for a very recent survey about this question.

    Note that it is not too difficult to see that one can do a small hole in any domain or add a "thin hair" without affecting the spectrum too much (easy part in Example 16 and more explanations in [**BC**], [**CGI**]). Therefore, it cannot be hoped for example, that Ω will be homeomorphic to a ball, or will be Hausdorff close to a ball. However, essentially, one can show that Ω is close to a ball in the *sense of the measure*, see Figure 1 and [**FMP**], [**BP**].

(2) **The spectral stability.** The next natural question is to see what this stability will imply: in [**BC**], we have shown that if Ω and B have the same volume, and if $\lambda_1(\Omega)$ is close to $\lambda_1(B)$ then, for all k, $\lambda_k(\Omega)$ is close to $\lambda_k(B)$ (but, of course, not uniformly in k). The difficulty is that the proximity of $\lambda_1(\Omega)$ and $\lambda_1(B)$ implies only that the domains are "close

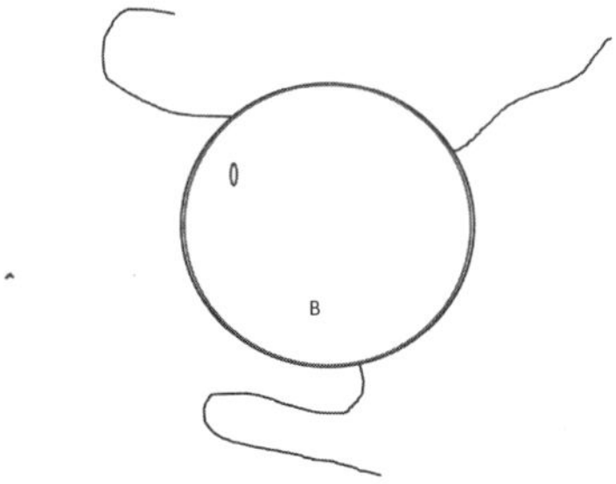

FIGURE 1. The domain Ω is close to the ball B in the sense of the measure

in the sense of the measure", and we have to show that this is enough to control all the eigenvalues.

(3) **The extremal domains.** We have seen that, among all domains having the same volume, the ball is the domain having the minimal λ_1. We can of course ask for domain(s) having the minimal λ_k. The various aspects of this problem are very complicated and most are far from being solved. For λ_2, it is well known that the solution is the union of two disjoint balls (see [**He**, Thm. 4.1.1]). Note that this domain is not regular in the sense that was expected. But in general, it is already difficult to find a right context where it can be shown that an extremal domain exists. It will be one of the goals of D. Bucur's lecture to explain this, and I do not develop the question more here. See also the contribution of D. Bucur in [**BF**].

It is interesting to sketch the proof for λ_2 as it is done, for example, in [**He**]. It uses the *Courant Nodal Theorem* (see the lecture of B. Helffer, [**BH**] or [**Ch1**, p. 19]) which says the following: if $\{f_i\}_{i=1}^{\infty}$ denotes an orthonormal basis of eigenfunctions for $\{\lambda_i(\Omega)\}_{i=1}^{\infty}$, then the number of *nodal domains* of f_k is less than or equal to k, for every $k \geq 1$, where a *nodal domain of* u_k is a connected component of $\bar{\Omega}/f_k^{-1}(0)$.

The first implication of the theorem of Courant is that any eigenfunction f_1 associated to the first eigenvalue λ_1 of a domain Ω has a constant sign (say it is positive) and has multiplicity one. The second eigenvalue λ_2 of Ω could have multiplicity. If f_2 is an eigenfuction associated to λ_2, it has to be orthogonal to f_1, and, as consequence, changes its sign. Let

$$A_1 = \{x \in \Omega : f_2(x) > 0\};\ A_2 = \{x \in \Omega : f_2(x) < 0\}.$$

The Courant Nodal Theorem says that A_1 and A_2 are connected. Thanks to this information and to the theorem of Faber-Krahn, we can prove that the extremal domain for λ_2 is the union of two balls of the same size. Let Ω be a domain, and f_2 an eigenfunction for λ_2.

The restriction of f_2 to A_1 and to A_2 satisfies the Laplace equation, and f_2 is an eigenfunction of eigenvalue λ_2. But on A_1 and A_2, f does not change its sign. This means that f_2 is an eigenfunction for the *first* eigenvalue of A_1 and A_2, and it follows

$$\lambda_1(A_1) = \lambda_1(A_2) = \lambda_2(\Omega).$$

Let B_1, B_2 two balls with $Vol(B_1) = Vol(A_1)$ and $Vol(B_2) = Vol(A_2)$. By Faber-Krahn, we have

$$\lambda_1(A_i) \geq \lambda_1(B_i),\ i = 1, 2,$$

with equality if A_i is congruent to B_i, so that

$$\lambda_2(\Omega) \geq max(\lambda_1(B_1), \lambda_1(B_2)).$$

If we consider the disjoint union B^* of B_1 and B_2, the spectrum of B^* is the union of both spectrum, and $Vol(B^*) = Vol(\Omega)$, so that $\lambda_2(B^*) \leq max(\lambda_1(B_1), \lambda_1(B_2))$.

We deduce $\lambda_2(B^*) = max(\lambda_1(B_1), \lambda_1(B_2))$. In order to have the smallest possible λ_2, we have to choose two balls of the same radius, and the equality case in the Faber-Krahn inequality implies that Ω is the disjoint union of two identical balls.

(4) **Numerical estimates.** Knowing about the existence of extremal domains from a theoretical viewpoint, one can try to investigate *the shape* of such domains. It is almost impossible to do this from a formal point of view, and this was investigated from a numerical point of view, in particular for domains of $\mathbb{R}^2$. But this is also a difficult numerical problem, in particular due to the fact that there are a lot of *local* extrema. This approach was initiated in the thesis of E. Oudet. Note that it gives us a candidate to be extremal, but we have no proof that the domain appearing as extremal is the right one. It is important to apply different numerical approaches, and to see if they give the same results. See the thesis of A. Berger [**Ber**] for a description of results.

REMARK 3. A question could be whether a domain of given fixed volume could have a very large first eigenvalue λ_1: The answer is yes. For example, think of a long and thin domain, and more generally of "thin" domains, that is domains with small inradius. However, formally, a small inradius does not imply large eigenvalue λ_1. We have to take into account the *connectivity* of the domain, see [**Cr**], where the following is shown: if Ω is a bounded connected domain in $\mathbb{R}^2$ with inradius ρ and k boundary components, then the first eigenvalue $\lambda_1(\Omega)$ for the Dirichlet boundary considitions satisfies

$$\lambda_1(\Omega) \geq \frac{1}{4\rho^2}$$

if $k = 1, 2$, and

$$\lambda_1(\Omega) \geq \frac{1}{2k\rho^2}$$

for $k \geq 2$. So, there is an intriguing relationship between k and ρ. For example, a ball with a lot of very small holes can have a first eigenvalue close to the first eigenvalue of the ball (the problem of the Crushed Ice described for example in [**Ch1**, p. 233]).

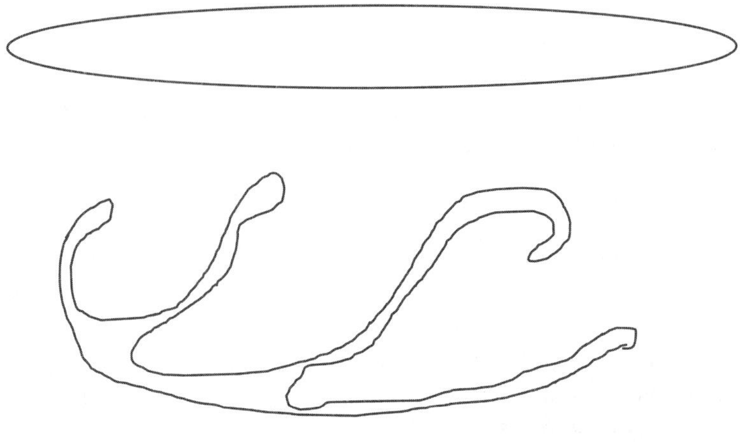

FIGURE 2. Examples with "large" Dirichlet eigenvalue

1.2. The Laplacian for Euclidean domains with Neumann boundary conditions. Let $\Omega \subset \mathbb{R}^n$ be a bounded, connected domain with a Lipschitz boundary. The *Laplacian* is given by

$$\Delta f = -\sum_{i=1}^{n} \frac{\partial^2 f}{\partial x_i^2}$$

where $f \in C^2(\Omega)$. What is investigated is the spectrum of the Laplacian Δ on Ω with the *Neumann boundary condition*, that is the eigenvalue problem

$$\Delta f = \lambda f \tag{3}$$

under the Neumann condition

$$(\frac{\partial f}{\partial n})_{|\partial\Omega} = 0. \tag{4}$$

where n denotes the exterior normal to the boundary.

This problem has a discrete and real spectrum

$$\lambda_0 = 0 < \lambda_1(\Omega) < \lambda_2(\Omega) \leq \lambda_3(\Omega) \leq ... \to \infty,$$

with the eigenvalues repeated according to their multiplicity.

EXAMPLE 4. If Ω is the interval $]0, \pi[\subset \mathbb{R}$, the Laplacian is given by $\Delta f = -f''$ and the spectrum, for the Neumann boundary condition, is given by $\lambda_k = k^2$, $k = 0, 1, 2, ...$ The eigenfunction corresponding to $\lambda_k = k^2$ is $f_k(x) = \cos kx$.

We also refer to [**Ber**] for the calculation of the spectrum of the ball in dimensions 2 and 3.

Some similarities between the spectrum for the Neumann boundary condition and Dirichlet boundary condition can be noticed. However, in this introduction, I will mainly focus on the differences.

A first obvious difference is that zero is always an eigenvalue, corresponding to the constant eigenfunction. This means that the first *interesting* eigenvalue is the second, or the first *nonzero* eigenvalue.

In Example 13, for the Dirichlet problem, we will see that if $\Omega_1 \subset \Omega_2$, then we have for each k that $\lambda_k(\Omega_1) \geq \lambda_k(\Omega_2)$ (we say that we have *monotonicity*).

On the contrary, in Example 18, we will see that we have no monotonicity for the Neumann problem. Indeed, in this case, the fact that $\Omega_1 \subset \Omega_2$ has no implication on the spectrum.

We will also see that the spectrum for the Neumann conditions is *very* sensitive to perturbations of the boundary. At this stage, I must clarify that, because the goal of these lectures was to present a geometric approach, I have chosen bounded domains with a *Lipschitz* boundary. This guarantees the discreteness of the spectrum, but this hypothesis may be relaxed, in particular for the Dirichlet problem (see the lectures of D. Bucur). In Example 19, we will construct a bounded domain, with a smooth boundary up to one singular point, and a non-discrete spectrum.

1.2.1. *The Szegö-Weinberger inequality.* For further details, please refer to [**As**, p. 103]. It is similar to the Faber-Krahn inequality, but is more delicate to prove, precisely because it concerns the second eigenvalue λ_1.

THEOREM 5. *Let Ω be an open bounded domain in $\mathbb{R}^n$ with Lipschitz boundary and $B \subset \mathbb{R}^n$ a ball with the same volume of Ω. If λ_1 denotes the first eigenvalue for the Neumann boundary conditions, then*

$$\lambda_1(\Omega) \leq \lambda_1(B),$$

with equality if and only if Ω is equal to B up to a displacement.

REMARK 6.

(1) In contrast with the case of the Dirichlet boundary condition, λ_1 cannot be very large for a domain of fixed volume when we take the Neumann boundary condition.
(2) We will see that there are domains of fixed volume with as many eigenvalues close to 0 as we want.
(3) There is no spectral stability in the Neumann problem. Indeed, we can perturb a ball by pasting a thin full cylinder of convenient length L: It does not affect the first nonzero eigenvalue but all the others. Using results in the spirit of [**An1**], the spectrum converges to the union of the spectrum of the ball and of the spectrum of $[0, L]$, with the Dirichlet boundary condition on 0 and the Neumann condition on L. It suffices to choose L in such a way that the first eigenvalue of the interval lies between the two first eigenvalues (without multiplicity) of the ball.

1.3. The Laplacian on a Riemannian manifold. Let (M, g) be a Riemannian manifold. If $f \in C^2(M)$, then let us define

$$\Delta f = -div\ grad\ f,$$

and look at the eigenvalue problem

$$\Delta f = \lambda\ f.$$

In local coordinates $\{x_i\}$, the Laplacian reads

$$\Delta f = -\frac{1}{\sqrt{det(g)}} \sum_{i,j} \frac{\partial}{\partial x_j}(g^{ij}\sqrt{det(g)}\frac{\partial}{\partial x_i} f).$$

In particular, in the Euclidean case, we recover the usual expression

$$\Delta f = -\sum_j \frac{\partial}{\partial x_j}\frac{\partial}{\partial x_j} f.$$

We will not use very often the expression of the Laplacian in local coordinates. People who are not familiar with the Riemannian geometry could think of a Riemannian manifold as a submanifold of the Euclidean space. Most of the operations we will make consist in "deforming" the Riemannian metric g in order to construct examples or counter-examples. These deformations can be viewed as deformations of the submanifold. However, this intuitive way of thinking has its limits: Some deformations are much easier to realize abstractly as deformations of the Riemannian metric, than to be viewed directly as deformations of a submanifold. This is the case of the *conformal deformation* which will be considered in the second part of this lecture.

When M is compact and connected, we have a discrete spectrum

$$0 = \lambda_0(M,g) < \lambda_1(M,g) \leq \lambda_2(M,g) \leq ... \to \infty.$$

The eigenvalue 0 corresponds to the constant eigenfunction.

EXAMPLE 7. Let us take for M the circle of radius 1 that we can identify with the interval $[0, 2\pi]$ with periodic condition. The spectrum is given by $\lambda_0 = 0$ and

$$\lambda_{2k-1} = \lambda_{2k} = k^2$$

for $k \geq 1$ corresponding to the eigenfuctions $f_{2k-1}(x) = \sin(kx)$, $f_{2k}(x) = \cos(kx)$.

Here as well, there are very few situations where the spectrum can be explicitly calculated. However, there are more examples in the context of Riemannian manifolds than for domains. In the book [**BGM**], the case of the n-dimensional round sphere, and of the flat tori in dimension 2 are studied.

Note that, in dimension greater than 1, the eigenvalues are generically of multiplicity 1 [**Uh**]. However, in the very few examples where the spectrum can be calculated, large multiplicity often arises. This comes from the fact that the examples where we can calculate explicitly the spectrum have a lot of symmetries, and this implies very often the emergence of multiplicity.

1.3.1. *Large and small eigenvalues.* We can address a similar question as that asked about domains. Given a compact connected differential manifold M without boundary, is it possible to find a metric g on M with $\lambda_1(M,g)$ arbitrarily large or small? First, we have to observe that some constraint is needed: for any Riemannian metric g, we have the relation

$$\lambda_k(M, t^2 g) = \frac{1}{t^2}\lambda_k(M,g).$$

This means that, thanks to a homothety of the metric, arbitrarily large or small eigenvalues can be produced. This is also true for Euclidean domains.

A possible constraint is to fix the volume, or, equivalently, to estimate $\lambda_k(M,g)Vol(M,g)^{2/n}$ rather than $\lambda_k(M,g)$, where $n = dim\ M$, because this expression is invariant by homothety.

Small eigenvalues. We will soon see that it is easy to produce a metric of given volume with as many small eigenvalues as we want. This leads to the question of finding lower bounds depending on the geometry.

Large eigenvalues. For large eigenvalues, the result is surprising and it leads to a lot of different types of questions.

The case $dim M \geq 3$. If M is a given compact differential manifold with $dim\ M \geq 3$, then it was proved in [**CD**] that we can choose g of given volume with λ_1 as large as we want. To prove this result:

- first, prove this for the sphere of odd dimension (see for example [**Bl**]) using that the sphere of dimension $(2n+1)$ is a S^1-bundle over $\mathbb{C}P^n$.

- extend the result to the even dimension sphere [**Mu**].

- prove it for every manifold M of dimension ≥ 3 [**CD**], using classical, but rather difficult results from spectral theory. The idea is to deform the metric of the manifold to make it "close" to the metric of a sphere with large eigenvalue, and then to conclude using results about the behavior of the spectrum under surgery.

The case of surfaces. For surfaces, there is an upper bound for λ_k which depends on the genus and on k. This will be proven in the second part of this lecture. But the case of the first nonzero eigenvalue λ_1 is of special interest, and I will conclude this first section with some consideration about this question.

1.3.2. *The case of the first nonzero eigenvalue for surfaces.* For this paragraph, please refer to the recent survey of R. Schoen [**Sc**] paragraph 3, where one can find precise references and explanations, and to [**CE1**].

A first result was proved by Hersch for the sphere in 1970 [**He**]: for any Riemannian metric g on the sphere S^2

$$\lambda_1(S^2,g)Vol(S^2,g) \leq 8\pi \tag{5}$$

with equality if and only if g is the canonical round metric. In 1980, Yang and Yau extended the result to every genus: if S is an orientable surface of genus γ and g a Riemannian metric on S

$$\lambda_1(S,g)Vol(S,g) \leq 8\pi E(\frac{\gamma+3}{2}) \tag{6}$$

where E denotes the integer part. This result is good, in the following sense: There exists a universal constant $C>0$ such that, for each γ, there exists a surface (S,g) of genus γ with $\lambda_1(S,g)Vol(S,g) \geq C\gamma$ (and this is not easy at all to construct). However, it is not optimal, in the sense that there is no equality case.

There are only a few surfaces where the maximum/extremum of $\lambda_1(S,g)Vol(S,g)$ is known:

- the projective space, where the maximum is 12π, reached for the metric with constant curvature;

- the torus, where the maximum is $\frac{8\pi^2}{\sqrt{3}}$, reached by the flat equilateral torus;

- the Klein bottle, where the maximum is $12\pi E(\frac{2\sqrt{2}}{3})$ with an equality case.

- the surface of genus 2. In this situation, the maximum is 16π and is reached by a family of singular metrics. At some point in the proof, there is a numerical estimate.

For surfaces with genus greater than 2, almost nothing is known about maximum/supremum for λ_1.

2. Variational characterization of the spectrum and simple applications

In this section, I give a variational characterization of the spectrum: Roughly speaking, this allows us to investigate the spectrum of the Laplacian without looking at the equation $\Delta u = \lambda u$ itself, but rather by considering some *test functions*.

Moreover, we have only to take into account the gradient of these test functions, and not their second derivative, which is much easier. One can say that this variational characterization is one of the fundamental tools allowing us to use the geometry in order to investigate the spectrum. To illustrate this, I will explain with some detail very elementary constructions *of small eigenvalues*: These constructions are well known by the specialists of the topic, and, in general, they are mentioned in one sentence. Although these are used here at an elementary level, they allow us to understand principles that will be used later in a more difficult context. Please, refer to the book of P. Bérard [**Be**] for more details about the theory.

Let (M,g) be a compact manifold with boundary ∂M. Let $f,h \in C^2(M)$. Then we have the well-known Green's Formula

$$\int_M \Delta f h dvol_g = \int_M \langle df, dh\rangle dvol_g - \int_{\partial M} h\frac{df}{dn}dA$$

where $\frac{df}{dn}$ denotes the derivative of f in the direction of the outward unit normal vector field n on ∂M. $dvol_g$ the volume form on (M,g) (associated to g) and dA the volume form on ∂M.

In particular, if one of the following conditions $\partial M = \emptyset$, $h_{|\partial M} = 0$ or $(\frac{df}{dn})_{|\partial M} = 0$ is satisfied, then we have the relation

$$(\Delta f, h) = (df, dh) = (f, \Delta h)$$

where $(,)$ denotes the L^2-scalar product.

In the sequel, we will study the following eigenvalue problems when M is compact:

- Closed Problem:

$$\Delta f = \lambda f \ in \ M; \ \partial M = \emptyset;$$

- Dirichlet Problem

$$\Delta f = \lambda f \ in \ M; \ f_{|\partial M=0};$$

- Neumann Problem:

$$\Delta f = \lambda f \ in \ M; \ (\frac{df}{dn})_{|\partial M} = 0.$$

The following standard result about the spectrum can be seen in [**Be**, p. 53].

THEOREM 8. *Let M be a compact connected manifold with boundary ∂M (which may be empty), and consider one of the above mentioned eigenvalue problems. Then:*

(1) *The set of eigenvalue consists of an infinite sequence $0 < \lambda_1 \le \lambda_2 \le \lambda_3 \le ... \to \infty$, where 0 is not an eigenvalue in the Dirichlet problem;*
(2) *Each eigenvalue has finite multiplicity and the eigenspaces corresponding to distinct eigenvalues are $L^2(M)$-orthogonal;*
(3) *The direct sum of the eigenspaces $E(\lambda_i)$ is dense in $L^2(M)$ for the L^2-norm. Furthermore, each eigenfunction is C^∞-smooth.*

REMARK 9. The Laplace operator depends only on the given Riemannian metric. If

$$F : (M,g) \to (N,h)$$

is an isometry, then (M, g) and (N, h) have the same spectrum, and if f is an eigenfunction on (N, h), then $f \circ F$ is an eigenfunction on (M, g) for the same eigenvalue.

As already mentioned, the spectrum cannot be computed explicitly, with a few exceptions. In general, it is only possible to get estimates of the spectrum, and these estimations are related to the geometry of the considered manifold (M, g). However, asymptotically, we know how the spectrum behaves. This is the Weyl law.

Weyl law: If (M, g) is a compact Riemannian manifold of dimension n (with or without boundary), then, for each of the above eigenvalue problems,

$$\lambda_k(M,g) \sim \frac{(2\pi)^2}{\omega_n^{2/n}} \left(\frac{k}{Vol(M,g)}\right)^{2/n} \tag{7}$$

as $k \to \infty$, where ω_n denotes the volume of the unit ball of $\mathbb{R}^n$.

This also means

$$\lim_{k\to\infty} \frac{\lambda_k(M,g)}{k^{2/n}} = \frac{(2\pi)^2}{\omega_n^{2/n}} \left(\frac{1}{Vol(M,g)}\right)^{2/n} \tag{8}$$

In particular, the spectrum of (M, g) determines the volume of (M, g).

It is important to stress that the result is asymptotic: We do not know in general for which k the asymptotic estimate becomes good! However, this formula is a guide when trying to get upper bounds.

To introduce some geometry on the study of the Laplacian, it is very relevant to use the variational characterization of the spectrum. To this aim, let us introduce the Rayleigh quotient. In order to do this, we have to consider functions in the *Sobolev space* $H^1(M)$ or $H_0^1(M)$. It is possible to find the definition of $H^1(M)$ or $H_0^1(M)$ in every book on PDE, but what we will really consider are functions which are of class C^1 by part and glue them continuously along a submanifold. Moreover, for $H_0^1(M)$, we consider only functions taking the value 0 on ∂M.

If a function f lies in $H^1(M)$ in the closed and Neumann problems, and in $H_0^1(M)$ for the Dirichlet problem, the Rayleigh quotient of f is

$$R(f) = \frac{\int_M |df|^2 dvol_g}{\int_M f^2 dvol_g} = \frac{(df, df)}{(f, f)}.$$

Note that in the case where f is an eigenfunction for the eigenvalue λ_k, then

$$R(f) = \frac{\int_M |df|^2 dvol_g}{\int_M f^2 dvol_g} = \frac{\int_M \Delta f \ f dvol_g}{\int_M f^2 dvol_g} = \lambda_k.$$

THEOREM 10. *(Variational characterization of the spectrum,* [**Be**, pp. 60–61]*) Let us consider one of the 3 eigenvalues problems.*

Min-Max formula: *we have*

$$\lambda_k = \inf_{V_k} \sup\{R(u) : u \neq 0, \ u \in V_k\}$$

where V_k runs through $k+1$-dimensional subspaces of $H^1(M)$ (k-dimensional subspaces of $H_0^1(M)$ for the Dirichlet eigenvalue problem).

This min-max formula is useless to calculate λ_k, but it is very useful to find an upper bound because of the following fact: For any given $(k+1)$ dimensional vector subspace V of $H^1(M)$, we have

$$\lambda_k(M,g) \leq sup\{R(u) : u \neq 0, \; u \in V\}.$$

This gives immediately an upper bound for $\lambda_k(M,g)$ if it is possible to estimate the Rayleigh quotient $R(u)$ of all the functions $u \in V_k$. Note that there is no need to calculate the Rayleigh quotient, it suffices to estimate it from above. Of course, this upper bound is useful if the vector space V is conveniently chosen.

It would be a delicate problem to estimate the Rayleigh quotient of all functions $u \in V$. A special situation is when V is generated by $k+1$ *disjointly supported functions* $f_1, ..., f_{k+1}$. In this case,

$$sup\{R(u) : u \neq 0, \; u \in V\} = sup\{R(f_i) : i = 1, ..., k+1\}, \tag{9}$$

which makes the estimation easier to do, because we have only to estimate from above the Rayleigh quotient of $(k+1)$ functions. We will use this fact in the sequel.

To see it, let $f = \alpha_1 f_1 + ... + \alpha_{k+1} f_{k+1}$. Then

$$(f,f) = \alpha_1^2 (f_1, f_1) + ... + \alpha_{k+1}^2 (f_{k+1}, f_{k+1}).$$

and

$$(df, df) = \alpha_1^2 (df_1, df_1) + ... + \alpha_{k+1}^2 (df_{k+1}, df_{k+1}).$$

so that $R(f)$ is bounded from above by the maximum of the Rayleigh quotients $R(f_i)$, $i = 1, ..., k+1$.

REMARK 11. We have indeed shown a little more: If the test functions $\{f_i\}_{i=1}^{k+1}$ are orthonormal *and* if the $\{df_i\}_{i=1}^{k+1}$ are orthogonal, then (9) is also true.

REMARK 12. We can see already two advantages to this variational characterization of the spectrum. First, there is no need to work with solutions of the Laplace equation, but only with "test functions", which is easier. Then, only one derivative of the test function has to be controlled, and not two, as in the case of the Laplace equation.

To see this concretely, let us give with some details a couple of simple examples.

EXAMPLE 13. **Monotonicity in the Dirichlet problem.** Let $\Omega_1 \subset \Omega_2 \subset (M,g)$, two domains of the same dimension n of a Riemannian manifold (M,g). Let us suppose that Ω_1 and Ω_2 are both compact connected manifolds with a smooth boundary. If we consider the Dirichlet eigenvalue problem for Ω_1 and Ω_2 with the induced metric, then for each k

$$\lambda_k(\Omega_2) \leq \lambda_k(\Omega_1).$$

The proof is very simple: Each eigenfunction of Ω_1 may be continuously extended by 0 on Ω_2 and may be used as a test function for the Dirichlet problem on Ω_2.

Let us construct an upper bound for $\lambda_k(\Omega_2)$: for V_k, we choose the vector subspace of $H_0^1(\Omega_2)$ generated by an orthonormal basis $f_1, ..., f_k$ of eigenfunctions of Ω_1 extended by 0 on Ω_2. Clearly, these functions vanish on $\partial\Omega_2$ and they are C^∞ on Ω_1 and $\Omega_2 \cap \bar{\Omega_1}^c$. They are continuous on $\partial\Omega_1$.

Let $f = \alpha_1 f_1 + ... + \alpha_k f_k$. We have

$$(f, f) = \alpha_1^2 + ... + \alpha_k^2.$$

We have

$$(df_i, df_j) = \int_{\Omega_2} \langle df_i, df_j \rangle dvol_g = \int_{\Omega_1} \langle df_i, df_j \rangle dvol_g$$
$$= \int_{\Omega_1} \langle \Delta f_i, f_j \rangle dvol_g = \lambda_i \int_{\Omega_1} f_i f_j dvol_g,$$

and it follows that $(df_i, df_i) = \lambda_i(\Omega_1)(f_i, f_i)$ and $(df_i, df_j) = 0$ if $i \neq j$. We have

$$(df, df) = \alpha_1^2 \lambda_1(\Omega_1) + ... + \alpha_k^2 \lambda_k(\Omega_1).$$

We conclude that $R(f) \leq \lambda_k(\Omega_1)$, and we have $\lambda_k(\Omega_2) \leq \lambda_k(\Omega_1)$. As this is true for each k, we have the result.

EXAMPLE 14. As a consequence of (9), if M is a compact Riemannian manifold without boundary, and if Ω_1,...,Ω_{k+1} are domains in M with disjoint interiors, then

$$\lambda_k(M, g) \leq max(\mu_1(\Omega_1), ..., \mu_1(\Omega_{k+1})),$$

where $\mu_1(\Omega)$ denotes the first eigenvalue of Ω for the Dirichlet problem.

Let us choose $(k+1)$ as test functions the eigenfunctions $u_1, ...u_{k+1}$ corresponding to $\mu_1(\Omega_1), ..., \mu_1(\Omega_{k+1})$ respectively, extended by 0 on M.

They have $\mu_1(\Omega_1), ..., \mu_1(\Omega_{k+1})$ as Rayleigh quotients, and this allows us to show the inequality.

EXAMPLE 15. Let us see how to deform a Riemannian manifold (keeping the volume fixed), in order to produce as many small eigenvalues as we want.

We first consider the cylinder $C_L = [0, L] \times S^{n-1}$, where the first Dirichlet eigenvalue satisfies

$$\lambda_1(C_L) \leq \frac{\pi^2}{L^2}$$

To verify that, it suffices to consider the function

$$f(r, x) = f(r) = \sin \frac{\pi r}{L}$$

which is an eigenfunction for $\frac{\pi^2}{L^2}$.

Then, on each manifold M, we can construct a family of Riemannian metrics of fixed volume, with as many small eigenvalues as we want. We just deform the metric without changing the topology as follows: we deform locally a small ball into a long and thin "nose", that is a cylinder $[0, L] \times S_\epsilon^{n-1}$ closed by a cap. We can divide this cylindrical part into $(k + 1)$ disjoint cylinders of length $\frac{L}{k+1}$, and, considering the Dirichlet problem on each of these cylinders, we get

$$\lambda_k \leq \frac{\pi^2 (k+1)^2}{L^2}$$

which is arbitrarily small for k fixed and $L \to \infty$.

In the sequel, we will explain how to produce arbitrarily small eigenvalues for a Riemannian manifold with fixed volume and *bounded diameter* (Cheeger's dumbbell construction and its applications). But let us first apply the min-max formula to an elementary situation of *surgery*.

EXAMPLE 16. **Elementary surgery.** We will explain in detail the already mentioned fact: *A small hole in a domain does not affect the spectrum "too much" (see (10) below).* Let $\Omega \subset \mathbb{R}^n$ a domain with smooth boundary. Let $x \in \Omega$, and $B(x,\epsilon)$ the ball of radius ϵ centered at the point x (ϵ is chosen small enough such that $B(x,\epsilon) \subset \Omega$). We denote by Ω_ϵ the subset $\Omega - B(x,\epsilon)$, that is we make a hole of radius ϵ on Ω.

We consider the two domains Ω and Ω_ϵ with the Dirichlet boundary conditions, and denote by $\{\lambda_k\}_{k=1}^{\infty}$ and by $\{\lambda_k(\epsilon)\}_{k=1}^{\infty}$ their respective spectrums.

Then, for each k, we have

$$\lim_{\epsilon \to 0} \lambda_k(\epsilon) = \lambda_k \tag{10}$$

Before showing this in detail, let us make a few remarks.

REMARK 17.

(1) The convergence is not uniform in k.
(2) This result is a very specific part of a much more general facts. We get this type of results on manifolds, with subset much more general than balls, for example tubular neighborhood of submanifolds of codimension greater than 1. For the interested reader, we refer to the paper of Courtois [**Cou**] and to the book of Chavel [**Ch1**].
(3) We can get very precise asymptotic estimates of $\lambda_k(\epsilon)$ in terms of ϵ. Again, we refer to [**Cou**] and references therein.
(4) We have also the convergence of the eigenspace associated to $\lambda_k(\epsilon)$ to the eigenspace associated to λ_k, but this has to be defined precisely: a problem occurs if the multiplicity of λ_k is not equal to the multiplicity of $\lambda_k(\epsilon)$, see [**Cou**].

In order to see the convergence, we first observe that by monotonicity, for all k

$$\lambda_k \leq \lambda_k(\epsilon).$$

Our goal is to show that

$$\lambda_k(\epsilon) \leq \lambda_k + c(\epsilon),$$

with $c(\epsilon) \to 0$ as $\epsilon \to 0$.

In order to use the min-max construction, we need to consider a family of test-functions. This family is constructed using a perturbation of the eigenfunctions of Ω. Note that we do the proof for $n \geq 3$, but the strategy is the same if $n = 2$.

Let $\{f_i\}_{i=1}^{\infty}$ be an orthonormal basis of eigenfuctions on Ω. We fix a C^∞-plateau function $\chi : \mathbb{R} \to \mathbb{R}$ defined by

$$\chi(r) = \begin{cases} 0 & \text{if } r \leq \frac{3}{2} \\ 1 & \text{if } r \geq 2 \\ 0 \leq \chi(r) \leq 1 & \text{if } \frac{3}{2} \leq r \leq 2 \end{cases}$$

The test function $f_{i,\epsilon}$ associated to f_i is defined by

$$f_{i,\epsilon}(p) = \chi(\frac{d(p,x)}{\epsilon}) f_i.$$

By construction, the function $f_{i,\epsilon}(p)$ takes the value 0 on the ball $B(x,r)$ and satisfies the Dirichlet boundary condition. So, it can be used as a test function in order to estimate $\lambda_{k,\epsilon}$.

Let f be a function on the vector space generated by $\{f_{i,\epsilon}\}_{i=1}^k$. In order to estimate its Rayleigh quotient, it makes a great simplification if the basis is orthonormal and the (df_i) are orthogonal. This is not the case here. However, the basis is *almost* orthonormal and the (df_i) are almost orthogonal: this is what we will first show and use. Note that this is a very common situation.

The basis $\{f_{i,\epsilon}\}_{i=1}^k$ is almost orthonormal. Let us denote by a_i (resp. b_i) the maximum of the function $|f_i|$ (resp. $|df_i|$) on Ω. Then

$$\int_{B(x,2\epsilon)} f_i^2 \leq a_i^2 2^n \omega_n \epsilon^n, \int_{B(x,2\epsilon)} |df_i|^2 \leq b_i^2 2^n \omega_n \epsilon^n \tag{11}$$

where ω_n is the volume of the unit ball in $\mathbb{R}^n$.

Let us show that

$$\delta_{ij} - C_k \epsilon^{n/2} \leq \langle f_{i,\epsilon}, f_{j,\epsilon} \rangle \leq \delta_{ij} + C_k \epsilon^{n/2},$$

where C_k depends on $a_1, ..., a_k$.

$$\langle f_{i,\epsilon}, f_{j,\epsilon}\rangle = \langle \chi_\epsilon f_i, \chi_\epsilon f_j\rangle = \langle (\chi_\epsilon - 1) f_i + f_i, (\chi_\epsilon - 1) f_j + f_j\rangle =$$
$$= \langle f_i, f_j\rangle + \langle (\chi_\epsilon - 1) f_i, f_j\rangle + \langle (\chi_\epsilon - 1) f_j, f_i\rangle + \langle (\chi_\epsilon - 1) f_i, (\chi_\epsilon - 1) f_j\rangle.$$

By (11), $\|(\chi_\epsilon - 1) f_i\|^2 \leq a_i^2 2^n \omega_n \epsilon^n$, and by Cauchy-Schwarz

$$\delta_{ij} - C_k \epsilon^{n/2} \leq \langle f_{i,\epsilon}, f_{j,\epsilon} \rangle \leq \delta_{ij} + C_k \epsilon^{n/2},$$

where C_k depends on $a_1, .., a_k$.

The set $\{df_{i,\epsilon}\}_{i=1}^k$ is almost orthogonal. Let us obverse that

$$df_{i,\epsilon} = d\chi_\epsilon f_i + \chi_\epsilon df_i,$$

and

$$\langle df_{i,\epsilon}, df_{j,\epsilon}\rangle = \langle d\chi_\epsilon f_i, d\chi_\epsilon f_j\rangle + \langle d\chi_\epsilon f_i, \chi_\epsilon df_j\rangle + \langle \chi_\epsilon df_i, d\chi_\epsilon f_j\rangle + \langle \chi_\epsilon df_i, \chi_\epsilon df_j\rangle.$$

This implies

$$\|d\chi_\epsilon f_i\|^2 \leq C \frac{1}{\epsilon^2} \int_{B(x,2\epsilon)} f_i^2 \leq C a_i^2 2^n \omega_n \epsilon^{n-2}$$

where C depends only on the derivative χ' of χ. This is the place where $n \geq 3$ is used in order to have a positive exponent to ϵ.

With the same considerations as before

$$|\langle df_{i,\epsilon}, df_{j,\epsilon}\rangle| \leq \langle df_i, df_j\rangle + C_i \epsilon^{n/2} = \lambda_i \delta_{ij} + C_k \epsilon^{n/2}.$$

where C_k depends on $a_1, ..., a_k, b_1, ..., b_k, C$.

Now, we can estimate the Rayleigh quotient of a function $f \in [f_{1,\epsilon}, ..., f_{k,\epsilon}]$. This is done exactly in the same spirit as the proof of the monotonicity, but we have to deal with the fact that the basis of test functions is only *almost*-orthonormal.

Let $f = \alpha_1 f_{1,\epsilon} + ... + \alpha_k f_{k,\epsilon}$. Thanks to the above considerations, we have

$$\|f\|^2 = \alpha_1^2 + ... + \alpha_k^2 + O(\epsilon^{n/2}),$$
$$\|df\|^2 = \alpha_1^2 \lambda_1 + ... + \alpha_k^2 \lambda_k + O(\epsilon^{\frac{n-2}{2}}).$$

This implies

$$R(f) \leq \lambda_k + O(\epsilon^{\frac{n-2}{2}})$$

and gives the result.

The next example explains how to produce arbitrarily small eigenvalues for Riemannian manifold with fixed volume and *bounded diameter*.

The Cheeger dumbbell construction for Riemannian manifolds. The idea is to consider two n-spheres of fixed volume A connected by a small cylinder C of length $2L$ and radius ϵ. We denote by M_ϵ this manifold. The first nonzero eigenvalue of M_ϵ converges to 0 as ϵ goes to 0. It is even possible to estimate very precisely the asymptotic of λ_1 in term of ϵ (see [**An2**]), but here, let us just shows that it converges to 0.

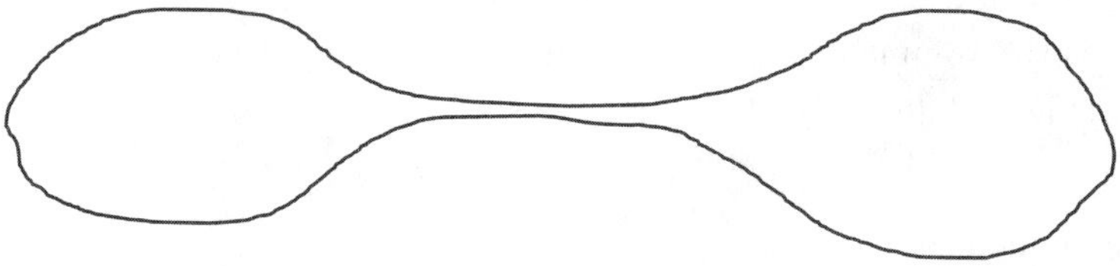

FIGURE 3. Cheeger Dumbell

Let f be a function with value 1 on the first sphere, -1 on the second and decreasing linearly along the cylinder.

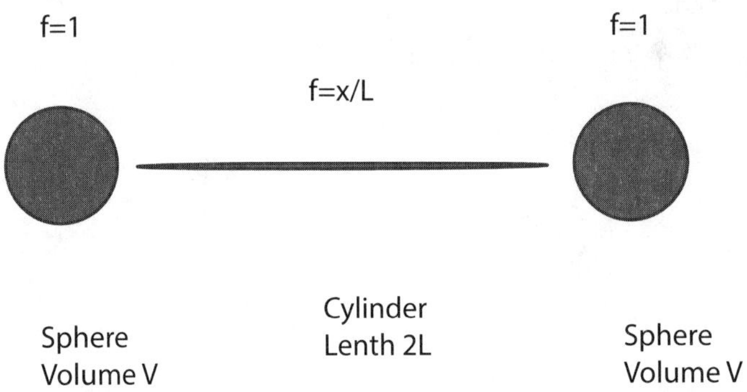

The maximum norm of its gradient is $\frac{1}{L}$. By construction (and because we can suppose for simplicity that the manifold is symmetric), we have $\int_{M_\epsilon} f dvol_{g_\epsilon} = 0$.

Let V be the vector space generated by f and by the constant function 1. If $h \in V$, we can write $h = a + bf$, $a, b \in \mathbb{R}$ and

$$\int_{M_\epsilon} h^2 dvol_{g_\epsilon} = a^2 Vol(M_\epsilon) + b^2 \int_{M_\epsilon} f^2 dvol_{g_\epsilon},$$

$$\int_{M_\epsilon} |dh|^2 dvol_{g_\epsilon} = b^2 \int_{M_\epsilon} |df|^2 dvol_{g_\epsilon}.$$

So, as $\lambda_1 = inf\{R(h) : h \in V\}$, we get $\lambda_1(M_\epsilon) \leq R(f)$.

The function f varies only on the cylinder C and its gradient has norm $\frac{1}{L}$. This implies

$$\int_{M_\epsilon} |df|^2 dvol_{g_\epsilon} = \frac{1}{L^2} Vol(C).$$

Moreover, because f^2 takes the value 1 on both spheres of volume A, we have

$$\int_{M_\epsilon} f^2 dvol_{g_\epsilon} \geq 2A.$$

This implies that the Rayleigh quotient of f is bounded above by

$$\frac{VolC/L^2}{2A}$$

which goes to 0 as ϵ does.

A similar construction with k spheres connected by thin cylinders shows that there exist examples with k arbitrarily small eigenvalues.

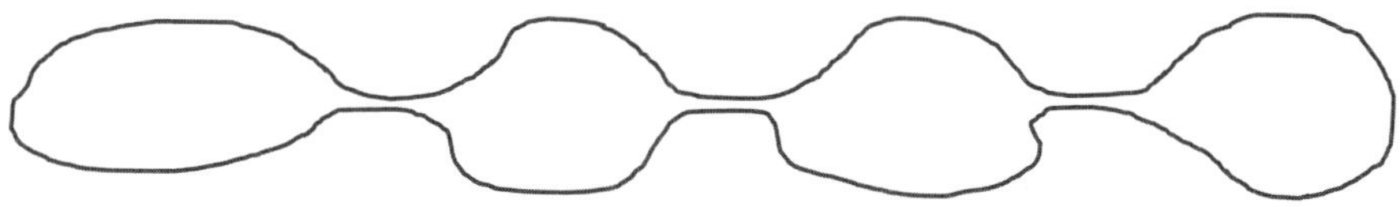

FIGURE 4. Examples with 3 "small" nonzero eigenvalues

Observe that we can easily fix the volume and the diameter in all these constructions: Thus to fix the volume and diameter is not enough to have a lower bound on the spectrum.

Cheeger dumbbell for the Neumann problem. The same construction as above may be done in the case of the Neumann problem for a domain in $\mathbb{R}^n$. A Cheeger dumbbell is simply given by two disjointed balls related by a thin full cylinder. This gives two interesting examples. The first shows that we have no monotonicity for the Neumann problem.

EXAMPLE 18. Let $\Omega \subset \mathbb{R}^n$ a domain. There exists a domain $\Omega_1 \subset \Omega$ with a smooth boundary such that the k first eigenvalues of Ω_1 are arbitrarily small.

To do this, choose Ω_1 to be a like a Cheeger dumbbell, with $k+1$ balls related by very thin cylinders. We see immediately that the k first eigenvalues can be made as small as we wish, with the same calculations as above.

Note that we have no monotonicity for the Neumann problem even when we restrict ourself to *convex* domains. For example, in dimension 2, we can consider a square $[0, \pi] \times [0, \pi]$. The first nonzero eigenvalue is 1. But we can construct inside this square a thin rectangle around the diagonal of the square of length almost $\sqrt{2}\pi$: the first eigenvalue is close to $\frac{1}{2}$.

Note, however, that we cannot find *convex* subsets of $[0, \pi] \times [0, \pi]$ with arbitrarily small first nonzero eigenvalue. By a result of Payne and Weinberger [**PW**], we have for $\Omega \subset \mathbb{R}^n$, convex, the inequality

$$\lambda_1(\Omega) \geq \frac{\pi^2}{diam(\Omega)^2}.$$

EXAMPLE 19. This example shows that a small, local perturbation of a domain may strongly affect the spectrum of the Laplacian for the Neumann conditions. The text gives only qualitative arguements, the calculations are left to the reader if he needs them to understand the examples.

We begin with a domain Ω (a ball in the picture) and show that a very small perturbation of the boundary may change drastically the spectrum for the Neumann boundary condition: A nonzero eigenvalue arbitrarily close to zero may appear as a consequence of a very small perturbation.

FIGURE 5. We want to perturb locally a domain Ω

We add a small ball close to Ω (but at a positive distance) and link it to Ω using a thin cylinder. The important point is not the size of the ball or of the cylinder, but the ratio. As on the picture, the radius of the cylinder must be much smaller than the radius of the ball. This creates a Cheeger dumbbell: the only difference with the above calculations is that the two "thick" parts do not have the same size, but it is easy to adapt the calculations and show that if the radius of the cylinder goes to zero, then the same is true for the first nonzero eigenvalue. The ball can be very small and very close to Ω, so the perturbation may be confined in an arbitrarily small region.

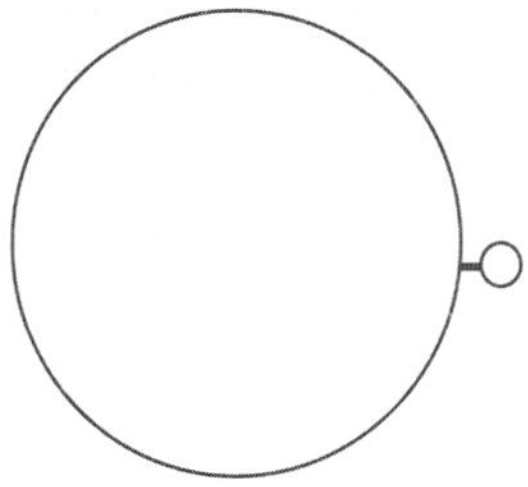

FIGURE 6. Add a small ball and link it to Ω with a thin cylinder

We can iterate this first deformation, constructing a new deformation on the first, a new one on the second, etc.

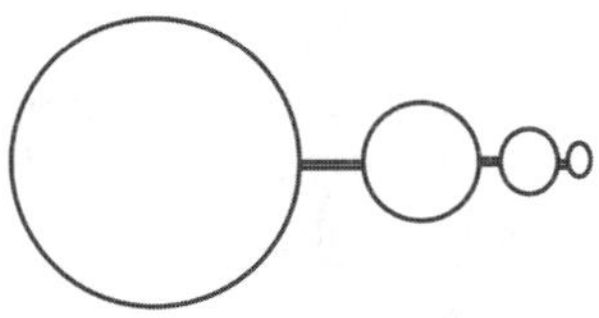

FIGURE 7. Add a small ball and link it to Ω with a thin cylinder

This can be understood as a family of balls B_k of radius $r_k = \frac{1}{2^{2k}}$, with center x_k. All the centers are on the same line, and the distance between x_k and x_{k+1} is $\frac{1}{2^k}$.

The balls B_k and B_{k+1} are joined using a cylinder of radius $\frac{1}{2^{2^k}}$. This radius is very thin in comparison with the radius of the ball.

The result of this construction is a domain with an infinite number of Cheeger dumbbells. The domain is not compact, but taking its adherence add only one point, which is of course a singular point. In conclusion, we get a domain with a smooth boundary up to one singular point, and infinitely many small eigenvalues: This implies that the spectrum is not discrete and shows that we must be careful with the smoothness of the boundary.

Conclusion: More generally, by a *Cheeger dumbbell*, we understand a manifold where two (or more) "thick parts" are separated by one (or more) "thin parts". In such situations, the presence of small eigenvalue(s) may be suspected.

FIGURE 8. "Generalized" Cheeger dumbbell

A very general question is to understand under which conditions we can get lower bounds for the spectrum, and in particular for the first nonzero eigenvalue λ_1.

3. Lower bounds for the first nonzero eigenvalue

As mentioned in the preamble, the second part of this lecture will be concerned with the subject *upper bounds for the spectrum*. One of the participants to the school asked me if it is more important or difficult to find upper bounds than lower bounds. The answer is no. The question about *lower bounds* is a world by itself, and the goal of this short section is to present *the tip of the iceberg*: Two different types of results are briefly explained.

In some sense, there are two ways to bound from below the first nonzero eigenvalue of a compact Riemannian manifold. After understanding which deformations of the Riemannian metric can produce small eigenvalues, we have the choice between two strategies.

- A comparison with a geometric constant *taking account* of such local or global deformations of the Riemannian metric

or

- To impose geometric constraints *in order to avoid* such local or global deformations of the Riemannian metric.

It has already been explained which deformations of the Riemannian metric can produce small eigenvalues:

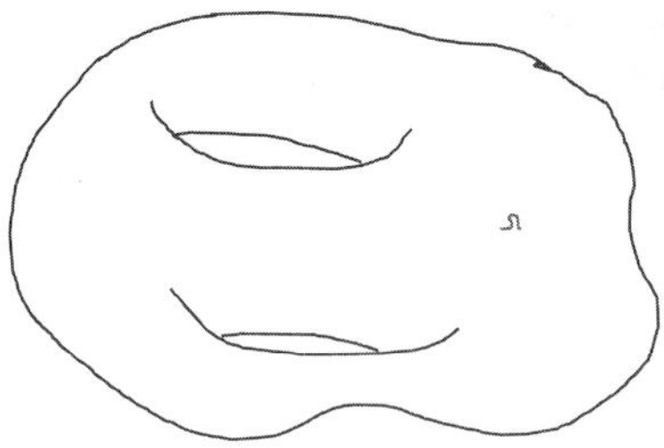

FIGURE 9. A local deformation of the Riemannian metric can produce small eigenvalues

FIGURE 10. "Small mushroom" or a local Cheeger dumbbell

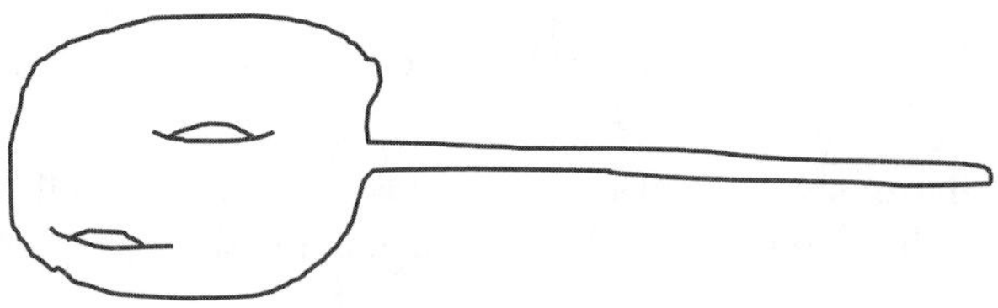

FIGURE 11. Presence of small eigenvalues coming from a global deformation of the metric

It can be local deformations, typically a deformation of the metric around a point producing a dumbbell (one says also sometimes that we construct a small *mushroom* on the manifold). It can be a global deformation, adding a *long nose* to the manifold.

Of course, it is not clear that these types of deformations are the only ones producing small eigenvalues, and the difficulty is to find constraints which allow us to control the spectrum from below.

3.1. A first method: Cheeger's inequality. The Cheeger inequality is in some sense the counter-part of the dumbbell example. It is presented here in the case of a compact Riemannian manifold without boundary, but it may be generalized to compact manifolds with boundary (for both Neumann or Dirichlet boundary conditions) or to non-compact, complete, Riemannian manifolds.

DEFINITION 20. Let (M, g) be an n-dimensional compact Riemannian manifold without boundary. The Cheeger's isoperimetric constant $h = h(M)$ is

$$h(M) = \inf_C \{J(C);\ J(C) = \frac{Vol_{n-1}C}{min(Vol_n M_1, Vol_n M_2)}\},$$

where C runs through all compact codimension one submanifolds which divide M into two disjoint connected open submanifolds M_1, M_2 with common boundary $C = \partial M_1 = \partial M_2$.

THEOREM 21. *(*Cheeger's inequality, 1978*). We have the inequality*

$$\lambda_1(M, g) \geq \frac{h^2(M, g)}{4}.$$

A proof may be found in Chavel's book [**Ch1**] and developments and other statement in Buser's paper [**Bu2**]. In particular, Buser shows that Cheeger's inequality is sharp ([**Bu2**, Thm. 1.19]).

This inequality is remarkable, because it relates an analytic quantity (λ_1) to a geometric quantity (h) without any other assumption on the geometry of the manifold. Note that the Cheeger constant becomes small in the presence of a Cheeger dumbbell or of a long cylinder. The Cheeger constant takes account of the deformations producing small eigenvalues. Note that it is not always easy to estimate the Cheeger constant h of a Riemannian manifold. Sometimes, it is easier to estimate the first nonzero eigenvalue λ_1 in order to get an estimate of h.

Under some geometrical assumptions there is an *upper bound* of λ_1 in terms of the Cheeger constant (see [**Bu2**]).

THEOREM 22. *(Buser, 1982) Let (M^n, g) be a compact Riemannian manifold with Ricci curvature bounded below $Ric(M, g) \geq -\delta^2(n-1)$, $\delta \geq 0$. Then we have*

$$\lambda_1(M, g) \leq C(\delta h + h^2),$$

where C is a constant depending only on the dimension and h is the Cheeger constant.

The condition about the Ricci curvature is necessary. In [**Bu2**], Buser constructs a surface with an arbitrarily small Cheeger constant, but with λ_1 uniformly bounded from below. It is easy to generalize it to any dimension. This example is very interesting, and we will describe the original construction of Buser in detail.

EXAMPLE 23. Let $S^1 \times S^1$ be a torus with its product metric g and coordinates $(x, y), -\pi \leq x, y \leq \pi$ and a conformal metric $g_\epsilon = \chi_\epsilon^2 g$.

The function χ_ϵ is an even function depending only on x, takes the value ϵ at $0, \pi$, 1 outside an ϵ-neighborhood of 0 and π.

It follows immediately that the Cheeger constant $h(g_\epsilon) \to 0$ as $\epsilon \to 0$ and it remains to show that $\lambda_1(g_\epsilon)$ is uniformly bounded from below.

Note that the example seems to be very close to the Cheeger dumbbell. The difference is that in the case of the dumbbell, the length of the cylinder joining the two "big" parts may be small but is fixed. Here, the length of the cylinder goes to 0 as $\epsilon \to 0$.

Let f be an eigenfunction for $\lambda_1(g_\epsilon)$. We have

$$\lambda_1(g_\epsilon) = R(f) = \frac{\int_T |df|_\epsilon^2 dvol_{g_\epsilon}}{\int_T f^2 dvol_{g_\epsilon}}.$$

Let $S_1 = \{p : f(p) \geq 0\}$ and $S_2 = \{p : f(p) \leq 0\}$ and let

$$F(p) = \begin{cases} f(p) & \text{if } p \in S_1 \\ af(p) & \text{if } p \in S_2 \end{cases}$$

where a is chosen such that $\int_T F dvol_g = 0$.

Let V be the vector space generated by the constant function 1 and the function F of integral 0. The situation is exactly the same as for the calculation around the Cheeger dumbbell and it follows $\lambda_1(g) \leq R_g(F)$.

So, it is enough to show that $R_g(F) \leq \lambda_1(g_\epsilon)$:

$$R_g(F) = \frac{\int_{S_1} |df|_g^2 dvol_g + a^2 \int_{S_2} |df|_g^2 dvol_g}{\int_{S_1} f^2 dvol_g + a^2 \int_{S_2} f^2 dvol_g}.$$

By the conformal invariance in dimension 2 (see Prop. 29),

$$\int_{S_i} |df|_{g_\epsilon}^2 dV_{g_\epsilon} dvol_{g_\epsilon} = \int_{S_i} |df|_g^2 dvol_g,$$

and by construction

$$\int_{S_i} f^2 dvol_{g_\epsilon} \leq \int_{S_i} f^2 dvol_g.$$

This implies

$$\lambda_1(g_\epsilon) = R_{g_\epsilon}(f) \geq R_g(F) \geq \lambda_1(g).$$

The geometrical idea behind this construction is the following: the geometry changes very quickly. This allows to get a small Cheeger constant, but the first eigenfunction has not enough place to vary, and the first eigenvalue remains essentially unchanged.

3.2. A second method: control of the curvature and of the diameter. An upper bound on the diameter is clearly a necessary condition to bound the spectrum from below.

A lower bound on the (Ricci) curvature allows avoiding local deformation such as "mushrooms". More precisely, the Ricci curvature allows us to control *the growth of the volume of the balls:* This is the Theorem of Bishop-Gromov that will explained in section 4, in particular Theorem 34.

Here is a lower bound obtained by Li and Yau in 1979:

THEOREM 24 (See [**LY**]). . *Let (M, g) be a compact n-dimensional Riemannian manifold without boundary. Suppose that the Ricci curvature satisfies $Ric(M, g) \geq (n-1)K$ and that d denotes the diameter of (M, g).*

Then, if $K < 0$,

$$\lambda_1(M, g) \geq \frac{exp - (1 + (1 - 4(n-1)^2 d^2 K)^{1/2})}{2(n-1)^2 d^2},$$

and if $K = 0$, then

$$\lambda_1(M, g) \geq \frac{\pi^2}{4d^2}.$$

This first inequality is difficult to read. It means essentially that, for large d,

$$\lambda_1(M, g) \geq C(n) \frac{e^{-(2(n-1)d\sqrt{-K})}}{d^2}.$$

This type of results was generalized in different directions, see for example [**BBG**].

Note that a control of the diameter and of the curvature also allows us to get *upper bounds* for the spectrum.

THEOREM 25 (Cheng Comparison Theorem, 1975, [**Che**]). *Let (M^n, g) be a compact n-dimensional Riemannian manifold without boundary. Suppose that the Ricci curvature satisfies $Ric(M, g) \geq (n-1)K$ and that d denotes the diameter of (M, g).*

Then

$$\lambda_k(M, g) \leq \frac{(n-1)^2 K^2}{4} + \frac{C(n)k}{d^2}$$

where $C(n)$ is a constant depending only on the dimension.

4. Estimates on the conformal class

This section is the more technical part of the text. I will present with some details the proof given by Korevaar of the existence of upper bounds for all the eigenvalues in a given conformal class of Riemannian metric. This is based on a text by Grigor'yan, Netrusov and Yau [**GNY**] that I find particularly enlightening.

4.1. Introduction. Let us begin by recalling the following result from [**CD**] already mentioned in the first part:

THEOREM 26. *Let M be any compact manifold of dimension $n \geq 3$ and $\lambda > 0$. Then there exists a Riemannian metric g on M with $Vol(M, g) = 1$ and $\lambda_1(M, g) \geq \lambda$.*

However, if we stay on the *conformal class* of a given Riemannian metric g_0, then, we get upper bounds for the spectrum on volume one metrics, and it is the goal of this section to explain this.

DEFINITION 27. If g_0 is a Riemannian metric on M, a metric g is said to be *conformal to the metric* g_0 if there is a differentiable function f on M, $f > 0$, such that $g(p) = f^2(p) g_0(p)$ for all $p \in M$.

We denote by $[g_0]$ the conformal class of g_0, that is the family of all Riemannian metrics g conformal to g_0

REMARK 28. Geometrically, if two metrics are conformal, the angle between two tangent vectors is preserved. However, it is difficult to see "intuitively" that two Riemannian metrics (for example two submanifolds) are conformal.

For the proof, only one specific property is needed:

PROPOSITION 29. *Let M be a manifold of dimension n and g a Riemannian metric. Let h be a differentiable function on M. Then, the expression*

$$|\nabla^g h(p)|_g^n dvol_g$$

is a conformal invariant, where $dvol_g$ denotes the volume form. This means that, if $g(p) = f^2(p)g_0(p)$, then, for each $p \in M$, we have

$$|\nabla^g h(p)|_g^n dvol_g = |\nabla^{g_0} h(p)|_{g_0}^n dvol_{g_0}$$

Proof. This is a purely linear algebra arguement. If $dimM = n$ and if $g(p) = f^2(p)g_0(p)$, then $dvol_g(p) = f^n(p)dvol_{g_0}$;

If h is a function, $|\nabla^g h(p)|_g^2 = \frac{1}{f^2(p)}|\nabla^{g_0} h(p)|_{g_0}^2$.

This implies that $|\nabla^g h(p)|_g^n dvol_g = |\nabla^{g_0} h(p)|_{g_0}^n dvol_{g_0}$, and the expression

$$|\nabla^g h(p)|_g^n dvol_g$$

is a conformal invariant.

REMARK 30.

(1) If a metric g_0 is conformally deformed, even keeping the volume equal to 1, we have neither control of the diameter nor of the curvature.
(2) It is easy to produce arbitrarily small eigenvalues on a conformal class keeping the volume fixed: the Cheeger dumbbell type construction may be done via a conformal deformation of the metric around a point (see [**CE1**]).
(3) For a more complete story of the question about "upper bounds on the conformal class", one can read the introduction of [**CE1**].

Our goal is to prove the following theorem from Korevaar [**Ko**]:

THEOREM 31. *Let (M^n, g_0) be a compact Riemannian manifold. Then, there exists a constant $C(g_0)$ depending on g_0 such that for any Riemannian metric $g \in [g_0]$*

$$\lambda_k(M, g)Vol(M, g)^{2/n} \leq C(g_0)k^{2/n}.$$

Moreover, if the Ricci curvature of g_0 is non-negative, we can replace the constant $C(g_0)$ by a constant depending only on the dimension n.

In the special case of surfaces, the bound depends only on the topology.

THEOREM 32. *Let S be an oriented surface of genus γ. Then, there exists a universal constant C such that for any Riemannian metric g on S*

$$\lambda_k(S, g)Vol(S) \leq C(\gamma + 1)k.$$

The approach of Korevaar for the proof of this theorem is very original and not easy to understand. Around 10 years after the publication of [**Ko**], Grigor'yan, Netrusov and Yau wrote a paper [**GNY**] where they explained in particular the main ideas of [**Ko**] from a more general and more conceptual viewpoint. This paper was used recently in a lot of different situations, in particular in order to find upper bounds for the spectrum of the Steklov problem [**CEG1**]. In this lecture, I will explain how to use one of the main results of [**GNY**].

REMARK 33.

(1) Recall that $\lambda_k(M,g)Vol(M,g)^{2/n}$ is invariant through homothety of the metric, and this control is equivalent to fixing the volume.
(2) The estimate is compatible with the Weyl law:

$$\lambda_k(M,g)Vol(M,g)^{2/n} \le C(g_0)k^{2/n} \text{ implies } \frac{\lambda_k(M,g)Vol(M,g)^{2/n}}{k^{2/n}} \le C(g_0).$$

But this leads to a natural question: Can we get a similar estimate depending asymptotically only on the dimension and on k, but not on g_0 or on the genus? This is part of the Ph.D. thesis of A. Hassannezhad (see Theorem 41 and Corollary 43 in this paper).
(3) These estimates are not sharp in general.
(4) These results were already known for $k = 1$, with different kinds of proofs and different authors (see for example the introduction of [**CE1**]). However, in order to make a proof for all k, Korevaar used a completely new approach.

4.2. The Bishop-Gromov estimate. Before going into the description of the proof, let us recall a classical result of Riemannian geometry which appears very often in such situation: the theorem of Bishop-Gromov.

The Bishop-Gromov inequality allows us to control the *growth of balls*. Let us begin with 3 simple examples:

The volume of a ball of radius r in $\mathbb{R}^n$ is $c_n r^n$ and we have

$$\frac{Vol(B(2r))}{Vol(B(r))} = 2^n.$$

The volume of a ball of radius r in the hyperbolic space $\mathbb{H}^n$ is $c_n e^{(n-1)r}$ asymptotically as $r \to \infty$, and we have

$$\frac{Vol(B(2r))}{Vol(B(r))} \sim e^{(n-1)r},$$

and the ratio grows to ∞ as $r \to \infty$.

In the hyperbolic space with curvature $-a^2$, the volume of a ball of radius r is $c_n e^{a(n-1)r}$ asymptotically as $a \to \infty$ and we have

$$\frac{Vol(B(2r))}{Vol(B(r))} \sim e^{a(n-1)r}.$$

The ratio growths to ∞ for a *fixed radius* as $a \to \infty$.

More generally, on a given manifold (M,g), what can be said about the ratio $\frac{Vol(B(2r))}{Vol(B(r))}$? How is it possible to control it, even for manifold with "non-simple" topology? The result of Bishop-Gromov says that the situations we have described in the hyperbolic spaces are the worst case.

THEOREM 34 (Bishop-Gromov, see [**Sa**] for a proof). *Let (M,g) be a complete Riemannian manifold (without boundary): if $Ricci(M,g) \ge -(n-1)a^2 g$, with $a \ge 0$, then for $x \in M$ and $0 < r < R$,*

$$\frac{VolB(x,R)}{VolB(x,r)} \le \frac{VolB^a(x,R)}{VolB^a(x,r)}$$

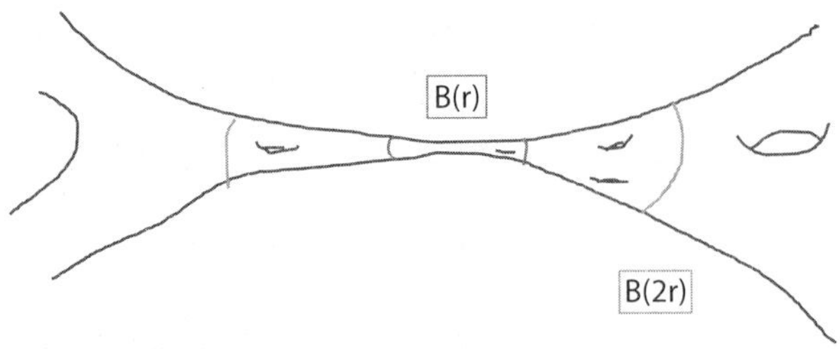

where B^a denotes the ball on the model space of constant curvature $-a^2$.

If $a = 0$, that is if $Ricci(M, g) \geq 0$, the ratio $\frac{VolB(x_i,2r)}{VolB(x_i,r)}$ is controlled by a similar ratio as in the Euclidean space, and this depends only on the dimension!

If $a > 0$, the control of the ratio $\frac{VolB(x_i,2r)}{VolB(x_i,r)}$ is exponential in r.

However, if M is compact, this ratio is controlled in function of the diameter of (M, g) and of a.

Another way to read this inequality is that

$$Vol(B(x, 2R)) \leq \frac{VolB^a(x, 2R)}{VolB^a(x, R)} Vol(B(x, R)).$$

This means that the volume of a ball of radius $2R$ is controlled by the volume of a ball of radius R. If the manifold is compact, this control depends only on a and on the diameter.

In particular, if (M, g) is compact, it is easy to see, using the Bishop-Gromov inequality, that the number of disjoint balls of radius $r/2$ contained in a ball of radius r is controlled by the lower bound a of the Ricci curvature and the diameter of (M, g) (see [**Zu**, Lemma 3.6, p. 230]).

DEFINITION 35. This number (maximal number of disjoint balls of radius R contained in a ball of radius $2R$) is called *the packing constant.*

Strategy of the proof of Korevaar's theorem. During the proof, the way to get upper bounds is to construct test functions, and, as said at point (9) of Theorem 10, it is nice to have disjointly supported functions. These test functions are associated to a *convenient* family of disjoint domains. We will see that the construction of Korevaar ([**Ko**], [**GNY**]) gives us a family of *disjoint annuli.* Let us first see how we can associate a test function to an annulus.

4.3. Test functions associated to an annulus. This is word-for-word the method of [**GNY**] as it is described in section 2 of [**CES**, Lemma 2.1].

Let us fix a reference metric $g_0 \in [g]$ and denote by d_0 the distance associated to g_0. An *annulus* $A \subset M$ is a subset of M of the form $\{x \in M : r < d_0(x, a) < R\}$ where $a \in M$ and $0 \leq r < R$ (if necessary, we will denote it $A(a, r, R)$). The annulus $2A$ is by definition the annulus $\{x \in M : r/2 < d_0(x, a) < 2R\}$.

To such an annulus we associate the function u_A supported in $2A$ and such that

$$u_A(x) = \begin{cases} 1 - \frac{2}{r} d_0(x, A) & \text{if } \frac{r}{2} \leq d_0(x, a) \leq r \\ 1 & \text{if } x \in A \\ 1 - \frac{1}{R} d_0(x, A) & \text{if } R \leq d_0(x, a) \leq 2R \end{cases}$$

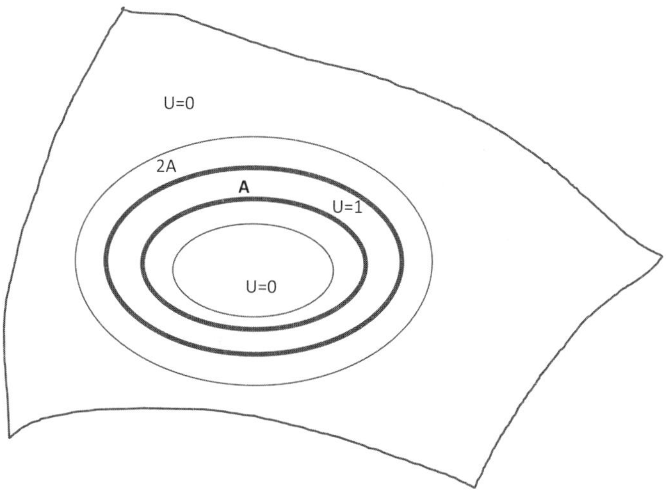

FIGURE 12. Test function associated to an annulus

REMARK 36. On a Riemannian manifold (M, g), we use frequently the distance d associated to g in order to construct new functions. It could be, like here, the distance to a subset A of M. Note that, even if the boundary of A is not smooth, the function $d(\partial A, \cdot)$ "distance to the boundary of A" is well known to be 1-Lipschitz on M. According to Rademacher's theorem (see Section 3.1.2, page 81–84 in [**EG**]), $d(\partial A, \cdot)$ is differentiable almost everywhere (since $dvol_g$ is absolutely continuous with respect to Lebesgue's measure), and its g-gradient satisfies $|\nabla d(\partial A, \cdot)|_g \leq 1$, almost everywhere.

We introduce the following constant:

$$\Gamma(g_0) = \sup_{x \in M, r>0} \frac{V_{g_0}(B(x,r))}{r^n}$$

where $B(x,r)$ stands for the ball of radius r centered at x in (M, d_0). Notice that since M is compact, the constant $\Gamma(g_0)$ is finite and depends only on g_0. This constant can be bounded from above in terms of a lower bound of the Ricci curvature Ric_{g_0} and an upper bound of the diameter $diam(M, g_0)$ (Bishop-Gromov inequality). In particular, if the Ricci curvature of g_0 is non-negative, then $\Gamma(g_0)$ is bounded above by a constant depending only on the dimension n.

LEMMA 37. *For every annulus $A \subset (M, d_0)$ one has*

$$\int_M |\nabla^g u_A|_g^2 dvol_g \leq 8\ \Gamma(g_0)^{\frac{2}{n}} \left(\int_{2A} dvol_g \right)^{1-\frac{2}{n}} = 8\ \Gamma(g_0)^{\frac{2}{n}} Vol_g(2A)^{1-\frac{2}{n}}.$$

PROOF. Let $A = A(a, r, R)$ be an annulus of (M, d_0). Since u_A is supported in $2A$, we get, using Hölder inequality,

$$\int_M |\nabla^g u_A|_g^2 dvol_g = \int_{2A} |\nabla^g u_A|_g^2 dvol_g \leq \left(\int_{2A} |\nabla^g u_A|_g^n dvol_g \right)^{\frac{2}{n}} \left(\int_{2A} dvol_g \right)^{1-\frac{2}{n}}.$$

From the conformal invariance of $\int_{2A} |\nabla^g u_A|_g^n dvol_g$ we have

$$\int_{2A} |\nabla^g u_A|_g^n dvol_g = \int_{2A} |\nabla^{g_0} u_A|_{g_0}^n dvol_{g_0}$$

with

$$|\nabla^{g_0} u_A| \stackrel{a.e.}{=} \begin{cases} \frac{2}{r} & \text{if } \frac{r}{2} \leq d_0(x,a) \leq r \\ 0 & \text{if } r \leq d_0(x,a) \leq R \\ \frac{1}{R} & \text{if } R \leq d_0(x,a) \leq 2R. \end{cases}$$

Hence,

$$\int_{2A} |\nabla^{g_0} u_A|_{g_0}^n dvol_{g_0} \leq \left(\frac{2}{r}\right)^n V_{g_0}(B(a,r)) + \left(\frac{1}{R}\right)^n V_{g_0}(B(a,2R)) \leq 2^{n+1}\Gamma(g_0)$$

where the last inequality follows from the definition of $\Gamma(g_0)$. Putting together all the previous inequalities, we obtain the result of the Lemma. □

In order to prove Theorem 31 and 32, we need to consider the Rayleigh quotient of the test-functions. It is given by

$$R(u_A) = \frac{\int_M |\nabla^g u_A|_g^2 dvol_g}{\int_M u_A^2 dvol_g},$$

and we have

$$R(u_A) \leq \frac{8\ \Gamma(g_0)^{\frac{2}{n}} Vol_g(2A)^{1-\frac{2}{n}}}{\int_{2A} u_A^2 dvol_g}.$$

So, in order to conclude, we need to control the term $Vol(2A)^{1-\frac{2}{n}}$ from above and the term $\int_{2A} u_A^2 dvol_g$ from below. The first point is easy, but for the second, we need to know about the existence of annuli of *rather large* measure, which is difficult, because we do not have a good geometrical understanding of the geometry under conformal deformations. This is precisely the essential contribution of Korevaar, revisited by Grigor'yan, Netrusov and Yau, to do this.

4.4. The construction of Korevaar and Grigor'yan-Netrusov-Yau, [Ko], [GNY]. The construction is metric and it is explained in the context of metric measured spaces.

DEFINITION 38. Let (X,d) be a metric space. The *annulus*, denoted by $A(a,r,R)$, (with $a \in X$ and $0 \leq r < R$) is the set

$$A(a,r,R) = \{x \in X : r \leq d(x,a) \leq R\}.$$

Moreover, if $\lambda \geq 1$, we will denote by λA the annulus $A(a, \frac{r}{\lambda}, \lambda R)$.

Let (X,d) be a metric space with a finite measure ν. We make the following hypothesis about this space:

(1) The balls are precompact (the closed balls are compact);
(2) The measure ν is non-atomic (Recall that an atom is a measurable set which has positive measure and contains no set of smaller but positive measure. A measure which has no atoms is called non-atomic; in particular, the points have measure 0);

(3) There exists $N > 0$ such that, for each r, a ball of radius r may be covered by at most N balls of radius $r/2$.

The last hypothesis plays, in some sense, the role of a control of the curvature, but, as we will see, it is much weaker. Note that it is purely metric, and has nothing to do with the measure, even if, in order to show its validity, we use the Bishop-Gromov estimate about the volume growth of balls.

If these hypotheses are satisfied, we have the following result

THEOREM 39. *For each positive integer k, there exists a family of annuli $\{A_i\}_{i=1}^k$ such that*

(1) *We have $\nu(A_i) \geq C(N)\frac{\nu(X)}{k}$, where $C(N)$ is an explicit constant depending only on N;*
(2) *The annuli $2A_i$ are disjoint from each other.*

4.5. Application. Proof of Theorem 31. The metric space X will be the manifold M with the Riemannian distance associated to g_0 and the *measure* ν will be the measure associated to the volume form $dvol_g$.

Note that this is *one of the crucial ideas of the proof*: we endowe M with the distance associated to the model Riemannian metric g_0, but with a measure associated to the Riemannian metric g to be studied.

As M is compact, the theorem of Bishop-Gromov gives us a constant $C(N) = C(g_0) > 0$, such that, for each $r > 0$ and $x \in M$,

$$\frac{Vol_{g_0}B(x,r)}{Vol_{g_0}B(x,r/2)} \leq C(g_0);$$

The constant $C(g_0)$ depends on the lower bound of $Ricci(g_0)$ and of the diameter of (M, g_0), and only on the dimension if the Ricci curvature is non-negative.

REMARK 40. In the sequel, different constants depending on the lower bound of $Ricci(g_0)$ and of the diameter of (M, g_0) will appear: they are denoted by $C(g_0)$. It would be an interesting exercise to make these constants really explicit.

The goal is to find an upper bound for $\lambda_k(g)$. To this aim, let us take a family of disjoint $2k+2$ annuli given by Theorem 39 and satisfying $Vol_g(A_i) \geq C(g_0)\frac{Vol_g(M)}{k}$ (note that the same constant $C(g_0)$ as in the previous step could be used without lost of generality).

Using for each of the annuli A the test function u_A defined above, we recall that

$$R(u_A) \leq \frac{8\,\Gamma(g_0)^{\frac{2}{n}} Vol(2A)^{1-\frac{2}{n}}}{\int_{2A} u_A^2 dv_g}, \quad R(u_A) \leq \frac{\Gamma(g_0)^{\frac{2}{n}} Vol_g(2A)^{1-\frac{2}{n}}}{Vol_g(A)}$$

Moreover, by Theorem 39,

$$Vol_g(A) \geq C(g_0)\frac{Vol_g(M)}{k}.$$

As we have $2k+2$ disjoint annuli, at least $k+1$ of them have a measure less than $\frac{Vol_g(M)}{k}$. So,

$$R(u_A) \leq \Gamma(g_0)^{\frac{2}{n}} \left(\frac{Vol_g(M)}{k}\right)^{1-\frac{2}{n}} \frac{k}{C(g_0)Vol_g(M)} = C(g_0)\left(\frac{k}{Vol_g(M)}\right)^{2/n},$$

and this allows us to prove Theorem (31)

Moreover, if the Ricci curvature of g_0 is bounded below by 0, $\Gamma(g_0)$ depends only on the dimension n of M and it is the same for $C(g_0)$.

Proof of Theorem 32. Let (S, g) be a compact orientable surface of genus γ. It is known as a corollary of the Riemann-Roch theorem (see [**YY**]) that (S, g) admits a conformal branched cover ψ over $(\mathbb{S}^2, g_0)$ with degree $\deg(\psi) \leq \gamma + 1$.

Let us endow $\mathbb{S}^2$ with the usual spherical distance d_0 associated to the canonical metric g_0, and with a measure associated to g, the push-forward measure $\nu = \psi_*(dvol_g)$. For any open set $\mathcal{O} \subset \mathbb{S}^2$,

$$\nu(\mathcal{O}) = \int_{\psi^{-1}(\mathcal{O})} dvol_g. \tag{12}$$

We apply Theorem 39 to the metric measure space $(\mathbb{S}^2, d_0, \nu)$: Note that the constant $c = c\left(N(\mathbb{S}^2, d_0)\right)$ arising from Theorem 39 depends now only on the canonical distance on the sphere S^2. It can be seen as a universal constant.

We deduce that there exist an absolute constant $c = c\left(N(\mathbb{S}^2, d_0)\right)$ and $k+1$ annuli $A_1, \ldots, A_{k+1} \subset \mathbb{S}^2$ such that the annuli $2A_1, \ldots, 2A_{k+1}$ are mutually disjoint and, $\forall i \leq k$,

$$\nu(A_i) \geq c\, \frac{\nu(\mathbb{S}^2)}{k}. \tag{13}$$

For each $i \leq k$, set $v_i = u_{A_i} \circ \psi$. From the conformal invariance of the energy and Lemma 37, one deduces that, for every $i \leq k$,

$$\int_S |\nabla_g v_i|_g^2 dvol_g, = \deg(\psi) \int_{\mathbb{S}^2} |\nabla_{g_0} u_{A_i}|_{g_0}^2\, dvol_{g_0} \leq 8\Gamma(\mathbb{S}^2, g_0)(\gamma + 1),$$

while, since u_{A_i} is equal to 1 on A_i,

$$\int_S v_i^2 dvol_g \geq Vol_g\left(\psi^{-1}(A_i)\right) = \nu(A_i) \geq c\, \frac{\nu(\mathbb{S}^2)}{k} = c\, \frac{Vol_g(S)}{k}.$$

Therefore,

$$R(v_i) \leq \frac{8\Gamma(\mathbb{S}^2, g_0)}{cVol_g(S)}(\gamma + 1)k \leq \frac{C(\gamma + 1)}{Vol_g(S)}\, k$$

where C is an absolute constant. Noticing that the $k+1$ functions $v_1, \ldots v_{k+1}$ are disjointly supported in S, we deduce the desired inequality for $\lambda_k(S, g)$.

4.6. A recent development: the result of A. Hassannezhad. The upper bounds obtained by N. Korevaar are good in the sense where they are compatible with the Weyl law: Asymptotically, they are of the type $c(g_0)k^{2/n}$ in dimension greater than 2 and $C(genus)k$ in dimension 2. By [**CD**],[**CE1**], some dependance on the geometry or in the topology is needed. On the other side, the Weyl law tells us that for a given compact Riemannian manifold of dimension n, the k-th eigenvalue is asymptotically of the type $C(n)k^{2/n}$. So, it is natural to ask if one can get uniform upper bounds, asymptotically of the type $C(n)k^{2/n}$. This is the main result of [**Ha**].

THEOREM 41. *For each $n \geq 2$, there exist two positive constants A_n, B_n such that, for every compact Riemannian manifold (M, g) of dimension n*

$$\lambda_k(M, g)Vol_g(M)^{2/n} \leq A_n V([g])^{2/n} + B_n k^{2/n}$$

The only dependence on the metric g is the term $V([g])$ called the min-conformal volume:

DEFINITION 42. Let (M, g) be a compact Riemannian manifold of dimension n. The *min-conformal volume* of (M, g) depends only on the conformal class $[g]$ of g and is defined by

$$V([g]) = inf\{Vol_{g_0}(M) : g_0 \in [g];\ Ric(g_0) \geq -(n-1)\}.$$

In particular, if there is $g_0 \in [g]$ with $Ric(g_0) \geq 0$, then $V([g]) = 0$.

Theorem (41) shows that the asymptotic in k is controlled by $B(n)k^{2/n}$:

$$\frac{\lambda_k(M, g)Vol_g(M)^{2/n}}{k^{2/n}} \leq A(n)\frac{V([g_0])^{2/n}}{k^{2/n}} + B_n,$$

and

$$\frac{V([g_0])^{2/n}}{k^{2/n}} \to 0$$

as $k \to \infty$.

In the case of surfaces, A. Hassannezhad got

COROLLARY 43. *There exist two constants A, B such that for every compact surface (S, g) of genus γ, we have*

$$\lambda_k(S, g)Vol_g(S) \leq A\gamma + Bk,$$

and, in particular, the asymptotic in k is Bk.

REMARK 44. Note that Corollary 43 applies for both orientable and non-orientable surfaces.

For the proof these theorems, the method consists in constructing disjointly supported test functions associated to disjoint subsets of the manifold. The new ingredient is to mix the method of Korevaar with a construction due to Colbois and Maerten [**CM**]. Roughly speaking, the method of Korevaar gives us annuli, and the estimates become bad when these annuli are too large. The main idea is to use the method of [**CM**] in such situations.

REMARK 45. Each time we have a result of the type

$$\lambda_k \leq C(geometry)\left(\frac{k}{Vol}\right)^{2/n}$$

one can ask if one can get a result of the type

$$\lambda_k Vol^{2/n} \leq A(n)C(geometry) + B(n)k^{2/n}.$$

Most of the questions of this type are open: An example will be given in section 5, Remark 49.

5. Another geometric method to construct upper bounds and applications.

In this section, I will present (with much less detail) another method to find upper bounds, which was established by D. Maerten and myself [**CM**], with one application to the spectrum of hypersurfaces. Roughly speaking, the method of [**Ko**], [**GNY**] is adequate for conformal metrics, but needs a comparison with one Riemannian metric. In the previous results, all the statements depend on metric g_0.

The method of [**CM**] does not require such a comparison, but it supposes that there is no concentration of the metric. Let us state the version of [**CEG1**]:

THEOREM 46. *Let (X, d, μ) be a complete, locally compact metric measured space, where μ is a finite measure. We assume that for all $r > 0$, there exists an integer $N(r)$ such that each ball of radius r can be covered by $N(r)$ balls of radius $r/2$.*

If there exist an integer $K > 0$ and a radius $r > 0$ such that, for each $x \in X$

$$\mu(B(x,r)) \leq \frac{\mu(X)}{4N^2(r)K},$$

then, there exist K μ-measurable subsets $A_1, ..., A_K$ of X such that, $\forall i \leq K$, $\mu(A_i) \geq \frac{\mu(X)}{2N(r)K}$ and, for $i \neq j$, $d(A_i, A_j) \geq 3r$.

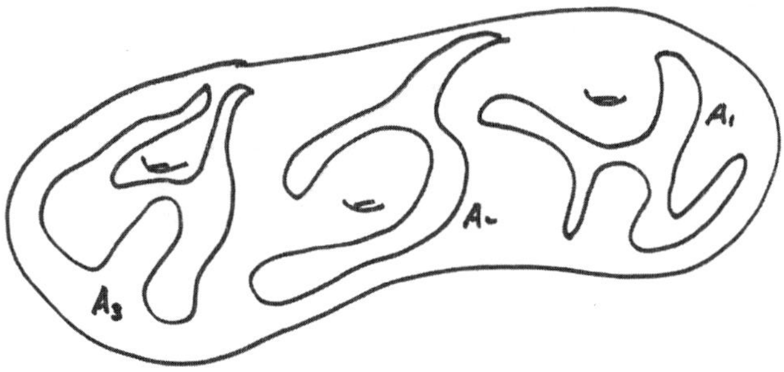

FIGURE 13. A surface with 3 subsets as in Theorem 46

REMARK 47.

(1) The first hypothesis is essentially the same as in the construction of Korevaar and suppose a control of the packing constant.
(2) In the version given in [**CM**], there is the hypothesis that the volume of the r-balls tends to 0 uniformly on X as $r \to 0$. This is not necessary; it is enough that the measure $\mu(B(x,r))$ of the ball is small enough.
(3) In order to get a bound for λ_k comparable with the Weyl law, r has to be of the size of $(\frac{C\mu(X)}{k})^{1/n}$, and $K = k + 1$.
(4) If r is chosen too small, the upper bounds we get are far from being optimal.

As in the previous construction we associate to each subset A_i the test function u_{A_i} which is 1 inside A_i and 0 outside the r-neighborhood A_i^r of A_i. If A is one of the subsets A_i and $A^r = \{p \in X : d(p, A) \leq r\}$

$$u_A(x) = \begin{cases} 1 - \frac{1}{r}d(x, A) & \text{if } x \in A^r \\ 1 & \text{if } x \in A \\ 0 & \text{if } d(x, A) \geq r \end{cases}$$

An application. Let us describe a situation where this method can be used.

Let $\Sigma \subset \mathbb{R}^{m+1}$ be a compact hypersurface. As a consequence of the result of [**CM**] and of a classical theorem of Nash-Kuiper, it is possible to deform Σ in $\mathbb{R}^{m+1}$ in order to have

$$\lambda_1(\Sigma)Vol(\Sigma)^{2/m}$$

arbitrarily large. See [**CDE**, paragraph 5], for a detailed explanation.

The upper bounds for Σ will depend of the *isoperimetric ratio* of the hypersurface. Let $\Omega \subset \mathbb{R}^{m+1}$ be a bounded domain with smooth boundary $\Sigma = \partial\Omega$. We denote by

$$I(\Omega) = \frac{Vol(\Sigma)}{Vol(\Omega)^{m/(m+1)}}$$

the isoperimetric ratio of Ω.

THEOREM 48 (C-El Soufi-Girouard, [**CEG2**]). *For any bounded domain $\Omega \subset \mathbb{R}^{m+1}$ with smooth boundary $\Sigma = \partial\Omega$, and all $k \geq 1$,*

$$\lambda_k(\Sigma)|\Sigma|^{2/m} \leq C_m I(\Omega)^{1+2/m}k^{2/m} \tag{14}$$

with C_m an explicit constant depending on m, and where $I(\Omega)$ denotes the isoperimetric ratio.

The proof, given in [**CEG1**], uses the construction of [**CM**]: First, we need to introduce (X, d, μ) be a complete, locally compact metric measure space, where μ is a finite measure satisfying the first hypothesis: For all $r > 0$, there exists an integer $N(r)$ such that each ball of radius r can be covered by $N(r)$ balls of radius $r/2$. In our situation, $X = \mathbb{R}^{m+1}$, d is the Euclidean distance. This implies that the packing constant N depends only on the dimension m. The measure μ is the measure associated to the hypersurface Σ:

$$\mu(U) = Vol(U \cap \Sigma).$$

The main difficulty for the proof is that the second hypothesis is not satisfied. It is not always true that there exists an integer $K > 0$ and a radius $r > 0$ such that, for each $x \in X$ $\mu(B(x, r)) \leq \frac{\mu(X)}{4N^2(r)K}$.. The reason is that the measure can concentrate some place.

Recall that for r_k of the type $\left(\frac{C\mu(\Sigma)}{k}\right)^{1/m}$, we hope to have

$$\mu(B(x, r_k)) \leq \frac{\mu(\Sigma)}{4C(m)k}.$$

The *idea* of the proof of Theorem 48 is as follows.

The difficult part of the proof (that I will not explain here) is to show that the hypothesis about the concentration is correct, but only *for a part of* Σ, proportional to the measure $\mu(\Sigma)$, with factor of proportionality $\frac{C(m)}{I(\Omega)}$.

This leads us to choose

$$r_k = \left(\frac{C_1(m)\mu(\Sigma)}{kI(\Omega)}\right)^{1/m}.$$

The Rayleigh quotient of a test function u_A can be estimated as follows. If dv_Σ denotes the volume form on Σ,

$$\int_\Sigma |\nabla u_A|^2 dv_\Sigma \le \frac{1}{r_k^2}\mu(A^{r_k})$$

and

$$\int_\Sigma u_A^2 dv_\Sigma \ge \frac{\mu(\Sigma)}{C_2(n)I(\Omega)k}$$

we get

$$R(u_A) \le \frac{1}{r_k^2}\frac{\mu(A^{r_k})}{\mu(\Sigma)}C_2(n)I(\Omega)k$$

and we have a problem with the term $\mu(A^{r_k})$... As in the proof of the theorem of Korevaar, we can begin with $2k+2$ subsets, so that, for at least $(k+1)$ of them, $\mu(A^{r_k}) \le \frac{\mu(\Sigma)}{k+1}$. This implies

$$R(u_A) \le \frac{1}{r_k^2}\frac{\mu(\Sigma)}{k+1}\frac{C_2(n)I(\Omega)k}{\mu(\Sigma)} \le C(n)I(\Omega)^{1+\frac{2}{m}}\left(\frac{k}{Vol(\Sigma)}\right)^{2/m}.$$

REMARK 49. This is a typical situation where the open question occurs: is it possible to establish an inequality of the type

$$\lambda_k(\Sigma)Vol(\Sigma)^{2/m} \le A_m I(\Omega)^{1+\frac{2}{m}} + B_m k^{2/m}$$

for two constant A_m, B_m depending only on the dimension m?

For this specific question the answer is no (thesis of Luc Pétiard, article in preparation for 2017).

6. The conformal spectrum

Having upper (or lower) bounds leads to investigate the spectrum from a qualitative or quantitative viewpoint. Let us give the example of the *conformal spectrum* and of the *topological spectrum* we developed in [**CE1**] with A. El Soufi (see also [**Co**] for a short survey).

DEFINITION 50. For any natural integer k and any conformal class of metrics $[g_0]$ on M, we define the *conformal k-th eigenvalue* of $(M,[g_0])$ to be

$$\lambda_k^c(M,[g_0]) = \sup\left\{\lambda_k(M,g)Vol(M,g)^{2/n} \mid g \text{ is conformal to } g_0\right\}.$$

The sequence $\{\lambda_k^c(M,[g_0])\}$ constitutes the *conformal spectrum* of $(M,[g_0])$.

In dimension 2, one can also define a *topological spectrum* by setting, for any genus γ and any integer $k \ge 0$,

$$\lambda_k^{top}(\gamma) = \sup\left\{\lambda_k(M,g)Vol(M,g)\right\},$$

where g describes the set of Riemannian metrics on the orientable compact surface M of genus γ.

Regarding the quantitative aspects, in some very special situations, the hope is to detect the maximum or the supremum in a conformal class. This concerns mainly the first nonzero eigenvalue. Note that for the topological spectrum on surfaces, it was already explained in (1.3.2) that it was a very difficult question. It is as well difficult to decide if the supremum is a maximum: Does it a Riemannian metric $g \in [g_0]$ exists such that $\lambda_k Vol(M,g)^{2/n}$ is maximum?

Regarding the conformal first eigenvalue, El Soufi and Ilias [**EI1**] gave a sufficient condition for a Riemannian metric g to maximize λ_1 in its conformal class $[g]$: if there exists a family $f_1, f_2, ..., f_p$ of first eigenfunctions satisfying $\sum_i df_i \otimes df_i = g$, then $\lambda_1^c(M,[g]) = \lambda_1(g)$. This condition is fulfilled in particular by the metric of any homogeneous Riemannian space with irreducible isotropy representation. For instance, the first conformal eigenvalues of the rank one symmetric spaces endowed with their standard conformal classes $[g_s]$, are given by

- $\lambda_1^c(\mathbb{S}^n,[g_s]) = n\omega_n^{2/n}$, where ω_n is the volume of the n-dimensional Euclidean sphere of radius one,
- $\lambda_1^c(\mathbb{R}P^n,[g_s]) = 2^{\frac{n-2}{n}}(n+1)\omega_n^{2/n}$,
- $\lambda_1^c(\mathbb{C}P^d,[g_s]) = 4\pi(d+1)d!^{-1/d}$,
- $\lambda_1^c(\mathbb{H}P^d,[g_s]) = 8\pi(d+1)(2d+1)!^{-1/2d}$,
- $\lambda_1^c(\mathbb{C}aP^2,[g_s]) = 48\pi(\frac{6}{11!})^{1/8} = 8\pi\sqrt{6}(\frac{9}{385})^{1/8}$.

REMARK 51. Note that this is a strong hypothesis to suppose that the maximum is reached by a *regular* Riemannian metric. This cannot be expected in general, and even in dimension 2, it is a fundamental question to understand what kinds of singularities may occurs for the maximal metrics (with respect to λ_1 or λ_k).

I will mainly describe the qualitative aspects of the problem and the first qualitative question is the following: On a compact manifold M, does a Riemannian metric g exists such that $\lambda_1^c[g]$ is arbitrarily small? The answer is no: Among all the possible conformal classes of metrics on manifolds, the standard conformal class of the sphere is the one having the lowest conformal spectrum.

THEOREM 52. *For any conformal class* $[g]$ *on* M *and any integer* $k \geq 0$,

$$\lambda_k^c(M,[g]) \geq \lambda_k^c(\mathbb{S}^n,[g_s]).$$

Although the eigenvalues of a given Riemannian metric may have nontrivial multiplicities, the conformal eigenvalues are all simple: The conformal spectrum consists of a strictly increasing sequence, and, moreover, the gap between two consecutive conformal eigenvalues is uniformly bounded. Precisely, we have the following theorem:

THEOREM 53. *For any conformal class* $[g]$ *on* M *and any integer* $k \geq 0$,

$$\lambda_{k+1}^c(M,[g])^{n/2} - \lambda_k^c(M,[g])^{n/2} \geq \lambda_1^c(\mathbb{S}^n,[g_s]) = n^{n/2}\omega_n,$$

where ω_n *is the volume of the* n*-dimensional Euclidean sphere of radius one.*

An immediate consequence of these two theorems is the following explicit estimate of $\lambda_k^c(M,[g])$:

COROLLARY 54. *For any conformal class* $[g]$ *on* M *and any integer* $k \geq 0$,

$$\lambda_k^c(M,[g]) \geq n\omega_n^{2/n}k^{2/n}.$$

Combined with the Hassannezhad estimates [**Ha**, Corollary 54] gives

$$n\omega_n^{2/n}k^{2/n} \le \lambda_k^c(M,[g]) \le A_n V([g])^{2/n} + B_n k^{2/n}$$

for some constants A_n, B_n depending only on n, and $V([g])$ depending on a lower bound of $Ric\ d^2$, where Ric is the Ricci curvature and d is the diameter of g or of another representative of $[g]$). This implies the relation

$$n\omega_n^{2/n} \le \frac{\lambda_k^c(M,[g])}{k^{2/n}} \le A_n \left(\frac{V([g])}{k}\right)^{2/n} + B_n.$$

Asymptotically, as $k \to \infty$, this shows that $\frac{\lambda_k^c(M,[g])}{k^{2/n}}$ is between $n\omega_n^{2/n}$ and B_n.

Corollary 54 implies also that, if the k-th eigenvalue $\lambda_k(g)$ of a metric g is less than $n\omega_n^{2/n}k^{2/n}$, then g does not maximize λ_k on its conformal class $[g]$. For instance, *the standard metric* g_s *of* $\mathbb{S}^2$*, which maximizes* λ_1*, does not maximize* λ_k *on* $[g_s]$ *for any* $k \ge 2$. This fact answers a question of Yau (see [**Y**, p. 686]).

El Soufi and Ilias have also shown that the property for a Riemannian metric to be critical (in a generalized sense) implies multiplicity. As a corollary of this and of the previous results, we get

COROLLARY 55. *If a Riemannian metric* g *maximizes* λ_1 *on its conformal class* $[g]$*, then it does not maximize* λ_2 *on* $[g]$*. More generally, a Riemannian metric* g *cannot maximize simultaneously three consecutive eigenvalues* $\lambda_k, \lambda_{k+1}, \lambda_{k+2}$ *on* $[g]$.

Note however that it is a very difficult question to decide if there exists a Riemannian metric $g_1 \in [g]$ such that $\lambda_k^c([g]) = \lambda_k(g_1)$.

Regarding the topological spectrum of surfaces, we have similar results:

THEOREM 56. *For any fixed genus* γ *and any integer* $k \ge 0$*, we have*

$$\lambda_{k+1}^{top}(\gamma) - \lambda_k^{top}(\gamma) \ge 8\pi,$$

and

$$\lambda_k^{top}(\gamma) \ge 8(k-1)\pi + \lambda_1^{top}(\gamma) \ge 8k\pi$$

However, we have good lower bounds for $\lambda_1^{top}(\gamma)$ (see for example [**BM**]) so that we can say that,

$$\lambda_1^{top}(\gamma) \ge \frac{4}{5}\pi(\gamma-1),$$

and it follows

$$\lambda_k^{top}(\gamma) \ge \frac{4}{5}\pi(\gamma-1) + 8(k-1)\pi.$$

Combined with Hassannezhad estimates [**Ha**], we get for an oriented surface of genus γ

$$\frac{4}{5}\pi(\gamma-1) + 8(k-1)\pi \le \lambda_k^{top}(\gamma) \le A(\gamma-1) + Bk.$$

for A, B constant.

We can also look at the behavior of $\lambda_k^c(\gamma)$ in terms of the genus γ.

THEOREM 57. *We have*

$$\lambda_k^{top}(\gamma+1) \ge \lambda_k^{top}(\gamma).$$

Note that it is an *open question* to know if the inequality is strict or not for each γ.

A few words about the proof. Locally, a Riemannian manifold is almost Euclidean and one can deform a small neighbourhood of a point into a (almost) round sphere (blow up). Then, we can use these deformations to get our results, using classical facts about the behavior of the spectrum under surgery. This explains the presence of the first eigenvalue of the round sphere in all these estimates.

In order to show $\lambda_k^{top}(\gamma+1) \geq \lambda_k^{top}(\gamma)$, we have to compare two surfaces with different topology and this needs another idea: to add a thin and short handle in order to pass from a surface of genus γ to a surface of genus $\gamma+1$. By classical surgery results, this neither affects the eigenvalues between λ_1 and λ_k (if the handle is short enough) nor the area. However, it cannot be proved with this method that the inequality is strict.

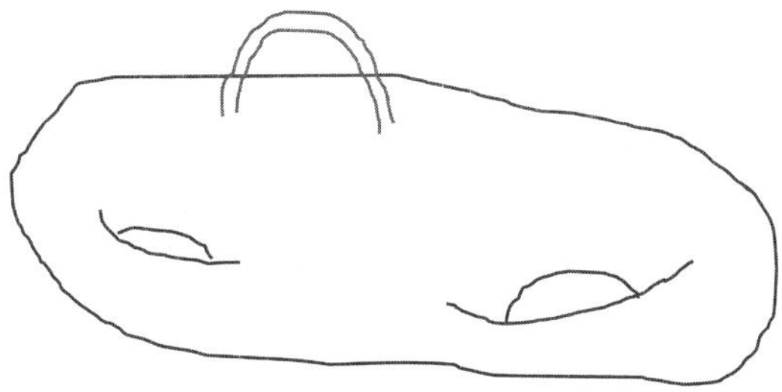

REMARK 58. Each time there are lower or upper bounds, it is possible to study the spectrum from a qualitative viewpoint. However, this is not always easy! Conside for example the following question in the case of hypersurfaces. For a positive number I (large enough), define

$$\lambda_k(I) = sup\{\lambda_k(\Sigma)Vol(\Sigma)^{2/m},\}$$

where $\Sigma = \partial\Omega$, Ω domain in $\mathbb{R}^{m+1}$ such that $I(\Omega) \leq I$.

What can be said about $\{\lambda_k(I)\}$?

For example, do we have $\lambda_{k+1}(I) > \lambda_k(I)$? What about the gap $\lambda_{k+1}(I) - \lambda_k(I)$?

Recent results about this topic.

(1) For the second conformal eigenvalue of the canonical metric on the sphere, asymptotically sharp upper bound were found in [**GNP**] and [**Pe1**].
(2) In [**Pe2**], Petrides proved the following result: let (M,g) be a compact Riemannian manifold of dimension $n \geq 3$. The first conformal eigenvalue is always greater than $n\omega_n^{2/n}$ (the value it takes for the round sphere) except if (M,g) is conformally diffeomorphic to the standard sphere.
(3) In the specific case of the first eigenvalue for compact surfaces, there have been several works recently published about the existence and the regularity of maximal metrics: Roughly speaking, the maximal metrics are not expected to be regular, but singular with very few singularities consisting only in conical points [**Kok**], [**Pe3**].

Acknowledgments

The author thanks the organizers of the summer school (especially Alexandre Girouard and Iosif Polterovich) for inviting me to Montréal and for the opportunity to write this article. The author also thank the referee for his very useful comments.

References

[An1] Colette Anné, *Spectre du laplacien et écrasement d'anses* (French, with English summary), Ann. Sci. École Norm. Sup. (4) **20** (1987), no. 2, 271–280. MR911759

[An2] Colette Anné, *A note on the generalized dumbbell problem*, Proc. Amer. Math. Soc. **123** (1995), no. 8, 2595–2599, DOI 10.2307/2161294. MR1257096

[As] Mark S. Ashbaugh, *Isoperimetric and universal inequalities for eigenvalues*, Spectral theory and geometry (Edinburgh, 1998), London Math. Soc. Lecture Note Ser., vol. 273, Cambridge Univ. Press, Cambridge, 1999, pp. 95–139, DOI 10.1017/CBO9780511566165.007. MR1736867

[BBG] P. Bérard, G. Besson, and S. Gallot, *Sur une inégalité isopérimétrique qui généralise celle de Paul Lévy-Gromov* (French), Invent. Math. **80** (1985), no. 2, 295–308, DOI 10.1007/BF01388608. MR788412

[BC] J. Bertrand and B. Colbois, *Capacité et inégalité de Faber-Krahn dans* $\mathbb{R}^n$ (French, with English and French summaries), J. Funct. Anal. **232** (2006), no. 1, 1–28, DOI 10.1016/j.jfa.2005.04.015. MR2200165

[Be] Pierre H. Bérard, *Spectral geometry: direct and inverse problems*, Lecture Notes in Mathematics, vol. 1207, Springer-Verlag, Berlin, 1986. With appendixes by Gérard Besson, and by Bérard and Marcel Berger. MR861271

[Ber] Berger, A.; Optimisation du spectre du Laplacien avec conditions de Dirichlet et Neumann dans $\mathbb{R}^2$ et $\mathbb{R}^3$, Thesis, Grenoble and Neuchâtel, (2015).

[BF] Bucur, D., Freitas P.; A free boundary approach to the Faber-Krahn inequality, to appear in this Volume.

[BGM] Marcel Berger, Paul Gauduchon, and Edmond Mazet, *Le spectre d'une variété riemannienne* (French), Lecture Notes in Mathematics, Vol. 194, Springer-Verlag, Berlin-New York, 1971. MR0282313

[BH] Bérard, P., Helffer B.; On the nodal patterns of the 2D isotropic quantum harmonic oscillator, arXiv:1506.02374, to appear in this Volume.

[Bl] David D. Bleecker, *The spectrum of a Riemannian manifold with a unit Killing vector field*, Trans. Amer. Math. Soc. **275** (1983), no. 1, 409–416, DOI 10.2307/1999029. MR678360

[BM] Robert Brooks and Eran Makover, *Riemann surfaces with large first eigenvalue*, J. Anal. Math. **83** (2001), 243–258, DOI 10.1007/BF02790263. MR1828493

[BP] Brasco, L., De Philippis, G.; Spectral inequalities in quantitative form, arXiv:1604.05072. This is a chapter of the forthcoming book "Shape Optimization and Spectral Theory", edited by Antoine Henrot and published by De Gruyter.

[Bu2] Peter Buser, *A note on the isoperimetric constant*, Ann. Sci. École Norm. Sup. (4) **15** (1982), no. 2, 213–230. MR683635

[CD] B. Colbois and J. Dodziuk, *Riemannian metrics with large* λ_1, Proc. Amer. Math. Soc. **122** (1994), no. 3, 905–906, DOI 10.2307/2160770. MR1213857

[CDE] Bruno Colbois, Emily B. Dryden, and Ahmad El Soufi, *Bounding the eigenvalues of the Laplace-Beltrami operator on compact submanifolds*, Bull. Lond. Math. Soc. **42** (2010), no. 1, 96–108, DOI 10.1112/blms/bdp100. MR2586970

[CE1] Bruno Colbois and Ahmad El Soufi, *Extremal eigenvalues of the Laplacian in a conformal class of metrics: the 'conformal spectrum'*, Ann. Global Anal. Geom. **24** (2003), no. 4, 337–349, DOI 10.1023/A:1026257431539. MR2015867

[CEG1] Bruno Colbois, Ahmad El Soufi, and Alexandre Girouard, *Isoperimetric control of the Steklov spectrum*, J. Funct. Anal. **261** (2011), no. 5, 1384–1399, DOI 10.1016/j.jfa.2011.05.006. MR2807105

[CEG2] Bruno Colbois, Ahmad El Soufi, and Alexandre Girouard, *Isoperimetric control of the spectrum of a compact hypersurface*, J. Reine Angew. Math. **683** (2013), 49–65. MR3181547

[CES] Bruno Colbois, Ahmad El Soufi, and Alessandro Savo, *Eigenvalues of the Laplacian on a compact manifold with density*, Comm. Anal. Geom. **23** (2015), no. 3, 639–670, DOI 10.4310/CAG.2015.v23.n3.a6. MR3310527

[CGI] Bruno Colbois, Alexandre Girouard, and Mette Iversen, *Uniform stability of the Dirichlet spectrum for rough outer perturbations*, J. Spectr. Theory **3** (2013), no. 4, 575–599, DOI 10.4171/JST/57. MR3122224

[Ch1] Isaac Chavel, *Eigenvalues in Riemannian geometry*, Pure and Applied Mathematics, vol. 115, Academic Press, Inc., Orlando, FL, 1984. Including a chapter by Burton Randol; With an appendix by Jozef Dodziuk. MR768584

[Ch2] Isaac Chavel, *On A. Hurwitz' method in isoperimetric inequalities*, Proc. Amer. Math. Soc. **71** (1978), no. 2, 275–279, DOI 10.2307/2042848. MR0493885

[Che] Shiu Yuen Cheng, *Eigenvalue comparison theorems and its geometric applications*, Math. Z. **143** (1975), no. 3, 289–297, DOI 10.1007/BF01214381. MR0378001

[CM] Bruno Colbois and Daniel Maerten, *Eigenvalues estimate for the Neumann problem of a bounded domain*, J. Geom. Anal. **18** (2008), no. 4, 1022–1032, DOI 10.1007/s12220-008-9041-z. MR2438909

[Co] Bruno Colbois, *Spectre conforme et métriques extrémales* (French, with French summary), Séminaire de Théorie Spectrale et Géométrie. Vol. 22. Année 2003–2004, Sémin. Théor. Spectr. Géom., vol. 22, Univ. Grenoble I, Saint-Martin-d'Hères, 2004, pp. 93–101. MR2136138

[CoHi] R. Courant and D. Hilbert, *Methods of mathematical physics. Vol. I*, Interscience Publishers, Inc., New York, N.Y., 1953. MR0065391

[Cou] Gilles Courtois, *Spectrum of manifolds with holes*, J. Funct. Anal. **134** (1995), no. 1, 194–221, DOI 10.1006/jfan.1995.1142. MR1359926

[Cr] Christopher B. Croke, *The first eigenvalue of the Laplacian for plane domains*, Proc. Amer. Math. Soc. **81** (1981), no. 2, 304–305, DOI 10.2307/2044213. MR593476

[EG] Lawrence C. Evans and Ronald F. Gariepy, *Measure theory and fine properties of functions*, Studies in Advanced Mathematics, CRC Press, Boca Raton, FL, 1992. MR1158660

[EHI] Ahmad El Soufi, Evans M. Harrell II, and Said Ilias, *Universal inequalities for the eigenvalues of Laplace and Schrödinger operators on submanifolds*, Trans. Amer. Math. Soc. **361** (2009), no. 5, 2337–2350, DOI 10.1090/S0002-9947-08-04780-6. MR2471921

[EI1] A. El Soufi and S. Ilias, *Immersions minimales, première valeur propre du laplacien et volume conforme* (French), Math. Ann. **275** (1986), no. 2, 257–267, DOI 10.1007/BF01458460. MR854009

[EI2] A. El Soufi and S. Ilias, *Majoration de la seconde valeur propre d'un opérateur de Schrödinger sur une variété compacte et applications* (French, with English summary), J. Funct. Anal. **103** (1992), no. 2, 294–316, DOI 10.1016/0022-1236(92)90123-Z. MR1151550

[FMP] Nicola Fusco, Francesco Maggi, and Aldo Pratelli, *Stability estimates for certain Faber-Krahn, isocapacitary and Cheeger inequalities*, Ann. Sc. Norm. Super. Pisa Cl. Sci. (5) **8** (2009), no. 1, 51–71. MR2512200

[GNP] Alexandre Girouard, Nikolai Nadirashvili, and Iosif Polterovich, *Maximization of the second positive Neumann eigenvalue for planar domains*, J. Differential Geom. **83** (2009), no. 3, 637–661. MR2581359

[GNY] Alexander Grigor′yan, Yuri Netrusov, and Shing-Tung Yau, *Eigenvalues of elliptic operators and geometric applications*, Surveys in differential geometry. Vol. IX, Surv. Differ. Geom., vol. 9, Int. Press, Somerville, MA, 2004, pp. 147–217, DOI 10.4310/SDG.2004.v9.n1.a5. MR2195408

[Go] Carolyn S. Gordon, *Survey of isospectral manifolds*, Handbook of differential geometry, Vol. I, North-Holland, Amsterdam, 2000, pp. 747–778, DOI 10.1016/S1874-5741(00)80009-6. MR1736857

[Ha] Asma Hassannezhad, *Conformal upper bounds for the eigenvalues of the Laplacian and Steklov problem*, J. Funct. Anal. **261** (2011), no. 12, 3419–3436, DOI 10.1016/j.jfa.2011.08.003. MR2838029

[He] Antoine Henrot, *Extremum problems for eigenvalues of elliptic operators*, Frontiers in Mathematics, Birkhäuser Verlag, Basel, 2006. MR2251558

[Ko] Nicholas Korevaar, *Upper bounds for eigenvalues of conformal metrics*, J. Differential Geom. **37** (1993), no. 1, 73–93. MR1198600

[Kok] Gerasim Kokarev, *Variational aspects of Laplace eigenvalues on Riemannian surfaces*, Adv. Math. **258** (2014), 191–239, DOI 10.1016/j.aim.2014.03.006. MR3190427

[La] Olivier Lablée, *Spectral theory in Riemannian geometry*, EMS Textbooks in Mathematics, European Mathematical Society (EMS), Zürich, 2015. MR3309800

[Lo] Joachim Lohkamp, *Discontinuity of geometric expansions*, Comment. Math. Helv. **71** (1996), no. 2, 213–228, DOI 10.1007/BF02566417. MR1396673

[LY] Peter Li and Shing Tung Yau, *Estimates of eigenvalues of a compact Riemannian manifold*, Geometry of the Laplace operator (Proc. Sympos. Pure Math., Univ. Hawaii, Honolulu, Hawaii, 1979), Proc. Sympos. Pure Math., XXXVI, Amer. Math. Soc., Providence, R.I., 1980, pp. 205–239. MR573435

[Mu] Hideo Mutô, *The first eigenvalue of the Laplacian on even-dimensional spheres*, Tôhoku Math. J. (2) **32** (1980), no. 3, 427–432, DOI 10.2748/tmj/1178229601. MR590038

[Pe1] Romain Petrides, *Maximization of the second conformal eigenvalue of spheres*, Proc. Amer. Math. Soc. **142** (2014), no. 7, 2385–2394, DOI 10.1090/S0002-9939-2014-12095-8. MR3195761

[Pe2] Romain Petrides, *On a rigidity result for the first conformal eigenvalue of the Laplacian*, J. Spectr. Theory **5** (2015), no. 1, 227–234, DOI 10.4171/JST/95. MR3340180

[Pe3] Romain Petrides, *Existence and regularity of maximal metrics for the first Laplace eigenvalue on surfaces*, Geom. Funct. Anal. **24** (2014), no. 4, 1336–1376, DOI 10.1007/s00039-014-0292-5. MR3248488

[PW] L. E. Payne and H. F. Weinberger, *Lower bounds for vibration frequencies of elastically supported membranes and plates*, J. Soc. Indust. Appl. Math. **5** (1957), 171–182. MR0092431

[Ro] Steven Rosenberg, *The Laplacian on a Riemannian manifold*, London Mathematical Society Student Texts, vol. 31, Cambridge University Press, Cambridge, 1997. An introduction to analysis on manifolds. MR1462892

[Sa] Takashi Sakai, *Riemannian geometry*, Translations of Mathematical Monographs, vol. 149, American Mathematical Society, Providence, RI, 1996. Translated from the 1992 Japanese original by the author. MR1390760

[San] G. Santhanam, *A sharp upper bound for the first eigenvalue of the Laplacian of compact hypersurfaces in rank-1 symmetric spaces*, Proc. Indian Acad. Sci. Math. Sci. **117** (2007), no. 3, 307–315, DOI 10.1007/s12044-007-0026-9. MR2352050

[Sc] Richard Schoen, *Existence and geometric structure of metrics on surfaces which extremize eigenvalues*, Bull. Braz. Math. Soc. (N.S.) **44** (2013), no. 4, 777–807, DOI 10.1007/s00574-013-0034-6. MR3167132

[ST] Brian Davies and Yuri Safarov (eds.), *Spectral theory and geometry*, London Mathematical Society Lecture Note Series, vol. 273, Cambridge University Press, Cambridge, 1999. Papers from the ICMS Instructional Conference held in Edinburgh, March 30–April 9, 1998. MR1736863

[Uh] K. Uhlenbeck, *Generic properties of eigenfunctions*, Amer. J. Math. **98** (1976), no. 4, 1059–1078, DOI 10.2307/2374041. MR0464332

[Y] Shing Tung Yau, *Problem section*, Seminar on Differential Geometry, Ann. of Math. Stud., vol. 102, Princeton Univ. Press, Princeton, N.J., 1982, pp. 669–706. MR645762

[YY] Paul C. Yang and Shing Tung Yau, *Eigenvalues of the Laplacian of compact Riemann surfaces and minimal submanifolds*, Ann. Scuola Norm. Sup. Pisa Cl. Sci. (4) **7** (1980), no. 1, 55–63. MR577325

[Zu] Shunhui Zhu, *The comparison geometry of Ricci curvature*, Comparison geometry (Berkeley, CA, 1993), Math. Sci. Res. Inst. Publ., vol. 30, Cambridge Univ. Press, Cambridge, 1997, pp. 221–262. MR1452876

Université de Neuchâtel, Institut de Mathématiques, Rue Emile-Argand 11, CH-2000, Neuchâtel, Suisse

E-mail address: bruno.colbois@unine.ch

Contemporary Mathematics
Volume **700**, 2017
http://dx.doi.org/10.1090/conm/700/14182

An elementary introduction to quantum graphs

Gregory Berkolaiko

Abstract. We describe some basic tools in the spectral theory of Schrödinger operator on metric graphs (also known as "quantum graphs") by studying in detail some basic examples. The exposition is kept as elementary and accessible as possible. In the later sections we apply these tools to prove some results on the count of zeros of the eigenfunctions of quantum graphs.

1. Introduction

Studying operators of Schrödinger type on metric graphs is a growing subfield of mathematical physics which is motivated both by direct applications of the graph models to physical phenomena and by use of graphs as a simpler setting in which to study complex phenomena of quantum mechanics, such as Anderson localization, universality of spectral statistics, nodal statistics, scattering and resonances, to name but a few.

The name "quantum graphs" is most likely a shortening of the title of the article "Quantum Chaos on Graphs" by Kottos and Smilansky [**36**]. The model itself has been studied well before the name appeared, for example in [**41**, **43**, **46**, **47**, **51**].

Several reviews and monographs cover various directions within the quantum graphs research [**29**, **40**, **45**]. However, when starting a research project with students, both (post-) graduate and undergraduate, the author felt that a more elementary introduction would be helpful. The present manuscript grew out of the same preparatory lecture repeated, at different points of time, to several students. It is basically a collection of minimal examples of quantum graphs which already exhibit behavior typical to larger graphs. We supply the examples with pointers to the more general facts and theorems. Only in the last sections we explore a research topic (the nodal statistics on graphs) in some depth.

For obvious reasons the pointers often lead to the monograph [**15**]; the notation is kept in line with that book, too.

2. Schrödinger equation on a metric graph

Consider a graph $\Gamma = (V, E)$, where V is the set of vertices and E is the set of edges. Each edge connects a pair of vertices; we allow more than one edge running between any two vertices. We also allow edges connecting vertices to themselves

---

2010 *Mathematics Subject Classification.* Primary 34B34, 35B05, 81Q35.

(*loops*). This freedom creates some notational difficulties, so we ask the reader to be flexible and forgiving.

Each edge e is assigned a positive length L_e and is thus identified with an interval $[0, L_e]$ (the direction is chosen arbitrarily and is irrelevant to the resulting theory). This makes Γ a *metric graph*. Now a function on a graph is just a collection of functions defined on individual edges.

The eigenvalue equation for the Schrödinger operator is

$$-\frac{d^2 f}{dx^2} + V(x)f(x) = \lambda f(x), \tag{1}$$

which is to be satisfied on every edge, in addition to the vertex matching conditions as follows

$$f(x) \text{ is continuous}, \tag{2}$$

$$\sum_{e\sim v} \frac{df}{dx}(v) = 0. \tag{3}$$

The continuity means that the values at the vertex agree among all functions living on the edges attached (or *incident*) to the vertex. In the second condition (often called *current conservation condition*), the sum is over all edges attached to the vertex and the derivative are all taken in the same direction: from the vertex into the edge. A looping edge contributes two terms to the sum, one for each end of the edge.

The function $V(x)$ is called the *electric potential* but we will set it identically to zero in all of the examples below. Vertex conditions (2)-(3) are called *Neumann conditions*[1]; they can be generalized significantly, but before we give any more theory, let us consider some examples.

2.1. Example: a trivial graph — an interval. An interval $[0, L]$ is the simplest example of a graph; it has two vertices (the endpoints of the interval) and one edge. The continuity condition is empty at every vertex since there is only one edge. The current conservation condition at the vertex 0 becomes

$$f'(0) = 0, \tag{4}$$

and at the vertex L becomes

$$-f'(L) = 0. \tag{5}$$

The minus sign appeared because we agreed to direct the derivatives into the edge; of course it is redundant in this particular case.

Let $V(x) \equiv 0$ and consider first the positive eigenvalues, $\lambda > 0$. The eigenvalue equation becomes

$$-f'' = k^2 f, \tag{6}$$

where for convenience we substituted $\lambda = k^2$. This is a second order linear equation with constant coefficients which for $k > 0$ is readily solved by

$$f(x) = C_1 \cos(kx) + C_2 \sin(kx). \tag{7}$$

[1]Other names present in the literature are "Kirchhoff", "Neumann-Kirchhoff", "standard", "natural" etc.

Applying the first vertex condition $f'(0) = 0$ we get $C_2 = 0$ and $f(x) = C_1 \cos(kx)$. The second vertex condition becomes

$$C_1 k \sin(kL) = 0, \tag{8}$$

which imposes a condition on k but does nothing to determine C_1 (naturally we are not interested in the trivial solution $f(x) \equiv 0$). We thus get the *eigenvalues* $\lambda = k^2 = (\pi n/L)^2$, $n = 1, 2, \ldots$ with the corresponding eigenfunctions $f(x) = \cos(\pi n x/L)$ defined up to an overall constant multiplier (as befits eigenvectors and eigenfunctions).

There is one other eigenvalue in the spectrum that we missed: $\lambda = 0$ with the eigenfunction $f(x) \equiv 1$. While this agrees with the above formulas with $n = 0$, the premise of equation (7) is no longer correct when $\lambda = 0$.

EXERCISE 2.1. Solve the eigenvalue equation with $\lambda < 0$ and show that the vertex conditions (4) and (5) are never satisfied simultaneously (ignore the trivial solution $f(x) \equiv 0$).

EXERCISE 2.2. Integrate by parts the scalar product

$$\langle f, -f'' \rangle = \int_0^L \overline{f(x)}\,(-f''(x))\,dx, \tag{9}$$

to obtain an expression that is obviously non-negative, and thus show that it is not necessary to solve (6) to conclude that there are no negative eigenvalues.

We did not try to look for complex eigenvalues. This is because the Schrödinger operator we defined is self-adjoint (see Thm 1.4.4 of [**15**]) and therefore has real spectrum. The spectrum in the above example is discrete: all eigenvalues are isolated and of finite multiplicity. This is true for any graph which is compact (has finitely many edges, all of which have finite length), see Thm 3.1.1 of [**15**]. The proof outlined in Exercise 2.2 works for general graphs with Neumann conditions at all vertices. The multiplicity of the eigenvalue 0 in the spectrum can be shown to equal the number of the connected components of the graph.

2.2. Example: a trivializable graph with a vertex of degree two. Consider now a graph consisting of two consecutive intervals, $[0, L_1]$ and $[L_1, L_1 + L_2]$. We do not really have to parametrize the edges starting from 0, so in this example we will employ the “natural” parametrization.

Denote the components of eigenfunction living on the two intervals by f_1 and f_2 correspondingly. Solving the equation on the first edge and enforcing the Neumann condition at 0 results in $f_1(x) = C \cos(kx)$. The conditions at the point L_1 are

$$f_1(L_1) = f_2(L_1), \tag{10}$$

$$-f_1'(L_1) + f_2'(L_1) = 0. \tag{11}$$

Now, by uniqueness theorem for second order differential equations, the solution on the second edge is fully determined by its value at L_1 and the value of its derivative. Thus the solution is still $f_2(x) = C \cos(kx)$ and there is no change in the solution happening at L_1. We could have considered the interval $[0, L_1 + L_2]$ without introducing the additional vertex at L_1. This obviously generalizes to the following rule: *having a Neumann vertex of degree 2 is equivalent to having an uninterrupted edge.*

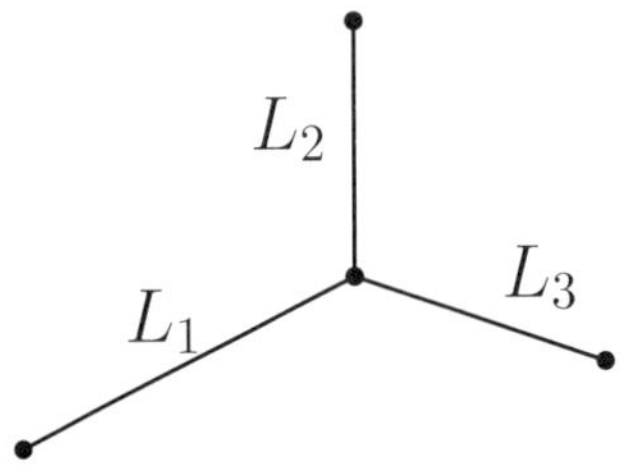

FIGURE 1. A star graph with three edges.

This rule is useful, for example, for when one wants to program a looping edge but is troubled by the notational difficulties of loops or multiple edges. In this case a looping edge can be implemented as a triangle with two "dummy" vertices of degree two.

2.3. Example: star graph with Neumann endpoints. Consider now a first non-trivial example: a star graph with 3 edges meeting at a central vertex, see Fig. 1. Parametrizing the edges from the endpoints towards the central vertex, we get

$$-f_1'' = k^2 f_1, \quad -f_2'' = k^2 f_2, \quad -f_3'' = k^2 f_3, \tag{12}$$

$$f_1'(0) = 0, \quad f_2'(0) = 0, \quad f_3'(0) = 0, \tag{13}$$

$$f_1(L_1) = f_2(L_2) = f_3(L_3), \tag{14}$$

$$-f_1'(L_1) - f_2'(L_2) - f_3'(L_3) = 0, \tag{15}$$

where in addition to the already familiar equations (12) and (13) (in three copies), we have continuity condition at the central vertex in equation (14) and current conservation at the central vertex in equation (15). Note that in equation (12), the eigenvalue k^2 is the same on all three edges.

Equations (12)-(13) are solved by

$$f_1(x) = A_1 \cos(kx), \quad f_2(x) = A_2 \cos(kx), \quad f_3(x) = A_3 \cos(kx), \tag{16}$$

for some constants A_1, A_2 and A_3. Now the remaining two equations become, after a minor simplification,

$$A_1 \cos(kL_1) = A_2 \cos(kL_2) = A_3 \cos(kL_3), \tag{17}$$

$$A_1 \sin(kL_1) + A_2 \sin(kL_2) + A_3 \sin(kL_3) = 0. \tag{18}$$

Dividing equation (18) by (17) cancels the unknown constants, resulting in

$$\tan(kL_1) + \tan(kL_2) + \tan(kL_3) = 0. \tag{19}$$

Squares of the roots k of this equation (which cannot be solved explicitly except when all Ls are equal) are the eigenvalues of the star graph.

EXERCISE 2.3. We ignored the possibility that one or more of the cosines in equation (17) are zero. Show that the more robust (but much longer!) version of equation (19) is

$$\begin{aligned} &\sin(kL_1)\cos(kL_2)\cos(kL_3) + \cos(kL_1)\sin(kL_2)\cos(kL_3) \\ &\qquad + \cos(kL_1)\cos(kL_2)\sin(kL_3) = 0. \end{aligned} \tag{20}$$

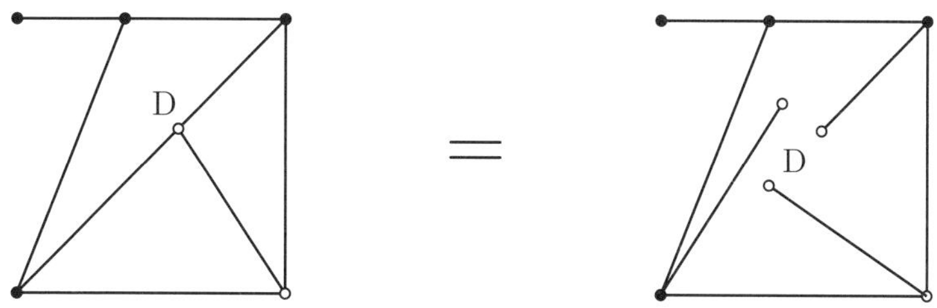

FIGURE 2. A Dirichlet condition imposed at a vertex of degree $d = 3$ (here and in subsequent figures, the Dirichlet vertices are denoted by empty circles) is equivalent to splitting the vertex into three and imposing the condition at every new vertex.

Moreover, the order of the root k of (20) is equal to the dimension of the corresponding eigenspace.

For example, if $L_1 = L_2 = L_3 = \pi/2$, the left-hand side of (20) vanishes at $k = 1$ to the second order. This corresponds to two linearly independent solutions,

$$(f_1, f_2, f_3) = (\cos(x), -\cos(x), 0) \quad \text{and} \quad (\cos(x), 0, -\cos(x)). \tag{21}$$

There is actually a lot more that can be (and will be said) about this simple graph, but we first need to extend the set of possible vertex conditions that we consider.

3. Dirichlet condition

Another possible vertex condition which is compatible with self-adjointness of the Schrödinger operator is the so-called Dirichlet condition,

$$f_e(v) = 0 \quad \text{for all } e \text{ incident to } v. \tag{22}$$

It is usually used only at vertices of degree 1 for the following reason. A Dirichlet condition imposed at a vertex of degree 2 or more fails to relate in any way the individual functions living on the incident edges. Thus a graph with a Dirichlet condition at a vertex v of degree d_v is equivalent to a graph with v substituted with d_v vertices of degree one, see Fig. 2.

Note that the difference between a Neumann and a Dirichlet condition at a vertex of degree d_v is minimal: the current conservation condition is substituted with the condition that *one* of the function values is equal to zero; the rest is taken care of by continuity.

EXERCISE 3.1. Show that the eigenvalues of the interval $[0, L]$ with Dirichlet conditions at both ends are given by $\lambda_n = (\pi n/L)^2$, $n = 1, 2, \ldots$ with the eigenfunctions $f^{(n)}(x) = \sin(\pi n x/L)$.

3.1. Example: a star graph with Dirichlet conditions at endpoints. Consider a star graph with N edges. We parametrize the edges from the endpoints towards the central vertex, as before. Solving the eigenvalue equation $-f'' = k^2 f$ and imposing the Dirichlet condition at $x = 0$ results in $f_i(x) = A_i \sin(kx)$, where the constant A_i depends on the edge.

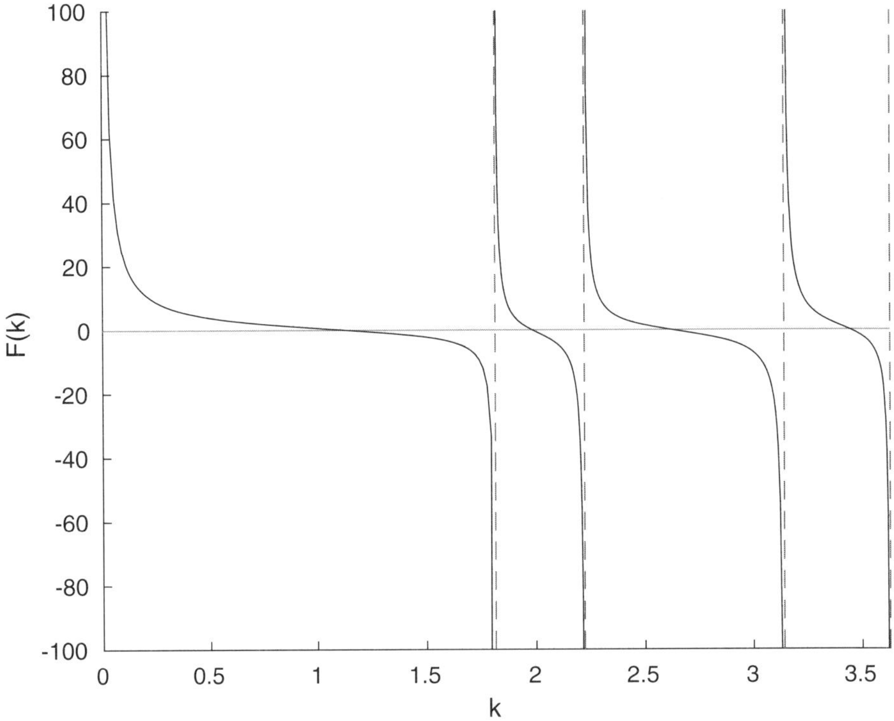

FIGURE 3. Plot of the right-hand side of (25) with 3 edges of lengths 1, $\sqrt{2}$ and $\sqrt{3}$. It is a function that decreases monotonely between each pair of its poles. The poles visible on the plot are 0, $\pi/\sqrt{3}$, $\pi/\sqrt{2}$, π and $2\pi/\sqrt{3}$.

At the central vertex we have

$$A_1 \sin(kL_1) = \ldots = A_N \sin(kL_N), \tag{23}$$

$$A_1 \cos(kL_1) + \ldots + A_N \cos(kL_N) = 0. \tag{24}$$

If we assume that the lengths L_i are incommensurate, we will not be missing any roots by dividing equation (24) by (23), leading to the eigenvalue condition

$$\sum_{i=1}^{N} \cot(kL_i) = 0. \tag{25}$$

This condition is very similar to equation (19) we derived for the star graph with Neumann conditions at the endpoints. However, it is now easier to see a connection between the star graph and the eigenvalue problem of an interval.

The left-hand side of equation (25) has derivative of constant sign (negative) except at the poles $k \in \{n\pi/L_i\}$, $i = 1, \ldots, N$, $n \in \mathbb{Z}$. Therefore, between each pair of consecutive poles there is a single root of equation (25), see Fig. 3. The poles can be interpreted as the square roots of the eigenvalues of the individual edges of the graph, see Exercise 3.1. Furthermore, the collection of the edges with Dirichlet conditions can be obtained from the original star graph by changing the central vertex condition from Neumann to Dirichlet, see Fig. 4. As we mentioned already,

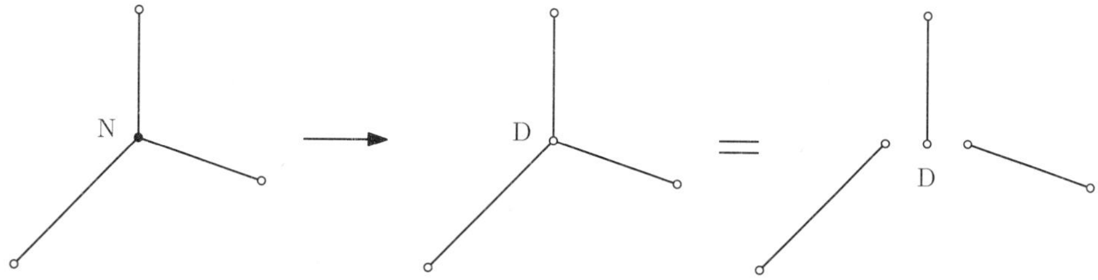

FIGURE 4. A star graph with the central vertex condition changed to Dirichlet splits into a collection of intervals.

this can be effected by changing only one equation in the Neumann conditions, which is a rank-one perturbation. To summarize, we found that there is exactly one eigenvalue of a star graph between any two consecutive eigenvalues of its rank 1 perturbation.

4. Interlacing inequalities

Naturally, the observation of Section 3.1 applies not only to star graphs but to any graphs with discrete spectrum.

LEMMA 4.1 (Neumann–Dirichlet interlacing). *Let Γ_0 be a quantum graph with a vertex v which is endowed with Neumann conditions. Let Γ_∞ denote the graph obtained by changing the conditions at v to Dirichlet. Numbering the eigenvalues of both graphs in ascending order starting from 1, we have*

$$\lambda_n(\Gamma_0) \le \lambda_n(\Gamma_\infty) \le \lambda_{n+1}(\Gamma_0) \le \lambda_{n+1}(\Gamma_\infty). \tag{26}$$

An equality between a Neumann and a Dirichlet eigenvalue is possible only if the eigenspace of the Neumann eigenvalue contains a function vanishing at v, or, equivalently, the eigenspace of the Dirichlet eigenvalue contains a function satisfying the current conservation condition.

The proof, which can be found in [**14**, **15**], uses the standard arguments built upon the minimax characterisation of eigenvalues of a self-adjoint operator. It is analogous to the proofs of Cauchy's Interlacing Theorem or rank-one perturbations for matrices, see, for example [**32**].

The following exercise contains an application of Lemma 4.1 to the nodal count of eigenfunctions.

EXERCISE 4.2. Show that if the n-th eigenvalue of a star graph with Dirichlet endpoints is simple and the corresponding eigenfunction is non-vanishing at the central vertex, the eigenfunction has precisely $n-1$ zeros in the interior of the graph.

This statement can be obtained by combining the strict version of inequality (26) with the following observation. If λ satisfies $\lambda_n(I) \le \lambda \le \lambda_{n+1}(I)$, where I is the interval $[0, L]$ with Dirichlet boundary conditions, then $f(x) = \sin(\sqrt{\lambda}x)$ has n zeros on the interval $(0, L)$.

A more general version of this statement holds for tree graphs. This theorem has a rich history, originally appearing in [**44**] and [**49**]; the shortest proof along the lines outlined in Exercise 4.2 appeared in [**14**] and in Section 5.2.2 of [**15**].

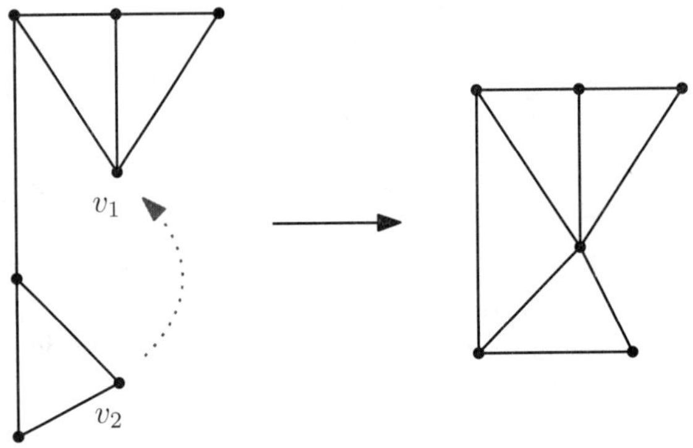

FIGURE 5. The operation of merging two vertices into one.

Another useful interlacing inequality arises when we join two Neumann vertices to form a single Neumann vertex, see Fig. 5. Since the change in the vertex conditions can be described as imposing *another* continuity equality[2], we expect the eigenvalues to increase as a result.

LEMMA 4.3. *Let Γ be a quantum graph (not necessarily connected) with two vertices v_1 and v_2 with Neumann conditions. Modify the graph by merging the two vertices into one, to obtain the graph Γ'. Then*

$$\lambda_n(\Gamma) \le \lambda_n(\Gamma') \le \lambda_{n+1}(\Gamma). \tag{27}$$

An equality between an eigenvalue of Γ and an eigenvalue of Γ' is only possible if the eigenspace of Γ contains an eigenfunction whose values at v_1 and v_2 are equal or, equivalently, the eigenspace of Γ' contains an eigenfunction which additionally satisfy the current conservation condition with respect to the subset E_{v_1} of the edges incident to vertex v_1 in the graph Γ.

This lemma and Lemma 4.1 have many applications to counting zeros of a graph's eigenfunctions, one of which will be presented in Section 7.3. Another application is to the eigenvalue counting which is the subject of the next section.

4.1. An application to eigenvalue counting: Weyl's law. Let us define the eigenvalue *counting function* $N_\Gamma(k)$ as the number of eigenvalues of the graph Γ which are smaller than k^2,

$$N_\Gamma(k) = \#\left\{\lambda \in \sigma(\Gamma) : \lambda \le k^2\right\}. \tag{28}$$

This number is guaranteed to be finite since the spectrum of a quantum graph is discrete and bounded from below (Sec 3.1.1 and Thm 1.4.19 of [**15**]). We count the eigenvalues in terms of $k = \sqrt{\lambda}$ as this is more convenient and can be easily related back to λ.

The counting function $N_\Gamma(k)$ grows linearly in k, with the slope proportional to the "size" of the graph. This type of result is known as the "Weyl's Law".

[2]This is not entirely correct, as the two current conservations conditions are also relaxed into one. However, in terms of quadratic forms, which impose the current conservation automatically, the change is indeed a one-dimensional reduction of the domain of the form.

LEMMA 4.4. *Let Γ be a graph with Neumann or Dirichlet conditions at every vertex. Then*

$$N(k) = \frac{\mathcal{L}}{\pi}k + O(1), \tag{29}$$

where $\mathcal{L} = L_1 + \ldots + L_{|E|}$ is the total length of the graph's edges and the remainder term is bounded above and below by constants independent of k.

PROOF. Let us first consider an interval of length L with Dirichlet conditions. We know the eigenvalues are $(\pi n/L)^2$, $n \in \mathbb{N}$, therefore we can express $N_L(k)$ using the integer part function,

$$N_L(k) = \left\lfloor \frac{kL}{\pi} \right\rfloor,$$

and thus bound it,

$$\frac{L}{\pi}k - 1 \le N_L(k) \le \frac{L}{\pi}k. \tag{30}$$

Let us now consider the setting of Lemma 4.1: Γ_0 is a quantum graph with a vertex v which is endowed with Neumann conditions and Γ_∞ is the graph obtained by changing the conditions at v to Dirichlet. Inequality (26) can be rewritten as

$$N_{\Gamma_\infty}(k) \le N_{\Gamma_0}(k) \le N_{\Gamma_\infty}(k) + 1. \tag{31}$$

Starting with a graph Γ, we can change conditions at every vertex to Dirichlet. Applying the interlacing inequality $|V|$ times (or less, if some vertices are already Dirichlet), we get

$$N_{\Gamma_D}(k) \le N_\Gamma(k) \le N_{\Gamma_D}(k) + |V|, \tag{32}$$

where by Γ_D we denote the graph with every vertex conditions changed to Dirichlet. The graph Γ_D is just a collection of disjoint intervals, each with Dirichlet conditions at the endpoints. The eigenvalue spectrum of Γ_D is the union (in the sense of multisets) of the spectra of the intervals; the counting function is the sum of the interval counting functions. By adding $|E|$ inequalities of type (30), we get

$$\frac{L_1 + \ldots + L_{|E|}}{\pi}k - |E| \le N_{\Gamma_D}(k) \le \frac{L_1 + \ldots + L_{|E|}}{\pi}k, \tag{33}$$

leading to the final estimate

$$\frac{\mathcal{L}}{\pi}k - |E| \le N_\Gamma(k) \le \frac{\mathcal{L}}{\pi}k + |V|. \tag{34}$$

□

REMARK 4.5. The bounds on the remainder term in the Weyl's law for a graph obtained in the proof are of order $|E|$. However, numerically it appears that the counting function follows the Weyl's term much more closely. Getting the optimal bound remains an open question at the time of writing.

5. Secular determinant

We will now describe another procedure for deriving an equation for the eigenvalues of a quantum graph. Before we describe the general case, we shall tackle a simple but useful example.

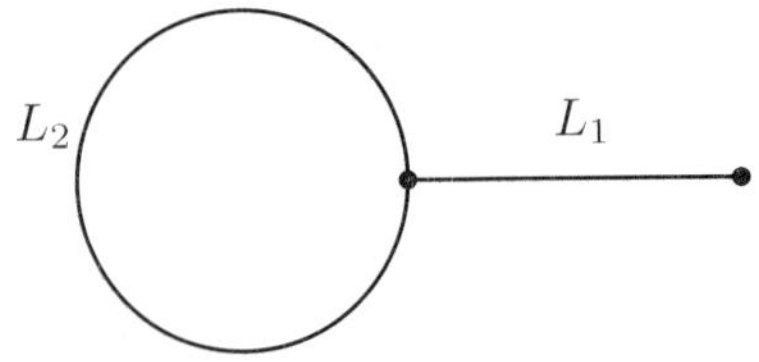

FIGURE 6. A lasso (or lollipop) graph, consisting of an edge and a loop.

5.1. Example: lasso (lollipop) graph. Consider the graph depicted in Fig. 6, an edge attached to a loop. We will impose Neumann conditions at both the attachment point and the endpoint of the edge.

Let the edge be parametrized by $[0, L_1]$ with 0 corresponding to the attachment point and the loop be parametrized by $[0, L_2]$. The solution of the eigenvalue equation $-f'' = k^2 f$ on the edge can be written as

$$f_1(x) = a_1 e^{ikx} + a_{\bar{1}} e^{ik(L_1 - x)}, \tag{35}$$

valid as long as $k \neq 0$ (we take care of this special case separately). The Neumann condition at the endpoint leads to

$$f_1'(L_1) = ika_1 e^{ikL_1} - ika_{\bar{1}} = 0, \tag{36}$$

and therefore

$$a_{\bar{1}} = a_1 e^{ikL_1}. \tag{37}$$

The solution on the loop we express similarly as

$$f_2(x) = a_2 e^{ikx} + a_{\bar{2}} e^{ik(L_2 - x)}, \tag{38}$$

At the attachment point, the continuity condition reads

$$a_1 + a_{\bar{1}} e^{ikL_1} = a_2 + a_{\bar{2}} e^{ikL_2} = a_{\bar{2}} + a_2 e^{ikL_2}, \tag{39}$$

while the current conservation is

$$f_1'(0) + f_2'(0) - f_2'(L_2) = 0, \tag{40}$$

which, after simplification, yields

$$a_1 - a_{\bar{1}} e^{ikL_1} + a_2 - a_{\bar{2}} e^{ikL_2} + a_{\bar{2}} - a_2 e^{ikL_2} = 0. \tag{41}$$

Rearranging equations (39) and (41) we get the system

$$a_1 = -\frac{1}{3} a_{\bar{1}} e^{ikL_1} + \frac{2}{3} a_{\bar{2}} e^{ikL_2} + \frac{2}{3} a_2 e^{ikL_2}, \tag{42}$$

$$a_2 = \frac{2}{3} a_{\bar{1}} e^{ikL_1} + \frac{2}{3} a_2 e^{ikL_2} - \frac{1}{3} a_{\bar{2}} e^{ikL_2}, \tag{43}$$

$$a_{\bar{2}} = \frac{2}{3} a_{\bar{1}} e^{ikL_1} - \frac{1}{3} a_2 e^{ikL_2} + \frac{2}{3} a_{\bar{2}} e^{ikL_2}. \tag{44}$$

This system has an interesting "dynamical" interpretation, see Fig. 7. Take, for example, the coefficient $a_{\bar{1}}$ and interpret it as the amplitude of the plain wave leaving the endpoint vertex in the direction of the loop. Traversing the edge (of length L_1), it acquires the phase factor of e^{ikL_1}. Hitting the vertex, it scatters in three directions: back into the edge with *back-scattering* amplitude $-1/3$ contributing to the right-hand side of equation (42), and forward into the two ends of the loop, with *forward scattering* amplitude $2/3$, contributing to equations (43) and (44).

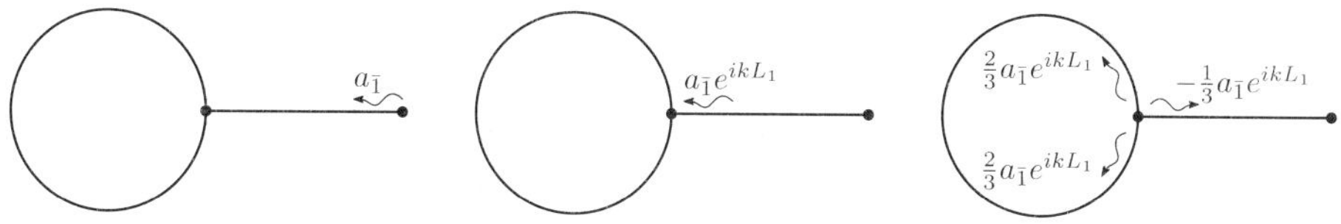

FIGURE 7. Scattering of a wave on a vertex. The waves leaves the endpoint with amplitude $a_{\bar{1}}$, acquires the phase e^{ikL_1} by traversing the edge and scatters in three directions on the vertex.

The amplitudes a_1, a_2 and $a_{\bar{2}}$ can be interpreted similarly and undergo the same process. Equations (37) and (42)-(44) can be interpreted as describing a *stationary state* of such a dynamical process. They can be written as

$$(45)\quad \begin{pmatrix} 0 & -\frac{1}{3} & \frac{2}{3} & \frac{2}{3} \\ 1 & 0 & 0 & 0 \\ 0 & \frac{2}{3} & \frac{2}{3} & -\frac{1}{3} \\ 0 & \frac{2}{3} & -\frac{1}{3} & \frac{2}{3} \end{pmatrix} \begin{pmatrix} e^{ikL_1} & 0 & 0 & 0 \\ 0 & e^{ikL_1} & 0 & 0 \\ 0 & 0 & e^{ikL_2} & 0 \\ 0 & 0 & 0 & e^{ikL_2} \end{pmatrix} \begin{pmatrix} a_1 \\ a_{\bar{1}} \\ a_2 \\ a_{\bar{2}} \end{pmatrix} = \begin{pmatrix} a_1 \\ a_{\bar{1}} \\ a_2 \\ a_{\bar{2}} \end{pmatrix}.$$

Defining two matrices

$$(46)\quad S = \begin{pmatrix} 0 & -\frac{1}{3} & \frac{2}{3} & \frac{2}{3} \\ 1 & 0 & 0 & 0 \\ 0 & \frac{2}{3} & \frac{2}{3} & -\frac{1}{3} \\ 0 & \frac{2}{3} & -\frac{1}{3} & \frac{2}{3} \end{pmatrix} \quad \text{and} \quad D = \begin{pmatrix} e^{ikL_1} & 0 & 0 & 0 \\ 0 & e^{ikL_1} & 0 & 0 \\ 0 & 0 & e^{ikL_2} & 0 \\ 0 & 0 & 0 & e^{ikL_2} \end{pmatrix},$$

we can interpret (45) as saying that the matrix $SD(k)$ has 1 as its eigenvalue. Moreover, each eigenvector of the eigenvalue 1 gives rise to a solution of the eigenvalue equation for the original differential operator, via equations (35) and (38). In other words, the geometric multiplicity of the eigenvalue 1 of the matrix $SD(k)$ is equal to the geometric multiplicity of the eigenvalue k^2 of the differential operator $-\frac{d^2}{dx^2}$. Furthermore, both matrices S and $D(k)$ are unitary, thus for their product $SD(k)$, the algebraic and geometric multiplicity coincide. The only point where this relationship can break down is at $k = 0$; this is because solutions (35) and (38) are not valid at this point.

To summarize, we have the following criterion: the value $k^2 \neq 0$ is an eigenvalue of the lasso quantum graph if and only if k is a root of the equation

$$(47)\qquad \Sigma(k) := \det\left(I - SD(k)\right) = 0.$$

The multiplicity of k^2 in the spectrum of the graph coincides with the multiplicity of k as a root of $\Sigma(k)$. The function $\Sigma(k)$ is called the *secular determinant* of the graph.

To finish this example, we mention that explicit evaluation results in

$$(48)\quad \Sigma(k) = \frac{1}{3}(z_2 - 1)(3z_1^2 z_2 - z_1^2 + z_2 - 3), \qquad \text{where } z_1 = e^{ikL_1},\ z_2 = e^{ikL_2}.$$

We will understand the reason for the factorization of $\Sigma(k)$ in Section 6. Note that the value $k = 0$ is a double root of $\Sigma(k)$ whereas $\lambda = 0$ is a simple eigenvalue of the graph (with constant as the eigenfunction).

5.2. Secular determinant for a general Neumann graph. Let us now consider a general vertex with Neumann conditions and d edges incident to it. Writing the solution on j-th edge as

$$f_j(x) = a_j e^{ikx} + a_{\bar{j}} e^{ik(L_j - x)}, \tag{49}$$

we get from the vertex conditions

$$a_1 + a_{\bar{1}} e^{ikL_1} = \ldots = a_d + a_{\bar{d}} e^{ikL_d}, \tag{50}$$

$$\sum_{j=1}^{d} a_j - \sum_{j=1}^{d} a_{\bar{j}} e^{ikL_j} = 0. \tag{51}$$

For any n, $1 \leq n \leq d$, equations (50) imply

$$\sum_{j=1}^{d} a_j + \sum_{j=1}^{d} a_{\bar{j}} e^{ikL_j} = d \left(a_n + a_{\bar{n}} e^{ikL_n} \right). \tag{52}$$

Subtracting from this equation (51) and solving for a_n results in

$$a_n = -a_{\bar{n}} e^{ikL_n} + \frac{2}{d} \sum_{j=1}^{d} a_{\bar{j}} e^{ikL_j}, \tag{53}$$

which is a generalization of both (37) and (42)-(44), with $d = 1$ and $d = 3$ correspondingly.

Now, it is clear how to generalize the matrices S and $D(k)$ in equation (46). Every edge of the graph gives rise to two directed edges which inherit the length of the edge. The two directed edges corresponding to the same undirected edge are *reversals* of each other. The reversal of a directed edge j is denoted by $\bar{j}$. Consider the $2|E|$-dimensional complex space, with dimensions indexed by the directed edges. The matrix $D(k)$ is diagonal with entries

$$D(k)_{j,j} = e^{ikL_j}, \tag{54}$$

while the matrix S has the entries

$$S_{j',j} = \begin{cases} \frac{2}{d_v} - 1, & \text{if } j' = \bar{j}, \\ \frac{2}{d_v}, & \text{if } j' \text{ follows } j \text{ and } j' \neq \bar{j}, \\ 0, & \text{otherwise.} \end{cases} \tag{55}$$

The edge j' *follows* j if the end-vertex of j is the start vertex of j'; d_v denotes the degree of the end-vertex of j. The matrix S is sometimes called the *bond scattering matrix*.

EXERCISE 5.1. Prove that the matrix S defined by (55) on a graph is unitary.

As before, every eigenvector of $SD(k)$ with $k \neq 0$ corresponds to an eigenfunction of the graph via equation (49). We therefore have the following theorem.

THEOREM 5.2. *Consider a graph with Neumann conditions at every vertex. The value $\lambda = k^2 \neq 0$ is an eigenvalue of the operator $-d^2/dx^2$ if and only if k is the solution of*

$$\Sigma(k) := \det \left(I - SD(k) \right) = 0, \tag{56}$$

where S and $D(k)$ are defined in equations (54) and (55).

EXERCISE 5.3. Incorporate vertices of degree 1 with Dirichlet conditions by showing that back-scattering from such a vertex has amplitude -1 (in contrast with 1 from a Neumann vertex, see the first case of (55) with $d = 1$). This matches with the classic reflection principle of the wave equation on an interval.

REMARK 5.4. Another method used to prove the Weyl's Law (Lemma 4.4) is to observe [**30**] that the eigenvalues of the matrix $SD(k)$ lie on the unit circle and move in the counter-clockwise direction as k is increased. There are $2|E|$ of the eigenvalues and their average angular speed can be calculated to be $\mathcal{L}/|E|$. Thus the frequency of an eigenvalue crossing the positive real axis is the average speed times the number of eigenvalues divided by the length of the circle, giving $2|E| \times \mathcal{L}/|E|/(2\pi) = \mathcal{L}/\pi$.

5.3. Example: secular determinant of star graphs with three edges. Consider again a star graph with 3 edges and Neumann conditions everywhere. Ordering the directed edges as $[1, 2, 3, \bar{1}, \bar{2}, \bar{3}]$, where j is directed away from the central vertex and $\bar{j}$ is directed towards the central vertex, the bond scattering matrix is

$$S = \begin{pmatrix} 0 & 0 & 0 & -1/3 & 2/3 & 2/3 \\ 0 & 0 & 0 & 2/3 & -1/3 & 2/3 \\ 0 & 0 & 0 & 2/3 & 2/3 & -1/3 \\ 1 & 0 & 0 & 0 & 0 & 0 \\ 0 & 1 & 0 & 0 & 0 & 0 \\ 0 & 0 & 1 & 0 & 0 & 0 \end{pmatrix}. \tag{57}$$

Evaluating the secular determinant $\Sigma(k)$ from equation (56), we get

$$\Sigma(k) = -z_1^2 z_2^2 z_3^2 - \frac{1}{3}\left(z_1^2 z_2^2 + z_2^2 z_3^2 + z_3^2 z_1^2\right) + \frac{1}{3}\left(z_1^2 + z_2^2 + z_3^2\right) + 1, \quad \text{where } z_j = e^{ikL_j}. \tag{58}$$

Dividing this expression by $iz_1 z_2 z_3 = ie^{ik(L_1+L_2+L_3)}$ and using the Euler's formula we can transform equation (58) to the form (20) obtained previously (up to a constant).

According to Exercise 5.3, supplying the star graph with Dirichlet conditions at the endpoints results in the bond scattering matrix

$$S = \begin{pmatrix} 0 & 0 & 0 & -1/3 & 2/3 & 2/3 \\ 0 & 0 & 0 & 2/3 & -1/3 & 2/3 \\ 0 & 0 & 0 & 2/3 & 2/3 & -1/3 \\ -1 & 0 & 0 & 0 & 0 & 0 \\ 0 & -1 & 0 & 0 & 0 & 0 \\ 0 & 0 & -1 & 0 & 0 & 0 \end{pmatrix}, \tag{59}$$

and the secular determinant

$$\Sigma(k) = z_1^2 z_2^2 z_3^2 - \frac{1}{3}\left(z_1^2 z_2^2 + z_2^2 z_3^2 + z_3^2 z_1^2\right) - \frac{1}{3}\left(z_1^2 + z_2^2 + z_3^2\right) + 1. \tag{60}$$

Again, dividing it by $z_1 z_2 z_3 = e^{ik(L_1+L_2+L_3)}$ brings it close to the previously obtained form, equation (25), namely to

$$\begin{aligned} e^{-ik(L_1+L_2+L_3)}\Sigma(k) &= \sin(kL_1)\sin(kL_2)\cos(kL_3) \\ &\quad + \cos(kL_1)\sin(kL_2)\sin(kL_3) + \sin(kL_1)\cos(kL_2)\sin(kL_3). \end{aligned} \tag{61}$$

5.4. Real secular determinant. Theorem 5.2 gives a handy tool for looking for the eigenvalues of a quantum graph. However, $\Sigma(k)$, as defined by equation (56) is a complex valued function (that needs to be evaluated on the real line — at least when looking for positive eigenvalues). A complex function is equal to zero when both real and imaginary part are equal to zero. It would be nicer to have one equation instead of two.

There are several indications that it should be possible. First, the fact that we do have roots of a complex function on the real line[3] is atypical; it suggests that the function has some symmetries. Second, in the two examples that we considered in Section 5.3 we succeeded in making the secular determinant real. It turns out that the same method works in general.

LEMMA 5.5. *Let*

$$\mathcal{L} = \sum_{e \in E} L_e \tag{62}$$

denote the total length of the graph. The analytic function

$$\zeta(k) = \frac{e^{-ik\mathcal{L}}}{\sqrt{\det S}} \det\left(I - SD(k)\right), \tag{63}$$

is real on the real line and has the same zeros as the secular determinant $\Sigma(k)$.

PROOF. We remark that

$$\det(D(k)) = e^{2ik\mathcal{L}}, \tag{64}$$

and the matrix $D(k)$ is unitary for real k. Denoting the unitary matrix $SD(k)$ by U, and using the identity $\det(AB) = \det A \det B$, we can rewrite

$$\zeta(k) = (\det U)^{-1/2} \det\left(I - U\right), \tag{65}$$

Using the unitarity of U, we now evaluate

$$\begin{aligned} \overline{\zeta(k)} &= (\det U)^{1/2} \det\left(I - U^*\right) \\ &= (\det U)^{1/2} \det\left(U - I\right) \det U^* = \zeta(k), \end{aligned}$$

where we used the identities

$$I - U^* = UU^* - U^* = (U - I)U^* \quad \text{and} \quad \det\left(U^*\right) = \left(\det U\right)^{-1}. \tag{66}$$

□

EXERCISE 5.6. Show that for a graph with Neumann conditions at every vertex except for n vertices of degree 1 where Dirichlet conditions are imposed, the determinant of S is $\det S = (-1)^{|E|-|V|+n}$.

A detailed study of the secular determinant, including the interpretation of the coefficients of the polynomials like (58) and (60) in terms of special closed paths on the graph, appears in [**6**].

[3]Since our operator is self-adjoint, the eigenvalues $\lambda = k^2$ must be real and therefore the roots of $\Sigma(k)$ are restricted to real and imaginary axes. Since the operator is bounded from below and unbounded from above, infinitely many of the eigenvalues must lie on the real axis

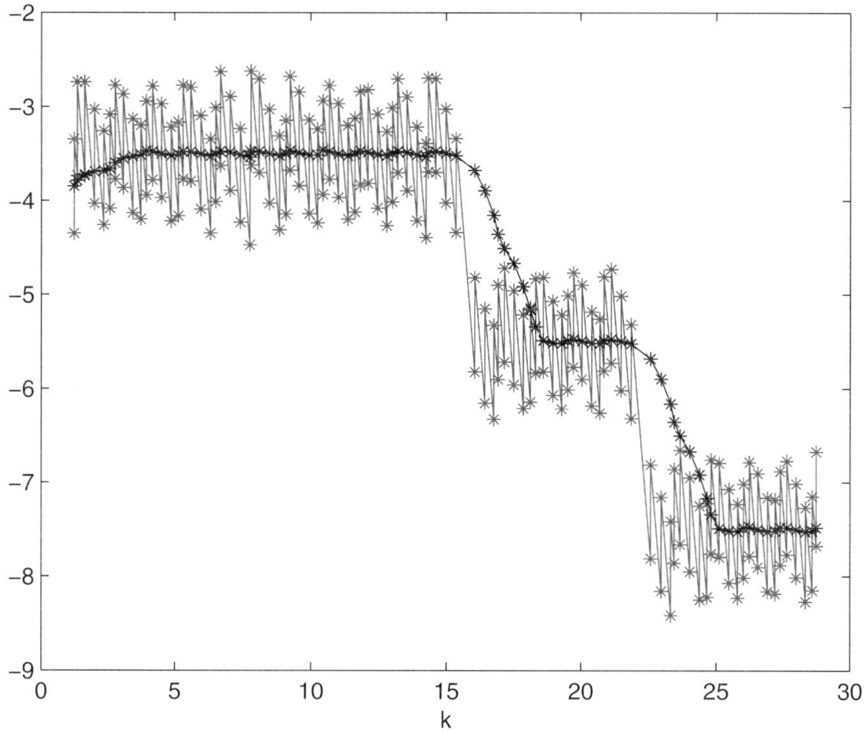

FIGURE 8. The difference between the counting function of the numerically found eigenvalue and the Weyl's estimate. The plot shows that two pairs of eigenvalues were missed, around $k = 15.5$ and $k = 22$.

5.5. Remarks on numerical calculation of graph eigenvalues. Expression (63) which is guaranteed to be real for real k allows for a simple way to compute eigenvalues of a quantum graph: find roots of a real function.

The naive method is to evaluate the function $\zeta(k)$ on a dense enough set of points to get bounds for the eigenvalues, within which the bisection method can be employed. The bisection method can be substituted by a more sophisticated tool such as Brent-Dekker method. For a small graph, the function $\zeta(k)$, which is a combination of trigonometric functions of incommensurate frequency, can be derived explicitly, giving access to its derivative and therefore Newton-like methods.

However, the initial evaluation may miss a pair of almost-degenerate eigenvalues. To check for this possibility, it is very effective to plot the difference between the counting function for the computed eigenvalues and the Weyl's Law. The approximate location of the missed eigenvalues (if any) can be seen very clearly, see Fig. 8 for a typical example. See also [**48**] for another method.

A smarter method for the initial step is to use the interlacing inequalities of Lemma 4.1 to bracket the eigenvalues. Unfortunately, this involves computing eigenvalues of another graph, but it may be much simpler, as in the case of the star graphs.

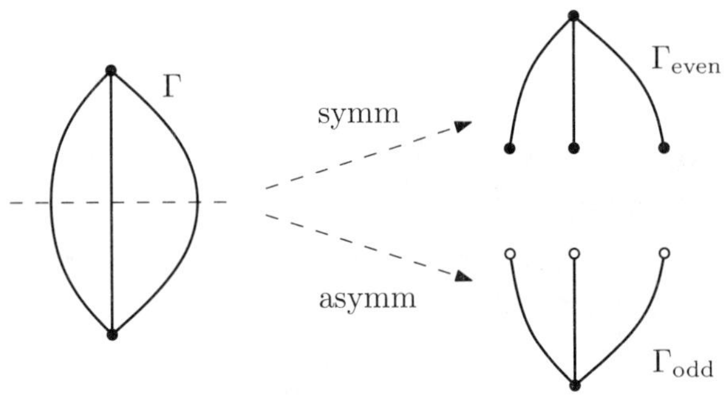

FIGURE 9. The mandarin graph with 3 edges (left) and its decomposition into the even and odd quotients (right). The Dirichlet vertices are distinguished as empty cicrles.

6. Symmetry and isospectrality

6.1. Example: 3-mandarin graph. The 3-mandarin graph is a graph with two vertices and three edges connecting them, see Fig. 9. If one is uncomfortable with multiple edges running between a pair of vertices, extra Neumann vertices of degree two may be placed on some edges, see Section 2.2.

Labelling the edges running down by 1, 2 and 3, and using the ordering $[1, 2, 3, \bar{1}, \bar{2}, \bar{3}]$, the matrix S becomes

$$S = \begin{pmatrix} 0 & 0 & 0 & -1/3 & 2/3 & 2/3 \\ 0 & 0 & 0 & 2/3 & -1/3 & 2/3 \\ 0 & 0 & 0 & 2/3 & 2/3 & -1/3 \\ -1/3 & 2/3 & 2/3 & 0 & 0 & 0 \\ 2/3 & -1/3 & 2/3 & 0 & 0 & 0 \\ 2/3 & 2/3 & -1/3 & 0 & 0 & 0 \end{pmatrix}. \tag{67}$$

Denoting, as before, $z_j = e^{ikL_j}$, $j = 1, 2, 3$, we get $D(k) = \mathrm{diag}(z_1, z_2, z_3, z_1, z_2, z_3)$. The secular determinant simplifies to

$$\begin{aligned} \Sigma(k) = &\left(-z_1z_2z_3 - \frac{1}{3}(z_1z_2 + z_2z_3 + z_3z_1) + \frac{1}{3}(z_1 + z_2 + z_3) + 1\right) \\ &\times \left(z_1z_2z_3 - \frac{1}{3}(z_1z_2 + z_2z_3 + z_3z_1) - \frac{1}{3}(z_1 + z_2 + z_3) + 1\right), \end{aligned} \tag{68}$$

where the factors coincide with the secular determinants we obtained for the star graphs with three edges and Neumann and Dirichlet conditions at the endpoints, correspondingly, see equations (58) and (60), modulo the change $z_j^2 \leftrightarrow z_j$.

The reason for this factorization is the symmetry. The graph, as shown in Fig. 9, is symmetric with respect to the vertical (up-down) reflection. This means that the reflected eigenfunction is still an eigenfunction. Denote by Rf the reflected version of an eigenfunction f. By linearity, $f_e = f + Rf$ and $f_o = f - Rf$ satisfy the eigenvalue equation with the same λ. They may be identically zero, but not both at the same time, since $(f_e + f_o)/2 = f \not\equiv 0$. And under the action of R, f_e is even and f_o is odd:

$$Rf_e = f_e, \qquad Rf_o = -f_o. \tag{69}$$

Using this idea one can show that every eigenspace has a basis of eigenfunctions each of which is either even or odd. Indeed, starting with an arbitrary basis of size m, we produce $2m$ even/odd combinations from them. These combinations span the eigenspace (since $f = (f_e + f_o)/2$), so it remains to choose m linearly independent vectors among them.

Consider an odd eigenfunction on the mandarin graph. Let x_m be the midpoint of the first edge. This point is fixed under the action of reflection, thus $(Rf)(x_m) = f(x_m)$. On the other hand, $Rf = -f$, therefore $f(x_m) = -f(x_m) = 0$. The same applies for the midpoint of every edge. Therefore every odd eigenfunction is the eigenfunction of the half of the mandarin with Dirichlet conditions at the midpoints. The converse is also true: starting from an eigenfunction of the half with Dirichlet boundary, we obtain an eigenfunction of the full graph by planting two copies and multiplying one of them by -1.

A similar reasoning for even eigenfunctions of the mandarin graph shows that they are in one-to-one correspondence with the eigenfunctions of the half of the graph with Neumann boundary. The half of a 3-mandarin is a star graph with three edges, see Fig. 9; the edge lengths are half of the mandarin's.

It turns out that this symmetry of the mandarin graph (and the corresponding factorization (68)) leads to interesting anomalies in the number of of zeros of the eigenfunctions. This subject will be visited again in Section 7.4.

6.2. Quotient graphs. To put the observations of the previous section on a more formal footing, the Hilbert space $H(\Gamma)$ of functions on the mandarin graph (that are sufficiently smooth and satisfy correct vertex conditions) can be decomposed into the direct sum of two orthogonal subspaces H_o and H_e, which are invariant with respect to operator $-d^2/dx^2$ acting on the graph. Restrictions of the operator to these subspaces can be identified with this operator acting on two smaller graphs, a star with Dirichlet ends and a star with Neumann ends.

Such a smaller graph, together with its vertex conditions, is called *quotient graph* and was introduced by Band, Parzanchevski and Ben-Shach [**9, 42**] to study isospectrality. To produce a quotient graph one needs a quantum graph, a group of symmetries (not necessarily the largest possible) and a representation of this group. We will not describe the full procedure, which can be learned from the already mentioned papers and the forthcoming article [**3**]. Instead we will briefly describe its consequences and explain one particular construction that leads to a pair of graphs with identical spectra (i.e. an *isospectral* pair).

Let Γ be a graph with a finite group of symmetries G. To each irreducible representation ρ there corresponds a subspace H_ρ of the Hilbert space $H(\Gamma)$. This is the subspace of functions that transform according to the representation ρ when acted upon by the symmetries from G. In some sources, such functions are called *equivariant vectors*; the subspace H_ρ is called the *isotypic component*. The subspaces corresponding to different irreducible representations are orthogonal, the space $H(\Gamma)$ is a direct sum of H_ρ over all irreps of the group G.

If ρ has dimension $d > 1$, then every eigenvalue of the Hamiltonian restricted to H_ρ has multiplicity which is a multiple of d. Moreover, the secular determinant $\Sigma(k)$ factorizes into factors that correspond to the irreps ρ of G. Each factor is raised to a power which is the dimension of the corresponding ρ (hence the degeneracy of

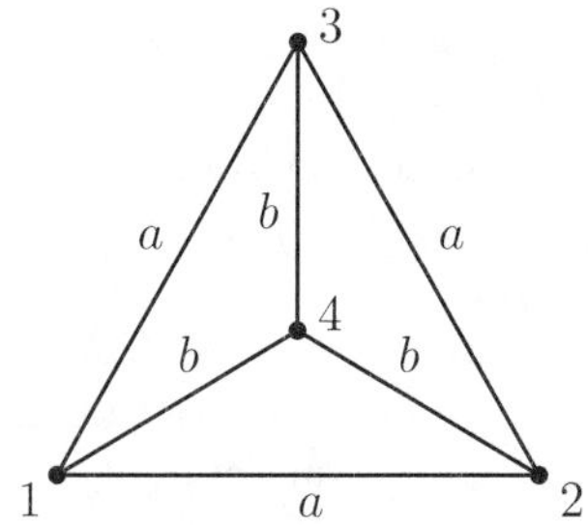

FIGURE 10. A tetrahedron graph which is invariant under rotation by $2\pi/3$ and horizontal reflection. Its group of symmetry is S_3: an arbitrary permutation of vertices 1, 2 and 3.

the corresponding eigenvalue),

$$\Sigma_\Gamma(k) = \prod_{\text{irreps } \rho} \Big(\Sigma_\rho(k)\Big)^{\dim(\rho)}. \tag{70}$$

EXAMPLE 6.1 (from [**3**]). Consider the tetrahedron graph from Fig. 10. This graph is symmetric under reflection and rotation by $2\pi/3$. The corresponding group of symmetries is S_3, the group of permutations of 3 objects; in this case it can be thought of as permuting the vertices number 1, 2 and 3. The group S_3 has three irreducible representations, *trivial*, *alternating* and $2d$. The first two are one-dimensional, while the latter is 2-dimensional (as suggested by its name). The secular determinant $\Sigma(k)$ has the corresponding factorization

$$\Sigma(k) = \frac{1}{27}(z_a - 1)(3z_a z_b^2 - z_b^2 + z_a - 3)(3z_a^2 z_b^2 + 2z_a z_b^2 - z_a^2 + z_b^2 - 2z_a - 3)^2. \tag{71}$$

Note that it may happen that for some ρ the subspace H_ρ is trivial. In this case the corresponding factor $\Sigma_\rho(k)$ is 1 and there are no eigenvalues corresponding to this representation.

6.3. Example: dihedral graphs. The present example originates from [**10**] and is the origin of the theory of [**9, 42**]. Consider the graph on Fig. 11(a). It has the symmetries of the square, thus its full group of symmetries is the dihedral group of degree four D_4 (and order eight, hence another notation, D_8, which causes much confusion).

We will first consider the subgroup generated by the vertical (up-down) reflection τ_1 and the horizontal (left-right) reflection τ_2. One of the irreducible representations of this subgroup is

$$\tau_1 \mapsto (1), \qquad \tau_2 \mapsto (-1), \tag{72}$$

where (1) (correspondingly (-1)) stands for the operation of multiplication by 1 (correspondingly -1).

To understand the functions that transform according to representation (72), we choose as the *fundamental domain* (a subgraph that covers the entire graph under the action of the subgroup) the top right quarter of the graph shown in Fig. 11(b), and plant there a function F. Applying the vertical reflection τ_1, we find that in the bottom right quarter of the graph, the function must be equal to F multiplied by 1 and suitably reflected. Applying the horizontal reflection τ_2, we

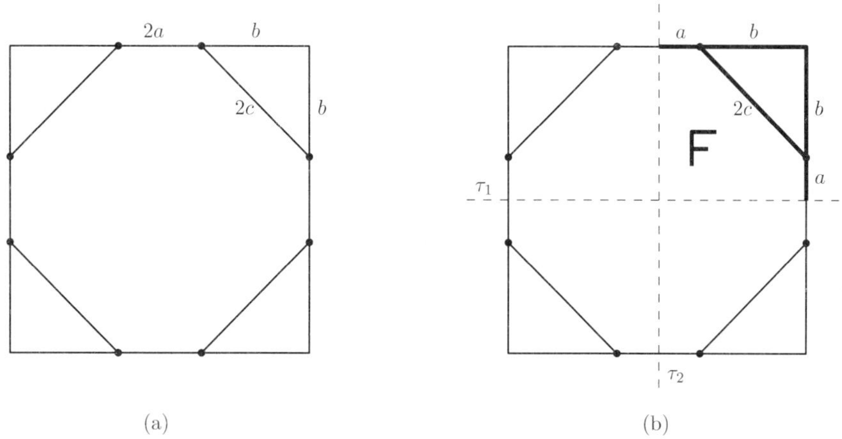

FIGURE 11. (a) A graph with symmetry group D_4, the dihedral group of degree 4; (b) symmetry axes of the first subgroup and a choice of fundamental domain.

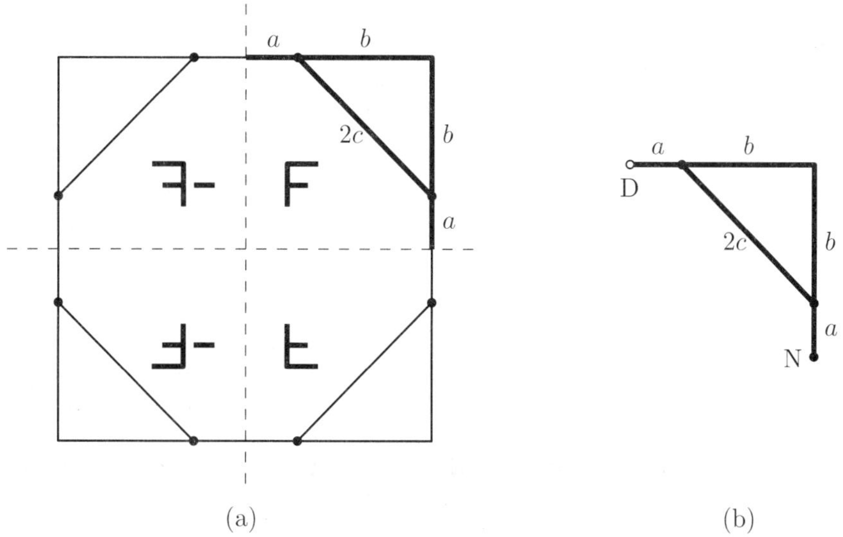

FIGURE 12. Constructing a quotient graph with respect to the representation (72).

find that the left side of the graph must be populated by the copies of the function F multiplied by -1, see Fig. 12(a).

We have already discovered in Section 6.1 that at the point where F meets $-F$, the function must vanish (i.e. have the Dirichlet condition), whereas at the point where F meets F the condition must be Neumann. Thus we obtain the quotient graph in Fig. 12(c).

Let us now repeat the same procedure but choose the diagonal reflections d_1 and d_2 as the generators of the subgroup, together with the representation

$$d_1 \mapsto (1), \qquad d_2 \mapsto (-1). \tag{73}$$

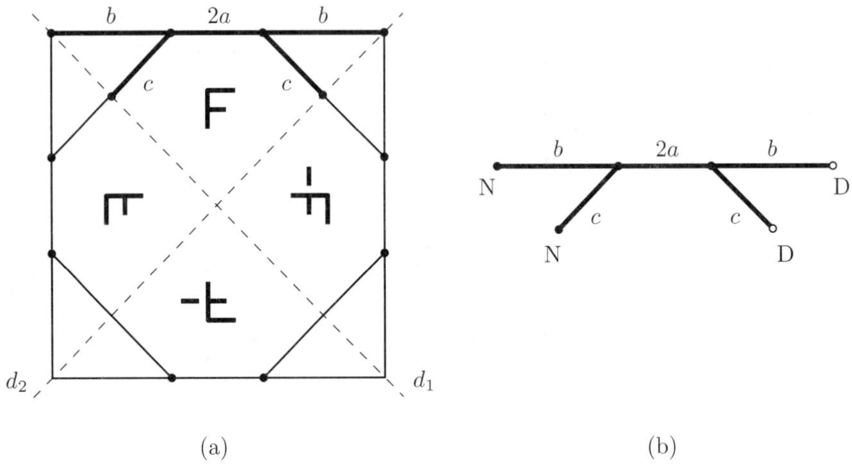

FIGURE 13. Constructing a quotient graph with respect to the representation (73).

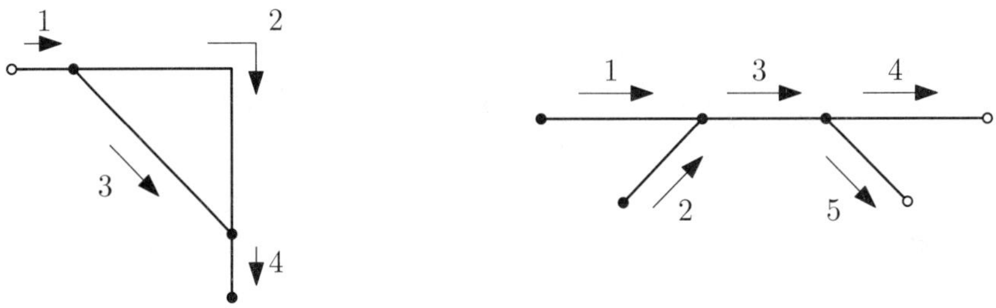

FIGURE 14. Numbering of edges of the two isospectral graph.

Starting with a fundamental domain, reflecting and multiplying it as prescribed by (73), we fill the entire graph as in Fig. 13(a). The corresponding conditions on the fundamental domain are shown in Fig. 13(b).

The most interesting feature of the two quotient subgraphs is that they are *isospectral*, i.e. have exactly the same eigenvalues. This can be shown by a transplantation procedure *a la* Buser [**18, 19**], which describes a unitary equivalence of the corresponding operators. Another possibility (admittedly more tedious) is to find the secular determinants of the two graphs.

To this end, number the edges of the two graphs as shown in Fig. 14. Starting with the graph with a cycle (which we will now call the *dihedral graph*, and its partner the *dihedral tree*), order its edges as $[1,2,3,4,\bar{1},\bar{2},\bar{3},\bar{4}]$. Then

$$S = \begin{pmatrix} 0 & 0 & 0 & 0 & -1 & 0 & 0 & 0 \\ 2/3 & 0 & 0 & 0 & 0 & -1/3 & 2/3 & 0 \\ 2/3 & 0 & 0 & 0 & 0 & 2/3 & -1/3 & 0 \\ 0 & 2/3 & 2/3 & 0 & 0 & 0 & 0 & -1/3 \\ -1/3 & 0 & 0 & 0 & 0 & 2/3 & 2/3 & 0 \\ 0 & -1/3 & 2/3 & 0 & 0 & 0 & 0 & 2/3 \\ 0 & 2/3 & -1/3 & 0 & 0 & 0 & 0 & 2/3 \\ 0 & 0 & 0 & 1 & 0 & 0 & 0 & 0 \end{pmatrix}, \tag{74}$$

and $D(k) = \mathrm{diag}(z_a, z_b^2, z_c^2, z_a, z_a, z_b^2, z_c^2, z_a)$, where $z_s = e^{iks}$, $s = a, b, c$. Evaluating the determinant, we obtain

(75)
$$\Sigma(k) = -z_a^4 z_b^4 z_c^4 + \frac{1}{9}\left(z_a^4 z_b^4 + z_b^4 z_c^4 + z_c^4 z_a^4\right) + \frac{8}{9}\left(z_a^4 - 1\right) z_b^2 z_c^2 - \frac{1}{9}\left(z_a^4 + z_b^4 + z_c^4\right) + 1.$$

Repeating the procedure for the dihedral tree, which has 10×10 matrices S and $D(k)$, we arrive to the secular determinant which is *again given by expression* (75). It is easy to check that 0 is eigenvalue of neither graph and therefore the graphs are isospectral.

The glimpse of the underlying reason for the isospectrality can be seen in the secular determinant of the original graph (that of Fig. 11(a)). As predicted by (70), it factorizes:

$$\begin{aligned}
\Sigma(k) = &\left(9z_a^4 z_b^4 z_c^4 - \left(z_a^4 z_b^4 + z_b^4 z_c^4 + z_c^4 z_a^4\right) - 8\left(z_a^4 - 1\right) z_b^2 z_c^2 + z_a^4 + z_b^4 + z_c^4 - 1\right)^2 \\
&\times \left(3z_a^2 z_b^2 z_c^2 + z_a^2 z_b^2 + z_b^2 z_c^2 + z_c^2 z_a^2 - z_a^2 - z_b^2 - z_c^2 - 3\right) \\
&\times \left(3z_a^2 z_b^2 z_c^2 + z_a^2 z_b^2 - z_b^2 z_c^2 + z_c^2 z_a^2 - z_a^2 + z_b^2 + z_c^2 + 3\right) \\
&\times \left(3z_a^2 z_b^2 z_c^2 - z_a^2 z_b^2 + z_b^2 z_c^2 - z_c^2 z_a^2 - z_a^2 + z_b^2 + z_c^2 - 3\right) \\
&\times \left(3z_a^2 z_b^2 z_c^2 - z_a^2 z_b^2 - z_b^2 z_c^2 - z_c^2 z_a^2 - z_a^2 - z_b^2 - z_c^2 + 3\right),
\end{aligned}$$

up to an overall factor. The last four terms correspond to the four one-dimensional representations of the group D_4, while the first one, squared, corresponds to the two-dimensional representation. The term inside the square also coincides with the secular determinant of the two quotient graphs. This suggests that although we constructed them as quotients by the (one-dimensional) representations of two different symmetry subgroups, they are both realizable as quotients by the two-dimensional representation of the whole group. This is indeed shown in [**9**], together with a general criterion for isospectrality involving induction of representations from subgroups to the whole group.

7. Magnetic Schrödinger operator and nodal count

Magnetic field is introduced into the Schrödinger equation via the magnetic *vector potential* usually denoted $A(x)$. In our case, $A(x)$ is a one-dimensional vector: it changes sign if the direction of the edge is reversed. The Schrödinger eigenvalue equation then takes the form

$$-\left(\frac{d}{dx} - iA(x)\right)^2 f(x) + V(x)f(x) = k^2 f(x), \tag{76}$$

where the square is interpreted in the sense of operators, i.e.

$$\begin{aligned}
\left(\frac{d}{dx} - iA(x)\right)^2 f(x) &= \left(\frac{d}{dx} - iA(x)\right)\Big(f'(x) - iA(x)f(x)\Big) \\
&= f''(x) - i\Big(A(x)f(x)\Big)' - iA(x)f'(x) - A^2(x)f(x).
\end{aligned} \tag{77}$$

To understand the "strange" definition of $A(x)$ a little better, consider the equation

$$-\left(\frac{d}{dx} - iA\right)^2 f(x) = k^2 f(x), \tag{78}$$

where A is a "normal" constant, on the interval $[0, L]$. Solutions of this equation, $e^{\pm ikx+iAx}$, under the change of variables $x \mapsto L - x$ become solutions of a slightly different equation,

$$-\left(\frac{d}{dx} + iA\right)^2 f(L-x) = k^2 f(L-x). \tag{79}$$

But this variable change is just a reparametrization of the interval in terms of the distance from the other end and should not affect the laws of physics. Letting A to be the "one-form" which transforms according to $A(L-x) = -A(x)$ addresses this problem.

To understand the effect of the magnetic potential $A(x)$ on the secular determinant derived in Section 5.2, we write the solution of (76) with $V \equiv 0$ on the j-th edge in the form

$$f_j(x) = a_j e^{ikx+i\int_0^x A(x)} + a_{\bar{j}} e^{ik(L_j-x)+i\int_{L_j}^x A(x)}. \tag{80}$$

Taking $A(x)$ to be the constant vector on the edge (as we will see, this results in no loss of generality), we obtain a somewhat more manageable form

$$f_j(x) = a_j e^{i(k+A)x} + a_{\bar{j}} e^{i(k-A)(L_j-x)}, \tag{81}$$

which also highlights the fact that the wave travelling in the negative direction (the second term) feels the magnetic potential as $-A$.

The vertex conditions also change with the introduction of the magnetic field. It is convenient to define the operator

$$D = \frac{d}{dx} - iA(x), \tag{82}$$

so that the Schrödinger operator can be written as $-D^2 + V$ and the Neumann vertex conditions become

$$f(x) \text{ is continuous}, \tag{83}$$

$$\sum_{e \sim v} Df(v) = 0, \tag{84}$$

which is to be compared to (2)-(3).

Applying these conditions to the solution form (81), we get

$$a_1 + a_{\bar{j}} e^{ikL_1+iA_{\bar{1}}L_1} = \ldots = a_d + a_{\bar{d}} e^{ikL_d+iA_{\bar{d}}L_d}, \tag{85}$$

$$\sum_{j=1}^{d} a_j - \sum_{j=1}^{d} a_{\bar{j}} e^{ikL_j+iA_{\bar{j}}L_j} = 0, \tag{86}$$

which assumes that all edges attached to v are oriented outward and also introduces the notation $A_{\bar{j}} = -A_j$ in agreement with the nature of A. In fact the same answer would be obtained had we started with equation (80) instead, and defined

$$A_j = \frac{1}{L_j}\int_0^{L_j} A(x), \qquad A_{\bar{j}} = \frac{1}{L_j}\int_{L_j}^{0} A(x). \tag{87}$$

Either way, the only change in the definition of the secular determinant $\Sigma(k) = \det(I - SD(k))$ is in the diagonal matrix $D(k)$ which becomes

$$D(k)_{b,b} = e^{ikL_b + i\int_b A(x)}. \tag{88}$$

As we just saw, the precise nature of $A(x)$ is not important; the only quantity that enters $\Sigma(k)$ is the integral of $A(x)$. In fact, even more is true: only the values of the integral of $A(x)$ around the *cycles* of the graph are important.

DEFINITION 7.1. The *flux* of the magnetic field given by $A(x)$ through an oriented cycle γ of Γ is the integral of $A(x)$ over the cycle,

$$\alpha_\gamma = \int_\gamma A(x). \tag{89}$$

THEOREM 7.2. *Consider two operators on the same quantum graph Γ differing only in their magnetic potentials $A_1(x)$ and $A_2(x)$. Then they are unitarily equivalent if their fluxes through every cycle on Γ are equal modulo 2π. In fact, it is enough to compute the fluxes through a fundamental set of $\beta = |E| - |V| + 1$ cycles. A magnetic perturbation of a Schrödinger operator on a graph Γ is thus fully specified by a set of β numbers between $-\pi$ and π.*

The proof of this simple theorem can be found in, for example, [**34**] or [**15**], Section 2.6.

7.1. Example: Dihedral graph. To study the influence of the magnetic perturbation on the eigenvalues of the dihedral graph, we put the magnetic flux α through its loop by using $D(k) = \operatorname{diag}(z_a, e^{i\alpha} z_b^2, z_c^2, z_a, z_a, e^{-i\alpha} z_b^2, z_c^2, z_a)$ together with the matrix S as given in (74). This results in the secular determinant

$$\begin{aligned} \Sigma(k) = &-z_a^4 z_b^4 z_c^4 + \frac{1}{9}\left(z_a^4 z_b^4 + z_b^4 z_c^4 + z_c^4 z_a^4\right) \\ &+ \frac{8}{9}\cos(\alpha)\left(z_a^4 - 1\right) z_b^2 z_c^2 - \frac{1}{9}\left(z_a^4 + z_b^4 + z_c^4\right) + 1. \end{aligned} \tag{90}$$

We plot the first few eigenvalues $\lambda_n(\alpha)$ of the resulting graph as a function of the magnetic flux α, Fig. 15. Since the flux is only important modulo 2π, we plot the eigenvalues over the interval $[-\pi, \pi]$. We observe that the eigenvalues are symmetric (even) functions with respect to $\alpha = 0$: this can be seen directly by complex conjugating equation (76): if $f(x)$ is an eigenfunction with potential $A(x)$ then $\overline{f(x)}$ is an eigenfunction with potential $-A(x)$ with the same eigenvalue. Sometimes the eigenvalue has a minimum at $\alpha = 0$ and sometimes a maximum. These events do not alternate as in the Hill's equation[4]; there is no strict periodicity there, but we will be able to extract some information about them.

7.2. Magnetic–nodal connection. Let us for a moment come back to the case of no magnetic field, $\alpha = 0$, and study the eigenfunctions of the dihedral graph, see Fig. 16. In Table 1 we give the results of a numerical calculation for one choice of the graph's lengths. We list the sequential number of the eigenvalue, starting from 1, its value, the number of zeros of the corresponding eigenfunction, and, somewhat arbitrarily, a description of the behavior of the eigenvalue of the magnetic dihedral graph (see Fig. 15), namely whether it has a maximum or a minimum at $\alpha = 0$.

A careful reader will observe a curious pattern: the magnetic eigenvalue $\lambda_n(\alpha)$ appears to have a minimum whenever the number of zeros of the eigenfunction,

[4] *Hill's differential equation* [**39**] is a Schrödinger equation on $\mathbb{R}^1$ with periodic potential; its Floquet reduction is equivalent to a quantum graph in the shape of a circle with a magnetic flux α through it. It is an important result of Hill's equation theory that the minima and maxima of $\lambda_n(\alpha)$ at $\alpha = 0$ alternate with n.

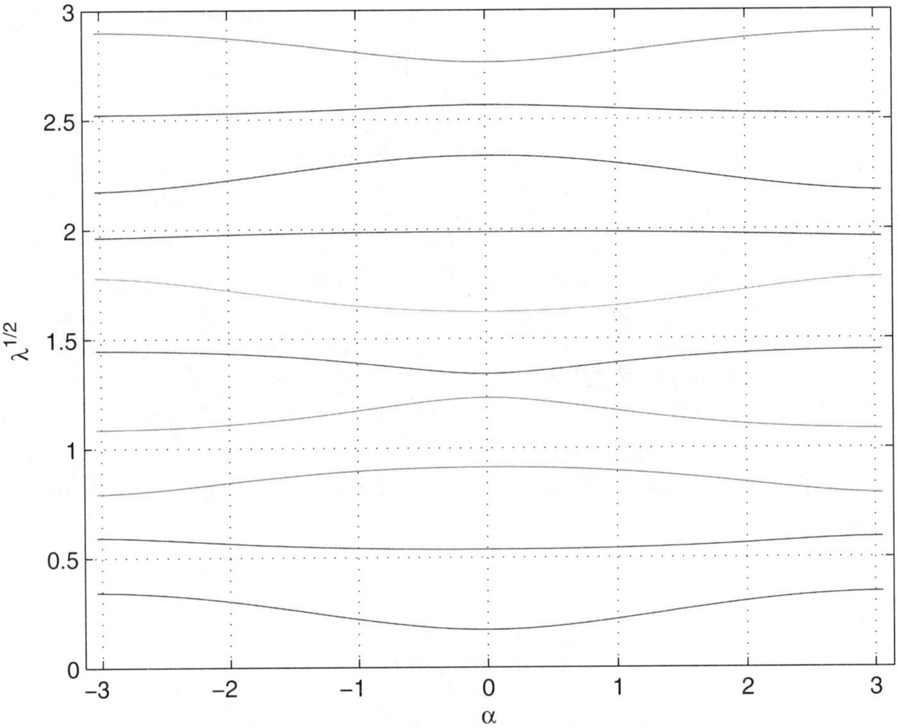

FIGURE 15. The square roots of the first few eigenvalues of the dihedral graph as function of the magnetic flux through the cycle. The lengths are $a = \pi$, $b = 1$, $c = \sqrt{2}$.

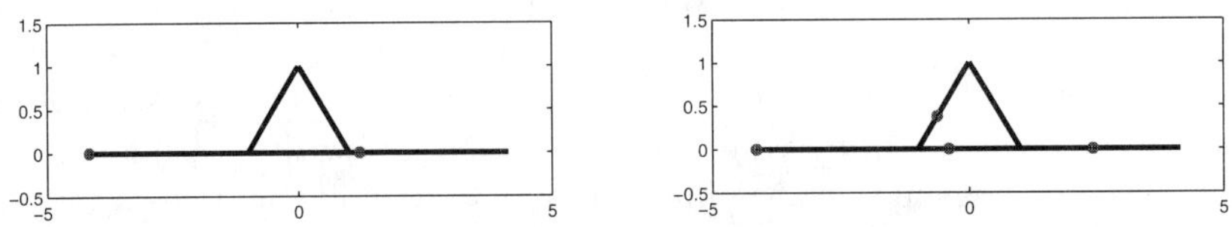

FIGURE 16. Location of zeros of two eigenfunctions of the dihedral graph. Eigenfunctions number $n = 2$ and $n = 3$ are displayed. The zero at the left endpoint is due to the Dirichlet condition; such zeros are not counted when we report the nodal count of an eigenfunction.

which we will denote ϕ_n is less than n and a maximum whenever $\phi_n = n$. The connection between the two was discovered in [**13**] for discrete Laplacians, an alternative proof given in [**20**] and an extension to quantum graphs proved in [**17**].

Before we formulate this result we need to recall some definitions from multivariate calculus.

DEFINITION 7.3. Let $F(x_1, \dots, x_\beta)$ be a twice differentiable function of β variables.

n	1	2	3	4	5	6	7	8	9
$\lambda_n(0)$	0.1708	0.5359	0.9126	1.2294	1.3398	1.6225	1.9877	2.3349	2.5680
# zeros	0	1	3	4	4	5	7	8	9
$\lambda_n(\alpha)$ at 0	min	min	max	max	min	min	max	max	max

TABLE 1. Eigenvalues of a dihedral graph with the lengths $a = \pi$, $b = 1$ and $c = \sqrt{2}$, the number of zeros of the corresponding eigenfunction, and the behavior of the magnetic eigenvalue around the point of no magnetic field.

- The point $x^* = (x_1^*, \ldots, x_\beta^*)$ is a *critical point* of the function F if all first derivatives of F vanish at x^*,
$$\frac{\partial F}{\partial x_j}(x_1^*, \ldots, x_\beta^*) = 0.$$
- The *Hessian* matrix of F at x^* is the matrix of all second derivatives of F,
$$\mathrm{Hess}(F) = \left(\frac{\partial^2 F}{\partial x_j \partial x_k}\right)_{j,k=1}^{\beta}.$$
The matrix $\mathrm{Hess}(F)$ is symmetric therefore all of its eigenvalues are real.
- A critical point is called *non-degenerate* if the Hessian evaluated at the point is a non-degenerate matrix (has no zero eigenvalues).
- The *Morse index* of a critical point is the number of the negative eigenvalues of its Hessian. The Second Derivative Test says that if the Morse index of a non-degenerate critical point is zero, the point is a local minimum; if it equals the dimension of the space, the point is a maximum.

THEOREM 7.4 (Berkolaiko–Weyand [**17**]). *Let $\Gamma^{\boldsymbol{\alpha}}$ be a quantum graph with magnetic Schrödinger operator characterized by magnetic fluxes $\boldsymbol{\alpha} = (\alpha_1, \ldots, \alpha_\beta)$ through a fundamental set of cycles. Let ψ be the eigenfunction of Γ^0 that corresponds to a simple eigenvalue $\lambda = \lambda_n(\Gamma^0)$ of the graph with zero magnetic field. We assume that ψ is non-zero on vertices of the graph.*

Then $\boldsymbol{\alpha} = (0, \ldots, 0)$ is a non-degenerate critical point of the function $\lambda_n(\boldsymbol{\alpha}) := \lambda_n(\Gamma^{\boldsymbol{\alpha}})$ and its Morse index is equal to the nodal surplus *$\phi - (n-1)$, where ϕ is the number of internal zeros of ψ on Γ.*

As a corollary we get a simple but useful bound on the number of zeros of n-th eigenfunction.

COROLLARY 7.5. *Let Γ be a quantum graph with a Schrödinger operator, λ_n be its n-th eigenvalue and ψ_n the corresponding eigenfunction. If λ_n is simple and ψ_n does not vanish on vertices, the number of zeros ϕ_n of the function ψ_n is a well-defined quantity which satisfies*

$$0 \le \phi_n - (n-1) \le \beta = |E| - |V| + 1. \tag{91}$$

REMARK 7.6. The result of Corollary 7.5 actually predates Theorem 7.4 by a considerable time. It goes back to the results on trees [**44, 49**], their extension to $\beta > 0$ for nodal domains [**12**] and to number of zeros [**4**]. But it also follows easily from Theorem 7.4 due to the Morse index being an integer between 0 and the dimension of the space of parameters.

EXERCISE 7.7. Let Γ be a quantum graph with a Schrödinger operator, λ be its simple eigenvalue and ψ the corresponding eigenfunction which does not vanish on vertices. Prove that ψ has an even number of zeros on every cycle of the graph Γ.

7.3. Nodal count of the dihedral graph. It turns out there is an explicit formula for the number of zeros of the n-th eigenfunction of the dihedral graph. This formula was discovered by Aronovitch, Band, Oren and Smilansky [**8**]. The discovery was remarkable as no explicit formula for the *eigenvalues* of the dihedral graph is known.

The formula was proved in [4] using a fairly involved construction of opening the graph by attaching two phase-synchronized infinite leads. It would be nice to be able to prove this result from Theorem 7.4 directly, but we know of no such proof. Instead, we will give here a relatively simple proof showcasing the power of the interlacing results of Section 4.1, Corollary 7.5 and the simple observation that the number of zeros on any cycle of the graph must be even. This proof has not previously appeared in any other source.

THEOREM 7.8 (Conjectured in [**8**], first proved in [4]). *Let n-th eigenvalue of a dihedral graph be simple and the corresponding eigenfunction not vanish at the vertices (except at the Dirichlet vertex). Then the number of zeros of the eigenfunction is*

$$\phi_n = n - \mathrm{mod}_2\left(\left\lfloor \frac{b+c}{a+b+c} n \right\rfloor\right). \tag{92}$$

REMARK 7.9. It can be shown that the hypothesis of the theorem is satisfied for all eigenvalues and eigenfunction for a generic choice of lengths a, b and c [**16**].

It is interesting to observe that the sequence of nodal counts $\{\phi_n\}$ contains the information about the relative length of the central loop in the graph.

Before we can prove the theorem, we need two auxiliary lemmas.

LEMMA 7.10. *Let λ_n denote the eigenvalue of the dihedral graph with parameters a, b and c and let $\tilde{\lambda}_n$ denote the ordered numbers from the set*

$$\tilde{\sigma} := \left\{\frac{\pi}{2a} n_1\right\}_{n_1 \in \mathbb{N}} \cup \left\{\frac{\pi}{2(b+c)} n_2\right\}_{n_2 \in \mathbb{N}}. \tag{93}$$

Then

$$\lambda_n \le \tilde{\lambda}_n \le \lambda_{n+1}, \qquad n = 1, 2, \ldots \tag{94}$$

PROOF. Denote by σ the spectrum of the dihedral graph. Consider the following sequence of modifications of the graph Γ consisting of two copies of the dihedral graph, Fig. 17(a). First we impose the Dirichlet condition on the left attachment point of one copy and the right attachment point of the other copy, obtaining the graph $\hat{\Gamma}$, see Fig. 17(b). Second we separate the right edge of the first dihedral graph and the left edge of the second dihedral graph, imposing Neumann conditions on the newly formed vertices, see Fig. 17(c). The first modification is covered by two applications of Lemma 4.1, while the second by two applications of Lemma 4.3 (in reverse).

Observe that the spectrum of the graph Γ is $\sigma \cup \sigma$ (in the sense of multisets) and the spectrum of the final graph $\widetilde{\Gamma}$ is $\{0\} \cup \tilde{\sigma} \cup \tilde{\sigma}$. We will denote the eigenvalues

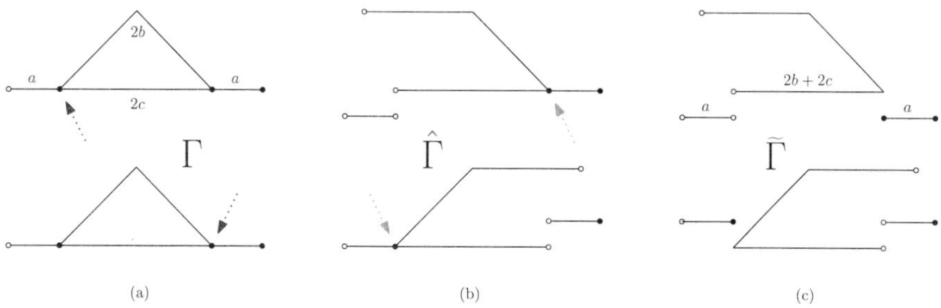

FIGURE 17. Modifications of the graph Γ, consisting of two copies of the dihedral graph, leading to interlacing inequalities (95) and (96). The Dirichlet vertices are distinguished as empty cicrles.

of the three stages by s_n, $\hat{s}_n$ and $\tilde{s}_n$ correspondingly. Because of the degeneracies in the spectrum and the interlacing Lemmas, we have the following inequalities,

$$0 < s_2 = s_1 \leq \hat{s}_1 \leq \hat{s}_2 \leq s_4 = s_3 \leq \hat{s}_3 \leq \hat{s}_4 \leq \dots \tag{95}$$

and

$$\tilde{s}_1 = 0 < \hat{s}_1 \leq \tilde{s}_3 = \tilde{s}_2 \leq \hat{s}_2 \leq \hat{s}_3 \leq \tilde{s}_5 = \tilde{s}_4 \leq \hat{s}_4 \leq \dots \tag{96}$$

Combining the two, we obtain

$$\tilde{s}_1 = 0 < s_2 = s_1 \leq \tilde{s}_3 = \tilde{s}_2 \leq s_4 = s_3 \leq \tilde{s}_5 = \tilde{s}_4 \leq \dots$$

Now the claim of the Lemma follows by observing that $s_1 = \lambda_2$, $\tilde{s}_2 = \tilde{\lambda}_1$, $s_4 = \lambda_2$, $\tilde{s}_4 = \tilde{\lambda}_2$ etc. □

LEMMA 7.11. *Let* $S_1 = \left\{\frac{n_1}{\alpha}\right\}_{n_1 \in \mathbb{N}}$ *and* $S_2 = \left\{\frac{n_2}{\beta}\right\}_{n_2 \in \mathbb{N}}$ *with positive* α *and* β. *If*

$$\#\{S_1 \cup S_2 \leq \lambda\} = n - 1 \qquad \text{then} \qquad \#\{S_1 \leq \lambda\} = \left\lfloor \frac{\alpha}{\alpha+\beta} n \right\rfloor. \tag{97}$$

REMARK 7.12. This Lemma was offered as an exercise to the attendees of 2015 Séminaire de Mathématiques Supérieures "Geometric and Computational Spectral Theory" at CRM, University of Montreal. At that time, the author did not know a good proof.

Several students, including Luc Petiard, Arseny Rayko, Lise Turner and Saskia Voß submitted proofs. The proof below is based on Arseny's proof with elements borrowed from other attendees' versions.

PROOF. Let

$$\#\{S_1 \leq \lambda\} = \lfloor \lambda\alpha \rfloor =: N_1, \qquad \#\{S_2 \leq \lambda\} = \lfloor \lambda\beta \rfloor =: N_2, \tag{98}$$

then $N_1 + N_2 = n - 1$ and also

$$N_1 \leq \lambda\alpha < N_1 + 1,$$
$$N_2 \leq \lambda\beta < N_2 + 1.$$

Multiplying the first inequality by β and the second by α and going through the middle term, we get

$$\beta N_1 < \alpha(N_2 + 1), \qquad \alpha N_2 < \beta(N_1 + 1).$$

Adding αN_1 to the first and $\alpha(N_1+1)$ to the second inequalities we get

$$(\alpha+\beta)N_1 < \alpha(N_1+N_2+1) < (\alpha+\beta)(N_1+1).$$

Dividing by $\alpha+\beta$ and using $N_1+N_2+1=n$ we get

$$N_1 < \frac{\alpha}{\alpha+\beta}n < N_1+1,$$

which implies the desired result. □

PROOF OF THEOREM 7.8. The eigenvalue λ_n of the dihedral graph has $n-1$ eigenvalues from $\tilde\sigma$ below it, so by Lemma 7.11, applied with $\alpha = 2a/\pi$ and $\beta = 2(b+c)/\pi$ it has $N_1 = \left\lfloor \frac{a}{a+b+c}n \right\rfloor$ eigenvalues from the sequence $\left\{\frac{\pi}{2a}\right\}$, which are precisely the eigenvalues of the side edges of the dihedral graph but with the Dirichlet conditions at the attachment points (i.e. the eigenvalues of the signle edge components of the graph $\hat\Gamma$).

By Sturm's theorem, the eigenfunction of the dihedral graph corresponding to λ_n has N_1 zeros on the side edges. Therefore $\phi_n - N_1$ zeros lie on the cycle and this quantity must be even. But we know from Corollary 7.5 that ϕ_n is either $n-1$ or n. To make $\phi_n - N_1$ even we must choose

$$\phi_n = n - \mathrm{mod}_2\,(n-N_1) = n - \mathrm{mod}_2\left(\left\lfloor \frac{b+c}{a+b+c}n \right\rfloor\right).$$

□

7.4. Nodal count of a mandarin graph. When the bounds of equation (91) were discovered, the following question arose: for an arbitrary graph, do all allowed numbers in the range $0, 1, \ldots, \beta$ appear as the nodal surplus $\phi_n - (n-1)$ of some eigenfunction? It turns out the answer is no.

THEOREM 7.13 (Band–Berkolaiko–Weyand [**5**]). *Let Γ be a mandarin graph of 2 vertices connected by d edges. If the eigenvalue number $n>1$, is simple and the corresponding eigenfunction does not vanish on vertices, then the nodal surplus σ_n satisfies*

$$1 \le \sigma_n \le \beta - 1. \tag{99}$$

In particular, the nodal surplus of the 3-mandarin graph is equal to 1 for all eigenfunctions except the first, whose nodal surplus is always 0.

It is interesting to combine this observation with the result of Theorem 7.4. The Morse index is never equal to 0 (for $n>1$) or to the dimension β, therefore the point $\boldsymbol{\alpha}=0$ is never a minimum or a maximum. But the space of all possible magnetic fluxes is a β-dimensional torus, which is compact. Therefore the extrema must be achieved somewhere!

There are other "standard" points where the eigenvalue $\lambda_n(\boldsymbol{\alpha})$ always have a critical point. It is relatively straightforward to extend Theorem 7.4 to points $(b_1, \ldots, b_\beta)$, where each b_i is 0 or π. But it is also straightforward to extend Theorem 7.13 (see [**5**] for both extensions) which will show that those critical point are also never extrema.

The missing extrema turn out to be achieved at singular points of $\lambda_n(\boldsymbol{\alpha})$, see Fig. 18 for an example. Such conical singularities are sometimes called the Dirac points and their appearance in 3-mandarin graphs is intimately related to their

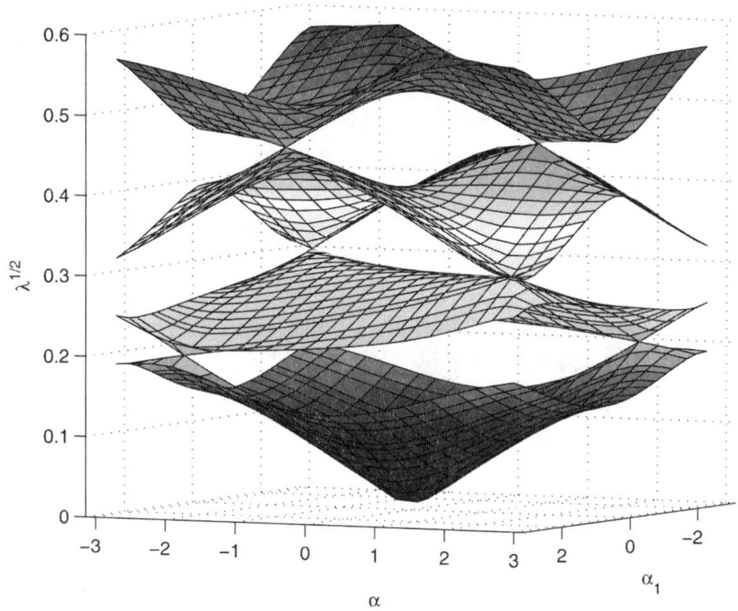

FIGURE 18. The first four eigenvalues of the mandarin graph as functions of two magnetic fluxes α_1 and α_2. The surfaces can be seen to be touching at conical singularities, the so-called Dirac points.

appearance in the dispersion relation of graphene [**38**]. This connection, however, lies outside the scope of this article.

8. Concluding remarks

There are many interesting topics within the area of spectral theory of metric graphs that we did not cover. A very partial list (heavily biased towards personal preferences of the author) is as follows:

- Generic properties of eigenfunctions and eigenvalues. Many results, such as Theorem 7.4 require the eigenvalue to be simple and the eigenfunction to be non-vanishing on vertices. These properties are generic with respect to small perturbations of the edge lengths (that need to break all symmetries of the graph). Results in this direction can be found in [**27**], [**21**](for eigenvalues) and [**16**] (for both eigenvalues and eigenfunctions).
- Ergodic flow on the secular manifold. Barra and Gaspard [**11**] introduced an interpretation of the secular determinant equation as an ergodic flow piercing a compact manifold (more precisely, an algebraic variety) given by solutions of an equation like (75) on a torus. This interpretation leads to many surprising and very general results, including those of [**2**] and [**21**].
- Spectral theory of infinite periodic graphs yields a fruitful connection to the theory of compact graphs with magnetic field. The background is covered in Chapter 4 of [**15**]; a sample of results can be found in [**23, 31**], [**38**], and [**2, 5**].

- Graphs make a very interesting setting to study resonances. Work in this direction has attracted many researchers from across the field [**37**], [**50**], [**22**], [**35**], [**28**], [**24–26**].
- There is an ongoing effort to find bounds on the graph eigenvalues (especially the lowest non-zero ones) in terms of the geometric properties of the graph, see [**1, 7, 33**] for the latest results and references.

References

[1] S. Ariturk. Eigenvalue estimates on quantum graphs. preprint `arXiv:1609.07471`, 2016.

[2] R. Band and G. Berkolaiko. Universality of the momentum band density of periodic networks. *Phys. Rev. Lett.*, 111:130404, Sep 2013.

[3] R. Band, G. Berkolaiko, C. Joyner, and W. Liu. Symmetry of quantum graphs and factorization of the spectral determinant. in preparation, 2016.

[4] R. Band, G. Berkolaiko, and U. Smilansky. Dynamics of nodal points and the nodal count on a family of quantum graphs. *Annales Henri Poincare*, 13(1):145–184, 2012.

[5] R. Band, G. Berkolaiko, and T. Weyand. Anomalous nodal count and singularities in the dispersion relation of honeycomb graphs. *J. Math. Phys.*, 56(12):122111, 2015.

[6] R. Band, J. M. Harrison, and C. H. Joyner. Finite pseudo orbit expansions for spectral quantities of quantum graphs. *J. Phys. A*, 45(32):325204, 19, 2012.

[7] R. Band and G. Lévy. Quantum graphs which optimize the spectral gap. preprint `arXiv:1608.00520`, 2016.

[8] R. Band, I. Oren, and U. Smilansky. Nodal domains on graphs—how to count them and why? In *Analysis on graphs and its applications*, volume 77 of *Proc. Sympos. Pure Math.*, pages 5–27. Amer. Math. Soc., Providence, RI, 2008.

[9] R. Band, O. Parzanchevski, and G. Ben-Shach. The isospectral fruits of representation theory: quantum graphs and drums. *J. Phys. A*, 42(17):175202, 42, 2009.

[10] R. Band, T. Shapira, and U. Smilansky. Nodal domains on isospectral quantum graphs: the resolution of isospectrality? *J. Phys. A*, 39(45):13999–14014, 2006.

[11] F. Barra and P. Gaspard. On the level spacing distribution in quantum graphs. *J. Statist. Phys.*, 101(1–2):283–319, 2000.

[12] G. Berkolaiko. A lower bound for nodal count on discrete and metric graphs. *Comm. Math. Phys.*, 278(3):803–819, 2008.

[13] G. Berkolaiko. Nodal count of graph eigenfunctions via magnetic perturbation. *Anal. PDE*, 6:1213–1233, 2013. preprint `arXiv:1110.5373`.

[14] G. Berkolaiko and P. Kuchment. Dependence of the spectrum of a quantum graph on vertex conditions and edge lengths. In *Spectral Geometry*, volume 84 of *Proceedings of Symposia in Pure Mathematics*. American Math. Soc., 2012. preprint `arXiv:1008.0369`.

[15] G. Berkolaiko and P. Kuchment. *Introduction to Quantum Graphs*, volume 186 of *Mathematical Surveys and Monographs*. AMS, 2013.

[16] G. Berkolaiko and W. Liu. Simplicity of eigenvalues and non-vanishing of eigenfunctions of a quantum graph. *J. Math. Anal. Appl.*, 445(1):803–818, 2017. preprint `arXiv:1601.06225`.

[17] G. Berkolaiko and T. Weyand. Stability of eigenvalues of quantum graphs with respect to magnetic perturbation and the nodal count of the eigenfunctions. *Philos. Trans. R. Soc. Lond. Ser. A Math. Phys. Eng. Sci.*, 372(2007):20120522, 17, 2014.

[18] P. Buser. Isospectral Riemann surfaces. *Ann. Inst. Fourier (Grenoble)*, 36(2):167–192, 1986.

[19] P. Buser, J. Conway, P. Doyle, and K.-D. Semmler. Some planar isospectral domains. *Internat. Math. Res. Notices*, (9):391–400, 1994.

[20] Y. Colin de Verdière. Magnetic interpretation of the nodal defect on graphs. *Anal. PDE*, 6:1235–1242, 2013. preprint `arXiv:1201.1110`.

[21] Y. Colin de Verdière. Semi-classical measures on quantum graphs and the Gauß map of the determinant manifold. *Annales Henri Poincaré*, 16(2):347–364, 2015. also `arXiv:1311.5449`.

[22] E.B. Davies and A. Pushnitski. Non-Weyl resonance asymptotics for quantum graphs. *Analysis & PDE*, 4:729–756, 2011.

[23] P. Exner, P. Kuchment, and B. Winn. On the location of spectral edges in $\mathbb{Z}$-periodic media. *J. Phys. A*, 43(47):474022, 8, 2010.

[24] P. Exner and J. Lipovský. Equivalence of resolvent and scattering resonances on quantum graphs. In *Adventures in mathematical physics*, volume 447 of *Contemp. Math.*, pages 73–81. Amer. Math. Soc., Providence, RI, 2007.
[25] P. Exner and J. Lipovský. Resonances from perturbations of quantum graphs with rationally related edges. *J. Phys. A*, 43(10):105301, 21, 2010.
[26] P. Exner and J. Lipovský. Non-Weyl resonance asymptotics for quantum graphs in a magnetic field. *Phys. Lett. A*, 375(4):805–807, 2011.
[27] L. Friedlander. Genericity of simple eigenvalues for a metric graph. *Israel J. Math.*, 146:149–156, 2005.
[28] S. Gnutzmann, H. Schanz, and U. Smilansky. Topological resonances in scattering on networks (graphs). *Phys. Rev. Lett.*, 110:094101, Feb 2013.
[29] S. Gnutzmann and U. Smilansky. Quantum graphs: Applications to quantum chaos and universal spectral statistics. *Adv. Phys.*, 55(5–6):527–625, 2006.
[30] Daniel Grieser. Monotone unitary families. *Proc. Amer. Math. Soc.*, 141(3):997–1005, 2013. preprint arXiv:0711.2869.
[31] J. M. Harrison, P. Kuchment, A. Sobolev, and B. Winn. On occurrence of spectral edges for periodic operators inside the Brillouin zone. *J. Phys. A*, 40(27):7597–7618, 2007.
[32] R. A. Horn and C. R. Johnson. *Matrix analysis*. Cambridge University Press, Cambridge, second edition, 2013.
[33] J. B. Kennedy, P. Kurasov, G. Malenová, and D. Mugnolo. On the spectral gap of a quantum graph. *Ann. Henri Poincaré*, 17(9):2439–2473, 2016.
[34] V. Kostrykin and R. Schrader. Quantum wires with magnetic fluxes. *Comm. Math. Phys.*, 237(1-2):161–179, 2003. Dedicated to Rudolf Haag.
[35] T. Kottos and H. Schanz. Statistical properties of resonance widths for open quantum graphs. *Waves Random Media*, 14(1):S91–S105, 2004. Special section on quantum graphs.
[36] T. Kottos and U. Smilansky. Quantum chaos on graphs. *Phys. Rev. Lett.*, 79(24):4794–4797, 1997.
[37] T. Kottos and U. Smilansky. Chaotic scattering on graphs. *Phys. Rev. Lett.*, 85(5):968–971, 2000.
[38] P. Kuchment and O. Post. On the spectra of carbon nano-structures. *Comm. Math. Phys.*, 275(3):805–826, 2007.
[39] Wilhelm Magnus and Stanley Winkler. *Hill's equation*. Interscience Tracts in Pure and Applied Mathematics, No. 20. Interscience Publishers John Wiley & Sons New York-London-Sydney, 1966.
[40] D. Mugnolo. *Semigroup methods for evolution equations on networks*. Understanding Complex Systems. Springer, Cham, 2014.
[41] S. Nicaise. Some results on spectral theory over networks, applied to nerve impulse transmission. In *Orthogonal polynomials and applications (Bar-le-Duc, 1984)*, volume 1171 of *Lecture Notes in Math.*, pages 532–541. Springer, Berlin, 1985.
[42] O. Parzanchevski and R. Band. Linear representations and isospectrality with boundary conditions. *J. Geom. Anal.*, 20(2):439–471, 2010.
[43] L. Pauling. The diamagnetic anisotropy of aromatic molecules. *J. Chem. Phys.*, 4(10):673–677, 1936.
[44] Yu. V. Pokornyĭ, V. L. Pryadiev, and A. Al′-Obeĭd. On the oscillation of the spectrum of a boundary value problem on a graph. *Mat. Zametki*, 60(3):468–470, 1996.
[45] O. Post. *Spectral Analysis on Graph-like Spaces*, volume 2039 of *Lecture Notes in Mathematics*. Springer Verlag, Berlin, 2012.
[46] J.-P. Roth. Spectre du laplacien sur un graphe. *C. R. Acad. Sci. Paris Sér. I Math.*, 296(19):793–795, 1983.
[47] K. Ruedenberg and C. W. Scherr. Free-electron network model for conjugated systems. i. *J. Chem. Phys.*, 21(9):1565–1581, 1953.
[48] H. Schanz. A relation between the bond scattering matrix and the spectral counting function for quantum graphs. In *Quantum graphs and their applications*, volume 415 of *Contemp. Math.*, pages 269–282. Amer. Math. Soc., Providence, RI, 2006.
[49] P. Schapotschnikow. Eigenvalue and nodal properties on quantum graph trees. *Waves Random Complex Media*, 16(3):167–178, 2006.
[50] C. Texier and G. Montambaux. Scattering theory on graphs. *J. Phys. A*, 34(47):10307–10326, 2001.

[51] J. von Below. A characteristic equation associated to an eigenvalue problem on c^2-networks. *Linear Algebra Appl.*, 71:309–325, 1985.

Department of Mathematics, Texas A&M University, College Station, Texas 77843-3368

Contemporary Mathematics
Volume **700**, 2017
http://dx.doi.org/10.1090/conm/700/14183

A free boundary approach to the Faber-Krahn inequality

Dorin Bucur and Pedro Freitas

Abstract. The purpose of this survey article is to present a complete, comprehensive, proof of the Faber-Krahn inequality for the Dirichlet Laplacian from the perspective of free boundary problems. The proof is of a purely variational nature, proceeding along the following steps: proof of the existence of a domain which minimizes the first eigenvalue among all domains of prescribed volume, proof of (partial) regularity of the optimal domain and usage of a reflection argument in order to prove radiality. As a consequence, no rearrangement arguments are used and, although not the simplest of proofs of this statement, it has the advantage of its adaptability to study the symmetry properties of higher eigenvalues and also to other isoperimetric inequalities (Faber-Krahn or Saint-Venant) involving Robin boundary conditions.

1. Introduction

It was conjectured by Rayleigh in 1877 that among all fixed membranes with a given area, the ball would minimize the first eigenvalue [**26**]. This assertion was proved by Faber and Krahn in the nineteen twenties using a rearrangement technique, and since then several proofs have appeared in the literature.

The purpose of this survey article is to give a comprehensive proof of the Rayleigh–Faber–Krahn inequality in the context of free boundary problems. It may be argued that, in spite of the fact that this is a basic result in the theory, no more proofs of this statement are needed, particularly if they are not simpler than other existing proofs. However, it is our belief that because the proof we propose here is somehow of a different nature, has applications to other problems, and follows a natural sequence of intuitive (but mathematically not easy) steps, it deserves some attention. These steps are the following: existence of an optimal shape, proof of its (partial) regularity, and use of its optimality in order to conclude that the optimizer must be radially symmetric.

One has in mind the incomplete proof of the isoperimetic inequality by Steiner in 1836 (see [**28**] and the survey article [**4**]). Steiner proved (in two–dimensional space) that if a *smooth* domain is not the ball, then there must exist another domain with the same area but lower perimeter. Of course, the missing step is precisely the proof of the existence of a sufficiently smooth set which minimizes the perimeter among all domains of fixed area! Moreover, existence *alone* is not enough,

This article surveys the lectures given by the first author at Université de Montréal in June 2015 in the framework of the "Geometric and Computational Spectral Geometry" summer school. P.F. was partially supported by FCT (Portugal) through project PTDC/MAT-CAL/4334/2014.

since in order to use his argument, Steiner implicitly needed some *smoothness*. In fact, Steiner provided no fewer than five *proofs* and some of these have since been completed by other mathematicians from Carathéodory (1909) to De Giorgi (1957), for instance – see [**4**] and [**15**], respectively. While Carathéodory's approach relied on proving convergence of the sequence of domains used in the proof, it is De Giorgi's approach which is more relevant to us here, as it consisted in proving that Steiner's argument could be carried out in the class where existence holds, precisely the sets which have a finite perimeter defined using functions of bounded variation.

We also refer to the open problem on the isoperimetric inequality for the buckling load of a clamped plate, where the same couple of questions remain unsolved. Willms and Weinberger (see [**19**, Theorem 11.3.7]) noticed that if a smooth, simply connected set would minimise the buckling load among all domains with fixed area (in two dimensions of the space), then necessarily the minimizer is the ball.

In the proof we give of the Faber–Krahn inequality, we use only variational arguments developed in the context of free boundary problems (see for instance [**1**, **6**, **29**]). Our purpose is to present the basic tools which allow to complete the sequence : existence-regularity-radiality and give the lecturer the fundamental ideas hidden behind this scheme. This approach has the advantage to be adaptable to other isoperimetric inequalities where rearrangement or mass transport techniques fail. We have in mind isoperimetric inequalities involving Robin boundary conditions, as for example the minimization of the first Robin eigenvalue or the maximization of the Robin torsional rigidity among domains of fixed volume [**9**, **10**]. In the Robin case, the techniques to prove existence-regularity-radiality steps are definitely more involved and require finer analysis arguments on special functions of bounded variations, developed in the framework of free discontinuity problems. In particular, it may even happen that the optimizer is no longer the ball, as was recently shown by David Krejčiřík and the second author [**16**].

Let $\Omega \subseteq \mathbb{R}^N$ be an open (or *quasi-open*) set of finite measure, but otherwise with no assumptions either on smoothness or on boundedness. Thanks to the compact embedding $H_0^1(\Omega) \hookrightarrow L^2(\Omega)$, the spectrum of Dirichlet-Laplacian on Ω is discrete and consists on a sequence of eigenvalues which can be ordered (counting multiplicities) as

$$0 < \lambda_1(\Omega) \leq \lambda_2(\Omega) \leq \cdots \leq \lambda_k(\Omega) \leq \ldots \to +\infty.$$

If Ω is open, $H_0^1(\Omega)$ is the classical Sobolev space consisting on the completion of $C_0^\infty(\Omega)$ for the L^2-norm of the gradients. The case where Ω is a quasi-open set will be considered in more detail in the next section.

The Faber–Krahn inequality asserts that

$$\lambda_1(\Omega) \geq \lambda_1(B),$$

where B is the ball having the same measure as Ω. Equality holds if and only if Ω is a ball (up to a negligible set of points, which may be expressed in terms of capacity).

Roughly speaking, the proof will be split into the following four steps:

Step 1. Prove that there exists a domain Ω^* which minimizes the first Dirichlet eigenvalue among all domains of fixed volume, i.e.

$$\exists \Omega^* \subseteq \mathbb{R}^N, |\Omega^*| = m, \ \forall \Omega \subseteq \mathbb{R}^N, |\Omega| = m \quad \lambda_1(\Omega^*) \leq \lambda_1(\Omega).$$

At this first step, the existence result is carried in the family of *quasi-open sets*. Proving existence among open sets requires special attention.

Step 2. Prove that the set Ω^* is *open* and connected. This result can be seen, by itself, as a first regularity result. No smoothness of the boundary is required by the next steps.

Step 3. Use a reflection argument in order to deduce that Ω^* is radially symmetric, hence it is one annulus.

Step 4. Prove that among all annuli of prescribed volume, the ball gives the lowest first eigenvalue.

It is clear that the proof of the Faber–Krahn inequality we propose in this note is not simple. The proof of Steps 1 and 2 requires some techniques developed in the context of free boundary problems, that we intend to present in a simplified way. Step 3 is done using an idea that may be traced to Steiner's original manuscript [**4**, **28**] and was named by Pólya the method of *alternative symmetrisation* [**25**, Section 16.13]. Following an idea of Payne and Weinberger, Pólya used this method to prove that the ball is the unique domain for which equality holds in the Faber-Krahn inequality. Alternative symmetrisation has also been used in the context of the minimization of integral functionals in H^1-Sobolev spaces [**22**, **23**]. We show in detail how this can be adapted to shape optimization in a functional context. Step 4 consists in a one dimensional analysis argument for which a precise computation can be carried out.

We note that if in Step 2 one is able to prove the smoothness of the boundary of $\partial\Omega^*$, by the Hadamard argument relying on the vanishing of the shape derivative, one can extract an *overdetermined* boundary condition. Precisely, one would get that $|\nabla u^*|$ is constant on $\partial\Omega^*$ and come to a Serrin problem which could be solved by moving plane techniques (see the pioneering paper [**27**]). Nevertheless, proving the smoothness of $\partial\Omega^*$ requires definitely more involved regularity techniques, as references [**1**, **12**, **29**] show. Proving only the openness of Ω^* is quite elementary, as shown in the sequel (see [**12**, **18**, **29**] for a complete analysis of the regularity question).

In the last section of the paper we discuss briefly the problem of minimizing the k-th eigenvalue of the Dirichlet Laplacian among all quasi-open sets of prescribed measure. We present some new results where, in particular, we focus on the symmetry of a minimizer of the k-th eigenvalue and show how our arguments may also be used there. We point out that although one might expect minimizers of this type of spectral problems to always have some symmetry, say at least for the reflection with respect to one hyperplane, recent numerical evidence on this problem has raised the issue of whether or not this is actually true [**2**]. More precisely, the planar domain found (numerically) in that paper which minimises the thirteenth Dirichlet eigenvalue of the Laplace operator does not have any such symmetry and, furthermore, if a restriction is imposed enforcing that the optimiser does have some symmetry, namely invariance under reflection with respect to an axis, the resulting value of the optimal eigenvalue is worse than the unrestricted case. Although a proof of such a statement, if true, is likely to be quite elusive, there has been some independent numerical confirmation of this observation given in [**3**, **5**]. In any case, these results do beg the question as to what is the minimum symmetry which we can guarantee these optimal domains will have. In this sense, the results presented here are a first step in this direction.

2. Setting the variational framework

Solving Step 1 requires to set up a very large framework for the existence question. As one cannot impose *a priori* constraints on the competing sets, in order to achieve existence the largest class of admissible shapes should be considered. This is a classical principle in shape optimization.

The most natural framework where the Dirichlet-Laplacian operator is well defined is the family of *quasi-open* sets. More precisely, $\Omega \subseteq \mathbb{R}^N$ is called quasi-open if for all $\varepsilon > 0$ there exists an open set U_ε such that the set $\Omega \cup U_\varepsilon$ is open, where

$$\operatorname{cap}(U_\varepsilon) := \inf\left\{ \int_{\mathbb{R}^N} |\nabla u|^2 + |u|^2 dx : u \in H^1(\mathbb{R}^N), u \geq 1 \text{ a.e. on } U_\varepsilon \right\} < \varepsilon.$$

Above, *cap*(U_ε) denotes the capacity of the set U_ε. Roughly speaking, quasi-open sets are precisely the level sets $\{\tilde{u} > 0\}$ of the "most continuous" representatives of Sobolev functions $u \in H^1(\mathbb{R}^N)$, i.e. the ones given by

$$\tilde{u}(x) = \lim_{r\to 0} \frac{\displaystyle\int_{B_r(x)} u(y)dy}{|B_r(x)|}. \tag{1}$$

The limit above exists for all points except a set of capacity zero.

If Ω is an open set, the Sobolev space $H^1_0(\Omega)$ is defined as the completion of the space of C^∞-functions with compact support in Ω, with respect to the norm $\|u\|_{L^2(\Omega)} + \|\nabla u\|_{L^2(\Omega,\mathbb{R}^N)}$. If Ω is a quasi-open set, then the Sobolev space $H^1_0(\Omega)$ associated to the quasi-open set Ω is defined as a subspace of $H^1(\mathbb{R}^N)$, by

$$H^1_0(\Omega) = \bigcap_{\varepsilon>0} H^1_0(\Omega \cup U_\varepsilon).$$

The definition above does not depend on the choice of the sets U_ε. Morover, if Ω is open, both definitions above lead to the same space.

If Ω is a quasi-open set of finite measure, the spectrum of the Dirichlet-Laplacian on Ω is defined in the same way as for open sets, being the inverse of the spectrum of the compact, positive, self-adjoint resolvent operator $R_\Omega : L^2(\Omega) \to L^2(\Omega)$, $R_\Omega f = u$, where $u \in H^1_0(\Omega)$ satisfies

$$\forall \varphi \in H^1_0(\Omega) \quad \int_\Omega \nabla u \nabla \varphi dx = \int_\Omega f \varphi dx. \tag{2}$$

In particular

$$\lambda_1(\Omega) := \min_{u \in H^1_0(\Omega)} \frac{\displaystyle\int_\Omega |\nabla u|^2 dx}{\displaystyle\int_\Omega |u|^2 dx}.$$

The minimizing function solves the equation

$$\begin{cases} -\Delta u = & \lambda_1(\Omega) u \text{ in } \Omega \\ u = & 0 \quad \text{ on } \partial\Omega \end{cases}$$

in the weak sense (2). Clearly, if Ω is open we find the classical definition of the first eigenvalue.

The following inequality, which holds for every quasi-open set of finite measure (see for instance [**14**, Example 2.1.8]), will be useful for the local study of the optimal sets

$$\|u\|_\infty \leq C_N \lambda_1(\Omega)^{\frac{N}{4}} \|u\|_{L^2}. \tag{3}$$

The problem we intend to solve is the following: given $m > 0$, prove that the unique solution of

$$\min\{\lambda_1(\Omega) : \Omega \subseteq \mathbb{R}^N \text{ quasi-open}, |\Omega| = m\} \tag{4}$$

is the ball. Uniqueness is understood up to a set of zero capacity, which is precisely the size of a set for which one cannot distinguish the "precise" values of a Sobolev function.

Since for every $t > 0$, one has $\lambda_1(t\Omega) = \frac{1}{t^2}\lambda_1(\Omega)$, there exists $C > 0$ such that problem (4) is equivalent to

$$\min\{\lambda_1(\Omega) + C|\Omega| : \Omega \subseteq \mathbb{R}^N \text{ quasi-open}\}. \tag{5}$$

Indeed, let us denote

$$\alpha(m) = \inf\{\lambda_1(\Omega) : \Omega \subseteq \mathbb{R}^N \text{ quasi-open}, |\Omega| = m\}.$$

From the Sobolev inequality, we know that $\alpha(m)$ is strictly positive. Indeed, we have for every $u \in H_0^1(\Omega)$

$$\int_{\mathbb{R}^N} |\nabla u^2| dx \geq C_N \Big(\int_{\mathbb{R}^N} |u|^{\frac{2N}{N-1}} \Big)^{\frac{N-1}{N}},$$

and so from Cauchy-Schwarz on the left hand side and Hölder on the right hand side

$$2\|u\|_{L^2(\mathbb{R}^N)} \|\nabla u\|_{L^2(\mathbb{R}^N)} \geq C_N \|u\|^2_{L^2(\mathbb{R}^N)} \frac{1}{|\Omega|^{\frac{1}{N}}},$$

which gives that

$$\lambda_1(\Omega) \geq \frac{C_N^2}{|\Omega|^{\frac{2}{N}}}.$$

Moreover,

$$\alpha(t^N m) = t^{-2}\alpha(m). \tag{6}$$

On the other hand, for every C, the minimizer Ω in (5) satisifies $2\lambda_1(\Omega) = CN|\Omega|$, as a consequence of the fact that the function $t \mapsto \lambda_1(t\Omega) + C|t\Omega|$ attains its minimum at $t = 1$. Consequently, $2\alpha(m) = CNm$, and so problems (4) and (5) are equivalent, as soon as

$$m = \Big(\frac{2\alpha(1)}{CN} \Big)^{\frac{N}{N+2}}. \tag{7}$$

The equivalence of (4) and (5) proved above plays a crucial role in the proof of the existence of an *open* minimizer, in Step 2 below. The fact that the constraint is penalized gives more freedom to perform local perturbations.

3. Proof of the Faber-Krahn inequality

PROPOSITION 3.1 (Step 1). *Problem* (4) *has a solution, i.e. there exists a quasi-open set* Ω^* *such that* $|\Omega^*| = m$ *and for every quasi-open set* $\Omega \subseteq \mathbb{R}^N$, $|\Omega| = m$ *we have*

$$\lambda_1(\Omega^*) \le \lambda_1(\Omega).$$

PROOF. The idea is very simple and is based on the concentration-compactness principle of P.L. Lions [**21**]. Assume that $(\Omega_n)_n$ is a minimizing sequence and let us denote $(u_n)_n$ a sequence of L^2-normalized, non negative, associated first eigenfunctions. Then the sequence $(u_n)_n \subseteq H^1(\mathbb{R}^N)$ is bounded. Since $H^1(\mathbb{R}^N)$ is not compactly embedded in $L^2(\mathbb{R}^N)$, for a subsequence (still denoted using the same index) one of the three possibilities below occurs:

i) compactness: $\exists y_n \in \mathbb{R}^N$ such that $u_n(\cdot + y_n) \longrightarrow u$ strongly in $L^2(\mathbb{R}^N)$ and weakly in $H^1(\mathbb{R}^N)$.

ii) dichotomy: there exists $\alpha \in (0,1)$ and two sequences $\{u_n^1\}, \{u_n^2\} \in H^1(\mathbb{R}^N)$, $\operatorname{supp} u_n^1 \cup \operatorname{supp} u_n^2 \subseteq \operatorname{supp} u_n$, such that

$$\|u_n - u_n^1 - u_n^2\|_{L^2(\mathbb{R}^N)} \to 0\,,$$

$$\int_{\mathbb{R}^N} |u_n^1|^2 dx \to \alpha \qquad \int_{\mathbb{R}^N} |u_n^2|^2 dx \to 1-\alpha\,,$$

$$\operatorname{dist}(\operatorname{supp} u_n^1, \operatorname{supp} u_n^2) \to +\infty\,,$$

and

$$\liminf_{n\to\infty} \int_{\mathbb{R}^N} |\nabla u_n|^2 - |\nabla u_n^1|^2 - |\nabla u_n^2|^2 dx \ge 0\,. \tag{8}$$

iii) vanishing: for every $0 < R < \infty$

$$\lim_{n\to+\infty} \sup_{y\in\mathbb{R}^N} \int_{B(y,R)} u_n^2 dx = 0\,.$$

Situations ii) and iii) cannot occur to a minimizing sequence.

Indeed, situation ii) leads to searching the minimizer in a class of domains of measure strictly lower than m. First, we notice that the measures of the sets $\{u_n^1 > 0\}, \{u_n^2 > 0\}$ cannot vanish as $n \to +\infty$. One of the two sequences $(\{u_n^1 > 0\})_n, (\{u_n^2 > 0\})_n$ has also to be minimizing for problem (4), in view of the algebraic inequality

$$\frac{a+b}{c+d} \ge \min\left\{\frac{a}{c}, \frac{b}{d}\right\}, \tag{9}$$

for positive numbers a, b, c, d. This allows to select (for a suitable subsequence, still denoted with the same index) either $(\{u_n^1 > 0\})_n$ or $(\{u_n^2 > 0\})_n$ as minimizing sequence of measure not larger than $m - \varepsilon$, for some $\varepsilon > 0$, in contradiction to the strict monotonicity (6).

Situation iii) can be excluded by an argument due to Lieb [**20**] which asserts that if iii) occurs then $\lambda_1(\Omega_n) \to +\infty$, in contradiction with the choice of a minimizing sequence (see also [**11**]). For the sake of the clearness, we shall provide a short argument to prove this fact. Without restricting the generality, we can assume that $\lambda_1(\Omega_n) \le M_1$, for some $M_1 > 0$ independent on n. As $u_n \ge 0$, we get

$$-\Delta u_n \le \lambda_1(\Omega_n) u_n \text{ in } \mathcal{D}'(\mathbb{R}^N),$$

and so (from (3))

$$-\Delta u_n \leq C_N \lambda_1(\Omega_n)^{\frac{N}{4}+1} \leq M_2.$$

This implies that for every $x_0 \in \mathbb{R}^N$, the function

$$u_n + M_2 \frac{|x-x_0|^2}{2N}$$

is subharmonic in $\mathbb{R}^N$. By direct computation we get that for every ball $B_x(r)$

$$u_n(x) \leq \frac{\displaystyle\int_{B_x(r)} u dx}{|B_x(r)|} + \frac{M_2 r^2}{2N}.$$

Choosing first r such that $\frac{M_2 r^2}{2N} = \frac{1}{3\sqrt{m}}$, and then n large enough such that for every $x \in \mathbb{R}^N$

$$\frac{\displaystyle\int_{B_x(r)} u dx}{|B_x(r)|} \leq \frac{1}{3\sqrt{m}},$$

we get that $\displaystyle\int_{\Omega_n} u_n^2 dx \leq \frac{4}{9}$, in contradiction with the L^2-normalization of u_n.

Only situation i) can occur and this leads to the existence of an optimal domain which is a quasi-open set. Indeed, we consider the set $\Omega := \{u > 0\}$. Then, if we choose the representative defined by (1), the set Ω is quasi-open and has a measure less than or equal to m. This latter assertion is a consequence of the strong L^2 convergence of u_n which has as a consequence that (at least for a subsequence) $1_\Omega(x) \leq \liminf_{n\to+\infty} 1_{\Omega_n}(x)$ a.e. $x \in \mathbb{R}^N$.

Moreover, we have

$$\lambda_1(\Omega) \leq \frac{\displaystyle\int_\Omega |\nabla u|^2 dx}{\displaystyle\int_\Omega |u|^2 dx} \leq \liminf_{n\to\infty} \frac{\displaystyle\int_\Omega |\nabla u_n|^2 dx}{\displaystyle\int_\Omega |u_n|^2 dx} = \liminf_{n\to\infty} \lambda_1(\Omega_n).$$

If necessary, taking a suitable dilation $\Omega^* = t\Omega$, for some $t \geq 1$ such that $|\Omega^*| = m$ and using the rescaling properties of λ_1, we conclude that Ω^* is a minimizing domain. □

PROPOSITION 3.2 (Step 2). *The optimal set Ω^* is open and connected.*

PROOF. Assuming one knows that Ω^* is open, the proof of the connectedness is immediate. Indeed, assume $\Omega^* = \Omega_1 \cup \Omega_2$ with Ω_1, Ω_2 open, disjoint and non-empty. Then $\lambda_1(\Omega^*)$ is either equal to $\lambda_1(\Omega_1)$ or to $\lambda_1(\Omega_2)$, hence one could find a set, say Ω_1, with the first Dirichlet eigenvalue equal to $\lambda_1(\Omega^*)$ but with measure strictly less than m. This is in contradiction to the strict monotonicity (6).

The proof of the openness has a technical issue and is obtained using a local perturbation argument developed by Alt and Caffarelli in the context of free boundary problems [**1**, Lemma 3.2]. The idea is to prove that u^* is at least continuous, so that $\Omega^* = \{u^* > 0\}$ is an open set. We refer the reader to [**29**, Theorem 3.2] and [**12**, Proposition 1.1] for a complete description of the method below.

Let $R > 0$ and $x_0 \in \mathbb{R}^N$. We introduce the harmonic extension of u^* in $B_R(x_0)$, by

$$\tilde{u}(x) = u^*(x) \text{ in } \Omega \setminus B_R(x_0),$$
$$\Delta\tilde{u}(x) = 0 \text{ in } B_R(x_0).$$

In view of (5), we have

$$\lambda_1(\Omega^*) + C|\Omega^*| \leq \frac{\int |\nabla\tilde{u}|^2 dx}{\int |\tilde{u}|^2 dx} + C|\{\tilde{u} > 0\}|,$$

or

$$\int_{\Omega^*} |\nabla u^*|^2 dx \leq \frac{\int_{\Omega^* \setminus B_R(x_0)} |\nabla u|^2 dx + \int_{B_R(x_0)} |\nabla\tilde{u}|^2 dx}{1 + \int_{B_R(x_0)} (|\tilde{u}|^2 - |u^*|^2) dx} + C|B_R(x_0) \setminus \Omega^*|.$$

From the L^∞ bound of the eigenfunction, we get $|\int_{B_R(x_0)} (|\tilde{u}|^2 - |u^*|^2) dx| \leq M_3 R^N$ so that after an easy computation and for R smaller than a suitable constant independent of the point, we get

$$\int_{B_R(x_0)} |\nabla u^*|^2 dx \leq \int_{B_R(x_0)} |\nabla\tilde{u}|^2 dx + M_4 R^N.$$

Since $\tilde{u}$ is harmonic and equal to u^* on ∂B_R, we get

$$\int_{B_R(x_0)} |\nabla u^*|^2 dx - \int_{B_R(x_0)} |\nabla\tilde{u}|^2 dx = \int_{B_R(x_0)} |\nabla(u^* - \tilde{u})|^2 dx.$$

Consequently, for every $0 < r < R$ we have

$$\int_{B_r(x_0)} |\nabla u^*|^2 dx \leq \int_{B_r(x_0)} |\nabla(u^* - \tilde{u})|^2 dx + \int_{B_r(x_0)} |\nabla\tilde{u}|^2 dx \leq$$
$$\leq \int_{B_R(x_0)} |\nabla(u^* - \tilde{u})|^2 dx + \left(\frac{r}{R}\right)^N \int_{B_R(x_0)} |\nabla\tilde{u}|^2 dx.$$

The last inequality is due to the fact that $|\nabla\tilde{u}|^2$ is subharmonic in $B_R(x_0)$, as a consequence of the harmonicity of $\tilde{u}$ in $B_R(x_0)$.

Finally, $\forall x_0 \in \mathbb{R}^N$, $\forall 0 < r < R \leq R_0$ we have

$$\int_{B_r(x_0)} |\nabla u^*|^2 dx \leq M_4 R^N + \left(\frac{r}{R}\right)^N \int_{B_R(x_0)} |\nabla u^*|^2 dx. \tag{10}$$

This inequality implies in a classical way that u^* is Hölder continuous. Indeed, one can prove in a first step that

$$\int_{B_r(x_0)} |\nabla u^*|^2 dx \leq M_5 r^{N-1}. \tag{11}$$

The proof of the passage from (10) to (11) is classical, see for instance [**17**, Lemma 2.1, Chapter 3]. The fact that u^* is Hölder continuous of order $\frac{1}{2}$ in $\mathbb{R}^N$ is a consequence of the Dirichlet growth theorem (see [**17**, Theorem 1.1, Chapter3]). For a detailed proof of all steps, we refer to [**29**] and the references therein. □

Analyzing the optimality of Ω^* by comparison with the sets $\Omega^* \setminus \overline{B}_R(x_0)$, one can deduce that Ω^* satisfies an inner density property and therefore has to be bounded. Comparing with the set $\{u^* > \varepsilon\}$, with vanishing ε, one can find an upper bound of the generalized perimeter. Further analysis, leads to the smoothness of the boundary. The precise smoothness depends on the dimension, but we do not insist on this point since *openness* alone is enough for our purposes.

PROPOSITION 3.3 (Step 3). *The optimal set Ω^* has radial symmetry.*

PROOF. As mentioned in the Introduction, the idea to prove radial symmetry for minimizers of integral functionals in $H^1(\mathbb{R}^N)$ has been used before (see, for instance, [**22, 23**]), while its usage in a geometrical setting appears in Steiner's arguments [**4, 28**]. Roughly speaking, if Ω^* is a minimizer then one can cut it by a hyperplane $\mathcal{H}$ in two pieces of equal measure. Up to a translation of Ω^*, we can assume that $\mathcal{H}$ is given by the equation $x_1 = 0$. Then both the left and right parts together with their respective reflections are admissible (they have the correct measure) and are also minimizers. Indeed, let u be a non-zero first eigenfunction on Ω^*. We put the indices l, r to the corresponding quantities on the left, right parts of Ω^*, respectively. We denote $\Omega_l = \Omega \cap \{x \in \mathbb{R}^N : x_1 \leq 0\}$.

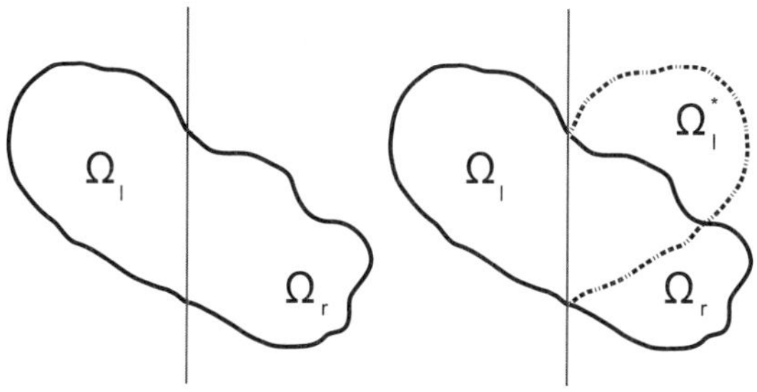

FIGURE 1. A region and one of its symmetrised counterparts with respect to a hyperplane

Then,

$$\lambda_1(\Omega^*) = \frac{\int_{\Omega_l^*} |\nabla u_l|^2 dx + \int_{\Omega_r^*} |\nabla u_r|^2 dx}{\int_{\Omega_l^*} u_l^2 dx + \int_{\Omega_r^*} u_r^2 dx}.$$

Using the algebraic inequality (9), we get (assuming for instance the left part is minimal)

$$\lambda_1(\Omega^*) \geq \frac{\int_{\Omega_l^*} |\nabla u_l|^2 dx}{\int_{\Omega_l^*} u_l^2 dx}.$$

Defining the reflection transformation $\mathcal{R} : \mathbb{R}^N \to \mathbb{R}^N$ $\mathcal{R}(x) = (-x_1, x_2, \ldots, x_N)$, we introduce the reflected domain

$$\Omega^l := \Omega_l^* \cup \mathcal{R}\Omega_l^*,$$

together with the reflected test function

$$\overline{u}(x) = u_l(x) \text{ if } x_1 \leq 0 \text{ and } \overline{u}(x) = u_l(\mathcal{R}x) \text{ if } x_1 \geq 0.$$

Then $|\Omega^l| = m$, $u^l \in H_0^1(\Omega^l)$ (this is immediate using the density of C_0^∞-function in H^1) and we get

$$\lambda_1(\Omega^*) \geq \frac{\int_{\Omega_l^*} |\nabla u_l|^2 dx}{\int_{\Omega_l^*} u_l^2 dx} = \frac{\int_{\Omega^l} |\nabla \overline{u}|^2 dx}{\int_{\Omega^l} |\overline{u}|^2 dx} \geq \lambda(\Omega^l).$$

Relying on the minimality of Ω^* and on the inequalities above, we conclude that Ω^l is also a minimizer and that $\overline{u}$ is an eigenfunction on Ω^l. Finally, this means that u_l has two analytic extensions: one in the open set Ω_r which is u_r and another one in $\mathcal{R}\Omega_l$ which is $\overline{u}$. Using the maximum principle, there cannot be a point of the complement of Ω_r where u_r is vanishing which is interior for $\mathcal{R}\Omega_l$, and vice-versa. Finally, this implies that $\Omega_r = \mathcal{R}\Omega_l$ and so Ω^* is symmetric with respect to $\mathcal{H}$.

We continue the procedure with the hyperplanes $\{x_i = 0\}$, for $i = 2, \ldots, N$. At this point, up to a translation, we know that the optimal domain Ω^* is symmetric with respect to all the hyperplanes $\{x_i = 0\}$, for $i = 1, \ldots, N$. Now, we can continue the procedure with an arbitrary hyperplane passing through the origin (without any translation), since such a hyperplane divides Ω^* in two pieces of equal measure. We conclude that Ω^* has to be radially symmetric. □

Let us point out that the *openness* of the optimal domain Ω^* was necessary in the proof above when using the analyticity of the eigenfunction. If the optimal set was only *quasi-open*, the analyticity would have failed, and so our reflection argument could not have been used.

Let us also say that in the proof above we implicitly obtained that the minimizer is radially symmetric, not only the domain Ω^*. This observation goes in the direction of [**22, 23**] where radial symmetry is proved for the minimizers of integral functionals, and can be successfully used in other situations.

PROPOSITION 3.4 (Step 4). *The optimal set Ω^* is the ball.*

PROOF. Since the optimal set is connected, using the proposition above, we know it is an annulus. Precisely, for some $t \geq 0$ this annulus can be written

$$\Omega^* = A(0, t, r(t)) := \{x \in \mathbb{R}^N : t < |x| < r(t)\},$$

where $\omega_{N-1}(r^N(t) - t^N) = m$. In order to prove that the solution of the Faber-Krahn inequality is the ball, it is enough to study the mapping $t \mapsto \lambda_1(A(0, t, r(t)))$ and to prove it is increasing. Using the the shape derivative formula for λ_1 (and denoting u an L^2-normalized eigenfunction on $A(0, t, r(t))$, we get

$$\frac{d}{dt}\lambda_1(A(0,t,r(t)))) = \int_{\partial B(0,t)} \left(\frac{\partial u}{\partial n}\right)^2 d\mathcal{H}^{N-1} - \frac{t^{N-1}}{r^{N-1}(t)} \int_{\partial B(0,r(t))} \left(\frac{\partial u}{\partial n}\right)^2 d\mathcal{H}^{N-1}.$$

Since u is radially symmetric, proving that $\frac{d}{dt}\lambda_1(A(0,t,r(t)))) > 0$ is equivalent to proving that $|u'(t)|^2 > |u'(r(t))|^2$ (in this notation u depends only on the radius).

The equation satisfied by the radial function u is

$$-u''(s) - \frac{N-1}{s}u'(s) = \lambda_1 u(s), \text{ on } (t, r(t)),$$

$$u(t) = u(r(t)) = 0.$$

Denoting $v(s) = |u'(s)|^2$, we get that

$$v'(s) = 2u'(s)u''(s) = -\frac{2(N-1)}{s}|u'(s)|^2 - 2\lambda_1 u'(s)u(s),$$

and summing between t and $r(t)$ we get

$$v(r(t)) - v(t) = -\frac{2(N-1)}{s} \int_t^{r(t)} |u'(s)|^2 ds < 0.$$

The last inequality is obvious since u is not constant, hence the mapping $t \mapsto \lambda_1(A(0,t,r(t)))$ is strictly increasing on $(0,+\infty)$. Consequently the ball, corresponding to $t=0$, is the global minimizer. □

4. Further remarks: higher order eigenvalues

For $k \geq 2$ one can also consider the isoperimetric problem

$$\min\{\lambda_k(\Omega) : \Omega \subseteq \mathbb{R}^N \text{ quasi-open}, |\Omega| = m\}. \tag{12}$$

When $k=2$ the minimizer consists of two equal and disjoint balls of measure $m/2$, this being a direct consequence of the inequality for the first eigenvalue and which was already considered by Krahn. For $k \geq 3$, and apart from numerical results (see, for instance, [**2**]) only few facts are known:

- A solution to problem (12) exists (let us call it Ω_k^*), it is a bounded set and has finite perimeter (see [**6**] and [**24**]).
- There exists an eigefunction u_k^* of the optimal set Ω_k^*, corresponding to the k-th eigenvalue $\lambda_k(\Omega_k^*)$ which is a Lipschitz function (see [**8**]). Note that this information does not imply that the optimal set Ω_k^* is open, because Ω_k^* contains both the open set $\{u_k^* \neq 0\}$ and the nodal set $\{u_k^* = 0\}$, which has a structure, not yet completely understood.

Relying on the reflection argument, one can get some more information on the symmetry of Ω_k^*, depending on the dimension of the space. Roughly speaking, the larger the space dimension is, the more symmetric must the minimizer be.

Assume that $u_1, \dots, u_k$ are L^2-normalized eigenfunctions corresponding to $\lambda_1(\Omega_k^*), \dots, \lambda_k(\Omega_k^*)$ such that

$$\forall i,j = 1,\dots,k, i \neq j, \quad \int u_i u_j dx = 0, \int \nabla u_i \nabla u_j = 0.$$

Problem (12) can be re-written as

$$\min_{|\Omega|=m} \min_{S_k \subset H_0^1(\Omega)} \max_{u \in S_k} \frac{\int_\Omega |\nabla u|^2 dx}{\int_\Omega |u|^2 dx},$$

where S_k denotes any subspace of dimension k.

Assume $\mathcal{H}$ is a hyperplane splitting Ω_k^* into Ω^l and Ω^r such that

$$|\Omega^l| = |\Omega^r|,$$

$$\forall i,j = 1,\dots,k, i \neq j, \int_{\Omega^l} u_i u_j dx = 0,$$

$$\forall i,j = 1,\dots,k, i \neq j, \int_{\Omega^l} \nabla u_i \nabla u_j dx = 0,$$

$$\forall i = 1,\dots,k-1, \quad \frac{\int_{\Omega^l} |\nabla u_i|^2 dx}{\int_{\Omega^l} |u_i|^2 dx} = \lambda_i(\Omega_k^*).$$

Notice that the number of constraints equals k^2.

Assuming that

$$\frac{\int_{\Omega^l} |\nabla u_k|^2 dx}{\int_{\Omega^l} |u_k|^2 dx} \leq \frac{\int_{\Omega^r} |\nabla u_k|^2 dx}{\int_{\Omega^r} |u_k|^2 dx},$$

and reflecting Ω^l together with the functions $u_1|_{\Omega^l}, \ldots, u_k|_{\Omega^l}$, we get

$$\lambda_k(\Omega^l \cup \mathcal{R}\Omega^l) \leq \max\{\lambda_{k-1}(\Omega_k^*), \frac{\int_{\Omega^l} |\nabla u_k|^2 dx}{\int_{\Omega^l} |u_k|^2 dx}\} \leq \lambda_k(\Omega_k^*).$$

Consequently, the set $\Omega^l \cup \mathcal{R}\Omega^l$ is also a minimizer and is symmetric with respect to $\mathcal{H}$.

If Ω_k^* were open, then we could conclude that $1_{\Omega_k^*} = 1_{\Omega^l \cup \mathcal{R}\Omega^l}$. Following the same arguments as [**23**, Theorem 2], we would get that the set Ω_k^* would be symmetric with respect to an affine subspace of dimension $k^2 - 1$. As Ω_k^* is not known to be open, we can only assert the existence of a minimizer which has $N - (k^2 - 1)$ hyperplanes of symmetry. In either case, we see that it is only for k equal to one that *full symmetry* may be obtained in this way.

REMARK 4.1. Similar existence questions can be raised for more general functions of eigenvalues. Let $F : \mathbb{R}^k \to \mathbb{R}$ be a lower semicontinuous function, non decreasing in each variable. Then, the following problem

$$\min \Big\{F(\lambda_1(\Omega), \ldots, \lambda_k(\Omega)) : \Omega \subseteq \mathbb{R}^N \text{ quasi-open}, |\Omega| = m\Big\}. \tag{13}$$

has a solution. If moreover F is strictly increasing in at least one variable, then any optimal set has to be bounded with finite perimeter. We refer the reader to [**6**, **7**, **13**, **24**]. A key argument is contained in the following surgery result, for which we refer the reader to [**7**].

Surgery result for the spectrum: for every $K > 0$, there exists $D, C > 0$ depending only on K and the dimension N, such that for every open (quasi-open) set $\tilde{\Omega} \subset \mathbb{R}^N$ there exists an open (quasi-open, respectively) set Ω satisfying

- the measure of Ω equals the measure of $\tilde{\Omega}$,
- diam $(\Omega) \leq D|\Omega|^{\frac{1}{N}}$ and $Per(\Omega) \leq \min\{Per(\tilde{\Omega}), C|\Omega|^{\frac{N-1}{N}}\}$,
- if for some $k \in \mathbb{N}$ it holds $\lambda_k(\tilde{\Omega}) \leq K|\tilde{\Omega}|^{-\frac{2}{N}}$, then $\lambda_i(\Omega) \leq \lambda_i(\tilde{\Omega})$ for all $i = 1, \ldots, k$.

The perimeter of a non-smooth set has to be understood in a weak sense (see [**7**] for the details).

Acknowledgements

The authors would like to thank the anonymous referee for a careful reading of the manuscript, and Mark Ashbaugh for pointing out Pólya's work [**25**] to us.

References

[1] H. W. Alt and L. A. Caffarelli, *Existence and regularity for a minimum problem with free boundary*, J. Reine Angew. Math. **325** (1981), 105–144. MR618549

[2] Pedro R. S. Antunes and Pedro Freitas, *Numerical optimization of low eigenvalues of the Dirichlet and Neumann Laplacians*, J. Optim. Theory Appl. **154** (2012), no. 1, 235–257, DOI 10.1007/s10957-011-9983-3. MR2931377

[3] Berger, A. Optimisation du spectre du Laplacien avec conditions de Dirichlet et Neumann dans $\mathbb{R}^2$ et $\mathbb{R}^3$, PhD thesis, University of Neuchâtel, May 2015.

[4] Viktor Blåsjö, *The isoperimetric problem*, Amer. Math. Monthly **112** (2005), no. 6, 526–566, DOI 10.2307/30037526. MR2142606

[5] Bogosel, B. Optimisation de formes et problèmes spectraux, PhD thesis, University of Grenoble, December 2015.

[6] Dorin Bucur, *Minimization of the k-th eigenvalue of the Dirichlet Laplacian*, Arch. Ration. Mech. Anal. **206** (2012), no. 3, 1073–1083, DOI 10.1007/s00205-012-0561-0. MR2989451

[7] Dorin Bucur and Dario Mazzoleni, *A surgery result for the spectrum of the Dirichlet Laplacian*, SIAM J. Math. Anal. **47** (2015), no. 6, 4451–4466, DOI 10.1137/140992448. MR3427044

[8] Dorin Bucur, Dario Mazzoleni, Aldo Pratelli, and Bozhidar Velichkov, *Lipschitz regularity of the eigenfunctions on optimal domains*, Arch. Ration. Mech. Anal. **216** (2015), no. 1, 117–151, DOI 10.1007/s00205-014-0801-6. MR3305655

[9] Dorin Bucur and Alessandro Giacomini, *Faber-Krahn inequalities for the Robin-Laplacian: a free discontinuity approach*, Arch. Ration. Mech. Anal. **218** (2015), no. 2, 757–824, DOI 10.1007/s00205-015-0872-z. MR3375539

[10] Dorin Bucur and Alessandro Giacomini, *The Saint-Venant inequality for the Laplace operator with Robin boundary conditions*, Milan J. Math. **83** (2015), no. 2, 327–343, DOI 10.1007/s00032-015-0243-0. MR3412286

[11] Dorin Bucur and Nicolas Varchon, *Global minimizing domains for the first eigenvalue of an elliptic operator with non-constant coefficients*, Electron. J. Differential Equations (2000), No. 36, 10. MR1764712

[12] Tanguy Briançon and Jimmy Lamboley, *Regularity of the optimal shape for the first eigenvalue of the Laplacian with volume and inclusion constraints*, Ann. Inst. H. Poincaré Anal. Non Linéaire **26** (2009), no. 4, 1149–1163, DOI 10.1016/j.anihpc.2008.07.003. MR2542718

[13] Giuseppe Buttazzo and Gianni Dal Maso, *An existence result for a class of shape optimization problems*, Arch. Rational Mech. Anal. **122** (1993), no. 2, 183–195, DOI 10.1007/BF00378167. MR1217590

[14] E. B. Davies, *Heat kernels and spectral theory*, Cambridge Tracts in Mathematics, vol. 92, Cambridge University Press, Cambridge, 1990. MR1103113

[15] Ennio De Giorgi, *Sulla proprietà isoperimetrica dell'ipersfera, nella classe degli insiemi aventi frontiera orientata di misura finita* (Italian), Atti Accad. Naz. Lincei. Mem. Cl. Sci. Fis. Mat. Nat. Sez. I (8) **5** (1958), 33–44. MR0098331

[16] Pedro Freitas and David Krejčiřík, *The first Robin eigenvalue with negative boundary parameter*, Adv. Math. **280** (2015), 322–339, DOI 10.1016/j.aim.2015.04.023. MR3350222

[17] Mariano Giaquinta, *Multiple integrals in the calculus of variations and nonlinear elliptic systems*, Annals of Mathematics Studies, vol. 105, Princeton University Press, Princeton, NJ, 1983. MR717034

[18] Mohammed Hayouni, *Sur la minimisation de la première valeur propre du laplacien* (French, with English and French summaries), C. R. Acad. Sci. Paris Sér. I Math. **330** (2000), no. 7, 551–556, DOI 10.1016/S0764-4442(00)00229-9. MR1760437

[19] Antoine Henrot, *Extremum problems for eigenvalues of elliptic operators*, Frontiers in Mathematics, Birkhäuser Verlag, Basel, 2006. MR2251558

[20] Elliott H. Lieb, *On the lowest eigenvalue of the Laplacian for the intersection of two domains*, Invent. Math. **74** (1983), no. 3, 441–448, DOI 10.1007/BF01394245. MR724014

[21] P.-L. Lions, *The concentration-compactness principle in the calculus of variations. The limit case. I*, Rev. Mat. Iberoamericana **1** (1985), no. 1, 145–201, DOI 10.4171/RMI/6. MR834360

[22] Orlando Lopes, *Radial symmetry of minimizers for some translation and rotation invariant functionals*, J. Differential Equations **124** (1996), no. 2, 378–388, DOI 10.1006/jdeq.1996.0015. MR1370147

[23] Mihai Mariş, *On the symmetry of minimizers*, Arch. Ration. Mech. Anal. **192** (2009), no. 2, 311–330, DOI 10.1007/s00205-008-0136-2. MR2486598

[24] Dario Mazzoleni and Aldo Pratelli, *Existence of minimizers for spectral problems*, J. Math. Pures Appl. (9) **100** (2013), no. 3, 433–453, DOI 10.1016/j.matpur.2013.01.008. MR3095209

[25] George Pólya, *Circle, sphere, symmetrization, and some classical physical problems.*, Modern mathematics for the engineer: Second series, McGraw-Hill, New York, 1961, pp. 420–441. MR0129169

[26] John William Strutt Rayleigh Baron, *The Theory of Sound*, Dover Publications, New York, N. Y., 1945. 2d ed. MR0016009

[27] James Serrin, *A symmetry problem in potential theory*, Arch. Rational Mech. Anal. **43** (1971), 304–318, DOI 10.1007/BF00250468. MR0333220

[28] J. Steiner, *Einfache Beweise der isoperimetrischen Hauptsätze* (German), J. Reine Angew. Math. **18** (1838), 281–296, DOI 10.1515/crll.1838.18.281. MR1578194

[29] Alfred Wagner, *Optimal shape problems for eigenvalues*, Comm. Partial Differential Equations **30** (2005), no. 7-9, 1039–1063, DOI 10.1081/PDE-200064443. MR2180294

Laboratoire de Mathématiques (LAMA), Université de Savoie, Campus Scientifique, 73376 Le-Bourget-Du-Lac, France
E-mail address: dorin.bucur@univ-savoie.fr

Departamento de Matemática, Instituto Superior Técnico, Universidade de Lisboa, Av. Rovisco Pais, 1049-001 Lisboa, Portugal — and — Grupo de Física Matemática, Faculdade de Ciências, Universidade de Lisboa, Campo Grande, Edifício C6, 1749-016 Lisboa, Portugal
E-mail address: psfreitas@fc.ul.pt

Contemporary Mathematics
Volume **700**, 2017
http://dx.doi.org/10.1090/conm/700/14184

Some nodal properties of the quantum harmonic oscillator and other Schrödinger operators in $\mathbb{R}^2$

Pierre Bérard and Bernard Helffer

ABSTRACT. For the spherical Laplacian on the sphere and for the Dirichlet Laplacian in the square, Antonie Stern claimed in her PhD thesis (1924) the existence of an infinite sequence of eigenvalues whose corresponding eigenspaces contain an eigenfunction with exactly two nodal domains. These results were given complete proofs respectively by Hans Lewy in 1977, and the authors in 2014 (see also Gauthier-Shalom–Przybytkowski, 2006). In this paper, we obtain similar results for the two dimensional isotropic quantum harmonic oscillator. In the opposite direction, we construct an infinite sequence of regular eigenfunctions with as many nodal domains as allowed by Courant's theorem, up to a factor $\frac{1}{4}$. A classical question for a 2-dimensional bounded domain is to estimate the length of the nodal set of a Dirichlet eigenfunction in terms of the square root of the energy. In the last section, we consider some Schrödinger operators $-\Delta + V$ in $\mathbb{R}^2$ and we provide bounds for the length of the nodal set of an eigenfunction with energy λ in the classically permitted region $\{V(x) < \lambda\}$.

1. Introduction and main results

Given a finite interval $]a,b[$ and a continuous function $q : [a,b] \mapsto \mathbb{R}$, consider the one-dimensional self-adjoint eigenvalue problem

$$-y'' + qy = \lambda y \text{ in }]a,b[,\ y(a) = y(b) = 0. \tag{1.1}$$

Arrange the eigenvalues in increasing order, $\lambda_1(q) < \lambda_2(q) < \cdots$. A classical theorem of C. Sturm [**22**] states that an eigenfunction u of (1.1) associated with $\lambda_k(q)$ has exactly $(k-1)$ zeros in $]a,b[$ or, equivalently, that the zeros of u divide $]a,b[$ into k sub-intervals.

In higher dimensions, one can consider the eigenvalue problem for the Laplace-Beltrami operator $-\Delta_g$ on a compact connected Riemannian manifold (M,g), with Dirichlet condition in case M has a boundary ∂M,

$$-\Delta u = \lambda u \text{ in } M,\ u|_{\partial M} = 0. \tag{1.2}$$

Arrange the eigenvalues in non-decreasing order, with multiplicities,

$$\lambda_1(M,g) < \lambda_2(M,g) \le \lambda_3(M,g) \le \dots$$

2010 *Mathematics Subject Classification.* Primary 35B05, 35Q40, 35P99, 58J50, 81Q05.
Key words and phrases. Quantum harmonic oscillator, Schrödinger operator, nodal lines, nodal domains, Courant nodal theorem.

Denote by M_0 the interior of M, $M_0 := M \setminus \partial M$.

Given an eigenfunction u of $-\Delta_g$, denote by

$$N(u) := \overline{\{x \in M_0 \mid u(x) = 0\}} \tag{1.3}$$

the *nodal set* of u, and by

$$\mu(u) := \#\{\text{ connected components of } M_0 \setminus N(u)\} \tag{1.4}$$

the number of *nodal domains* of u i.e., the number of connected components of the complement of $N(u)$.

Courant's theorem [**12**] states that if $-\Delta_g u = \lambda_k(M, g)u$, then $\mu(u) \leq k$.

In this paper, we investigate three natural questions about Courant's theorem in the framework of the 2D isotropic quantum harmonic oscillator.

QUESTION 1. *In view of Sturm's theorem, it is natural to ask whether Courant's upper bound is sharp, and to look for lower bounds for the number of nodal domains, depending on the geometry of (M, g) and the eigenvalue. Note that for orthogonality reasons, for any $k \geq 2$ and any eigenfunction associated with $\lambda_k(M, g)$, we have $\mu(u) \geq 2$.*

We shall say that $\lambda_k(M, g)$ is Courant-sharp *if there exists an eigenfunction u, such that $-\Delta_g u = \lambda_k(M, g)u$ and $\mu(u) = k$. Clearly, $\lambda_1(M, g)$ and $\lambda_2(M, g)$ are always Courant-sharp eigenvalues. Note that if $\lambda_3(M, g) = \lambda_2(M, g)$, then $\lambda_3(M, g)$ is not Courant-sharp.*

The first results concerning Question 1 were stated by Antonie Stern in her 1924 PhD thesis [**36**] written under the supervision of R. Courant.

THEOREM 1.1 (A. Stern, [**36**]).

(1) *For the square $[0, \pi] \times [0, \pi]$ with Dirichlet boundary condition, there is a sequence of eigenfunctions $\{u_r, r \geq 1\}$ such that*

$$-\Delta u_r = (1 + 4r^2)u_r, \text{ and } \mu(u_r) = 2.$$

(2) *For the sphere $\mathbb{S}^2$, there exists a sequence of eigenfunctions $u_\ell, \ell \geq 1$ such that*

$$-\Delta_{\mathbb{S}^2} u_\ell = \ell(\ell + 1)u_\ell, \text{ and } \mu(u_\ell) = 2 \text{ or } 3,$$

depending on whether ℓ is odd or even.

Stern's arguments are not fully satisfactory. In 1977, H. Lewy [**25**] gave a complete independent proof for the case of the sphere, without any reference to [**36**] (see also [**4**]). More recently, the authors [**2**] gave a complete proof for the case of the square with Dirichlet boundary conditions (see also Gauthier-Shalom–Przybytkowski [**17**]).

The original motivation of this paper was to investigate the possibility to extend Stern's results to the case of the two-dimensional isotropic quantum harmonic oscillator $\widehat{H} := -\Delta + |x|^2$ acting on $L^2(\mathbb{R}^2, \mathbb{R})$ (we will say "harmonic oscillator" for short). After the publication of the first version of this paper [**3**], T. Hoffmann-Ostenhof informed us of the unpublished master degree thesis of J. Leydold [**26**].

An orthogonal basis of eigenfunctions of the harmonic oscillator $\widehat{H}$ is given by

$$\phi_{m,n}(x,y) = H_m(x)H_n(y)\exp(-\frac{x^2+y^2}{2}), \tag{1.5}$$

for $(m,n) \in \mathbb{N}^2$, where H_n denotes the Hermite polynomial of degree n. For Hermite polynomials, we use the definitions and notation of Szegö [**37**, §5.5].

The eigenfunction $\phi_{m,n}$ corresponds to the eigenvalue $2(m+n+1)$,

$$\widehat{H}\phi_{m,n} = 2(m+n+1)\,\phi_{m,n}\,. \tag{1.6}$$

It follows that the eigenspace $\mathcal{E}_n$ of $\widehat{H}$ associated with the eigenvalue $\hat{\lambda}(n) = 2(n+1)$ has dimension $(n+1)$, and is generated by the eigenfunctions $\phi_{n,0}, \phi_{n-1,1}, \ldots, \phi_{0,n}$.

We summarize Leydold's main results in the following theorem.

THEOREM 1.2 (J. Leydold, [**26**]).

(1) *For $n \geq 2$, and for any nonzero $u \in \mathcal{E}_n$,*

$$\mu(u) \leq \mu_n^L := \frac{n^2}{2} + 2. \tag{1.7}$$

(2) *The lower bound on the number of nodal domains is given by*

$$\min\{\mu(u) \mid u \in \mathcal{E}_n, u \neq 0\} = \begin{cases} 1 & \text{if } n = 0, \\ 3 & \text{if } n \equiv 0 \pmod 4, n \geq 4, \\ 2 & \text{if } n \not\equiv 0 \pmod 4. \end{cases} \tag{1.8}$$

REMARK. *When $n \geq 3$, the estimate (1.7) is better than Courant's bound which is $\mu_n^C := \frac{n^2}{2} + \frac{n}{2} + 1$. The idea of the proof is to apply Courant's method separately to odd and to even eigenfunctions (with respect to the map $x \mapsto -x$). A consequence of (1.7) is that the only Courant-sharp eigenvalues of the harmonic oscillator are the first, second and fourth eigenvalues. The same ideas work for the sphere as well* [**26, 27**]. *For the analysis of Courant-sharp eigenvalues of the square with Dirichlet boundary conditions, see* [**2, 30**].

Leydold's proof that there exist eigenfunctions of the harmonic oscillator satisfying (1.8) is quite involved. In this paper, we give a simple proof that, for any odd integer n, there exists a one-parameter family of eigenfunctions with exactly two nodal domains in $\mathcal{E}_n$. More precisely, for $\theta \in [0,\pi[$, we consider the following curve in $\mathcal{E}_n$,

$$\Phi_n^\theta := \cos\theta\,\phi_{n,0} + \sin\theta\,\phi_{0,n}, \tag{1.9}$$

$$\Phi_n^\theta(x,y) = (\cos\theta\,H_n(x) + \sin\theta\,H_n(y))\exp(-\frac{x^2+y^2}{2}).$$

We prove the following theorems (Sections 4 and 5).

THEOREM 1.3. *Assume that n is odd. Then, there exists an open interval $I_{\frac{\pi}{4}}$ containing $\frac{\pi}{4}$, and an open interval $I_{\frac{3\pi}{4}}$, containing $\frac{3\pi}{4}$, such that for*

$$\theta \in I_{\frac{\pi}{4}} \cup I_{\frac{3\pi}{4}} \setminus \{\frac{\pi}{4}, \frac{3\pi}{4}\},$$

the nodal set $N(\Phi_n^\theta)$ is a connected simple regular curve, and the eigenfunction Φ_n^θ has two nodal domains in $\mathbb{R}^2$.

THEOREM 1.4. *Assume that n is odd. Then, there exists $\theta_c > 0$ such that, for $0 < \theta < \theta_c$, the nodal set $N(\Phi_n^\theta)$ is a connected simple regular curve, and the eigenfunction Φ_n^θ has two nodal domains in $\mathbb{R}^2$.*

REMARK. *The value θ_c and the intervals can be computed numerically. The proofs of the theorems actually show that $]0, \theta_c[\cap I_{\frac{\pi}{4}} = \emptyset$.*

QUESTION 2. *How good/bad is Courant's upper bound on the number of nodal domains? Consider the eigenvalue problem (1.2). Given $k \geq 1$, define $\mu(k)$ to be the maximum value of $\mu(u)$ when u is an eigenfunction associated with the eigenvalue $\lambda_k(M,g)$. Then,*

$$\limsup_{k \mapsto \infty} \frac{\mu(k)}{k} \leq \gamma(n) \tag{1.10}$$

where $\gamma(n)$ is a universal constant which only depends on the dimension n of M. Furthermore, for $n \geq 2$, $\gamma(n) < 1$. The idea of the proof, introduced by Pleijel in 1956, is to use a Faber-Krahn type isoperimetric inequality and Weyl's asymptotic law. Note that the constant $\gamma(n)$ is not sharp. For more details and references, see [**14**, **30**].

As a corollary of the above result, the eigenvalue problem (1.2) has only finitely many Courant-sharp eigenvalues.

The above result gives a quantitative improvement of Courant's theorem in the case of the Dirichlet Laplacian in a bounded open set of $\mathbb{R}^2$. When trying to implement the strategy of Pleijel for the harmonic oscillator, we get into trouble because of the absence of a reasonable Faber-Krahn inequality. P. Charron [**9**, **10**] has obtained the following theorem.

THEOREM 1.5. *If (λ_n, u_n) is an infinite sequence of eigenpairs of $\widehat{H}$, then*

$$\limsup \frac{\mu(u_n)}{n} \leq \gamma(2) = \frac{4}{j_{0,1}^2}, \tag{1.11}$$

where $j_{0,1}$ is the first positive zero of the Bessel function of order 0.

This is in some sense surprising that the statement is exactly the same as in the case of the Dirichlet realization of the Laplacian in a bounded open set in $\mathbb{R}^2$. The proof does actually not use the isotropy of the harmonic potential, can be extended to the n-dimensional case, but strongly uses the explicit knowledge of the eigenfunctions. We refer to [**11**] for further results in this direction.

A related question concerning the estimate (1.10) is whether the order of magnitude is correct. In the case of the 2-sphere, using spherical coordinates, one can find decomposed spherical harmonics u_ℓ of degree ℓ, with associated eigenvalue $\ell(\ell+1)$, such that $\mu(u_\ell) \sim \frac{\ell^2}{2}$ when ℓ is large, whereas Courant's upper bound is equivalent to ℓ^2. These spherical harmonics have critical zeros and their nodal sets have self-intersections. In [**16**, Section 2], the authors construct spherical harmonics v_ℓ, of degree ℓ, without critical zeros i.e., whose nodal sets are disjoint closed regular curves, such that $\mu(v_\ell) \sim \frac{\ell^2}{4}$. These spherical harmonics v_ℓ have as many nodal domains as allowed by Courant's theorem, up to a factor $\frac{1}{4}$. Since the v_ℓ's are regular, this property is stable under small perturbations in the same eigenspace.

In Section 6, in a direction opposite to Theorems 1.3 and 1.4, we construct eigenfunctions of the harmonic oscillator $\widehat{H}$ with "many" nodal domains.

THEOREM 1.6. *For the harmonic oscillator $\widehat{H}$ in $L^2(\mathbb{R}^2)$, there exists a sequence of eigenfunctions $\{u_k, k \geq 1\}$ such that $\widehat{H}u_k = \hat{\lambda}(k)u_k$, with $\hat{\lambda}(4k) = 2(4k+1)$, u_k as no critical zeros (i.e. has a regular nodal set), and*

$$\mu(u_k) \sim \frac{(4k)^2}{8}.$$

REMARKS. *1. The above estimate is, up to a factor $\frac{1}{4}$, asymptotically the same as the upper bounds for the number of nodal domains given by Courant and Leydold. 2. A related question is to analyze the zero set when θ is a random variable. We refer to* [**18**] *for results in this direction. The above questions are related to the question of spectral minimal partitions* [**19**]. *In the case of the harmonic oscillator similar questions appear in the analysis of the properties of ultracold atoms (see for example* [**33**]*).*

QUESTION 3. *Consider the eigenvalue problem* (1.2), *and assume for simplicity that M is a bounded domain in $\mathbb{R}^2$. Fix any small number r, and a point $x \in M$ such that $B(x,r) \subset M$. Let u be a Dirichlet eigenfunction associated with the eigenvalue λ and assume that $\lambda \geq \frac{\pi j_{0,1}^2}{r^2}$. Then $N(u) \cap B(x,r) \neq \emptyset$. This fact follows from the monotonicity of the Dirichlet eigenvalues, and indicates that the length of the nodal set should tend to infinity as the eigenvalue tends to infinity. The first results in this direction are due to Brüning and Gromes* [**6, 7**] *who show that the length of the nodal set $N(u)$ is bounded from below by a constant times $\sqrt{\lambda}$. For further results in this direction (Yau's conjecture), we refer to* [**15, 28, 29, 34, 35**].

In Section 7, we investigate this question for the harmonic oscillator.

THEOREM 1.7. *Let $\delta \in]0,1[$ be given. Then, there exists a positive constant C_δ such that for λ large enough, and for any nonzero eigenfunction of the isotropic 2D quantum harmonic oscillator,*

$$\widehat{H} := -\Delta + |x|^2, \ \widehat{H}u = \lambda u, \tag{1.12}$$

the length of $N(u) \cap B\left(\sqrt{\delta\lambda}\right)$ is bounded from below by $C_\delta\, \lambda^{\frac{3}{2}}$.

As a matter of fact, we prove a lower bound for more general Schrödinger operators in $\mathbb{R}^2$ (Propositions 7.2 and 7.8), shedding some light on the exponent $\frac{3}{2}$ in the above estimate. In Section 7.3, we investigate upper and lower bounds for the length of the nodal sets, using the method of Long Jin [**29**].

2. A reminder on Hermite polynomials

We use the definition, normalization, and notation of Szegö's book [**37**]. With these choices, the Hermite polynomial H_n has the following properties, [**37**, § 5.5 and Theorem 6.32].

(1) H_n satisfies the differential equation

$$y''(t) - 2t\, y'(t) + 2n\, y(t) = 0.$$

(2) H_n is a polynomial of degree n which is even (*resp.* odd) for n even (*resp.* odd).
(3) $H_n(t) = 2t\, H_{n-1}(t) - 2(n-1)\, H_{n-2}(t),\ n \geq 2,\ H_0(t) = 1,\ H_1(t) = 2t.$
(4) H_n has n simple zeros $t_{n,1} < t_{n,2} < \cdots < t_{n,n}$.
(5)

$$H_n(t) = 2t\, H_{n-1}(t) - H'_{n-1}(t).$$

(6)

$$H'_n(t) = 2nH_{n-1}(t). \tag{2.1}$$

(7) The coefficient of t^n in H_n is 2^n.
(8)

$$\int_{-\infty}^{+\infty} e^{-t^2} |H_n(t)|^2\, dt = \pi^{\frac{1}{2}}\, 2^n\, n!.$$

(9) The first zero $t_{n,1}$ of H_n satisfies

$$t_{n,1} = (2n+1)^{\frac{1}{2}} - 6^{-\frac{1}{2}}(2n+1)^{-\frac{1}{6}}(i_1 + \epsilon_n), \tag{2.2}$$

where i_1 is the first positive real zero of the Airy function, and $\lim_{n\to+\infty} \epsilon_n = 0$.

The following result (Theorem 7.6.1 in Szegö's book [**37**]) will also be useful.

LEMMA 2.1. *The successive relative maxima of* $t \mapsto |H_n(t)|$ *form an increasing sequence for* $t \geq 0$.

PROOF. It is enough to observe that the function

$$\Theta_n(t) := 2nH_n(t)^2 + H'_n(t)^2$$

satisfies

$$\Theta'_n(t) = 4t\,(H'_n(t))^2.$$

□

3. Stern-like constructions for the harmonic oscillator in the case n-odd

3.1. The case of the square. Consider the square $[0,\pi]^2$, with Dirichlet boundary conditions, and the following families of eigenfunctions associated with the eigenvalues $\hat{\lambda}(1,2r) := 1 + 4r^2$, where r is a positive integer, and $\theta \in [0, \pi/4]$,

$$(x,y) \mapsto \cos\theta\, \sin x\, \sin(2ry) + \sin\theta\, \sin(2rx)\, \sin y.$$

According to [**36**], for any given $r \geq 1$, the typical evolution of the nodal sets when θ varies is similar to the case $r = 4$ shown in Figure 1 [**2**, Figure 6.9]. Generally speaking, the nodal sets deform continuously, except for *finitely many* values of θ, for which self-intersections of the nodal set appear or disappear or, equivalently, for which critical zeros of the eigenfunction appear/disappear.

We would like to get similar results for the isotropic quantum harmonic oscillator.

FIGURE 1. Nodal sets for the Dirichlet eigenvalue $\hat{\lambda}(1,8)$ of the square.

3.2. Symmetries. Recall the notation,

$$\Phi_n^\theta(x,y) := \cos\theta\,\phi_{n,0}(x,y) + \sin\theta\,\phi_{0,n}(x,y). \tag{3.1}$$

More simply,

$$\Phi_n^\theta(x,y) = \exp\left(-\frac{x^2+y^2}{2}\right)\left(\cos\theta\,H_n(x) + \sin\theta\,H_n(y)\right).$$

Since $\Phi_n^{\theta+\pi} = -\Phi_n^\theta$, it suffices to vary the parameter θ in the interval $[0,\pi[$.

Assuming n is odd, we have the following symmetries.

$$\begin{cases} \Phi_n^\theta(-x,y) &= \Phi_n^{\pi-\theta}(x,y), \\ \Phi_n^\theta(x,-y) &= -\Phi_n^{\pi-\theta}(x,y), \\ \Phi_n^\theta(y,x) &= \Phi_n^{\frac{\pi}{2}-\theta}(x,y). \end{cases} \tag{3.2}$$

When n is odd, it therefore suffices to vary the parameter θ in the interval $[0,\frac{\pi}{4}]$. The case $\theta = 0$ is particular, so that we shall mainly consider $\theta \in]0,\frac{\pi}{4}]$.

3.3. Critical zeros. A *critical zero* of Φ_n^θ is a point $(x, y) \in \mathbb{R}^2$ such that both Φ_n^θ and its differential $d\Phi_n^\theta$ vanish at (x, y). The critical zeros of Φ_n^θ satisfy the following equations.

$$\begin{cases} \cos\theta\, H_n(x) + \sin\theta\, H_n(y) &= 0, \\ \cos\theta\, H_n'(x) &= 0, \\ \sin\theta\, H_n'(y) &= 0. \end{cases} \tag{3.3}$$

Equivalently, using the properties of the Hermite polynomials, a point (x, y) is a critical zero of Φ_n^θ if and only if

$$\begin{cases} \cos\theta\, H_n(x) + \sin\theta\, H_n(y) &= 0, \\ \cos\theta\, H_{n-1}(x) &= 0, \\ \sin\theta\, H_{n-1}(y) &= 0. \end{cases} \tag{3.4}$$

The only *possible* critical zeros of the eigenfunction Φ_n^θ are the points $(t_{n-1,i}, t_{n-1,j})$ for $1 \le i, j \le (n-1)$, where the coordinates are the zeros of the Hermite polynomial H_{n-1}. The point $(t_{n-1,i}, t_{n-1,j})$ is a critical zero of Φ_n^θ if and only if $\theta = \theta(i, j)$, where $\theta(i, j) \in]0, \pi[$ is uniquely determined by the equation,

$$\cos(\theta(i, j))\, H_n(t_{n-1,i}) + \sin(\theta(i, j))\, H_n(t_{n-1,j}) = 0. \tag{3.5}$$

The values $\theta(i, j)$ will be called *critical values* of the parameter θ, the other values *regular values*. Here we have used the fact that H_n and H_n' have no common zeros. We have proved the following lemma.

LEMMA 3.1. *For $\theta \in [0, \pi[$, the eigenfunction Φ_n^θ has no critical zero, unless θ is one of the critical values $\theta(i, j)$ defined by equation* (3.5). *In particular Φ_n^θ has no critical zero, except for finitely many values of the parameter $\theta \in [0, \pi[$. Given a pair $(i_0, j_0) \in \{1, \dots, n-1\}$, let $\theta_0 = \theta(i_0, j_0)$, be defined by* (3.5) *for the pair $(t_{n-1,i_0}, t_{n-1,j_0})$. Then, the function $\Phi_n^{\theta_0}$ has finitely many critical zeros, namely the points $(t_{n-1,i}, t_{n-1,j})$ which satisfy*

$$\cos\theta_0\, H_n(t_{n-1,i}) + \sin\theta_0\, H_n(t_{n-1,j}) = 0, \tag{3.6}$$

among them the point $(t_{n-1,i_0}, t_{n-1,j_0})$.

REMARKS. *From the general properties of nodal lines* [**2**, Properties 5.2], *we derive the following facts.*

(1) *When $\theta \notin \{\theta(i, j) \mid 1 \le i, j \le n-1\}$, the nodal set $N(\Phi_n^\theta)$ of the eigenfunction Φ_n^θ, is a smooth 1-dimensional submanifold of $\mathbb{R}^2$ (a collection of pairwise distinct connected simple regular curves).*

(2) *When $\theta \in \{\theta(i, j) \mid 1 \le i, j \le n-1\}$, the nodal set $N(\Phi_n^\theta)$ has finitely many singularities which are double crossings*[1]. *Indeed, the Hessian of the function Φ_n^θ at a* critical zero *$(t_{n-1,i}, t_{n-1,j})$ is given by*

$$\mathrm{Hess}_{(t_{n-1,i}, t_{n-1,j})} \Phi_n^\theta = \exp\Big(-\frac{t_{n-1,i}^2 + t_{n-1,j}^2}{2}\Big) \begin{pmatrix} \cos\theta\, H_n''(t_{n-1,i}) & 0 \\ 0 & \sin\theta\, H_n''(t_{n-1,j}) \end{pmatrix},$$

and the assertion follows from the fact that H_{n-1} has simple zeros.

[1] This result is actually general for any eigenfunction of the harmonic oscillator, as stated in [**26**], on the basis of Euler's formula and Courant's theorem.

3.4. General properties of the nodal set $N(\Phi_n^\theta)$. Denote by $\mathcal{L}$ the finite lattice

$$\mathcal{L} := \{(t_{n,i}, t_{n,j}) \mid 1 \leq i, j \leq n\} \subset \mathbb{R}^2, \tag{3.7}$$

consisting of points whose coordinates are the zeros of the Hermite polynomial H_n.

The horizontal and vertical lines $\{y = t_{n,i}\}$ and $\{x = t_{n,j}\}$, $1 \leq i, j \leq n$, form a checkerboard like pattern in $\mathbb{R}^2$ which can be colored according to the sign of the function $H_n(x)\, H_n(y)$ (grey where the function is positive, white where it is negative). We will refer to the following properties as *the checkerboard argument*, compare with [**2, 36**].

For symmetry reasons, we can assume that $\theta \in]0, \frac{\pi}{4}]$.

(i) We have the following inclusions for the nodal sets $N(\Phi_n^\theta)$,

$$\mathcal{L} \subset N(\Phi_n^\theta) \subset \mathcal{L} \cup \big\{(x,y) \in \mathbb{R}^2 \mid H_n(x)\, H_n(y) < 0\big\}\,. \tag{3.8}$$

(ii) The nodal set $N(\Phi_n^\theta)$ does not meet the vertical lines $\{x = t_{n,i}\}$, or the horizontal lines $\{y = t_{n,i}\}$ away from the set $\mathcal{L}$.

(iii) The lattice point $(t_{n,i}, t_{n,j})$ is not a critical zero of Φ_n^θ (because H_n and H_n' have no common zero). As a matter of fact, near a lattice point, the nodal set $N(\Phi_n^\theta)$ is a single arc through the lattice point, with a tangent which is neither horizontal, nor vertical.

Figure 2 shows the evolution of the nodal set of Φ_n^θ, for $n = 7$, when θ varies in the interval $]0, \frac{\pi}{4}]$. The pictures in the first column correspond to regular values of θ whereas the pictures in the second column correspond to critical values of θ. The form of the nodal set is stable in the open interval between two consecutive critical values of the parameter θ. In the figures, the thick curves represent the nodal sets $N(\Phi_7^\theta)$, the thin lines correspond to the zeros of H_7, and the grey lines to the zeros of H_7', i.e. to the zeros of H_6.

We now describe the nodal set $N(\Phi_n^\theta)$ outside a large enough square which contains the lattice $\mathcal{L}$. For this purpose, we give the following two *barrier lemmas* which describe the intersections of the nodal set with horizontal and vertical lines.

LEMMA 3.2. *Assume that $\theta \in]0, \frac{\pi}{4}]$. For n odd, define $t_{n-1,0}$ to be the unique point in $]-\infty, t_{n,1}[$ such that $H_n(t_{n-1,0}) = -H_n(t_{n-1,1})$. Then,*

(1) *$\forall t \leq t_{n,1}$, the function $y \mapsto \Phi_n^\theta(t,y)$ has exactly one zero in the interval $[t_{n,n}, +\infty[$;*
(2) *$\forall t < t_{n-1,0}$, the function $y \mapsto \Phi_n^\theta(t,y)$ has exactly one zero in the interval $]-\infty, +\infty[$.*

Using the symmetry with respect to the vertical line $\{x = 0\}$, one has similar statements for $t \geq t_{n,n}$ and for $t > -t_{n-1,0}$.

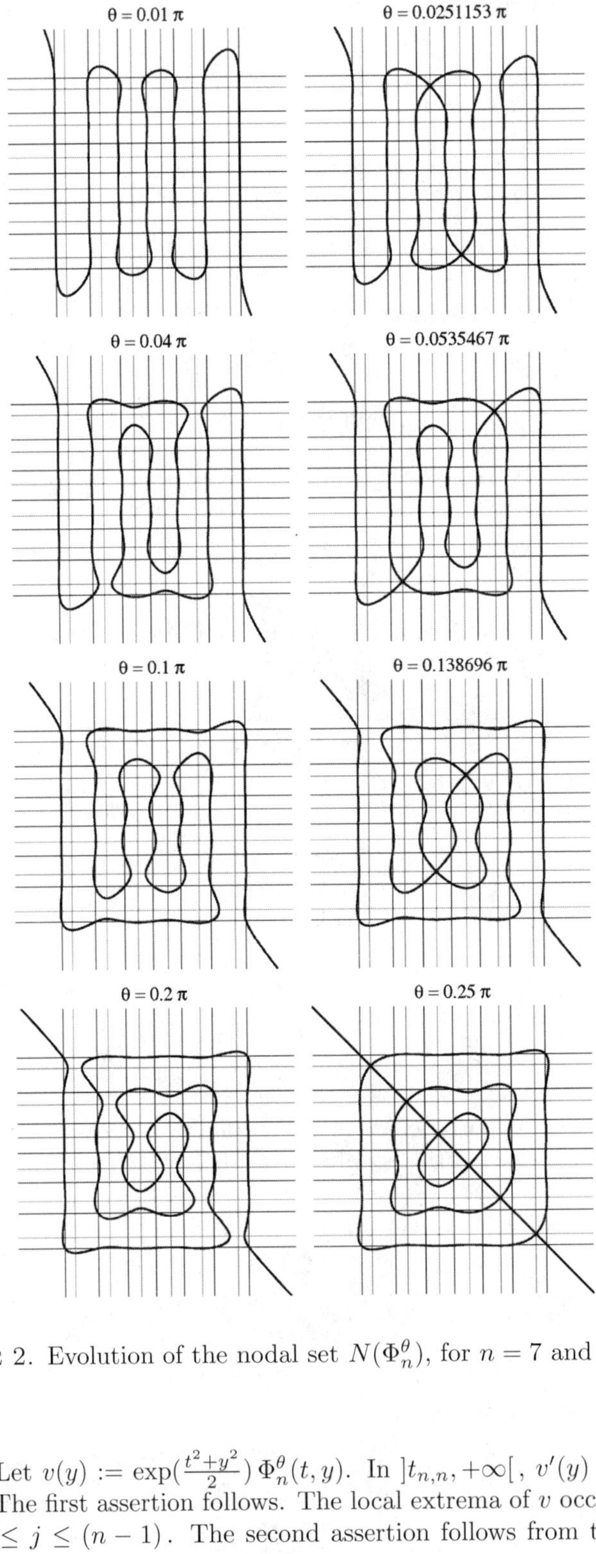

FIGURE 2. Evolution of the nodal set $N(\Phi_n^\theta)$, for $n = 7$ and $\theta \in]0, \frac{\pi}{4}]$.

PROOF. Let $v(y) := \exp(\frac{t^2+y^2}{2})\, \Phi_n^\theta(t, y)$. In $]t_{n,n}, +\infty[$, $v'(y)$ is positive, and $v(t_{n,n}) \leq 0$. The first assertion follows. The local extrema of v occur at the points $t_{n-1,j}$, for $1 \leq j \leq (n-1)$. The second assertion follows from the definition of

$t_{n-1,0}$, and from the inequalities,

$$\cos\theta\, H_n(t) + \sin\theta\, H_n(t_{n-1,j}) \le \frac{1}{\sqrt{2}}\Big(H_n(t) + |H_n|(t_{n-1,j})\Big)$$
$$< -\frac{1}{\sqrt{2}}\Big(H_n(t_{n-1,1}) - |H_n|(t_{n-1,j})\Big) \le 0,$$

for $t < t_{n-1,0}$, where we have used Lemma 2.1. □

LEMMA 3.3. *Let $\theta \in]0, \frac{\pi}{4}]$. Define $t^\theta_{n-1,n} \in]t_{n,n}, \infty[$ to be the unique point such that $\tan\theta\, H_n(t^\theta_{n-1,n}) = H_n(t_{n-1,1})$. Then,*

1. *$\forall t \ge t_{n,n}$, the function $x \mapsto \Phi^\theta_n(x,t)$ has exactly one zero in the interval $]-\infty, t_{n,1}]$;*
2. *$\forall t > t^\theta_{n-1,n}$, the function $x \mapsto \Phi^\theta_n(x,t)$ has exactly one zero in the interval $]-\infty,\infty[$.*
3. *For $\theta_2 > \theta_1$, we have $t^{\theta_2}_{n-1,n} < t^{\theta_1}_{n-1,n}$.*

Using the symmetry with respect to the horizontal line $\{y = 0\}$, one has similar statements for $t \le t_{n,1}$ and for $t < -t^\theta_{n-1,n}$.

PROOF. Let $h(x) := \exp(\frac{x^2+t^2}{2})\, \Phi^\theta_n(x,t)$. In the interval $]-\infty, t_{n,1}]$, the derivative $h'(x)$ is positive, $h(t_{n,1}) > 0$, and $\lim_{x\to-\infty} h(x) = -\infty$, since n is odd. The first assertion follows. The local extrema of h are achieved at the points $t_{n-1,j}$. Using Lemma 2.1, for $t \ge t^\theta_{n-1,n}$, we have the inequalities,

$$H_n(t_{n-1,j}) + \tan\theta\, H_n(t) \ge \tan\theta\, H_n(t^\theta_{n-1,n}) - |H_n(t_{n-1,j})|$$
$$= H_n(t_{n-1,1}) - |H_n(t_{n-1,j})| \ge 0.$$ □

As a consequence of the above lemmas, we have the following description of the nodal set far enough from $(0,0)$.

PROPOSITION 3.4. *Let $\theta \in]0, \frac{\pi}{4}]$. In the set $\mathbb{R}^2 \backslash] - t^\theta_{n-1,n}, t^\theta_{n-1,n}[\times]t_{n-1,0}, |t_{n-1,0}|[$, the nodal set $N(\Phi^\theta_n)$ consists of two regular arcs. The first arc is a graph $y(x)$ over the interval $]-\infty, t_{n,1}]$, starting from the point $(t_{n,1}, t_{n,n})$ and escaping to infinity with,*

$$\lim_{x\to-\infty} \frac{y(x)}{x} = -\sqrt[n]{\cot\theta}.$$

The second arc is the image of the first one under the symmetry with respect to $(0,0)$ in $\mathbb{R}^2$.

3.5. Local nodal patterns. As in the case of the Dirichlet eigenvalues for the square, we study the possible local nodal patterns taking into account the fact that the nodal set contains the lattice points $\mathcal{L}$, can only visit the connected components of the set $\{H_n(x)\, H_n(y) < 0\}$ (colored white), and consists of a simple arc at the lattice points. The following figure summarized the possible nodal patterns in the interior of the square [**2**, Figure 6.4],

Except for nodal arcs which escape to infinity, the local nodal patterns for the quantum harmonic oscillator are similar (note that in the present case, the connected components of the set $\{H_n(x)\, H_n(y) < 0\}$ are rectangles, no longer equal squares). The checkerboard argument and the location of the possible critical zeros determine the possible local patterns: (A), (B) or (C). Case (C) occurs near a critical zero.

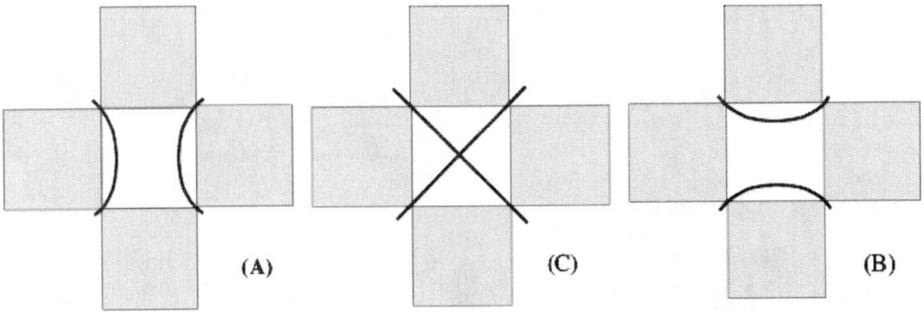

FIGURE 3. Local nodal patterns for Dirichlet eigenfunctions of the square.

Following the same ideas as in the case of the square, in order to decide between cases (A) and (B), we use the barrier lemmas, Lemma 3.2 or 3.3, the vertical lines $\{x = t_{n-1,j}\}$, or the horizontal lines $\{y = t_{n-1,j}\}$.

4. Proof of Theorem 1.3

Note that

$$\phi_{n,0}(x,y) - \phi_{0,n}(x,y) = -\sqrt{2}\,\Phi_n^{\frac{3\pi}{4}}(x,y) = -\sqrt{2}\Phi_n^{\frac{\pi}{4}}(x,-y).$$

Hence, up to symmetry, it is the same to work with $\theta = \frac{\pi}{4}$ and the anti-diagonal, or to work with $\theta = \frac{3\pi}{4}$ and the diagonal. For notational convenience, we work with $\frac{3\pi}{4}$.

4.1. The nodal set of $\Phi_n^{\frac{3\pi}{4}}$. The purpose of this section is to prove the following result which is the starting point for the proof of Theorem 1.3.

PROPOSITION 4.1. *Let $\{t_{n-1,i}, 1 \le i \le n-1\}$ denote the zeroes of H_{n-1}. For n odd, the nodal set of $\phi_{n,0} - \phi_{0,n}$ consists of the diagonal $x = y$, and of $\frac{n-1}{2}$ disjoint simple closed curves crossing the diagonal at the $(n-1)$ points $(t_{n-1,i}, t_{n-1,i})$, and the anti-diagonal at the $(n-1)$ points $(t_{n,i}, -t_{n,i})$.*

To prove Proposition 4.1, we first observe that it is enough to analyze the zero set of

$$(x,y) \mapsto \Psi_n(x,y) := H_n(x) - H_n(y).$$

4.1.1. *Critical zeros.* The only possible critical zeros of Ψ_n are determined by

$$H_n'(x) = 0,\ H_n'(y) = 0.$$

Hence, they consist of the $(n-1)^2$ points $(t_{n-1,i}, t_{n-1,j})$, for $1 \le i,j \le (n-1)$, where $t_{n-1,i}$ is the i-th zero of the polynomial H_{n-1}.

The zero set of Ψ_n contains the diagonal $\{x = y\}$. Since n is odd, there are only n points belonging to the zero set on the anti-diagonal $\{x + y = 0\}$. On the diagonal, there are $(n-1)$ critical points. We claim that there are no critical zeros outside the diagonal. Indeed, let $(t_{n-1,i}, t_{n-1,j})$ be a critical zero. Then, $H_n(t_{n-1,i}) = H_n(t_{n-1,j})$. Using Lemma 2.1 and the parity properties of Hermite polynomials, we see that $|H_n(t_{n-1,i})| = |H_n(t_{n-1,j})|$ occurs if and only if $t_{n-1,i} = \pm t_{n-1,j}$. Since n is odd, we can conclude that $H_n(t_{n-1,i}) = H_n(t_{n-1,j})$ occurs if and only if $t_{n-1,i} = t_{n-1,j}$.

4.1.2. *Existence of disjoint simple closed curves in the nodal set of* $\Phi_n^{\frac{3\pi}{4}}$. The second part in the proof of the proposition follows closely the proof in the case of the Dirichlet Laplacian for the square (see Section 5 in [**2**]). Essentially, the Chebyshev polynomials are replaced by the Hermite polynomials. Note however that the checkerboard is no more with equal squares, and that the square $[0,\pi]^2$ has to be replaced in the argument by the rectangle $[t_{n-1,0}, -t_{n-1,0}] \times [-t^{\theta}_{n-1,n}, t^{\theta}_{n-1,n}]$, for some $\theta \in]0, \frac{3\pi}{4}[$, see Lemmas 3.2 and 3.3.

The checkerboard argument holds, see (3.8) and the properties at the beginning of Section 3.4.

The separation lemmas of our previous paper [**2**] must be substituted by Lemmas 3.2 and 3.3, and similar statements with the lines $\{x = t_{n-1,j}\}$ and $\{y = t_{n-1,j}\}$, for $1 \le j \le (n-1)$.

One needs to control what is going on at infinity. As a matter of fact, outside a specific rectangle centered at the origin, the zero set is the diagonal $\{x = y\}$, see Proposition 3.4.

Hence in this way (like for the square), we obtain that the nodal set of Ψ_n consists of the diagonal and $\frac{n-1}{2}$ disjoint simple closed curves turning around the origin. The set $\mathcal{L}$ is contained in the union of these closed curves.

4.1.3. *No other closed curve in the nodal set of* $\Phi_n^{\frac{3\pi}{4}}$. It remains to show that there are no other closed curves which do not cross the diagonal. The "energy" considerations of our previous papers [**2, 4**] work here as well. Here is a simple alternative argument.

We look at the line $y = \alpha x$ for some $\alpha \neq 1$. The intersection of the zero set with this line corresponds to the zeroes of the polynomial $x \mapsto H_n(x) - H_n(\alpha x)$ which has at most n zeroes. But in our previous construction, we get at least n zeroes. So the presence of extra curves would lead to a contradiction for some α. This argument solves the problem at infinity as well. □

4.2. Perturbation argument. Figure 4 shows the desingularization of the nodal set $N(\Phi_n^{\frac{3\pi}{4}})$, from below and from above. The picture is the same as in the case of the square (see Figure 1), all the critical points disappear at the same time and in the same manner, i.e. all the double crossings open up horizontally or vertically depending whether θ is less than or bigger than $\frac{3\pi}{4}$.

As in the case of the square, in order to show that the nodal set can be desingularized under small perturbation, we look at the signs of the eigenfunction $\Phi_n^{\frac{3\pi}{4}}$ near the critical zeros. We use the cases (I) and (II) which appear in Figure 5 below (see also [**2**, Figure 6.7]).

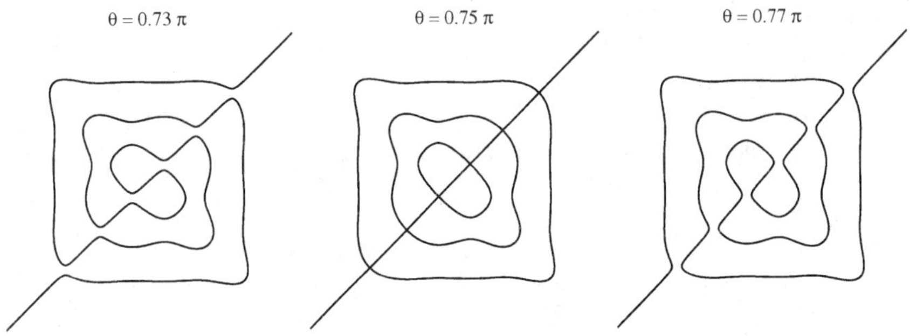

FIGURE 4. The nodal set of $N(\Phi_n^\theta)$ near $\frac{3\pi}{4}$ (here $n = 7$).

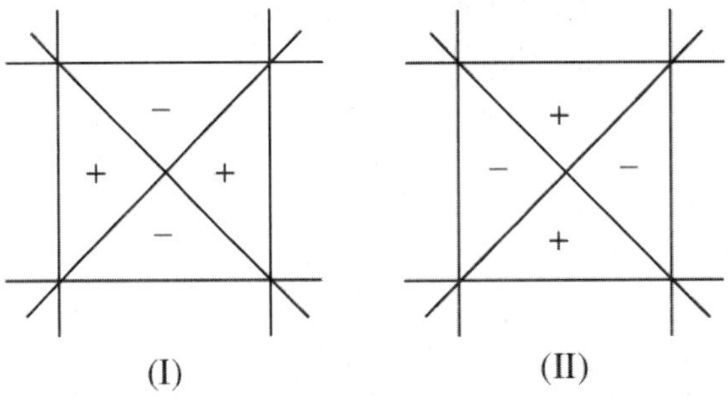

FIGURE 5. Signs near a critical zero.

The sign configuration for $\phi_{n,0}(x, y) - \phi_{0,n}(x, y)$ near the critical zero $(t_{n-1,i}, t_{n-1,i})$ is given by Figure 5

$$\begin{cases} \text{case (I), if } i \text{ is even,} \\ \text{case (II), if } i \text{ is odd.} \end{cases}$$

Looking at the intersection of the nodal set with the vertical line $\{y = t_{n-1,i}\}$, we have that

$$(-1)^i \left(H_n(t) - H_n(t_{n-1,i})\right) \geq 0, \text{ for } t \in]t_{n,i}, t_{n,i+1}[.$$

For positive ϵ small, we write

$$\begin{aligned} (-1)^i \left(H_n(t) - (1+\epsilon)H_n(t_{n-1,i})\right) = \\ (-1)^i \left(H_n(t) - H_n(t_{n-1,i})\right) + \epsilon(-1)^{i+1} H_n(t_{n-1,i}), \end{aligned}$$

so that

$$(-1)^i \left(H_n(t) - (1+\epsilon)H_n(t_{n-1,i})\right) \geq 0, \text{ for } t \in]t_{n,i}, t_{n,i+1}[.$$

A similar statement can be written for horizontal line $\{x = t_{n-1,i}\}$ and $-\epsilon$, with $\epsilon > 0$, small enough. These inequalities describe how the crossings all open up at the same time, and in the same manner, vertically (case I) or horizontally (case II), see Figure 6, as in the case of the square [**2**, Figure 6.8].

We can then conclude as in the case of the square, using the local nodal patterns, Section 3.5.

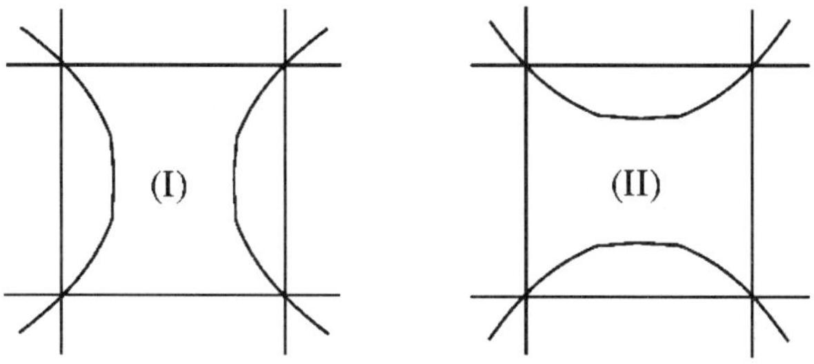

FIGURE 6. Desingularization at a critical zero.

REMARK. *Because the local nodal patterns can only change when θ passes through one of the values $\theta(i,j)$ defined in* (3.5), *the above arguments work for $\theta \in J \setminus \{\frac{3\pi}{4}\}$, for any interval J containing $\frac{3\pi}{4}$ and no other critical value $\theta(i,j)$.*

5. Proof of Theorem 1.4

PROPOSITION 5.1. *The conclusion of Theorem* 1.4 *holds with*

$$\theta_c := \inf \{\theta(i,j) \mid 1 \leq i,j \leq n-1\}, \tag{5.1}$$

where the critical values $\theta(i,j)$ are defined by (3.5).

PROOF. The proof consists in the following steps. For simplicity, we call N the nodal set $N(\Phi_n^\theta)$.

- Step 1. By Proposition 3.4, the structure of the nodal set N is known outside a large coordinate rectangle centered at $(0,0)$ whose sides are defined by the ad hoc numbers in Lemmas 3.2 and 3.3. Notice that the sides of the rectangle serve as barriers for the arguments using the local nodal patterns as in our paper for the square.
- Step 2. For $1 \leq j \leq n-1$, the line $\{x = t_{n-1,j}\}$ intersects the set N at exactly one point $(t_{n-1,j}, y_j)$, with $y_j > t_{n,n}$ when j is odd, *resp.* with $y_j < t_{n,1}$ when j is even. The proof is given below, and is similar to the proofs of Lemmas 3.2 or 3.3.
- Step 3. Any connected component of N has at least one point in common with the set $\mathcal{L}$. This follows from the argument with $y = \alpha x$ or from the energy argument (see Subsection 4.1.3).
- Step 4. Follow the nodal set from the point $(t_{n,1}, t_{n,n})$ to the point $(t_{n,n}, t_{n,1})$, using the analysis of the local nodal patterns as in the case of the square.

Proof of Step 2. For $1 \leq j \leq (n-1)$, define the function v_j by

$$v_j(y) := \cos\theta \, H_n(t_{n-1,j}) + \sin\theta \, H_n(y).$$

The local extrema of v_j are achieved at the points $t_{n-1,i}$, for $1 \leq i \leq (n-1)$, and we have

$$v_j(t_{n-1,i}) = \cos\theta \, H_n(t_{n-1,j}) + \sin\theta \, H_n(t_{n-1,i}),$$

which can be rewritten, using (3.5), as

$$v_j(t_{n-1,i}) = \frac{H_n(t_{n-1,j})}{\sin\theta(j,i)} \sin\left(\theta(j,i) - \theta\right).$$

The first term in the right-hand side has the sign of $(-1)^{j+1}$ and the second term is positive provided that $0 < \theta < \theta_c$. Under this last assumption, we have

$$(-1)^{j+1}\, v_j(t_{n-1,i}) > 0,\ \forall i,\ 1 \le i \le (n-1). \tag{5.2}$$

The assertion follows. □

6. Eigenfunctions with "many" nodal domains, proof of Theorem 1.6

This section is devoted to the proof of Theorem 1.6 i.e., to the constructions of eigenfunctions of $\widehat{H}$ with regular nodal sets (no self-intersections) and "many" nodal domains. We work in polar coordinates. An orthogonal basis of $\mathcal{E}_\ell$ is given by the functions $\Omega^{\pm}_{\ell,n}$,

$$\Omega^{\pm}_{\ell,n}(r,\varphi) = \exp(-\frac{r^2}{2})\, r^{\ell-2n}\, L_n^{(\ell-2n)}(r^2)\, \exp\left(\pm i(\ell-2n)\varphi\right), \tag{6.1}$$

with $0 \le n \le \left[\frac{\ell}{2}\right]$, see [**26**, Section 2.1]. In this formula $L_n^{(\alpha)}$ is the generalized Laguerre polynomial of degree n and parameter α, see [**37**, Chapter 5]. Recall that the Laguerre polynomial L_n is the polynomial $L_n^{(0)}$.

ASSUMPTION 6.1. *From now on, we assume that $\ell = 4k$, with k even.*

Since ℓ is even, we have a rotation invariant eigenfunction $\exp(-\frac{r^2}{2})\, L_{2k}(r^2)$ which has $(2k+1)$ nodal domains. We also look at the eigenfunctions $\omega_{\ell,n}$,

$$\omega_{\ell,n}(r,\varphi) = \exp(-\frac{r^2}{2})\, r^{\ell-2n}\, L_n^{(\ell-2n)}(r^2)\, \sin\left((\ell-2n)\varphi\right), \tag{6.2}$$

with $0 \le n < \left[\frac{\ell}{2}\right]$.
The number of nodal domains of these eigenfunctions is $\mu(\omega_{\ell,n}) = 2(n+1)(\ell-2n)$, because the Laguerre polynomial of degree n has n simple positive roots. When $\ell = 4k$, the largest of these numbers is

$$\mu_\ell := 4k(k+1), \tag{6.3}$$

and this is achieved for $n = k$.

When k tends to infinity, we have $\mu_\ell \sim \frac{\ell^2}{4}$, the same order of magnitude as Leydold's upper bound $\mu_\ell^L \sim \frac{\ell^2}{2}$.

We want now to construct eigenfunctions $u_k \in \mathcal{E}_\ell, \ell = 4k$ with *regular* nodal sets, and "many" nodal domains (or equivalently, "many" nodal connected components), more precisely with $\mu(u_k) \sim \frac{\ell^2}{8}$.

The construction consists of the following steps.

(1) Choose $A \in \mathcal{E}_\ell$ such that $\mu(A) = \mu_\ell$.
(2) Choose $B \in \mathcal{E}_\ell$ such that for a small enough, the perturbed eigenfunction $F_a := A + a\,B$ has no critical zero except the origin, and a nodal set with many components. Fix such an a.

(3) Choose $C \in \mathcal{E}_\ell$ such that for b small enough (and a fixed), $G_{a,b} := A + a\,B + b\,C$ has no critical zero.

From now on, we fix some ϵ, $0 < \epsilon < 1$. We assume that a is positive (to be chosen small enough later on), and that b is non zero (to be chosen small enough, either positive or negative later on).

In the remaining part of this section, we skip the exponential factor in the eigenfunctions since it is irrelevant to study the nodal sets.

Under Assumption 6.1, define

$$\begin{aligned} A(r,\varphi) &:= r^{2k}\, L_k^{(2k)}(r^2)\, \sin(2k\varphi), \quad B(r,\varphi) := r^{4k}\, \sin(4k\varphi - \epsilon\pi), \\ C(r,\varphi) &:= L_{2k}(r^2). \end{aligned} \tag{6.4}$$

We consider the deformations $F_a = A + a\,B$ and $G_{a,b} = A + a\,B + b\,C$. Both functions are invariant under the rotation of angle $\frac{\pi}{k}$, so that we can restrict to $\varphi \in [0, \frac{\pi}{k}]$.

For later purposes, we introduce the angles $\varphi_j = \frac{j\pi}{k}$, for $0 \le j \le 4k-1$, and $\psi_m = \frac{(m+\epsilon)\pi}{4k}$, for $0 \le m \le 8k-1$. We denote by $t_i, 1 \le i \le k$ the zeros of $L_k^{(2k)}$, listed in increasing order. They are simple and positive, so that the numbers $r_i = \sqrt{t_i}$ are well defined. For notational convenience, we denote by $\dot{L}_k^{(2k)}$ the derivative of the polynomial $L_k^{(2k)}$. This polynomial has $(k-1)$ simple zeros, which we denote by $t_i', 1 \le i \le k-1$, with $t_i < t_i' < t_{i+1}$. We define $r_i' := \sqrt{t_i'}$.

6.1. Critical zeros. Clearly, the origin is a critical zero of the eigenfunction $F_a = A + a\,B$, while $G_{a,b} = A + a\,B + b\,C$ does not vanish at the origin.

Away from the origin, the critical zeros of F_a are given by the system

$$\begin{aligned} F_a(r,\varphi) &= 0, \\ \partial_r F_a(r,\varphi) &= 0, \\ \partial_\varphi F_a(r,\varphi) &= 0. \end{aligned} \tag{6.5}$$

The first and second conditions imply that a critical zero (r,φ) satisfies

$$\sin(2k\varphi)\, \sin(4k\varphi - \epsilon\pi)\, \Big(kL_k^{(2k)}(r^2) - r^2 \dot{L}_k^{(2k)}(r^2)\Big) = 0, \tag{6.6}$$

where $\dot{L}$ is the derivative of the polynomial L.

The first and third conditions imply that a critical zero (r,φ) satisfies

$$2\sin(2k\varphi)\, \cos(4k\varphi - \epsilon\pi) - \cos(2k\varphi)\, \sin(4k\varphi - \epsilon\pi) = 0. \tag{6.7}$$

It is easy to deduce from (6.5) that when (r,φ) is a critical zero, $\sin(2k\varphi)\, \sin(4k\varphi - \epsilon\pi) \neq 0$. It follows that, away from the origin, a critical zero (r,φ) of F_a satisfies the system

$$\begin{aligned} &kL_k^{(2k)}(r^2) - r^2 \dot{L}_k^{(2k)}(r^2) = 0, \\ &2\sin(2k\varphi)\, \cos(4k\varphi - \epsilon\pi) - \cos(2k\varphi)\, \sin(4k\varphi - \epsilon\pi) = 0. \end{aligned} \tag{6.8}$$

The first equation has precisely $(k-1)$ positive simple zeros $r_{c,i}$, one in each interval $]r_i, r_i'[$, for $1 \le i \le (k-1)$. An easy analysis of the second shows that it has $4k$ simple zeros $\varphi_{c,j}$, one in each interval $]\varphi_j, \psi_{2j+1}[$, for $0 \le j \le 4k-1$.

PROPERTY 6.2. *The only possible critical zeros of the function F_a, away from the origin, are the points $(r_{c,i}, \varphi_{c,j})$, for $1 \le i \le k-1$ and $0 \le j \le 4k-1$, with corresponding finitely many values of a given by (6.5). In particular, there exists some $a_0 > 0$ such that for $0 < a < a_0$, the eigenfunction F_a has no critical zero away from the origin.*

The function $G_{a,b}$ does not vanish at the origin (provided that $b \neq 0$). Its critical zeros are given by the system

$$\begin{aligned} G(r,\varphi) &= 0,\\ \partial_r G(r,\varphi) &= 0,\\ \partial_\varphi G(r,\varphi) &= 0. \end{aligned} \tag{6.9}$$

We look at the situation for r large. Write

$$\begin{aligned} L_k^{(2k)}(t) &= \tfrac{(-1)^k}{k!}\, t^k + P_k(t),\\ L_{2k}(t) &= \tfrac{1}{(2k)!}\, t^{2k} + Q_k(t), \end{aligned} \tag{6.10}$$

where P_k and Q_k are polynomials with degree $(k-1)$ and $(2k-1)$ respectively.

The first and second equations in (6.9) are equivalent to the first and second equations of the system

$$\begin{aligned} 0 &= \tfrac{(-1)^k}{k!}\, \sin(2k\varphi) + a\, \sin(4k\varphi - \epsilon\pi) + \tfrac{b}{(2k)!} + O(\tfrac{1}{r^2}),\\ 0 &= \tfrac{(-1)^k}{k!}\, \cos(2k\varphi) + 2a\cos(4k\varphi - \epsilon\pi) + O(\tfrac{1}{r^2}), \end{aligned} \tag{6.11}$$

where the $O(\frac{1}{r^2})$ are uniform in φ and a, b (provided they are initially bounded).

PROPERTY 6.3. *There exist positive numbers $a_1 \le a_0$, b_1, R_1, such that for $0 < a < a_1$, $0 < |b| < b_1$, and $r > R_1$, the function $G_{a,b}(r,\varphi)$ has no critical zero. It follows that for fixed $0 < a < a_1$, and b small enough (depending on a), the function $G_{a,b}$ has no critical zero in $\mathbb{R}^2$.*

PROOF. Let $\alpha := \frac{(-1)^k}{k!}\, \sin(2k\varphi) + a\, \sin(4k\varphi - \epsilon\pi)$, $\beta := \frac{b}{(2k)!}$ and

$$\gamma := \frac{(-1)^k}{k!}\, \cos(2k\varphi) + 2a\cos(4k\varphi - \epsilon\pi).$$

Compute $(\alpha+\beta)^2 + \gamma^2$. For $0 < a < \frac{1}{2k!}$, one has

$$(\alpha+\beta)^2 + \gamma^2 \le \frac{1}{(2k!)^2} - \frac{4a}{k!} - \frac{4|b|}{k!(2k)!}.$$

The first assertion follows. The second assertion follows from the first one and from Property 6.2. □

6.2. The checkerboard. Since a in positive, the nodal set of F_a satisfies

$$\mathcal{L} \subset N(F_a) \subset \mathcal{L} \cup \{AB < 0\}\,, \tag{6.12}$$

where $\mathcal{L}$ is the finite set $N(A) \cap N(B)$, more precisely,

$$\mathcal{L} = \{(r_i, \psi_m) \mid 1 \le i \le k,\ 0 \le m \le 8k-1\}\,. \tag{6.13}$$

Let $p_{i,m}$ denote the point with polar coordinates (r_i, ψ_m). It is easy to check that the points $p_{i,m}$ are regular points of the nodal set $N(F_a)$. More precisely the nodal set $N(F_a)$ at these points is a regular arc transversal to the lines $\{\varphi = \psi_m\}$ and

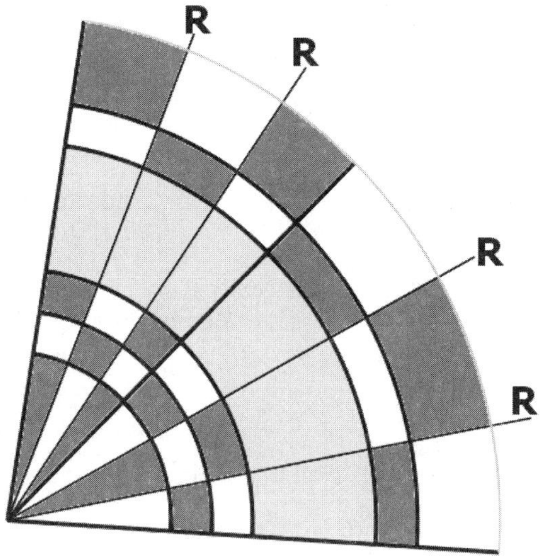

FIGURE 7. $\ell = 4k$, k even.

$\{r = r_i\}$. Note also that the nodal set $N(F_a)$ can only cross the nodal sets $N(A)$ or $N(B)$ at the points in $\mathcal{L}$.

The connected components of the set $\{AB \neq 0\}$ form a "polar checkerboard" whose white boxes are the connected components in which $AB < 0$. The global aspect of the checkerboard depends on the parity of k. Recall that our assumption is that $\ell = 4k$, with k even. Figure 7 displays a partial view of the checkerboard, using the invariance under the rotation of angle $\frac{\pi}{k}$. The thin lines labelled "R" correspond to the angles ψ_m, with $m = 0, 1, 2, 3$. The thick lines to the angles φ_j, with $j = 0, 1, 2$. The thick arcs of circle correspond to the values r_i, with $i = 1, 2, 3$ and then $i = k-1, k$. The light grey part represents the zone r_i with $i = 4, \ldots, k-2$. The intersection points of the thin lines "R" with the thick arcs are the point in $\mathcal{L}$, in the sector $0 \leq \varphi \leq \varphi_2$. The outer arc of circle (in grey) represents the horizon.

6.3. Behavior at infinity. We now look at the behavior at infinity of the functions F_a and $G_{a,b}$. We restrict our attention to the sector $\{0 \leq \varphi \leq \varphi_2\}$.

Recall that k is even.

For $r > r_k$, the nodal set $N(F_a)$ can only visit the white sectors $\mathcal{S}_0 := \{\varphi_0 < \varphi < \psi_0\}$, $\mathcal{S}_1 := \{\psi_1 < \varphi < \varphi_1\}$, and $\mathcal{S}_2 := \{\psi_2 < \varphi < \psi_3\}$, issuing respectively from the points $p_{k,0}, p_{k,1}$ or $p_{k,2}, p_{k,3}$.

As above, we can write

$$F_a(r, \varphi) = r^{4k} g(\varphi) + \sin(2k\varphi) P_k(r^2), \tag{6.14}$$

with

$$g(\varphi) = \frac{1}{k!} \sin(2k\varphi) + a \sin(4k\varphi - \epsilon\pi),$$

where we have used the fact that k is even.

• **Analysis in $\mathcal{S}_0$.** We have $0 < \varphi < \frac{\epsilon\pi}{4k}$. Note that $g(0)\,g(\frac{\epsilon\pi}{4k}) < 0$. On the other-hand, $g'(\varphi)$ satisfies

$$g'(\varphi) \geq 2k\left\{\frac{1}{k!}\cos(\frac{\epsilon\pi}{2}) - 2a\right\}.$$

It follows that provided that $0 < a < \frac{1}{2\,k!}\cos(\frac{\epsilon\pi}{2})$, the function g has exactly one zero θ_0 in the interval $]0, \frac{\epsilon\pi}{4k}[$.

It follows that for r big enough, the equation $F_a(r,\varphi) = 0$ has exactly one zero $\varphi(r)$ in the interval $]0, \frac{\epsilon\pi}{4k}[$, and this zero tends to θ_0 when r tends to infinity. Looking at (6.14) again, we see that $\varphi(r) = \theta_0 + O(\frac{1}{r^2})$. It follows that the nodal set in the sector $\mathcal{S}_0$ is a line issuing from $p_{k,0}$ and tending to infinity with the asymptote $\varphi = \theta_0$.

• **Analysis in $\mathcal{S}_1$.** The analysis is similar to the analysis in $\mathcal{S}_0$.

• **Analysis in $\mathcal{S}_2$.** In this case, we have that $\frac{(2+\epsilon)\pi}{4k} < \varphi < \frac{(3+\epsilon)\pi}{4k}$. It follows that $-\sin(2k\varphi) \geq \min\{\sin(\frac{\epsilon\pi}{2}), \cos(\frac{\epsilon\pi}{2})\} > 0$. If $0 < a < \frac{1}{k!}\min\{\sin(\frac{\epsilon\pi}{2}), \cos(\frac{\epsilon\pi}{2})\}$, then $F_a(r,\varphi)$ tends to negative infinity when r tends to infinity, uniformly in $\varphi \in]\psi_2, \psi_3[$. It follows that the nodal set of $N(F_a)$ is bounded in the sector $\mathcal{S}_2$.

6.4. The nodal set $N(F_a)$ and $N(G_{a,b})$.

PROPOSITION 6.4. *For $\ell = 4k$, k even, and a positive small enough, the nodal set of F_a consists of three sets of "ovals"*

1. *a cluster of $2k$ closed (singular) curves, with a common singular point at the origin,*
2. *$2k$ curves going to infinity, tangentially to lines $\varphi = \vartheta_{a,j}$ (in the case of the sphere, they would correspond to a cluster of closed curves at the south pole),*
3. *$2k(k-1)$ disjoint simple closed curves (which correspond to the white cases at finite distance of Stern's checkerboard for A and B).*

PROOF. Since B vanishes at higher order than A at the origin, the behavior of the nodal set of F_a is well determined at the origin. More precisely, the nodal set of F_a at the origin consists of $4k$ semi-arcs, issuing from the origin tangentially to the lines $\varphi = j\pi/2k$, for $0 \leq j \leq 4k-1$. At infinity, the behavior of the nodal set of F_a is determined for a small enough in Subsection 6.3. An analysis à la Stern, then shows that for a small enough there is a cluster of ovals in the intermediate region $\{r_2 < r < r_{k-1}\}$, when $k \geq 4$. ☐

Fixing a small enough so that the preceding proposition holds, in order to obtain a regular nodal set, it suffices to perturb F_a into $G_{a,b}$, with b small enough, choosing its sign so that the nodal set F_a is desingularized at the origin, creating $2k$ ovals.

Figure 8 displays the cases $\ell = 8$ (i.e. $k = 2$).

Finally, we have constructed an eigenfunction $G_{a,b}$ with $2k(k+1)$ nodal component so that $\mu(G_{a,b}) \sim 2k^2 = \frac{\ell^2}{8}$.

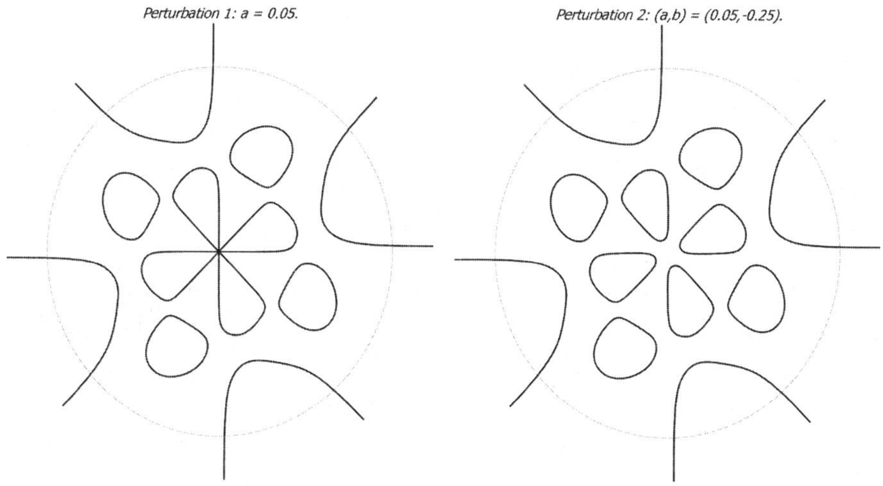

FIGURE 8. Ovals for $\ell = 8$.

7. On bounds for the length of the nodal set

In Subsection 7.1, we obtain Theorem 1.7 as a corollary of a more general result, Proposition 7.2, which sheds some light on the exponent $\frac{3}{2}$. The proof is typically 2-dimensional, à la Brüning-Gromes [**6**, **7**]. We consider more general potentials in Subsection 7.3. In Subsection 7.3, we extend the methods of Long Jin [**29**] to some Schrödinger operators. We obtain both lower and upper bounds on the length of the nodal sets in the classically permitted region, Proposition 7.10.

7.1. Lower bounds, proof à la Brüning-Gromes. Consider the eigenvalue problem on $L^2(\mathbb{R}^2)$

$$H_V := -\Delta + V(x),\ H_V\, u = \lambda\, u, \tag{7.1}$$

for some suitable non-negative potential V such that the operator has discrete spectrum (see [**24**, Chapter 8]). More precisely, we assume:

ASSUMPTION 7.1. *The potential V is positive, continuous and tends to infinity at infinity.*

Introduce the sets

$$B_V(\lambda) := \left\{x \in \mathbb{R}^2 \mid V(x) < \lambda\right\}, \tag{7.2}$$

and, for $r > 0$,

$$B_V^{(-r)}(\lambda) := \left\{x \in \mathbb{R}^2 \mid B(x,r) \subset B_V(\lambda)\right\}, \tag{7.3}$$

where $B(x,r)$ is the open ball with center x and radius r.

PROPOSITION 7.2. *Fix $\delta \in]0,1[$ and $\rho \in]0,1]$. Under Assumption 7.1, for λ large enough, and for any nonzero eigenfunction u of H_V, $H_V u = \lambda u$, the length of $N(u) \cap B_V(\delta\lambda)$ is not less than*

$$\frac{2(1-\delta)}{9\pi^2 j_{0,1}}\sqrt{\lambda}\, A\left(B_V^{(-2\rho)}(\delta\lambda)\right). \tag{7.4}$$

Proof of Proposition 7.2

LEMMA 7.3. *Choose some radius* $0 < \rho \leq 1$, *and let*

$$\rho_\delta := \frac{j_{0,1}}{\sqrt{1-\delta}}. \tag{7.5}$$

Then, for $\lambda > \left(\frac{\rho_\delta}{\rho}\right)^2$, *and for any* $x \in B_V^{(-\rho)}(\delta\lambda)$, *the ball* $B(x, \frac{\rho_\delta}{\sqrt{\lambda}})$ *intersects the nodal set* $N(u)$ *of the function* u.

Proof of Lemma 7.3. Let $r := \frac{\rho_\delta}{\sqrt{\lambda}}$. If the ball $B(x,r)$ did not intersect $N(u)$, then it would be contained in a nodal domain D of the eigenfunction u. Denoting by $\sigma_1(\Omega)$ the least Dirichlet eigenvalue of the operator H_V in the domain Ω, by monotonicity, we could write

$$\lambda = \sigma_1(D) \leq \sigma_1\left(B(x,r)\right).$$

Since $x \in B_V^{(-\rho)}(\delta\lambda)$ and $\lambda > \left(\frac{\rho_\delta}{\rho}\right)^2$, the ball $B(x,r)$ is contained in $B_V(\delta\lambda)$, and we can bound V from above by $\delta\lambda$ in this ball. It follows that $\sigma_1\left(B(x,r)\right) < \frac{j_{0,1}^2}{r^2} + \delta\lambda$. This leads to a contradiction with the definition of ρ_δ. ☐

Consider the set $\mathcal{F}$ of finite subsets $\{x_1, \ldots, x_n\}$ of $\mathbb{R}^2$ with the following properties,

$$\begin{cases} x_i \in N(u) \cap B_V^{(-\rho)}(\delta\lambda), \ 1 \leq i \leq n, \\ B(x_i, \frac{\rho_\delta}{\sqrt{\lambda}}), \ 1 \leq i \leq n, \text{ pairwise disjoint.} \end{cases} \tag{7.6}$$

For λ large enough, the set $\mathcal{F}$ is not empty, and can be ordered by inclusion. It admits a maximal element $\{x_1, \ldots, x_N\}$, where N depends on δ, ρ, λ and u.

LEMMA 7.4. *The balls* $B(x_i, \frac{3\rho_\delta}{\sqrt{\lambda}}), 1 \leq i \leq N$, *cover the set* $B_V^{(-2\rho)}(\delta\lambda)$.

Proof of Lemma 7.4. Assume the claim in not true, i.e. that there exists some $y \in B_V^{(-2\rho)}(\delta\lambda)$ such that $|y - x_i| > \frac{3\rho_\delta}{\sqrt{\lambda}}$ for all $i \in \{1, \ldots, N\}$. Since $y \in B_V^{(-\rho)}(\delta\lambda)$, by Lemma 7.3, there exists some $x \in N(u) \cap B(y, \frac{\rho_\delta}{\sqrt{\lambda}})$, and we have $x \in B_V^{(-\rho)}(\delta\lambda)$. Furthermore, for all $i \in \{1, \ldots, N\}$, we have $|x - x_i| \geq \frac{2\rho_\delta}{\sqrt{\lambda}}$. The set $\{x, x_1, x_2, \ldots, x_N\}$ would belong to $\mathcal{F}$, contradicting the maximality of $\{x_1, x_2, \ldots, x_N\}$. ☐

Lemma 7.4 gives a lower bound on the number N,

$$N \geq \frac{\lambda}{9\pi^2\rho_\delta^2} A\left(B_V^{(-2\rho)}(\delta\lambda)\right), \tag{7.7}$$

where $A(\Omega)$ denotes the area of the set Ω.

LEMMA 7.5. *For any* $\alpha < j_{0,1}$, *the ball* $B(x, \frac{\alpha}{\sqrt{\lambda}})$ *does not contain any closed connected component of the nodal set* $N(u)$.

Proof of Lemma 7.5. Indeed, any closed connected component of $N(u)$ contained in $B(x, \frac{\alpha}{\sqrt{\lambda}})$ would bound some nodal domain D of u, contained in $B(x, \frac{\alpha}{\sqrt{\lambda}})$, and we would have

$$\lambda = \sigma_1(D) \geq \sigma_1\left(B(x, \frac{\alpha}{\sqrt{\lambda}}\right) \geq \frac{j_{0,1}^2}{\alpha^2}\lambda,$$

contradicting the assumption on α. □

Take the maximal set $\{x_1, \ldots, x_N\} \subset N(u) \cap B_V^{(-\rho)}(\delta\lambda)$ constructed above. The balls $B(x_i, \frac{\rho_\delta}{\sqrt{\lambda}})$ are pairwise disjoint, and so are the balls $B(x_i, \frac{\alpha}{\sqrt{\lambda}})$ for any $0 < \alpha < j_{0,1}$. There are at least two nodal arcs issuing from a point x_i, and they must exit $B(x_i, \frac{\alpha}{\sqrt{\lambda}})$, otherwise we could find a closed connected component of $N(u)$ inside this ball, contradicting Lemma 7.5. The length of $N(u) \cap B(x_i, \frac{\alpha}{\sqrt{\lambda}})$ is at least $\frac{2\alpha}{\sqrt{\lambda}}$. Finally, the length of $N(u) \cap B_V(\delta\lambda)$ is at least $N\frac{2\alpha}{\sqrt{\lambda}}$ which is bigger than

$$\frac{2\alpha}{9\pi^2\rho_\delta^2}\sqrt{\lambda}A\left(B_V^{(-2\rho)}(\delta\lambda)\right).$$

Since this is true for any $\alpha < j_{0,1}$. □

PROOF OF THEOREM 1.7. We apply the preceding proposition with $V(x) = |x|^{2k}$ and $\rho = 1$. Then, $B_V(\lambda) = B(\lambda^{\frac{1}{2k}})$ and $B_V^{(-r)}(\lambda) = B(\lambda^{\frac{1}{2k}} - r)$. In this case, the length of the nodal set is bounded by some constant times $\lambda^{\frac{1}{2}+\frac{1}{k}} \approx \lambda^{\frac{1}{2}} A\left(B_V(\delta\lambda)\right)$. When $k = 1$, we obtain Proposition 1.7. □

REMARK. *The above proof sheds some light on the exponent* $\frac{3}{2}$ *in Proposition* 1.7.

7.2. More general potentials. We reinterpret Proposition 7.2 for more general potentials $V(x)$, under natural assumptions which appear in the determination of the Weyl's asymptotics of H_V (see [**32**], [**23**]).

After renormalization, we assume:

ASSUMPTION 7.6. *V is of class C^1, $V \geq 1$, and there exist some positive constants ρ_0 and C_1 such that for all $x \in \mathbb{R}^2$,*

$$|\nabla V(x)| \leq C_1 V(x)^{1-\rho_0}. \tag{7.8}$$

Note that under this assumption there exist positive constants r_0 and C_0 such that

$$x, y \text{ satisfy } |x-y| \leq r_0 \Rightarrow V(x) \leq C_0\, V(y). \tag{7.9}$$

The proof is easy. We first write

$$V(x) \leq V(y) + |x-y| \sup_{z\in[x,y]} |\nabla V(z)|.$$

Applying (7.8) (here we only use $\rho_0 \geq 0$), we get

$$V(x) \leq V(y) + C_1|x-y| \sup_{z\in[x,y]} V(z).$$

We now take $x \in B(y, r)$ for some $r > 0$ and get

$$\sup_{x\in B(y,r)} V(x) \leq V(y) + C_1\, r \sup_{x\in B(y,r)} V(x),$$

which we can rewrite, if $C_1 r < 1$, in the form

$$V(y) \leq \sup_{x \in B(y,r)} V(x) \leq V(y)(1 - C_1 r)^{-1}.$$

This is more precise than (7.9) because we get $C_0(r_0) = (1 - C_1 r_0)^{-1}$, which tends to 1 as $r_0 \to 0$.

We assume

ASSUMPTION 7.7. *For any $\delta \in]0,1[$, there exists some positive constants A_δ and λ_δ such that*

$$1 < A(B_V(\lambda))/A(B_V(\delta\lambda)) \leq A_\delta,\ \forall \lambda \geq \lambda_\delta. \tag{7.10}$$

PROPOSITION 7.8. *Fix $\delta \in (0,1)$, and assume that V satisfies the previous assumptions. Then, there exists a positive constant C_δ (depending only on the constants appearing in the assumptions on V) and λ_δ such that for any eigenpair (u, λ) of H_V with $\lambda \geq \lambda_\delta$, the length of $N(u) \cap B_V(\delta\lambda)$ is larger than $C_\delta \lambda^{\frac{1}{2}} A(B_V(\lambda))$.*

PROOF. Using (7.10), it is enough to prove the existence of r_1 such that, for $0 < r < r_1$, there exists $C_2(r)$ and $M(r)$ s.t.

$$B_V(\mu - C_2 \mu^{1-\rho_0}) \subset B_V^{-r}(\mu),\ \forall \mu > M(r).$$

But, if $x \in B_V(\mu - C_2\mu^{1-\rho_0})$, and $y \in B(x,r)$, we have

$$V(y) \leq V(x) + C_1 C_0(r)^{1-\rho_0} r V(x)^{1-\rho_0} \leq \mu - C_2 \mu^{1-\rho_0} + C_1 C_0(r)^{1-\rho_0} r \mu^{1-\rho_0}.$$

Taking $C_2(r) = C_1 C_0(r)^{1-\rho_0} r$ and $M(r) \geq (C_2(r) + 1)^{\frac{1}{\rho_0}}$ gives the result. □

REMARKS.

(1) *The method of proof of Proposition 7.2, which is reminiscent of the proof by Brüning* [**7**] *(see also* [**6**]*) is typically 2-dimensional.*

(2) *The same method could be applied to a Schrödinger operator on a complete noncompact Riemannian surface, provided one has some control on the geometry, the first eigenvalue of small balls, etc..*

(3) *If we assume that there exist positive constants $m_0 \leq m_1$ and C_3 such that for any $x \in \mathbb{R}^2$,*

$$\frac{1}{C_3} < x >^{m_0} \leq V(x) \leq C_3 < x >^{m_1}, \tag{7.11}$$

where $< x > := \sqrt{1 + |x|^2}$, then $A(B_V(\lambda))$ has a controlled growth at ∞.

(4) *If $m_0 = m_1$ in (7.11), then (7.10) is satisfied. The control of A_δ as $\delta \to +1$ can be obtained under additional assumptions.*

7.3. Upper and lower bounds on the length of the nodal set: the semi-classical approach of Long Jin. In [**29**], Long Jin analyzes the same question in the semi-classical context for a Schrödinger operator

$$H_{W,h} := -h^2 \Delta_g + W(x),$$

where Δ_g is the Laplace-Beltrami operator on the compact connected analytic Riemannian surface (M, g), with W analytic. In this context, he shows that if (u_h, λ_h) is an h-family of eigenpairs of $H_{W,h}$ such that $\lambda_h \to E$, then the length of the zero set of u_h inside the classical region $W^{-1}(] - \infty, E])$ is of order h^{-1}.

Although not explicitly done in [**29**], the same result is also true in the case of $M = \mathbb{R}^2$ under the condition that $\liminf W(x) > E \geq \inf W$, keeping the assumption that W is analytic. Let us show how we can reduce the case $M = \mathbb{R}^2$ to the compact situation.

PROPOSITION 7.9. *Let us assume that W is continuous and that there exists E_1 such that $W^{-1}(]-\infty, E_1])$ is compact. Then the bottom of the essential spectrum of $H_{W,h}$ is bigger than E_1. Furthermore, if (λ_h, u_h) is a family ($h \in]0, h_0]$) of eigenpairs of $H_{W,h}$ such that $\lim_{h\to 0} \lambda_h = E_0$ with $E_0 < E_1$ and $||u_h|| = 1$, then given K a compact neighborhood of $W^{-1}(]-\infty, E_0])$, there exists $\epsilon_K > 0$ such that*

$$||u_h||_{L^2(K)} = 1 + \mathcal{O}\left(\exp(-\epsilon_K/h)\right),$$

as $h \to 0$.

This proposition is a consequence of Agmon estimates (see Helffer-Sjöstrand [**21**] or Helffer-Robert [**20**] for a weaker result with a remainder in $\mathcal{O}_K(h^\infty)$) measuring the decay of the eigenfunctions in the classically forbidden region. This can also be found in a weaker form in the recent book of M. Zworski [**38**] (Chapter 7), which also contains a presentation of semi-classical Carleman estimates.

Observing that in the proof of Long Jin the compact manifold M can be replaced by any compact neighborhood of $W^{-1}(]-\infty, E_0])$, we obtain:

PROPOSITION 7.10. *Let us assume in addition that W is analytic in some compact neighborhood of $W^{-1}(]-\infty, E_0])$, then the length of the zero set of u_h inside the classical region $W^{-1}(]-\infty, E_0])$ is of order h^{-1}. More precisely, there exist $C > 0$ and $h_0 > 0$ such that for all $h \in]0, h_0]$ we have*

$$\frac{1}{C} h^{-1} \leq \text{length}\left(N(u_h) \cap W^{-1}(]-\infty, E_0])\right) \leq C\, h^{-1}. \tag{7.12}$$

REMARK 7.11. *As observed in* [**29**] *(Remark 1.3), the results of* [**18**] *suggest that the behavior of the nodal sets in the classically forbidden region could be very different from the one in the classically allowed region.*

We can by scaling recover Proposition 1.7, and more generally treat the eigenpairs of $-\Delta_x + |x|^{2k}$. Indeed, assume that $(-\Delta_x + |x|^{2k})u(x) = \lambda u(x)$. Write $x = \rho y$. Then, $(-\rho^{-2}\Delta_y + \rho^{2k}|y|^{2k} - \lambda)u(\rho y) = 0$. If we choose $\rho^{2k} = \lambda$, $h = \rho^{-k-1} = \lambda^{-\frac{k+1}{2k}}$ and let $v_h(y) = h^{\frac{1}{2(k+1)}}y)\, u(h^{\frac{1}{k+1}}y)$, then, $(-h^2\Delta_y + |y|^{2k} - 1)v_h(y) = 0$. Applying (7.12) to the family v_h and rescaling back to the variable x, we find that

$$\frac{1}{C}\lambda^{\frac{k+2}{2k}} \leq \text{length}\left(N(u) \cap \{x \in \mathbb{R}^2 \mid |x|^{2k} < \lambda\}\right) \leq C\,\lambda^{\frac{k+2}{2k}}. \tag{7.13}$$

With this extension of Long Jin's statement, when $V = |x|^{2k}$, we also obtain an upper bound of the length of $N(u)$ in $B_V(\lambda)$. Note that when $k \to +\infty$, the problem tends to the Dirichlet problem in a ball of size 1. We then recover that the length of $N(u)$ is of order $\sqrt{\lambda}$.

The above method can also give results in the non-homogeneous case, at least when (7.11) is satisfied with $m_0 = m_1$. We can indeed prove the following generalization.

PROPOSITION 7.12. *Let us assume that there exist $m \geq 1$, $\epsilon_0 > 0$ and $C > 0$ such that V is holomorphic in*

$$\mathcal{D} := \{z = (z_1, z_2) \in \mathbb{C}^2,\ |\Im z| \leq \epsilon_0 < \Re z >\}$$

and satisfies

$$|V(z)| \leq C < \Re z >^m,\ \forall z \in \mathcal{D}. \tag{7.14}$$

Suppose in addition that we have the ellipticity condition

$$\frac{1}{C'} < x >^m \leq V(x),\ \forall x \in \mathbb{R}^2. \tag{7.15}$$

Then, for any $\epsilon > 0$, the length $N(u) \cap (B_V(\lambda) \setminus B_V(\epsilon\lambda))$ for an eigenpair (u, λ) of H_V, is of the order of $\lambda^{\frac{1}{2}+\frac{2}{m}}$ as $\lambda \to +\infty$. Moreover, one can take $\epsilon = 0$ when V is a polynomial.

PROOF. The lower bound was already obtained by a more general direct approach in Proposition 7.8. One can indeed verify using Cauchy estimates that (7.14) and (7.15) imply (7.8) and (7.11), with $\rho_0 = 1/2m$. Under the previous assumptions, we consider

$$W_\lambda(y) = \lambda^{-1} V(\lambda^{\frac{1}{m}} y),\ v_\lambda(y) = \lambda^{\frac{1}{4m}} u(\lambda^{\frac{1}{m}} y).$$

We observe that with

$$h = \lambda^{-\frac{1}{2}-\frac{1}{m}}, \tag{7.16}$$

the pair $(v_\lambda, 1)$ is an eigenpair for the semi-classical Schrödinger operator $-h^2\Delta_y + W_\lambda(y)$:

$$(-h^2\Delta + W_\lambda)v_\lambda = v_\lambda.$$

It remains to see if we can extend the result of Long Jin to this situation. We essentially follow his proof, whose basic idea goes back to Donnelly-Feffermann [**15**]. The difference being that W_λ depends on h through (7.16).
The inspection of the proof[2] shows that there are three points to control.

Analyticity
What we need is to have for any y_0 in $\mathbb{R}^2 \setminus \{0\}$ a complex neighborhood $\mathcal{V}$ of y_0, $h_0 > 0$ and C such that, for any $h \in]0, h_0]$, v_λ admits an holomorphic extension in $\mathcal{V}$ with

$$\sup_{\mathcal{V}} |v_\lambda| \leq C \exp\left(\frac{C}{h}\right) ||v_\lambda||_{L^\infty(\mathbb{R}^2)}. \tag{7.17}$$

This can be done by using the FBI transform, controlling the uniformity when W is replaced by W_λ. But this is exactly what is given by Assumption (7.14). Notice that this is not true in general for $y_0 = 0$. We cannot in general find a λ-independent neighborhhod of 0 in $\mathbb{C}^2$ where W_λ is defined and bounded.
Note here that $||v_\lambda||_{L^\infty(\mathbb{R}^2)}$ is by standard semiclassical analysis $\mathcal{O}(h^{-N})$ for some N.
When V is in addition a polynomial:

$$V(x) = \sum_{j=0}^{m} P_j(x)$$

[2] We refer here to the proof of (2.20) in [**29**].

where P_j is an homogeneous polynomial of degree j, we get

$$W_\lambda(y) = P_m(y) + \sum_{\ell=1}^{m} \lambda^{-\frac{\ell}{m}} P_{m-\ell}(y),$$

and we can verify the uniform analyticity property for any y_0.

Uniform confining
As we have mentioned before, Long Jin's paper was established in the case of a compact manifold (in this case and for Laplacians, it is worth to mention the papers of Sogge-Zelditch [**34, 35**]) but it can be extended to the case of $\mathbb{R}^2$ under the condition that the potential is confining, the length being computed in a compact containing the classically permitted region. This is the case with W_λ. Note that if $W_\lambda(y) \leq C_1$, then we get

$$\lambda^{-1} V(\lambda^{\frac{1}{m}} y) \leq C_1,$$

which implies by the ellipticity condition $\frac{1}{C'}\lambda^{-1}|\lambda^{\frac{1}{m}}|^m |y|^m \leq C_1$, that is

$$|y| \leq (C' C_1)^{\frac{1}{m}}.$$

Uniform doubling property
Here instead of following Long Jin's proof, it is easier to refer to the results of Bakri-Casteras [**1**], which give an explicit control in term of the C^1 norm of W_λ. As before, we have to use our confining assumption in order to establish our result in any bounded domain Ω in $\mathbb{R}^2$ containing uniformly the classically permitted area $W_\lambda^{-1}(]-\infty, +1])$. This last assumption permits indeed to control the L^2-norm of v_λ from below in Ω. We actually need the two following estimates (we assume (7.16)): Given Ω like above, for any $R > 0$, there exists C_R such that, for any (x, R) such that $B(x, R) \subset \Omega$,

$$||v_\lambda||_{L^2(B(x,R))} \geq \exp\left(-\frac{C_R}{h}\right). \tag{7.18}$$

Given Ω like above, there exists C such that, for any (x, r) such that $B(x, 2r) \subset \Omega$,

$$||v_\lambda||_{L^2(B(x,2r))} \leq \exp\left(\frac{C}{h}\right) ||v_\lambda||_{L^2(B(x,r))}. \tag{7.19}$$

Here we have applied Theorem 3.2 and Proposition 3.3 in [**1**] with electric potential $h^{-2}(W_\lambda - 1)$. These two statements involve the square root of the C^1 norm of the electric potential in $\overline{\Omega}$, which is $\mathcal{O}(h^{-1})$ in our case.

End of the proof
Hence, considering an annulus $A(\epsilon_0, R_0)$ we get following Long Jin that the length of the nodal set of v_λ in this annulus is indeed of order $\mathcal{O}(h^{-1})$ and after rescaling we get the proposition for the eigenpair (u, λ). In the polynomial case, we get the same result but in the ball $B(0, R_0)$. □

REMARKS.

(1) *Long Jin's results hold in dimension n, not only in dimension 2. The above extensions work in any dimension as well, replacing the length by the $(n-1)$-Hausdorff measure.*

(2) *As observed in* [**29**], *the results in* [**18**] *suggest that the behavior of nodal sets in the classically forbidden region could be very different from the one in the classically allowed region.*

(3) *Under the assumptions of Proposition* 7.12, *one gets from Theorem 1.1 in* [**1**] *that the order of a critical point of the zero set of an eigenfunction of* H_V *associated with* λ *in the classically permitted region is at most of order* $\lambda^{\frac{1}{2}+\frac{1}{m}}$. *Let us emphasize that here no assumption of analyticity for* V *is used. On the other hand, note that using Courant's theorem and Euler's and Weyl's formulas, one can prove that the number of critical points in the classically allowed region is at most of order* $\lambda^{1+\frac{2}{m}}$. *When* $m = 2$, *we can verify from the results in Section* 6 *that this upper bound cannot be improved in general.*

(4) *For nodal sets in forbidden regions, see* [**8**].

Acknowledgements

The authors would like to thank P. Charron for providing an earlier copy of [**9**], T. Hoffmann-Ostenhof for pointing out [**26**], J. Leydold for providing a copy of his master degree thesis [**26**], Long Jin for enlightening discussions concerning [**29**] and Section 7, I. Polterovich for pointing out [**9**], as well as D. Jakobson and M. Persson-Sundqvist for useful comments. During the preparation of this paper, B. H. was Simons foundation visiting fellow at the Isaac Newton Institute in Cambridge. Finally, the authors would like to thank the referee for his remarks which helped improve the paper.

References

[1] Laurent Bakri and Jean-Baptiste Casteras, *Quantitative uniqueness for Schrödinger operator with regular potentials*, Math. Methods Appl. Sci. **37** (2014), no. 13, 1992–2008, DOI 10.1002/mma.2951. MR3245115

[2] Pierre Bérard and Bernard Helffer, *Dirichlet eigenfunctions of the square membrane: Courant's property, and A. Stern's and Å. Pleijel's analyses*, Analysis and geometry, Springer Proc. Math. Stat., vol. 127, Springer, Cham, 2015, pp. 69–114, DOI 10.1007/978-3-319-17443-3_6. MR3445517

[3] P. Bérard and B. Helffer. On the number of nodal domains for the 2D isotropic quantum harmonic oscillator, an extension of results of A. Stern. arXiv:1409.2333v1 (September 8, 2014).

[4] P. Bérard and B. Helffer, *A. Stern's analysis of the nodal sets of some families of spherical harmonics revisited*, Monatsh. Math. **180** (2016), no. 3, 435–468, DOI 10.1007/s00605-015-0788-6. MR3513215

[5] P. Bérard and B. Helffer. Edited extracts from Antonie Stern's thesis. Séminaire de Théorie spectrale et géométrie, Institut Fourier, Grenoble, 32 (2014-2015), 39–72.

[6] Jochen Brüning and Dieter Gromes, *Über die Länge der Knotenlinien schwingender Membranen* (German), Math. Z. **124** (1972), 79–82, DOI 10.1007/BF01142586. MR0287202

[7] Jochen Brüning, *Über Knoten von Eigenfunktionen des Laplace-Beltrami-Operators* (German), Math. Z. **158** (1978), no. 1, 15–21, DOI 10.1007/BF01214561. MR0478247

[8] Yaiza Canzani and John A. Toth, *Nodal sets of Schrödinger eigenfunctions in forbidden regions*, Ann. Henri Poincaré **17** (2016), no. 11, 3063–3087, DOI 10.1007/s00023-016-0488-3. MR3556516

[9] P. Charron. On Pleijel's theorem for the isotropic harmonic oscillator. Mémoire de Maîtrise, Université de Montréal (June 2015).

[10] P. Charron. A Pleijel type theorem for the quantum harmonic oscillator. To appear in Journal of Spectral Theory. arXiv:1512.07880.

[11] P. Charron, B. Helffer and T. Hoffmann-Ostenhof. Pleijel's theorem for Schrödinger operators with radial potentials. To appear in Annales mathématiques du Québec. arXiv:1604.08372.

[12] R. Courant. Ein allgemeiner Satz zur Theorie der Eigenfunktionen selbstadjungierter Differentialausdrücke. Nachr. Ges. Göttingen (1923), 81-84.

[13] R. Courant and D. Hilbert. Methods of Mathematical Physics. Volume 1. First English edition. Translated and revised from the German original, Winheim 2004.

[14] Harold Donnelly, *Counting nodal domains in Riemannian manifolds*, Ann. Global Anal. Geom. **46** (2014), no. 1, 57–61, DOI 10.1007/s10455-013-9408-7. MR3205801

[15] Harold Donnelly and Charles Fefferman, *Nodal sets of eigenfunctions on Riemannian manifolds*, Invent. Math. **93** (1988), no. 1, 161–183, DOI 10.1007/BF01393691. MR943927

[16] Alexandre Eremenko, Dmitry Jakobson, and Nikolai Nadirashvili, *On nodal sets and nodal domains on S^2 and $\mathbb{R}^2$* (English, with English and French summaries), Ann. Inst. Fourier (Grenoble) **57** (2007), no. 7, 2345–2360. Festival Yves Colin de Verdière. MR2394544

[17] G. Gauthier-Shalom and K. Przybytkowski. Description of a nodal set on $\mathbb{T}^2$. McGill University Research Report 2006 (unpublished).

[18] Boris Hanin, Steve Zelditch, and Peng Zhou, *Nodal sets of random eigenfunctions for the isotropic harmonic oscillator*, Int. Math. Res. Not. IMRN **13** (2015), 4813–4839, DOI 10.1093/imrn/rnu071. MR3439093

[19] B. Helffer, T. Hoffmann-Ostenhof, and S. Terracini, *Nodal domains and spectral minimal partitions*, Ann. Inst. H. Poincaré Anal. Non Linéaire **26** (2009), no. 1, 101–138, DOI 10.1016/j.anihpc.2007.07.004. MR2483815

[20] B. Helffer and D. Robert, *Calcul fonctionnel par la transformation de Mellin et opérateurs admissibles* (French, with English summary), J. Funct. Anal. **53** (1983), no. 3, 246–268, DOI 10.1016/0022-1236(83)90034-4. MR724029

[21] B. Helffer and J. Sjöstrand, *Multiple wells in the semiclassical limit. I*, Comm. Partial Differential Equations **9** (1984), no. 4, 337–408, DOI 10.1080/03605308408820335. MR740094

[22] Don Hinton, *Sturm's 1836 oscillation results evolution of the theory*, Sturm-Liouville theory, Birkhäuser, Basel, 2005, pp. 1–27, DOI 10.1007/3-7643-7359-8_1. MR2145075

[23] Lars Hörmander, *On the asymptotic distribution of the eigenvalues of pseudodifferential operators in* $\mathbf{R}^n$, Ark. Mat. **17** (1979), no. 2, 297–313, DOI 10.1007/BF02385475. MR608322

[24] R.S. Laugesen. Spectral Theory of Partial Differential Equations. University of Illinois, Urbana-Champain 2014. `https://wiki.cites.illinois.edu/wiki/display/MATH595STP/Math+595+STP`

[25] Hans Lewy, *On the minimum number of domains in which the nodal lines of spherical harmonics divide the sphere*, Comm. Partial Differential Equations **2** (1977), no. 12, 1233–1244, DOI 10.1080/03605307708820059. MR0477199

[26] J. Leydold. Knotenlinien und Knotengebiete von Eigenfunktionen. Diplomarbeit 1989, University of Vienna, Austria. Unpublished, available at `http://othes.univie.ac.at/34443/`

[27] Josef Leydold, *On the number of nodal domains of spherical harmonics*, Topology **35** (1996), no. 2, 301–321, DOI 10.1016/0040-9383(95)00028-3. MR1380499

[28] A. Logunov and E. Malinnikova. Nodal sets of Laplace eigenfunctions: estimates of the Hausdorff measure in dimension two and three. arXiv:1605.02595.

[29] Long Jin, *Semiclassical Cauchy estimates and applications*, Trans. Amer. Math. Soc. **369** (2017), no. 2, 975–995, DOI 10.1090/tran/6715. MR3572261

[30] Åke Pleijel, *Remarks on Courant's nodal line theorem*, Comm. Pure Appl. Math. **9** (1956), 543–550, DOI 10.1002/cpa.3160090324. MR0080861

[31] Iosif Polterovich, *Pleijel's nodal domain theorem for free membranes*, Proc. Amer. Math. Soc. **137** (2009), no. 3, 1021–1024, DOI 10.1090/S0002-9939-08-09596-8. MR2457442

[32] D. Robert, *Propriétés spectrales d'opérateurs pseudo-différentiels* (French), Comm. Partial Differential Equations **3** (1978), no. 9, 755–826, DOI 10.1080/03605307808820077. MR504628

[33] Jimena Royo-Letelier, *Segregation and symmetry breaking of strongly coupled two-component Bose-Einstein condensates in a harmonic trap*, Calc. Var. Partial Differential Equations **49** (2014), no. 1-2, 103–124, DOI 10.1007/s00526-012-0571-7. MR3148108

[34] Christopher D. Sogge and Steve Zelditch, *Lower bounds on the Hausdorff measure of nodal sets*, Math. Res. Lett. **18** (2011), no. 1, 25–37, DOI 10.4310/MRL.2011.v18.n1.a3. MR2770580

[35] Christopher D. Sogge and Steve Zelditch, *Lower bounds on the Hausdorff measure of nodal sets II*, Math. Res. Lett. **19** (2012), no. 6, 1361–1364, DOI 10.4310/MRL.2012.v19.n6.a14. MR3091613

[36] A. Stern. Bemerkungen über asymptotisches Verhalten von Eigenwerten und Eigenfunktionen. Inaugural-Dissertation zur Erlangung der Doktorwürde der Hohen Mathematisch-Naturwissenschaftlichen Fakultät der Georg August-Universität zu Göttingen (30 Juli 1924). Druck der Dieterichschen Universitäts-Buchdruckerei (W. Fr. Kaestner). Göttingen, 1925. Partial extracts in the above reference [**5**].

[37] Gábor Szegő, *Orthogonal polynomials*, 4th ed., American Mathematical Society, Providence, R.I., 1975. American Mathematical Society, Colloquium Publications, Vol. XXIII. MR0372517

[38] Maciej Zworski, *Semiclassical analysis*, Graduate Studies in Mathematics, vol. 138, American Mathematical Society, Providence, RI, 2012. MR2952218

Institut Fourier, Université Grenoble Alpes and CNRS, B.P.74, F38402 Saint Martin d'Hères Cedex, France

E-mail address: pierrehberard@gmail.com

Laboratoire Jean Leray, Université de Nantes and CNRS, F44322 Nantes Cedex France — and — Laboratoire de Mathématiques, Univ. Paris-Sud 11

E-mail address: Bernard.Helffer@univ-nantes.fr

Contemporary Mathematics
Volume **700**, 2017
http://dx.doi.org/10.1090/conm/700/14185

Numerical solution of linear eigenvalue problems

Jessica Bosch and Chen Greif

Abstract. We review numerical methods for computing eigenvalues of matrices. We start by considering the computation of the dominant eigenpair of a general dense matrix using the power method, and then generalize to orthogonal iterations and the QR iteration with shifts. We also consider divide-and-conquer algorithms for tridiagonal matrices. The second part of this survey involves the computation of eigenvalues of large and sparse matrices. The Lanczos and Arnoldi methods are developed and described within the context of Krylov subspace eigensolvers. We also briefly present the idea of the Jacobi–Davidson method.

1. Introduction

Eigenvalue problems form one of the central problems in Numerical Linear Algebra. They arise in many areas of sciences and engineering. In this survey, we study linear eigenvalue problems. The standard algebraic eigenvalue problem has the form

$$\boldsymbol{Ax} = \lambda \boldsymbol{x}.$$

We consider real eigenvalue problems, i.e., $\boldsymbol{A} \in \mathbb{R}^{n \times n}$. In some places we will use the notion of complex matrices, as they are crucial in mathematical as well as computational aspects of eigenvalue solvers. There is a wide range of publications dealing with numerical methods for solving eigenvalue problems, e.g., [**22, 32, 39, 47, 54, 55, 62, 66**]. Typically, eigensolvers are classified into methods for symmetric (or Hermitian) and nonsymmetric (or non-Hermitian) matrices, or methods for small, dense matrices and large, sparse matrices.
This survey reviews popular methods for computing eigenvalues of a given matrix. It follows a minicourse presented by the second author at the 2015 Summer School on "Geometric and Computational Spectral Theory" at the Université de Montréal, and can be viewed as a set of comprehensive lecture notes.

When it comes to numerical computation of eigenvalues, it is reasonable to classify eigensolvers by the size and the nonzero pattern of the matrix. As opposed to the solution of linear systems, where it is possible to obtain a solution within a finite number of steps, most eigenvalue computations (except trivial cases such as a diagonal or a triangular matrix) require an iterative process. For matrices that are not particularly large and do not have a specific nonzero structure, eigensolvers are

2010 *Mathematics Subject Classification.* Primary 65F15.

often based on matrix decompositions. One may be interested in a small number of the eigenvalues and/or eigenvectors, or all of them, and there are methods that are available for accomplishing the stated goal. On the other hand, when the matrix is large and sparse, it is rare to seek the entire spectrum; in most cases we are interested in just a few eigenvalues and eigenvectors, and typical methods are based on matrix-vector products rather than matrix decompositions. Interestingly, despite the fact that all processes of eigenvalue computations are iterative, methods that are based on matrix decompositions are often referred to as *direct*, whereas methods that are based on matrix-vector products are termed *iterative*. This slight abuse of terminology is nonetheless widely understood and typically does not cause any confusion.

It is a bit ambitious to talk in general terms about a recipe for solution of eigenvalue problems, but it is legitimate to identify a few main components. A typical eigensolver starts with applying similarity transformations and transforming the matrix into one that has an appealing nonzero structure: for example tridiagonal if the original matrix was symmetric. Once this is accomplished, an iterative process is pursued, whereby repeated orthogonal similarity transformations are applied to get us closer and closer to a diagonal or triangular form. For large and sparse matrices, an additional component, generally speaking, in state of the art methods, is the transformation of the problem to a small and dense one on a projected subspace.

This survey devotes a significant amount of space to elaborating on the above principles. It is organized as follows. In Section 2, we briefly review basic concepts of Numerical Linear Algebra that are related to eigenvalue problems. We start with presenting methods for computing a few or all eigenvalues for small to moderate-sized matrices in Section 3. This is followed by a review of eigenvalue solvers for large and sparse matrices in Section 4. Conclusions complete the paper.

2. Background in Numerical Linear Algebra

2.1. Theoretical basics. We begin our survey with a review of basic concepts in Numerical Linear Algebra. We introduce some notation used throughout the survey.

Let $\boldsymbol{A} \in \mathbb{C}^{m\times n}$. The *kernel* or *nullspace* of $\boldsymbol{A}$ is given as

$$\ker(\boldsymbol{A}) = \{\boldsymbol{x} \in \mathbb{C}^n \colon \boldsymbol{A}\boldsymbol{x} = \boldsymbol{0}\}.$$

Another important subspace, which is often related to the kernel, is the *range* of $\boldsymbol{A}$, which is given as

$$\operatorname{ran}(\boldsymbol{A}) = \{\boldsymbol{A}\boldsymbol{x} \colon \boldsymbol{x} \in \mathbb{C}^n\}.$$

The *rank* of $\boldsymbol{A}$ is the maximal number of linearly independent columns (or rows), i.e.,

$$\operatorname{rank}(\boldsymbol{A}) = \dim\left(\operatorname{ran}(\boldsymbol{A})\right).$$

It holds $n = \operatorname{rank}(\boldsymbol{A}) + \dim\left(\ker(\boldsymbol{A})\right)$. $\boldsymbol{A}$ is called *rank-deficient* if $\operatorname{rank}(\boldsymbol{A}) < \min\{m, n\}$.

In what follows, we consider real matrices $\boldsymbol{A} \in \mathbb{R}^{n\times n}$ if not stated otherwise.

DEFINITION 2.1 (Invertibility). $\boldsymbol{A}$ is called *invertible* or *nonsingular* if there exists a matrix $\boldsymbol{B} \in \mathbb{R}^{n\times n}$ such that

$$\boldsymbol{A}\boldsymbol{B} = \boldsymbol{B}\boldsymbol{A} = \boldsymbol{I}.$$

Here, $\boldsymbol{I} \in \mathbb{R}^{n\times n}$ is the *identity matrix*. The *inverse* of $\boldsymbol{A}$ is uniquely determined, and we denote it by $\boldsymbol{A}^{-1}$.

Related to the inverse and a matrix norm $\|\cdot\|$ is the *condition number*, which is defined for a general square matrix $\boldsymbol{A}$ as

$$\kappa(\boldsymbol{A}) = \|\boldsymbol{A}\|\,\|\boldsymbol{A}^{-1}\|.$$

In general, if $\kappa(\boldsymbol{A})$ is large[1], then $\boldsymbol{A}$ is said to be an *ill-conditioned* matrix. Useful matrix norms include the well-known *p-norms* or the *Frobenius norm* $\|\cdot\|_F$, which is given as

$$\|\boldsymbol{A}\|_F = \sqrt{\sum_{i=1}^{n}\sum_{j=1}^{n} |a_{i,j}|^2},$$

where $a_{i,j}$ is the (i,j) entry of $\boldsymbol{A}$.
Let us come to the heart of this paper. The *algebraic eigenvalue problem* has the following form:

DEFINITION 2.2 (Algebraic Eigenvalue Problem). $\lambda \in \mathbb{C}$ is called an *eigenvalue* of $\boldsymbol{A}$ if there exists a vector $\boldsymbol{0} \neq \boldsymbol{x} \in \mathbb{C}^n$ such that

$$\boldsymbol{A}\boldsymbol{x} = \lambda\boldsymbol{x}.$$

The vector $\boldsymbol{x}$ is called a (right) *eigenvector* of $\boldsymbol{A}$ associated with λ. We call the pair $(\lambda, \boldsymbol{x})$ an *eigenpair* of $\boldsymbol{A}$. The set of all eigenvalues of $\boldsymbol{A}$ is called the *spectrum* of $\boldsymbol{A}$ and is denoted by $\lambda(\boldsymbol{A})$.

Note from the above definition that real matrices can have complex eigenpairs. Geometrically, the action of a matrix $\boldsymbol{A}$ expands or shrinks any vector lying in the direction of an eigenvector of $\boldsymbol{A}$ by a scalar factor. This scalar factor is given by the corresponding eigenvalue of $\boldsymbol{A}$.

REMARK 2.3. Similarly, a left eigenvector of $\boldsymbol{A}$ associated with the eigenvalue λ is defined as a vector $\boldsymbol{0} \neq \boldsymbol{y} \in \mathbb{C}^n$ that satisfies $\boldsymbol{y}^*\boldsymbol{A} = \lambda\boldsymbol{y}^*$. Here, $\boldsymbol{y}^* = \bar{\boldsymbol{y}}^T$ is the *conjugate transpose* of $\boldsymbol{y}$.

Throughout the survey, we use the term *eigenvector* for a right eigenvector.
The eigenvalues of $\boldsymbol{A}$ can be used to determine the invertibility of $\boldsymbol{A}$.

DEFINITION 2.4 (Determinant). If $\lambda(\boldsymbol{A}) = \{\lambda_1, \ldots, \lambda_n\}$, then the *determinant of* $\boldsymbol{A}$ *is given as*

$$\det(\boldsymbol{A}) = \prod_{i=1}^{n} \lambda_i.$$

$\boldsymbol{A}$ is nonsingular if and only if $\det(\boldsymbol{A}) \neq 0$.
Another way to define eigenvalues is the following:

DEFINITION 2.5 (Characteristic Polynomial). The polynomial

$$p_{\boldsymbol{A}}(x) = \det(\boldsymbol{A} - x\boldsymbol{I})$$

is called the *characteristic polynomial* of $\boldsymbol{A}$. It is a polynomial of degree n. The roots of $p_{\boldsymbol{A}}(x)$ are the eigenvalues of $\boldsymbol{A}$.

---

[1] Of course, this depends on the definition of "large"; see, e.g., [**22**, Chap. 3.5].

A useful concept for eigenvalues solvers is the *Rayleigh quotient*:

DEFINITION 2.6 (Rayleigh Quotient). Let $\mathbf{0} \neq \boldsymbol{z} \in \mathbb{C}^n$. The *Rayleigh quotient* of $\boldsymbol{A}$ and $\boldsymbol{z}$ is defined by

$$R_{\boldsymbol{A}}(\boldsymbol{z}) = \frac{\boldsymbol{z}^* \boldsymbol{A} \boldsymbol{z}}{\boldsymbol{z}^* \boldsymbol{z}}.$$

Note that if $\boldsymbol{z}$ is an eigenvector of $\boldsymbol{A}$, then the Rayleigh quotient is the corresponding eigenvalue.
Another way to express the eigenvalue problem in Definition 2.2 is that $(\lambda, \boldsymbol{x})$ is an eigenpair of $\boldsymbol{A}$ if and only if $\mathbf{0} \neq \boldsymbol{x} \in \ker(\boldsymbol{A} - \lambda \boldsymbol{I})$. Based on this kernel, we can define the *eigenspace* of $\boldsymbol{A}$:

DEFINITION 2.7 (Eigenspace).

$$\mathcal{E}_\lambda(\boldsymbol{A}) = \ker(\boldsymbol{A} - \lambda \boldsymbol{I})$$

is the *eigenspace* of $\boldsymbol{A}$ corresponding to λ.

The following concept of *invariant subspaces* bears similarities to the eigenvalue problem.

DEFINITION 2.8 (Invariant Subspace). A subspace $\mathcal{S} \subset \mathbb{C}^n$ is said to be *invariant* under a matrix $\boldsymbol{A} \in \mathbb{C}^{n \times n}$ ($\boldsymbol{A}$-invariant) if $\boldsymbol{A}\mathcal{S} \subset \mathcal{S}$.

DEFINITION 2.9. Let $\boldsymbol{A} \in \mathbb{C}^{n \times n}$, $\mathcal{S} \subset \mathbb{C}^n$, and $\boldsymbol{S} \in \mathbb{C}^{n \times k}$ with $k = \operatorname{rank}(\boldsymbol{S}) = \dim(\mathcal{S}) \leq n$ and $\mathcal{S} = \operatorname{ran}(\boldsymbol{S})$. Then, $\mathcal{S}$ is $\boldsymbol{A}$-invariant if and only if there exists a matrix $\boldsymbol{B} \in \mathbb{C}^{k \times k}$ such that

$$\boldsymbol{A}\boldsymbol{S} = \boldsymbol{S}\boldsymbol{B}.$$

REMARK 2.10. Using Definition 2.9, it is easy to show the following relations:

- If $(\lambda, \boldsymbol{x})$ is an eigenpair of $\boldsymbol{B}$, then $(\lambda, \boldsymbol{S}\boldsymbol{x})$ is an eigenpair of $\boldsymbol{A}$. Hence, $\lambda(\boldsymbol{B}) \subset \lambda(\boldsymbol{A})$.
- If $k = n$, then $\boldsymbol{S}$ is invertible and hence

  $$\boldsymbol{A} = \boldsymbol{S}\boldsymbol{B}\boldsymbol{S}^{-1}.$$

  This means $\boldsymbol{A}$ and $\boldsymbol{B}$ are *similar* and $\lambda(\boldsymbol{B}) = \lambda(\boldsymbol{A})$. This concept is introduced next.

Most of the presented algorithms will transform a matrix $\boldsymbol{A}$ into simpler forms, such as diagonal or triangular matrices, in order to simplify the original eigenvalue problem. Transformations that preserve the eigenvalues of matrices are called *similarity transformations.*

DEFINITION 2.11 (Similarity Transformation). Two matrices $\boldsymbol{A}, \boldsymbol{B} \in \mathbb{C}^{n \times n}$ are said to be *similar* if there exists a nonsingular matrix $\boldsymbol{C} \in \mathbb{C}^{n \times n}$ such that

$$\boldsymbol{A} = \boldsymbol{C}\boldsymbol{B}\boldsymbol{C}^{-1}.$$

The mapping $\boldsymbol{B} \to \boldsymbol{A}$ is called a *similarity transformation.* The similarity of $\boldsymbol{A}$ and $\boldsymbol{B}$ implies that they have the same eigenvalues. If $(\lambda, \boldsymbol{x})$ is an eigenpair of $\boldsymbol{B}$, then $(\lambda, \boldsymbol{C}\boldsymbol{x})$ is an eigenpair of $\boldsymbol{A}$.

The simplest form to which a matrix can be transformed is a diagonal matrix. But as we will see, this is not always possible.

DEFINITION 2.12 (Diagonalizability). If $\boldsymbol{A} \in \mathbb{C}^{n \times n}$ is similar to a diagonal matrix, then $\boldsymbol{A}$ is said to be *diagonalizable.*

A similarity transformation in which $\boldsymbol{C}$ is orthogonal (or unitary), i.e., $\boldsymbol{C}^T\boldsymbol{C} = \boldsymbol{I}$ (or $\boldsymbol{C}^*\boldsymbol{C} = \boldsymbol{I}$), is called *orthogonal (or unitary) similarity transformation.* Unitary/orthogonal similarity transformations play a key role in numerical computations since $\|\boldsymbol{C}\|_2 = 1$. Considering the calculation of similarity transformations, it can be shown (cf. [**22**, Chap. 7.1.5]) that the roundoff error $\boldsymbol{E}$ satisfies

$$\|\boldsymbol{E}\| \approx \epsilon_{\text{machine}}\, \kappa_2\,(\boldsymbol{C})\|\boldsymbol{A}\|_2.$$

Here, $\epsilon_{\text{machine}}$ is the *machine precision*[2] and $\kappa_2(\boldsymbol{C})$ the condition number of $\boldsymbol{C}$ with respect to the 2-norm. In particular, $\kappa_2(\boldsymbol{C})$ is the error gain. Therefore, if the similarity transformation is unitary, we get

$$\|\boldsymbol{E}\| \approx \epsilon_{\text{machine}}\|\boldsymbol{A}\|_2$$

and hence no amplification of error.

THEOREM 2.13 (Unitary Diagonalizability; see [**22**, Cor. 7.1.4].). *$\boldsymbol{A} \in \mathbb{C}^{n\times n}$ is unitarily diagonalizable if and only if it is normal ($\boldsymbol{A}^*\boldsymbol{A} = \boldsymbol{A}\boldsymbol{A}^*$).*

Now, let us show the connection between a similarity transformation of a matrix $\boldsymbol{A}$ and its eigenpairs: It follows from Definition 2.5 and the Fundamental Theorem of Algebra that $\boldsymbol{A}$ has n (not necessarily distinct) eigenvalues. If we denote the n eigenpairs by $(\lambda_1, \boldsymbol{x}_1), \ldots, (\lambda_n, \boldsymbol{x}_n)$, i.e. $\boldsymbol{A}\boldsymbol{x}_i = \lambda_i\boldsymbol{x}_i$ for $i = 1, \ldots, n$, we can write

$$\boldsymbol{A}\boldsymbol{X} = \boldsymbol{X}\boldsymbol{\Lambda}, \tag{2.1}$$

where $\boldsymbol{\Lambda} = \operatorname{diag}(\lambda_i)_{i=1,\ldots,n} \in \mathbb{C}^{n\times n}$ is a diagonal matrix containing the eigenvalues, and $\boldsymbol{X} = [\boldsymbol{x}_1|\ldots|\boldsymbol{x}_n] \in \mathbb{C}^{n\times n}$ is a matrix whose columns are formed by the eigenvectors. This looks almost as a similarity transformation. In fact, the "only" additional ingredient we need is the invertibility of $\boldsymbol{X}$. Under the assumption that $\boldsymbol{X}$ is nonsingular, we obtain $\boldsymbol{X}^{-1}\boldsymbol{A}\boldsymbol{X} = \boldsymbol{\Lambda}$, and hence, $\boldsymbol{A}$ and $\boldsymbol{\Lambda}$ are similar. But when can we expect of $\boldsymbol{X}$ to be nonsingular? To discuss this, we introduce some terminology:

DEFINITION 2.14 (Multiplicity). Let λ be an eigenvalue of $\boldsymbol{A}$.

- λ has *algebraic multiplicity* m^a, if it is a root of multiplicity m^a of the characteristic polynomial $p_{\boldsymbol{A}}$.
- If $m^a = 1$, then λ is called *simple*. Otherwise, λ is said to be *multiple*.
- The *geometric multiplicity* m^g of λ is defined as the dimension of the associated eigenspace, i.e., $m^g = \dim(\mathcal{E}_\lambda(\boldsymbol{A}))$. It is the maximum number of independent eigenvectors associated with λ.
- It holds $m^g \le m^a$.
- If $m^g < m^a$, then λ and $\boldsymbol{A}$ are called *defective* or *non-diagonalizable*.

Note that if all eigenvalues of $\boldsymbol{A}$ are simple, then they are distinct. Now, we can state a result about the nonsingularity of the eigenvector matrix $\boldsymbol{X}$ in (2.1):

THEOREM 2.15 (Diagonal Form; see [**22**, Cor. 7.1.8].). *Let $\boldsymbol{A} \in \mathbb{R}^{n\times n}$ with eigenvalues $\lambda_1, \ldots, \lambda_n \in \mathbb{C}$. $\boldsymbol{A}$ is nondefective if and only if there exists a nonsingular matrix $\boldsymbol{X} \in \mathbb{C}^{n\times n}$ such that*

$$\boldsymbol{X}^{-1}\boldsymbol{A}\boldsymbol{X} = \operatorname{diag}(\lambda_i)_{i=1,\ldots,n}.$$

[2]The machine precision is $\epsilon_{\text{machine}} = 2^{-53} \approx 1.11 \cdot 10^{-16}$ in the double precision IEEE floating point format and $\epsilon_{\text{machine}} = 2^{-24} \approx 5.96 \cdot 10^{-6}$ in the single precision IEEE floating point format. For more details, we refer to, e.g., [**27, 37, 66**].

The similarity transformation given in Theorem 2.15 transforms $\boldsymbol{A}$ into a diagonal matrix whose entries reveal the eigenvalues of $\boldsymbol{A}$.
We have seen that a similarity transformation to a diagonal matrix is not always possible. Before we come to the next similarity transformation, we introduce the concept of *deflation* – the process of breaking down an eigenvalue problem into smaller eigenvalue problems.

THEOREM 2.16 (See [**22**, Lemma 7.1.3].). *Let* $\boldsymbol{A} \in \mathbb{C}^{n\times n}$, $\boldsymbol{S} \in \mathbb{C}^{n\times k}$ *with* $\mathrm{rank}(\boldsymbol{S}) = k < n$ *and* $\boldsymbol{B} \in \mathbb{C}^{k\times k}$ *such that*

$$\boldsymbol{AS} = \boldsymbol{SB},$$

i.e., $\mathrm{ran}(\boldsymbol{S})$ *is an* $\boldsymbol{A}$*-invariant subspace. Then, there exists a unitary* $\boldsymbol{Q} \in \mathbb{C}^{n\times n}$ *such that*

$$\boldsymbol{Q}^*\boldsymbol{AQ} = \boldsymbol{T} = \begin{bmatrix} \boldsymbol{T}_{11} & \boldsymbol{T}_{12} \\ \boldsymbol{0} & \boldsymbol{T}_{22} \end{bmatrix}$$

and

$$\begin{aligned} \lambda(\boldsymbol{T}) &= \lambda(\boldsymbol{T}_{11}) \cup \lambda(\boldsymbol{T}_{22}), \\ \lambda(\boldsymbol{T}_{11}) &= \lambda(\boldsymbol{A}) \cap \lambda(\boldsymbol{B}) \end{aligned}$$

with $\boldsymbol{T}_{11} \in \mathbb{C}^{k\times k}$.

From Theorem 2.16, we obtain a similarity transformation that transforms a matrix $\boldsymbol{A}$ into an upper triangular matrix whose diagonal entries reveal the eigenvalues of $\boldsymbol{A}$. Such a decomposition always exists.

THEOREM 2.17 (Schur Decomposition; see [**22**, Theor. 7.1.3].). *Given* $\boldsymbol{A} \in \mathbb{C}^{n\times n}$ *with eigenvalues* $\lambda_1, \ldots, \lambda_n \in \mathbb{C}$. *Then, there exists a unitary matrix* $\boldsymbol{Q} \in \mathbb{C}^{n\times n}$ *such that*

$$\boldsymbol{Q}^*\boldsymbol{AQ} = \boldsymbol{T} = \boldsymbol{D} + \boldsymbol{N},$$

where $\boldsymbol{D} = \mathrm{diag}(\lambda_i)_{i=1,\ldots,n}$, *and* $\boldsymbol{N} \in \mathbb{C}^{n\times n}$ *is strictly upper triangular. Moreover,* $\boldsymbol{Q}$ *can be chosen such that the eigenvalues* λ_i *appear in any order in* $\boldsymbol{D}$.

The transformation in Theorem 2.17 deals with a complex matrix $\boldsymbol{Q}$ even when $\boldsymbol{A}$ is real. A slight variation of the Schur decomposition shows that complex arithmetic can be avoided in this case. This is based on the fact that complex eigenvalues always occur in complex conjugate pairs, i.e., if $(\lambda, \boldsymbol{x})$ is an eigenpair of $\boldsymbol{A} \in \mathbb{R}^{n\times n}$, then $(\bar{\lambda}, \bar{\boldsymbol{x}})$ is an eigenpair of $\boldsymbol{A}$.

THEOREM 2.18 (Real Schur Decomposition; see [**22**, Theor. 7.4.1].). *Let* $\boldsymbol{A} \in \mathbb{R}^{n\times n}$ *with eigenvalues* $\lambda_1, \ldots, \lambda_n \in \mathbb{C}$. *Then, there exists an orthogonal matrix* $\boldsymbol{Q} \in \mathbb{R}^{n\times n}$ *such that*

$$\boldsymbol{Q}^T\boldsymbol{AQ} = \boldsymbol{T} = \begin{bmatrix} \boldsymbol{T}_{1,1} & \cdots & \boldsymbol{T}_{1,m} \\ & \ddots & \vdots \\ & & \boldsymbol{T}_{m,m} \end{bmatrix},$$

where $\boldsymbol{T} \in \mathbb{R}^{n\times n}$ *is quasi-upper triangular. The diagonal blocks* $\boldsymbol{T}_{i,i}$ *are either* 1×1 *or* 2×2 *matrices. A* 1×1 *block corresponds to a real eigenvalue* $\lambda_j \in \mathbb{R}$. *A* 2×2 *block corresponds to a pair of complex conjugate eigenvalues. For a complex conjugate eigenvalue pair* $\lambda_k = \mu + \imath\nu$, $\lambda_l = \mu - \imath\nu$, $\boldsymbol{T}_{i,i}$ *has the form*

$$\boldsymbol{T}_{i,i} = \begin{bmatrix} \mu & \nu \\ -\nu & \mu \end{bmatrix}.$$

Moreover, $\boldsymbol{Q}$ can be chosen such that the diagonal blocks $\boldsymbol{T}_{i,i}$ appear in any order in $\boldsymbol{T}$.

The next similarity transformation we present transforms a matrix $\boldsymbol{A}$ into *upper Hessenberg* form. Such a decomposition always exists and will play an important role in eigenvalue solvers for nonsymmetric matrices.

THEOREM 2.19 (Hessenberg Decomposition). *Let $\boldsymbol{A} \in \mathbb{C}^{n\times n}$. Then, there exists a unitary matrix $\boldsymbol{Q} \in \mathbb{C}^{n\times n}$ such that*

$$\boldsymbol{Q}^*\boldsymbol{A}\boldsymbol{Q} = \boldsymbol{H} = \begin{bmatrix} h_{1,1} & h_{1,2} & h_{1,3} & \cdots & h_{1,n} \\ h_{2,1} & h_{2,2} & h_{2,3} & \cdots & h_{2,n} \\ 0 & h_{3,2} & h_{3,3} & \ddots & \vdots \\ \vdots & \ddots & \ddots & \ddots & h_{n-1,n} \\ 0 & \cdots & 0 & h_{n,n-1} & h_{n,n} \end{bmatrix}.$$

$\boldsymbol{H}$ is called an upper Hessenberg matrix. Further, $\boldsymbol{H}$ is said to be unreduced if $h_{j+1,j} \neq 0$ for all $j = 1, \ldots, n-1$.

From a theoretical point of view, one of the most important similarity transformations is the *Jordan decomposition*, or *Jordan Canonical Form*.

THEOREM 2.20 (Jordan Decomposition; see [**22**, Theor. 7.1.9].). *Let $\boldsymbol{A} \in \mathbb{C}^{n\times n}$ with exactly p distinct eigenvalues $\lambda_1, \ldots, \lambda_p \in \mathbb{C}$ for $p \leq n$. Then, there exists a nonsingular matrix $\boldsymbol{X} \in \mathbb{C}^{n\times n}$ such that*

$$\boldsymbol{X}^{-1}\boldsymbol{A}\boldsymbol{X} = \begin{bmatrix} \boldsymbol{J}_1(\lambda_1) & & \\ & \ddots & \\ & & \boldsymbol{J}_p(\lambda_p) \end{bmatrix}.$$

Each block $\boldsymbol{J}_i(\lambda_i)$ has the block diagonal structure

$$\boldsymbol{J}_i(\lambda_i) = \begin{bmatrix} \boldsymbol{J}_{i,1}(\lambda_i) & & \\ & \ddots & \\ & & \boldsymbol{J}_{i,m_i^g}(\lambda_i) \end{bmatrix} \in \mathbb{C}^{m_i^a \times m_i^a}$$

with

$$\boldsymbol{J}_{i,k}(\lambda_i) = \begin{bmatrix} \lambda_i & 1 & & \\ & \ddots & \ddots & \\ & & \lambda_i & 1 \\ & & & \lambda_i \end{bmatrix} \in \mathbb{C}^{m_{i,k} \times m_{i,k}},$$

where m_i^a and m_i^g are the algebraic and geometric multiplicity of the eigenvalue λ_i. Each of the subblocks $\boldsymbol{J}_{i,k}(\lambda_i)$ is referred to as a Jordan block.

Unfortunately, from a computational point of view, the computation of the Jordan Canonical Form is numerically unstable.
An important and practical factorization is the *QR decomposition*:

DEFINITION 2.21 (QR Decomposition; see [**22**, Theor. 5.2.1].). Let $\boldsymbol{A} \in \mathbb{R}^{m\times n}$. Then, there exists an orthogonal $\boldsymbol{Q} \in \mathbb{R}^{m\times m}$ and an upper triangular $\boldsymbol{R} \in \mathbb{R}^{m\times n}$ such that

$$\boldsymbol{A} = \boldsymbol{Q}\boldsymbol{R}.$$

This concludes the theoretical part of the background study. Next, we are getting started with computational aspects.

2.2. First computational aspects. This section quickly reviews aspects of perturbation theory and illustrates possible difficulties in computing eigenvalues accurately. This is followed by a brief overview of different classes of methods for solving eigenvalue problems. Details about all mentioned methods are given in the upcoming sections.

First of all, it should be clear that in general we must iterate to find eigenvalues of a matrix: According to Definition 2.5, the eigenvalues of a matrix $\boldsymbol{A}$ are the roots of the characteristic polynomial $p_{\boldsymbol{A}}(x)$. In 1824, Abel proved that for polynomials of degree $n \geq 5$, there is no formula for its roots in terms of its coefficients that uses only the operations of addition, subtraction, multiplication, division, and taking kth roots. Hence, even if we could work in exact arithmetic, no computer would produce the exact roots of an arbitrarily polynomial in a finite number of steps. (This is different than direct methods for solving systems of linear equations such as Gaussian elimination.) Hence, computing the eigenvalues of any $n \times n$ matrix $\boldsymbol{A}$ requires an iterative process if $n \geq 5$.

As already indicated in the previous section, many methods are based on repeatedly performing *similarity transformations* to bring $\boldsymbol{A}$ into a simpler equivalent form. This typically means generating as many zero entries in the matrix as possible. The goal is eventually to perform a Schur decomposition. If the matrix is normal, then the Schur decomposition simplifies to a diagonal matrix (not only an upper triangular matrix), and this has implications in terms of stability of numerical computations. As part of the process, we often aim to reduce the matrix into tridiagonal form (symmetric case) or upper Hessenberg form (nonsymmetric case). *Deflation*, *projection*, and other tools can be incorporated and are extremely valuable.

Now, let us focus on the reduction of a matrix $\boldsymbol{A}$ to upper Hessenberg form. One way to accomplish this is the use of *Householder reflectors* (also called *Householder transformations*). They can be used to zero out selected components of a vector. Hence, by performing a sequence of Householder reflections on the columns of $\boldsymbol{A}$, we can transform $\boldsymbol{A}$ into a simpler form. Householder reflectors are matrices of the form

$$\boldsymbol{P} = \boldsymbol{I} - \frac{2}{\boldsymbol{v}^*\boldsymbol{v}}\boldsymbol{v}\boldsymbol{v}^*,$$

where $\boldsymbol{v} \in \mathbb{C}^n \setminus \{\boldsymbol{0}\}$. Householder matrices are Hermitian ($\boldsymbol{P} = \boldsymbol{P}^*$), unitary, and numerically stable. Geometrically, $\boldsymbol{P}$ applied to a vector $\boldsymbol{x}$ reflects it about the hyperplane $\text{span}\{\boldsymbol{v}\}^{\perp}$.

Assume we want to bring $\boldsymbol{A}$ into upper Hessenberg form. Then, the first step is to introduce zeros into all except the first two entries of the first column of $\boldsymbol{A}$. Let us denote by $\boldsymbol{x} = [a_{2,1}, \ldots, a_{n,1}]^T$ the part of the first column of $\boldsymbol{A}$ under consideration. We are looking for a vector $\boldsymbol{v} \in \mathbb{C}^{n-1} \setminus \{\boldsymbol{0}\}$ such that $\boldsymbol{P}\boldsymbol{x}$ results in a multiple of the first unit vector $\boldsymbol{e}_1$. This can be achieved with the ansatz $\boldsymbol{v} = \boldsymbol{x} \pm \|\boldsymbol{x}\|_2\boldsymbol{e}_1$, since this yields

$$\boldsymbol{P}\boldsymbol{x} = \mp\|\boldsymbol{x}\|_2\boldsymbol{e}_1.$$

Let us illustrate the action of $\boldsymbol{P}$ to the first column of $\boldsymbol{A}$:

$$\begin{bmatrix} a_{1,1} & a_{1,2} & \cdots & a_{1,n} \\ a_{2,1} & a_{2,2} & \cdots & a_{2,n} \\ a_{3,1} & a_{3,2} & \cdots & a_{3,n} \\ \vdots & \vdots & \ddots & \vdots \\ a_{n,1} & a_{n,2} & \cdots & a_{n,n} \end{bmatrix} \rightarrow \begin{bmatrix} a_{1,1} & a_{1,2} & \cdots & a_{1,n} \\ \mp\|\boldsymbol{x}\|_2 & a_{2,2} & \cdots & a_{2,n} \\ 0 & a_{3,2} & \cdots & a_{3,n} \\ \vdots & \vdots & \ddots & \vdots \\ 0 & a_{n,2} & \cdots & a_{n,n} \end{bmatrix}.$$

Note that the first step is not complete yet: Remember that, for a similarity transformation, we need to apply the Householder matrix twice, i.e., $\boldsymbol{P}^*\boldsymbol{A}\boldsymbol{P}$. Note that the right multiplication with $\boldsymbol{P}$ does not destroy the zeros:

$$\underbrace{\begin{bmatrix} * & * & \cdots & * \\ * & * & \cdots & * \\ * & * & \cdots & * \\ \vdots & \vdots & \ddots & \vdots \\ * & * & \cdots & * \end{bmatrix}}_{\boldsymbol{A}} \xrightarrow{\boldsymbol{P}^*\cdot} \underbrace{\begin{bmatrix} * & * & \cdots & * \\ * & * & \cdots & * \\ 0 & * & \cdots & * \\ \vdots & \vdots & \ddots & \vdots \\ 0 & * & \cdots & * \end{bmatrix}}_{\boldsymbol{P}^*\boldsymbol{A}} \xrightarrow{\cdot\boldsymbol{P}} \underbrace{\begin{bmatrix} * & * & \cdots & * \\ * & * & \cdots & * \\ 0 & * & \cdots & * \\ \vdots & \vdots & \ddots & \vdots \\ 0 & * & \cdots & * \end{bmatrix}}_{\boldsymbol{P}^*\boldsymbol{A}\boldsymbol{P}}.$$

Let us denote the Householder matrix in the first step by $\boldsymbol{P}_1$. The above procedure is repeated with the Householder matrix $\boldsymbol{P}_2$ to the second column of $\boldsymbol{P}_1^*\boldsymbol{A}\boldsymbol{P}_1$, then to the third column of $\boldsymbol{P}_2^*\boldsymbol{P}_1^*\boldsymbol{A}\boldsymbol{P}_1\boldsymbol{P}_2$ with the Householder matrix $\boldsymbol{P}_3$, and so on, until we end up with a matrix in upper Hessenberg form as given in Definition 2.19. Let us denote the Householder matrix in step i by $\boldsymbol{P}_i$. After $n-2$ steps, we obtain the upper Hessenberg form:

$$\underbrace{\boldsymbol{P}_{n-2}^*\cdots\boldsymbol{P}_1^*}_{\boldsymbol{P}^*}\,\boldsymbol{A}\,\underbrace{\boldsymbol{P}_1\cdots\boldsymbol{P}_{n-2}}_{\boldsymbol{P}} = \boldsymbol{H} = \begin{bmatrix} * & * & * & \cdots & * \\ * & * & * & \cdots & * \\ 0 & * & * & \ddots & \vdots \\ \vdots & \ddots & \ddots & \ddots & * \\ 0 & \cdots & 0 & * & * \end{bmatrix}.$$

REMARK 2.22. Here are a few additional comments about the process:

- In practice, one choses $\boldsymbol{v} = \boldsymbol{x} + \operatorname{sign}(x_1)\|\boldsymbol{x}\|_2\boldsymbol{e}_1$, where x_1 is the first entry of the vector $\boldsymbol{x}$ under consideration.
- Note that in each step i, the corresponding vector $\boldsymbol{x}_i$, and hence $\boldsymbol{v}_i$ and $\boldsymbol{P}_i$, shrink by one in size.
- The reduction of an $n \times n$ matrix to upper Hessenberg form via Householder reflections requires $\mathcal{O}(n^3)$ operations.

One may ask why do we first bring $\boldsymbol{A}$ to upper Hessenberg form and not immediately to triangular form using Householder reflections? In that case, the right multiplication with $\boldsymbol{P}$ would destroy the zeros previously introduced:

$$\underbrace{\begin{bmatrix} * & * & \cdots & * \\ * & * & \cdots & * \\ \vdots & \vdots & \ddots & \vdots \\ * & * & \cdots & * \end{bmatrix}}_{\boldsymbol{A}} \xrightarrow{\boldsymbol{P}^*\cdot} \underbrace{\begin{bmatrix} * & * & \cdots & * \\ 0 & * & \cdots & * \\ \vdots & \vdots & \ddots & \vdots \\ 0 & * & \cdots & * \end{bmatrix}}_{\boldsymbol{P}^*\boldsymbol{A}} \xrightarrow{\cdot\boldsymbol{P}} \underbrace{\begin{bmatrix} * & * & \cdots & * \\ * & * & \cdots & * \\ \vdots & \vdots & \ddots & \vdots \\ * & * & \cdots & * \end{bmatrix}}_{\boldsymbol{P}^*\boldsymbol{A}\boldsymbol{P}}.$$

This should not come as a surprise: we already knew from Abel (1824) that it is impossible to obtain a Schur form of $\boldsymbol{A}$ in a finite number of steps; see the beginning of this Section.

REMARK 2.23. If $\boldsymbol{A}$ is symmetric, the reduction to upper Hessenberg form turns into a tridiagonal matrix. That is because the right multiplication with $\boldsymbol{P}_i$ also introduces zeros above the diagonal:

$$\underset{\boldsymbol{A}}{\begin{bmatrix} * & * & * & \cdots & * \\ * & * & * & \cdots & * \\ * & * & * & \cdots & * \\ \vdots & \vdots & \vdots & \ddots & \vdots \\ * & * & * & \cdots & * \end{bmatrix}} \xrightarrow{\boldsymbol{P}_1^* \cdot} \underset{\boldsymbol{P}_1^*\boldsymbol{A}}{\begin{bmatrix} * & * & * & \cdots & * \\ * & * & * & \cdots & * \\ 0 & * & * & \cdots & * \\ \vdots & \vdots & \vdots & \ddots & \vdots \\ 0 & * & * & \cdots & * \end{bmatrix}} \xrightarrow{\cdot \boldsymbol{P}_1} \underset{\boldsymbol{P}_1^*\boldsymbol{A}\boldsymbol{P}_1}{\begin{bmatrix} * & * & 0 & \cdots & 0 \\ * & * & * & \cdots & * \\ 0 & * & * & \cdots & * \\ \vdots & \vdots & \vdots & \ddots & \vdots \\ 0 & * & * & \cdots & * \end{bmatrix}}.$$

Later on, we will discuss fast algorithms for eigenvalue problems with symmetric tridiagonal matrices.

REMARK 2.24. The Hessenberg reduction via Householder reflections is backward stable, i.e., there exists a small perturbation $\delta\boldsymbol{A}$ of $\boldsymbol{A}$ such that

$$\hat{\boldsymbol{H}} = \hat{\boldsymbol{P}}^*(\boldsymbol{A} + \delta\boldsymbol{A})\hat{\boldsymbol{P}}, \quad \|\delta\boldsymbol{A}\|_F \leq cn^2\epsilon_{\text{machine}}\|\boldsymbol{A}\|_F.$$

Here, $\hat{\boldsymbol{H}}$ is the computed upper Hessenberg matrix, $\hat{\boldsymbol{P}} = \hat{\boldsymbol{P}}_1 \cdots \hat{\boldsymbol{P}}_{n-2}$ is a product of exactly unitary Householder matrices based on computed vectors $\hat{\boldsymbol{v}}_i$, and $c > 0$ a constant. For more details, we refer to [**66**, p. 351] and [**27**, Sec. 19.3].

During the next sections, we will see how the upper Hessenberg form (or the tridiagonal form in case of symmetric matrices) is used within eigenvalue solvers.
Before we talk about algorithms, we need to understand when it is difficult to compute eigenvalues accurately. The following example shows that eigenvalues of a matrix are continuous (but not necessarily differentiable) functions of it.

EXAMPLE 2.25. Consider the perturbed Jordan block

$$\boldsymbol{A}(\varepsilon) = \begin{bmatrix} 0 & 1 & & \\ & \ddots & \ddots & \\ & & \ddots & 1 \\ \varepsilon & & & 0 \end{bmatrix} \in \mathbb{R}^{n \times n}.$$

The characteristic polynomial is given as $p_{\boldsymbol{A}(\varepsilon)}(x) = (-1)^n(x^n - \varepsilon)$. Hence, the eigenvalues are $\lambda_j(\varepsilon) = \varepsilon^{\frac{1}{n}} \exp(\frac{2\imath j\pi}{n})$ for $j = 1, \ldots, n$. None of the eigenvalues is differentiable at $\varepsilon = 0$. Their rate of change at the origin is infinite. Consider for instance the case $n = 20$ and $\varepsilon = 10^{-16}$ (machine precision), then $\lambda_1(\varepsilon) = 0.1507 + 0.0490\imath$ whereas $\lambda(0) = 0$.

Let us quickly address the issue of estimating the quality of computed eigenvalues. The question here is: How do eigenvalues and eigenvectors vary when the original matrix undergoes small perturbations? We start with considering the sensitivity of simple eigenvalues.

THEOREM 2.26 (See, e.g. [**22**, Chap. 7.2.2].). *Let $\boldsymbol{A} \in \mathbb{C}^{n\times n}$ with a simple eigenvalue λ, a right (unit norm) eigenvector $\boldsymbol{x}$, and a left (unit norm) eigenvector $\boldsymbol{y}$. Let*

$\boldsymbol{A} + \delta\boldsymbol{A}$ be a perturbation of $\boldsymbol{A}$ and $\lambda + \delta\lambda$ the corresponding perturbed eigenvalue. Then

$$\delta\lambda = \frac{\boldsymbol{y}^*\delta\boldsymbol{A}\boldsymbol{x}}{\boldsymbol{y}^*\boldsymbol{x}} + \mathcal{O}\left(\|\delta\boldsymbol{A}\|_2^2\right).$$

The condition number of λ is defined as $s(\lambda) = \frac{1}{|\boldsymbol{y}^*\boldsymbol{x}|}$. It can be shown that

$$s(\lambda) = \frac{1}{\cos\left(\theta(\boldsymbol{x}, \boldsymbol{y})\right)},$$

where $\theta(\boldsymbol{x}, \boldsymbol{y})$ is the angle between $\boldsymbol{x}$ and $\boldsymbol{y}$.

In general, $\mathcal{O}(\varepsilon)$ perturbations in $\boldsymbol{A}$ can induce $\frac{\varepsilon}{s(\lambda)}$ changes in an eigenvalue. Thus, if $s(\lambda)$ is small, then λ is ill-conditioned, and $\boldsymbol{A}$ is "close to" a matrix with multiple eigenvalues. If $\boldsymbol{A}$ is normal, then every simple eigenvalue satisfies $s(\lambda) = 1$, which means that these eigenvalues are well-conditioned. In the case of a multiple eigenvalue λ, $s(\lambda)$ is not unique anymore. For a defective eigenvalue λ, it holds in general that $\mathcal{O}(\varepsilon)$ perturbations in $\boldsymbol{A}$ can result in $\mathcal{O}\left(\varepsilon^{\frac{1}{p}}\right)$ changes in λ, where p denotes the size of the largest Jordan block associated with λ. This is the effect we have observed in Example 2.25: $\boldsymbol{A}(0)$ has the effective eigenvalue zero with algebraic multiplicity n and geometric multiplicity one. Hence, $\mathcal{O}(10^{-16})$ perturbations in $\boldsymbol{A}$ can result in $\mathcal{O}\left(10^{-\frac{16}{20}}\right) = \mathcal{O}(0.1585)$ changes in the eigenvalue. In other words, small perturbations in the input data caused a large perturbation in the output. This can lead to numerical instabilities of eigenvalue solvers.
In the following, we start with algorithms for computing a few up to all eigenvalues for small to moderate-sized matrices. Then, we continue with large and sparse matrices.

3. Small to moderate-sized matrices

In general, as previously stated, we may separate methods into ones that are based on matrix decompositions vs. ones that are based on matrix-vector products. The power method, which we start with in the sequel, is an important building block for both classes of methods. It is based on matrix-vector products, but it is invaluable for eigensolvers based on decompositions. We choose to include it in this section, noting that it is relevant also for eigensolvers for large and sparse matrices.

3.1. Power method.

The power method is one of the oldest techniques for solving eigenvalue problems. It is used for computing a *dominant eigenpair*, i.e., the eigenvalue of maximum modulus of a matrix $\boldsymbol{A}$ and a corresponding eigenvector. The algorithm consists of generating a sequence of matrix-vector multiplications $\{\boldsymbol{A}^k\boldsymbol{v}_0\}_{k=0,1,\ldots}$, where $\boldsymbol{v}_0$ is some nonzero initial vector.
Let $\boldsymbol{A} \in \mathbb{R}^{n\times n}$ with $\boldsymbol{A}\boldsymbol{x}_j = \lambda_j\boldsymbol{x}_j$ for $j = 1, \ldots, n$. Assume that the eigenvectors $\boldsymbol{x}_j, j = 1, \ldots, n$, are linearly independent, i.e., $\boldsymbol{A}$ is nondefective. Given $\boldsymbol{0} \neq \boldsymbol{v}_0 \in \mathbb{C}^n$, we can expand it using the eigenvectors of $\boldsymbol{A}$ to

$$\boldsymbol{v}_0 = \sum_{j=1}^{n} \beta_j\boldsymbol{x}_j,$$

where $\beta_j \in \mathbb{C}$ for $j = 1, \dots, n$. Applying $\boldsymbol{A}$ to $\boldsymbol{v}_0$ yields

$$\boldsymbol{A}\boldsymbol{v}_0 = \sum_{j=1}^{n} \beta_j \boldsymbol{A}\boldsymbol{x}_j = \sum_{j=1}^{n} \beta_j \lambda_j \boldsymbol{x}_j.$$

Hence, the eigenvectors corresponding to eigenvalues of larger modulus are favored. The above procedure can be repeated. In fact, for any $k \in \mathbb{N}$, we have

$$\boldsymbol{A}^k\boldsymbol{v}_0 = \sum_{j=1}^{n} \beta_j \boldsymbol{A}^k\boldsymbol{x}_j = \sum_{j=1}^{n} \beta_j \lambda_j^k \boldsymbol{x}_j.$$

In order for the following algorithm to converge, we need the following assumptions: $|\lambda_1| > |\lambda_2| \geq |\lambda_3| \geq \dots \geq |\lambda_n|$. Since we are interested in the eigenvalue of maximum modulus, we need some distance to the remaining eigenvalues. λ_1 is called the *dominant eigenvalue*. We further need $\boldsymbol{v}_0$ to have a component in the direction of the eigenvector corresponding to λ_1, i.e., $\beta_1 \neq 0$. Note that this assumption is less concerning in practice since rounding errors during the iteration typically introduce components in the direction of $\boldsymbol{x}_1$. However, we need it for the following theoretical study. Due to $\beta_1 \neq 0$, we can write

$$\boldsymbol{A}^k\boldsymbol{v}_0 = \beta_1\lambda_1^k\boldsymbol{x}_1 + \sum_{j=2}^{n} \beta_j \lambda_j^k \boldsymbol{x}_j = \beta_1\lambda_1^k\left(\boldsymbol{x}_1 + \sum_{j=2}^{n} \frac{\beta_j}{\beta_1}\left(\frac{\lambda_j}{\lambda_1}\right)^k \boldsymbol{x}_j\right).$$

Since λ_1 is a dominant eigenvalue, we get $\left(\frac{\lambda_j}{\lambda_1}\right)^k \overset{k\to\infty}{\longrightarrow} 0$ for all $j = 2, \dots, n$. Hence, it can be shown (cf. [**47**, Theor. 4.1]) that $\boldsymbol{A}^k\boldsymbol{v}_0$, as well as the scaled version $\boldsymbol{v}_k = \frac{\boldsymbol{A}^k\boldsymbol{v}_0}{\|\boldsymbol{A}^k\boldsymbol{v}_0\|_2}$ which is used in practice to avoid overflow/underflow, converges linearly to a multiple of $\boldsymbol{x}_1$ with a convergence rate proportional to $\frac{|\lambda_2|}{|\lambda_1|}$. A value of $\frac{|\lambda_2|}{|\lambda_1|} \approx 1$ indicates a slow convergence behavior. Algorithm 3.1 shows the power method. The approximated eigenvalue in step k

$$\lambda_1^{(k)} = \boldsymbol{v}_k^T\boldsymbol{A}\boldsymbol{v}_k$$

is computed using the *Rayleigh quotient*; see Definition 2.6. This is based on the following: Given a vector $\hat{\boldsymbol{x}}_1$ that approximates the eigenvector $\boldsymbol{x}_1$. Then, $\hat{\lambda}_1 = \hat{\boldsymbol{x}}_1^T\boldsymbol{A}\hat{\boldsymbol{x}}_1$ is the best eigenvalue approximation in the least-squares sense, i.e.,

$$\hat{\lambda}_1 = \arg\min_{\mu} \|\boldsymbol{A}\hat{\boldsymbol{x}}_1 - \mu\hat{\boldsymbol{x}}_1\|_2^2. \tag{3.1}$$

We can solve this minimization problem by solving the *normal equation*

$$\begin{aligned} \hat{\boldsymbol{x}}_1^T\hat{\boldsymbol{x}}_1\,\mu &= \hat{\boldsymbol{x}}_1^T\boldsymbol{A}\hat{\boldsymbol{x}}_1 \\ \Leftrightarrow \mu &= \frac{\hat{\boldsymbol{x}}_1^T\boldsymbol{A}\hat{\boldsymbol{x}}_1}{\hat{\boldsymbol{x}}_1^T\hat{\boldsymbol{x}}_1}; \end{aligned}$$

see, e.g., [**46**, Chap. 5.3.3]. Since we normalize the computed eigenvectors in the power method, i.e., $\|\hat{\boldsymbol{x}}_1\|_2 = 1$, we get the desired result. The cost for k iterations is $\mathcal{O}(2kn^2)$ floating point operations (flops).

Algorithm 3.1: Power method

Choose $\boldsymbol{v}_0 = \frac{\boldsymbol{v}}{\|\boldsymbol{v}\|_2}$
for $k = 1, 2, \dots,$ *until termination* **do**
  $\tilde{\boldsymbol{v}} = \boldsymbol{A}\boldsymbol{v}_{k-1}$
  $\boldsymbol{v}_k = \frac{\tilde{\boldsymbol{v}}}{\|\tilde{\boldsymbol{v}}\|_2}$
  $\lambda_1^{(k)} = \boldsymbol{v}_k^T \boldsymbol{A}\boldsymbol{v}_k$
end

The power method can be applied to large, sparse, or implicit matrices. It is simple and basic but can be slow. We assumed for the convergence that $\boldsymbol{A}$ is nondefective. For the case of a defective $\boldsymbol{A}$, the power method can still be applied but converges even more slowly; see, e.g., [**28**]. Moreover, we want to emphasize again that the power method only works if the matrix under consideration has *one* dominant eigenvalue. This excludes the case of, e.g., a dominant complex eigenvalue[3] or of dominant eigenvalues of opposite signs. The power method is rather used as a building block for other, more robust and general algorithms. We refer to [**66**, Chap. 10] for a detailed discussion of the power method. Next, we discuss a method that overcomes the mentioned difficulties.

3.2. Inverse power method. We have seen that the power method is in general slow. Moreover, it is good only for one well-separated dominant eigenvalue. How can we accelerate it, and what about the more general case of looking for a non-dominant eigenpair? The inverse power method uses *shift and invert* techniques to overcome these limitations of the power method. It aims to compute the eigenvalue of $\boldsymbol{A}$ that is closest to a certain scalar (shift) and a corresponding eigenvector. It also enhances the convergence behavior. The price for these improvements is the solution of a linear system in each iteration.
The idea is the following: Assume $\boldsymbol{A} \in \mathbb{R}^{n \times n}$ has eigenpairs $(\lambda_j, \boldsymbol{x}_j)_{j=1,\dots,n}$ with $|\lambda_1| \geq \ldots \geq |\lambda_n|$. Let $\alpha \in \mathbb{R}$ with $\alpha \neq \lambda_j$ for $j = 1, \dots, n$. This will be the *shift* in the inverse power method. In practice, we choose $\alpha \approx \lambda_i$ for some i depending on which (real) eigenvalue λ_i we want to find. Hence, in order for the method to work, we need to know approximately the value of the eigenvalue we are interested in. Then, $\boldsymbol{A} - \alpha\boldsymbol{I}$ has eigenpairs $(\lambda_j - \alpha, \boldsymbol{x}_j)_{j=1,\dots,n}$, and $(\boldsymbol{A} - \alpha\boldsymbol{I})^{-1}$ has eigenpairs $(\mu_j, \boldsymbol{x}_j)_{j=1,\dots,n}$ with $\mu_j = (\lambda_j - \alpha)^{-1}$. Let λ_i and λ_j be the two eigenvalues that are closest to α with $|\lambda_i - \alpha| < |\lambda_j - \alpha|$. Then, the two largest eigenvalues μ_1 and μ_2 of $(\boldsymbol{A} - \alpha\boldsymbol{I})^{-1}$ are

$$\mu_1 = \frac{1}{\lambda_i - \alpha}, \quad \mu_2 = \frac{1}{\lambda_j - \alpha}.$$

Hence, the power method applied to $(\boldsymbol{A} - \alpha\boldsymbol{I})^{-1}$ converges to μ_1 and an eigenvector of μ_1 with convergence rate

$$\frac{|\mu_2|}{|\mu_1|} = \frac{\frac{1}{|\lambda_j - \alpha|}}{\frac{1}{|\lambda_i - \alpha|}} = \frac{|\lambda_i - \alpha|}{|\lambda_j - \alpha|}.$$

[3]As noted in Section 2.1, eigenvalues of real matrices always occur in complex conjugate pairs.

We know from the previous section that we need a small value of $\frac{|\mu_2|}{|\mu_1|}$ in order to converge fast. Hence, we desire $|\lambda_i - \alpha| \ll |\lambda_j - \alpha|$, which requires a "good" choice of the shift α. If we are interested for instance in the dominant eigenvalue, estimations based on norms of $\boldsymbol{A}$ can be used; see, e.g., [**22**, Chap. 2.3.2].

Algorithm 3.2: Inverse power method

```
Choose v_0 = v / ||v||_2
for k = 1, 2, ..., until termination do
    Solve (A − αI)ṽ = v_{k−1}
    v_k = ṽ / ||ṽ||_2
    λ^(k) = v_k^T A v_k
end
```

As already mentioned at the beginning of this section, the price for overcoming difficulties of the power method by using a shift and invert approach is the solution of a linear system in every iteration. If α is fixed, then we have to solve linear systems with one matrix and many right-hand sides: If a direct method can be applied, then we form an LU decomposition of $\boldsymbol{A} - \alpha\boldsymbol{I}$ once. The cost for solving the two triangular systems arising from the LU decomposition is $\mathcal{O}(n^2)$. For huge problems, iterative methods have to be employed to solve the linear systems. This pays off only if the inverse iteration converges very fast.

In summary, we have seen that we can apply the inverse power method to find different eigenvalues using different shifts. During the whole iteration, the inverse power method uses a fixed shift α. The next method involves a dynamic shift α_k.

3.3. Rayleigh quotient iteration. The idea of the Rayleigh quotient iteration is to learn the shift as the iteration proceeds using the calculated eigenvalue $\lambda^{(k-1)}$ from the previous step $k-1$. Now, each iteration is potentially more expensive since the linear systems involve different matrices in each step. However, the new algorithm may converge in many fewer iterations. In the Hermitian case, we potentially obtain a cubic convergence rate; see, e.g., [**39**].

Note that the matrix $(\boldsymbol{A} - \lambda^{(k-1)}\boldsymbol{I})$ may be singular. This is the case when the shift hits an eigenvalue of $\boldsymbol{A}$. The cost for solving the linear system with $(\boldsymbol{A} - \lambda^{(k-1)}\boldsymbol{I})$ is $\mathcal{O}(n^3)$ if $\boldsymbol{A}$ is full. For an upper Hessenberg matrix, it reduces to $\mathcal{O}(n^2)$, and for a tridiagonal matrix even to $\mathcal{O}(n)$.

Next, we discuss a technique that uses information of a computed dominant eigenpair for the approximation of a second-dominant eigenpair.

3.4. Deflation. Let $\boldsymbol{A} \in \mathbb{R}^{n \times n}$ have eigenvalues $|\lambda_1| > |\lambda_2| \geq \ldots \geq |\lambda_n|$, right eigenvectors $\boldsymbol{x}_1, \ldots, \boldsymbol{x}_n$, and left eigenvectors $\boldsymbol{y}_1, \ldots, \boldsymbol{y}_n$. Note that $(\lambda_1, \boldsymbol{x}_1)$ is a dominant eigenpair. Suppose we have approximated the dominant eigenvector $\boldsymbol{x}_1$ of $\boldsymbol{A}$ by $\hat{\boldsymbol{x}}_1$ with $\|\hat{\boldsymbol{x}}_1\|_2 = 1$. Now, we are interested in approximating the next eigenvalue λ_2.

Deflation is based on a simple rank-one modification of $\boldsymbol{A}$, as follows: Compute $\boldsymbol{A}_1 = \boldsymbol{A} - \alpha\hat{\boldsymbol{x}}_1\boldsymbol{w}^T$, where $\alpha \in \mathbb{R}$ is an appropriate shift and $\boldsymbol{w} \in \mathbb{R}^n$ an arbitrary vector such that $\boldsymbol{w}^T\hat{\boldsymbol{x}}_1 = 1$.

THEOREM 3.1 (Wielandt; see [**65**].). *In the case* $\hat{\boldsymbol{x}}_1 = \boldsymbol{x}_1$, *the eigenvalues of* $\boldsymbol{A}_1$ *are* $\lambda_1 - \alpha, \lambda_2, \ldots, \lambda_n$. *Moreover, the right eigenvector* $\boldsymbol{x}_1$ *and the left eigenvectors* $\boldsymbol{y}_2, \ldots, \boldsymbol{y}_n$ *are preserved.*

PROOF.

$$\left(\boldsymbol{A} - \alpha \boldsymbol{x}_1 \boldsymbol{w}^T\right) \boldsymbol{x}_1 = \boldsymbol{A}\boldsymbol{x}_1 - \alpha \boldsymbol{x}_1 \boldsymbol{w}^T \boldsymbol{x}_1 = \lambda_1 \boldsymbol{x}_1 - \alpha \boldsymbol{x}_1$$

since $\boldsymbol{w}^T \boldsymbol{x}_1 = 1$. For $i = 2, \ldots, n$, we have

$$\boldsymbol{y}_i^* \left(\boldsymbol{A} - \alpha \boldsymbol{x}_1 \boldsymbol{w}^T\right) = \boldsymbol{y}_i^* \boldsymbol{A} - \alpha \boldsymbol{y}_i^* \boldsymbol{x}_1 \boldsymbol{w}^T = \boldsymbol{y}_i^* \boldsymbol{A} = \lambda_i \boldsymbol{y}_i^*$$

since $\boldsymbol{y}_i^* \boldsymbol{x}_1 = 0$ for $i = 2, \ldots, n$. □

Hence, a modification of $\boldsymbol{A}$ to $\boldsymbol{A}_1 = \boldsymbol{A} - \alpha \hat{\boldsymbol{x}}_1 \boldsymbol{w}^T$ displaces the dominant eigenvalue of $\boldsymbol{A}$. The rank-one modification should be chosen such that λ_2 becomes the dominant eigenvalue of $\boldsymbol{A}_1$. We can then proceed for instance with the power method applied to $\boldsymbol{A}_1$ in order to obtain an approximation of λ_2. This technique is called *Wielandt deflation.*

There are many ways to choose $\boldsymbol{w}$. A simple choice (due to Hotelling [**29**]) is to choose $\boldsymbol{w} = \boldsymbol{y}_1$ the first left eigenvector (or an approximation of it) or $\boldsymbol{w} = \boldsymbol{x}_1$ or rather its approximation $\boldsymbol{w} = \hat{\boldsymbol{x}}_1$. It can be shown (cf. [**47**, Chap. 4.2.2]) that if $\boldsymbol{x}_1$ is nearly orthogonal to $\boldsymbol{x}_2$ or if $\frac{\lambda_1 - \lambda_2}{\alpha} \ll 1$, the choice $\boldsymbol{w} = \boldsymbol{x}_1$ is nearly optimal in terms of eigenvalue conditioning.

Note that we never need to form the matrix $\boldsymbol{A}_1$ explicitly. This is important since $\boldsymbol{A}_1$ is a dense matrix. For calculating the matrix-vector product $\boldsymbol{y} = \boldsymbol{A}_1 \boldsymbol{x}$, we just need to perform $\boldsymbol{y} \leftarrow \boldsymbol{A}\boldsymbol{x}$, $\beta = \alpha \boldsymbol{w}^T \boldsymbol{x}$, and $\boldsymbol{y} \leftarrow \boldsymbol{y} - \beta \hat{\boldsymbol{x}}_1$. We can apply this procedure recursively without difficulty. However, keep in mind that, for a long deflation process, errors accumulate.

So far, the discussed algorithms compute only one eigenpair at once, i.e., a one-dimensional invariant subspace. Next, we consider another generalization of the power and inverse power method that can be used to compute higher-dimensional invariant subspaces.

3.5. Orthogonal iteration. Let $\boldsymbol{A} \in \mathbb{R}^{n \times n}$ have eigenpairs $(\lambda_j, \boldsymbol{x}_j)_{j=1,\ldots,n}$ with $|\lambda_1| \geq \ldots \geq |\lambda_n|$. From the real Schur decomposition in Theorem 2.18, we know there exists an orthogonal $\boldsymbol{Q} \in \mathbb{R}^{n \times n}$ such that

$$\boldsymbol{Q}^T \boldsymbol{A} \boldsymbol{Q} = \boldsymbol{T},$$

where the diagonal blocks of $\boldsymbol{T}$ correspond to the eigenvalues of $\boldsymbol{A}$ in real form. Assume that the eigenvalues λ_i, represented in $\boldsymbol{T}$ in real form, are ordered from λ_1 to λ_n. Let $1 \leq r < n$. Then, we can do the following partitioning:

$$\boldsymbol{Q} = [\boldsymbol{Q}^{(r)}, \boldsymbol{Q}^{(n-r)}], \quad \boldsymbol{T} = \begin{bmatrix} \boldsymbol{T}^{(r,r)} & \boldsymbol{T}^{(r,n-r)} \\ \boldsymbol{0} & \boldsymbol{T}^{(n-r,n-r)} \end{bmatrix},$$

where $\boldsymbol{Q}^{(r)} \in \mathbb{R}^{r \times r}$ and $\boldsymbol{T}^{(r,r)} \in \mathbb{R}^{r \times r}$. Note that r should be chosen such that the $(r+1, r)$ entry in $\boldsymbol{T}$ is zero, i.e., we do not split a complex conjugate eigenpair to $\boldsymbol{T}^{(r,r)}$ and $\boldsymbol{T}^{(n-r,n-r)}$. Then,

$$\boldsymbol{A}\boldsymbol{Q}^{(r)} = \boldsymbol{Q}^{(r)} \boldsymbol{T}^{(r,r)},$$

i.e., $\operatorname{ran}(\boldsymbol{Q}^{(r)})$ is an $\boldsymbol{A}$-invariant subspace corresponding to the r largest (in modulus) eigenvalues. Due to this property, this subspace is also called *dominant.*

Now, we are interested in computing such a dominant r-dimensional invariant subspace. Hence, instead of dealing with a matrix-vector product as in the algorithms before, we go over to a matrix-matrix product, i.e., we apply $\boldsymbol{A}$ to a few vectors simultaneously. This can be achieved by the orthogonal iteration presented in Algorithm 3.3.

Algorithm 3.3: Orthogonal iteration

1 Choose $\boldsymbol{Q}_0 \in \mathbb{R}^{n \times r}$ with orthonormal columns
2 **for** $k = 1, 2, \ldots,$ *until termination* **do**
3 $\quad \boldsymbol{Z}_k = \boldsymbol{A}\boldsymbol{Q}_{k-1}$
4 $\quad \boldsymbol{Q}_k\boldsymbol{R}_k = \boldsymbol{Z}_k$ (QR factorization)
5 **end**

The QR factorization in Line 4 refers to the QR decomposition in Definition 2.21. It can be computed by, e.g., the modified Gram–Schmidt algorithm in $\mathcal{O}\left(2nr^2\right)$ flops [**22**, Chap. 5.2.8], Householder reflections in $\mathcal{O}\left(2r^2\left(n - \frac{r}{3}\right)\right)$ flops [**22**, Chap. 5.2.2], or Givens transformations in $\mathcal{O}\left(3r^2\left(n - \frac{r}{3}\right)\right)$ flops [**22**, Chap. 5.2.5]. Note that the complexity can be reduced if the corresponding matrix is of upper Hessenberg form. We will discuss this further below. Note that Line 3 and 4 yield

$$\boldsymbol{A}\boldsymbol{Q}_{k-1} = \boldsymbol{Q}_k\boldsymbol{R}_k,$$

where $\boldsymbol{R}_k$ is upper triangular. Now, if $|\lambda_r| > |\lambda_{r+1}|$ and $\boldsymbol{Q}_0$ has components in the desired eigendirections, then we have

$$\operatorname{ran}(\boldsymbol{Q}_k) \stackrel{k\to\infty}{\longrightarrow} \operatorname{ran}(\boldsymbol{Q}^{(r)})$$

with a convergence rate proportional to $\frac{|\lambda_{r+1}|}{|\lambda_r|}$. For more details, we refer to [**22**, Chap. 7.3.2].

REMARK 3.2. By replacing the QR factorization in Line 4 of Algorithm 3.3 with $\boldsymbol{Q}_k = \boldsymbol{Z}_k$, we obtain the *subspace iteration*, also called *simultaneous iteration*. Under the same conditions as before, it holds

$$\operatorname{ran}(\boldsymbol{Z}_k) \stackrel{k\to\infty}{\longrightarrow} \operatorname{ran}(\boldsymbol{Q}^{(r)}).$$

However, the columns of $\boldsymbol{Z}_k$ form an increasingly ill-conditioned basis for $\boldsymbol{A}^k\operatorname{ran}(\boldsymbol{Q}_0)$ since each column of $\boldsymbol{Z}_k$ converges to a multiple of the dominant eigenvector. The orthogonal iteration overcomes this difficulty by orthonormalizing the columns of $\boldsymbol{Z}_k$ at each step.

From the orthogonal iteration, we can derive the QR iteration, a method for finding all eigenvalues of a matrix $\boldsymbol{A}$.

3.6. QR iteration. We obtain the QR iteration from the orthogonal iteration if we set $r = n$, i.e., we want to compute all eigenvalues, and $\boldsymbol{Q}_0 = \boldsymbol{I}$.
We can rewrite Algorithm 3.4 by using the following equivalence:

$$\boldsymbol{A}_{k-1} \stackrel{\text{Line 5}}{=} \boldsymbol{Q}_{k-1}^T\boldsymbol{A}\boldsymbol{Q}_{k-1} \stackrel{\text{Line 3}}{=} \boldsymbol{Q}_{k-1}^T\boldsymbol{Z}_k \stackrel{\text{Line 4}}{=} \boldsymbol{Q}_{k-1}^T\boldsymbol{Q}_k\boldsymbol{R}_k =: \tilde{\boldsymbol{Q}}_k\boldsymbol{R}_k, \tag{3.2}$$

$$\boldsymbol{A}_k \stackrel{\text{Line 5}}{=} \boldsymbol{Q}_k^T\boldsymbol{A}\boldsymbol{Q}_k = \boldsymbol{Q}_k^T\boldsymbol{A}\boldsymbol{Q}_{k-1}\boldsymbol{Q}_{k-1}^T\boldsymbol{Q}_k \stackrel{\text{Line 3}}{=} \boldsymbol{Q}_k^T\boldsymbol{Z}_k\boldsymbol{Q}_{k-1}^T\boldsymbol{Q}_k$$

$$\stackrel{\text{Line 4}}{=} \boldsymbol{R}_k\boldsymbol{Q}_{k-1}^T\boldsymbol{Q}_k \stackrel{(3.2)}{=} \boldsymbol{R}_k\tilde{\boldsymbol{Q}}_k.$$

Algorithm 3.4: Prelude to QR iteration

Choose $\boldsymbol{Q}_0 = \boldsymbol{I}$ (orthogonal)
for $k = 1, 2, \ldots,$ *until termination* **do**
    $\boldsymbol{Z}_k = \boldsymbol{A}\boldsymbol{Q}_{k-1}$
    $\boldsymbol{Q}_k\boldsymbol{R}_k = \boldsymbol{Z}_k$ (QR factorization)
    $\boldsymbol{A}_k = \boldsymbol{Q}_k^T\boldsymbol{A}\boldsymbol{Q}_k$
end

Note that the product of two orthogonal matrices is orthogonal. Hence, $\tilde{\boldsymbol{Q}}_k$ is orthogonal. Therefore, $\boldsymbol{A}_k$ is determined by a QR decomposition of $\boldsymbol{A}_{k-1}$. This form of the QR iteration is presented in Algorithm 3.5. Note that $\boldsymbol{Q}_0$ does not have to be the identity matrix.

Algorithm 3.5: QR iteration

1 $\boldsymbol{A}_0 = \boldsymbol{Q}_0^T\boldsymbol{A}\boldsymbol{Q}_0$ (real Schur form, $\boldsymbol{Q}_0 \in \mathbb{R}^{n\times n}$ orthogonal)
2 **for** $k = 1, 2, \ldots,$ *until termination* **do**
3     $\boldsymbol{Q}_k\boldsymbol{R}_k = \boldsymbol{A}_{k-1}$ (QR factorization)
4     $\boldsymbol{A}_k = \boldsymbol{R}_k\boldsymbol{Q}_k$
5 **end**

From Line 3 and 4 of Algorithm 3.5 we get

$$\boldsymbol{A}_k = (\boldsymbol{Q}_0 \cdots \boldsymbol{Q}_k)^T \boldsymbol{A} (\boldsymbol{Q}_0 \cdots \boldsymbol{Q}_k) =: \hat{\boldsymbol{Q}}_k^T \boldsymbol{A} \hat{\boldsymbol{Q}}_k,$$

where $\hat{\boldsymbol{Q}}_k$ is orthogonal. Hence, $\operatorname{ran}(\hat{\boldsymbol{Q}}_k)$ is an $\boldsymbol{A}$-invariant subspace and $\lambda(\boldsymbol{A}) = \lambda(\boldsymbol{A}_k)$. If $|\lambda_1| > \ldots > |\lambda_n|$ and $\boldsymbol{Q}_0$ has components in the desired eigendirections, then we have

$$\operatorname{ran}(\hat{\boldsymbol{Q}}_k(:, 1:l)) \overset{k\to\infty}{\longrightarrow} \operatorname{ran}(\boldsymbol{Q}(:, 1:l)) \quad \forall 1 \le l \le n$$

with a convergence rate proportional to $\frac{|\lambda_{l+1}|}{|\lambda_l|}$. Hence, $\boldsymbol{A}_k \overset{k\to\infty}{\longrightarrow} \boldsymbol{T}$, where $\boldsymbol{Q}^T\boldsymbol{A}\boldsymbol{Q} = \boldsymbol{T}$ is a real Schur decomposition of $\boldsymbol{A}$. For more details, we refer to [**22**, Chap. 7.3.3]. Overall, the QR iteration computes the Schur form of a matrix. As in the previous section, we considered the real Schur form here. But note that if we allow complex arithmetic, we get the same results with a (complex) Schur form. For further readings on the QR iteration we refer to, e.g., [**32, 55, 62**].
As already mentioned in the previous section, in this form the cost of each step of the QR iteration is $\mathcal{O}(n^3)$. But we can reduce the complexity if we start with $\boldsymbol{A}_0$ in upper Hessenberg form. Moreover, we can speed up the convergence using shifts.

3.7. QR iteration with shifts. If we choose $\boldsymbol{Q}_0$ such that $\boldsymbol{A}_0$ is in upper Hessenberg form, the cost of each step of the QR iteration reduces to $\mathcal{O}(n^2)$. If $\boldsymbol{A}$ is symmetric, then the cost per step is $\mathcal{O}(n)$. It can be shown that each $\boldsymbol{A}_k$ is upper Hessenberg. This is the first modification. Second, shifts $\zeta_k \in \mathbb{R}$ are introduced in order to accelerate the deflation process (see Theorem 2.16). Deflation occurs every time $\boldsymbol{A}_k$ is reduced, i.e., at least one of its subdiagonal entries is zero. In such a case, we continue with two smaller subproblems. The matrices $\boldsymbol{A}_{k-1}$ and $\boldsymbol{A}_k$ in Algorithm 3.6 are orthogonally similar since

$$\boldsymbol{A}_k = \boldsymbol{R}_k\boldsymbol{Q}_k + \zeta_k\boldsymbol{I} = \boldsymbol{Q}_k^T\left(\boldsymbol{Q}_k\boldsymbol{R}_k + \zeta_k\boldsymbol{I}\right)\boldsymbol{Q}_k = \boldsymbol{Q}_k^T\boldsymbol{A}_{k-1}\boldsymbol{Q}_k,$$

and $\boldsymbol{Q}_k$ from the QR decomposition is orthogonal.

Algorithm 3.6: QR iteration with shifts

1 $\boldsymbol{A}_0 = \boldsymbol{Q}_0^T\boldsymbol{A}\boldsymbol{Q}_0$ upper Hessenberg form (Tridiagonal if $\boldsymbol{A}$ is symmetric)
2 **for** $k = 1, 2, \ldots,$ *until termination* **do**
3 $\quad\boldsymbol{Q}_k\boldsymbol{R}_k = \boldsymbol{A}_{k-1} - \zeta_k\boldsymbol{I}$ (QR factorization)
4 $\quad\boldsymbol{A}_k = \boldsymbol{R}_k\boldsymbol{Q}_k + \zeta_k\boldsymbol{I}$
5 **end**

Why does the shift strategy work? If ζ_k is an eigenvalue of the unreduced Hessenberg matrix $\boldsymbol{A}_{k-1}$, then $\boldsymbol{A}_{k-1} - \zeta_k\boldsymbol{I}$ is singular. This implies $\boldsymbol{R}_k$ is singular, where the (n, n) entry of $\boldsymbol{R}_k$ is zero. Then, the last row of the upper Hessenberg matrix $\boldsymbol{A}_k = \boldsymbol{R}_k\boldsymbol{Q}_k + \zeta_k\boldsymbol{I}$ consists of zeros except for the (n, n) entry which is ζ_k. So we have converged to the form

$$\boldsymbol{A}_k = \begin{bmatrix} \boldsymbol{A}' & \boldsymbol{a} \\ \boldsymbol{0}^T & \zeta_k \end{bmatrix},$$

and can now work on a smaller matrix (deflate) and continue the QR iteration. We can accept the (n, n) entry as ζ_k as it is presumably a good approximation to the eigenvalue. In summary, we obtain deflation after one step in exact arithmetic if we shift by an exact eigenvalue.

If $\zeta = \zeta_k$ for all $k = 1, 2, \ldots,$ and we order the eigenvalues λ_i of $\boldsymbol{A}$ such that

$$|\lambda_1 - \zeta| \geq \ldots \geq |\lambda_n - \zeta|,$$

then the pth subdiagonal entry in $\boldsymbol{A}_k$ converges to zero with rate $\frac{|\lambda_{p+1}-\zeta|}{|\lambda_p-\zeta|}$. Of course, we need $|\lambda_{p+1} - \zeta| < |\lambda_p - \zeta|$ in order to get any convergence result.

In practice, deflation occurs whenever a subdiagonal entry $a_{p+1,p}^{(k)}$ of $\boldsymbol{A}_k$ is small enough, e.g., if

$$|a_{p+1,p}^{(k)}| \leq c\epsilon_{\text{machine}}(|a_{p,p}^{(k)}| + |a_{p+1,p+1}^{(k)}|)$$

for a small constant $c > 0$.

Let us quickly summarize some shift strategies: The single-shift strategy uses $\zeta_k = a_{n,n}^{(k-1)}$. It can be shown (cf. [**22**, Chap. 7.5.3]) that the convergence $a_{n,n-1}^{(k)} \overset{k\to\infty}{\longrightarrow} 0$ is even quadratic. When we deal with complex eigenvalues, then $\zeta_k = a_{n,n}^{(k-1)}$ tends to be a poor approximation. Then, the double-shift strategy is preferred which performs two single-shift steps in succession, i.e., Lines 3–4 in Algorithm 3.6 are repeated a second time with a second shift. Using implicit QR factorizations, one double-shift step can be implemented with $\mathcal{O}(n^2)$ flops ($\mathcal{O}(n)$ flops in the symmetric case); see e.g., [**22**, Chap. 7.5.5]. This technique was first described by Francis [**18, 19**] and refers to a *Francis QR step.*

The overall QR algorithm requires $\mathcal{O}(n^3)$ flops. For more details about the QR iteration, we refer to, e.g., [**33, 35, 42, 60, 63, 64**]. Further readings concerning shift strategies include [**15, 17, 61**].

We know that the Hessenberg reduction of a symmetric matrix leads to a tridiagonal matrix. In the following, we review methods for this special case.

3.8. Algorithms for symmetric (tridiagonal) matrices. Before we consider eigenvalue problems for the special case of symmetric tridiagonal matrices, we review one of the oldest methods for symmetric matrices $\boldsymbol{A}$ — *Jacobi's method.* For general symmetric eigenvalue problems, we refer the reader to [**11**, Chap. 5] — it contains important theoretic concepts, e.g., gaps of eigenvalues and the related perturbation theory, and gives a nice overview of direct eigenvalue solvers.

3.8.1. *Jacobi's method.* Jacobi's method is one of the oldest algorithms [**30**] for eigenvalue problems with a cost of $\mathcal{O}(cn^3)$ flops with a large constant c. However, it is still of current interest due to its parallelizability and accuracy [**12**].
The method is based on a sequence of orthogonal similarity transformations

$$\ldots \boldsymbol{Q}_3^T \boldsymbol{Q}_2^T \boldsymbol{Q}_1^T \boldsymbol{A} \boldsymbol{Q}_1 \boldsymbol{Q}_2 \boldsymbol{Q}_3 \ldots, \tag{3.3}$$

such that each transformation becomes closer to diagonal form. We can write (3.3) as

$$\boldsymbol{A}_{k+1} = \boldsymbol{Q}_{k+1}^T \boldsymbol{A}_k \boldsymbol{Q}_{k+1}, \; k = 0, 1, 2, \ldots$$

with $\boldsymbol{A}_0 = \boldsymbol{A}$. In particular, the orthogonal matrices $\boldsymbol{Q}_i$ are chosen such that the Frobenius norm of the off-diagonal elements

$$\operatorname{off}(\boldsymbol{A}_k) = \sqrt{\sum_{i=1}^{n} \sum_{\substack{j=1 \\ j \neq i}}^{n} \left(a_{i,j}^{(k)} \right)^2}$$

is reduced with each transformation. This is done using *Jacobi rotations* (*Givens rotations*)

$$\boldsymbol{J}(p,q,\theta) = \begin{bmatrix} 1 & & & & & & & & & \\ & \ddots & & & & & & & & \\ & & 1 & & & & & & & \\ & & & c & 0 & \cdots & 0 & s & & \\ & & & 0 & 1 & & & 0 & & \\ & & & \vdots & & \ddots & & \vdots & & \\ & & & 0 & & & 1 & 0 & & \\ & & & -s & 0 & \cdots & 0 & c & & \\ & & & & & & & & 1 & \\ & & & & & & & & & \ddots \\ & & & & & & & & & & 1 \end{bmatrix} \begin{matrix} \\ \\ \\ p \\ \\ \\ \\ q \\ \\ \\ \\ \end{matrix}$$

$$\qquad\qquad p \qquad\qquad\qquad q$$

where $1 \leq p < q \leq n$, $c = \cos(\theta)$, and $s = \sin(\theta)$. Givens rotations are orthogonal. The application of $\boldsymbol{J}(p,q,\theta)^T$ to a vector rotates the vector counterclockwise in the (p,q) coordinate plane by θ radians. In order to make $\boldsymbol{A}_{k+1}$ iteratively more diagonal, $\boldsymbol{Q}_{k+1} = \boldsymbol{J}(p,q,\theta)$ is chosen to make one pair of off-diagonal entries of $\boldsymbol{A}_{k+1} = \boldsymbol{Q}_{k+1}^T \boldsymbol{A}_k \boldsymbol{Q}_{k+1}$ zero at a time. Thereby, θ is chosen such that the (p,q) and

(q,p) entry of $\boldsymbol{A}_{k+1}$ become zero. To determine θ, we can consider the corresponding 2×2 system

$$\begin{bmatrix} c & s \\ -s & c \end{bmatrix}^T \begin{bmatrix} a_{p,p}^{(k)} & a_{p,q}^{(k)} \\ a_{q,p}^{(k)} & a_{q,q}^{(k)} \end{bmatrix} \begin{bmatrix} c & s \\ -s & c \end{bmatrix} = \begin{bmatrix} a_{p,p}^{(k+1)} & 0 \\ 0 & a_{q,q}^{(k+1)} \end{bmatrix},$$

where $a_{p,p}^{(k+1)}$ and $a_{q,q}^{(k+1)}$ are the eigenvalues of

$$\begin{bmatrix} a_{p,p}^{(k)} & a_{p,q}^{(k)} \\ a_{q,p}^{(k)} & a_{q,q}^{(k)} \end{bmatrix}.$$

One can show (cf. [**11**, Chap. 5.3.5]) that $\tan(2\theta) = \frac{2a_{p,q}^{(k)}}{a_{q,q}^{(k)} - a_{p,p}^{(k)}}$ and using this, we can compute c and s. Using the fact that the Frobenius norm is preserved by orthogonal transformations, we obtain (cf. [**11**, Lemma 5.4])

$$\text{off}(\boldsymbol{A}_{k+1})^2 = \text{off}(\boldsymbol{A}_k)^2 - 2\left(a_{p,q}^{(k)}\right)^2, \tag{3.4}$$

i.e., $\boldsymbol{A}_{k+1}$ moves closer to diagonal form with each Jacobi step. In order to maximize the reduction in (3.4), p and q should be chosen such that $|a_{p,q}^{(k)}|$ is maximal. With this choice, we get after k Jacobi steps (cf. [**11**, Theor. 5.11])

$$\text{off}(\boldsymbol{A}_k)^2 \le \left(1 - \frac{2}{n(n-1)}\right)^k \text{off}(\boldsymbol{A}_0)^2,$$

i.e., convergence at a linear rate. This scheme is the original version from Jacobi in 1846 and is referred to as *classical Jacobi algorithm*. It even can be shown that the asymptotic convergence rate is quadratic (cf. [**11**, Theor. 5.12]); see [**49**, **58**]. While the cost for an update is $\mathcal{O}(n)$ flops, the search for the optimal (p,q) costs $\mathcal{O}(n^2)$ flops. For a simpler method, we refer the reader to the *cyclic Jacobi method*; see e.g. [**66**, p. 270] or [**22**, Chap. 8.5.3]. In general, the cost of the cyclic Jacobi method is considerably higher than the cost of the symmetric QR iteration. However, it is easily parallelizable.

Again we want to emphasize that we do not need to tridiagonalize in Jacobi's method. In the following, we discuss two methods that need to start by reducing a symmetric matrix $\boldsymbol{A}$ to tridiagonal form: *bisection* and *divide-and-conquer*. Another method is *MR*^{3} or *MRRR* (Algorithm of Multiple Relatively Robust Representations) [**13**] — a sophisticated variant of the inverse iteration, which is efficient when eigenvalues are close to each other.

3.8.2. *Bisection.* For the rest of Section 3, we consider eigenvalue problems for symmetric tridiagonal matrices of the form

$$\boldsymbol{A} = \begin{bmatrix} a_1 & b_1 & & & \\ b_1 & a_2 & b_2 & & \\ & b_2 & a_3 & \ddots & \\ & & \ddots & \ddots & b_{n-1} \\ & & & b_{n-1} & a_n \end{bmatrix}. \tag{3.5}$$

We begin with bisection, a method that can be used to find a subset of eigenvalues, e.g., the largest/smallest eigenvalue or eigenvalues within an interval. Let $\boldsymbol{A}^{(k)} =$

$\boldsymbol{A}(1:k,1:k)$ be the leading $k \times k$ principal submatrix of $\boldsymbol{A}$ with characteristic polynomial

$$p^{(k)}(x) = \det(\boldsymbol{A}^{(k)} - x\boldsymbol{I})$$

for $k = 1, \ldots, n$. If $b_i \neq 0$ for $i = 1, \ldots, n-1$, then

$$\det(\boldsymbol{A}^{(k)}) = a_k \det(\boldsymbol{A}^{(k-1)}) - b_{k-1}^2 \det(\boldsymbol{A}^{(k-2)}),$$

which yields

$$p^{(k)}(x) = (a_k - x)p^{(k-1)}(x) - b_{k-1}^2 p^{(k-2)}(x)$$

with $p^{(-1)}(x) = 0$ and $p^{(0)}(x) = 1$. Hence, $p^{(n)}(x)$ can be evaluated in $\mathcal{O}(n)$ flops. Given $y < z \in \mathbb{R}$ with $p^{(n)}(y)p^{(n)}(z) < 0$ (Hence, there exists a $w \in (y, z)$ with $p^{(n)}(w) = 0$.), we can use the *method of bisection* (see, e.g., [**22**, Chap. 8.4.1]) to find an approximate root of $p^{(n)}(x)$ and hence an approximate eigenvalue of $\boldsymbol{A}$. The method of bisection converges linearly in the sense that the error is approximately halved at each step.

Assume that the eigenvalues $\lambda_j(\boldsymbol{A}^{(k)})$ of $\boldsymbol{A}^{(k)}$ are ordered as

$$\lambda_1(\boldsymbol{A}^{(k)}) \geq \ldots \geq \lambda_k(\boldsymbol{A}^{(k)}).$$

For computing, e.g., $\lambda_k(\boldsymbol{A})$ for a given k or the largest eigenvalue that is smaller than a given $\mu \in \mathbb{R}$, then we need the following theorem:

THEOREM 3.3 (Sturm Sequence Property; see [**22**, Theor. 8.4.1].). *If $\boldsymbol{A}$ is unreduced, i.e., $b_i \neq 0$ for $i = 1, \ldots, n-1$, then the eigenvalues of $\boldsymbol{A}^{(k-1)}$ strictly separate the eigenvalues of $\boldsymbol{A}^{(k)}$:*

$$\begin{aligned}\lambda_k(\boldsymbol{A}^{(k)}) &< \lambda_{k-1}(\boldsymbol{A}^{(k-1)}) < \lambda_{k-1}(\boldsymbol{A}^{(k)}) \\ &< \lambda_{k-2}(\boldsymbol{A}^{(k-1)}) < \lambda_{k-2}(\boldsymbol{A}^{(k)}) < \ldots \\ &< \lambda_2(\boldsymbol{A}^{(k)}) < \lambda_1(\boldsymbol{A}^{(k-1)}) < \lambda_1(\boldsymbol{A}^{(k)}).\end{aligned}$$

Moreover, if $a(\mu)$ denotes the number of sign changes in the sequence

$$\{p^{(0)}(\mu), p^{(1)}(\mu), \ldots, p^{(n)}(\mu)\},$$

where $p^{(k)}(\mu)$ has the opposite sign from $p^{(k-1)}(\mu)$ if $p^{(k)}(\mu) = 0$, then $a(\mu)$ equals the number of $\boldsymbol{A}$'s eigenvalues that are less than μ.

In order to find an initial interval for the method of bisection, we make use of the following simplified version of the *Gershgorin theorem*:

THEOREM 3.4 (Gershgorin). *If $\boldsymbol{A} \in \mathbb{R}^{n \times n}$ is symmetric, then*

$$\lambda(\boldsymbol{A}) \subseteq \cup_{i=1}^{n} [a_{i,i} - r_i, a_{i,i} + r_i],$$

where $r_i = \sum_{\substack{j=1 \\ j \neq i}}^{n} |a_{i,j}|$.

The more general version of the Gershgorin theorem can be found, e.g., in [**22**, Theor. 8.1.3]. Suppose we want to compute $\lambda_k(\boldsymbol{A})$, where $\boldsymbol{A}$ is symmetric tridiagonal as in (3.5). Then, from Theorem 3.4, we get $\lambda_k(\boldsymbol{A}) \in [y, z]$ with

$$y = \min_{1 \leq i \leq n} a_i - |b_i| - |b_{i-1}|, \quad z = \max_{1 \leq i \leq n} a_i + |b_i| + |b_{i-1}|$$

and $b_0 = b_n = 0$. Hence, with this choice of y and z, we can reformulate the method of bisection to converge to $\lambda_k(\boldsymbol{A})$; see, e.g., [**22**, Chap. 8.4.2]. Another version of this scheme can be used to compute subsets of eigenvalues of $\boldsymbol{A}$; see [**3**]. For a variant that computes specific eigenvalues, we refer to [**39**, p. 46].

The cost of bisection is $\mathcal{O}(nk)$ flops, where k is the number of desired eigenvalues. Hence, it can be much faster than the QR iteration if $k \ll n$. Once the desired eigenvalues are found, we can use the *inverse power method* (Section 3.2) to find the corresponding eigenvectors. The inverse power method costs in the best case (well-separated eigenvalues) $\mathcal{O}(nk)$ flops. In the worst case (many clustered eigenvalues), the cost is $\mathcal{O}(nk^2)$ flops and the accuracy of the computed eigenvectors is not guaranteed. Next, we review a method that is better suited for finding all (or most) eigenvalues and eigenvectors, especially when the eigenvalues may be clustered.

3.8.3. *Divide-and-conquer.* The idea of divide-and-conquer is to recursively divide the eigenvalue problem into smaller subproblems until we reach matrices of dimension one, for which the eigenvalue problem is trivial. The method was first introduced in 1981 [**9**] while its parallel version was developed in 1987 [**14**]. The starting point is to write the symmetric tridiagonal matrix $\boldsymbol{A}$ in (3.5) as a sum of a block diagonal matrix of two tridiagonal matrices $\boldsymbol{T}_1$ and $\boldsymbol{T}_2$, plus a rank-1 correction:

$$\boldsymbol{A} = \begin{bmatrix} \boldsymbol{T}_1 & \boldsymbol{0} \\ \boldsymbol{0} & \boldsymbol{T}_2 \end{bmatrix} + b_m \boldsymbol{v}\boldsymbol{v}^T,$$

where $\boldsymbol{v} \in \mathbb{R}^n$ is a column vector whose mth and $(m+1)$st entry is equal to one $(1 \le m \le n-1)$ and all remaining entries are zero. Suppose we have the real Schur decompositions of $\boldsymbol{T}_1$ and $\boldsymbol{T}_2$, i.e., $\boldsymbol{T}_i = \boldsymbol{Q}_i\boldsymbol{D}_i\boldsymbol{Q}_i^T$ for $i = 1, 2$ with $\boldsymbol{Q}_1 \in \mathbb{R}^{m\times m}$ and $\boldsymbol{Q}_2 \in \mathbb{R}^{(n-m)\times(n-m)}$ orthogonal. Then,

$$\boldsymbol{A} = \begin{bmatrix} \boldsymbol{Q}_1 & \boldsymbol{0} \\ \boldsymbol{0} & \boldsymbol{Q}_2 \end{bmatrix} \left(\begin{bmatrix} \boldsymbol{D}_1 & \boldsymbol{0} \\ \boldsymbol{0} & \boldsymbol{D}_2 \end{bmatrix} + b_m \boldsymbol{u}\boldsymbol{u}^T \right) \begin{bmatrix} \boldsymbol{Q}_1^T & \boldsymbol{0} \\ \boldsymbol{0} & \boldsymbol{Q}_2^T \end{bmatrix},$$

where

$$\boldsymbol{u} = \begin{bmatrix} \boldsymbol{Q}_1^T & \boldsymbol{0} \\ \boldsymbol{0} & \boldsymbol{Q}_2^T \end{bmatrix} \boldsymbol{v} = \begin{bmatrix} \text{last column of } \boldsymbol{Q}_1^T \\ \text{first column of } \boldsymbol{Q}_2^T \end{bmatrix}.$$

Hence, $\lambda(\boldsymbol{A}) = \lambda(\boldsymbol{D} + b_m\boldsymbol{u}\boldsymbol{u}^T)$ where $\boldsymbol{D} = \begin{bmatrix} \boldsymbol{D}_1 & \boldsymbol{0} \\ \boldsymbol{0} & \boldsymbol{D}_2 \end{bmatrix} = \operatorname{diag}(d_i)_{i=1,\dots,n}$ is a diagonal matrix. Hence, the problem now reduces to finding the eigenvalues of a diagonal plus a rank-1 matrix. This can be further simplified to finding the eigenvalues of the identity matrix plus a rank-1 matrix, using simply the characteristic polynomial: In particular, under the assumption that $\boldsymbol{D} - \lambda\boldsymbol{I}$ is nonsingular, and using

$$\det(\boldsymbol{D} + b_m\boldsymbol{u}\boldsymbol{u}^T - \lambda\boldsymbol{I}) = \det(\boldsymbol{D} - \lambda\boldsymbol{I})\det\left(\boldsymbol{I} + b_m\left(\boldsymbol{D} - \lambda\boldsymbol{I}\right)^{-1}\boldsymbol{u}\boldsymbol{u}^T\right),$$

we obtain

$$\lambda \in \lambda(\boldsymbol{A}) \Leftrightarrow \det\left(\boldsymbol{I} + b_m\left(\boldsymbol{D} - \lambda\boldsymbol{I}\right)^{-1}\boldsymbol{u}\boldsymbol{u}^T\right) = 0.$$

The matrix $\boldsymbol{I} + b_m\left(\boldsymbol{D} - \lambda\boldsymbol{I}\right)^{-1}\boldsymbol{u}\boldsymbol{u}^T$ is of special structure, and its determinant can be computed using the following lemma:

LEMMA 3.5 (See [**11**, Lemma 5.1].). *Let $\boldsymbol{x}, \boldsymbol{y} \in \mathbb{R}^n$. Then*

$$\det\left(\boldsymbol{I} + \boldsymbol{x}\boldsymbol{y}^T\right) = 1 + \boldsymbol{y}^T\boldsymbol{x}.$$

In our case, we get

$$\det\left(\boldsymbol{I} + b_m\left(\boldsymbol{D} - \lambda\boldsymbol{I}\right)^{-1}\boldsymbol{u}\boldsymbol{u}^T\right) = 1 + b_m\sum_{i=1}^{n}\frac{u_i^2}{d_i - \lambda} \equiv f(\lambda),$$

and the eigenvalues of $\boldsymbol{A}$ are the roots of the *secular equation* $f(\lambda) = 0$. This can be solved, e.g., by Newton's method, which converges in practice in a bounded number of steps per eigenvalue. Note that solving the secular equation needs caution due to possible deflations ($d_i = d_{i+1}$ or $u_i = 0$) or small values of u_i. For more details on the function f and on solving the secular equation, we refer to [**11**, Chap. 5.3.3]. The cost for computing all eigenvalues is $\mathcal{O}(n^2 \log(n))$ flops by using the above strategy of recursively dividing the eigenvalue problem into smaller subproblems. Hence, the pure eigenvalue computation (without eigenvectors) is more expensive than in the QR iteration. However, the eigenvectors can be computed more cheaply:

LEMMA 3.6 (See [**11**, Lemma 5.2].). *If* $\lambda \in \lambda(\boldsymbol{D} + b_m \boldsymbol{u}\boldsymbol{u}^T)$, *then* $(\boldsymbol{D} - \lambda \boldsymbol{I})^{-1}\boldsymbol{u}$ *is a corresponding eigenvector.*

The cost for computing all eigenvectors is $\mathcal{O}(n^2)$ flops. However, the eigenvector computation from Lemma 3.6 is not numerically stable. If λ is too close to a diagonal entry d_i, we obtain large roundoff errors since we divide by $d_i - \lambda$. If two eigenvalues λ_i and λ_j are very close, the orthogonality of the computed eigenvectors can get lost. For a numerical stable computation, we refer to [**24**], which requires in practice $\mathcal{O}(cn^3)$ flops where $c \ll 1$.

Here, we finish the discussion of eigenvalue problems for small to moderate-sized matrices. We now move to discuss problems where the matrix is large and sparse.

4. Large and sparse matrices

In this section, $\boldsymbol{A} \in \mathbb{R}^{n \times n}$ is considered to be large and sparse. Sparse matrices are matrices with very few nonzero entries. Sparse often means that there are $\mathcal{O}(1)$ nonzero entries per row. We note that matrices that are not necessarily sparse but give rise to very fast matrix-vector products (for example, via the Fast Fourier Transform) often also allow for applying the methods discussed in this section.

The meaning of "large matrices" is relative. Let us say we consider matrices of size millions. In order to take advantage of the large number of zero entries, special storage schemes are required; see, e.g., [**47**, Chap. 2]. We will assume that it is not easy to form a matrix decomposition such as the QR factorization. In particular, similarity transformations would destroy the sparsity. Hence, we will mainly rely on matrix-vector products, which are often computable in $\mathcal{O}(n)$ flops instead of $\mathcal{O}(n^2)$.

In this chapter, we review methods for computing a few eigenpairs of $\boldsymbol{A}$. In fact, in practice, one often needs the k smallest/largest eigenvalues or the k eigenvalues closest to $\mu \in \mathbb{C}$ for a small k and their corresponding eigenvectors. In the following, we introduce *orthogonal projection methods*, from which we can derive the state-of-the-art *Krylov methods*, which make use of cheap matrix-vector products. Note that projection methods even play a role for the methods discussed in Section 3.

4.1. Orthogonal projection methods. Suppose we want to find an approximation $(\hat{\lambda}, \hat{\boldsymbol{x}})$ of an eigenpair $(\lambda, \boldsymbol{x})$ of $\boldsymbol{A} \in \mathbb{R}^{n \times n}$. The idea of *projection techniques* is to extract $\hat{\boldsymbol{x}}$ from some subspace $\mathcal{K}$. This is called the *subspace of approximants* or the *right subspace*. The uniqueness of $\hat{\boldsymbol{x}}$ is typically realized via the imposition of orthogonality conditions. We denote by

$$\boldsymbol{r} = \boldsymbol{A}\hat{\boldsymbol{x}} - \hat{\lambda}\hat{\boldsymbol{x}}$$

the residual vector. It is a measure for the quality of the approximate eigenpair $(\hat{\lambda}, \hat{\boldsymbol{x}})$. The orthogonality conditions consist of constraining the residual $\boldsymbol{r}$ to be orthogonal to some subspace $\mathcal{L}$, i.e.,

$$\boldsymbol{r} \perp \mathcal{L}.$$

$\mathcal{L}$ is called the *left subspace*. This framework is commonly known as the *Petrov-Galerkin conditions* in diverse areas of mathematics, e.g., the finite element method. The case $\mathcal{L} = \mathcal{K}$ leads to the *Galerkin conditions* and gives an *orthogonal projection*, which we discuss next. The case where $\mathcal{L}$ is different from $\mathcal{K}$ is called *oblique projection*, and we quickly have a look into this framework at the end of this section. Let us assume that $\boldsymbol{A}$ is symmetric. Let $\mathcal{K}$ be a k-dimensional subspace of $\mathbb{R}^n$. An *orthogonal projection* technique onto $\mathcal{K}$ seeks an approximate eigenpair $(\hat{\lambda}, \hat{\boldsymbol{x}})$ such that $\hat{\boldsymbol{x}} \in \mathcal{K}$ and

$$\boldsymbol{A}\hat{\boldsymbol{x}} - \hat{\lambda}\hat{\boldsymbol{x}} \perp \mathcal{K},$$

or equivalently

$$\left(\boldsymbol{A}\hat{\boldsymbol{x}} - \hat{\lambda}\hat{\boldsymbol{x}}, \boldsymbol{v}\right) = 0 \quad \forall \boldsymbol{v} \in \mathcal{K}. \tag{4.1}$$

Let $\{\boldsymbol{q}_1, \ldots, \boldsymbol{q}_k\}$ be an orthonormal basis of $\mathcal{K}$ and $\boldsymbol{Q}_k = [\boldsymbol{q}_1 | \ldots | \boldsymbol{q}_k] \in \mathbb{R}^{n \times k}$. Then, (4.1) becomes

$$\left(\boldsymbol{A}\hat{\boldsymbol{x}} - \hat{\lambda}\hat{\boldsymbol{x}}, \boldsymbol{q}_i\right) = 0 \quad \forall i = 1, \ldots, k.$$

If we express $\hat{\boldsymbol{x}}$ in terms of the basis of $\mathcal{K}$, i.e., $\hat{\boldsymbol{x}} = \boldsymbol{Q}_k \boldsymbol{y}$, we get

$$\left(\boldsymbol{A}\boldsymbol{Q}_k\boldsymbol{y} - \hat{\lambda}\boldsymbol{Q}_k\boldsymbol{y}, \boldsymbol{q}_i\right) = 0 \quad \forall i = 1, \ldots, k,$$

and due to $\boldsymbol{Q}_k^T \boldsymbol{Q}_k = \boldsymbol{I}$, we obtain

$$\boldsymbol{Q}_k^T \boldsymbol{A} \boldsymbol{Q}_k \boldsymbol{y} = \hat{\lambda}\boldsymbol{y}.$$

This is the basis for *Krylov subspace methods*, which we discuss in the next section. The matrix $\boldsymbol{Q}_k^T \boldsymbol{A} \boldsymbol{Q}_k \in \mathbb{R}^{k \times k}$ will often be smaller than $\boldsymbol{A}$ and is either upper Hessenberg (nonsymmetric case) or tridiagonal (symmetric case). The *Rayleigh–Ritz procedure* presented in Algorithm 4.1 computes such a Galerkin approximation.

Algorithm 4.1: Rayleigh–Ritz procedure

1. Compute an orthonormal basis $\{\boldsymbol{q}_1, \ldots, \boldsymbol{q}_k\}$ of the subspace $\mathcal{K}$. Set $\boldsymbol{Q}_k = [\boldsymbol{q}_1 | \ldots | \boldsymbol{q}_k]$.
2. Compute $\boldsymbol{T}_k = \boldsymbol{Q}_k^T \boldsymbol{A} \boldsymbol{Q}_k$.
3. Compute j eigenvalues of $\boldsymbol{T}_k$, say $\theta_1, \ldots, \theta_j$.
4. Compute the corresponding eigenvectors $\boldsymbol{v}_j$ of $\boldsymbol{T}_k$. Then, the corresponding approximate eigenvectors of $\boldsymbol{A}$ are $\hat{\boldsymbol{x}}_j = \boldsymbol{Q}_k \boldsymbol{v}_j$.

The θ_i are called *Ritz values* and $\hat{\boldsymbol{x}}_i$ are the *Ritz vectors*. We will see that the Ritz values and Ritz vectors are the best approximate eigenpairs in the least-squares sense. But first, let us put the presented framework into a similarity transformation of $\boldsymbol{A}$: Suppose $\boldsymbol{Q} = [\boldsymbol{Q}_k, \boldsymbol{Q}_u] \in \mathbb{R}^{n \times n}$ is an orthogonal matrix with $\boldsymbol{Q}_k \in \mathbb{R}^{n \times k}$ being the matrix above that spans the subspace $\mathcal{K}$. We introduce

$$\boldsymbol{T} := \boldsymbol{Q}^T \boldsymbol{A} \boldsymbol{Q} = \begin{bmatrix} \boldsymbol{Q}_k^T \boldsymbol{A} \boldsymbol{Q}_k & \boldsymbol{Q}_k^T \boldsymbol{A} \boldsymbol{Q}_u \\ \boldsymbol{Q}_u^T \boldsymbol{A} \boldsymbol{Q}_k & \boldsymbol{Q}_u^T \boldsymbol{A} \boldsymbol{Q}_u \end{bmatrix} =: \begin{bmatrix} \boldsymbol{T}_k & \boldsymbol{T}_{uk} \\ \boldsymbol{T}_{ku} & \boldsymbol{T}_u \end{bmatrix}.$$

Let $\boldsymbol{T}_k = \boldsymbol{V}\boldsymbol{\Theta}\boldsymbol{V}^T$ be the eigendecomposition of $\boldsymbol{T}_k$. Note that for $k = 1$, $\boldsymbol{T}_1$ is just the Rayleigh quotient (see Definition 2.6).
Now, we can answer the question on the "best" approximation to an eigenvector in $\mathcal{K}$. Similar to the observation in Section 3.1 that the Rayleigh quotient is the best eigenvalue approximation in the least-squares sense, we have the following useful result.

THEOREM 4.1 (See [**11**, Theor. 7.1].). *The minimum of* $\|\boldsymbol{A}\boldsymbol{Q}_k - \boldsymbol{Q}_k\boldsymbol{R}\|_2$ *over all* $k \times k$ *symmetric matrices* $\boldsymbol{R}$ *is attained by* $\boldsymbol{R} = \boldsymbol{T}_k$, *in which case* $\|\boldsymbol{A}\boldsymbol{Q}_k - \boldsymbol{Q}_k\boldsymbol{R}\|_2 = \|\boldsymbol{T}_{ku}\|_2$. *Let* $\boldsymbol{T}_k = \boldsymbol{V}\boldsymbol{\Theta}\boldsymbol{V}^T$ *be the eigendecomposition of* $\boldsymbol{T}_k$. *The minimum of* $\|\boldsymbol{A}\boldsymbol{P}_k - \boldsymbol{P}_k\boldsymbol{D}\|_2$ *over all* $n \times k$ *orthogonal matrices* $\boldsymbol{P}_k$ $(\boldsymbol{P}_k^T\boldsymbol{P}_k = \boldsymbol{I})$ *where* $\operatorname{span}(\boldsymbol{P}_k) = \operatorname{span}(\boldsymbol{Q}_k)$ *and over diagonal matrices* $\boldsymbol{D}$ *is also* $\|\boldsymbol{T}_{ku}\|_2$ *and is attained by* $\boldsymbol{P}_k = \boldsymbol{Q}_k\boldsymbol{V}$ *and* $\boldsymbol{D} = \boldsymbol{\Lambda}$.

In practice, the columns of $\boldsymbol{Q}_k$ will be computed by, e.g., the *Lanczos algorithm* or *Arnoldi algorithm*, which we discuss in Section 4.3 and 4.4.
Now, let us have a quick look at the *oblique projection* technique in which $\mathcal{L}$ is different from $\mathcal{K}$. Let $\mathcal{K}$ and $\mathcal{L}$ be k-dimensional subspaces of $\mathbb{R}^n$. An *oblique projection* technique onto $\mathcal{K}$ seeks an approximate eigenpair $(\hat{\lambda}, \hat{\boldsymbol{x}})$ such that $\hat{\boldsymbol{x}} \in \mathcal{K}$ and

$$\boldsymbol{A}\hat{\boldsymbol{x}} - \hat{\lambda}\hat{\boldsymbol{x}} \perp \mathcal{L},$$

or equivalently

$$\left(\boldsymbol{A}\hat{\boldsymbol{x}} - \hat{\lambda}\hat{\boldsymbol{x}}, \boldsymbol{v}\right) = 0 \quad \forall \boldsymbol{v} \in \mathcal{L}. \tag{4.2}$$

Let $\{\boldsymbol{q}_1, \ldots, \boldsymbol{q}_k\}$ be an orthonormal basis of $\mathcal{K}$, $\{\boldsymbol{p}_1, \ldots, \boldsymbol{p}_k\}$ an orthonormal basis of $\mathcal{L}$, $\boldsymbol{Q}_k = [\boldsymbol{q}_1|\ldots|\boldsymbol{q}_k] \in \mathbb{R}^{n\times k}$, and $\boldsymbol{P}_k = [\boldsymbol{p}_1|\ldots|\boldsymbol{p}_k] \in \mathbb{R}^{n\times k}$. Further, we assume biorthogonality, i.e., $\boldsymbol{P}_k^T\boldsymbol{Q}_k = \boldsymbol{I}$. Then, (4.2) becomes

$$\left(\boldsymbol{A}\hat{\boldsymbol{x}} - \hat{\lambda}\hat{\boldsymbol{x}}, \boldsymbol{p}_i\right) = 0 \quad \forall i = 1, \ldots, k.$$

If we express $\hat{\boldsymbol{x}}$ in terms of the basis of $\mathcal{K}$, i.e., $\hat{\boldsymbol{x}} = \boldsymbol{Q}_k\boldsymbol{y}$, we get

$$\left(\boldsymbol{A}\boldsymbol{Q}_k\boldsymbol{y} - \hat{\lambda}\boldsymbol{Q}_k\boldsymbol{y}, \boldsymbol{p}_i\right) = 0 \quad \forall i = 1, \ldots, k,$$

and due to $\boldsymbol{P}_k^T\boldsymbol{Q}_k = \boldsymbol{I}$, we obtain

$$\boldsymbol{P}_k^T\boldsymbol{A}\boldsymbol{Q}_k\boldsymbol{y} = \hat{\lambda}\boldsymbol{y}.$$

Oblique projection techniques form the basis for the *non-Hermitian Lanczos process* [**25**, **26**, **41**], which belongs to the class of *Krylov subspace solvers*. Krylov subspace solvers form the topic of the next section. For a further discussion on the oblique projection technique, we refer to, e.g., [**47**, Chap. 4.3.3].

4.2. Krylov subspace methods. Let $\boldsymbol{A} \in \mathbb{R}^{n\times n}$. Krylov subspace methods are used to solve linear systems or eigenvalue problems of sparse matrices. They only require that $\boldsymbol{A}$ be accessible via a "black-box" subroutine which describes the application of $\boldsymbol{A}$ to a vector. A k-dimensional *Krylov subspace* associated with a matrix $\boldsymbol{A}$ and a vector $\boldsymbol{v}$ is the subspace given by

$$\mathcal{K}_k(\boldsymbol{A}; \boldsymbol{v}) = \operatorname{span}\{\boldsymbol{v}, \boldsymbol{A}\boldsymbol{v}, \boldsymbol{A}^2\boldsymbol{v}, \ldots, \boldsymbol{A}^{k-1}\boldsymbol{v}\}.$$

The corresponding *Krylov matrix* is denoted by

$$\boldsymbol{K}_k(\boldsymbol{A}; \boldsymbol{v}) = [\boldsymbol{v}|\boldsymbol{A}\boldsymbol{v}|\boldsymbol{A}^2\boldsymbol{v}|\ldots|\boldsymbol{A}^{k-1}\boldsymbol{v}].$$

Using a Krylov subspace as *right subspace* $\mathcal{K}$ in projection methods has proven to be efficient. Various Krylov subspace methods arose from different choices of the *left subspaces* $\mathcal{L}$. The Krylov subspace $\mathcal{K}_k(\boldsymbol{A};\boldsymbol{v})$ arises naturally if we refer to it as the subspace generated by $k-1$ steps of the power iteration (see Section 3.1) with initial guess $\boldsymbol{v}$. Similarly, for the inverse power iteration (see Section 3.2), we obtain the subspace

$$\mathcal{K}_k\left((\boldsymbol{A}-\alpha\boldsymbol{I})^{-1};\boldsymbol{v}\right).$$

Both iterations produce a sequence of vectors $\boldsymbol{v}_1,\ldots,\boldsymbol{v}_k$ that span a Krylov subspace and take $\boldsymbol{v}_k$ as the approximate eigenvector. Now, rather than taking $\boldsymbol{v}_k$, it is natural to use the whole sequence $\boldsymbol{v}_1,\ldots,\boldsymbol{v}_k$ in searching for the eigenvector. In fact, we saw in the previous section (Theorem 4.1 for the symmetric case) that we can even use $\mathcal{K}_k$ to compute the k best approximate eigenvalues and eigenvectors. There are three basic algorithms for generating a basis for the Krylov subspace: the *Lanczos process* for symmetric matrices, which we discuss next, the *Arnoldi process* for nonsymmetric matrices (Section 4.4), and the *nonsymmetric Lanczos process*. The latter computes matrices $\boldsymbol{Q}$ and $\boldsymbol{P}$ with $\boldsymbol{P}^T\boldsymbol{Q}=\boldsymbol{I}$ such that $\boldsymbol{P}^T\boldsymbol{A}\boldsymbol{Q}$ is tridiagonal; see, e.g., [**25**, **26**, **41**]. Moreover, there exist *block versions* of the Arnoldi and Lanczos process; see, e.g., [**8**, **48**], which may exploit the block structure of a matrix in some situations. They are basically an acceleration technique of the *subspace iteration*, similar to the way the subspace iteration generalizes the power methods.

4.3. The Lanczos process. Let $\boldsymbol{A}\in\mathbb{R}^{n\times n}$ be symmetric. The *Lanczos process* computes an orthogonal basis for the Krylov subspace $\mathcal{K}_k(\boldsymbol{A};\boldsymbol{v})$ for some initial vector $\boldsymbol{v}$, and approximates the eigenvalues of $\boldsymbol{A}$ by the Ritz values.
Recall that the Hessenberg reduction of a symmetric matrix $\boldsymbol{A}$ reduces to a tridiagonal matrix, i.e., there exists an orthogonal $\boldsymbol{Q}\in\mathbb{R}^{n\times n}$ such that

$$\boldsymbol{T}=\boldsymbol{Q}^T\boldsymbol{A}\boldsymbol{Q}=\begin{bmatrix}\alpha_1 & \beta_1 & & & \\ \beta_1 & \alpha_2 & \beta_2 & & \\ & \beta_2 & \alpha_3 & \ddots & \\ & & \ddots & \ddots & \beta_{n-1} \\ & & & \beta_{n-1} & \alpha_n\end{bmatrix}. \tag{4.3}$$

The connection between the tridiagonalization of $\boldsymbol{A}$ and the QR factorization of $\boldsymbol{K}_k(\boldsymbol{A};\boldsymbol{q}_1)$, where $\boldsymbol{q}_1=\boldsymbol{Q}\boldsymbol{e}_1$ is given as follows:

THEOREM 4.2 (See [**22**, Theor. 8.3.1].). *Let (4.3) be the tridiagonal decomposition of a symmetric matrix $\boldsymbol{A}\in\mathbb{R}^{n\times n}$ with $\boldsymbol{q}_1=\boldsymbol{Q}\boldsymbol{e}_1$. Then:*

(1) $\boldsymbol{Q}^T\boldsymbol{K}_n(\boldsymbol{A};\boldsymbol{q}_1)=\boldsymbol{R}$ *is upper triangular.*
(2) *If $\boldsymbol{R}$ is nonsingular, then $\boldsymbol{T}$ is unreduced.*
(3) *If $k=\arg\min_{j=1,\ldots,n}\{r_{j,j}=0\}$, then $k-1=\arg\min_{j=1,\ldots,n-1}\{\beta_j=0\}$.*

It follows from (1) in Theorem 4.2 that $\boldsymbol{Q}\boldsymbol{R}$ is the QR factorization of $\boldsymbol{K}_n(\boldsymbol{A};\boldsymbol{q}_1)$. In order to preserve the sparsity, we need an alternative to similarity transformations in order to compute the tridiagonalization. Let us write $\boldsymbol{Q}=[\boldsymbol{q}_1|\ldots|\boldsymbol{q}_n]$. Considering the kth column of $\boldsymbol{A}\boldsymbol{Q}=\boldsymbol{Q}\boldsymbol{T}$, we obtain the following three-term recurrence:

$$\boldsymbol{A}\boldsymbol{q}_k=\beta_{k-1}\boldsymbol{q}_{k-1}+\alpha_k\boldsymbol{q}_k+\beta_k\boldsymbol{q}_{k+1}. \tag{4.4}$$

Since the columns of $\boldsymbol{Q}$ are orthonormal, multiplying (4.4) from the left by $\boldsymbol{q}_k$ yields

$$\alpha_k = \boldsymbol{q}_k^T \boldsymbol{A} \boldsymbol{q}_k.$$

This leads to the method in Algorithm 4.2 developed by Lanczos in 1950 [**34**].

Algorithm 4.2: Lanczos process

Given $\boldsymbol{q}_0 = \boldsymbol{0}$, $\boldsymbol{q}_1 = \frac{\boldsymbol{v}}{\|\boldsymbol{v}\|_2}$, $\beta_0 = 0$
for $k = 1, 2, \ldots$ **do**
  $\boldsymbol{z}_k = \boldsymbol{A}\boldsymbol{q}_k$
  $\alpha_k = \boldsymbol{q}_k^T \boldsymbol{z}_k$
  $\boldsymbol{z}_k = \boldsymbol{z}_k - \beta_{k-1}\boldsymbol{q}_{k-1} - \alpha_k \boldsymbol{q}_k$
  $\beta_k = \|\boldsymbol{z}_k\|_2$
  if $\beta_k = 0$ **then**
    quit
  end
  $\boldsymbol{q}_{k+1} = \frac{\boldsymbol{z}_k}{\beta_k}$
end

The vectors $\boldsymbol{q}_k$ computed by the Lanczos algorithm are called *Lanczos vectors*. The Lanczos process stops before the complete tridiagonalization if $\boldsymbol{q}_1$ is contained in an exact $\boldsymbol{A}$-invariant subspace:

THEOREM 4.3 (See [**22**, Theor. 10.1.1].). *The Lanczos Algorithm* 4.2 *runs until* $k = m$, *where*

$$m = \operatorname{rank}(\boldsymbol{K}_n(\boldsymbol{A}, \boldsymbol{q}_1)).$$

Moreover, for $k = 1, \ldots, m$, *we have*

$$\boldsymbol{A}\boldsymbol{Q}_k = \boldsymbol{Q}_k \boldsymbol{T}_k + \beta_k \boldsymbol{q}_{k+1} \boldsymbol{e}_k^T, \tag{4.5}$$

where $\boldsymbol{T}_k = \boldsymbol{T}(1:k, 1:k)$, $\boldsymbol{Q}_k = [\boldsymbol{q}_1 | \ldots | \boldsymbol{q}_k]$ *has orthonormal columns with*

$$\operatorname{span}\{\boldsymbol{q}_1, \ldots, \boldsymbol{q}_k\} = \mathcal{K}_k(\boldsymbol{A}, \boldsymbol{q}_1).$$

In particular, $\beta_m = 0$, *and hence*

$$\boldsymbol{A}\boldsymbol{Q}_m = \boldsymbol{Q}_m \boldsymbol{T}_m.$$

The eigenvalues of the tridiagonal $\boldsymbol{T}_m$ can then be computed via, e.g., the QR iteration. A corresponding eigenvector can be obtained by using the inverse power iteration with the approximated eigenvalue as shift.

We can show that the quality of the approximation after k Lanczos steps depends on β_k and on parts of the eigenvectors of $\boldsymbol{T}_k$ (cf. [**22**, Chap. 10.1.4]): Therefore, let $(\theta, \boldsymbol{y})$ be an eigenpair of $\boldsymbol{T}_k$. Applying (4.5) to $\boldsymbol{y}$ yields

$$\begin{aligned} \boldsymbol{A}\boldsymbol{Q}_k\boldsymbol{y} &= \boldsymbol{Q}_k\boldsymbol{T}_k\boldsymbol{y} + \beta_k \boldsymbol{q}_{k+1}\boldsymbol{e}_k^T\boldsymbol{y} \\ &= \theta\boldsymbol{Q}_k\boldsymbol{y} + \beta_k \boldsymbol{q}_{k+1}\boldsymbol{e}_k^T\boldsymbol{y} \end{aligned}$$

and hence the following error estimation (cf. Theorem 4.1)

$$\|\boldsymbol{A}\boldsymbol{Q}_k\boldsymbol{y} - \theta\boldsymbol{Q}_k\boldsymbol{y}\|_2 = |\beta_k|\,|\boldsymbol{e}_k^T\boldsymbol{y}|.$$

Hence, we want to accomplish $\beta_k = 0$ fast. Regarding the convergence theory, we refer to [**31**, **38**, **43**] and [**22**, Chap. 10.1.5]. In summary, the Ritz values converge

fast to the extreme eigenvalues. Using shift and invert strategies (as in the inverse power method in Section 3.2), we can obtain convergence to interior eigenvalues. In practice, rounding errors have a significant effect on the behavior of the Lanczos iteration. If the computed β_k are close to zero, then the Lanczos vectors lose their orthogonality. Reorthogonalization strategies provide a remedy; see, e.g., [**6**, **21**, **38**, **40**, **50**, **67**]. Nevertheless, we know from the last section that the Ritz values and vectors are good approximations.
So far, we have assumed that $\boldsymbol{A}$ is symmetric. Next, we consider the nonsymmetric case.

4.4. The Arnoldi process. For a nonsymmetric $\boldsymbol{A} \in \mathbb{R}^{n\times n}$, we know that there exists a Hessenberg decomposition, i.e., there exists an orthogonal $\boldsymbol{Q} \in \mathbb{R}^{n\times n}$ such that

$$\boldsymbol{H} = \boldsymbol{Q}^T\boldsymbol{A}\boldsymbol{Q} = \begin{bmatrix} h_{1,1} & h_{1,2} & h_{1,3} & \cdots & h_{1,n} \\ h_{2,1} & h_{2,2} & h_{2,3} & \cdots & h_{2,n} \\ 0 & h_{3,2} & h_{3,3} & \ddots & \vdots \\ \vdots & \ddots & \ddots & \ddots & h_{n-1,n} \\ 0 & \cdots & 0 & h_{n,n-1} & h_{n,n} \end{bmatrix}. \tag{4.6}$$

The connection between the Hessenberg reduction of $\boldsymbol{A}$ and the QR factorization of $\boldsymbol{K}_k(\boldsymbol{A};\boldsymbol{q}_1)$, where $\boldsymbol{q}_1 = \boldsymbol{Q}\boldsymbol{e}_1$ is given as follows (cf. the symmetric case in Theorem 4.2)

THEOREM 4.4 (See [**22**, Theor. 7.4.3].). *Suppose $\boldsymbol{Q} \in \mathbb{R}^{n\times n}$ is orthogonal and let $\boldsymbol{q}_1 = \boldsymbol{Q}\boldsymbol{e}_1$ and $\boldsymbol{A} \in \mathbb{R}^{n\times n}$. Then, $\boldsymbol{Q}^T\boldsymbol{A}\boldsymbol{Q} = \boldsymbol{H}$ is an unreduced upper Hessenberg matrix if and only if $\boldsymbol{Q}^T\boldsymbol{K}_n(\boldsymbol{A};\boldsymbol{q}_1) = \boldsymbol{R}$ is nonsingular and upper triangular.*

It follows from Theorem 4.4 that $\boldsymbol{Q}\boldsymbol{R}$ is the QR factorization of $\boldsymbol{K}_n(\boldsymbol{A};\boldsymbol{q}_1)$. As before, in order to preserve the sparsity, we need an alternative to similarity transformations in order to compute the Hessenberg reduction. Let us write $\boldsymbol{Q} = [\boldsymbol{q}_1|\cdots|\boldsymbol{q}_n]$. Considering the kth column of $\boldsymbol{A}\boldsymbol{Q} = \boldsymbol{Q}\boldsymbol{H}$, we obtain the following recurrence:

$$\boldsymbol{A}\boldsymbol{q}_k = \sum_{i=1}^{k+1} h_{i,k}\boldsymbol{q}_i. \tag{4.7}$$

Since the columns of $\boldsymbol{Q}$ are orthonormal, multiplying (4.7) from the left by $\boldsymbol{q}_i$ yields

$$h_{i,k} = \boldsymbol{q}_i^T\boldsymbol{A}\boldsymbol{q}_k$$

for $i = 1, \dots, k$. This leads to the method in Algorithm 4.3 developed by Arnoldi in 1951 [**1**]. It can be viewed as an extension of the Lanczos process to nonsymmetric matrices.
Note that, in contrast to the symmetric case, we have no three-term recurrence anymore. Hence, we have to store all computed vectors $\boldsymbol{q}_k$. These vectors are called *Arnoldi vectors*. The Arnoldi process can be seen as a modified Gram-Schmidt orthogonalization process (cf. [**22**, Chap. 5.2.8]) since in each step k we orthogonalize $\boldsymbol{A}\boldsymbol{q}_k$ against all previous $\boldsymbol{q}_i$ — ths requires $O(kn)$ flops. Hence, the computational cost grows rapidly with the number of steps. After k steps of the Arnoldi Algorithm 4.3, we have

$$\boldsymbol{A}\boldsymbol{Q}_k = \boldsymbol{Q}_k\boldsymbol{H}_k + h_{k+1,k}\boldsymbol{q}_{k+1}\boldsymbol{e}_k^T, \tag{4.8}$$

Algorithm 4.3: Arnoldi process

Given $\boldsymbol{q}_1 = \frac{\boldsymbol{v}}{\|\boldsymbol{v}\|_2}$
for $k = 1, 2, \ldots$ **do**
  $\boldsymbol{z}_k = \boldsymbol{A}\boldsymbol{q}_k$
  for $i = 1, \ldots, k$ **do**
    $h_{i,k} = \boldsymbol{q}_i^T \boldsymbol{z}_k$
    $\boldsymbol{z}_k = \boldsymbol{z}_k - h_{i,k}\boldsymbol{q}_i$
  end
  $h_{k+1,k} = \|\boldsymbol{z}_k\|_2$
  if $h_{k+1,k} = 0$ **then**
    quit
  end
  $\boldsymbol{q}_{k+1} = \frac{\boldsymbol{z}_k}{h_{k+1,k}}$
end

where $\boldsymbol{H}_k = \boldsymbol{H}(1:k, 1:k)$ and

$$\operatorname{span}\{\boldsymbol{q}_1, \ldots, \boldsymbol{q}_k\} = \mathcal{K}_k(\boldsymbol{A}, \boldsymbol{q}_1). \tag{4.9}$$

We can show that the quality of the approximation depends on the magnitude of $h_{k+1,k}$ and on parts of the eigenvectors of $\boldsymbol{H}_k$ (cf. [**22**, Chap. 10.5.1]): Therefore, let $(\theta, \boldsymbol{y})$ be an eigenpair of $\boldsymbol{H}_k$. Applying (4.8) to $\boldsymbol{y}$ yields

$$\begin{aligned} \boldsymbol{A}\boldsymbol{Q}_k\boldsymbol{y} &= \boldsymbol{Q}_k\boldsymbol{H}_k\boldsymbol{y} + h_{k+1,k}\boldsymbol{q}_{k+1}\boldsymbol{e}_k^T\boldsymbol{y} \\ &= \theta\boldsymbol{Q}_k\boldsymbol{y} + h_{k+1,k}\boldsymbol{q}_{k+1}\boldsymbol{e}_k^T\boldsymbol{y} \end{aligned}$$

and hence the following error estimation (cf. Theorem 4.1)

$$\|\boldsymbol{A}\boldsymbol{Q}_k\boldsymbol{y} - \theta\boldsymbol{Q}_k\boldsymbol{y}\|_2 = |h_{k+1,k}|\,|\boldsymbol{e}_k^T\boldsymbol{y}|.$$

Hence, we want $h_{k+1,k} = 0$ fast. As the Lanczos process, the Arnoldi process has a (lucky) breakdown at step $k = m$ if $h_{m+1,m} = 0$ since $\mathcal{K}_m(\boldsymbol{A}, \boldsymbol{q}_1)$ is an $\boldsymbol{A}$-invariant subspace in this case. In the following, we discuss accelerating techniques for the Arnoldi and Lanczos process.

4.5. Restarted Arnoldi and Lanczos. Note that with each Arnoldi step we have to store one additional Arnoldi vector. A remedy is restarting the Arnoldi process with carefully chosen restarts after a certain maximum of steps is reached. Acceleration techniques (mainly of a polynomial nature) generate an initial guess with small components in the unwanted parts of the spectrum. The strategies we present are called *polynomial acceleration* or *filtering techniques*. They exploit the powers of a matrix similar as the power method in the sense that they generate iterations of the form

$$\boldsymbol{z}_r = p_r(\boldsymbol{A})\boldsymbol{z}_0,$$

where p_r is a polynomial of degree r. In the case of the power method, we have $p_r(t) = t^r$. Filtering methods have been successfully combined with the subspace iteration. When combined with the Arnoldi process, they are often called *implicitly restarted methods*, which we discuss next. Selecting a good polynomial often relies on some knowledge of the eigenvalues or related quantities (e.g., Ritz values).

Suppose $\boldsymbol{A} \in \mathbb{R}^{n\times n}$ is diagonalizable and has eigenpairs $\{(\lambda_i, \boldsymbol{x}_i)\}_{i=1,\dots,n}$ with $\lambda_1 \geq \dots \geq \lambda_n$. Let

$$\boldsymbol{q}_1 = \sum_{i=1}^{n} \alpha_i \boldsymbol{x}_i$$

be an initial guess for the Arnoldi process. After running r steps of the Arnoldi process, we do a restart. We may seek a new initial vector from the span of the Arnoldi vectors $\boldsymbol{q}_1, \dots, \boldsymbol{q}_r$, which has, due to (4.9), the form

$$\begin{aligned}\boldsymbol{q}_+ &= \sum_{j=1}^{r} \beta_j \boldsymbol{A}^{j-1}\boldsymbol{q}_1 = \sum_{j=1}^{r} \beta_j \sum_{i=1}^{n} \alpha_i \boldsymbol{A}^{j-1}\boldsymbol{x}_i = \sum_{j=1}^{r} \beta_j \sum_{i=1}^{n} \alpha_i \lambda_i^{j-1}\boldsymbol{x}_i \\ &= \sum_{i=1}^{n} \alpha_i p_{r-1}(\lambda_i)\boldsymbol{x}_i.\end{aligned}$$

Suppose we are interested in the eigenvalue λ_j. If $|\alpha_j p_{r-1}(\lambda_j)| \gg |\alpha_l p_{r-1}(\lambda_l)|$ for all $l \neq j$, then $\boldsymbol{q}_+$ has large components in the eigendirection $\boldsymbol{x}_j$. Note that the α_i are unknown. Hence, with an appropriate constructed polynomial, we can amplify the components in the desired parts of the spectrum. For instance, we are seeking for a polynomial that satisfies $p_{r-1}(\lambda_j) = 1$ and $|p_{r-1}(\lambda_l)| \ll 1$ for all $l \neq j$. However, the eigenvalues λ_i are unknown as well. Hence we need some approximation. Let Ω be a domain (e.g., an ellipse) that contains $\lambda(\boldsymbol{A}) \setminus \{\lambda_j\}$, and suppose we have an estimate of λ_j. Then, we can aim to solve

$$\min_{\substack{p_{r-1}\in P_{r-1},\\ p_{r-1}(\lambda_j)=1}} \max_{t\in\Omega} |p_{r-1}(t)|.$$

Suitable polynomials include the shifted and scaled Chebyshev polynomials, and in the symmetric case, we can exploit the three-term recurrence for fast computation; see, e.g., [**45**].

An alternative to Chebyshev polynomials is the following: Given $\{\theta_i\}_{i=1,\dots,r-1}$, then one natural idea is to set

$$p_{r-1}(t) = (t-\theta_1)(t-\theta_2)\cdots(t-\theta_{r-1}); \tag{4.10}$$

see [**22**, Chap. 10.5.2]. If $\lambda_i \approx \theta_l$ for some l, then $\boldsymbol{q}_+$ has small components in the eigendirection $\boldsymbol{x}_i$. Hence, the θ_i are all unwanted values. For θ_i we can use the Ritz values, which presumably approximate the eigenvalues of $\boldsymbol{A}$. For further heuristics, we refer to [**44**].

The above strategies are *explicit restarting* techniques, which use only one vector for the restart. The following *implicit restarting* strategy uses k vectors from the previous Arnoldi process for the new restarted Arnoldi process and throws away the remaining $r-k =: p$ vectors. The procedure was developed in 1992 [**53**]. It implicitly determines a polynomial of the form (4.10) using the QR iteration with shifts. Suppose we have performed r steps of the Arnoldi iteration with starting vector $\boldsymbol{q}_1$. Due to (4.8), we have

$$\boldsymbol{A}\boldsymbol{Q}_r = \boldsymbol{Q}_r\boldsymbol{H}_r + h_{r+1,r}\boldsymbol{q}_{r+1}\boldsymbol{e}_r^T, \tag{4.11}$$

where $\boldsymbol{H}_r \in \mathbb{R}^{r\times r}$ is upper Hessenberg, $\boldsymbol{Q}_r \in \mathbb{R}^{n\times r}$ has orthonormal columns, and $\boldsymbol{Q}_r\boldsymbol{e}_1 = \boldsymbol{q}_1$. Next, we apply p steps of the QR iteration with shifts $\theta_1, \dots, \theta_p$

(Algorithm 3.6), i.e., in step i we compute

$$V_i R_i = H^{(i-1)} - \theta_i I, \tag{4.12}$$

$$H^{(i)} = R_i V_i + \theta_i I, \tag{4.13}$$

where $H^{(0)} = H_r$. After p steps, we have

$$H^{(p)} = R_p V_p + \theta_p I = V_p^T (V_p R_p + \theta_p I) V_p = V_p^T H^{(p-1)} V_p = \ldots = V^T H^{(0)} V$$

with $V = V_1 \cdots V_p$. We use the notation

$$H_+ := H^{(p)} = V^T H^{(0)} V = V^T H_r V. \tag{4.14}$$

The relationship to a polynomial of the form (4.10) is the following:

THEOREM 4.5 (See [**22**, Theor. 10.5.1].). *If $V = V_1 \cdots V_p$ and $R = R_p \cdots R_1$ are defined by (4.12)–(4.13), then*

$$VR = (H_r - \theta_1 I) \cdots (H_r - \theta_p I).$$

Using (4.14), we get in (4.11)

$$AQ_r = Q_r V H_+ V^T + h_{r+1,r} q_{r+1} e_r^T. \tag{4.15}$$

Multiplying (4.15) from the right by V yields

$$AQ_+ = Q_+ H_+ + h_{r+1,r} q_{r+1} e_r^T V \tag{4.16}$$

with $Q_+ = Q_r V$. It can be shown that $V_1, \ldots, V_p$ from the shifted QR iteration are upper Hessenberg. Hence, $V(r, 1 : r - p - 1) = 0^T$ and therefore $e_r^T V = [0 \cdots 0\, \alpha \, * \cdots *]$ is a row vector of length r whose first $r - p - 1$ entries are zero. Now, using the notation $Q_+ = [\hat{Q}_{r-p}, \hat{Q}_p]$ with $\hat{Q}_{r-p} \in \mathbb{R}^{n \times (r-p)}$ we can write (4.16) as

$$A[\hat{Q}_{r-p}, \hat{Q}_p] = [\hat{Q}_{r-p}, \hat{Q}_p] \begin{bmatrix} \hat{H}_{r-p} & * \\ \beta e_1 e_{r-p}^T & * \end{bmatrix} + h_{r+1,r} q_{r+1} [\underbrace{0 \cdots 0}_{r-p-1} \alpha * \cdots *]. \tag{4.17}$$

Now, we throw away the last p columns in (4.17) and obtain an $(r-p)$-step Arnoldi decomposition

$$\begin{aligned} A\hat{Q}_{r-p} &= \hat{Q}_{r-p} \hat{H}_{r-p} + \beta \hat{Q}_p e_1 e_{r-p}^T + h_{r+1,r} q_{r+1} [\underbrace{0 \cdots 0}_{r-p-1} \alpha] \\ &= \hat{Q}_{r-p} \hat{H}_{r-p} + \left(\beta \hat{Q}_p e_1 + \alpha h_{r+1,r} q_{r+1} \right) e_{r-p}^T \\ &=: \hat{Q}_{r-p} \hat{H}_{r-p} + \hat{v}_{r+1} e_{r-p}^T. \end{aligned}$$

This is the Arnoldi recursion we would have obtained by restarting the Arnoldi process with the starting vector $q_+ = Q_+ e_1$. Hence, we do not need to restart the Arnoldi process from step one but rather from step $r - p + 1$. For further details, we refer to [**22**, Chap. 10.5.3] and the references therein.

REMARK 4.6. It can be shown (cf. [**22**, Chap. 10.5.3]) that

$$q_+ = c\,(A - \theta_1 I) \cdots (A - \theta_p I)\, Q_r e_1$$

for some scalar c and is hence of the form (4.10).

For further reading on the Arnoldi process we refer to, e.g., [**47, 54, 55, 62**].
Next we present another acceleration technique which is very popular for solving linear systems.

4.6. Preconditioning. In the following, we quickly review the preconditioning concept for solving large and sparse systems of linear equations of the general form

$$\boldsymbol{Az} = \boldsymbol{b}. \tag{4.18}$$

Here, $\boldsymbol{A} \in \mathbb{R}^{n \times n}$ is the given coefficient matrix, $\boldsymbol{z} \in \mathbb{R}^n$ is the unknown solution vector, and $\boldsymbol{b} \in \mathbb{R}^n$ is the given right-hand side vector. In order for the Equation (4.18) to have a unique solution, we assume that $\boldsymbol{A}$ is nonsingular. Systems of the form (4.18) arise after the discretization of a continuous problem like partial differential equations such as the time-harmonic Maxwell equations. Other applications arise in incompressible magnetohydrodynamics as well as constrained optimization. As already mentioned in Section 4.2, Krylov subspace solvers are also used for solving linear systems. In fact, they are state-of-the-art iterative solvers. However, they are usually only efficient in combination with an accelerator, which is called a *preconditioner*. The aim of a preconditioner is to enhance the convergence of the iterative solver. In our case, we want to accelerate the speed of convergence of Krylov subspace solvers. The basic idea is to construct a nonsingular matrix $\boldsymbol{P} \in \mathbb{R}^{n \times n}$ and solve

$$\boldsymbol{P}^{-1}\boldsymbol{Az} = \boldsymbol{P}^{-1}\boldsymbol{b} \tag{4.19}$$

instead of $\boldsymbol{Az} = \boldsymbol{b}$. In order for $\boldsymbol{P}$ to be efficient, it should approximate $\boldsymbol{A}$, and at the same time, the action of $\boldsymbol{P}^{-1}$ should require little work. The construction process of $\boldsymbol{P}$ should incorporate the goal of eigenvalue clustering. That means, $\boldsymbol{P}^{-1}\boldsymbol{A}$ is aimed to have a few number of eigenvalues or eigenvalue clusters. This is bases on the following: In a nutshell, for linear systems the residual of a Krylov subspace solver $\boldsymbol{r}_k = \boldsymbol{b} - \boldsymbol{Az}_k$ satisfies $\boldsymbol{r}_k = p_k(\boldsymbol{A})\boldsymbol{r}_0$, and one approach would be to minimize the norm of the residual, which amounts to requiring that $\|p_k(\lambda_i)\boldsymbol{v}_i\|_2$ be as small as possible for all $i = 1, \ldots, n$. Here, $\{(\lambda_i, \boldsymbol{v}_i)\}_{i=1,\ldots,n}$ are the eigenpairs of $\boldsymbol{A}$. Therefore, replacing $\boldsymbol{A}$ by $\boldsymbol{P}^{-1}\boldsymbol{A}$ such that $\boldsymbol{P}^{-1}\boldsymbol{A}$ has more clustered eigenvalues is one way to go. This typically results in outstanding performances of Krylov subspace solvers. For an overview of iterative solvers and preconditioning techniques, we refer to [**2, 4, 5, 16, 20, 23, 46, 59**].
Preconditioning plays an important role in eigenvalue problems as well. Taken in the same spirit as seeking an operator that improves the spectrum, we can think of the inverse power iteration (see Section 3.2) as a preconditioning approach: The operator $(\boldsymbol{A} - \theta\boldsymbol{I})^{-1}$ has a much better spectrum than $\boldsymbol{A}$ for a suitable chosen shift θ. So, we can run Arnoldi on $(\boldsymbol{A} - \theta\boldsymbol{I})^{-1}$ rather than $\boldsymbol{A}$ since the eigenvectors of $\boldsymbol{A}$ and $(\boldsymbol{A} - \theta\boldsymbol{I})^{-1}$ are identical. Another idea is to incorporate polynomial preconditioning, i.e., replace $\boldsymbol{A}$ by $p_k(\boldsymbol{A})$. As a guideline, we want to transform the k wanted eigenvalues of $\boldsymbol{A}$ to k eigenvalues of $p_k(\boldsymbol{A})$ that are much larger than the other eigenvalues, so as to accelerate convergence. Preconditioning also plays a role in solving *generalized eigenvalue problems*

$$\boldsymbol{Ax} = \lambda\boldsymbol{Bx}.$$

They can be solved, e.g., by the *Jacobi–Davidson method*, whose idea we briefly discuss in Section 4.8 for solving the standard algebraic eigenvalue problem $\boldsymbol{Ax} = \lambda\boldsymbol{x}$. The discussion of generalized eigenproblems is out of the scope of this survey. We refer the reader to [**56, 57, 62**] for a background to these problems.

4.7. Davidson method. Davidson's method is basically a preconditioned version of the Lanczos process, but the amount of work increases similarly to Arnoldi, due to increased orthogonalization requirements. Let $\boldsymbol{A} \in \mathbb{R}^{n\times n}$ and $\mathcal{K}_k = \mathcal{K}_k(\boldsymbol{A};\boldsymbol{v})$ be a Krylov subspace with respect to some vector $\boldsymbol{v}$. Let $\{\boldsymbol{q}_1,\dots,\boldsymbol{q}_k\}$ be an orthonormal basis of $\mathcal{K}_k$. In the orthogonal projection technique, we are seeking for an $\hat{x} \in \mathcal{K}_k$ such that

$$\left(\boldsymbol{A}\hat{\boldsymbol{x}} - \hat{\lambda}\hat{\boldsymbol{x}}, \boldsymbol{q}_i\right) = 0 \quad \forall i = 1,\dots,k,$$

Suppose, we have a Ritz pair $(\theta_i, \boldsymbol{u}_i)$. Then, the residual is given by

$$\boldsymbol{r}_i = \boldsymbol{A}\boldsymbol{u}_i - \theta_i\boldsymbol{u}_i = (\boldsymbol{A} - \theta_i\boldsymbol{I})\boldsymbol{u}_i.$$

Now, we can improve the eigenpair approximation by precondition the residual, i.e., by solving

$$(\boldsymbol{P} - \theta_i\boldsymbol{I})\,\boldsymbol{t} = \boldsymbol{r}_i,$$

and define $\boldsymbol{t}$ as a new search direction, enriching the subspace. That is, $\boldsymbol{t}$ is orthogonalized against all basis vectors $\boldsymbol{q}_1,\dots,\boldsymbol{q}_k$, and the resulting vector $\boldsymbol{q}_{k+1}$ enriches $\mathcal{K}_k$ to $\mathcal{K}_{k+1}$.

Davidson [**10**] originally proposed to precondition with the diagonal matrix of $\boldsymbol{A}$, i.e., $\boldsymbol{P} = \text{diag}(\boldsymbol{A})$, since he dealt with a diagonal dominant matrix $\boldsymbol{A}$. Additionally, diagonal preconditioning offers a computationally cheap iteration. For the use of other preconditioners, we refer to [**7**]. Further references on Davidson's method include [**36, 54, 55**].

Next, we consider an extension of Davdison's method, which has the potential of working better for matrices that are not diagonally dominant.

4.8. Jacobi–Davidson method. The idea is to extend the strategy of preconditioning the residual. If $(\hat{\lambda}, \hat{\boldsymbol{x}})$ with $\|\hat{\boldsymbol{x}}\|_2 = 1$ is an approximate eigenpair of $\boldsymbol{A}$, then the residual is $\boldsymbol{r} = \boldsymbol{A}\hat{\boldsymbol{x}} - \hat{\lambda}\hat{\boldsymbol{x}}$. Now, we look for $(\hat{\lambda} + \delta\hat{\lambda}, \hat{\boldsymbol{x}} + \delta\hat{\boldsymbol{x}})$ to improve the eigenpair. We write

$$\boldsymbol{A}(\hat{\boldsymbol{x}} + \delta\hat{\boldsymbol{x}}) = (\hat{\lambda} + \delta\hat{\lambda})(\hat{\boldsymbol{x}} + \delta\hat{\boldsymbol{x}}),$$

which is equivalent to

$$(\boldsymbol{A} - \hat{\lambda}\boldsymbol{I})\delta\hat{\boldsymbol{x}} - \delta\hat{\lambda}\hat{\boldsymbol{x}} = -\boldsymbol{r} + \delta\hat{\lambda}\delta\hat{\boldsymbol{x}}.$$

By neglecting the second-order term, we obtain

$$(\boldsymbol{A} - \hat{\lambda}\boldsymbol{I})\delta\hat{\boldsymbol{x}} - \delta\hat{\lambda}\hat{\boldsymbol{x}} = -\boldsymbol{r}.$$

This is an underdetermined system and a constraint must be added, e.g., $\|\hat{\boldsymbol{x}} + \delta\hat{\boldsymbol{x}}\|_2 = 1$. With $\|\hat{\boldsymbol{x}}\|_2 = 1$ and neglecting the second-order term, this condition becomes

$$\hat{\boldsymbol{x}}^T\delta\hat{\boldsymbol{x}} = 0.$$

If $\hat{\lambda} = \hat{\boldsymbol{x}}^T\boldsymbol{A}\hat{\boldsymbol{x}}$, then we obtain $\delta\hat{\boldsymbol{x}}$ by solving the projected system

$$\begin{aligned}
\left(\boldsymbol{I} - \hat{\boldsymbol{x}}\hat{\boldsymbol{x}}^T\right)(\boldsymbol{A} - \hat{\boldsymbol{\lambda}}\boldsymbol{I})\left(\boldsymbol{I} - \hat{\boldsymbol{x}}\hat{\boldsymbol{x}}^T\right)\delta\hat{\boldsymbol{x}} &= -\left(\boldsymbol{I} - \hat{\boldsymbol{x}}\hat{\boldsymbol{x}}^T\right)(\boldsymbol{r} - \delta\hat{\boldsymbol{\lambda}}\hat{\boldsymbol{x}}) \\
&= -\left(\boldsymbol{I} - \hat{\boldsymbol{x}}\hat{\boldsymbol{x}}^T\right)\boldsymbol{r} \\
&= -\left(\boldsymbol{I} - \hat{\boldsymbol{x}}\hat{\boldsymbol{x}}^T\right)(\boldsymbol{A}\hat{\boldsymbol{x}} - \hat{\boldsymbol{\lambda}}\hat{\boldsymbol{x}}) \\
&= -\left(\boldsymbol{I} - \hat{\boldsymbol{x}}\hat{\boldsymbol{x}}^T\right)\boldsymbol{A}\hat{\boldsymbol{x}} \\
&= -(\boldsymbol{A}\hat{\boldsymbol{x}} - \hat{\boldsymbol{\lambda}}\hat{\boldsymbol{x}}) = -\boldsymbol{r}
\end{aligned}$$

subject to the constraint $\hat{\boldsymbol{x}}^T\delta\hat{\boldsymbol{x}} = 0$. As in the previous section, we replace $\boldsymbol{A}$ by a preconditioner $\boldsymbol{P}$, such that we have to solve an approximate projected system

$$\left(\boldsymbol{I} - \hat{\boldsymbol{x}}\hat{\boldsymbol{x}}^T\right)(\boldsymbol{P} - \hat{\lambda}\boldsymbol{I})\left(\boldsymbol{I} - \hat{\boldsymbol{x}}\hat{\boldsymbol{x}}^T\right)\delta\hat{\boldsymbol{x}} = -\boldsymbol{r}$$

subject to the constraint $\hat{\boldsymbol{x}}^T\delta\hat{\boldsymbol{x}} = 0$.
The connection of the described method to Jacobi is given in Remark 4.7.

REMARK 4.7. Given an approximate eigenpair $(\hat{\lambda}, \hat{\boldsymbol{x}})$ of $\boldsymbol{A}$, Jacobi [**30**] proposed to solve an eigenvalue problem $\boldsymbol{A}\boldsymbol{x} = \lambda\boldsymbol{x}$ by finding a correction $\boldsymbol{t}$ such that

$$\boldsymbol{A}(\hat{\boldsymbol{x}} + \boldsymbol{t}) = \lambda(\hat{\boldsymbol{x}} + \boldsymbol{t}), \quad \hat{\boldsymbol{x}} \perp \boldsymbol{t}.$$

This is called the *Jacobi Orthogonal Component Correction (JOCC)*.

The Jacobi–Davidson framework can also be connected with Newton's method; see, e.g., [**47**, Chap. 8.4].
The debate over the advantaged and disadvantages of Jacobi–Davidson versus other approaches such as the Arnoldi process (with shift and invert) is delicate. Sleijpen and van der Vorst [**51**] relate it to whether the new direction has a strong component in previous directions. It is a fairly technical argument, and not much theory is available. For more details about the Jacobi–Davidson method, we refer to [**51, 52, 54**].

5. Conclusions

The numerical solution of eigenvalue problems is an extremely active area of research. Eigenvalues are very important in many areas of applications, and challenges keep arising. The survey covers only some basic principles, which have established themselves as the fundamental building blocks of eigenvalue solvers. We have left out some important recent advances, which are extremely important but also rather technical. Generalized eigenvalue problems are also very important, but there is not enough room to cover them in this survey.
One of the main messages of this survey is the distinction between important *mathematical* observations about eigenvalues, and practical *computational* considerations. Objects such as the Jordan Canonical Form or determinants are classical mathematical tools, but they cannot be easily utilized in practical computations. On the other hand, sparsity of the matrix and the availability of matrix decompositions are often overlooked when a pure mathematical discussion of the problem ensues, but they are absolutely essential in the design of numerical methods.
Altogether, this topic is satisfyingly rich and challenging. Efficiently and accurately computing eigenvalues and eigenvectors of matrices continues to be one of the most important problems in mathematical sciences.

References

[1] W. E. Arnoldi, *The principle of minimized iteration in the solution of the matrix eigenvalue problem*, Quart. Appl. Math. **9** (1951), 17–29, DOI 10.1090/qam/42792. MR0042792

[2] O. Axelsson, *A survey of preconditioned iterative methods for linear systems of algebraic equations*, BIT **25** (1985), no. 1, 166–187, DOI 10.1007/BF01934996. MR785811

[3] W. Barth, R. S. Martin, and J. H. Wilkinson, *Handbook Series Linear Algebra: Calculation of the eigenvalues of a symmetric tridiagonal matrix by the method of bisection*, Numer. Math. **9** (1967), no. 5, 386–393, DOI 10.1007/BF02162154. MR1553954

[4] M. Benzi, *Preconditioning techniques for large linear systems: a survey*, J. Comput. Phys. **182** (2002), no. 2, 418–477, DOI 10.1006/jcph.2002.7176. MR1941848

[5] M. Benzi, G. H. Golub, and J. Liesen, *Numerical solution of saddle point problems*, Acta Numer. **14** (2005), 1–137, DOI 10.1017/S0962492904000212. MR2168342

[6] D. Calvetti, L. Reichel, and D. C. Sorensen, *An implicitly restarted Lanczos method for large symmetric eigenvalue problems*, Electron. Trans. Numer. Anal. **2** (1994), no. March, 1–21. MR1270124

[7] M. Crouzeix, B. Philippe, and M. Sadkane, *The Davidson method*, SIAM J. Sci. Comput. **15** (1994), no. 1, 62–76, DOI 10.1137/0915004. MR1257154

[8] J. Cullum and W. E. Donath, *A block Lanczos algorithm for computing the q algebraically largest eigenvalues and a corresponding eigenspace of large, sparse, real symmetric matrices*, 1974 IEEE Conference on Decision and Control, 1974, pp. 505–509.

[9] J. J. M. Cuppen, *A divide and conquer method for the symmetric tridiagonal eigenproblem*, Numer. Math. **36** (1980/81), no. 2, 177–195, DOI 10.1007/BF01396757. MR611491

[10] E. R. Davidson, *The iterative calculation of a few of the lowest eigenvalues and corresponding eigenvectors of large real-symmetric matrices*, J. Computational Phys. **17** (1975), 87–94. MR0381271

[11] J. W. Demmel, *Applied numerical linear algebra*, Society for Industrial and Applied Mathematics (SIAM), Philadelphia, PA, 1997. MR1463942

[12] J. Demmel and K. Veselić, *Jacobi's method is more accurate than QR*, SIAM J. Matrix Anal. Appl. **13** (1992), no. 4, 1204–1245, DOI 10.1137/0613074. MR1182723

[13] I. S. Dhillon and B. N. Parlett, *Multiple representations to compute orthogonal eigenvectors of symmetric tridiagonal matrices*, Linear Algebra Appl. **387** (2004), 1–28, DOI 10.1016/j.laa.2003.12.028. MR2069265

[14] J. J. Dongarra and D. C. Sorensen, *A fully parallel algorithm for the symmetric eigenvalue problem*, SIAM J. Sci. Statist. Comput. **8** (1987), no. 2, S139–S154, DOI 10.1137/0908018. Parallel processing for scientific computing (Norfolk, Va., 1985). MR879400

[15] A. A. Dubrulle and G. H. Golub, *A multishift QR iteration without computation of the shifts*, Numer. Algorithms **7** (1994), no. 2-4, 173–181, DOI 10.1007/BF02140681. MR1283096

[16] H. C. Elman, D. J. Silvester, and A. J. Wathen, *Finite elements and fast iterative solvers: with applications in incompressible fluid dynamics*, Numerical Mathematics and Scientific Computation, Oxford University Press, New York, 2005. MR2155549

[17] E. X. Jiang, *A note on the double-shift QL algorithm*, Linear Algebra Appl. **171** (1992), 121–132, DOI 10.1016/0024-3795(92)90254-8. MR1165449

[18] J. G. F. Francis, *The QR transformation: a unitary analogue to the LR transformation. I*, Comput. J. **4** (1961/1962), 265–271, DOI 10.1093/comjnl/4.3.265. MR0130111

[19] J. G. F. Francis, *The QR transformation. II*, Comput. J. **4** (1961/1962), 332–345, DOI 10.1093/comjnl/4.4.332. MR0137289

[20] R. W. Freund, G. H. Golub, and N. M. Nachtigal, *Iterative solution of linear systems*, Acta numerica, 1992, Acta Numer., Cambridge Univ. Press, Cambridge, 1992, pp. 57–100. MR1165723

[21] G. H. Golub, R. R. Underwood, and J. H. Wilkinson, *The Lanczos algorithm for the symmetric $Ax = \lambda Bx$ problem*, Tech. report, Dep. Comput. Sci., Stanford Univ., Stanford, CA, 1972.

[22] G. H. Golub and C. F. Van Loan, *Matrix computations*, 4th ed., Johns Hopkins Studies in the Mathematical Sciences, Johns Hopkins University Press, Baltimore, MD, 2013. MR3024913

[23] A. Greenbaum, *Iterative methods for solving linear systems*, Frontiers in Applied Mathematics, vol. 17, Society for Industrial and Applied Mathematics (SIAM), Philadelphia, PA, 1997. MR1474725

[24] M. Gu and S. C. Eisenstat, *A divide-and-conquer algorithm for the symmetric tridiagonal eigenproblem*, SIAM J. Matrix Anal. Appl. **16** (1995), no. 1, 172–191, DOI 10.1137/S0895479892241287. MR1311425

[25] M. H. Gutknecht, *A completed theory of the unsymmetric Lanczos process and related algorithms. I*, SIAM J. Matrix Anal. Appl. **13** (1992), no. 2, 594–639, DOI 10.1137/0613037. MR1152770

[26] M. H. Gutknecht, *A completed theory of the unsymmetric Lanczos process and related algorithms. II*, SIAM J. Matrix Anal. Appl. **15** (1994), no. 1, 15–58, DOI 10.1137/S0895479890188803. MR1257615

[27] N. J. Higham, *Accuracy and stability of numerical algorithms*, 2nd ed., Society for Industrial and Applied Mathematics (SIAM), Philadelphia, PA, 2002. MR1927606

[28] L. Hogben, *Elementary linear algebra*, West, St. Paul, MN, 1987.

[29] H. Hotelling, *Analysis of a complex of statistical variables into principal components*, J. Educ. Psychol. **24** (1933), 417–441.

[30] C. G. J. Jacobi, *Über ein leichtes Verfahren die in der Theorie der Säcularstörungen vorkommenden Gleichungen numerisch aufzulösen* (German), J. Reine Angew. Math. **30** (1846), 51–94, DOI 10.1515/crll.1846.30.51. MR1578455

[31] S. Kaniel, *Estimates for some computational techniques in linear algebra*, Math. Comp. **20** (1966), 369–378, DOI 10.2307/2003590. MR0234618

[32] D. Kressner, *Numerical methods for general and structured eigenvalue problems*, Lecture Notes in Computational Science and Engineering, vol. 46, Springer-Verlag, Berlin, 2005. MR2164298

[33] V. N. Kublanovskaja, *Some algorithms for the solution of the complete problem of eigenvalues* (Russian), Ž. Vyčisl. Mat. i Mat. Fiz. **1** (1961), 555–570. MR0136058

[34] C. Lanczos, *An iteration method for the solution of the eigenvalue problem of linear differential and integral operators*, J. Research Nat. Bur. Standards **45** (1950), 255–282. MR0042791

[35] R. S. Martin, G. Peters, and J. H. Wilkinson, *Handbook Series Linear Algebra: The QR algorithm for real hessenberg matrices*, Numer. Math. **14** (1970), no. 3, 219–231, DOI 10.1007/BF02163331. MR1553971

[36] R. B. Morgan and D. S. Scott, *Generalizations of Davidson's method for computing eigenvalues of sparse symmetric matrices*, SIAM J. Sci. Statist. Comput. **7** (1986), no. 3, 817–825, DOI 10.1137/0907054. MR848565

[37] M. L. Overton, *Numerical computing with IEEE floating point arithmetic*, Society for Industrial and Applied Mathematics (SIAM), Philadelphia, PA, 2001. Including one theorem, one rule of thumb, and one hundred and one exercises. MR1828597

[38] C. C. Paige, *The computation of eigenvalues and eigenvectors of very large sparse matrices*, PhD thesis, Univ. London, 1971.

[39] B. N. Parlett, *The symmetric eigenvalue problem*, Classics in Applied Mathematics, vol. 20, Society for Industrial and Applied Mathematics (SIAM), Philadelphia, PA, 1998. Corrected reprint of the 1980 original. MR1490034

[40] B. N. Parlett and D. S. Scott, *The Lanczos algorithm with selective orthogonalization*, Math. Comp. **33** (1979), no. 145, 217–238, DOI 10.2307/2006037. MR514820

[41] B. N. Parlett, D. R. Taylor, and Z. A. Liu, *A look-ahead Lánczos algorithm for unsymmetric matrices*, Math. Comp. **44** (1985), no. 169, 105–124, DOI 10.2307/2007796. MR771034

[42] H. Rutishauser, *Solution of eigenvalue problems with the LR-transformation*, Nat. Bur. Standards Appl. Math. Ser. **1958** (1958), no. 49, 47–81. MR0090118

[43] Y. Saad, *On the rates of convergence of the Lanczos and the block-Lanczos methods*, SIAM J. Numer. Anal. **17** (1980), no. 5, 687–706, DOI 10.1137/0717059. MR588755

[44] Y. Saad, *Variations on Arnoldi's method for computing eigenelements of large unsymmetric matrices*, Linear Algebra Appl. **34** (1980), 269–295, DOI 10.1016/0024-3795(80)90169-X. MR591435

[45] Y. Saad, *Chebyshev acceleration techniques for solving nonsymmetric eigenvalue problems*, Math. Comp. **42** (1984), no. 166, 567–588, DOI 10.2307/2007602. MR736453

[46] Y. Saad, *Iterative methods for sparse linear systems*, 2nd ed., Society for Industrial and Applied Mathematics, Philadelphia, PA, 2003. MR1990645

[47] Y. Saad, *Numerical methods for large eigenvalue problems*, Classics in Applied Mathematics, vol. 66, Society for Industrial and Applied Mathematics (SIAM), Philadelphia, PA, 2011. Revised edition of the 1992 original [1177405]. MR3396212

[48] M. Sadkane, *A block Arnoldi-Chebyshev method for computing the leading eigenpairs of large sparse unsymmetric matrices*, Numer. Math. **64** (1993), no. 2, 181–193, DOI 10.1007/BF01388686. MR1199284

[49] A. Schönhage, *Zur quadratischen Konvergenz des Jacobi-Verfahrens* (German), Numer. Math. **6** (1964), 410–412, DOI 10.1007/BF01386091. MR0174171

[50] H. D. Simon, *Analysis of the symmetric Lanczos algorithm with reorthogonalization methods*, Linear Algebra Appl. **61** (1984), 101–131, DOI 10.1016/0024-3795(84)90025-9. MR755252

[51] G. L. G. Sleijpen and H. A. Van der Vorst, *A Jacobi-Davidson iteration method for linear eigenvalue problems*, SIAM J. Matrix Anal. Appl. **17** (1996), no. 2, 401–425, DOI 10.1137/S0895479894270427. MR1384515

[52] G. L. G. Sleijpen and H. A. Van der Vorst, *A Jacobi-Davidson iteration method for linear eigenvalue problems*, SIAM Rev. **42** (2000), no. 2, 267–293, DOI 10.1137/S0036144599363084. MR1778354

[53] D. C. Sorensen, *Implicit application of polynomial filters in a k-step Arnoldi method*, SIAM J. Matrix Anal. Appl. **13** (1992), no. 1, 357–385, DOI 10.1137/0613025. MR1146670

[54] D. C. Sorensen, *Numerical methods for large eigenvalue problems*, Acta Numer. **11** (2002), 519–584, DOI 10.1017/S0962492902000089. MR2009379

[55] G. W. Stewart, *Matrix algorithms. Vol. II*, Society for Industrial and Applied Mathematics (SIAM), Philadelphia, PA, 2001. Eigensystems. MR1853468

[56] G. W. Stewart, *Introduction to matrix computations*, Academic Press [A subsidiary of Harcourt Brace Jovanovich, Publishers], New York-London, 1973. Computer Science and Applied Mathematics. MR0458818

[57] G. W. Stewart and J. G. Sun, *Matrix perturbation theory*, Computer Science and Scientific Computing, Academic Press, Inc., Boston, MA, 1990. MR1061154

[58] H. P. M. van Kempen, *On the quadratic convergence of the special cyclic Jacobi method*, Numer. Math. **9** (1966), 19–22, DOI 10.1007/BF02165225. MR0202291

[59] A. J. Wathen, *Preconditioning*, Acta Numer. **24** (2015), 329–376, DOI 10.1017/S0962492915000021. MR3349311

[60] D. S. Watkins, *Understanding the* QR *algorithm*, SIAM Rev. **24** (1982), no. 4, 427–440, DOI 10.1137/1024100. MR678561

[61] D. S. Watkins, *The transmission of shifts and shift blurring in the QR algorithm*, Proceedings of the Fourth Conference of the International Linear Algebra Society (Rotterdam, 1994), Linear Algebra Appl. **241/243** (1996), 877–896, DOI 10.1016/0024-3795(95)00545-5. MR1400468

[62] D. S. Watkins, *The matrix eigenvalue problem*, Society for Industrial and Applied Mathematics (SIAM), Philadelphia, PA, 2007. *GR* and Krylov subspace methods. MR2383888

[63] D. S. Watkins, *The QR algorithm revisited*, SIAM Rev. **50** (2008), no. 1, 133–145, DOI 10.1137/060659454. MR2403061

[64] D. S. Watkins, *Francis's algorithm*, Amer. Math. Monthly **118** (2011), no. 5, 387–403, DOI 10.4169/amer.math.monthly.118.05.387. MR2805025

[65] H. Wielandt, *Das Iterationsverfahren bei nicht selbstadjungierten linearen Eigenwertaufgaben* (German), Math. Z. **50** (1944), 93–143, DOI 10.1007/BF01312438. MR0017460

[66] J. H. Wilkinson, *The algebraic eigenvalue problem*, Clarendon Press, Oxford, 1965. MR0184422

[67] K. Wu and H. Simon, *Thick-restart Lanczos method for large symmetric eigenvalue problems*, SIAM J. Matrix Anal. Appl. **22** (2000), no. 2, 602–616, DOI 10.1137/S0895479898334605. MR1781506

Department of Computer Science, The University of British Columbia, Vancouver, BC, V6T 1Z4, Canada
E-mail address: `jbosch@cs.ubc.ca, greif@cs.ubc.ca`

Department of Computer Science, The University of British Columbia, Vancouver, BC, V6T 1Z4, Canada
E-mail address: `greif@cs.ubc.ca`

Contemporary Mathematics
Volume **700**, 2017
http://dx.doi.org/10.1090/conm/700/14186

Finite element methods for variational eigenvalue problems

Guido Kanschat

Contents

1. Introduction

The discretization of the eigenvalue problem through finite elements relies on two independent concepts: first, the abstract idea of a Galerkin discretization in Section 3, which describes projections to general finite dimensional subspaces of Hilbert spaces, and second, the choice of these subspaces by piecewise polynomials and the resulting concrete approximation error estimates in Section 4.

These notes are only a short overview over the theory of finite element approximation of eigenvalue problems, and to a large extend a compilation of results found in [**Bof10**, **BO87**, **BO89**]. They are also content with discussing the approximation theory and giving a pointer to a software package for experiments. After discretization, we always obtain a matrix eigenvalue problem of the form

$$Ax = \lambda Mx,$$

where A is the matrix of the discretized differential operator and M is the so-called mass matrix, which generates the bilinear form of the L^2-inner product on the finite element space. Methods for the computation of eigenvalues and eigenvectors of the discretized problem are discussed in the chapter by Chen Greif in this volume.

2010 *Mathematics Subject Classification.* Primary 65N25, 65N30.

2. Problem setting

2.1. Source and eigenvalue problems for the Laplacian. We begin by shortly reviewing the most simple differential operator in this framework and its setting in Hilbert spaces. We are beginning with the so-called *source problem*, the Dirichlet problem for Poisson's equation. Let Ω be a domain in $\mathbb{R}^d$, where the dimension d is typically 2 or 3, but not restricted to those values. The boundary $\partial\Omega$ is assumed to be Lipschitz in the sense that there is a finite covering of $\partial\Omega$ of open sets B_i and a family of Lipschitz continuous mappings Φ_i, which map the open unit ball $B \subset \mathbb{R}^d$ to Ω_i, such that $\Phi^{-1}(\Omega \cap B_i) \subset \{x \in B | x_0 > 0\}$ with x_0 being the first component of the vector x. On such a domain, we search for the solution of

$$\begin{aligned} -\Delta u &= f \text{ in } \Omega, \\ u &= 0 \text{ on } \partial\Omega. \end{aligned}$$

In order to develop a reasonable solution theory for this problem, we multiply with a test function v and integrate by parts to obtain the weak formulation

$$\int_\Omega \nabla u \cdot \nabla v \,\mathrm{d}x = \int_\Omega f v \,\mathrm{d}x \quad \forall v \in V, \tag{1}$$

where V is a suitable test function space, here $V = H_0^1(\Omega)$, the Sobolev space obtained by completing the space $C_0^\infty(\Omega)$ of infinitely often differentiable functions with compact support in Ω with respect to the norm

$$\|v\|_V = \sqrt{\int_\Omega |\nabla v|^2 \,\mathrm{d}x}.$$

The Riesz representation theorem guarantees that this equation has a unique solution in $u \in V$ for any suitable right hand side f, see for instance '¡[**Eva98, GT98**]. Indeed, while the right hand side in (1) suggests $f \in L^2(\Omega)$, we can actually relax this requirement to f being a continuous linear functional in $V' = H^{-1}(\Omega)$, such that the right hand side of (1) becomes $f(v)$. Then, the weak form redefines the Laplacian as an operator

$$-\Delta : H_0^1(\Omega) \to H^{-1}(\Omega).$$

Now, we tend to the eigenvalue problem of finding $u \in V$ and $\lambda \in \mathbb{C}$ such that

$$-\Delta u = \lambda u.$$

With the above understanding of the operator $-\Delta$, this equation does not make sense, since the object on the right is in V, the object on the left in V'. Thus, we transform this problem into weak form as well. First, we require a second space H, which in basic examples is typically chosen $L^2(\Omega)$. Then, invoke the Riesz representation theorem again, this time in H, yielding the *variational eigenvalue problem*

$$\int_\Omega \nabla u \cdot \nabla v \,\mathrm{d}x = \lambda \int_\Omega u v \,\mathrm{d}x \quad \forall v \in V. \tag{2}$$

Since $H_0^1(\Omega)$ is continuously embedded into $L^2(\Omega)$, the equation above is well defined.

Due to the existence and uniqueness of solutions, we can define the inverse of the Laplacian as an operator

$$(-\Delta)^{-1} : L^2(\Omega) \to H_0^1(\Omega).$$

Indeed, since the Laplacian contains two derivatives, it might be suggested that the range is contained in $H^2(\Omega)$. Nevertheless, the regularity theory of solutions on Lipschitz domains does not admit this conclusion [**Gri85**]. On the other hand, $H_0^1(\Omega)$ as the domain of the Laplacian is just what we need.

Since the embedding of $H_0^1(\Omega)$ into $L^2(\Omega)$ is not only continuous, but also compact, see for instance [**AF03**], $(-\Delta)^{-1}$ is a compact operator.

The spectral theorem for compact operators says that $(-\Delta)^{-1}$ has a point spectrum of at most countably many eigenvalues λ_k^{-1}, which may not have any accumulation point in $\mathbb{C}$ except zero. Consequently, we deduce that the spectrum of the Laplacian as an operator on $H_0^1(\Omega)$ consists of at most countably many eigenvalues $\lambda_k \neq 0$ which do not have an accumulation point in $\mathbb{C}$.

Furthermore, the Laplacian in its weak form is self-adjoint, see for instance [**GT98**], such that its spectrum is contained in $\mathbb{R}^+$. Thus, we conclude

THEOREM 1. *The spectrum of the Laplacian defined as the values λ such that there is a function $u \in V$ such that equation* (2) *holds contains at most countably many real values*

$$0 < \lambda_1 \leq \lambda_2 \leq \cdots \leq \lambda_k \leq \ldots$$

2.2. Abstraction from the Laplacian. The eigenvalue problem for the Laplacian is only a model problem. Therefore, we generalize the ideas from the preceding paragraphs and introduce some notation. First, we introduce

DEFINITION 1. A bilinear form $a(.,.)$ is bounded and elliptic on a vector space V if there are positive constants $\overline{C}$ and $\underline{C}$ such that

$$\begin{aligned} a(u,v) &\leq \overline{C}\|u\|_V\|v\|_V & \forall u,v \in V \quad &\text{(boundedness)}\\ a(u,u) &\geq \underline{C}\|u\|_V^2 & \forall u \in V \quad &\text{(ellipticity)}. \end{aligned}$$

If in addition the bilinear form is symmetric, it defines a norm on V by

$$\|v\| = \sqrt{a(v,v)}.$$

We introduce the oprator A associated to this bilinear form defined by

$$\langle Av, w\rangle_{V^*\times V} = a(v,w) \qquad \forall v,w \in V.$$

If the form $a(.,.)$ is bounded, then $A : V \to V^*$ is a bounded operator.

DEFINITION 2 (Source problem). Given a bilinear form $a(.,.)$ on V and f in the normed dual V^*, find a function $u \in V$ such that

$$a(u,v) = f(v) \quad \forall v \in V. \tag{4}$$

For the class of bilinear forms introduced above, the well-posedness[1] is established in the elliptic case by

[1]Well-posedness in the context of numerical approximation follows the definition of Hadamard [**Had02**], namely that the solution shall exist, be unique, and shall depend continuously on the parameters.

Lemma 1 (Lax-Milgram). *Let $a(.,.)$ be symmetric, bounded and elliptic on V. Then a unique solution $u \in V$ of equation (4) exists with the estimate*

$$\|u\|_V \le \frac{\overline{C}}{\underline{C}}\|f\|_{V^*}, \tag{5}$$

where

$$\|f\|_{V^*} = \sup_{v\in V} \frac{|f(v)|}{\|v\|_V}$$

is the operator norm of f on the space V.

In the general case, we use a version of Banach's closed range theorem which is particularly amenable to the study of numerical approximation

Lemma 2 (Inf-sup condition). *Let $a(.,.)$ be bounded and let there be a constant $\underline{C} > 0$ such that*

$$\inf_{\substack{u\in V\\ \|u\|=1}} \sup_{\substack{v\in V\\ \|v\|=1}} |a(u,v)| \ge \underline{C}, \qquad \inf_{\substack{v\in V\\ \|v\|=1}} \sup_{\substack{u\in V\\ \|u\|=1}} |a(u,v)| \ge \underline{C}. \tag{6}$$

Then, equation (4) has a unique solution $u \in V$ admitting the estimate (5).

Obviously, Lemma 2 implies Lemma 1 for symmetric bilinear forms.

We proceed by generalizing (2) to

Definition 3 (Variational eigenvalue problem). A pair $(\lambda, u) \in \mathbb{C} \times V$ with $u \neq 0$ is an eigenpair of the operator A associated with the bilinear form $a(.,.)$, if there holds

$$a(u,v) = \lambda \langle u, v\rangle \quad \forall v \in V. \tag{7}$$

Here, $\langle .,. \rangle$ is the inner product in a Hilbert space H with norm $\|.\|$ and $V \subset H$ is the domain of A.

If the bilinear form $a(.,.)$ is nonsymmetric, we also introduce the

Definition 4 (Adjoint variational eigenvalue problem). A pair $(\lambda^*, u^*) \in \mathbb{C}\times V$ with $u \neq 0$ is an adjoint eigenpair of the operator A associated with the bilinear form $a(.,.)$, if there holds

$$a(v,u^*) = \lambda^* \langle v, u^*\rangle \quad \forall v \in V. \tag{8}$$

Here, $\langle .,. \rangle$ is the inner product in a Hilbert space H with norm $\|.\|$ and $V \subset H$ is the domain of A.

It is a well known fact, that the eigenvalues λ in (7) and λ^* in (8) coincide (note that u^* is on the right hand side of the sesquilinear form $\langle .,. \rangle$). Thus, we speak of the eigenfunction u and the adjoint eigenfunction u^* with eigenvalue λ.

We point out that while the source problem was solely defined on the space V, typically the domain of the operator associated with the bilinear form, this definition of an eigenvalue problem makes use of an additional space H containing V.

An immediate consequence of ellipticity is the fact that the real parts of all eigenvalues of the variational eigenvalue problem (7) are positive and bounded from below by $\underline{C}$. If additionally the bilinear form is symmetric (Hermitean in the complex case), the eigenvalues are even real and positive, and $a(.,.)$ forms an inner product on its domain.

Let $a(.,.)$ be such that either Lemma 1 or Lemma 2 holds. Then, we define a solution operator $T : H \to V$ for the source problem such that for any $w \in H$ there holds

$$a(Tw, v) = \langle w, v \rangle \quad \forall v \in V.$$

Then, by entering Tu into (7), the eigenvalue problem is equivalent to

$$\lambda T u = u.$$

Throughout the remainder of this chapter, we impose

ASSUMPTION 1. The solution operator T is compact, that is, the embedding $V \hookrightarrow H$ is compact.

As a consequence, the spectral theorem for compact operators holds. We denote that by this assumption, we exclude bilinear forms with zero eigenvalues, a problem which can be easily fixed by adding a shift of the form $\mu \langle u, v \rangle$ to $a(u, v)$ and computing the eigenvalues $\lambda + \mu$ of the new form.

Let $a(.,.)$ be an inner product on its domain V and V compactly embedded in H. Then, Theorem 1 holds for this variational eigenvalue problem, and thus all eigenvalues are real and positive. Thus, the spectrum can be ordered and we have two important results

THEOREM 2 (Minimum principle). *The eigenpairs (λ_k, u_k) of the symmetric variational eigenvalue problem* (7) *are recursively characterized by*

$$u_k = \operatorname*{argmin}_{\substack{u \in V \\ a(u,u_j)=0 \ \forall j<k}} \frac{a(u,u)}{\langle u, u \rangle}$$

$$\lambda_k = \frac{a(u_k, u_k)}{\langle u_k, u_k \rangle}$$

Moreover, we have

THEOREM 3 (Minimum-maximum theorem). *The eigenvalues λ_k of the symmetric variational eigenvalue problem* (7) *are characterized by*

$$\lambda_k = \min_{\substack{W \subset V \\ \dim W = k}} \max_{v \in W} \frac{a(v,v)}{\langle v, v \rangle}. \tag{9}$$

This theorem not only provides a condition that a number $\lambda \in \mathbb{R}$ be an eigenvalue, it furthermore assigns an ordering to these values:

$$0 < \lambda_1 \leq \lambda_2 \leq \cdots \leq \lambda_k \leq \cdots.$$

We close this section by defining the eigenspace

$$E_k = \{u \in V \setminus \{0\} \big| a(u, v) = \lambda_k \langle u, v \rangle \ \forall v \in V\},$$

2.3. Well-posedness and stability. An important concept whenever approximating the solution of a problem is well-posedness. This concept was introduced by Hadamard in [**Had02**] and cast in the famous three conditions:

DEFINITION 5 (Well-posedness). A problem, that assigns to a set of data x a solution $y = f(x)$ is well-posed, if

(1) A solution y exists
(2) The solution y is unique for given x

(3) The solution y depends continuously on variations of the data x

We remark that the crucial condition is the third one and that it is very vague, since neither the topology for x, nor that of y is defined. These are an important part of the model used.

The necessity of the third condition stems from the fact, that we typically cannot solve the problem with exact data, because

- data may be related to a physical configuration and is measured with some error,
- the approximation of the problem involves projected or interpolated data, and
- numbers cannot be represented exactly in a computer and must be rounded.

While the third condition of well-posedness is qualitative, it is important for the judgment of the results of a computation as well as for the evaluation of solution algorithms to quantify this continuity, basically replacing it by a Lipschitz condition:

DEFINITION 6 (Condition number). Let $y = f(x)$ be the solution of the same abstract problem depending on data x as before, then the *condition number* κ of this problem is the smallest number, possibly infinity, such that for any data x_1, x_2 in a required set there holds

$$\|f(x_1) - f(x_2)\| \le \kappa \|x_2 - x_1\|.$$

A problem is called well-conditioned, if κ is "small" and ill-conditioned, if it is not. Here, small is defined by the requirements of the application.

Remark that even in this definition, the choice of the norms is up to its user and typically mandated by the information we require from the solution y.

As discussed in [**GW76**], the eigenvalue problem is in general ill-conditioned. Let us investigate the famous example of the $n \times n$-matrix

$$\mathfrak{A}_{n,\varepsilon} = \begin{pmatrix} 0 & 1 & & & \\ & 0 & 1 & & \\ & & \ddots & \ddots & \\ & & & 0 & 1 \\ \varepsilon & & & & 0 \end{pmatrix},$$

which has the only eigenvalue zero if $\varepsilon = 0$. Perturbing this matrix by a tiny positive number ε, we see that the characteristic polynomial becomes $\lambda^n + \varepsilon$. Thus, the perturbed matrix $\mathfrak{A}_{n,\varepsilon}$ has n different eigenvalues $\lambda_k(\varepsilon) = \sqrt[n]{\varepsilon} e^{ik/n}$. First, we see from this that the problem "determine the multiplicity of an eigenvalue" is ill-posed, since even the tiniest perturbation of a matrix may separate a single multiple eigenvalue into multiple single eigenvalues. The problem "determine the value of the eigenvalue" is ill-posed as well, since we do not specify which one and the solution is not unique. "Determine the eigenvalue with greatest positive real part and nonnegative imaginary part" has a unique solution, and since the formula for $\lambda_k(\varepsilon)$ is continuous, is also well-posed. But, since this formula is not Lipschitz, the condition number is infinite. Indeed, let us assume there are no other errors and numbers in a computer are stored with 16 digits accuracy. Let $n = 16$ in the definition of the matrix $\mathfrak{A}_n$ above. Then, rounding of the data may perturb the solution by the value $1/10$, which is way above the accuracy of the computer.

It is important to realize that the concepts of well-posedness and conditioning above are related to the original problem, not to the particular algorithm used for their solution. In fact, the condition number above determines the condition number of the best possible algorithm for the solution of the problem. Obviously, we may also have devised a bad algorithm. In order to judge this, we introduce as a final concept

DEFINITION 7 (Stability of algorithms). Let $y = f(x)$ be the solution of a problem with data x and let κ be its condition number. Let $\tilde{y} = \tilde{f}(x)$ be an approximation to this solution by an algorithm $\tilde{f}$, and let $\tilde{\kappa}$ be the condition number of this problem. Then, we call an algorithm *stable*, if the constant c in $\tilde{\kappa} \leq c\kappa$ is of moderate size.

Since no algorithm can have a better condition number than the original problem, we can consider the numerical solution of the example above as not computable. In fact, Golub and Wilkinson suggest in [**GW76**] to reevaluate the emphasis the Jordan normal form receives for this very reason.

Wilkinson showed [**GW76, Wil72**] on the other hand the following remarkable result for matrices

THEOREM 4. *Let $A \in \mathbb{C}^{n\times n}$ and $B \in \mathbb{C}^{n\times n}$ with $\|B\|_2 = 1$. Let λ be a simple eigenvalue of A with right eigenvector x and left eigenvector y, both of norm unity. Then, the corresponding eigenvalue $\lambda(\varepsilon)$ of the perturbed matrix $A + \varepsilon B$ admits the estimate*

$$\left|\frac{d}{d\varepsilon}\lambda(\varepsilon)\right| \leq \frac{1}{y^H x}.$$

Thus, at least for very small perturbations, the conditioning of the problem of finding this eigenvalue λ depends on the angle between the right and left eigenvector. And, as an immediate corollary, we obtain that the eigenvalue problem for any simple eigenvalue of a normal matrix is well-posed, since for such matrices right and left eigenvectors coincide.

3. Galerkin approximation

The beauty and the power of Galerkin[2] methods lies in their simplicity: replace the infinite dimensional space V in which the weak formulation of differential equation problem is posed by a finite dimensional subspace, say[3] V_n. Then, we define the discrete analogues to the source and eigenvalue problems in definitions 2 and 3, respectively.

DEFINITION 8 (Discrete source problem). Find $u_n \in V_n$ such that there holds

$$a(u_n, v_n) = \langle f, v_n\rangle \quad \forall v_n \in V_n. \tag{10}$$

DEFINITION 9 (Discrete variational eigenvalue problem). A pair $(\lambda_n, u_n) \in \mathbb{C} \times V_n$ is a discrete eigenpair to the operator A associated with the bilinear form $a(.,.)$ if there holds

$$a(u_n, v_n) = \lambda_n \langle u_n, v_n\rangle \quad \forall v_n \in V_n. \tag{11}$$

[2]Boris Grigoryevich Galerkin (Борис Григорьевич Галёркин), 1871-1945, Russian engineer

[3]We will use the subscript n as an indicator of discretized values without giving it a defined meaning. Intuitively, it may be seen as the dimension of the finite dimensional space, but later on this will not be sufficient.

The discrete adjoint eigenvalue problem consists of finding pairs $\lambda_n^*, u_n^* \in \mathbb{C} \times V_n$ such that there holds

$$a(v_n, u_n^*) = \lambda_n^* \langle v_n, u_n^* \rangle \quad \forall v_n \in V_n.$$

Since the space V_n is finite dimensional of dimension n, we can choose a basis $\{\varphi_j\}_{j=1,\dots,n}$ and expand the solution u_n with respect to the basis functions as

$$u_n(x) = \sum_{j=1}^{n} \mathfrak{u}_j \varphi_j(x).$$

Thus, testing (11) with each φ_j, we obtain the rows of the algebraic eigenvalue problem

$$\mathfrak{A}\mathfrak{u} = \lambda_n \mathfrak{M}\mathfrak{u},$$

where we denote $\mathfrak{u} = (\mathfrak{u}_1, \dots, \mathfrak{u}_n)^T$ and the so called stiffness and mass matrices are

$$\mathfrak{A} = \Bigl(a(\varphi_j, \varphi_i)\Bigr)_{i,j=1,\dots,n}, \qquad \mathfrak{M} = \Bigl(\langle \varphi_j, \varphi_i \rangle\Bigr)_{i,j=1,\dots,n}.$$

For numerical solution methods of this problem, we refer to the chapter by Chen Greif in this volume. Here, we only remind the reader of the:

THEOREM 5 (spectral theorem for normal matrices). *Let $\mathfrak{A} \in \mathbb{C}^{n\times n}$ be a normal matrix. Then, $\mathfrak{A}$ is diagonalizable and there exists an orthogonal matrix $\mathfrak{X} \in \mathbb{C}^{n\times n}$, such that*

$$\mathfrak{A} = \mathfrak{X} \begin{pmatrix} \lambda_1 & & \\ & \ddots & \\ & & \lambda_n \end{pmatrix} \mathfrak{X}^T.$$

The column vectors of $\mathfrak{X}$ are the eigenvectors of $\mathfrak{A}$ and left and right eigenvectors for each eigenvalue coincide.

If in addition, $\mathfrak{A}$ is Hermitean, all eigenvalues are real.

3.1. The source problem. We begin our study of the properties of Galerkin approximations with the source problem and summarize analysis found in basic courses on finite element methods, for instance early chapters in [**Bra97**, **BS02**, **Cia78**, **GRS07**, **SF73**].

LEMMA 3 (Discrete Lax-Milgram). *Let $a(.,.)$ be symmetric, bounded and elliptic on V. Then a unique solution $u_n \in V_n$ of equation* (10) *exists with the estimate* (5).

PROOF. If the bilinear form $a(.,.)$ is elliptic, the Lax-Milgram Lemma 1 transfers to V_n immediately, since $V_n \subset V$. □

In the nonsymmetric case we have to assume that Lemma 2 holds in V_n as well:

LEMMA 4 (Discrete inf-sup condition). *Let $a(.,.)$ be bounded and let there be a constant $\underline{C} > 0$ such that for any n there holds*

$$\inf_{\substack{u_n \in V_n \\ \|u_n\|=1}} \sup_{\substack{v_n \in V_n \\ \|v_n\|=1}} |a(u_n, v_n)| \ge \underline{C}, \qquad \inf_{\substack{v_n \in V_n \\ \|v_n\|=1}} \sup_{\substack{u_n \in V_n \\ \|u_n\|=1}} |a(u_n, v_n)| \ge \underline{C}. \tag{12}$$

Then, equation (10) *has a unique solution $u_n \in V_n$ admitting the estimate* (5).

In principle, the constants $\underline{C}$ and $\overline{C}$ in Lemmas 2 and 4, respectively may be different. By taking the worse pair, we can keep the presentation simple and consider them equal. Indeed, Lemma4 would even hold with constants depending on n. We do not consider this case because it leads to suboptimal convergence estimates.

We assume unique solvability of the discrete problem either by Lemma 3 or by Lemma 4. Thus, let $u \in V$ and $u_n \in V_n$ be the unique solutions of

$$\begin{aligned} a(u, v) &= f(v) && \forall v \in V \\ a(u_n, v_n) &= f(v_n) && \forall v_n \in V_n. \end{aligned}$$

An immediate consequence obtained by testing with $v \in V_n \subset V$ in the first equation and subtracting the second is

LEMMA 5 (Galerkin orthogonality). *There holds*

$$a(u - u_n, v_n) = 0 \quad \forall v \in V_n.$$

From this result, we immediately obtain

LEMMA 6 (Céa's lemma). *Let $a(.,.)$ be bounded and elliptic such that equations* (3) *hold. Let furthermore u and u_n be the solutions in equations* (13). *Then, there holds the quasi-best approximation result*

$$\|u - u_n\|_V \leq \frac{\overline{C}}{\underline{C}} \inf_{v \in V_n} \|u - v\|_V.$$

PROOF. From the assumptions there holds for arbitrary $w_n \in V_n$:

$$\begin{aligned} \frac{1}{\underline{C}} \|u - u_n\|_V^2 &\leq a(u - u_n, u - u_n) && \text{ellipticity} \\ &= a(u - u_n, u - w_n) && \text{Galerkin orthogonality} \\ &\leq \overline{C} \|u - u_n\|_V \, \|u - w_n\|_V && \text{boundedness.} \end{aligned}$$

Dividing by $\|u - u_n\|_V$ and making use of the fact that w_n was chosen arbitrarily in V_n yields the lemma. □

Thus, the error between the continuous solution $u \in V$ and the discrete solution $u_n \in V_n$ is reduced to the approximability of the function $u \in V$ by a function in V_n. This is now simply a property of the approximation space and independent of the bilinear form $a(.,.)$. Thus, we introduce the notation

$$\overline{\eta}_u(V_n) = \inf_{v \in V_n} \|u - v\|_V,$$

which describes the approximation accuracy of u by elements of V_n. The estimate in Céa's lemma thus becomes

$$\|u - u_n\|_V \leq \frac{\overline{C}}{\underline{C}} \overline{\eta}_u(V_n).$$

3.2. The discrete eigenvalue problem. The results on eigenvectors and eigenspaces in this section will all be of the same type. The choice of finite element spaces for V_n and their approximation properties are deferred to Section 4. Here, we assume that the sequence of spaces $\{V_n\}$ is exhausting V, that is,

$$\forall u \in V \ \inf_{v \in V_n} \|u - v\|_V \to 0 \qquad \text{as } n \to \infty. \tag{14}$$

We introduce two operators important for the analysis of eigenvalue problems. First, the Ritz projection $P_n : V \to V_n$ is defined such that for any $w \in V$ there holds

$$a(P_n w, v_n) = a(w, v_n) \quad \forall v_n \in V_n.$$

In addition, we define the discrete solution operator T_n, such that for any $w_n \in V_n$ there holds

$$a(T_n w_n, v_n) = (w_n, v_n) \quad \forall v_n \in V_n.$$

Let P_n^* be the $a(.,.)$-adjoint of P_n, $P_n = P_n^*$ for a symmetric bilinear form. For any $v \in V$ there holds

$$a(T_n w_n, v) = a(T_n w_n, P_n^* v) = (w_n, P_n^* v) = a(T w_n, P_n^* v) = a(P_n w_n, v).$$

Thus, we obtain the relation

$$T_n = P_n T.$$

Entering $T_n u_n$ into (11), we obtain the equivalent eigenvalue problem

$$\lambda_n P_n T u_n = u_n.$$

In this context, the assumption that the sequence of discrete spaces exhausts V in (14) translates into

$$\|T - P_n T\| = \sup_{\|u\|_V = 1} \|Tu - P_n Tu\|_V \to 0 \qquad \text{as } n \to \infty. \tag{15}$$

3.3. A single eigenpair. In this section, we derive error estimates for one solution of equation (11) in comparison to those of equation (7). We first follow [**Fix73**] for the general, non-selfadjoint problem[4]. We assume that (6) holds for the space V as well as for the finite dimensional subspace V_n with the same constant $\underline{C}$ independent of n. For an eigenvalue λ of the continuous problem (7), its eigenspace E_λ, and its adjoint eigenspace E_λ^*, we characterize approximation by V_n by

$$\begin{aligned}
\overline{\eta}_\lambda(V_n) &= \sup_{\substack{u \in E_\lambda \\ \|u\|=1}} \inf_{v \in V_n} \|u - v\|_V, \\
\overline{\eta}_\lambda^*(V_n) &= \sup_{\substack{u^* \in E_\lambda^* \\ \|u^*\|=1}} \inf_{v \in V_n} \|u^* - v\|_V,
\end{aligned}$$

that is, we measure the best approximation of the unit vector worst approximated in this eigenspace. From [**Fix73**, Theorem 1], we obtain the following estimates

THEOREM 6. *Let the inf-sup condition* (6)*, the discrete inf-sup condition* (12)*, and the uniform convergence* (15) *hold. Let λ be an eigenvalue of* (7)*. Then, there is an eigenvalue λ_n of* (11)*, such that*

$$|\lambda_n - \lambda| \le C \overline{\eta}_\lambda(V_n) \overline{\eta}_\lambda^*(V_n). \tag{17}$$

Furthermore, if $u_n \in V_n$ with $\|u_n\| = 1$, there is a function $u \in E_\lambda$ such that

$$\|u_n - u\|_V \le C \overline{\eta}_\lambda(V_n). \tag{18}$$

In both estimates, the constant C depends on the bilinear forms, but not on n.

[4] We only consider the case of diagonalizable operators here. See [**Fix73**] for the general case.

From estimate (18), we deduce that eigenvectors are approximated with the same accuracy as solutions to the source problem. Eigenvalues, as (17) shows, typically converge twice as fast as $n \to \infty$.

3.4. Multiple eigenvalues and their eigenspaces. The result in the previous section covers multiple eigenvalues, but it does not make any predictions how a multidimensional eigenspace is approximated. Such a theory was developed in [**BO87**, **BO89**]. It makes much stronger statements on the approximation of eigenvectors, but it assumes an order relation on the spectrum. Thus, here we assume a real symmetric bilinear form and real eigenvalues.

In the case of a multiple eigenvalue of the continuous problem, the approximating eigenvalues may be either simple or or multiple. Obviously, we have the

THEOREM 7 (Discrete min-max condition).

$$\lambda_{n,k} = \min_{\substack{W \subset V_n \\ \dim E = k}} \max_{v \in W} \frac{a(v,v)}{\langle v, v \rangle}. \tag{19}$$

Since the maximum in this equation only depends on the choice of the space W and the minimum is taken over a smaller set than in equation (9), we always have $\lambda_{k,n} \geq \lambda_k$.

We now consider the case of a q-fold eigenvalue of the continuous problem, that is,

$$\lambda_{k-1} < \lambda_k = \cdots = \lambda_{k+q-1} < \lambda_{k+q}.$$

Due to the operator approximation (15), each discrete eigenvector converges to its continuous counterpart. Thus, if n is sufficiently large, we have the situation

$$\lambda_k \leq \lambda_{n,k} \leq \cdots \leq \lambda_{n,k+q-1} < \lambda_{k+q}.$$

We have (see e.g. [**BO89**]) the following quasi-orthogonality condition, which relates the error of the eigenvalue to the residual of the eigenvalue problem:

LEMMA 7. *Assume that (λ, u) is an eigenpair according to Definition* 3 *and $w \in V$ arbitrary with $\|w\|_H = 1$. Furthermore, let*

$$\mu = a(w, w).$$

Then,

$$\mu - \lambda = a(w - u, w - u) - \lambda \|w - u\|^2.$$

PROOF. From the variational eigenvalue problem, we obtain $a(u,u) = \lambda \|u\|^2$ and by symmetry

$$a(v, u) = \lambda \langle v, u \rangle \quad \forall v \in V.$$

Thus, entering the assumptions, we obtain

$$\begin{aligned} a(w-u, w-u) - \lambda \|w-u\|^2 =& a(w,w) - 2a(w,u) + a(u,u) \\ & - \lambda \|w\|^2 + 2\lambda \langle w, u \rangle - \lambda \|u\|^2 \\ =& \mu \|w\|^2 + \lambda \|u\|^2 - \lambda \|w\|_2 - \lambda \|u\|^2 \\ =& \mu - \lambda. \end{aligned}$$

□

Next we refine the notion of approximability of eigenvectors. In (15) and consequently in (17) and (18), only the worst approximation within the eigenspace E_λ was used in the estimate. Here, we define recursively and begin with

$$\eta_{k,0}(V_n) = \inf_{\substack{u \in E_{\lambda_k} \\ \|u\|=1}} \inf_{v \in V_n} \|u - v\|_V \,.$$

Let u_0 be a vector for which this infimum is achieved, and similarly u_j below. Define for $j = 1, \dots, q-1$

$$E^j_{\lambda_k} = \bigl\{ u \in E_{\lambda_k} \bigm| \langle u, u_i \rangle = 0,\ i = 0, \dots, j-1 \bigr\}.$$

Then, define

$$\eta_{k,j}(V_n) = \inf_{\substack{u \in E^j_{\lambda_k} \\ \|u\|=1}} \inf_{v \in V_n} \|u - v\|_V \,.$$

Clearly, $\eta_{k,j}(V_n) \le \overline{\eta}_{\lambda_k}(V_n)$, such that estimates involving these quantities are sharper than the previous ones. We obtain the estimate [**BO87**, Theorem 3.1]:

THEOREM 8. *For every eigenvalue λ_k of (9) of multiplicity q, there is an n_0 and a constant C such that for any $n \ge n_0$ and any discrete eigenvalue $\lambda_{n,k+j}$ of (19) with $0 \le j < q$ there holds*

$$\lambda_{n,k+j} - \lambda_k \le C\eta^2_{k,j}(V_n).$$

Furthermore, for each discrete eigenfunction $u_{n,k+j}$ solving (11) for $\lambda_{n,k+j}$, there is a continuous eigenfunction u_{k+j}, such that

$$\|u_{n,k+j} - u_{k+j}\|_V \le C\eta_{k,j}(V_n).$$

First, this theorem shows that the eigenvalue estimate in the previous section may be pessimistic and it should be possible to obtain an error bounded by $\eta^2_{\lambda_k,0}$ instead of $\overline{\eta}^2_{\lambda_k}$. But the consequences of this theorem are reaching farther. It predicts, that the kth discrete eigenvalue approximates the kth continuous eigenvalue, therefore preserving the structure of the spectrum. Furthermore, in the case that a continuous multiple eigenvalue is "split" into different discrete eigenvalues, the order of these is determined by the approximability of the corresponding eigenfunction. Thus, the method will in fact compute approximations for the functions $u_0, \dots, u_{q-1}$ in the definition of $\eta_{k,j}$ above in exactly this order. See Problem 5 in Section B.1.

4. The finite element method

In this section, we give a cursory introduction to finite element spaces and their approximation properties. We will not present the method in all detail and refer the reader to the textbooks [**Bra97, BS02, Cia78, GRS07, SF73**].

The fundamental property of the finite element method as a Galerkin scheme consists in defining a discrete subspace for approximation. Thus, in this section we construct the spaces and provide estimates for the right hand sides of the quasi best approximation results of the previous section.

4.1. Finite element spaces. Finite element spaces consist of three components:

(1) A mesh consisting of mesh cells
(2) A shape function space for each mesh cell
(3) Node functionals

4.1.1. *Meshes and mesh cells.* A mesh[5] T_h is a covering[6] of the computational domain Ω by nonoverlapping cells of simple geometry. Here, simple typically means simplices[7] or smooth images of hypercubes in any dimension. We assume that for each topology type of a mesh cell T there is a reference cell $\hat{T}$. For simplices, this might be the simplex with the origin and the unit vectors e_i as its corners. For hypercubes, this might be the reference hypercube $[0,1]^d$. For each cell of the mesh T_h, there is a one-to-one mapping $\Phi : \hat{T} \to T$. The inverse of this mapping can be decomposed into the following parts:

(1) A fixed body movement Φ_F^{-1} (translation and rotation) such that the longest edge of T is a subset of the positive x_1-axis and the barycenter has only positive coordinates.
(2) An isotropic scaling Φ_S^{-1} by the scaling factor $1/h_T$ such that this longest edge is mapped to $[0,1]$.
(3) A warping operation Φ_W^{-1}.

We compose

$$\Phi = \Phi_F \circ \Phi_S \circ \Phi_W, \qquad \nabla\Phi = \nabla\Phi_F \nabla\Phi_S \nabla\Phi_W.$$

By construction, $\nabla\Phi_F$ is orthogonal and $\Phi_S = h_T\mathbb{I}$. The "shape" of T is encoded in Φ_W. We call a family of meshes $\{T_h\}$ shape regular, if there is a constant C such that for any cell T of any of the meshes we can find such a decomposition such that for the singular values $\sigma_i(\hat{x})$ of $\Phi_W(\hat{x})$ holds

$$\max_{\hat{x}\in\hat{T}} \max_{i=1,\dots,d} \sigma_i(\hat{x}) \le C \min_{\hat{x}\in\hat{T}} \min_{i=1,\dots,d} \sigma_i(\hat{x}).$$

Several sufficient geometric conditions for this have been introduced in the literature, namely for simplices, that the circumference is bounded uniformly by the radius of the inscribed sphere. For quadrilaterals, all angles should be uniformly bounded away from π and two vertices should not get too close to each other.

4.1.2. *Shape functions.* Shape functions form the local function spaces on each mesh cell. In almost all finite element methods, they are polynomial spaces or derived from such. It is convenient to derive them on the reference cell $\hat{T}$ and define them on the mesh cell T by pull-back through the mapping Φ. Standard spaces are the space P_k of multivariate polynomials of degree k, namely (for example in three dimensions)

$$P_k = \operatorname{span}\{x^\alpha y^\beta z^\gamma \,|\, 0 \le \alpha,\beta,\gamma \;\wedge\; \alpha+\beta+\gamma \le k\},$$

[5]The index h is used to be able to denote sequences of meshes. It is loosely understood to mean mesh size. On the other hand, modern finite element methods do not use a fixed mesh size, such that the meaning of h is somewhat diffuse.

[6]A favorite discussion in finite element expositions is whether cells should be open or closed. When we consider a covering or the intersection of cells, they should be closed. When we write nonoverlapping, they should be open. In this text we decide to be undecided, they may be open or closed, whatever is befitting at the moment. The context and a second of thought will provide the right meaning.

[7]deal.II and thus Amandus do not provide simplicial meshes. Other software does.

and the space of tensor product polynomials of degree k, namely

$$Q_k = \operatorname{span}\{x^\alpha y^\beta z^\gamma | 0 \le \alpha, \beta, \gamma \le k\}.$$

4.1.3. *Node functionals.* Node functionals establish continuity over cell boundaries. For instance, in order that a piecewise polynomial function be in the space $H^1(\Omega)$, it must be continuous. This can be achieved by the following mechanism: if the mesh cell is a cube, the trace of a polynomial in Q_k on one of its faces is again in Q_k, just of one dimension lower. The trace on one of its edges is again Q_k, but only in dimension one. Thus, in order to establish continuity of functions between sharing a face, it is sufficient to establish interpolation conditions on the face and require that they are equal for the functions on both cells. In order to achieve continuity, we have to do this for vertices, edges, and faces. A very instructive graphical representation can be found in [**AL14**].

Node functionals define the continuity between cells, but they also determine the topology of the global (in the sense of "on the whole mesh") finite element space V_n. In particular, the number of node functionals scattered over the mesh is the dimension of the finite element space.

4.1.4. *Approximation properties.* Error estimates for finite element functions can be derived either by averaged Taylor expansion of Sobolev functions [**BS02**] or by an abstract argument [**Cia78**]. They use an interpolation operator based on node functionals and the degree of the shape function spaces to

LEMMA 8. *Let $u \in H^s(\Omega)$, and let $\mathbb{T}_n$ be a mesh of mesh size $h = \max h_T$. Let V_n be a finite element space on $\mathbb{T}_n$ based on a shape function space containing P_k. Then, there is a function $v_n \in V_n$, such that*

$$|u - v_n|_{H^m} \le C h^{\min s-1,k+1-m} |u|_{H^s}.$$

From this estimate follows immediately that the quantities $\overline{\eta}_\lambda(V_n)$ and $\eta_{k,j}(V_n)$ defined in (16) and (20), respectively, are of order k if the eigenfunctions are sufficiently smooth. On the other hand, since eigenfunctions become more and more oscillatory for larger eigenvalues, this estimate also implies, that these values grow for higher eigenvalues. The largest eigenvalues of the discrete problem correspond to functions oscillating with a period corresponding to the grid spacing, and are thus determined more by mesh geometry and shape function spaces than by the shape of continuous eigenfunctions. Thus, only smaller eigenvalues and their eigenfunctions are approximated reliably.

5. Saddle point problems

So far we have only considered elliptic problems. In this section, we are going to extend our theory to problems with constraints. The two model problems we consider with increasing difficulty are the Stokes and the Maxwell eigenvalue problem. In both cases, the mathematical formulation is based on Lagrange multipliers and leads to saddle point problems. We provide their basic theory first and then study the two applications. The material in this section can be found for instance in [**BFB13**].

5.1. Saddle point problems. Consider a symmetric, positive definite bilinear form $a(.,.)$ on the space V. Consider a second bilinear form $b(v, q)$ with the arguments $v \in V$ and q from a second space Q. Now, we formulate the minimization problem: find $u \in V$, such that

$$a(u,u) = \min_{v\in V}\left[a(v,v) - \langle f,v\rangle_V\right], \qquad \text{subject to } b(v,q) = \langle g,q\rangle_Q\,, \quad \forall q \in Q,$$

that is, the bilinear form $b(.,.)$ constrains the original minimization problem in V. The Lagrange multiplier rule says, that the solution u of this constrained minimization problem is a stationary point of the Lagrange functional

$$\mathcal{L}(u,p) = \left[a(u,u) - \langle f,u\rangle_V\right] - \left[b(u,p) - \langle g,p\rangle_Q\right].$$

Closer analysis reveals that locally it is the minimum with respect to variations of u and the maximum with respect to variations of p, hence the term saddle point problem. The Euler-Lagrange equations of this system can be written as: find $(u,p) \in V \times Q$ such that for all $v \in V$ and $q \in Q$ there holds

$$a(u,v) - b(v,p) - b(u,q) = \langle f,v\rangle_V + \langle g,q\rangle_Q\,. \tag{21}$$

Here, we already have the immediate analogue of the weak formulation (6), the source problem for a saddle point formulation. It is customary to consider (21) more in the form of a system of equations for the vector $(u,p)^T$, yielding the equivalent formulation

$$\begin{array}{lclcl} a(u,v) & - & b(v,p) & = \langle f,v\rangle_V & \forall v \in V \\ b(u,q) & & & = \langle g,q\rangle_Q & \forall q \in Q. \end{array} \tag{22}$$

In order to simplify the presentation, we will assume $g = 0$, which is also the physically relevant situation in both our examples.

Since we have already established that the solution is a saddle point, the system must be indefinite and therefore cannot be elliptic. Thus, well-posedness must be derived by the inf-sup condition. For saddle point problems, this condition takes a special form. To this end, let us first define the space of functions which obey the constraint, namely

$$V^0 = \left\{v \in V \middle| b(v,q) = 0\ \forall q \in Q\right\}.$$

Then, u is a solution of either (21) or (22) if and only if it is a solution to the reduced problem: find $u \in V^0$ such that

$$a(u,v) = \langle f,v\rangle \qquad \forall v \in V^0. \tag{23}$$

Thus, we can derive unique existence of u without considering p. In a second step, we can determine p from the equation

$$b(v,p) = \langle f,v\rangle_V - a(u,v) \qquad \forall v \in V.$$

Thus, we need an inf-sup condition for u on the subspace V^0 and one for p with respect to the form $b(.,.)$.

LEMMA 9 (Mixed inf-sup condition). *Let $a(.,.)$ be bounded on $V \times V$ and $b(.,.)$ be bounded on $V \times Q$. Let $a(.,.)$ admit the inf-sup condition (6) on the space V^0. Assume furthermore that for $b(.,.)$ there holds*

$$\inf_{\substack{q\in Q\\ \|u\|=1}} \sup_{\substack{v\in V\\ \|v\|=1}} |b(v,q)| \geq \underline{B}. \tag{24}$$

Then, there exists a unique solution $(u,p) \in V \times Q$ of equations (21) and (22), respectively.

Considering eigenvalue problems of equations in saddle point form we will adopt the variational setting of Section 2. But, here we are faced with two options, depending on whether we consider eigenvalues of the whole operator on the left of (22) with associated eigenvalues in $V \times Q$ or eigenvalues of the constrained problem (23). Accordingly, we define

DEFINITION 10 (Eigenvalue problem for the saddle point operator). A triplet $(\lambda, u, p) \in \mathbb{C} \times V \times Q$ with $(u,p) \neq 0$ is an eigenpair of the operator associated with the saddle point problem (22), if there holds

$$a(u,v) - b(v,p) - b(u,q) = \lambda\big[\langle u,v\rangle_H + \langle p,q\rangle_Q\big], \qquad \forall v \in V, q \in Q. \tag{25}$$

DEFINITION 11 (Constrained eigenvalue problem). A pair $(\lambda, u) \in \mathbb{C} \times V$ with $u \neq 0$ is an eigenpair of the operator A associated with the bilinear form $a(.,.)$ on the subspace V^0, if there is a function $p \in Q$ such that there holds

$$a(u,v) - b(v,p) - b(u,q) = \lambda \langle u,v\rangle_H, \qquad \forall v \in V, q \in Q. \tag{26}$$

Note that in the first definition $(u,p) \in V \times Q$ is considered the eigenfunction, while in the second definition, $u \in V$ is the eigenfunction and $p \in Q$ is just the Lagrange multiplier for the constraint. Note also that the two variational formulations only differ by the inner products on the right hand side.

5.2. The Stokes equations. The Stokes equations for incompressible flow are formulated for a vector valued velocity u and a scalar pressure. We choose the simplest setting here and refer to [**BFB13**] for more details: the boundary condition is no-slip, that is, all velocities vanish at the boundary of the domain. Thus, the velocity space is $V = H^1_0(\Omega;\mathbb{R}^d)$. The matching pressure space in the sense of (24) is

$$Q = \left\{ q \in L^2(\Omega) \middle| \int_\Omega q\,dx = 0 \right\}.$$

The incompressibility constraint is $\nabla \cdot u = 0$, such that we choose

$$b(v,q) = \int_\Omega q \nabla \cdot v\,dx.$$

Finally, the bilinear form $a(.,.)$ of our abstract framework has to be defined. While the form should involve the strain tensor for reasons of frame invariance, it turns out that no-slip boundary conditions allow for a simpler form: let u_i be the components of the velocity vector, then

$$a(u,v) = \sum_{i=1}^d \int_\Omega \nabla u_i \cdot \nabla v_i\,dx.$$

The next step involves finding discrete spaces. Like in Section 2, we have to require that the inf-sup condition holds in the discrete setting. The operator $a(.,.)$ is elliptic on V, thus, the inf-sup condition (6) holds for any subspace. It remains to guarantee (24). In order to find conditions on the spaces V_n and Q_n, we rephrase (24) to

$$\forall q \in Q_h\ \exists v \in V_h\ : \|v\|_V = \|q\|_Q \ \wedge\ b(v,q) \geq \underline{B}\|q\|^2_Q.$$

In this form, we see that (24) is among others a condition that the velocity is "big enough" to control the pressure. Many pairs of spaces have been proposed over the last decades. Here, we point out the Hood/Taylor pair Q_{k+1}/Q_k and the divergence conforming discontinuous Galerkin method, see [**CKS07**, **KS14**]. Both of them are implemented in the programs described in Section A.

From the subspace property $V^0 \subset V$, it is clear that constrained eigenvalues of an elliptic bilinear form are greater than unconstrained ones. Otherwise, after obeying the mixed inf-sup condition, the Stokes problem does not pose any more challenges than the problems we considered before. In particular, we do not have to expect spurious eigenvalues inserted into the spectrum and the theory of subsection 3.4 holds.

5.3. The Maxwell equations. Maxwell's equations have a similar setup as Stokes equations in the way that they also compute a vector field, here the magnetic field, under a divergence constraint. But, the bilinear form $a(.,.)$ is changed to one based on the curl of the vector field.

$$a(u,v) = \int_\Omega \nabla \times u \cdot \nabla \times v \, dx.$$

The natural space for solutions is the graph space

$$V = H_0^{\text{curl}}(\Omega) = \left\{ v \in L^2(\Omega;\mathbb{R}^d) \middle| \nabla \times v \in L^2(\Omega;\mathbb{R}^d) \ \wedge v \times n = 0 \text{ on } \partial\Omega \right\}.$$

The difficulties arising are two-fold: first, the divergence of a vector field in $H_0^{\text{curl}}(\Omega)$ is not well-defined. Thus, we have to integrate the divergence condition by parts to obtain

$$b(v,q) = \int_\Omega v \cdot \nabla q \, dx. \tag{27}$$

The natural space for the so-called pseudo pressure p is thus $Q = H_0^1(\Omega)$. The second difficulty results from the fact that the curl operator has a big kernel, namely all gradients, plus additional functions if the domain is not simply connected. For a thorough study of the involved topics of cochain complexes of Hilbert- and finite element spaces, we refer the reader to [**AFW06**, **AFW10**], where the analytical framework is derived. Here, we just note that we have the Hodge decomposition of $H_0^{\text{curl}}(\Omega)$ into

$$V = H_0^{\text{curl}}(\Omega) = \underbrace{\nabla Q \oplus \mathcal{H}}_{=\ker \nabla \times} \oplus V^\perp.$$

Here, $\mathcal{H}$ are the harmonic forms, which are computed in Problem 4 in Appendix B. This decomposition is in fact orthogonal in $L^2(\Omega;\mathbb{R}^d)$, and the bilinear form $a(.,.)$ is elliptic just on $V^\perp$.

We surely do not want to compute a basis for the kernel of the curl operator. What we are interested in is the dimension of $\mathcal{H}$, since it is equal to the Betti numbers and determines the topology of the domain. Furthermore, we are interested in the nonzero eigenvalues when we constrain the problem to $V^\perp$. Thus, we are in the framework of the constrained eigenvalue problem (26) and the space V_0 is defined by the form $b(.,.)$ in equation (27).

When we investigated the Stokes problem, we concluded that the discrete velocity space had to be big enough to control the discrete pressure. Here now, we also need the opposite mechanism: the discrete space for the pseudo pressure must be big enough to guarantee that for any $v \in V_h$ there holds

$$b(v,q) = 0 \; \forall q \in Q_h \quad \Rightarrow \quad b(v,q) = 0 \; \forall q \in Q. \tag{28}$$

Thus, the spaces V_h and Q_h must match exactly, which can be achieved by the mechanisms in [**AFW06, AFW10**].

But, does it actually matter? The results of problem 3 in Appendix B.2 indicate that the spectrum may be completely destroyed and spurious eigenvalues may be inserted at any point of the spectrum. How can this happen?

Let $u_n \in V_n$ be an eigenfunction with eigenvalue

$$\lambda_n = \frac{a(u_n, u_n)}{\langle u_n, u_n \rangle},$$

such that the left hand side of (28) holds, but not the right. Then, we can split orthogonally $u_n = u_n^0 + u_n^\perp$, where the right hand side of (28) holds for u_n^0. Thus

$$\lambda_n = \frac{a(u_n^0, u_n^0)}{\langle u_n^0, u_n^0 \rangle + \langle u_n^\perp, u_n^\perp \rangle}.$$

We see that even a high frequency function can produce a small eigenfunction, if its part in V^0 is sufficiently small.

Appendix A. Programs for experiments

Basic experiments with the finite element method for solving source and aigenvalue problems can be conducted with our sofware package Amandus. Amandus in turn is based on the finite element library deal.II available at `www.dealii.org`.

Note that the instructions below require a Unix system like Linux or MAC OSX. Neither deal.II nor Amandus work reliably on native Windows as of now. If you only have a Windows computer available, either use a virtual box or consider a dual boot installation with Linux.

A.1. The Amandus program package. Amandus is a collection of a few classes which simplify the usage of the quite complex finite element libary deal.II combined with a set of example applications. It can be cloned from the git archive at `https://bitbucket.org/guidokanschat/amandus`.

A.1.1. *Installation.* First, you have to install a recent version of deal.II. When configuring with cmake, make sure that the Arpack library is picked up. The configuration output lists all configured options at the end. if you see a line

```
DEAL_II_WITH_ARPACK set up with external dependencies
```

you have it. If you see instead

```
( DEAL_II_WITH_ARPACK = OFF )
```

check your system installation. For instance, on Debian and related system, you have to install the developer package of libarpack as well.

cmake and deal.II use three different directory: the source directory which you downloaded, the build directory in which you configure and build the library, and an install directory into which you install the library. A reasonable layout for these might be

```
$HOME/dealii/deal.II (source)
$HOME/dealii/build
$HOME/dealii/install
```

How do we get there? First, in your home directory, make a subdirectory `dealii`. Change into this directory, create a subdirectory `build`, and unpack deal.II, either the download of a release or the clone from github into the subdirectory `deal.II`. Change to the directory `build` created before and run cmake ../deal.II.

`Note:` Amandus is currently under co-development with some functionality of deal.II. Therefore, we recommend to clone the developer version of deal.II (see the deal.II web site for this).

You are free to delete the build directory after make install, and even the source directory, if you are not planning to rebuild deal.II.

Installation of Amandus follows the same concept, except that you might skip the installation and run code in the build directory right away. Given the above directories for deal.II and the structure

```
$HOME/amandus/amandus (source)
$HOME/amandus/build
```

for Amandus, you can configure Amandus in the build directory with

```
cmake -DDEAL_II_DIR=$HOME/dealii/install ../amandus
```

In order to try if everything is installed correctly, do in the build directory

```
make laplace_eigen
./laplace/eigen
```

You should get approximations of the eigenvalues of the Laplacian on the square $[-1,1]^2$.

A.1.2. *Experimenting with eigenvalue problems.* The Amandus source directory contains subdirectories for different partial differential equations and some of them contain code for eigenvalue problems. Check for files `eigen.h` and `eigen.cc`. By the time of writing these notes, they exist in the subdirectories `laplace`, `stokes`, and `maxwell`. Replace `XXX` below for any of these. All of these directories contain a file `eigen.prm`, which is copied by cmake into the corresponding subdirectory of the build directory.

In the file `amandus/build/XXX/eigen.prm`, change the number of eigenvalues or the number of refinement iterations (`Steps`). Use the output section to output eigenfunctions in gnuplot or VTK format; visualize them with gnuplot or a VTK viewer (check out paraview or visit). Experiment with different finite elements (`FE`). All these can be tried without recompiling the program.

Try different domains and coarse meshes. In order to do this, you must change the file `amandus/amandus/XXX/eigen.cc` and recompile afterwards. Compilation can always be done in the build directory with

```
make XXX_eigen
```

Find the line which contains the word GridGenerator and change the function, for instance to GridGenerator::simplex. More ideas to get started are in Appendix B.

Appendix B. Selected problems

B.1. The Laplacian. As a basis for these problems, use the programs in `amandus/laplace` referring to eigenvalue problems, in particular `eigen.cc`. See Appendix A for compiling, running, and modifying them.

(1) Verify the theoretical convergence estimates by computing on a sequence of meshes, where each mesh is obtained by global refinement of the previous one.

(a) If the exact eigenvalue λ is known, by computing the error $\lambda_h - \lambda$ on each mesh. Use the assumption

$$\lambda_h - \lambda = Ch^p$$

on consecutively refined meshes to estimate C and p. How do they depend on the mesh size and the eigenvalue?

(b) If the exact eigenvalue is not known, use the "intrinsic convergence rate" generated by terms of the form $\|\lambda_h - \lambda_{h/2}\|$ instead of $\lambda_h - \lambda$ and conclude with properties of the geometric series.

(2) Change the polynomial order (`build/laplace/eigen.prm`) and check how the results of the previous exercise change.

(3) Create your own program file `my.cc` in the subdirectory `laplace` and run `cmake .` in the build directory to add it to the compilation list.

(4) Use GridTools::distort_random() to break the symmetry of the mesh and see how multiple eigenvalues separate.

(5) The code in `eigen.cc` uses regular divisions of a mesh for a square with a single cell obtained by GridGenerator::hyper_cube(). Change this to an anisotropic mesh by using GridGenerator::subdivided_hyper_rectangle() and see how the approximations of eigenvalues 2 and 3 and their eigenfunctions changes.

(6) Change the domain from a square to
  (a) an L-shaped and a slit domain, a triangle
  (b) a circle (Hint: dealii tutorial step 6)
  (c) a cube (Hint: dealii tutorial step 4) and experiment with paraview visualization of functions in 3D

(7) Introduce a variable coefficient
  (a) First, select cells with a certain criterion and add a factor to the call of the Laplace:: cell_matrix (). Example:

```
double factor = 1.;
if (dinfo.cell->center()(0) < 0.5 &&
      dinfo.cell->center()(0) < 0.5)
   factor = 10.;
Laplace::cell_matrix(dinfo.matrix(0,false).matrix,
   info.fe_values(0), factor);
```

  (b) Find out how to use continuously varying coefficients (requires some more programming)

(8) Implement error estimation and adaptive refinement (big exercise)

B.2. Mixed problems.

(1) Change the code for the Stokes eigenvalue problem such that it solves the eigenvalue problem (25) of the saddle point operator instead of the constrained eigenvalue problem (26).

(2) Compute eigenvalues of the Oseen equation by adding an advection term (namespace LocalIntegrators :: Advection) to the bilinear form $a(u, v)$.

(3) For the Maxwell eigenvalue problem, check how the eigenvalues change if you replace FE_Nedelec in the parameter file by FE_System[FE_Q(1)^d]

(4) Compute the zero eigenvalues of the Maxwell operator and of the Stokes operator on a domain with holes generated with GridGenerator::cheese() and compare.

References

[AF03] Robert A. Adams and John J. F. Fournier, *Sobolev spaces*, 2nd ed., Pure and Applied Mathematics (Amsterdam), vol. 140, Elsevier/Academic Press, Amsterdam, 2003. MR2424078

[AFW06] Douglas N. Arnold, Richard S. Falk, and Ragnar Winther, *Finite element exterior calculus, homological techniques, and applications*, Acta Numer. **15** (2006), 1–155, DOI 10.1017/S0962492906210018. MR2269741

[AFW10] Douglas N. Arnold, Richard S. Falk, and Ragnar Winther, *Finite element exterior calculus: from Hodge theory to numerical stability*, Bull. Amer. Math. Soc. (N.S.) **47** (2010), no. 2, 281–354, DOI 10.1090/S0273-0979-10-01278-4. MR2594630

[AL14] D. N. Arnold and A. Logg. Periodic table of the finite elements. *SIAM News*, 47(9), 2014. www.femtable.org.

[BFB13] Daniele Boffi, Franco Brezzi, and Michel Fortin, *Mixed finite element methods and applications*, Springer Series in Computational Mathematics, vol. 44, Springer, Heidelberg, 2013. MR3097958

[BO87] I. Babuška and J. E. Osborn, *Estimates for the errors in eigenvalue and eigenvector approximation by Galerkin methods, with particular attention to the case of multiple eigenvalues*, SIAM J. Numer. Anal. **24** (1987), no. 6, 1249–1276, DOI 10.1137/0724082. MR917451

[BO89] I. Babuška and J. E. Osborn, *Finite element-Galerkin approximation of the eigenvalues and eigenvectors of selfadjoint problems*, Math. Comp. **52** (1989), no. 186, 275–297, DOI 10.2307/2008468. MR962210

[Bof10] Daniele Boffi, *Finite element approximation of eigenvalue problems*, Acta Numer. **19** (2010), 1–120, DOI 10.1017/S0962492910000012. MR2652780

[Bra97] Dietrich Braess, *Finite elements*, Cambridge University Press, Cambridge, 1997. Theory, fast solvers, and applications in solid mechanics; Translated from the 1992 German original by Larry L. Schumaker. MR1463151

[BS02] Susanne C. Brenner and L. Ridgway Scott, *The mathematical theory of finite element methods*, 2nd ed., Texts in Applied Mathematics, vol. 15, Springer-Verlag, New York, 2002. MR1894376

[Cia78] Philippe G. Ciarlet, *The finite element method for elliptic problems*, North-Holland Publishing Co., Amsterdam-New York-Oxford, 1978. Studies in Mathematics and its Applications, Vol. 4. MR0520174

[CKS07] Bernardo Cockburn, Guido Kanschat, and Dominik Schötzau, *A note on discontinuous Galerkin divergence-free solutions of the Navier-Stokes equations*, J. Sci. Comput. **31** (2007), no. 1-2, 61–73, DOI 10.1007/s10915-006-9107-7. MR2304270

[Eva98] Lawrence C. Evans, *Partial differential equations*, Graduate Studies in Mathematics, vol. 19, American Mathematical Society, Providence, RI, 1998. MR1625845

[Fix73] George J. Fix, *Eigenvalue approximation by the finite element method*, Advances in Math. **10** (1973), 300–316, DOI 10.1016/0001-8708(73)90113-8. MR0341900

[Gri85] P. Grisvard, *Elliptic problems in nonsmooth domains*, Monographs and Studies in Mathematics, vol. 24, Pitman (Advanced Publishing Program), Boston, MA, 1985. MR775683

[GRS07] Christian Grossmann and Hans-Görg Roos, *Numerical treatment of partial differential equations*, Universitext, Springer, Berlin, 2007. Translated and revised from the 3rd (2005) German edition by Martin Stynes. MR2362757

[GT98] David Gilbarg and Neil S. Trudinger, *Elliptic partial differential equations of second order*, Springer-Verlag, Berlin-New York, 1977. Grundlehren der Mathematischen Wissenschaften, Vol. 224. MR0473443

[GW76] G. H. Golub and J. H. Wilkinson, *Ill-conditioned eigensystems and the computation of the Jordan canonical form*, SIAM Rev. **18** (1976), no. 4, 578–619, DOI 10.1137/1018113. MR0413456

[Had02] J. Hadamard. Sur les problemes aux derivees partielles et leur signification physique. *Princeton University Bulletin*, 1902.

[KS14] Guido Kanschat and Natasha Sharma, *Divergence-conforming discontinuous Galerkin methods and C^0 interior penalty methods*, SIAM J. Numer. Anal. **52** (2014), no. 4, 1822–1842, DOI 10.1137/120902975. MR3240852

[SF73] Gilbert Strang and George J. Fix, *An analysis of the finite element method*, Prentice-Hall, Inc., Englewood Cliffs, N. J., 1973. Prentice-Hall Series in Automatic Computation. MR0443377

[Wil72] J. H. Wilkinson, *Note on matrices with a very ill-conditioned eigenproblem*, Numer. Math. **19** (1972), 176–178, DOI 10.1007/BF01402528. MR0311092

Interdisciplinary Center for Scientific Computing, Heidelberg University, Mathematikon, Klaus-Tschira-Platz 1, 69120 Heidelberg, Germany

E-mail address: kanschat@uni-heidelberg.de

Contemporary Mathematics
Volume **700**, 2017
http://dx.doi.org/10.1090/conm/700/14187

Computation of eigenvalues, spectral zeta functions and zeta-determinants on hyperbolic surfaces

Alexander Strohmaier

ABSTRACT. These are lecture notes from a series of three lectures given at the summer school "Geometric and Computational Spectral Theory" in Montreal in June 2015. The aim of the lecture was to explain the mathematical theory behind computations of eigenvalues and spectral determinants in geometrically non-trivial contexts.

1. The method of particular solutions

The method of particular solutions is a method to find eigenvalues for domains with Dirichlet boundary conditions. It goes back to an idea by Fox-Henrici-Moler from 1967 ([**11**]) and was revived by Betcke and Trefethen [**6**] essentially by modifying it to make it numerically stable.

1.1. A high accuracy eigenvalue solver in one dimension. In order to illustrate the method, let us look at it in the simple case of a differential operator on an interval. Let $[-L, L] \subset \mathbb{R}$ be a compact interval. As usual, let $-\Delta = -\frac{\partial^2}{\partial x^2}$ be the Laplace operator and assume that $V \in C^\infty([-L, L])$ is a potential. Then the operator $-\Delta + V$ subject to Dirichlet boundary conditions has discrete spectrum. This means there exists a discrete set of values $(\lambda_i)_{i\in\mathbb{N}}$ such that the equation

$$(-\Delta + V - \lambda)u = 0, \quad u(-L) = 0, \quad u(L) = 0.$$

admits a non-trivial solution $u = \phi_i$. The eigenvalues (λ_i) can be computed as follows.

STEP 1. Solve the initial value problem.

For each $\lambda \in \mathbb{C}$ we can solve the initial value problem

$$(-\Delta + V - \lambda)u_\lambda = 0, \quad u_\lambda(-L) = 0, \quad \frac{d}{dx}u_\lambda(-L) = 1.$$

This can be done either analytically or numerically depending on the type of differential equation. Then $u_\lambda(+L)$ as a function of λ is entire in λ. The function does not vanish identically as for example can be shown using integration by parts at $\lambda = \mathrm{i}$. The eigenvalues are precisely the zeros of this function. This provides a direct proof that the eigenvalues form a discrete set.

STEP 2. Find the zeros of the function $\lambda \mapsto u_\lambda(+L)$ for example using the secant method or Newton's method. This will converge rather fast because the function is analytic.

This algorithm is implemented in the following Mathematica script in the case

$$V(x) = 5(1 - x^2)$$

on the interval $[-1, 1]$.

```
(*Define a potential on an interval. Will
 impose Dirichlet boundary conditions*)
L = 1; (*boundary of the interval*)
V[x_] = 5 (L^2 - x^2); (*Potential as a function of x*)
Plot[V[x], {x, -L, L}]
```

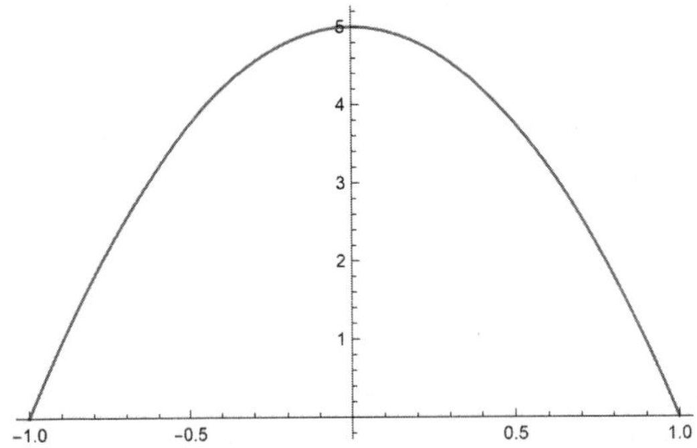


```
(*Numerically solve the ODE with Dirichlet initial conditions at -L*)
G[λ_] :=
  NDSolve[{-u''[x] + V[x] u[x] == λ u[x], u[-L] == 0, u'[-L] == 1}, u, {x, -L, L}][[1]];

(*This is the value of the function at x=L*)
uval[λ_] := (g = u /. G[λ];
   g[L]);

(*Example for lambda=1.3*)
uval[1.34]
```

```
7.45023
```

```
(*As a function on lambda this has zeros*)
Plot[uval[λ], {λ, 0, 100}]
```

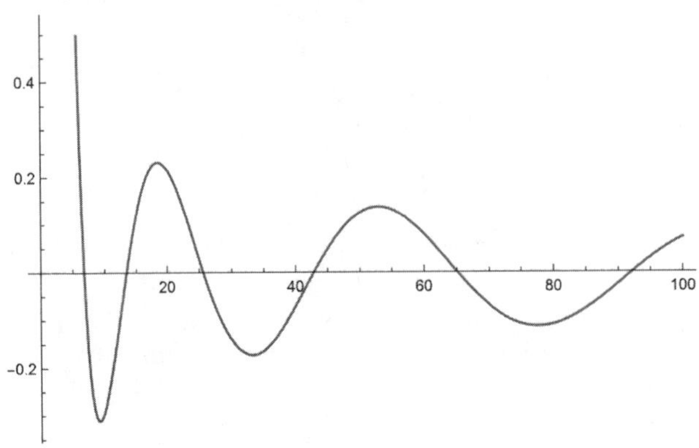


```
secante[xx_] := {xx[[2]],
   xx[[1]] - uval[xx[[1]]] (xx[[1]] - xx[[2]]) / (uval[xx[[1]]] - uval[xx[[2]]])};
```

```
(*Apply the secant method to "zoom in"*)
λ1 = Nest[secante, {5, 6}, 7] [[2]] ;
λ2 = Nest[secante, {12, 15}, 7] [[2]] ;
λ3 = Nest[secante, {25, 30}, 7] [[2]] ;
λ4 = Nest[secante, {40, 45}, 7] [[2]] ;
λ5 = Nest[secante, {60, 66}, 7] [[2]] ;
λ6 = Nest[secante, {90, 95}, 7] [[2]] ;
λlarge = Nest[secante, {1000, 1010}, 7] [[2]] ;

(*Display the eigenvalues and the
 corresponding values of uval with a certain precision*)
{SetPrecision[λ1, 7], uval[λ1]}
{SetPrecision[λ2, 7], uval[λ2]}
{SetPrecision[λ3, 7], uval[λ3]}
{SetPrecision[λ4, 7], uval[λ4]}
{SetPrecision[λ5, 7], uval[λ5]}
{SetPrecision[λ6, 7], uval[λ6]}
{SetPrecision[λlarge, 7], uval[λlarge]}
```

$\{6.782757, -6.63898 \times 10^{-16}\}$

$\{13.42803, -1.1453 \times 10^{-15}\}$

$\{25.65992, -3.36428 \times 10^{-16}\}$

$\{42.88313, -5.023 \times 10^{-15}\}$

$\{65.06532, 2.90012 \times 10^{-15}\}$

$\{92.19290, -8.13911 \times 10^{-14}\}$

$\{990.2968, -3.70806 \times 10^{-15}\}$

```
(*Plot the corresponding eigenfunctions,
the first one is compared to the Cos function for comparison*)
f1 = u /. G[λ1] [[1]] ;
factor =
  Sqrt[NIntegrate[f1[x]^2, {x, -L, L}] / NIntegrate[Cos[Pi x / 2]^2, {x, -L, L}]]
Plot [{f1[x], factor * Cos[Pi x / 2]}, {x, -L, L}]
f2 = u /. G[λ2] [[1]] ;
Plot[f2[x], {x, -L, L}]
f3 = u /. G[λ3] [[1]] ;
Plot[f3[x], {x, -L, L}]
f4 = u /. G[λ4] [[1]] ;
 (*Plot [f4 [x] ,{x,-L,L}]
  f5=u /.G[λ5] [[1]] ;
Plot [f5[x] ,{x,-L,L}]
  f6=u /.G[λ6] [[1]] ;
Plot [f6[x] ,{x,-L,L}]
  flarge=u /.G[λlarge] [[1]] ;
Plot[flarge[x] ,{x,-L,L}]*)
```

```
0.557479
```

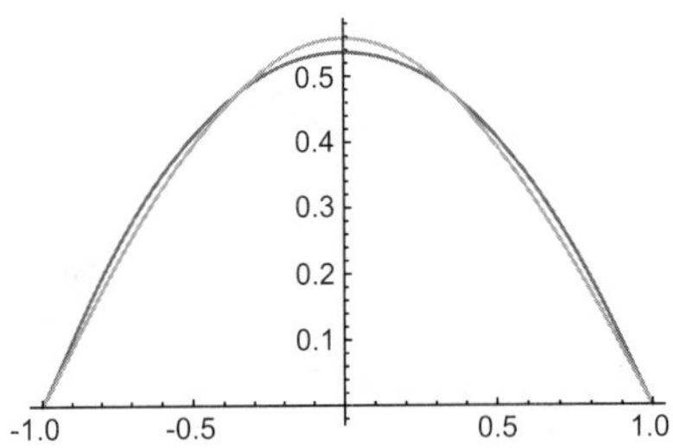

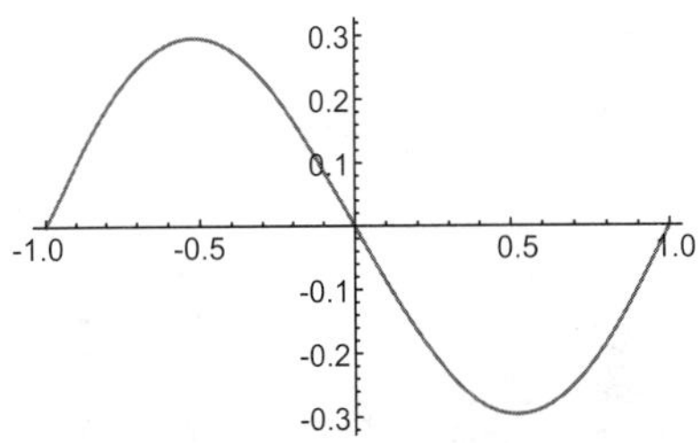

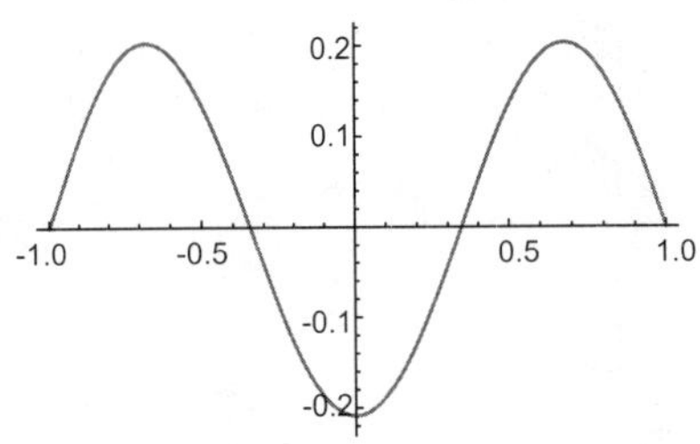

```
(*Up to here the code works for any potential. For certain potentials
 the ODE can be solved "analytically" by special functions*)
Gh[λ_] :=
  DSolve [{-u''[x] + V[x] u[x] == λ u[x], u[-L] == 0, u'[-L] == 1}, u, {x, -L, L}] [[1]] ;
TraditionalForm[Simplify[u /. Gh[λ]]]
uvalh[λ_] :=(g = u /. Gh[λ];
   Re[g[L]]);
secanteh[xx_] :={xx[[2]], xx[[1]]-
    uvalh[xx[[1]]] (xx[[1]] - xx[[2]]) / (uvalh[xx[[1]]] - uvalh[xx[[2]]])} ;
```

$$x \mapsto -\left(\left(\left(\frac{1}{2}-\frac{i}{2}\right)\left(D_{\frac{1}{10}i\left(\sqrt{5}\,\lambda-5\sqrt{5}+5i\right)}\left((1-i)\sqrt[4]{5}\right)D_{-\frac{i\lambda+\sqrt{5}-5i}{2\sqrt{5}}}\left((1+i)\sqrt[4]{5}\,x\right)-D_{-\frac{i\lambda+\sqrt{5}-5i}{2\sqrt{5}}}\left((-1-i)\sqrt[4]{5}\right)D_{\frac{1}{10}i\left(\sqrt{5}\,\lambda-5\sqrt{5}+5i\right)}\left((-1+i)\sqrt[4]{5}\,x\right)\right)\right)\Big/\left(\sqrt[4]{5}\left(D_{\frac{1}{10}\left(-i\sqrt{5}\,\lambda+5i\sqrt{5}+5\right)}\left((-1-i)\sqrt[4]{5}\right)D_{\frac{1}{10}i\left(\sqrt{5}\,\lambda-5\sqrt{5}+5i\right)}\left((1-i)\sqrt[4]{5}\right)+D_{-\frac{i\lambda+\sqrt{5}-5i}{2\sqrt{5}}}\left((-1-i)\sqrt[4]{5}\right)\left((1+i)\sqrt[4]{5}\,D_{\frac{1}{10}i\left(\sqrt{5}\,\lambda-5\sqrt{5}+5i\right)}\left((1-i)\sqrt[4]{5}\right)-i\,D_{\frac{1}{10}\left(i\sqrt{5}\,\lambda-5i\sqrt{5}+5\right)}\left((1-i)\sqrt[4]{5}\right)\right)\right)\right)\right)$$

```
(*...which allows the computation of eigenvalues with ridiculous precision*)
λ1 = SetPrecision[Nest[secanteh, SetPrecision[{6, 7}, 200], 11][[2]], 200]
uvalh[λ1]
```

```
6.7827572685741140189448252100179145880084157865005913492791603655832714240228\
 4638245403495657397373582167784872566527677589482071652819972843602272314541\
 5862001872806077519617712103286847433763966236
```

```
5.3899340426842098098587113087448983390346204164232530445289084348503078045 2×
 10^-116
```

```
(*Check that we indeed seem to have at least 150 digits of of precision*)
eps = 10^-110;
1. Table[{uvalh[λ1 + nn * eps]}, {nn, {-3, 3}}]
```

$\{\{9.32355\times 10^{-111}\}, \{6.21572\times 10^{-111}\}, \{3.10789\times 10^{-111}\}, \{5.38993\times 10^{-116}\}, \{-3.10778\times 10^{-111}\}, \{-6.21561\times 10^{-111}\}, \{-9.32344\times 10^{-111}\}\}$

1.2. Dirichlet eigenvalues for domains in $\mathbb{R}^n$. The following is a classical result by Fox-Henrici-Moler from 1967 ([**11**]). Suppose that $\Omega \subset \mathbb{R}^n$ is an open bounded domain in $\mathbb{R}^n$. Then, the Laplace operator $-\Delta$ with Dirichlet boundary conditions can be defined as the self-adjoint operator obtained from the quadratic form

$$q(f, f) = \langle \nabla f, \nabla f \rangle_{L^2(\Omega)}$$

with form domain $H^1_0(\Omega)$. Since the space $H^1_0(\Omega)$, by Rellich's theorem, is compactly embedded in $L^2(\Omega)$ the spectrum of this operator is purely discrete and has ∞ as its only possible accumulation point. Hence, there exists an orthonormal basis $(u_j)_{j\in\mathbb{N}}$ in $L^2(\Omega)$ consisting of eigenfunctions with eigenvalues λ_j, which we assume to be ordered, i.e.

$$\begin{aligned} -\Delta u_j &= \lambda_j u_j, \\ \|u_j\|_{L^2(\Omega)} &= 1, \\ u_j|_{\partial\Omega} &= 0, \\ 0 < \lambda_1 \le \lambda_2 &\le \cdots \end{aligned} \tag{1}$$

Suppose that $u \in C^\infty(\overline{\Omega})$ is a smooth function on the closure $\overline{\Omega}$ of Ω satisfying

$$-\Delta u = \lambda u,$$

and assume that

$$\|u\|_{L^2(\Omega)} = 1,$$

$$\epsilon = \sqrt{|\Omega|} \cdot \|u|_{\partial\Omega}\|_\infty < 1. \tag{2}$$

Then the theorem of Fox-Henrici-Moler states that there exists an eigenvalue λ_j of the Dirichlet Laplace operator $-\Delta_D$ such that

$$\frac{|\lambda - \lambda_j|}{\lambda} \leq \frac{\sqrt{2}\epsilon + \epsilon^2}{1 - \epsilon^2}. \tag{3}$$

This estimate can be used to obtain eigenvalue inclusions as follows. Choose a suitable set of functions $(\phi_j)_{j=1,\dots,N}$ satisfying

$$-\Delta\phi_j = \lambda\phi_j.$$

Such functions could for example be chosen to be plane waves $\phi_j = \exp(\mathrm{i}\mathbf{k}_j \cdot x)$, where $\mathbf{k}_j \in \mathbb{R}^n$ are vectors such that $\|\mathbf{k}_j\| = \lambda$. Then one tries to find a linear combination $u = \sum_{j=1}^N v_j\phi_j$, $v_j \in \mathbb{R}$ such that $\|u|_{\partial\Omega}\|_\infty$ is very small. If one approximates the boundary by a finite set of points this reduces to a linear algebra problem. This strategy was quite successful to find low lying eigenvalues for domains in $\mathbb{R}^2$, but was thought to be unstable for higher eigenvalues and for greater precision when more functions were used. The reason for this unstable behavior is that with too many functions being used, i.e. N being very large, there might be more linear combinations of the functions ϕ_j whose L^2-norm is rather small, despite the fact that the ℓ^2-norm of the coefficient vector a_j is not small.

Betcke and Trefethen ([**6**]) managed to stabilize the method of particular solutions by preventing the function u from becoming small in the interior. A simple way to implement a stable method of particular solutions is as follows.

Let $(\phi_k)_{k=1,\dots,N}$ be functions as before. Let $(x_j)_{j=1,\dots,M}$ be a family of points on the boundary $\partial\Omega$, and let $(y_j)_{j=1,\dots,Q}$ be a sufficiently large family of internal points in Ω, say randomly distributed.

We are looking for a linear combination $u = \sum_{k=1}^N v_k\phi_k$ that is small at the boundary, but that does not vanish in the interior of Ω. Thus, roughly, we are seeking to minimize $\sum_{j=1}^M |u(x_j)|^2$ whilst keeping $\sum_{j=1}^Q |u(y_j)|^2$ constant. Using the matrices

$$A = (a_{ij}), \quad a_{ij} = \phi_j(x_i),$$
$$B = (b_{ij}), \quad b_{ij} = \phi_j(y_i),$$

we are thus looking for a vector $v = (v_1, \dots, v_N) \in \mathbb{C}^N$ such that the quotient $\frac{\|Av\|}{\|Bv\|}$ is minimal. Minimizing this quotient is the same as finding the smallest generalized singular vector of the pair (A, B). The minimal quotient is the smallest singular value of the pair (A, B). This value can then be plotted as a function of λ.

The following simple Mathematica code implements this for in the interior of an ellipse. This is done for the interior

$$\Omega = \{(x, y) \in \mathbb{R}^2 \mid \frac{1}{4}x^2 + y^2 < 1\}.$$

The code illustrates that the first Dirichlet eigenvalues can be computed with a remarkable precision.

```
In[364]:= (* Ω is an ellipse. First take boundary points*)
NN = 30;
δ = 0.02;
X = Table[{ 2 Cos[ϕ], Sin[ϕ]}, {ϕ, 0, 2 Pi, δ}];
 (*Table of random internal points.*)
Y = Table[Random[] {2 Cos[ϕ], Sin[ϕ]}, {ϕ, 0, 2 Pi, δ}];
Show[ListPlot[Y, PlotRange →   {2.1, 2.1}, {-1.1, 1.1}}],
 ListPlot{X, PlotRange → {{-2.1, 2.1}, {-1.1, 1.1}}]]
```

Out[368]=

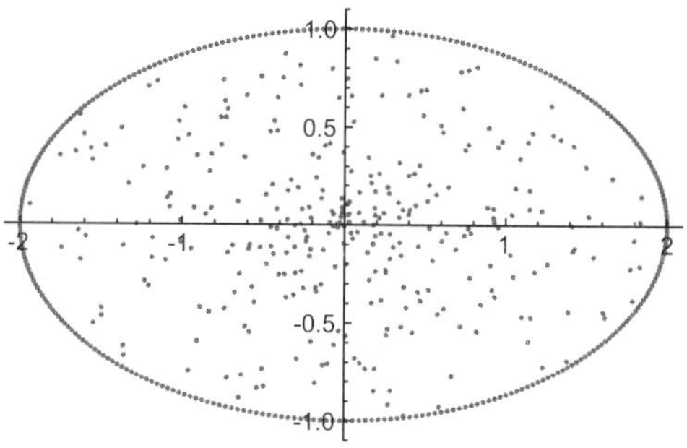

```
In[369]:= (*smallest singular value of the pair A,B as a function of λ*)
smallestsingval[λ_] : = (
    (*let's use a plane wave basis for simplicity*)
   F[x_, k_] := Exp[I Sqrt[λ] x.{Cos[2 k π / NN], Sin[2 k π / NN]}];
    (*Matrix A*)
   A = Table[F[X[[j]], k], { j, 1, Length[Y]}, { k, 1, NN}];
   B = Table[F[Y[[j]], k], { j, 1, Length[Y]}, { k, 1, NN}];
   smallest = First[Sort[SingularValueList[{A, B}, Tolerance → 0]]];
   smallest);
```

```
In[370]:= (*Plot the smallest singular value as a function of λ for a range*)
singlist = ParallelTable[{λ, smallestsingval[λ]}, {λ, 0, 20, 0.05}];
ListPlot[singlist]
```

Out[371]=

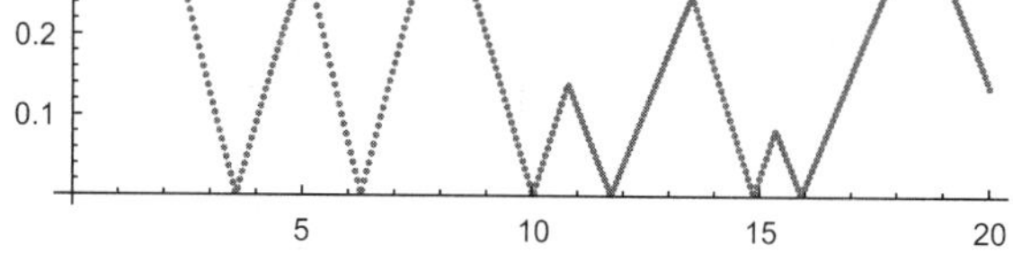

In[372]:=
```
(*zoom in near an eigenvalue*)
singlist =
  ParallelTable[{λ, smallestsingval[λ]}, {λ, 3.5667, 3.56675, 0.0000002}];
ListPlot[singlist]
```

Out[373]=

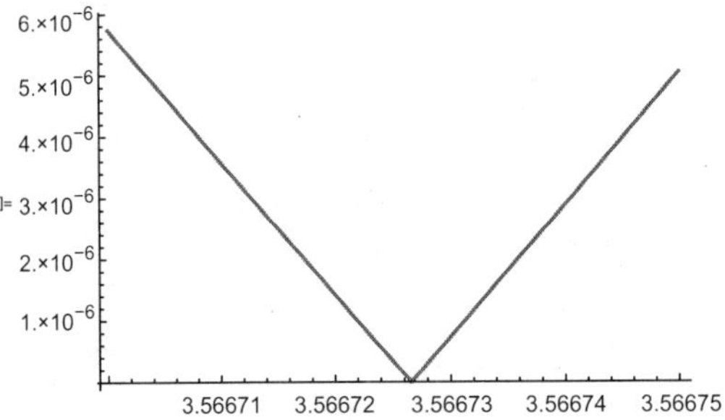

In[389]:=
```
(*Search for the minimum using some kind of secant method*)
λ0 = 3.56;
ϵ = 0.01;
Do[{x1 = λ0 - ϵ,
  x2 = λ0,
  x3 = λ0 + ϵ,
  y1 = smallestsingval[x1],
  y2 = smallestsingval[x2],
  y3 = smallestsingval[x3],
  newvalue = x1 + (y1) (x3 - x1) / (y3 + y1),
  newsmall = smallestsingval[newvalue],
  Print[{SetPrecision[newvalue, 15], newsmall, y1, y3, y2}],
  λ0 = newvalue,
  ϵ = ϵ / 100}, {runvar, 1, 4}]
```

{3.56672966693890, 6.60517 × 10^{-7}, 0.00360918, 0.000705525, 0.00145062}

{3.56672660348964, 1.20887 × 10^{-10}, 0.0000208969, 0.0000222177, 6.60517 × 10^{-7}}

{3.56672660292893, 1.21517 × 10^{-14}, 2.15452 × 10^{-7}, 2.15694 × 10^{-7}, 1.20887 × 10^{-10}}

{3.56672660292887, 1.92787 × 10^{-16}, 2.15572 × 10^{-9}, 2.15574 × 10^{-9}, 1.21517 × 10^{-14}}

In[398]:=
```
λ0 = 6.27;
ϵ = 0.01;
Do[{x1 = λ0 - ϵ,
  x2 = λ0,
  x3 = λ0 + ϵ,
  y1 = smallestsingval[x1],
  y2 = smallestsingval[x2],
  y3 = smallestsingval[x3],
  newvalue = x1 + (y1) (x3 - x1) / (y3 + y1),
  newsmall = smallestsingval[newvalue],
  Print[{SetPrecision[newvalue, 15], newsmall, y1, y3, y2}],
  λ0 = newvalue,
  ϵ = ϵ / 100}, {runvar, 1, 4}]
```

{6.27543312851491, 5.8749 × 10^{-7}, 0.00361608, 0.00107005, 0.00127218}

{6.27543062054181, 8.35045 × 10^{-11}, 0.0000228342, 0.000024009, 5.8749 × 10^{-7}}

{6.27543062018532, 8.61361 × 10^{-15}, 2.34132 × 10^{-7}, 2.34299 × 10^{-7}, 8.35045 × 10^{-11}}

{6.27543062018528, 1.42285 × 10^{-15}, 2.34215 × 10^{-9}, 2.34217 × 10^{-9}, 8.61361 × 10^{-15}}

Once the numerical part is successful and we have a singular vector for the smallest singular value, we are left with two analytical challenges to establish an eigenvalue inclusion in an interval $[\lambda - \epsilon, \lambda + \epsilon]$:

(1) Prove that the function u is small on the boundary, i.e. estimate $\|u|_{\partial\Omega}\|_\infty$.
(2) Prove that the L^2-norm of the function u is not too small, i.e. estimate $\|u\|_{L^2(\Omega)}$.

The first point is easy to deal with, for example by Taylor expanding the function u at the boundary (in case the boundary is smooth) and using Taylor's remainder estimate. The second point is more tricky. Since however even any bad bound from below will do the job, numerical integration with a remainder term can be used to check directly that the L^2-norm is not very small.

Once a list of eigenvalues is established there is another analytical challenge.

(3) Prove that the method does not miss any eigenvalue if the step-size is chosen small enough.

This point is the most difficult one. It requires a proof that the set of functions is sufficiently large in a quantified sense. It is often easier to first compute a list of eigenvalues and then check afterwards, using other methods, that this list is complete.

The method of particular solutions for domains has been further improved beyond what is presented here (see for example [**4**] and references therein) and a software package MPS-pack ([**3**]) exists that makes it possible to compute eigenvalues with very high accuracy for domains in $\mathbb{R}^2$.

2. The Method of Particular Solutions in a Geometric Context

Instead of the Dirichlet problem for a domain, we will now consider the problem of finding the spectral resolution of the Laplace operator on a closed Riemannian manifold M with metric g and dimension n. Then the metric Laplace operator $-\Delta : C^\infty(M) \to C^\infty(M)$ is given in local coordinates by

$$-\Delta = -\sum_{i,k=1}^{n} \frac{1}{\sqrt{|g|}} \frac{\partial}{\partial x^i} \sqrt{|g|} g^{ik} \frac{\partial}{\partial x^k}. \tag{4}$$

The space $C^\infty(M)$ is equipped with the metric inner product

$$\langle f_1, f_2 \rangle = \int_M f_1(x) \overline{f_2(x)} \sqrt{|g|} dx.$$

The completion of $C^\infty(M)$ is the space $L^2(M)$. The Laplace operator is essentially self-adjoint as an unbounded operator in $L^2(M)$ and the domain of the closure is equal to the second Sobolev space $H^2(M)$. By Rellich's theorem this space is compactly embedded in $L^2(M)$ and therefore the Laplace operator has compact resolvent, i.e. its spectrum is purely discrete with ∞ as the only possible accumulation point. Moreover, $-\Delta$ is a non-negative operator, and the zero eigenspace consists of locally constant functions. Because of elliptic regularity the eigenfunctions are smooth on M. Summarizing, we therefore know that there exists an orthonormal basis (u_j) in $L^2(M)$ such that

$$\begin{gathered} -\Delta u_j = \lambda_j u_j, \\ u_j \in C^\infty(M), \\ 0 \leq \lambda_1 \leq \lambda_2 \leq \cdots \end{gathered} \tag{5}$$

We will be applying the idea of the method of particular solutions to manifolds (see [**18**]). We start by describing this in a very general setting. Suppose that M is a compact Riemannian manifold and suppose this manifold is glued from a finite number of closed subsets M_j along their boundaries so that

$$M = \cup_{j=1}^q M_j.$$

We assume here that M_j are manifolds that have a piecewise smooth Lipschitz boundary.

EXAMPLE 2.1. The n-torus T^n can be obtained from the cube $[0,1]^n$ by identifying opposite boundary components. In this case we have only one component M_1 and its boundary ∂M_1.

EXAMPLE 2.2. A surface of genus 2 can be glued from two pair of pants, or alternatively, from 4 hexagons. This will be discussed in detail in Section 3.

If $f \in C^\infty(M)$ is a function on M then we can of course restrict this function to each of the components M_j and we thus obtain a natural map

$$R : C^\infty(M) \to C^\infty(\sqcup_j M_j). \tag{6}$$

Since the interior of M_j is naturally a subset in M, and its boundary has zero measure, we can also understand functions in $C^1(\sqcup_j M_j)$ as (equivalence classes of) functions on M that have jump type discontinuities along the boundaries of M_j. In this way we obtain a map

$$E : C^\infty(\sqcup_j M_j) \to L^\infty(M). \tag{7}$$

By construction, we have $E \circ R = \mathbb{1}$. Given a function in $C^\infty(\sqcup_j M_j)$, we can also measure its jump behavior as follows. After gluing the boundaries $\sqcup_j \partial M_j$ form a piecewise smooth Lipschitz hypersurface Σ in M. Suppose x is a point in Σ. Then x arises from gluing points in $\sqcup_j \partial M_j$. We will assume that there are precisely two such points $x_+ \in \partial M_{j_1}$ and $x_- \in \partial M_{j_2}$ that form the point x after gluing. We will also assume that the normal outward derivatives $\partial_{n(x_+)}$ and $\partial_{n(x_-)}$ are well defined at these points. These two assumption are satisfied on a set of full measure in Σ. Note that there is freedom in the choice of x_+ and x_- for a given x. We assume here that such a choice has been made and that this choice is piecewise continuous. Given $f \in C^\infty(\sqcup_j M_j)$ we define

$$\begin{aligned} Df(x) &= f(x_+) - f(x_-), \\ D_n f(x) &= \partial_{n(x_+)} f + \partial_{n(x_-)} f. \end{aligned} \tag{8}$$

These functions are then functions in $L^\infty(\Sigma)$. Df measures the extent to which f fails to be continuous and $D_n f$ measures the extent to which f fails to be differentiable.

The significance of the functions Df and $D_n f$ is in the fact that they naturally appear in Green's identity as follows. Suppose that (f_j) is a collection of smooth functions on M_j and f is the assembled function $f = E(f_j)$. Then, by Green's formula, for any test function $g \in C_0^\infty(M)$ we have

$$\begin{aligned} \int_M f(x)(\Delta g)(x)dx &= \sum_j \left(\int_{M_j} (\Delta f_j)(x) g(x) dx \right) \\ &+ \sum_j \left(- \int_{\partial M_j} (\partial_n f)(x) g(x) dx + \int_{\partial M_j} f(x)(\partial_n g)(x) dx \right). \end{aligned} \tag{9}$$

The last two terms can be re-written as

$$\sum_j \left(-\int_{\partial M_j} (\partial_n f)(x) g(x) dx + \int_{\partial M_j} f(x)(\partial_n g)(x) dx \right)$$

$$= -\int_\Sigma (D_n f)(x) g(x) dx + \int_\Sigma (Df)(x)(\partial_n g)(x) dx \tag{10}$$

if the normal vector field ∂_n at the point x is chosen to be $\partial_{n(x_+)}$. In other words, in the sense of distributional derivatives $-\Delta f$ is the distribution

$$E(-\Delta f_j) + (D_n f) \otimes \delta_\Sigma + (Df) \otimes \delta'_\Sigma. \tag{11}$$

Here the distributions δ_Σ and δ'_Σ are the Dirac delta masses and the corresponding normal derivative along the hypersurface Σ. The tensor product here is understood in the sense that pairing with test functions is defined as follows

$$(h \otimes \delta_\Sigma)(g) := \int_\Sigma h(x) g(x) dx \tag{12}$$

and

$$(h \otimes \delta'_\Sigma)(g) := -\int_\Sigma h(x)(\partial_n g)(x) dx. \tag{13}$$

In particular, if the functions f_j satisfy the eigenvalue equation $(\Delta + \lambda) f_j = 0$ on each component M_j then we have in the sense of distributions

$$(-\Delta - \lambda) f = (D_n f) \otimes \delta_\Sigma + (Df) \otimes \delta'_\Sigma. \tag{14}$$

Since Σ was assumed to be piecewise smooth and Lipschitz, the Sobolev spaces $H^s(\Sigma)$ are well defined for any $s \in \mathbb{R}$.

THEOREM 2.3. *There exists a constant $C > 0$ which can be obtained explicitly for a given Riemannian manifold M and decomposition (M_j) once the Sobolev norms are defined in local coordinates, such that the following statement holds. Suppose that (ϕ_j) is a collection of smooth functions on M_j, and denote by ϕ the corresponding function $E(\phi_j)$ on M. Suppose furthermore that*

(1) $\|\phi\|_{L^2(M)} = 1$,
(2) $-\Delta\phi - \lambda\phi = \chi$ *on* $M \backslash \Sigma$,
(3) $\|\chi\|_{L^2(M)} = \eta$,
(4) $C \left(\|D\phi\|^2_{H^{-\frac{1}{2}}(\Sigma)} + \|D_n\phi\|^2_{H^{-\frac{3}{2}}(\Sigma)} \right)^{\frac{1}{2}} = \epsilon < 1.$

Then there exists an eigenvalue λ_j of $-\Delta$ in the interval

$$[\lambda - \frac{(1+\lambda)\epsilon + \eta}{1-\epsilon}, \lambda + \frac{(1+\lambda)\epsilon + \eta}{1-\epsilon}].$$

PROOF. By the Sobolev restriction theorems the distributions $(D_n f) \otimes \delta_{\partial\Sigma}$ as well as $(Df) \otimes \delta'_{\partial\Sigma}$ are in $H^{-2}(M)$ and we have

$$\|D\phi \otimes \delta'_\Sigma\|_{H^{-2}(M)} \leq C_1 \|D\phi\|_{H^{-1/2}(\Sigma)},$$
$$\|D_n\phi \otimes \delta_\Sigma\|_{H^{-2}(M)} \leq C_2 \|D_n\phi\|_{H^{-3/2}(\Sigma)}.$$

Loosely speaking this follows since restriction to a co-dimension one Lipschitz hypersurface is continuous as a map from H^s to $H^{s-\frac{1}{2}}$ for $s > \frac{1}{2}$ and the corresponding dual statement. These estimates can also be obtained in local coordinates using the Fourier transform. The constants C_1 and C_2 can therefore be estimated once local charts are fixed.

Let us define the distribution $g := (-\Delta+1)^{-1}((D_n f)\otimes\delta_\Sigma + (Df)\otimes\delta'_\Sigma)$. Then, by elliptic regularity, $g \in L^2(M)$ and

$$\|g\|_{L^2(M)} = \epsilon \leq C\left(\|D\phi\|^2_{H^{-\frac{1}{2}}(\Sigma)} + \|D_n\phi\|^2_{H^{-\frac{3}{2}}(\Sigma)}\right)^{\frac{1}{2}}.$$

One checks by direct computation that

$$(-\Delta-\lambda)(\phi-g) = \chi + (1+\lambda)g.$$

Using

$$\|\chi + (1+\lambda)g\|_{L^2(M)} \leq \eta + |1+\lambda|\|g\|_{L^2(M)},$$
$$\|\phi - g\| \geq 1 - \|g\|_{L^2(M)},$$

one obtains

$$\|(-\Delta-\lambda)^{-1}\|_{L^2(M)} \geq \frac{1-\|g\|_{L^2(M)}}{\eta + |1+\lambda|\|g\|_{L^2(M)}}.$$

This implies the statement as the resolvent norm is bounded by the distance to the spectrum. □

Of course, $\|g\|^2_{H^s(\Sigma)} \leq \|g\|^2_{L^2(\Sigma)}$ for any $s \leq 0$ so, one also obtains a bound in terms of $\left(\|D\phi\|^2_{L^2(\Sigma)} + \|D_n\phi\|^2_{L^2(\Sigma)}\right)^{\frac{1}{2}}$, although this bound does not take into account the different microlocal properties of $D_n\phi$ and $D\phi$, i.e. their behaviour for large frequencies.

3. Hyperbolic Surfaces and Teichmüller Space

The following section is a brief description of the construction and theory of hyperbolic surfaces. In the same way as the sphere S^2 admits a round metric and the torus T^2 admits a two dimensional family of flat metrics, a two dimensional compact manifold M of genus $\mathrm{g} \geq 2$ admits a family of metrics of constant negative curvature -1. By the theorem of Gauss-Bonnet all these metrics yield the same volume

$$\mathrm{Vol}(M) = 4\pi(\mathrm{g}-1).$$

For an introduction into hyperbolic surfaces and their spectral theory, we would like to refer to the reader to the excellent monograph [**8**]. We start by describing some two dimensional spaces of constant curvature -1.

- **The upper half space**

  The hyperbolic upper half space $\mathbb{H}$ is defined as $\mathbb{H} := \{x+iy \in \mathbb{C} \mid y > 0\}$ with metric

  $$g = y^{-2}(dx^2+dy^2).$$

  The Laplace operator with respect to this metric is then given by

  $$-\Delta = -y^2\left(\frac{\partial^2}{\partial x^2} + \frac{\partial^2}{\partial y^2}\right).$$

  The geodesics in this space are circles that are perpendicular to the real line. The group of isometries of the space is the group $PSL(2,\mathbb{R})$. The

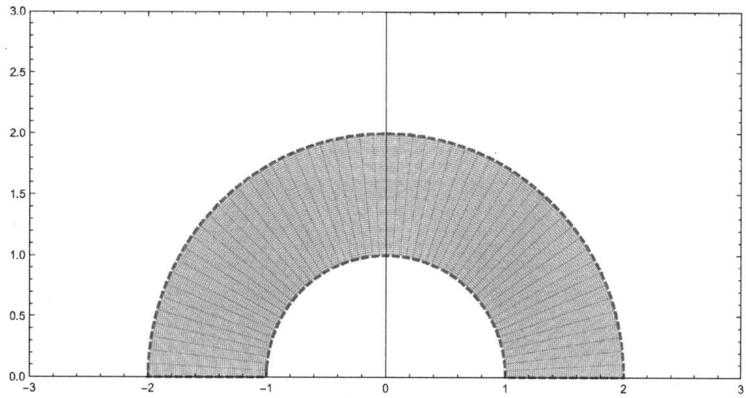

FIGURE 1. Fundamental domain for a hyperbolic cylinder

action of $PSL(2,\mathbb{R})$ derives from the action of $SL(2,\mathbb{R})$ on $\mathbb{H}$ by fractional linear transformations as follows.

$$\begin{pmatrix} a & b \\ c & d \end{pmatrix} z = \frac{az+b}{cz+d}.$$

Since $\begin{pmatrix} -1 & 0 \\ 0 & -1 \end{pmatrix}$ acts trivially, this factors to an action of $PSL(2,\mathbb{R}) = SL(2,\mathbb{R})/\{-1,1\}$. It is easy to check that this acts as a group of isometries.

- **The Poincaré disc**

  The Poincare disc $\mathbb{D}$ is defined as $\mathbb{D} := \{x+iy \in \mathbb{C} \mid x^2+y^2<1\}$ with metric

$$g = \frac{4}{(1-x^2-y^2)^2}(dx^2+dy^2).$$

  Geodesics in this model are circles perpendicular to the unit circle and straight lines through the origin. This space has constant negative curvature -1 and is simply connected. It therefore is isometric to the hyperbolic plane. An isometry from $\mathbb{D}$ to $\mathbb{H}$ is for example the Moebius transformation

$$z \mapsto \mathrm{i}\frac{1+z}{1-z}.$$

- **Hyperbolic cylinders**

  Let $\ell > 0$. Then the hyperbolic cylinder can be defined as the quotient $Z_\ell := \Gamma\backslash\mathbb{H}$ of $\mathbb{H}$ by the group $\Gamma \subset SL(2,\mathbb{R})$ defined by

$$\Gamma = < \begin{pmatrix} e^{\ell/2} & 0 \\ 0 & e^{-\ell/2} \end{pmatrix} > = \left\{ \begin{pmatrix} e^{\ell k/2} & 0 \\ 0 & e^{-\ell k/2} \end{pmatrix} \mid k \in \mathbb{Z} \right\}.$$

  A fundamental domain is depicted in the Figure 1. Using the angle $\varphi = \arctan(x/y)$ and $t = \frac{1}{2}\log(x^2+y^2)$ as coordinates the metric becomes

$$g = \frac{1}{\cos^2\varphi}(d\varphi^2+dt^2).$$

  We can also use Fermi coordinates (ρ, t), where t is as before and $\cosh\rho = \frac{1}{\cos\varphi}$. The coordinate ρ is the oriented hyperbolic distance from the y-axis in $\mathbb{H}$. On the quotient Z_ℓ the y-axis projects to a closed geodesic of length ℓ. This is the unique simple closed geodesic on Z_ℓ. Using Fermi coordinates we can see that the hyperbolic cylinder Z_ℓ is isometric to $\mathbb{R} \times (\mathbb{R}/\ell\mathbb{Z})$ with metric

$$d\rho^2 + \cosh^2 \rho \, dt^2.$$

The Laplace operator in these coordinates

$$-\frac{1}{\cosh\rho}\frac{\partial}{\partial\rho}\cosh\rho\frac{\partial}{\partial\rho} - \frac{1}{\cosh^2\rho}\frac{\partial^2}{\partial t^2}. \tag{15}$$

A large set of solutions of the eigenvalue equation $(-\Delta - \lambda)\Phi = 0$ can then be obtained by separation of variables. Namely, if we assume that

$$\Phi(\rho, t) = \Phi_k(\rho)\exp(2\pi i\frac{t}{\ell})$$

for some $k \in \mathbb{Z}$ then the eigenvalue equation is equivalent to

$$(-\frac{1}{\cosh\rho}\frac{d}{d\rho}\cosh\rho\frac{d}{d\rho} + \frac{4\pi^2k^2}{\ell^2\cosh^2\rho} - \lambda)\Phi_k(\rho) = 0 \tag{16}$$

A fundamental system of (non-normalized) solutions of this equation, consisting of an even and an odd function, can be given explicitly for each $k \in \mathbb{Z}$ in terms of hypergeometric functions

$$\Phi_k^{even}(\rho) = (\cosh\rho)^{\frac{2\pi ik}{\ell}}\, {}_2\mathrm{F}_1(\frac{s}{2} + \frac{\pi ik}{\ell}, \frac{1-s}{2} + \frac{\pi ik}{\ell}; \frac{1}{2}; -\sinh^2\rho), \tag{17}$$

$$\Phi_k^{odd}(\rho) = \sinh\rho(\cosh\rho)^{\frac{2\pi ik}{\ell}}\, {}_2\mathrm{F}_1(\frac{1+s}{2} + \frac{\pi ik}{\ell}, \frac{2-s}{2} + \frac{\pi ik}{\ell}; \frac{3}{2}; -\sinh^2\rho),$$

where $\lambda = s(1-s)$ (see [**7**], where these functions are analysed). Normalization gives the corresponding solutions to the initial value problems.

- **Hyperbolic pair of pants**

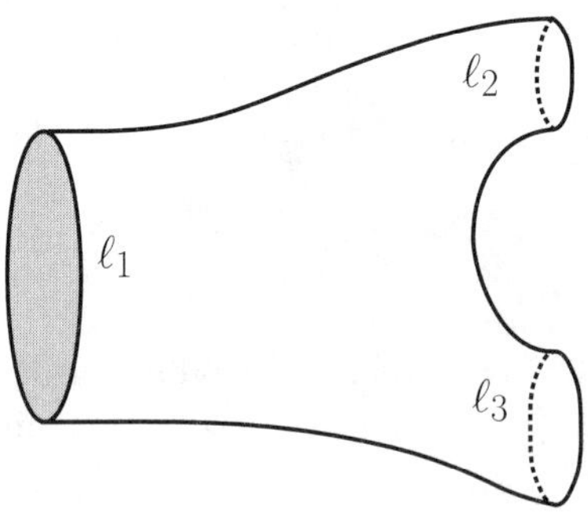

FIGURE 2. Y-piece with boundary geodesics

For any given $\ell_1, \ell_2, \ell_3 > 0$ one can construct a right angled geodesic hexagon in the hyperbolic plane such that the length of every second side is $\ell_1/2, \ell_2/2$ and $\ell_3/2$. Two such hexagons can then be glued along the other sides to form a hyperbolic surface with three geodesic boundary components of lengths ℓ_1, ℓ_2, ℓ_3. A hyperbolic pair of pants can also be glued from a subset of a hyperbolic cylinder as depicted in the figure.

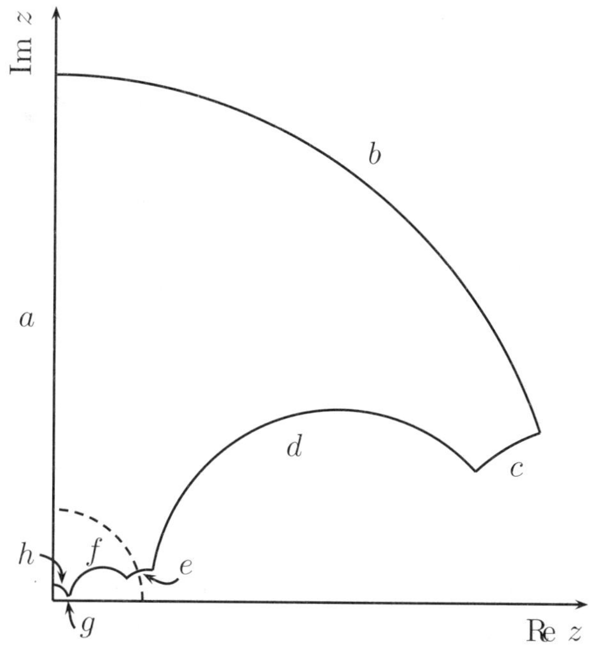

FIGURE 3. Two hyperbolic hexagons together form an octagon which can be glued into a pair of pants

- **General surfaces of genus** g

Let $g > 2$ be an integer. Suppose we are given $2g - 2$ pairs of pants, and a three-valent graph together with a map that associates with each vertex a pair of pants, and with each edge associated with that vertex a boundary component of that pair of pants. So each edge of the graph will connect two vertices and will therefore correspond to two different boundary components of that pair of pants. Suppose that these boundary components have the same length. So each edge of the graph will have a length ℓ_j associated to it. There are $3g - 3$ such edges. We can then glue the hyperbolic pair of pants together along the boundary components using a gluing scheme that identifies each collar neighborhood of the boundary component with a subset of the corresponding hyperbolic cylinder. Such a gluing is unique up to a twist angle $\alpha_j \in S^1$. Once such a twist angle is fixed we obtain a surface of genus g equipped with a hyperbolic metric. It is known that each oriented hyperbolic surface can be obtained in this way. The parameters ℓ_j and α_j then constitute the Fenchel-Nielsen parameters of that construction. For each given three-valent graph and $6g - 6$ Fenchel-Nielsen parameters there is a hyperbolic surface constructed. Of course, it may happen that different Fenchel-Nielsen parameters yield an isometric surface. It can be shown that there is a discrete group, the mapping class group, acting on the Teichmüller space $\mathbb{R}^{6g-6}$ such that the quotient coincides with the set of hyperbolic metrics on a given two dimensional oriented surface.

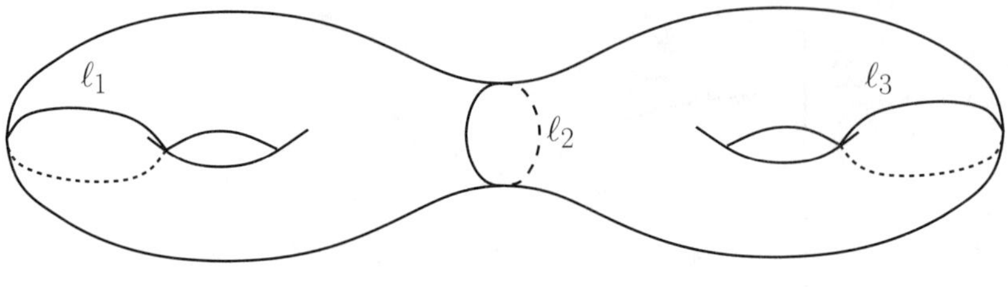

FIGURE 4. Genus two hyperbolic surface glued from two pairs of pants

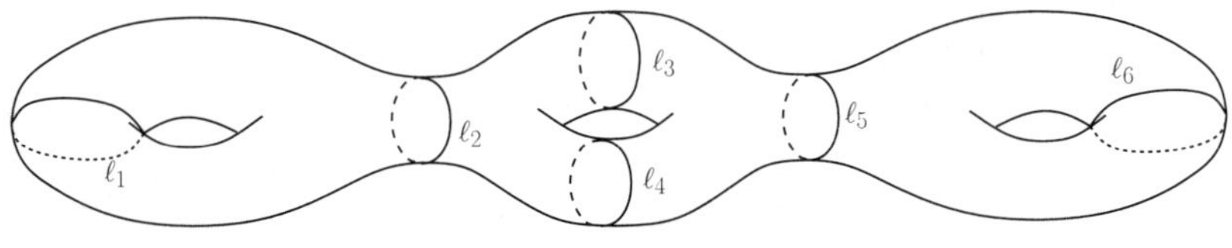

FIGURE 5. Genus three hyperbolic surface glued from four pair of pants

4. The Method of Particular Solutions for Hyperbolic Surfaces

In the following, we will describe a very efficient way to implement the method of particular solutions for hyperbolic surfaces. Each surface can be decomposed into 2g − 2 pairs of pants. Each pair of pants can then be cut open along one geodesic connecting two boundary components to obtain a subset of a hyperbolic cylinder. Our surface M can therefore be glued from 2g−2 subsets M_j of hyperbolic cylinders.

$$M = \cup_j M_j.$$

This gives a decomposition of M as discussed before and the hypersurface Σ will consist of geodesic segments. On each piece M_j we have a large set of functions satisfying the eigenvalue equation $(-\Delta - \lambda)\Phi = 0$ by restricting the functions constructed on the hyperbolic cylinder to M_j. If we let k vary between $-N$ and $+N$ we obtain a $2(2N+1)$-dimensional space of functions with a canonical basis. We can assemble these into a $2(2N+1)(2\mathrm{g}-2)$-dimensional subspace $\mathcal{W}_N^{(\lambda)}$ in $L^\infty(M)$. Basis elements in this subspace are indexed by $j \in \{1, \ldots, 2\mathrm{g}-2\}$, by $k \in \{-N, -N+1, \ldots, N-1, N\}$ and by $\{e, o\}$ where the last index distinguishes between even and odd solutions of the ODE. We will assemble all these indices into a larger index α. So we have a set of basis function $\Phi_\alpha^{(\lambda)}$ on $\sqcup_j M_j$ and we would like to apply the estimate MPS in order to find eigenvalues.

A simple strategy is as follows. Discretize the geodesic segments of Σ into a finite set of Q points $(x_j)_{j=1,\ldots,Q}$. In order to keep things simple let us avoid corners. So every point x_j will be contained in the boundary of precisely two components, so there are exactly two points y_j and $\tilde{y}_j$ in $\sqcup_j \partial M_j$ that correspond to this point. A simple strategy of MPS for these surfaces is therefore to form the matrices

$$A_\lambda = (a_{j\alpha}), \quad a_{j\alpha} = \Phi_\alpha^{(\lambda)}(y_j),$$
$$\tilde{A}_\lambda = (\tilde{a}_{j\alpha}), \quad \tilde{a}_{j\alpha} = \Phi_\alpha^{(\lambda)}(\tilde{y}_j),$$
$$B_\lambda = (b_{j\alpha}), \quad b_{j\alpha} = \partial_n \Phi_\alpha^{(\lambda)}(y_j)$$
$$\tilde{B}_\lambda = (\tilde{b}_{j\alpha}), \quad \tilde{b}_{j\alpha} = \partial_n \Phi_\alpha^{(\lambda)}(\tilde{y}_j).$$

We assemble $Q_\lambda := (A_\lambda - \tilde{A}_\lambda) \oplus (B_\lambda + \tilde{B}_\lambda)$ and also $R_\lambda := A_\lambda \oplus \tilde{A}_\lambda \oplus B_\lambda \oplus \tilde{B}_\lambda$. Then the smallest singular value

$$s_\lambda = \inf_{v \neq 0} \frac{\|Q_\lambda v\|}{\|R_\lambda v\|}$$

of the pair (Q_λ, R_λ) is then a measure of how close we are to an eigenvalue.

For a quantitative statement see [**18**] where this method is described and analysed in great detail. The idea behind this is easily explained as follows. Suppose that λ is an eigenvalue. Then there exists a corresponding eigenfunction ϕ. This eigenfunction can be restricted to each piece M_j and can then be expanded in our basis functions. Since the eigenfunction is analytic, the Fourier series with respect to the circle action on the hyperbolic cylinder converges exponentially fast. This means the eigenfunction is approximated exponentially well by the chosen basis functions Φ_α. Cutting off at a Fourier mode will produce an error in the C^1-norm that is exponentially small as N becomes large. Since the actual eigenfunction satisfies $D\phi = 0$ and $D_n\phi = 0$ its approximation by our basis functions ϕ_N will satisfy the same equation up to an exponentially small error. Therefore, if v is the coefficient vector of ϕ_N with respect to our basis Φ_α, the norm of $Q_\lambda v$ is very small. On the other hand, by Green's formula, the boundary data of ϕ does not vanish on ∂M_j but merely gives a measure for its L^2-norm. So the norm of $R_\lambda v$ will be comparable to the L^2-norm of ϕ. We conclude that s_λ is exponentially small as N gets large if λ is an eigenvalue.

Conversely, since $Q_\lambda v$ roughly approximates the L^2-norm of $D\phi \oplus D_n\phi$ and $R_\lambda v$ roughly approximates the L^2 norm of ϕ, the quotient will not be small if λ is not a eigenvalue.

Hence, if we plot s_λ as a function of λ we will be able to find the eigenvalues. In a similar way, multiplicities can be found by looking at higher singular values.

4.1. The Bolza surface. In the following, we would like to illustrate this method and some results for the case of the Bolza surface. The Bolza surface is the unique oriented hyperbolic surface of genus 2 with maximal group of orientation preserving isometries of order 48. It can be described in several different ways.

The easiest way uses the Poincare disk model. Define the regular geodesic octagon with corner points $2^{-\frac{1}{4}} \exp(\frac{\pi i k}{4})$. In order to obtain the Bolza surface, opposite sides are identified by means of hyperbolic isometries using the identification scheme as in the figure.

The group of orientation preserving isomtries is $GL(2, \mathbb{Z}_3)$ which is a double cover of S_4. The full isometry group $GL(2, \mathbb{Z}_3) \rtimes \mathbb{Z}_2$ has 13 isomorphism classes of irreducible representations: four one-dimensional, two two-dimensional, four three-dimensional, and three four-dimensional ones. The representation theory of this group and its connection to boundary conditions on subdomains has been worked out in detail by Joe Cook in his thesis ([**10**]). It was claimed by Jenni in his PhD thesis that the first non-zero eigenspace is a three dimensional irreducible representation. The proof seems to rely on some numerical input as well. Jenni also gives the bound for the first non-zero eigenvalue $3.83 < \lambda_1 < 3.85$.

The Bolza surface was also investigated by Aurich and Steiner in the context of quantum chaos (see for example [**1, 2**]), where it was referred to as the Hadamard-Gutzwiller model. A finite element method was applied to the surface and the first non-zero eigenvalue was indeed found to be of multiplicity three and was given by

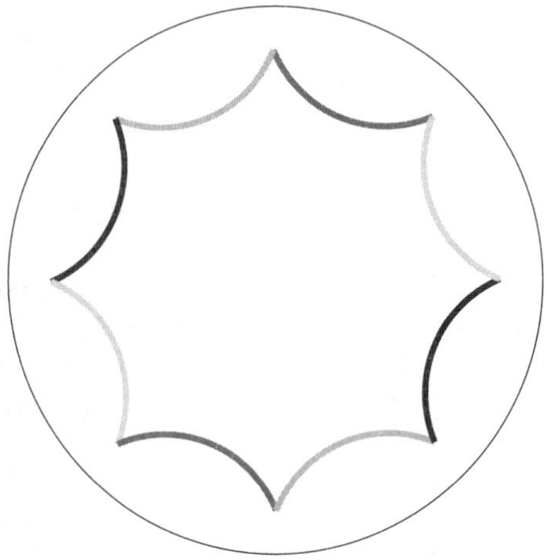

FIGURE 6. The Bolza surface obtained from a regular octagon in the hyperbolic plane

$\lambda_1 = 3.838$. Nowadays, it is not difficult to code the Bolza surface in the available finite element frameworks. It can be done rather quickly in the freely available FreeFEM++ ([**12**]). Its Fenchel-Nielsen m-w-coordinates can be worked out to be

$$(\ell_1, t_1; \ell_2, t_2; \ell_3, t_3) =$$
$$= (2\,\mathrm{arccosh}(3 + 2\sqrt{2}), \frac{1}{2}; 2\,\mathrm{arccosh}(1 + \sqrt{2}), 0; 2\,\mathrm{arccosh}(1 + \sqrt{2}), 0).$$

Another more symmetric decomposition of the Bolza surface into pairs of pants [1] is one with Fenchel Nielsen paramaters given by

$$(\ell_1, t_1; \ell_2, t_2; \ell_3, t_3) = (\ell_s, t; \ell_s, t; \ell_s, t),$$
$$\ell_s = 2\,\mathrm{arccosh}(1 + \sqrt{2}),$$
$$t = \frac{\mathrm{arccosh}\left(\sqrt{\frac{2}{7}}\,(3 + \sqrt{2})\right)}{\mathrm{arccosh}\left(1 + \sqrt{2}\right)}.$$

Note that the Bolza surface is also extremal in the sense that it is the unique maximizer for the length of the systole.

The method of particular solutions can now be applied to the Bolza surface as well. The general code for genus 2 surfaces was written by Ville Uski (see [**18**]). Based on our paper,

with high precision, one finds a multiplicity three eigenvalue at

$$\lambda_1 = 3.8388872588421995185866224504354645970819150157.$$

The programme as well as further computed eigenvalues can be found at `http://www-staff.lboro.ac.uk/~maas3/publications/eigdata/datafile.html`. Numerical evidence suggests that this is the global maximum for constant negative curvature genus 2 surfaces. The reason for it being locally maximal is however its degeneracy. For an analytic one parameter family of perturbations in Teichmüller

[1] derived by Lucy McCarthy in a project

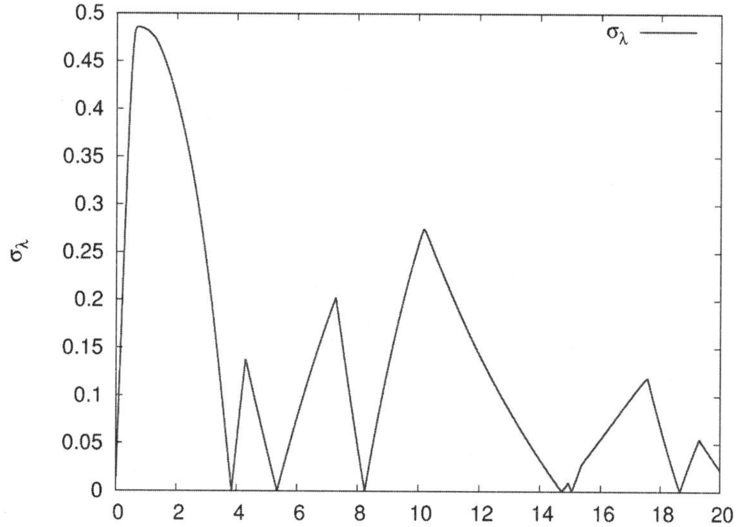

FIGURE 7. Smallest singular value as a function of λ

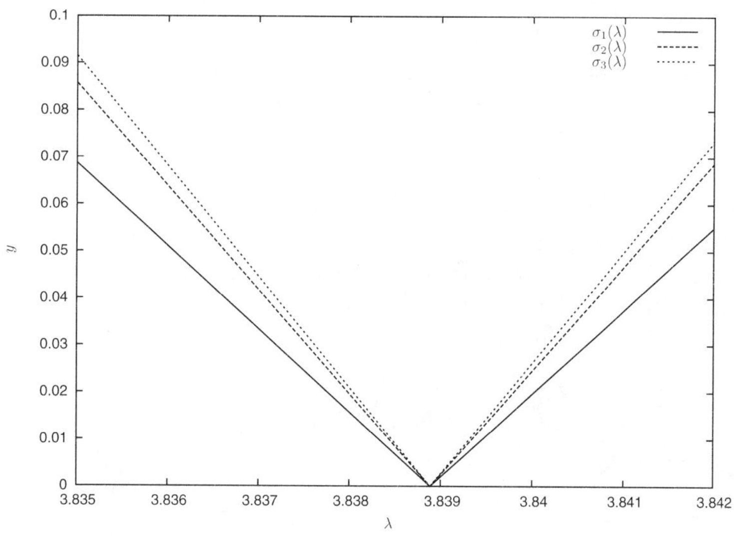

FIGURE 8. Smallest three singular value as a function of λ

space one can choose the eigenvalues λ_1, λ_2 and λ_3 to depend analytically on the perturbation parameter. Numerically one can see that no matter what perturbation one chooses, none of the eigenvalues λ_1, λ_2 and λ_3 has an extremal value at the Bolza surface. The Bolza surface is also the unique global maximum of the length of the systole. This was shown by Schmutz-Schaller in [**17**], where more properties of the Bolza surface are discussed.

The following is a list of the first 38 non-zero eigenvalues computed using the method of particular solutions in the implementation described in the paper by Uski and the author in [**18**].

λ_n	multiplicity
3.8388872588421995185866224504354 6	3
5.35360134118905041091804831103144	4
8.24955481520065812189010645068245	2
14.72621678778883204128931844218 48	4
15.04891613326704874618158434025 88	3
18.65881962726019380629623466134 09	3
20.51985973414200200114977126064 20	4
23.07855848138163515507520629957 45	1
28.07960573767772908156220794500 11	3
30.83304273793254967424395756047 01	4
32.67364961607880802483588170810 14	1
36.23839168215309025254109747525 83	2
38.96181576240495442900789740841 24	4

5. Heat Kernels, Spectral Asymptotics, and Zeta functions

Let us start again with general statements. Let M be a n-dimensional closed Riemannian manifold and let $-\Delta$ be the Laplace operator acting on functions on M. Assume that M is connected. Then the zero eigenspace is one-dimensional and we can arrange the eigenvalues such that

$$0 = \lambda_0 < \lambda_1 \leq \lambda_2 \leq \dots$$

The fundamental solution $k_t(x, y)$ of the heat equation, i.e. the integral kernel of the operator $e^{t\Delta}$ is well known to be a smoothing operator for all $t > 0$. It is hence of trace class and, by Mercer's theorem, we have

$$\operatorname{tr}(e^{t\Delta}) = \sum_{j=0}^{\infty} e^{-t\lambda_j} = \int_M k_t(x, x)dx. \tag{18}$$

For large t one obtains

$$\operatorname{tr}(e^{t\Delta}) - 1 = O(e^{-ct}), \tag{19}$$

for some $c > 0$. From the construction of a short time parametrix for the heat equation (see for example [**9**]) one obtains that as $t \to 0^+$:

$$\operatorname{tr}(e^{t\Delta}) = t^{-\frac{n}{2}} \sum_{j=0}^{N} a_j \, t^j + O(t^{N-n/2+1}), \tag{20}$$

for any natural number N. The coefficients a_j are integrals of functions $a_j(x)$ that are locally computable from the metric, i.e.

$$a_j = \int_M a_j(x)dx. \tag{21}$$

The first couple of terms are well known

$$a_0(x) = \frac{1}{(4\pi)^{n/2}},$$

$$a_1(x) = \frac{1}{(4\pi)^{n/2}} r(x)/6,$$

where r is the scalar curvature. In two dimensions, the scalar curvature is twice the Gauss curvature so that we have $a_1(x) = -\frac{1}{12\pi}$ in the case of a hyperbolic surface, and by Gauss-Bonnet $a_1 = \frac{g-1}{3}$.

An application of Ikehara's Tauberian theorem to the heat expansion yields Weyl's law that the counting function

$$N(\lambda) = \#\{\lambda_j \leq \lambda\}$$

satisfies

$$N(\lambda) \sim C_n \mathrm{Vol}(M) \lambda^{n/2},$$

where C_n depends only on n.

5.1. Zeta functions. Because of Weyl's asymptotic formula, the following zeta function is well defined and holomorphic in s for $\mathrm{Re}(s) > \frac{n}{2}$:

$$\zeta_\Delta(s) := \sum_{j=1}^{\infty} \lambda_j^{-s}.$$

This can easily be rewritten as

$$\zeta_\Delta(s) = \frac{1}{\Gamma(s)} \int_0^\infty t^{s-1} \left(\mathrm{tr}(e^{t\Delta}) - 1\right) dt.$$

We can now split this integral into two parts to obtain

$$\Gamma(s)\zeta_\Delta(s) = \int_0^1 t^{s-1} \left(\mathrm{tr}(e^{t\Delta}) - 1\right) dt + \int_1^\infty t^{s-1} \left(\mathrm{tr}(e^{t\Delta}) - 1\right) dt = I_1(s) + I_2(s).$$

Note that $I_2(s)$ is entire in s. The integral $I_1(s)$ can be rewritten using the asymptotic expansion

$$I_1(s) = \int_0^1 t^{s-1} \left(\mathrm{tr}(e^{t\Delta}) - t^{-\frac{n}{2}} \sum_{j=0}^{N} a_j\, t^j \right) dt + \sum_{j=0}^{N} \int_0^1 a_j\, t^{j+s-1-\frac{n}{2}} dt - \int_0^1 t^{s-1} dt.$$

The last two terms together yield

$$-\frac{1}{s} + \sum_{j=0}^{N} \frac{a_j}{s + j - \frac{n}{2}},$$

and the first integral is holomorphic for $\mathrm{Re}\, s > \frac{n}{2} - N$. This can be done for any natural number N. Therefore, $I_1(s)$ has a meromorphic extension to the entire complex plane with simple poles at $\frac{n}{2} - j$ and at 0. Hence, we showed that ζ admits a meromorphic extension to the complex plane. Since $\Gamma(s)$ has a pole at the non-positive integers this shows that ζ is regular at all the non-positive integers. In particular zero is not a pole of ζ. The above shows that $\zeta_\Delta(0) = -1$ if n is odd and $\zeta_\Delta(0) = -1 + a_{\frac{n}{2}}$ if n is even. The value $\zeta'_\Delta(0)$ is therefore well defined and is used to define the zeta-regularized determinant $\det_\zeta(-\Delta)$ of $-\Delta$ as follows

$$\zeta'_\Delta(0) = -\log \det_\zeta(-\Delta).$$

The motivation for this definition is the formula

$$\log\det(A) = \sum_{j=1}^{N} \log\lambda_j = \left(-\frac{d}{ds}\sum_{j=1}^{N}\lambda_j^{-s}\right)|_{s=0},$$

for a non-singular Hermitian $N \times N$-matrix with eigenvalues $\lambda_1, \dots, \lambda_N$.

The computation of this spectral determinant is quite a challenge. The method of meromorphic continuation for the zeta function also is a method of computation for the spectral determinant.

6. The Selberg Trace Formula

Suppose that M is an connected oriented hyperbolic surface. Then there is an intriguing formula connecting the spectrum of the Laplace operator to the length spectrum. Suppose that $g \in C_0^\infty(\mathbb{R})$ is an even real valued test function. Then its Fourier transform $h = \hat{g}$ is an entire function defined on the entire complex plane. It is also in the Schwartz space $\mathcal{S}(R)$ and real valued on the real axis. As usual, we use the notation $\lambda_j = r_j^2 + \frac{1}{4}$, where for eigenvalues smaller than $\frac{1}{4}$ we choose r_j to have positive imaginary part. Hence, by Weyl's law, the sum

$$\sum_{\lambda_j} h\left(\sqrt{\lambda_j - \frac{1}{4}}\right) = \sum_j h(r_j)$$

converges and depends continuously on g. It therefore defines an even distribution

$$\operatorname{Tr}\cos\left(t\sqrt{\Delta - \frac{1}{4}}\right)$$

in $\mathcal{D}'(\mathbb{R})$. Selberg's trace formula reads

$$\sum_{n=0}^{\infty} h(r_n) \quad = \quad \frac{\operatorname{Vol}(M)}{4\pi}\int_{-\infty}^{\infty} rh(r)\tanh(\pi r)dr + \sum_{k=1}^{\infty}\sum_{\gamma}\frac{\ell(\gamma)}{2\sinh(k\ell(\gamma)/2)}g(k\ell(\gamma)),$$

where the second sum in the second term is over the set of primitive closed geodesics γ, whose length is denoted by $\ell(\gamma)$. We would like to refer to Iwaniec's monograph [**14**] for an introduction and a derivation. In the sense of distributions this reads as follows.

$$\begin{aligned}\operatorname{Tr}\cos\left(t\sqrt{\Delta - \frac{1}{4}}\right) &= -\frac{\operatorname{Vol}(M)}{8\pi}\frac{\cosh(t/2)}{\sinh^2(t/2)} \\ &+ \sum_{k=1}^{\infty}\sum_{\gamma}\frac{\ell(\gamma)}{4\sinh(k\ell(\gamma)/2)}(\delta(|t| - k\ell(\gamma))).\end{aligned}$$

Note that this is not a tempered distribution. Therefore, we may not pair either side with a general Schwartz functions. One can however still apply it to the function $h(x) = e^{-tx^2}$ and obtain

$$\operatorname{tr}(\mathrm{e}^{\Delta t}) = \frac{\operatorname{Vol}(M)\mathrm{e}^{-\frac{t}{4}}}{4\pi t}\int_0^\infty \frac{\pi \mathrm{e}^{-r^2 t}}{\cosh^2(\pi r)}dr + \sum_{n=1}^{\infty}\sum_{\gamma}\frac{\mathrm{e}^{-t/4}}{\sqrt{4\pi t}}\frac{\ell(\gamma)\mathrm{e}^{-\frac{n^2\ell(\gamma)^2}{4t}}}{2\sinh\frac{n\ell(\gamma)}{2}}.$$

Note that the second term is of order $O(e^{-\frac{\ell_0^2}{4t}})$ as $t \to 0^+$, where ℓ_0 is the length of the shortest closed geodesic (the systole length). The first term can therefore be thought of as a much more refined version of the heat asymptotics.

EXERCISE 6.1. Derive the heat asymptotics from the first term in Selberg's trace formula by asymptotic analysis. Derive the first three heat coefficients.

The formula

$$\zeta_\Delta(s) = \frac{1}{\Gamma(s)} \int_0^\infty t^{s-1} \left(\mathrm{tr}(\mathrm{e}^{\Delta t}) - 1\right) dt$$

can now directly be used with the Selberg trace formula. In order to perform the analytic continuation, one can again split the integral into integrals over $(0, 1]$ and over $(1, \infty)$. For numerical purposes it is however convenient to instead split into $(0, \epsilon]$ and (ϵ, ∞) for a suitably chosen $\epsilon > 0$. This means

$$\zeta_\Delta(s) = \frac{1}{\Gamma(s)} \int_0^\epsilon t^{s-1} \left(\mathrm{tr}(\mathrm{e}^{\Delta t}) - 1\right) dt + \frac{1}{\Gamma(s)} \int_\epsilon^\infty t^{s-1} \left(\mathrm{tr}(\mathrm{e}^{\Delta t}) - 1\right) dt.$$

We now compute the first term from the Selberg trace formula and the second term from the spectrum. Using the same unique continuation process as described earlier, one obtains the following representation of the spectral zeta function for $\mathrm{Re}(s) > -N$:

$$\zeta_\Delta(s) = \frac{1}{\Gamma(s)} (T_1^\epsilon(s) + T_2^{\epsilon,N}(s) + T_3^{\epsilon,N}(s) + T_4^{\epsilon,N}(s)),$$

where

$$T_1^\epsilon(s) = \sum_{i=1}^\infty \lambda_i^{-s} \Gamma(s, \epsilon\lambda_i),$$

$$T_2^{\epsilon,N}(s) = \sum_{k=0}^N \frac{a_k \epsilon^{s+k-1}}{s+k-1},$$

$$T_3^{\epsilon,N}(s) = \frac{\mathrm{Vol}(M)}{4\pi} \int_0^\infty I_N^\epsilon(r) dr,$$

$$T_4^{\epsilon,N}(s) = \sum_{n=1}^\infty \sum_\gamma \int_0^\epsilon t^{s-1} \frac{\mathrm{e}^{-t/4}}{\sqrt{4\pi t}} \frac{\ell(\gamma) \mathrm{e}^{-\frac{n^2 \ell(\gamma)^2}{4t}}}{2 \sinh \frac{n\ell(\gamma)}{2}} dt.$$

Here

$$I_N^\epsilon(r) = \int_0^\epsilon t^{s-2} \left(\mathrm{e}^{-(r^2+\frac{1}{4})t} - \sum_{k=0}^N \frac{(-1)^k}{k!} (r^2 + \frac{1}{4})^k t^k \right) dt,$$

and the coefficients a_k are the heat coefficients of the expansion of $\mathrm{tr}(\mathrm{e}^{\Delta t}) - 1$, which are given by

$$a_k = \frac{\mathrm{Vol}(M)}{4\pi} \int_0^\infty \frac{(-1)^k}{k!} \frac{\pi(r^2 + 1/4)^k}{\cosh^2(\pi r)} dr - \delta_{1,k}.$$

As usual $\Gamma(x, y)$ denotes the incomplete Gamma function

$$\Gamma(x, y) = \int_y^\infty t^{x-1} \mathrm{e}^{-t} dt.$$

Differentiation gives the following formula for the spectral determinant.

$$-\log \det_\zeta \Delta = \zeta_\Delta'(0) = L_1^\epsilon + L_2^\epsilon + L_3^\epsilon$$

where

$$L_1^\epsilon = \sum_{i=1}^{\infty} \Gamma(0, \epsilon\lambda_i),$$

$$L_2^\epsilon = -\frac{\mathrm{Vol}(M)}{4\pi\epsilon} - \left(\frac{\mathrm{Vol}(M)}{12\pi} + 1\right)(\gamma + \log(\epsilon)) + \frac{\mathrm{Vol}(M)}{4} \times$$

$$\int_0^\infty \mathrm{sech}^2(\pi r)\left(\frac{1 - \mathrm{E}_2\left(\epsilon(r^2 + \frac{1}{4})\right)}{\epsilon} + (r^2 + \frac{1}{4})\left(\gamma - 1 + \log(\epsilon(r^2 + 1/4))\right)\right) dr,$$

$$L_3^\epsilon = \sum_{n=1}^{\infty}\sum_{\gamma}\int_0^\epsilon \mathrm{e}^{-t/4}\frac{\ell_i \mathrm{e}^{-\frac{n^2\ell(\gamma)^2}{4t}}}{4\sqrt{\pi}t^{3/2}\sinh\left(\frac{1}{2}n\ell(\gamma)\right)} dt,$$

and $\mathrm{E}_2(x)$ is the generalized exponential integral which equals $x\,\Gamma(-1, x)$. All the integrals have analytic integrands and can be truncated with exponentially small error. They can therefore be evaluated to high accuracy using numerical integration.

For fixed s and $\epsilon > 0$ not too small the sums over the eigenvalues converge very quickly and therefore $T_1^\epsilon(s)$ and L_1^ϵ can be computed accurately from the first eigenvalues only.

If ϵ is small compared to ℓ_0^2 the terms $T_4^{\epsilon,N}(s)$ and L_3^ϵ are very small. The terms L_1^ϵ and $T_1^\epsilon(s)$ involve the spectrum but the sums converge rapidly, so that only a finite proportion of the spectrum is needed to numerically approximate these values. A detailed error analysis of these terms is carried out in [**15**].

In order to illustrate the idea behind this method, let us look at the function

$$R_N(t) = \sum_{j=0}^{N} e^{-\lambda_j t} - \frac{\mathrm{Vol}(M)\mathrm{e}^{-\frac{t}{4}}}{4\pi t}\int_0^\infty \frac{\pi \mathrm{e}^{-r^2 t}}{\cosh^2(\pi r)} dr.$$

By Selberg's trace formula we have

$$R_N(t) = -\sum_{j=N+1}^{\infty} e^{-\lambda_j t} + \sum_{n=1}^{\infty}\sum_{\gamma}\frac{\mathrm{e}^{-t/4}}{\sqrt{4\pi t}}\frac{\ell(\gamma)\mathrm{e}^{-\frac{n^2\ell(\gamma)^2}{4t}}}{2\sinh\frac{n\ell(\gamma)}{2}}.$$

The first term is negative and dominant when t is small. The second term is positive and dominates when t is large. Figure 9 shows this function for the Bolza surface. Here the first 500 eigenvalues were computed numerically using the method outlined in the previous paragraphs. The integral in the zero term of the Selberg trace formula is computed numerically.

One can now clearly see the regions in which each term dominates. There is a clearly visible region between $t = 0.05$ and $t = 0.2$ where the function is very small. In fact its value at $t = 0.1$ is of order smaller than 10^{-9}.

In order to compute the spectral zeta function one can therefore choose $\epsilon = 0.1$ and estimate the errors of the contributions of T_4 and L_3, as well as the error from cutting off the spectrum and considering only the first 500 eigenvalues. One obtains for example for the Bolza surface

$$\det_\zeta(\Delta) \approx 4.72273,$$
$$\zeta_\Delta(-1/2) \approx -0.650006.$$

To compute the first 500 eigenvalues of the Bolza surface to a precision of 12 digits, about 10000 λ-evaluations of generalized singular value decomposition were needed.

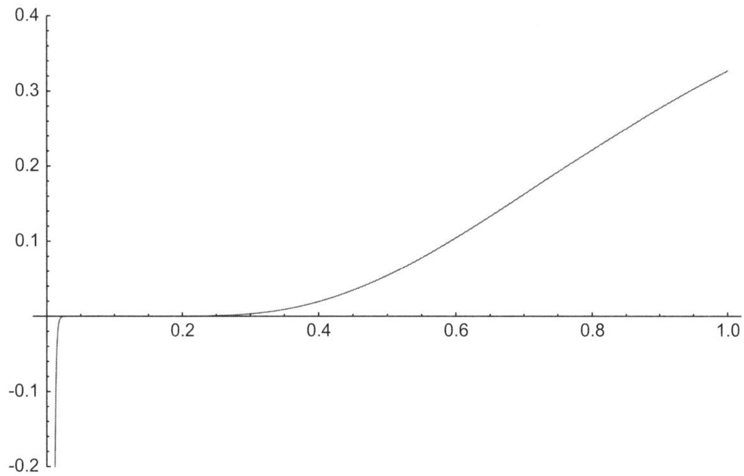

FIGURE 9. The function R_N for the Bolza surface with $N = 500$

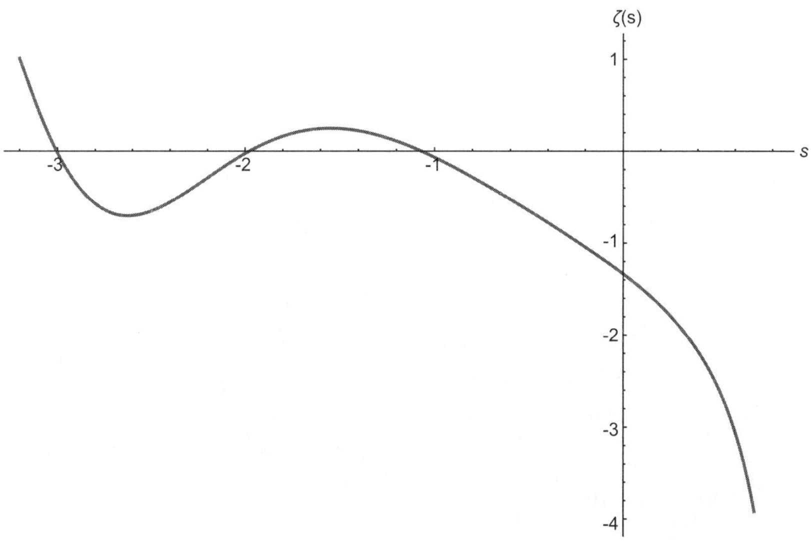

FIGURE 10. $\zeta_\Delta(s)$ as a function of s for the Bolza surface

This took about 10 minutes on a 2.5 GHz Intel Core i5 quad core processor (where parallelization was used).

Numerical evidence suggests that the spectral determinant is maximized in genus 2 for the Bolza surface. One can see quite clearly from perturbing in Teichmüller space that the Bolza surface is indeed a local maximum for the spectral determinant. Note that the Bolza surface is known to be a critical point by symmetry considerations.

7. Completeness of a Set of Eigenvalues

The method of particular solution on oriented hyperbolic surfaces is able to produce quite quickly a list of eigenvalues. Once such a list is computed and error bounds are established, one would like to check that this list is complete and one has not missed an eigenvalue, for example because the step-size in the search algorithm was chosen too small, or an eigenvalue had a higher multiplicity. In [**18**] it was proved that the step size can always be chosen small enough so that no eigenvalues are missed. Choosing the step-size according to these bounds does however slow down the speed of computation significantly. In this section we discuss two methods by which completeness of a set of eigenvalues can be checked.

7.1. Using the heat kernel and Selberg's trace formula. Suppose that $\{\mu_0, \dots, \mu_N\}$ is a list of computed eigenvalues. We would like to use this list and check that there are no additional eigenvalues in an interval $[0, \lambda]$, where λ is possibly smaller than μ_N. As before consider the function

$$R_N(t) = \sum_{j=0}^{N} e^{-\lambda_j t} - \frac{\mathrm{Vol}(M)\mathrm{e}^{-\frac{t}{4}}}{4\pi t} \int_0^\infty \frac{\pi \mathrm{e}^{-r^2 t}}{\cosh^2(\pi r)} dr,$$

and recall that

$$R_N(t) = -\sum_{j=N+1}^{\infty} e^{-\lambda_j t} + \sum_{n=1}^{\infty} \sum_{\gamma} \frac{\mathrm{e}^{-t/4}}{\sqrt{4\pi t}} \frac{\ell(\gamma)\mathrm{e}^{-\frac{n^2 \ell(\gamma)^2}{4t}}}{2\sinh\frac{n\ell(\gamma)}{2}}.$$

For $t < T < \sqrt{\ell_0^2 + 1} - 1$ the second term is bounded by

$$F_T(t) = \sqrt{\frac{T}{t}} \mathrm{tr}(e^{-\Delta T}) e^{\frac{T}{4} + \frac{l^2}{4T}} e^{\frac{-l^2}{4t}},$$

In [**15**] Fourier Tauberian theorems were used to establish the bound

$$F_T(t) \leq \frac{\mathrm{Vol}(M)}{4\pi} \frac{1}{\sqrt{t}} e^{\frac{T}{4} + \frac{\ell_0^2}{4T} - \frac{\ell_0^2}{4t}} \left(\frac{1}{\sqrt{T}} + \frac{2\nu^2 + \nu\pi}{\sqrt{\pi}\ell_0} + \sqrt{T} \left(\frac{4\nu^3 + 2\nu^2\pi}{\pi \ell_0^2} \right) \right),$$

where $\nu \approx 4.73$ is the first non-zero solution to the equation $\cos(\lambda)\cosh(\lambda) = 1$, and ℓ_0 is the systole length. Hence,

$$R_N(t) \leq F_T(t).$$

Therefore, if we compute

$$\tilde{R}_N(t) = \sum_{j=0}^{N} e^{-\mu_j t} - \frac{\mathrm{Vol}(M)\mathrm{e}^{-\frac{t}{4}}}{4\pi t} \int_0^\infty \frac{\pi \mathrm{e}^{-r^2 t}}{\cosh^2(\pi r)} dr$$

and

$$F_T(t) - \tilde{R}_N \leq \epsilon,$$

then there can not be any additional eigenvalues in the interval $[0, -\frac{\log F_T(t) - \tilde{R}_N}{t}]$ as otherwise we would have

$$R_N(t) > F_T(t).$$

For the Bolza surface we have $\ell_0 \approx 3.05714$ and we can choose for instance $T = 2$.

Using the list of the first 200 eigenvalues one can see from Fig. 11 that choosing t near 0.1 maximizes the function $-\frac{\log F_T(t) - \tilde{R}_N}{t}$. For $t = 0.095$ one gets that there

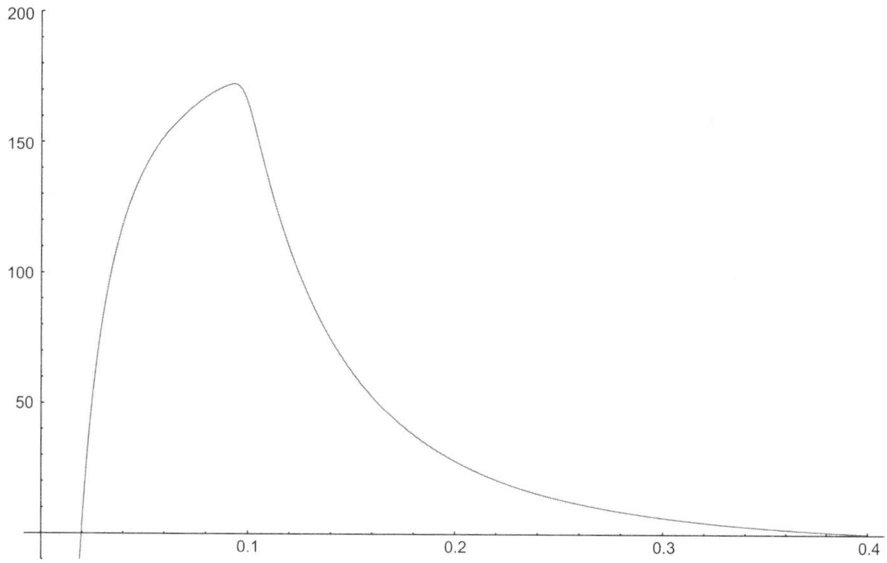

FIGURE 11. $-\frac{\log F_T(t)-\tilde{R}_N}{t}$ as a function of t for the Bolza surface, $N = 200$

are no additional eigenvalues smaller than 172. Note that $\lambda_{200} \approx 200.787$. So we had to compute roughly 30 more eigenvalues to make sure our list is complete. This method in principle can be made rigorous by using interval arithmetics. Its disadvantage is that for larger lists it requires the low lying eigenvalues to be known with very high accuracy.

7.2. Using the Riesz mean of the counting function. It is sometimes convenient to reparametrize in terms of square roots of eigenvalues. Let us define the local counting function

$$\tilde{N}(t) = N(t^2) = \#\{\lambda_j \leq t^2\} = \#\{\sqrt{\lambda_j} \leq t\}.$$

For a general negatively curved two dimensional compact Riemannian manifold one has (see [**5**])

$$\tilde{N}(t) \sim \frac{\mathrm{Vol}(M)}{4\pi} t^2 + O(\frac{t}{\log(t)}),$$

as $t \to \infty$. Because of the growing error term this is unsuitable to detect missed eigenvalues from the spectrum. However, the so-called Riesz means of the counting functions are known to have improved asymptotic expansions. In our case define the first Riesz mean as

$$(R_1\tilde{N})(t) := \frac{1}{t}\int_0^t \tilde{N}(r)dr.$$

Then for two dimensional compact surfaces of negative curvature one has

$$(R_1\tilde{N})(t) = \frac{\mathrm{Vol}(M)}{12\pi} t^2 + \frac{1}{12\pi}\int \kappa(x)dx + O(\frac{1}{\log(t)^2}),$$

where $\kappa(x)$ is the scalar curvature at the point $x \in M$. This can be inferred in the case of constant curvature hyperbolic surfaces from Selberg's trace formula (see

[**13**]), but also can be shown to hold true in the case of negative variable curvature ([**16**]). In the case of hyperbolic surfaces one obtains

$$(R_1\tilde{N})(t) = \frac{\mathrm{Vol}(M)}{12\pi}\left(t^2 - 1\right) + O(\frac{1}{\log(t)^2}).$$

The strategy is to compute the Riesz means from a set of computed eigenvalues. That is, if $\{\mu_0, \dots, \mu_N\}$ is a set of eigenvalues we compute the function

$$\tilde{N}_{test}(t) := \#\{\sqrt{\mu_j} \leq t\}$$

and plot

$$F_{test(t)} := (R_1\tilde{N}_{test})(t) - \frac{\mathrm{Vol}(M)}{12\pi}\left(t^2 - 1\right).$$

This is done in Fig. 12 for the Bolza surface. The red line was computed with an eigenvalue missing. One can clearly see this in the plot, and this also allows one to say roughly where the missing eigenvalue was. If an eigenvalue is missing somewhere this will result in the function not going to zero. In this way one can even detect roughly where the missed eigenvalue is located and how many eigenvalues may be missing.

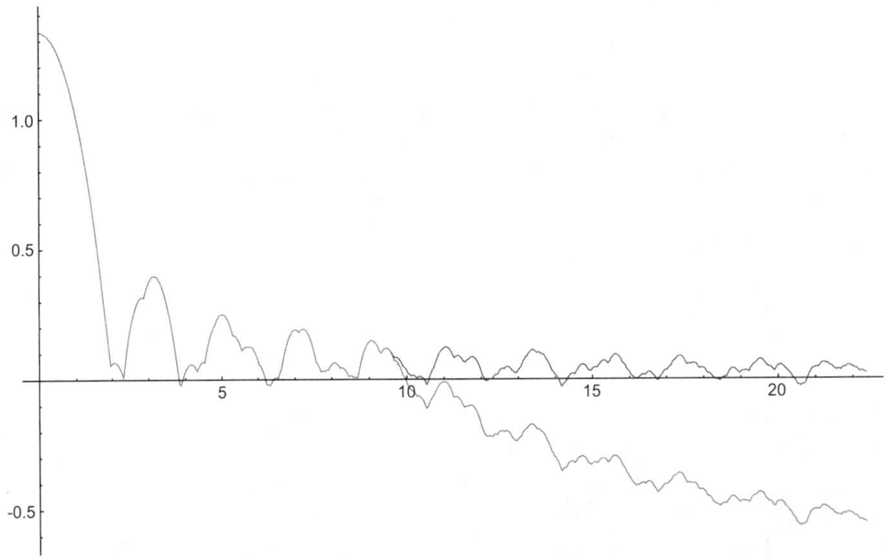

FIGURE 12. $F_{test(t)}$ as a function of t for the Bolza surface, the red line is the function with $\lambda_{89} \approx (9.563)^2$ missing

Acknowledgements

The author would like to thank the organizers of the summer school for the perfect organization and the hospitality. The author is also grateful to Joseph Cook for carefully reading these notes and for providing some numerical work on the Bolza surface as well as diagrams.

References

[1] R. Aurich and F. Steiner, *Periodic-orbit sum rules for the Hadamard-Gutzwiller model*, Phys. D **39** (1989), no. 2-3, 169–193, DOI 10.1016/0167-2789(89)90003-1. MR1028714

[2] R. Aurich and F. Steiner, *Energy-level statistics of the Hadamard-Gutzwiller ensemble*, Phys. D **43** (1990), no. 2-3, 155–180, DOI 10.1016/0167-2789(90)90131-8. MR1067908

[3] A.H. Barnett and T. Betcke. MPSpack: A MATLAB toolbox to solve Helmholtz PDE, wave scattering, and eigenvalue problems, 2008–2012.

[4] A. H. Barnett and A. Hassell, *Boundary quasi-orthogonality and sharp inclusion bounds for large Dirichlet eigenvalues*, SIAM J. Numer. Anal. **49** (2011), no. 3, 1046–1063, DOI 10.1137/100796637. MR2812557

[5] Pierre H. Bérard, *On the wave equation on a compact Riemannian manifold without conjugate points*, Math. Z. **155** (1977), no. 3, 249–276, DOI 10.1007/BF02028444. MR0455055

[6] Timo Betcke and Lloyd N. Trefethen, *Reviving the method of particular solutions*, SIAM Rev. **47** (2005), no. 3, 469–491, DOI 10.1137/S0036144503437336. MR2178637

[7] David Borthwick, *Sharp upper bounds on resonances for perturbations of hyperbolic space*, Asymptot. Anal. **69** (2010), no. 1-2, 45–85. MR2732192

[8] Peter Buser, *Geometry and spectra of compact Riemann surfaces*, Modern Birkhäuser Classics, Birkhäuser Boston, Inc., Boston, MA, 2010. Reprint of the 1992 edition. MR2742784

[9] Isaac Chavel, *Eigenvalues in Riemannian geometry*, Pure and Applied Mathematics, vol. 115, Academic Press, Inc., Orlando, FL, 1984. Including a chapter by Burton Randol; With an appendix by Jozef Dodziuk. MR768584

[10] J. Cook *PhD-thesis*, in preparation.

[11] L. Fox, P. Henrici, and C. Moler, *Approximations and bounds for eigenvalues of elliptic operators*, SIAM J. Numer. Anal. **4** (1967), 89–102, DOI 10.1137/0704008. MR0215542

[12] F. Hecht, *New development in freefem++*, J. Numer. Math. **20** (2012), no. 3-4, 251–265. MR3043640

[13] Dennis A. Hejhal, *The Selberg trace formula for* PSL$(2, R)$. *Vol. I*, Lecture Notes in Mathematics, Vol. 548, Springer-Verlag, Berlin-New York, 1976. MR0439755

[14] Henryk Iwaniec, *Spectral methods of automorphic forms*, 2nd ed., Graduate Studies in Mathematics, vol. 53, American Mathematical Society, Providence, RI; Revista Matemática Iberoamericana, Madrid, 2002. MR1942691

[15] Kamil Mroz and Alexander Strohmaier, *Explicit bounds on eigenfunctions and spectral functions on manifolds hyperbolic near a point*, J. Lond. Math. Soc. (2) **89** (2014), no. 3, 917–940, DOI 10.1112/jlms/jdu010. MR3217656

[16] Kamil Mroz and Alexander Strohmaier, *Riesz means of the counting function of the Laplace operator on compact manifolds of non-positive curvature*, J. Spectr. Theory **6** (2016), no. 3, 629–642, DOI 10.4171/JST/134. MR3551179

[17] P. Schmutz, *Riemann surfaces with shortest geodesic of maximal length*, Geom. Funct. Anal. **3** (1993), no. 6, 564–631, DOI 10.1007/BF01896258. MR1250756

[18] Alexander Strohmaier and Ville Uski, *An algorithm for the computation of eigenvalues, spectral zeta functions and zeta-determinants on hyperbolic surfaces*, Comm. Math. Phys. **317** (2013), no. 3, 827–869, DOI 10.1007/s00220-012-1557-1. MR3009726

School of Mathematics, University of Leeds, Leeds, LS2 9JT, United Kingdom
E-mail address: a.strohmaier@leeds.ac.uk

Contemporary Mathematics
Volume **700**, 2017
http://dx.doi.org/10.1090/conm/700/14188

Scales, blow-up and quasimode constructions

Daniel Grieser

ABSTRACT. In this expository article we show how the concepts of manifolds with corners, blow-ups and resolutions can be used effectively for the construction of quasimodes, i.e. of approximate eigenfunctions of the Laplacian on certain families of spaces, mostly exemplified by domains $\Omega_h \subset \mathbb{R}^2$, that degenerate as $h \to 0$. These include standard adiabatic limit families and also families that exhibit several types of scaling behavior. An introduction to manifolds with corners and resolutions, and how they relate to the ideas of (multiple) scales and matching, is included.

CONTENTS

1. Introduction

This article gives an introduction to the ideas of blow-up and resolution, and how they can be used for the construction of quasimodes for the Laplacian in singular perturbation problems. Blow-up is a rigorous geometric tool for describing multiple scales, which appear in many analytic problems in pure and applied mathematics. The construction of quasimodes is a low-tech yet non-trivial problem where this tool can be used effectively.

The idea of scales. One of the fundamental ideas in analysis is scale. As an illustration consider the function

$$f_h(x) = \frac{x}{x+h}, \quad x \in [0,1] \tag{1.1}$$

where h is a 'small' positive number, see Figure 1 for $h = 0.1$ and $h = 0.01$. Observe that at $x = 0$ the function takes the value 0 while for 'most' values of x it is 'close'

1991 *Mathematics Subject Classification.* Primary 35-02; Secondary 35B25, 35P05, 58J37.

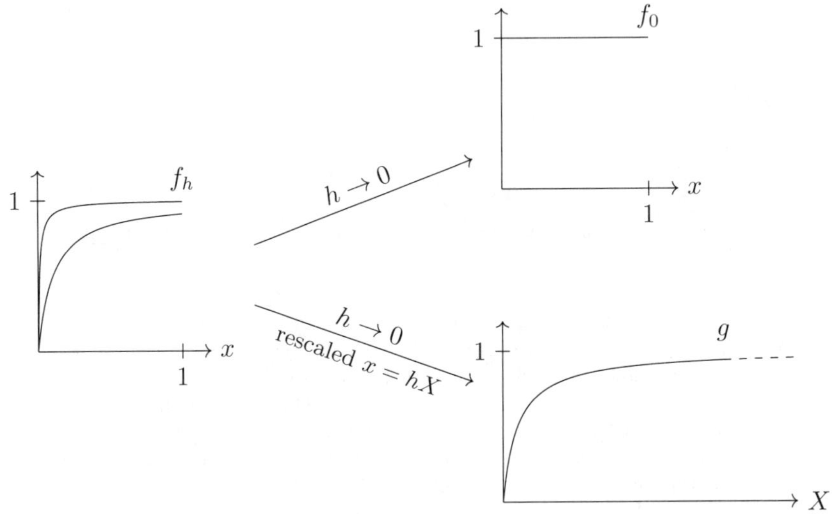

FIGURE 1. Graph of f_h for $h = 0.1$ and $h = 0.01$, and limits at two scales

to 1. On the other hand, taking $x = h$ we get $f_h(h) = \frac{1}{2}$, and more generally if x is 'on the order of h' then $f_h(x)$ will be somewhere 'definitely between 0 and 1'.

This may be the way a physicist describes the function f_h, even without the quotation marks; to a mathematician the quotes create a sense of uneasiness, so we search for a precise statement. We then realize that we are really talking about the *family* of functions $(f_h)_{h>0}$ and its limiting behavior as $h \to 0$. More precisely, we first have the pointwise limit

$$\lim_{h\to 0} f_h(x) = f_0(x) := \begin{cases} 0 & \text{if } x = 0 \\ 1 & \text{if } x > 0. \end{cases} \tag{1.2}$$

On the other hand, we have the *rescaled limit* where we set $x = hX$ and fix X while letting $h \to 0$:

$$\lim_{h\to 0} f_h(hX) = g(X) := \frac{X}{X+1}, \quad X \geq 0\,. \tag{1.3}$$

The function g shows how the transition from the value 0 to almost 1 happens in f_h. We call this the limit of f_h at the scale $x \sim h$, while (1.2) is the limit at the scale $x \sim 1$. We could also consider other scales, i.e. limits $\lim_{h\to 0} f_h(h^a X)$ with $a \in \mathbb{R}$, but they don't give new insights in this case: if $a < 1$ then we get the jump function f_0 while for $a > 1$ we just get zero.

Summarizing, we see that the family (f_h) has non-trivial behavior at two scales, $x \sim 1$ and $x \sim h$, for $h \to 0$.

Geometric resolution analysis and matched asymptotic expansions. This rough first explanation of scales will be made more precise in Section 2. But let us now turn to real problems: Consider a differential equation whose coefficients depend on a parameter h, and have non-trivial behavior at several scales as $h \to 0$. We then ask how the solutions behave as $h \to 0$. Of course we expect them to exhibit several scales also.[1] The same phenomenon arises in so-called singular perturbation problems, where the type of the equation changes at $h = 0$.[2] Similarly, we could think of a partial differential equation on a domain which depends on h and has parts that scale in different ways, or which degenerates to a lower-dimensional domain as $h \to 0$, or both. For examples see Figures 13 and 15. Such problems arise frequently in global and geometric analysis as well as in applied analysis (sometimes under the name of boundary layer problems). We will call them *singular problems*.

There is a standard method to attack such problems, called *matched asymptotic expansions* (MAE) and commonly used in applied analysis since the mid-1900s (see e.g. [**31**]): Roughly speaking, for each scale appearing in the problem you make an ansatz for the Taylor expansion (in h) of the solution at this scale and plug it into the equation. This yields recursive sets of equations for the Taylor coefficients. The fact that the solutions at different scales must 'fit together' yields boundary conditions that make these equations well-posed (and often explicitly solvable).

Of more recent origin is a different but closely related method, which has been used frequently in global and geometric analysis and which we call *geometric resolution analysis*[3] (GRA): the starting point is a shift in perspective, which in the example above is to consider $f : (x, h) \mapsto f_h(x)$ as a function of two variables rather than as a family of functions of one variable. Then f has singular behavior at $(x, h) = (0, 0)$, and the scaling considerations above can be restated as saying that this singularity can be *resolved by blowing up* the point $(0, 0)$ in (x, h)-space, as will be explained in Section 2. In order to analyze the solutions of a singular differential equation we first resolve its singularities by suitably blowing up (x, h)-space; then the asymptotic behavior of solutions is obtained by solving model problems at the $h = 0$ boundary faces of the blown-up space. The model problems are simpler than the original problem and correspond to the recursive sets of equations of MAE.

Eigenfunctions and quasimodes. The purpose of this article is to introduce the concepts needed for geometric resolution analysis and apply them to problems in spectral theory. The needed concepts are manifolds with corners, blow-up and resolution. The spectral problem is to analyze solutions $\lambda \in \mathbb{R}$, $u : \Omega \to \mathbb{R}$ of the equation

$$-\Delta u = \lambda u$$

where Δ is the Laplacian on a bounded domain $\Omega \subset \mathbb{R}^2$, and the Dirichlet boundary condition $u = 0$ at $\partial\Omega$ is imposed. This problem has natural generalizations to higher dimensions, manifolds and other boundary conditions, some of which will occasionally also be considered. The eigenvalues form a sequence $0 < \lambda_1 \leq \lambda_2 \leq \cdots \to \infty$ and can usually not be calculated explicitly. But if we look at families of domains Ω_h which degenerate to a line segment as $h \to 0$ then we have a chance to analyze the asymptotic behavior of $\lambda_k(h)$ (and associated eigenfunctions) as $h \to 0$. Here we fix k while letting $h \to 0$. Other regimes are also interesting, e.g. k going

[1] Although it is not essential for this article, as a warm-up exercise you may analyze the behavior as $h \to 0$ of the solution of the differential equation $u' + f_h(x)u = 0$, $u(0) = 1$, or (more difficult) of $u'' + f_h(x)u = 0$, $u(0) = 0, u'(0) = 1$.

[2] As an example, consider the equation $hu' + u = 0$, $u(0) = 1$. At $h = 0$ this is not even a differential equation! For $h > 0$ it has the solution $u_h(x) = e^{-x/h}$, which exhibits scaling behavior as $h \to 0$ similar to f_h.

[3] As far as I know, no name has been coined for the method in the literature. This name must not be confused with the so-called geometric multi-resolution analysis, a method for the analysis of high dimensional data.

to ∞ like h^{-1}, but we don't consider them here. One expects that the leading term in the asymptotics can be calculated by solving a one-dimensional (ODE) problem. This is indeed the case also for higher order terms, but the details of how this works depend crucially on *how* Ω_h degenerates (the 'shape' of Ω_h). We will analyze several interesting cases of such degenerations.

A standard approach to analyzing such eigenvalue problems is to first construct so-called *quasimodes*, i.e. pairs (λ, u) which solve the eigenvalue equation up to a small, i.e. $O(h^N)$, error, and then to show that the quasimodes are close to actual solutions. The construction yields the full asymptotics (i.e. up to errors $O(h^N)$ for any N) of quasimodes, and then of actual eigenvalues and eigenfunctions as $h \to 0$. It is in the construction of quasimodes where GRA (or MAE) is used, and we will focus on this step in this article. The second step is quite straight-forward if the operator is scalar and the limit problem is one-dimensional, as is the case for all problems considered here. See Remark 5.5, [**12**], [**20**], [**53**] and point (V) below. For higher dimensional limit problems quasimodes need not be close to modes, see [**4**].

Why GRA? The methods of geometric resolution analysis and matched asymptotic expansions are closely related: they are really different ways to encode the same calculational base. GRA requires you to learn and get used to some new concepts, like manifolds with corners and blow-up, while MAE is very 'down-to-earth'. Here are some points why it may be worth to invest the effort to learn about GRA. I hope they will become clear while you read this article.

(I) GRA provides a rigorous framework for the powerful idea of MAE. For example, the 'expansions at different scales' of a putative solution $u(x, h)$ are simply Taylor expansions at different faces of u when considered on (i.e. pulled back to) the blown-up space.

(II) GRA provides conceptual clarity. In GRA the 'singular' aspects of a problem are dealt with in the geometric operation of blow-up. Then the analysis (solution of differential equations) is reduced to non-singular model problems, and to a version of the standard Borel lemma. In this way essential structures of a problem are clearly visible, while notationally messy (but essentially trivial) calculations involving multiple Taylor series run invisibly in the background. This also helps to identify common features of seemingly different problems.

(III) GRA helps to stay sane in complex settings. Often more than two model problems appear, and remembering how they fit together (the 'matching conditions' of MAE) may be a torturous task. In GRA each model problem corresponds to a boundary face of the resolved space, and their relations can be read off from how these faces intersect.

(IV) GRA may guide the intuition. The true art in solving singular problems is to identify the scales that can be expected to appear in the solutions. The geometric way of thinking about singularities often helps to 'see' how to proceed, see Section 7 for a nice example. An added complication is that sometimes solutions exhibit more scales than the data (i.e. the coefficients or the domains), as the setting in Section 6 shows. It is desirable to have systematic methods to find these. These are beyond the scope of this article however, and we refer to [**51**].

(V) GRA can be refined to provide a systematic way to extend modern PDE methods like the pseudodifferential calculus to singular problems, and embeds them in a larger mathematical framework, see [**50**], [**51**], [**14**]. In this way one may also carry out the second step mentioned above, proving that quasimodes are close to actual solutions, in the framework of GRA, by analyzing the resolvent on a blown-up double space, see e.g. [**43**].

In this article we use simple examples to explain structures which also arise in more elaborate contexts. We consider planar domains and the scalar Laplacian, but the methods generalize without much extra work to manifolds and systems of elliptic PDEs (for example the Hodge Laplacian on differential forms). This is indicated at the end of each section. The methods can also be extended to study many other types of singular degenerations (with more work!), for example families of triangles degenerating to a line (ongoing work with R. Melrose, see also [**7**], [**53**]), domains from which a small ball is removed etc.

The results presented here are not new, and in some cases more precise or more general results have been obtained by other methods, as is indicated in the subsections on generalizations. In the PDE literature blow-up methods have mostly been used in the context of microlocal analysis. Our purpose here is to illustrate their use on a more elementary level, and to introduce a systematic setup for applying them to quasimode constructions. A minor novelty seems to be the use of the quasimode and remainder spaces $\mathcal{E}(M), \mathcal{R}(M)$ and their associated leading part maps, see Section 3 and Definitions 5.1, 7.1 and 7.3, although it is reminiscent of and motivated by the rescaled bundles used for example in [**43**].

Outline of the paper. In Section 2 we introduce the main objects of geometric resolution analysis (manifolds with corners, blow-up and resolution) and explain how they relate to the idea of scales. If you are mostly interested in quasimode constructions it will suffice to skim this section and only use it for reference; however, for Section 7 more of this material will be needed. In the remaining sections we show how quasimodes can be constructed using geometric resolution analysis. The examples are ordered to have increasing complexity, so that later examples use ideas introduced in previous examples plus additional ones. For easier reading the main steps of the constructions are outlined in Section 3. To set the stage, we first consider regular perturbation problems in Section 4. All further problems are eigenvalue problems on families of domains Ω_h which degenerate to a line segment as $h \to 0$. Such problems are sometimes called 'adiabatic limit problems'. The simplest setting for these, where the cross section has constant lowest eigenvalue, is considered in Section 5. The treatment is general enough to apply to fibre bundles with Riemannian submersion metrics. Variable eigenvalues of the cross section, which occur for example when Ω_h is an ellipse with half axes 1 and h, will introduce new scales, and this is analyzed in Section 6. Then in Section 7 we consider a problem where Ω_h scales differently in some parts than in others. Here it will be especially apparent how the geometric way of thinking guides us to the solution. The quasimode results are formulated in Theorems 4.3, 5.4, 6.1, 7.6. In Section 8 we summarize the main points of the various quasimode constructions.

Related literature. The book [**51**] (unfinished, available online) introduces and discusses in great generality and detail manifolds with corners and blow-ups and their use in analysis. The big picture is outlined in [**48**]. The focus in the present article is on problems depending on a parameter h, where singularities only appear as $h \to 0$ (so-called singular perturbation problems). Closely related are problems which do not depend on a parameter but where the underlying space (or operator) is singular, and the methods of geometric resolution analysis can be and have been applied extensively in this context. A basic introduction to this is given by the author in [**14**], with applications to microlocal analysis, including many references to the literature. Other frameworks for manifolds with corners have been proposed, see for example [**33**] and references there.

Blow-up methods have also been used in the context of dynamical systems, e.g. in celestial mechanics [**46**], for analyzing geodesics on singular spaces [**13**] or in multiple time scale analysis, see for example [**8**], [**38**], [**57**] and the book [**37**], which gives an excellent overview and many more references.

The survey [**17**] discusses various types of 'thin tube' problems including the ones discussed here; their origin as well as various methods and results are explained. The books [**41**], [**42**] discuss many singular perturbation problems of geometric origin and their solution by a method called 'compound asymptotic expansions' there, which is similar to matched asymptotic expansions.

More references are given at the end of each section.

Acknowledgements. These notes are based on a series of lectures that I gave at the summer school 'Geometric and Computational Spectral Theory' at the Centre de Recherches Mathématiques in Montreal. I am grateful to the organizers of the school for inviting me to speak and for suggesting to write lecture notes. I thank Leonard Tomczak for help with the pictures and D. Joyce, I. Shestakov, M. Dafinger and the anonymous referee for useful comments on previous versions of these notes. My biggest thanks go to Richard Melrose for introducing many of the concepts discussed here, and for many inspiring discussions.

2. A short introduction to manifolds with corners and resolutions

In this section the basic concepts of geometric resolution analysis are introduced: manifolds with corners, polyhomogeneous functions, blow-up, resolutions. We emphasize ideas and introduce concepts mostly by example or picture (after all, we are talking geometry here!), hoping that the interested reader will be able to supply precise definitions and proofs herself, if desired. Many details can be found in [**50**] and [**51**].

To see where we're heading consider the example from the introduction:

$$f(x,h) = \frac{x}{x+h}, \quad x,h \geq 0,\ (x,h) \neq (0,0)\,.$$

Recall its $h \to 0$ limits at two scales:

$$f_0(x) = \lim_{h\to 0} f(x,h) = \begin{cases} 0 & (x=0) \\ 1 & (x>0) \end{cases}, \qquad g(X) = \lim_{h\to 0} f(hX,h) = \frac{X}{X+1},$$

see Figure 1. The 'geometry' (of geometric resolution analysis) resides in the spaces on which these functions are defined, i.e. their domains:

$$\operatorname{dom} f = \mathbb{R}^2_+,\ \operatorname{dom} f_0 = \mathbb{R}_+,\ \operatorname{dom} g = [0,\infty]$$

where

$$\mathbb{R}_+ := [0,\infty)\,.$$

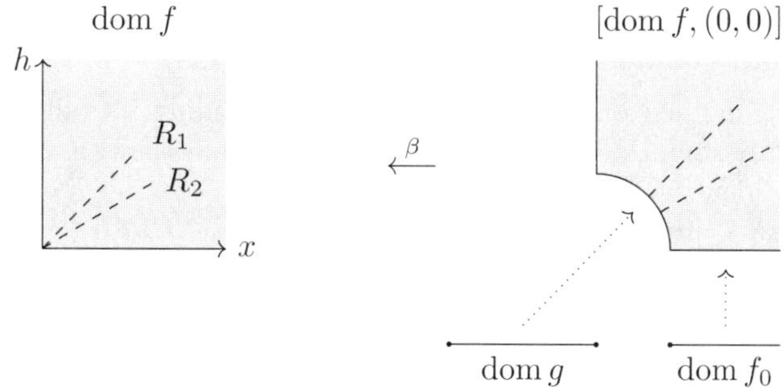

FIGURE 2. Domains of f and of its rescaled limits f_0 and g, and how they relate to each other. Dotted arrows mean 'identify with'.

See Figure 2. Actually, f is not defined at $(0, 0)$, but we ignore this for the moment. For g we have added ∞ to its domain, where we set $g(\infty) = \lim_{X\to\infty} g(X) = 1$. We'll see in a moment why this makes sense.

These spaces are simple examples of manifolds with corners. We ask:

> *Can we understand f_0 and g as restrictions of f to suitable subsets of its domain?*

For f_0 this is easy: if we identify $\operatorname{dom} f_0$ with the lower edge of $\operatorname{dom} f$ then f_0 is simply the restriction of f. (Again we should exclude the point $(0, 0)$.)

How about understanding g as a restriction of f? Can we reasonably identify $\operatorname{dom} g$ as a subset of $\operatorname{dom} f$? This is less obvious. Note that, for any $X \geq 0$, $h \mapsto f(hX, h)$ is the restriction of f to the ray

$$R_X := \{(x, h) \in \operatorname{dom} f : x = hX,\ h > 0\}.$$

By definition, $g(X)$ is the limit of this restriction as $h \to 0$, so it should be the value of f at the endpoint of R_X. This remains true for $X = \infty$ if we set $R_\infty = \{(x, 0) : x > 0\}$. Now this endpoint is $(0, 0)$, so we have two problems: First, f is not defined there, and second, the endpoints of all rays R_X (with different X) coincide.

That's why we don't find $\operatorname{dom} g$ in $\operatorname{dom} f$. But there is a way out, and this is *the idea of blow-up: we simply add a separate endpoint for each ray R_X to the picture.*

That is, we remove $(0, 0)$ from $\operatorname{dom} f$ and replace it by a quarter circle as in Figure 2. This produces a new space, denoted $[\operatorname{dom} f, (0, 0)]$ and called the blow-up of $(0, 0)$ in $\operatorname{dom} f$. A precise definition is given in Section 2.3. It involves polar coordinates, and the quarter circle corresponds to $r = 0$. We denote the quarter circle by ff ('front face'). Each point of the blown-up space corresponds to a point of $\operatorname{dom} f$, as is indicated in Figure 2 by the dashed rays. We encode this by a map

$$\beta : [\operatorname{dom} f, (0, 0)] \to \operatorname{dom} f$$

which maps ff to $(0, 0)$ and is bijective between the complements of these sets. Under this correspondence, f translates into the function $\beta^* f := f \circ \beta$ on $[\operatorname{dom} f, (0, 0)]$.

Essentially, we will see that $\beta^* f$ is 'f written in polar coordinates'. This simple construction solves all our problems:

- $\beta^* f$ is defined on all of $[\operatorname{dom} f, (0,0)]$, including its full boundary. It is actually smooth, once we define what smoothness means on $[\operatorname{dom} f, (0,0)]$.
- If we identify ff with $[0,\infty]$ (the endpoint of the ray R_X being identified with $X \in [0,\infty]$) then g is the restriction of $\beta^* f$ to ff.
- The pointwise limit $f_0(x) = \lim_{h\to 0} f(x,h)$ is, for $x > 0$, still the restriction of f to the lower part of the boundary of $[\operatorname{dom} f, (0,0)]$.

In addition, as we will see later, $\beta^* f$ also encodes how f_0 and g relate to each other (so-called 'matching').

Summarizing, the multiple scales behavior of f is completely encoded by the behavior of $\beta^* f$ near the boundary of $[\operatorname{dom} f, (0,0)]$, and different scales correspond to different segments (later called boundary hypersurfaces) of the boundary.

2.1. Manifolds with corners. Even if we wanted to study problems on domains in $\mathbb{R}^n$ only, the natural setting for our theory is that of manifolds, for (at least) two reasons:

(1) Just as finite dimensional vector spaces are like $\mathbb{R}^n$ without choice of a basis, manifolds are locally like $\mathbb{R}^n$ without choice of a (possibly non-linear) coordinate system – and foregoing such a choice leads to greater conceptual clarity. To put it more mundanely, it will be useful to use different coordinate systems (e.g. polar coordinates, projective coordinates), and it is reassuring to know that all constructions are independent of such choices.

(2) Globally, a manifold represents how various local objects fit together – and one of our goals is to fit different scales together. In fact, even if the problem to be studied is topologically trivial, there may be non-trivial topology (or combinatorics) in the way that different scales relate to each other.

To get an idea what a manifold with corners is, look at Figure 3. The most complicated specimen appearing in this text is on the right in Figure 16.

Recall that a manifold is a space which can locally be parametrized by coordinates. For a manifold with corners some coordinates will be restricted to take only non-negative values. As before we use the notation

$$\mathbb{R}_+ := [0,\infty)$$

and write $\mathbb{R}^k_+ = (\mathbb{R}_+)^k$.

DEFINITION 2.1. *A* ***manifold with corners (mwc)*** *of dimension n is a space M which can locally be parametrized by open subsets of the* ***model spaces*** $\mathbb{R}^k_+ \times \mathbb{R}^{n-k}$, *for various $k \in \{0,\dots,n\}$.*

In addition, we require that the boundary hypersurfaces be embedded, as explained below.

The model space condition is meant as in the standard definition of manifolds, for which only $k = 0$ is allowed. So for each point $p \in M$ there is $k \in \{0,\dots,n\}$ and a neighborhood U of p with a coordinate map $U \to \tilde{U}$, with $\tilde{U} \subset \mathbb{R}^k_+ \times \mathbb{R}^{n-k}$ open,

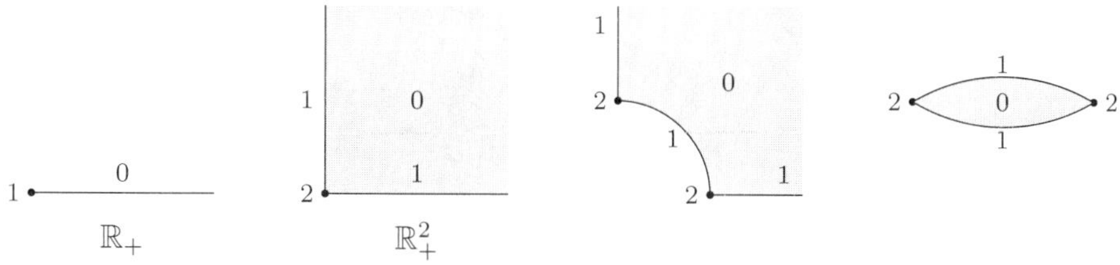

FIGURE 3. Examples of manifolds with corners, with codimensions of points indicated

and it is required that coordinate changes are smooth.[4] The smallest k which works for a fixed p is called the **codimension** of p. See Figures 3, 4 for some examples and non-examples of mwc.

The set of points of codimension 0 is the interior $\text{int}(M)$ of M. The closure of a connected component of the set of points of codimension k is called a **boundary hypersurface (bhs)** if $k = 1$, and a **corner of codimension** k if $k \geq 2$. So the examples in Figure 3 have 1, 2, 3, 2 boundary hypersurfaces.

It is clear that each boundary hypersurface itself satisfies the local model condition, with n replaced by $n - 1$. However, as in the example on the right in Figure 4, it may happen that a boundary hypersurface 'intersects itself', that is, it is an immersed rather than an embedded submanifold (with corners). So according to our definition it is not a manifold with corners.

The embeddedness requirement is equivalent to the existence of a **boundary defining function** for each bhs H, i.e. a smooth function $x : M \to \mathbb{R}_+$ which vanishes precisely on H and whose differential at any point of H is non-zero. A boundary defining function x can be augmented to a **trivialization near** H, i.e. an identification of a neighborhood U of H with $[0, \varepsilon) \times H$ for some $\varepsilon > 0$, where x is the first component and each $y \in H \subset U$ corresponds to $(0, y)$.

Each bhs and each corner of a mwc M is a mwc. But if M has corners then its full boundary is not a manifold with corners.

Some authors, e.g. D. Joyce [**32**], define manifolds with corners without the embeddedness condition on boundary hypersurfaces. Also, Joyce defines the notion of boundary of a mwc differently, so that it is also a mwc.

Taylor's theorem implies the following simple fact which we need later.

LEMMA 2.2. *Let M be a manifold with corners and $\mathcal{S}$ a finite set of boundary hypersurfaces of M. Let h be a total boundary defining function for $\mathcal{S}$, i.e. the product of defining functions for all $H \in \mathcal{S}$.*

Then any $u \in C^\infty(M)$ which vanishes at each $H \in \mathcal{S}$ can be written as $u = h\tilde{u}$ with $\tilde{u} \in C^\infty(M)$.

---

[4] Open means relatively open, that is, there is an open subset $\tilde{U}' \subset \mathbb{R}^n$ with $\tilde{U}' \cap (\mathbb{R}^k_+ \times \mathbb{R}^{n-k}) = \tilde{U}$. For example, $[0, 1)$ is open in $\mathbb{R}_+$. A **smooth function** on an open subset $\tilde{U} \subset \mathbb{R}^k_+ \times \mathbb{R}^{n-k}$ is a function which extends to a smooth function on such a $\tilde{U}'$. A map $\tilde{U} \to \mathbb{R}^k_+ \times \mathbb{R}^{n-k}$ is smooth if each component function is smooth. The space of smooth functions on M (which are sometimes called 'smooth up to the boundary' for emphasis) is denoted by $C^\infty(M)$.

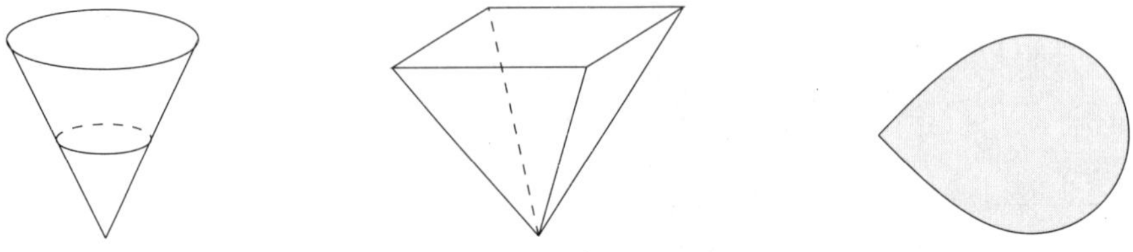

FIGURE 4. Not manifolds with corners. The cone and pyramid are understood as 3-dimensional bodies. The teardrop satisfies the local condition of a mwc, but the boundary line is not embedded.

Exercise: Prove this. Show that the analogous statement would not be true for the pyramid in Figure 4.[5]

REMARK 2.3. ***The corners of a mwc should not be considered as a problem, but as (part of) a solution*** *– of all kinds of problems involving singularities. They should not be thought of as corners in a metric sense, only in a differential sense (i.e. some coordinates are ≥ 0).*

For example, suppose you want to analyze the behavior of harmonic functions near the vertex of $\mathbb{R}^2_+$ or of a cone or of the pyramid in Figure 4 (where the Laplacian is the standard Laplacian for the Euclidean metric on these spaces). The essential first step towards a solution would be to introduce polar coordinates around the vertex, and in the case of the pyramid also cylindrical coordinates around the edges. Geometrically this corresponds to the operation of blow-up, discussed below. This results in manifolds with corners. The fact that the original (metric) $\mathbb{R}^2_+$ happens to be a mwc also is irrelevant.

REMARK 2.4. *Manifolds with corners are an oriented analogue of manifolds with normal crossings divisors as used in real algebraic geometry. 'Oriented' means that the boundary hypersurfaces, which correspond to the components of the divisor, have a relative orientation, i.e. possess a transversal vector field. The use of manifolds with corners allows for greater flexibility in many analytic problems. See also Remark* 2.12.

2.2. Polyhomogeneous functions. All functions we consider will be smooth in the interior of their domains. Our interest will lie in their boundary behavior – partly because we have a much better chance to analyze their boundary behavior than their interior properties. Functions smooth up to the boundary (see Footnote 4) have the following important properties:

1. A smooth function on $\mathbb{R}_+$ has a Taylor expansion $f(x) \sim \sum_{k=0}^{\infty} a_k x^k$ as $x \to 0$, i.e. at $\partial\mathbb{R}_+$.

2a. A smooth function on $\mathbb{R}^2_+$ has Taylor expansions

$$f(x,y) \sim \sum_{k=0}^{\infty} a_k(y) x^k \text{ as } x \to 0, \quad f(x,y) \sim \sum_{l=0}^{\infty} b_l(x) y^l \text{ as } y \to 0 \tag{2.1}$$

at the boundary hypersurfaces $x = 0$ and $y = 0$ of $\mathbb{R}^2_+$, with a_k, b_l smooth on $\mathbb{R}_+$.

[5]If you understand this then you understand one of the main points about manifolds with corners!

2b. (Matching) For each $k, l \in \mathbb{N}_0$ the l-th Taylor coefficient of a_k at $y = 0$ equals ('matches') the k-th Taylor coefficient of b_l at $x = 0$. This corresponds to the Taylor expansion of f at the corner $(0,0)$.

2c. (Borel lemma) Conversely, given $a_k, b_l \in C^\infty(\mathbb{R}_+)$ satisfying these matching (or compatibility) conditions for all k, l, there is a function $f \in C^\infty(\mathbb{R}^2_+)$ satisfying (2.1), and it is unique modulo functions vanishing to infinite order at the boundary of $\mathbb{R}^2_+$.

It turns out that requiring smoothness up to the boundary is too restrictive for many purposes. The class of polyhomogeneous functions[6] is obtained by replacing the powers x^m, $m \in \mathbb{N}_0$ in these expansions by terms $x^z \log^j x$ where $z \in \mathbb{C}$ and $j \in \mathbb{N}_0$, and is big enough for many problems.

Apart from this, polyhomogeneous functions enjoy the analogous properties as listed above. Properties 2b. and 2c. will be essential for our purpose of analyzing multiple scale solutions of PDEs.

2.2.1. *Definition and examples.* We will define the space of polyhomogeneous functions on a manifold with corners M. The essence of the definition can be grasped from two special cases: $M = \mathbb{R}_+ \times \mathbb{R}^n$ where $n \in \mathbb{N}_0$ and $M = \mathbb{R}^2_+$. The terms permitted in an expansion are characterized by a set $E \subset \mathbb{C} \times \mathbb{N}_0$ satisfying

$$\{(z,j) \in E : \ \operatorname{Re} z \leq r\} \quad \text{is finite for every } r \in \mathbb{R}\,. \tag{2.2}$$

This guarantees that the expansion (2.3) below makes sense.

DEFINITION 2.5. *A* ***polyhomogeneous function*** *on $M = \mathbb{R}_+ \times \mathbb{R}^n$ or $M = \mathbb{R}^2_+$ is a smooth function u on* int(M) *satisfying:*

(a) For $M = \mathbb{R}_+ \times \mathbb{R}^n$: u has an asymptotic expansion

$$u(x,y) \sim \sum_{(z,j)\in E} a_{z,j}(y)\, x^z \log^j x \qquad \text{as } x \to 0 \tag{2.3}$$

for each $y \in \mathbb{R}^n$, for a set E as above, where each $a_{z,j} \in C^\infty(\mathbb{R}^n)$.

The set of these functions with E fixed is denoted $\mathcal{A}^E(\mathbb{R}_+ \times \mathbb{R}^n)$.

(b) For $M = \mathbb{R}^2_+$: u has an asymptotic expansion (2.3) *for each $y > 0$, where each $a_{z,j} \in \mathcal{A}^F(\mathbb{R}_+)$, for sets $E, F \subset \mathbb{C} \times \mathbb{N}_0$ satisfying* (2.2).

Also, the same condition is required to hold with x, E and y, F interchanged.

The set of these functions with E, F fixed is denoted $\mathcal{A}^{E,F}(\mathbb{R}^2_+)$.

By definition, we understand asymptotic expansions always 'with derivatives', i.e. $\partial_x u$ has the asymptotic series with each term differentiated, and similarly for $\partial_y u$ and higher derivatives. In addition, certain uniformity conditions are required.

All asymptotic expansions occuring in the problems in this article have no logarithms, so $E \subset \mathbb{C} \times \{0\}$.[7]

---

[6] These are called 'nice functions' in [**14**].

[7] However, logarithms are included in the definition since they appear in the solutions of many differential equations even if they don't appear in their coefficients. For example, the equation $u' = f_h$, $u(0) = 0$ with f_h as in (1.1) has solution $u_h(x) = x - h \log\left(\frac{x}{h} + 1\right)$ which for fixed positive x has the expansion

$$u_h(x) \sim x + h \log h - h \log x + O(h^2)$$

as $h \to 0$. The appearance of the log term here can be predicted without calculating integrals, using geometric resolution analysis via the push-forward theorem of Melrose [**49**], as is explained in [**14**] for the related example where $f_h(x) = \sqrt{x^2 + h^2}$, see also [**18**].

The 'asymptotics with derivatives' condition is equivalent to

$$\left|(x\partial_x)^\alpha \partial_y^\beta \left(u(x,y) - \sum_{(z,j)\in E, \operatorname{Re} z \le r} a_{z,j}(y)\, x^z \log^j x \right)\right| \le C_{r,\alpha,\beta}\, x^r \tag{2.4}$$

for all $r \in \mathbb{R}$ and all $\alpha \in \mathbb{N}_0, \beta \in \mathbb{N}_0^n$. Here $C_{r,\alpha,\beta}$ may depend on y. For $M = \mathbb{R}_+ \times \mathbb{R}^n$ the local uniformity condition is that for any compact $K \subset \mathbb{R}^n$ the same constant can be chosen for all $y \in K$.
For $M = \mathbb{R}^2_+$ this is required for all compact $K \subset (0, \infty)$, plus a local uniformity near $(x, y) = (0, 0)$: there is $N \in \mathbb{R}$ so that estimate (2.4) holds for all $y \in (0, 1)$, with ∂_y replaced by $y\partial_y$ and $C_{r,\alpha,\beta}$ by $C_{r,\alpha,\beta} y^{-N}$.

We now give examples and then formulate the general definition.

EXAMPLES 2.6.

(1) $u(x) = \frac{1}{x}$ *is in* $\mathcal{A}^E(\mathbb{R}_+)$ *for* $E = \{(-1, 0)\}$.

(2) If $E = F = \mathbb{N}_0 \times \{0\}$ *then* $u \in \mathcal{A}^{E,F}(\mathbb{R}^2_+)$ *if and only if* u *extends smoothly to the boundary of* $\mathbb{R}^2_+$.[8]

(3) $u(x, y) = \frac{x}{x+y}$ *is smooth on* $\mathbb{R}^2_+ \setminus \{(0, 0)\}$, *but not polyhomogeneous (for any index sets) on* $\mathbb{R}^2_+$. *To see this, we expand* u *as* $x \to 0$ *for fixed* $y > 0$:

$$u(x,y) = \frac{x}{x+y} = \frac{1}{y}\frac{x}{1+\frac{x}{y}} = \frac{1}{y}x - \frac{1}{y^2}x^2 + \frac{1}{y^3}x^3 - + \cdots \tag{2.5}$$

We see that u *has an expansion as in* (2.3), *but the coefficients* $a_{k,0}(y) = (-1)^k y^{-k}$ *become more and more singular (for* $y \to 0$*) as* k *increases, so there is no index set* F *for which all coefficients lie in* $\mathcal{A}^F(\mathbb{R}_+)$.

Note that this is precisely our first example (1.1).

A set $E \subset \mathbb{C} \times \mathbb{N}_0$ satisfying (2.2) and in addition $(z, j) \in E, l \le j \Rightarrow (z, l) \in E$ is called an **index set**. This condition guarantees that $\mathcal{A}^E(\mathbb{R}_+ \times \mathbb{R}^n)$ is invariant under the operator $x\partial_x$. If, in addition, $(z, j) \in E \Rightarrow (z+1, j) \in E$ then E is called a **smooth (or C^∞) index set**. This guarantees coordinate independence, i.e. any self-diffeomorphism of $\mathbb{R}_+ \times \mathbb{R}^n$ preserves the space $\mathcal{A}^E(\mathbb{R}_+ \times \mathbb{R}^n)$. The index set E in Example 2.6.1 is not smooth; the smallest smooth index set containing E is $\{-1, 0, 1, \dots\} \times \{0\}$.

We now consider general manifolds with corners. Of course we want to say a function is polyhomogeneous if it is so in any coordinate system. Since we want to allow corners of higher codimension, we give an inductive definition.

An **index family** for M is an assignment $\mathcal{E}$ of a C^∞ index set $\mathcal{E}(H)$ to each boundary hypersurface H of M. Recall that there is a trivialization near each H, i.e. we may write points near H as pairs (x, y) where $x \in [0, \varepsilon)$ and $y \in H$, for some $\varepsilon > 0$.

DEFINITION 2.7. *Let* M *be a manifold with corners and* $\mathcal{E}$ *an index family for* M. *A* ***polyhomogeneous function*** *on* M *with index family* $\mathcal{E}$ *is a smooth function* u *on* $\operatorname{int}(M)$ *which has an expansion as in* (2.3) *at each boundary hypersurface* H, *in some trivialization near* H, *where* $E = \mathcal{E}(H)$ *and the functions* $a_{z,j}$ *are polyhomogeneous on* H *with the induced index family for* H.[9]

[8] Exercise: prove this.

[9] The index family $\mathcal{E}$ for M induces an index family $\mathcal{E}_H$ for the mwc H as follows: Any boundary hypersurface H' of H is a component of a set $H \cap G$ where G is boundary hypersurface

The set of these functions is denoted $\mathcal{A}^{\mathcal{E}}(M)$.

Again, if $\mathcal{E}(H) = \mathbb{N}_0 \times \{0\}$ for all H then $u \in \mathcal{A}^{\mathcal{E}}(M)$ if and only if u extends to a smooth function on all of M.

REMARK 2.8. *In our terminology a 'polyhomogeneous function on a manifold with corners* M*' needs to be defined on the interior* $\operatorname{int}(M)$ *only. The terminology is justified since its behavior near the boundary is prescribed;* $C^\infty(\operatorname{int}(M))$ *is the much larger space of functions without prescribed boundary behavior. More formally,* $\mathcal{A}^{\mathcal{E}}$ *defines a sheaf over* M*, not over* $\operatorname{int}(M)$.

2.2.2. *Matching conditions and Borel lemma.* A central point of polyhomogeneity is to have 'product type' asymptotic expansions at corners. This is most clearly seen in the case of $\mathbb{R}^2_+$. To ease notation we formulate this only for the case without logarithms.

LEMMA 2.9 (Matching conditions). *Let* $E, F \subset \mathbb{C} \times \{0\}$ *be index sets for* $\mathbb{R}^2_+$. *Suppose* $u \in \mathcal{A}^{E,F}(\mathbb{R}^2_+)$, *and assume* u *has expansions*

$$\begin{aligned} u(x,y) &\sim \sum_{(z,0)\in E} a_z(y)\, x^z \qquad \text{as } x \to 0 \\ u(x,y) &\sim \sum_{(w,0)\in F} b_w(x)\, y^w \qquad \text{as } y \to 0 \end{aligned} \tag{2.6}$$

where $a_z \in \mathcal{A}^F(\mathbb{R}_+)$, $b_w \in \mathcal{A}^E(\mathbb{R}_+)$ *for each* $(z,0) \in E$, $(w,0) \in F$. *Expand*

$$a_z(y) \sim \sum_{(w,0)\in F} c_{z,w}\, y^w, \qquad b_w(x) \sim \sum_{(z,0)\in E} c'_{z,w}\, x^z \tag{2.7}$$

as $y \to 0$ *resp.* $x \to 0$. *Then*

$$c_{z,w} = c'_{z,w} \qquad \text{for all } z, w. \tag{2.8}$$

This has a converse, which is a standard result:

LEMMA 2.10 (Borel lemma). *Let* E, F *be as in the previous lemma, and assume that functions* a_z, b_w *satisfying* (2.7) *are given.*

If (2.8) *holds then there is* $u \in \mathcal{A}^{E,F}(\mathbb{R}^2_+)$ *satisfying* (2.6). *It is uniquely determined up to errors vanishing to infinite order at the boundary.*

This will be a central tool in our analysis since it allows us to construct approximate solution of a PDE from solutions of model problems.

2.3. Blow-up and resolution. We now introduce blow-up, which is what makes the whole manifolds with corners business interesting. Here are the most important facts about blow-up. They will be explained in this section:

- **Blow-up is a geometric and coordinate free way to introduce polar coordinates.**
- **Blow-up serves to desingularize singular objects.**

---

of M uniquely determined by H'. Then we let $\mathcal{E}_H(H') := \mathcal{E}(G)$. We require $a_{z,j} \in \mathcal{A}^{\mathcal{E}_H}(H)$ for each $(z,j) \in \mathcal{E}(H)$ and each H. If this is true in one trivialization then it is true in any other, since each $\mathcal{E}(H)$ is a C^∞ index set. Local uniformity is also required, analogous to the explanation after equation (2.4).

This definition is inductive over the highest codimension of any point in M.

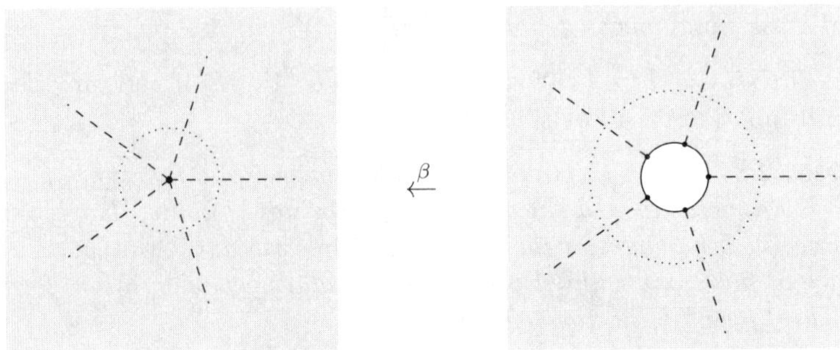

$\mathbb{R}^2$ $[\mathbb{R}^2, 0]$

FIGURE 5. Blow-up of 0 in $\mathbb{R}^2$, with a few rays (dashed) and a pair of corresponding circles (dotted) drawn; the white disk is not part of $[\mathbb{R}^2, 0]$; its inner boundary circle is the front face

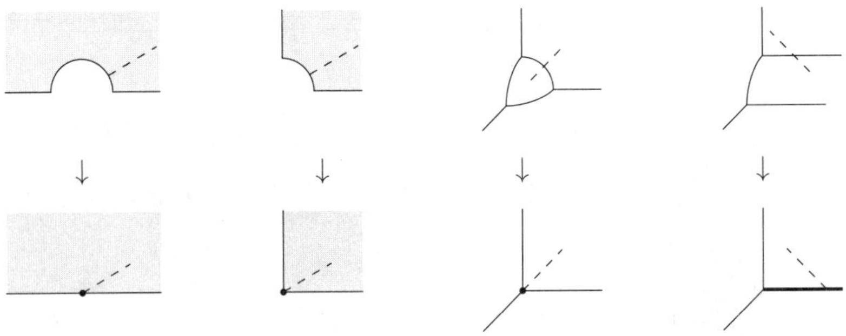

(a) (b) (c) (d)

FIGURE 6. Some examples of blow-up; in each bottom picture the submanifold being blown up is drawn fat, and the blown-up space is in the top picture. The vertical arrow is the blow-down map. The third and fourth example are 3-dimensional, and only the edges are drawn.

- **Blow-up helps to understand scales and transitions between scales – and therefore to solve PDE problems involving different scales.**

We first explain the idea in the case of blow-up of 0 in $\mathbb{R}^2$ and then give the general definition in Subsection 2.3.2. After discussing resolutions and projective coordinates we return to our motivating example (1.1) in Example 2.18. There is also a short discussion of quasihomogeneous blow-up, which occurs naturally in Section 6.

2.3.1. *The idea.* We first explain the idea in the case of blowing up the point 0 in $\mathbb{R}^2$, see Figure 5: Consider the set of rays (half lines) in $\mathbb{R}^2$ emanating from 0. They are pairwise disjoint except that they all share the common endpoint 0. *The* ***blow-up of 0 in*** $\mathbb{R}^2$ *is the space constructed from* $\mathbb{R}^2$ *by removing 0 and replacing it by one separate endpoint for each ray.* This space is denoted by $[\mathbb{R}^2, 0]$. So we replace 0 by a circle, and each point on the circle corresponds to a direction of approach to 0. This circle is called the **front face** of the blow-up. Thus, blowing-up 0 in $\mathbb{R}^2$ means taking out 0 from $\mathbb{R}^2$ and then choosing a new 'compactification at 0' of $\mathbb{R}^2 \setminus 0$, by adding the front face instead of 0.

Here is a concrete mathematical model realizing this idea: As a space we take $[\mathbb{R}^2, 0] = \mathbb{R}_+ \times S^1$, where $S^1 = \{\omega \in \mathbb{R}^2 : |\omega| = 1\}$ is the unit circle. The front face is $\text{ff} := \{0\} \times S^1$. In Figure 5 the rays are the sets $\omega = \text{const}$, the unbroken circle is ff and the dotted circle is $\{1\} \times S^1$. We then need to specify how points of $[\mathbb{R}^2, 0]$ correspond to points of $\mathbb{R}^2$. This is done using the map

$$\beta : [\mathbb{R}^2, 0] \to \mathbb{R}^2, \quad \beta(r, \omega) = r\omega$$

called the **blow-down map.** Note that β is a diffeomorphism from $(0, \infty) \times S^1$ to $\mathbb{R}^2 \setminus \{0\}$; this means that it provides an identification of $[\mathbb{R}^2, 0] \setminus \text{ff}$ with $\mathbb{R}^2 \setminus \{0\}$. The sets $\omega = \text{const}$ are mapped to rays, and two different such sets have different endpoints on ff. All these endpoints are mapped to 0 by β. Thus, this model and β do precisely what they were supposed to do.

In addition, the model gives $[\mathbb{R}^2, 0]$ a differentiable structure, making it a smooth manifold with boundary and β a smooth map.

Note that if we parametrize S^1 by $\omega = (\cos\varphi, \sin\varphi)$ then β is just the polar coordinates map

$$(r, \varphi) \mapsto (x, y), \quad x = r\cos\varphi, \ y = r\sin\varphi\,. \tag{2.9}$$

Recall that 'polar coordinates on $\mathbb{R}^2$' are not coordinates at the origin. So $[\mathbb{R}^2, 0]$ is the space on which polar coordinates are actual coordinates – also at $r = 0$.

EXERCISE 2.11. *Show that points of* ff *correspond to directions at 0 not only of rays, but of any regular curve. That is: Let $\gamma : [0, 1) \to \mathbb{R}^2$ be a smooth curve with $\gamma(0) = 0$, $\dot\gamma(0) \neq 0$ and $\gamma(t) \neq 0$ for $t \neq 0$. Show that there is a unique smooth curve $\tilde\gamma : [0, 1) \to [\mathbb{R}^2, 0]$ lifting γ, i.e. satisfying $\beta \circ \tilde\gamma = \gamma$, and that $\tilde\gamma(0) = \frac{\dot\gamma(0)}{\|\dot\gamma(0)\|}$.*

2.3.2. *Definition and examples.* The general operation of blow-up associates to any manifold X and submanifold $Y \subset X$ a manifold with boundary, denoted $[X, Y]$, and a surjective smooth map $\beta : [X, Y] \to X$. We say that $[X, Y]$ is obtained from **blowing up Y in X** and call β the **blow-down map.**[10] X, Y may also be manifolds with corners, then a local product assumption (see below) must be placed on Y, and $[X, Y]$ is a manifold with corners. The preimage $\beta^{-1}(Y)$ is called the **front face** ff of the blow-up. It is a boundary hypersurface of $[X, Y]$, and β maps diffeomorphically $[X, Y] \setminus \text{ff} \to X \setminus Y$. See Figure 6 for some examples.

To define blow-up we use local models as in the previous subsection, but you should always keep the original idea of adding endpoints of rays in mind. We start with blow-up of an interior point, then generalize this in two ways: blow-up of a point on the boundary, and blow-up of a subspace (by taking products). Finally both generalizations are combined to yield the most general case.

[10]For this to be defined Y must have codimension at least one. We will always assume that the codimension is at least two, the other case being less interesting.

Definition of blow-up for the local models.

Recall that a *model space* is a space of the form $\mathbb{R}^{n-k} \times \mathbb{R}^k_+$ (or $\mathbb{R}^k_+ \times \mathbb{R}^{n-k}$). We consider these first.

(1) Blow-up of[11] 0 in $\mathbb{R}^n$: Define

$$[\mathbb{R}^n, 0] := \mathbb{R}_+ \times S^{n-1}, \quad \beta(r,\omega) = r\omega$$

where $S^{n-1} = \{\omega \in \mathbb{R}^n : |\omega| = 1\}$ is the unit sphere, $n \geq 1$.

Note that $[\mathbb{R}^n, 0]$ is a manifold with boundary.

(2) Blow-up of 0 in the upper half plane $\mathbb{R} \times \mathbb{R}_+$: Define

$$[\mathbb{R} \times \mathbb{R}_+, 0] := \mathbb{R}_+ \times S^1_+, \; \beta(r,\omega) = r\omega$$

where $S^1_+ = S^1 \cap (\mathbb{R} \times \mathbb{R}_+)$ is the upper half circle. See Figure 6(a).

This is simply the upper half of case (1) with $n = 2$. This generalizes in an obvious way to the blow-up of zero in any model space:

$$[\mathbb{R}^{n-k} \times \mathbb{R}^k_+, 0] := \mathbb{R}_+ \times S^{n-1}_k, \; \beta(r,\omega) = r\omega$$

where $S^{n-1}_k := S^{n-1} \cap (\mathbb{R}^{n-k} \times \mathbb{R}^k_+)$. See Figure 6(b) for $n = k = 2$ and Figure 6(c) for $n = k = 3$.

Note that $[\mathbb{R}^{n-k} \times \mathbb{R}^k_+, 0]$ has corners if $k \geq 1$.

(3) Blow-up of the x-axis $\mathbb{R} \times \{0\}$ in $\mathbb{R}^3$: Define

$$[\mathbb{R}^3, \mathbb{R} \times \{0\}] := \mathbb{R} \times [\mathbb{R}^2, 0], \; \beta(x,y,z) = (x, \beta_0(y,z))$$

with $\beta_0 : [\mathbb{R}^2, 0] \to \mathbb{R}^2$ from case (1). So the line $Y = \mathbb{R} \times \{0\}$ is blown up to a cylinder, the front face of this blow-up. Any point $p \in Y$ is blown up to a circle $\beta^{-1}(p)$. Points on the front face correspond to a pair consisting of a point $p \in Y$ and a direction of approach to p, modulo directions tangential to Y.

This generalizes in an obvious way to the blow-up of $\mathbb{R}^{n-m} \times \{0\}$ in $\mathbb{R}^n$:

$$[\mathbb{R}^n, \mathbb{R}^{n-m} \times \{0\}] = \mathbb{R}^{n-m} \times [\mathbb{R}^m, 0]$$

(write $\mathbb{R}^n = \mathbb{R}^{n-m} \times \mathbb{R}^m$ and take out the common factor $\mathbb{R}^{n-m}$).

(4) Blow-up of $\mathbb{R}_+ \times \{0\}$ in $\mathbb{R}^3_+$. Combining cases (2) and (3) we define

$$[\mathbb{R}^3_+, \mathbb{R}_+ \times \{0\}] = \mathbb{R}_+ \times [\mathbb{R}^2_+, 0]$$

see Figure 6(d).

The main point here is the product structure. In general, for model spaces X, W, Z,

$$\text{for } X = W \times Z,\; Y = W \times \{0\} \quad \text{define} \quad [X,Y] = W \times [Z,0] \tag{2.10}$$

with $[Z,0]$ defined in (2). In the example, $X = \mathbb{R}^3_+$, $W = \mathbb{R}_+$, $Z = \mathbb{R}^2_+$.

Definition of blow-up for manifolds (possibly with corners). It can be shown (see [**47**], [**51**]) that these constructions are invariant in the following sense: for model spaces X, Y as in case (4), any self-diffeomorphism of X fixing Y pointwise lifts to a unique self-diffeomorphism of $[X,Y]$.[12] Now if X is a manifold and $Y \subset X$

[11] To simplify notation we often write 0 instead of $\{0\}$. Also 0 denotes the origin in any $\mathbb{R}^k$.

[12] In the case of $[\mathbb{R}^2, 0]$ this can be rephrased as follows: let x, y be standard cartesian coordinates and r, φ corresponding polar coordinates. Let x', y' be some other coordinate system defined near 0 (possibly non-linearly related to x, y), with $x' = y' = 0$ corresponding to the point 0. Define polar coordinates in terms of x', y', i.e. $x' = r' \cos\varphi'$, $y' = r' \sin\varphi'$. Then $(r,\varphi) \mapsto (r', \varphi')$ is a smooth coordinate change on $[\mathbb{R}^2, 0]$.

a submanifold, then $Y \subset X$ is locally $\mathbb{R}^{n-m} \times \{0\} \subset \mathbb{R}^n$, in suitable coordinates. Therefore, the blow-up $[X, Y]$ is well-defined as a manifold, along with the blow-down map $\beta : [X, Y] \to X$.[13]

If X is a manifold with corners then a subset $Y \subset X$ is called a **p-submanifold** if it is everywhere locally like the models (2.10) (p is for product). Therefore, the blow-up $[X, Y]$ is defined for p-submanifolds $Y \subset X$. For example, the fat subsets in the bottom line of Figure 6 are p-submanifolds, as are the dashed rays in the top line. However, the dashed rays in (b), (c) and (d) in the bottom line are not p-submanifolds.

Put differently, a subset $Y \subset X$ is a p-submanifold if near every $q \in Y$ there are local coordinates centered at q so that Y and every face of X containing q is a coordinate subspace, i.e. a linear subspace spanned by some coordinate axes, locally.

The preimage $\beta^{-1}(Y) \subset [X, Y]$ is a boundary hypersurface of $[X, Y]$, called the **front face** of the blow-up. The other boundary hypersurfaces of $[X, Y]$ are in 1-1 correspondence with those of X.

REMARK 2.12. *This notion of blow-up, sometimes called* ***oriented blow-up****, is closely related to (unoriented) blow-up as defined in real algebraic geometry, where one 'glues in' a real projective space instead of a sphere. Unoriented blow-up can be obtained from oriented blow-up by identifying pairs of antipodal points of this sphere. This results in an interior hypersurface (usually called exceptional divisor) rather than a new boundary hypersurface as front face. Compare Remark* 2.4.

Unoriented blow-up has the virtue of being definable purely algebraically, so it extends to other ground fields, e.g. to complex manifolds. See [**24**]*, where also a characterization of blow-up by a universal property is given (Proposition 7.14).*

2.3.3. *Multiple blow-ups.* Due to the geometric nature of the blow-up operation, it can be iterated. So if X is a manifold with corners and Y a p-submanifold, we can first form the blow-up $\beta_1 : [X, Y] \to X$. Next, if Z is a p-submanifold of $[X, Y]$ then we can form the blow-up $\beta_2 : [[X, Y], Z] \to [X, Y]$. The **total blow-down map** is then the composition

$$\beta = \beta_1 \circ \beta_2 : [[X, Y], Z] \to X .$$

See Figure 7 for a simple example. Of course one may iterate any finite number of times.

2.3.4. *Resolutions via blow-up.* The main use of blow-ups is that they can be used to resolve singular objects, for example functions and sets.

It is in this sense that blow-up is a coordinate free way of introducing polar coordinates: the result does not depend on the (cartesian) coordinates chosen initially. This is important, for example, for knowing that we may choose coordinates at our convenience. For example, when doing an iterated blow-up we may choose projective coordinates after the first blow-up, or polar coordinates, and will get the same mathematics in the end.

[13]The original idea that points on the front face correspond to directions at 0 can be used directly as an invariant definition: Let M be a manifold and $p \in M$. The set of directions at p is $S_pM := (T_pM \setminus \{0\})/\mathbb{R}_{>0}$ where T_pM is the tangent space and $\mathbb{R}_{>0}$ acts by scalar multiplication. Then $[M, p] = (M \setminus \{p\}) \cup S_pM$, with β the identity on $M \setminus \{p\}$ and mapping S_pM to p. One still needs local coordinates to define the differentiable structure on $[M, p]$.

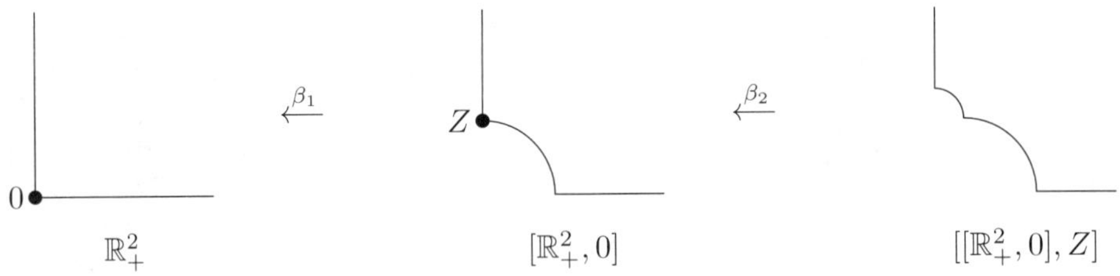

FIGURE 7. A double blow-up

DEFINITION 2.13 (Resolving functions). *Let $\beta : X' \to X$ be a (possibly iterated) blow-down map of manifolds with corners and $f : \operatorname{int}(X) \to \mathbb{C}$ a function. We say that f **is resolved by** β if $\beta^* f$ is a polyhomogeneous function on X'. Here $\beta^* f := f \circ \beta$ is the pull-back.*

Recall that $\beta^* f$ need only be defined on the interior of X', compare Remark 2.8. In Example 2.18 we will see that the function $f(x, y) = \frac{x}{x+y}$ on $\mathbb{R}^2_+ \setminus \{0\}$ is resolved by blowing up zero.

For subsets we need a slight generalization of p-submanifolds. A **d-submanifold** of a manifold with corners X is a subset $Y \subset X$ which is everywhere locally modelled on

$$X = W \times Z \times \mathbb{R}^l, \quad Y = W \times \{0\} \times \mathbb{R}^l_+ \tag{2.11}$$

for some $l \geq 0$ and model spaces W, Z (d means decomposable). This is a p-submanifold iff $l = 0$, see (2.10). For example, $\mathbb{R}^2_+ \subset \mathbb{R}^2$ is a d-submanifold which is not a p-submanifold.

DEFINITION 2.14 (Resolving subsets). *Let $\beta : X' \to X$ be a (possibly iterated) blow-down map of manifolds with corners and $S \subset X$ a subset. We say that S **is resolved by** β if $\beta^* S$ is a d-submanifold of X'. Here the **lift**[14] $\beta^* S$ under a blow-down map $[X, Y] \to X$ is defined as*

$$\beta^* S = \overline{\beta^{-1}(S \setminus Y)} \ \text{ if } S \not\subset Y, \quad \beta^* S = \beta^{-1}(S) \ \text{ if } S \subset Y.$$

For an iterated blow-down map $\beta = \beta_1 \circ \cdots \circ \beta_k$ we define $\beta^* S = \beta_k^* \dots \beta_1^* S$.

For example, the solid cone $S \subset \mathbb{R}^3$ (left picture in Figure 4) is resolved by blowing up 0 in $\mathbb{R}^3$. Here $\beta^* S \subset [\mathbb{R}^3, 0]$ is a manifold with corners, the local model at the corner is (2.11) with $W = \mathbb{R} \times \mathbb{R}_+$, $Z = \{0\}$ and $l = 1$. The boundary of the cone is also resolved by β, its lift is even a p-submanifold.

Note that in general the lift $\beta^* S$ is almost the preimage, but not quite. In the cone example, the preimage $\beta^{-1} S$ would be the union of $\beta^* S$ and the front face of the blow-up, which is a 2-sphere. We consider $\beta^* S$ since it contains the only interesting information about S.

See Figure 8(d) for another example (dashed lines) and Figure 16 for an example of a resolution by a multiple blow-up. Both of them will be used later.

Of course we can combine Definitions 2.14 and 2.13: If $S \subset X$ then a function f on $S \cap \operatorname{int}(X)$ is resolved by $\beta : X' \to X$ if S is resolved and $\beta^* f$ is polyhomogeneous on $\beta^* S$.

[14]The lift is also called the **strict transform** in the algebraic geometry literature.

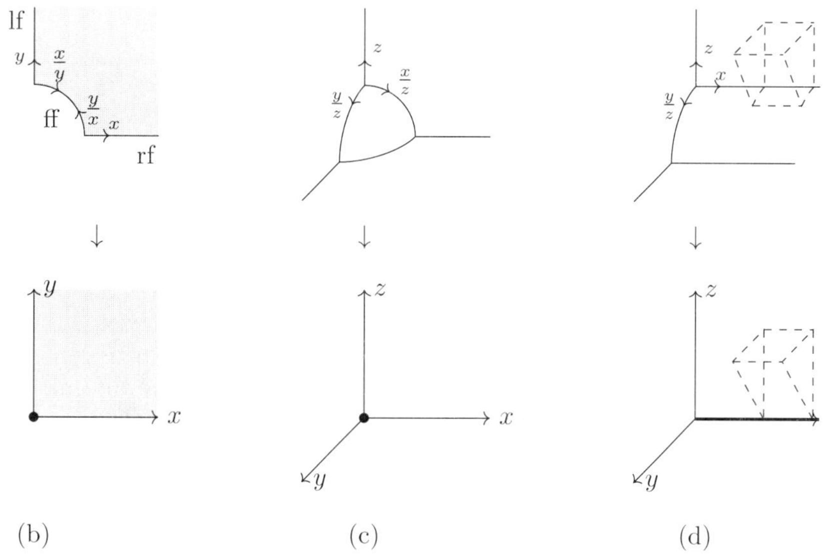

FIGURE 8. Projective coordinates for examples (b), (c), (d) of Figure 6. Dashed lines in (d) indicate a singular subset (below) and its resolution (above).

Note that in these definitions we consider polyhomogeneous functions and d-submanifolds as 'regular' and more general functions resp. subsets as 'singular'. Regular objects in this sense remain regular after blow-up, as is easy to see using projective coordinates, introduced below.[15]

REMARK 2.15. *By a deep famous theorem of Hironaka every algebraic variety $S \subset \mathbb{C}P^n$ can be resolved by a sequence of blow-ups (in the algebraic geometric sense, see Remark* 2.12*). Similar statements hold for algebraic (or even semi- or subalgebraic) subsets of $\mathbb{R}^n$, see* **[30]** *and* **[27]** *for a more entertaining and low-tech survey.*

REMARK 2.16. *There is a generalization of blow-up which is sometimes useful when resolving several scales simultaneously, see* **[32]**, **[36]**.

2.3.5. *Projective coordinates.* Projective coordinates simplify calculations with blow-ups and also provide the link of blow-ups to the discussion of scales.

We first discuss this for the space $[\mathbb{R}^2_+, 0]$, see Figure 8(b). Recall that points of $[\mathbb{R}^2_+, 0]$ correspond to pairs consisting of a ray (in $\mathbb{R}^2_+$, emanating from 0) and a point on that ray. Now, with x, y standard coordinates on $\mathbb{R}^2_+$,

$$\text{rays} \leftrightarrow \text{values of } \frac{y}{x}, \qquad \text{points on a ray} \leftrightarrow \text{values of } x$$

except if the ray is the y-axis (which would correspond to $\frac{y}{x} = \infty$). Here $\frac{y}{x} \geq 0$ and $x \geq 0$, and $x = 0$ is the endpoint of the ray.

[15]For a d-submanifold $S \subset X$ to lift to a d-submanifold under blow-up of $Y \subset X$ we must require that S and Y intersect *cleanly* (which might be called 'normal crossings' by algebraic geometers), i.e. near every intersection point there are coordinates in which X, S and Y are given by model spaces.

This means that $\frac{y}{x}$ and x provide a coordinate system for $[\mathbb{R}^2_+, 0] \setminus \mathrm{lf}$, where lf ('left face') is the lift of the y-axis:[16]

$$(x, \frac{y}{x}) : [\mathbb{R}^2_+, 0] \setminus \mathrm{lf} \to \mathbb{R}^2_+ \tag{2.12}$$

We need to check that this is a smooth coordinate system. This means:

1. The function $\frac{y}{x}$, which is defined and smooth on $[\mathbb{R}^2_+, 0] \setminus (\mathrm{lf} \cup \mathrm{ff})$, extends smoothly to $[\mathbb{R}^2_+, 0] \setminus \mathrm{lf}$.
2. The map (2.12) is a diffeomorphism.

Both statements refer to the differentiable structure on $[\mathbb{R}^2_+, 0]$, which was defined by writing $[\mathbb{R}^2_+, 0] = \mathbb{R}_+ \times S^1_{++}$ where S^1_{++} is the quarter circle. If we use the angle coordinate $\varphi \in [0, \frac{\pi}{2}]$ on S^1_{++} then we need to check that the map $(r, \varphi) \to (x, \frac{y}{x})$ extends smoothly from $r > 0, \varphi < \frac{\pi}{2}$ to $r \geq 0, \varphi < \frac{\pi}{2}$ and is a diffeomorphism $\mathbb{R}_+ \times [0, \frac{\pi}{2}) \to \mathbb{R}_+ \times \mathbb{R}_+$. This can be seen from the explicit formulas $x = r\cos\varphi$, $\frac{y}{x} = \tan\varphi$, and for the inverse map $r = x\sqrt{1 + \left(\frac{y}{x}\right)^2}$, $\varphi = \arctan\frac{y}{x}$.

By symmetry, we have another smooth coordinate system given by $\frac{x}{y}$ and y on the set $[\mathbb{R}^2_+, 0] \setminus \mathrm{rf}$, where rf ('right face') is the lift of the x-axis.

Note that in the coordinate system $x, \frac{y}{x}$ the boundary defining function of the front face is x, and in the coordinate system $y, \frac{x}{y}$ it is y.

Projective coordinates can be used to check that a function is resolved under a blow-up:

LEMMA 2.17. *A function f on $\mathbb{R}^2_{>0}$ is resolved by the blow up of 0 if and only if f is polyhomogeneous as a function of $\frac{x}{y}, y$ and as a function of $x, \frac{y}{x}$.*

This is clear since polyhomogeneity (or smoothness) of a function on a manifold means polyhomogeneity (or smoothmess) in each coordinate system of an atlas.

EXAMPLE 2.18. *We consider the function $f(x, y) = \frac{x}{x+y}$ on $\mathbb{R}^2_+ \setminus 0$ again. We saw in Example 2.6(3) that f is not polyhomogeneous at 0. However,*

$$\text{in coordinates } X = \frac{x}{y},\ y: \quad \beta^* f = \frac{X}{X+1}$$

$$\text{in coordinates } x,\ Y = \frac{y}{x}: \quad \beta^* f = \frac{1}{1+Y}$$

and both of these functions are smooth for $(X, y) \in \mathbb{R}^2_+$ resp. $(x, Y) \in \mathbb{R}^2_+$, the respective ranges of these coordinates. So f is resolved by β, and $\beta^* f$ is even smooth on $[\mathbb{R}^2_+, 0]$.

As another example, consider $f_2(x, y) = \frac{x}{x+y+xy}$. Here $\beta^* f_2 = \frac{X}{X+1+Xy}$ and $\beta^* f_2 = \frac{1}{1+Y+xY}$ in the two coordinate systems, so f_2 is also resolved by β. Note that these agree with $\beta^* f$ at $y = 0$ and $x = 0$ respectively, which means $\beta^* f_2 = \beta^* f$ at the front face. This is clear a priori since xy vanishes to second order at $x = y = 0$.

REMARK 2.19 (Relation of projective coordinates to scaled limit). *Suppose a function f on $\mathbb{R}^2_{>0}$ is resolved by $\beta : [\mathbb{R}^2_+, 0] \to \mathbb{R}^2_+$, and assume $\beta^* f$ is even smooth. To emphasize the relation to the discussion of scales, we denote coordinates by x, h and write $f_h(x) = f(x, h)$.*

---

[16]It would be formally better to write $\frac{\beta^* y}{\beta^* x}$ and $\beta^* x$ instead of $\frac{y}{x}$ and x, but this quickly becomes cumbersome. Note that $\beta^* x$ vanishes on $\mathrm{lf} \cup \mathrm{ff}$ and $\beta^* y$ vanishes on $\mathrm{ff} \cup \mathrm{rf}$.

(1) *The rescaled limit $g(X) = \lim_{h\to 0} f_h(hX)$ is simply the restriction of $\beta^* f$ to the front face* ff*, when parametrizing* ff *by the projective coordinate X.*
To see this, note that in the projective coordinate system X, h the map β is given by $\beta(X, h) = (hX, h)$ (this is the meaning of writing $X = \frac{x}{h}$), so $(\beta^* f)(X, h) = f(hX, h)$, and $h = 0$ is the front face.
(2) *That f is resolved by β contains additional information beyond existence of this scaled limit: information on derivatives as well as information on the behavior of $g(X)$ as $X \to \infty$. Note that $X = \infty$ corresponds to the 'lower' corner in $[\mathbb{R}^2_+, 0]$. More precisely, g is smooth at ∞ in the sense that $\eta \mapsto g(\frac{1}{\eta})$ is smooth at $\eta = 0$. Here η is the coordinate $\frac{h}{x}$ in the second projective coordinate system.*

For more general blow-ups it is useful to have:

Quick practical guide to finding projective coordinate systems:

Point blow-up of 0 in $\mathbb{R}^k_+ \times \mathbb{R}^{n-k}$: Near the (lift of the) x-axis projective coordinates are x and $\frac{y_j}{x}$, where y_j are the variables other than x. These are coordinates except on the (lift of the) set $\{x = 0\}$. Similarly for any other axis.

Blow-up of coordinate subspace $Y \in \mathbb{R}^k_+ \times \mathbb{R}^{n-k}$: Apply the previous to variables x, y_j vanishing on Y. Other variables remain unchanged.

It may be useful to think of x as 'dominant' variable on the coordinate patch: for any compact subset of the patch there is a constant C so that $|y_j| \le Cx$. So $\frac{y_j}{x}$ is bounded there. Note:

dominant variable = boundary defining function of front face

For the examples in Figure 6(a),(c),(d) we get the projective coordinate systems, see also Figure 8(c),(d) (where only one system is indicated):

(a) $[\mathbb{R} \times \mathbb{R}_+, 0]$: near the interior of the front face: $y, \frac{x}{y}$; in a neighborhood of the lift of the x-axis: $x, \frac{y}{x}$.[17]
(c) $[\mathbb{R}^3_+, 0]$: outside the left boundary hypersurface: $x, \frac{y}{x}, \frac{z}{x}$; outside the back boundary hypersurface: $y, \frac{x}{y}, \frac{z}{y}$; outside the bottom boundary hypersurface: $z, \frac{x}{z}, \frac{y}{z}$.
(d) $[\mathbb{R}^3_+, \mathbb{R}_+ \times \{0\}]$: outside the back boundary hypersurface: $x, y, \frac{z}{y}$; outside the bottom boundary hypersurface: $x, z, \frac{y}{z}$.

EXERCISE 2.20. *Show that the function $f(x, y) = \sqrt{x^2 + xy + y^3}$ on $\mathbb{R}^2_+$ is resolved by the double blow-up in Figure 7, but not by the simple blow-up of $0 \in \mathbb{R}^2_+$.*[18]

[17]The latter are really two coordinate patches, one for $x \ge 0$ (near right corner) and one for $x \le 0$ (near left corner). Near the left corner it is more customary to use $|x|, \frac{y}{|x|}$ instead so the dominant variable is positive.

[18]Solution: In coordinates $x, Y = \frac{y}{x}$ the function $\beta_1^* f = x\sqrt{1 + Y + xY^3}$ is polyhomogeneous since it is smooth. In coordinates $X = \frac{x}{y}, y$ the function $\beta_1^* f = y\sqrt{X^2 + X + y}$ is polyhomogeneous outside $X = y = 0$, but not at this point.
Therefore we blow up $X = y = 0$, which is the point Z in Figure 7. Let $\beta = \beta_1 \circ \beta_2$. In coordinates $X, \eta = \frac{y}{X}$ the function $\beta^* f = X^{3/2}\eta\sqrt{X + 1 + \eta}$ is polyhomogeneous. In coordinates $\xi = \frac{X}{y}, y$ the function $\beta^* f = y^{3/2}\sqrt{\xi^2 y + \xi + 1}$ is polyhomogeneous. So f is resolved by β.

2.3.6. *Quasihomogeneous blow-up.* In many problems scalings other than $x \sim y$ appear, for example $x \sim \sqrt{y}$ in the function $f(x,y) = \frac{1}{x^2+y}$. These can be understood either by multiple blow-ups, as in Exercise 2.20, or by the use of quasihomogeneous blow-up.

This occurs, for example, in Section 6, and also for the heat kernel (where y is time), see e.g. [**50**], [**15**], [**45**].

For simplicity we only consider the quasihomogeneous blow-up of 0 in $\mathbb{R}^2_+$, with x scaling like $\sqrt{y}$. We denote it by $[\mathbb{R}^2_+, 0]_q$. This is sometimes called parabolic blow-up. The idea is analogous to regular blow-up, except that the rays in $\mathbb{R}^2_+$ through 0 are replaced by 'parabolas', by which we mean the sets $\{y = Cx^2\}$ including the cases $C = 0$, i.e. the x-axis, and $C = \infty$, i.e. the y-axis. Then the blown-up space is constructed by removing 0 and replacing it by one separate endpoint for each parabola. These endpoints can be thought of as forming a quarter circle again, so the blown-up space looks just like, and in fact will be diffeomorphic to, $[\mathbb{R}^2_+, 0]$. However, the blow-down map β will be different.

Here is a local model realizing this idea: Let $r(x,y) = \sqrt{x^2+y}$ and $S^1_q = \{(\omega,\eta) \in \mathbb{R}^2_+ : r(\omega,\eta) = 1\}$. Then we let $[\mathbb{R}^2_+, 0]_q = \mathbb{R}_+ \times S^1_q$ with blow-down map

$$\beta(r, (\omega,\eta)) = (r\omega, r^2\eta).$$

This is constructed so that β maps each half line $\{(\omega,\eta) = \text{const}\}$ to a parabola, so that indeed endpoints of parabolas correspond to points of $\text{ff} := \{0\} \times S^1_q$. Also, β maps $\text{ff} \subset [\mathbb{R}^2_+, 0]_q$ to $0 \in \mathbb{R}^2_+$ and is a diffeomorphism between the complements of these sets.[19]

Projective coordinates are as shown in Figure 9. The coordinates near A seem quite natural: x smoothly parametrizes the points on each parabola $\{y = Cx^2\}$ (except $C = \infty$), and the parabolas are parametrized by the value of $C = \frac{y}{x^2}$, so pairs $(\frac{y}{x^2}, x)$ parametrize pairs (parabola, point on this parabola). On the other hand, the coordinates near B require explanation. One way to understand them is to check in the model that these are indeed coordinates (compare the explanation after (2.12); do it!). Without reference to the model the exponents that occur can be understood from three principles:

(a) The coordinate 'along the front face' should reflect the scaling $x \sim \sqrt{y}$.
(b) β should be smooth, so both x and y must be expressible as monomials in the coordinates,[20] near A and near B
(c) The smooth structure on $[\mathbb{R}^2_+, 0]_q$ should be the minimal one satisfying (a) and (b), i.e. the exponents should be maximal possible.

So for the system near A, (b) implies that in the coordinate along ff the exponent of y must be $\frac{1}{m}$ for some $m \in \mathbb{N}$, and then (c) implies $m = 1$. Hence the coordinate must be $\frac{y}{x^2}$ by (a). The exponent of x in the other coordinate must be 1 by (b) and (c). Similarly, near B in the coordinate along ff we need x in first power by

[19]Maybe you ask: why this model, not another one? In fact, the precise choice or r and S^1_q are irrelevant – any choice of positive smooth function r which is 1-homogeneous when giving x the weight 1 and y the weight 2, and any section transversal to all parabolas which stays away from the origin will do, with the same definition of β. Choosing $S^1_q = r^{-1}(1)$ has the nice feature that use of the letter r is consistent in that $r(\beta(R,(\omega,\eta))) = R$.

[20]This means that we require β to be a b-map, a condition stronger than smoothness, see [**51**].

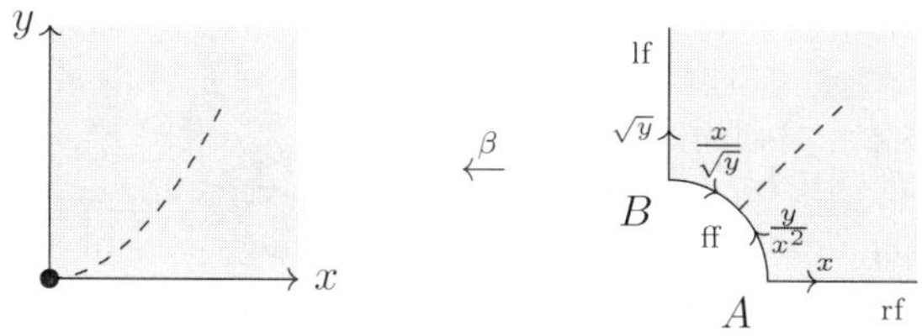

FIGURE 9. Projective coordinate systems for quasihomogeneous blow-up $[\mathbb{R}^2_+, 0]_q$

(b) and (c), and (a) gives $\frac{x}{\sqrt{y}}$. Then (b) and (c) leave no choice but to have $\sqrt{y}$ as the other coordinate.[21]

Projective coordinates can be used as in Lemma 2.17 to check whether quasi-homogeneous blow-up resolves a function.

For more details, including the question of coordinate invariance, see [**9**] and [**51**]; see also [**19**]. A more general blow-up procedure is introduced in [**36**], see also [**32**], [**35**]. This is closely related to blow-up in toric geometry, see [**5**].

2.4. Summary on blow-up and scales; further examples. We first summarize our discussion of the function $f(x,h) = \frac{x}{x+h}$: f is smooth on $\mathbb{R}^2_+ \setminus 0$ but has no continuous extension to 0. The behavior of f near 0 can be described by saying that the scaling limit $\lim_{h\to 0} f(hX, h) = g(X)$ exists for all X. This can be restated in terms of the blow-up of 0 in $\mathbb{R}^2_+$ with blow-down map $\beta : [\mathbb{R}^2_+, 0] \to \mathbb{R}^2_+$ and front face $\mathrm{ff} = \beta^{-1}(0)$: the function $\beta^* f$, defined on $[\mathbb{R}^2_+, 0] \setminus \mathrm{ff}$, extends continuously to ff, and g is the restriction of this extension to ff when ff is parametrized by X. Here $X = \frac{x}{h}$ is part of the projective coordinate system X, h.

In fact, we saw that the extension of $\beta^* f$ is not only continuous but even smooth on $[\mathbb{R}^2_+, 0]$. That is, f is resolved by β in the sense of Definition 2.13.

The fact that g is not constant leads to the discontinuity of f at 0.

The example suggests that the vague idea of scaling behavior is captured by the notion of resolution, which is defined rigorously in Definition 2.13. We note a few details of this definition:

(1) The resolved function $\beta^* f$ is required to be polyhomogeneous, which means in particular:
   - the asymptotics holds with all derivatives
   - full asymptotics is required, not just leading order asymptotics

   To include derivatives is natural since we want to deal with differential equations. To require full asymptotics is then natural since for example smoothness at a boundary point means having a full asymptotic series (the Taylor series). Only the combination of both conditions yields a unified theory.[22]

---

[21]A different way to understand the coordinates $\frac{y}{x^2}$, $\frac{x}{\sqrt{y}}$ along ff is to note that $\frac{y}{x^2}$ is a defining function of rf in its interior $x > 0$, and $\frac{x}{\sqrt{y}}$ is a defining function of lf in its interior $y > 0$.

This reflects the fact that only the point $0 \in \mathbb{R}^2_+$ is affected by the blow-up, that is, that β is a diffeomorphism between the complements of $\beta^{-1}(0)$ and $\{0\}$. In particular, quasihomogeneous blow-up is *not* the same as first replacing the variable y by $\sqrt{y}$ and then doing a standard blow-up.

[22]Of course one could define finite order (in number of derivatives or number of asymptotic terms) theories, and this may be useful for some problems. However, many problems do admit

(2) On the other hand, requiring $\beta^* f$ to be smooth would be too restrictive (compare Footnote 7). What really matters is the product structure near corners as explained in Section 2.2.2.
(3) Of course any function can be 'over-resolved', for example if f is smooth on $\mathbb{R}^2_+$ then we may still look at $\beta^* f$ which is still smooth. This would correspond to 'looking at f at scale $x \sim h$'.[23]

We give some more examples to illustrate these points.

EXAMPLES 2.21. *In these examples we denote coordinates on $\mathbb{R}^2_+$ by x, h to emphasize the relation to scaling. β is always the blow-down map for the blow-up of 0 in $\mathbb{R}^2_+$.*

(1) $f(x,h) = x + h$ is smooth on $\mathbb{R}^2_+$. In scaled coordinates $f(hX, h) = h(X+1)$ is the expansion of $\beta^* f$ at the front face.
(2) $f(x,h) = \sqrt{x+h}$ is not polyhomogeneous on $\mathbb{R}^2_+$ as can be seen from the Taylor expansion as $h \to 0$ for fixed $x > 0$:

$$\sqrt{x+h} = \sqrt{x}\sqrt{1+\frac{h}{x}} = \sum_{k=0}^{\infty} \binom{\frac{1}{2}}{k} x^{\frac{1}{2}-k} h^k$$

compare (2.5). However, note that $f_h = f(\cdot, h)$ converges uniformly to f_0 on $\mathbb{R}_+$. But already f_h' does not converge uniformly to f_0'. The same is true for $f_2(x,h) = \sqrt{x^2+h^2}$ even though f_0 is smooth.

Both f and f_2 are resolved by blowing up 0 in $\mathbb{R}^2_+$.

These examples show that non-trivial scaling behavior may only be visible in the derivatives.
(3) $f(x,h) = \sqrt{x^2 + xh + h^3}$ is resolved by the double blow-up in Figure 7, see Exercise 2.20. The two front faces correspond to the scales $x \sim h$ and $x \sim h^2$. Any problem involving f needs to take into account both of these scales.

To end this section we consider an example in three dimensions where a set is resolved by two blow-ups. This will be used in Section 7.

Consider the family of plane domains $\Omega_h \subset \mathbb{R}^2$, $h > 0$, shown in Figure 10: The $1 \times h$ rectangle $[0,1) \times (0,h)$ with a fixed triangle (e.g. a right-angled isosceles triangle), scaled to have base h, attached at one end. Again we want to describe the behavior of Ω_h as $h \to 0$. As in the first example, different features emerge at different scales:

(1) We can consider $B := \lim_{h\to 0} \Omega_h$. This is just an interval.[24] Many features of Ω_h are lost in the limit: the thickness h, the triangular shape at the end.

---

infinite order asymptotics – once the scales are correctly identified. Requiring less than the best possible sometimes obfuscates the view towards the structure of a problem.

[23]So really we should not say that a function 'exhibits the scale $x \sim h$', since every function does. More appropriate may be 'f requires scale $x \sim h$', or 'The scale $x \sim h$ is relevant for f'. In any case, 'f is resolved by β' is a well-defined statement giving an upper bound on the 'badness' of f.

[24]The precise meaning of the limit is irrelevant for this motivational discussion. You may think of Hausdorff limits.

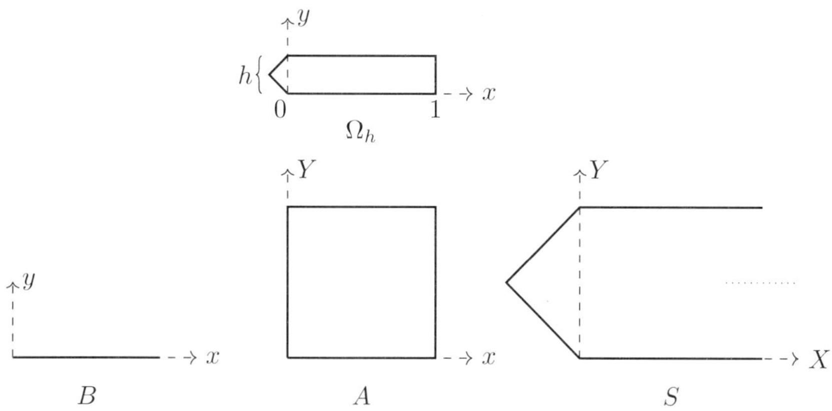

FIGURE 10. A family of domains Ω_h and three rescaled limits as $h \to 0$

(2) More information is retained by noting that y scales like h, hence considering

$$A_h := \{(x, Y) : \; (x, hY) \in \Omega_h\}, \tag{2.13}$$

the domain obtained from stretching by the factor h^{-1} in the y-direction. Then $A := \lim_{h\to 0} A_h$ is the square $(0,1) \times (0,1)$. This still forgets the triangular shape at the end.

(3) At the left end, both x and y scale like h. So we consider

$$S_h := \{(X, Y) : \; (hX, hY) \in \Omega_h\} = h^{-1}\Omega_h\,. \tag{2.14}$$

Then $S := \lim_{h\to 0} S_h$ is a half infinite strip of width one with a triangle attached at the left end. This limit remembers the triangle, but not that Ω_h has essentially length 1 in the x-direction.

For the asymptotic analysis of the eigenvalue problem on Ω_h in Section 7 it will be essential to understand A and S as parts of one bigger space, which arises as resolution of the closure of $\Omega = \bigcup\limits_{h>0} \Omega_h \times \{h\} \subset \mathbb{R}^3$. This resolution is shown in Figure 16 and explained there. Note that A and S are boundary hypersurfaces. The limit interval B occurs as the base of a natural fibration of the face A.

3. Generalities on quasimode constructions; the main steps

In this section we give an outline of the main steps of the quasimode constructions that will be carried out in the following sections.

For each $h > 0$ let Ω_h be a bounded domain in $\mathbb{R}^2$, and let $P_h = -\Delta$ be the Laplacian on Ω_h, acting on functions that vanish at the boundary $\partial\Omega_h$. We assume that $\partial\Omega_h$ is piecewise smooth.[25]

[25] More generally one can consider families of compact manifolds with (or without) boundary and differential operators on them which are elliptic and self-adjoint with respect to given measures and for given boundary conditions. The methods are designed to work naturally in this context. Non-smooth boundary may require extra work.

A **quasimode** for the family $(\Omega_h)_{h>0}$ is a family $(\lambda_h, u_h)_{h>0}$ where $\lambda_h \in \mathbb{R}$ and u_h is in the domain of P_h (in particular, $u_h = 0$ at $\partial\Omega_h$), so that

$$(P_h - \lambda_h)u_h = O(h^\infty) \quad \text{as } h \to 0. \tag{3.1}$$

Here $O(h^\infty)$ means $O(h^N)$ for each N. We are ambitious in that we require these estimates to hold uniformly, also for all derivatives with respect to $x \in \Omega_h$ and with respect to h.

We reformulate this as follows: Consider the **total space**

$$\Omega = \bigcup_{h>0} \Omega_h \times \{h\} \subset \mathbb{R}^2 \times \mathbb{R}_+.$$

We assume that Ω_h depends continuously on h in the sense that Ω is open. A family of functions u_h on Ω_h corresponds to a single function u on Ω defined by $u(x, h) = u_h(x)$. The operators P_h define a single operator P on Ω via

$$(Pu)(\cdot, h) = P_h(u_h).$$

The operator P differentiates only in the Ω_h directions, not in h. Then a quasimode is a pair of functions $\lambda : \mathbb{R}_{>0} \to \mathbb{R}$, $u : \Omega \to \mathbb{R}$ satisfying the boundary conditions and

$$(P - \lambda)u = O(h^\infty) \quad \text{as } h \to 0.$$

How can we find quasimodes? Since the only issue is the behavior as $h \to 0$, one expects that finding λ and u reduces to solving PDE problems 'at $h = 0$', along with an iterative construction: first solve with $O(h)$ as right hand side, then improve the solution so the error is $O(h^2)$ etc.

This is straightforward in the case of a regular perturbation, i.e. if the family $(\Omega_h)_{h>0}$ has a limit Ω_0 at $h = 0$, and the resulting family is smooth for $h \geq 0$. This essentially means that the closure $\overline{\Omega}$ of the total space Ω is a manifold with corners, see Section 4.1 for details. In particular, Ω_0 is still a bounded domain in $\mathbb{R}^2$. Then the problem at $h = 0$ is the **model problem**

$$(P_0 - \lambda_0)v = g \quad \text{on } \Omega_0, \quad v = 0 \text{ at } \partial\Omega_0$$

where $P_0 = -\Delta$ on Ω_0. Solving the model problem is the only analytic input in the quasimode construction. As we recall in Section 4 the iterative step reduces to solving this equation, plus some very simple algebra.

However, our main focus will be on **singular perturbations**, where a limit Ω_0 exists but Ω_h does not depend smoothly on h at $h = 0$, so $\overline{\Omega}$ has a singularity at $h = 0$. For example, if Ω_0 is an interval or a curve, then this singularity looks approximately like an edge, see Figures 12, 14 and 16. We will consider several concrete such families. Their common feature is that this singularity can be resolved by (possibly several) blow-ups, yielding a manifold with corners M and a smooth map

$$\beta : M \to \overline{\Omega}.$$

As explained in Section 2 this corresponds to a certain scaling behavior in the family $(\Omega_h)_{h>0}$ as $h \to 0$. The boundary hypersurfaces of M at $h = 0$, whose union is

$$\partial_0 M := \beta^{-1}(\overline{\Omega} \cap \{h = 0\}),$$

will now take the role of Ω_0, i.e. they will carry the model problems whose solution is used for constructing quasimodes.

Since in the singular case several model problems are involved, the algebra needed for the quasimode construction is more complicated than in the regular case. However, this can be streamlined, and unified, by cleverly defining function spaces $\mathcal{E}(M)$ and $\mathcal{R}(M)$ which will contain putative quasimodes u and remainders $f = (P-\lambda)u$, respectively, along with suitable notions of **leading part** (at $h = 0$). The leading parts will lie in spaces $\mathcal{E}(\partial_0 M)$ and $\mathcal{R}(\partial_0 M)$, and are, essentially, functions on $\partial_0 M$. All model problems together define the **model operator** $(P - \lambda)_0 : \mathcal{E}(\partial_0 M) \to \mathcal{R}(\partial_0 M)$. Denoting for the moment by LP the leading part map, the needed algebra will be summarized in a *Leading part and model operator lemma*, which states[26]

a) the exactness of the sequences

$$\begin{array}{ccccccccc} 0 & \to & h\mathcal{E}(M) & \to & \mathcal{E}(M) & \xrightarrow{\text{LP}} & \mathcal{E}(\partial_0 M) & \to & 0 \\ 0 & \to & h\mathcal{R}(M) & \to & \mathcal{R}(M) & \xrightarrow{\text{LP}} & \mathcal{R}(\partial_0 M) & \to & 0; \end{array} \tag{3.2}$$

The main points here are exactness at $\mathcal{R}(M)$ and at $\mathcal{E}(\partial_0 M)$, explicitly:

$$f \in \mathcal{R}(M),\ \text{LP}(f) = 0 \Rightarrow f \in h\mathcal{R}(M),$$

and any $v \in \mathcal{E}(\partial_0 M)$ is the leading part of some $u \in \mathcal{E}(M)$;

b) the commutativity of the diagram

$$\begin{array}{ccc} \mathcal{E}(M) & \xrightarrow{\quad\text{LP}\quad} & \mathcal{E}(\partial_0 M) \\ \Big\downarrow{\scriptstyle P-\lambda} & & \Big\downarrow{\scriptstyle (P-\lambda)_0} \\ \mathcal{R}(M) & \xrightarrow{\quad\text{LP}\quad} & \mathcal{R}(\partial_0 M) \end{array} \tag{3.3}$$

That is, $(P - \lambda)_0$ encodes the leading behavior of $P - \lambda$ at $h = 0$.

Summarizing, the main steps of the quasimode constructions are:

(1) Resolve the geometry, find the relevant scales
(2) Find the correct spaces for eigenfunctions and remainders
(3) Find the correct 'leading part' definition for eigenfunctions and remainders. Identify model operators, prove Leading part and model operator lemma.
(4) Study model operators (solvability of homogeneous/non-homogeneous PDE problems)
(5) Carry out the construction: Initial step, inductive step

The examples are progressively more complex, so that some features will occur only in later examples. Of course the process of finding the correct spaces etc. may be non-linear, as usual.

The 'meat' is in step 4. After this, step 5 is easy. Steps 1-3 are the conceptual work needed to reduce the construction of quasimodes to the study of model operators.

The results are formulated in Theorems 4.3, 5.4, 6.1, 7.6. They all have the same structure: given data for λ and u at $h = 0$ there is a unique quasimode having this data. For λ the data is the first or first two asymptotic terms, for u the data

[26]This is analogous to the algebra needed for the parametrix construction in the classical pseudodifferential calculus, as explained in **[14]**: LP corresponds to the symbol map, the model operator is the constant coefficient operator obtained by freezing coefficients at any point. Invertibility of the model operator (which amounts to ellipticity) allows construction of a parametrix, which is the analogue of the construction of a quasimode.

is the restriction to the boundary hypersurfaces of M at $h = 0$. Both cannot be freely chosen but correspond to a boundary eigenvalue problem.

There are many other types of singular perturbations which can be treated by the same scheme. For example, Ω_0 could be a domain with a corner and Ω_h be obtained from Ω_0 by rounding the corner at scale h. Or Ω_h could be obtained from a domain Ω_0 by removing a disk of radius h.

REMARK 3.1 (Are the blow-ups needed?). *Our constructions yield precise asymptotic information about u as a function of h, x, y. Different boundary hypersurfaces of M at $h = 0$ correspond to different asymptotic regimes in the family Ω_h. This is nice, but is it really needed if we are only interested in λ, say?*

The leading asymptotic term for λ and u as $h \to 0$ is often easier to come by and does not usually require considering different regimes. But in order to obtain higher order terms of λ, it is necessary to obtain this detailed information about u along the way. As we will see, all regimes of the asymptotics of u will 'influence' the asymptotics of λ, often starting at different orders of the expansion. Another mechanism is that justifying a formal expansion up to a certain order usually requires knowing the expansion to a higher order (as is explained in [**20**]*, for example).*

4. Regular perturbations

To set the stage we first consider the case of a regular perturbation. Here basic features of any quasimode construction are introduced: the reduction to an initial and an inductive step, the identification of a model operator, and the use of the solvability properties of the model operator for carrying out the initial and inductive steps.

4.1. Setup. Let Ω_h, $h \geq 0$ be a family of bounded domains in $\mathbb{R}^2$ with smooth boundary.[27] We say that this family is a regular perturbation of Ω_0 if one of the following equivalent conditions is satisfied:

(A) There are diffeomorphisms $\Phi_h : \overline{\Omega}_0 \to \overline{\Omega}_h$ so that Φ_h is smooth in $x \in \overline{\Omega}_0$ and $h \geq 0$, and $\Phi_0 = \mathrm{Id}_{\overline{\Omega}_0}$.

(B) The closure of the total space

$$M = \overline{\Omega} = \bigcup_{h \geq 0} \overline{\Omega}_h \times \{h\} \subset \mathbb{R}^2 \times \mathbb{R}_+$$

is a manifold with corners, with boundary hypersurfaces

$$X := \overline{\Omega}_0, \quad \partial_{\mathrm{D}} M := \bigcup_{h \geq 0} \partial \overline{\Omega}_h.$$

See Figure 11.[28] Note that the two boundary hypersurfaces play different roles: At $\partial_{\mathrm{D}} M$, the 'Dirichlet boundary', we impose Dirichlet boundary conditions. The

[27] Everything works just as well in $\mathbb{R}^n$ or in a smooth Riemannian manifold. Also the smoothness of the boundary can be relaxed, for example the Ω_h could be domains with corners, then the requirement (B) below is that M be a d-submanifold of $\mathbb{R}^n \times \mathbb{R}_+$, as defined before Definition 2.14.

[28] To prove the equivalence of (A) and (B) note that $\overline{\Omega}_0 \times \mathbb{R}_+$ is a manifold with corners and that the Φ_h define a trivialization (diffeomorphism) $\Phi : \overline{\Omega}_0 \times \mathbb{R}_+ \to \overline{\Omega}, (x, h) \mapsto (\Phi_h(x), h)$, and conversely a trivialization defines Φ_h.

(B) could also be reformulated as: M is a p-submanifold of $\mathbb{R}^2 \times \mathbb{R}_+$

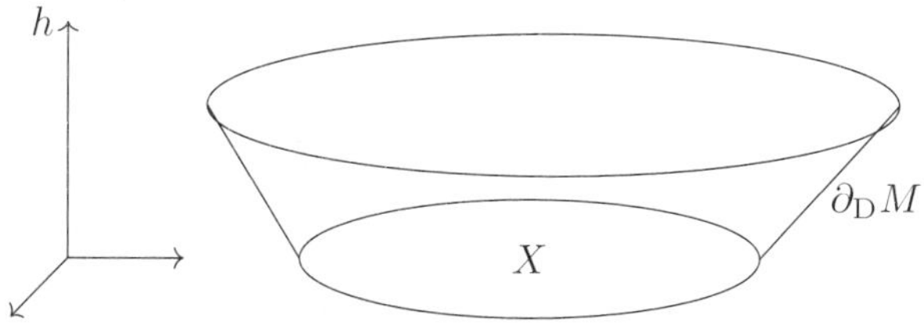

FIGURE 11. The total space M for a regular perturbation

quasimode construction proceeds at $X = \{h = 0\}$. To unify notation, we denote the boundary of X by $\partial_{\mathrm{D}}X$.

In the geometric spirit of this article, and to prepare for later generalization, we use condition (B). For explicit calculations the maps Φ_h in (A) are useful, as we indicate in Subsection 4.3.

As explained in Section 3 the quasimode construction problem is to find u and λ satisfying $(P-\lambda)u = O(h^\infty)$, where u is required to satisfy Dirichlet boundary conditions. Here $P = -\Delta$ on each Ω_h.

4.2. Solution. The idea is this: Rather than solve $(P-\lambda)u = O(h^\infty)$ directly, we proceed inductively with respect to the order of vanishing of the right hand side:

Initial step:	Find λ, u satisfying	$(P-\lambda)u = O(h)$.
Inductive step:	Given λ, u satisfying	$(P-\lambda)u = O(h^k)$ where $k \geq 1$,
	find $\tilde{\lambda}, \tilde{u}$ satisfying	$(P-\tilde{\lambda})\tilde{u} = O(h^{k+1})$.

Before carrying this out, we prepare the stage. We structure the exposition of the details so that it parallels the later generalizations.

4.2.1. *Function spaces, leading part and model operator.* For a regular perturbation we expect λ and u to be smooth up to $h = 0$. Therefore we introduce the function spaces

$$C^\infty_{\mathrm{D}}(M) = \{u \in C^\infty(M) : \ u = 0 \text{ at } \partial_{\mathrm{D}}M\}$$
$$C^\infty_{\mathrm{D}}(X) = \{v \in C^\infty(X) : \ v = 0 \text{ at } \partial_{\mathrm{D}}X\}$$

and

$$h^k C^\infty(M) = \{h^k f : \ f \in C^\infty(M)\}, \quad h^\infty C^\infty(M) = \bigcap_{k\in\mathbb{N}} h^k C^\infty(M).$$

So $h^\infty C^\infty(M)$ is the space of smooth functions on M vanishing to infinite order at the boundary $h = 0$. For simplicity we always consider real-valued functions.

We seek $u \in C^\infty_{\mathrm{D}}(M)$ for which the remainders $f = (P-\lambda)u$ lie in $h^k C^\infty(M)$ for $k = 1, 2, 3, \ldots$. Our final goal is:

$$\text{Find } \lambda \in C^\infty(\mathbb{R}_+), \ u \in C^\infty_{\mathrm{D}}(M) \text{ so that } (P-\lambda)u \in h^\infty C^\infty(M).$$

The **leading part** of $u \in C^\infty_{\mathrm{D}}(M)$ and of $f \in C^\infty(M)$ is defined to be the restriction to $h = 0$:

$$u_X := u_{|X}, \quad f_X := f_{|X}.$$

The following lemma is obvious. In (a) use Taylor's theorem.

LEADING PART AND MODEL OPERATOR LEMMA (regular perturbation).

a) If $f \in C^\infty(M)$ *then*

$$f \in h\,C^\infty(M) \quad \text{if and only if} \quad f_X = 0.$$

b) For $\lambda \in C^\infty(\mathbb{R}_+)$ *we have*

$$P - \lambda : C^\infty_{\mathrm{D}}(M) \to C^\infty(M)$$

and

$$[(P-\lambda)u]_X = (P_0 - \lambda_0)u_X$$

where $P_0 = -\Delta$ *is the Laplacian on* Ω_0 *and* $\lambda_0 = \lambda(0)$.

We call

$$P_0 - \lambda_0 : C^\infty_{\mathrm{D}}(X) \to C^\infty(X)$$

the **model operator** of $P - \lambda$, since it models its action at $h = 0$. Thus, the leading part of $(P-\lambda)u$ is obtained by applying the model operator to the leading part of u.

REMARK 4.1. *In the uniform notation of Section* 3, *see* (3.2), (3.3), *we have* $\partial_0 M = X$ *and* $\mathcal{E}(M) = C^\infty_{\mathrm{D}}(M), \mathcal{E}(\partial_0 M) = C^\infty_{\mathrm{D}}(X), \mathcal{R}(M) = C^\infty(M), \mathcal{R}(\partial_0 M) = C^\infty(X)$ *and* $\mathrm{LP}(u) = u_X$, $\mathrm{LP}(f) = f_X$, $(P-\lambda)_0 = P_0 - \lambda_0$.

4.2.2. *Analytic input for model operator.* The core analytic input in the construction of quasimodes is the following fact about P_0.

LEMMA 4.2. *Let* $\lambda_0 \in \mathbb{R}$ *and* $g \in C^\infty(X)$. *Then there is a unique* $\gamma \in \mathrm{Ker}(P_0 - \lambda_0)$ *so that the equation*

$$(P_0 - \lambda_0)v = g + \gamma \tag{4.1}$$

has a solution $v \in C^\infty_{\mathrm{D}}(X)$. *Also,* $\gamma = 0$ *if and only if* $g \perp \mathrm{Ker}(P_0 - \lambda_0)$.

The solution v *is unique up to adding an element of* $\mathrm{Ker}(P_0 - \lambda_0)$.

Note that the lemma is true for any elliptic, self-adjoint elliptic operator on a compact manifold with boundary.

PROOF. By standard elliptic theory, self-adjointness of P_0 in $L^2(X)$ and elliptic regularity imply the orthogonal decomposition $C^\infty(X) = \mathrm{Ran}(P_0 - \lambda_0) \oplus \mathrm{Ker}(P_0 - \lambda_0)$. This implies the lemma. □

4.2.3. *Inductive construction of quasimodes.*

Initial step We want to solve

$$(P-\lambda)u \in hC^\infty(M). \tag{4.2}$$

By the leading part and model operator lemma this is equivalent to $[(P-\lambda)u]_X = 0$ and then to

$$(P_0 - \lambda_0)u_X = 0.$$

Therefore we choose

$$\begin{aligned} \lambda_0 &= \text{ an eigenvalue of } P_0 \\ u_0 &= \text{ a corresponding eigenfunction} \end{aligned}$$

then any u having $u_X = u_0$ will solve (4.2). For simplicity we make the[29]

(4.3) **Assumption:** the eigenspace $\mathrm{Ker}(P_0 - \lambda_0)$ is one-dimensional.

Inductive step

INDUCTIVE STEP LEMMA (regular perturbation). *Let λ_0, u_0 be chosen as in the initial step, and let $k \geq 1$. Suppose $\lambda \in C^\infty(\mathbb{R}_+)$, $u \in C^\infty_{\mathrm{D}}(M)$ satisfy*

$$(P - \lambda)u \in h^k C^\infty(M)$$

and $\lambda(0) = \lambda_0$, $u_X = u_0$. Then there are $\mu \in \mathbb{R}$, $v \in C^\infty_{\mathrm{D}}(M)$ so that

$$(P - \tilde{\lambda})\tilde{u} \in h^{k+1} C^\infty(M)$$

for $\tilde{\lambda} = \lambda + h^k\mu$, $\tilde{u} = u + h^k v$. The number μ is unique, and v_X is unique up to adding constant multiples of u_0.

More precisely, μ and v_X (modulo $\mathbb{R}u_0$) are uniquely determined by λ_0, u_0 and the leading part of $h^{-k}(P - \lambda)u$.

PROOF. Writing $(P - \lambda)u = h^k f$ and $\tilde{\lambda} = \lambda + h^k\mu$, $\tilde{u} = u + h^k v$ we have

$$(P - \tilde{\lambda})\tilde{u} = h^k[f - \mu u + (P - \lambda)v - h^k \mu v]$$

This is in $h^{k+1}C^\infty(M)$ if and only if the term in brackets is in $hC^\infty(M)$, which by the leading part and model operator lemma (and by $k \geq 1$) is equivalent to $f_X - \mu u_X + (P_0 - \lambda_0)v_X = 0$, i.e. (using $u_X = u_0$) to

(4.4) $$(P_0 - \lambda_0)v_X = -f_X + \mu u_0 \,.$$

This equation can be solved for μ, v_X by applying Lemma 4.2 to $g = -f_X$, since $\mathrm{Ker}(P_0 - \lambda_0) = \{\mu u_0 : \mu \in \mathbb{R}\}$ by (4.3). Having v_X we extend it to a smooth function v on M. Lemma 4.2 also gives the uniqueness of μ and the uniqueness of v_X modulo multiples of u_0. □

The initial and inductive steps give eigenvalues and quasimodes to any order h^N, and this is good enough for all purposes. It is still nice to go to the limit and also consider uniqueness. We get the final result:

THEOREM 4.3 (quasimodes for regular perturbation). *Assume the setup of a regular perturbation as described in Section 4.1. Given a simple eigenvalue λ_0 and associated eigenfunction u_0 of P_0, there are $\lambda \in C^\infty(\mathbb{R}_+)$, $u \in C^\infty_{\mathrm{D}}(M)$ satisfying*

$$(P - \lambda)u \in h^\infty C^\infty(M)$$

and

$$\lambda(0) = \lambda_0, \quad u_X = u_0 \,.$$

Furthermore, λ and u are unique in Taylor series at $h = 0$, up to replacing u by $a(h)u$ where a is smooth and $a(0) = 1$.

Clearly, u cannot be unique beyond what is stated.

[29]The method can be adjusted to the case $\dim \mathrm{Ker}(P_0 - \lambda_0) > 1$. The main difference is that generically, not every eigenfunction u_0 of P_0 will arise as a limit of quasimodes u_h with $h > 0$.

PROOF. Let $u_{(k)}$, $\lambda_{(k)}$ be as obtained in the initial step (if $k = 0$) or the inductive step (if $k \geq 1$), respectively. Then $u_{(k+1)} = u_{(k)} + O(h^k)$, $\lambda_{(k+1)} = \lambda_{(k)} + O(h^k)$ for all k by construction, so by asymptotic summation (Borel Lemma, cf. Lemma 2.10) we obtain λ, u as desired.

To prove uniqueness, we show inductively that for λ, λ' and u, u' having the same leading terms, the assumptions $(P-\lambda)u \in h^k C^\infty(M)$, $(P-\lambda')u' \in h^k C^\infty(M)$ imply that $\lambda - \lambda' = O(h^k)$ and $u - a_{(k)}(h)u' \in h^k C^\infty_{\mathrm{D}}(M)$ for a smooth function $a_{(k)}$, $a_{(k)}(0) = 1$.

For $k = 1$ there is nothing to prove. Suppose the claim is true for k, and let $(P - \lambda)u \in h^{k+1}C^\infty(M)$, $(P - \lambda')u' \in h^{k+1}C^\infty(M)$. By the inductive hypothesis, we have $\lambda - \lambda' = O(h^k)$ and $u - a_{(k)}(h)u' \in h^k C^\infty_{\mathrm{D}}(M)$. Since the leading terms of $h^{-k}(P - \lambda)u$ and $h^{-k}(P - \lambda')u'$ both vanish, the uniqueness statement in the inductive step lemma implies that $\lambda - \lambda' = O(h^{k+1})$ and $u - a_{(k)}(h)u' - ch^k u_0 \in h^{k+1}C^\infty_{\mathrm{D}}(M)$ for some $c \in \mathbb{R}$. Then $a_{(k+1)}(h) = a_{(k)}(h) + ch^k$ satisfies $u - a_{(k+1)}(h)u' \in h^{k+1}C^\infty_{\mathrm{D}}(M)$. Now define a from the $a_{(k)}$ by asymptotic summation.

□

4.3. Explicit formulas. The proof of Theorem 4.3 is constructive: it gives a method for finding $u(x, h)$ and $\lambda(h)$ to any order in h, under the assumption that the model problem (4.1) can be solved. We present two standard alternative ways of doing the calculation.

We use the maps $\Phi_h : X \to \overline{\Omega}_h$, see (A) in Section 4.1, where $X = \overline{\Omega}_0$. In fact, only the restriction of Φ_h to $\partial_{\mathrm{D}}X$ is needed, as will be clear from the first method presented below.

4.3.1. *Boundary perturbation.* We will compute $\dot{\lambda}$, where the dot denotes the first derivative in h at $h = 0$. This is the first order perturbation term since $\lambda(h) = \lambda(0) + h\dot{\lambda} + O(h^2)$. Differentiating the equation $(P - \lambda)u \in h^2 C^\infty(M)$ in h at $h = 0$ we obtain

$$(\dot{P} - \dot{\lambda})u_0 + (P_0 - \lambda_0)\dot{u} = 0 \,. \tag{4.5}$$

In our case $\dot{P} = 0$. The boundary condition is $u(x, h) = 0$ for all $x \in \partial_{\mathrm{D}}\Omega_h$ and all h, so $u(\Phi_h(y), h) = 0$ for $y \in \partial_{\mathrm{D}}X$. Differentiating in h yields the boundary condition for $\dot{u}$:

$$Vu_0 + \dot{u} = 0 \quad \text{on } \partial_{\mathrm{D}}X$$

where Vu_0 is the derivative of u_0 in the direction of the vector field $V = (\partial_h \Phi_h)_{|h=0}$. Now take the $L^2(X)$ scalar product of (4.5) with u_0. We write the second summand using Green's formula as

$$\langle (P_0 - \lambda_0)\dot{u}, u_0\rangle = \int_{\partial_{\mathrm{D}}X} (-\partial_n \dot{u} \cdot u_0 + \dot{u} \cdot \partial_n u_0)\, dS + \langle \dot{u}, (P_0 - \lambda_0)u_0\rangle$$

where ∂_n denotes the outward normal derivative. Using $u_{0|\partial_{\mathrm{D}}X} = 0$, $(P_0 - \lambda_0)u_0 = 0$ we obtain

$$\dot{\lambda} = -\frac{1}{\|u_0\|^2} \int_{\partial_{\mathrm{D}}X} Vu_0 \cdot \partial_n u_0 \, dS$$

where $\|u_0\|$ is the $L^2(X)$-norm of u_0. Commonly one chooses Φ_h so that $V = a\partial_n$ for a function a on $\partial_{\mathrm{D}}X$. This means that the boundary is perturbed in the vertical direction at velocity a. For L^2-normalized u_0 this yields Hadamard's formula (see [**23**]) $\dot{\lambda} = -\int_{\partial_{\mathrm{D}}X} a(\partial_n u_0)^2\, dS$. Higher order terms are computed in a similar way.

Note that we did not need to solve the model problem. Its solution is only needed to compute $\dot{u}$ or higher derivatives of λ and u.

4.3.2. *Taylor series ansatz.* Here is a different method where in a first step all operators are transferred to the h-independent space X. Using the maps $\Phi_h : X \to \Omega_h$ pull back the operator P_h to X:

$$P'_h = \Phi_h^* P_h \, .$$

Now P'_h is a smooth family of elliptic operators on X, so we can write

$$P'_h \sim P_0 + hP_1 + \dots$$

Here P_0 is the Laplacian on X since Φ_0 is the identity. We also make the ansatz

$$u \sim u_0 + hu_1 + \dots, \qquad \lambda \sim \lambda_0 + h\lambda_1 + \dots$$

where all $u_i \in C^\infty_{\mathrm{D}}(X)$, multiply out the left side of

$$(P_0 + hP_1 + \dots - \lambda_0 - h\lambda_1 - \dots)(u_0 + hu_1 + \dots) \sim 0,$$

order by powers of h and equate each coefficient to zero. The h^0 term gives the initial equation

$$(P_0 - \lambda_0)u_0 = 0 \tag{4.6}$$

and the h^k term, $k \geq 1$, gives the recursive set of equations

$$\begin{aligned} (P_0 - \lambda_0)u_k &= -(P_1 - \lambda_1)u_{k-1} - \dots - (P_k - \lambda_k)u_0 \\ &=: -f_k + \lambda_k u_0 \end{aligned} \tag{4.7}$$

where f_k is determined by $u_0, \dots, u_{k-1}$ and $\lambda_0, \dots, \lambda_{k-1}$. This is the decomposition of Lemma 4.2 for $g = f_k$, so it can be solved for λ_k, u_k.

We can solve (4.7) explicitly as follows: Taking the scalar product with u_0 and using $\langle (P_0 - \lambda_0)u_k, u_0\rangle = \langle u_k, (P_0 - \lambda_0)u_0\rangle = 0$ we get

$$\lambda_k = \frac{\langle f_k, u_0\rangle}{\|u_0\|^2}, \tag{4.8}$$

for example

$$\lambda_1 = \frac{\langle P_1 u_0, u_0\rangle}{\|u_0\|^2}, \quad \lambda_2 = \frac{\langle (P_1 - \lambda_1)u_1 + P_2 u_0, u_0\rangle}{\|u_0\|^2}$$

Here u_1, u_2 etc. are computed as

$$u_k = (P_0 - \lambda_0)^{-1}(-f_k + \lambda_k u_0)$$

where $(P_0 - \lambda_0)^{-1}$ is a generalized inverse of $P_0 - \lambda_0$, i.e. a left inverse defined on $\mathrm{Ran}(P_0 - \lambda_0)$. The choice (4.8) of λ_k guarantees that $-f_k + \lambda_k u_0 \in \mathrm{Ran}(P_0 - \lambda_0)$.

REMARK 4.4. *This method seems simpler and more effective than the one presented in Section 4.2. However, in the context of singular perturbations, where several model problems occur, it will pay off to have a geometric view and not to have to write down asymptotic expansions.*

The relation between these two methods becomes clearer if we formulate the present one in terms of the operator P' on the space $\overline{\Omega}' = X \times \mathbb{R}_+$. The product structure of $\overline{\Omega}'$ allows us to extend functions on X to functions on $\overline{\Omega}'$ in a canonical way (namely, constant in h). This yields the explicit formulas. In comparison, for $\overline{\Omega}$ there is no such canonical extension.

4.4. Generalizations. Theorem 4.3 generalizes to any smooth family of uniformly elliptic operators P_h with elliptic boundary conditions on a compact manifold with boundary, supposing P_0 is self-adjoint. Note that P_h for $h > 0$ need not be self-adjoint. If P_h has complex coefficients then u and λ will be complex valued, and if all P_h are self-adjoint then λ can be chosen real-valued.

The method in Subsection 4.3.2 can be formulated abstractly for any family of operators P'_h on a Hilbert space which has a regular Taylor expansion in h as $h \to 0$. Using contour integration one may find the asymptotics of eigenfunctions and eigenvalues, not just quasimodes, directly and show that they vary smoothly in the parameter h under the simplicity assumption (4.3). See [**34**].

5. Adiabatic limit with constant fibre eigenvalue

The adiabatic limit[30] is a basic type of singular perturbation which will be part of all settings considered later. Its simplest instance is the Laplacian on the family of domains

$$\Omega_h = (0,1) \times (0,h) \subset \mathbb{R}^2 . \tag{5.1}$$

Since the domain of the variable y is $(0,h)$ it is natural to use the variable $Y = \frac{y}{h} \in (0,1)$ instead. Then

$$\Delta = \partial_x^2 + \partial_y^2 = h^{-2}\partial_Y^2 + \partial_x^2 . \tag{5.2}$$

Although it is not strictly needed for understanding the calculations below, we explain how this is related to blow-up, in order to prepare for later generalizations: The closure of the total space $\Omega = \bigcup_{h>0} \Omega_h \times \{h\} \subset \mathbb{R}^2 \times \mathbb{R}_+$ has a singularity (an edge) at $h = 0$.[31] This singularity can be resolved by blowing up the x-axis $L = \{y = h = 0\}$ in $\mathbb{R}^2 \times \mathbb{R}_+$. If $\beta : [\mathbb{R}^2 \times \mathbb{R}_+, L] \to \mathbb{R}^2 \times \mathbb{R}_+$ is the blow-down map then the lift

$$M = \beta^* \overline{\Omega}$$

is contained in the domain of the projective coordinates system $x, Y = \frac{y}{h}, h$, compare Figure 8(d). In these coordinates the set M is given by $x \in [0,1], Y \in [0,1], h \in \mathbb{R}_+$. See Figure 12. Note that the operators Δ turn into the 'singular' family of operators (5.2) on M.

This example, and the generalization needed in Section 6, motivates considering the following setting. See Section 5.4 for more examples where this setup occurs.

5.1. Setup. Suppose B, F are compact manifolds, possibly with boundary. For the purpose of this article you may simply take B, F to be closed intervals (but see Subsection 5.5 for a generalization needed later). We consider a family of differential operators depending on $h > 0$

$$P(h) \sim h^{-2}P_F + P_0 + hP_1 + \dots \tag{5.3}$$

on $A = B \times F$. We assume

$$P_F \text{ is a self-adjoint elliptic operator on } F \tag{5.4}$$

---

[30]The word adiabatic originally refers to physical systems that change slowly. In their quantum mechanical description structures similar to the ones described here occur, where x corresponds to time and h^{-1} to the time scale of unit changes of the system. This motivated the use of the word adiabatic limit in global analysis in this context.

[31] The precise meaning of this is that $\overline{\Omega}$ is not a d-submanifold of $\mathbb{R}^2 \times \mathbb{R}_+$, as defined before Definition 2.14. This is what distinguishes it from a regular perturbation. Note that $\overline{\Omega}$ happens to be a submanifold with corners of $\mathbb{R}^3$, but this is irrelevant here.

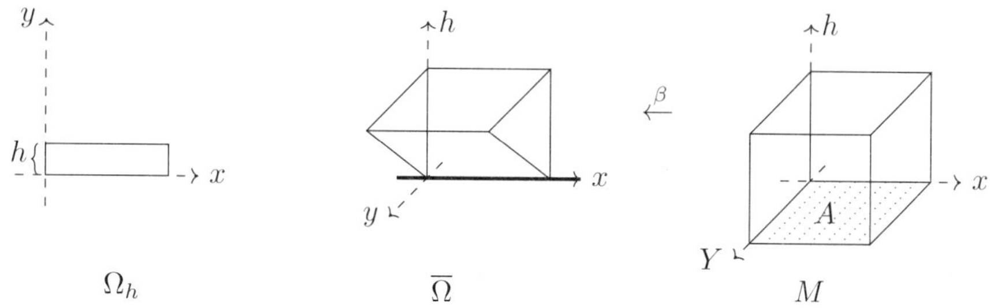

FIGURE 12. Domain Ω_h, total space $\overline{\Omega}$ and resolution M of $\overline{\Omega}$ for adiabatic limit. Compare Figure 8(d). On the right only the part of the blown-up space $[\mathbb{R}^2 \times \mathbb{R}_+, \{y = h = 0\}]$ where the 'top' projective coordinates $h, Y = \frac{y}{h}$ are defined is shown. Dotted lines are fibres of the natural fibration of the front face A.

where boundary conditions are imposed if F has boundary.[32] For example, if $F = [0,1]$ then we could take $P_F = -\partial_Y^2$ with Dirichlet boundary conditions. $P_0, P_1, \dots$ are differential operators on A. A condition on P_0 will be imposed below, see equations (5.11), (5.12).

One should think of A as the union of the fibres (preimages of points) of the projection $\pi : A = B \times F \to B$, i.e. $A = \bigcup_{x \in B} \{x\} \times F$, see also Remark 5.6 below. We call F the fibre and B the base. The analysis below generalizes to the case of fibre bundles $A \to B$, see Section 5.5. The letter A is used for 'adiabatic limit'.

We will denote coordinates on B by x and on F by Y. This may seem strange but serves to unify notation over the whole article, since this notation is natural in the following sections.

5.2. What to expect: the product case. To get an idea what happens, we consider the case of a product operator, i.e.

$$P(h) = h^{-2} P_F + P_B$$

where P_B, P_F are second order elliptic operators on B and F, self-adjoint with given boundary conditions. An example is (5.1), (5.2) where $B = F = [0,1]$ and $P_B = -\partial_x^2$, $P_F = -\partial_Y^2$. More generally, P_B, P_F could be the Laplacians on compact Riemannian manifolds (B, g_B), (F, g_F). Then P would be the Laplacian on A with respect to the metric $h^2 g_F \oplus g_B$ in which the lengths in F-direction are scaled down by the factor h.

By separation of variables $P(h)$ has the eigenvalues $\lambda_{k,l} = h^{-2}\lambda_{F,k} + \lambda_{B,l}$ where $\lambda_{F,k}$, $\lambda_{B,l}$ are the eigenvalues of P_F, P_B respectively, with eigenfunctions[33] $\phi_k \otimes \psi_l$.

Although we have solved the problem, we now rederive the result using formal expansions, in order to distill from it essential features that will appear in the general case. We make the ansatz

$$u = u_0 + hu_1 + \dots, \quad \lambda = h^{-2}\lambda_{-2} + \dots$$

[32] Formally it would be more correct to write $\mathrm{Id}_B \otimes P_F$ instead of P_F in (5.3), but here and in the sequel we will use the simplified notation.

[33] For functions $\phi : B \to \mathbb{R}$ and $\psi : F \to \mathbb{R}$ we write $\phi \otimes \psi : B \times F \to \mathbb{R}$, $(x, Y) \mapsto \phi(x)\psi(Y)$.

and plug in

$$(h^{-2}P_F + P_B - h^{-2}\lambda_{-2} - h^{-1}\lambda_{-1} - \lambda_0 - \dots)(u_0 + hu_1 + h^2u_2 + \dots) = 0. \tag{5.5}$$

The h^{-2} term gives

$$(P_F - \lambda_{-2})u_0 = 0 \tag{5.6}$$

so λ_{-2} must be an eigenvalue of P_F. Suppose it is simple and let ψ be a normalized eigenfunction. It follows that

$$u_0(x, Y) = \phi(x)\psi(Y)$$

for some yet unknown function ϕ. How can we find ϕ? The h^{-1} term gives $(P_F - \lambda_{-2})u_1 = \lambda_{-1}u_0$. Taking the scalar product with u_0 and using self-adjointness of P_F we get $\lambda_{-1} = 0$. The h^0 term then gives

$$(P_F - \lambda_{-2})u_2 = -(P_B - \lambda_0)u_0.$$

By Lemma 4.2, applied to P_F for fixed $x \in B$, this has a solution u_2 if and only if

$$(P_B - \lambda_0)u_0(x, \cdot) \perp \psi \quad \text{in } L^2(F) \text{ for each } x \in B. \tag{5.7}$$

Now the left side is $[(P_B - \lambda_0)\phi(x)]\,\psi$, so we get

$$(P_B - \lambda_0)\phi = 0 \text{ on } B.$$

Thus, λ_0 is an eigenvalue of P_B with eigenfunction ϕ. This solves the problem since $\phi \otimes \psi$ is clearly an eigenfunction of $P(h)$ with eigenvalue $h^{-2}\lambda_{-2} + \lambda_0$.

From these considerations, we see basic features of the adiabatic problem:

- λ_{-2} is an eigenvalue of the fibre operator P_F.
- λ_0 is an eigenvalue of the base operator P_B.
- The leading term of the eigenfunction, u_0, is the tensor product of the eigenfunctions on fibre and base. It is determined from the two 'levels', h^{-2} and h^0 of (5.5).

For a general operator (5.3) we cannot separate variables since P_0 (and the higher P_i) may involve Y-derivatives (or Y-dependent coefficients). However, the 'adiabatic' structure of $P(h)$ still allows separation of variables to leading order: The h^{-2} term of (5.5) still yields $u_0 = \phi \otimes \psi$ and the h^{-1} term yields $\lambda_{-1} = 0$. The h^0 term now yields condition (5.7) with P_B replaced by P_0. This shows that ϕ must be an eigenfunction of the operator

$$U \mapsto (\Pi \circ P_0)(U \otimes \psi)$$

where $\Pi u = \langle u, \psi \rangle_F$ is the $L^2(F)$ scalar product with ψ. This motivates the definition of the horizontal operator P_B below.

5.3. Solution. The solution of the formal expansion equation (5.5) is complicated by the fact that a single u_i is only determined using several h^k. It is desirable to avoid this, in order to easily progress to more complex problems afterwards. Thus, we need a procedure where consideration of a fixed h^k gives full information on the corresponding next term in the u expansion.

This can be achieved by redefining the function space containing the remainders $f = (P - \lambda)u$ in the iteration, as well as their notion of leading part.

As before, we consider a family $(u_h)_{h \geq 0}$ of functions on $B \times F$ as one function on the total space

$$M = B \times F \times \mathbb{R}_+$$

and consider a differential operator P acting on functions on M and having an expansion as in (5.3). Let

$$A := B \times F \times \{0\}$$

be the boundary at $h = 0$ of M.

5.3.1. *A priori step: Fixing a vertical mode. The horizontal operator.* A priori we fix

$$\begin{aligned} \lambda_{-2} &= \text{a simple eigenvalue of } P_F \\ \psi &= \text{an } L^2(F)\text{-normalized corresponding eigenfunction.} \end{aligned} \tag{5.8}$$

We will seek (quasi-)eigenvalues of P of the form $h^{-2}\lambda_{-2} + C^\infty(\mathbb{R}_+)$.

Every $f \in C^\infty(F)$ may be decomposed into a ψ component and a component perpendicular to ψ:

$$f = \langle f, \psi\rangle_F \, \psi + f^\perp, \quad f^\perp \perp_F \psi \tag{5.9}$$

where $\langle\ ,\ \rangle_F$ is the $L^2(F)$ scalar product. The same formula defines a fibrewise decomposition of f in $C^\infty(A)$ or in $h^k C^\infty(M)$, $k \in \mathbb{Z}$. The coefficient of ψ defines projections

$$\begin{aligned} \Pi &: C^\infty(A) \to C^\infty(B) \\ \Pi &: h^k C^\infty(M) \to h^k C^\infty(B \times \mathbb{R}_+) \end{aligned} \qquad f \mapsto \langle f, \psi\rangle_F$$

By self-adjointness of P_F

$$\Pi \circ (P_F - \lambda_{-2}) = 0 \tag{5.10}$$

on the domain of P_F. Motivated by the consideration at the end of the previous section we define the **horizontal operator**[34]

$$P_B : C^\infty_{\mathrm{D}}(B) \to C^\infty(B), \quad U \mapsto \Pi P_0(U \otimes \psi). \tag{5.11}$$

We can now formulate the assumption on P_0:

$$P_B \text{ is a self-adjoint elliptic differential operator on } B \tag{5.12}$$

where self-adjointness is with respect to some fixed density on B and given boundary conditions. This notation is consistent with the use of P_B in the product case.

5.3.2. *Function spaces, leading part and model operator.* We will seek quasimodes u in the **solution space** $C^\infty_{\mathrm{D}}(M)$, the space of smooth functions on M satisfying the boundary conditions. The **leading part** of $u \in C^\infty_{\mathrm{D}}(M)$ is defined to be

$$u_A := u_{|h=0} \in C^\infty_{\mathrm{D}}(A).$$

The following definition captures the essential properties of the remainders $f = (P - \lambda)u$ arising in the iteration.

DEFINITION 5.1. *The* **remainder space** *for the adiabatic limit is*

$$\begin{aligned} \mathcal{R}(M) &:= \{f \in h^{-2}C^\infty(M) : \Pi f \textit{ is smooth at } h = 0\} \\ &= \{f = h^{-2}f_{-2} + h^{-1}f_{-1} + \cdots : \ \Pi f_{-2} = \Pi f_{-1} = 0\}. \end{aligned}$$

The **leading part** *of $f \in \mathcal{R}(M)$, $f = h^{-2}f_{-2} + h^{-1}f_{-1} + \dots$ is*[35]

$$f_{AB} := \begin{pmatrix} f_{-2} \\ \Pi f_0 \end{pmatrix} \in C^\infty(A)_{\Pi^\perp} \oplus C^\infty(B)$$

[34] P_B is also called the *effective Hamiltonian*, e.g. in **[56]**.

[35] The notation f_{AB} is meant to indicate that the leading part has components which are functions on A and on B.

where

$$C^\infty(A)_{\Pi^\perp} := \{v \in C^\infty(A) : \Pi v = 0\}.$$

For functions in the solution space we clearly have:

$$\text{Let } u \in C^\infty_{\mathrm{D}}(M). \text{ Then } u \in hC^\infty_{\mathrm{D}}(M) \iff u_A = 0.$$

The definition of the leading part of $f \in \mathcal{R}(M)$ is designed to make the corresponding fact for f true:

LEADING PART AND MODEL OPERATOR LEMMA (adiabatic limit).

a) If $f \in \mathcal{R}(M)$ then

$$f \in h\mathcal{R}(M) \quad \textit{if and only if} \quad f_{AB} = 0.$$

b) For $\lambda \in h^{-2}\lambda_{-2} + C^\infty(\mathbb{R}_+)$ we have

$$P - \lambda : C^\infty_{\mathrm{D}}(M) \to \mathcal{R}(M) \tag{5.13}$$

and

$$[(P-\lambda)u]_{AB} = \begin{pmatrix} (P_F - \lambda_{-2})u_A \\ \Pi(P_0 - \lambda_0)u_A \end{pmatrix} \tag{5.14}$$

where λ_0 is the constant term of λ.

The operator $(P-\lambda)_A := \begin{pmatrix} P_F - \lambda_{-2} \\ \Pi(P_0 - \lambda_0) \end{pmatrix}$ is called the **model operator** for $P - \lambda$ at A.

PROOF.

a) Let $f = h^{-2}f_{-2} + h^{-1}f_{-1} + f_0 + \dots$ with $\Pi f_{-2} = \Pi f_{-1} = 0$. Suppose $f_{AB} = 0$, so $f_{-2} = 0$ and $\Pi f_0 = 0$. Then $f = h^{-1}f_{-1} + f_0 + O(h)$ with $\Pi f_{-1} = \Pi f_0 = 0$, so $f \in h\mathcal{R}(M)$. The converse is obvious.

b) If $u \in C^\infty_{\mathrm{D}}(M)$ then $(P-\lambda)u = h^{-2}(P_F - \lambda_{-2})u + (P_0 - \lambda_0)u + O(h)$ is in $\mathcal{R}(M)$ by (5.10), and then the definition of leading part implies (5.14). □

REMARK 5.2. *In the uniform notation of Section 3, see (3.2), (3.3), we have $\partial_0 M = A$ and $\mathcal{E}(M) = C^\infty_{\mathrm{D}}(M)$, $\mathcal{E}(\partial_0 M) = C^\infty_{\mathrm{D}}(A)$, $\mathcal{R}(M)$ is defined in Definition 5.1, $\mathcal{R}(\partial_0 M) = C^\infty(A)_{\Pi^\perp} \oplus C^\infty(B)$, and $\mathrm{LP}(u) = u_A$, $\mathrm{LP}(f) = f_{AB}$, $(P-\lambda)_0 = (P-\lambda)_A$.*

5.3.3. *Analytic input for model operator.* For the iterative construction of quasimodes we need the solution properties of the model operator, analogous to Lemma 4.2. The main additional input is the triangular structure of the model operator, equation (5.16) below.

By definition

$$(P-\lambda)_A : C^\infty_{\mathrm{D}}(A) \to C^\infty(A)_{\Pi^\perp} \oplus C^\infty(B)$$

In the proof below it will be important to decompose functions $v \in C^\infty_{\mathrm{D}}(A)$ into their fibrewise $\Pi^\perp$ and Π components. More precisely, the decomposition (5.9) defines an isomorphism

$$C^\infty_{\mathrm{D}}(A) \cong C^\infty_{\mathrm{D}}(A)_{\Pi^\perp} \oplus C^\infty_{\mathrm{D}}(B), \quad v \mapsto (v^\perp, \Pi v) \tag{5.15}$$

so that $v = v^\perp + (\Pi v) \otimes \psi$.

LEMMA 5.3. *Let P be an operator on M having an expansion as in* (5.3), (5.4), *and assume P and $\lambda_{-2} \in \mathbb{R}$, $\psi \in C^\infty_{\mathrm{D}}(F)$ satisfy* (5.8), (5.12).

Then for each $g \in C^\infty(A)_{\Pi^\perp} \oplus C^\infty(B)$ and $\lambda_0 \in \mathbb{R}$ there is a unique $\gamma \in \operatorname{Ker}(P_B - \lambda_0) \subset C^\infty_{\mathrm{D}}(B)$ so that the equation

$$(P-\lambda)_A v = g + \begin{pmatrix} 0 \\ \gamma \end{pmatrix}$$

has a solution $v \in C^\infty_{\mathrm{D}}(A)$. This solution is unique up to adding $w \otimes \psi$ where $w \in \operatorname{Ker}(P_B - \lambda_0)$.

PROOF. Decompose $v \in C^\infty_{\mathrm{D}}(M)$ as in (5.15). Then $(P_F - \lambda_{-2})v = (P_F - \lambda_{-2})v^\perp$ and $\Pi(P_0 - \lambda_0)v = \Pi P_0 v^\perp + (P_B - \lambda_0)\Pi v$ since $\Pi v^\perp = 0$ and by definition of P_B. Therefore, we may write $(P-\lambda)_A$ as a 2×2 matrix:

$$(5.16)\qquad (P-\lambda)_A = \begin{pmatrix} P_F - \lambda_{-2} & 0 \\ \Pi P_0 & P_B - \lambda_0 \end{pmatrix} : \begin{matrix} C^\infty_{\mathrm{D}}(A)_{\Pi^\perp} \\ \oplus \\ C^\infty_{\mathrm{D}}(B) \end{matrix} \to \begin{matrix} C^\infty(A)_{\Pi^\perp} \\ \oplus \\ C^\infty(B) \end{matrix}$$

In order to solve $(P-\lambda)_A v = g + \begin{pmatrix} 0 \\ \gamma \end{pmatrix}$ we write $v = \begin{pmatrix} v^\perp \\ v_\Pi \end{pmatrix}$ and $g = \begin{pmatrix} g^\perp \\ g_\Pi \end{pmatrix}$ and get the system

$$\begin{aligned} (P_F - \lambda_{-2})v^\perp &= g^\perp \\ \Pi P_0 v^\perp + (P_B - \lambda_0)v_\Pi &= g_\Pi + \gamma \end{aligned}$$

The first equation has a unique solution $v^\perp$ by Lemma 4.2 applied to P_F. Then by Lemma 4.2 applied to P_B, there is a unique $\gamma \in \operatorname{Ker}(P_B - \lambda_0)$ so that the second equation has a solution v_Π, and v_Π is unique modulo $\operatorname{Ker}(P_B - \lambda_0)$. □

5.3.4. *Inductive construction of quasimodes.* We now set up the iteration.

Initial step: We want to solve

$$(5.17)\qquad (P-\lambda)u \in h\mathcal{R}(M).$$

By the leading part and model operator lemma this is equivalent to $[(P-\lambda)u]_{AB} = 0$ and then to

$$(P_F - \lambda_{-2})u_A = 0, \quad \Pi(P_0 - \lambda_0)u_A = 0.$$

By (5.8) the first equation implies $u_A = \phi \otimes \psi$ for some function ϕ on B, and then the second equation is equivalent to $(P_B - \lambda_0)\phi = 0$ by (5.11), so if we choose

$$\begin{aligned} \lambda_0 &= \text{an eigenvalue of } P_B \\ \phi &= \text{a corresponding eigenfunction of } P_B \end{aligned}$$

then any u having $u_A = \phi \otimes \psi$ satisfies (5.17). Again, we make the

(5.18) **Assumption:** the eigenvalue λ_0 of P_B is simple

From now on, we fix the following data:

$$\lambda_{-2},\ \lambda_0 \in \mathbb{R}, \quad u_0 := \phi \otimes \psi \in C^\infty_{\mathrm{D}}(A).$$

Inductive step:

INDUCTIVE STEP LEMMA (adiabatic limit). *Let* λ_{-2}, λ_0 *and* u_0 *be as above, and let* $k \geq 1$. *Suppose* $\lambda \in h^{-2}C^\infty(\mathbb{R}_+)$, $u \in C^\infty_{\mathrm{D}}(M)$ *satisfy*

$$(P-\lambda)u \in h^k\mathcal{R}(M)$$

and $\lambda = h^{-2}\lambda_{-2}+\lambda_0+O(h)$, $u_A = u_0$. *Then there are* $\mu \in \mathbb{R}$, $v \in C^\infty_{\mathrm{D}}(M)$ *so that*

$$(P-\tilde{\lambda})\tilde{u} \in h^{k+1}\mathcal{R}(M)$$

for $\tilde{\lambda} = \lambda + h^k\mu$, $\tilde{u} = u + h^k v$. *The number* μ *is unique, and* v_A *is unique up to adding constant multiples of* u_0.

PROOF. Writing $(P-\lambda)u = h^k f$ and $\tilde{\lambda} = \lambda + h^k\mu$, $\tilde{u} = u + h^k v$ we have

$$(P-\tilde{\lambda})\tilde{u} = h^k[f - \mu u + (P-\lambda)v - h^k\mu v]$$

This is in $h^{k+1}\mathcal{R}(M)$ if and only if the term in brackets is in $h\mathcal{R}(M)$, which by the initial step and model operator lemma is equivalent to $[f - \mu u + (P-\lambda)v]_{AB} = 0$ and then to

$$(P-\lambda)_A v_A = -f_{AB} + \begin{pmatrix} 0 \\ \mu\phi \end{pmatrix}$$

where we used $(h^2u)_{h=0} = 0$ and $\Pi u_A = \Pi u_0 = \phi$. Now Lemma 5.3 gives the result. □

We obtain the following theorem.

THEOREM 5.4 (quasimodes for adiabatic limit). *Suppose the operator* P *in* (5.3) *satisfies* (5.4) *and* (5.12), *where* P_B *is defined in* (5.11). *Given simple eigenvalues* λ_{-2}, λ_0 *of* P_F, P_B *with eigenfunctions* ψ, ϕ *respectively, there are* $\lambda \in h^{-2}C^\infty(\mathbb{R}_+)$, $u \in C^\infty_{\mathrm{D}}(M)$ *satisfying*

$$(P-\lambda)u \in h^\infty C^\infty(M)$$

and

$$\lambda = h^{-2}\lambda_{-2} + \lambda_0 + O(h), \quad u_A = \phi \otimes \psi\,.$$

Furthermore, λ *and* u *are unique in Taylor series at* $h = 0$, *up to replacing* u *by* $a(h)u$ *where* a *is smooth and* $a(0) = 1$.

PROOF. This follows from the initial and inductive step as in the proof of Theorem 4.3. □

REMARK 5.5 (Quasimodes vs. modes). *This construction works for any simple eigenvalues* λ_{-2}, λ_0 *of* P_F, P_B *respectively. However, when we ask whether a quasimode* (λ, u) *is close (for small* h*) to an actual eigenvalue/eigenfunction pair we need to be careful: while* λ *will still be close to a true eigenvalue,* u *may not be close to an eigenfunction unless* λ_{-2} *is the* smallest *eigenvalue of* P_F *('first vertical mode'). This is in contrast to the case of a regular perturbation where this problem does not arise.*

The reason is that closeness of u *to an eigenfunction can only be proved (and in general is only true) if we have some a priori knowledge of a spectral gap, i.e. separation of eigenvalues. Such a separation is guaranteed for small* h *only for the smallest* λ_{-2}. *For example, in the case of intervals* $B = F = [0, \pi]$ *we have eigenvalues* $\lambda_{l,m} = h^{-2}l^2+m^2$, $k,l \in \mathbb{N}$. *Then for each* m *there are* $h_i \to 0$ *and* $m'_i \in \mathbb{N}$ *so that* $\lambda_{2,m} = \lambda_{1,m'_i}$ *for each* i. *Then besides* $u_{2,m}$ *also* $au_{2,m} + bu_{1,m'}$, $a, b \in \mathbb{R}$ *are eigenfunctions for these eigenvalues, and in fact under small perturbations (i.e. if* $P_1 \neq 0$*) only the latter type may 'survive'.*

If one fixes k *and considers the* k*th eigenvalue* $\lambda_k(h)$ *of* Ω_h *then, for sufficiently small* h*, it will automatically correspond to the first vertical mode. This is clear for the rectangle but follows in general from the arguments that show that such a quasimode is close to an eigenfunction.*

REMARK 5.6 (Why fibres?). *Why is it natural to think of the subsets* $F_x := \{x\} \times F$ *of* $A = B \times F$ *as 'fibres' (and not the sets* $B \times \{Y\}$*, for example)? The reason is that these sets are inherently distinguished by the operator* P*: if* u *is a smooth function on* $M = A \times \mathbb{R}_+$ *then* Pu *is generally of order* h^{-2}*. But it is bounded as* $h \to 0$ *if and only if* u *and* $\partial_h u$ *are constant on each set* F_x*. Put invariantly,* P *determines the fibres* F_x *to second order at the boundary* $h = 0$.

In the geometric setup of the problem, which is sketched in Figure 12*, the fibres arise naturally as fibres (i.e. preimages of points) of the blow-down map* β *restricted to the front face.*

EXERCISE 5.7. *Find a formula for the first non-trivial perturbation term* λ_1.

5.4. Examples. We already looked at the trivial example of a rectangle. A non-trivial example will be given in Section 6. Tubes around curves provide another interesting example: Let $\gamma : I \to \mathbb{R}^2$ be a smooth simple curve in the plane parametrized by arc length, where $I \subset \mathbb{R}$ is a compact interval. The tube of width $h > 0$ around γ is

$$T_h = \{\gamma(x) + hYn(x) \, : \, x \in I, Y \in [-\tfrac{1}{2}, \tfrac{1}{2}]\}$$

where $n(x)$ is a unit normal at $\gamma(x)$. For h small the given parametrization is a diffeomorphism, and in coordinates x, Y the euclidean metric on T_h is $a^2dx^2+h^2dY^2$ where $a(x,Y) = 1 - hY\kappa(x)$ with κ the curvature of γ, so the Laplacian is $\Delta = a^{-1}\partial_x a^{-1}\partial_x + h^{-2}a^{-1}\partial_Y a \partial_Y$, which is selfadjoint for the measure $adxdY$. This does not have the desired form. However, the operator $P = -a^{1/2}\Delta a^{-1/2}$ is unitarily equivalent to $-\Delta$ and self-adjoint in $L^2(I \times [-\frac{1}{2}, \frac{1}{2}], dxdY)$, and short calculation gives

$$P = -h^{-2}\partial_Y^2 - \partial_x^2 - \frac{1}{4}\kappa^2 + O(h).$$

Theorem 5.4 now yields quasimodes where $\lambda_{-2} = \pi^2 k^2$ and λ_0 is a Dirichlet eigenvalue of the operator $-\partial_x^2 - \frac{1}{4}\kappa^2$ on I. See [**17**] and [**11**] for details.

In all previous examples (and also in the example of Section 6) the operators P_F and P_0 commute. Here is a simple example where this is not the case. Take $B = F = [0,1]$, $P_F = -\partial_Y^2$ and $P_0 = -\partial_x^2 + b(x,Y)$ for some smooth function b. Then $P_B = -\partial_x^2 + c(x)$ where $c(x) = \langle b(x,Y)\psi(Y), \psi(Y)\rangle_F = \frac{1}{2}\int_0^1 b(x,Y)\sin^2 \pi Y \, dY$ if $\lambda_{-2} = \pi^2$ is the lowest eigenvalue of P_F. Here P_0 commutes with P_F iff $b = b(x)$, and then $c = b$.

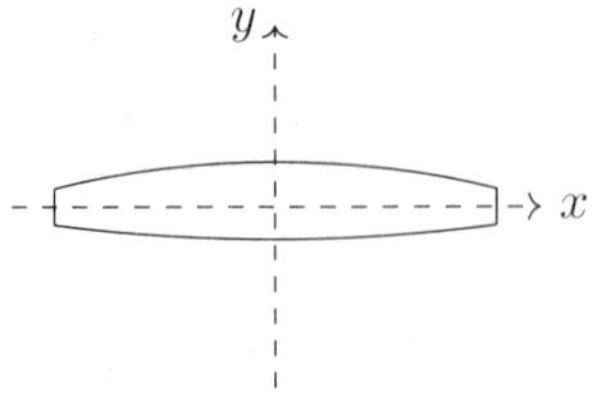

FIGURE 13. Thin domain Ω_h of variable thickness

5.5. Generalizations.

Fibre bundles. The product $B \times F$ can be replaced by a fibre bundle $\pi : A \to B$ with base B and fibres $F_x = \pi^{-1}(x)$. We assume P is given as in (5.3), where P_F differentiates only in the fibre directions. That is, for each $x \in B$ there is an operator P_{F_x} on the fibre F_x. We assume that P_{F_x} has *the same* eigenvalue λ_{-2} for each $x \in B$, with one-dimensional eigenspace K_x. Under this assumption there are no essential changes, mostly notational ones:

The K_x form a line bundle K over B. Sections of $K \to B$ may be identified with functions on A which restricted to F_x are in K_x, for each x, so

$$C^\infty(B, K) \subset C^\infty(A).$$

The line bundle $K \to B$ may not have a global non-vanishing section (replacing ψ). We deal with this by replacing functions on B by sections of $K \to B$. The projections $C^\infty(F_x) \to K_x$ fit together to a map

$$\Pi : C^\infty(M) \to C^\infty(B \times \mathbb{R}_+, K)$$

and then

$$P_B = \Pi P_0 i : C^\infty_{\mathrm{D}}(B, K) \to C^\infty(B, K)$$

where $i : C^\infty_{\mathrm{D}}(B, K) \to C^\infty_{\mathrm{D}}(A)$ is the inclusion. We replace $C^\infty(B)$ by $C^\infty(B, K)$ and $\phi \otimes \psi$ by $u_0 \in C^\infty_{\mathrm{D}}(B, K) \subset C^\infty_{\mathrm{D}}(A)$, an eigensection of P_B, everywhere. Then the construction of formal eigenvalues and eigenfunctions works as before.

The adiabatic limit for fibre bundles has been considered frequently in the global analysis literature, see for example [**43**], [**6**].

Multiplicities. The construction can be generalized to the case where λ_{-2} and λ_0 are multiple eigenvalues. In the case of fibre bundles it is important that the multiplicity of λ_{-2} is independent of the base point, otherwise new analytic phenomena arise.

Noncompact base. The base (or fibre) need not be compact as long as P_B (resp. P_F) has compact resolvent (hence discrete spectrum) and the higher order (in h) terms of P behave well at infinity.

For example, the case $B = \mathbb{R}$ with $P_B = -\partial_x^2 + V(x)$ where $V(x) \to \infty$ as $|x| \to \infty$ arises in Section 6.

6. Adiabatic limit with variable fibre eigenvalue

In this section we consider thin domains of variable thickness, see Figure 13. We will see that the nonconstancy of the thickness makes a big difference to the behavior of eigenfunctions and hence to the construction of quasimodes. However, using a suitable rescaling, reflected in the second blow-up in Figure 14, we can reduce the problem to the case considered in the previous section.

We consider a family of domains $\Omega_h \subset \mathbb{R}^2$ defined as follows. Let $I \subset \mathbb{R}$ be a bounded open interval and $a_-, a_+ : I \to \mathbb{R}$ be functions satisfying $a_-(x) < a_+(x)$ for all $x \in I$. Let

$$\Omega_h = \{(x,y) \in \mathbb{R}^2 : ha_-(x) < y < ha_+(x),\ x \in I\} \tag{6.1}$$

for $h > 0$. We assume that the height function $a := a_+ - a_-$ has a unique, non-degenerate maximum, which we may assume to be at $0 \in I$. More precisely

$$\begin{aligned} &\text{for each } \varepsilon > 0 \text{ there is a } \delta > 0 \text{ so that } |x| > \varepsilon \Rightarrow a(x) < a(0) - \delta, \text{ and} \\ &a \text{ is smooth near } 0 \text{ and } a''(0) < 0 \end{aligned} \tag{6.2}$$

The conditions in the second line sharpen the first condition near 0. See Section 6.3 for generalizations.

As before, we want to construct quasimodes (λ_h, u_h) for the Laplacian on Ω_h with Dirichlet boundary conditions, as $h \to 0$. Our construction will apply to 'low' eigenvalues, see Remark 6.2 below.

As in the previous section we rescale the y-variable to lie in a fixed interval, independent of x: Let

$$Y = \frac{y - ha_-(x)}{ha(x)} \in (0,1). \tag{6.3}$$

The change of variables $(x,y) \to (x,Y)$ transforms the vector fields ∂_x, ∂_y to[36]

$$\begin{aligned} \partial_x &\rightsquigarrow \partial_x + b(x,Y)\partial_Y, \quad b = \frac{\partial Y}{\partial x} = -\frac{a_-'}{a} - Y\frac{a'}{a} \\ \partial_y &\rightsquigarrow \frac{\partial Y}{\partial y}\partial_Y = h^{-1}a^{-1}\partial_Y \end{aligned}$$

Therefore

$$\Delta = h^{-2}a^{-2}\partial_Y^2 + (\partial_x + b\partial_Y)^2$$

This is reminiscent of the adiabatic limit considered in Section 5, but the fibre operator $a^{-2}\partial_Y^2$ has first eigenvalue $\pi^2 a(x)^{-2}$ depending on x, so the analysis developed there is not directly applicable.

We deal with this by expanding around $x = 0$ and rescaling the x-variable.

6.1. Heuristics: Finding the relevant scale. The assumption $a''(0) < 0$ implies that the Taylor series of a^{-2} around 0 is

$$a^{-2}(x) \sim c_0 + c_2x^2 + \dots, \quad c_0 > 0,\ c_2 > 0 \tag{6.4}$$

so

$$\Delta = c_0h^{-2}\partial_Y^2 + c_2h^{-2}x^2\partial_Y^2 + \dots + (\partial_x + b\partial_Y)^2 \tag{6.5}$$

near $x = 0$.

Which behavior do we expect for the eigenfunctions with small eigenvalues, say the first? Such an eigenfunction u will minimize the Rayleigh-quotient

$$R(u) = \frac{\langle -\Delta u, u\rangle}{\|u\|^2}$$

[36]This is common but terrible notation. For calculational purposes it helps to write (x', Y) for the new coordinates, related to (x,y) via $x' = x$ and (6.3). Then $\frac{\partial}{\partial x} = \frac{\partial x'}{\partial x}\frac{\partial}{\partial x'} + \frac{\partial Y}{\partial x}\frac{\partial}{\partial Y} = \frac{\partial}{\partial x'} + b(x', Y)\frac{\partial}{\partial Y}$ and similarly for $\frac{\partial}{\partial y}$. In the end replace x' by x to simplify notation.

Put differently, $\rightsquigarrow$ means push-forward under the map $F(x,y) = (x, Y(x,y))$.

among functions satisfying Dirichlet boundary conditions. Let us see how the different terms in (6.5) contribute to $R(u)$:

- The $h^{-2}\partial_Y^2$ term contributes at least $c_0\pi^2 h^{-2}$, since $\langle -\partial_Y^2\psi,\psi\rangle_{[0,1]} \geq \pi^2\|\psi\|^2_{[0,1]}$ for any $\psi:[0,1]\to\mathbb{R}$ having boundary values zero.[37]
- The $h^{-2}x^2\partial_Y^2$ term contributes a positive summand which is $O(h^{-2})$, but can be much smaller if the eigenfunction is large only for x near zero. Specifically, if u concentrates near $x=0$ on a scale of L, i.e.

$$u(x,Y)\approx \phi(\frac{x}{L})\psi(Y)$$

for a function ϕ on $\mathbb{R}$ that is rapidly decaying at infinity then this term will be of order

$$h^{-2}L^2$$

since $x^2\phi(\frac{x}{L}) = L^2\tilde\phi(\frac{x}{L})$ for $\tilde\phi(\xi)=\xi^2\phi(\xi)$ and $\tilde\phi$ is bounded[38]. If $L\to 0$ for $h\to 0$ then this is much smaller than h^{-2}.
- On the other hand, the ∂_x^2 term will be of order L^{-2} if u concentrates on a scale of L near $x=0$.
- The other terms are smaller.

We can now determine the scale L (as function of h) for which the sum of the $h^{-2}x^2\partial_Y^2$ and ∂_x^2 terms is smallest: For fixed h the sum $h^{-2}L^2+L^{-2}$ is smallest when $h^{-2}L^2=L^{-2}$ (since the product of $h^{-2}L^2$ and L^{-2} is constant), i.e.

$$L=h^{1/2}.$$

The expectation of concentration justifies using the Taylor expansions around $x=0$.

The heuristic considerations of this section are justified by the construction of quasimodes in the next section.

6.2. Solution by reduction to the adiabatic limit with constant fibre. The scaling considerations suggest to introduce the variable

$$\xi = \frac{x}{h^{1/2}} \tag{6.6}$$

in (6.5). Expanding also $b(x,Y)$ in Taylor series around $x=0$ and substituting $x=\xi h^{1/2}$ we obtain

$$\Delta \sim h^{-2}c_0\partial_Y^2 + h^{-1}\left(\partial_\xi^2+\xi^2c_2\partial_Y^2\right)+\sum_{j=-1}^{\infty} h^{j/2}P_j \tag{6.7}$$

where P_j are second order differential operators in ξ, Y whose coefficients are polynomial in ξ (of degree at most $j+4$) and linear in Y.

The right hand side of (6.7) is a formal series of differential operators which are defined for $Y\in(0,1)$ and $\xi\in\mathbb{R}$. Now we may apply the constructions of Section 5, with $F=[0,1]$ and $B=\mathbb{R}$. More precisely, $-\Delta = h^{-1}P$ where, with $t=h^{1/2}$,

$$P\sim t^{-2}P_F+P_0+tP_1+\dots$$

[37] This is just the fact that the smallest eigenvalue of the Dirichlet Laplacian on $[0,1]$ is π^2.
[38] It is useful to think of this as follows: '$\phi(\frac{x}{L})$ contributes only for $x\approx L$, and then $x^2\approx L^2$'.

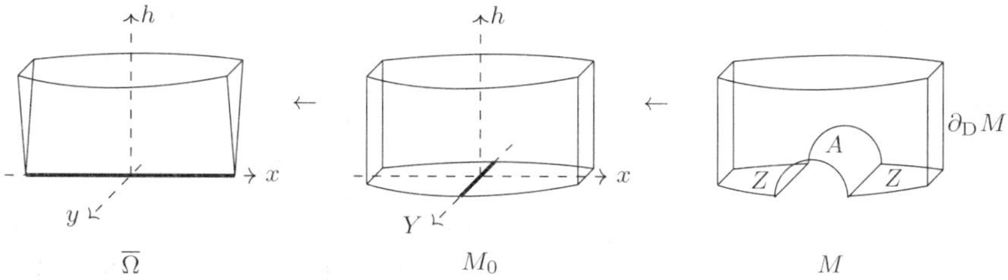

FIGURE 14. Total space for adiabatic limit with variable thickness and its resolution

with $P_F = -c_0\partial_Y^2$ and $P_0 = -\partial_\xi^2 - \xi^2 c_2 \partial_Y^2$. These operators act on bounded functions satisfying Dirichlet boundary conditions at $Y = 0$ and $Y = 1$. Using the first eigenvalue, $\lambda_{-2} = c_0\pi^2$, of P_F we get the horizontal operator (see (5.11))

$$P_B = -\partial_\xi^2 + \omega^2\xi^2, \quad \omega = \sqrt{c_0 c_2}\pi.$$

This is the well-known quantum harmonic oscillator, with eigenvalues $\mu_m = \omega(2m+1)$, $m = 0, 1, 2, \ldots$, and eigenfunctions

$$\psi_m(\xi) = H_m(\sqrt{\omega}\xi)e^{-\frac{1}{2}\omega\xi^2} \tag{6.8}$$

where H_m is the mth Hermite polynomial.

The exponential decay of ψ_m as $|\xi| \to \infty$ justifies a posteriori the scaling limit considerations above. It means that quasimodes concentrate on a strip around $x = 0$ whose width is of order $h^{1/2}$.

By Theorem 5.4 in Section 5 the operator P has quasimodes $\sin \pi Y \psi_m(\xi) + O(t)$. To get quasimodes for $-\Delta$ on Ω_h we simply substitute the coordinates Y, ξ as in (6.3), (6.6). In addition, we should introduce a cutoff near the ends of the interval I so that Dirichlet boundary conditions are satisfied there.

We state the result in terms of resolutions. Introducing the singular coordinates Y and ξ corresponds to a resolution of the total space $\Omega = \bigcup_{h>0} \Omega_h \times \{h\}$ by two blow-ups as shown in Figure 14:

$$\overline{\Omega} \longleftarrow [\overline{\Omega}, \{y = h = 0\}] =: M_0 \longleftarrow [M_0, \{x = h = 0\}]_q =: M\,.$$

The blow-up of $\overline{\Omega}$ in the x axis corresponds to introducing Y, as in Section 5, and results in the space M_0. The quasihomogeneous blow-up (see Subsection 2.3.6) of M_0 in the Y-axis corresponds to introducing $\xi = \frac{x}{\sqrt{h}}$. Compare Figure 9 (with y replaced by h): ξ and $\sqrt{h} = t$, the variables used for the operator P, are precisely the 'top' projective coordinates defined away from the right face. Denote the total blow-down map by

$$\beta : M \to \overline{\Omega}\,.$$

Each of the two blow-ups creates a boundary hypersurface of M at $h = 0$: the first blow-up creates Z, the second blow-up creates A (for 'adiabatic'). In addition, M has the Dirichlet boundary $\partial_D M$ which is the lift of $\bigcup_{h>0}(\partial\Omega_h) \times \{h\} \subset \overline{\Omega}$.

The essence of these blow-ups is that we can construct quasimodes as smooth functions on M.[39] Their expansion at A is the one obtained using the analysis of

[39] Of course this means that we construct quasimodes on Ω so that their pull-backs to M extend smoothly to the boundary of M.

P. Since the quasimodes of P are exponentially decaying as $\xi \to \pm\infty$, we may just take the zero expansion at Z (hence the letter Z).

Summarizing, we obtain the following theorem. We denote

$$C^\infty_{1/2}(\mathbb{R}_+) = \{\mu : \mathbb{R}_+ \to \mathbb{R} : \mu(h) = \tilde{\mu}(\sqrt{h}) \text{ for some } \tilde{\mu} \in C^\infty(\mathbb{R}_+)\}.$$

THEOREM 6.1 (quasimodes for adiabatic limit with variable fibre eigenvalue). *Consider the family of domains Ω_h defined in* (6.1) *and satisfying* (6.2). *Define M as above. Then for each $m \in \mathbb{N}$ there are $\lambda_m \in h^{-2}C^\infty_{1/2}(\mathbb{R}_+)$, $u_m \in C^\infty_{\mathrm{D}}(M)$ satisfying*

$$(-\Delta - \lambda_m)u_m \in h^\infty C^\infty(M)$$

and

$$\begin{aligned} \lambda_m &\sim c_0\pi^2 h^{-2} + \sqrt{c_0c_2}\pi(2m+1)h^{-1} + O(h^{-1/2}) \\ u_m &= \sin \pi Y \psi_m(\xi) \text{ at } A, \quad u_m = 0 \text{ at } Z \end{aligned}$$

where $c_0 = a(0)^{-2}$, $c_2 = -a''(0)a(0)^{-1}$. In addition, u_m vanishes to infinite order at Z.

In the original coordinates on Ω_h the conditions on u_m translate to

$$u_m(h,x,y) = \sin \pi \frac{y - ha_-(x)}{ha(x)}\, \psi_m(\frac{x}{h^{1/2}}) + O(h^{1/2}\left(1+\tfrac{x^2}{h}\right)^{-N}) \tag{6.9}$$

for all N. There is also a uniqueness statement similar to the one in Theorem 5.4.

PROOF. Choose a function u_m on M satisfying the following conditions: The expansion of u_m at the face A is given by the expansion for the quasimodes of P discussed above. The expansion of u_m at the face Z is identically zero; and u_m is zero at the Dirichlet boundary of M. Since ψ_m is exponentially decaying and all P_j have coefficients which are polynomial in ξ, all terms in the expansion at A are exponentially decaying as $\xi \to \infty$. Since $\xi = \infty$ corresponds to the corner $A \cap Z$, the matching conditions of the Borel Lemma 2.10 are satisfied, so $u_m \in C^\infty_{\mathrm{D}}(M)$ exists having the given expansions. Since both expansions satisfy the eigenvalue equation to infinite order, so does u_m. The extra decay factor in the error term of u_m in (6.9) corresponds to the infinite order vanishing at Z, since $\frac{x^2}{h}$ defines Z near $A \cap Z$, see Figure 9. □

REMARK 6.2. *The scaling considerations depended on the assumption that u concentrates near $x = 0$ as $h \to 0$, and this was justified a posteriori by Theorem* 6.1. *On the other hand, it can also be shown a priori using Agmon estimates that eigenfunctions for eigenvalues $\lambda_k(h)$, where k is fixed as $h \to 0$, behave in this way (and this can be used to prove closeness of quasimodes to eigenfunctions, see* [**1**], [**7**] *for example).*

Quasimodes can also be constructed for higher vertical modes, i.e. taking $\lambda_{-2} = l^2c_0\pi^2$ for any $l \in \mathbb{N}$. However, the same caveat as in Remark 5.5 *applies.*

EXERCISE 6.3. *Compute the next term in the expansion of λ_m, i.e. the coefficient of $h^{-1/2}$.*

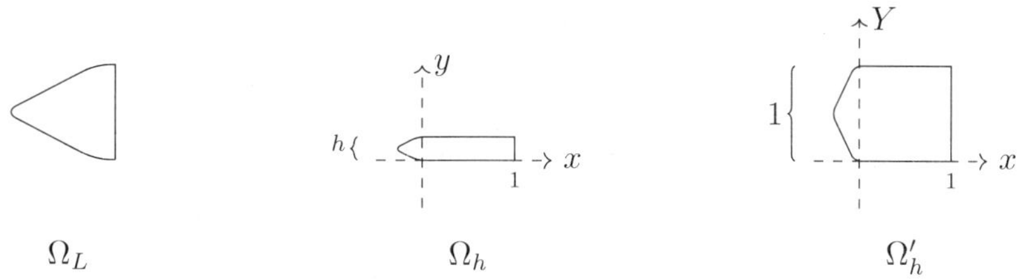

FIGURE 15. Example of domains Ω_L and Ω_h, and rescaling after first blow-up

6.3. Generalizations.

Degenerate maximum. A very similar procedure works if a has a finitely degenerate maximum, i.e. if the condition $a''(0) < 0$ in (6.2) is replaced by

$$a^{(j)}(0) = 0 \ \text{ for } j < 2p, \quad a^{(2p)}(0) < 0 \tag{6.10}$$

for some $p \in \mathbb{N}$. The order is even by smoothness. The expansion (6.4) is replaced by $a^{-2}(x) \sim c_0 + c_{2p}x^{2p} + \dots$ with $c_{2p} > 0$, and then the correct scaling is found from the equation $h^{-2}L^{2p} = L^{-2}$, so $L = h^{\frac{1}{p+1}}$. So we set $\xi = \frac{x}{t}$ where $t = h^{\frac{1}{p+1}}$, then $-\Delta = t^{-2}P$ where

$$P = t^{-2p}(-c_0\partial_Y^2) + (-\partial_\xi^2 - c_{2p}\xi^{2p}\partial_Y^2) + tP_1 + \dots$$

The adiabatic limit analysis works just as well with t^{-2p} as with t^{-2} in the leading term (do it!), and the eigenfunctions of the operator $-\partial_\xi^2 + \omega^2\xi^{2p}$ are still rapidly decaying at infinity, so we obtain

$$\lambda_m \sim c_0\pi^2h^{-2} + \sum_{j=-2}^{\infty} d_{jm}h^{\frac{j}{p+1}}$$

and a similar statement for u_m.

This problem with weaker regularity assumptions (and also allowing half-integer p in (6.10)) was analyzed in [**12**], by a different method.

Several maxima. If the height function a has several isolated maxima then each one will contribute quasimodes. For instance, consider the case of two maxima at $x = x_1$ and $x = x_2$, with $a_i = a(x_i)$, and let $\lambda_k(h)$ be the kth eigenvalue of Ω_h for fixed $k \in \mathbb{N}$. If $a_1 > a_2$ then the leading term of the quasi-eigenvalue constructed at a_1 is smaller than the one at a_2, and therefore the aymptotics of $\lambda_k(h)$ as $h \to 0$ is determined from the Taylor series of a around x_1, and the eigenfunction concentrates near x_1 alone. On the other hand, if $a_1 = a_2$ then both maxima will generally contribute, and it is interesting to analyze their interaction (so-called tunnelling). A special case of this was analyzed in [**53**], and a detailed study of tunnelling for Schrödinger operators with potentials was carried out in [**29**] and [**28**].

Other approaches. A different, more operator-theoretic approach to the problem considered here (and more general ones, e.g. higher dimensions) is taken in [**40**], [**22**], [**39**], see also the book [**56**].

7. Adiabatic limit with ends

We consider the following problem, see Figure 15 left and center: Let $\Omega_L \subset \mathbb{R}^2$ be a bounded domain contained in the left half plane $x < 0$, having $\{0\} \times [0, 1]$ as part of its boundary. For $h > 0$ consider the domain

$$\Omega_h = h\Omega_L \cup R_h \subset \mathbb{R}^2, \quad R_h = [0, 1) \times (0, h) \tag{7.1}$$

i.e. a $1 \times h$ rectangle with the 'end' Ω_L, scaled down by the factor h, attached at its left boundary. To simplify notation we assume that Ω_L is such that the boundary of Ω_h is smooth, except for the right angles at the right end; however, this is irrelevant for the method.

We denote coordinates on Ω_h by x, y. We will construct quasimodes (λ_h, u_h) for the Laplacian $\Delta_h = \partial_x^2 + \partial_y^2$ on Ω_h, with Dirichlet boundary conditions, as $h \to 0$.

The central difficulty, and new aspect compared to the adiabatic limit, is the fact that there are two different scalings in the problem:

- in the rectangular part of Ω_h only the y-direction scales like h,
- in the left end both x- and y-directions scale like h.

This leads to different ways in which these two parts of Ω_h influence eigenvalues and eigenfunctions.

This is a simple case of a much more general setup arising in contexts such as surgery in global analysis and 'fat graph' analysis, see Section 7.4. The essential structures, however, already appear in this simple case. An explicit analysis using matched asymptotic expansions was carried out in [**20**]. We will rederive the quasimode expansions in a more conceptual way using the idea of resolutions.

7.1. Resolution. First, we construct a space on which we may hope the eigenfunctions (and quasimodes) to be smooth. We start with the total space on which these are functions, which is

$$\Omega = \bigcup_{h>0} \Omega_h \times \{h\} \subset \mathbb{R}^3$$

see the left picture in Figure 16. Really we want to consider the closure $\overline{\Omega}$ since we are interested in the behavior of quasimodes as $h \to 0$, compare Remark 2.8. This set is not a manifold with corners, let alone a d-submanifold of $\mathbb{R}^2 \times \mathbb{R}_+$ (compare Footnote 31). At $y = h = 0$ the set $\overline{\Omega}$ has an adiabatic limit type singularity as in the case of Section 5. In addition, it has a conical singularity (with singular base) at the point $x = y = h = 0$.

So we blow up these two submanifolds of $\mathbb{R}^3$ and find the lift (see Definition 2.14) of $\overline{\Omega}$: The blow up of $\{y = h = 0\}$ results in the space M_0 in the center of Figure 16. Projective coordinates are x, $Y = \frac{y}{h}$ and h, globally on M_0 since $|y| \leq Ch$ on $\overline{\Omega}$.[40] The bottom face of M_0 is $h = 0$, and the preimage of the point $x = y = h = 0$ is the bold face line $x = h = 0$ in M_0. So we blow up this line and define M to be the lift of M_0.[41]

---

[40]To make sense of the picture for M_0 it may help to note that M_0 is the closure of $\bigcup_{h>0} \Omega'_h \times \{h\}$ where $\Omega'_h = \{(x, Y) : (x, y) \in \Omega_h, Y = \frac{y}{h}\}$ is depicted on the right in Figure 15.

[41]You may wonder if we would have obtained a different space if had first blown up the point $x = y = h = 0$ and then the (lift of the) line $y = h = 0$. It can easily be checked that this results in the same space M – more precisely that the identity on the interiors of this space

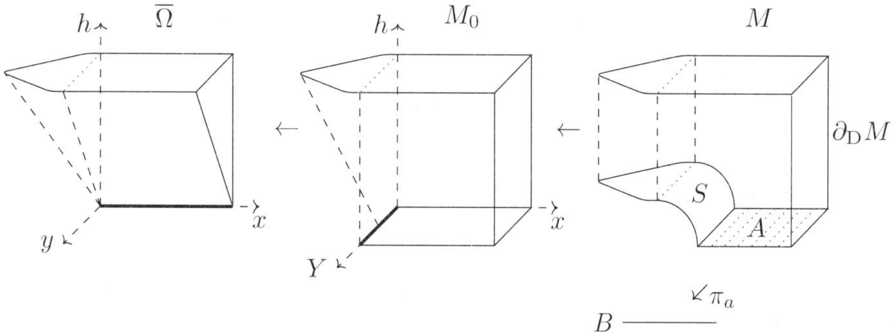

FIGURE 16. Total space and its resolution for adiabatic limit with ends, with fibration of the adiabatic face A; solid lines are codimension 2 corners of M, dashed or dotted lines are not

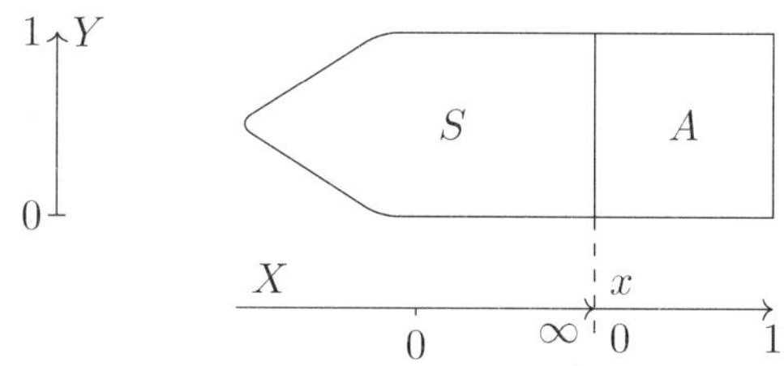

FIGURE 17. 'Flattened' picture of $h = 0$ boundary of resolved total space M, with coordinates for each face

As always we will use x, y, h to denote the pull-backs of the coordinate functions x, y, h on $\overline{\Omega}$ to M. Projective coordinate systems for the second blow-up give coordinates $h, X = \frac{x}{h}, Y$ on $M \setminus A$ and $\frac{h}{x}, x, Y$ in a neighborhood of A. The space M has two types of boundary hypersurfaces:

- The 'Dirichlet boundary' $\partial_D M$, which corresponds to the boundary of Ω_h. This is the union of the two 'vertical' faces in the right picture of Figure 16:

$$\partial_D M = \beta^{-1}\overline{\left(\bigcup_{h>0} \partial\Omega_h \times \{h\}\right)}$$

  where $\beta : M \to \overline{\Omega}$ is the total blow-down map.
- The boundary at $h = 0$,

$$\partial_0 M = S \cup A$$

  where A and S are the front faces of the two blow-ups, which meet in the corner $S \cap A$.[42]

Our interest lies in the behavior of quasimodes at A and S. All functions will be smooth at the Dirichlet boundary.

---

and of M extends to the boundary as a diffeomorphism. This also follows from the fact that $\{x = y = h = 0\} \subset \{y = h = 0\}$ and a general theorem about commuting blow-ups, see [**51**].

[42] A is for adiabatic and S is for surgery, see Section 7.4 for an explanation.

The faces A and S are rescaled limits of Ω_h, see the discussion at the end of Section 2.4. The adiabatic face A is naturally a rectangle

$$A \equiv [0,1] \times [0,1] \text{ with coordinates } x \text{ and } Y = \frac{y}{h}.$$

It is the limit as $h \to 0$ of $\{(x, \frac{y}{h}) : (x,y) \in \overline{R}_h\}$ – this is precisely what the blow-up means, in terms of projective coordinates. The Laplacian in these coordinates is

$$\Delta = h^{-2}\partial_Y^2 + \partial_x^2.$$

Thus, we have an adiabatic problem, with base $B = [0,1]_x$ and fibre $F = [0,1]_Y$ and $P_F = -\partial_Y^2$, $P_B = -\partial_x^2$. The corresponding projection is

$$\pi_A : U_A \to U_B, \quad (x, Y, h) \mapsto (x, h) \tag{7.2}$$

where $U_B = B \times [0, \varepsilon)$ for some $\varepsilon > 0$ and U_A is a neighborhood of A. There is a difference to the setup in Section 5 in that h is not a defining function for A. This leads to various issues below.

The interior of the surgery face S can be identified with the plane domain Ω^∞ obtained by taking $h^{-1}\Omega_h$ and letting $h \to 0$ (again, by definition of the blowup):

$$\text{int}(S) \equiv \Omega^\infty := \Omega_L \cup ([0,\infty) \times (0,1)) \text{ with coordinates } X = \frac{x}{h} \text{ and } Y = \frac{y}{h}, \tag{7.3}$$

and the Laplacian is

$$\Delta = h^{-2}(\partial_X^2 + \partial_Y^2).$$

The corner $S \cap A$ is the interval $[0,1]$ and corresponds to $x = 0$ in A and to $X = \infty$ in S. Coordinates near the corner are x, defining S locally, and $\frac{h}{x} = X^{-1}$, defining A locally and even globally.

Note that the face A carries naturally a non-trivial fibration, compare Remark 5.6, but the face S does not: locally near any point of S no direction is distinguished.

7.2. Solution. The construction of quasimodes builds on the construction for the adiabatic limit in Section 5. The presence of the extra scale, i.e. the left end of Ω_h, leads to a number of new features.

To emphasize the relation with previous sections and motivated by the considerations above we will use the notation

$$\begin{aligned} P &= -\Delta = -\partial_x^2 - \partial_y^2 \\ P_F &= -\partial_Y^2,\ P_B = -\partial_x^2,\ P_S = -\partial_X^2 - \partial_Y^2 \end{aligned} \tag{7.4}$$

7.2.1. *A priori step: Fixing the vertical mode.* Since an adiabatic limit is involved, we fix a priori

λ_{-2} = a simple eigenvalue of P_F on $[0,1]$, with Dirichlet boundary conditions

ψ = an L^2-normalized corresponding eigenfunction.

Here we take the lowest fibre eigenvalue[43]

$$\lambda_{-2} = \pi^2, \quad \psi(Y) = \sqrt{2}\sin \pi Y$$

We will seek (quasi-)eigenvalues of P of the form $\lambda(h) \in h^{-2}\lambda_{-2} + C^\infty(\mathbb{R}_+)$.

[43]One could also consider higher fibre modes, but this would change the analysis at S, see also Remark 5.5.

7.2.2. *Function spaces, leading parts and model operators.* We want to define spaces $\mathcal{E}(M)$ and $\mathcal{R}(M)$ which will contain the eigenfunctions/quasimodes and remainders in the construction, respectively.

Our resolution was chosen so that eigenfunctions have a chance of being smooth on M, so $\mathcal{E}(M) \subset C^\infty(M)$. Since $\frac{h}{x}$ is a defining function for A, functions $u \in C^\infty(M)$ have an expansion at A

$$u \sim \sum_{j=0}^{\infty} \left(\frac{h}{x}\right)^j \tilde{u}_j(x,Y), \quad \tilde{u}_j \in C^\infty(A).$$

In the sequel it will be convenient[44] to write this as

$$u \sim \sum_{j=0}^{\infty} h^j u_j(x,Y) \tag{7.5}$$

where $u_j = x^{-j}\tilde{u}_j$. Note that u_j may be not smooth at $x = 0$, i.e. at $S \cap A$, even though $u \in C^\infty(M)$. We posit that quasimodes satisfy the stronger condition that u_j be smooth on A (including $S \cap A$) and define

$$C^{\infty,\mathrm{tr}}(M) = \{u \in C^\infty(M) : \; u_j \in C^\infty(A) \text{ in the expansion (7.5)}\} \tag{7.6}$$

See Remark 7.5 below for an explanation why we expect quasimodes to satisfy this condition. This can be reformulated as a 'triangular' condition on the indices in the expansion at the corner $S \cap A$:

$$\begin{gathered}\text{If } u \in C^\infty(M),\; u \sim \sum_{j,l=0}^{\infty} a_{jl}(Y) \left(\frac{h}{x}\right)^j x^l \quad \text{near } S \cap A \\ \text{then } u \in C^{\infty,\mathrm{tr}}(M) \iff (a_{jl} \neq 0 \Rightarrow l \geq j)\,.\end{gathered} \tag{7.7}$$

In addition, quasimodes should vanish at the Dirichlet boundary $\partial_{\mathrm{D}}M$. As before, we indicate this by the index D in the function spaces. For functions on the faces A, S, $S \cap A$ we use a similar notation. For example, $C^\infty_{\mathrm{D}}(A)$ is the space of smooth functions on A vanishing on the Dirichlet boundary of A, which consists of the three sides $x = 1$, $Y = 0$, $Y = 1$.

DEFINITION 7.1. *The* **space of quasimodes** *for the adiabatic limit with ends is defined as*

$$\mathcal{E}(M) = C^{\infty,\mathrm{tr}}_{\mathrm{D}}(M)$$

i.e. smooth functions on M satisfying Dirichlet boundary conditions and the triangular condition explained above. The **leading parts** *of $u \in \mathcal{E}(M)$ are defined as*

$$u_S := u_{|S}, \quad u_A := u_{|A}.$$

What are the restrictions of elements of $\mathcal{E}(M)$ to $\partial_0 M = S \cup A$? Define

(7.8)
$$C^{\infty,\mathrm{tr}}_{\mathrm{D}}(S) := \{u_s \in C^\infty_{\mathrm{D}}(S) : \; u_s = a(Y) + O(X^{-\infty}) \text{ as } X \to \infty, \; \in C^\infty_{\mathrm{D}}(S \cap A)\}$$

(7.9)
$$\mathcal{E}(\partial_0 M) := \{(u_s, u_a) : \; u_s \in C^{\infty,\mathrm{tr}}_{\mathrm{D}}(S), \; u_a \in C^\infty_{\mathrm{D}}(A), \; u_s = u_a \text{ at } S \cap A\}$$

Here we use the coordinate X on S. Recall that X^{-1} defines the face $S \cap A$ of S.

[44]In order to have $Pu \sim \sum_j h^j P u_j$. But note that h is not a defining function of A.

LEMMA 7.2 (leading parts of quasimodes, adiabatic limit with ends). *If $u \in \mathcal{E}(M)$ then $(u_S, u_A) \in \mathcal{E}(\partial_0 M)$. Conversely, given $(u_s, u_a) \in \mathcal{E}(\partial_0 M)$ there is $u \in \mathcal{E}(M)$ satisfying $(u_S, u_A) = (u_s, u_a)$, and u is unique modulo $h\mathcal{E}(M)$.*

This could be formulated as existence of a short exact sequence:

$$0 \to h\mathcal{E}(M) \to \mathcal{E}(M) \to \mathcal{E}(\partial_0 M) \to 0 \tag{7.10}$$

where the left map is inclusion and the right map is restriction.

PROOF. It is clear that the restrictions of $u \in \mathcal{E}(M)$ to S, A are smooth and agree at $S \cap A$. Write the expansion of u at the corner as in (7.7). The $l = 0$ terms give the expansion of u_S at $S \cap A$, i.e. as $\frac{h}{x} \to 0$. The only such term is $j = 0$, so $u_S = a_{00}(Y) + O((\frac{h}{x})^\infty)$. From $\frac{h}{x} = X^{-1}$ we get $(u_S, u_A) \in \mathcal{E}(\partial_0 M)$.

Given $(u_s, u_a) \in \mathcal{E}(\partial_0 M)$ one constructs $u \in \mathcal{E}(M)$ having this boundary data using the Borel Lemma 2.10, as follows. We write $\eta = X^{-1}$ for the function defining A and suppress the Y-coordinate. Write $u_a(x) \sim \sum_{l \geq 0} a_{0l} x^l$, $x \to 0$. We choose u having complete expansions

$$u(x, \eta) \sim u_s(\eta) + \sum_{l=1}^{\infty} a_{0l} x^l \qquad \text{as } x \to 0, \quad \text{i.e. at } S$$

$$u(x, \eta) \sim u_a(x) \qquad \text{as } \eta \to 0, \quad \text{i.e. at } A$$

(with error $O(\eta^\infty)$ in the second case). Such a $u \in C^\infty_{\mathrm{D}}(M)$ exists by the Borel Lemma – the matching conditions at $x = \eta = 0$ are satisfied since $\frac{\partial a_{0l}}{\partial \eta} = 0$ for all l. Also, the expansions satisfy the triangular condition in (7.7), hence $u \in C^{\infty,\mathrm{tr}}_{\mathrm{D}}(M)$.

Finally, we need to show that if $u \in \mathcal{E}(M)$, $(u_S, u_A) = 0$ then $u \in h\mathcal{E}(M)$. Now $h = \frac{h}{x} x$ is a total boundary defining function for $\{S, A\}$, so $u = h\tilde{u}$ for some $\tilde{u} \in C^\infty_{\mathrm{D}}(M)$ by Lemma 2.2. In the expansion (7.5) all u_j are smooth and $u_0 = u_A = 0$, so $\tilde{u} = \sum_{j \geq 1} h^{j-1} u_j$ is in $C^{\infty,\mathrm{tr}}_{\mathrm{D}}(M)$. □

The definition of the remainder space combines the triangular condition with the remainder space for the adiabatic limit. First, the choice of λ_{-2} defines a projection type map related to the projection $\pi : U_A \to U_B$, see (7.2),

$$\Pi : C^\infty(M) \to C^\infty(U_B), \quad f \mapsto \langle f_{|U_A}, \psi \rangle_F .$$

Then

$$\Pi \circ (P_F - \lambda_{-2}) = 0 \tag{7.11}$$

where this is defined.

DEFINITION 7.3. *The* **remainder space** *for the adiabatic limit with ends is defined as*

$$\mathcal{R}(M) = \{f \in h^{-2} C^{\infty,\mathrm{tr}}(M) : \ \Pi f \text{ is smooth at } B\}.$$

where $B := B \times \{0\} \subset U_B$. The **leading parts** *of $f \in \mathcal{R}(M)$ are*

$$f_{-2,S} := (h^2 f)_{|S}, \quad f_{AB} := \begin{pmatrix} f_{-2,A} \\ \Pi f_{0,A} \end{pmatrix}$$

where $f_{-2,A} = (h^2 f)_{|A}$, $\Pi f_{0,A} = (\Pi f)_{|B}$.

Thus, a function $f \in h^{-2}C^\infty(M)$ is in $\mathcal{R}(M)$ iff it has an expansion $f \sim h^{-2}f_{-2,A} + h^{-1}f_{-1,A} + f_{0,A} + \dots$ at A with $f_{j,A} \in C^\infty(A)$ analogous to (7.5), and $\Pi f_{-2,A} = \Pi f_{-1,A} = 0$. This defines $f_{-2,A}$ and $f_{0,A}$ in the definition of f_{AB}. Note that $f \in \mathcal{R}(M)$ implies that

$$f_{-2,S} \in C^{\infty,\mathrm{tr}}(S), \quad \Pi f_{-2,S} = 0 \text{ at } S \cap A. \tag{7.12}$$

The first statement follows as in the proof of Lemma 7.2 and the second from $\Pi(h^2 f)_A = 0$ and $(h^2 f)_A = (h^2 f)_S$ at $S \cap A$.

As usual, the remainder space and leading part definitions are justified by the following properties. Recall the definition of the operators P, P_F, P_B, P_S in (7.4).

LEADING PART AND MODEL OPERATOR LEMMA (adiabatic limit with ends).

a) If $f \in \mathcal{R}(M)$ then

$$f \in h\mathcal{R}(M) \text{ if and only if } f_{-2,S} = 0, \ f_{AB} = 0.$$

b) For $\lambda \in h^{-2}\lambda_{-2} + C^\infty(\mathbb{R}_+)$ we have

$$P - \lambda : \mathcal{E}(M) \to \mathcal{R}(M)$$

and

$$[(P-\lambda)u]_{-2,S} = (P-\lambda)_S u_S \qquad \text{where } (P-\lambda)_S = P_S - \lambda_{-2} \tag{7.13}$$

$$[(P-\lambda)u]_{AB} = (P-\lambda)_A u_A \qquad \text{where } (P-\lambda)_A = \begin{pmatrix} P_F - \lambda_{-2} \\ \Pi(P_B - \lambda_0) \end{pmatrix} \tag{7.14}$$

where λ_0 is the constant term of λ.

The operators $(P-\lambda)_S$, $(P-\lambda)_A$ are called the **model operators** of $P - \lambda$ at S and at A. There is also a short exact sequence like (7.10) for $\mathcal{R}(M)$, but we need only what is stated as a).

PROOF.

a) "$\Rightarrow$" is obvious. "$\Leftarrow$": If $f \in \mathcal{R}(M)$ then $h^2 f \in C^{\infty,\mathrm{tr}}(M)$, and $f_{-2,S} = 0$, $f_{AB} = 0$ imply $(h^2 f)_S = 0$, $(h^2 f)_A = 0$, so Lemma 7.2 gives $h^2 f \in hC^{\infty,\mathrm{tr}}(M)$, so $f = h\tilde{f}$ with $\tilde{f} \in h^{-2}C^{\infty,\mathrm{tr}}(M)$. Furthermore, $f_{AB} = 0$ implies $f_{-2,A} = 0$ and $\Pi f_{0,A} = 0$, so $\Pi\tilde{f}$ is smooth at B, hence $\tilde{f} \in \mathcal{R}(M)$.

b) If $u \in \mathcal{E}(M)$ then $(P-\lambda)u = h^{-2}(P_S - \lambda_{-2} + O(h^2))u$ near S and $(P-\lambda)u = h^{-2}(P_F - \lambda_{-2})u + (P_B - \lambda_0)u + O(h)$ near A. This is clearly in $h^{-2}C^{\infty,\mathrm{tr}}(M)$, and even in $\mathcal{R}(M)$ by (7.11). The definition of leading parts directly implies (7.13), (7.14).

□

7.2.3. *Analytic input for model operators.* At the face A, i.e. for the operators $P_F = -\partial_Y^2$ and $P_B = -\partial_x^2$ on $F = [0,1]_Y$ resp. $B = [0,1]_x$, with Dirichlet boundary conditions, we have the standard elliptic solvability result, Lemma 4.2.

The solvability properties of the model operator $(P-\lambda)_S$ are of a different nature, essentially since this operator has essential spectrum.

Recall from (7.3) that the interior of S can be identified with the unbounded domain $\Omega^\infty \subset \mathbb{R}^2$, see Figure 17. This set is the union of a compact set and an infinite strip, hence an example of a space with infinite cylindrical ends, and we can use the standard theory for such spaces. We assume:

$$\textbf{Non-resonance assumption:}\ \text{The resolvent } z \mapsto (P_S - z)^{-1} \text{ of the Laplacian } P_S \text{ on } \Omega^\infty \text{ has no pole at } z = \lambda_{-2} = \pi^2. \tag{7.15}$$

It is well-known that this condition is equivalent to the non-existence of bounded solutions of $(P_S - \lambda_{-2})v = 0$, and also to the unique solvability of $(P_S - \lambda_{-2})v = f$ for compactly supported f, with bounded v, see [**50**, Proposition 6.28]. Also, this condition is satisfied for convex sets Ω^∞, see [**20**, Lemma 7], and holds for generic Ω_L.

LEMMA 7.4. *Assume $\Omega^\infty \subset \mathbb{R}^2$ satisfies the non-resonance assumption* (7.15). *If $f_s \in C^{\infty,\mathrm{tr}}(S)$, $\Pi f_s = 0$ at $S \cap A$ then the equation*

$$(P_S - \lambda_{-2})v_s = f_s \tag{7.16}$$

has a unique bounded solution v_s, and $v_s \in C^{\infty,\mathrm{tr}}_{\mathrm{D}}(S)$.

PROOF. Uniqueness holds since $(P_S - \lambda_{-2})v = 0$ has no bounded solution. For existence, we first reduce to the case of compactly supported f_s, then use the non-resonance assumption to get a bounded solution v_s and then show that $v_s \in C^{\infty,\mathrm{tr}}_{\mathrm{D}}(S)$. The first and third step can be done by developing f_s and v_s for each fixed $X > 0$ in eigenfunctions $\psi_k(Y) = \sqrt{2}\sin k\pi Y$ of the 'vertical' operator $-\partial_Y^2$ on $[0,1]$ with Dirichlet conditions: $f_s(X,Y) = \sum_{k=1}^\infty f_k(X)\psi_k(Y)$. Then (7.16) is equivalent, in $X > 0$, to the ODEs $(-\frac{d^2}{dX^2} + \mu_k)v_k = f_k$ where $\mu_k = (k^2-1)\pi^2$, and these can be analyzed explicitly. For example, if $k > 1$ and $f_k(X) = 0$ for large X then any bounded solution v_k must be exponentially decaying. For details see [**20**, Lemma 6 and Lemma 9 (with $p = 0$)]. □

REMARK 7.5. *This lemma explains why we expect the 'triangular' condition on the Taylor series of quasimodes: for compactly supported f_s the solution v_s lies in $C^{\infty,\mathrm{tr}}_{\mathrm{D}}(S)$. This leads to the definition of $\mathcal{E}(\partial_0 M)$. Then $\mathcal{E}(M)$ must be defined so that the sequence* (7.10) *is exact.*

7.2.4. *Inductive construction of quasimodes.*

Initial step We want to solve

$$(P-\lambda)u \in h\mathcal{R}(M), \quad u \in \mathcal{E}(M).$$

By the leading part and model operator lemma this means

$$(P_S - \lambda_{-2})u_S = 0 \tag{7.17}$$

$$(P_F - \lambda_{-2})u_A = 0 \tag{7.18}$$

$$(P_B - \lambda_0)\Pi u_A = 0 \tag{7.19}$$

where we used that Π commutes with $P_B = -\partial_x^2$.

Also, $(u_S, u_A) \in \mathcal{E}(\partial_0 M)$, defined in (7.9).

First, Lemma 7.4 implies $u_S = 0$.

Therefore $u_A = 0$ at $S \cap A$, hence u_A satisfies Dirichlet boundary conditions at all four sides of the square A. Thus we have an adiabatic problem as treated in Section 5, so λ_0 must be a Dirichlet eigenvalue of $-\partial_x^2$ on $B = [0,1]$, i.e.

$$\lambda_0 = \pi^2 m^2, \quad u_A = u_0 := \phi \otimes \psi,\ \phi(x) = \sqrt{2}\sin \pi m x$$

for some $m \in \mathbb{N}$. Since B is one-dimensional, λ_0 is a simple eigenvalue as required in (5.18).

From now on we fix m, ϕ, $\lambda_{-2} = \pi^2$, λ_0, and $u_0 = \phi \otimes \psi$.

Inductive step

INDUCTIVE STEP LEMMA (adiabatic limit with ends). *Let λ_{-2}, λ_0 and u_0 be chosen as above in the initial step, and let $k \geq 1$. Suppose $\lambda \in h^{-2}C^\infty(\mathbb{R}_+)$, $u \in \mathcal{E}(M)$ satisfy*

$$(P - \lambda)u \in h^k \mathcal{R}(M)$$

and $\lambda = h^{-2}\lambda_{-2} + \lambda_0 + O(h)$ and $u_S = 0, u_A = u_0$. Then there are $\mu \in \mathbb{R}$, $v \in \mathcal{E}(M)$ so that

$$(P - \tilde{\lambda})\tilde{u} \in h^{k+1}\mathcal{R}(M)$$

for $\tilde{\lambda} = \lambda + h^k\mu$, $\tilde{u} = u + h^k v$. The number μ and the restriction v_S are unique, and v_A is unique up to adding constant multiples of u_0.

PROOF. Writing $(P - \lambda)u = h^k f$, $f \in \mathcal{R}(M)$ we have

$$(P - \tilde{\lambda})\tilde{u} = h^k[f - \mu u + (P - \lambda)v - h^k \mu v]$$

This is in $h^{k+1}\mathcal{R}(M)$ if and only if the term in brackets is in $h\mathcal{R}(M)$, which by the leading part and model operator lemma is equivalent to

$$(P_S - \lambda_{-2})v_S = -f_{-2,S} \tag{7.20}$$

$$(P_F - \lambda_{-2})v_A = -f_{-2,A} \tag{7.21}$$

$$(P_B - \lambda_0)\Pi v_A = -\Pi f_{0,A} + \mu\phi \tag{7.22}$$

where we have used that $(h^2 u)_S = 0$, $(h^2 u)_A = 0$ and $\Pi u_A = \Pi u_0 = \phi$.

We first solve at S: We have $f \in \mathcal{R}(M)$, so by (7.12) we can apply Lemma 7.4 with $f_s = -f_{-2,S}$ and obtain $v_S \in C_{\mathrm{D}}^{\infty,\mathrm{tr}}(S)$ solving (7.20). This determines in particular $v_{|S\cap A}$, i.e. the boundary value of v_A at $S \cap A$.

Now at A we need to solve an adiabatic problem, but with an inhomogeneous boundary condition at $S \cap A$. To this end we extend $v_{|S\cap A}$ to $v' \in C_{\mathrm{D}}^\infty(A)$. Writing $v_A = v' + v''$ we then need to find v'' satisfying homogeneous boundary conditions also at $S \cap A$, and solving (7.21), (7.22) with $f_{-2,A}$ modified to $f_{-2,A} + (P_F - \lambda_{-2})v'$ and $f_{0,A}$ modified to $f_{0,A} + (P_B - \lambda_0)v'$.

This is an adiabatic problem, so Lemma 5.3 guarantees the existence of a solution v''. Note that since Π commutes with P_B there is no off-diagonal term in (5.16) (where $P_0 = P_B$ in current notation).

The uniqueness follows directly from (7.20)-(7.22): The difference between two solutions v would satisfy the same equations with $f = 0$, so would have to vanish at S and therefore solve the adiabatic problem at A with homogeneous boundary condition at $S \cap A$, for which we have already shown that μ is unique and v_A is unique up to multiples of u_0. □

Now by the same arguments as for Theorem 4.3 we obtain from the initial and inductive steps:

THEOREM 7.6 (quasimodes for adiabatic limit with ends). *Consider the family of domains Ω_h defined in (7.1). Suppose the non-resonance assumption (7.15) is satisfied. Then for each $m \in \mathbb{N}$ there are $\lambda_m \in h^{-2}C^\infty(\mathbb{R}_+)$, $u_m \in C^{\infty,\mathrm{tr}}_{\mathrm{D}}(M)$ satisfying*

$$(P - \lambda_m)u_m \in h^\infty C^\infty(M)$$

and

$$\lambda_m = h^{-2}\pi^2 + m^2\pi^2 + O(h)$$
$$u_A = 2\sin m\pi x \,\sin \pi Y\,, \quad u_S = 0$$

There is also a uniqueness statement similar to the one in Theorem 5.4.

REMARK 7.7 (Quasimodes vs. modes). *It is shown in* [**20**] *that for convex Ω_h all eigenfunctions are captured by this construction. That is, for each $m \in \mathbb{N}$ there is $h_0 > 0$ so that for $h < h_0$ the mth eigenvalue of Ω_h is simple, and both eigenvalue and (suitably normalized) eigenfunction are approximated by λ_m, u_m with error $O(h^\infty)$. However, if Ω_h is not convex then there may be an additional finite number of eigenvalues not captured by this construction. Essentially, these arise from L^2-eigenvalues of the Laplacian on Ω^∞ below the essential spectrum. See* [**16**] *and references there for a detailed discussion.*

7.3. Explicit formulas. The inductive step yields a method for finding any number of terms in the expansions of λ_m and u_m as $h \to 0$ in terms of solutions of the model problems. In [**20**] the next two terms for λ_m are computed:

$$\lambda_m = h^{-2}\pi^2 + m^2\pi^2(1+ah)^{-2} + O(h^3)$$

where $a > 0$ is determined by the scattering theory of $-\Delta$ on Ω^∞ at the infimum of the essential spectrum, which equals π^2. More precisely, there is, up to scalar multiples, a unique polynomially bounded solution v of $(\Delta + \pi^2)v = 0$ on Ω^∞, and it has the form

$$v(X,Y) = (X + a)\sin \pi Y + O(e^{-X}) \text{ as } X \to \infty.$$

This fixes a. Another description is $a = \frac{1}{2}\gamma'(0)$ where $\gamma(s)$ is the scattering phase at frequency $\pi^2 + s^2$.

7.4. Generalizations. The structure of Ω_h may be described as 'thin cylinder with end attached'. A natural general setup for this structure is obtained by replacing the Y-interval $[0,1]$ by a compact Riemannian manifold N, of dimension $n-1$, and the end Ω_L by another compact Riemannian manifold, of dimension n, which has an isometric copy of N as part of its boundary. One may also add another Riemannian manifold as right end. This is studied in global analysis (where it is sometimes called 'analytic surgery') as a tool to study the glueing behavior of spectral invariants, see [**25**], [**26**], [**44**] for example. Other degenerations which have been studied by similar methods include conic degeneration [**21**], [**54**], [**55**] and degeneration to a (fibred) cusp [**2**], [**3**].

Another generalization is to have several thin cylinders meeting in prescribed ways, so that in the limit $h = 0$ one obtains a graph-like structure instead of an interval. This is called a 'fat graph'. For example, consider a finite graph embedded in $\mathbb{R}^n$ with straight edges, and let Ω_h be the set of points of $\mathbb{R}^n$ having distance at most h from this graph. This was studied in detail in [**10**], [**16**] and [**52**], see also [**17**] for a discussion and many more references. The methods in these papers actually yield a stronger result: $\lambda_m(h)$ is given by a power series in h which converges for small h, plus an exponentially small error term.

8. Summary of the quasimodes constructions

We summarize the essential points of the quasimode constructions, continuing the outline given in Section 3.

In the case of a regular perturbation we introduced the iterative setup that allowed us to reduce the quasimode construction to the solution of a model problem (Lemma 4.2). It involves spaces of quasimodes and remainders and notions of leading part. In this case these are simply smooth functions and their restriction to $h = 0$.

For the adiabatic limit problem with constant fibre eigenvalue this needs to be refined: the different scaling in fibre and base directions requires a new definition of remainder space and leading part of remainders (Definition 5.1). The model operator combines fibre and horizontal operators, and its triangular structure with respect to the decomposition of functions in fibrewise λ_{-2} modes and other modes, Equation (5.16), enables us to solve the model problem.

The adiabatic limit problem with variable fibre eigenvalue can be reduced to the previous case by expanding the fibre eigenvalue (as function on the base) around its maximum and by rescaling the base variable. This rescaling balances the leading non-constant term in the expansion of the eigenvalue with the leading term of the base operator. The rescaling is encoded geometrically by a blow-up of the total space.

The adiabatic limit problem with ends carries the new feature of having two regions with different scaling behavior. Geometrically this corresponds to two boundary hypersurfaces, A and S, at $h = 0$ in the resolved total space. The model problem at A is the same as for the adiabatic limit with constant fibre eigenvalue. The model problem at S is a scattering problem, i.e. a spectral problem on a non-compact domain. The properties of the solutions of the scattering problem lead to the triangular condition on the Taylor series at the corner $S \cap A$ in the spaces of quasimodes and remainders. Once this setup is installed the construction proceeds in a straight-forward way as in the other cases.

References

[1] Shmuel Agmon, *Bounds on exponential decay of eigenfunctions of Schrödinger operators*, Schrödinger operators (Como, 1984), Lecture Notes in Math., vol. 1159, Springer, Berlin, 1985, pp. 1–38, DOI 10.1007/BFb0080331. MR824986

[2] Pierre Albin, Frédéric Rochon, and David Sher. *Analytic torsion and R-torsion of Witt representations on manifolds with cusps.* Preprint math.DG/1411.1105 at arxiv.org, 2014.

[3] Pierre Albin, Frédéric Rochon, and David Sher. *Resolvent, heat kernel, and torsion under degeneration to fibered cusps.* Preprint math.DG/1410.8406 at arxiv.org, 2014.

[4] V. I. Arnol′d, *Modes and quasimodes* (Russian), Funkcional. Anal. i Priložen. **6** (1972), no. 2, 12–20. MR0297274

[5] David A. Cox, John B. Little, and Henry K. Schenck, *Toric varieties*, Graduate Studies in Mathematics, vol. 124, American Mathematical Society, Providence, RI, 2011. MR2810322

[6] Xianzhe Dai and Richard B. Melrose, *Adiabatic limit, heat kernel and analytic torsion*, Metric and differential geometry, Progr. Math., vol. 297, Birkhäuser/Springer, Basel, 2012, pp. 233–298, DOI 10.1007/978-3-0348-0257-4_9. MR3220445

[7] Monique Dauge and Nicolas Raymond, *Plane waveguides with corners in the small angle limit*, J. Math. Phys. **53** (2012), no. 12, 123529, 34, DOI 10.1063/1.4769993. MR3405919

[8] Freddy Dumortier and Robert Roussarie, *Canard cycles and center manifolds*, Mem. Amer. Math. Soc. **121** (1996), no. 577, x+100, DOI 10.1090/memo/0577. With an appendix by Cheng Zhi Li. MR1327208

[9] C. L. Epstein, R. B. Melrose, and G. A. Mendoza, *Resolvent of the Laplacian on strictly pseudoconvex domains*, Acta Math. **167** (1991), no. 1-2, 1–106, DOI 10.1007/BF02392446. MR1111745

[10] Pavel Exner and Olaf Post, *Convergence of spectra of graph-like thin manifolds*, J. Geom. Phys. **54** (2005), no. 1, 77–115, DOI 10.1016/j.geomphys.2004.08.003. MR2135966

[11] P. Freitas and D. Krejčiřík, *Location of the nodal set for thin curved tubes*, Indiana Univ. Math. J. **57** (2008), no. 1, 343–375, DOI 10.1512/iumj.2008.57.3170. MR2400260

[12] Leonid Friedlander and Michael Solomyak, *On the spectrum of the Dirichlet Laplacian in a narrow strip*, Israel J. Math. **170** (2009), 337–354, DOI 10.1007/s11856-009-0032-y. MR2506330

[13] Vincent Grandjean and Daniel Grieser. *The exponential map at a cuspidal singularity.* J. R. Angew. Math., 2015. DOI 10.1515/crelle-2015-0020. arXiv:1205.4554v2.

[14] Daniel Grieser, *Basics of the b-calculus*, Approaches to singular analysis (Berlin, 1999), Oper. Theory Adv. Appl., vol. 125, Birkhäuser, Basel, 2001, pp. 30–84. MR1827170

[15] Daniel Grieser. *Notes on heat kernel asymptotics.* Unpublished notes, www.uni-math.gwdg.de/iwitt/SpecGeo2014/heat.pdf, 2004.

[16] Daniel Grieser, *Spectra of graph neighborhoods and scattering*, Proc. Lond. Math. Soc. (3) **97** (2008), no. 3, 718–752, DOI 10.1112/plms/pdn020. MR2448245

[17] Daniel Grieser, *Thin tubes in mathematical physics, global analysis and spectral geometry*, Analysis on graphs and its applications, Proc. Sympos. Pure Math., vol. 77, Amer. Math. Soc., Providence, RI, 2008, pp. 565–593, DOI 10.1090/pspum/077/2459891. MR2459891

[18] Daniel Grieser and Michael J. Gruber, *Singular asymptotics lemma and push-forward theorem*, Approaches to singular analysis (Berlin, 1999), Oper. Theory Adv. Appl., vol. 125, Birkhäuser, Basel, 2001, pp. 117–130. MR1827172

[19] Daniel Grieser and Eugénie Hunsicker, *Pseudodifferential operator calculus for generalized $\mathbb{Q}$-rank 1 locally symmetric spaces. I*, J. Funct. Anal. **257** (2009), no. 12, 3748–3801, DOI 10.1016/j.jfa.2009.09.016. MR2557724

[20] Daniel Grieser and David Jerison, *Asymptotics of eigenfunctions on plane domains*, Pacific J. Math. **240** (2009), no. 1, 109–133, DOI 10.2140/pjm.2009.240.109. MR2485476

[21] Colin Guillarmou and David A. Sher, *Low energy resolvent for the Hodge Laplacian: applications to Riesz transform, Sobolev estimates, and analytic torsion*, Int. Math. Res. Not. IMRN **15** (2015), 6136–6210, DOI 10.1093/imrn/rnu119. MR3384474

[22] Stefan Haag, Jonas Lampart, and Stefan Teufel, *Generalised quantum waveguides*, Ann. Henri Poincaré **16** (2015), no. 11, 2535–2568, DOI 10.1007/s00023-014-0374-9. MR3411741

[23] Jacques Hadamard. *Mémoire sur le problème d'analyse relatif à l'équilibre des plaques élastiques encastrées.* Mém. Sav. étrang. (2) 33, Nr. 4, 128 p, 1908.

[24] Robin Hartshorne, *Algebraic geometry*, Springer-Verlag, New York-Heidelberg, 1977. Graduate Texts in Mathematics, No. 52. MR0463157

[25] Andrew Hassell, *Analytic surgery and analytic torsion*, Comm. Anal. Geom. **6** (1998), no. 2, 255–289, DOI 10.4310/CAG.1998.v6.n2.a2. MR1651417

[26] Andrew Hassell, Rafe Mazzeo, and Richard B. Melrose, *Analytic surgery and the accumulation of eigenvalues*, Comm. Anal. Geom. **3** (1995), no. 1-2, 115–222, DOI 10.4310/CAG.1995.v3.n1.a4. MR1362650

[27] Herwig Hauser, *The Hironaka theorem on resolution of singularities (or: A proof we always wanted to understand)*, Bull. Amer. Math. Soc. (N.S.) **40** (2003), no. 3, 323–403, DOI 10.1090/S0273-0979-03-00982-0. MR1978567

[28] B. Helffer and J. Sjöstrand, *Multiple wells in the semiclassical limit. I*, Comm. Partial Differential Equations **9** (1984), no. 4, 337–408, DOI 10.1080/03605308408820335. MR740094

[29] Bernard Helffer, *Semi-classical analysis for the Schrödinger operator and applications*, Lecture Notes in Mathematics, vol. 1336, Springer-Verlag, Berlin, 1988. MR960278

[30] Heisuke Hironaka, *Resolution of singularities of an algebraic variety over a field of characteristic zero. I, II*, Ann. of Math. (2) **79** (1964), 109–203; ibid. (2) **79** (1964), 205–326. MR0199184

[31] Mark H. Holmes, *Introduction to perturbation methods*, 2nd ed., Texts in Applied Mathematics, vol. 20, Springer, New York, 2013. MR2987304

[32] Dominic Joyce, *A generalization of manifolds with corners*, Adv. Math. **299** (2016), 760–862, DOI 10.1016/j.aim.2016.06.004. MR3519481

[33] Dominic Joyce, *A generalization of manifolds with corners*, Adv. Math. **299** (2016), 760–862, DOI 10.1016/j.aim.2016.06.004. MR3519481

[34] Tosio Kato, *Perturbation theory for linear operators*, Die Grundlehren der mathematischen Wissenschaften, Band 132, Springer-Verlag New York, Inc., New York, 1966. MR0203473

[35] Chris Kottke. *Blow-up in manifolds with generalized corners.* arXiv:1509.03874, 2015.

[36] Chris Kottke and Richard B. Melrose, *Generalized blow-up of corners and fiber products*, Trans. Amer. Math. Soc. **367** (2015), no. 1, 651–705, DOI 10.1090/S0002-9947-2014-06222-3. MR3271273

[37] Christian Kuehn, *Multiple time scale dynamics*, Applied Mathematical Sciences, vol. 191, Springer, Cham, 2015. MR3309627

[38] Christian Kuehn and Peter Szmolyan, *Multiscale geometry of the Olsen model and non-classical relaxation oscillations*, J. Nonlinear Sci. **25** (2015), no. 3, 583–629, DOI 10.1007/s00332-015-9235-z. MR3338451

[39] Jonas Lampart and Stefan Teufel, *The adiabatic limit of Schrödinger operators on fibre bundles*, Math. Ann. **367** (2017), no. 3-4, 1647–1683, DOI 10.1007/s00208-016-1421-2. MR3623234

[40] Jonas Lampart, Stefan Teufel, and Jakob Wachsmuth, *Effective Hamiltonians for thin Dirichlet tubes with varying cross-section*, Mathematical results in quantum physics, World Sci. Publ., Hackensack, NJ, 2011, pp. 183–189, DOI 10.1142/9789814350365_0018. MR2885171

[41] Vladimir Maz′ya, Serguei Nazarov, and Boris Plamenevskij, *Asymptotic theory of elliptic boundary value problems in singularly perturbed domains. Vol. I*, Operator Theory: Advances and Applications, vol. 111, Birkhäuser Verlag, Basel, 2000. Translated from the German by Georg Heinig and Christian Posthoff. MR1779977

[42] Vladimir Maz′ya, Serguei Nazarov, and Boris Plamenevskij, *Asymptotic theory of elliptic boundary value problems in singularly perturbed domains. Vol. II*, Operator Theory: Advances and Applications, vol. 112, Birkhäuser Verlag, Basel, 2000. Translated from the German by Plamenevskij. MR1779978

[43] Rafe R. Mazzeo and Richard B. Melrose, *The adiabatic limit, Hodge cohomology and Leray's spectral sequence for a fibration*, J. Differential Geom. **31** (1990), no. 1, 185–213. MR1030670

[44] R. R. Mazzeo and R. B. Melrose, *Analytic surgery and the eta invariant*, Geom. Funct. Anal. **5** (1995), no. 1, 14–75, DOI 10.1007/BF01928215. MR1312019

[45] Rafe Mazzeo and Julie Rowlett, *A heat trace anomaly on polygons*, Math. Proc. Cambridge Philos. Soc. **159** (2015), no. 2, 303–319, DOI 10.1017/S0305004115000365. MR3395373

[46] Richard McGehee, *Singularities in classical celestial mechanics*, Proceedings of the International Congress of Mathematicians (Helsinki, 1978), Acad. Sci. Fennica, Helsinki, 1980, pp. 827–834. MR562695

[47] R. B. Melrose. *Real blow up.* Notes for lectures at MSRI. http://www-math.mit.edu/~rbm/InSisp/InSiSp.html, 2008.

[48] Richard B. Melrose, *Pseudodifferential operators, corners and singular limits*, Proceedings of the International Congress of Mathematicians, Vol. I, II (Kyoto, 1990), Math. Soc. Japan, Tokyo, 1991, pp. 217–234. MR1159214

[49] Richard B. Melrose, *Calculus of conormal distributions on manifolds with corners*, Internat. Math. Res. Notices **3** (1992), 51–61, DOI 10.1155/S1073792892000060. MR1154213

[50] Richard B. Melrose, *The Atiyah-Patodi-Singer index theorem*, Research Notes in Mathematics, vol. 4, A K Peters, Ltd., Wellesley, MA, 1993. MR1348401

[51] Richard B. Melrose. *Differential analysis on manifolds with corners.* Book in preparation. http://www-math.mit.edu/~rbm/book.html, 1996.

[52] S. Molchanov and B. Vainberg, *Scattering solutions in networks of thin fibers: small diameter asymptotics*, Comm. Math. Phys. **273** (2007), no. 2, 533–559, DOI 10.1007/s00220-007-0220-8. MR2318317

[53] Thomas Ourmières-Bonafos, *Dirichlet eigenvalues of asymptotically flat triangles*, Asymptot. Anal. **92** (2015), no. 3-4, 279–312. MR3371117

[54] Julie Rowlett, *Spectral geometry and asymptotically conic convergence*, Comm. Anal. Geom. **16** (2008), no. 4, 735–798, DOI 10.4310/CAG.2008.v16.n4.a2. MR2471369

[55] David A. Sher, *Conic degeneration and the determinant of the Laplacian*, J. Anal. Math. **126** (2015), 175–226, DOI 10.1007/s11854-015-0015-3. MR3358031

[56] Stefan Teufel, *Adiabatic perturbation theory in quantum dynamics*, Lecture Notes in Mathematics, vol. 1821, Springer-Verlag, Berlin, 2003. MR2158392

[57] S. van Gils, M. Krupa, and P. Szmolyan, *Asymptotic expansions using blow-up*, Z. Angew. Math. Phys. **56** (2005), no. 3, 369–397, DOI 10.1007/s00033-004-1021-y. MR2142930

Institut für Mathematik, Carl von Ossietzky Universität Oldenburg, 26111 Oldenburg

E-mail address: daniel.grieser@uni-oldenburg.de

Contemporary Mathematics
Volume **700**, 2017
http://dx.doi.org/10.1090/conm/700/14189

Scattering for the geodesic flow on surfaces with boundary

Colin Guillarmou

Abstract. These are lecture notes based on a mini-course given in the 2015 summer school *Théorie spectrale géométrique et computationnelle* in CRM, Montréal.

1. Introduction

In these notes, we discuss some geometric inverse problems in 2-dimension that have been studied since the eighties, and we review some results on these questions.

The problem we consider consists in recovering a Riemannian metric on a surface with boundary from measurements at the boundary: the lengths of geodesics relating boundary points and their tangent directions at the boundary. This is a non-linear problem called the *lens rigidity problem*, which has a gauge invariance (pull-backs by diffeomorphisms fixing the boundary). The associated linear problem consists in the analysis of the kernel of the geodesic X-ray transform, a curved version of the Radon transform.

The tools to study the X-ray transform are of analytic nature, more precisely a combination of analysis of transport equations with some energy identity. Microlocal methods have also been very powerful in that study, but we won't review this aspect in these notes. The techniques presented in these notes are quite elementary and give a short introduction to that area of research.

2. Geometric background

Let (M, g) be a smooth oriented compact Riemannian surface with boundary ∂M and let M° be its interior. In local coordinates $x = (x_1, x_2)$ the metric will be written

$$g = \sum_{i,j=1}^{2} g_{ij}(x) dx_i dx_j,$$

where $(g_{ij}(x))_{ij}$ are symmetric positive definite matrices smoothly depending on x. We will write ∇ the Levi-Civita connection of g on M. The tangent bundle of M is denoted TM and the projection on the base is written

$$\pi_0 : TM \to M.$$

The second fundamental form II is the symmetric tensor

$$\mathrm{II} : T\partial M \times T\partial M \to \mathbb{R}, \quad \mathrm{II}(u, w) := -g(\nabla_u \nu, w),$$

2010 *Mathematics Subject Classification.* Primary 35R30.

where ν is the interior pointing unit normal vector to ∂M. We say that ∂M is *strictly convex* for g if II is positive definite and we will assume along this course that this property holds.

Exercise: Show that a neighborhood of ∂M in M is isometric to $[0,\epsilon]_r \times \partial M$ with metric $dr^2 + h_r$ where h_r is a smooth 1-parameter family of metrics on ∂M. In these *geodesic normal coordinates*, we have $\nu = \partial_r|_{r=0}$ and $\mathrm{II} = -\frac{1}{2}\partial_r h_r|_{r=0}$.

2.1. Geodesic flow. A *geodesic* on M is a C^2 curve on M such that $\nabla_{\dot{x}}\dot{x} = 0$ where $\dot{x}(t) \in T_{x(t)}M$ is the tangent vector to the curve, i.e $\dot{x}(t) := \partial_t x(t)$. In local coordinates $x = (x_1, x_2)$, we can write $\nabla_{\partial_{x_i}}\partial_{x_j} = \sum_{k=1}^2 \Gamma_{ij}^k \partial_{x_k}$ for some smooth functions Γ_{ij}^k called *Christoffel symbols.* The geodesic equation in these coordinates is

$$\ddot{x}_j(t) = -\sum_{k,\ell=1}^{2} \Gamma_{k\ell}^j(x(t))\dot{x}_k(t)\dot{x}_\ell(t), \quad j = 1, 2.$$

By standard arguments of ordinary differential equations – Cauchy-Lipschitz–, this second order equation has a solution $x(t)$ in some interval $t \in [0,\epsilon)$ if we fix an initial condition $(x(0),\dot{x}(0)) = (x_0, v_0) \in TM^\circ$, and the solution can be extended until $x(t)$ reaches ∂M.

The geodesics are minimizers of the *energy* and of the *length functionals*: if p,q are two points in M and if $\gamma : [0,1] \to M$ is a C^2 curve such that $\gamma(0) = p$ and $\gamma(1) = q$, then the energy $E_{p,q}(\gamma)$ and the length $L_{p,q}(\gamma)$ are defined by

$$E_{p,q}(\gamma) = \int_0^1 |\dot{\gamma}(t)|^2_{g(\gamma(t))} dt, \quad L_{p,q}(\gamma) = \int_0^1 |\dot{\gamma}(t)|_{g(\gamma(t))} dt.$$

Then the minimum of $E_{p,q}(\gamma)$ and $L_{p,q}(\gamma)$ among curves as above are obtained by a geodesic. In fact, one can show using variational methods and a compactness argument that in each homotopy class of curves with endpoints p,q, there is a mimimizer for $E_{p,q}$ and $L_{p,q}$ which is a geodesic. The miminizer is in general not unique.

DEFINITION 2.1. *The geodesic flow at time $t \in \mathbb{R}$ is the map φ_t defined by*

$$\varphi_t : U(t) \to TM, \quad \varphi_t(x,v) := (x(t), \dot{x}(t)),$$

if $x(t)$ is the geodesic with initial condition $(x(0),\dot{x}(0)) = (x,v)$, where $U(t) \subset TM$ is the set of points $(x,v) \in TM$ such that the geodesic $x(s)$ with initial condition (x,v) exists in M for all $s \in [0,t]$.

The *exponential map* at a point $x \in M$ is the map

$$\exp_x : U_x \subset T_xM \to M, \quad \exp_x(v) = \pi_0(\varphi_1(x,v)),$$

where U_x is the set of vector $v \in T_xM$ so that $\varphi_t(x,v) \in M$ for all $t \in [0,1)$. The map $\exp_x$ is a local diffeomorphism near $v = 0$ at each $x \in M^\circ$.

Notice that for $x(t)$ a geodesic on M,

$$\partial_t(g_{x(t)}(\dot{x}(t),\dot{x}(t))) = 2g_{x(t)}(\nabla_{\dot{x}(t)}\dot{x}(t),\dot{x}(t)) = 0$$

and therefore φ_t acts on the unit tangent bundle

$$SM := \{(x,v) \in TM; g_x(v,v) = 1\}.$$

The vector field generating the flow φ_t is a smooth vector field on SM defined by

$$Xf(x,v) = \partial_t f(\varphi_t(x,v))|_{t=0}.$$

The manifold SM is compact and has boundary $\partial SM = \pi_0^{-1}(\partial M)$. This boundary splits into the disjoint parts

$$\partial_- SM := \{(x,v) \in SM; x \in \partial M, g_x(v,\nu) > 0\},$$
$$\partial_+ SM := \{(x,v) \in SM; x \in \partial M, g_x(v,\nu) < 0\},$$
$$\partial_0 SM := \{(x,v) \in SM; x \in \partial M, g_x(v,\nu) = 0\}.$$

We call $\partial_- SM$ the *incoming boundary*, $\partial_+ SM$ the *outgoing boundary* and $\partial_0 SM$ the *glancing boundary*.

2.2. Hamiltonian approach. The cotangent bundle T^*M is a symplectic manifold, with symplectic form $\omega = d\alpha$ where $\alpha \in C^\infty(T^*M, T^*(T^*M))$ is the Liouville 1-form defined by $\alpha_{(x,\xi)}(W) = \xi(d\pi_0(x,\xi).W)$ if $\pi_0 : SM \to M$ is the projection on the base. In local coordinates $x = (x_1, x_2)$, $\xi = \xi_1 dx_1 + \xi_2 dx_2$, we have

$$\alpha = \sum_{i=1}^{2} \xi_i dx_i, \quad \omega = \sum_{i=1}^{2} d\xi_i \wedge dx_i.$$

The function $p : T^*M \to \mathbb{R}$ defined by $p(x,\xi) = \frac{1}{2} g_x^{-1}(\xi,\xi)$ where g^{-1} is the metric induced on T^*M by g has a Hamiltonian vector field X_p defined by $\omega(X_p, \cdot) = dp$ and X_p is tangent to $S^*M := p^{-1}(1/2)$.

Exercise: Show that the duality isomorphism $SM \to S^*M$ given by the metric g conjugates $\varphi_t = e^{tX}$ to e^{tX_p}.

2.3. Geometry of SM. There are particular sets of coordinates $x = (x_1, x_2)$ near each points $x_0 \in M$, called *isothermal coordinates*, such that in these coordinates, the metric has the form

$$g = e^{2\rho}(dx_1^2 + dx_2^2)$$

in these coordinates, for some smooth function $\rho(x)$ near x_0. The metric is conformal to the Euclidean metric in these coordinates, which will be a useful fact for what follows. These coordinates can be obtained by solving an elliptic equation, and more precisely a Beltrami equation (see [**Ta**, Chapter 5.10]). These coordinates induce a diffeomorphism

$$\Omega \times \mathbb{R}/2\pi\mathbb{Z} \to \pi_0^{-1}(\Omega) \subset SM, \quad (x,\theta) \mapsto (x, v = e^{-\rho(x)}(\cos(\theta)\partial_{x_1} + \sin(\theta)\partial_{x_2})),$$

where Ω is the neighborhood of x_0 where the isothermal coordinates are valid. In these coordinates, the vector field X becomes

$$X = e^{-\rho}\Big(\cos(\theta)\partial_{x_1} + \sin(\theta)\partial_{x_2} + (-\sin(\theta)\partial_{x_1}\rho + \cos(\theta)\partial_{x_2}\rho)\partial_\theta\Big). \tag{2.1}$$

We start by analyzing the flow of X near the boundary, under the assumption that ∂M is strictly convex.

LEMMA 2.2. *Geodesics in M° intersect ∂M transversally, i.e. a geodesic coming from M° and touching ∂M at a point x can not be tangent to ∂M*

PROOF. There are isothermal coordinates $x = (x_1, x_2)$ near each $x_0 \in \partial M$ such that a neighborhood of x_0 in M correspond to a neighborhood of 0 in the half-plane $\{x_2 \geq 0\}$ and the metric is of the form $e^{2\rho}(dx_1^2 + dx_2^2)$, and we can assume that x_0 is mapped to $x = 0$ by this chart. One has $\partial_{x_2}\rho|_{x_2=0} < 0$ if ∂M is strictly convex. If $x(t)$ is a geodesic for $t \leq t_0$ with $x_2(t) > 0$ for $t < t_0$ and $x_2(t_0) = 0$, then if $\dot{x}_2(t_0) = 0$, we get by (2.1) that $\theta(t_0) = 0$ (or π) and $\dot{\theta}(t_0) = e^{-\rho(0)}(\cos(\theta_0)\partial_{x_2}\rho(0))$.

Let us consider the case $\theta(t_0) = 0$ (the case $\theta(t_0) = \pi$ is similar): then $\dot{\theta}(t_0) < 0$ and θ decreases as $t \to t_0$, and since $\dot{x}_2(t) = e^{-\rho} \sin \theta(t)$, we get $\ddot{x}_2(t_0) = e^{\rho(0)} \dot{\theta}(t_0) < 0$. A Taylor expansion gives

$$x_2(t) = \tfrac{1}{2}(t - t_0)^2 \ddot{x}_2(t_0) + \mathcal{O}((t - t_0)^3),$$

which is negative near t_0, leading to a contradiction. $\square$

Define Θ_t the rotation of angle $+t$ in the fibers of SM; in the coordinates above Θ_t is just $(x, \theta) \mapsto (x, \theta + t)$. This smooth 1-parameter family of diffeomorphisms of SM induces a smooth vector field V defined by

$$Vf(x, v) = \partial_t f(\Theta_t(x, v))|_{t=0}, \quad \forall f \in C^\infty(SM).$$

In the coordinates (x, θ), $V = \partial_\theta$. Next we define another vector field

$$X_\perp := [X, V],$$

which in the coordinates (x, θ), is given by

$$X_\perp = -e^{-\rho}\Big(-\sin(\theta)\partial_{x_1} + \cos(\theta)\partial_{x_2} - (\cos(\theta)\partial_{x_1}\rho + \sin(\theta)\partial_{x_2}\rho)\partial_\theta \Big).$$

It it an elementary computation to check that the three vector fields $(X, X_\perp, V)$ form a global basis of $T(SM)$ (we recover that SM is trivialisable) and satisfy the commutation relations

$$[X_\perp, V] = -X, \quad [X, X_\perp] = -\kappa(x)V, \tag{2.2}$$

where $\kappa(x)$ is the Gaussian curvature of g at x. In isothermal coordinates, a computation yields

$$\kappa(x) = e^{-2\rho(x)} \Delta_x \rho(x)$$

where $\Delta_x = -(\partial_{x_1}^2 + \partial_{x_2}^2)$.

We define the *Sasaki metric* of g as the metric G on SM so that $(X, X_\perp, V)$ is an orthonormal basis, and its volume form dv_G is also equal to the Liouville measure $d\mu_L$ obtained from the symplectic form $\omega = d\alpha$ by setting $d\mu_L = |\alpha \wedge d\alpha|$ when we use the identification $S^*M \to SM$. In isothermal coordinates, one has

$$d\mu_L(x, \theta) = e^{2\rho(x)} dx d\theta.$$

If $W = aX + bX_\perp + cV$, we have

$$G(W, W) = a^2 + b^2 + c^2 = g(d\pi_0(W), d\pi_0(W)) + c^2.$$

The Sasaki metric is usually defined using the splitting of the vertical bundle and horizontal bundle (see [**Pa**]), but it coincides in our case with the definition above. Here $(X, X_\perp)$ span the horizontal bundle while V span the vertical bundle of the fibration $\pi_0 : SM \to M$.

Exercise: Check, using Cartan formula, that the following Lie derivatives vanish:

$$\forall Z \in \{X, X_\perp, V\}, \ \mathcal{L}_Z d\mu_L = 0.$$

As a consequence, we have $X^* = -X$, $V^* = -V$ and $X_\perp^* = -X_\perp$ on $C_0^\infty(SM)$ with respect to the $L^2(SM, d\mu_L)$ product, where $C_0^\infty(SM)$ is the set of smooth functions on SM vanishing at the boundary $\partial(SM)$ of SM.

On $SM \subset TM$, we can consider functions which are restrictions to SM of homogeneous polynomials of order $m \in \mathbb{N}_0$ in the fibers of TM, i.e. symmetric tensors defined as sections of $\otimes_S^m T^*M$. There is a natural map for each $m \in \mathbb{N}_0$

$$\pi_m^* : C^\infty(M, \otimes_S^m T^*M) \to C^\infty(SM), \quad \pi_m^* f(x, v) := f(x)(\otimes^m v). \tag{2.3}$$

2.4. Conjugate points. Geodesic flows can have 1-parameter families of geodesics with the same endpoints x_-, x_+: this is related to the existence of *conjugate points*. We say that $x_\pm \in M$ are conjugate points if there exist $v_\pm \in S_{x_\pm}M$ and t_0 so that $\varphi_{t_0}(x_-, v_-) = (x_+, v_+)$, and if

$$d\varphi_{t_0}(x_-, v_-).V \in \mathbb{R}V$$

where V is the vertical vector field. Equivalently, we say that $x_\pm$ are conjugate if there is an *orthogonal Jacobi field* $J = J(t)$ along the geodesic $(x(t))_{t\in[0,t_0]}$ vanishing at x_- and x_+. Recall that an orthogonal Jacobi field is a vector field along $x(t)$, orthogonal to $\dot{x}(t) = v(t)$. If we write $v^\perp(t) = R_{\pi/2}(v(t))$ the unit orthogonal vector obtained by a rotation of angle $\pi/2$ of $v(t)$, such a field would be of the form $J(t) = a(t)v^\perp(t)$, and for it to be a Jacobi field the function $a(t)$ has to satisfy:

$$a(0) = a(t_0) = 0, \quad \ddot{a}(t) + \kappa(x(t))a(t) = 0.$$

Exercise: Show that when the Gauss curvature κ is non-positive, there are no conjugate points.

By Gauss-Bonnet theorem, for a geodesic triangle with interior angles $\alpha_1, \alpha_2, \alpha_3$, one has

$$\int_M \kappa\, \mathrm{dvol}_g + \pi = \sum_{i=1}^{3} \alpha_i.$$

If two geodesics have the same endpoints x_-, x_+, we obtain a triangle with angles π, α_2, α_3, and this forces by Gauss-Bonnet to have some positive curvature somewhere. In fact, it can be proved that absence of conjugate points implies that between two points x_-, x_+, there is a unique geodesic – this is done using the *index form*, see [**Mi**, Sections 14 & 15].

3. Scattering map, length function and X-ray transform

3.1. Lens rigidity problem. We start by making the *non-trapping* assumption on the geodesic flow. That is, for each $(x, v) \in SM^\circ$ there is a unique $\ell_+(x, v) \geq 0$ and $\ell_-(x, v) \leq 0$ so that $\varphi_{\ell_\pm(x,v)}(x, v) \in \partial SM$, which means that each geodesic of SM has finite length.

Exercise: Prove, using the strict convexity of ∂M and the implicit function theorem, that $\ell_\pm$ are smooth in SM° and that they extend smoothly to $SM\backslash\partial_0 SM$. Show also that $\ell_\pm$ extend continuously to SM in a way that $\ell_\pm|_{\partial_\pm SM\cup\partial_0 SM} = 0$. We will still call $\ell_\pm$ these continous extensions.

DEFINITION 3.1. *The function ℓ_+ is called the length function and $\ell_g := \ell_+|_{\partial SM}$ is called the* boundary length function. *The map*

$$S_g : \partial_- SM \to \partial_+ SM, \quad S_g(x, v) = \varphi_{\ell_+(x,v)}(x, v)$$

is called the scattering map *of g.*

We introduced these objects to formulate some questions in the realm of inverse problems. They are quantities that can be measured from the boundary. The boundary length function contains the set of Riemannian distances between boundary points, but it does contain a priori more information in the case where there are several geodesics between boundary points. The scattering map tells where geodesics leave SM.

DEFINITION 3.2. *The X-ray transform on functions on SM is defined as the operator*

$$I : C^\infty(SM) \to C^\infty(\partial_- SM), \quad If(x,v) = \int_0^{\ell_+(x,v)} f(\varphi_t(x,v))dt.$$

The X-ray on symmetric tensors of order m is the operator

$$I_m := I\pi_m^* : C^\infty(M, \otimes_S^m T^*M) \to C^\infty(\partial_- SM).$$

The two main inverse problems related to these objects are:

Problem 1: Determine the kernel of I_m and invert I_m on $\mathrm{Ran}(I_m|_{(\ker I_m)^\perp})$.

Problem 2: Do (S_g, ℓ_g) determine the metric g up to Gauge invariance ?

The natural *Gauge invariance* in Problem 2 is the diffeomorphism action: let $\mathrm{Diff}_{\partial M}(M)$ be the group of diffeomorphism of M which are equal to the identity on ∂M, then one has for each $\psi \in \mathrm{Diff}(M)$

$$S_{\psi^* g} = S_g, \quad \ell_{\psi^* g} = \ell_g.$$

Problem 2 is called the *lens rigidity problem* and (S_g, ℓ_g) is the *lens data.*

There is a link between these inverse problems. Indeed, one has

LEMMA 3.3. *Let $g_s = e^{2\rho_s} g_0$ be some smooth 1-parameter family of non-trapping metrics with strictly convex boundary and no conjugate points, where ρ_s is a smooth family of smooth functions on M such that $\rho_0 = 0$. If $(\ell_{g_s}, S_{g_s}) = (\ell_{g_0}, S_{g_0})$ for each $s \in (-\epsilon, \epsilon)$, then $I_0(\rho_0') = 0$ if I_0 is the X-ray transform on functions for g_0 and $\rho_0' := \partial_s \rho_s|_{s=0}$.*

PROOF. Fix $(x,v) \in \partial_- SM$ and $(x', v') = S_{g_0}(x,v) = S_{g_s}(x,v)$. We differentiate

$$\ell_{g_s}(x,v) = \int_0^{\ell_{g_0}(x,v)} e^{\rho_s(\gamma_s(t,x,v))} |\dot\gamma_s(t,x,v)|_{g_0(\gamma_s(t,x,v))} dt$$

with respect to s, where $\gamma_s(t,x,v)$ is the unique geodesic for g_s relating x and x'. Using the fact that $\gamma_0(t,x,v)$ is the unique geodesic for g_0 relating x and x', it minimizes the length functional among curves with endpoints x, x' and thus it is direct to see that

$$0 = \int_0^{\ell_{g_0}(x,v)} \rho_0'(\gamma_0(t,x,v))dt + \partial_s(L^{g_0}_{x_-,x_+}(\gamma_s))|_{s=0} = I_0(\rho_0')(x,v)$$

where $L^{g_0}_{p,q}(\gamma)$ denotes the length of a curve γ joining p, q for the metric g_0. □

This corresponds to analyzing *deformation lens rigidity* within a conformal class. More generally we have (with essentially the same proof):

LEMMA 3.4. *Let g_s be some smooth 1-parameter family of non-trapping metrics with strictly convex boundary and no conjugate points. If $(\ell_{g_s}, S_{g_s}) = (\ell_{g_0}, S_{g_0})$ for each $s \in (-\epsilon, \epsilon)$, then $I_2(g_0') = 0$ if I_2 is the X-ray transform on symmetric 2-tensors for g_0 and $g_0' := \partial_s g_s|_{s=0} \in C^\infty(M; \otimes_S^2 T^*M)$.*

These two lemmas are folklore and the ideas appear already in Guillemin-Kazhdan [**GuKa**] and the Siberian school (Mukhometov, Anikonov, Sharafutdinov, etc).

Remark that if $\psi_s : M \to M$ is a smooth family of diffeomorphisms which are equal to Id on ∂M, we have an associated vector field $Z(x) = \partial_s \psi_s(x)|_{s=0}$ with $Z|_{\partial M} = 0$ and, according to Lemma 3.4, $\mathcal{L}_Z g_0 = \partial_s(\psi_s^* g_0)|_{s=0}$ satisfies $I_2(\mathcal{L}_Z g_0) = 0$ if I_2 is the X-ray transform for g_0 on symmetric 2-tensors. The natural question about the kernel of X-ray transform is then: under which conditions on g_0 do we have

$$\ker I_0 = 0 \text{ ? and } \ker I_2 = \{\mathcal{L}_Z g_0; Z \in C^\infty(M, TM), Z|_{\partial M} = 0\} \text{ ?}$$

3.2. Boundary rigidity problem. When the metric g has strictly convex boundary, is non-trapping and satisfies that between each pair of points $x, x' \in M$ there is a unique geodesic, we say that g is *simple*. In this case, knowing the lens data is equivalent to knowing the restriction $d_g|_{\partial M \times \partial M}$ of the Riemannian distance $d_g : M \times M \to \mathbb{R}^+$. The lens rigidity problem is called *boundary rigidity problem* in that setting.

4. Resolvents and boundary value problems for transport equations

For a general metric g on SM with strictly convex boundary, we define the incoming tail Γ_- and outgoing tails as the sets

$$\Gamma_- := \{(x,v) \in SM; \ell_+(x,v) = +\infty\}, \quad \Gamma_+ := \{(x,v) \in SM; \ell_-(x,v) = -\infty\}.$$

These sets correspond to the set of points which are on geodesics that are trapped inside SM° in forward (for Γ_-) and backward (for Γ_+) time. They are closed sets in SM°. The trapped set is defined by

$$K := \Gamma_+ \cap \Gamma_-,$$

it corresponds to trajectories contained entirely in the interior SM°. It is a closed set in SM, invariant by the geodesic flow, and by the strict convexity of the boundary ∂M, we actually have $K \subset SM^\circ$, since each point $(x,v) \in \partial_\mp SM$ is not in $\Gamma_\pm$ and each point $(x,v) \in \partial_0 SM$ has $\ell_+(x,v) = \ell_-(x,v) = 0$.

4.1. Resolvents in physical half-planes. Assume that $\Gamma_\pm = \emptyset$, i.e the metric is non-trapping. There are two natural boundary value problems for the transport equations associated to X. For $f \in C^\infty(SM)$, find $u_\pm$ in some fixed functional space solving (in the distribution sense)

$$\begin{cases} -Xu_\pm = f \\ u_\pm|_{\partial_\pm SM} = 0 \end{cases}$$

One is an incoming Dirichlet type boundary condition and the other one is an ougoing Dirichlet type boundary condition. Moreover, it is easy to check that

$$u_+(x,v) = \int_0^{\ell_+(x,v)} f(\varphi_t(x,v))dt, \quad u_-(x,v) = -\int_{\ell_-(x,v)}^0 f(\varphi_t(x,v))dt$$

are solutions, and in fact they are the only continuous solutions: indeed the difference of two solutions would be constant along flow lines and, under the non-trapping condition each point in SM is on a flow line with two endpoints in $\partial_+ SM$ and $\partial_- SM$. We see in particular that

$$f \in C^\infty(SM) \Longrightarrow u_\pm \in C^\infty(SM \setminus \partial_0 SM).$$

Without assuming the non-trapping condition, we can proceed using the resolvent of X.

LEMMA 4.1. *For* $\mathrm{Re}(\lambda) > 0$, *there exist two operators* $R_\pm(\lambda) : C^\infty(SM) \to C^0(SM)$ *satisfying for all* $f \in C^\infty(SM)$ *(in the distribution sense)*

$$\begin{cases} (-X \pm \lambda)R_\pm(\lambda)f = f, \\ R_\pm(\lambda)f|_{\partial_\pm SM} = 0. \end{cases}$$

They are given by the expressions

$$\begin{aligned} R_+(\lambda)f(x,v) &= \int_0^{\ell_+(x,v)} e^{-\lambda t} f(\varphi_t(x,v))dt, \\ R_-(\lambda)f(x,v) &= -\int_{\ell_-(x,v)}^0 e^{\lambda t} f(\varphi_t(x,v))dt. \end{aligned} \tag{4.1}$$

PROOF. Lebesgue theorem shows directly that $R_\pm(\lambda)f$ are continuous if f is continuous. The fact that they solve the desired boundary value problem for $\mathrm{Re}(\lambda)$ large enough follows from the fact that $X(f(\varphi_t(x,v))) = \partial_t(f(\varphi_t(x,v))$ and the estimate

$$|d(f\circ\varphi_t)|_G \le |df|_G |d\varphi_t|_G, \quad |d\varphi_t|_G \le Ce^{Ct}$$

for some $C > 0$ depending on X. Then, we get that for each $f' \in C_c^\infty(SM^\circ)$ and $\mathrm{Re}(\lambda) > 0$

$$\langle (-X \pm \lambda)R_\pm(\lambda)f, f'\rangle = \langle R_\pm(\lambda)f, (X \pm \lambda)f'\rangle$$

where the pairing uses the measure μ_L, and the left hand side is equal to $\langle f, f'\rangle$ for $\mathrm{Re}(\lambda) > C$, thus by using that the right hand side is analytic in $\mathrm{Re}(\lambda) > 0$, the right hand side is equal to $\langle f, f'\rangle$ in that half-plane. $\square$

Exercise: Show that the operators $R_\pm(\lambda)$ extend analytically in $\lambda \in \mathbb{C}$ as operators

$$R_\pm(\lambda) : C_c^\infty(SM^\circ \setminus \Gamma_\pm) \to C^\infty(SM).$$

If we assume that $\mu_L(\Gamma_\pm) = 0$, we can then expect to extend $R_\pm(0)$ to some L^p space by some density argument. In fact, observe that

$$|R_+(0)f(x,v)| \le ||f||_{L^\infty}\ell_+(x,v),$$

thus $\ell_+ \in L^p(SM)$ implies that $R_+(0) : C^0(SM) \to L^p(SM)$ is bounded.

4.2. Santalo formula. The Santalo formula describes the desintegration of the measure μ_L along flow lines.

LEMMA 4.2. *Assume that* $\mu_L(\Gamma_\pm) = 0$ *and let* $f \in L^1(SM)$, *then the following formula holds*

$$\int_{SM} f d\mu_L = \int_{\partial_- SM}\int_0^{\ell_+(x,v)} f(\varphi_t(x,v))dt\, d\mu_\nu(x,v),$$

where $d\mu_\nu(x,v) = \langle v,\nu\rangle_g \iota_{\partial SM}^* \mathrm{dv}_G$ *is a measure on* ∂SM, dv_G *being the Riemannian measure of the Sasaki metric viewed as a* 3*-form.*

PROOF. We first take $f \in C_c^\infty(SM^\circ \setminus \Gamma_+)$ and write $f = -XR_+(0)f$ with $R_+(0)f = 0$ on $\partial_+ SM$. Thus using Green's formula

$$\int_{SM} f d\mu_L = -\int_{SM} X(R_+(0)f)d\mu_L = \int_{\partial SM} (R_+(0)f)|_{\partial SM}\langle X, N\rangle_G\, \iota_{\partial SM}^*\mathrm{dv}_G$$

if N is the unit inward pointing normal to ∂SM for G. The unit normal N satisfies $d\pi_0(N) = \nu$ and $G(N,V) = 0$ if ν is the exterior pointing unit normal to ∂M for g, since the vertical bundle $\mathbb{R}V = \ker d\pi_0$ is tangent to ∂SM. Then we get

$\langle N, X\rangle_G = \langle \nu, v\rangle_g$ and we use a density argument for the general case to end the proof. Note that an alternative definition of $d\mu_\nu$ is $d\mu_\nu = \iota^*_{\partial SM} i_X d\mu_L$. □

4.3. Boundedness in (weighted) L^2 spaces and limiting absorbtion principle. The operators $R_\pm(\lambda)$ are also bounded on $L^2(SM)$ for $\mathrm{Re}(\lambda) > 0$. Indeed, using the Santalo formula and defining $f(\varphi_t(x,v)) := 0$ when $t \geq \ell_+(x,v)$, we have

$$\begin{aligned}\int_{SM} |f(\varphi_t(x,v))|^2 d\mu_L(x,v) &= \int_{\partial_- SM} \int_0^{\ell_+(x,v)} |f(\varphi_{t+s}(x,v))|^2 ds\, d\mu_\nu(x,v)\\ &= \int_{\partial_- SM} \int_t^{\ell_+(x,v)} |f(\varphi_u(x,v))|^2 du\, d\mu_\nu(x,v)\\ &\leq ||f||_{L^2(SM)}.\end{aligned}$$

We can write using Minkowski inequality

$$\begin{aligned}||R_+(\lambda)f||_{L^2(SM)} &\leq \Big(\int_{SM} \Big(\int_0^{+\infty} e^{-\mathrm{Re}(\lambda)t}|f(\varphi_t(x,v))|dt\Big)^2 d\mu_L(x,v)\Big)^{\frac{1}{2}}\\ &\leq \int_0^{+\infty} e^{-\mathrm{Re}(\lambda)t}||f\circ\varphi_t||_{L^2(SM)}dt \leq \frac{||f||_{L^2(SM)}}{\mathrm{Re}(\lambda)}.\end{aligned}$$

The question of the extension of $R_\pm(\lambda)$ up to the imaginary line in a certain functional space is very similar to the so-called *limiting absorbtion principle* in quantum scattering theory. To make the parallel, recall that the Laplacian on $L^2(\mathbb{R}^3)$ is self-adjoint as an unbounded operator, its spectrum is $[0,\infty)$ and its resolvent is the operator defined for $\mathrm{Im}(\lambda) > 0$ by

$$R_\Delta(\lambda) = (\Delta - \lambda^2)^{-1} : L^2(\mathbb{R}^3) \to L^2(\mathbb{R}^3)$$

and there is an explicit formula for its integral kernel

$$R_\Delta(\lambda; x, x') = C\frac{e^{i\lambda|x-x'|}}{|x-x'|}$$

for some explicit constant $C \in \mathbb{R}$. Now when $\lambda \in \mathbb{R}$, this is not anymore a bounded operator on L^2 but it makes sense as an operator

$$R_\Delta(\lambda) : \langle x\rangle^{-1/2-\epsilon}L^2(\mathbb{R}^3) \to \langle x\rangle^{1/2+\epsilon}L^2(\mathbb{R}^3) \tag{4.2}$$

and both $R_\Delta(\lambda)$ and $R_\Delta(-\lambda)$ are inverses for $(\Delta - \lambda^2)$ (here $\langle x\rangle := (1+x^2)^{1/2}$). They are called the incoming and outgoing resolvents on the spectrum, and they need to be applied on functions which have some decay near infinity. Such property also holds in higher dimension. A result of Kenig-Ruiz-Sogge [**KRS**] shows that for $\lambda \in \mathbb{R}^*$

$$R_\Delta(\lambda) : L^p(\mathbb{R}^n) \to L^q(\mathbb{R}^n), \quad p = \frac{2n}{n+2}, \quad \frac{1}{p} + \frac{1}{q} = 1.$$

We will discuss similar properties for the resolvent of the flow vector field $-X$. The first boundedness property we describe is comparable to (4.2).

LEMMA 4.3. *For each $\lambda \in i\mathbb{R}$ and $\epsilon > 0$, the resolvent $R_\pm(\lambda)$ is bounded as a map*

$$R_\pm(\lambda) : \langle \ell_+\rangle^{-1/2-\epsilon}L^2(SM) \to \langle \ell_+\rangle^{1/2+\epsilon}L^2(SM).$$

Proof. We do the case $R_+(0)$, the other frequencies λ are similar. First we notice that $\ell_+(\varphi_s(y)) = \ell_+(y) - s$. Then for $f \in C^\infty(SM)$ and $\widetilde{f} := \langle \ell_+\rangle^{-1/2-\epsilon} f$ we have

$$\begin{aligned}
&\int_{SM} |R_+(0)\widetilde{f}(y)|^2 \langle \ell_+(y)\rangle^{-1-2\epsilon} d\mu_L(y)\\
&\leq \int_{\partial_- SM}\int_0^{\ell_+(y)} \langle \ell_+(y)-s\rangle^{-1-2\epsilon}\Big(\int_0^{\ell_+(y)-s} \widetilde{f}(\varphi_{t+s}(y))dt\Big)^2 ds d\mu_\nu(y)\\
&\leq \int_{\partial_- SM}\int_0^{\ell_+(y)} \langle \ell_+(y)-s\rangle^{-1-2\epsilon}\int_0^{\ell_+(y)-s} \langle \ell_+(y)-s-t\rangle^{-1-2\epsilon} dt\\
&\quad\times \int_0^{\ell_+(y)-s} |f(\varphi_{t+s}(y))|^2 dt d\mu_\nu(y) ds\\
&\leq C\int_{\partial_- SM}\int_0^{\ell_+(y)} \langle \ell_+(y)-s\rangle^{-1-2\epsilon}\int_0^{\ell_+(y)-s} |f(\varphi_{t+s}(y))|^2 dt d\mu_\nu(y) ds\\
&\leq C\int_{\partial_- SM}\int_0^{\ell_+(y)} \langle \ell_+(y)-s\rangle^{-1-2\epsilon}\int_0^{\ell_+(y)} |f(\varphi_u(y))|^2 du d\mu_\nu(y) ds\\
&\leq C^2\int_{\partial_- SM}\int_0^{\ell_+(y)} |f(\varphi_u(y))|^2 du d\mu_\nu(y) \leq C^2 ||f||^2_{L^2(SM)}
\end{aligned}$$

where we have used that there is $C > 0$ depending only on ϵ so that

$$\int_0^{a-s} \langle a-s-t\rangle^{-1-2\epsilon} dt \leq C.$$

To complete the proof, we use the density of smooth functions in L^2. □

A priori, it is not clear that the space $\langle \ell_+\rangle^{1/2+\epsilon} L^2(SM)$ can be embedded into the space of distributions on SM, since the function ℓ_+ could explode quite drastically at Γ_-. To quantify this, we define the *non-escaping mass function*:

$$V(T) := \mathrm{Vol}_{\mu_L}(\{y \in SM^\circ; \varphi_t(y) \in SM^\circ, \forall t \in [0,T]\}) = \mathrm{Vol}_{\mu_L}(\ell_+^{-1}([T,+\infty]))$$

which is like the repartition function of ℓ_+. The Cavalieri principle gives

$$||\ell_+||^p_{L^p} \leq C\Big(1 + \int_1^\infty t^{p-1}V(t)dt\Big).$$

Recall that $\ell_+(x,-v) = -\ell_-(x,v)$ thus the L^p norms of ℓ_+ and ℓ_- are the same since the involution $(x,v) \to (x,-v)$ preserves μ_L.

Lemma 4.4. *For $p \in [1,\infty)$ we have the boundedness properties*

$$R_\pm(0) : C^0(SM) \to L^p(SM) \text{ if } \int_1^\infty V(t)t^{p-1}dt < \infty,$$

and for $p > 1$

$$R_\pm(0) : L^p(SM) \to L^1(SM) \text{ if } \int_1^\infty V(t)t^{1/(p-1)}dt < \infty.$$

Proof. Left as an exercise. Use Hölder and Santalo formula. □

4.4. Return on X-ray transform. First we remark that the X-ray transform can be defined also in the trapping case as a map

$$I : C_c^\infty(SM \setminus \Gamma_+) \to C^\infty(\partial_- SM);$$

and for a function $f \in C_c^\infty(SM \setminus \Gamma_+)$ this can be written as

$$If(x, v) = (R_+(0)f)(x, v) \quad (x, v) \in \partial_- SM.$$

If $\widetilde{f} = \langle \ell_+ \rangle^{-1/2-\epsilon/2} f$, we have

$$\begin{aligned}\int_{\partial_- SM} |I\widetilde{f}(y)|^2 d\mu_\nu(y) &= \int_{\partial_- SM} \Big| \int_0^{\ell_+(y)} \langle \ell_+(y) - t \rangle^{-1/2-\epsilon/2} f(\varphi_t(y)) dt \Big|^2 d\mu_\nu(y) \\ &\leq C \int_{\partial_- SM} \int_0^{\ell_+(y)} |f(\varphi_t(y))|^2 dt d\mu_\nu(y) = C ||f||^2_{L^2(SM)}\end{aligned}$$

and therefore

$$I : \langle \ell_+ \rangle^{-1/2-\epsilon} L^2(SM) \to L^2(\partial_- SM, d\mu_\nu)$$

is bounded for each $\epsilon > 0$. It is a straightforward consequence of Santalo formula that

$$I : L^1(SM) \to L^1(\partial_- SM, d\mu_\nu)$$

is bounded. We get, just as for $R_\pm(0)$, the following boundedness property

LEMMA 4.5. *When $p > 2$, the X-ray transform is bounded as a map $L^p(SM) \to L^2(\partial_- SM, d\mu_\nu)$ if $\int_1^\infty t^{p/(p-2)} V(t) dt < \infty$*

PROOF. Use the Hölder and Santalo formulas. □

As a consequence, taking the adjoint, we obtain the boundedness

$$I^* : L^2(\partial_- SM, d\mu_\nu) \to L^{p'}(SM)$$

under the assumption $\int_1^\infty t^{p/(p-2)} V(t) dt < \infty$ and in general the boundedness of

$$I^* : L^2(\partial_- SM, d\mu_\nu) \to \langle \ell_+ \rangle^{1/2+\epsilon} L^2(SM)$$

holds for all $\epsilon > 0$. We would like to characterize what operator is I^*. For f, f' smooth supported oustide $\Gamma_- \cup \Gamma_+$, we have

$$\begin{aligned}\int_{\partial_- SM} If.f' d\mu_\nu &= \int_{\partial_- SM} R_+(0)f.f' d\mu_\nu \\ &= \int_{SM} -X(R_+(0)f).\mathcal{E}_-(f') d\mu_L = \langle f, \mathcal{E}_-(f') \rangle\end{aligned}$$

where $\mathcal{E}_-(f')$ solves

$$\begin{cases} X\mathcal{E}_-(f') = 0, \\ \mathcal{E}_-(f')|_{\partial_- SM} = f' \end{cases}$$

We thus get $I^* = \mathcal{E}_-$. Notice that $\mathcal{E}_-(f')(y) = f'(\varphi_{\ell_-(y)}(y))$ is constant on flow lines.

4.5. The normal operator. Assume that $\mu_L(\Gamma_-\cup\Gamma_+)=0$. We define the normal operator on SM as the operator given by the expression

$$\Pi:\langle\ell_+\rangle^{-1/2-\epsilon}L^2(SM)\to\langle\ell_+\rangle^{1/2+\epsilon}L^2(SM),\quad \Pi:=I^*I.$$

By Lemma 4.5, we see that if $\int_1^\infty V(t)t^{p/(p-2)}dt<\infty$ for some $p>2$, then Π extends as a bounded operator

$$\Pi:L^p(SM)\to L^{p'}(SM).$$

We can relate Π to the operators $R_\pm(0)$.

LEMMA 4.6. *The following identity holds true if* $\mu_L(\Gamma_-\cup\Gamma_+)=0$

$$\Pi=R_+(0)-R_-(0).$$

PROOF. Note that as operators acting on $C_c^\infty(SM^\circ)$, we have $R_+(0)^*=-R_-(0)$ thus we need to prove

$$\langle I^*If,f\rangle=2\langle R_+(0)f,f\rangle.$$

But we have for each $f\in C_c^\infty(SM\setminus\Gamma_+)$

$$\int_{SM}R_+(0)f.fd\mu_L=-\int_{SM}X(R_+(0)f).R_+(0)fd\mu_L=-\frac{1}{2}\int_{SM}X((R_+(0)f)^2)d\mu_L$$
$$=\frac{1}{2}\int_{\partial SM}|R_+(0)f|^2d\mu_\nu=\frac{1}{2}\int_{\partial_-SM}|If|^2d\mu_\nu.$$

and we complete the proof using a density argument. □

Using this, let us characterize the kernel of I:

LEMMA 4.7. *Assume* $\int_1^\infty V(t)t^{p/(p-2)}dt<\infty$ *for some* $p>2$, *then* $f\in\ker I\cap C^0(SM)$ *if and only there exists a unique* $u\in L^p(SM)\cap C^0(SM\setminus K)$ *such that*

$$Xu=f,\quad u|_{\partial SM}=0,$$

K being the trapped set. If $K=\emptyset$ and if $f\in C^\infty(SM)$ vanishes to infinite order at ∂SM, then $u\in C^\infty(SM)$ and u vanishes to infinite order at ∂SM.

PROOF. Assume that $If=0$. Set $u=-R_+(0)f$, then $Xu=f$, $u\in C^0(SM\setminus\Gamma_-)$ and satisfies $u|_{\partial_+SM}=0$. We have $\Pi f=0$, thus by Lemma 4.6, $u=-R_+(0)f=-R_-(0)f$. Thus u is actually in $C^0(SM\setminus\Gamma_-)$ and vanishes on ∂_-SM. Since there is no solution of $Xu=0$ with $u|_{\partial SM}=0$ and $u\in L^1(SM)\cap C^0(SM\setminus K)$, we have proved one direction. Conversely, if $u\in L^1(SM)\cap C^0(SM\setminus K)$ satisfies $Xu=f$ in the distribution sense, then $u=-R_+(0)f$ by uniqueness of solutions with $u|_{\partial_+SM}=0$, and similarly $u=-R_-(0)f$. Thus $I^*If=\Pi f=0$ and therefore $If=0$ since $\langle\Pi f,f\rangle=|If|^2_{L^2}$. The fact that u is smooth when g has no trapped set and $f\in C^\infty(SM)$ vanishes to infinite order at ∂SM is direct from the expression (4.1). Notice that if f is smooth but does not vanish to infinite order at ∂SM, then it is not clear that u is smooth at ∂_0SM. □

We have just seen that f being in $\ker I$ can be interpreted in terms of properties of solutions of the transport equation $Xu=f$. In fact, the regularity of the solutions u to $Xu=f$ will be very important for what follows, and this leads us to define the following

DEFINITION 4.8. *We shall say that a metric g with strictly convex boundary has the smooth Livsic property if for each $f\in C^\infty(SM)$ satisfying $If=0$, there exists a unique $u\in C^\infty(SM)$ such that $Xu=f$ and $u|_{\partial SM}=0$.*

Pestov-Uhlmann [**PeUh**] show the following result

THEOREM 1. *If g is a non-trapping metric on a surface M with and strictly convex boundary, then it satisfies the smooth Livsic property.*

The main difficulty is the regularity at the glancing region $\partial_0 SM$, which is studied in the work of Pestov-Uhlmann using fold theory - we refer to [**PeUh**] for the interested reader (where fold theory is recalled). We notice that the presence or absence of conjugate points is not relevant here, since this result is really a property on the flow on SM and has not much to do with the fact that we are working with a geodesic flow.

In the recent work [**Gu**], we show the following result by using techniques of microlocal analysis and anisotropic Sobolev spaces:

THEOREM 2. *If the curvature of g near the trapped set K is negative (or more generally if K is a hyperbolic set for the geodesic flow of g), then g has the smooth Livsic property.*

We notice that $V(t) = \mathcal{O}(e^{-Qt})$ for some $Q > 0$ if K is a hyperbolic set by [**BoRu**] (see [**Gu**, Proposition 2.4]), and this implies that $\ell_\pm \in L^p$ for all $p < \infty$.

5. Injectivity of X-ray transform for tensors

In this section, we use the Pestov identity (that we will explain below) as in [**PSU1**] and the results of previous section to prove the injectivity of X-ray transform on functions and divergence-free 1-forms when the metric has no conjugate points. For 2-tensors, we use the method of [**GuKa**] to determine the kernel of I_2 when the curvature κ is non-positive.

First, we denote by D the symmetrized covariant derivative mapping 1-forms to symmetric 2-tensors by

$$Dw(Y_1, Y_2) := \tfrac{1}{2}((\nabla_{Y_1} w)(Y_2) + (\nabla_{Y_2} w)(Y_1)). \tag{5.1}$$

Its L^2-adjoint is denoted D^* and is called the divergence operator on symmetric 2-tensors. We notice that if $w^\sharp$ is the vector field dual to w, then Dw can be written in terms of Lie derivative of the metric

$$Dw = \tfrac{1}{2}\mathcal{L}_{w^\sharp} g. \tag{5.2}$$

It will be convenient to use the Fourier decomposition in the circle fibers of SM. Using the vertical vector field, we can decompose each function $u \in C^\infty(SM)$ uniquely as a converging sum (in any C^k norms)

$$u = \sum_{k\in\mathbb{Z}} u_k, \qquad \text{with } Vu_k = iku_k$$

where $u_k \in C^\infty(SM)$. This gives an orthogonal (with respect to L^2) decomposition

$$C^\infty(SM) = \bigoplus_{k\in\mathbb{Z}} \Omega_k$$

where $\Omega_k = \ker(V - ik)$. In isothermal coordinates $x = (x_1, x_2)$ near a point x_0, one has associated coordinates (x, θ) on SM near $S_{x_0}M$ with $\theta \in \mathbb{R}/2\pi\mathbb{Z}$, see Section 2.3. Then the functions u_k can be written locally as $u_k(x, \theta) = \tilde{u}_k(x)e^{ik\theta}$ for some $\tilde{u}_k$ smooth on M. In fact, when $k \geq 0$, Ω_k can be identified to the space of smooth sections of the k-th tensor power of the complex line bundle $\mathcal{K} := (T^*M)^{1,0} \subset$

$\mathbb{C}T^*M$ in the sense that $u_k = \pi_k^* s_k$ for some section $s_k \in C^\infty(M; \otimes_S^k \mathcal{K})$ where π_k^* is the map (2.3). Similalry when $k < 0$, Ω_k can be identitifed as the space of smooth sections of the k-th tensor power of the bundle $\overline{\mathcal{K}} := (T^*M)^{0,1}$.

There are two natural operators on $C^\infty(SM)$ called raising and lowering operators, introduced by [**GuKa**], and defined by

$$\eta_+ := \tfrac{1}{2}(X + iX_\perp), \quad \eta_- := \tfrac{1}{2}(X - iX_\perp).$$

They satisfy $\eta_\pm : \Omega_k \to \Omega_{k\pm 1}$, $X = \eta_+ + \eta_-$ and $\eta_+^* = -\eta_-$ when acting on smooth functions vanishing at ∂SM.

THEOREM 3. *Assume that (M, g) has strictly convex boundary and that g has the smooth Livsic property and no conjugate points. Then we have:*
1) I_0 is injective on $C^\infty(M)$.
2) If $a \in C^\infty(M; T^*M)) \cap \ker I_1$, then there exists $f \in C^\infty(M)$ such that $a = df$ and $f|_{\partial M} = 0$.
3) Assume that $\kappa \leq 0$. If $h \in C^\infty(M; \otimes_S^2 T^*M) \cap \ker I_2$, then there exists a 1-form $w \in C^\infty(M; T^*M)$ such that $h = Dw$ and $w|_{\partial M} = 0$, where D is the symmetrized covariant derivative.

PROOF. If $f \in \ker I_0$, by Theorem 2 there is $u \in C^\infty(SM)$ such that $u|_{\partial SM} = 0$ and $Xu = \pi_0^* f$. Thus $VXu = 0$ since $d\pi_0(V) = 0$. We have $(VX)^* = XV$ on smooth functions vanishing at ∂SM by using that V, X preserve μ_L and that V is tangent to ∂SM. Then we get

$$||VXu||_{L^2}^2 = ||XVu||_{L^2}^2 + \langle [XV, VX]u, u\rangle$$

and

$$\begin{aligned}[XV, VX] =& XV^2X - VX^2V = VXVX + X_\perp VX - VXVX - VXX_\perp \\ =& V[X_\perp, X] - X^2 = -X^2 + V\kappa V.\end{aligned}$$

This implies the *Pestov identity* for each $u \in C^\infty(SM)$ vanishing at ∂SM

$$||XVu||_{L^2}^2 - \langle \kappa Vu, Vu\rangle + ||Xu||_{L^2}^2 - ||VXu||_{L^2}^2 = 0. \tag{5.3}$$

We conclude that since $VXu = 0$, $\kappa \leq 0$ implies $Xu = \pi_0^* f = 0$. In fact, if there are no conjugate points, we claim that for each smooth function h on SM vanishing on ∂SM

$$||Xh||_{L^2}^2 - \langle \kappa h, h\rangle \geq 0$$

and this is equal to 0 only if $h = 0$. This is proved by using Santalo formula to decompose the integral along geodesics with initial points on $\partial_- SM \setminus \Gamma_-$ and then by using that the index form is non-negative for each of these geodesics, when there is no conjugate points along these geodesics (see for example [**PSU2**, Lemma 11.2]). This completes the proof of the injectivity of I_0 by taking $h = Vu$.

Now if $I_1 a = 0$, we have $u \in C^\infty(SM)$ such that $Xu = \pi_1^* a$ and $u|_{\partial SM} = 0$. We apply the Pestov identity (5.3): since a is a 1-form and V acts as the Hodge operator on pull-backs of 1-forms, we have $||V\pi_1^* a||_{L^2(SM)}^2 = ||\pi_1^* a||_{L^2(SM)}^2$ and (5.3) becomes

$$||XVu||_{L^2(SM)}^2 - \langle \kappa Vu, Vu\rangle = 0.$$

This implies that $Vu = 0$ and thus $u = \pi_0^* f$ for some $f \in C^\infty(M)$ vanishing on ∂M. Then $Xu = \pi_1^* df$ and this completes the proof since this is equal to $\pi_1^* a$.

Let $h \in C^\infty(M; \otimes_S^2 T^*M)$, then $\pi_2^* h = h_0 + h_2 + h_{-2}$ with $h_k \in \Omega_k$. If $I_2 h = 0$, there is $u \in C^\infty(SM)$ such that $Xu = \pi_2^* h$ and, after possibly replacing u by $\frac{1}{2}(u(x,v) - u(x,-v))$, we can always assume that u is odd with respect to the involution $A : (x,v) \mapsto (x,-v)$. Indeed, X maps even functions with respect to A to odd functions, and conversely. We will write $u = \sum_k u_k$ with $u_k \in \Omega_k$ and $u_{2k} = 0$ for all $k \in \mathbb{Z}$. Since $X = \eta_+ + \eta_-$, we have $\eta_+ u_{k-1} + \eta_- u_{k+1} = 0$ if $k \notin \{-2, 0, 2\}$. Next, using the commutation relation

$$\eta_- \eta_+ = \eta_+ \eta_- - \tfrac{1}{2} \kappa i V$$

which follows from (2.2), the fact that $u_k|_{\partial SM} = 0$ for all k and $\eta_+^* = -\eta_-$, we obtain

$$\begin{aligned}||\eta_+ u_{k+1}||_{L^2}^2 &= -\langle \eta_- \eta_+ u_{k+1}, u_{k+1}\rangle = -\langle \eta_+ \eta_- u_{k+1}, u_{k+1}\rangle - \tfrac{1}{2}(k+1)\langle \kappa u_{k+1}, u_{k+1}\rangle \\ &\geq ||\eta_- u_{k+1}||^2\end{aligned}$$

for $k+1 \geq 0$, since $\kappa \leq 0$. For $k \geq 3$, this implies that $||\eta_+ u_{k+1}||_{L^2} \geq ||\eta_+ u_{k-1}||_{L^2}$ and therefore $c_k := ||\eta_+ u_k||_{L^2}$ is a non-decreasing series which converges to 0, that is $c_k = 0$ for all $k \geq 2$. A similar argument shows that $\eta_- u_k = 0$ for all $k \leq -2$. This shows that $u = u_1 + u_{-1}$ and $u = \pi_1^* w$ for some smooth 1-form w vanishing at ∂M. Now it is easy to check that $Xu = \pi_2^*(Dw)$. □

Remark that the proof given in 3) actually works as well for $\ker I_m$ with $m \geq 3$, and we obtain that $h \in \ker I_m$ if and only if $h = Dw$ for some $w \in C^\infty(M, \otimes_S^{m-1} T^*M)$ and D is the symmetrized covariant derivative, defined similarly to (5.1). Acting by X on a pull-back (by π_m^*) of an m-symmetric tensor w is equivalent to pull-back Dw on SM by π_{m+1}^*. A proof of the injectivity of I_m on divergence-free tensors for simple metrics was provided recently in [**PSU1**], without assuming $\kappa \leq 0$.

Combining Theorem 3 with Theorem 2 and Lemma 3.4, we deduce the

COROLLARY 5.1. *Let g_s be a smooth family of metrics on a surface M with strictly convex boundary, non-positive curvature and with either no trapped set or hyperbolic set. If the lens data (ℓ_{g_s}, S_{g_s}) is constant in s, then one has $g_s = \phi_s^* g_0$ where ϕ_s is a smooth family of diffeomorphism equal to Identity on ∂M.*

PROOF. Let $q_s := \partial_s g_s$. By Lemma 3.4, Theorem 3 and Theorem 2, we know that there is w_s so that $q_s = \mathcal{L}_{w_s^\sharp} g_s$ (with $w_s^\sharp$ the dual vector field to w_s though g_s). We claim that $w_s = (\Delta_{D_s})^{-1} D_s^* q_s$ if D_s is the operator D on 1-forms for g_s, D_s^* its adjoint with respect to the L^2-product of g_s and $\Delta_{D_s} := D_s^* D_s$ with Dirichlet condition. Indeed $\Delta_{D_s} w_s = D_s^* q_s = \Delta_{D_s}(\Delta_{D_s})^{-1} D_s^* q_s$ and the Laplacian Δ_{D_s} with Dirichlet condition has no kernel since $\langle \Delta_{D_s} u, u\rangle = ||D_s u||_{L^2}^2$ if $u|_{\partial M} = 0$, and $D_s u = 0$ with $u|_{\partial M} = 0$ implies $u = 0$ (check this as an exercise). Then, since g_s is smooth in s, it can be shown by elliptic theory that the inverse $\Delta_{D_s}^{-1}$ maps smooth functions of (s,x) to smooth functions of (s,x), if x is the variable on M. This implies that w_s is a smooth family in s of smooth 1-forms on M. Integrating the dual vector field $w_s^\sharp$, we can construct a smooth family of diffeomorphism which are the Identity on ∂M by $\partial_s \phi_s(x) = w_s^\sharp(\phi_s(x))$ and $\phi_0(x) = x$. Then ϕ_s satisfies $g_s = \phi_s^* g_0$. □

6. Some references

We haved worked in dimension 2 for simplicity but many results described here are also valid in higher dimension.

We provide a few references on the subject, this is not a comprehensive list.

We first recommend the lecture notes of Merry-Paternain [**Pa**] and the lecture notes of Sharafutdinov [**Sh**], which contain a lot of material on the subject. The survey of Croke [**Cr3**] also contains a nice overview of the subject (up to 2004).

The following articles deal with the boundary rigidity problem or the analysis of X-ray transform.

- For simple metrics in a fixed conformal class, Mukhometov [**Mu2**] proved that the boundary distance function determines the metric, with a stability estimate (see also the previous works [**Mu1**, **MuRo**]). This result was proved later with a simpler method by Croke [**Cr2**]. These works show the injectivity of the X-ray transform on functions for simple metrics (any dimension).
- The paper of Michel [**Mi**] established that simple metrics with constant curvature are boundary rigid in dimension 2. Gromov [**Gr**] proved the same result in higher dimension for flat metrics.
- Croke [**Cr1**] and Otal [**Ot**] proved boundary ridAfter for simple negatively curved surfaces (dimension 2).
- Pestov-Uhlmann [**PeUh**] proved boundary rigidity for all simple surfaces. More particularly, they proved that the scattering data determines the conformal class of the surface by relating the scattering map of the geodesic flow to the Dirichlet-to-Neumann map for the Laplacian. Using Mukhometov result, this shows the full boundary rigidity.
- Burago-Ivanov [**BuIv**] proved that metrics close to flat ones are boundary rigid (any dimension).
- Anikonov-Romanov [**AnRo**] proved injectivity of the X-ray transform on the space of divergence-free 1-forms for simple metrics (any dimension).
- Pestov-Sharafutdinov [**PeSh**] proved the injectivity of the X-ray transform on the space of divergence-free symmetric tensors for simple non-positively curved metrics (any dimension). This uses the so-called Pestov identity.
- Stefanov-Uhlmann [**StUh**] proved injectivity of the X-ray transform on tensors for analytic simple metrics and deduce a local boundary rigidity result for generic metrics.
- Paternain-Salo-Uhlmann [**PSU1**] proved injectivity of the X-ray transform on all divergence-free symmetric tensors for simple surfaces (dimension 2).
- Guillarmou [**Gu**] proved injectivity of the X-ray transform on functions and on the space of divergence-free 1-forms for metrics with strictly convex boundary, hyperbolic trapped set and no conjugate points; this setting contains all negatively curved metrics with strictly convex boundary. When the curvature is in addition non-positive, the injectivity on tensors is also proved (any dimension). The same result as Pestov-Uhlmann is shown also in that class of metrics.
- Uhlmann-Vasy [**UhVa**] proved injectivity of the X-ray transform on functions for manifolds admitting a foliation by convex hypersurfaces (any

dimension ≥ 3), and injectivity for the local X-ray transform (i.e. integrals along geodesics almost tangent to boundary)

Acknowledgement

The author's thank the anonymous referee for a careful reading and useful comments.

References

[AnRo] Yu. E. Anikonov and V. G. Romanov, *On uniqueness of determination of a form of first degree by its integrals along geodesics*, J. Inverse Ill-Posed Probl. **5** (1997), no. 6, 487–490 (1998), DOI 10.1515/jiip.1997.5.6.487. MR1623603

[BoRu] Rufus Bowen and David Ruelle, *The ergodic theory of Axiom A flows*, Invent. Math. **29** (1975), no. 3, 181–202, DOI 10.1007/BF01389848. MR0380889

[BuIv] Dmitri Burago and Sergei Ivanov, *Boundary rigidity and filling volume minimality of metrics close to a flat one*, Ann. of Math. (2) **171** (2010), no. 2, 1183–1211, DOI 10.4007/annals.2010.171.1183. MR2630062

[Cr1] Christopher B. Croke, *Rigidity for surfaces of nonpositive curvature*, Comment. Math. Helv. **65** (1990), no. 1, 150–169, DOI 10.1007/BF02566599. MR1036134

[Cr2] Christopher B. Croke, *Rigidity and the distance between boundary points*, J. Differential Geom. **33** (1991), no. 2, 445–464. MR1094465

[Cr3] Christopher B. Croke, *Rigidity theorems in Riemannian geometry*, Geometric methods in inverse problems and PDE control, IMA Vol. Math. Appl., vol. 137, Springer, New York, 2004, pp. 47–72, DOI 10.1007/978-1-4684-9375-7_4. MR2169902

[DKSU] David Dos Santos Ferreira, Carlos E. Kenig, Mikko Salo, and Gunther Uhlmann, *Limiting Carleman weights and anisotropic inverse problems*, Invent. Math. **178** (2009), no. 1, 119–171, DOI 10.1007/s00222-009-0196-4. MR2534094

[DaSh] Nurlan S. Dairbekov and Vladimir A. Sharafutdinov, *Some problems of integral geometry on Anosov manifolds*, Ergodic Theory Dynam. Systems **23** (2003), no. 1, 59–74, DOI 10.1017/S0143385702000822. MR1971196

[Gr] Mikhael Gromov, *Filling Riemannian manifolds*, J. Differential Geom. **18** (1983), no. 1, 1–147. MR697984

[Gu] Colin Guillarmou, *Lens rigidity for manifolds with hyperbolic trapped sets*, J. Amer. Math. Soc. **30** (2017), no. 2, 561–599, DOI 10.1090/jams/865. MR3600043

[GuKa] V. Guillemin and D. Kazhdan, *Some inverse spectral results for negatively curved 2-manifolds*, Topology **19** (1980), no. 3, 301–312, DOI 10.1016/0040-9383(80)90015-4. MR579579

[KRS] C. E. Kenig, A. Ruiz, and C. D. Sogge, *Uniform Sobolev inequalities and unique continuation for second order constant coefficient differential operators*, Duke Math. J. **55** (1987), no. 2, 329–347, DOI 10.1215/S0012-7094-87-05518-9. MR894584

[MePa] W.J. Merry, G. Paternain, *Inverse Problems in Geometry and Dynamics.* Lecture notes. Available at https://www.dpmms.cam.ac.uk/~gpp24

[Mi] René Michel, *Sur la rigidité imposée par la longueur des géodésiques* (French), Invent. Math. **65** (1981/82), no. 1, 71–83, DOI 10.1007/BF01389295. MR636880

[Mil] J. Milnor, *Morse theory*, Based on lecture notes by M. Spivak and R. Wells. Annals of Mathematics Studies, No. 51, Princeton University Press, Princeton, N.J., 1963. MR0163331

[Mu1] R. G. Muhometov, *The reconstruction problem of a two-dimensional Riemannian metric, and integral geometry* (Russian), Dokl. Akad. Nauk SSSR **232** (1977), no. 1, 32–35. MR0431074

[MuRo] R. G. Muhometov and V. G. Romanov, *On the problem of finding an isotropic Riemannian metric in an n-dimensional space* (Russian), Dokl. Akad. Nauk SSSR **243** (1978), no. 1, 41–44. MR511273

[Mu2] R. G. Muhometov, *On a problem of reconstructing Riemannian metrics* (Russian), Sibirsk. Mat. Zh. **22** (1981), no. 3, 119–135, 237. MR621466

[Ot] Jean-Pierre Otal, *Sur les longueurs des géodésiques d'une métrique à courbure négative dans le disque* (French), Comment. Math. Helv. **65** (1990), no. 2, 334–347, DOI 10.1007/BF02566611. MR1057248

[Pa] Gabriel P. Paternain, *Geodesic flows*, Progress in Mathematics, vol. 180, Birkhäuser Boston, Inc., Boston, MA, 1999. MR1712465

[PSU1] Gabriel P. Paternain, Mikko Salo, and Gunther Uhlmann, *Tensor tomography on surfaces*, Invent. Math. **193** (2013), no. 1, 229–247, DOI 10.1007/s00222-012-0432-1. MR3069117

[PSU2] Gabriel P. Paternain, Mikko Salo, and Gunther Uhlmann, *Invariant distributions, Beurling transforms and tensor tomography in higher dimensions*, Math. Ann. **363** (2015), no. 1-2, 305–362, DOI 10.1007/s00208-015-1169-0. MR3394381

[PeSh] L. N. Pestov and V. A. Sharafutdinov, *Integral geometry of tensor fields on a manifold of negative curvature* (Russian), Sibirsk. Mat. Zh. **29** (1988), no. 3, 114–130, 221, DOI 10.1007/BF00969652; English transl., Siberian Math. J. **29** (1988), no. 3, 427–441 (1989). MR953028

[PeUh] Leonid Pestov and Gunther Uhlmann, *Two dimensional compact simple Riemannian manifolds are boundary distance rigid*, Ann. of Math. (2) **161** (2005), no. 2, 1093–1110, DOI 10.4007/annals.2005.161.1093. MR2153407

[Sh] V.A. Sharafutdinov, *Ray transform on Riemannian manifolds*, Eight lectures on integral geometry. available at http://www.math.nsc.ru/~sharafutdinov

[StUh] Plamen Stefanov and Gunther Uhlmann, *Boundary rigidity and stability for generic simple metrics*, J. Amer. Math. Soc. **18** (2005), no. 4, 975–1003, DOI 10.1090/S0894-0347-05-00494-7. MR2163868

[Ta] Michael E. Taylor, *Partial differential equations I. Basic theory*, 2nd ed., Applied Mathematical Sciences, vol. 115, Springer, New York, 2011. MR2744150

[UhVa] Gunther Uhlmann and András Vasy, *The inverse problem for the local geodesic ray transform*, Invent. Math. **205** (2016), no. 1, 83–120, DOI 10.1007/s00222-015-0631-7. MR3514959

E-mail address: `cguillar@dma.ens.fr`

DMA, U.M.R. 8553 CNRS, École Normale Superieure, 45 rue d'Ulm, 75230 Paris cedex 05, France

Published Titles in This Subseries

700 **Alexandre Girouard, Dmitry Jakobson, Michael Levitin, Nilima Nigam, Iosif Polterovich, and Frédéric Rochon, Editors,** Geometric and Computational Spectral Theory, 2017

680 **Sergei Gukov, Mikhail Khovanov, and Johannes Walcher, Editors,** Physics and Mathematics of Link Homology, 2016

655 **A. C. Cojocaru, C. David, and F. Pappalardi, Editors,** SCHOLAR—a Scientific Celebration Highlighting Open Lines of Arithmetic Research, 2015

654 **Carlo Gasbarri, Steven Lu, Mike Roth, and Yuri Tschinkel, Editors,** Rational Points, Rational Curves, and Entire Holomorphic Curves on Projective Varieties, 2015

638 **Javad Mashreghi, Emmanuel Fricain, and William Ross, Editors,** Invariant Subspaces of the Shift Operator, 2015

630 **Pierre Albin, Dmitry Jakobson, and Frédéric Rochon, Editors,** Geometric and Spectral Analysis, 2014

622 **S. Ejaz Ahmed, Editor,** Perspectives on Big Data Analysis, 2014

606 **Chantal David, Matilde Lalín, and Michelle Manes, Editors,** Women in Numbers 2, 2013

605 **Omid Amini, Matthew Baker, and Xander Faber, Editors,** Tropical and Non-Archimedean Geometry, 2013